CHAPTER 1 — THE STRATEGIC CONTEXT

LEARNING OBJECTIVES

After reading Chapter 1, students should be able to answer the following questions:

1. What is the definition of management accounting?
2. How does management accounting form part of the management control system?
3. What is strategy and what is the role of management accounting in strategy?
4. How does management accounting facilitate the accomplishment of strategy through the value creation chain?
5. What is new with management accounting?

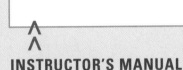

INSTRUCTOR'S MANUAL

Learning Objectives

1. What is the definition of management accounting?
2. How does management accounting form part of the management control system?
3. What is strategy and what is the role of management accounting in strategy?
4. How does management accounting facilitate the accomplishment of strategy through the value creation chain?
5. What is new with management accounting?

© 2008 by Nelson, a division of Thomson Nelson Limited.

MICROSOFT® POWERPOINT® SLIDES

Chapter 1 The Strategic Context

**CHAPTER 1
THE STRATEGIC CONTEXT**

CHAPTER OVERVIEW

This chapter introduces managerial accounting in context of its role in gathering information for planning purposes, making decisions, evaluating performance, and controlling an organization. Managerial accounting is distinguished from financial accounting in that managerial accounting tends to provide information for users internal to an organization while financial accounting focuses on external users. Meanwhile, cost accounting overlaps both management and financial accounting in providing cost measurements for financial reporting purposes as well as providing cost-based information for managers for various operational decisions.

Managerial accounting is an organizational control; it is one of many controls that try to ensure that the various employees and business units within an organization work towards a common goal and do what is required of them.

Managerial accounting provides useful information in order to formulate, implement, and evaluate the success (or failure) of organizational strategies. Companies should establish mission statements on which to base their strategic planning. Plans should include goals and objectives. Several kinds of constraints may affect a company's goals and objectives.

Organizational structure shows the distribution of responsibility and authority within an organization. Core competencies indicate the organization's internal strengths and capabilities and, therefore, help select appropriate business functions to do internally or to outsource.

Strategic management involves the deployment of resources in achieving the company's strategic objectives. The main focus of strategic management is the value chain, which is the series of activities that convert inputs into products and services. Managerial accounting facilitates effective analysis of a company's value chain and, consequently, effective strategic management by providing financial and nonfinancial information required to plan, control, and evaluate performance at each stage of a company's value chain.

As a discipline, managerial accounting evolves over time based on the requirements of its users. Two of the more significant changes are the change from manual accounting systems to enterprise resource planning (ERP) systems, and the increased focus on ethical standards and ethical behaviour on the part of companies and their employees.

CHAPTER STUDY GUIDE

For a business to operate effectively in the global economy, it must meet two requirements. First, managers must understand the factors that affect international markets to identify the locations in which the company has the strengths and desire to compete. Second, managers must devise a business strategy to achieve the company's goals and objectives within the company's operating markets.

This chapter introduces management accounting for use in both the traditional and the new global organizations, and shows how, as an organizational control, management accounting assists with the implementation of an organization's strategy.

Learning Objective 1: What is the definition of management accounting?

Management accounting is defined as the gathering and application of information used to plan, make decisions, evaluate performance, and control an organization. Management accounting has two-way interactions

1

STUDY GUIDE

CHAPTER 1: THE STRATEGIC CONTEXT

MULTIPLE CHOICE

1. In which order do the following activities take place in an organization?

	Setting goals	Setting objectives	Setting strategy
a.	first	second	third
b.	third	first	second
c.	second	third	first
d.	third	second	first

   ANS: C   REF: page 10   OBJ: LO3

2. Strategy
   a. reflects the day-to-day activities needed to satisfy customers' needs or wants.
   b. focuses on how to eliminate competitors to gain market share.
   c. links an organization's internal skills and resources to external opportunities.
   d. is the art of assessing the value of an organization's products and services to potential consumer markets.

   ANS: C   REF: page 8   OBJ: LO3

3. For empowerment to be effective, employees must be
   a. able to negotiate their own reward package.
   b. trained to perform all functions in a given production area.
   c. able to trust management and be trusted by management.
   d. provided the most technologically advanced equipment.

   ANS: C   REF: page 10   OBJ: LO3

4. _____ are the roots of competitive advantage and competitiveness.
   a. Strategies
   b. Core competencies
   c. Key variables
   d. Confrontation strategies

   ANS: B   REF: page 11   OBJ: LO3

5. A firm with a core competency in after-sale service would
   a. perform this activity better than its competitors.
   b. perform this activity better than all other companies.
   c. perform this activity less expensively than all other companies.
   d. consider this an acceptable function to outsource.

TEST BANK

MANAGERIAL ACCOUNTING

Third Canadian Edition

BRENDA M. MALLOUK
University of Toronto

GARY SPRAAKMAN
York University

CECILY A. RAIBORN
Texas State University–San Marcos

JESSE T. BARFIELD
Loyola University–New Orleans

MICHAEL R. KINNEY
Texas A&M University

NELSON / EDUCATION

NELSON EDUCATION

Managerial Accounting, Third Canadian Edition

by Brenda M. Mallouk, Gary Spraakman,
Cecily A. Raiborn, Jesse T. Barfield, and
Michael R. Kinney

**Associate Vice President,
Editorial Director:**
Evelyn Veitch

Marketing Manager:
Kathaleen McCormick

Developmental Editor:
Jim Polley

Photo Researcher:
Melody Tolson

Permissions Coordinator:
Melody Tolson

Content Production Manager:
Christine Gilbert

Production Service:
Pre-Press PMG

Copy Editor:
Matthew Kudelka

Proofreader:
Pre-Press PMG

Indexer:
Pre-Press PMG

**Manufacturing Manager –
Higher Education**
Joanne McNeil

Design Director:
Ken Phipps

Managing Designer:
Katherine Strain

Interior Design:
ArtPlus Design and Communications

Cover Concepts:
Jim Polley

Cover Design:
Peter Papayanakis

Cover Image:
GJS/Shutterstock

Compositor:
Pre-PressPMG

Printer:
Courier

**Library and Archives Canada
Cataloguing in Publication**

Managerial accounting / Brenda
M. Mallouk … [et al.]. — 3rd
Canadian ed.

Includes index.
ISBN 978-0-17-650060-3

1. Managerial accounting—
Textbooks. I. Mallouk, Brenda M.
II. Title.

HF5657.4.M348 2008
658.15'11   C2008-902617-9

ISBN-13: 978-0-17-650060-3
ISBN-10: 0-17-650060-X

PHOTO CREDITS:
P. 3: © 2007 Dell Inc. All Rights Reserved; 11: Lisa F. Young/Shutterstock; 20: Courtesy of Dell Inc.; P. 35, 48, 49, 66: Courtesy of Brenda Mallouk; 54: viZualStudio/Shutterstock; P. 97, 129: Courtesy of United Online; 99: salamanderman/Shutterstock; 107, 113: Courtesy of Brenda Mallouk; Chapter 4. David Papazian Photography Inc./Jupiter; 173: Courtesy of Brenda Mallouk; 178: © Leslie Garland Picture Library / Alamy; 186: Courtesy of Brenda Mallouk; 206: Courtesy of Brenda Mallouk; 243: Courtesy of Ganong Bros. Ltd.; 244: Kristiina Paul; 245: Courtesy of Ganong Bros. Ltd.; 251: Greg Pease/Stone/Getty Images; 269: Cheryl Hewitt/Ganong Chocolates; 299: Brian Mackie/The Hospital for Sick Children; 318: Phil Date/Shutterstock; 341: Brian Mackie/The Hospital for Sick Children; 358: By permission of Famous Players, a division of Viacom Limited; 381: Courtesy of Connie Reed; 383: Courtesy of Brenda Mallouk; 385: Courtesy of Brenda Mallouk; 415: Courtesy of Brenda Mallouk; 451: © Denton Anthony; 453: Courtesy of Karina Hope; 458: Courtesy of Gary Spraakman; 491: Copyright Corel; 525: PR NEWSWIRE / ASSOCIATED PRESS; 535: Kraft; 536: Courtesy of Brenda Mallouk; 538: Courtesy of Brenda Mallouk; 548: Courtesy of Brenda Mallouk; 548: Courtesy of MaxiAids; 548: Stockbyte/PictureQuest; 561: Courtesy of The Gillette Company; 599: Courtesy Air Canada; 605: Courtesy of WestJet; 622: By permission of General Motors of Canada; 627: © Corel; 635: Adrian Wyld/CP Picture Archive; 661: University of Toronto Strategic Communications; 672: James Polley; 675: Heather Spraakman; 679: Courtesy of McCain Foods Limited; 689: Aron Brand/Shutterstock; 723: Phil Carpenter, The Gazette (Montreal); 724: Clive Watkins/Shutterstock; 748: Photodisc Blue/Getty Images; 750: Courtesy of Gary Spraakman; 751: CP PHOTO/Francois Roy; 779: Dick Hemingway; 794: Heather Spraakman; 798: The Hudson's Bay Company corporate logo is a registered trademark, and reproduced with the permission of Hudson's Bay Company; W14-3: Courtesy of Brenda Mallouk; W14-6: By permission of Petro Canada; W14-22: © Corel; W14-26: By permission of General Motors of Canada; W14-32: By permission of Petro Canada.

BRENDA M. MALLOUK

Brenda Mallouk has been a member of the accounting faculty at the University of Toronto for more than twenty years. She is currently on the faculty at the Centre for Industrial Relations and Human Resources, University of Toronto, where she teaches Accounting for Human Resource Professionals. Brenda is known for her energetic teaching style and her popularity with students and is also involved in professional accounting education. She has taught at both the undergraduate and graduate levels. Brenda has authored many books and articles in the field of accounting and education. Her research work has appeared in conference proceedings and journals. Her research interests include cost control, teaching methodology, and management control issues. She is actively involved in professional activities with the Human Resources Professionals Association of Ontario where she serves on the Discipline Committee and the Education Committee. In addition to her teaching experience at the University of Toronto, she has taught extensively in Central America, the Caribbean, Cuba, The People's Republic of China, Taiwan, and Hong Kong. She is actively involved on many university committees and has received several Excellence in Teaching Awards at the University of Toronto. Her greatest passion is travelling to exotic locales.

GARY SPRAAKMAN

Gary Spraakman is an associate professor of management accounting at the Atkinson Faculty of Liberal and Professional Studies, York University. In addition to his CMA, in 2007 he was made a Fellow of the Society of Management Accountants of Canada and awarded the FMCA. He has a Ph.D. in accounting from Concordia University. Prior to pursuing his Ph.D. studies, he worked as a senior consultant at Coopers and Lybrand, as a manager at Molson's, and as director at Alberta Social Services. He has frequently received his university's annual merit award. Also, he received his faculty's major teaching excellence award, which was adjudicated by the alumni association. In 2002 he received a certificate of appreciation from the Ontario Ministry of Enterprise, Opportunities and Innovation for his contribution to the Ministry's biotechnology convergence and network cluster team. Gary's research focus is management accounting, broadly from historical accounting, to questioning theory, to information technology, data mining, to innovation. Recently, he published academic articles in *Critical Perspectives on Accounting*, the *Journal of Management Accounting Research* and the *Accounting Historians Journal*, and teaching cases in the *Journal of Accounting Case Research* and other publications. He is on the editorial boards of two journals, *Canadian Accounting Perspectives* and the *Journal of Accounting and Organizational Change*.

CECILY A. RAIBORN

Dr. Cecily A. Raiborn is Professor of Accounting at Texas State University-San Marcos. She received her Ph.D. from Louisiana State University in 1975. Professor Raiborn teaches cost, managerial, intermediate, and advanced accounting at the undergraduate level, and financial and managerial accounting, cost management, and performance measurement at the graduate level. Her research interests include cost management, international, quality, and ethics issues. She has published articles in accounting, law, and ethics journals including *Management Accounting, Advances in Management Accounting, Journal of Accounting Case Research, Labor Law Journal*, and *Journal of Business Ethics*. She serves on the editorial board of *Advances in Management Accounting*. In 1991, she received the AICPA/Louisiana CPA Society Outstanding Educator Award. Her interests outside the classroom include travelling, reading, water activities, fishing, decorating, and cooking.

JESSE T. BARFIELD

Dr. Jesse T. Barfield is a Professor of Accounting at Loyola University—New Orleans. He received his Ph.D. from Louisiana State University in 1971. He earned an undergraduate degree in accounting and a masters in accounting at Florida State University. He has practiced as a CPA and is licensed to practice in Florida and Louisiana. His research and professional interests include managerial and cost accounting, total quality management, and quality assessments for managers. He teaches accounting, quality management, and auditing in Loyola's undergraduate program and also teaches graduate courses in the MBA and MQM programs. He was chosen by the Loyola CBA undergraduates to receive the 1998 Award for Outstanding Teaching. He has published in the *Journal of Accountancy, Management Accounting, The Florida Certified Public Accountant,* and *The Louisiana CPA*.

MICHAEL R. KINNEY

Dr. Michael Kinney is a native of the rural, sandhills area of Nebraska and received a BA degree from Hastings College, Hastings, Nebraska in 1978. Following graduation, Professor Kinney worked as an insurance agent and broker and later as a commodity futures broker. He returned to graduate school in 1984, earning an MS in accounting from the University of Wyoming and a Ph.D. from the University of Arizona. Professor Kinney joined the faculty of accounting at Texas A&M in 1989, and is currently the Price Waterhouse Teaching Excellence Professor of accounting. He teaches undergraduate courses in cost and management accounting and graduate courses in management control systems, corporate tax, and tax strategies. He has received numerous teaching awards including the outstanding teacher of the Texas A&M College of Business from the College of Business Honors Society (twice), and Delta Iota Chapter's Beta Alpha Psi teaching excellence award in accounting (twice). Professor Kinney also received the Southwest Chapter of the Academy of International Business' Distinguished Paper Award for international research. Professor Kinney has authored and co-authored numerous articles in accounting, taxation, and finance. Professor Kinney is married with four children, and he spends his free time sailing the Gulf of Mexico.

BRIEF TABLE OF CONTENTS

TABLE OF CONTENTS

TABLE OF CONTENTS

TABLE OF CONTENTS

TABLE OF CONTENTS

TABLE OF CONTENTS

TABLE OF CONTENTS

TABLE OF CONTENTS

TABLE OF CONTENTS

TABLE OF CONTENTS

TABLE OF CONTENTS

Accounting is often referred to as the *language of business*. However, managers must be able to communicate their information needs to accountants and understand the resulting answers. This text provides a context for dialogue among all the business disciplines and emphasizes the practical rather than the theoretical. Thus, it stresses the techniques of greatest managerial importance. More specifically, the focus is on techniques for management accounting and not just techniques with calculations. The perspective taken by *Managerial Accounting* is that managers and accountants must have a common understanding of the organizational role of accounting information. They need to understand what techniques are available to provide that information, what data are needed for various techniques, and the benefits and limitations of the information provided by those various techniques in response to managers' needs. This integrated approach to information flow will create an atmosphere of trust, sharing, and cooperation.

We believe that it is critical for readers to understand that accounting is a cross-functional discipline that provides information useful to all management areas. It is also essential that readers recognize that managerial accounting information is necessary in all types of organizations (manufacturing, service, and not-for-profit), regardless of their size. Substantial effort has been taken to illustrate all of these enterprise types, in both domestic and international operations. Rapid changes in the global business environment, such as the introduction of profit-making operations into those countries that were previously communist, will create new demands for management information, and this information will be prepared in the international language of business: accounting.

MAJOR CHANGES IN THE THIRD CANADIAN EDITION

Numerous changes have been made to increase the text's teachability, student orientation, and relevance based on comments from Canadian adopters and reviewers. The basic management accounting techniques have been kept within a sharpened strategic context that emphasizes Canadian and global organizations. The underlying belief is that Canadian organizations have to compete globally, or at least that global competition affects all Canadian organizations.

The most notable change has been to separate out Job Costing and Process Costing. Thus, Chapter 4 has been divided into two chapters. Chapter 4 (present) covers overhead allocation, which was previously covered in Chapter 2. These two topics are now combined as one chapter. Process Costing is now covered on its own in Chapter 5. The result is that there are now 14 chapters rather than 13. Chapter 14 is located on the text website at www.mallouk3e.nelson.com. Also, the order of the chapters has been changed in response to adopters and reviews.

There are two other important changes. The end-of-the chapter case assignments are new mini-cases. The previous cases were basically long problems. The mini-cases require students to exhibit higher-level learning. The cases test students on that chapter's content; they also integrate content from earlier chapters. Case writing instructions in Appendix B are provided to assist students with the mini case assignments. Another change is that the ethics assignments have been entirely rewritten. Students are to use the CMA (Canada) Code of Ethics to evaluate situations with ethical concerns. This change advances the usefulness of the text in view of ethical realities.

The third edition continues to be set within the context of a computerized or information technology-intensive organization. This recognizes that management accounting is only one part of an organization's numerous computerized information systems. In other words, management accounting in terms of budgeting and control is just one of numerous systems maintained and used by medium-sized and larger firms. The textbook examines enterprise resource planning (ERP) systems, which are a means of integrating all systems through a common relational database. From a practical point of view, students should understand how management accounting is part of an ERP system. The discussion of SAP, the dominant international ERP vendor, has been expanded in this edition to reflect accounting realities.

Consistent with the importance of ERP systems for contemporary management accounting, the order of the chapters has been changed to allow the book to conclude with the chapter "Management Accounting Systems." This chapter discusses how major aspects of management accounting can be included in an ERP system, and also highlights how management accounting can be enhanced with ERP systems. Also, a discussion has been added about how ERP systems developed from computer technology to improve inventory planning and ordering. As capital budgeting is generally not handled with the course level of management accounting intended by this book, the chapter on capital budgeting has been taken from the hardcopy text and placed on the Web page for the text. For those instructors wanting to include the chapter on capital budgeting, it is now Chapter 14 on the textbook's website: www.mallouk3e.nelson.com.

For better flow, the budgeting chapter is now Chapter 6 instead of Chapter 9, and the material on controlling costs has been moved from Chapter 8 to Chapter 10. As previously mentioned, Chapter 4 has been divided. New Chapter 4 now covers overhead (from Chapter 2) and job order costing, while Chapter 5 deals only with process costing. Of course, all chapters have been updated and detected errors have been removed.

The third edition can be best described as a strategically focused management accounting textbook set in the context of contemporary information technology. It has a full set of end-of-chapter materials, as well as a unique set of mini-cases to expand testing to higher educational objectives.

CHAPTER COVERAGE

- Chapter 1 sets the stage for future chapters by carefully and thoroughly defining management accounting and explaining how it is a part of control. This chapter also explains strategy and how management accounting assists with implementing strategy. The importance of the value creation chain in implementing strategy is discussed, along with how management accounting relates to both the value creation chain and strategy. The chapter then addresses the enterprise resource planning (ERP) systems environment in which businesses operate. ERP is revisited in other chapters. In summary, Chapter 1 is designed to help students understand the numerous forces that must be considered by businesspeople today and how those forces affect management accounting and decision making.

- Chapter 2 provides an introduction to basic cost terminology and cost flows. This chapter allows students to understand the varying but basic informational needs of managers and how that information can be captured, analyzed, and used in an organization with a well-designed cost management system.

- Chapter 3 discusses cost behaviour and cost–volume–profit analysis. This chapter discusses the basic and traditional management accounting techniques and practices. It includes a discussion of variable and absorption costing methodology.

- Chapter 4 provides a basic discussion of overhead application and job order costing.

- Chapter 5 is now devoted entirely to Process Costing.

- Chapter 6 discusses traditional budgeting and the behavioural consequences that may result from the use of various budgeting techniques. The chapter also examines the role of continuous budgeting and discusses the recommendations of the Beyond Budgeting Round Table group.

- Chapter 7 discusses the basic management accounting technique of standard costs. This topic is discussed for both a service and a manufacturing operation. A discussion of sales variances is also included in this chapter.

- Chapter 8 discusses the contemporary techniques of activity-based costing and activity-based management. ABC is compared to other costing techniques.

- Chapter 9 discusses relevant revenues and costs. In decision making, it is important to understand which costs are relevant and which are not.

- Chapter 10 is a unique chapter that focuses on managing costs in a changing workplace. This chapter includes contemporary, thoughtful, and wide-ranging techniques for controlling costs.

- Chapter 11 covers management accounting in decentralized organizations. It includes a discussion of transfer pricing and how it can be used to set prices.

- Chapter 12 covers the processes of measuring and rewarding performance. Traditional and contemporary techniques are covered.

- Chapter 13 discusses both cost management systems and performance measurement systems, and comments on the advantages of integrating these two systems with an ERP system.

- Web Chapter 14 looks at capital investment and return measurements. In the appendix to this chapter the Canadian method of capital budgeting and its tax implications are discussed complete with an example. The complete chapter is available on the text's website: www.mallouk3.nelson.com.

PEDAGOGY

This text is very student-oriented, and aims to anticipate and provide the features needed by introductory management accounting students. The following text features have been designed to promote ease of learning and provide a high interest level.

On Site

Each chapter begins with a vignette about a relevant aspect of a real-world organization. These openers show students how the chapter topics affect an operating business on a daily basis. The On Sites feature organizations such as Bright Pearl Seafood Restaurant Inc., Ganong Bros. Ltd., Dell Incorporated, Air Canada, WestJet, Swiss Chalet, Canadian National Railway, Bank Canadian National, and Petro-Canada. The theme of each chapter-opening vignette is often carried throughout the chapter using a fictitious company within a related industry. Because of the need to maintain confidentiality of proprietary information, the On Site company's actual data are not used, but example data are reflective of reality.

Key Terms

When a new term is introduced within a chapter, it is listed in boldface type, indicated in a margin annotation, and defined at that point. All key terms in each chapter are presented at the end of the chapter with page references for the definition. Additionally, a complete end-of-text glossary is provided.

News Notes

News Notes in the chapters provide selections from the popular business press and reflect the contemporary world of business activity. Two themes (general business and international) are used to illustrate how managerial accounting concepts affect business. There are more than 60 references to organizations such as the Bank of Montreal, Celestica, Dell Computer, Canadian Tire, Levi Strauss & Co., PeopleSoft, and Wal-Mart.

Internet Links

Website addresses for many real-world companies are listed on the book's website: **www.mallouk3e.nelson.com**.

Site Analysis

This chapter section continues the discussion of the On Site company's reaction to, or resolution of, the opening topic.

Chapter Summary

A summary of the most important concepts in each chapter is provided to promote student retention.

Points to Remember

When relevant, students are provided with all relevant formulas and major computational formats from the chapter. These strategies may be used as guides to work end-of-chapter materials or to refresh one's memory.

Demonstration Problems

At the end of appropriate chapters, demonstration problems and solutions are shown so that students can check their understanding of chapter computations before doing end-of-chapter assignments.

End-of-Chapter Materials

Each chapter contains a variety of end-of-chapter materials at different levels of difficulty. Materials include self-test questions (with answers), questions, exercises, problems, cases, and ethics and quality discussions. Students are encouraged to do the self-test questions on their own to signal their comprehension of the chapter content. If their test scores are low, students may want to reread the chapter before proceeding. Some of the end-of-chapter materials are specifically designed to provide the opportunity for students to use their writing skills and/or to emphasize the needs of different individuals in an organization (for instance, the marketing manager, finance officer, production supervisor, or human resource manager). Many of the ethics and quality discussions are taken from the popular business press and relate to actual business situations. These two sets provide an additional avenue for written expression and logical thought.

Many of the end-of-chapter items ask the student to act as if he or she had a particular position at the firm. This approach promotes analysis and discussion from alternative perspectives. Journal entries are included in chapter. Their particular placement allows instructors to include or exclude this accounting process information without interrupting the flow of materials in each of the chapters.

Numerical end-of-chapter materials that are computer-solvable are indicated with a **spreadsheet icon.**

Web Resources

This text's supporting website at **www.mallouk3e.nelson.com** provides downloadable versions of key instructor supplements, as well as Web Links, Web Cases, Check Figures, Internet Exercises, Test Yourself Questions, Supplementary Learning Objectives, Communication Activities, Microsoft® Excel® spreadsheets, and more.

Supplementary Learning Objectives

In addition to the learning objectives in the chapter, additional learning objectives are provided to correspond to the additional parts of Chapters 1, 10, 11, and 14, that appear on the book's website:

- Web Chapter 1: The Strategic Context
- Web Chapter 10: Controlling Costs
- Web Chapter 11: Responsibility Accounting and Transfer Pricing in Decentralized Operations
- Web Chapter 12: Measuring and Rewarding Performance

If there are additional learning objectives for the chapter, they are indicated at the end of the chapter, before the End-of-Chapter Materials. For example, the first chapter has two additional learning objectives: How did management accounting develop? How does information technology affect management accounting? For the full text, see **www.mallouk3e.nelson.com**

End-of-Text Appendices

Appendix A is a brief overview of the various ethical theories to help students analyze ethics situations and answer the chapter ethics discussion questions. Appendix B provides the same for the end-of-chapter cases.

Glossary

The end-of-text glossary includes all of the key terms in the text and their definitions. Key term definitions are shown in the margin where the terms appear in the text.

INSTRUCTOR SUPPORT MATERIALS

The text is accompanied by the following full range of support materials for the instructor:

Instructor's Solutions Manual

This volume, prepared by the authors, has been independently reviewed and checked for accuracy. It contains complete solutions to each question, exercise, problem, and case in the text, as well as suggested answers for the ethics and quality discussions and the communications activities. The Instructor's Solutions Manual is available on the Instructor's CD-ROM.

Test Bank

The test bank, which has been prepared by Kathy Falk, University of Toronto, contains more than one thousand multiple-choice, short exercise, and short discussion questions with related solutions. The test bank can be found on the Instructor's CD-ROM.

ExamView®

A computerized version of the test bank includes editing and word-processing features that allow test customization through the addition, deletion, and scrambling of test selections. ExamView can be found on the Instructor's CD-ROM.

Instructor's Manual

This manual, developed by Ann Clarke Okah, Carleton University, contains sample syllabi, a listing of chapter learning objectives and terminology, chapter lecture outlines, and some exam multiple-choice questions for use as additional test material or for quizzes. The manual is available on the Instructor's CD-ROM and the Instructor's portion of the text's website at www.mallouk3e.nelson.com.

Microsoft® PowerPoint® Teaching Transparency Slides

Microsoft® PowerPoint® files, prepared by Elliott Currie, University of Guelph, provide entertaining and informative graphics and text for full-colour electronic presentations. These files are available on the Instructor's CD-ROM and on the Instructor's portion of the text's website at www.mallouk3e.nelson.com.

Instructor's CD-ROM

The Instructor's CD-ROM contains the Instructor's Solutions Manual, the Test Bank, the Computerized Test Bank, the Instructor's Manual, and the Microsoft® Teaching Transparency Slides. ISBN: 978-0-17-647498-0

Turning Point: JoinIn™ on TurningPoint®

Now you can author, deliver, show, assess, and grade all in PowerPoint . . . with NO toggling back and forth between screens! **JoinIn on TurningPoint** is the only classroom response software tool that gives you **true** PowerPoint integration. With **JoinIn,** you are no longer tied to your computer . . . you can walk about your classroom as you lecture, showing slides and collecting and displaying responses with ease. There is simply no easier or more effective way to turn your lecture hall into a personal, fully interactive experience for your students. If you can use PowerPoint, you can use **JoinIn on TurningPoint!** Resources for this text have been prepared by Rick Bates, University of Guelph, and can be found on the Instructor's CD-ROM.

Course Management With CengageNOW™

Specifically designed to ease the time-consuming task of grading homework, iLrn™ 5.0 lets students complete their assigned homework from the text or practise on unassigned homework online. The results are instantly entered into a grade book. Enhanced with annotated spreadsheets and complete grade book functionality, iLrn™ 5.0 provides an unprecedented real-time, guided, self-correcting learning reinforcement system outside the classroom. Use this resource as an integrated solution for your distance learning and traditional course. iLrn™ 5.0 features:

- **Questions**: Students can get help entering their answers in the proper format and even run a spell check on their answers. On selected questions, they can complete additional, similar questions for extra practice. Optional algorithmic questions are also included.
- **Grade book**: The flexible grade book can display and download any combination of student work, chapters, or activities. Capture grades on demand or set a particular time for grades to be automatically captured. Mark questions as required or excluded, so students can only access the questions you want them to complete.
- **Hints**: Students can get up to three hints per activity. These hints can be PowerPoint® slides, video clips, images, and more—and instructors can add their own hints.
- **Flexibility**: iLrn™ 5.0 can easily be integrated within WebCT™ and Blackboard™.

Web Resources

This text's supporting website at **www.mallouk3e.nelson.com** provides downloadable versions of key instructor supplements, as well as Web Links, Web Cases, Check Figures, Internet Exercises, Test Yourself Questions, Supplementary Learning Objectives, Chapter 14, Capital Asset Selection and Capital Budgeting, Communication Activities, Microsoft® Excel® spreadsheets, and more.

STUDENT SUPPORT MATERIALS

Students are also provided with a comprehensive support package to enhance their learning experience.

Study Guide

The student study guide, prepared by Prem Lobo, York University, contains chapter learning objectives, chapter overview, detailed chapter notes, and self-test questions. (ISBN: 978-0-17-647494-2)

Spreadsheet Applications for Managerial Accounting

Spreadsheet Applications are available on www.mallouk3e.nelson.com and allow students to use Microsoft® Excel® spreadsheets to solve the many in-text problems (which have been indicated with a spreadsheet icon).

Student's Solutions Manual

The Student's Solutions Manual contains solutions to Exercises and Problems in the text. (ISBN: 978-0-17-647501-7)

Homework Management With Cengage Now

Specifically designed to ease the time-consuming task of completing homework, iLrn™ 5.0 lets students complete their assigned homework from the text or practise on unassigned homework online.

ACKNOWLEDGMENTS

We would like to thank the many people who have helped us during the preparation of all editions of this textbook. The constructive comments and suggestions made by the following reviewers were instrumental in developing, rewriting, and improving the quality and readability of this book.

Philip Beaulicu	University of Calgary
Hilary Becker	Carleton University
Ann Bigelow	University of Western Ontario
Robert Biscontri	University of Manitoba
Carole Bowman	Sheridan College
Ted Carney	Humber College
Anthony Moung Yin Chan	Ryerson University
Suzanne Coombs	Kwantlen University College
Angela Downey	University of Lethbridge
D.H. Drury	McGill University
Fathi Elloumi	Athabasca University
Ian Feltmate	Acadia University
Michael Favere-Marchesi	Simon Fraser University
Clinton Free	Queen's University
Ilene Gilborn	Mount Royal College
Larry Goldsman	McGill University
Rob Harvey	Algonquin College

Jeffrey Kantor	University of Windsor
Valerie Kinnear	Mount Royal College
Glen Kobussen	University of Saskatchewan
Michael Maingot	University of Ottawa
Winston Marcellin	George Brown College
R.C. Nichols	British Columbia Institute of Technology
Mary Oxner	St. Francis Xavier University
Connie Reed	University of Toronto, Rotman School of Management
Paul Roy	York University
Naqi Sayed	Lakehead University
Wendy Schultz	University of Manitoba
Lawrence Shum	Seneca College
Bob Sproule	University of Waterloo
Nelson Waweru	York University
Shu-Lun Wong	Memorial University

Special thanks must also be made to the Institute of Management Accountants and the Certified General Accountants Association of Canada. These organizations have been extremely generous in granting their permission to use numerous problems and excerpts from their publications. Permission has been received from the Institute of Management Accountants to use questions and/or unofficial answers from past CMA examinations. We also want to acknowledge the many publishers who granted permission for use of their materials as On Site/Site Analysis/News Note excerpts.

Sincere appreciation is extended to Drs. Howard L. Price and Keith H. Wong who are on a constant quest to find solutions to problems. This is what sets these individuals apart from others. Special mention must be given to Lawrence Chung, Ida Copelovici, Gamon Gomes, Rochelle Gordon, Ambrus Kecskés, Brian Mackie, Amy Nijmeh, Rose G. Reed, and Fred Shearer, as well as to the many other individuals who provided information related to the On Sites and Site Analyses. Very special thanks must be given to Gamon Gomes for his extensive research assistance.

The authors would like to thank those at Nelson Education who have toiled long hours to help both of us with this project. We would especially like to thank our families and friends, who have encouraged and supported us in this endeavour.

Dr. Brenda Mallouk
Dr. Gary Spraakman

Chapter 1

The Strategic Context

LEARNING OBJECTIVES

After reading this chapter, you should be able to answer the following questions:

1 What
is the definition of management accounting?

2 How
does management accounting form part of the management control system?

3 What
is strategy and what is the role of management accounting in strategy?

4 How
does management accounting facilitate the accomplishment of strategy through the value creation chain?

5 What
is new with management accounting?

ON SITE

www.dell.com

Dell Incorporated

Management accounting serves management in a global market, which has in recent decades transcended local and national markets with the assistance of information technology. Just as information technology is changing the way firms organize and interact with their customers and suppliers, it is changing management accounting.

DELL INCORPORATED has a business model that is at the leading edge of this information technology-based change. It is a model that other firms study and emulate, and that management accountants should understand in their role as advisers to management.

At 19, while a student at the University of Texas in 1984, Michael Dell started Dell Incorporated. The often-repeated story is that he started by selling PC components from his residence room. The products in the first years were surplus random-access memory chips and disk drives, which he acquired from IBM dealers and sold through newspaper advertisements. He expanded into buying and reselling surplus PCs, which he enhanced with more powerful disk drives, memories, and graphics cards. Dell sought to bypass wholesalers and retailers to sell directly to end users.

This Dell PC business model has three dominant and related characteristics. First, all Dell PCs are custom-built or assembled to order and then shipped directly to customers; thus, bypassing wholesalers and retailers. Direct interaction with customers ensures quality service and lower costs. Second, Dell uses on-demand assembly to avoid the need for and cost of carrying large stocks of parts, components, and finished goods. On-demand assembly reduces costs, particularly with model or technology changes. Third, although Dell assembles the PCs (and now other products) it sells, most parts are outsourced to firms that are the best in the world in what they produce. Michael Dell explains the advantages of outsourcing with the following (paraphrased) illustration: If you have a race with 20 players all vying to make the fastest graphics chip in the world, do you want to be the 21st player, or do you want to evaluate the field of 20 and pick the best player? Clearly, Dell chose to evaluate the suppliers and to pick the world's best for long-term partnerships. This strategy has two advantages. First, name-brand processors, disk drives, modems, speakers, and multimedia components increase quality and performance. Second, Dell obtains timely deliveries of components because of its commitment to purchasing specific percentages from each of its long-term suppliers.

Dell depends on its ability to optimize its procedures and systems and its relationships with employees, suppliers, investors, and customers. The clarity of this approach for implementing its strategy is reflected in Dell's above-average financial performance.

Dell has been losing market share to Hewlett-Packard in recent years. In 2005, Dell had dominated with an 18.2% market share compared to HP's 15.7%. According to research firm IDC, by June 30, 2007, Dell's worldwide PC market share had fallen to 16.1% for the quarter ending June 30, 2007, compared to HP's 19.3%. So in June 2007 Dell began complementing its direct PC sales model by selling to retailers such as Wal-Mart and Sam's Club. In addition, to compete with Apple, Michael Dell announced that the company would focus more on product design to attract consumers who wanted products to serve as fashion accessories: "We are kind of in the fashion business. We have been putting quite a bit more energy into this. It will be reflected in future products."

Dell's supply chain efficiency and direct build-to-order sales do not provide as big an advantage as they once did. Its competitors have reduced Dell's supply chain edge. In 1997, for example, in selling a PC that cost $1,000 to make, Dell incurred about $20 in inventory costs compared to HP's $160. By 2005 those costs were $10 for Dell compared to $70 for HP. In other words, the $140 advantage had fallen to $60—though still an advantage.

If Dell hopes to keeping growing and competing with HP and Apple, it will have to target consumers more efficiently and expand its expertise beyond direct sales and supply chain management. These are normal expectations for Dell in a competitive environment. Will Dell continue to succeed? The world will be watching.

SOURCES: "Dell Jacks Into the Digital Hub," *BusinessWeek* online, Special Report: Consumer Electronics, December 9, 2003; Geoffrey Downey, "Dell Adds Services to Enterprise Menu," *Computing Canada*, January 31, 2003, pp. 1; Adam Lashinsky, "Where Dell Is Going Next," *Fortune*, October 18, 2004, p. 115; Andrew Park, "Dude, You're Getting a Printer," *BusinessWeek*, April 19, 2004, p. 87, www.dell.com; www.knowledge.wharton.upenn.edu/article.cfm?articleid=1794 (Feb. 25, 2007)

*T*his first chapter introduces management accounting as a service of providing information to management. Management is responsible for the success of organizations, and this means formulating and implementing effective strategies, which are particularly important for setting the direction an organization takes. Management accounting provides information to management in determining direction and in reporting on how well an organization is doing in pursuing that direction.

There are several reasons why we selected Dell Incorporated for the opening chapter vignette of the Canadian edition. First, Dell has been very successful with a unique strategy of dealing directly with customers by eliminating retailers and wholesalers. Second, Dell has been innovative in using information technology to interact with its customers and suppliers. Third, Dell's strategy is being copied to various degrees by other organizations. Fourth, Dell's strategy continues to change to meet market conditions. In brief, Dell's strategy is one that will be increasingly prevalent in the future, and it is best to consider management accounting in terms of what will occur in the future rather than what has happened in the past.

This textbook shows how organizations are proceeding with their strategies, which allow management accounting to be explained as it will be used by students in their future careers.

Chapter 1 introduces management accounting for use in both traditional and the new global organizations, and shows how, as an organizational control, management accounting assists with the implementation of an organization's strategy. The chapter links strategy creation and implementation to control and management accounting. To help readers fully understand how management accounting assists with implementing strategy, the value creation chain is used to explain the organization as a series of processes and activities that create value for customers. The main point is *that the value creation chain[1] underlies both strategy and management accounting. Also, the history of management accounting and its partner, information technology, are discussed on the Web page for Chapter 1 to provide a more insightful understanding of management accounting in global organizations such as Dell.*

In other words, this chapter defines and explains management accounting and the organizational context within which it functions. It deals with how management accounting fits with management per se, strategy, controls, activities, and information technology.

The other chapters will address the techniques and systems of management accounting, which will be more understandable once the context is already understood. There are two overriding themes. First, management accounting assists managers with developing and implementing strategy. Second, management accounting is increasingly computerized as a component of enterprise resource planning systems. Chapter 2 introduces and defines basic terminology for management accounting. Chapter 3 describes some very basic management accounting analytical techniques, including cost–volume–profit analysis. Chapter 4 discusses overhead and job order costing. The latter is one of the two traditional costing systems. Chapter 5 explains the other traditional costing system, process costing. Budgeting is the main topic of Chapter 6. Standard costs and variances—necessary concepts for management accounting—are discussed in Chapter 7. Activity-based management and activity-based costing are the main topics for Chapter 8. Chapter 9 provides techniques for assessing the relevance of various costs when different decisions are being made. Within the framework of managing costs, Chapter 10 discusses a number of today's innovative techniques. Responsibility accounting and related transfer pricing are the dominant topics in Chapter 11. Chapter 12 discusses the approaches that management accounting takes for measuring and rewarding performance. Chapter 13, the final chapter of this text, is groundbreaking in that it provides new material on both cost management and performance measurement for creating management accounting systems. (Chapter 14, on capital budgeting, is on the textbook's Web page.)

MANAGEMENT ACCOUNTING DEFINED

LEARNING OBJECTIVE **1**

What is the definition of management accounting?

Before we proceed, management accounting needs to be defined. Other important terms will be defined in this and the other chapters. **Management accounting** is defined as the gathering and application of information used to plan, make decisions, evaluate performance, and control an organization. This definition makes it clear that management accounting deals with the use of information, which may be financial or nonfinancial (i.e., operational). The definition also makes it clear that the information is for managers to use for their work in terms of planning, decision making, performance evaluation, and in general the control of the activities that occur in an organization.

Management accounting has two-way interactions with other organizational units. The management accounting unit gathers information from other units about their activities. The management accounting unit also provides information to other units to allow them to manage their activities, particularly for coordination among units. For example, the management accounting unit would gather sales information from sales units and then provide that information to the production unit, and vice versa.

Management accounting gathers two time-based types of information: "expected" and "what happened." "Expected" information includes what might or

management accounting
the gathering and application of information used to plan, make decisions, evaluate performance, and control an organization

should be. For example, standards and budgets specify information in terms of what should exist in the future. "What happened" information reports what has already taken place, as with financial accounting statements reporting events that have already occurred. More will be said about each of these types of information in this and other chapters of the book.

Management accounting can be understood more precisely when it is compared to financial accounting.

Financial Accounting

financial accounting
generation of accounting information for external reporting

Financial accounting focuses on external users and is generally required for obtaining loans, preparing tax returns, and reporting to the investment community on how well or poorly the business is performing. The information used in financial accounting must comply with generally accepted accounting principles (GAAP). Financial accounting information is usually quite aggregated and relates to the entire organization. In some cases, a regulatory agency (such as a provincial securities commission) or an industry commission (such as in banking or insurance) may prescribe specific financial accounting practices.

Management Accounting

In contrast to financial accounting, management accounting can be applied in all types of organizations to provide information for internal users. Exhibit 1-1 details the differences between financial and management accounting.

EXHIBIT 1-1

Financial and Management Accounting Differences

	Financial	Management
Primary users	External	Internal
Primary organizational focus	Whole (aggregated)	Parts (segmented)
Information characteristics	Must be:	May be:
	Historical	Forecasted
	Quantitative	Quantitative or qualitative
	Monetary	Monetary or nonmonetary
	Accurate	Timely and, at a minimum, a reasonable estimate
Overriding criteria	Generally accepted accounting principles	Situational relevance (usefulness)
	Consistency	Benefits exceed costs
	Verifiability/Objectivity	Flexibility
Recordkeeping	Formal	Combination of formal and informal

Managers are often concerned with individual parts or segments of the business rather than with the organization as a whole. Therefore, management accounting information often focuses on particular segmental aspects of an entity rather than the big picture of financial accounting. Management accounting is flexible because it is not regulated by any organization or regulatory body. Often, management accountants provide forecasted, qualitative, and nonmonetary information. For instance, a manager debating whether to sell a piece of land now or in three years is not likely to use the land's historical cost to make the decision. Instead, he or she will need estimates about expected changes in land prices for the next three years as well as information about expected events, such as the possibility that a shopping centre will be built on property adjoining the land.

A primary criterion for internal information is that it serves management's needs. A related criterion is the cost/benefit consideration that information should be developed and provided only if the cost of producing it is less than the benefit gained from using the information.

Cost Accounting

Cost accounting bridges the financial accounting and management accounting functions as shown in Exhibit 1-2. As part of financial accounting, cost accounting provides product cost measurements for inventories and cost of goods sold on the financial statements. As part of management accounting, cost accounting provides some of the quantitative, cost-based information managers need to assess product profitability, prepare budgets, and make investment decisions. Cost accounting measurements often depend on classification of costs as product or period costs. These topics will be elaborated upon in a later chapter.

cost accounting
tools and methods applied to determine the cost of making products or performing services

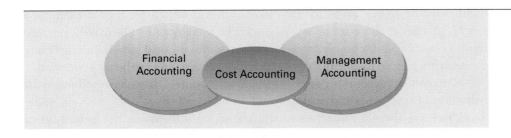

EXHIBIT 1-2
Financial, Management, and Cost Accounting Overlap

Management Accountants

Management accounting provides satisfying careers to many Canadians. It is not entirely necessary to have accounting credentials to work as a management accountant. However, certification by one of the three Canadian accounting associations may assist in developing the necessary abilities to effectively function as a management accountant. There are three accounting designations in Canada: CA (chartered accountant), CGA (certified general accountant), and CMA (certified management accountant). The Canadian Institute of Chartered Accountants sponsors the CA; the Certified General Accountants' Association of Canada sponsors the CGA; while the Society of Management Accountants of Canada sponsors the CMA. Each designation requires students to have a university degree and to successfully complete other studies. The CA program focus is on external audit and financial accounting. The CMA is the only one of the three to emphasize only management accounting. The CGA program has a number of specialties, one of which includes management accounting. Web sites for these professional associations contain more information for students considering becoming certified accountants (see, for example, www.cica.ca, www.cga-canada.org, and www.cma-canada.org).

The United States has two accounting designations: the CPA or certified public accountant is sponsored by the American Institute of Certified Public Accountants, and the American CMA is sponsored by the Institute of Management Accountants.

With the prevalence of international trade, many Canadian accountants are obtaining the American CPA credentials to better understand American accounting and business practices.

How does management
accounting form part of the
management control system?

control
exertion of managerial influence on
operations so that they will conform
to plans

MANAGEMENT ACCOUNTING: A COMPONENT OF MANAGEMENT CONTROL

Where does management accounting fit within an organization. In the context of an entire organization, management accounting is one of many **controls** that ensure, with varying degrees of success, that employees (and managers) do what is required. The control problem is that employees do not always do what the organization requires (i.e., "individuals are sometimes unable or unwilling to act in the organization's best interest, and a set of controls must be implemented to guard against undesirable behaviour and to encourage desirable actions"[2]).

There are two reasons why employees and even managers might not do what would be deemed appropriate by the organization. First, employees may not always understand what is expected or how best to perform jobs, as they may lack the necessary ability, training, or information. Controls are needed to compensate for personal limitations. Second, employees may lack goal congruence with the organization. In other words, the organization may want the employees to undertake certain activities, but the employees may prefer to undertake a different set of activities. For example, a retail organization may want sales personnel to be friendly and polite to all customers; this may be difficult for poorly trained employees who are paid minimum wage rates. Controls are needed to ensure that only appropriate activities are being performed.

Management accounting is an organizational control. It seeks to influence the behaviour of employees and managers.

There are three approaches to controlling or influencing the behaviour of employees: specify appropriate activities, specify appropriate results, and recruit or develop appropriate personnel. These controls relate to management accounting information in numerous ways.

Specific activity controls attempt to ensure that employees perform certain **activities** and/or do not perform others. Undesirable activities can be precluded with behavioural constraints such as locks, separate rooms, fences, and the separation of duties. The physical controls prevent entry to areas, while the separation of duties has a similar effect over activities. Action control specifies the appropriate activities to be undertaken, via work rules, policies and procedures, and codes of conduct. Activities are, in effect, preprogrammed, and the managerial accounting information reporting on the activities would be nonfinancial.

activities
repetitive actions, movements, or
work sequences performed to fulfill a
business function

The results approach to control is less specific. Instead of specifying activities through action controls, a result control specifies what must be accomplished, leaving the selection of activities to the employees and managers. This type of control is particularly reasonable when the overseeing manager does not know the most appropriate activities under unseen circumstances (such as a salesperson being unobservable). Results accountability can be accomplished through setting expectations for performance (e.g., for sales, costs, and profits) with standards, budgets, and management by objectives, which will be discussed in subsequent chapters. Briefly, standards include expectations about what should be produced in terms of quantity and/or quality. An example of a quantitative measure would be the number of purchase orders to be processed by a clerk; the qualitative measure would be the number of errors per, say, 1,000 purchase orders processed, with lower numbers of errors indicating higher quality. Budgets are commitments that are equated to dollars of sales, costs, profits, or profitability. Management accounting information reporting on the results could be financial or nonfinancial.

The third approach to control is personnel. The control is placed on getting employees to do what the organization desires without using action or result controls. To control via personnel, the capabilities of employees can be upgraded through selective hiring of only those who are likely to do what the organization desires. Relatedly, the employees and managers are more likely to do what the organization desires if communication is effective. This can be ensured by clarification of what is desired and by detailed coordination of employees and managers. Finally, personnel control can be accomplished by creating an organizational culture that compels or forces employees to do what is organizationally correct. Personnel control does not require management accounting information.

Management accounting is a control. It is used to specify and monitor activities and results. Nevertheless, there are other controls that need to be carefully considered when developing management accounting practices. These other controls include financial accounting, management information systems, employee and manager performance evaluation systems, and **organizational culture**. For example, an organization with a strong culture of performance will not be as dependent on management accounting for ensuring activity performance as will an organization whose culture considers performance to be onerous.

organizational culture
the set of basic assumptions about the organization, its goals, and its business practices; describes an organization's norms in internal and external, as well as formal and informal, transactions

MANAGEMENT ACCOUNTING: IMPLEMENTING STRATEGY

LEARNING OBJECTIVE 3

What is strategy and what is the role of management accounting in strategy?

To understand how management accounting assists an organization in effectively implementing its strategy, we must first understand **strategy**. What follows is a brief primer on strategy, particularly on the basic terms and components.

An organization should begin its strategy formulation with a mission statement. The mission statement should (1) clearly state what the organization wants to accomplish and (2) express how that organization uniquely meets its targeted customers' needs with its products and services. This statement may change over time. For example, a few pages ago it was noted that Dell has had to modify its strategy of selling only directly to customers. It now sells to retailers. Dell's supply chain, in particular its scheduling, will need to be adjusted to produce PCs for retailers.

Strategy links an organization's mission to its actual activities. In other words, activities implement strategy. Strategy can also be defined as follows:

> Strategy is the art of creating value. It provides the intellectual frameworks, conceptual models, and governing ideas that allow an organization's managers to identify opportunities for bringing value to customers and for delivering value at a profit. In this respect, strategy is the way a company defines its business and links together with the only two resources that really matter in today's economy: knowledge and relationships or an organization's competencies and its customers.[3]

strategy
a long-term dynamic plan that fulfills organizational goals and objectives through satisfaction of customer needs or wants within the company's acknowledged operating markets

An organization's **business model** tries to match its strategy with its internal skills and resources to the opportunities found in the external environment.[4] Although small organizations may have a single strategy, larger organizations often have an overall entity strategy as well as individual strategies for each business unit (such as a division). The business units' strategies should flow from the overall strategy to ensure that effective and efficient resource allocations are made, an overriding corporate culture is developed, and organizational direction is enhanced. Senior management needs to question the appropriateness of a strategy.[5] Profitability by product line should be compared to that of major competitors. This comparability should extend to product line sales, prices, and customers. It should include determination of the product line source of the organization's profits.

business model
a description of a business's distinguishing operations or mechanisms, functions, and revenues and expenses

Management accounting serves managers in designing, implementing, and evaluating the organization's strategy by providing information about expectations of what a strategy will accomplish and cost, and the strategy's actual past performance.

Strategy should dominate the activities within an organization. All activities should support the strategy. The News Note provides an example of how Loblaws is changing its strategy and business model to meet the competition from Wal-Mart.

Organizational Structure

organizational structure
the way in which authority and responsibility for making decisions is distributed in an organization

goal
a desired result or condition that is expressed in qualitative terms

objective
a quantitatively expressed result that can be achieved during a pre-established period or by a specified date; should logically measure progress in achieving goals

Organizational structure is designed to implement the organization's strategy. The structure must be appropriate for doing the job of implementing strategy, or in other words, structure follows strategy.[6] An organization should be understood as being composed of people, resources, and commitments that are acquired and arranged to achieve results specified by the strategy via goals and objectives. **Goals** are desired results expressed in qualitative terms. For example, in profit-oriented organizations, one typical goal is to maximize shareholder wealth. Goals are also likely to be formulated for other major stakeholders such as customers, employees, and suppliers. In contrast, **objectives** are quantitatively expressed results that can be achieved during a pre-established period or by a specified date. Objectives should logically measure progress in achieving goals. For example, Coca-Cola had a goal of being the soft-drink sponsor of a recent Summer Olympic Games and reportedly spent $40 million for that right. The objective following from that goal was to emphasize the drink's "universal appeal" and thus, the company had daily themes for each of the 17 days. Coca-Cola developed 100 different commercials to fit the daily themes and paid approximately $62 million for television advertising time during the Games' telecast.[7]

Management accounting provides information for setting the goals and objectives. Subsequently, management accounting provides information on the organization's success with accomplishing those goals and objectives. Of course, there is more data precision with objectives than with goals.

GENERAL NEWS NOTE

Loblaws Struggles for Survival Against Wal-Mart

There have been some great rivalries over the years: Ali versus Frazier, the Maple Leafs versus the Canadiens, the Yankees versus the Red Sox. And now you can add LOBLAWS versus WAL-MART. It may not be as thrilling as the grudge matches from the world of sports, but the two retailers are still fighting tooth and nail for your shopping dollars. And after taking more than a few kicks while it was down, Loblaws has just thrown a counterpunch in the form of a new and improved superstore in Milton that it hopes will help even the score.

Loblaws has suffered from flagging sales and fierce competition from Wal-Mart, but the new store could turn the tides. Shoppers who hit the aisles for the official opening on Wednesday seemed impressed.

"It's beautiful inside," said Maxine Brownhenry. "The set-up is great. The people are friendly. It's the first day but it's absolutely fantastic."

Store manager Chris Shewchyk explained some of the upgrades. "We want to be very unique. We've introduced the wider aisles, better fixtures, a brighter look to the store."

More important, prices are about 15% lower than at a regular Loblaws, and plastic bags have been outlawed. Loblaws is now the first national retailer to go bagless.

"I think it's the only way to get it going . . . This way it forces people," says shopper Diane Roberts-Scarfone.

Loblaws plans to test the store over the next few months with the aim of opening more like it next year.

SOURCE: August 29, 2007, CityNews.ca staff, www.citynews.ca/news/news_14212.aspx.

The organizational structure reflects the distribution of authority and responsibility for making decisions in an organization. The right—usually by virtue of position or rank—to use resources to accomplish an activity or to achieve an objective is called **authority**. The obligation to accomplish an activity or achieve an objective is called **responsibility**. The organizational structure normally evolves from its mission, goals, and managerial responsibilities.

Management accounting information is prepared in order to help managers carry out their responsibilities. At the same time, management accounting reports on how well these managers have fulfilled their responsibilities.

authority
the right (usually by virtue of position or rank) to use resources to accomplish a task or achieve an objective; can be delegated or assigned to others

responsibility
the obligation to accomplish a task or achieve an objective; cannot be delegated to others

Core Competencies

A **core competency** is any critical function or activity in which one organization has a higher proficiency than its competitors. Core competencies are the roots of competitiveness and competitive advantage. "Core competencies are different for every organization; they are, so to speak, part of an organization's personality."[8] Technological innovation, engineering, product development, and after-sale service are some examples of core competencies. For instance, the Japanese electronics industry is viewed as having a core competency in the miniaturization of electronics. Bell Canada Enterprises and Disney believe that they have core competencies in communications and entertainment, respectively.

core competency
any critical function or activity in which one organization has a higher proficiency than its competitors; the roots of competitiveness and competitive advantage

Couriers are very important for contemporary firms that outsource to domestic or international suppliers.

Generic Strategies

In determining its strategy or strategies to meet the needs of targeted customers, an organization may choose differentiation or cost leadership.[9] A company deciding to compress its competitive scope focuses on a specific market segment to the exclusion of others. Many companies producing or selling luxury goods (such as Rolex watches) adopt this strategy. The same approach has, however, been adopted by some nonluxury entities, such as Harvey's hamburger restaurants, which allow the customer to select from a range of toppings.

A company choosing a **differentiation** strategy distinguishes its product or service from that of competitors by adding enough value (including quality and/or

differentiation
a competitive strategy in which an organization distinguishes its products or services from those of competitors by adding enough value (including quality and/or features) that customers are willing to pay a higher price

features) that customers are willing to pay a higher price. Differentiation can be "based on the product itself, the delivery system by which it is sold, the marketing approach, or other factors."[10]

Competition may also be avoided by establishing a position of **cost leadership**, that is, by becoming the low-cost producer/provider and, therefore, being able to charge low prices that emphasize cost efficiencies. In this strategy, competitors cannot compete on price and must differentiate their products/services from the cost leader. Wal-Mart excels at cost leadership, which is only possible with extensive information systems and control over its multitude of suppliers who are located around the world.

Dell competes both on low price and differentiation. This provides Dell with a competitive edge over all of its competitors.

A final factor affecting strategy is the environment in which the organization operates. An **environmental constraint** is any limitation on strategy caused by external cultural, fiscal (such as taxation structures), legal/regulatory, or political situations and by competitive market structures. Because environmental constraints cannot be directly controlled by an organization's management, these factors tend to have long-run rather than short-run effects. Managerial actions and organizational culture influence the firm and may work to affect the operating environment through numerous activities, including attempts to change laws.

The food industry provides many excellent examples of the influence of culture as one environmental constraint on organizational strategy. Many companies have recognized that culture may affect strategy because products and services that sell well in one locale may not be appropriate in another locale. For instance, Coca-Cola has not attempted to sell its fermented milk drink in Canada and, although pigs' feet, oxtails, and pork ears may be popular staples in many Hispanic, Haitian, and Jamaican diets, these items are not available at most local Canadian grocery stores.

Management Accounting Provides Information

Management accounting provides information important in formulating, implementing, and evaluating strategies. In formulating a strategy, management accounting provides information on prospective customers such as their numbers, locations, spending patterns, and profitability. These data provide the basis for detailed forecasts and plans upon which to make decisions about whether to pursue the strategy. Once the strategy is implemented, management accounting provides information for effectively accomplishing the strategy, and then for evaluating its success and its effectiveness among competitors.

Management accounting provides both financial and nonfinancial or operational data for designing, implementing, and assessing strategies. A particularly important focus of management accounting is on costs involved with strategies, including unit costs and total costs, as well as the costs for organizational units.

In financial accounting, financial measures generated from the income statement are highly important. Management accounting goes beyond those measures both internally and externally. The literature recently identified 17 strategic management accounting techniques, which are listed below in alphabetical order:
- attribute costing
- benchmarking
- brand valuation

cost leadership
a competitive strategy in which an organization becomes the low-cost producer/provider and is thus able to charge low prices that emphasize cost efficiencies

environmental constraint
any limitation on strategy caused by external cultural, fiscal (such as taxation structures), legal/regulatory, or political situations or by competitive market structures; tends to have long-run rather than short-run effects

- capital budgeting
- competitor cost assessment
- competitive position monitoring
- competitor appraisal based on published financial statements (called competitor performance appraisal)
- customer profitability analysis
- integrated performance measurement
- life cycle costing
- lifetime customer profitability analysis
- quality costing
- strategic costing
- strategic pricing
- target costing
- valuation of customers or customer groups as assets, *and*
- value chain costing[11]

Many of these techniques are covered in this book. The other techniques are covered in more advanced textbooks.

MANAGEMENT ACCOUNTING'S CONTRIBUTION TO THE VALUE CREATION CHAIN

LEARNING OBJECTIVE   4

How does management accounting facilitate the accomplishment of strategy through the value creation chain?

Strategic management involves organizational planning for deployment of resources (such as fixed assets, employees, and working capital) to create value for customers and shareholders. The strategic management of resources is concerned with the following issues:[12]

- how to deploy resources to support strategies
- how resources are used in, or recovered from, change processes
- how customer value and shareholder value will serve as guides to the effective use of resources
- how resources are to be deployed and redeployed over time

These areas cannot be measured by financial accounting because they often relate to nonmonetary information and measurements. Thus, management accounting provides the necessary estimates to help managers address these issues and focus on strategic objectives.

The foundation of the strategic management of resources is the **value creation chain (VCC)**[13] or the set of processes and activities that convert resources into products and services that have value to the organization's customers. The value creation chain includes suppliers, internal processes, and customers. Managers can use the value creation chain to determine which activities create customer value as reflected in product/service prices and thus, revenues earned. By reducing or eliminating activities that do not add value within the value creation chain, organizations can become more efficient and effective. Management accounting provides information to managers on value creation.

For their contributions to the value creation chain, employees are compensated and suppliers earn revenues. Successful organizations will gain the cooperation of everyone in the value creation chain and communicate a perspective that today's competition is more between value creation chains than between individual businesses. Once this concept is accepted, members of the value creation chain become aware that information must be shared among all entities in the chain.

value creation chain
the set of processes and activities that convert inputs into products and services that have value to the organization's customers

Exhibit 1-3 presents a simple model of the VCC. It reflects that organizations can either undertake the activities themselves or, like Dell, outsource to suppliers.

EXHIBIT 1-3
The Value Creation Chain

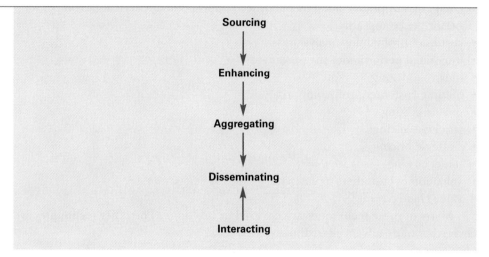

SOURCE: Robert J. Fong and Gary Spraakman, *Fusion: The Creation of Innovation*, Working Paper, School of Administrative Studies, York University 2004.

The VCC in Exhibit 1-3 is premised on the belief that value is created for customers in goods and services by activities. Although organizations are accountable for many activities, Exhibit 1-3 divides those activities into five major categories that apply to an organization conducting all activities itself or largely outsourcing the required activities to create value. The exhibit also recognizes that one set of activities in creating value includes the interaction required from the customer in obtaining the good or service, for example, whether physically or via the Internet. The stages of the VCC are briefly defined.

- **Sourcing:** obtaining raw or crudely produced materials in order to add value at later stages. A dairy or producer of milk must obtain raw milk from farmers.
- **Enhancing:** making basic products from raw materials. The conversion of crude oil into gasoline and other petroleum products is an example of enhancing.
- **Aggregating:** putting together various enhanced products to produce a complex product. An automobile is an example of aggregating, as it is the production result of assembling numerous parts or products. A Dell computer is another example, as the company assembles parts from suppliers into a custom PC for the customer order.
- **Disseminating:** distributing products or services to customers or consumers. Disseminating includes wholesale and retail activities.
- **Interacting:** the only stage conducted by the customer. It is the activities undertaken by the customer in obtaining the good or service being produced by the value creation chain. We drive to a movie theatre and wait in line to see a movie; or we rent a video or DVD to see a movie at home; or, soon, we will download a movie to see it at home.

The VCC can be demonstrated with an automotive assembly operation such as that of General Motors of Canada, which, according to the VCC, operates at the "aggregating" and "disseminating" stages. General Motors' aggregating would consist of assembling cars from parts and subassemblies acquired from suppliers such as Magna International who have "enhanced" or produced parts or subassemblies from raw materials or less processed parts that were obtained by "sourcing" from suppliers of more basic components. Once General Motors has assembled the cars, it must "disseminate" those cars through its dealer network, which interfaces directly with customers, the car buyers. The "interacting" stage comprises the activities that the customers undertake in acquiring a car.

Brand value is the result of value creation and extends beyond physical assets on the balance sheet. Financial accounting in Canada does not capture the development of brand value. However, management must, as it represents part of a company's overall value. The following table lists some U.S. companies with recognizable brands and the basis of value in those brands:[14]

Company	Brand known for ...
Wal-Mart	Always low prices
FedEx	Absolutely, positively, doing whatever it takes
Lexus	Pursuit of perfection
Procter & Gamble	Brands you know and trust
McKinsey	Being a CEO's trusted adviser
Boeing	People working together as a global enterprise for aerospace leadership
Apple	Innovation and design

In contrast to General Motors, Wal-Mart's strategy is focused on the disseminating stage. Explicitly, Wal-Mart has pursued a strategy of fusing product lines such as men's clothing, drugs and toiletries, automotive, food, and so on. It offers customers a wide range of products from its outlets at the lowest possible prices. Wal-Mart influences and exerts control over suppliers at the aggregating and enhancing stages, but it does not perform those activities.

The Canadian company Fish Products International Limited (FPI) provides a vivid example of the importance of examining the value creation chain for strategic opportunities.[15] Similarly, it demonstrates that management accounting must be used to analyze the viability of those anticipated opportunities.

Up to the early 1990s when the Canadian groundfish stocks collapsed, FPI was involved nearly completely with catching fish, the initial sourcing stage, allowing others to conduct the enhancement, aggregation, and dissemination stages. Others were involved with buying fish from FPI and transforming that fish into a product for consumption. With the overfishing of groundfish, FPI's Canadian catch was decimated. FPI faced a decision point: (1) to give up and become bankrupt, or (2) to change and survive. FPI chose to change.

There are various value creation stages with numerous players between the many suppliers of fish and various types of consumers. Briefly, the fish can be wild or farmed. There are also numerous processors who convert raw fish into various stages in preparation for final cooking. Some processors merely deliver the raw fish, in fresh form, to restaurants. Others prepare the fish in various ways, quick-freeze it, and send frozen fish to retailers, restaurants, and institutions.

When deciding to "change and survive," FPI found profitable opportunities to undertake more of the enhancing, aggregating, and disseminating. Also, FPI found that it could buy from others wild and/or farmed fish sources to add value along with its own catch from its fish quotas in Atlantic Canada. Enhancing, aggregating, and disseminating fish required a substantial investment to upgrade and modernize plants, equipment, and vessels. Identified brands and constant innovation are essential. Moreover, to make strategic VCC decisions, substantial management accounting information was needed to ascertain expected revenues, costs, and, most important, profits.

Regardless of their VCC stage or stages, organizations require management accounting information in order to manage their activities. Customer information is necessary to determine which products and services are desired and how many units of each must be produced, and to project demand levels for existing and future products and services. Information on the effectiveness of supplier relationships (e.g., on-time deliveries) is necessary for acquiring the parts, materials, and services needed in producing goods and services that create value for customers.

Managers require management information so they may plan, control, evaluate performance, and make VCC decisions. In planning, managers describe outcomes they hope to achieve in the future. Managers exert control by acting to bring operations into compliance with the plans. Performance is evaluated by measuring actual outcomes against plans, past performance levels, and other performance benchmarks. Managers make decisions in the process of executing plans and controlling operations.

It was noted that a value creation chain is the set of all activities that convert materials into products and services for the final consumer. In this regard, **vertical integration** is a measure of the extent to which the value creation chain resides within a single organization. Organizations that are highly vertically integrated have more in-house links to the value creation chain than links to other firms. Firms with low vertical integration depend on their suppliers or customers to contribute more links to the value creation chain. The very successful Dell has low vertical integration, as it contracts out most activities. One of the most significant choices managers make for their organizations is the role to be played in the value creation chain in which they are located. Many of the headlines in the financial press today relate to value creation chain role decisions. For example, decisions involving **strategic alliances**, restructuring, outsourcing, and mergers are driven by value creation chain considerations. To remain competitive, firms must monitor not only their own costs and quality, but also the operations of suppliers, customers, and competitors.

vertical integration
the extent to which the value creation chain resides within a single firm

strategic alliance
an agreement involving two or more firms with complementary core competencies to contribute jointly to the value creation chain

GENERAL NEWS NOTE

Measuring Shareholder Value

Discounted cash flow (DCF) is a company's preferred method for measuring shareholder value. With the DCF method, a forecast is made of the company's discretionary cash flow for (usually) the next three to seven years. DCF represents the cash that the providers of business capital can readily withdraw without impairing ongoing operations or growth prospects. In simple terms, DCF can be calculated as follows:

Projected earnings before interest and taxes (EBIT)
Less: income taxes
Equals: after-tax income
Add back: depreciation and amortization expenses
Deduct: capital expenditure requirements
Deduct: incremental working capital requirements
Equals: DCF (before financing costs).

The future flows of DCF for three to seven years are then discounted by a discount rate (the company's weighted average cost of capital) to ascertain the present value of those cash flows. Then an estimate is made of the average DCF for all subsequent years beyond the three to seven years; this is then divided by the capitalization rate (reflecting the risk of maintaining DCF at the forecasted level into the future). This terminal value is also discounted. These discounted cash flows are added to get the enterprise value, from which debt is subtracted to equal the value of equity, or shareholder value.

SOURCE: H. Johnson, "Strategies for Shareholder Value Enhancement," *CMA Management,* December–January 2007, pp. 29–32.

RECENT DEVELOPMENTS AND THEIR IMPACT ON MANAGEMENT ACCOUNTING

A discipline such as management accounting evolves over time based on the needs and demands of its users. Its evolution is also influenced by the profession of management accounting or, in other words, the practitioners of management accounting.

The demand for management accounting is being influenced by the needs of its organizational users. With globalization, these organizations are either expanding globally or being affected by global competitors. The global economy encompasses the international trade of goods and services, movement of labour, and flows of capital and information.[16] The world has essentially become smaller through improved modes of communication and transportation as well as trade agreements that promote, rather than hinder, the international movement of goods and services among countries. The overall result is more complexity because of global considerations. Management accounting is being called upon to provide additional information for managers to plan, make decisions, evaluate performance, and control organizations within a complex business environment.

Information Technology

These same globally affected organizations are also influenced by information technology in terms of computerized transaction processing and electronic telecommunication such as that done with the Internet, intranet, and extranet. Management accounting has had to change in order to "fit" within this new context. The first step has been to change from manual and then mainframe accounting systems to **enterprise resource planning** (ERP) systems. ERP systems provide management accounting with accounting information as well as a wide range of processing activities and operational information. ERP systems integrate all information systems, enabling management accounting access to a range of data previously impossible to obtain. The second step, made possible by ERP systems, has been a general shift to manage at the activity level rather than at the more abstract level of financial transactions. This greater level of detail with activities has resulted in increased complexity. Management accounting has its focus on activities, and it can be most effective when it is used with ERP systems to incorporate the activity level for costing and performance measurements. ERP systems allow management accounting to deal with the complexity of global competition with management at the detailed activity level.

enterprise resource planning
a fully integrated, full-service suite of software with a common database that can be used to plan and control resources across an entire organization

The Dell example highlights the new environment for management accounting. Improved differentiation and lower costs must exist together. These apparently conflicting demands must be accomplished. Management accounting practitioners must be constantly on the outlook for improving product or service quality while at the same time reducing costs. Information technology is an integral component of this new environment. The Canadian company Research in Motion is assisting with information technology management.

Brand Values

A topic close to value creation is the value of brands. Customers are willing to pay more for a company's products and services if there is brand value, which is comparable to a guarantee of something special. As noted on page 15, Wal-Mart has brand value because its prices are always low. Similarly, customers are willing to pay more for an Apple laptop because they believe they are acquiring superior innovation and design.

In Canada, the value of the brand created by a company such as RBC is not included in the GAAP-based financial statement. However, the brand value is included in the stock price, and the CEO and board of directors are responsible for preserving and increasing that value, even though it is not included in the financial accounting records. Management accountants make it a concern to record and monitor brand value. How can you record and monitor something that is not included in the financial statements?

Interbrand is a consulting firm that specializes in calculating brand value for major companies. To arrive at brand value, it asks the same question as for any other asset: What amount is it likely to earn for the company?[17] Using analysts' projections, the company's financial statements, and its own quantitative and qualitative research, Interbrand applies a three-step method:

1. It calculates how much of a company's sales relate to the brand and then forecasts the brand's sales and earnings for the next five years.
2. It calculates the proportion of earnings that results from the brand's power. Operating costs, taxes, and charges for capital employed are deducted from brand sales to yield the earnings related to the brand for the same five years.

GENERAL NEWS NOTE

Management Accounting in the 21st Century

According to the INTERNATIONAL FEDERATION OF ACCOUNTANTS (IFAC), changes are happening in the environment in which management accountants serve. The degree of sophistication needed is much greater than it was in the mid-1980s. More opportunities are available for management accountants to advance. For example:

- Information systems have advanced to the point that accounting systems depend heavily on nonfinancial operating systems in order to function. Indeed, ERP systems are highly oriented to management accounting requirements, more so than we have experienced in the past.
- Analytical software now permits data to be gathered, manipulated, projected, and reported in ways that were unimaginable 10 years ago.
- Shareholders' interests have shifted, from prior-period profits to value creation premised on the expected future cash value of inherent advantages.
- More dynamic, externally driven forecasting methods are replacing insensitive and misguided budgets.
- Accounting knowledge is being "decentred" as the financial impact of operational decisions is better understood by non-accountants.
- It is now recognized that managers need to apply better, more quantitative methods in order to simulate various profit scenarios.

Perhaps most important, accountants are recognizing the changes taking place in management accounting. IFAC has changed its definition of management accounting in International Management Accounting Practice Statement (IMAPS) I: "Management Accounting Concepts," since it was first issued in 1988. The revised version (1998) provides management accounting with a rich and complex set of guidelines, the central theme of which is resource utilization.

Paragraph 28 of IMAPS I states: "Management Accounting refers to that part of the management process which is focused on organization resource use. Thus, it refers to managerial processes and technologies that are focused on adding value to organizations by attaining the effective use of resources in dynamic and competitive contexts."

IFAC has a complete definition of management accounting on its website at http://www.ifac.org.

SOURCE: Paul A. Sharman, "The Case for Management Accounting," *Management Accounting*, November–December 2005, pp. 24–27.

3. The brand earnings for the next five years are discounted to the present, using a discount rate that reflects the company's risk profile. The present value of the cash flows for five years is the value of the brand as a financial asset.

At U.S.\$65 billion, Coca-Cola was assessed by Interbrand to have the most valuable brand in the world. Microsoft was second at U.S.\$59 billion.

For a brand to be managed, its value must be calculated. Each year the brand should be valued by an independent and objective specialist. The company should have plans for maintaining and increasing the brand's value. This would include, in the case of Apple, continuing to provide customers with products that are innovative and whose designs break industry norms. In the case of the consulting firm McKinsey, it would need to maintain and even enhance its success at being a trusted adviser to CEOs. These two companies would also need to monitor their performance with regard to those attributes.

It is very important to recognize that brands are developed over years. The long-term value arises from the end customer's willingness to purchase the product or service. Companies must continue to provide extra value. Companies such as Coca-Cola and Microsoft understand that they must make decisions and take actions so as to preserve the long-term value of their brand. There are three reasons why companies might become short-term oriented:

> An abundance of real-time sales data that make short-term promotional effects more apparent, thus pushing [companies] to overdiscount; a corresponding dearth of usable information to help assess the effect of long-term investments in brand equity, new products, and distribution; and the short tenure of brand managers.[18]

Measuring and monitoring brand values is a challenge for management accounting.

Automated data collection tools (ADCs), when added to ERP systems, can raise an organization's management information to a higher level of strategic importance.[19] ADCs are the product barcodes that are read by wireless scanners in order to seamlessly update ERP systems. When data are captured using ADC tools, the work of management accountants changes.

ERP systems have increased the demand for strategic staff and reduced it for clerical staff. Given how transaction processes are connected to ERP systems, users need to understand at least one step before and one step after their own job functions, both inside and outside the ERP system. ERP systems are configured around key business processes outside the system itself, which means that users have to understand these connections and work with them to create an efficient organization.

ADC with ERP systems is a way for a company to leverage its employees. Such systems allow for real-time reporting. Timely and accurate tracking of supplier and customer activities is possible. The rule that there must be a trade-off between the relevance (timeliness) and the reliability (accuracy) of management accounting information is no longer valid. The trade-off no longer exists; you can have both. Management accounting information is now broader than traditional cost accounting. It now provides information about assets, quality/services, time (e.g., cycle times), and outputs.

This new ERP environment produces more information for measuring costs and performance. That information provides opportunities for improving performance. Adeptness at measuring does much to explain the success of Toyota, the world's largest automobile maker.[20]

ethical standards
norms that represent beliefs about moral and immoral behaviours; norms for individual conduct in making decisions and engaging in business transactions

Ethics

More than ever, adherence to ethical standards is required. In contrast to laws, **ethical standards** represent beliefs about moral and immoral behaviours. Because beliefs are inherently personal, some differences in moral perspectives exist among individuals. However, the moral perspective is generally more homogeneous within a given society than it is across societies. In a business context, ethical standards are norms for individual conduct in making decisions and engaging in business transactions.

Managers in global businesses are very aware that legal and ethical standards differ from one country to another. Although, in general, both legal and ethical standards for business conduct are higher in most industrialized and economically developed countries, the standards and their enforcement vary greatly from one industrialized country to another. Therefore, because of varying standards of ethical behaviour and varying international laws, a company should develop internal norms for conduct, such as a code of ethics, to ensure that behaviour is consistent in all of its geographical operating segments.

The code of Ethics for Canadian CMAs is shown in Appendix A. These ethical standards will be considered when doing the "Ethics" questions at the end of each chapter.

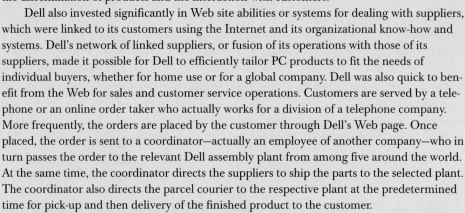

SITE ANALYSIS

Dell Incorporated

In providing management accounting information on business models, it is best to start with an outstanding business model that many other firms are expecting to imitate. Dell has such a business model.

To understand Dell's business model, it is necessary to use the value creation chain (VCC). Dell does not distribute through wholesalers and retailers, and it does not require customers to physically interact. In this way, Dell fuses the interaction and dissemination stages of the VCC by the use of its telephone and Web-based ordering abilities. More specifically, Dell developed the abilities or systems to redefine the dissemination of products and the interaction with customers.

Dell also invested significantly in Web site abilities or systems for dealing with suppliers, which were linked to its customers using the Internet and its organizational know-how and systems. Dell's network of linked suppliers, or fusion of its operations with those of its suppliers, made it possible for Dell to efficiently tailor PC products to fit the needs of individual buyers, whether for home use or for a global company. Dell was also quick to benefit from the Web for sales and customer service operations. Customers are served by a telephone or an online order taker who actually works for a division of a telephone company. More frequently, the orders are placed by the customer through Dell's Web page. Once placed, the order is sent to a coordinator—actually an employee of another company—who in turn passes the order to the relevant Dell assembly plant from among five around the world. At the same time, the coordinator directs the suppliers to ship the parts to the selected plant. The coordinator also directs the parcel courier to the respective plant at the predetermined time for pick-up and then delivery of the finished product to the customer.

Complete fusion at Dell is dependent on low-cost information. Moreover, low-cost information was used by Dell to make its inventories traceable and trackable throughout the entire logistical operations, even with outsourced activities. Every activity is connected (e.g., truck

SITE ANALYSIS

drivers report deliveries by wireless technology). Executing a supply chain with full visibility gives Dell better information to work with and a more flexible system. Dell's customers are able to track their own orders, from assembly and testing to shipment. Moreover, by producing custom products at a rapid pace, Dell receives payments from customers before it pays suppliers. Dell can do this because there is a very short lapsed time between receiving and shipping an order. Fusion has been good for Dell's customers and shareholders.

During its first 20 years Dell singularly focused on selling PCs directly to businesses, consumers, and government agencies, and doing it more cheaply than anyone else. Now with PC market growth slowing, Dell has had to apply its successful business model elsewhere for opportunities to maintain growth and profitability. In addition to desktop and laptop PCs, Dell now has the following products and services:

- servers
- storage
- printing and imaging systems
- workstations
- network products
- software and peripheral products
- professional services
- deployment services
- support services
- training and certification services
- flat-panel TVs and iPod-like portable music players
- online music download service

Dell believes that its low-cost, direct-sales approach will allow it to reduce prices in the printer market, especially for ink cartridges, which can cost as much in a year as the printer itself. Diversification, as with the PC business, calls for developing a strategy that has two purposes: (1) to help customers, and (2) to hurt competitors.

Another example of diversification is storage computers, the complex multi-unit systems that businesses use to store corporate data. In the past, storage hardware was often unique or specially produced. This is the opposite to Dell, which prefers to sell standard products that are often called commoditized as many firms can make them. Dell's entry into the storage market will emphasize commoditized products and lower costs for consumers.

Dell's business model is a significant competitive threat for the new markets being entered. Its business model will set the standards for costs and processes in those markets. Management accountants will need to understand that model in order to advise managers successfully.

SOURCES: "Dell Jacks Into the Digital Hub," *BusinessWeek* online, Special Report: Consumer Electronics, December 9, 2003; Geoffrey Downey, "Dell Adds Services to Enterprise Menu," *Computing Canada*, January 31, 2003, Vol. 29, Issue 2, pp. 1+; Adam Lashinsky, "Where Dell is Going Next: After Eating Everyone's Lunch in the U.S. PC Biz, They're Now Aiming at Printers, Storage—and the World. Is Anyone Scared Yet?" *Fortune*, October 18, 2004, Volume 150, Issue 8, p. 115; Andrew Park, "Dude, You're Getting a Printer," *BusinessWeek*, April 19, 2004, p. 87, www.dell.com.

CHAPTER SUMMARY

1 **What is the definition of management accounting?**

Management accounting is defined as the gathering and application of information used to plan, make decisions, evaluate, and control an organization. Management accountants provide information for managers' planning, controlling, performance evaluation, and decision-making needs. Much broader than management accounting, controls are needed to encourage employees and managers to perform numerous functions including planning, controlling, and decision making. Control includes, but is much broader than, management accounting. Controls are needed to encourage employees and managers to perform appropriate actions and to discourage inappropriate actions. There are three approaches or alternatives to influence the behaviour of employees and managers—actions, results, and personnel.

2 **How does management accounting form part of the management control system?**
Management accounting uses certain types of information to control organizations. Management accounting is only one of numerous alternatives for controlling organizations and is used as organizations become complex because of large-scale operations or uncertainty. The greater the complexity, the more developed will be the management accounting. Simpler organizations can be operated satisfactorily with only financial accounting and managers' general understanding of operations. With greater complexity, there is a need for management accounting to assist managers in understanding operations.

3 **What is strategy and what is the role of management accounting in strategy?**
Strategy should be based on a mission statement that indicates what the organization wants to accomplish. Goals and objectives should flow from that statement. Strategy options may be constrained by internal or external factors. Organizational structure indicates the distribution of authority and responsibility in the entity. Core competencies indicate the organization's internal strengths and capabilities and, thus, help select appropriate business functions to do internally or to outsource. Management style and organizational culture provide a foundation for normal business practices and protocol for interactions among employees, customers, and suppliers.

4 **How does management accounting facilitate the accomplishment of strategy through the value creation chain?**
Management practices today are increasingly recognizing the need to develop systems for managing costs and activities through the value creation chain. The value creation chain consists of all processes both internal and external to the firm. The external processes are provided by vendors, and possibly customers. The more a firm relies on suppliers, the greater is the need to have systems in place to manage the costs and activities of its vendors.

5 **What is new with management accounting?**
Information technology in the form of enterprise resource planning (ERP) systems and other systems for dealing with suppliers and customers can greatly enhance the ability of managers. Management accounting, as part of ERP systems, can be much more valuable in assisting with the management of complex and global organizations.

Key Terms

Activities (p. 8)

Authority (p. 11)

Business model (p. 9)

Control (p. 8)

Core competency (p. 11)

Cost accounting (p. 7)

Cost leadership (p. 12)

Differentiation (p. 11)

Enterprise resource planning (p. 17)

Environmental constraint (p. 12)

Ethical standards (p. 20)

Financial accounting (p. 6)

Goal (p. 10)

Management accounting (p. 5)

Objective (p. 10)

Organizational culture (p. 9)

Organizational structure (p. 10)

Responsibility (p. 11)

Strategic alliance (p. 16)

Strategy (p. 9)

Value creation chain (p. 13)

Vertical integration (p. 16)

End-of-Chapter Materials

SELF-TEST QUESTIONS

(SOLUTIONS APPEAR AT THE END OF THE CHAPTER.)

1. Which of the following does the definition of management accounting not include?
   a. Planning
   b. Making decisions
   c. Ordering inventory
   d. Controlling

2. All of the following except one is an object of control. Which is not an object of control?
   a. Specific actions
   b. Profits
   c. Results
   d. Personnel

3. The value creation chain consists of:
   a. Activities
   b. Dollars
   c. Assets
   d. Liabilities

4. Information can be either financial or nonfinancial. Both financial and nonfinancial information can also be internal or external. Which of the following possible combinations of information has historically been the focus of management accounting systems?
   a. Nonfinancial and external information
   b. Financial and external information
   c. Financial and internal information
   d. Nonfinancial and internal information

   Extract from *Management Accounting 2 Examination*, published by the Certified General Accountants Association of Canada (© CGA-Canada, 2000). Reprinted with permission.

5. Which of the following does *not* describe managerial accounting?
   a. It draws heavily upon other disciplines.
   b. It emphasizes the segments of an organization rather than just looking at the organization as a whole.
   c. It is optional.
   d. It is governed by generally accepted accounting principles.

   Extract from *Management Accounting 1 Examination*, published by the Certified General Accountants Association of Canada (© CGA-Canada, 1999). Reprinted with permission.

6. What is not new in management accounting?
   a. Enterprise resource planning systems
   b. Globalization
   c. Public confidence
   d. Controls

7. What is common with both management and financial accounting?
   a. An enterprise resource planning system
   b. Cost accounting
   c. Controls
   d. Strategy

8. What is not a control?
   a. An accounting report
   b. An expectation
   c. A reporting relationship
   d. A calculator

9. Which of the following does not relate to the major thrust of management accounting?
   a. Internal   c. Timely
   b. Historical   d. Flexible

10. Strategy is primarily concerned with
    a. Creating value
    b. Expansion
    c. Customers
    d. Employees

QUESTIONS

1. What is the role of information in decision making?

2. Why would operating in a global (rather than a strictly domestic) marketplace create a need for additional information? Discuss some of the additional information you think managers would need and why such information would be valuable.

3. Discuss the validity of the following statement: "Only large companies (such as those that are publicly held and listed on a major stock exchange) have the opportunity to operate in a global marketplace."

4. Why is an effective management information system a key element of an effective management control system?

5. Why do managers require both internal and external information to manage effectively?

6. Why would an organization have multiple control systems in place?

7. Why is cost control different from cost minimization?

8. How is managerial accounting related to financial accounting? to cost accounting?

QUESTIONS

9. Why is the choice of organizational structure a cost management decision?

10. Why is a mission statement important to an organization?

11. What is organizational strategy? Why would each organization have a unique strategy or set of strategies?

12. Distinguish between goals and objectives. What goals do you hope to achieve by taking this course? What objectives can you establish to measure the degree to which you achieve these stated goals?

13. Differentiate between authority and responsibility. Can you have one without the other? Explain.

14. What is a core competency and how do core competencies impact the feasible set of alternative organizational strategies?

15. Define each of the two generic strategies an organization may pursue, and discuss the attributes of each type of strategy.

16. Define and differentiate among the primary management functions. Provide several examples of instances in which a manager would need different information in order to perform these functions.

17. Are the financial implications of strategic planning more important in a business than in a not-for-profit organization? Why or why not?

18. "Most organizations determine product or service price by adding a reasonable profit margin to costs incurred." Is this statement true or false? Provide a rationale for your answer.

19. What is the value creation chain of an organization and how does it interface with strategic resource management?

20. Why is it especially necessary to achieve a balance between short-term and long-term considerations in today's business environment?

21. Changes in organizational environment have emphasized ethical considerations.
    Required:
    a. When discussing the role of ethics, an individual can consider a proposed rule from at least *two* perspectives. Identify and describe these *two* perspectives.
    b. Why should accountants be concerned about ethical issues?

    Extract from *Management Accounting 2 Examination*, published by the Certified General Accountants Association of Canada (© CGA-Canada, 2000). Reprinted with permission.

22. Strategic alliances are popular today for exploiting new market opportunities. What are strategic alliances and why are managers using this organizational structure so frequently today?

23. How does the exchange of information by firms in a value creation chain increase the opportunities for the value creation chain to become more competitive?

EXERCISES

1. (LO 1) The following words and phrases describe or are associated with either financial or managerial accounting. Indicate for each item whether it is more closely associated with financial (F) or management (M) accounting.

a.	Verifiable	h.	Focus is on organizational segments
b.	Largely historical	i.	Cost/benefit analysis
c.	Relevant	j.	Focus is on serving external users
d.	Internally focused	k.	Emphasis is on timeliness
e.	*CICA Handbook*	l.	Emphasis is on consistency
f.	Forecasted	m.	Largely future oriented
g.	Formal	n.	Flexible

2. (LO 3) Match the following lettered items with the appropriate numbered description.

a.	Authority	1.	A target expressed in quantitative terms
b.	Core competency		
c.	Goal	2.	The right to use resources to accomplish something
d.	Objective		

EXERCISES

e. Responsibility
f. Decision making
g. Effectiveness
h. Planning
i. Efficiency

3. A process that an organization does better than other organizations
4. A process of choosing among alternatives
5. A desired result, expressed qualitatively
6. The obligation to accomplish something
7. A measure of success of an endeavour
8. The process of determining long-term and short-term strategy
9. A measure of output achieved relative to resources consumed

3. (LO 3) Match the following lettered items with the appropriate numbered description.

a. Strategy
b. Value creation chain
c. Organizational culture
d. Cost leadership
e. Differentiation
f. Organizational structure

1. Basic assumptions about an organization, its goals, and its practices
2. A long-term plan related to organizational goals and objectives
3. The way in which authority and responsibility are distributed in an organization
4. The attribute of being the low-cost producer or service provider
5. The processes of an organization and its suppliers to convert inputs into products and services
6. The attribute of avoiding competition by distinguishing a product or service from that of competitors

4. (LO 3) Obtain a copy of your university or college's mission statement. Draft a mission statement for this class that supports the school's mission statement.
   a. How does your mission statement reflect the goals and objectives of the school's mission statement?
   b. How can you measure the successful accomplishment of your objectives?
   c. Is there a difference between the effective and the efficient accomplishment of your objectives? Provide the rationale for your answer.

5. (LO 3) Early this year, you started a house-cleaning service and now have 20 customers. Because of other obligations (including classes), you have had to hire three employees.
   a. What types of business activities would you allow these employees to handle and why?
   b. What types of business activities would you keep for yourself and why?

6. (LO 3) As part of a team, make a list of the core competencies of your university or college and explain why you believe these items to be core competencies. Make an appointment with a professor and, without sharing your list, ask what he or she believes the core competencies are and why. Prepare a written report contrasting the two lists, and explain the basis of the differences.

7. (LO 4) You are the manager of an exclusive jewellery store that sells primarily on credit. The majority of your customers use the store's credit card rather than a bank or other major credit card.
   a. What would you consider to be the primary benefits of outsourcing the store's accounts collection function?
   b. What would you consider to be the primary risks of outsourcing the store's accounts collection function?

8. (LO 3) Choose a company that might utilize each of the following strategies relative to its competitors and discuss the benefits that might be realized from that strategy.
   a. Differentiation
   b. Cost leadership

9. (LO 3) You are the manager of the local store. Make a list of 10 factors that you believe to be critical to your organization. How would each of your key variables affect your strategic planning?

EXERCISES

10. (LO 3) You are the manager of a small restaurant in your hometown.
    a. What information would you want to have in making the decision whether to add chicken fajitas and Boston clam chowder to your menu?
    b. Why would each of the above information items be significant?

11. (LO 5) The 2007 annual report of Calgary Oil Company (headquartered in Calgary) was slightly untraditional in that the opening "letter" to shareholders was given not only in English but also in German, French, Spanish, Japanese, and Chinese.
    a. Discuss the costs and benefits to a Canadian-based company in taking the time to provide such translations.
    b. What additional information would you want to have to assess how such translations are related to Calgary Oil's strategic plans?

12. (LO 2) As the marketing manager for a small copying company, you have requested that your boss purchase a new high-speed, colour copier that collates up to 50 sets of copies. The current colour copier operates at approximately one-third the speed of the new one and only collates 25 sets of copies.
    a. How might you present the costs and benefits of this purchase to your boss?
    b. What additional information might you request from the marketing manager if you were the accounting or finance manager?

13. (LO 3) In their annual reports, companies provide brief descriptions of their most important contracts. These descriptions include strategic alliances. Select a large, publicly traded company and obtain a copy of its most recent annual report. Review the portions of the annual report that discuss strategic alliances. (Annual reports can be found on the Internet at www.sedar.com.)
    Required:
    Based on your review, prepare an oral report in which you discuss the following points.
    a. Motivations for establishing strategic alliances
    b. The extent to which strategic alliances are used to conduct business
    c. The relative financial success of the strategic alliances

14. (LO 4) Following are descriptions of four companies. Based on the descriptions given, discuss the relative extent to which each company might benefit from conducting value creation chain cost analysis as a tool to become more cost competitive.
    a. Car dealer. This firm is a typical Ford dealership that handles the entire Ford/Mercury/Lincoln product line.
    b. Small manufacturing company. This small company manufactures ceramic lawn furniture that is sold through a wholesaling firm to lawn and garden retail stores.
    c. Large manufacturer of paper products. This firm makes hundreds of household and commercial products from a variety of stock and custom inputs.
    d. Large personal computer company. This firm manufactures no components; instead, it purchases all required components in large volume. The components are custom-assembled into products sold to mail-order customers. The firm competes principally on the basis of price.

15. (LO 5) Why are there changes in the environment in which management accountants work?

16. (LO 4) Consider the management accounting course you are now taking. You have your activities for the course. The instructor and other members of the college or university also have their activities. Specify and describe the activities of the instructor and other members of the college or university for your management accounting course.

17. (LO 4) The value creation chain applies to retail firms, such as Wal-Mart and the Hudson's Bay Company. For a retail firm of your choice, specify its value creation chain. Also, specify with the value creation chain a merger of the retail firm with another retail firm that has a different product line.

18. (LO4) In recent decades, the North American automotive industry has increasingly contracted out work to parts suppliers. For example, GM and Ford have continued to assemble cars and trucks while increasingly depending on such firms as Magna to make the parts and components. Show these two conditions at GM and Ford with the use of the value creation chain.

19. (LO 4) Use the value creation chain to explain Dell's business model for PCs. Dell's value creation chain has a very different shape.

20. (LO 4) Why do management accountants have a code of ethics?

EXERCISES

21. (LO 3) You have owned Lee Construction for 15 years and employ 100 people. Business has been profitable, but you are concerned that the locale in which your business is based may soon experience a downturn in growth. As one way to help prepare for such an event, you have decided to engage in a higher level of strategic planning, beginning with a mission statement for your company.
    a.   How does a mission statement add strength to the strategic planning process?
    b.   Who should be involved in developing a mission statement and why?
    c.   What factors should be considered in the development of a mission statement? Why are these factors important?
    d.   Prepare a mission statement for Lee Construction and discuss how your mission statement will provide benefits to tactical as well as strategic planning.

22. (LO 3) Successful business organizations appear to be those that have clearly defined long-range goals and a well-planned strategy for reaching those goals. These successful organizations understand their markets as well as their internal strengths and weaknesses, and take advantage of this knowledge to grow, through internal development or acquisitions, in a consistent and disciplined manner.
    a.   Discuss business organizations' need for long-range goals.
    b.   Discuss how long-range goals are set.
    c.   Define the concepts of strategic planning and management control. Discuss how they relate to each other and contribute to progress toward the attainment of long-range goals.

    (CMA adapted)

23. (LO 3) Four common organizational constraints involve monetary capital, intellectual capital, technology, and organizational structure. Additionally, the environment in which the organization operates may present one or more types of constraints (cultural, fiscal, legal/regulatory, or political).
    Required:
    a.   Discuss whether each of these constraints might or might not be influential in the following types of organizations:
        i.   City Hall in a major metropolitan city
        ii.   A franchised quick-copy business
        iii. A newly opened firm of lawyers, all of whom recently graduated from law school
        iv.   An international oil exploration and production company
        Explain the rationale for each of your answers.
    b.   For each of the previously listed organizations, discuss your perceptions of which of the constraints would be most critical and why.
    c.   For each of the previously listed organizations, discuss your perceptions of whether human or structural capital would be most important and why.

24. (LO 3) Canada provides an ethnically, racially, and culturally diverse workplace. It has been argued that this plurality may be a competitive handicap for Canadian businesses. For example, communicating may be difficult because some workers do not speak English; motivating workers may be complicated because workers have diverse work ethics; and work scheduling may be difficult because of differing religions and ethnic holidays. Conversely, it has been argued that Japan has a competitive advantage because its population is much more homogeneous.
    Required:
    a.   What are the advantages of a pluralistic society in the global marketplace?
    b.   On balance, does Canada's plurality give it a competitive advantage or place it at a competitive disadvantage? Discuss.

25. (LO 3) You have recently come into a very large inheritance and have decided to buy an existing business or open a new one. Given your interests, you have narrowed your choices to the following:
    • Purchase the existing cable company in your regional area
    • Purchase an airline that operates in most areas of the country
    • Open a plant to manufacture and sell hot sauce domestically and in Central and South America
    • Buy franchises for and open 15 locations of a fast-food restaurant in areas of the former Soviet Union
    Required:
    a.   Discuss the competitive influences that will affect each of your potential businesses.

b. How would product/service differentiation or cost leadership work in each of your potential businesses?

c. Which business would you open and why?

26. (LO 4) Strategic alliances are important parts of the value creation chain. In many organizations, suppliers are beginning to provide more and more input into customer activities. For example, in 1997 Chrysler announced that supplier ideas were expected to result in approximately $325 million in cost savings and, thus, increased profits.

a. In Canada, when would a strategic alliance be considered illegal?

b. What would you perceive to be the primary reasons for pursuing a strategic alliance?

c. You are the manager of a catalogue company that sells flowers and plants. With whom would you want to establish strategic alliances? What issues might you want to specify prior to engaging in the alliance?

CASES

1. This is your first summer after taking introductory management accounting but your third summer working for Aabo Lawn Grass Installation. You have always enjoyed the money and getting into good physical condition, but you have become more critical about how Aabo is managed. You reflect on the management of Aabo.

Mr. Aabo started the company 35 years ago. He worked as an ice maker for the NHL arena during the winter, and he needed something for the non-hockey months. Lawn installation provided him with a good living, allowing him to provide for a family of four children. All of his daughters and sons worked for the company in the past. Now only one son is employed, but there must be six or more grandchildren, and even more relatives. Mr. Aabo just died. His son, Bob Aabo, has just started running the firm.

The business is lawn grass installation, which mainly involves laying sod for tracts of new homes. Builders contact lawn grass installers such as Aabo. The request for bids is accompanied by plans of the physical layout of the housing tracts, with detailed specifications for the square metres of grass required. Each job has a range of days for laying the grass, usually five days. However, the required time is usually two days. Bob bids for these jobs, and if his bids are accepted, the grass is purchased, the crew is hired, and the grass is laid.

The average job is for 60,000 metres of grass or sod. There are, on average, 120 jobs in a summer. Each labourer can lay 200 metres per hour. A supervisor is needed for each group of eight to 10 labourers. The grass must be ordered eight or more working days prior to when it is actually needed.

There have been some problems this year. For some jobs, the grass was laid late, to the great dissatisfaction of clients. One job was lost because the grass was not laid as per the schedule. For some jobs, not enough labourers were hired; for other jobs, too many labourers were hired. For two jobs, the crew was ready to go, but the grass had not been ordered.

Mr. Aabo had been able to ensure that the jobs were done properly, on schedule, and to the satisfaction of clients. Bob has been asking you how his father was so successful.

Required:

Using the case approach, advise Bob.

2. Your family has been in the hotel business for more than a century. Your ancestors followed the Canadian Pacific Railway west in 1885 to start one of Calgary's first hotels. From that one hotel the family business grew gradually, or, as it is said by family members, "two steps forward and one step back." The first hotel was relocated and expanded three times over its first 30 years. Later, over the next 15 years, the family business pursued growth by developing hotels in seven other prairie cities. In the 1930s, instead of expanding, two of the hotels were closed and these properties were sold. In 1948 three hotels were bought in British Columbia. A hotel was built in Toronto in 1952, but it was a cash drain and not profitable until 1965. Then, with a change in management, 13 hotels were purchased or built between 1967 and 1980. The recession of the early 1980s put a brake on growth. Fortunately, the family business had not been heavily in debt. Only five of the hotels were sold.

There were 18 hotels in the family chain, Best Canadian Hotels, in 1985 when your uncle became the CEO. In 1988 he acquired a chain of Ontario and Quebec hotels with about 75 percent of the number of rooms that your family's hotel business had at the time. This acquisition added 13 hotels and also got your family into the resort business. Previously the hotels had catered to business travellers, but with the resort hotels, vacation travellers were now also being pursued.

CASES

Maintaining family control had always been important. Only family members held shares. To finance the 1988 acquisition, bank loans had to be obtained, and as interest rates increased in the late 1980s, interest costs became unbearable. At the same time, the recession of 1989 to 1991 reduced revenues. Profits became negative, and to survive, seven hotels had to be sacrificed. Twenty-four hotels remained by 1991, and that number has only increased by one since then.

The focus over the past decade has been on developing better hotels rather than owning more hotels. There are plans to expand, but first, your uncle wants to create successful hotels that provide superior returns to shareholders and to all other stakeholders. He has asked you for help.

You start by asking your uncle about the general managers at the hotels. He tells you that the approach has been to place a "good" person on profit sharing and let that person sink or swim. Usually that has meant family members, who have varied greatly in their management abilities. A few family members have been great managers, but even they have not been outstanding for their entire tenure. Most members have been mediocre or downright poor managers.

In interviewing existing and former guests, you find that the repeat rate is less than for comparable hotels. You ask why. These people over and over again have said that they are not completely happy with the service. They have not complained about the room or food prices.

You then ask your uncle why the hotels cannot provide the guests with a higher level of satisfaction. You also ask two other uncles, three cousins, and a grandfather to explain the dissatisfaction of guests. They are nearly unanimous in saying that the problem is with guests' unrealistic demands. To this, you reply that guests rate their experiences with competitive hotels higher than with Best Canadian Hotels and Resorts.

To get a better understanding of guest satisfaction, you work for a summer in two of the Toronto hotels, doing nearly all of the entry-level jobs at one time or another. Within a month you realize that only a handful of tasks need to be done correctly in order to satisfy customers. For example, there is a set of tasks that need to be done correctly when cleaning rooms. Also, there is a set of tasks for correctly checking guests into their rooms. Similarly, there are predetermined tasks for ensuring that the hotel has been subject to appropriate maintenance. Based on these insights, you conclude that guest satisfaction will come from determining the proper procedures and then carrying those procedures out.

You again meet with your two other uncles, three cousins, and grandfather to explain how to increase customer satisfaction. You tell each of them that guest satisfaction will come from determining the proper procedures for all tasks and then carrying out those tasks according to the procedures.

The reaction from all of them is the same: according to them, the employees are so new to their jobs that they have not learned the proper procedures. By the time they have learned the proper procedures, they have moved on to higher paying jobs elsewhere.

You go back to your uncle to explain what you have learned. He tells you that the turnover rate for Best Canadian Hotels and Resorts is 120 percent per year, which is about double the average among competing hotels. Your uncle says he is aware of the problem with inexperienced employees and that ten years ago he introduced two weeks of mandatory training for all new employees, which was double the industry rate.
Required:
Using the case approach, undertake the assignment given to you by your uncle.

3. Deep Sleep, an income trust, is one of the two leading retailers of mattresses in Canada and is the number one retailer of mattresses in the three provinces in which it operates. Deep Sleep believes that it commands a 16% national market share and an average regional market share of approximately 40% across the six regional markets it serves. Since 1999, sales have grown at a compound annual growth rate of 33% and, since 2000, earnings before interest expense, income taxes, depreciation, and amortization (EBITDA) have grown at 39%. In 2007, Deep Sleep generated $151.3 million in sales and $19.4 million in EBITDA. Mattress sets accounted for 94% of the company's sales in 2007. The remaining 6% of the company's sales were generated from third-party warranty protection products and a limited assortment of headboards, footboards, pillows, mattress pads, bed frames, and sheets. The company has been able to fund this historic growth from internal cash flow due to the low capital expenditure requirements of its business model, new stores' quickly contributing positive cash flow, and the company's ability to generate cash from working capital as its business grows.

CASES

The North American mattress industry is characterized by stable long-term growth and recession-resistant demand. Deep Sleep estimates that the mattress industry has exhibited a long-term growth rate of approximately 5% to 6% in both Canada and the United States. The company believes that the North American retail mattress industry has exhibited stable growth characteristics for the following reasons:
- Mattresses are a necessity rather than a fashion purchase
- Customers typically replace their mattresses every 11 to 12 years
- Increased unit demand is driven by steady long-term demographic trends
- Prices have been increasing at a rate consistent with inflation
- Consumer demand is evolving towards larger and better quality products

Deep Sleep has successfully capitalized on a substantial market opportunity to create a specialty retailer focused exclusively on mattresses and designed to provide a high level of customer service throughout the purchase and delivery experience. This focus has resulted in a number of competitive advantages that the company believes make its performance sustainable and provide the platform for future growth.

Deep Sleep is the number one retailer of mattresses in all of the regional markets it serves, as illustrated by the table below. Deep Sleep believes that this regional scale creates economic advantages that have allowed the company to continually strengthen its competitive position and to generate increased cash flow.

	Market Share	Market Standing
BC Lower Mainland/Vancouver Island	45%	#1
Greater Toronto Area	35%	#1
Southwestern Ontario	43%	#1
Calgary	56%	#1
Edmonton	38%	#1
Ottawa	27%	#1

Regional market share is particularly critical to operating successfully in the mattress retailing industry in Canada. The retail mattress industry is characterized by the existence of substantial regional fixed costs (advertising, management and distribution), which are independent of the number of stores in a particular region. Deep Sleep believes its strategy of becoming a regional market leader with multiple stores brings regional fixed costs to an effective level on a per-store basis, which allows the company to invest in creating competitive advantages.

The company invests significantly in advertising and brand development to create "top of mind" brand awareness. Through a combination of radio and television advertising—which features the company's trademark, "Your Mattress Professional"—Deep Sleep strives to convey that it is a trustworthy, enjoyable place to purchase a mattress. As well, the company prominently positions the Sealy, Serta, and Simmons brands in its advertising to build on the strength and popularity of these brands, and to take advantage of supplier advertising arrangements.

The company believes that it distinguishes itself by creating a superior in-store experience that generates a high rate of sales, repeat sales, positive word-of-mouth advertising and low staff turnover. This in-store experience is anchored in five operational pillars:
- *Convenient and highly visible locations.* The company has strategically located stores in each of its existing regional markets close to residential areas, in high-traffic, highly visible locations with prominent signage and convenient access.
- *Effective salesforce.* Deep Sleep provides knowledgeable, friendly, and helpful salespeople (not pushy or intrusive) to assist customers in choosing the right product at the best value. Deep Sleep's employees participate in a comprehensive training program that is focused on exceeding customer expectations through a low pressure, informative sales approach. Deep Sleep currently experiences less than 5% annual salesforce turnover, which is substantially lower than many retail salesforces, thereby allowing Deep Sleep to consistently offer a high level of experienced service.
- *Enterprisewide IT system.* Deep Sleep has a real-time, enterprisewide inventory management system that enables the salesforce to assess the available inventory and arrange optimal delivery times for customers.
- *Differentiated, multi-vendor product mix.* The company offers a wide variety of the best mattress sets available, including several models that are exclusive to Deep Sleep, to

ensure that customers have a large selection of mattresses to choose from at each price point.
- *Customer-oriented policies.* Deep Sleep strives to take the worry out of the customer's purchase decision. Deep Sleep offers 60-day price and "comfort" guarantees and convenient payment methods and terms.

Deep Sleep believes that its approach to home delivery and ongoing customer relationships is a significant differentiation for the customer. Deep Sleep offers free delivery seven days a week, delivering within a specified three-hour time frame. The company recruits people with positive attitudes and then teaches them critical customer service and delivery skills. Delivery personnel are uniformed, wear "booties" over their shoes to protect the customer's home, and are trained to be very courteous. New mattresses are set up and old mattresses are removed without charge; the old mattresses that are in good condition are then offered for re-use to charities. In addition to the delivery force, Deep Sleep maintains a well-trained in-house customer service department and a complete enterprisewide IT system to support the inventory and delivery logistics. This system allows the company to manage its distribution centres and optimize delivery routes, ensuring customers get the right mattress at the right time. Based on an analysis of customer response cards, 98% of responding customers would recommend Deep Sleep to their friends and family.

The company's overall size, regional market leadership, and approach to vendor relations result in strong relationships with its leading suppliers (Sealy, Serta, and Simmons) that yield many advantages. These advantages include better product cost than most of its smaller competitors, and the ability of the company to obtain unique product features and high service levels from suppliers.

Since its inception, Deep Sleep has grown to become a leader in the retail mattress industry in Canada. It has developed a leading regional market strategy, a strong brand, a reputation for excellence in customer service, and favourable supplier relationships. Now that this infrastructure has been established, Deep Sleep believes that it is well positioned to take advantage of the positive trends in the Canadian retail mattress industry to continue to grow revenue and cash flow in a low capital expenditure environment. Deep Sleep intends to build on its leading market position and enhance distributions by continuing to grow comparable store sales, adding new stores in existing markets, and evaluating expansion opportunities beyond the six regional markets in the three provinces it currently serves. The company also plans to eventually expand into the U.S. market.

The business model has been relatively successful in entering new markets. Senior management wants to expand at a more rapid rate, but that would be dependent on a higher level of profitability. Various methods for improving profitability have been considered. Presently, Deep Sleep senior management has requested three courier companies to provide proposals for delivering mattresses. It is recognized that delivery is important for customer experience, but at about $115 per mattress for 300,000 mattresses sold in 2007, delivery costs are sizable. Of the total delivery costs, about $4 million comes from General and Administrative Expenses while the remainder is contained in Cost of Sales.

Delivery involves all costs to bring the mattresses from the manufacturers to regional warehouses and then to the stores and customer homes. The trips from manufacturers are done by various trucking firms, whereas shipments from warehouses to customers are done by Deep Sleep's own trucks and drivers. The costs of operating regional warehouses is also included in the $115 cost per mattress.

All three courier companies have said they will bid on this delivery contract. To date, only one firm has submitted a proposal, which is for a 10-year contract under which the courier company would charge an average cost of $65 per mattress, with a guarantee of three-day delivery, seven days a week. Deep Sleep would need to terminate employees and acquire special software for arranging delivery, etc., for a total cost of about $1 million.

Required:
As Deep Sleep's assistant controller, prepare a report using the case approach that analyzes the advantages and disadvantages of this proposal from both quantitative and qualitative perspectives. Be sure to include the impact of this proposal on Deep Sleep's value creation chain. In addition, specify the conditions to be followed by the courier company if it were to be awarded the 10-year contract in order to maintain Deep Sleep's favourable customer relationship.

Consolidated Statements of Operations and Deficits
Year Ending December 31
($000s)

	2007	2006	2005
Sales	151,348	127,041	112,883
Cost of sales*	107,037	90,320	77,713
Gross profit	44,311	36,721	35,170
Gross profit as a percent of sales	29.3%	28.9%	31.2%
General and administrative expenses	24,945	20,790	19,156
EBITDA**	19,366	15,931	16,014
EBITDA as a percent of sales	12.8%	12.5%	14.2%
Net income (loss) for the year	303	(4,194)	(3,585)
Consolidated Balance Sheet			
Current assets	20,650	14,658	16,357
Goodwill***	80,587	80,587	85,064
Fixed and other assets	12,060	11,035	10,913
Total assets	113,297	106,280	112,334
Current liabilities	26,227	20,329	18,749
Deferred lease inducement	2,415	1,493	1,141
Interest payable on long-term debt	13,564	13,990	14,285
Long-term debt	61,180	61,859	69,247
	103,386	97,671	101,140
Shareholders' equity (deficiency)			
Capital stock	17,608	16,609	15,000
Deficit	(7,697)	(8,000)	(3,806)
	9,911	8,609	11,194
	113,297	106,280	112,334

* Includes operating lease costs.

** EBITDA are earnings before interest expense, income taxes, depreciation, and amortization. EBITDA is a metric used by many investors to compare companies on the basis of ability to generate cash from operations. EBITDA is not a recognized measure under Canadian generally accepted accounting principles (GAAP) and is not intended to be representative of cash flow or results of operations determined in accordance with GAAP or cash available for distribution. Deep Sleep believes that EBITDA is a better measure from which to make adjustments to determine the distributable cash.

*** Effective January 1, 2005, adopted the new provision of *CICA Handbook*, Section 3062, "Goodwill and Other Intangible Assets." In accordance with the requirements of Section 3062, this change in accounting policy has been applied prospectively.

SOURCE: Sleep Country, Initial Public Offering, April 2003, with numerous changes.

ETHICS

1. You are the management accountant for the Trenday's consumer products group, which has six manufacturing divisions. You report to the group vice president. A major part of your job involves analyzing the financial performance of each of the divisions and then reporting those results to the group vice president. A particularly important part of your job is to examine the entertainment expenses of general managers of those six manufacturing divisions.

   Your partner's father is one of the general mangers who reports to the group vice president. What should you do? Why?

2. As the controller for a major retailer, you allow one of the suppliers to take you to lunch at an expensive restaurant. Years ago, this supplier was in some of your undergraduate accounting classes. You were friends but not close friends. Because of these lunches, she has a tendency to call you to discuss when her company will be paid and to ask whether the cheque could be processed earlier than the regular policy. You instruct your accounts payable staff to pay vendors in 30 days, but your friend is requesting payment in 20 or even fewer days.

   What should you do? Why?

ETHICS

3. You work for a medium-sized consulting firm as a management accountant. Your area of expertise is all areas of management and strategy, especially the planning and implementing of strategically appropriate management accounting systems. A partner in your firm has included you in a proposal, but to your surprise he had added to your credentials: "ERP expert with seven successful implementations." These added credentials are entirely false.

   What should you do? Why?

   Alter the scenario. Consider that you did not learn of the erroneous inclusion until after the proposal had been accepted by the client. What should you do? Why?

SOLUTIONS TO SELF-TEST QUESTIONS

1. c, 2. b, 3. a, 4. c, 5. d, 6. d, 7. b, 8. d, 9. b, 10. a.

ENDNOTES

1. "Value creation chain" will be used instead of the more common "value chain" to emphasize that processes and activities must create value.

2. Kenneth A. Merchant, "The Control Function of Management," *Sloan Management Review,* Summer 1982, pp. 43–55.

3. Richard Normann and Rafael Ramirez, "From Value Chain to Value Constellation: Designing Interactive Strategy," *Harvard Business Review,* July–August 1993, p. 65.

4. Thomas S. Bateman and Scott A. Snell, *Management: Building Competitive Advantage,* Chicago: Irwin, 1996, p. 117.

5. Richard Koch, *The Financial Times Guide to Management and Finance,* London: Financial Times/Pitman Publishing, 1994, p. 39.

6. Alfred D. Chandler, Jr., *Strategy and Structure,* Boston: MIT Press, 1962.

7. Associated Press, "100 Different Ads, Most Running Only Once, Is Coke's Plan," *New Orleans Times–Picayune,* July 16, 1996, p. C2.

8. Peter F. Drucker, "The Information Executives Truly Need," *Harvard Business Review,* January–February 1995, p. 60.

9. Michael Porter, *Competitive Advantage: Creating and Sustaining Superior Performance,* New York: Free Press, 1985, p. 17.

10. Richard J. Palmer, "Strategic Goals and Objectives and the Design of Strategic Management Accounting," *Advances in Management Accounting,* Vol. 1, 1992, p. 187.

11. Simon Cadez, "A Cross-Industry Comparison of Strategic Management Accounting Practices: An Exploratory Study," *Economic and Business Review* 3 (2006): 279–98.

12. W.P. Birkett, "Management Accounting and Knowledge Management," *Management Accounting,* November 1995, pp. 44–48.

13. The value creation chain is also known as the value chain.

14. Dave Ulrich and Norm Smallwood, "Building a Leadership Brand," Harvard Business Review, July–August 2007, pp. 93–100.

15. Derrick Rowe, Canadian Aquaculture Industry Alliance Summit, Ottawa, Ontario, March 23, 2005; www.fpil.com; Mr. Rowe is the CEO of Fish Products International Limited.

16. Paul Krugman, *Peddling Prosperity,* quoted by Alan Farnham in "Global—or Just Globaloney," *Fortune,* June 27, 1994, p. 98,

17. David Kiley "The 100 top brands," *Business Week,* August 6, 2007, pp. 59–64.

18. Leonard M. Lodish and Carl F. Mela, "If Brands Are Built over Years, Why Are They Managed over Quarters?" *Harvard Business Review,* July–August 2007, pp. 104–12.

19. Rod Rego, "Strategic Application," CMA Management, December–January 2007, pp. 19–21.

20. Katsuaki Watanabe, "Lesson from Toyota's Long Drive," *Harvard Business Review,* July–August 2007, pp. 74–83.

Chapter 2

Cost Terminology and Cost Flows

LEARNING OBJECTIVES

After reading this chapter, you should be able to answer the following questions:

1 **What**
is the relationship between cost objects and direct costs?

2 **How**
does the conversion process work in manufacturing and service companies?

3 **What**
assumptions do accountants make about cost behaviour and why are these assumptions necessary?

4 **How**
can mixed costs be analyzed using the high–low method, scattergraph method, and least-squares regression analysis (Appendix 2A)?

5 **How**
is cost of goods manufactured calculated? Cost of goods sold?

ON SITE

www.swisschalet.com

Swiss Chalet

Since Confederation times, Cara, the parent company of Swiss Chalet, has been adapting to the changing Canadian landscape. It has developed menus and technology and acquired new businesses, and just as important, it has constantly revitalized itself with new talent. In 2003, Gail Regan, Rosemary Phelan, and Holiday Phelan-Jonson—daughters of Cara's modern founder, P.J. Phelan—reacquired Cara's shares, returning control of the company to the Phelan family.

"Cara is the leading branded full-service restaurant company in Canada," says CEO Don Robinson. Currently it is number three on *Foodservice and Hospitality*'s Top 100 list. Cara plans to take advantage of today's favourable dining-out trends across all its brands. Canadians want to eat healthy and are more time starved than ever. Providing fast, convenient, and great-tasting meals is at the heart of Cara's strategy.

In the foodservice world, few Canadian companies carry more historical clout than Cara. The Canada Railway News Co., founded in 1883, sold newspapers and food to travelling Canadians. Over the years, the company branched into restaurants and airline catering, forming today's Cara Operations Limited in 1961. In 1968 the company went public. By the time it was privatized again it had grown its annual revenues to almost $2 billion.

The 1950s marked the era of the dutiful homemaker, the ducktail hairdo, and, if you are Canadian, **SWISS CHALET'S** rotisserie chicken.

While slick greaser 'dos have gone the way of the dodo bird and homemakers have morphed into modern mavens, we still love our quarter quicken dinner. Succulent, spit-cooked, and very Canadian, Swiss Chalet has been attending to chicken cravings for 50 years. The company's first restaurant opened on April 15, 1954, on Toronto's Bloor Street West, but—after one exterior and four interior renovations—it no longer stands there. After 52 years, the original Swiss Chalet barbecued-chicken eatery that spawned today's 191-store chain has closed to make way for ... what else? A luxury condominium tower, the One Bedford. The humble Swiss Chalet had a prime location across from the Royal Conservatory of Music, just west of the Royal Ontario Museum's new Crystal addition and a mere stone's throw from the University of Toronto.

When Swiss Chalet first opened in 1954, the menu was simple and rotisserie chicken was the only entrée. Guests could visit the Swiss-style dining room or use the convenient take-out service to enjoy a quarter chicken dinner with zesty dipping sauce and an order of Swiss Chalet's famous fresh-cut fries, all prepared to the strictest standards of freshness. Today, although the menu has been greatly expanded, the rotisserie is still the heart of every Swiss Chalet restaurant. Swiss Chalet's unique, crispy rotisserie chicken was inspired by a secret Swiss recipe and the cooking process, wherein the bird slowly roasts in its juices in an open-flame brick oven, has become almost synonymous with the brand itself.

SOURCES: Alistair Kyte, *Foodservice and Hospitality,* July 2007, pp. 60–62; Anthony Reinhart, "The Little Eatery That Cooked Up an Empire," *Globe and Mail,* September 9, 2006, A15; Iris Benarioa, "Dreams," *Foodservice and Hospitality,* July 2004, pp. 65–68; "Swiss Chalet: Celebrating 50 Years of Wholesome Meals," *Canada Newswire,* Ottawa, March 25, 2004, p. 1.

C̲ost is a major factor both in achieving strategic success through competing effectively and in operating profitably. It is of interest to everyone. A student is concerned about the cost of a Saturday-night dinner and a movie. Parents are concerned about the cost of their child's postsecondary education. University administrators are concerned about the costs associated with equipping and updating high-tech classrooms. The management at Swiss Chalet is concerned about the cost of ingredients, equipment, and product quality assurance.

However, simply referring to "the cost" is inappropriate because numerous conditions must be specified before the cost can be determined. Is the student considering a fast-food or a four-star restaurant? Will the child want to attend a public or private school, in the home city or away? Will the classrooms be updated annually or as technology changes? At Swiss Chalet, how many meals are to be prepared and what does it cost the company to prepare and serve each meal?

*To be strategically effective, managers must be able to understand and communicate about costs using common management accounting terms. **Cost** is an often-used word and reflects a monetary measure of the resources given up to acquire a good or service. But the term "cost" is seldom used without a preceding adjective to specify the type of cost being considered. Different types of costs are used in different situations. For instance, an asset's historical or acquisition cost is used to prepare a balance sheet, but its replacement cost is used to estimate its insurance value.*

Before being able to communicate information to others effectively, accountants must clearly understand the differences among the various types of costs, their computations, and their usage. This chapter provides the terminology that is necessary to understand and articulate cost and management accounting information. The chapter also presents cost flows and accumulation in a production environment.

COMPONENTS OF PRODUCT COST

A **cost object** is anything to which management desires to attach costs or to which costs are related. A cost object can be a product or service, a department, a division, or a territory. Any cost that is clearly traceable to the cost object is called a **direct cost**. Costs that cannot be traced are **indirect** (or common) **costs** and these costs can only be **allocated**, or assigned, to cost objects by the use of one or more appropriate drivers, predictors, or arbitrarily chosen bases. Different cost objects may be designated for different decisions. As the cost object changes, the costs that are direct and indirect to it may also change. For instance, if a production division is specified as the cost object, the production division manager's salary is direct. If instead the cost object is a sales territory and the production division operates in more than one territory, the production division manager's salary is indirect.

Costs can also be classified as either period or product costs. **Period costs** are incurred in the nonproduction area. They are related to business functions such as selling and administration, while **product costs** are all the costs incurred to produce a product or provide a service. These costs are either direct or indirect to a particular cost object. Product costs are also called inventoriable costs and include the costs of direct material, direct labour, and overhead (a set of indirect costs).

cost
a monetary measure of the resources given up to acquire a good or service

LEARNING OBJECTIVE 1

What is the relationship between cost objects and direct costs?

cost object
anything to which costs attach or are related

direct cost
a cost that is clearly, conveniently, and economically traceable to a particular cost object

indirect cost
a cost that cannot be clearly traced to a particular cost object

allocate
assign indirect or overhead costs based on the use of a cost driver, a predictor, or an arbitrary method

period cost
a cost that is incurred during an accounting period to support the activities of the company; the cost of resources consumed during the period—an expense

product cost
a cost associated with making or acquiring inventory or providing a service—an asset

Direct Material

Any readily identifiable, physical part of a product that is clearly, conveniently, and economically traceable to that product is a **direct material**. Direct materials may be purchased raw materials or manufactured components.[1] Direct materials cost should theoretically include the cost of all materials used in manufacturing a product or performing a service. For example, the cost of cornstarch, salt, tomato powder, chicken fat, spice, dextrose, caramel colour, onion powder, garlic powder, silicon dioxide, and water would theoretically make up the direct materials cost for Swiss Chalet's dipping sauce.

Because direct costs are so expensive to record, management may decide that the benefit of treating an insignificant cost as direct is not worth the clerical cost involved. Such costs are treated and classified as indirect costs. For instance, most accountants would agree that the costs of the salt and water are neither economically traceable nor monetarily significant to the sauce's production cost. Thus, these costs would probably be deemed indirect materials and therefore would be included as part of overhead.

Similarly in a service business, some materials that could be traced to a cost object may have such an insignificant cost that they are not considered direct. For instance, a marketing firm needs to separately accumulate costs of each advertising campaign for each one of its clients. When dummy boards, or mock-ups, of possible ads are created, artists use a variety of coloured pens and pencils for design purposes. The firm would probably not attempt to trace the costs of these items to a particular advertising campaign. The costs would be too insignificant and thus would be charged to overhead.

Managers try to keep the cost of raw materials at the very lowest price and in some cases try to form partnerships with their suppliers.

Rick George, Suncor's president and chief executive officer, said that costs from subcontractors and other suppliers would be the single largest source of savings in cutting the cash operating cost of a barrel (of oil) to $9 by the end of 2003 from the then-current $10.50. He said, "We're looking for partners and suppliers who want to work with us for a very long time. We're looking for suppliers who want to help us reduce those costs."[2]

The International News Note on page 38 shows the same theme in the automobile industry.

To remain competitive in the parts business, companies will have to know their cost structures and understand why and how they exist. This means that companies will have to review their costs on a continuous basis.

direct material
a readily identifiable, physical part of a product that is clearly, conveniently, and economically traceable to that product

Direct Labour

Direct labour refers to the individuals who work specifically on a cost object (i.e., manufacturing a product or performing a service). Their labour transforms raw materials or supplies into finished goods or completed services. Another perspective on direct labour is that it directly *adds* value to the final product or service. The food preparer and the chef at Swiss Chalet represent direct labour.

Direct labour cost consists of wages or salaries paid to employees who work directly on a cost object (usually on a product or in the performance of a service). Direct labour cost should include basic compensation, production efficiency bonuses, and the employer's share of employment taxes. In addition, when a company's operations are relatively stable, direct labour cost should include all employer-paid insurance costs, holiday and vacation pay, and pension and other retirement benefits.

direct labour
the time spent by individuals who work specifically on manufacturing a product or performing a service and whose efforts are conveniently and economically traceable to that product or service; can also be viewed as the cost of the direct labour time

Price Reductions Demanded

Supplier price cuts are demanded by auto makers on a regular basis. Generally, suppliers give in: the average annual supplier price reduction over the next few years is expected to be about 3.3%.

The auto-parts sector, a key Ontario economic engine, says it is at "the breaking point." And it blames the Big Three auto makers in North America who, the group says, continue to demand price cuts instead of taking a more collaborative Japanese approach on cost reductions.

The president of the AUTOMOTIVE PARTS MANUFACTURERS' ASSOCIATION says that some suppliers are on the "brink of bankruptcy while others are preparing to exit the industry altogether" because of continuing demands from the Big Three—GENERAL MOTORS CORP., FORD MOTOR CO. LTD., and DAIMLERCHRYSLER AG. The association says that Japanese-based auto makers HONDA and TOYOTA, which assemble autos here, have worked hard with suppliers to reduce costs through elimination of waste and finding better ways to produce components.

"The Japanese will never give you business, ever, without multiple, multiple, visits" to a parts operation, says Frank O'Brien, vice president of Asia operations for Magna. He goes on to say that "one key to winning business is remembering that Japanese automakers maintain a strict purchasing, quality control, and manufacturing system that has been established over decades. Only the people change."

He calls it the chopsticks approach. "You hold one chopstick firm and it doesn't move at all. The *other* one moves." The Japanese companies also make sure the entire supply chain is in sync, not just direct suppliers.

Historically there have been two schools of supplier management in the automotive industry. The United States-based auto makers over the years gained a reputation for focusing on price reductions from suppliers and the slumping automotive market in recent years has intensified some of that pressure. Japanese car makers like Honda and Toyota, however, became known for building long-term, close-knit relationships with top suppliers under the keiretsu system, which had original equipment manufacturers owning a percentage of their top suppliers.

In the Japanese system, central firms in a relationship called keiretsu own a majority share of other firms (e.g., Toyota, MITSUBISHI, and MITSUI), which also include suppliers of parts and services needed by the central firms. The members of the keiretsu often share key executives who meet periodically during the year to share information with one another and to renew contracts of service.

In keiretsu, suppliers are considered family members and, although price reductions may be requested, Japanese auto companies would try to make certain that those reductions would not produce significant financial harm to the suppliers.

Given the history of a relationship in which car makers have long been able to dictate pricing to their suppliers through collective purchasing power, suppliers have had no choice but to adopt cost-cutting measures of their own. The knock-on effect of their actions is being felt down the supplier chain to the smallest component makers.

Japanese auto makers want long-term supplier relationships. They select suppliers as a person would a mate. The Japanese are equally tough on price but are committed to maintaining supplier continuity. So if Toyota or Honda finds that GREEN'S [a supplier] price exceeds the target cost, both sides look for savings.

When it comes to selecting suppliers, the Big Three choose on the basis of lowest price and annual price reductions, says Neil DeKoker, president of the ORIGINAL EQUIPMENT SUPPLIERS ASSOCIATION. "They look globally for the lowest parts prices from the lowest cost countries."

Mr. DeKoker and other parts industry officials have praised the Japan-based auto makers for a more collaborative approach to cost cutting and a greater willingness to help suppliers improve their cost and quality rather than simply demanding lower prices.

SOURCES: David Hannon, "The Automotive Buy–Suppliers: Friend or Foe?" *Purchasing,* February 6, 2003; Tony Van Alphen, "Auto-Parts Firms Send Dire Warning," *Toronto Star,* December 22, 2004; Mike Osheroff, "A Look at Corporate Governance Worldwide," *Strategic Finance,* April 2004, Vol. 85, p. 18; Brian Milligan, "Automakers Keep Demanding Price Cuts From Suppliers," *Purchasing,* March 9, 2000, pp. 87–89; Jeremy Grant, "Supplier Industry: Parts Companies Feel Knock-On Effect," FT.com London, March 3, 2003; Robert Sherefkin and Amy Wilson, "Why the Big 3 Can't Be Japanese," *Automotive News,* February 10, 2003; Greg Keenan, "Ford Yanks Contract From Decoma; Dispute Over Parts Prices Behind Move," *Auto Industry Reporter,* December 20, 2003.

Even though direct labour cost is clearly traceable to a particular cost object, a given cost must also be conveniently and economically traceable to the product or service to be considered direct. As with some materials, some labour costs that should theoretically be considered direct are treated as indirect for two reasons.

First, it might be cost inefficient to trace the labour costs. For example, some employee fringe benefits should conceptually be treated as direct labour cost, but many companies do not have stable workforces and cannot develop a reasonable estimate of fringe benefit costs. Thus, the time, effort, and cost of trying to trace the fringe benefit costs might not be worth the additional accuracy that would be provided. In contrast, when fringe benefit costs are extremely high (such as for professional staff in a service organization), tracing them to products and services may provide more useful management information.

Second, erroneous information about product or service costs might result from handling such costs in the theoretically correct manner. An assumed payroll for one week for the six production workers who make dipping sauce at Swiss Chalet can illustrate this possibility. If each of these employees earns $8 per hour, their overtime pay would be $12 per hour (time-and-a-half). One week prior to a holiday, the employees worked a total of 300 hours, including 60 hours of overtime to complete all the orders. Exhibit 2-1 presents the determination of how much of this portion of Swiss Chalet's weekly payroll is direct labour and how much is an indirect factory cost known as overhead and will be discussed later.

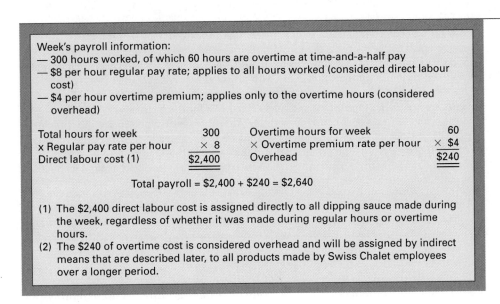

EXHIBIT 2-1

Payroll Analysis for Direct Labour and Overhead

Dipping sauce production is scheduled based on the expected current demand. If the $4 per hour overtime premium were assigned to the sauce produced during the overtime hours, the labour cost for this sauce would appear to be 50% greater than that for sauce manufactured during regular working hours. Since scheduling is random, the sauce made during overtime hours should not be forced to bear the overtime charges. Therefore, amounts incurred for costs such as overtime or shift premiums are usually considered overhead rather than direct labour cost and are allocated to all products.

There are occasions, however, when allocating costs such as overtime to overhead (all units) is not appropriate. If a catering request by a customer is to be scheduled during overtime hours or comes in as a rush request that requires overtime to be worked, then the overtime or shift premiums incurred should be considered direct labour and be attached to the particular job that created the costs.

Direct labour cost in proportion to total product cost has been declining in many industries, especially over the past 15 years. Now, in many highly automated production environments, it is not uncommon to find that direct labour accounts for a very small proportion of total cost at many manufacturers. Eventually, managers may find that almost all direct labour cost is replaced with a new cost of production—the cost of robots and other fully automated machinery. Thus, although labour may still be an essential element of production in some industries, managers should avoid overestimating the importance of labour cost in a technically advanced setting.

We tend to look at direct labour as a variable cost. However, we can see from the following News Note that this is not always the case.

GENERAL NEWS NOTE

When Is Labour Considered a Fixed Cost?

For those who are worried about where the money is going at FORD MOTOR CO., the answer is "fixed costs." Where is the money going? Gross margins (or revenue minus the cost of goods sold) fell during the quarter to 9.4% from 14.1% in the same period a year earlier. Revenue fell to US$41.9 billion in the second quarter from $44.5 billion in the previous year. Revenue per vehicle sold was down slightly to $22,987 from $23,123 in the prior year. Ford also sold 28,000 fewer cars in the second quarter in North America than in the same period a year earlier.

In such an environment it is vital to make up for the decline by better cost management. That keeps gross margins up; then, as sales revive, so does profitability. That didn't happen at Ford because its fixed costs were too large. Fixed costs, such as rent, property taxes, and insurance, don't vary with production levels. Variable costs, such as steel, aluminum, freight, taxes, and incentive payments, do vary with production levels. Health care is a form of insurance and thus a fixed cost for the company. Ordinarily, labour is a variable cost. But contracts with the Auto Workers Union require the company to pay a large share of salary and benefits if it idles a worker, so labour is essentially a fixed cost as well. Because of plummeting sales and the existence of fixed costs, Ford had no choice but to accelerate its cost cutting, slash its salaried workforce, and expand its buyout program for hourly workers.

SOURCE: Stephen D. Jones, "Fixed Costs Gobbling Up Ford Cash," Dow Jones News Service, September 19, 2006. Copyright ©2006. Dow Jones & Company Inc.

At Dell Inc.'s plant in Nashville, online orders go directly to assembly-line robots, which fetch all the parts to create a custom-built PC. The company's one-year-old system automatically loads software onto the hard drives and tests the machines before an army of robots boxes them up for shipping.

Dell's new set-up requires half as many workers as before, and it runs at three times the speed. It churns out one computer every four seconds. Dell is hurrying to automate its eight other plants.[3]

The News Note on page 41 shows how the introduction of robotics can save on labour costs.

Robots Save Time and Money for Companies

GENERAL
NEWS NOTE

Not only are robots used in the manufacturing industry, but they are also used heavily in the practice of surgery. At ST. MICHAEL'S HOSPITAL in Toronto, Canada, Ken Pace, a surgeon, now has four arms, instead of two, helping him patch up his patients. His new assistant's limbs are made of sleek grey plastic. They belong to a $4.5 million robot with the brand name da Vinci, which crouches over the operating table like a giant crab. The robot helps surgeons perform minimally invasive surgery more quickly and safely. The robot's full range of motion helps surgeons manoeuvre the curved suture needles at tricky angles and gives them more precision during delicate procedures. Doctors feel that patients who get robot-assisted surgery will recover more quickly and have less post-op pain and chance of infection.

SUPERIOR ROBOTICS—a new company in Sault Ste Marie, Ontario—engineers and installs high-performance robots for the jewellery industry. This technology takes raw jewellery, fresh from the casting mould, and grinds off the excess metal using robotic systems similar to those used in the automotive industry. Traditionally, jewellery polishing and finishing is carried out manually, with a skilled craftsperson sitting behind a grinding wheel for hours on end. "It is a dirty job," says Blaine Wallace, owner of Superior Robotics. Trainees need two months of instruction to obtain proficiency. The turnover rate is high and repetitive strain injuries are common. That is why companies are eager to explore automated alternatives. Superior Robotics sells the R 100-G used for grinding rings or the R 100-P used for polishing rings. "With these you can program a ring style within a half hour and it will produce a high quality ring every time."

Flexibility is at the heart of auto makers' and suppliers' manufacturing strategies. A combination of falling hardware prices and more capable software is enabling robots and automated systems to play a larger role in manufacturing.

At the GENERAL MOTORS Cadillac body shop, the robotic fixtures that hold the steel panels in place for welding are smart enough to construct a Cadillac CTS in one cycle and follow it with a Cadillac SRX in the next—all this without a long and expensive changeover.

With the addition of vision and force-sensing technologies, robots can handle more complex assembly tasks than before and cost savings from robots make companies more competitive, which can counter the push to move jobs to low-wage countries such as China.

In the body shop at the SUBARU Indiana Automotive plant in Lafayette, Indiana, a robot arm fits doors for the Legacy, Outback, and Baja. When a body rolls into place on the line, a robot arm scans a bar-code tag on the carrier to determine the body style. A camera mounted on the robot arm looks at the hole pattern among three piles of door panels to find the correct front or rear door, then holds it in place while hinges are attached to the body with automated nut drivers.

General Motors introduced the first industrial robots in 1961. Since then, Japan's largest companies have competed to make robots as human as possible. The carmaker uses robots throughout its manufacturing process. Robotics solved a major industrial problem. "Japan has no visa category in place for low-skilled workers," notes Jessie Wilson of an investment bank. "To manufacturers needing extra hands, robots were a gift from heaven." According to the INTERNATIONAL FEDERATION OF ROBOTICS, Japan bought 37,000 robots in 2006, between three and four times more than its nearest rivals, America, Germany, and South Korea.

MARUTI, which is still majority owned by Suzuki, has plans to increase its already highly automated processes, with the goal of cutting its production time in half and trimming costs. Already, giant swivelling robots are doing much of the welding. Manpower is employed mostly to check for errors.

The jewel in FORD'S crown is the new $55 million wide-body press line where sheet metal is fed by huge robots into the stamping machine to create car panels and other components. It is capable of producing a single-piece body side panel—a first for Ford in Australia. It is serviced by six robots and five automated guided vehicles and will eventually produce up to 520 parts per hour. The press will be used for the 2008 Falcon and Focus. One press weighs 2,400 tonnes and it's an impressive sight.

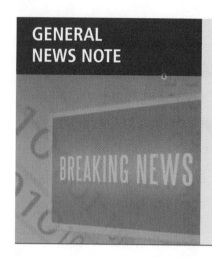

At HONDA if one robot is forced to leave a job unfinished because its battery is running low, another robot can take up the work where it left off. A wireless network links the robots together. The robots automatically plug themselves into recharging stations when they are running out of power.

SOURCES: Megan Ogilvie, "Robot 'the Future of Surgery,'" *Toronto Star*, March 28, 2008; Ian Ross, "Robot Maker Returns to Sault to Set Up Shop," *Northern Ontario Business*, April 2004, p. 19; Dale Jewett, "Rise of the Machines, Lower Costs and Better Software Enable Robots to Play a Larger Manufacturing Role," *Automotive News*, August 2, 2004; "Robots to the Rescue; Carmaker Toyota Says Robotics Will Become a Core Business," *The Economist*, December 15, 2007; Heather Timmons and Saher Mahood, "In India, a $2,500 Pace Car," *New York Times*, October 12, 2007; Murray Hubbard, "Ford in Overdrive: Good Vibrations in Quest for Smooth Running," *Gold Coast Sun*, December 19, 2007; Simon Burns, "Robot Teamwork Demonstrated by Honda," *VNUNet United Kingdom*, December 14, 2007.

Overhead

overhead
the expenses of a business such as rent, insurance, and utilities consumed in the production of a product or consumed in the supplying of a service

Overhead is any manufacturing or production cost that is not directly or conveniently traceable to manufacturing a product or providing a service. Overhead, therefore, needs to be allocated to the products produced or services rendered during the period. Overhead is considered indirect and, accordingly, does not include direct material and direct labour. Manufacturing overhead costs are essential to the process of converting raw materials into finished goods. "The greatest part of most companies' costs (other than those for purchased materials) typically occurs in overhead categories. In manufacturing, more than two-thirds of all nonmaterial costs tend to be indirect or overhead expenses."[4] Direct labour cost has become a progressively smaller proportion of product cost in recent years while overhead has become a much larger portion; therefore, it requires much more attention than in the past.

The following examples from both Chrysler and Pirelli Tire show that increased costs for capital investment (machinery)—which translate into lower labour costs but higher depreciation costs, which in turn increase overhead costs.

At the Chrysler plant in Illinois, the use of robots and better production processes have eliminated more than 1,000 jobs in the new factory.[5] At Pirelli Tire, a new production process has been designed to cut the cost of its products by 25%, while raising the quality and lowering costs by as much as 15% for some models. Pirelli's new technology, called a modular integrated robotized system, or MIRS, is an automated process that allows for high-speed production in an area about one-fifth the floor space required for traditional tire-making methods, thus creating minifactories that can be located next to car manufacturing plants. Through the use of robots and specialized software, Pirelli says that it will be able to reduce the steps in manufacturing a tire from 14 to just three, while cutting the lead time from six days to just 72 minutes.[6]

The sum of direct materials, direct labour, and overhead costs comprises total product cost.[7] According to generally accepted accounting principles, product costs are inventoriable until the products are sold or otherwise disposed of.

Stage of Production

Production processing or conversion can be viewed as existing in three stages: (1) work not yet started (raw materials), (2) work in process, and (3) finished goods. The stages of production in a manufacturing firm and some costs associated with each stage are illustrated in Exhibit 2-2. In the first stage of processing, the cost incurred reflects the prices paid for raw materials and/or supplies. As work progresses through the second stage, accrual-based accounting requires that costs related to the conversion of raw materials or supplies be accumulated and attached to the product. These costs include wages paid to people producing the goods as well as overhead charges. The total costs incurred in stages 1 and 2 are equal to the total production cost of finished goods in stage 3.

Cost accounting provides the means for accumulating the processing costs and allocating the costs to the goods produced. The primary accounts involved in the cost accumulation process are (1) Raw Materials, (2) Work in Process, and (3) Finished Goods. These accounts relate to the three stages of production shown in Exhibit 2-2 and form a common database for cost, management, and financial accounting.

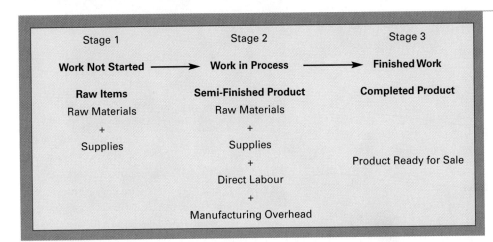

EXHIBIT 2-2
Stages of Production

Service firms, ordinarily, do not have the same degree of cost complexity as manufacturers. The work-not-started stage of processing normally consists of the cost of supplies necessary for performing the services. Supplies are inventoried until they are placed into a work-in-process stage. At that point, labour and overhead are added to achieve finished results. Developing the cost of services is extremely important and useful in service-oriented businesses. For instance, cost accounting is very useful in hospitals that need to accumulate the costs incurred by patients in their hospital stays, in architectural firms that need to accumulate the costs incurred for designs and models of individual projects, and in legal firms that need to accumulate all costs incurred for a legal case until it is completed.

The product and service costs accumulated in the inventory accounts are composed of three cost components—direct materials, direct labour, and overhead. Each of these components was discussed in the preceding section of this chapter. Precise classification of some costs into one of these categories may be difficult and judgment may be required in the classification process.

Prime and Conversion Costs

The total cost of direct materials and direct labour is referred to as **prime cost** because these costs are most convincingly associated with, and traceable to, a specific product. **Conversion cost** is defined as the sum of direct labour and overhead that is directly or indirectly necessary for transforming direct (raw) materials and purchased parts into a saleable finished product. Because direct labour is included as part of both prime cost and conversion cost, prime cost plus conversion cost does not sum to product cost, as direct labour would be double-counted. Exhibits 2-3 and 2-4 show the typical components of product cost for a manufacturing company in terms of prime and conversion costs.

prime cost
the total cost of direct materials and direct labour; so called because these costs are most convincingly associated with and traceable to a specific product

conversion cost
the sum of direct labour and manufacturing overhead that is directly or indirectly necessary for transforming direct (raw) materials and purchased parts into a saleable finished product

EXHIBIT 2-3
Components of Product Cost

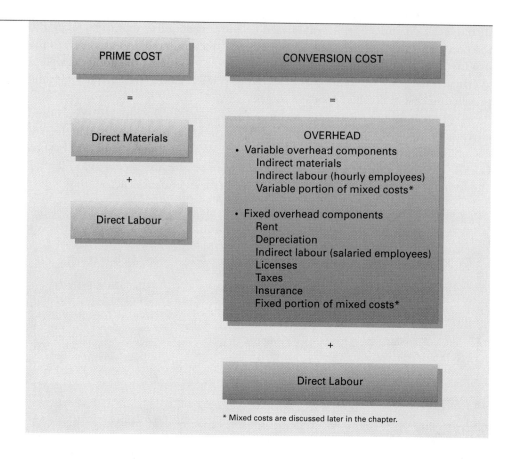

The cost of a completed product will include the following costs as shown in Exhibit 2-4.

EXHIBIT 2-4
Product Cost

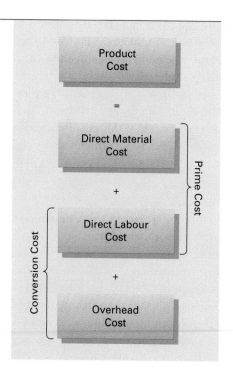

COST BEHAVIOUR

What assumptions do accountants make about cost behaviour and why are these assumptions necessary?

A cost may change from a prior period because of changes in activity. The way a cost responds to a change in activity is known as its cost behaviour. For Swiss Chalet, activity measures can include sales, production volume, machine hours, the number of purchase orders sent, or the number of grocery stores selling Swiss Chalet's products using Swiss Chalet's dipping sauce. The way a *total* (rather than unit) cost reacts to a change in activity reflects that cost's behaviour pattern. Every cost will change if enough time passes or if extreme shifts in activity occur. Therefore, for **cost behaviour** information to be properly identified, analyzed, and used, a time frame must be specified to indicate how far into the future a cost should be examined, and a particular range of activity must be assumed. The time frame generally encompasses the operating cycle or a year, whichever is longer. The assumed activity range usually reflects the company's normal operating range and is referred to as the **relevant range**.

To understand how costs will behave under various conditions, accountants need to find the underlying cost driver for cost changes. A **cost driver** is an activity or occurrence that has a direct cause–effect relationship with a cost. For example, a production volume has a direct effect on the total cost of raw materials used and so can be said to drive that cost. A change in production volume causes a similar change in the cost of raw materials.

In most situations, the cause–effect relationship is less clear because costs are commonly affected by multiple factors. For example, quality assurance costs are affected by volume of production, quality of materials used, skill level of workers, and level of automation. Although determining which factor actually caused a specific change in quality assurance cost might be difficult, managers could choose any one of these factors to predict that cost, if they were confident about the factor's relationship with cost changes. When a change in an activity measure is accompanied by a consistent, observable change in a cost item, that activity measure is a **predictor**. To be used as a predictor, the activity measure need only change with the cost in a foreseeable manner.

In contrast to a cost driver, a predictor does not necessarily cause the change in the related item; the two items simply need to change in the same manner. The difference between a cost driver and a predictor is important. A cost driver reflects the actual cause–effect relationship; a predictor reflects a possible relationship or perhaps even a totally random occurrence that simply seems to be related. However, managers often use both cost drivers and predictors to estimate how changes in activity will influence cost behaviour.

cost behaviour
the manner in which a cost responds to a change in a related level of activity

relevant range
the specified range of activity over which a variable cost remains constant per unit and a fixed cost remains fixed in total

cost driver
a factor that has a direct cause–effect relationship to a cost

predictor
an activity measure that is accompanied by a consistent, observable change in a cost item

Variable and Fixed Costs

Cost behaviour patterns will be referred to throughout the text because they are so helpful in many management accounting situations requiring analysis and decision making. The two types of cost behaviours are variable and fixed. The respective total cost and unit cost definitions for variable and fixed cost behaviours are presented in Exhibit 2-5.

Variable Cost

A cost that varies in total in direct proportion to changes in activity is classified as a **variable cost.** Because the total cost varies in direct proportion to the changes in activity, a variable cost is a constant amount per unit.[8]

Some examples of variable costs and their drivers include raw material costs and production volume, units-of-production depreciation and production volume,

variable cost
a cost that varies in total in direct proportion to changes in activity

EXHIBIT 2-5
Comparative Total and Unit Cost Behaviour Definitions

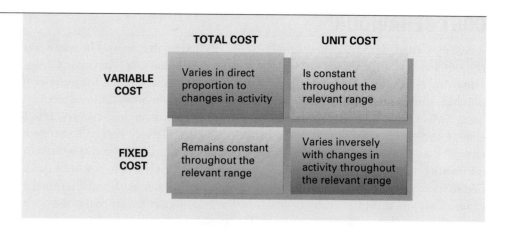

	TOTAL COST	UNIT COST
VARIABLE COST	Varies in direct proportion to changes in activity	Is constant throughout the relevant range
FIXED COST	Remains constant throughout the relevant range	Varies inversely with changes in activity throughout the relevant range

sales commissions and number or price of products sold, and gasoline cost and kilometres driven. Variable costs are extremely important to a company's total profit picture because every time a particular activity takes place, a specific amount of variable cost is incurred.

When direct labour cost is treated as a variable cost, during an economic downturn there are numerous layoffs. We can see this at Canadian Pacific Railway Ltd. The company is giving greater clout to senior branch managers in a decentralization strategy designed to boost employee productivity and streamline its rail network. Industry and labour officials say that CPR, as part of its productivity drive, also plans to cut nearly 400 staff (15 percent of its non-unionized workforce) in North America. David Newman, an analyst with National Bank Financial Inc., expects the job cuts to come mostly through attrition with buyouts and early retirement packages; however, there could be some "involuntary moves."[9]

In Western cultures, direct labour cost is commonly viewed as a variable cost, and during an economic downturn there are numerous layoffs in all industries. However, this is not the case everywhere. In Japan, for example, many workers have lifelong employment contracts; thus companies often treat direct labour costs as fixed. Because of a downturn in the Japanese economy, some companies are trying to modify this situation and trade these fixed costs for variable ones, as indicated in the following International News Note.

INTERNATIONAL NEWS NOTE

Lifetime Contracts Make Labour Cost Fixed

Because lifetime employment is still so prevalent in Japan and mid-career job changes are still not common, workers are placed at a disadvantage if they cannot protest an acquisition that will lessen the terms of employment. Recent business publications contend that Japan's current economic woes have been compounded by lifetime employment practices, which render companies unable to reduce their workforces.

In China, a new labour law called the Labour Contract Law, which took effect on January 1, 2008, gives employees who have worked at a company for more than 10 years the right to sign contracts protecting them from being fired without a legitimate reason. Some companies worry that the law might restore the "iron rice bowl" of lifetime employment practised by China's state sector during the era of central planning that followed the 1949 Communist Revolution, says Ken Kedl, general manager of the consulting firm Technomic Asia.

SOURCES: "Labour Group Urges Protection for Workers After Buyouts," *Nikkei Report*, October 11, 2007; "Some US Cos Say China May Be Losing Edge as Costs, Wages Rise," *Dow Jones Chinese Financial Wire*, December 14, 2007.

Fixed Cost

In contrast, a cost that remains constant in total within the relevant range of activity is a **fixed cost**. Many fixed costs are incurred to provide a firm with production capacity. Fixed costs include depreciation,[10] property taxes, and insurance. On a per-unit basis, a fixed cost varies inversely with changes in activity: the per-unit fixed cost decreases with increases in activity and increases with decreases in activity. In other words with increased activity, the fixed costs are spread over more units and thus fixed costs per unit are lower. The following News Note discusses the problem of labour costs being fixed and why North American vehicles are more expensive than foreign imports.

fixed cost
a cost that remains constant in total within a specified range of activity

GENERAL NEWS NOTE

Canada Is the Most Expensive Place to Produce Cars

Canada is now the most expensive country in the world for car makers to operate according to the Canadian Vehicle Manufacturers Association, an industry trade group that represents Ford, Chrysler LLC, and GM in Canada. And that new reality has forced the six auto makers with a local presence to ask themselves a simple question: What does it make sense to build and do here?

The Detroit wage and benefit costs have been reduced to about U.S.$50 per hour from roughly $75 an hour. That compares with little more than C$70 an hour at Chrysler, Ford, and GM's Canadian operations.

The health care change in the U.S. has almost no relevance in Canada because of the taxpayer-financed health care system. The historic shift to let new workers be paid a lower wage and benefits than existing workers will be a serious pressure point for Mr. Hargrove. Mr. Hargrove says, "We're not agreeing to a second-class group of workers at our plants that come in at half pay and never get top pay. That just isn't going to happen."

In May 2008, Ford workers ratified an early contract that froze wages of employees for three years; suspended a cost-of-living allowance (COLA) until the end of 2009; cut vacation pay; and raised benefit expenses such as for prescription drugs. New retirees also lost inflation protection on their pensions for one year. It will also take longer for new workers to get full pay. They will start employment at 70% of the top wage rate and reach 100% after three years. They will not receive a COLA until the end of the contract.

On May 15, 2008, Chrysler and GM agreed to match the wages and benefits in the three-year contract agreed to by Ford of Canada, said Buzz Hargrove, the CAW president. However, the contract for Chrysler and GM differs from that of Ford in that their deal freezes wages for three years but provides a COLA in the second and third years. According to Hargrove, the fact the union has got out with what it still has intact, while avoiding a two-tier wage structure forced on the UAW in the United States, makes this CAW deal "historic."

It is interesting to note that most domestic (North American) manufacturing and assembly plants still use complex systems of restrictive work rules that strictly define the jobs a worker can or cannot do. Combined with the difference in paid time off, unexcused absences, and relief time, the result is that GM, Ford, and Chrysler must employ more workers per vehicle produced.

SOURCES: Greg Keenan, "CAW Gears Up for Toughest Fight in 2008," *Globe and Mail*, December 31, 2007, B3; Nicolas Van Praet, "What to Build in Canada?" *Financial Post*, January 2, 2008; Tony Van Alphen, "Ford Workers Accept Deal to Freeze Wages," *Toronto Star*, May 5, 2008; Chris Vander Doelen, "CAW Settles with Both Chrysler and GM," *National Post*, May 16, 2008; Harbour Felax Group, Executive Summary, "Automotive Competitive Challenges Going Beyond Lean," October 2006.

While direct materials and direct labour are generally variable in relation to production volume, overhead costs may be variable, mixed, or fixed. Variable manufacturing overhead includes the cost of indirect materials and indirect labour paid on an hourly basis, such as wages for material handlers and for others who support the production, assembly, or service processes. Also included in variable manufacturing overhead are the costs of oil and grease used for machine maintenance and of paper towels used in factory restrooms, as well as the variable portion of utility charges for the conversion area. Depreciation calculated using the units-of-production method is a variable manufacturing overhead cost.

For Wokking on Wheels, the fixed cost of depreciation is taken not on a "fixed" asset, but rather on a movable restaurant and its equipment. The gas used to move the restaurant back and forth to the site is treated as a variable cost.

Fixed overhead comprises costs such as straight-line and declining balance depreciation and insurance and property taxes on production/service-providing assets. Fixed indirect manufacturing labour cost includes salaries for production supervisors, shift superintendents, and service managers. The fixed portion of maintenance and utilities incurred in the conversion area is also part of fixed manufacturing overhead.

Each fixed cost is basically independent of production or sales volume as long as a relevant range is specified. However, if production or sales volume were to rise to a point at which additional supervisors, plant space, or equipment was needed, the related salaries, depreciation, and insurance costs would also rise.

When the manufacturers can't sell as many vehicles as they can build, the fixed costs of the assembly plants drive up the cost of each vehicle. Thus, the auto makers use incentives so they can sell more cars and thus keep production up and unit costs down.[11] The following News Note discusses the incentives being offered by the North American auto makers to get cars off the dealership lots.

GENERAL NEWS NOTE

Rebates Help Sell Cars

The deep discounts that auto makers are offering on new cars in Canada are triggering trouble in the used-car market and leading to major financial losses, a leading auto broker warns. Auto makers are offering thousands of dollars worth of rebates to better reflect the strength of the Canadian dollar and to woo buyers to their showrooms. The average price to purchase or lease a vehicle fell 6.8% in February (2008) from a year ago, the sharpest decline since 1956, according to Statistics Canada.

GENERAL NEWS NOTE

CHRYSLER, which has boosted cash incentives across its vehicle line-up, said that it would lower prices further. It said its deals will include a further $3,750 discount on its Ram heavy-duty pickups and a $4,000 additional discount on its Charger sedans.

Chrysler, credited with inventing the minivan in the early 1980s, is slashing the price of its next-generation family haulers by as much as $6,570 per vehicle while packing them with more features in a bid to keep a stranglehold on that slumping segment.

Pricing announcements of new vehicles are always closely watched events in the auto industry, and recently, Chrysler priced its upcoming Dodge Caravan and Chrysler Town and Country models, starting at $26,495 and $35,995 respectively, in Canada. That's significantly below the prices of the models that they will replace, and it makes the base-model Caravan—the country's third most popular vehicle—cheaper than almost all its direct rivals.

The automobile manufacturers use zero-percent financing, cash back rebates, and employee pricing to help dealers clear their inventories.

Chrysler says that the reduced prices and new features should help it jump-start van sales and extend its leadership position in the minivan market. The company is also trying to better reflect the true cost of the vehicle up front without having to offer discounts later on.

Reid Bigland, Chrysler's president and CEO, said that the company is increasing the overall value of its incentive packages from present sweeteners, which already totalled thousands of dollars on several models. Chrysler Canada is now also offering free gas for six months to "shake up" the market.

GM boosted spending on incentives in an effort to lift sales, only to be "surprised" by the incentive spending at some rivals. TOYOTA, for example, offered rebates in June 15, 2007, of as much as $3,500 or no-interest loans on the new Tundra pickup truck. This resulted in sales of 21,727 Tundras, which is more than double their previous sales of the vehicle.

While it is no secret that car prices are falling in Canada, even those paid to track such data were taken aback to learn yesterday (March 18, 2008) that the last time conditions were so good to buy a car it likely had tailfins on it.

SOURCES: Nicolas Van Praet, "New-Car Deals Are Hurting Used-Car Sales, Values Plummet," *Financial Post*, March 28, 2008, FP6; Nicolas Van Praet, "Automaker in Giving Spirit to End Year," *Financial Post*, December 4, 2007, FP6; Nicolas Van Praet, "Chrysler Cuts Van Price to Drive Sales; $6,570 Off New Models," *Financial Post*, July 13, 2007, FP3; Nicolas Van Praet "Dealers Try Free-Gas Gambit," *Financial Post*, July 4, 2008; Tony Van Alphen, "Ring Out a Good Year, Brace for Bad," *Toronto Star*, January 4, 2008, B1; Grant Surridge, "Dramatic Decline in Car Prices, Steepest Since 1956," *Financial Post*, March 19, 2008.

While many of the North American car makers need to discount prices, Toyota Motors rarely has to. Perhaps it is because it is uniquely profitable. Toyota's innovations tend to be of the incremental variety. Yet over the long haul the venerable Japanese car maker has shown a remarkable ability to produce the best cars in the fastest growing market segments. In 2001, Toyota launched the Prius—the first mass-market hybrid gas and electric car. It remains the most fuel-efficient car on the market. The car incorporates several key innovations, including the hybrid synergy drive engine, a light and durable nickel metal hydride battery, air conditioning that runs off its own electric motor, a flexible resin gasoline tank, and a vacuum flask to keep coolant hot when the car is parked.[12]

We see, at Toyota Motor Corp.'s Motomachi factory in Japan, workers scurrying to fit the right parts in the correct sequence before a swiftly moving conveyor can bear the half-assembled cars away to the next stage of production. Although practised, the workers' movements are hurried and their faces are set in concentration. There is none of the constant banter that sustains factory employees elsewhere in the world; none of the practical jokes. The foundation of Toyota's success is its production system, imitated by companies all over the world but seldom matched. At the heart of that system lies a handful of basic, common-sense ideas. For example, each employee is responsible for quality control. If there is a defect during the production process, the individual worker must ensure it is corrected immediately. As a result, vehicles leave Toyota factories with remarkably few defects. The cost of such vigilance is remarkably low.[13]

Variable Versus Fixed Costs: The Tradeoff

Shifting from costs exhibiting one type of cost behaviour to costs exhibiting a different type of cost behaviour changes a company's basic cost structure and can significantly affect profits.

Manufacturers must adopt more advanced and leaner business practices, possibly outsourcing more of their production, to survive the current profit crunch in a "new industrial age," according to a Canadian consulting firm. "Reports are showing that manufacturers are feeling the pinch ... increasing revenues and reduced profitability are telling indicators," Grant Thornton LLP says. Rising costs in nearly every facet of business are chipping away at companies' bottom lines, with half expecting further increases in their already soaring costs and for transportation and raw materials.

"The higher cost of wages, commodities, energy and transportation ... has in turn been responsible for increased costs of production and distribution," says John Copeland. Compounding the problem is the relative strength displayed by the Canadian dollar against most major currencies, including the U.S. dollar, over the past four years.

The Grant Thornton report suggests that manufacturers themselves are not doing enough, with one in five having no plan in place to improve their plants, nearly half not planning any change in their capital investment plans, and less than one in 10 investing a minimum of 10 percent of their revenue in innovation.[14]

Many companies are looking at ways to decrease costs and increase profits. One way is the adoption of lean production. The following International News Note shows how Jefferson Pilot Financial uses this system.

Using Lean Production at Jefferson Pilot Financial to Increase Profits

In contrast to traditional mass-production operations, a lean company emphasizes eliminating waste, boosting inventory turnover, and reducing inventory levels. The focus is on achieving the shortest possible production cycle and producing only to meet customer demand. The benefits generally are lower costs, higher product quality, and shorter lead times. The principles of lean production can also be applied to firms other than those in manufacturing.

JEFFERSON PILOT FINANCIAL (JPF) knew it needed to do something to differentiate itself from its competitors. It was clear that management could significantly increase revenue by improving operations.

Management investigated the concept of lean production, which had been introduced by manufacturing companies in the '90s. Lean production is built around the concept of continuous-flow processing—a departure from traditional production systems, in which large batches are processed at each step and are passed along only after an entire batch has been processed. At any given time, most of a batch in a traditional system is sitting waiting to be processed—in other words, it is costly excess inventory. As well, errors cannot be caught or addressed quickly, because if they occur, they tend to occur on a large scale.

JPF believed that its business could benefit from lean production because its operations involved the processing of an almost tangible "service product." Like an automobile on the assembly line, an insurance policy goes through a series of processes, from initial application to underwriting, or risk assessment, to policy issuance. With each step, value is added to the work in progress—just as a car gets doors or a coat of paint.

The initiative has delivered impressive results. The company halved the average time from receipt of a Premier Partner application to issuance of a policy, reduced labour costs by 26%, and trimmed the rate of reissues due to errors by 40%. These outcomes contributed to a remarkable 60% increase in new annualized life premiums in the company's core individual-life-insurance business in just two years.

The application of lean principles throughout JPF is not only delivering direct productivity gains, but it is also helping the firm make more cost-effective capital investments.

SOURCES: Karen M. Kroll, "The Lowdown on Lean Accounting," *Journal of Accountancy*, Vol. 198, Issue 1 (2004); Cynthia Karen Swank, "The Lean Service Machine," *Harvard Business Review*, October 2003.

Airlines are decreasing frills that they once offered free in order to reduce costs. So far, no airline has plans to install pay toilets. But just about every other possible action aimed at reducing costs or increasing revenues is on the table as the world's major scheduled carriers grapple with combined losses of nearly $50 billion over the past five years.

With $140 US a barrel of oil, the balancing act becomes crucial. Raise fares too high, and planes burn precious fuel to fly empty seats around. Keep them too low, and you risk cutting your anorexic profit margins.[15] Cost-saving moves proposed by the IATA include reducing the weight of items carried on board, greater use of technology through an increase in electronic tickets and self-check-in machines, reducing the number of airlines through mergers, slashing labour costs, and lobbying for cost reductions at the world's most expensive airports. Other suggestions include reducing on-board weight—for example, removing old magazines and newspapers, galley containers, ovens, excess duty-free items, and pillows and blankets—and even dumping the slop from toilets more frequently. Another saving could involve shortening flying times from point A to point B. This could save an airline $140 for every minute saved. For example, flying over Washington DC instead of around it would cut 30 nautical miles off flight times and save carriers $21 million a year.

A growing number of fliers are finding there's a price to pay for checking bags. Airlines are now charging for bags that once were free to check and raising prices for fliers with lots of luggage, overweight bags, and oversize bags. Most airlines now allow only one free checked bag, but this will not be the case for long.

Air Canada is now charging $25 to check a second bag. American Airlines is now charging $15 for the first bag. Air Canada has also persuaded you to check yourself in and print your own boarding pass, and the country's largest airline wants you to take care of your own bags. Consumers will save time by "self-tagging" luggage after using electronic check-in kiosks.

Airlines face high fuel bills and fierce fare competition domestically and internationally, so it makes sense to stay competitive by expanding the use of kiosks to reduce labour costs. In speeding up the check-in process, the airlines are hoping to improve "turnaround" times for their aircraft. Better on-time performance does not just bolster the mood of travellers—it's also good for the bottom line, because planes that depart and arrive as scheduled eliminate the need to pay overtime to employees.[16]

In the long run, however, even fixed costs will not remain constant. Business will increase or decrease sufficiently that production capacity may be added or sold. Alternatively, management may make a strategic decision to "trade" fixed and variable costs for each other. For example, if a company installs new highly computerized equipment rather than employing labourers, an additional large fixed cost for depreciation is generated and the variable cost of hourly production workers is eliminated.

Ford built the Dearborn, Michigan, plant around the labour-saving properties of machines. Automation lowers production costs, which bolsters profits. Companies spend these profits on improving what they sell, and on building more labour-saving machines. As technology advances, these improvements make products more complex.[17]

Empowering Employees to Make Changes That Help Cut Costs

Darcy Ste. Marie hasn't reinvented the wheel. But he can take a little credit for changing the way they are made. About a year ago, the man in charge of the assembly at GM's auto assembly facility in Oshawa, Ontario, noticed a problem on the production line.

The flow of parts, the lifeblood of every manufacturing operation, was off kilter. When cars passed by on the line to be fitted with new tires and rims, the wheels required for the various models being built weren't always ready. The disruptions left crews scrambling to make up for lost time. "I've got 45 seconds to build five tires for each car," Mr. Ste. Marie says over the steady noise of the plant. "That's not a lot if something goes wrong. And you don't want to stop the line." The solution was a simple fix: better communication between the line and the wheel crews. In the end, it probably shaved a few seconds from the time it takes to make a car. In the modern auto sector, where a new car rolls off the line in Oshawa every 45 seconds like clockwork, even the smallest efforts can be counted as major victories.

"We're not landing a man on the moon any more," says Mike Quinton, the plant manager in Oshawa, Canada's largest auto assembly facility, which produces more than 2,600 cars a day. "Eliminating the need to walk around to get parts, eliminating wasted movements, having the parts right there when you need them—it all adds up."[18]

Outsourcing and Its Impact on Cost

Until recently, Japanese tech companies rejected the notion of outsourcing. They preferred to control quality by keeping the majority of operations in-house, and they perceived cost reduction through labour arbitrage to be at odds with Japanese employment customs. Japanese employees are often promised lifetime employment.

Resource actions, such as layoffs, are typically not an option. But today the slowing economic climate, the aging Japanese workforce, and the declining pool of skilled IT and business university graduates are challenging the country's executives to find appropriate solutions.

Japanese companies are engaging in strategic outsourcing arrangements that retain employee commitment, augment internal technology and business process skills, and improve IT business processes, all while reducing operating costs. The success of these arrangements hinges on developing innovative outsourcing agreements and selecting a provider with the right capabilities.[19]

This process of "outsourcing" can create another type of cost. In such cases, there is a trade-off of costs. Oftentimes, substantial fixed costs are eliminated and are replaced by a variable cost. Whether a company exchanges variable for fixed, or fixed for mixed costs (a combination of fixed and variable costs), shifting costs from one type of cost behaviour to another changes the basic cost structure of the company and can have a significant impact on profits.

As industries advance, manufacturers manage the growing complexity of their products by outsourcing: they share with others the work of making the products. This enables each company in the production chain to specialize in part of the complicated task. The car industry, for instance, relies on parts companies that make nothing but electrical systems, brakes, or transmissions. These parts companies, in turn, depend on the work of other suppliers to make individual components. At each level of production, outsourcing divides up growing complexity into more manageable pieces.[20]

Some firms hire other firms to do their IT work. For example, Shoppers Drug Mart Corp. is outsourcing some of its information technology jobs under a five-year agreement with Keane Canada Inc., which will manage the retail company's software applications.[21] GM plans to bid out a $3 billion IT contract. The company is under pressure to cut costs and accelerate product development and the auto maker hopes to boost productivity while reducing the redundancies and computer systems and processes on which it relies.[22]

HSBC (Hong Kong and Shanghai Banking Corporation), for instance, carries out credit card and loan processing from India and both Allstate Corp. and Prudential Property & Casualty Insurance Co. have application designers and call-centre personnel working out of Ireland. General Electric Co.—arguably one of the pioneers in understanding this shift—has over 15,000 people in India alone carrying out a variety of knowledge-work business processes.[23]

India is outsourcing. One of the constants of the global economy has been companies moving their tasks—and jobs—to India. But rising wages here, a stronger currency, a demand for workers who speak languages other than English, and competition from countries looking to emulate India's success as a back office—including China, Morocco, and Mexico—are challenging that model.

Ashok Vemuri, an Infosys senior vice president, explains that the future of outsourcing is "to take the work from any part of the world and do it in any part of the world."

Infosys says that its outsourcing experience in India has taught it to carve up a project, apportion each slice to suitable workers, double-check quality, and then export a final, reassembled product to clients. The company contends that it can clone its Indian back office, grooming Chinese, Mexican, or Czech employees to be more productive than local outsourcing firms could make them.

Some analysts compare the strategy to the Japanese penetration of auto manufacturing in the United States in the 1970s. Just as the Japanese learned to make cars without Japanese workers, Indian vendors are learning to outsource without Indians, said Dennis McGuire, chairman of TPI, a Texas-based consultancy that focuses on outsourcing.[24]

Although direct materials and direct labour are generally variable in relation to production volume, overhead costs may be variable, mixed, or fixed. Variable overhead includes the cost of indirect materials and indirect labour paid on an hourly basis, such as wages for forklift operators, material handlers, and others who support the production, assembly, or service process. Depreciation calculated using the units-of-production method is a variable manufacturing overhead cost.

Fixed manufacturing overhead comprises costs such as straight-line depreciation on manufacturing plant assets, and insurance and property taxes on production/service-providing assets. Fixed indirect manufacturing labour cost includes salaries for production supervisors, janitorial workers, shift superintendents, and service managers. The fixed portion of mixed costs (such as maintenance and utilities) incurred in the manufacturing area is also part of fixed manufacturing overhead. Investments in new equipment may create significantly large fixed overhead costs but may also improve product or service quality—and thus reduce another overhead cost: that of poor quality. This is borne out by the following example.

Alwin Thompson is passionate about his products. His big fascination is fruit pies: "Just look at those cherries. You don't get many pies like that anymore," he says, surveying his products in the sampling room of Inter Link Foods' Blackburn bakery.

Mr. Thompson founded Inter Link Foods in 1994. "If you make 40 products you will not do any of them efficiently," he says. He now concentrates on making a handful of core "quality" products at low unit cost and high volume. When he first bought the bakery, it was making a lot of products for the catering trade and losing money. It operated old machinery and much of the work was done by hand. Inter Link swiftly rationalized the product line and invested in automation. Many products were dropped in order to concentrate on a narrow range of "mainstream" cakes and pastries for sale to the big supermarkets as "own-label" products and "in-store baked items." As a result, productivity has been improved.[25]

Mixed Costs

Some costs are not strictly variable or fixed; they are a combination of both. This type of cost is called a **mixed cost**. It is said to have both a variable and a fixed component. This type of cost does not fluctuate in direct proportion to changes in activity, nor does it remain constant with changes in activity. Electricity is a good example of a mixed cost. Electricity bills are commonly computed as a flat charge (the fixed component) for basic service plus a stated rate for each kilowatt hour (kwh) of electricity used (the variable component). Exhibit 2-6 on the following page shows a graph for Swiss Chalet's electricity charge, which consists of a flat rate

mixed cost
a cost that has both a variable and a fixed component; it does not fluctuate in direct proportion to changes in activity, nor does it remain constant with changes in activity

of \$100 per month plus \$0.02 per kwh consumed. If Swiss Chalet uses 20,000 kwh of electricity in a month, its total electricity bill is \$500 [\$100 + (\$0.02 × 20,000)]. If the company uses 30,000 kwh, the electricity bill is \$700. Management accountants generally separate mixed costs into their variable and fixed components so that the behaviour of these costs is more readily apparent and can be analyzed in greater detail.

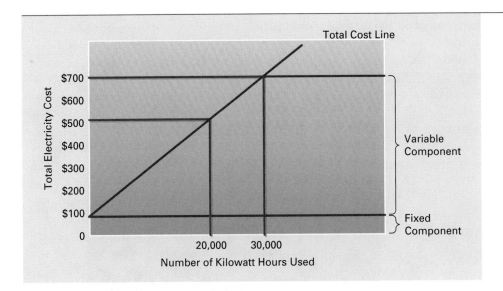

EXHIBIT 2-6
Graph of a Mixed Cost

Step Cost

Another type of cost shifts upward or downward when activity changes by a certain interval or "step." A **step cost** can be variable or fixed. Step variable costs have small steps. Exhibit 2-7 illustrates an example of a step-variable cost. If Swiss Chalet's purchasing agent buys tomato powder in lots of less than 2,000 grams, the price per

step cost
a variable or fixed cost that shifts upward or downward when activity changes by a certain interval or step

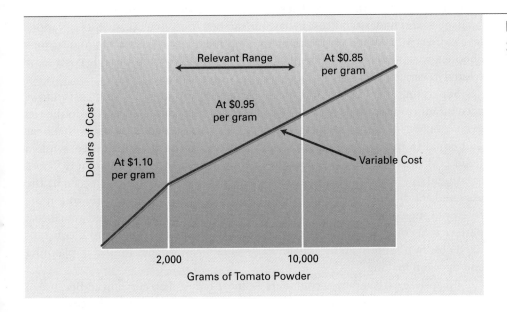

EXHIBIT 2-7
Step Variable Cost

gram is $1.10. If tomato powder is purchased in lots between 2,000 and 10,000 grams, the price falls to $0.95 per gram. Quantities over 10,000 grams may be purchased for only $0.85 per gram. Therefore, if Swiss Chalet buys 4,000 grams, it will pay $3,800 for its purchases; if it buys 11,000 grams, the price will be $9,350. In contrast, an example of a step-fixed cost is shown in Exhibit 2-8. At Swiss Chalet, the salary cost for a delivery person who can service 2,000 customers per month is $3,200 per month. If delivery volume increases from the current 8,000 customers to 10,000 customers, Swiss Chalet will need five drivers rather than the four that are presently employed. An additional 2,000 customers will result in an additional step fixed cost of $3,200 for a total for $6,400.

EXHIBIT 2-8

Step Fixed Cost

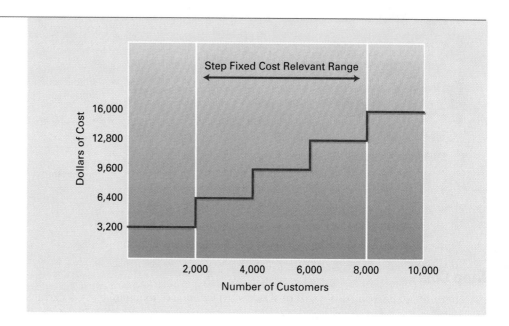

Although all costs do not strictly conform to the categories just described, the categories represent the types of cost behaviour typically encountered in business. Managers who understand cost behaviour can better estimate total costs at various levels of activity. When step variable or step fixed costs exist, accountants must choose a specific relevant range of activity that will allow step variable costs to be treated as variable and step fixed costs to be treated as fixed.

Separating mixed costs and specifying a relevant range for step costs allows accountants to treat their perceptions of the cost behaviours that occur in the relevant range as if they were fact. A variable cost is assumed to be perfectly linear and equal to the average variable unit cost within the relevant range, while a fixed cost is assumed to be constant in total within the relevant range. These treatments of variable and fixed costs are justified for two reasons. First, the assumed conditions approximate reality; if the company operates only within the relevant range of activity, the cost behaviours reflect the expected and actual cost patterns. Second, selection of a constant variable cost per unit and a constant fixed cost in total provides a convenient, stable measurement for use in planning and decision making.

All costs are treated by accountants as linear rather than curvilinear. Because of this treatment, the general formula for a straight line is used to describe any type of cost (variable, fixed, or mixed) within a relevant range of activity. The straight-line formula is:

$$y = a + bx$$

where

y = total cost

a = fixed portion of total cost

b = variable portion of total cost (the rate at which total cost changes in relation to changes in x; when a graph is prepared to depict the straight line, b represents the slope of the line)

x = activity base (or cost driver) to which y is being related

Exhibit 2-9 illustrates the use of the straight-line formula for each type of cost behaviour. An entirely variable cost is represented as $y = \$0 + bx$. Zero is shown as the value for a because there is no fixed cost. A purely fixed cost is formulated as $y = a + \$0x$. Zero is the b-term in the formula since no cost component varies with activity. A mixed cost has formula values for both the a and b unknowns.

Since mixed costs contain amounts for both values, mixed costs must be separated into their variable and fixed components before separate overhead rates (fixed and variable) can be calculated. The simplest method of separation is the high–low method.

EXHIBIT 2-9

Uses of the Straight-Line Cost Formula

Variable Cost

To explain or predict a variable cost such as indirect materials when the cost per unit is $2:

$$y = \$0 + \$2x$$

where y = Total indirect materials cost
x = Number of units produced

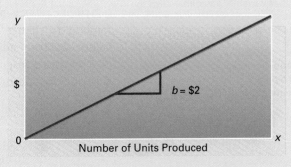

Fixed Cost

To explain or predict a fixed cost such as building rent of $80,000 per year:

$$y = \$80,000 + \$0x$$

where y = Total annual building rent

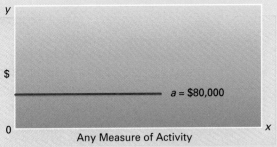

Mixed Cost

To explain or predict a mixed cost such as repairs and maintenance when the fixed element is $14,000 per year and the variable element is $0.60 per machine hour

$$y = \$14,000 + \$0.60x$$

where y = Total annual repairs and maintenance cost
x = Number of machine hours incurred

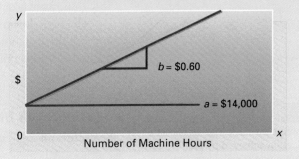

high–low method
a technique for separating mixed costs that uses actual observations of a total cost at the highest and lowest levels of activity and calculates the change in both activity and cost; the levels chosen must be within the relevant range

outlier
a nonrepresentative point that falls outside of the relevant range of activity or that is a distortion of normal costs within the relevant range

independent variable
a variable that, when changed, will cause consistent, observable changes in another variable; a variable used as the basis of predicting the value of a dependent variable

dependent variable
an unknown variable that is to be predicted by use of one or more independent variables

scattergraph
a graphic representation of the relationship between variables within a population achieved by plotting each magnitude or item against the coordinates provided

High–Low Method

The **high–low method** is a cost estimation technique for separating a mixed cost into its variable and fixed components. The high–low method uses activity and cost information from an actual set of cost observations to calculate the variable and fixed cost estimates. The highest and lowest activity levels are selected from the data set if these two levels are within the relevant range. The reason for selecting the high and low activity levels rather than high and low costs is that the analysis is undertaken to estimate how costs change in relation to activity changes. Activities cause costs to change; costs do not cause activities to change.

A nonrepresentative point that falls outside of the relevant range of activity or that is a distortion of normal costs within the relevant range is known as an **outlier**. These outliers should be disregarded when analyzing mixed costs under the high–low method.

The high–low method is used to develop an equation that predicts the unknown values of a dependent variable (y-term) from the known values of one or more independent variables (x-term). An **independent variable** is an amount that, when changed, will cause consistent, observable changes in another variable. A **dependent variable** is an unknown amount that can be predicted by the use of one or more independent variables.

Total mixed cost increases or decreases with changes in activity. The change in cost is equal to the change in activity multiplied by the unit variable cost; the fixed cost element does not fluctuate with changes in activity. The variable cost per unit of activity reflects the average change in cost for each additional unit of activity. Finding the changes in activity and cost simply involves subtracting the observation values of activity and cost at the lowest level of activity from the observation values of activity and cost at the highest level of activity. These differences are then used to calculate the b-term in the $y = a + bx$ formula as follows:

$$b = \frac{\text{Cost at highest activity level} - \text{Cost at lowest activity level}}{\text{Highest activity level} - \text{Lowest activity level}}$$
$$= \frac{\text{Change in the total cost}}{\text{Change in activity level}}$$

The b-term represents the unit variable cost per measure of activity. At either the lowest or the highest level of activity, the b-value can be multiplied by the activity level to determine the amount of total variable cost contained in the total mixed cost at either the highest or lowest level of activity.

Since a mixed cost has both a variable (b) and a fixed component (a), the latter is found by subtracting total variable cost from total cost: $y - bx = a$. Either the highest or the lowest level of activity can be used to determine the fixed portion of the mixed cost. Both activity levels are assumed to be on the same straight line and, thus, fixed cost would be constant at all activity levels within the relevant range.

The high–low method illustrated in Exhibit 2-10 shows the cost of supplies used and the direct labour hours for a Swiss Chalet take-out counter. The restaurant's normal cost of supplies is between $1,600 and $2,300 per month. For this store, the variable cost is $15.555 per direct labour hour and the fixed cost is $978 per month.

Scattergraph Method

Scattergraph analysis is an attempt to overcome the deficiencies of the high–low method. All the observations are considered rather than just the high and low as is done in the high–low method. A scattergraph requires the plotting of points

EXHIBIT 2-10

High–Low Analysis of Supplies
Cost

The following information on direct labour hours and supplies cost is available from the prior year:

Month	Labour Hours	Supplies Cost
January	40	$1,600
February	60	1,650
March	64	2,000
April	50	1,750
May	33	1,300
June	90	2,350
July	80	2,280
August	83	2,210
September	62	1,950
October	85	2,300
November	75	2,000
December	70	1,890

Note that the May data appears to be out of the relevant range; this unusually low activity was analyzed and found to be caused by closing the restaurant due to an electricity shutdown.

Step 1: Select the highest and lowest levels of activity within the relevant range and obtain the costs associated with those levels. The highest activity level, 90 direct labour hours, cost $2,350. The lowest activity level, 40 direct labour hours, cost $1,600. (The May data is considered an outlier and thus is omitted from the analysis.)

Step 2: Calculate the change in activity level and the change in cost.

	Labour Hours	Cost of Supplies
High activity (June)	90	$2,350
Low activity (January)	40	1,600
Changes	50	$ 750

Step 3: Determine the relationship of cost change to activity change to find the variable cost element.

$$b = \frac{\text{Change in total cost}}{\text{Change in activity level}} = \frac{\$750}{50} = \$15.00 \text{ per hour}$$

Step 4: Compute total variable cost (TVC) at either level of activity.

Highest level of activity: TVC = $15.00(90) = $1,350
              or
Lowest level of activity: TVC = $15.00(40) = $ 600

Step 5: Subtract total variable cost from total cost at either level of activity to determine fixed cost.

Highest level of activity: $a = \$2{,}350 - \$1{,}350$
                          = $1,000

Lowest level of activity: $a = \$1{,}600 - \$ 600$
                          = $1,000

Step 6: Substitute the fixed and variable cost values in the straight-line formula to get an equation that can be used to estimate total cost at any level of activity within the relevant range.

$y = \$1{,}000 + \$15.00x$ (where x = number of direct labour hours)

representing both cost and activity observations on a graph. The scattergraph method basically discloses the trend line of the points from these two sets of data. The vertical axis of the graph is normally used to represent dollars of cost, and the horizontal axis represents the activity measure that is causing a change in the total cost amount. This graphical illustration should provide insight into how well the cost is driven (correlated) by the activity measure on the horizontal axis.

An appropriate "fit" tries to have an equal number of observations above and below the line such that the fit represents an "average" of all the observations. In this particular case, the fit connects two of the twelve observations. However, a different person might fit a slightly different straight line through the twelve observations.

When preparing a scattergraph, the first step is to plot the points on the diagram, as is shown in Exhibit 2-11. The data should cover a range of volume that is wide enough to include both the lowest and highest volumes likely to be experienced in the near future. Monthly data are generally used as this is the timing for accounting reports and records.

EXHIBIT 2-11

Scattergraph Analysis of
Supplies Cost

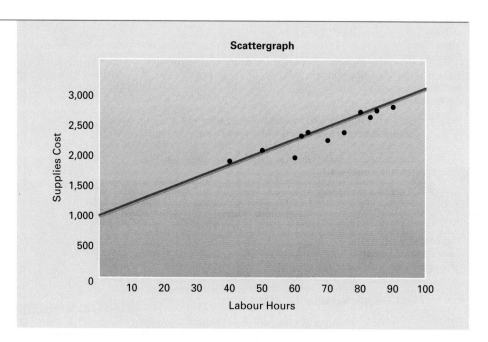

Using the same information as presented in the high–low example shown on page 59, plot the number of direct labour hours (activity) on the horizontal axis and the cost of supplies in dollars on the vertical axis.

In the second step, a straight line is drawn through the points in such a way that it represents the trend of the points. This line is sketched in by inspection and generally provides sufficiently accurate results for forecasting the variability of costs. This line represents the path along which costs move with an increasing level of activity. By reading from the graph, the indicated amount of supplies cost may be determined for any volume within the range of the graph.

When the cost line on the graph in Exhibit 2-11 is extended out to the left where it crosses the vertical axis of the graph, the indicated fixed portion of the cost is obtained. Reading from the graph, the fixed cost is thus found to be $1,000 per month. The amount of variable cost at any given volume can be determined by reading the total cost from the graph and then subtracting the amount of fixed cost.[26]

regression analysis
a statistical procedure used to determine and measure a predictive relationship between one dependent variable and one or more other variables

Regression analysis is another technique used to separate mixed costs into their variable and fixed cost elements. Regression often results in a better estimate of the cost formula than does the high–low method. Performing it by hand is tedious; however, many software packages are available to do regression analysis. Regression analysis often results in a more reliable estimate of the cost formula than does the high–low method. Unlike the high–low method, this method uses all of the data points to calculate the cost formula.

Regardless of which method is used to separate mixed costs, it is important to recognize the following three points. First, high–low, scattergraph, and regression are simply cost estimation techniques; none provides exact costs of future activities. Second, the appropriateness of the cost formula depends on the validity of the activity measure chosen to predict the variable cost. The activity base selected should be logically related to the incurrence of overhead cost and should reflect significant **correlation**. (Correlation is a statistical measure of the strength of the relationship between two variables.) Third, when significant changes are occurring in a business (such as the introduction of new production techniques or new product lines or expansion into new locales), historical information may not be very useful in attempting to predict future costs.

correlation
a statistical measure of the strength of the relationship between two variables

As has been discussed earlier, overhead costs are essential to the conversion process but simply cannot be traced directly to output. Overhead is any manufacturing or production cost that is indirect to manufacturing a product or providing a service and, accordingly, does not include direct material and direct labour. It does include indirect material and indirect labour as well as any and all other costs incurred in the production area. The greater part of most companies' costs (other than those for purchased materials) typically occurs in overhead categories. Even in manufacturing, more than two-thirds of all nonmaterial costs tend to be indirect or overhead expenses.

Cost containment is a key item for businesses today. It is important for all businesses to keep track of costs. The following News Note shows how ERP systems help companies do this.

The Use of an ERP System Improves Profitability

GENERAL NEWS NOTE

ERP stands for enterprise resource planning. ERP is a way to integrate the data and processes of an organization into a single system. Most ERP systems utilize many components, including hardware and software, in order to achieve integration. Typically, ERP systems use a unified database to store data for various functions found throughout the organization.

Once an ERP system is in place, all aspects of an organization can usually work in harmony instead of every single system needing to be compatible with each of the others. For large organizations, increased productivity and fewer types of software are a result.

There are many advantages to implementing an ERP system. Here are a few of them:
- A totally integrated system.
- The ability to streamline different processes and workflows.
- The ability to easily share data across various departments in an organization.
- Improved efficiency and productivity levels.
- Better tracking and forecasting.
- Lower costs.
- Improved customer service.

UNICORN CHEMICAL, a British-based chemicals firm with 20 employees, had been running its business using Tas Books, a basic accounting package. In 2001, SAGE, a British-based vendor of accounting and business software products, announced that it would be buying TAS SOFTWARE, which makes Tas Books. Unicorn worried how the deal would affect users of Tas Books. "We were never contacted by the vendor since it was taken over," says Tim Kilpatrick, managing director of Unicorn. As a result, Unicorn decided to switch to a modern resource planning package that did more than keep the books.

"I decided I wanted to bring in CRM [Customer Relationship Management] capability because before we had no knowledge of how our customers used our products," says Mr. Kilpatrick, who was also keen to get better control of the firm's supply chain.

According to Donna Troy, vice president for SME business at SAP (Systems Applications and Products), a German software firm, this is a common problem for small and medium-sized enterprises (SMEs) that use stand-alone products such as accounting packages and spreadsheets. "They find they have no visibility into their business so they cannot link customers to supply."

Unicorn bought BUSINESS ONE, a recent ERP offering from SAP that is aimed at businesses with fewer than 100 employees. The package of hardware, software, and consulting cost $34,272. Mr. Kilpatrick says that it has already proved its worth: the software's supply chain management capabilities have enabled Unicorn to free up $12,000 of inventory.

BUSINESS ONE, acquired from an Israeli company, represents a radical shift for SAP, which had always developed everything in-house. The package is also an attempt to shake off the perception that you need deep pockets, lots of time, and a team of well-paid system analysts to install and run the software. "Business One was priced competitively and the project was completed in three weeks," Mr. Kilpatrick says.

Quick implementation and ease-of-use are what really set SME offerings apart from mainstream ERP software. "Most Business One customers do not have any IT staff," Mr. Shepherd says.

SOURCE: Tech-FAQ, all rights reserved, Copyright 2007; Geoffrey Nairn, "Taking Account of Packages," *FT-IT Review*, March 23, 2005.

ACCUMULATION OF PRODUCT COSTS—A REVIEW

Product costs are accumulated for inventory purposes and expensed to Cost of Goods Sold using either a periodic or a perpetual inventory system. In either system, all product costs flow through Work in Process Inventory to Finished Goods Inventory and, ultimately, to Cost of Goods Sold. The perpetual inventory control system continuously provides current inventory and cost of goods sold information for financial statement preparation and for inventory planning, cost control, and decision making. The costs of maintaining a perpetual inventory system have fallen significantly as computerized production, bar coding, and information processing have become more pervasive. This text will assume that all companies discussed use the perpetual inventory method.

The following hypothetical information for Red River Rotisserie Ltd. is used to illustrate the flow of product costs in a manufacturing organization. The June 1 inventory account balances for the company are as follows: Raw Materials (all direct), $2,500; Work in Process, $6,000; and Finished Goods, $9,000. The company uses separate variable and fixed accounts to record the incurrence of overhead. Such separation of information improves the accuracy of tracking and controlling costs. Overhead costs are transferred at the end of the month to the Work in Process Inventory account. The following transactions, keyed to the journal entries in Exhibit 2-12, represent Red River Rotisserie's activity for the month of June.

Entry #	Description
1	During June, Red River Rotisserie's purchasing agent bought $85,000 of raw materials on account.
2	Transferred $81,600 of materials into the production area; of these, $69,000 represented direct materials and $12,600 represented indirect materials.
3	Production wages for the month totalled $18,800; direct labour accounted for $5,000 of that amount.

4   The June salaries for production supervisors totalled $7,500.

5   The total utility cost for June was $1,870; analyzing this cost indicated that $1,200 of this amount was variable and $670 was fixed.

6   Contract maintenance in the amount of $2,692 was paid.

7   Red River Rotisserie recorded depreciation on the manufacturing assets in the amount of $8,333.

8   Red River recorded an entry for the expiration of $355 of prepaid insurance on the manufacturing assets.

9   During June, $122,150 of goods were completed and transferred to Finished Goods Inventory.

10   Items sold during the month of June were transferred from finished goods. The cost of the finished goods that were sold amounted to $120,150.

11   The total sales for the month amounted to $242,000. All sales are on credit.

EXHIBIT 2-12

Flow of Product Costs Through the Accounts

(1)	Raw Materials Inventory	85,000	
	Accounts Payable		85,000
	To record cost of raw materials purchased on account.		
(2)	Work in Process Inventory	69,000	
	Variable Overhead	12,600	
	Raw Materials Inventory		81,600
	To record transfer of direct and indirect materials.		
(3)	Work in Process Inventory	5,000	
	Variable Overhead	13,800	
	Salaries and Wages Payable		18,800
	To accrue manufacturing wages for direct and indirect labour.		
(4)	Fixed Overhead	7,500	
	Salaries and Wages Payable		7,500
	To accrue production supervisors' salaries.		
(5)	Variable Overhead	1,200	
	Fixed Overhead	670	
	Utilities Payable		1,870
	To record mixed utility cost in its variable and fixed proportions.		
(6)	Fixed Overhead	2,692	
	Cash		2,692
	To record payments for contract maintenance for the period.		
(7)	Fixed Overhead	8,333	
	Accumulated Depreciation—Manufacturing Equipment		8,333
	To record depreciation on manufacturing assets for the period.		
(8)	Fixed Overhead	355	
	Prepaid Factory Insurance		355
	To record expiration of prepaid insurance on manufacturing assets.		
(9)	Work in Process Inventory	47,150	
	Variable Overhead		27,600
	Fixed Overhead		19,550
	To record the transfer of predetermined fixed and variable overhead costs to Work in Process Inventory.		
(10)	Finished Goods Inventory	122,150	
	Work in Process Inventory		122,150
	To record the transfer of work completed during the period.		
(11)	Cost of Goods Sold	120,150	
	Finished Goods Inventory		120,150
	To record cost of goods sold for the period.		
(12)	Accounts Receivable	242,000	
	Sales		242,000
	To record the sale of goods on account during the period.		

As illustrated in the T-accounts below in Exhibit 2-13, the perpetual inventory system provides detailed information about the cost of raw materials used, goods completed, and goods sold. From this information, financial statements can be prepared.

EXHIBIT 2-13
Cost Flow Overview—
T Accounts

Raw Materials Inventory

Beginning balance	2,500	Raw material	(2)	81,600
Purchase	(1) 85,000			
	87,500			
Ending balance	5,900			

Salaries and Wages Payable

	Direct & indirect	(3)	18,800
	Supervisors	(4)	7,500
			26,300

Variable Overhead

Indirect material	(2)	12,600	Transfer to WIP	(9)	27,600
Indirect labour	(3)	13,800			
Variable utilities	(5)	1,200			
		27,600			

Fixed Overhead

Supervisor salaries	(4)	7,500	Transfer to WIP	(9)	19,550
Fixed utilities	(5)	670			
Fixed maintenance	(6)	2,692			
Depreciation	(7)	8,333			
Insurance	(8)	355			
		19,550			19,550

Accounts Payable

	Purchase	(1)	85,000

Utilities Payable

	Variable and fixed overhead	(5)	1,870

Accounts Receivable

Credit Sales	(12) 242,000	

Accumulated Depreciation—Manufacturing Equipment

	Depreciation	(7)	8,333

Work in Process Inventory

Beginning balance	6,000	Complete	(9)	122,150
Direct material	(2) 69,000			
Direct labour	(3) 5,000			
To close overhead (variable and fixed)	(9) 47,150			
	127,150			
Ending balance	5,000			

Finished Goods Inventory

Beginning balance	9,000	Sold	(10)	120,150
Complete	(10) 122,150			
	131,150			
Ending balance	11,000			

Cost of Goods Sold

Sold	(11) 120,150	
	120,150	

Sales

	Sold	(11)	242,000

Prepaid Factory Insurance

	Expired insurance	(8)	355

Cash

	Maintenance	(6)	2,692

The first schedule that must be prepared in a manufacturing concern is a Schedule of Cost of Goods Manufactured. The information from this schedule is then transferred to the Schedule of Cost of Goods Sold, the total of which is then transferred to the Corporation's Income Statement.

COST OF GOODS MANUFACTURED AND SOLD

LEARNING OBJECTIVE 5

How is cost of goods manufactured calculated? Cost of goods sold?

In merchandising businesses, cost of goods sold (CGS) is presented as the beginning merchandise inventory plus net purchases minus ending merchandise inventory. Manufacturing businesses cannot use such a simplistic approach to calculate cost of goods sold. The production costs incurred during the period relate both to goods that were completed and to goods that are still in process. Therefore, a manufacturer prepares a schedule of cost of goods manufactured as a preliminary step to the presentation of cost of goods sold. **Cost of goods manufactured** (CGM) represents the total production cost of the goods that were completed and transferred to Finished Goods Inventory during the period. This amount does not include the cost of work still in process at the end of the period. The schedule of cost of goods manufactured allows managers to see the relationships among the various production costs and to know the results of the cost flows through the inventory accounts. It is prepared only as an internal schedule and is not provided to external parties.

cost of goods manufactured
the total manufacturing costs attached to units produced during an accounting period

cost of goods manufactured statement
the total cost of the goods that were completed and transferred to Finished Goods Inventory during the period

Using the information from Exhibit 2-13, a cost of goods manufactured schedule is presented in Exhibit 2-14 and a cost of goods sold schedule is presented in Exhibit 2-15. The cost of goods manufactured schedule reflects the manufacturing activity as summarized in the Work in Process Inventory (WIP) account. The statement starts with the calculation of the cost of raw materials used in the production process during the period. This figure is calculated as beginning raw materials inventory plus raw materials purchased during the period minus the ending balance of raw materials inventory. Direct labour cost is determined from payroll records of the period and is added to the cost of direct materials used. All charges for direct labour during the period become part of Work in Process Inventory. Variable and fixed overhead are added to the prime cost of direct materials used and direct labour incurred to arrive at the total current period manufacturing costs.

Red River Rotisserie Ltd. Schedule of Cost of Goods Manufactured For Month Ended June 30, 2011		
Manufacturing costs for the period:		
Raw Materials Used:		
Beginning raw materials balance	$ 2,500	
Plus: Purchases of raw materials	85,000	
Raw materials available for use	$87,500	
Less: Ending raw materials balance	5,900	
Total raw materials used	$81,600	
Less: Indirect materials	12,600	
Total direct materials used		$ 69,000
Direct Labour		5,000
Variable overhead		27,600
Fixed overhead		19,550
Total current period manufacturing costs		$121,150
Plus: Beginning work in process inventory, June 1, 2011		6,000
Total costs to account for		$127,150
Less: Ending work in process inventory, June 30, 2011		5,000
Cost of goods manufactured		$122,150

EXHIBIT 2-14

Schedule of Cost of Goods Manufactured

Adding the beginning Work in Process Inventory cost to total current period manufacturing costs provides a subtotal amount that is referred to as "total costs to account for." The value of ending Work in Process Inventory is subtracted from this subtotal to provide the Cost of Goods Manufactured during the period.

To calculate the Cost of Goods Sold, the Cost of Goods Manufactured (CGM) (from Exhibit 2-14) is added to the beginning balance of Finished Goods (FG) Inventory to determine the cost of goods available for sale during the period. The ending Finished Goods Inventory is then deducted from the cost of goods available for sale during the period to arrive at the **cost of goods sold**. In a perpetual inventory system, the actual amount of ending Finished Goods Inventory, which is arrived at by taking a physical inventory, can be compared to the amount that is listed in the Finished Goods Inventory account at the end of the period. Any differences can be attributed to losses that might have arisen from theft, breakage, evaporation, or accounting errors. Major differences between the amount of inventory shown in the accounting records and the actual amount of inventory on hand should be investigated.

cost of goods sold
the cost of the products or services sold during the period

EXHIBIT 2-15

Schedule of Cost of Goods Sold

Red River Rotisserie Ltd.	
Schedule of Cost of Goods Sold	
For Month Ended June 30, 2011	
Beginning Balance of Finished Goods Inventory, June 1, 2011	$ 9,000
Plus: Cost of Goods Manufactured	122,150
Cost of Goods Available for Sale	$131,150
Less: Ending Balance of Finished Goods Inventory, June 30, 2011	11,000
Cost of Goods Sold	$120,150

SITE ANALYSIS

Swiss Chalet

Cara, which got its start as the Canada Railway News Co. in 1883, was built on the business of a few entrepreneurial Phelans who were selling apples and newspapers on trains leaving Toronto. As people found new ways to travel, the company kept pace. But by the time P.J. Phelan came along, in the mid-1950s, Cara's ownership structure was a mess, as were its business divisions. As the company's history books like to boast, P.J. "awoke the sleeping giant" when he consolidated ownership and shifted Cara's focus from transportation to restaurants.

The company that returned to family control in February 2004 is hardly the same one that the Phelans took public 35 years ago, when sales amounted to just $33 million. Cara has morphed from an airline caterer to an operator of Swiss Chalet (with 190 units in Canada and five in the United States) and other major restaurant chains such as Harvey's, Second Cup, Kelsey's, and Milestone's.

It's fitting that Swiss Chalet is the sort of place where everybody knows your name. It's a reliable, nostalgic Canadian tradition. The quarter chicken dinner, a bestseller since 1954, is one of those dishes that you intensely crave. The sauce hasn't changed, the chicken hasn't changed, and the fresh-cut fries haven't changed. What has changed is the advent of website ordering, launched in July 2003 in conjunction with the call-ahead service, which receives an astounding 15,000 orders per month and accounts for about 8% of the total off-premises sales. As well, Swiss Chalet has improved on its takeout packaging—it's now a deluxe doggy bag with an emphasis on form and function. Consumers are becoming more conscious of the health consequences of the foods they eat; foodservice companies are responding to the resulting trends. For example, Swiss Chalet has announced that it has switched to transfat-free canola oil. Furthermore, detailed nutritional information is available for all its restaurants online and in printed form.

Time-starved guests, like our couple pictured, are demanding healthier fare that is also good tasting. This couple has found that Swiss Chalet is a reliable and enjoyable oasis in which to dine.

The company has declared: "Cara is dedicated to providing fresh and healthy meal choices for Canadians. In our efforts to provide the perfect Guest experience, we believe that our Guests shouldn't have to be concerned with excessive hydrogenated oils and fats. And we believe making this change right now, is the right thing to do."

Swiss Chalet instinctively knows it should do what it does best: make succulently delicious chicken served in a casual, comfortable environment.

SOURCES: "Dreams," *Foodservice and Hospitality*, July 2004, pp. 65–68; Mark Brown, "Inside an Empire," *Canadian Business*, May 24–June 6, 2004, p. 61. "New at Swiss Chalet," *Foodservice News*, February, 2005; J. Stewart, "Restaurant Chain Keen to Go Lean," *Mississauga News*, December 21, 2007.

SITE ANALYSIS

APPENDIX 2A

Least-Squares Regression Analysis

The chapter illustrates the high–low method and the scattergraph method of separating mixed costs into their variable and fixed elements. A potential weakness of the high–low method is that outliers may be inadvertently used in the calculation. Outliers are not representative of actual costs and are generally not good predictors of future costs. Thus, a cost formula derived from outlier data will probably not be very useful.

This appendix introduces a statistical technique known as **least-squares regression analysis**, another method of mixed cost analysis. The least-squares method makes it possible to mathematically determine the cost formula of a mixed cost by considering the best fit to all representative data points rather than only two points. (Outliers should be excluded from the set of data points.)

Like the high–low method, least-squares separates the variable and fixed cost elements of any type of mixed cost. When multiple independent variables exist, least-squares regression also helps managers to select the independent variable that

LEARNING OBJECTIVE 4

How can mixed costs be analyzed using the high–low method, scattergraph method, and least-squares regression analysis?

least-squares regression analysis
a statistical technique for mathematically determining the cost line of a mixed cost that best fits the data set by considering all representative data points; allows the user to investigate the relationship between or among dependent and independent variables

has the strongest correlation with—and thus is the best predictor of—the dependent variable. For example, least-squares can be used by managers trying to decide if machine hours, direct labour hours, or number of parts per product best explains and predicts changes in a certain manufacturing overhead cost pool.

All chapter examples assume that a linear relationship exists between the independent and dependent variables. Thus, each one-unit change in an independent variable produces a specific unit change in the dependent variable. When only one independent variable is used to predict the dependent variable, the process is known as **simple regression** analysis. In **multiple regression**, two or more independent variables are used.

Simple linear regression employs the same straight-line formula ($y = a + bx$) used in the high–low method. First, the available data set consisting of the actual values of the independent variable (x) and actual values of the dependent variable (y) is analyzed for outliers, which are eliminated from consideration. Next, a **regression line** is mathematically developed that represents the line that best fits the data observations. This line minimizes the sum of the squares of the vertical deviations between it and the actual observation points.

Exhibit 2-16 graphically illustrates least-squares regression. Graph A of the exhibit presents a set of actual observations. These observed values from the data set are designated as y values. Graph B indicates that many lines could be drawn through the data set, but most would provide a poor fit. The y values are used, along with the actual activity levels (x values), to mathematically determine the regression line of best fit. This regression line represents values computed for the dependent variable for all actual activity levels. The dependent values that comprise the regression line are designated as y_c values.

The vertical line segments from the actual observation points (y values) to the regression line (y_c values) in Graph B of Exhibit 2-16 are called deviations. The amount of a deviation is determined by subtracting the y_c value at an activity level from its related y value. Deviations above the regression line are positive amounts, while deviations below the line are negative. By squaring the deviations, the negative signs are eliminated. The positive sum of the squared deviations [$(y - y_c)^2$] can be mathematically manipulated to yield the regression line of best fit. This regression line minimizes the sum of the squared deviations (hence, the name least-squares). The least-squares regression line can then be used to estimate cost formula values for fixed (a) and variable (b) terms. This equation can then be used by the cost analyst to make predictions and analyses.

EXHIBIT 2-16

Illustration of Least-Squares
Regression Line

simple regression
regression analysis using only one independent variable to predict the dependent variable

multiple regression
regression analysis using two or more independent variables

regression line
a line that represents the cost formula for a set of cost observations fit to those observations in a mathematically determined manner

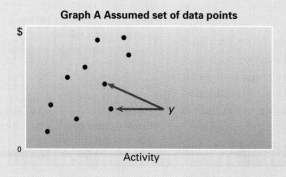

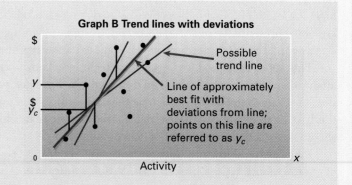

The following information on cups of coffee and utility cost is available from the records of Crimson Lights Café for seven months of the current fiscal year.

Month	Level of Activity in Cups of Coffee	Utility Cost
January	11,300	$1,712
February	11,400	1,716
March	9,000	1,469
April	11,500	1,719
May	11,200	1,698
June	10,100	1,691
July	14,200	2,589

The above information is used to illustrate the calculation of the least-squares regression line. The equations necessary to compute b- and a-values using the method of least squares are as follows.[27]

$$b = \frac{\Sigma xy - n\bar{x}\bar{y}}{\Sigma x^2 - n\bar{x}^2}$$

$$a = \bar{y} - b\bar{x}$$

where

$\bar{x}$ = mean (or arithmetic average) of the independent variable
$\bar{y}$ = mean (or arithmetic average) of the dependent variable
n = number of observations

The Crimson Lights Café data must be restated in an appropriate form for substitution into the equations for b and a. Because of the magnitude of the x values, calculations are made for each 100 cups of coffee to avoid working with extremely large numbers. At the completion of the calculations, the resulting values are converted to a per-unit b value by dividing by 100. These restatements are as follows:

x	y	xy	x^2
113	$ 1,712	$ 193,456	12,769
114	1,716	195,624	12,996
90	1,469	132,210	8,100
115	1,719	197,685	13,225
112	1,698	190,176	12,544
101	1,691	170,791	10,201
645	$10,005	$1,079,942	69,835

(Note that the outlier for July of 12,200 cups of coffee has been ignored.) The mean value for the data in the x-column is 107.5 (or 645 ÷ 6) and the mean value for the data in the y-column is $1,667.50 (or $10,005 ÷ 6).

Substituting appropriate amounts into the formulas yields the b (variable) and a (fixed) cost values. The b value is calculated first, since it is used to compute a.

$$b = \frac{\Sigma xy - n\bar{x}\bar{y}}{\Sigma x^2 - n\bar{x}^2}$$

$$= \frac{\$1,079,942 - 6(107.5)(\$1,667.50)}{69,835 - 6(107.5)(107.5)}$$

$$= \frac{\$4,404.50}{497.5} = \$8.85 \text{ per hundred or } \$0.09 \text{ per cup of coffee}$$

$$a = \bar{y} - b\bar{x}$$

$$= \$1,667.50 - \$8.85(107.5)$$

$$= \$1,667.50 - \$951.38$$

$$= \$716.12$$

Thus, the cost formula under least-squares regression is:

Total utility cost = $716.12 + $0.09 per cup of coffee

Regression information yields more reliable results—a characteristic that is very important to managers seeking to understand and control costs based on changes in activity. Because of the many computer packages that are able to do least-squares regression quickly and accurately, it has become virtually costless to do this type of analysis using a variety of possibilities as the independent variable.

CHAPTER SUMMARY

This chapter is premised on the belief that managers must understand their organizations' costs if they are to achieve strategic successes. Accordingly, it introduces terminology used by managers and management accountants and presents the flow of costs in manufacturing and service environments.

1 **What is the relationship between cost objects and direct costs?**
Direct costs are so defined because they are traceable to a specific cost object. Although indirect costs cannot be explicitly traced to a cost object, allocation techniques can be used to assign such costs to related cost objects. Materials and labour may be directly or indirectly related to particular products, but manufacturing overhead costs are indirect and must be allocated to the products produced.

2 **How does the conversion process work in manufacturing and service companies?**
Converting raw product to a finished good requires the addition of direct material, direct labour, and manufacturing overhead. Prime costs include raw material and direct labour. Conversion costs include direct labour and manufacturing overhead. Raw products are transformed into finished products by the addition of direct labour and manufacturing overhead. The costs of raw material, direct labour, and manufacturing overhead are transferred to work in process and, when completed, the costs are transferred to finished goods.

3 **What assumptions do accountants make about cost behaviour and why are these assumptions necessary?**
Variable costs are constant per unit but fluctuate in total with changes in activity levels within the relevant range. Fixed costs are constant in total as activity levels change within the relevant range, but vary inversely on a per-unit basis with changes in activity levels. The relevant range is generally the company's normal operating range. Step variable costs have small steps and are treated as variable costs; step fixed costs have large steps and are treated as fixed costs. Mixed costs have both a variable and a fixed element.

A predictor is an activity measure that changes in a consistent, observable way with changes in a cost. A cost driver is an activity measure that has a direct causal effect on a cost.

How can mixed costs be analyzed using the high–low method, scattergraph method, and least-squares regression analysis (Appendix 2A)?

All mixed costs must be separated into their variable and fixed elements using either the high–low method, scattergraph method, or regression analysis. The high–low method uses two points of actual activity data (the highest and lowest) to determine the change in cost and activity. Dividing the cost change by the activity change gives the per-unit variable cost portion of the mixed cost. Fixed cost is found by subtracting total variable cost from total cost at either the high or the low level of activity.

The scattergraph method discloses the trend line for two sets of data. The data is plotted on the graph and a straight line is then drawn through the points in such a way as to show a trend of the points. Normally the points do not fall in a straight line but are scattered along a trend.

The least-squares regression analysis is based on an equation for a straight line: $y = a + bx$. It is a precise mathematical measurement. This method is not subjective and includes all observations.

How is cost of goods manufactured calculated? Cost of goods sold?

A cost of goods manufactured statement is the total cost of the goods completed and transferred to finished goods during the period. This cost of goods manufactured computation is prepared for internal management information and is presented on a statement that supports the cost of goods sold computation on the income statement. It includes the cost of direct materials used, the cost of direct labour incurred and the cost of overhead incurred for the period. This statement provides the necessary information to carry forward to the income statement in order to prepare the cost of goods sold section of a manufacturer's income statement.

Key Terms

Allocate (p. 36)

Conversion cost (p. 43)

Correlation (p. 61)

Cost (p. 36)

Cost behaviour (p. 45)

Cost driver (p. 45)

Cost object (p. 36)

Cost of goods manufactured (p. 65)

Cost of goods manufactured
 statement (p. 65)

Cost of goods sold (p. 66)

Dependent variable (p. 58)

Direct cost (p. 36)

Direct labour (p. 37)

Direct material (p. 37)

Fixed cost (p. 47)

High–low method (p. 58)

Independent variable (p. 58)

Indirect cost (p. 36)

Least-squares regression analysis
 (p. 67)

Mixed cost (p. 54)

Multiple regression (p. 68)

Outlier (p. 58)

Overhead (p. 42)

Period cost (p. 36)

Predictor (p. 45)

Prime cost (p. 43)

Product cost (p. 36)

Regression analysis (p. 60)

Regression line (p. 68)

Relevant range (p. 45)

Scattergraph (p. 58)

Simple regression (p. 68)

Step cost (p. 55)

Variable cost (p. 45)

Points to Remember

High–Low Method (example using assumed amounts)

	(Independent Variable) Activity	(Dependent Variable) Associated Total Cost		Total Variable Cost (Rate × Activity)		Total Fixed Cost
High level of activity	28,000	$36,000	=	$22,400	+	$13,600
Low level of activity	18,000	28,000	=	14,400	+	13,600
Differences	10,000	$ 8,000				

$0.80 variable cost per unit of activity

Flow of Costs

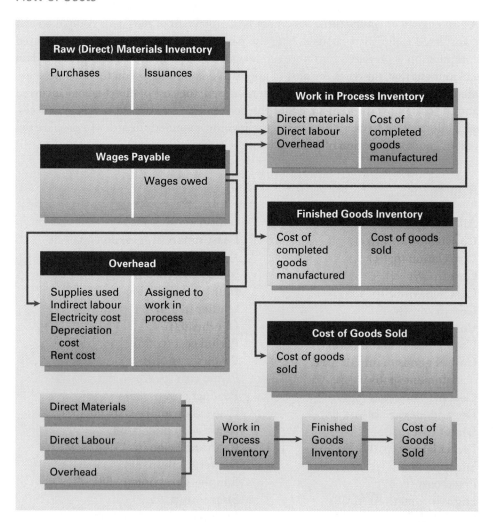

Schedule of Cost of Goods Manufactured

Cost of Goods Manufactured		
Manufacturing Cost for the Period		
Raw materials:		
Beginning raw materials balance	XX	
Plus: Purchases of direct raw materials	+ XX	
Raw materials available for use	XXX	
Less: Ending direct raw materials balance	– XX	
Total raw materials used		XXX
Direct labour		+ XX
Variable overhead		+ XX
Fixed overhead		+ XXX
Total current period manufacturing costs		XXX
Plus: Beginning work in process inventory		+ XX
Total costs to account for		XXXX
Less: Ending work in process inventory		– XX
Cost of Goods Manufactured		XXXX

Schedule of Cost of Goods Sold

Beginning Finished Goods Inventory	XX
Plus: Cost of Goods Manufactured	+XXXX
Cost of Goods Available for Sale	XXXX
Less: Ending Finished Goods Inventory	– XX
Cost of Goods Sold	XXXX

DEMONSTRATION PROBLEMS

Problem 1

Kathy Falk Company Ltd. had the following account balances as of April 1, 2011.

Raw materials (direct and indirect)	$19,300
Work in Process Inventory	43,000
Finished Goods Inventory	28,000
Prepaid Insurance	9,600

Transactions during April were:

1. Purchased $92,000 of raw materials on account.
2. Issued $80,000 of raw materials, of which $57,000 were direct to the product.
3. Factory payroll of $54,000 was accrued; $37,000 was for direct labour and the rest was for supervisors.
4. Utility costs were accrued at $4,900; of these costs, $1,000 were fixed.
5. Property taxes on the factory building were accrued in the amount of $1,500.
6. Prepaid insurance in the amount of $800 on the manufacturing equipment expired in April.
7. Straight-line depreciation on manufacturing equipment was $10,000.
8. Overhead was applied to Work in Process Inventory.
9. Transferred finished products from Work in Process Inventory to Finished Goods Inventory.
10. Sales on account totalled $230,000.
11. Cost of goods sold was $151,000.
12. Selling and administrative costs were $43,575 (credit "Various Accounts").

   End of year information: Ending Work in Process Inventory is $24,500; Ending Indirect Materials Inventory is $2,500; and Ending Direct Materials Inventory $28,800.

Required:

a. Journalize the transactions for April.
b. Prepare a schedule of cost of goods manufactured for April.
c. Prepare an income statement, including a detailed schedule of cost of goods sold.
d. What is the total prime cost? Conversion cost?

Problem 2

Victoria Hospital installed a new scanning machine last year. The controller, in trying to estimate the expected cost of operating and maintaining the scanner in the current year, has been reviewing cost and use data for each of the past four quarters, shown below:

Quarter	Number of Patients	Number of Hours Used	Total Cost
1st	100	75	$10,750
2nd	350	200	12,500
3rd	400	550	15,000
4th	250	300	13,000

Required:

a. Prepare two scattergraphs, one based on number of patients and the other on number of hours used.
b. Use the high–low method to calculate the variable rate and the fixed cost using the information given.
c. Use the least squares method to determine the fixed and variable elements of total cost.

Solutions to Demonstration Problems

Problem 1

a.	(1)	Raw Materials Inventory	92,000	
		Accounts Payable		92,000
		To record purchases of raw materials.		
	(2)	Work in Process Inventory	57,000	
		Variable Overhead	23,000	
		Raw Materials Inventory		80,000
		To record issuance of raw materials from the storeroom.		
	(3)	Work in Process Inventory	37,000	
		Fixed Overhead	17,000	
		Salaries and Wages Payable		54,000
		To record manufacturing payroll.		
	(4)	Variable Overhead	3,900	
		Fixed Overhead	1,000	
		Utilities Payable		4,900
		To record the utilities cost.		
	(5)	Fixed Overhead	1,500	
		Property Taxes Payable		1,500
		To accrue property taxes on factory building.		
	(6)	Fixed Overhead	800	
		Prepaid Insurance		800
		To record expired insurance on manufacturing equipment.		
	(7)	Fixed Overhead	10,000	
		Acc. Depreciation–Manufacturing Equipment		10,000
		To record depreciation on manufacturing equipment.		

(8)	Work in Process Inventory	57,200	
	Variable Overhead		26,900
	Fixed Overhead		30,300
	To apply overhead to work in process.		
(9)	Finished Goods Inventory	169,700*	
	Work in Process Inventory		169,700
	To record cost of goods transferred from Work in Process Inventory to Finished Goods Inventory.		

* from schedule of cost of goods manufactured

(10)	Cost of Goods Sold	151,000	
	Finished Goods Inventory		151,000
	To record cost of goods sold.		
(11)	Accounts Receivable	230,000	
	Sales		230,000
	To record sales on account.		
(12)	Selling and Administrative Expenses	43,575	
	Cash**		43,575
	To record selling and administrative expenses.		

** No cash T-account is shown

Posting of the Journal Entries

Raw Materials Inventory

Bal	19,300	(2)	80,000
(1)	92,000		
Bal	31,300		

Work in Process Inventory

Bal	43,000	(9)	169,700
(2)	57,000		
(3)	37,000		
(8)	57,200		
	194,200		
Bal	24,500		

Finished Goods Inventory

Bal	28,000	(10)	151,000
(9)	169,700		
	197,700		
Bal	46,700		

Prepaid Insurance

Bal	9,600	(6)	800
Bal	8,800		

Accumulated Depreciation–Mfg. Equipment

		(7)	10,000

Various Payables

		(1)	92,000
		(3)	54,000
		(4)	4,900
		(5)	1,500
		Bal	152,400

Fixed Overhead

(3)	17,000	(8)	30,300
(4)	1,000		
(5)	1,500		
(6)	800		
(7)	10,000		
	30,300		

Variable Overhead

(2)	23,000	(8)	26,900
(4)	3,900		
	26,900		

Cost of Goods Sold

(10)	151,000		

Accounts Receivable

(11)	230,000		

Sales

		(11)	230,000

Selling Admin. Expenses

(12)	43,575		

b.

Kathy Falk Company Ltd.
Schedule of Cost of Goods Manufactured
For the Month Ended April 30, 2011

Raw Materials		
Beginning raw materials inventory, April 1, 2011		$ 19,300
Plus: Purchases of raw materials		92,000
Raw materials available for use		$ 111,300
Less: Indirect materials used	$23,000	
Ending balance indirect materials	2,500	25,500
Total direct materials		$ 85,800
Less: Ending direct materials inventory, April 30, 2011		28,800
Total direct materials used		$ 57,000
Direct labour		37,000
Variable overhead	$26,900	
Fixed overhead	30,300	57,200
Total current period manufacturing costs		$ 151,200
Plus: Beginning Work in Process Inventory, April 1, 2011		43,000
Total cost to account for		$ 194,200
Less: Ending Work in Process Inventory, April 30, 2011		24,500
Cost of goods manufactured this period		$ 169,700

c.

Kathy Falk Company Ltd.
Schedule of Cost of Goods Sold
For the Month Ended April 30, 2011

Beginning Finished Goods Inventory, April 1, 2011	$ 28,000
Plus: Cost of Goods Manufactured in April	169,700
Cost of Goods Available for Sale	$197,700
Less: Ending Finished Goods Inventory, April 30, 2011	46,700
Cost of Goods Sold	$151,000

Kathy Falk Company Ltd.
Income Statement
For the Month Ended April 30, 2011

Sales	$230,000
Less: Cost of Goods Sold	151,000
Gross Profit	$ 79,000
Less: Selling and Administrative Expenses	43,575
Profit (Loss) from Operations (before taxes)	$ 35,425

d. Prime cost—$94,000 (Direct material $57,000 + Direct labour $37,000)
Conversion cost—$94,200 (Direct labour $37,000 + Overhead $57,200)

Problem 2

a.

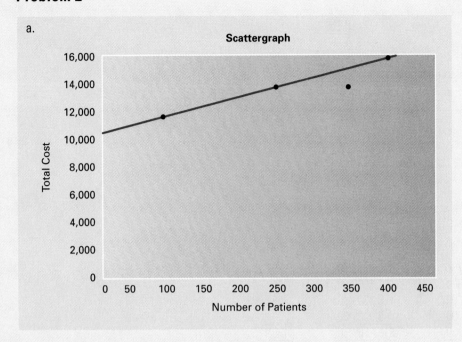

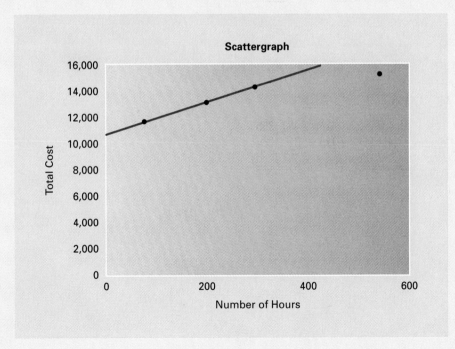

b.

	Number of Hours	Total Cost
3rd quarter (high)	550	$15,000
1st quarter (low)	75	10,750
Difference	475	$ 4,250

Variable rate = $4,250 ÷ 475 hours = $8.947 per hour

Total cost = Fixed cost + Variable cost
Therefore in the high quarter of activity –
$15,000 = Fixed cost + ($8.947 × 550 hours)
$15,000 = Fixed cost + $4,921[1]
Fixed cost = $15,000 − $4,921 = $10,079 per quarter

[1] Rounded to nearest dollar

c.

Quarter	Total Number of Hours	Total Cost y	xy	x^2
1st	75	$10,750	$ 806,250	5,625
2nd	200	12,500	2,500,000	40,000
3rd	550	15,000	8,250,000	302,500
4th	300	13,000	3,900,000	90,000
	1,125	$51,250	$15,456,250	438,125

1. $\Sigma xy = a\Sigma x + b\Sigma x^2$

$$\$15,456,250 = 1,125a + 438,125b$$

2. $\Sigma y + na + b\Sigma x^2$

$$\$51,250 = 4a + 1,125b$$

Equation 1:	$15,456,250 = 1,125a + 438,125b
Multiply equation 2 by 281.25 (1,125 ÷ 4)	14,414,062 = 1,125a + 316,406b
Subtract Equation 2 from Equation 1	$ 1,042,188 = 121,719b

Therefore: b = $8,562 ($1,042,188 ÷ 121,719)
Substituting $8,562 for b in original Equation 2:
$51,250 = 4a + 1,125 ($8,562)
$51,250 = 4a + $9,632[1]
4a = $51,250 − $9,632
4a = $41,618
 a = $41,618 ÷ 4 = $10,405 per quarter

[1] Rounded to nearest dollar

End-of-Chapter Materials

SELF-TEST QUESTIONS

(SOLUTIONS APPEAR AT THE END OF THE CHAPTER.)

Self-Test Questions 1–3 are based on the following information.

Barbara Didona's Friendly Kitchens Ltd. produces dumplings, which are shipped all over the world. All materials are added at the start of production. The following is information pertaining to the corporation's manufacturing operations:

Inventories	January 1	December 31
Direct materials	$35,000	$25,000
Work in process	45,000	20,000
Finished goods	28,000	35,000

Additional information for the current year:

Direct materials purchased	$75,000
Direct labour	85,000
Direct labour rate per hour	10
Overhead rate per direct labour hour	8

1. What was the prime cost?
   a. $ 85,000
   b. $ 75,000
   c. $170,000
   d. $160,000

2. What was the conversion cost?
   a. $ 85,000
   b. $153,000
   c. $165,000
   d. $160,000

3. What was the cost of goods manufactured?
   a. $205,000
   b. $234,000
   c. $263,000
   d. $274,000

Self-Test Questions 1–3 are extracted by the authors from *Management Accounting Examination*, published by the Certified General Accountants Association of Canada (© CGA-Canada, 1999). Reprinted with permission.

4. Which of the following costs should be included as part of overhead in the production of a wooden table?
   a. The amount paid to the individual who stains the table
   b. The commission paid to the salesperson who sells the table
   c. The cost of glue used in the table
   d. The cost of wood used in the table

5. Alpha Co. has the following estimated costs for next year.

Direct materials	$ 6,000
Direct labour	20,000
Rent on factory building	15,000
Sales salaries	25,000
Depreciation on factory equipment	8,000
Indirect labour	12,000
Production supervisor's salary	15,000

Alpha estimates that 20,000 direct labour hours will be worked during the year. If manufacturing overhead is applied on the basis of direct labour hours, what will be the overhead rate per hour?
   a. $2.50
   b. $3.50
   c. $3.75
   d. $5.05

6. Omega Co. had the following data for the first five months of the current year:

	Machine Hours (x)	Lubrication Cost (y)
January	120	$750
February	160	800
March	200	870
April	150	790
May	170	840

Omega Co. expects to work 180 machine hours in June.

What would be the variable rate per machine hour expected in June, using the high–low method?
   a. $0.67
   b. $1.25
   c. $1.40
   d. $1.50

Self-Test Questions 4–6 are extracted by the authors from *Management Accounting Examination*, published by the Certified General Accountants Association of Canada (© CGA-Canada, 2000). Reprinted with permission.

7. David Faber Inc. had the following activities and costs during 2011:

Direct materials:	
Beginning inventory	$ 50,000
Purchases	154,000
Ending inventory	26,000
Direct labour	40,000
Overhead	30,000
Work in process, beginning inventory	2,000
Work in process, ending inventory	10,000
Finished goods, beginning inventory	60,000
Finished goods, ending inventory	40,000

What is the cost of raw materials used by Faber Inc. in 2011?
a. $ 24,000
b. $128,000
c. $178,000
d. $204,000

Self-Test Question 7 is extracted by the authors from *Management Accounting Examination*, published by the Certified General Accountants Association of Canada (© CGA-Canada 2001). Reprinted with permission.

8. The following information for BNN Corp. is available:

	Highest	Lowest
Machine hours	24,000	15,000
Cost per month	$39,200	$32,000

Using the high–low method, what is the estimated variable cost per machine hour?
a. $ 1.25
b. $12.50
c. $ 0.80
d. $ 0.08

9. Grey's Anatomy Ltd. incurred the following costs last year:

Direct materials	$85,000
Direct labour	24,000
Indirect labour	2,500
Indirect materials	3,000

Other operating expenses pertaining to factory operations were the following:

Utilities	$3,200
Maintenance	4,600
Supplies	1,800
Depreciation	15,100
Property taxes	2,900

The only inventory was $6,800 of finished goods at year-end. What was the cost of goods sold?
a. $127,000
b. $135,300
c. $142,100
d. $148,900

10. Which of the following statements is true?
a. Indirect costs can be identified specifically with a given cost object in an economically feasible way.
b. Direct costs cannot be identified specifically with a given cost object in an economically feasible way.
c. Managers prefer to classify costs as indirect rather than direct.
d. A cost may be simultaneously direct and indirect to different cost objects.

Self-test Questions 8 to 10 are extracted by the authors from *Management Accounting Examination*, published by the Certified General Accountants Association of Canada (© CGA Canada, December 2004). Used with permission.

Self-Test Questions 11 and 12 are based on the following information.

Pear Ltd. reports the following cost information for the month of July:

	July 1	July 31
Inventories:		
Direct materials	$13,000	$18,000
Work in process	5,000	4,000
Finished goods	24,000	32,000

Additional costs incurred in July:	
Purchases of direct material	$75,000
Direct manufacturing payroll	$37,500
Direct labour rate per hour	$15.00
Overhead application rate per direct labour hour	$6.00

11. What was the prime cost incurred in July?
a. $ 52,500
b. $107,500
c. $112,500
d. $113,500

12. What was the cost of goods manufactured in July?
a. $108,500
b. $115,500
c. $122,500
d. $123,500

Self-test questions 11 and 12 are extracted by the authors from *Management Accounting Examination*, published by the Certified General Accountants Association of Canada (© CGA Canada, June 2005). Used with permission.

13. Quality Products incurred the following costs last year:

Direct materials	$85,000
Direct labour	$24,000
Indirect labour	$ 2,500
Indirect materials	$ 3,000

Other operating expenses pertaining to factory operations were the following:

Utilities	$ 3,200
Maintenance	$ 4,600
Supplies	$ 1,800
Depreciation	$15,100
Property taxes	$ 2,900

The only inventory was $6,800 of finished goods at year-end. What was the cost of goods sold?
a. $127,000
b. $135,300
c. $142,100
d. $148,900

Self-test question 13 is extracted by the authors from *Management Accounting Examination*, published by the Certified General Accountants Association of Canada (© CGA Canada, December 2004). Used with permission.

QUESTIONS

1. With respect to a specific cost object, what is the difference between a direct cost and an indirect cost?

2. What is a product cost? What are the three general categories of product costs?

3. What specific costs are usually included in direct labour cost?

4. "Prime costs and conversion costs are components of product cost; therefore, the sum of these two cost categories is equal to product cost." Is this statement true or false? Explain.

5. At year-end, where on the balance sheet would the costs appear for products that had been placed into production but were not finished?

6. Why is the relevant range important to managers?

7. What is the distinction between a fixed cost and a variable cost?

8. How do predictors and cost drivers differ? Why is the distinction important?

9. What is a mixed cost? How do mixed costs behave with changes in the activity measure?

10. What is a step cost? Explain the distinction between a step-fixed and a step-variable cost.

11. What are the two major types of overhead costs? Which of these categories has been increasing in recent years?

12. Why is it necessary to separate mixed costs into their variable and fixed cost elements for product costing purposes?

13. What is meant by the term conversion cost, and what product costs does the term include?

14. What is the difference between an expired and an unexpired product cost? Where should each type of cost appear in the financial statements at year-end?

15. Describe the major difference between Cost of Goods Manufactured and Cost of Goods Sold.

16. What is included on the schedule of cost of goods manufactured? Why is it said that this statement shows the flow of costs in a manufacturing company?

17. (Appendix 2A) How does the least-squares regression method improve upon the high–low method for separating mixed costs into their fixed and variable components?

18. (Appendix 2A) Differentiate between an independent and a dependent variable.

EXERCISES

1. (LO 1, 2, 3, 4)

   a. Cost of goods manufactured
   b. Expired cost
   c. Overhead
   d. Conversion cost
   e. Mixed cost
   f. Unexpired cost
   g. Indirect cost
   h. Product cost
   i. Period cost
   j. Direct cost
   k. Prime cost
   l. Cost driver

   1. The sum of direct labour and overhead
   2. A cost outside the conversion area
   3. A factor that causes a cost to be incurred
   4. A cost that has both a variable and a fixed component
   5. The sum of direct materials and direct labour
   6. A cost that cannot be traced to a particular cost object
   7. A cost that has no future benefit
   8. The total cost of products finished during the period
   9. A cost that is clearly traceable to a particular object
   10. The total of all nontraceable costs necessary to make a product or perform a service
   11. An expense or a loss
   12. An inventoriable cost

EXERCISES

Required:

Match the definitions on the right with the terms on the left. Definitions may be used more than once or not at all.

2. (LO 2) Leah Carter Plastic Containers, Inc., purchased a plastic extruding machine for $400,000 to make plastic pill bottles. During its first operating year, the machine produced 500,000 bottles and depreciation was calculated to be $50,000. The company sold 450,000 bottles.

    Required:
    a. What part of the $400,000 machine cost is expired at year-end?
    b. What are the amounts related to this machine and where do these amounts appear on the financial statements at year-end?

3. (LO 2) This year Logan Fashions completed its first year of operations. The company generated sales of $4,000,000 and net income of $600,000. For this same period the firm's gross margin was $2,100,000. Total manufacturing cost incurred this year was $3,200,000.

    Required:
    a. How much period cost did the firm incur this year?
    b. How much product cost did this firm charge against its revenues this year?
    c. How much unexpired manufacturing cost would be shown on the balance sheet at year-end?

4. (LO 2) Classify the following costs incurred in manufacturing potato chips as direct materials, direct labour, or manufacturing overhead.
    a. Hourly wages of a packaging machine operator
    b. Wages of maintenance and clean-up person
    c. Potato costs
    d. Cooking oil costs (considered to be significant)
    e. Seasoning costs (considered to be significant)
    f. Packaging material costs
    g. Packing carton costs
    h. Heating and energy costs
    i. Potato storage costs
    j. Production supervisor's salary

5. (LO 2) Chancellor Canoe Company manufactures aluminum canoes. The following are some costs incurred in the manufacturing process:

    Material Costs

Aluminum	$371,000
Oil and grease for equipment	6,000
Chrome rivets to assemble canoes	3,600
Wooden ribbing and braces	18,400

    Labour Costs

Equipment operators	$120,000
Equipment mechanics	54,000
Manufacturing supervisors	28,000

    Required:
    a. What is the direct material cost?
    b. What is the direct labour cost?
    c. What are the indirect labour and indirect materials costs?

6. (LO 2) Gina's Finest Ltd. is a catering operation that operates two shifts. The company pays a late-shift premium of 10% and an overtime premium of 50%. Labour premiums are included in service overhead.

    The May manufacturing payroll is as follows:

Total wages for May for 7,000 hours	$66,000
Normal hourly wage for early-shift employees	$8
Total regular hours worked, split evenly between the early and late shifts	5,000

    All overtime was worked by the early shift during May.

    Required:
    a. How many overtime hours were worked in May?
    b. How much of the total labour cost should be charged to direct labour? to service overhead?

EXERCISES

c. What amount of service overhead was for late-shift premiums? for overtime premiums?

7. (LO 3) The accounting records of Carlton Ltd., a small construction company, showed the following construction and operating costs for this fiscal year:

Direct materials	$718,000
Direct labour	421,000
Indirect materials	102,000
Indirect labour	129,000
Construction utilities	103,000
Selling and administrative expenses	317,000

Required:
a. What amount of prime cost was incurred?
b. What amount of conversion cost was incurred?
c. What was total product cost?

8. (LO 3) Classify the following costs incurred in the production of bicycles as direct materials, direct labour, or overhead. Indicate whether each cost is most likely fixed, mixed, or variable. Use number of units produced as the activity measure.
a. Manufacturing supervision
b. Aluminum tubing
c. Rims
d. Emblem
e. Gearbox
f. Crew supervisor's salary
g. Fenders
h. Inventory clerk's salary
i. Inspector's salary
j. Handlebars
k. Metalworkers' wages (assume wages are hourly)
l. Roller chain
m. Spokes (assume costs are considered significant)
n. Paint (assume costs are considered significant)

9. (LO 3) Amanda Lang Incorporated produces croquet sets. The company incurred the following costs to produce 2,000 sets last month:

Wooden cases (1 per set)	$ 4,000
Balls (6 per set)	6,000
Mallets	12,000
Wire hoops (12 per set including extras)	4,800
Straight-line depreciation	2,400
Supervisors' salaries	4,400
Total	$33,600

Required:
The firm's accountant has requested that you assist her by answering the following:
a. What did each croquet set component cost? What did each croquet set cost?
b. What type of behaviour would you expect each of these costs to exhibit?
c. This month the company expects to produce 2,500 sets. Would you expect each type of cost to increase or decrease relative to last month? Why? What will be the total cost of 2,500 sets?

10. (LO 4) Better Cheddar Ltd. specializes in making cheese. Management wants to improve its planning of overhead costs and provides you with the following data:

Month	Monthly Production in Kilos of Cheese	Cheese-Making Facility Overhead
January	1,000	$12,000
February	1,250	10,900
March	2,000	13,300
April	1,500	12,100
May	2,125	16,500
June	1,750	13,000
July	1,800	13,700

EXERCISES

Required:
Determine a- and b-values for the equation $y = a + bx$ using the high–low method.

11. (LO 4) Sammy Brady Appliances Ltd. incurred the following expenses for utilities during the first six months:

Month	Sales Volume	Utilities
January	$60,000	$600
February	35,000	350
March	40,000	400
April	50,000	450
May	30,000	150
June	42,500	425

Required:
a. Using the high–low method, develop a formula for utilities expense.
b. Describe any unusual features of your solution in part (a). Give a probable explanation for the result.

12. (LO 4) Smielauskas Printers Ltd. pays $200 per month for a photocopy machine maintenance contract. In addition, variable charges average $0.04 per page copied.
Required:
a. Determine the total cost and the cost per page if the company makes the following number of photocopies (pages):
    i. 1,000
    ii. 2,000
    iii. 4,000
b. Why is the cost per page different in each of the above three cases?

13. (LO 4) The owner of the Winters Fishery Restaurant wants to estimate a cost function for supplies expense. The restaurant has been operating for six months and has had the following activity (customer volume) and costs:

Month	Customer Volume	Supplies
March	3,400	$6,100
April	3,100	5,850
May	3,400	6,200
June	3,600	6,400
July	3,000	5,500
August	2,800	5,400

Required:
a. In a restaurant, what types of supplies are in the variable expense category? the fixed expense category?
b. Using the high–low method, estimate the cost equation for supplies expense.
c. What amount of supplies expense would the company expect to incur in a month in which 3,300 customers were served?

14. (LO 5) Neal Winters Machine Shop had the following inventory balances at the beginning and end of September:

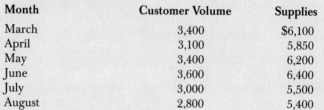

	September 1	September 30
Raw Materials Inventory	$ 16,000	$ 18,000
Work in Process Inventory	94,000	72,000
Finished Goods Inventory	36,000	22,000

All raw materials are direct to the production process. The following information is available about manufacturing costs incurred during September:

Cost of raw materials used	$ 94,000
Direct labour costs	181,000
Manufacturing overhead	258,000

Required:
As the company accountant, you have been asked to
a. Calculate the cost of goods manufactured for September.
b. Determine the cost of goods sold for September.

EXERCISES

15. (LO 2, 5) The following information is related to the Painless Animal Clinic for April, the firm's first month in operation:

Veterinary salaries for April	$23,000
Assistants' salaries for April	7,200
Medical supplies purchased in April	3,200
Utilities for month (80% related to animal treatment)	900
Office salaries for April (50% of time spent in animal treatment)	3,400
Medical supplies at April 30	1,800
Depreciation on medical equipment for April	2,100
Building rental (80% related to animal treatment)	1,700

Required:
Compute the cost of services rendered.

16. (LO 5) The December cost of goods sold at Mark Haines Custom Mirrors amounted to $900,000. The December 31 work in process was 80% of the December 1 work in process. Overhead was 100% of direct labour cost. During December, $220,000 of raw materials was purchased. All raw materials are direct to the production process. Other December information follows:

	December 1	December 31
Raw Materials Inventory	$108,000	$ 95,400
Work in Process Inventory	180,000	?
Finished Goods Inventory	419,000	411,200

Required:
a. Prepare the December cost of goods manufactured statement.
b. What was the amount of prime cost incurred in December?
c. What was the amount of conversion cost incurred in December?
d. Prepare a cost of goods sold schedule for December.

PROBLEMS

1. (LO 1) One of your co-workers (at the manufacturing firm where you are employed) feels that it does not matter if a cost is classified as a period or product cost. She maintains that, as long as the cost is included in one of the financial statements, how it is classified will have no impact on the operating results of the company.

   She is aware that some members of the accounting department have been debating how a particular expenditure of $150,000 should be classified. Some feel that it should be a period cost, whereas others feel it should be a product cost.
   Required:
   a. Briefly define period costs and product costs.
   b. Explain to your co-worker why it is or is not important to classify the $150,000 expenditure properly as either a period or product cost. Include in your discussion the specific circumstances under which your co-worker's assertion might be correct or incorrect.

   Extract from *Management Accounting Examination*, published by the Certified General Accountants Association of Canada (© CGA-Canada 1995). Reprinted with permission.

2. (LO 1, 2, 3) David, a painter, incurred the following costs during September when he painted three houses. He spent $600 on paint, $50 on paint thinner, and $65 on brushes. He also bought two pairs of coveralls for $12 each; he wears coveralls only while he works. During the first week of September, David placed a $10 ad for his business in the classifieds. David had to hire an assistant for one of the painting jobs; he paid her $8 per hour, and she worked 25 hours.

   Being a very methodical person, David keeps detailed records of his mileage to and from each painting job. The average operating cost per kilometre for his van is $0.25. He found a $15 receipt in his van for a map that he purchased in September; he uses it to find addresses when he is first contacted to give an estimate on a painting job. He also has road toll receipts for $6 for a painting job he did. David charges his customers for travel costs related to painting their homes.

PROBLEMS

Near the end of September, David decided to go camping, and he turned down a job on which he had bid $1,800. He called the homeowner long-distance (at a cost of $3.60) to explain his reasons for declining the job.

Required:

Using the following headings, you are asked to indicate how each of the September costs incurred by David would be classified. Assume that the cost object is a house-painting job.

Cost
Variable
Fixed
Direct
Indirect
Period
Product

3. (LO 1) Abbott Contractors had the following inventory balances at the beginning and end of May:

	May 1	May 31
Raw Materials	$16,900	$21,700
Work in Process	32,100	29,600
Finished Goods	25,800	22,600

During May, the company purchased $90,000 of raw materials. All raw materials are considered direct materials. Total labour payroll for the month was $78,000. Direct labour employees were paid $9 per hour and worked 6,800 hours in May. Total manufacturing overhead charges for the period were $109,300. Mr. Abbott, the company president, has asked for your help.

Required:

a. Determine the prime cost added to production during May.
b. Determine the conversion cost added to production in May.
c. Determine the cost of goods manufactured in May.
d. Determine the cost of goods sold in May.

4. (LO 2, 3) A company's cost structure may contain many different cost behaviour patterns. Descriptions of several different costs follow.

1. Cost of raw materials, where the cost decreases by $0.06 per unit for each of the first 150 units purchased, after which it remains constant at $2.75 per unit.
2. City water bill, which is computed as follows:

First 750,000 litres or less	$1,000 flat fee
Next 15,000 litres	$0.002 per litre used
Next 15,000 litres	$0.005 per litre used
Next 15,000 litres	$0.008 per litre used
Etc.	Etc.

3. Rent on a manufacturing building donated by the city, where the agreement provides for a fixed-fee payment, unless 250,000 labour hours are worked, in which case no rent needs to be paid.
4. Cost of raw materials used.
5. Electricity bill—a flat fixed charge of $250 plus a variable cost after 150,000 kilowatt hours are used.
6. Salaries of maintenance workers if one maintenance worker is needed for every 1,000 hours or less of machine time.
7. Depreciation of equipment using the straight-line method.
8. Rent on a manufacturing building donated by the province, where the agreement provides for a monthly rental of $100,000 less $1 for each labour hour worked in excess of 200,000 hours. However, a minimum rental payment of $20,000 must be made each month.
9. Rent on a machine that is billed at $1,000 for up to 500 hours of machine time. After 500 hours of machine time, an additional charge of $1 per hour is paid up to a maximum charge of $2,500 per period.

PROBLEMS

Required:

Identify, by letter, the graph below that illustrates each of the cost behaviour patterns. Graphs may be used more than once. On each graph, the vertical axis represents cost and the horizontal axis represents level of activity or volume.

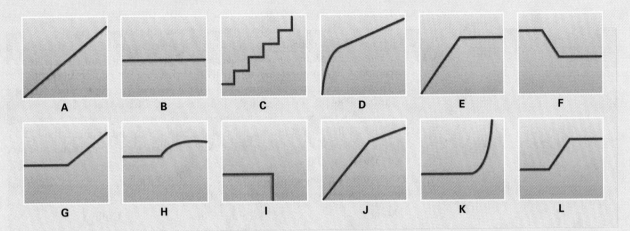

SOURCE: Material from the *Uniform CPA Examination Questions and Unofficial Answers*, copyright by the American Institute of Certified Public Accountants, Inc., is adapted with permission.

5. (LO 3) Ken Lavin has been elected to handle the local Grande Theatre summer play. He is trying to determine the price to charge Grande Theatre members for attendance at this year's presentation of "My Fair Lady." He has developed the following cost estimates associated with the play:
   - Cost of printing invitations will be $260 for 100 to 500; cost to print between 500 and 600 will be $280.
   - Cost of readying and operating the theatre for three evenings will be $1,000 if attendance is below 500; this cost rises to $1,200 if attendance is 500 or above.
   - Postage to mail invitations will be $0.30 each.
   - Cost of building stage sets will be $1,215.
   - Cost of printing up to 1,000 programs will be $250.
   - Cost of security will be $110 per night plus $30 per hour; five hours will be needed each night.
   - Costumes will be donated by several local businesses.

   The Grande Theatre has 200 members, and each member is allowed two guests. Ordinarily, only 75% of the members attend the summer offering, and each member brings the two allowed guests. The play will be presented from 8 P.M. to 11 P.M. Invitations are mailed to those members who call to say they plan to come and also to each of the guests they specify.

   Required:
   a. Indicate the type of behaviour exhibited by all the items Ken needs to consider.
   b. If the ordinary attendance occurs, what will be the total cost of the summer offering of the play?
   c. If the ordinary attendance occurs, what will be the cost per person attending?
   d. If 90% of the members attend and each invites two guests, what will be the total cost of the play? the cost per person?

6. (LO 3) Didona Delights prepares dinners for several airlines, and sales average 300,000 meals per month. The significant costs of each dinner prepared are for the meat, vegetables, plastic trays, and utensils. (No desserts are provided, because passengers are more calorie-conscious than in the past.) The company prepares meals in batches of 1,000. The following data are shown in the company's accounting records for April:

Cost of meat for 1,000 dinners	$900
Cost of vegetables for 1,000 dinners	360
Cost of plastic trays and utensils for 1,000 dinners	120
Direct labour cost for 1,000 dinners	950

PROBLEMS

Overhead charges total $1,200,000 per month; these are considered fully fixed for purposes of cost estimation.

Required:

Company management has asked you to address the following:

a. What is the cost per dinner based on average sales and April prices?

b. If sales increase to 400,000 dinners per month, what will the cost per dinner be (assuming that cost behaviour patterns remain the same as in April)?

c. If sales are 400,000 dinners per month but the company does not want the cost per dinner to exceed its current level (based on part (a)), what amount can the company pay for meat, assuming all other costs are the same as in April?

d. The company's major competitor has bid a price of $10.96 per dinner to the airlines. The profit margin in the industry is 100% of total cost. If Didona Delights is to retain the airlines' business, how many dinners must the company produce each month to reach the bid price of the competitor and maintain the 100% profit margin? Assume April cost patterns will not change and dinners must be produced in batches of 1,000.

7. (LO 4) Sandra Chowfen Enterprises has compiled the following data to analyze its utility costs in an attempt to improve cost control:

Month	Machine-Hours	Utility Cost
January	200	$150
February	325	220
March	400	240
April	410	245
May	525	310
June	680	395
July	820	420
August	900	450

Required:

a. Determine the a- and b-values for the utility cost formula using the high–low method.

b. Determine the a- and b-values for the utility cost formula using least-squares regression analysis.

c. Assuming September's machine hours are expected to be 760, what is the expected utility cost for September based on your answer to part (a)? based on your answer to part (b)? Why do these answers differ?

d. Which of the answers—part (a) or part (b)—is preferable, and why?

e. As a manager, what questions might you ask about the data just compiled?

8. (LO 4) Danny Romalotti Corporation is a manufacturer of electric guitars. Judith Poë, the management accountant at the firm, has been having some difficulty estimating overhead costs. She wishes to determine a systematic method for associating overhead costs with production levels. To facilitate this association, she has assembled data on the monthly overhead costs and monthly production levels for the current year.

Month	Production (Units)	Overhead Cost
1	75,000	$ 925,800
2	90,000	876,000
3	65,000	910,000
4	80,000	946,000
5	55,000	879,000
6	50,000	825,000
7	85,000	960,000
8	105,000	1,055,000
9	102,000	1,020,000
10	68,000	905,000
11	75,000	938,000
12	95,000	995,000

Required:

a. Using the high–low method, calculate next month's overhead costs, assuming the company is planning to produce 100,000 units.

PROBLEMS

b.   Sketch a scattergraph showing the overhead costs plotted against the production in units.

c.   Briefly describe the relationship you observe in the scattergraph between overhead costs and units produced.

(Extract from *Management Accounting Examination* published by the Certified General Accountants' Association of Canada (© CGA-Canada). Reprinted with permission.)

9.   (LO 5) Chretien Inc. produces Canadian flags for department stores. The raw materials account includes both direct and indirect materials. The account balances at the beginning and end of July are as follows:

	July 1	July 31
Raw Materials Inventory	$18,000	$16,700
Work in Process Inventory	24,500	19,200
Finished Goods Inventory	8,000	9,200

During the month, the firm purchased $92,000 of raw materials; direct materials consumption in July was $47,900. Manufacturing payroll costs for July were $95,000, of which 87% was related to direct labour. Overhead charges for depreciation, insurance, utilities, and maintenance were $69,400 for the month.

Required:

a.   Determine total actual overhead for July.

b.   Prepare a cost of goods manufactured statement.

c.   Prepare a schedule of the cost of goods sold.

10.   (LO 5) NPV Custom Products had the following inventory balances at the beginning and end of October:

	October 1	October 31
Raw Materials Inventory	$16,900	$21,700
Work in Process Inventory	32,100	29,600
Finished Goods Inventory	25,800	22,600

During October, the company purchased $90,000 of raw materials. All raw materials are considered direct materials. Total labour payroll for the month was $78,000. Direct labour employees were paid $9 per hour and worked 6,800 hours in October. Total manufacturing overhead for the period was $109,300.

Required:

a.   Determine the prime cost added to production during October.

b.   Determine the conversion cost added to production in October.

c.   Determine the cost of goods manufactured in October.

d.   Determine the cost of goods sold in October.

11.   (LO 5) Newman Ltd. manufactures a single product—mailboxes. The following data represent transactions and balances for December, the company's first month of operations.

Direct materials purchased on account	$124,000
Direct materials issued to production	93,000
Direct production labour payroll accrued	67,000
Manufacturing insurance expired	1,800
Manufacturing utilities accrued	8,100
Manufacturing depreciation recorded	7,900
Ending work in process (6,000 units)	18,000
Sales ($12 per unit)	324,000
Ending finished goods	3,000 units

Required:

As a consulting accountant, you have been asked to address the following:

a.   How many units were sold in December? How many units were completed?

b.   What was the total cost of goods manufactured in December?

c.   What was the per unit cost of goods manufactured in December?

d.   Prepare the journal entries to record the flow of costs in the company for December using the perpetual inventory system.

PROBLEMS

12. (LO 5) Boniface Metal Customworks had the following inventory balances at the beginning and end of June:

	June 1	June 30
Raw Materials Inventory	$16,000	$18,000
Work in Process Inventory	94,000	72,000
Finished Goods Inventory	36,000	22,000

All raw materials are direct to the production process. The following information is also available about manufacturing costs incurred during June:

Cost of raw materials used	$94,000
Direct labour costs	181,000
Factory overhead	258,000

Required:
a. Calculate the cost of goods manufactured for June.
b. Determine the cost of goods sold for June.

13. (LO 7) Lotsa Pull began business in late December of last year and makes home vacuum cleaners. The following data are taken from the firm's accounting records that pertain to its first year of operation.

Direct materials purchased on account	$213,000
Direct materials issued to production	192,000
Direct labour payroll accrued	114,000
Indirect labour payroll paid	45,300
Manufacturing insurance expired	2,700
Manufacturing utilities paid	8,900
Manufacturing depreciation recorded	18,700
Ending work in process inventory	32,000
Ending finished goods inventory (80 units)	12,800
Sales on account ($210 per unit)	442,050

Required:
a. How many units did the company sell in its first year? How many units were manufactured in the first year?
b. What was the total cost of goods manufactured?
c. What was the per unit cost of goods manufactured?
d. What was the cost of goods sold in the first year?
e. Did the company post a positive gross profit in its first year of operations?

CASES

1. You are the manager of the main Regina branch of the Bank of Saskatchewan, the seventh largest bank in Canada. The Bank of Saskatchewan began business as a trust company in 1920. It became a bank in 1972 in order to increase its leverage so as to compete with banks and to expand across Canada and internationally. Though the Bank is a relatively small Canadian bank, it has the largest international presence among all Canadian banks.

Your branch is located in downtown Regina in the city's most prestigious building, the Bank of Saskatchewan building. The branch is particularly well appointed as it is intended to demonstrate the bank's capabilities to its many affluent national and international clients, who fly in by private jet. Compared to other Regina branches, the main branch is more spacious; all employee offices are larger and better equipped. You have always considered being the manager at this branch to be a pleasure. Well, until recently.

The Saskatchewan regional controller has developed a technique to compare teller services among branches by area. Regina's main branch has not done as well as the other branches (see Exhibit 2-1). You are now required to reduce your costs. You are not sure whether your branch is being treated fairly. As your tellers are competent and always busy, you are somewhat confused about the "cost per teller" measure. You ask for details on the number of teller transactions with clients for the year as used in Exhibit 2-1. You are told that your branch carried out 470,000 transactions that year; all the Regina branches together carried out 3,600,000.

Your superior, the vice president for Saskatchewan, has asked you to reduce the number of tellers to get your teller costs in line with those of the other branches in the Regina area.

CASES

Required:
Using the case approach, respond to the vice president for Saskatchewan.

	Main Branch	All Regina Branches
Personnel costs	$420,000	3,210,000
Personnel benefits	75,600	577,800
Supplies	14,000	107,000
Rent	280,000	931,000
Utilities	28,000	102,400
Depreciation	21,000	67,500
Total costs	$838,600	4,995,700
Number of tellers	14	107
Cost per teller	$ 59,900	46,689

EXHIBIT 2-1
Costs per Teller

2. Sidco builds business intelligence (BI) software for firms with ERP systems. Their client firms want specialized software to create business intelligence software. They have ERP systems such as Peoplesoft and SAP that integrate all aspects of organizations, but the reports from these systems fall short in assisting management decision making. As a result, firms such as Hyperion and Sidco have stepped in to provide BI software to produce reports containing information for management decision making. Hyperion sells largely standardized BI software; Sidco makes customized BI software but limits its clientele to retail firms around the world.

Sidco employs highly skilled programmers, who write the code for its customized BI software. The programming can be divided into two parts: basic and customized. The basic programming is largely the same for each client. The customizing programming is based on the number of products in the firm's product line. The basic programming comes from stock programs with some modifications. The customization is done by studying and understanding the client firm's context and ERP system; additional code can then be written to provide the required BI for the client.

Last year, Sidco had 10 jobs. Exhibit 2-1 shows the actual costs for these jobs. Actual costs were very close to planned costs. None of the customers objected to the quoted prices. Revenue from these jobs totalled $49 million. The CEO was not pleased with the profitability from these jobs. He wants to ensure a higher level of profitability by instituting a new pricing model. Specifically, he wants to cover all programming costs and earn 20% for overhead and 10% for profit on each job.

Required:
The CEO wants you, the management accountant, to determine a method for pricing customized BI software. Use the case approach to respond to the CEO.

Job	Stock Program, $	Customization, $	Total, $	Number of Products
1	405,000	3,967,000	4,372,000	60,000
2	396,000	3,575,000	3,971,000	55,000
3	403,000	2,560,000	2,963,000	40,000
4	401,000	2,112,000	2,513,000	32,000
5	394,000	5,850,000	6,244,000	90,000
6	398,000	5,568,000	5,966,000	87,000
7	404,000	3,015,000	3,419,000	45,000
8	395,000	3,328,000	3,723,000	52,000
9	401,000	5,082,000	5,483,000	77,000
10	403,000	2,405,000	2,808,000	37,000
	4,000,000	37,462,000	41,462,000	

EXHIBIT 2-1
Costs for Recent
BI Software Jobs

CASES

3. Price Reducer (PR) is a mid-sized grocery chain that operates stores in various Canadian towns. These communities are too small for the major chains such as Safeway, Loblaws, and Sobey's to enter with any of their business models. PR stores operate from 8 am to 8 pm, six days a week.

    Costs at PR stores can be divided roughly into two types, as shown in Exhibit 2-1: (1) Cost of goods sold and (2) Store selling and administration costs. The CEO is content with the cost of goods sold but is very dissatisfied with the level of store selling and administration (S&A) costs. The CEO is requesting a 4% reduction in S&A costs. There is confusion about what costs to cut in the short term.

    A 4% reduction implies that these costs are too high, and you are not sure that it is true for all times of day and all days of the week. You know that store employees are busier at some times during the week and less busy at other times. You, as the management accountant, are very skeptical about the reasonableness of cutting all S&A costs.

    You examine a sample of stores. All stores are located in rental spaces, which have leases with terms from 5 to 20 years. Each lease would be expensive to break; alternative space would not be any cheaper.

    Managers and full-time employees would be expensive to terminate as the company would need to give advance notice and to provide severance pay. Casual employees could be eliminated quickly and with little difficulty.

    As you examine the various stores, you observe that at certain times of the week the employees are very busy, e.g., Thursday evening, Friday evening, and Saturday.

EXHIBIT 2-1
Operating Statement (000s)

Revenues		$765,213
Cost of goods sold		436,946
Gross margin		$328,267
S & A:		
Full time employees' wages and benefits	97,301	
Casual employees' wages and benefits	47,832	
Head office and Management salary and benefits	25,324	
Amortization of leasehold improvements	10,764	
Rental of store space	82,801	
Rental of office space	11,885	
Supplies	24,015	
		299,922
Net income		$28,345

Employees are able to cope with the demand and provide customers with fully satisfactory service. You estimate that the employees are about 90% utilized during the above time periods.

At the other times of the week, the employees are underutilized. You estimate employee utilization to be 65% at these times. Restocking shelves is done at night with dedicated and fully utilized employees.

Required:

As the management accountant, address the CEO's request for cost cutting. Be sure to use the case approach.

ETHICS

1. You are the chief financial officer for a small manufacturing company that has applied for a bank loan. In speaking with the bank loan officer, Barbara Didona, you are told that two minimum criteria for granting loans are (1) a 40% gross profit and (2) income of at least 15% of sales. Looking at the last four months' income statements, you find that gross profit has been between 30% and 33% and income has ranged from 18% to 24% of sales. You discuss these relationships with the company president, who suggests

CASES

that some of the product costs included in Cost of Goods Sold be moved to the selling, general, and administrative categories so that the income statement will conform to the bank's criteria.

Required:

a. Which types of product costs might most easily be reassigned to period cost classifications?

b. Since the president is not suggesting that any expenses be kept off the income statement, do you see any ethical problems with the request? Discuss.

c. Write a short memo to convince the banker to lend the company the funds in spite of its noncompliance with the loan criteria.

2. A cost of operating any organization in the contemporary business environment is computer software. Most software can be purchased on either a per-unit basis (making it a variable cost) or a site-licence basis (making it a fixed cost). You are the manager of Manley Marketing, a company that engages in a great deal of market research. You have asked that the company acquire a copy of a statistical analysis package that would cost $400 per package for each of the 20 people in your department. Alternatively, the software company will give a site licence at a cost of $12,000. The package is essential to the organization's ability to perform research, but the controller does not have funds in the budget for 20 copies. Therefore, the controller purchases four copies and tells you to duplicate the other necessary copies. You resist, saying that to do so would violate the copyright law, which allows only one copy to be made for backup purposes.

Required:

a. Since the fixed cost for the site licence exceeds the cost for 20 copies, can you think of any reason to incur that $12,000 cost? Discuss.

b. Assume you are currently working on a marketing research project for Triton Publishing Company. Proper analysis requires the use of this software package. Is the cost of the software a direct or an indirect cost to the Triton project? If direct, what amount do you believe could be attached to the project? If indirect, should the cost be allocated to the project in some way? If so, how?

c. How would you handle this situation? What might be the consequences of your actions?

3. It was a company on the rise. Then the company dropped a bombshell. Pressberger Ltd. said it would start expensing indirect costs related to developing landfill sites. The company had heretofore been capitalizing these costs, which included public relations and legal costs to obtain permits for landfills. The change resulted in a $27 million charge to earnings, which wiped out more than half the company's income and more than $1.4 billion of its market valuation.

Required:

a. How does the issue of capitalizing versus expensing relate to the conceptual difference between expired and unexpired cost?

b. Why would a company's market value drop because of a simple change in an accounting practice such as this?

c. What ethical obligations do accountants and managers bear in deciding whether to "expense" or "capitalize" a cost item?

SOLUTIONS TO SELF-TEST QUESTIONS

1. c: Prime cost = Direct materials used + Direct labour
   = ($35,000 + $75,000 − $25,000) + $85,000
   = $85,000 + $85,000
   = $170,000

2. b: Conversion cost = Direct labour + Overhead
   = $85,000 + [($85,000 ÷ 10) × 8]
   = $85,000 + $68,000
   = $153,000

ETHICS

3. c: Cost of goods manufactured
    = Beginning work in process + Direct materials used + Direct labour +
      Overhead − Ending work in process
    = $45,000 + $85,000 + $85,000 + $68,000 − $20,000
    = $263,000

4. c: Glue is an insignificant part of the table; therefore, it is treated as overhead and not as direct material.

5. a: [($15,000 + $8,000 + $12,000 + $15,000) ÷ 20,000] = $2.50

6. d: ($870 − $750) ÷ (200 − 120) = $1.50

7. c: $50,000 + $154,000 − $26,000 = $178,000

8. c: Change in total cost ÷ Change in machine hours
    = $7,200 ÷ 9,000
    = $0.80 variable cost per unit

9. b: $85,000 + $24,000 + 2,500 + $3,000 + $3,200 + $4,600 + $1,800 + $15,100 + $2,900 − $6,800 = $135,300

10. d.

11. b: DM $75,000 + $13,000 − $18,000 $ 70,000
    DL   37,500
                                          $107,500

12. d: OH ($37,500 ÷ $15) × $6.00 $ 15,000
    DM   70,000
    DL   37,500
                                          $122,500
    Change in WIP   1,000
                                          $123,500

13. b: $85,000 + $24,000 + 2,500 + $3,000 + $3,200 + $4,600 + $1,800 + $15,100 + $2,900 − $6,800 = $135,300

ENDNOTES

1. Outside processing cost may also be considered a direct material cost. For example, a furniture manufacturer may want a special plastic laminate on tables. Rather than buying the necessary equipment, the manufacturer may send the tables to another company that specializes in this process. The amount paid for this process may be considered a direct material cost by the manufacturer.

2. Patrick Brethour, "Suncor to Squeeze Suppliers to Cut Costs," *Globe and Mail*, June 18, 2002, B5.

3. Andrew Park, "Dell," *Business Week*, November 24, 2003, 104.

4. James Brian Quinn et al., "Beyond Products: Services-Based Strategy," *Harvard Business Review*, March–April 1990, p. 65.

5. "Robots Cut Jobs at Jeep Factory," *Star Tribune*, April 30, 2001, 7D.

6. Deborah Ball, "Pirelli Unveils New Tire-Making Process," *Wall Street Journal*, December 3, 1999, p. 3.

7. This definition of product cost is traditionally accepted and is also referred to as absorption costing. Another product costing method, called variable costing, excludes the fixed manufacturing overhead component from inventories. Absorption and variable costing are discussed in Chapter 3.

8. An accountant's view of a variable cost is, in fact, a slight distortion of reality. Variable costs usually increase at a changing rate until a range of activity is reached in which U, the average variable cost rate per unit, becomes fairly constant. Within this range, the slope of the cost line becomes less steep because the firm benefits from operating efficiencies such as price discounts on materials, improved worker skills, and increased productivity. Beyond this range, the slope becomes quite steep as the firm enters an

ENDNOTES

activity range in which some operating inefficiencies (such as worker crowding and material shortages) cause the average variable cost rate to trend sharply higher. Because of the curves on each end of the graph, accountants choose as the relevant range that range of activity in which the variable costs per unit are constant.

9. Brent Jang, "CPR Signals Switch in Strategy to Narrow Competitive Gap with CN," *Globe and Mail*, January 20, 2006, B3.

10. Section 3060 of the *CICA Handbook* uses the term "amortization." In practice, however, the term "depreciation" is still used, therefore "depreciation" will be used in this text.

11. Al Haas, "Falling Prices Make It a Vintage Year for Used-Car Buying," *The (New Orleans) Times-Picayune*, July 3, 1998, p. Fl.

12. "Disruption, Innovation," *Globe and Mail*, December 31, 2007, B4.

13. Tom Holland, "Car Makers," *Far Eastern Economic Review*, August 12, 2004.

14. Eric Beauchesne, "Get Leaner, Consultant Tells Manufacturers: Outsourcing Among Practices Suggested to Beat Profit Crunch," *Ottawa Citizen*, June 1, 2007, E7.

15. Derek DeCloet, "West Jet Is on the Horns or a Dilema," *Globe and Mail*, July 12, 2008, PB2.

16. Brent Jang, "Airlines Want to Help You Help Yourself," *Globe and Mail*, December 27, 2007, A1.

17. Ben Edwards, "Men and Machines," *The Economist*, November 19, 2004.

18. Grant Robertson, "In the Boardroom at the General Motors Oshawa Plant Is a Baseball Bat . . ." *Globe and Mail*, September 15, 2005, pg. B16.

19. Michael Heideman and Shinji Igarashi, "Japan Warms to Outsourcing," *Electronic Engineering Times*, November 26, 2007.

20. Ibid.

21. "Shoppers Outsourcing IT Jobs to Keane," *Globe and Mail*, October 6, 2004.

22. Associated Press, "GM Plans to Bid Out $3 billion IT Contract," *Toronto Star*, October 4, 2004.

23. N. Venkat Venkatraman, "Offshoring Without Guilt," *MIT Sloan Management Review*, Spring 2004.

24. Anand Giridharadas, "Novel Passage to India," *National Post*, September 26, 2007, WK3.

25. Sheila James, "Taking a Small but Toothsome Slice of the Bakery Market," *Financial Times*, October 5, 1999, p. 35.

26. The least-squares method (discussed later) is a more refined mathematical procedure; however, the visual method is the one generally used in practice because it is simple and yields sufficiently accurate results.

27. These equations are derived from mathematical computations beyond the scope of this text but are found in many statistics books. The symbol Σ means "the summation of."

Chapter 3

Cost–Volume–Profit Analysis

LEARNING OBJECTIVES

After reading this chapter, you should be able to answer the following questions:

1 What does the breakeven point represent and how is it computed?

2 How can cost–volume–profit (CVP) analysis be used by a business?

3 What is the purpose of breakeven and profit–volume graphs?

4 How do cost–volume–profit (CVP) analyses in single-product and multiproduct firms differ?

5 What are the underlying assumptions of CVP analysis and how do these assumptions create a short-run managerial perspective?

6 How are the margin of safety and operating leverage concepts used in business?

7 What are the cost accumulation and cost presentation approaches to product costing?

8 How do changes in sales and/or production levels affect net income as computed under absorption and variable costing?

9 What are the mathematical approaches to CVP analysis? (Appendix)

ON SITE

http://www.untd.com

United Online

NETZERO was started in 1998 to provide free and value-priced Internet connectivity. It has since become UNITED ONLINE, INC., after a merger with Juno Online Services. NetZero sought to grow rapidly while maximizing the return on every dollar it spent. United Online features NetZero and Juno Online Services Inc. access that offers value-priced access services on a monthly subscription basis.

Within 20 months of the merger, NetZero was able to meet one of its greatest challenges, breaking even at the gross margin level. It was able to turn one of its major *fixed* costs, telecommunications, into *variable* costs by contracting with numerous national providers.

Historically, the company's Classmates Media cost of revenues has been relatively fixed; however, as a result of its loyalty marketing service, acquired in April 2006, its cost of revenues has become more variable as the costs associated with the service tend to fluctuate with revenues.

United Online is a leading provider of consumer Internet and media services through a number of brands, including Classmates, My Points, NetZero, and Juno. The company's Classmates Media services offer online social networking and online loyalty marketing. Its primary communication services are Internet access and e-mail. The company has a base of more than 60 million registered accounts. This large online audience enables the company to offer a broad array of Internet marketing products and services for advertisers. Advertising revenues have increased from $99.1 million (19% of total revenues) in 2006 to $134.0 million (26.1% of total revenues) in 2007. These results reflect the record growth in its core subscription business, the expansion of its product offerings, and the significant operating leverage of United Online's business model. Many advertisers recognize that consumers are spending an increasing amount of time online and view social networking websites as an attractive medium through which to market their products and services. An independent Internet industry research firm expects advertising spending on social networking websites to increase more than 600% between 2006 and 2011, from $350 million to $2.7 billion.

Historically, the company has focused on providing value-priced dial-up Internet access in the United States and Canada. Its strategy is to continue to leverage its resources and core competencies to further expand its businesses beyond dial-up Internet access services, through internal development and acquisitions.

SOURCES: Adapted from Press Release, Prime Newswire, April 20, 2007; Press Release, "United Online Reports Third-Quarter Results," Form 10K, United Online, Inc., March 20, 2008.

*B*reakeven point—does the term ring a bell? It should. That's the magic number that tells you when your revenue will cover your expenses. Although entrepreneurs often fail to realize the significance of recognizing and reaching the breakeven point, understanding what it takes to break even is critical to making any business profitable.

Incorporating accurate and thorough breakeven analysis as a routine part of your financial planning will keep you abreast of how your business is really faring. Determining how much business is needed to keep the door open will help improve your cash flow management and your bottom line.[1]

Understanding the impact that competitor decisions, pricing, changes in market demand, input costs, business activity, and your firm's overall efficiency has on revenue, costs, and net income can be quite challenging. The dynamic interaction of these factors can be especially complicated for new businesses in planning, forecasting, and making business decisions. Fortunately, breakeven analysis (also known as cost–volume–profit analysis) can be an invaluable tool in making sense of these complex and changing factors and in performing informed and objective business planning.[2]

To be strategically successful, managers must ensure that their organizations are achieving the right combination and volume of products and selling prices that will generate enough revenue to cover all variable and fixed costs. This is a problem faced by all organizations. Covering costs is a matter of operational survival regardless of whether you manage Chapters–Indigo Bookstores or the Toronto Raptors, are a promoter of a concert to be held at the National Arts Centre, or are a physician with your own practice.

Every business planner needs to know the breakeven point, that point or level of sales at which the firm neither earns a profit nor incurs a loss, and how this point changes as costs and volumes change. Armed with such information, managers can answer other questions as well, such as what effect increases in capacity have on profitability, what the effect of changing salaried workers over to commission would be, and what income level is needed to justify a given increase in advertising.[3]

Tata Motors has spent years developing a new small car, the Nano. Emerging markets are its main target for sales. Tata's new car is expected to transform driving in India, allowing a new generation of drivers to graduate from motorcycles to automobiles. India's economy is roaring ahead, with annual growth averaging about 8.6% over the past four years. Even so, Tata is taking a risk with its new product, because a serious global slowdown could dent consumer spending in the country. Tata plans to start production of its new car in 2008.

Tata touts the Nano as the most inexpensive car in the world at just 100,000 rupees (U.S. $2,500, or 1,600 Euros). The price of an entire Nano is roughly equivalent to the price of a DVD player option in a Western luxury car. The Nano looks very similar to Daimler's Smart car and has a small, rear-mounted engine. It has no air conditioning, no electric windows, and no power steering; however, two deluxe versions will be available.

Tata says it will initially produce about 250,000 Nanos; however, it expects eventually to produce one million. The car could become available in Europe in the future.

The company is considering online ordering and selling, which could well change the rules of more than one game. A look at the Tata Nano website reveals that the Pune-based auto maker is embracing the idea of an e-dealership for the people's car.

How can Tata Motors manufacture a car so cheaply? It started by looking at everything from scratch, applying what some analysts have described as "Gandhian engineering" principles—that is, deep frugality along with a willingness to challenge conventional wisdom. The engineers strived to do more with less. A lot of features that

The Nano will cost only 100,000 rupees and will transform driving in India.

Western consumers take for granted are missing from the entry-level model. The Nano is much lighter and has rear-wheel drive and an all-aluminum, two-cylinder, 623 cc multipoint fuel-injection gas engine. It has a maximum speed of about 65 mph. The fuel efficiency is attractively high—50 miles to the gallon.

Emerging markets are a fertile ground for innovation. The challenge of reaching dispersed low-income consumers in emerging markets often spurs significant innovation.

Analysts say that even with a vibrant Indian economy and a successful launch, it could take more than four years for the project to break even because of high development costs.[4]

Another example of the use of breakeven analysis is the Oberoi Group's commissioning of an eight-cabin, 16-passenger double-decker cruising catamaran. The boat cost the Oberoi Group U.S.$40 million, including the impeccable interior detailing complete with air conditioning, attached luxury baths, wood floors and panelling, and facilities such as cable TV when docked, and in-cabin DVD players. "We are already booked for 40 percent of the season," reflects general manager Visheshwar Raj Singh, "but hope to achieve at least 60 percent occupancy." For now, the sailing season stretches from October 1 to April 30, with the boat lifting anchor every alternate day for the two-day cruise. In effect, this means 106 sailings before it anchors for the rainy season (May–September). Breakeven point is three occupied cabins, which means the boat should more than cover its cost during its first full season of sailing.[5]

The first part of this chapter discusses methodology for calculating an organization's breakeven point. At breakeven, a company experiences neither profits nor losses on its operating activities. As a manager, promoter, or physician, however, you would most likely not want to operate at a volume level that simply covers costs; you would want to make profits. Knowing the breakeven level of operations provides a point of reference from which you will be better able to plan for volume goals that generate income rather than produce losses.

Breakeven analysis is very important for medical practices. The following News Note discusses the use of breakeven analysis in a radiology practice (a service industry).

GENERAL NEWS NOTE

Using Breakeven Analysis in Medicine

Radiology practices face serious challenges to their financial health. Reimbursement is under almost continuous attack, with government cutbacks and with threats of worse to come in the near future. In the United States, competition is increasing from within and from outside the specialty, with increasing numbers of imaging centres and new entrants into imaging from other specialties. This competition is chipping away at revenue, especially in the more lucrative forms of imaging.

The ability to respond to these challenges is hampered by the high-fixed-cost structure of most practices and by a lack of flexibility within those cost structures. This is a particular challenge for medical practices that own expensive assets.

These challenges require a variety of efforts at the practice and national levels to preserve and protect the profession. One approach that should be used in any organization is to examine costs and their relationship to how the business is being managed. Are sound principles being applied, or is the management philosophy to simply "wing it" and treat the business as a black box?

Many managers lack insight about their costs. While they know how much they pay for machines and salaries, most imaging centres don't have a detailed understanding of how those resources are used. This is often particularly true of larger, more complex centres.

If you walk into most practices and ask the cost of a myelogram, the answer too often is "I don't know," or even worse, a made-up number that doesn't reflect what is actually occurring within the enterprise. Businesses need to know how costs are matched to productivity. One of the great strengths of managerial accounting is that it can pry open the black box and show what is really going on inside.

Costs differ—not all costs are the same in terms of how they affect practice decisions. What do you think it costs to perform one more brain MRI at the end of the day? First, there is the cost of the machine. Let's assume it was purchased for $2 million and that it will be used for 10 years before it is replaced. The MRI machine is a fixed cost of the business. At first glance, it appears that performing one more scan won't change that cost. We will ignore wear-and-tear issues and assume that MRI scanners don't wear out twice as fast if you use them twice as much—unlike cars, for example. This means that the MRI device is a fixed cost and doesn't scale with the number of studies performed.

Now consider a contrast-enhanced study. The MRI scanner is used in the same way as in the example above, and the machine remains a fixed cost just as with the noncontrast exam. But now it is slightly more interesting. Items like the needle, the dose of contrast, and the bandage are all true variable costs. If you didn't do the extra study, you wouldn't incur these costs.

Sometimes variable costs are referred to as marginal costs; these terms are often used interchangeably even though there are some technical differences. What's important is to keep the differences between fixed and variable costs in mind, as they can have a significantly different impact on how you do business.

Marginal revenue is another item that requires attention when analyzing a radiology practice. Marginal revenue represents how much the practice is paid for a particular service such as government or insurance reimbursement for that additional MRI, myelogram, or brain angiography case. The contribution per procedure is calculated as marginal revenue minus marginal cost.

Another analysis that can be useful, particularly with expensive equipment, involves calculating the number of procedures that are needed in order to achieve the breakeven point. This type of arithmetic is standard in purchase-versus-lease calculations. Put simply, the number of procedures needed to cover a fixed cost is that cost divided by the marginal contribution per case. This calculation only works with procedures that make a positive contribution. You can't pay for an expensive PET or CT if you lose money every time you use it.

SOURCE: Frank James Lexa, "Radiology Practices Must Understand Costs of Doing Business to Achieve Profitability," *Diagnostic Imaging*, January 2007.

The latter part of the chapter looks at cost accumulation and cost presentation of data. The method of accumulation specifies which manufacturing cost components are recorded as part of the product cost. The method of presentation focuses on how costs are shown on external financial statements or internal management reports. Accumulation and presentation procedures are accomplished using one of two methods: absorption or variable costing. Each method uses the same basic data but structures and processes it differently.

THE BREAKEVEN POINT

Cost–volume–profit analysis is one of the most powerful tools that management and the board of directors can use. This type of analysis helps them understand the interrelationships among costs, volumes, and profit. The five elements of this type of analysis are as follows: prices of products, volume or level of activity, per unit variable costs, fixed costs, and the mix of products sold.

Two methods—the equation method or the unit contribution method—may be used. Similarly, a graphic presentation may be used to analyze the impact of decisions, showing, for example, the "profit area" or the "loss area."[6]

The level of activity, in units or dollars, at which total revenues equal total costs is called the **breakeven point** (BEP). Although most business managers hope to do better than just break even, the breakeven point is an important point of reference by which the manager can measure both the company's level of risk of not exceeding the BEP and the company's level of comfort in exceeding the BEP. Managers make this determination by comparing the magnitude of the company's current or planned sales with the BEP. Finding the breakeven point requires an understanding of an organization's revenue and cost functions.

The following News Note illustrates the use of contribution margin analysis in Germany.

LEARNING OBJECTIVE 1

What does the breakeven point represent and how is it computed?

breakeven point
that level of activity, in units or dollars, at which total revenues equal total costs

How German Firms Use Costing Systems

INTERNATIONAL NEWS NOTE

Why are German firms much more satisfied with their costing systems? It isn't just because they tend to use more advanced costing practices. We found through our survey and interviews that Germany's culture, long-term thinking, stronger information systems, and stronger focus on management accounting all contribute to this higher satisfaction.

Almost every German firm uses a very detailed contribution margin income statement, which it uses for most management decisions. Our survey found that 71% of German firms use contribution margin accounting compared to only 48% of North American firms. Of course, generating accurate contribution margin statements is contingent on accurate segmentation of variable and fixed costs.

Surprisingly, we found that similar percentages of German and North American firms distinguish cost behaviour. Even German firms with hundreds or even thousands of cost areas don't necessarily segment fixed and variable costs within each cost area. Both German and North American firms also transfer costs from support cost areas to primary cost areas while maintaining the distinction between fixed and variable costs at about the same rate. The main difference? Typically, German firms separate fixed from variable costs for a much larger number of cost centres, whereas North American firms tend to simplify things by assuming that a cost centre is entirely fixed or entirely variable. One company that separates fixed from variable costs is juice producer CLIFFSTAR CORPORATION. It differentiates labour cost behaviour by examining how closely the workers are tied to actual production. Cliffstar considers production line workers a variable cost, so distinguishing payroll and work centre costs as variable or fixed helps the company communicate about cost drivers. For utilities, it looks at periodic consumption rates. The company considers most utilities to be variable, but it has added meters for different parts of the plant and uses a formula to break out the utility bills.

SOURCE: Kip Krumwuide and Augustin Suessmair, "Getting Down to Specifics on RCA," *Strategic Finance*, June 2007.

Basic Assumptions

Certain assumptions are made about cost behaviour so that cost information can be used in accounting computations. The following list summarizes these simplifying assumptions about revenue and cost functions.

- *Relevant range*: A primary assumption is that the company is operating within the relevant range of activity specified in determining the revenue and cost information used in each of the following assumptions.[7]
- *Revenue*: Total revenue fluctuates in direct proportion to units sold. Revenue per unit is assumed to remain constant, and fluctuations in per-unit revenue for factors such as quantity discounts are ignored.
- *Variable costs*: Total variable costs fluctuate in direct proportion to the level of activity or volume. On a per-unit basis, variable costs are assumed to remain constant within the relevant range. This assumed variable cost behaviour is the same as assumed revenue behaviour. Variable production costs include direct material, direct labour, and variable overhead; variable selling costs include charges for items such as commissions and shipping. Variable administrative costs may exist in areas such as purchasing.
- *Fixed costs*: Total fixed costs remain constant within the relevant range; thus, per-unit fixed costs decrease as volume increases and increase as volume decreases. Fixed costs include both fixed manufacturing overhead and fixed selling and administrative expenses.
- *Mixed costs*: Mixed costs must be separated into their variable and fixed elements before they can be used in CVP analysis. Any method (such as high–low or regression analysis) that validly separates these costs in relation to one or more predictors may be used.

Because these basic assumptions treat selling prices and costs as known and constant, any analysis based on these assumptions is valid for only the short term. Long-range planning must recognize the possibilities of price and cost fluctuations.

An important amount in breakeven and CVP analysis is **contribution margin** (CM), which can be defined on either a per-unit or total basis. On a per-unit basis, contribution margin (CM) is equal to unit selling price minus per-unit variable production, selling, and administrative costs $(R - VC = CM)$. Contribution margin reflects the revenue remaining after all variable costs have been covered. Contribution margin per unit is constant, because both revenue and variable costs per unit have been defined as being constant. Total contribution margin fluctuates in direct proportion to sales volume.

contribution margin
selling price per unit minus all variable production, selling, and administrative costs per unit

Leveraging Contribution Margin

Financial institutions are increasingly utilizing contribution margin, not only as a means of measuring profitability performance but also as a tool to assist in making daily pricing decisions. When used as a measurement of profitability reporting, contribution margin shows more clearly how cost behaviour impacts profitability. Since many of the functions an operational manager performs depend on a clear understanding of costs, taking a contribution margin approach when reporting profitability focuses the user directly on fixed and variable cost behaviour. When utilizing contribution margin to facilitate pricing decisions, a user can pinpoint the exact price point that must be achieved to cover variable costs, which can contribute toward covering fixed costs and ultimately creating profits.

The classification of expenses as fixed, variable, or semivariable defines how an expense will behave over a relevant range of volume during a predefined time period (usually one year). It can be argued that when the concepts of relevant volume ranges and time are discarded, all expenses are semivariable. In other words, at some volume level during some period of time all expenses will increase (or decrease) as volume increases (or decreases).

Contribution margin assumes only variable and fixed cost classifications and defines what remains from total sales revenues after variable costs are deducted. The remainder can contribute toward covering fixed expenses as well as toward profits for the period. The semivariable component is key to business analyses, such as staffing models and capacity planning. However, for ongoing profitability measurement in a monthly production environment, the semivariable component can be associated with the variable and fixed components to simplify analysis, including the contribution margin calculation. Typically, the semivariable component can be split 60% fixed and 40% variable unless a detailed analysis determines an alternative split. With the contribution margin calculation, it is important to understand that revenue is not always required in order to cover the fixed cost component.[8]

As an example let's visit the sleepy little town of Creaking Springs in the weeks before Christmas. At the end of Main St. is Walter's market stall, where he sells Christmas trees. He buys them for $15 and sells them for $25, thus his variable costs are $15 per tree and his margin is $10 each time he sells one. We call this difference between selling price and variable costs the "contribution." It is not a profit yet because he has a fixed cost to pay, which is the stall he rents from the market owner. The market owner charges Walter $50 per day, making the weekly fixed costs $300 (he works all day Saturday). He has to sell 30 trees a week (each generating $10 per sale) before he has amassed enough contribution to pay his fixed costs. Then come the profits. The 31st tree he sells will allow him to keep the contribution from this sale as a profit of $10. Every additional tree he sells will generate an additional $10. If he sells 50 trees a week, then 20 will generate $10 each, bringing his total weekly profit to $200 (16% of total sales of $1,250). His variable cost is the price of each tree and his fixed cost is his stall rent.

As another example, the most expensive option for diners at the critically acclaimed New York restaurant Abacus is a nine-course tasting menu, which goes for a fixed price of $90. One of the menu's main ingredients: fish scraps.

The scraps are leftovers after Abacus cuts up fish into larger à la carte portions. They could have been thrown away. Instead, chef Tre Wilcox turns them into culinary gold: minute portions for his tasting menu. The menu, which changes frequently and recently included Kobe beef carpaccio and Alaskan king crab ravioli, yields about a 75% contribution margin, the difference between his menu price and ingredient prices and labour costs, says Mr. Wilcox. That's compared with a 66% margin on his à la carte menu.

Another reason diners are seeing so many of these menus lately is that the fixed-price route often delivers a better contribution margin to the restaurant. Chefs can buy fewer ingredients for the more limited menus and save money ordering them in bulk. In the kitchen, it can mean fewer staff, fewer stations, and the chance to use food that might otherwise be thrown out. At the table, revenue becomes plentiful and predictable as customers spend a substantial amount each time they dine.[9]

BASIC CALCULATIONS TO USE IN BREAKEVEN ANALYSIS

To illustrate computation of the breakeven point, the current year income statement information for Aspinall Computer Corporation is presented in Exhibit 3-1 below. The current relevant range of production and sales for the company is between 10,000 and 30,000 SCSI drives. The costs given in the exhibit are costs for all product elements.

EXHIBIT 3-1

Aspinall Computer Corporation
Income Statement for the Current
Year

	Total	Contribution Per Unit	Contribution Margin Ratio Percentage
Sales (15,000 units)	$6,750,000	$ 450	100%
Variable costs:			
Production	$4,725,000	$ 315	70
Selling	270,000	18	4
Total variable cost	(4,995,000)	$(333)	(74)
Contribution margin	$1,755,000	$ 117	26%
Fixed costs:			
Production	$ 550,000		
Selling and administrative expenses	700,000		
Total fixed costs	(1,250,000)		
Profit before income taxes	$ 505,000		

Contribution Margin and Calculating the Breakeven Point

Breakeven volume is equal to total fixed cost divided by the difference between revenue per unit and variable cost per unit. Since revenue minus variable cost equals contribution margin, the breakeven point in units can be calculated as follows:

$$\text{Fixed costs} \div \text{Contribution margin} = \text{Breakeven point in units}$$
$$\$1,250,000 \div \$117 \ (\$450 - \$333) = 10,684 \ (\text{rounded})$$

To calculate the breakeven point in dollars, multiply the breakeven point in units by the selling price per unit:

$$\text{Breakeven point in units} \times \text{Selling price per unit}$$
$$10,684 \times \$450 = \$4,807,800$$

Contribution Margin Ratio

The contribution margin ratio indicates the proportion of the revenue dollar remaining to go toward covering fixed costs and increasing profits. It is calculated as contribution margin divided by revenue. The contribution margin ratio can be computed with either per-unit or total cost information. Thus, if the unit selling price and unit variable costs are not known, the breakeven point can still be calculated. Dividing total fixed cost by the contribution margin ratio gives the breakeven point in sales dollars.

contribution margin ratio
contribution margin divided by
revenue; indicates what proportion of
selling price remains after variable
costs have been covered

$$\text{Contribution margin ratio} = (\text{Revenue} - \text{Variable cost}) \div \text{Revenue}$$
$$26\% = \$117 \ (\$450 - \$333) \div \$450$$

TARGET NET PROFIT

Fixed Net Profit

Assume that Aspinall Computer Corporation wants to earn $444,000 of profit after taxes and that the company's marginal tax rate is 30%:

In dollars:
Profit before tax = Profit after tax ÷ (1 − Tax rate)
$$= \$444{,}000 \div (1 - 0.30)$$
$$= \$634{,}286 \text{ (rounded)}$$

In units:
Fixed costs + Profit before tax ÷ Contribution margin
$$\$1{,}250{,}000 + \$634{,}286 \div \$117$$
$$= \$1{,}884{,}286 \div 117$$
$$= 16{,}106 \text{ units (rounded)}$$

Incremental Analysis for Short-Run Changes

The breakeven point may increase or decrease, depending on the particular changes that occur in the revenue and cost factors.

In densely populated Japan, convenience stores are continually adding products and services that attract customers, even if these activities do not contribute directly to the bottom line. One must assume that bringing customers into the stores will increase sales of other items that do contribute to the bottom line.[10]

Other things being equal, the breakeven point will increase if there is an increase in the total fixed cost, a decrease in selling price per unit, or an increase in variable costs. As well, a decrease in selling price, an increase in variable costs, or a combination of the two will cause a decrease in unit contribution margin. These relationships are illustrated in Exhibit 3-2. The breakeven point will decrease if there is a decrease in total fixed cost or an increase in unit (or percentage) contribution margin. A change in the breakeven point will also cause a shift in total profits or losses at any level of activity.

EXHIBIT 3-2

Effects of Changes From Original Data

Original Data: (from Exhibit 3-1)	Revenue per unit	$450
	Variable cost per unit	333
	Contribution margin per unit	$117

Fixed costs   = $1,250,000
Breakeven point = 10,684 units

If fixed costs increase to $2,340,000, BEP rises to 20,000 units

$$\$117X = \$2{,}340{,}000$$
$$X = \$2{,}340{,}000 \div \$117$$
$$X = 20{,}000$$

If revenue per unit falls to $433, BEP rises to 12,500 units

$$\$433 - \$333 = \$100 \text{ new CM}$$
$$\$100X = \$1{,}250{,}000$$
$$X = 12{,}500$$

If variable costs rise to $340, BEP rises to 11,364 units

$$\$450 - \$340 = \$110 \text{ new CM}$$
$$\$110X = \$1{,}250{,}000$$
$$X = 11{,}364 \text{ (rounded)}$$

incremental analysis
a technique used in decision analysis that compares alternatives by focusing on the differences in their projected revenues and costs

Incremental analysis is a process focusing only on factors that change from one course of action or decision to another. As related to CVP situations, incremental analysis is based on changes occurring in revenues, costs, and/or volume. The following are some examples of changes that may occur in a company and the incremental computations that can be used to determine the effects of those changes on the breakeven point or profits.

The following cases use the basic facts presented for Aspinall Computer Corporation in Exhibit 3-1. All of the following examples use before-tax information to simplify the computations. After-tax analysis would require the application of a $(1 - \text{Tax rate})$ factor to all profit figures.

Case 1

The company wishes to earn a before-tax profit of $702,000. How many units does it need to sell?

Since the breakeven point is known, answering this question requires simply determining how many units above the breakeven point are needed to generate before-tax profits of $702,000. Each dollar of contribution margin generated by product sales goes first to cover fixed costs and then to produce profits. Thus, after the breakeven point is reached, each dollar of contribution margin is a dollar of profit. To achieve $702,000 in desired profit requires Aspinall Computer Corporation to sell 6,000 units over the breakeven point (10,684 units), with each drive providing $117 of contribution margin:

$702,000 ÷ $117 = 6,000 units above BEP
∴ Total units = 10,684 + 6,000 = 16,684

Case 2

Aspinall Computer Corporation estimates that it can sell an additional 40 units if it spends $4,200 more on advertising. Should the company incur this extra fixed cost?

The contribution margin from the additional units must first cover the additional fixed cost before profits can be generated.

Increase in contribution margin	
40 units × $117 CM per unit	$ 4,680
Less: Increase in fixed cost	(4,200)
Equals: Net incremental benefit	$ 480

Since the net incremental benefit is $480, the advertising campaign would result in an additional profit and, thus, should be undertaken.

Case 3

The company estimates that, if the selling price of each unit is reduced to $440, an additional 1,000 units per year can be sold. Should the company reduce the price of the units? Current sales volume, given in Exhibit 3-1, is 15,000 units.

If the selling price (SP) is reduced, the contribution margin per unit will decrease to $107 per drive ($440 SP − $333 VC). Sales volume is estimated to increase to 16,000 units (15,000 + 1,000).

Total new contribution margin

(16,000 units × $107 CM per unit)	$ 1,712,000
Less: Total fixed costs (unchanged)	(1,250,000)
Equals: New profit before taxes	$ 462,000
Less: Current profit before taxes (from Exhibit 3-1)	(505,000)
Equals: Reduction in profit before taxes	$ (43,000)

Based on the new computation, the company will have less profit before taxes than is currently being generated; therefore, the company should not reduce its selling price. It is possible, however, that the reduction in price might increase sales by more than 1,000 units, and this might make the reduction worthwhile.

A DVD is installed after undergoing testing by Patrick Aspinall, the expert.

Case 4

Aspinall Computer Corporation has the opportunity on a one-time basis to sell 5,000 units to a foreign company. This sale will not disturb existing Canadian sales. The foreign company is offering to pay $375 per drive. The drives will be packaged and sold using the foreign company's own logo. Packaging costs will increase by $10.00 per unit. If the order is accepted, an additional $10,000 will be incurred by Aspinall to ship the product, but no other variable selling costs will be incurred by the company. Should Aspinall Computer Corporation make this sale?

The new total variable cost per drive is $343 ($333 total current variable costs + $10.00 additional variable packaging costs). The $375 selling price minus the $343 new total variable cost provides a contribution margin of $32 per drive sold to the foreign company.

Total contribution margin provided by this sale (5,000 units × $32 CM per drive)	$160,000
Less: Additional fixed cost related to this sale	10,000
Net incremental benefit	$150,000

The total contribution margin generated by the sale covers the additional fixed cost of the packaging, but also provides a net incremental benefit or profit to the firm; therefore, the deal should be made.

These are just a few examples of changes that might occur in a company's revenue and cost structure. In most situations, a complete income statement need not be prepared to determine the effects of changes. The contribution margin or incremental approach will often be sufficient to decide on the monetary merits of proposed or necessary changes. In making decisions, however, management must also consider the qualitative and long-run effects of the changes.

The contribution approach is often used to evaluate alternative pricing strategies in economic downturns. In such times, companies must recognize the reality that they will be unable to sell a normal volume of goods at normal prices. With this understanding, they can choose to maintain normal prices and sell a lower volume of goods, or reduce prices and attempt to maintain market share and normal volume.

We have seen this in the automobile industry. Imports of autos from the United States are on its way to breaking a record. Canadians imported 151,169 vehicles as of June 30, 2008, more than double the amount for the same period a year earlier. This prompted auto makers in Canada to offer record incentives on new autos. These incentives lowered contribution margin and raised the breakeven point; however, they did cover some of the fixed costs incurred.[11]

In the News Note below, we can see what changes firms are making in today's economy in order to improve their bottom line.

GENERAL
NEWS NOTE

Operating in Tough Times

Times are tough. For many firms, the margins are decreasing and costs of materials, labour, and benefits are increasing. Competition does not allow for sales price increases.

The most important thing that one has to understand is the difference between variable and fixed costs. Variable costs are those that increase with the filling of every order while fixed costs do not vary with sales but with the basic decisions put into place by management in operating the infrastructure. Although the term "fixed" seems to imply that these costs cannot be modified, this is not the case. "Fixed" actually indicates that these costs must be closely monitored.

Increasing sales is one way of increasing profits, however, in today's times, markets are shrinking and it may be difficult to maintain the current sales level, much less achieve more.

Rising fuel costs are forcing AIR CANADA and WESTJET to raise their fares and consolidate routes. An Air Canada spokesperson noted: "Fuel is our single largest expense. Last year we spent $2.5 billion on fuel." Air Canada, he added, calculates "that about every $1 change in the price of a barrel of oil impacts our operating income by $26 million." At WestJet, a $1 change in the price of a barrel of oil has about a $5 million impact on the bottom line.

Calgary-based WestJet announced on May 18, 2008, that it would begin charging an additional $20, $30, or $45 per one-way ticket for short, medium, and long-haul flights. This move followed a similar decision by Air Canada to implement a one-way surcharge of $20, $40, or $60 for tickets sold within Canada and to the United States.

What remains to be seen, analysts say, is whether the most recent price increases by Air Canada and WestJet will curtail demand by forcing price-sensitive travellers to cancel travel plans or look for alternative forms of transportation such as driving or taking the train. This could mean smaller fleets, fewer routes, and an increased focus on "premium" traffic such as business travellers. Air Canada and other carriers have announced decreased flights and frequencies.

JETBLUE AIRWAYS CORP., the low-cost carrier partly owned by Germany's DEUTSCHE LUFTHANSA AG, has said it doesn't expect oil prices to decline soon and has reaffirmed plans to cut capacity in the fourth quarter of 2008.

And it is not just airlines that are adding fuel surcharges—in Toronto, TTC officials aren't ruling out the possibility of adding a fuel surcharge to the price of a ride in 2009. A 10-cent increase in fares would raise about $25 million annually.

The above has described the impact of increased revenues and expenses on the breakeven point and contribution margin. Cutting capacity will reduce the number of fare-paying passengers, and thus revenues will go down. It is important to make sure there is sufficient cost cutting in both variable costs and fixed costs to ensure that there is not a great change in the breakeven volume.

Cost of sales, on the other hand, is a major target for savings. This is made up of material, labour, and overhead. You might be able to improve plant efficiency by reducing scrap or outsourcing. Labour is important to control. For example, companies can use temporaries during volume surges. They can look at alternatives to underutilized operations in-house and outsource (i.e., IT or accounting). However it is important not to remove operations that contribute profits toward covering overhead.

Certain other expenses are worth revisiting. Perhaps insurance coverage has not been reviewed for years and some coverage may no longer be needed. Reallocating facility space and maintaining leaner inventories can free up areas for sale or for subletting.

By applying these thoughts to reducing its infrastructure, one company in the prototyping industry, particularly hard hit by declining product development, was able to reduce its breakeven sales from $600,000 per month to approximately $100,000. This change in infrastructure came about from reductions in direct labour, utilities, insurance, and administrative salaries. The company also reduced its dependence on certain vendors by creating a greater share of tooling in-house.

CHRYSLER aims to cut its supply chain costs by 25 per cent in the next three years, and improve its relationship with suppliers. The Chrysler VP of procurement has named its supplier of choice: Japan's Denso Corp., which would enable the company to win future Chrysler business. The purchasing chief said it would achieve the targeted cost-cuts in a number of ways including reducing complexity and parts, and maintaining a stable production schedule.

At FORD, revenue fell to $41.9 billion in the second quarter from $44.5 billon in the prior year. Revenue per vehicle sold was down slightly to $22,987 from $23,123 in the prior year. Ford also sold 28,000 fewer cars in the second quarter in North America than in the same period a year ago.

In such an environment, it is vital to make up for the decline by managing costs better. At Ford, the problem is that fixed costs are too large.

Fixed costs, such as rent, property taxes, and insurance, don't vary depending on production levels. Variable costs, such as steel, aluminum, freight, taxes, and incentive payments, do. Health care is insurance and therefore a fixed cost for the company. Ordinarily, labour is a variable cost. But contracts with the UNITED AUTO WORKERS require the company to pay a large share of salary and benefits if it idles a worker, so labour is essentially a fixed cost as well.

Times as tough as they have been over the past three years are rare. For most, margins are decreasing. Companies face rising costs and do not have the ability to raise selling prices. Random desperate cost cutting is not the solution. Rather, the impact of reductions must be carefully weighed. Right-sizing has a special meaning to companies in trouble. It takes planning.

SOURCES: Adapted from "Operating in a Service Business in Tough Times," from the November 2003 issue of *Electrical Apparatus*, copyright 2003 by Barks Publications, Inc., Chicago, IL, USA; Canadian Press, "Air Canada, WestJet Up Fares to Offset Fuel Cost," *Toronto Star*, March 18, 2008, B7; Chris Sorenson, "WestJet, Porter Hike Fares," *Toronto Star*, May 13, 2008; Sherwin and Williams, "JetBlue Clips Wings as Fuel Costs Soar," *Toronto Star*, May 16, 2008; Tess Kalinowski, "Fuel Costs May Spike TTC Fares," *Toronto Star*, May 16, 2008; "Chrysler Seeks Better Relations with Suppliers," Reuters News Agency, Detroit, *Toronto Star*, Business, Economy, and Automotive. August 16, 2008 Pg. B3; Stephen D. Jones, "In the Money: Fixed Costs Gobbling Up Ford Cash," *Dow Jones*, September 19, 2006.

GENERAL NEWS NOTE

LEARNING OBJECTIVE 3

What is the purpose of breakeven and profit–volume graphs?

breakeven graph
a graphical depiction of the relationships among revenues, variable costs, fixed costs, and profits (or losses)

Solutions to breakeven problems are determined in this chapter using a formula approach. In some situations, however, information is clearer when presented in a more visual format, such as a graph. A breakeven graph may be used to graphically depict the relationships among revenues, variable costs, fixed costs, and profits (or losses). The breakeven point on a breakeven graph is located at the point where the total cost and total revenue lines cross. The following steps are necessary in preparing a **breakeven graph**.

Step 1.   Label the *x*-axis as volume and the *y*-axis as dollars. Plot the variable cost line as a linear function with a slope equal to total variable cost per unit. Next, plot the revenue line with a slope equal to the unit sales price. The area between the variable cost and revenue lines represents total contribution margin at each level of volume. The result of this step is shown in Exhibit 3-3 on page 110.

Step 2.   To graph total cost, add a line parallel to the total variable cost line. The distance between the total and variable cost lines is the amount of fixed cost.

EXHIBIT 3-3

Step One in Breakeven Graph
Preparation

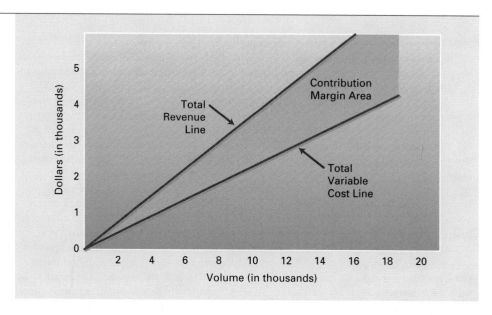

The total cost line is above and to the left of the total variable cost line. The breakeven point is located where the revenue and total cost lines intersect. If exact readings could be taken on the graph shown in Exhibit 3-4 below, the breakeven point for Aspinall Computer Corporation, based on the original information in Exhibit 3-1, and is shown as $4,807,800 of sales and 10,684 units (both figures are rounded).

EXHIBIT 3-4

Breakeven Graph

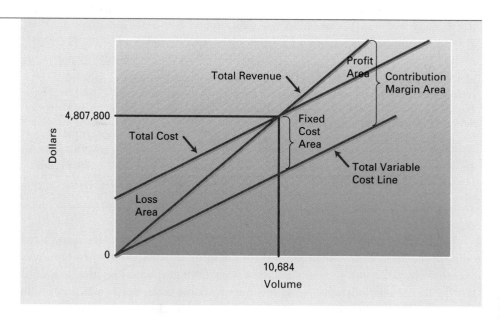

The format of the breakeven graph in Exhibit 3-4 allows the following important observations to be made.

1. Contribution margin is created by the excess of revenues over variable costs. If variable costs are greater than revenues, no quantity of volume will allow a profit to be made.
2. Total contribution margin is equal to total fixed cost plus profit or minus loss.
3. Before profits can be generated, contribution margin must exceed fixed costs.

Another method of visually presenting income statement information is the **profit–volume** (PV) **graph**, which reflects the amount of profit or loss at each sales level. The horizontal axis on the PV graph represents unit sales volume, and the vertical axis represents dollars. Amounts shown above the horizontal axis are positive and represent profits, while amounts shown below the horizontal axis are negative and represent losses.

profit–volume graph
a graphical presentation of the profit or loss associated with each level of sales

To draw the graph, first locate two points: total fixed costs and breakeven point. Total fixed costs are shown on the vertical axis as a negative amount (or below the sales volume line). If no units were sold, fixed costs would still be incurred, and a loss would result. The location of the breakeven point may be determined either by use of a breakeven graph or algebraically. The breakeven point in units is shown on the horizontal axis because there is no profit or loss at that point. With these two points plotted, a line is drawn that passes between them and extends through the breakeven point. This line can be used to read, from the vertical axis, the amount of profit or loss for any sales volume. This line represents total contribution margin, and its slope is determined by the unit contribution margin. The line shows that no profit is earned until the contribution margin covers the fixed costs.

The PV graph for Aspinall Computer Corporation is shown in Exhibit 3-5 below. Total fixed costs are $1,250,000 and the breakeven point is 10,684 units. The profit line reflects the original Exhibit 3-1 income statement data that, at sales of 15,000 SCSI drives, the company earns a profit of $505,000.

Although graphic approaches to breakeven point, cost–volume–profit analysis, and profit–volume relationships provide detailed visual displays, they may not yield precise answers to questions asked by mangers. Such solutions must be found using an algebraic formula approach because exact numerical points cannot always be read from the graphs.

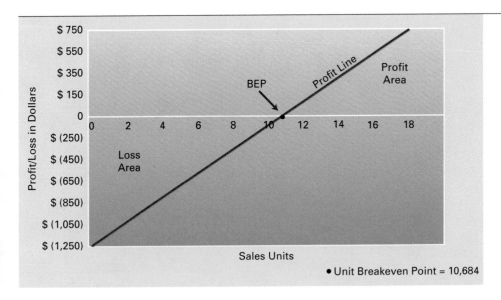

EXHIBIT 3-5
Profit–Volume Graph

If we refer back to page 100 and the discussion of radiology practices, we can analyze and display data graphically rather than in the form of equations or spreadsheets.

One way to understand these concepts is to combine them into a cost–volume–profit diagram (see Exhibit 3-6). All of the action that occurs can be seen in this figure. Total costs are the sum of the fixed costs and marginal costs per procedure. Revenue is the sum of the individual marginal revenues from each procedure. In this case, the procedure volume is yielding a net profit (revenue minus total costs).

EXHIBIT 3-6

Cost–Volume–Profit Diagram
Business A

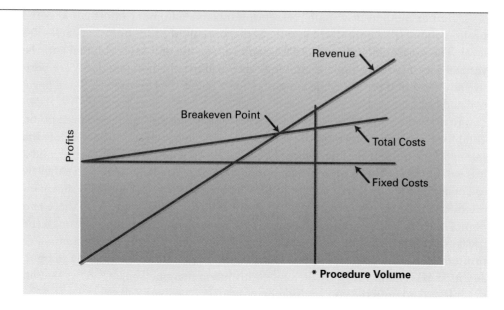

With the graphical approach, you can also see obvious ways to make the service more effective. Lowering fixed costs will reduce risk by decreasing the number of procedures necessary to surpass the breakeven point (see Exhibit 3-7). In Exhibits 3-6 and 3-7, this is the point where the total revenue line intersects with the total cost line. The service in Exhibit 3-6 is riskier—the practice must guarantee more procedures per week to break even. With the service structure, of lowered fixed cost, shown in Exhibit 3-7, a practice could tolerate a worse slump in procedure volume. Once the breakeven point is surpassed, the marginal revenue is almost all profit.

EXHIBIT 3-7

Cost–Volume–Profit Diagram
with Lowered Fixed Costs

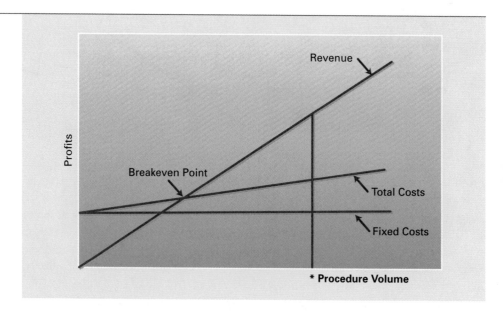

LEARNING OBJECTIVE 4

How do cost–volume–profit (CVP) analyses in single-product and multiproduct firms differ?

CVP ANALYSIS IN A MULTIPRODUCT ENVIRONMENT

The breakeven point for many companies is influenced by the mix of products sold. For example, the daily breakeven attendance at the National Arts Centre depends on how many tickets are sold in the various price ranges for each performance. Likewise, the breakeven point for an Air Canada overseas flight will be influenced by the number of first-class, business-class, and economy-class tickets sold for the flight.

"Air Canada is very competitive at the low end," says Rick Erickson, a Calgary-based airline consultant, referring to the airline's popular discounted "Tango" fare class. Indeed, several observers have speculated that Air Canada may even be willing to operate the bulk of its domestic routes on a breakeven basis, relying on its higher margin international flights to make up for the shortfall.[12]

Companies typically produce and sell a variety of products or services. To perform CVP analysis in a multiproduct company, it is necessary to assume a constant product sales mix or an average contribution margin ratio. The constant mix assumption can be referred to as the "bag" or "package" assumption. This analogy compares the sales mix to a bag or package of items that are sold together. For example, whenever some of Product A is sold, specified quantities of Products B and C are also sold.

Use of the constant sales mix assumption allows the computation of a weighted average contribution margin ratio. The CM ratio is *weighted* on the basis of the quantity of each item included in the bag. The contribution margin ratio of the item that makes up the largest proportion of the bag has the greatest impact on the average contribution margin of the bag mix. Without the assumptions of a constant sales mix, the breakeven point cannot be calculated, nor can CVP analysis be used effectively.[13]

Patrick Aspinall explains to a satisfied customer that only the best quality parts are used at Aspinall Computer Corporation.

The Aspinall Computer Corporation example continues. Because of the success of the SCSI drives, company management has decided to produce DVD drives. Vice-president of marketing Ambrus Kesckes estimates that, for every five SCSI drives sold, the company will sell two DVD drives. Therefore, the "bag" of products has a 5:2 ratio. The company will incur an additional $150,000 in fixed costs related to plant assets (depreciation, insurance, and so on) to support a higher relevant range of production and additional licensing fees. Exhibit 3-8 on page 114 provides relevant company information and shows the breakeven computations.

The weighted average contribution margin ratio is calculated by multiplying the sales mix percentage (relative to sales dollars)* by the CM ratio** for each product and summing the results. According to the note at the bottom of Exhibit 3-8, the relationship of dollars of SCSI drive sales to dollars of DVD drive sales is 90% to 10%. Based on this information, the CM ratio for the "bag" of products is computed by multiplying these percentages by the contribution margin ratios of the respective individual products (also from Exhibit 3-8) and adding the results as follows:

SCSI drives	$90\% \times 26\%$ =	0.234
DVD drives	$10\% \times 20\%$ =	0.020
Total CM ratio		0.254

*For SCSI drives this is calculated as $2,250 ÷ $2,500, which is 90%, and for DVD drives as $250 ÷ $2,500, which is 10%.

**The contribution margin ratio for SCSI drives is calculated as $585 ÷ $2,250, which is 26% and for DVDs as $50 ÷ $250, which is 20%.

EXHIBIT 3-8

CVP Analysis—Multiple Products

Product cost information	SCSI Drives		DVD	
Selling price	$450	100%	$125	100%
Total variable cost	(333)	(74%)	(100)	(80%)
Contribution margin	$117	26%	$ 25	20%

Total Fixed Costs ($1,250,000 previous + $150,000 additional new costs) = **$1,400,000**

	SCSI Drives		DVD		Per Bag Total	Percent
Number of products per bag		5		2		
Revenue per product	$450		$125			
Total revenue per "bag"		$2,250		$250	$2,500	100.0%
Variable cost per unit	(333)		(100)			
Total variable cost per "bag"		(1,665)		(200)	(1,865)	(74.6)%
Contribution margin—product	$117		$ 25			
Contribution margin—"bag"		$ 585		$ 50	$ 635	25.4%

BEP in *units* (where B = "bags" of products)

$$CM(B) = FC$$
$$\$2,500 - \$1,865 = 1,400,000$$
$$\$635B = \$1,400,000$$
$$B = 2,205 \text{ bags to break even (rounded)}$$

Note: Each bag is made up of 5 SCSI drives; thus, it will take 11,025 (5 × 2,205) SCSI drives and 4,410 (2 × 3,205) DVD drives to break even, assuming the constant 5:2 sales mix.

BEP in *sales dollars* (where CM ratio = Weighted average CM for each "bag" of products):

$$B_{\$} = FC ÷ CM \text{ ratio}$$
$$B_{\$} = \$1,400,000 ÷ 0.254$$
$$B_{\$} = \$5,511,811 \text{ (rounded)}$$

Note: The breakeven sales dollars also represent the assumed constant sales mix of $2,205 of sales of SCSI drives to $250 of sales of DVD drives to represent a 90% ($2,250 ÷ $2,500) to 10% ($250 ÷ $2,500) ratio. Thus, the company must have approximately $4,960,630 ($5,511,811 × 90%) of sales of SCSI drives and $551,181 ($5,511,811 × 10%) in sales of DVDs to break even.

Proof of the computations in Exhibit 3-8 using the income statement approach is shown below:

	SCSI Drives	DVD Drives	Total
Sales	$ 4,960,630	$ 551,181	$5,511,811[1]
Variable costs[2]	(3,670,866)	(440,945)	(4,111,811)
Contribution margin	$ 1,289,764	$ 110,236	$1,400,000
Fixed costs			(1,400,000)
Income before income taxes			$ 0

[1]From Exhibit 3-8.
[2]These amounts are determined by taking the previously calculated variable cost percentages of 74% for SCSI drives (0.74 × $4,960,630) and 80% for DVDs (0.80 × $551,181) (Exhibit 3-8).

Any shift in the proportion of sales mix of products will change the weighted average contribution margin and the breakeven point. If the sales mix shifts toward products with lower contribution margins, there will be an increase in the BEP; furthermore, there will be a decrease in profits unless there is a corresponding increase in total revenues. A shift toward higher-margin products without a corresponding decrease in revenues will cause increased profits and a lower breakeven point.

To break even at the level indicated, Aspinall Computer Corporation must sell the products in exactly the relationships specified in the original sales mix. If sales are at the specified level but not in the specified mix, the company will experience either a profit or a loss, depending on whether the mix is shifted toward the product with the higher or lower contribution margin ratio.

As seen in our example of Aspinall Computer Corporation, sales mix has a profound effect on the bottom line. Other companies are using bundling as a means to increase sales and profit. The News Note below shows how companies are doing this.

Bundling Products Together

GENERAL NEWS NOTE

Companies can increase sales by bundling various services, a growing trend in Canada, but the strategy isn't as simple as throwing a couple of products together and slapping on a discounted price.

A bundle can be as basic as a MCDONALD'S value meal, combining a burger, fries, and drink. MICROSOFT CORP. used bundling to great success in the 1990s by bundling its word-processing program Word® with its spreadsheet program Excel®, and stamping out a competitive threat from rival program WordPerfect®.

In the communications sector, from cable television to telephone service, bundles are increasingly popular. BELL CANADA is making its move, too. Canada's largest phone company, wants to offer all its services—telephone, mobile telephone, satellite television, and Internet—in one package. The Company's aim is to "deepen relationships . . . while simplifying choice," said the annual report of BCE. Mr. Sabia [BCE Inc.'s prior president and chief executive] said a key element of BCE's new bundling approach is the realization consumers are more loyal if they have at least two services. This suggests consumers like the convenience of dealing with one supplier as much or more than discounts. As a result Mr. Sabia said BCE will focus on upselling one-service households. "It appears the propensity to switch is markedly lower with just one additional product," he said. "So the payback is greater from taking a customer from one to two products than from three to four."

ROGERS has expanded on the range of bundled products available to allow customers to find bundles for every need. With the aptly named Incredible Rogers Bundles, customers can enjoy the benefits of high-speed Internet access, no upfront hardware costs, ROD, and 24/7 support from Canada's most advanced digital network. Rogers Business Solutions specializes in providing smart and flexible cable, Internet, and wireless services to a much neglected sector—home based businesses and small businesses—as well as to the growing population of telecommuters. They are also personalizing the "My Home Advantage" bundle to meet a family's unique needs.

Those who subscribe to bundles are less likely to cancel services. It is an advantage because it reduces the so-called churn, the number of customers cancelling a service, which is costly for companies. Rogers said that the churn rate of customers buying a bundle is far lower than for customers buying only one service.

SOURCE: Dave Ebner, "Strategic Bundling of Services Offers Prospect of Higher Sales," *The Globe and Mail,* August 1, 2003; Mark Evans, BCE to shift sales strategy: Bell aims to sell more services to single-use clients, *Financial Post,* August 4, 2005; *Hot Stuff,* a special advertising supplement, Rogers. Your home is unique, a special advertising supplement." Rogers Communications Inc., July 2008.

UNDERLYING ASSUMPTIONS OF CVP ANALYSIS

The CVP model is a useful planning tool that can provide information on how profits are affected when changes are made in the costing system or in sales levels. Like any

LEARNING OBJECTIVE 5

What are the underlying assumptions of CVP analysis and how do these assumptions create a short-run managerial perspective?

model, however, it reflects reality but does not duplicate it. Cost–volume–profit analysis is a tool that focuses on the short run, partially because of the assumptions that underlie the computations. Although these assumptions are necessary, they limit the results' accuracy. These assumptions follow; some of them were also provided at the beginning of the chapter.

1. All variable cost and revenue behaviour patterns are constant per unit and linear within the relevant range.
2. Total contribution margin (Total revenue – Total variable cost) is linear within the relevant range and increases proportionally with output. This assumption follows directly from assumption 1.
3. Total fixed cost is a constant amount within the relevant range.
4. Mixed costs can be accurately separated into their fixed and variable elements. Such accuracy is particularly unrealistic, but estimates can be developed from the high–low method or regression analysis (discussed in Chapter 2).
5. Sales and production are equal; thus, there is no material fluctuation in inventory levels. This assumption is necessary because of the allocation of fixed costs to inventory at potentially different rates each year.
6. There will be no capacity additions during the period under consideration. If such additions were made, fixed (and possibly variable) costs would change. Any changes in fixed or variable costs would invalidate assumptions 1 to 3.
7. In a multiproduct firm, the sales mix will remain constant. If this assumption were not made, no useful weighted average contribution margin could be computed for the company for purposes of CVP analysis.
8. There is no inflation, or inflation affects all cost factors equally, or if factors are affected unequally, the appropriate effects are incorporated into the CVP figures.
9. Labour productivity, production technology, and market conditions will not change. If any of these changes occurred, costs would change correspondingly, and it is possible that selling prices would change. Such changes would invalidate assumptions 1 to 3.

The nine assumptions are the traditional ones associated with cost–volume–profit analysis and reflect a basic disregard of possible (and probable) future changes. Accountants generally assume that cost behaviour, once classified, remains constant over periods of time as long as operations remain within the relevant range and in the absence of evidence to the contrary. Thus, for example, once a cost is determined to be fixed, it is fixed next year, the year after, and from then on.

As mentioned in Chapter 2, however, it may be more realistic to regard fixed costs as long-term variable costs. Companies can, over the long run and through managerial decisions, lay off supervisors and sell plant and equipment items. Alternatively, companies may grow and increase their fixed investments in people, plant, and equipment. Fixed costs are not fixed forever. In many companies, some costs considered to be fixed "have been the most variable and rapidly increasing costs."[14] Part of this cost "misclassification" problem has occurred because of improper specification of cost drivers. As companies become less focused on production and sales volumes as cost drivers, they will begin to recognize that fixed costs only exist under a short-term reporting period perspective.

In addition, certain costs may arise that are variable in the first year of providing a product or service to a customer but will not recur in future years. Customer acquisition costs for a pure-play Internet operation is $82 per customer. On-line customer acquisition costs may continue to rise in the short term but they should eventually drop as on-line companies become more recognized by buyers. It is a fact that pure-play Internet companies spend 20% to 40% more than those companies that do not have Internet presence.[15]

With the typical off-Broadway show now taking about $500,000 just to get to opening night (compared to a minimum of $2 million for a Broadway play), it's becoming almost impossible to break even when you've only got about 350 seats to sell. (Union regulations state that off-Broadway houses must have fewer than 499 seats; many have far fewer.)

Back in February, the *New York Times* ran an eye-opening chart analyzing the costs of *Bug*, an off-Broadway sensation that has since been adapted as a feature film by director William Friedkin. The play ran for about a year at the Barrow Street Theater and only just managed to recoup its $2 million costs, which included both preopening and weekly running charges.

From one perspective, it's understandable: Why pay up to $65 for an off-Broadway show with no stars when you can pick up discounted tickets to a Broadway show for the same price? And since off-Broadway producers have far less to spend on advertising, it's getting harder to grab the fickle attention of audiences. (Do the math: You'd have to sell out five nights' worth of 400-seat houses at $50 a pop in order to pay for a single one-page $100,000 ad in the *Sunday Times*.)[16]

Differing current and future period costs are very important concerns in various service businesses. Getting new customers requires a variety of one-time costs for things such as advertising, mailing, and checking customers' credit histories.

As companies and customers become more familiar with one another, services can be provided more efficiently or higher prices can be charged for the trusted relationship. Failure to consider such changes in costs can provide a very distorted picture of how profits are generated and, therefore, can lead to an improper analysis of the relationships of costs, volume, and profits.

MARGIN OF SAFETY AND OPERATING LEVERAGE

LEARNING OBJECTIVE 6

How are the margin of safety and operating leverage concepts used in business?

The breakeven point is the lowest level of sales volume at which an organization would want to operate. As sales increase from that point, managers become less concerned about whether decisions will cause the company to lose money. Thus, when making decisions about various business opportunities, managers often consider the company's margin of safety and operating leverage.

Margin of Safety

The **margin of safety** is the excess of a company's estimated (budgeted) or actual sales over its breakeven point. It is the amount that sales can drop before reaching the breakeven point and thus provides a measure of the amount of "cushion" from losses. It helps management to determine how close to the danger level the company is operating and provides an indication of risk. The lower the margin of safety, the more carefully management must watch sales figures and control costs so that a net loss will not be generated. At low margins of safety, managers are less likely to take advantage of opportunities that could send the company into a loss position.

The margin of safety can be expressed as units, dollars, or a percentage. The following formulas are applicable:

margin of safety
the excess of the estimated (budgeted) or actual sales of a company over its breakeven point; can be calculated in units or sales dollars, or as a percentage

Margin of safety in units = Estimated (Actual) units − Breakeven units

Margin of safety in dollars = Estimated (Actual) sales dollars − Breakeven sales dollars

Margin of safety percentage = Margin of safety in units or dollars ÷ Estimated (Actual) sales in units or dollars

The breakeven point for Aspinall Computer Corporation (using the original, single-product data in Exhibit 3-1 page 104) is 10,684 SCSI drives or $4,807,800 of sales. The income statement for the company presented in Exhibit 3-1 shows actual sales for the current year of 15,000 SCSI drives and sales revenue of $6,750,000. The margin of safety for Aspinall Computer Corporation is calculated in Exhibit 3-9 below. The margin is high, since the company is operating far above its breakeven point.

EXHIBIT 3-9
Margin of Safety

In units:	15,000 actual − 10,684 BEP = 4,316 SCSI drives
In sales dollars:	$6,750,000 actual − $4,807,800 BEP = $1,942,200
In percentage:	(15,000 − 10,684) ÷ 15,000 = 0.288, or 29% rounded
	or
	($6,750,000 − $4,807,800) ÷ $6,750,000 = 0.288 or 29% (rounded)

Operating Leverage

operating leverage
a factor that reflects the relationship of a company's variable and fixed costs; measures the change in profits expected to result from a specified percentage change in sales

Another measure that is closely related to the margin of safety and also provides useful management information is the company's degree of **operating leverage**. The relationship of a company's variable and fixed costs is reflected in its operating leverage. Typically, highly labour-intensive organizations, such as McDonald's and Pizza Pizza, have high variable costs and low fixed costs and thus have a low operating leverage and a relatively low breakeven point. (An exception to this rule is sports teams, which are highly labour-intensive but have labour costs that are fixed rather than variable.) Companies with a low operating leverage can show a profit even when they experience wide swings in volume levels. Many companies choose to outsource certain of their functions. For example, BP Amoco PLC is contracting out the accounting services at its Canadian petroleum subsidiary, a U.S.$200 million agreement. This is the largest business process outsourcing deal in Canada and the first of its kind in the oilpatch. PricewaterhouseCoopers will look after the accounting and associated information technology for BP Amoco, the largest natural gas producer in Canada.[17] This philosophy allows companies to eliminate some fixed costs and, therefore, reduce the probability of losses if business volume declines.

Conversely, organizations that are highly capital-intensive, such as Air Canada, have a cost structure that includes very high fixed costs. Such a structure reflects high operating leverage. Because fixed costs are high, the breakeven point is relatively high; if selling prices are predominantly set by the market, volume has the primary impact on profitability. As companies become more automated, they will face this type of cost structure and will be increasingly dependent on volume to add profits.

Companies with high operating leverage have high contribution margin ratios. Although such companies have to establish fairly high sales volumes initially to cover fixed costs, once those costs are covered, each unit sold after breakeven produces large profits. Thus, a small increase in sales can have a major impact on a company's profits.

Recently, the long-distance business of Bell Canada, fell 7% in a single quarter, average revenue per user declined, and sales of local services remained flat. Like other former telecom monopolies, Bell faces growing competition in both the cable and telecommunications markets as cable companies and smaller telecom competitors move in, offering wireless or Internet-based services. Their chief financial officer said, "Pressure on margins continues to come from long distance and data, and the challenge for us for the second half of the year is going to be to offset that type of erosion with improved margins in our growth businesses."

As discussed earlier, bundling is one means by which the company hopes to increase revenues and thus profits. This change in methodology affects the sales mix of most companies. In the quarter ended June 2004, 70,000 new customers signed up with Bell for bundled products, bringing the total number to 200,000. Growth was boosted by a new long-distance package introduced in June that offers 1,000 minutes in Canada and the United States for $5 to customers who have at least two of Bell's high-speed Internet, wireless or ExpressVu services; 45% of customers who are opting for a package are purchasing at least one new product.[18]

Rogers Communications Inc. may be headed for difficult times. The latest cause for concern came in December 2007, when the company reported a fourth-quarter cellphone subscriber figure that fell short of what was anticipated. Three wireless cellphone carriers control an industry in Canada that adds more than a million customers each year. With Ottawa setting aside some wireless airwaves for new entrants to bid on later in 2008, there is a concern that market share will be stolen from existing carriers. In the first nine months of 2007, Rogers grabbed the biggest share of wireless subscribers. Rogers also announced an increase of 20,000 subscribers for basic cable in the fourth quarter of 2007.[19]

Companies also attempt to manage their levels of operating leverage as economic conditions change. This is discussed in the following News Note.

Managing Operating Leverage

GENERAL NEWS NOTE

Electronics manufacturer CELESTICA INC. will cut 10% to 15% of its workforce—as many as 6,000 jobs—as it copes with falling revenue and a continuing industrywide slowdown, the company said on July 17, 2002.

Celestica, which manufactures equipment sold by major telecommunication companies such as LUCENT TECHNOLOGIES INC. and computer companies such as INTERNATIONAL BUSINESS MACHINES CORP., said it is reducing its manufacturing capacity to deal with a slump in the worldwide telecom sector.

Celestica, which is controlled by conglomerate ONEX CORP., has also been on an efficiency drive for much of the last year.

"Over the past 15 months, we have rebalanced our manufacturing footprint and have been focused on driving greater efficiency from our operations.

We [Celestica] have made significant progress on these initiatives, resulting in stable profitability, and as a result believe that we can undertake this action without compromising our growth opportunities or limiting our customers' potential growth needs."

SOURCE: David Paddon, Canadian Press, *Toronto Star*, July 18, 2002, D4.

The **degree of operating leverage** (DOL) indicates how sensitive the company is to sales increases and decreases by measuring how a percentage change in sales affects company profits. The computation for the degree of operating leverage is:

Degree of operating leverage = Contribution margin ÷ Profit before tax

The calculation assumes that fixed costs do not increase when sales increase.

Assume that Aspinall Computer Corporation is currently selling 12,000 SCSI drives. Using the basic facts from Exhibit 3-1, Exhibit 3-10 provides the income

degree of operating leverage
a measure of how a percentage change in sales will affect profits; calculated at a specified sales level as contribution margin divided by income before tax

statement that reflects this sales level. As shown in this exhibit, the company has an operating leverage factor of 9.12 at this level of sales. If the company increases sales by 20%, the change in profits is equal to the degree of operating leverage multiplied by the percentage change in sales, or 182%! If sales decrease by the same 20%, there is a negative 182% impact on profits.

EXHIBIT 3-10

Degree of Operating Leverage

	12,000 Drives Current	14,400 Drives 20% Increase	9,600 Drives 20% Decrease
Sales	$ 5,400,000	$ 6,480,000	$ 4,320,000
Variable costs ($333 per drive)	(3,996,000)	(4,795,200)	(3,196,800)
Contribution margin	$ 1,404,000	$ 1,684,800	$ 1,123,200
Fixed costs	(1,250,000)	(1,250,000)	(1,250,000)
Profit before tax	$ 154,000	$ 434,800	$ (126,800)

Degree of operating leverage:

Contribution margin ÷ Profit before tax

$1,404,000 ÷ $ 154,000	9.12	
$1,684,800 ÷ $ 434,800		3.87
$1,123,200 ÷ $(126,800)		Can't be calculated

Profit increase at 14,400 drives = $434,800 − $154,000
= $280,800 or 182% of original income

Profit decrease at 9,600 drives = $(126,800) − $154,000
= $(280,800) or −182% of original income

The degree of operating leverage decreases the further a company moves from its breakeven point. When the margin of safety is small, the degree of operating leverage is large. In fact, at breakeven, the degree of operating leverage is infinite, because any increase from zero is an infinite percentage change. If a company is operating close to the breakeven point, each percentage increase in sales can make a dramatic impact on net income. As the company moves away from breakeven sales, the margin of safety increases, but the degree of operating leverage declines.

The following example discusses the newest airbus A380 and the aircraft sales needed to breakeven.

Singapore Airlines raised the bar in the global race to pamper premium passengers on October 25, 2007, with its first commercial flight of the A380, from Singapore to Sydney. The 12 first-class passengers nestle in fully enclosed cabins reminiscent of a luxury yacht. Each suite boasts a private coat closet, a 23-inch video screen, and ergonomically designed reclining seats, in addition to a built-in bed, which is expandable to double size for travelling couples who want to nap.

The 60 seats in business class are 86 centimetres wide—twice as wide as typical 48-centimetre economy seats.

Almost half the cabin space on the A380 is reserved for the 72 premium passengers. A key question for the industry is whether allotting so much space to a carrier's best customers is the wisest use of this plane's voluminous real estate.

Singapore Airlines is providing just 471 seats on the aircraft, which has 50% more floor space than the previous record holder, Boeing's 747-400. Even the 399 economy-class passengers on Singapore Airlines' A380 will have their own USB computer ports, with full miniature keyboards, as well as seats that recline 115 degrees.

SIA is charging a premium for all this luxury. First-class fares on the A380 between Singapore and Sydney are 20% higher than for the same route on the airline's 747-400s, bringing the one-way fare to around $6,000, excluding taxes and extra charges. Business-class passengers pay a 15% premium, about $4,140 one-way, excluding taxes and charges.

SIA is among the world's most profitable airlines. A company spokesman says that it is able to charge above-market rates for its products because "if you want to live in Trump Tower, you've got to expect to pay a bit more." (There will be no premium on economy-class seats, where at least eight different fare levels apply that can vary from month to month.)

Demand for first-class service probably is "recession proof," agrees Shukor Yusof of Standard and Poor's Asia Equity Research in Singapore. But he notes that corporate demand for business-class seats on the A380 could dry up in a severe economic downturn and that an external event such as the terrorist attacks of September 2001 or the 2003 outbreak of severe acute respiratory syndrome (SARS) could pinch profits.

Airbus has received firm orders for 165 A380s from 14 different customers and needs to sell about 420 of them to break even.[20]

Absorption and Variable Costing

Knowing the cost to produce a product or provide a service is important to all businesspeople. But, as discussed in Chapter 2, cost may be defined in a variety of ways. A company's costing system and inventory measurement method provide necessary, but not sufficient, information for determining product cost. Two additional dimensions must be considered: cost accumulation and cost presentation. The method of presentation focuses on how costs are shown on external financial statements or internal management reports. Accumulation and presentation procedures use either absorption or variable costing. These methods are discussed and contrasted. The methods use the same basic data but structure and process these data differently.

The most common approach to product costing is **absorption costing**, which is also known as full costing. This approach treats the costs of all manufacturing components (direct material, direct labour, variable manufacturing overhead, and fixed manufacturing overhead) as inventoriable or product costs. Exhibit 3-11 depicts the absorption costing model.

LEARNING OBJECTIVE 7

What are the cost accumulation and cost presentation approaches to product costing?

absorption costing
a cost accumulation method that treats the costs of all manufacturing components (direct materials, direct labour, variable overhead, and fixed overhead) as inventoriable or product costs; also known as full costing

EXHIBIT 3-11
Absorption Costing Model

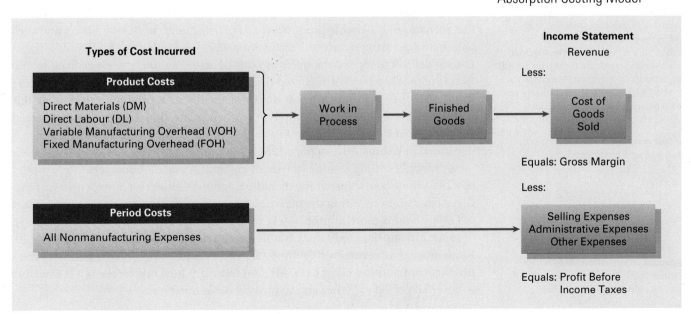

An organization incurs costs for direct material (DM), direct labour (DL), variable manufacturing overhead (VOH) and fixed manufacturing overhead (FOH) to produce products. However, when one thinks about the costs of production, it can be said that direct material (DM), direct labour (DL), and variable manufacturing overhead (VOH) are incurred when goods are produced or services are rendered. Since total DM, DL, and VOH costs increase with each additional product made or unit of service rendered, these costs are considered product costs and are inventoried until the product or service is sold. Fixed manufacturing overhead (FOH) cost, on the other hand, may be incurred even when production or service facilities are idle. Although total FOH cost does not vary with units of production or level of service, this cost provides the basic capacity necessary for production or service to occur. Because production could not take place without the incurrence of fixed manufacturing overhead, absorption costing considers this cost to be inventoriable.

Thus, when absorption costing is used, the financial statements show the Work in Process Inventory, Finished Goods Inventory, and Cost of Goods Sold accounts as including variable per-unit production costs as well as a per-unit allocation of fixed manufacturing overhead. Absorption costing also presents expenses on an income statement according to their functional classifications. A **functional classification** is a grouping of costs that were all incurred for the same basic purpose. Functional classifications include categories such as cost of goods sold, selling expenses, and administrative expenses.

functional classification
a grouping of costs incurred for the same basic purpose

The actual Work in Process Inventory cost that is transferred to Finished Goods Inventory is computed as follows:

Direct materials	$xxx
Direct labour	xxx
Variable manufacturing overhead	xxx
Fixed manufacturing overhead	xxx
Production cost for period	$xxx
Plus: Beginning Work in Process	xxx
Total cost to account for this period	$xxx
Less: Ending Work In Process*	xxx
Cost of Goods Manufactured	$xxx

* Calculation of this amount is covered in a later chapter.

variable costing
a cost accumulation method that includes only variable production costs (direct materials, direct labour, and variable manufacturing overhead) as product or inventoriable costs and treats fixed manufacturing overhead as a period cost; also known as direct costing

Variable costing, also known as **direct costing**,[21] is a cost accumulation method that includes only variable production costs (direct material, direct labour, and variable manufacturing overhead) as inventoriable or product costs. Thus, variable costing defines product costs solely as costs of *actual production*. Since fixed manufacturing overhead will be incurred even if there is no production, variable costing proponents believe that this cost does not qualify as a product cost. Under this method the fixed manufacturing overhead costs are therefore treated as period costs (expenses) and are charged against revenue as incurred. Variable costing is illustrated in Exhibit 3-12 on page 123.

direct costing
see *variable costing*

A variable costing income statement and management report separates costs by cost behaviour (variable and fixed), although it may also present expenses by functional classifications within the behavioural categories. Under variable costing, Cost of Goods Sold is more appropriately called *Variable* Cost of Goods Sold (VCGS), because it comprises only the variable production costs related to the units sold. Remember that revenue (R) minus variable cost of goods sold (VCGS) is called **product contribution margin** (PCM), and indicates how much revenue is available to cover all period expenses and to provide net income.

product contribution margin
revenue minus variable cost of goods sold

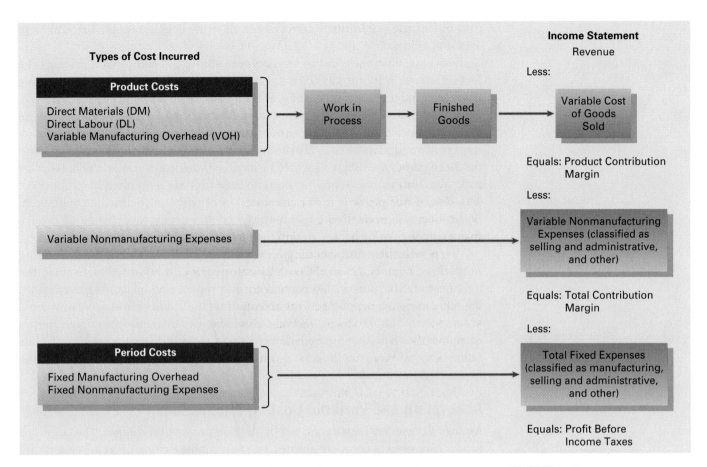

EXHIBIT 3-12
Variable Costing Model

total contribution margin
revenue minus all variable costs
regardless of the area of incurrence
(production or nonproduction)

Variable nonmanufacturing period expenses (such as a sales commission set at 10% of product selling price) are deducted from product contribution margin to determine the amount of **total contribution margin** (TCM). Total contribution margin is the difference between total revenues and total variable expenses. This amount represents the dollar figure available to "contribute" to the coverage of all fixed expenses, both manufacturing and nonmanufacturing. After fixed expenses are covered, any remaining contribution margin provides income to the company. Variable costing financial statements are also known as contribution income statements.

Major authoritative bodies of the accounting profession, such as the Canadian Institute of Chartered Accountants (CICA) and the Financial Accounting Standards Board (FASB) in the United States, believe that absorption costing provides external parties with the most informative picture of earnings. The rationale for this position reflects the importance of the matching concept in that absorption costing expenses all product costs in the period that the related revenue is recognized.

Cost behaviour (relative to changes in activity) cannot be observed from an absorption costing income statement. Managers attempting to use absorption costing information for internal decision making find that combining costs into functional classifications obscures important cost behaviour patterns. Therefore, although companies must prepare external statements using absorption costing, internal reports are also often prepared to show cost behaviours to facilitate management analysis and decision making. Cost behaviour is extremely important for a variety of managerial activities including cost–volume–profit analysis, relevant costing, and budgeting.[22] Whether the perspective is of the short run or long run, one of the preeminent concerns of all firms is generation of revenues in excess of all costs.

Two basic differences can be seen between absorption and variable costing. The first difference is in the way fixed overhead (FOH) is treated for product costing purposes. Under absorption costing, FOH is considered a product cost; under variable costing, it is considered a period cost. Absorption costing advocates contend that products cannot be made without the capacity provided by fixed manufacturing costs and so these costs are product costs. Variable costing advocates contend that fixed manufacturing costs would be incurred whether or not production occurs and, therefore, cannot be product costs because they are not caused by production. The second difference is in the presentation of costs on the income statement. Absorption costing classifies expenses by function, whereas variable costing categorizes expenses first by behaviour and then may further classify them by function.

Even with their differences, the two costing methods have some underlying similarities. First, both methods use the same basic cost information. Second, the treatment of direct material, direct labour, and variable manufacturing overhead is the same under absorption and variable costing; these costs are always considered product costs. Third, selling and administrative expenses are considered period costs under both costing methods. Fourth, there are no differences among accounts other than in Work in Process Inventory, Finished Goods Inventory, and the expense accounts under the two methods.

Absorption and Variable Costing Illustrations

Aspinall Computer Corporation is a small drive-production company. Data for this product are used to compare absorption and variable costing procedures and presentations. Exhibit 3-13 gives the production costs per unit, the annual budgeted nonmanufacturing costs, and other basic operating data for the company. All costs are assumed to remain constant over the next three years and, for simplicity, the company is assumed to have no Work in Process Inventory at the end of a period. Actual costs are assumed to equal the estimated (budgeted costs) for the years presented. Exhibit 3-14 on page 125, compares actual unit production with actual unit sales to determine the change in inventory for each of the three years.

EXHIBIT 3-13

Basic Data for Three Years

Sales price per unit	$ 6.00
Direct material cost per unit	$ 2.040
Direct labour	1.500
Variable manufacturing overhead	0.180
Total variable manufacturing cost per unit	$ 3.720
Fixed overhead based on expected activity level of 30,000 units	$16,020
Fixed overhead applied per unit = $16,020 ÷ 30,000	$ 0.534
Total absorption cost per unit:	
Variable manufacturing cost	$ 3.720
Fixed manufacturing overhead	0.534
Total absorption cost per unit	$ 4.254
Estimated (budgeted) nonmanufacturing expenses:	
Variable selling expenses per unit	$ 0.24
Fixed selling and administrative expenses	$2,340.00
Total estimated (budgeted) nonmanufacturing expenses = ($0.24 per unit sold + $2,340)	

	2009	2010	2011	Total
Actual units made	30,000	29,000	31,000	90,000
Actual units sold	30,000	27,000	33,000	90,000
Change in Finished Goods Inventory	0	+2,000	−2,000	0

EXHIBIT 3-14

What Happened Over the Three Years?

Since the company began operations in 2009, there is no beginning Finished Goods Inventory. The next year, 2010, also has a zero beginning inventory because all units produced in 2009 were also sold in 2009. In 2010 and 2011, production and sales quantities differ, which is a common situation because production frequently "leads" sales so that inventory can be stockpiled for a later period. The illustration purposefully has no beginning inventory and equal cumulative units of production and sales for the three years to demonstrate that, regardless of whether absorption or variable costing is used, the cumulative income before taxes will be the same ($128,520 in Exhibit 3-15) under these conditions. Also, for any particular year in which there is no change in inventory levels from the beginning of the year to the end of the year, both methods will result in the same net income. An example of this occurs in 2009, as is demonstrated in Exhibit 3-15.

EXHIBIT 3-15

Absorption and Variable Costing Income Statements for 2009, 2010, and 2011

Absorption Costing Presentation

	2009	2010	2011	Total
Sales ($6 per unit)	$ 180,000	$ 162,000	$ 198,000	$ 540,000
CGS ($4.254 per unit)	(127,620)	(114,858)	(140,382)	(382,860)
Gross Margin	$ 52,380	$ 47,142	$ 57,618	$ 157,140
Deduct: Underapplied Fixed Overhead*		(534)		(534)
Add: Overapplied Fixed Overhead*			534	534
Adjusted Gross Margin	$ 52,380	$ 46,608	$ 58,152	$ 157,140
Operating Expenses				
Selling and Administrative	(9,540)	(8,820)	(10,260)	(28,620)
Income Before Income Taxes	$ 42,840	$ 37,788	$ 47,892	$ 128,520

*Underapplied overhead means that the cost of goods sold is too low and thus the gross margin is overstated; therefore, it must be deducted from the gross margin. In the case of overapplied overhead the opposite happens.

Variable Costing Presentation

	2009	2010	2011	Total
Sales ($6 per unit)	$ 180,000	$ 162,000	$ 198,000	$ 540,000
Variable CGS ($3.72 per unit)	(111,600)	(100,440)	(122,760)	(334,800)
Product Contribution Margin	$ 68,400	$ 61,560	$ 75,240	$ 205,200
Variable Selling Expenses ($0.24 × units sold)	(7,200)	(6,480)	(7,920)	(21,600)
Total Contribution Margin	$ 61,200	$ 55,080	$ 67,320	$ 183,600
Fixed Expenses				
Manufacturing	$ 16,020	$ 16,020	$ 16,020	$ 48,060
Selling and Administrative	2,340	2,340	2,340	7,020
Total Fixed Expenses	$ (18,360)	$ (18,360)	$ (18,360)	$ (55,080)
Income Before Income Taxes	$ 42,840	$ 36,720	$ 48,960	$ 128,520

Because all actual production and operating costs are assumed to be equal to the budgeted costs for the years 2009 through 2011, the only item that requires an adjustment is the under- and overapplied overhead, which occurs in years 2010 and 2011. The amounts are immaterial (not significant) and are reflected as adjustments to the gross margins for 2010 and 2011 in Exhibit 3-15.

The underapplied fixed overhead occurs because the units produced were different from the number of units that were estimated (budgeted). In 2009 the estimated (budgeted) and the actual production are equal. For 2010, the underapplied fixed overhead of $534 is calculated as the difference between the applied fixed overhead and the actual fixed overhead. (Actual fixed overhead $16,020 minus applied fixed overhead [$0.534 × 29,000 units] $15,486 equals $534.) In 2011 the production was greater than the estimated amount (the amount used to set the fixed overhead rate), and therefore the fixed overhead is overapplied. Variable costing does not have over- or underapplied fixed overhead because all fixed manufacturing overhead is not applied to units produced but is written off in its entirety as a period expense.

In Exhibit 3-15, income before tax for 2010 for absorption costing exceeds that of variable costing by $1,068. This difference is caused by the positive change in inventory (2,000 units shown in Exhibit 3-14, to which the absorption costing method applies the predetermined fixed manufacturing overhead to each unit (2,000 units × $0.534* = $1,068). This $1,068 is the fixed manufacturing overhead added to absorption costing inventory and therefore not expensed in 2010. Critics of absorption costing refer to this phenomenon as one that creates illusory or phantom profits. Phantom profits are temporary absorption-costing profits caused by producing more inventory than is sold. When sales increase to eliminate the previously produced inventory, the phantom profits disappear. In contrast, all fixed manufacturing overhead, including the $1,068, is expensed in its entirety in variable costing.

Exhibit 3-14 on page 125 shows that in 2011 inventory decreased by 2,000 drives. This decrease, multiplied by the predetermined fixed overhead ($0.534) applied, explains the $1,068 by which 2011 absorption costing income falls short of variable costing income in Exhibit 3-15. This is because the fixed manufacturing overhead written off in absorption costing through the cost of goods sold at $0.534 per drive for all units sold in excess of production ((sales) 33,000 − (production) 31,000 = 2,000) results in the $1,068 by which absorption costing income is lower than variable costing income in 2011.

Variable costing income statements are more useful internally for short-term planning, controlling, and decision making than absorption costing statements. To carry out their functions, managers need to understand and be able to project how different costs will change in reaction to changes in activity levels. Variable costing, through its emphasis on cost behaviour, provides that necessary information.

The income statements in Exhibit 3-15 show that absorption and variable costing tend to provide different income figures in some years. Comparing the two sets of statements illustrates that the difference in income arises solely from which production component costs are included in or excluded from product cost for each method. If no beginning or ending inventories exist, cumulative total income under both methods will be identical. For Aspinall Computer Corporation over the three-year period, 90,000 drives are produced and 90,000 are sold. Thus, all the costs incurred (whether variable or fixed) are expensed in one year or another under either method. The income difference in each year is caused solely by the timing of the expensing of fixed manufacturing overhead.

*From Exhibit 3-13.

COMPARISON OF THE TWO APPROACHES

LEARNING OBJECTIVE 8

How do changes in sales and/or production levels affect net income as computed under absorption and variable costing?

Variable costing income statements are more useful internally for planning, controlling, and decision making than absorption costing statements are. This benefit exists because, to carry out their various functions effectively, mangers need to understand and be able to project how different costs will change in reaction to changes in activity levels. "Systems designed mainly to value inventory for financial and tax statements are not giving managers the accurate and timely information they need to promote operating efficiencies and measure product costs."[23]

Absorption and variable costing provide different income figures when sales are not equal to production. These income differences arise solely from what components are included in or excluded from the product cost under each of the two methods rather than from the method of presentation. That is, the differences are caused by including fixed manufacturing overhead as a product cost under absorption costing but considering it a period cost under variable costing.

When sales equal production, no differences will occur in net income under each of the two methods. However when production and sales differ, there will be a difference in profit under the two methods.

Under variable costing, when production is greater than sales, inventory is being accumulated for sales in the next period. Under variable costing, the cost of the unsold inventory is made up of direct material, direct labour, and variable manufacturing costs. All fixed manufacturing costs are written off in the period in which they were incurred. Thus, total expenses under variable costing will be higher than those under absorption costing and lead to a lower net income in that period.

Under absorption costing when production is greater than sales, the cost of the unsold inventory is made up of direct material, direct labour, variable manufacturing overhead, and fixed manufacturing overhead. Because of the inclusion of fixed manufacturing overhead, the cost of the unsold inventory is valued higher under this method than under variable costing; therefore, because some of the fixed manufacturing overhead is included in the unsold inventory, this method will show a greater net income than under variable costing in the period.

The amount of fixed manufacturing overhead included in product cost under absorption costing will ultimately be taken into account in computing net income when the products are sold. Product sales, however, may take place in a time period different from the one in which the costs are actually incurred.

Exhibit 3-16 summarizes the differences between absorption and variable costing according to four categories: composition of product cost, structure of the chart of accounts, process of accumulating costs, and format of the income statement. Although four categories are presented, only two real differences exist between the methods. The primary difference lies in the treatment of fixed manufacturing overhead. Fixed manufacturing overhead is a product cost for absorption costing and a period cost for variable costing. The other difference is that absorption costing requires different charts of accounts, processes of accumulating costs, and formats for income statements.

Information must be gathered and recorded somewhat differently under these two costing methods. Thus, the accounting process is affected, although maintaining two sets of accounting records is unnecessary. Often, the accounting system is kept on a variable costing basis, and working paper entries are made at year-end to convert the internal information to an appropriate external format.

Because absorption costing uses a process of deferring and releasing fixed overhead costs to and from inventory, income manipulation is possible under absorption costing by adjusting production of inventory relative to sales. For this reason, some people believe that variable costing might be more useful for external purposes than absorption costing. For internal reporting, keeping the accounting records on a variable costing basis will allow managers to have information available about the behaviour of various product and period costs. This information can be used in computing the breakeven point and analyzing a variety of cost–volume–profit relationships.

EXHIBIT 3-16

Differences Between Absorption and Variable Costing

Absorption Costing	Variable Costing
(1) Composition of Product Cost	
Fixed manufacturing overhead is attached, in separate measurable amounts, to units produced. Only if the firm sells all inventory produced in a period as well as all inventory on hand at the beginning of the period will all previously incurred fixed manufacturing overhead be recognized on the income statement as part of Cost of Goods Sold.	Fixed manufacturing overhead is recognized as a period cost (expense) when it is incurred. It does not attach in separate measurable amounts to the units produced. Each period, all fixed manufacturing overhead incurred is recognized on the income statement as an expense, but not through Cost of Goods Sold.
(2) Structure of the Chart of Accounts	
Costs are classified according to functional categories such as production, selling, and administrative.	Costs are classified according to both types of cost behaviour (fixed or variable) and functional categories (manufacturing and non-manufacturing). Mixed costs are separated into their fixed and variable components.
(3) Process of Accumulating Costs	
Costs are assigned to functional categories without analysis of behaviour. All manufacturing costs are considered product costs. All nonmanufacturing costs are considered period costs.	Costs are classified and accumulated by cost behaviour. Only variable manufacturing costs are considered product costs. Fixed manufacturing costs are considered period costs. All nonmanufacturing costs are considered period costs.
(4) Format of the Income Statement	
Costs are presented on the income statement by functional categories, which allows gross margin to be highlighted. The various functional categories present costs without regard to cost behaviour. Nonmanufacturing period costs are deducted from gross margin to determine income before taxes.	Costs are presented on the income statement separately by cost behaviour, which allows the contribution margin to be highlighted. Fixed costs are deducted from the contribution margin to determine income before taxes. Costs may be further categorized by functional classifications.

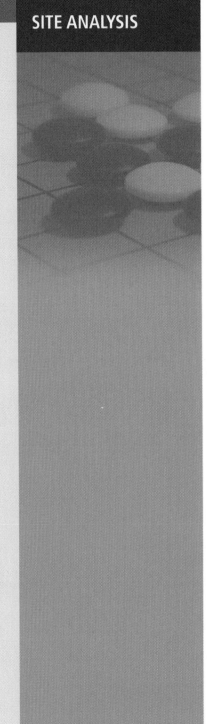

SITE ANALYSIS

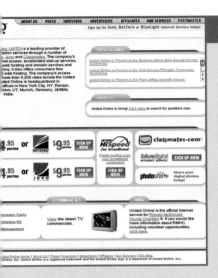

United Online

United Online has invested heavily in expanding its social networking services into several international markets, primarily Sweden, Germany, France, and Austria, and international accounts now constitute a significant part of its pay account growth. It plans to continue expanding its social networking services into international markets. Its international operations, in total, are not currently profitable; however, United Online intends to continue to invest in international operations by expanding its services into new markets.

Consolidated billable services revenues decreased by $44.9 million (or 10%) to $379.5 million for the year ended December 31, 2007, compared to $423.6 million for the year ended December 31, 2006. The decrease in billable services revenues for the year ended December 31, 2007, was due to a decrease in revenues from the Communications segment, partially offset by an increase in revenues from the Classmates Media segment.

The company's dial-up Internet access services are provided on both a free and a pay basis, with the free services subject to hourly and other limitations. Its dial-up Internet services are available in more than 10,000 cities across the United States and Canada. The cost of free services includes direct costs incurred in providing certain telephone technical support services to the free access users as well as costs that have been allocated to free services. Allocated costs consist primarily of telecommunications and data centre costs, personnel and overhead-related costs associated with operating the network and data centres, and depreciation of the network.

On October 25, 2007, Scott H. Ray, executive vice president and CFO, said: "I am encouraged that our operating income as a percentage of revenues increased in both segments versus the year-ago third quarter. We remain confident in our ability to again deliver strong adjusted Operating Income before Depreciation and Amortization in the fourth quarter, reflecting the company's disciplined financial management and continued focus on enhancing shareholder value."

United Online, while its business model has had to adapt to the constant flux of the dynamic new economy, remains firmly positioned in the value corner of the market. It fears little competition to its rather unique value-approach pricing method.

United Online has come a long way from its free-lunch offer, which drew salivating consumers in droves. However, only time will tell whether this company will be able to survive next to its more powerful peers.

SOURCE: Adapted from United Online Overview, http://www.irconnect.com/untd/pages/ newsreleases; NetZero Web page; United Online, Inc., Form 10K filing with the SEC for the periods ended December 31, 2007, and March 20, 2008; Press Release, October 25, 2007.

APPENDIX 3A

CVP Analysis: Algebraic Formulas

LEARNING OBJECTIVE 9

What are the mathematical approaches to cost–volume–profit (CVP) analysis using algebraic formulas?

MATHEMATICAL APPROACHES

This approach uses an algebraic equation to calculate the breakeven point. However, the answer to the equation is not always acceptable and may need to be rounded to a whole number. For instance, partial units cannot be sold, and some items may be sold only in specified lot sizes.

Algebraic breakeven computations use an equation representing the income statement. This equation groups costs by behaviour and shows the relationships among revenue, volume, variable cost, fixed cost, and profit as follows:

$$R(X) - VC(X) - FC = PBT$$

where

R = revenue (selling price) per unit
X = number of units sold or to be sold
$R(X)$ = total revenue
VC = variable cost per unit
$VC(X)$ = total variable cost
FC = fixed cost
PBT = profit before tax

Since the equation represents an income statement, profit (P) can be set equal to zero so that the formula indicates a breakeven situation. At the point where $P = \$0$, total revenues are equal to total costs and the breakeven point (BEP) in units can be found by solving the equation for X.

$$R(X) - VC(X) - FC = \$0$$
$$R(X) - VC(X) = FC$$
$$(R - VC)(X) = FC$$
$$X = FC \div (R - VC)$$

Breakeven volume is equal to total fixed cost divided by the difference between revenue per unit and variable cost per unit. Since revenue minus variable cost equals contribution margin, the formula can be abbreviated as follows:

$$(R - VC)X = FC$$
$$(CM)X = FC$$
$$X = FC \div CM$$

where
CM = contribution margin per unit.

For Aspinall Computer Corporation, Exhibit 3-17 indicates a unit selling price of $450, a unit variable cost of $333, and total fixed costs of $1,250,000. The contribution margin is $117 per unit ($450 – $333). Substituting these values into the equation yields the following breakeven point:

$$\$450X - \$333X = \$1,250,000$$
$$\$117X = \$1,250,000$$
$$X = \$1,250,000 \div \$117$$
$$X = 10,684 \text{ units*}$$

*This answer is rounded up from 10,683.76.

	Total	Contribution Per Unit	Contribution Margin Ratio Percentage
Sales (15,000 units)		$6,750,000	$ 450	100%
Variable costs:				
Production	$4,725,000		$ 315	70
Selling	270,000		18	4
Total variable cost		(4,995,000)	$(333)	(74)
Contribution margin		$1,755,000	$ 117	26%
Fixed costs:				
Production	$ 550,000			
Selling and administrative expenses	700,000			
Total fixed costs		(1,250,000)		
Profit before income taxes		$ 505,000		

EXHIBIT 3-17

Aspinall Computer Corporation Income Statement for the Current Year

As mentioned, the breakeven point can be expressed either in units or in dollars of revenue. One way to convert a unit breakeven point to dollars is to multiply the breakeven point in units by the selling price per unit. For Aspinall Computer Corporation, the breakeven point in sales dollars is $4,807,800 (10,684 units $\times$ $450 per unit).

Another method of computing the breakeven point in sales dollars requires the computation of a contribution margin ratio. The contribution margin ratio (CM ratio, or CM%) is calculated as contribution margin divided by revenue and indicates what proportion of revenue remains after variable costs have been covered. The contribution margin ratio represents that portion of the revenue dollar remaining to go toward covering fixed costs and increasing profits. The contribution margin ratio can be computed with either per-unit or total cost information; thus, if unit selling price and unit variable cost are not known, the breakeven point can still be calculated. Dividing total fixed cost by the CM ratio gives the breakeven point in sales dollars.

$$X_\$ = \text{FC} \div \text{CM ratio}$$

where

$X_\$$ = breakeven point in sales dollars

CM% = contribution margin ratio or (R − VC) ÷ R

The contribution margin ratio for Aspinall Computer Corporation is given in Exhibit 3-17 as 26% ($117 ÷ $450). Thus, based on the CM ratio, the company's breakeven point in dollars equals $1,250,000 ÷ 0.26 = $4,807,692—virtually the same amount shown in the earlier calculation (rounding caused the slight difference). The company's breakeven point in units can be determined by dividing the BEP in sales dollars by the unit selling price $4,807,692 ÷ $450 = 10,684 (rounded up from 10,683.76).

Another measure that can be used is the **variable cost** (VC) **ratio.** This is found by subtracting the CM ratio from 100 percent, and it represents the variable cost proportion of each revenue dollar.

Knowledge of the BEP can help managers plan for future operations. Managers want to earn profits, not just cover costs. Substituting an amount other than zero for the profit (P) term converts the breakeven formula to cost–volume–profit analysis.

variable cost ratio
100% minus the CM ratio; represents the variable cost proportion of each revenue dollar

Using Cost–Volume–Profit Analysis

This analysis is the process of examining the relationships among revenues, costs, and profits for a relevant range of activity and for a particular time period. This technique is applicable in all economic sectors (manufacturing, wholesaling, retailing, and service industries) because the same types of managerial functions are performed in all types of organizations.

When known amounts are used for selling price per unit, variable cost per unit, volume of units, and fixed costs, the algebraic equation given in the previous section can be solved to give the amount of profit generated under specified conditions. A more frequent and significant application of **cost–volume–profit** (CVP) **analysis** is to set a desired target profit and focus on the relationships between that target and specified income statement amounts to find an unknown. Volume is a common unknown because managers want to achieve a particular level of profit and need to know what quantity of sales must be generated for this objective to be accomplished. Managers may want to use CVP analysis to determine how high variable cost can increase (given fixed costs, selling price, and volume) and still provide a given profit level. Variable cost may be increased or decreased by modifying product design specifications, the manufacturing process, or the grade of material.

Profits may be stated as either a fixed or a variable amount and on either a before-tax or an after-tax basis. The following examples continue to use the Aspinall Computer Corporation data using different amounts of target profit.

cost–volume–profit analysis
the process of examining the relationships among revenues, costs, and profits for a relevant range of activity and for a particular time period

Fixed Amount of Profit Before Tax

If the desired profit is stated as a before-tax amount, it is treated in CVP analysis simply as an additional cost to be covered. The following equation yields before-tax profit in units:

$$R(X) - VC(X) - FC = PBT$$
$$R(X) - VC(X) = FC + PBT$$
$$X = (FC + PBT) \div (R - VC)$$
$$X = (FC + PBT) \div CM$$

where PBT = profit before tax.

If sales dollars are desired, the formula is as follows:

$$R(X) = (FC + PBT) \div CM\%$$

Assume that Aspinall Computer Corporation wants to generate a before-tax profit of $622,000. To do so, the company must sell 16,000 units, which will generate $7,200,000 of revenue. These calculations are shown in Exhibit 3-18.

EXHIBIT 3-18
CVP Analysis—Fixed Amount of Profit Before Tax

PBT desired = $622,000

In Units:

$$R(X) - VC(X) = FC + PBT$$
$$CM(X) = FC + PBT$$
$$(\$450X - \$333X) = \$1,250,000 + \$622,000$$
$$X = \$1,872,000 \div \$117$$
$$X = 16,000 \text{ units}$$

In Sales Dollars:

$$Sales = (FC + PBT) \div CM \text{ ratio}$$
$$= \$1,872,000 \div 0.26$$
$$= \$7,200,000$$

Fixed Amount of Profit After Tax

Both production costs and income taxes are important factors in analyzing organizational profitability. Income taxes represent a significant influence on business decision making. Managers need to be aware of the income tax effects when choosing a target profit amount.

A company desiring a particular amount of after-tax net income must first determine the equivalent amount on a before-tax basis, given the applicable tax rate. The CVP formulas needed to calculate a desired after-tax net income amount are as follows:

$$R(X) - VC(X) - FC = PBT$$
$$[(PBT)(TR)] = \text{Tax expense}$$

Thus, the profit after tax (PAT) is equal to the profit before tax minus the applicable tax. Defined as such, PAT can be integrated into the original before-tax CVP formula above:

$$PBT - (PBT)(TR) = PAT$$
$$PBT(1 - TR) = PAT$$
$$PBT = PAT \div (1 - TR)$$

where
PBT = fixed amount of profit before tax
PAT = fixed amount of profit after tax
 TR = tax rate

Assume that Aspinall Computer Corporation wants to earn $444,000 of profit after taxes and the company's marginal tax rate is 30%. The number of units and dollars of sales needed are calculated in Exhibit 3-19.

EXHIBIT 3-19

CVP Analysis—Fixed Amount of Profit After Tax

PAT desired = $444,000; tax rate = 30%

In Units:

$$PBT = PAT \div (1 - \text{Tax rate})$$
$$= \$444,000 \div (1 - 0.30)$$
$$= \$444,000 \div 0.70$$
$$= \$634,286 \text{ necessary profit before income tax (rounded)}$$
$$R(X) - VC(X) = FC + PBT$$
$$CM(X) = FC + PBT$$
$$\$117X = \$1,250,000 + \$634,286 \text{ (rounded)}$$
$$\$117X = \$1,884,286$$
$$X = \$1,884,286 \div \$117$$
$$= 16,106 \text{ units (rounded)}$$

In Sales Dollars:

$$\text{Sales} = (FC + PBT) \div CM \text{ ratio}$$
$$= (\$1,250,000 + \$634,286) \div 0.26$$
$$= \$1,884,286 \div 0.26$$
$$= \$7,247,254 \text{ (rounded)}$$

Rather than specifying a fixed amount of profit to be earned, managers may state profit as a variable amount. Then, as units sold or sales dollars increase, profit will increase proportionally. Variable profit may be stated on either a before-tax or an after-tax basis and either as a percentage of revenues or a per-unit amount. If the variable amount is stated as a percentage, it is convenient to convert that percentage into a per-unit amount. When variable profit is used, the CVP formula must be adjusted to recognize that the profit is related to volume of activity.

Variable Amount of Profit Before Tax

Managers may want desired profit to be equal to a specified variable amount of sales. The CVP formula for computing the unit volume of sales necessary to earn a specified variable rate or per-unit profit before income tax is as follows:

$$R(X) - VC(X) - FC = P_uBT(X)$$

where P_uBT = profit per unit before income tax.

Solving for X (or volume) gives the following:

$$R(X) - VC(X) - P_uBT(X) = FC$$
$$CM(X) - P_uBT(X) = FC$$
$$X(CM - P_uBT) = FC$$
$$X = FC \div (CM - P_uBT)$$

The variable profit is treated in the CVP formula as if it were an additional variable cost to be covered. If the profit is viewed in this manner, the original contribution margin and contribution margin ratio are effectively adjusted downward to reflect the desired net margin or profit per unit.

When the desired profit is set as a percentage of selling price, that percentage cannot exceed the contribution margin ratio. If it does, an infeasible problem is created, because the "adjusted" contribution margin is negative. In such a case, the variable cost percentage plus the desired profit percentage would exceed 100% of the selling price—a condition that cannot occur.

Assume that Patrick Aspinall, the president of Aspinall Computer Corporation, wants to know what level of sales (in units and dollars) would be required to earn an 8% before-tax profit on sales. The calculations in Exhibit 3-20 provide the answer.

EXHIBIT 3-20

CVP Analysis—Variable Amount of Profit Before Tax

P_uBT desired = 8% on sales revenues
P_uBT per unit = 0.08($450)
= $36

In Units:

$$(R(X) - VC(X)) - P_uBT(X) = FC$$
$$CM(X) - P_uBT(X) = FC$$
$$(\$450X - \$333X) - \$36X = \$1,250,000$$
$$X = \$1,250,000 \div (\$117 - \$36)$$
$$= \$1,250,000 \div \$81$$
$$= 15,433 \text{ units (rounded)}$$

In Sales Dollars:
The following relationships exist:

	Per Unit	Percent of Sales
Selling price	$450	100%
Variable costs	(333)	(74%)
Variable profit before income tax	(36)	(8%)
"Adjusted" contribution margin	$ 81	18%

Sales = FC ÷ "Adjusted" CM ratio*
= $1,250,000 ÷ 0.18
= $6,944,444**

* Note that it is not necessary to have per-unit data; all computations can be made with percentage information only.
**15,433 units @ $450 selling price = $6,944,850. Difference due to rounding.

Variable Amount of Profit After Tax

Adjusting the CVP formula to determine the return on sales on an after-tax basis involves stating profits in relation to both the volume and the tax rate. The algebraic manipulations are as follows:

$$(R(X) - VC(X) - FC = P_uBT(X)$$
$$[P_uBT(X)](TR) = \text{Tax expense}$$

$$P_uBT(X) - [P_uBT(X)](TR) = P_uAT(X)$$
$$P_uBT(X)(1 - TR) = P_uAT(X)$$
$$P_uBT(X) = P_uAT(X) \div (1 - TR)$$

$$R(X) - VC(X) - FC = P_uBT(X)$$
$$R(X) - VC(X) - P_uBT(X) = FC$$
$$CM(X) - P_uBT(X) = FC$$
$$X(CM - P_uBT) = FC$$
$$X = FC \div (CM - P_uBT)$$

where

P_uBT = desired profit per unit before tax

P_uAT = desired profit per unit after tax

Assume that Aspinall Computer Corporation wishes to earn a profit after tax of 14% of revenue and has a 30% tax rate. The necessary sales in units and dollars are computed in Exhibit 3-21.

EXHIBIT 3-21

CVP Analysis—Variable Amount of Profit After Tax

$$P_uAT \text{ desired} = 14\% \text{ of revenue}$$
$$= 0.14(\$450)$$
$$= \$63$$
$$\text{Tax rate} = 30\%$$

In Units:

$$P_uBT(X) = [\$63 \div (1 - 0.30)](X)$$
$$= (\$63 \div 0.70)X$$
$$= \$90X$$
$$R(X) - VC(X) - P_uBT(X) = FC$$
$$CM(X) - P_uBT(X) = FC$$
$$\$450X - \$333X - \$90X = \$1,250,000$$
$$\$27X = \$1,250,000$$
$$X = \$1,250,000 \div \$27$$
$$= 46,297 \text{ units (rounded)}$$

Note that the necessary number of units (46,297 units) is beyond the current maximum of Aspinall's relevant range of activity (30,000 units). Thus, it is highly unlikely that such a high rate of profit could be generated under the current cost structure.

In Sales Dollars:

	Per Unit	Percent of Sales
Selling price	$450	100
Variable costs	(333)	(74)
Variable profit before taxes	(90)	(20)
"Adjusted" contribution margin	$ 27	6%

$$\text{Sales} = FC \div \text{"Adjusted" CM ratio}$$
$$= \$1,250,000 \div 0.06$$
$$= \$20,833,333 \text{ (rounded)}*$$

*46,297 units @ $450 selling price = $20,833,650. The difference between the answer in units and the answer in sales dollars results from rounding in both the unit answer and the contribution margin percentage answer.

All the previous illustrations of CVP analysis were made using a variation of the formula approach. Solutions were not accompanied by mathematical proofs. The income statement model is an effective means of developing and presenting solutions and/or proofs for solutions to CVP applications.

The answers provided by breakeven and CVP analysis are valid only in relation to specific selling prices and cost relationships. Changes in the company's selling price or cost structure will cause changes in the breakeven point and in the sales needed for the company to achieve a desired profit figure.

The Income Statement Approach

The income statement approach to CVP analysis allows the preparation of pro forma statements. Income statements can be used to prove the accuracy of computations made using the formula approach to CVP analysis, or the statements can be prepared to determine the impact of various sales levels on profits either before or after tax. Since the formula and income statement approaches are based on the same relationships, each should be able to prove the other.[24] Exhibit 3-22 proves each of the computations made in Exhibits 3-18 through 3-21 for Aspinall Computer Corporation. The answers provided by breakeven or cost–volume–profit analysis are valid only in relation to specific selling prices and cost relationships. Changes that occur in the company's selling price or cost structure will cause a change in the breakeven point or in the sales needed to obtain a desired profit figure. How revenue and cost changes will affect a company's breakeven point or sales volume required to realize desired profits can be determined through incremental analysis.

EXHIBIT 3-22

Income Statement Approach to CVP—Proof of Computations

Previous computations:

Exhibit 3-2—Breakeven point: 10,684 units
Exhibit 3-18—Fixed profit ($622,000) before tax: 16,000 units
Exhibit 3-19—Fixed profit ($444,000) after tax: 16,106 units
Exhibit 3-20—Variable profit (8% of revenues) before tax: 15,433 units
Exhibit 3-21—Variable profit (14% of revenues) after tax: 46,297 units

R = $450 per unit; VC = $333 per unit; FC = $1,250,000;
Tax rate = 30% for Exhibits 3-19 and 3-21.

	Basic Breakeven Data	Ex. 3-18	Ex. 3-19	Ex. 3-20	Ex. 3-21
Units sold	10,684[3]	16,000	16,106[3]	15,433[3]	46,297[3]
Sales	$ 4,807,800	$ 7,200,000[5]	$ 7,247,254	$ 6,944,850	$ 20,833,333[2]
Total variable costs	(3,557,772)	(5,328,000)	(5,363,298)	(5,139,189)	(15,416,901)
Contribution margin	$ 1,250,028	$ 1,872,000	$ 1,883,956	$ 1,805,661	$ 5,416,432
Total fixed costs	(1,250,000)	(1,250,000)	(1,250,000)	(1,250,000)	1,250,000)
Profit before income taxes	$ 28[1]	$ 622,000	$ 633,956	$ 555,661[4]	$ 4,166,432
Income taxes (30%)			(190,187)		(1,249,930)
Profit after income taxes (NI)			$ 443,769		$ 2,916,502[6]

[1] Difference due to rounding
[2] Rounded ($450 × 46,297 = $20,833,650)
[3] Rounded
[4] Desired profit before tax = 8% on revenue; (0.08 × $6,944,850) = $555,588 (difference due to rounding)
[5] Rounded ($450 × 16,106 = $7,247,700)
[6] Desired profit after tax = 14% of revenue; (0.14 × $20,833,333) = $2,916,667 (Difference due to rounding)

CHAPTER SUMMARY

Management planning for company success includes planning for price, volume, fixed and variable costs, contribution margins, and breakeven points. The interrelationships of these factors are studied when applying breakeven (BEP) and cost–volume–profit (CVP) analysis. Management should understand these interrelationships and combine them effectively and efficiently for company success.

What does the breakeven point represent and how is it computed?

The breakeven point (BEP) is that quantity of sales volume at which the company will experience zero profit or loss. Total contribution margin (sales minus all variable costs) is equal to total fixed costs at the BEP. The BEP can be calculated using a cost–volume–profit formula that reflects basic income statement relationships. The BEP will change if the company's selling price(s) or costs change.

How can cost–volume–profit (CVP) analysis be used by a business?

Since most companies want to operate above breakeven, CVP analysis extends the BEP computation by introducing a desired profit factor. A company can determine the sales necessary to generate a desired amount of profit by adding the desired profit to fixed costs and dividing that total by the contribution margin or contribution margin ratio. The sales necessary to generate a desired amount of profit are computed by adding the desired profit to fixed costs and dividing that total by contribution margin. Profit can be stated as a fixed or a variable amount on a before- or after-tax basis. After fixed costs are covered, each dollar of contribution margin generated by company sales will produce a dollar of before-tax profit.

What is the purpose of breakeven and profit–volume graphs?

A breakeven graph is used to graph the relationships among revenue, volume, and the various costs. A profit–volume graph reflects the amount of profit or loss at each sales level. It has been said that information may be much clearer when presented in a more visual format, such as a graph.

How do cost–volume–profit (CVP) analyses in single-product and multiproduct firms differ?

In a multiproduct firm, all breakeven and cost–volume–profit analyses are performed using an assumed constant sales mix of products or services. This sales mix is referred to as the "bag" assumption. Use of the "bag" assumption requires the computation of a weighted average contribution margin (and, thus, contribution margin ratio) for the "bag" of products being sold by the company. Answers to breakeven or CVP computations are in units or dollars of "bags" of products; these "bag" amounts can be converted to individual products by using the sales mix relationship.

What are the underlying assumptions of CVP analysis and how do these assumptions create a short-run managerial perspective?

CVP analysis is short-range in focus because it assumes linearity of all functions. Managers need to include in their considerations the effects of changes in both current and future costs to make better, more realistic decisions. While CVP analysis provides one way for a manager to reduce the risk of uncertainty, the model is based on several assumptions that limit its ability to reflect reality.

How are the margin of safety and operating leverage concepts used in business?

The margin of safety (MS) of a firm indicates how far (in units, sales dollars, or a percentage) a company is operating from its breakeven point. A company's degree of operating leverage (DOL) shows what percentage change in profit would occur given a specified percentage change in sales from the current level.

7   **What are the cost accumulation and cost presentation approaches to product costing?**
Two methods by which business can determine product costs are absorption and variable costing. Under absorption costing, all manufacturing costs, both variable and fixed, are treated as product costs. The absorption costing income statement reflects a full production cost approach for cost of goods sold, computes gross margin, and classifies nonmanufacturing costs according to functional areas rather than by cost behaviour.

Variable costing computes product costs by including only the variable costs of production (direct material, direct labour, and variable manufacturing overhead). Fixed manufacturing overhead is considered to be a period expense in the period of occurrence under variable costing. The variable costing income statement presents cost of goods sold as composed of only the variable production cost per unit, shows product and total contribution margin figures, and classifies costs according to their cost behaviour (variable or fixed). Variable costing provides management with better information for internal purposes than absorption costing.

8   **How do changes in sales and/or production levels affect net income as computed under absorption and variable costing?**
Under absorption costing, net income will tend to vary with production because the fixed costs are included in inventory, whereas under variable costing net income will vary with sales.

9   **What are the mathematical approaches to cost–volume–profit (CVP) analysis using algebraic formulas?***
Using an algebraic approach, a company can determine the sales necessary to generate a desired amount of profit by adding the desired profit to fixed costs and dividing that total by the contribution margin or the contribution margin ratio. The sales necessary to generate a desired amount of profit by are computed by adding the desired profit to fixed costs and dividing that total by the contribution margin. Profit can be stated as a fixed or a variable amount on a before- or after-tax basis. After fixed costs are covered, each dollar of contribution margin generated by company sales will produce a dollar of before-tax profit.

*Appendix

Key Terms

Absorption costing (p. 121)
Breakeven graph (p. 109)
Breakeven point (p. 101)
Contribution margin (p. 102)
Contribution margin ratio (p. 104)
Cost–volume–profit analysis (p. 132)
Degree of operating leverage (p. 119)
Direct costing (p. 122)

Functional classification (p. 122)
Incremental analysis (p. 106)
Margin of safety (p. 117)
Operating leverage (p. 118)
Product contribution margin (p. 122)
Profit–volume graph (p. 111)
Total contribution margin (p. 123)
Variable costing (p. 122)
Variable cost ratio (p. 131)

Points to Remember

Cost–Volume–Profit

CVP problems can be solved by using a numerator/denominator approach. All numerators and denominators and the type of problem to which each relates are listed below. The formulas relate to both single-product and multiproduct firms, but results for multiproduct firms are per bag and must be converted to units of individual products.

Problem Situation	Numerator	Denominator
Simple BEP in units	FC	CM
Simple BEP in dollars	FC	CM%
CVP with fixed profits in units	FC + P	CM
CVP with fixed profit in dollars	FC + P	CM%
CVP with variable profit in units	FC	$CM - P_u$
CVP with variable profit in dollars	FC	$CM\% - P_u\%$

where

FC = fixed cost

CM = contribution margin per unit

CM% = contribution margin percentage

P = total profit (on a before-tax basis)

P_u = profit per unit (on a before-tax basis)

$P_u\%$ = profit percentage per unit (on a before-tax basis)

To convert after-tax profit to before-tax profit, divide after-tax profit by (1 − Tax rate).

Margin of Safety

Margin of safety in units   = Actual units − Breakeven units

Margin of safety in dollars   = Actual sales $ − Breakeven sales $

Margin of safety percentage = Margin of safety in units or dollars ÷ Estimated (Actual) sales in units or dollars

Degree of Operating Leverage

Degree of operating leverage = Contribution margin ÷ Profit before tax

Predicted additional profit   = Degree of operating leverage × Percent change in sales × Current profit

Absorption Versus Variable Costing

1. Which method is being used: absorption or variable?
   a. If absorption:
      • What is the fixed overhead application rate?
      • What capacity was used in the denominator in determining the fixed manufacturing overhead application rate?
      • What is the cost per unit of product? (DM + DL + VOH + FOH)
   b. If variable:
      • What is the cost per unit of product? (DM + DL + VOH)
      • What is the total manufacturing overhead? Assign to the income statement as a period cost.
2. What is the relationship of production to sales? If:
   a. Production = Sales
      Absorption costing income = Variable costing income
   b. Production > Sales
      Absorption costing income > Variable costing income
   c. Production < Sales
      Absorption costing income < Variable costing income
3. How is the difference in income measured?
   Dollar difference between absorption costing income and variable costing income = FOH application rate × Change in inventory units.
4. How are dollar differences in fixed costs used to explain profit differences?

Profit Impacts—Why?	
Production = Sales	Income is the same under both methods
Production > Sales	Fixed costs are hidden in ending inventory under absorption costing so profit is greater under absorption costing than under variable costing where the total fixed cost incurred in the period is written off in the period.

| Production < Sales | Profit under variable costing is greater than under absorption costing because cost of sales contains fixed costs from the prior period under absorption costing. |

Note: The effects of the relationships presented here are based on two qualifying assumptions:
(1) that unit costs are constant over time, and
(2) that any fixed cost variances are written off when incurred rather than being prorated to inventory balances.

DEMONSTRATION PROBLEMS

Problem 1

Anderson Corporation, a small manufacturer run by CEO Tom Anderson, makes and sells jar lid openers. Cost information for one unit is as follows:

Direct material	$	1.00
Direct labour		0.50
Variable manufacturing overhead		0.25
Variable selling expenses		0.05
Total variable costs	$	1.80
Total fixed manufacturing expenses	$194,400	

Each lid opener sells for $4.50. Current annual production and sales volume is 150,000 lid openers. A predetermined fixed manufacturing overhead rate can be computed based on this activity level.

Required:

a. Compute the unit contribution margin and contribution margin ratio for Anderson Corporation's product.
b. Compute the breakeven point in units for Anderson Corporation, using contribution margin.
c. Compute the breakeven point in sales dollars for Anderson Corporation, using contribution margin ratio.
d. If Anderson Corporation wants to earn $43,200 of before-tax profits, how many openers will it have to sell?
e. If Anderson Corporation wants to earn $40,500 after taxes and is subject to a 25% tax rate, how many units will it have to sell?
f. If Anderson Corporation's fixed manufacturing costs increased by $7,560, how many units would it need to sell to break even? (Use original data.)
g. Anderson Corporation can sell an additional 12,000 openers overseas for $3.50. Variable costs will increase by $0.20 for shipping expenses, and fixed manufacturing costs will increase by $25,000 because of the purchase of a new machine. This is a one-time-only sale and will not affect domestic sales this year or in the future. Should Anderson Corporation sell the additional units?

Problem 2

Kevin O'Leary Ltd. makes and sells scratch posts for cats. Cost information for one scratch post is as follows:

Direct material	$	2.00
Direct labour		1.00
Variable manufacturing overhead		0.50
Variable selling expenses		0.10
Total variable costs	$	3.60
Total fixed manufacturing expenses	$388,800	

Each scratch post sells for $9. Current annual production and sales volume is 75,000 posts. The company uses this activity level to set the predetermined fixed manufacturing overhead rate. The company incurs no fixed selling and administrative expenses.

Required:

a. Compute the contribution margin and contribution margin ratio for O'Leary Ltd.'s product.
b. Compute the breakeven point in units for O'Leary Ltd.'s, using contribution margin.
c. Compute the breakeven point in sales dollars for O'Leary Ltd., using contribution margin ratio.
d. What is O'Leary Ltd.'s margin of safety in units? In sales dollars?
e. What is O'Leary Ltd.'s degree of operating leverage? If sales increase by 20%, by how much will before-tax profit increase?
f. If O'Leary Ltd. wants to earn $43,200 of before-tax profits, how many posts will it have to sell?
g. If O'Leary Ltd. wants to earn $40,500 after taxes and is subject to a 25% tax rate, how many units will it have to sell?
h. If O'Leary Ltd. fixed manufacturing costs increased by $7,560, how many units would it need to sell to break even? (Use original data.)
i. O'Leary Ltd. can sell an additional 6,000 scratch posts overseas for $8.50. Variable costs will increase by $0.30 for shipping expenses, and fixed manufacturing costs will increase by $25,000 because of the purchase of a new machine. This is a one-time-only sale and will not affect domestic sales this year or in the future. Should O'Leary Ltd. sell the additional units?
j. What is the inventoriable absorption costing per unit?
k. What is the inventoriable variable costing per unit?

Problem 3

The Gamon Gomes Corporation began operations on January 14, year 1. The firm manufactures a computer keyboard, which it sells to various computer producers. The firm's product costing system is based on actual costs and assumes a FIFO cost flow. Work in Process inventories are always minimal and are ignored for product costing purposes. Following are the firm's published income statements (based on absorption costing) for its first two years of operations.

		Year 1		Year 2
Sales		$625,000		$891,000
Cost of Goods Sold				
Beginning FG	$ 0		$ 60,000	
Plus cost of goods manufactured	300,000		382,500	
Goods available	$300,000		$442,500	
Less: ending FG	60,000	240,000	25,500	417,000
Gross Margin		$385,000		$474,000
Less: SG&A expenses				
Selling	$ 90,000		$126,000	
General & administrative	145,000	235,000	180,000	306,000
Net income		$150,000		$168,000

With regard to the year 1 and year 2 operations, other information from the records indicated the following:

	Year 1	Year 2
Production in units	25,000	30,000
Sales in units	20,000	33,000
Production costs:		
Direct materials per unit	$4.00	$4.00
Direct labour per unit	$3.00	$3.50
Variable overhead per unit	$1.00	$1.50
Other variable costs:		
Selling costs per unit	$2.00	$2.00
Other fixed costs:		
Annual selling costs	$ 50,000	$ 60,000
Annual G&A costs	$145,000	$180,000
Annual fixed overhead cost	$100,000	$112,500

Required:

a. Based on the previous data, recast the year 1 and year 2 income statements using the variable costing format.

b. Reconcile the costs assigned to the ending inventories for year 1 and year 2 in part (a) with the costs assigned to the ending inventories in the income statements presented earlier.

c. Reconcile the net incomes determined in part (a) with the net incomes shown in the original income statements.

Solutions to Demonstration Problems

Problem 1

a. CM = Selling price − Variable cost = $4.50 − $1.80 = $2.70
   CM% = Selling price − Variable cost ÷ Selling price = $2.70 ÷ $4.50 = 60%
b. BEP = Fixed cost ÷ CM = $194,400 ÷ $2.70 = 72,000
c. BEP = Fixed cost ÷ CM% = $194,400 ÷ 60% = $324,000
   (Note: This answer is also equal to 72,000 units × $4.50 per unit selling price.)
d. BEP = (FC + Desired profit) ÷ CM = ($194,400 + $43,200) ÷ $2.70 = 88,000 units
e. Profit after tax ÷ (1 − Tax rate) = Profit before tax $40,500 ÷ 0.75 = $54,000
   BEP = (FC + Desired profit) ÷ CM = ($194,400 + $54,000) ÷ $2.70 = 92,000 units
f. Additional units to break even = Increase in FC ÷ CM = $7,560 ÷ $2.70 = 2,800;
   New BEP = 72,000 + 2,800 = 74,800 units
g. New CM for these units = $3.50 − $2.00 = $1.50; 12,000 × $1.50 = $18,000, which is $7,000
   below the additional $25,000 fixed costs. Anderson Corporation should not sell the additional units.

Problem 2

a. CM = Selling price − Variable cost = $9.00 − $3.60 = $5.40
   CM% = (Selling price − Variable cost) ÷ Selling price = $5.40 ÷ $9.00 = 60%
b. BEP = Fixed cost ÷ CM = $388,800 ÷ $5.40 = 72,000
c. BEP = Fixed cost ÷ CM% = $388,800 ÷ 0.6 = $648,000
   (Note: This answer is also equal to 72,000 units × $9 per unit selling price.)
d. Margin of safety = Current units of sales − Breakeven sales = 75,000 − 72,000 = 3,000 units
   Current revenues = Current sales volume × Unit selling price = 75,000 × $9 = $675,000
   Margin of safety = Current revenues − Breakeven revenues = $675,000 − $648,000 = $27,000
e.* Current CM = 75,000 × $5.40 = $405,000;
   Current before-tax profit = $405,000 − $388,800 = $16,200
   Degree of operating leverage = $405,000 ÷ $16,200 = 25
   Increase in income = 25 × 20% = 500%
   Proof: 75,000 × 1.2 = 90,000 units; 90,000 × $5.40 = $486,000 CM − $388,800 FC = $97,200 PBT;
   ($16,200 current PBT × 500%) + $16,200 = $97,200
f. BEP = (FC + Desired Profit) ÷ CM = ($388,800 + $43,200) ÷ $5.40 = 80,000 units
g.* Profit after tax ÷ (1 − Tax rate) = Profit before tax
   $40,500 ÷ 0.75 = $54,000
   BEP = (FC + Desired Profit) ÷ CM = ($388,800 + $54,000) ÷ $5.40 = 82,000 units
h. Additional units to break even = Increase in FC ÷ CM = $7,560 ÷ $5.40 = 1,400;
   New BEP = 72,000 + 1,400 = 73,400
i. New CM for these units = $8.50 − $3.90 = $4.60; 6,000 × $4.60 = 27,600, which is $2,600
   above the additional $25,000 fixed cost. Yes, Kevin O'Leary Ltd. should sell the additional units.
j. Absorption cost = $3.50 + ($388,800 ÷ 75,000) = $3.60 + ≈ $5.18 = $8.68
k. Variable cost = $3.50

*Appendix

Problem 3

a.   Recast the income statements for year 1 and year 2:

	Year 1		Year 2	
Sales		$625,000		$891,000
Cost of Goods Sold				
Beginning Finished Goods	$ 0		$ 40,000	
Plus: cost of goods manufactured	200,000		270,000	
Goods available	$200,000		$310,000	
Less: ending Finished Goods	40,000	160,000	18,000	292,000
Production contribution margin		$465,000		$599,000
Less variable selling expenses		40,000		66,000
Total contribution margin		$425,000		$533,000
Less: fixed expenses				
Overhead	$100,000		$112,500	
Selling	50,000		60,000	
General & administrative	145,000	295,000	180,000	352,500
Net income		$130,000		$180,500

b.   Reconcile ending Finished Goods Inventory costs:

	Year 1	Year 2
Ending inventory (variable costing)	$40,000	$18,000
Add back inventoriable portion of fixed factory overhead under the use of absorption costing:		
Year 1: ($100,000 ÷ 25,000) x 5,000	20,000	
Year 2: ($112,500 ÷ 30,000) x 2,000		75,000
Ending inventory (absorption costing)	$60,000	$25,500

c.   Reconcile the net income for year 1 and year 2 under variable costing with the reported net income reported under absorption costing:

	Year 1	Year 2
Net income variable costing, part a	$130,000	$180,500
For year 1, add back the portion of fixed overhead that would be inventoried under absorption costing [($100,000 ÷ 25,000) x 5,000]	20,000	
For year 2, deduct the portion of fixed overhead that would be charged against this period's income under absorption costing[1]		(12,000)
Net income (absorption costing)	$150,000	$168,000
[1]Fixed overhead deducted under variable costing		$112,500
Fixed overhead deducted under absorption costing with a FIFO cost flow:		
First 5,000 units sold (from beginning inventory)	$ 20,000	
Next 28,000 units sold [($112,500 ÷ 30,000) x 28,000]	105,000	$125,000
Additional fixed overhead deducted under absorption costing		$ 12,500

[1]Fixed overhead deducted under variable costing

End-of-Chapter Materials

SELF-TEST QUESTIONS

(SOLUTIONS APPEAR AT THE END OF THE CHAPTER.)

1. A company is forecasting the following operating results:

Production and sales	2,000 units
Total revenues	$100,000
Total manufacturing costs	$35,000 + $15 per unit
Selling and administrative expenses	$20,000 + $5 per unit
Interest and principal payments	$5,000

   What is the breakeven point in units?
   a. 1,333 units
   b. 2,000 units
   c. 3,000 units
   d. 3,333 units

2. Cooka Cooler Ltd. is considering adding a new type of beverage to its list of products. This beverage would have the following price and costs:

Selling price per bottle	$32
Variable costs per bottle	12
Annual fixed costs associated with the new beverage	45,000
Income tax rate	40%

   How many bottles would Cooka Cooler Ltd. have to sell in order to earn $90,000 after taxes?
   a. 2,250 bottles
   b. 6,750 bottles
   c. 9,750 bottles
   d. 14,750 bottles

3. Under which of the following conditions would the breakeven point not change?
   a. The selling price per unit increases by 10%, the variable costs per unit increase by 10%, and fixed costs per unit remain the same
   b. The total sales increase by 10%, the total variable costs increase by 10%, and total fixed costs increase by 10%
   c. The selling price per unit increases by 10%, the variable costs per unit increase by 10%, and total fixed costs increase by 10%
   d. The total sales increase by 10%, the total variable costs increase by 10% and fixed costs per unit increase by 10%

   Self-Test Questions 1–3 are extracted from *Management Accounting 2 Examination*, published by the Certified General Accountants Association of Canada (© CGA-Canada 2000). Reprinted with permission.

4. Gaetane Labelle Maraj Ltd. presents you with the following information and asks you to calculate its operating leverage.

Revenue	$1,000,000
Variable costs	350,000
Contribution margin	$ 650,000
Fixed costs	210,000
Profit before taxes	$ 440,000

   The operating leverage is:
   a. 0.8
   b. 2.27
   c. 1.48
   d. 0.48

Use the following information about Wiggles to answer Questions 5 and 6:

Sales (50,000 units)	$750,000
Raw materials	150,000
Direct labour	100,000
Variable overhead	60,000
Fixed overhead	65,000
Variable selling and administrative costs	6,000
Fixed selling and administrative costs	24,000

5. What is the company's approximate breakeven point in units?
   a. 5,933   c. 10,254
   b. 10,114   d. 89,000

6. What is the company's approximate breakeven point in units if the company wants to earn a net profit of $50,000?
   a. 9,194   c. 16,014
   b. 11,693   d. 16,360

   Self-Test Questions 4–6 are extracted from *Management Accounting 2 Examination*, published by the Certified General Accountants Association of Canada (© CGA-Canada 2004). Reprinted with permission.

7. Linda Ondrack Corp., a manufacturer of widgets, had the following data for year 1:

Sales	2,400 units
Sales price	$40 per unit
Variable costs	$14.00 per unit
Fixed costs	$19,500

   If the company wishes to increase its total dollar contribution margin by 40% in year 2, all other factors remaining constant, by how much will it need to increase its sales?
   a. $17,160   c. $26,400
   b. $24,960   d. $38,400

   Self-Test Question 7 is extracted from *Management Accounting 1 Examination*, published by the Certified General Accountants Association of Canada (© CGA-Canada 2000). Reprinted with permission.

SELF-TEST QUESTIONS

8. Ambrus Corporation produces two products, X and Y. The following information is presented for both products:

	X	Y
Selling price per unit	$9	$6
Variable cost per unit	7	3

Total fixed costs are $117,000.

What will be the breakeven point for Ambrus Corporation in units of X and Y if the ratio of sales is expected to be 3X:1Y?
   a.   X = 13,000 units : Y = 13,000 units
   b.   X = 26,000 units : Y = 78,000 units
   c.   X = 39,000 units : Y = 13,000 units
   d.   X = 78,000 units : Y = 26,000 units

9. Brittany Ltd. manufactures top-quality microphones. The selling price per microphone is $160 and the variable cost per microphone is $95. A sales volume of $1,552,000 is necessary to produce a net income of $201,500 before taxes. What are Brittany Ltd.'s total fixed costs?
   a. $201,500
   b. $429,000
   c. $535,000
   d. $635,500

Self-Test Questions 8 and 9 are extracted from *Management Accounting 1 Examination*, published by the Certified General Accountants Association of Canada (© CGA-Canada 2003). Reprinted with permission.

10. Petersen Products has an expense category called Occupancy Expense. For the current year, this expense is projected to cost $7.50 per unit at an activity level of 4,500 units manufactured and sold, and $5.00 per unit at a level of 6,750 units.

What is the best approximated description of Occupancy Expense within the relevant range of 4,500 to 6,750 units of activity?
   a.   Variable cost
   b.   Fixed cost
   c.   Semi-variable or mixed cost
   d.   Non-linear cost

Self-Test Question 10 is extracted from *Management Accounting Examination*, published by the Certified General Accountants Association of Canada (© CGA-Canada 1999). Reprinted with permission.

11. Wolfe Blitzer Ltd. produces and sells two products marbles and rables. Revenue and cost data are shown below:

	Marbles	Rables
Product mix	40%	60%
Selling price	$21.00	$10.00
Markup on variable cost	50%	60%
Total Fixed Cost	$100,000	

If a boxed set containing 10 marbles and rables in total contained the normal product mix, what would be the contribution margin per boxed set?
   a. $28.50
   b. $43.00
   c. $50.50
   d. $55.00

12. Below is the selling and cost information concerning Paul Stephen Co.'s only product:

Selling price per unit	$100.00
Costs per unit	
Direct material	20.00
Direct labour	30.00
Variable overhead	15.00
Fixed overhead	5.00
Commission	10% of sales

What is the contribution margin ratio?
   a.   25%   b.   30%
   c.   35%   d.   50%

Self-test Questions 11 to 12 are extracted by the authors from *Management Accounting Examination*, published by the Certified General Accountants Association of Canada (© CGA Canada, June, 2005). Used with permission.

13. If fixed expenses were to double and contribution margin ratio per unit were to double, what would the effect be on the breakeven point?
   a.   The breakeven point would be reduced to half.
   b.   The breakeven point would not change.
   c.   The breakeven point would double.
   d.   The breakeven point would quadruple.

Note: Use the following information to answer parts (14) and (15):

A company manufactures baby products. The company has just launched a new product with the following prime costs: $10 of raw materials and $15 of direct labour. Overhead costs are applied at a rate of 100% of direct labour cost. Assume that 45% of overhead costs are variable. All costs are based on an expected level of production and sales of 12,000 units.

14. The company requires a minimum contribution margin of 22% for all its products. What should be the minimum sale price of the new product?
   a. $24.77   b. $40.71
   c. $42.63   d. $51.28

15. What must the selling price of the new product be to break even?
   a. $23.50
   b. $31.75
   c. $33.25
   d. $40.00

16. Spring Company is developing a quality improvement program that would reduce its cost of goods sold by $1,000 at the present level of sales. The following is the company's income statement.

SPRING COMPANY
Income Statement
year ended March 31, Current Year

Sales	$ 30,000
Cost of goods sold	25,000
Gross margin	5,000
Selling and administrative expenses	2,000
Income before taxes	$ 3,000

Of the total costs (cost of goods sold plus selling and administrative expenses), 60% are variable and the remainder are fixed.

What is the breakeven point in sales dollars for Spring Company?

a. $10,800   c. $20,000
b. $16,200   d. $23,478

17. What is the breakeven point stated in sales dollars equal to?
   a. Fixed costs divided by contribution margin per unit
   b. Fixed costs divided by contribution margin percentage
   c. Variable costs divided by contribution margin percentage
   d. Variable costs divided by contribution margin per unit

(Self-Test questions 16 and 17 are adapted by the authors from Management Accounting examinations published by the Certified General Accountants Association of Canada © CGA-Canada, June 2005, used by permission)

Use the following information from Yun Company's records for the year ended December 31 to answer Questions 18 to 21.

Sales	$1,400,000
Cost of goods manufactured	
Variable	$ 630,000
Fixed	315,000
Operating expenses	
Variable	$ 98,000
Fixed	140,000
Units manufactured	70,000 units
Units sold	60,000 units
Finished goods inventory, January 1	0

There were no work in process inventories at the beginning or end of the year.

18. What would be the cost of the ending finished goods inventory under variable costing?
   a. $90,000
   b. $104,000
   c. $105,000
   d. $135,000

19. What would be the cost of the ending finished goods inventory under absorption costing?
   a. $90,000
   b. $104,000
   c. $105,000
   d. $135,000

20. What would be the operating profit before taxes for the current fiscal year under absorption costing?
   a. $217,000
   b. $307,000
   c. $352,000
   d. $374,000

21. What would be the profit before taxes for the current fiscal year under variable costing?
   a. $135,000
   b. $217,000
   c. $307,000
   d. $352,000

QUESTIONS

1. Since managers in commercial entities aspire to make a profit, why do they care about the breakeven point?

2. What is contribution margin and how is it used?

3. How can contribution margin be used to determine breakeven in both units and dollars?

4. Of what value is cost–volume–profit analysis to managers?

5. Why does contribution margin fluctuate in direct proportion to sales volume?

6. Define product contribution margin and total contribution margin. What is the difference between the product and total contribution margins?

7. How is breakeven analysis related to CVP?

8. If the variable costs that are associated with a product increase per unit but selling price and fixed costs remain constant, what will happen to (a) contribution margin, and (b) breakeven point? Explain.

9. What do you think are the three most fundamental CVP assumptions? Why should managers who use CVP analysis keep these assumptions in mind when using the answers provided by the model?

10. What effect would specifying the quality of a product be likely to have on each of the CVP factors?

11. Tony Soprano, the president of Tony's Waste Management Ltd., has just been informed that his business is operating at 4% above the breakeven point. What should his course of action be and why?

QUESTIONS

12. Why is it necessary to consider qualitative factors when solving problems using CVP?

13. Why is the perspective of managers using CVP a short-term one, and what are the implications of such a perspective?

14. What is meant by the term "bundling"?

15. What is a breakeven graph? How is it similar to and different from a profit–volume graph?

16. What is the bag assumption and why is it necessary in a multiproduct company?

17. In allocating a scarce production resource in a multiproduct corporation whose goal is to maximize the total corporate contribution margin, why would management not simply produce the product that generates the highest contribution margin per unit?

18. Why are some direct costs irrelevant to the decision to eliminate a product line?

19. What is meant by the term "incremental" as it applies to costs and revenues?

20. Which approach, variable or absorption, is required by the CICA for external financial reporting? Why does this requirement exist?

21. For each of the terms that follow, indicate whether the term would be found on an absorption costing income statement (A), a variable costing income statement (V), or both (B).
    a. Cost of goods sold
    b. Contribution margin
    c. Gross margin
    d. Selling expenses
    e. Variable expenses
    f. Administrative expenses
    g. Fixed expenses

22. Which of the following statements are true?
    a. Net income under absorption costing is a function of both sales volume and production volume.
    b. Net income under absorption costing is a function of sales volume only.
    c. Net income under variable costing is a function of both sales volume and production volume.
    d. Net income under variable costing is a function of sales volume only.

23. Which of the following are defined as product costs when absorption costing is used? when variable costing is used?
    a. Direct material
    b. Variable manufacturing overhead
    c. Selling expenses
    d. Direct labour
    e. Fixed manufacturing overhead
    f. Administrative expenses

24. For a specific firm in a year in which production and sales volume are equal, both absorption and variable costing income statements are prepared. Would you normally expect that the gross margin on the absorption costing statement would be equal to the total contribution margin on the variable costing statement? Explain.

25. Which costing approach (variable or absorption) provides the clearer picture as to how costs will change as activity changes? Explain.

26. If the net incomes for a company computed under the variable and absorption approaches are different, which of the following cost(s) is (are) responsible for the difference?
    a. the variable cost of direct materials
    b. the variable cost of factory overhead
    c. the variable selling expenses
    d. the fixed selling expenses
    e. the fixed factory overhead

27. Describe a circumstance in which net income computed under the absorption costing method will exceed the net income computed under the variable costing method. Why does this condition exist?

28. Evaluate the merits of the following statement: "Relative to variable costing, absorption costing is a superior product costing method."

29. Why do proponents of variable costing view fixed factory overhead as a period cost?

30. Which approach (variable or absorption) classifies costs by behaviour? Which classifies costs by functional categories? Are these mutually exclusive?

31. What is the difference between absorption and variable costing in the treatment of fixed manufacturing overhead? Why is this difference important?

EXERCISES

1. (LO 1) The Didona Co. has the following revenue and cost functions:
   Revenue = $15 per unit
   Fixed costs = $400,000
   Variable costs = $11 per unit
   Required:
   Determine the breakeven point, both in units and in dollars.

2. (LO 2) Leah Carter Enterprises has the following revenue and cost functions:
   Revenue = $60 per unit
   Fixed costs = $200,000
   Variable costs = $8 per unit
   Required:
   What is the breakeven point in units? In dollars?

3. (LO 1) The following information is available for Pat Bollen Ltd.
   a. Total fixed costs are $45,000, and the unit contribution margin is $9.
   b. Unit selling price is $8, unit variable cost is $5, and total fixed costs are $48,000.
   c. Unit selling price is $12, contribution margin is 25% of revenue, and total fixed costs are $30,000.
   d. Unit variable cost is 80% of the unit selling price, total fixed costs are $48,000, and unit selling price is $12.
   e. Unit variable cost is $5, contribution margin per unit is $3, and total fixed costs are $24,000. Compute total sales at the breakeven volume in addition to the total number of units.
   Required:
   For each of the above situations, determine how many units must be sold for the company to break even.

4. (LO 2) Sandra Chowfen Ltd. manufactures and sells a toy train set called Woo-Woo. The company's annual fixed costs are $340,000. Its variable cost is $62 per Woo-Woo, and each set is sold for $190.
   Required:
   a. What is the breakeven point in units and dollars?
   b. How many units must be sold for the company to earn $1,000,000 in before tax profit?

5. (LO 2) Radford Corporate Supplies Ltd. is planning to make and sell 10,000 computer disk trays. Fixed costs are $40,000, and variable costs are 60% of the selling price.
   Required:
   Your neighbour, Anne Cowan, works for the firm and she wants you to help her determine what the selling price must be for the company to earn $10,000 of before-tax profit on the trays.

6. (LO 2) Ida's Dog House Builders is planning to make and sell 10,000 of its finest canine palaces. The fixed costs are $400,000, and the variable costs are 60% of the selling price.
   Required:
   What must the selling price be to earn $100,000 profit before tax?

7. (LO 2) Domestic Steel, Inc., manufactures furnace air filters that sell for $1,000. The unit costs are:

Direct material	$375
Direct labour	250
Variable manufacturing overhead	130
Variable selling expense	45

EXERCISES

Annual fixed manufacturing overhead is $100,000 and fixed selling and administrative expenses are $120,000. The company is in a 30% tax bracket.
Required:
Determine how many furnace air filters the company needs to make and sell to earn $140,000 in after-tax profit.

8. (LO 2) Jeff Walker manufactures riding lawnmowers that sell for $800. The unit costs are:

Direct materials	$275
Direct labour	150
Variable overhead	70
Variable selling expense	45

Fixed factory overhead is $100,000 annually. Fixed general, selling, and administrative expenses are $120,000. Jeff is in a 30% tax bracket.
Required:
a. How many lawnmowers does Mr. Walker have to make and sell to earn $140,000 in after-tax income?
b. How much revenue is needed to earn an after-tax income of 12% of sales?

9. (LO 2) Joanne Steinman has learned about the CVP model but has not yet gained confidence in using it.
Required:
You have been asked to help her compute the number of units that must be sold and the total sales in each of the following situations:

a. The company's profit goal is $40,000. Total fixed costs are $80,000, unit contribution margin is $5, and unit selling price is $8.
b. The company's profit goal is $25,000 after tax, and its tax rate is 40%. Unit variable cost is $6, unit contribution margin is $4, and total fixed costs are $40,000.
c. The company's after-tax profit goal is $54,000, and the tax rate is 40%. Unit variable cost is 70% of the $10 unit selling price, and total fixed costs are $60,000.
d. The company's after-tax profit goal is $30,000, and the tax rate is 50%. Unit contribution margin is $3, unit variable cost is 70% of the unit selling price, and total fixed costs are $60,000.
e. The company's after-tax profit goal is $40,000 and the tax rate is 50%. Unit variable cost is $9, unit contribution margin is 25% of the selling price, and total fixed costs are $25,000.

10. (LO 2) Exotic Rugs has annual sales of $2,000,000, variable expenses of 60% of sales, and fixed expenses of $80,000 monthly.
Required:
How much will sales have to increase so that Exotic Rugs will have before-tax profit of 20% of sales?

11. Triton Publishing Ltd. publishes paperback comic books. The following operational data relate to a typical month:

Unit sales price	$10.00
Unit variable cost	$4.60
Fixed costs	$16,200
Current volume of books	3,200

The company is considering an expansion that would increase monthly fixed costs by $5,400. If it does expand, production and sales will increase by 2,000 books.
Required:
As the company's newest employee and the only employee who has had a course in managerial accounting, you have been asked to do the following:
a. Without considering the expansion, calculate the firm's breakeven point and its monthly before-tax profit.
b. Recalculate the breakeven point in books and Triton's monthly before-tax profit assuming that the company undertakes the expansion.

12. (LO 2) Nicol Walker Ltd., a large, diversified corporation, is considering the acquisition of two firms that manufacture electric razors. Victor Ltd. has a variable unit cost of $11 and total fixed costs of $2,500,000. Brandon Ltd. has a variable unit cost of $14 and total fixed

EXERCISES

costs of $500,000. The wholesale price for the electric razors is $16, and each firm has an annual capacity of 800,000 razors.

Required:

Which firm would you recommend that the corporation acquire if the estimated demand for electric razors is:

a. 400,000 units per year?
b. 600,000 units per year?
c. 800,000 units per year?

13. (LO 3) Yun Candy Co. makes and sells boxes of Cajun candies. The firm's income statement for current fiscal year follows:

Sales (25,000 boxes @ $12)		$300,000
Variable costs		
Production (25,000 @ $3)	$75,000	
Sales commissions (25,000 @ $1.20)	30,000	(105,000)
Contribution margin		$195,000
Fixed costs		
Production	$58,000	
General, selling, and administrative	20,000	(78,000)
Profit before tax		$117,000

Required:

a. Prepare a cost–volume–profit graph for Yun Candy Co.
b. Prepare a profit–volume graph for Yun Candy Co.

14. (LO 4) William Chan Ltd. sells flags and sun visors at the entrances to local sporting events. The firm sells two flags for each sun visor. A flag sells for $3 and costs $1. A sun visor sells for $1.50 and costs $1. The company's monthly fixed costs are $4,500.

Required:

Calculate the number of flags that the company will sell at the breakeven point (BEP). Prove your answer.

15. (LO 4) David Rosenberg Golf World manufactures two types of golf carts, which are sold to golfers throughout the country. The compact cart is sold for an average price of $2,000 per unit; variable manufacturing costs are $1,800 per unit. The standard-size cart is sold for an average price of $3,500 per unit; variable manufacturing costs are $3,000 per unit. Total fixed costs are estimated to be $360 million per year.

Required:

a. Determine the breakeven volume for the company if the expected sales mix is one-third compact carts and two-thirds standard carts.
b. Because of a battery shortage, the management team expects the sales mix to shift to 50% compact carts and 50% standard carts. Determine the breakeven volume based on the new sales mix, and explain why your answer differs from the one you gave in part (a).
c. It is expected that if the firm produced more than 50% compact carts, fixed costs would increase by $65 million. Determine the breakeven volume based on a sales mix of 60% compact carts and 40% standard carts.

16. (LO 4) Brooke Logan sells flashlights and batteries at the entrance to a local cave. The firm sells two batteries to each flashlight. The flashlight sells for $3.00 and costs $1.00. Each battery sells for $0.50 and costs $0.20. The company's monthly fixed costs are $2,400.

Required:

How many batteries will the company sell at the BEP? Prove your answer.

17. (LO 6) Abe Carver has a street lunch-vending business in which he sells quiche and a can of pop as a package for $3. The variable costs of each package lunch are $1.20. His annual fixed costs are $27,000.

Required:

a. What is his breakeven point in revenue and number of lunches?
b. If the business is currently selling 18,000 lunches annually, what is Carver's margin of safety in units, percentage, and dollars?

EXERCISES

18. (LO 6) Picante Hot Sauce Inc. sells its small bottle of pepper sauce for $2.90. Variable costs are $0.52 per bottle, and fixed costs are $288,000 annually. The firm is currently selling 320,000 bottles annually.
Required:
a. What is the company's margin of safety in units?
b. Calculate the degree of operating leverage.
c. If the company can increase sales by 25%, by what percentage will its income increase? Prove your answer.

19. (LO 6) Tom Anderson Tool and Die Company is considering acquiring new equipment to set up a production line to produce a newly designed locking wrench. Demand for this wrench is estimated at 100,000 units a year, and the selling price is to be $10. One production line being considered uses primarily manual labour. Estimated variable production cost per unit on this line is $7, and total fixed production cost for the line is $150,000. The other possible production line is more automated; its estimated variable production cost per unit is $3, and total fixed production cost for the line is $630,000.
Required:
a. Which production line would you recommend that the firm use? What is the margin of safety for each production line?
b. If the demand were estimated to be 120,000 units, would your recommendation change?
c. If the demand were estimated to be 150,000 units, would your recommendation change?
d. Assume that the firm has an after-tax profit goal of $60,000. If the tax rate is 40% and estimated demand is 100,000 units, what will the selling price have to be for both production lines?

20. (LO 6) Paula Freeman's Pet-Do specializes in washing and grooming pets. Paula charges $12 per pet visit and has the following costs:

Variable costs per visit	
Direct materials	$0.50
Direct labour	2.00
Fixed monthly costs	
Shop rent	$400
Limo insurance	50
Licences	25
Equipment depreciation	50
Promotion	100
Utilities	150

Required:
a. How many pet visits are needed to break even? How many dollars of revenue?
b. Paula feels that she should earn 25% of revenues before tax. How many pet visits would this require?
c. If Paula has 140 pet visits a month, what is her operating leverage?
d. Paula can increase pet visits 20% over the current 140 visits. How much would income increase? What would be the new total income? Prove your answer.

21. (LO 7) The Alison Ground Electric Company is considering switching to variable costing. In an effort to better understand the significance of the possible change, the management team has asked that ending inventories be costed on both an absorption and a variable costing basis. Production for the year was 200,000 units, of which 25,000 units remained in ending inventory. Additional information concerning production follows:

Direct material costs	$600,000
Direct labour costs	450,000
Manufacturing overhead costs	600,000

Manufacturing overhead has not been separated into fixed and variable components, but the fixed manufacturing overhead rate approximates $6 per direct labour hour. The current direct labour rate is $10 per hour.
Required:
As consultant to the team, you have been asked to calculate the total costs to be assigned to ending inventory under both absorption and variable costing.

EXERCISES

22. (LO 7) The Blue Suede Shoe Company produced 100,000 pairs of shoes and sold 70,000 in its first year of operations. There was no Work in Process Inventory at year-end. Its costs for that year were as follows:

Direct materials	$ 400,000
Direct labour	300,000
Variable manufacturing overhead	150,000
Variable selling and administrative expenses	210,000
Fixed manufacturing overhead	250,000
Fixed selling and administrative expense	175,000
Total	$1,485,000

Required:
a. Compute the cost of one unit of product if the company uses variable costing.
b. Compute the cost of one unit of product if the company uses absorption costing.

23. (LO 7) Shortly after the end of its first year of operations, thieves stole or destroyed nearly all cost and production records of the Fred Shearer Products Company, a producer of high-quality burglar alarms. Having been hired to piece together the fragments of the records that were salvaged from the scene, you have determined the following regarding the first-year operations:

Production in units	?
Sales in units	9,500
Total sales	$109,250
Gross margin	54,625
Total fixed manufacturing overhead costs incurred	22,500
Total selling and administrative costs	38,000
Variable production costs (per unit)	3.50

Required:
a. How many units were produced in the first year?
b. From the previous information, prepare an income statement using absorption costing.

24. (LO 8) Josiah Bartlett Corporation has been in operation for two years. It is a privately held firm and produces no external financial information. It employs the variable costing method for preparing internal financial statements. Selected information from its first two years of operations follows:

	Year 1	Year 2
Litres of product produced	500,000	500,000
Litres of product sold	450,000	525,000
Fixed production costs	$2,000,000	$2,000,000
Variable production costs	2,500,000	2,500,000
Net income (variable costing)	500,000	1,600,000

Required:
a. Had the company used absorption costing in year 1, how much net profit would it have reported?
b. Had the company used absorption costing in both years, how much net profit would it have reported in year 2?

25. (LO 7, 8) After Jia Chen Co.'s first year of operations, the finished goods inventory consisted of 1,200 units. Variable costs per unit consist of $15 manufacturing and $10 selling and administrative. Fixed costs per unit consist of $50 manufacturing and $20 selling and administrative. During the period the company sold 18,800 units.

Required:
If Jia Chen Co. used absorption costing rather than variable costing, would its net income be higher or lower and by how much than if it had used variable costing? Briefly explain your answer.

26. (LO 8) Renee Chu Co. prepares its income statements using both the variable and absorption costing methods. The manufacturing cost applied last year is the same as this year. However, the fixed selling and administrative expense is $2 per unit higher than last year. This year's variable costing income statement showed a profit, whereas this year's absorption costing income statement reported a loss.

Required:
Explain under what circumstances this could have occurred.

27. (LO 8) Schwarzenegger Manufacturing Ltd. uses the following accounts: Sales Revenue, Cost of Goods Sold, Gross Profit, Variable Expenses, Contribution Margin, Fixed Expenses, and Net Income. The company produces both absorption costing and variable costing income statements. Schwarzenegger Manufacturing Ltd.'s income statement for the year ended March 31, 2008, showed that its actual sales revenues, its total gross profit, and its total contribution margin were very close to the planned figures. However, its net income was substantially greater than the planned amount.

Required:

Explain under what circumstances this could have occurred.

Exercises 25, 26, and 27 are extracted from *Management Accounting 1 Examination*, published by the Certified General Accountants Association of Canada (© CGA-Canada 1998). Reprinted with permission.

28. (LO 7, 8) The Kevin O'Leary Company Ltd. produces telephones that it sells to a variety of electronics wholesalers. Its operating costs for the current year are summarized:

Variable costs	
Selling & administration (per unit sold)	$2
Production (per unit produced)	8
Fixed Costs	
Selling & administration	$1,000,000
Production	2,000,000
Selling price (per unit)	$50

In the current year, the company produced 100,000 units and sold 80,000. It had no beginning inventories at the start of the current year and no ending Work in Process Inventory.

Required:

a. If the company uses absorption costing, compute the cost assigned to the ending inventory.

b. If the company uses variable costing, compute the cost assigned to the ending inventory.

29. (LO 7, 8) The following information pertains to the operations of the George Bush Manufacturing Company for the current year:

Sales (2,000 units @ $20)	$40,000
Variable costs of production	10,000
Fixed costs of production	5,000
Variable selling costs (per unit Sold)	1
Fixed selling costs	3,000
Beginning WIP and Finished Goods Inventories (units)	0
Ending WP Inventory (Units)	0
Total number of units produced	2,500

Required:

a. net income if absorption costing is used,

b. net income if variable costing is used, and

c. reconcile your answers in parts (a) and (b).

PROBLEMS

1. (LO 1, 2) High School Traditions operates a shop that makes and sells class rings for local high schools. Operating statistics follow:

Average selling price per ring	$ 250
Variable costs per ring	
Rings and stones	90
Sales commissions	18
Variable manufacturing overhead	8
Annual fixed costs	
Selling expenses	42,000
Administrative expenses	56,000
Production expenses	30,000

The company's tax rate is 30%.

PROBLEMS

Required:

a. What is the firm's breakeven point in rings? in revenue?
b. How much revenue is needed to yield $140,000 in before-tax profit?
c. How much revenue is needed to yield an after-tax profit of $120,000?
d. How much revenue is needed to yield an after-tax profit of 20% of revenue?
e. The firm's marketing manager believes that by spending an additional $12,000 in advertising and lowering the price by $20 per ring, he can increase the number of rings sold by 25%. He is currently selling 2,200 rings. Should he make these changes?

2. (LO 1, 2) Crestor Manufacturing Co. incurred the following costs to produce a new product:

Direct materials per unit	$6
Direct labour per unit	0.8 DLH @ $15/DLH
Variable overhead per unit	2/3 of direct labour costs
Fixed manufacturing costs	$1,200,000
Fixed selling and administrative costs	$2,000,000
Selling price per unit	$40
Variable selling costs per unit	$2

The production manager feels that savings could be achieved by automating the plant. Under automation, the costs would shift as follows:

Direct materials cost per unit	$5.50
Direct labour per unit	0.5 DLH @ $20/DLH
Variable overhead per unit	1/2 of direct labour costs
Fixed manufacturing costs	$1,600,000

There would be no change to any other costs or to the selling price.

Required:

a. Calculate the breakeven point in annual units of sales of the new product if Crestor Manufacturing Co. uses the:
   i. present method of production
   ii. automated method of production
b. Calculate the annual number of units of sales up to which Crestor Manufacturing Co. would be indifferent about which manufacturing method is used. If demand exceeds this amount, which method of production should be used?
c. Identify four factors that Crestor Manufacturing Co. might consider before selecting either the current method of production or the automated method of production.

3. (LO 2) Because of the opportunities created for competition by the merger between Air Canada and Canadian Airlines, Onexa Air is about to introduce a daily round-trip flight on the Toronto-to-Vancouver route. Onexa offers only one seat class on all its flights, comfort class, which provides lots of leg room. No other airline offers this kind of seat. Onexa is in the process of determining how it should price its round-trip tickets. The following information is available.

Seating capacity per plane	360
Maximum expected demand for seats on any flight	300
Food and beverage service cost for a round trip per passenger (no additional charge to passenger)	$40
Commission to travel agents paid by Onexa on each ticket (assume all tickets are booked by travel agents)	8% of fare
Fuel cost for a round-trip flight	$24,000
Fixed annual lease cost allocated to a round-trip flight	$100,000
Fixed ground services costs (maintenance, check-in, baggage handling) allocated to a round-trip flight	$10,000
Fixed flight crew salaries allocated to a round-trip flight	$8,000

For simplicity, assume that fuel costs are not affected by the actual number of passengers on a flight.

The market research group at Onexa segments the market into two groups, business travellers and pleasure travellers, and provides the following information on the effect of different price levels on the estimated demand for seats on any given flight:

PROBLEMS

	Price Charged	Number of Seats Expected to be Sold
Business travellers	$ 500	200
	2,000	190
Pleasure travellers	500	100
	2,000	20

Assume these prices are the only choices available to Onexa. The market research team offers one additional piece of information: pleasure travellers usually begin their travel in one week, spend at least a weekend at their destination, and return in a following week. Business travellers usually begin and complete their travel within the same week and do not stay over a weekend.

Required:

a. Prepare an analysis of the total contribution margin that would be obtained from each of the two types of travellers at each of the two fares.

b. Explain the key factor or factors that should be considered in determining which fare or fares to charge.

c. If Onexa wishes to charge different prices for the two types of travellers, explain how it might achieve such a policy.

4. (LO 2) The company for which you work as a managerial accountant engages independent agents to sell the company's products. These agents are currently being paid a commission of 15% based on sales price but are asking for an increase to 20% of sales made during the coming year. You had already prepared the following pro forma income statement for the company based on the 15% commission.

Forrester Creations Corporation
Pro Forma Income Statement
For the Year Ending April 30

Sales		$1,000,000
Cost of goods sold (all variable)		600,000
Gross profit		$ 400,000
Selling and administrative:		
Variable (commission only)	$150,000	
Fixed	10,000	160,000
Income before taxes		$ 240,000
Income tax expense (25%)		60,000
Net income		$ 180,000

Management wants to examine the possibility of employing the company's own sales staff: a sales manager at an annual salary of $60,000, and three salespeople at an annual salary of $30,000 each plus a commission of 5% of sales. All other fixed costs as well as the variable cost percentages would remain the same as in the above pro forma income statement.

Required:

a. Based on the pro forma income statement above, what is the breakeven point in sales dollars for Forrester Creations Corporation for the year ending April 30?

b. If Forrester Creations Corporation employed its own sales staff, what would be the breakeven point in sales dollars for the year ending April 30?

c. What would be the volume of sales dollars required for the year ending April 30, to yield the same net income as projected in the pro forma income statement if Forrester Creations Corporation continued to use the independent sales agents and agreed to their demand for a 20% sales commission?

d. Compute the estimated sales volume in sales dollars that would generate an identical net income for the year ending April 30, regardless of whether Forrester Creations Corporation employed its own sales staff or continued to use the independent sales agents and paid them a 20% commission.

5. (LO 2) G. Spraakman and Son, Ltd., build custom-made pleasure boats that range in price from $10,000 to $250,000. For the past 30 years, Mr. Spraakman, Sr., has determined the selling price of each boat by estimating the cost of material, labour, and a prorated portion of overhead. He adds 20% to estimated costs for profits.

PROBLEMS

For example, a recent price quotation was determined as follows:

Direct materials	$ 50,000
Direct labour	80,000
Manufacturing overhead	20,000
	$150,000
Plus 20%	30,000
Selling price	$180,000

The overhead figure was determined by estimating total overhead for the year and allocating it at 25% of direct labour costs.

If a customer rejected the price and business was slow, Mr. Spraakman, Sr., might be willing to reduce his markup to as little as 5% over estimated costs. Thus, average markup for the year was estimated at 15%. Mr. Spraakman, Jr., has just completed a managerial accounting course that dealt with pricing, and he believes that the firm could use some of the techniques discussed in the course. The course emphasized the contribution margin approach to pricing and Mr. Spraakman, Jr., feels that such an approach would be helpful in determining an appropriate price for the boats.

Total overhead, which includes selling and administrative expenses for the year, has been estimated at $1,500,000, of which $900,000 is fixed and the remainder is variable in direct proportion to direct labour.

Required:

a. Assume that the customer rejected the $180,000 quotation and also rejected a $157,500 (5% markup) quotation during a slack period. The customer countered with a $150,000 offer.

   i. What is the minimum selling price Mr. Spraakman, Sr., could have quoted without reducing or increasing company net income?

   ii. What is the difference in company net income for the year between accepting or rejecting the customer's offer?

b. Identify and briefly explain one advantage and one disadvantage of the contribution approach to pricing compared to the approach previously used by G. Spraakman and Son, Ltd.

6. (LO 2) The following income statement for Hall Company shows the results for the current fiscal year.

Hall Company
Income Statement
Year Ended December 31

Sales (90,000 units @ $4.00)			$360,000
Cost of goods sold:			
Direct materials		$90,000	
Direct labour		90,000	
Manufacturing overhead:			
Variable	$18,000		
Fixed	80,000	98,000	278,000
Gross margin (profit)			$ 82,000
Selling expenses:			
Variable:			
✷Sales commissions*	$18,000		
Shipping	3,600	$21,600	
Fixed:			
Advertising		40,000	$61,600	
Administrative expenses:			
Variable		$ 4,500	
Fixed		20,400	24,900	86,500
Net profit (loss)			$ (4,500)

*Based on sales dollars, not physical units.

Required:

Answer the following independent questions.

PROBLEMS

a. Assuming the relationship between advertising dollars spent and sales achieved remains constant, how much may advertising be increased to bring production and sales to 130,000 units and earn a target net income of 5% of sales?

b. For the current year, a mail-order firm is willing to buy 60,000 units of product "if the price is right." Assume that the present market of 90,000 units at $4 each will not be disturbed. Hall will not pay any sales commissions on these 60,000 units. Variable administration costs will continue at the same rate. The mail-order firm will pick up the units directly at the Hall factory. However, Hall must refund $24,000 of the total sales price as a promotional and advertising allowance for the mail-order firm. In addition, special packaging will increase manufacturing costs on these 60,000 units by $0.10 per unit. At what unit price must the mail-order firm's business be quoted for Hall to break even on total operations in the current year?

c. The president suspects that a fancy new package will aid consumer sales and, ultimately, Hall's sales. Present packaging costs per unit are all variable and consist of $0.05 for direct materials and $0.04 for direct labour; new packaging costs will be $0.30 and $0.13 for direct materials and direct labour, respectively. Assuming no other changes in cost behaviour, how many units must be sold to earn a net income of $20,000?

(Problems 1, 2, 3, 4, and 6 are adapted by the authors from Management Accounting examinations published by the Certified General Accountants Association of Canada © CGA-Canada, #1(c) 1994, #3 and #6(c) 2001, #2 1999, #4(c) 2000 used with permission)

7. (LO 2) McCain Fashion Shoes Inc. has created a new type of sandal that is expected to be very popular with active people. There are two models available—the Clintoon and the Obama. Cost and production data are as follows:

	Clintoon	Obama
Selling price	$29.99	$49.99
Cost to produce 50,000 units of each product:		
Direct materials	$350,000	$400,000
Direct labour	75,000	75,000
Variable overhead	500,000	550,000
Fixed overhead allocation	356,000	400,000
Selling and administrative costs:		
Shipping costs per unit	$1.99	$1.99
Advertising budget allocated	$100,000	$150,000

Required:

a. Calculate the breakeven point in units for the Clintoon model, assuming the allocations of fixed costs given above.

b. Total unit sales are estimated at 100,000 units, the allocated fixed overhead amounts are as given, and the Clintoon model is expected to account for 70% of unit sales and the Obama model 30%. Calculate the breakeven sales level in dollars for the products combined.

c. What would be the breakeven sales level in dollars for the products combined if the fixed overhead were allocated to the two models in proportion to their sales— that is, 70% of fixed overhead allocated to Clintoon and 30% of fixed overhead allocated to Obama? Briefly explain your response.

(Problem 7 is adapted by the authors from Management Accounting examinations published by the Certified General Accountants Association of Canada © CGA-Canada, June 2005, used by permission)

8. (LO 1, 2, 3) Ping Zhang Company wishes to present its operating results for the year ended December 31, in the form of a contribution margin income statement. Ping Zhang Company produces a single product and has a relevant range between 20,000 units and 80,000 units. Total production costs range from $321,875 to $966,875 at the low and high ends of the relevant range, respectively. Sales volume in the current year was 32,000 units, and net income was $45,125. Ping Zhang Company's product is highly specialized; therefore, no units are kept in inventory.

Required:

a. Prepare a contribution income statement for the year ended December 31. Include columns for total dollars, per-unit dollars, and percentage of sales.

b. Draw a rough cost–volume–profit graph for this situation. Label all points and lines, including the breakeven point.

PROBLEMS

Problem 8 is extracted from *Management Accounting 1 Examination*, published by the Certified General Accountants Association of Canada (© CGA-Canada 2003). Reprinted with permission.

9. (LO 3) The Senior Citizens' Club has enlisted you to help in developing a presentation for a group of local business executives who have previously given generously to support the club's efforts. An investigation reveals that each member pays dues of $8 per month, monthly variable costs per member are $1, and the club's monthly fixed expenses are $2,100. Most of the club's workers are volunteers.

   Required:
   a. Prepare a breakeven graph for the club.
   b. Prepare a profit–volume graph for the club.
   c. Which graph would you recommend that the club use in its presentation?

10. (LO 1, 2, 4) Brooke Logan Ltd. produces two products, Xenon and Yuon. This year, for every 4 units of Xenon that were sold, 1 unit of Yuon was sold. Xenon's sales price was $50 and variable costs were $20. Yuon's sales price was $120 and its variable costs were $48. Sales volume for 2007 was $6,400,000 and fixed costs were $840,000.

   Required:
   a. How many units of each product were sold this year?
   b. What is the breakeven point in dollars and in units?
   c. If the sales mix were to change next year to three units of Xenon to two units of Yuon, what would be the new breakeven point in dollars and in units? (All other items will remain unchanged.)
   d. If sales volume remained at $6,400,000, what net income would Brooke Logan Ltd. have using the sales mix in part (c)? What was the net income this year based on the original sales mix?
   e. If Brooke Logan Ltd.'s desired income (before taxes) is $3,600,000, what sales revenue in dollars would be required to generate this income if the original sales mix of 4 Xenon to 1 Yuon prevailed? How many units of each product would be required to generate that income before taxes?

Problem 10 is extracted from Management Accounting Examinations, published by the Certified General Accountants Association of Canada © CGA-Canada, 1998. Reprinted with permission.

11. (LO 4) Della Computers Ltd. manufactures three types of computers, all of which are sold at wholesale to dealers throughout the world. Laptop models manufactured by Della sell at an average price of $2,200, and variable costs per unit total $1,900. Standard-size Della computers sell at an average price of $3,700, and variable costs per unit equal $3,000. Luxury models manufactured by Della sell at an average price of $6,000, and the variable costs per unit are $5,000. Fixed costs for the company are estimated at $1,080,000,000.

   Required:
   a. The company's marketing department estimates that next year's unit sales mix will be 30% laptop, 50% standard, and 20% luxury. What is the breakeven point in units for the firm?
   b. If the company has an after-tax profit goal of $1 billion and the tax rate is 50%, how many units of each type of computer must be sold for the goal to be reached?
   c. Assume the sales mix shifts to 50% laptop, 40% standard, and 10% luxury. How does this mix affect your answer to part (b)?
   d. If the company sold more luxury computers and fewer laptop computers, how would your answers to parts (a) and (b) change?

12. (LO 4) Enchanting Sounds makes portable CD players, CDs, and batteries, which follow a normal sales mix pattern of 1:3:6. The following are the company's costs:

	CD Players	CDs	Batteries
Variable product costs	$ 62	$1.20	$0.22
Variable selling expenses	14	0.50	0.10
Variable administrative expenses	3	0.05	0.03
Selling prices	140	5.00	0.50

Annual fixed manufacturing overhead	$110,000
Annual fixed selling expenses	60,000
Annual fixed administrative expenses	16,290

PROBLEMS

The firm is in a 40% income tax bracket. As the new owner of the firm, you are interested in fine-tuning the performance of the company and need to devote some attention to the questions listed below.

Required:

a.   What is the annual dollar breakeven point?

b.   How many CD players, CDs, and batteries are expected to be sold at the breakeven point?

c.   If the firm desires a before-tax profit of $114,640, how much total revenue is required and how many units of each item must be sold?

d.   If the firm desires an after-tax profit of $103,176, how much total revenue is required and how many units of each item must be sold?

13. (LO 4) The Gaetane Labelle Maraj Emporium makes carved wooden mallard ducks and ducklings. For every duck the firm sells, it sells two ducklings. Information on the two products is as follows:

	Ducks	Ducklings
Selling price	$12	$6
Variable cost	4	4
Contribution margin	$ 8	$2

Monthly fixed costs are $12,000. You have just purchased the firm.

Required:

a.   What is the average contribution margin ratio?

b.   What is the breakeven point? At the breakeven point, identify the total units of each product sold and sales dollars of each product.

c.   If the company wants to earn $24,000 in before-tax profit per month, how many ducks and how many ducklings must it sell?

d.   The company, which is in a 40% tax bracket, specifies $9,000 of after-tax profit as its objective. You believe that the mix has changed to five ducklings for every duck. How much total revenue is needed, and in what product proportions, to achieve this profit objective?

14. (LO 4, 5) Alan Guiliford owns a travel agency. He receives commission revenue based on the total dollar volume of business he generates for various client firms in the travel and entertainment industries. His rates of commission currently are 20% of total hotel fees, 15% of total car rental fees, and 10% of airline ticket fees. Alan is your friend and has asked for your help. Data for a normal month's operations are as follows:

Costs		Fees Generated for Clients	
Advertising	$1,000	Hotel fees	$10,800
Rent	800	Car rental fees	3,600
Utilities	300	Airline ticket fees	14,200
Other expenses	1,400		$28,600

Required:

a.   Given the stated commission percentages, what is Alan's normal total monthly commission? What is the normal monthly before-tax profit?

b.   Alan can increase the amount of hotel fees he generates by 40% if he spends an additional $200 on advertising. Should he do this?

c.   Connie Reed has offered to merge her bookings with Alan's and become his employee. She would receive a base salary of $600 a month plus 20% of the commissions on client fees she generates, which, for a normal month, are:

Hotel fees	$5,000
Car rental fees	2,000
Airline ticket fees	2,000

Should Alan accept the proposal?

d.   Use the information in part (c). During Connie's first month, she generated $10,000 of total fees, but they were as follows:

Hotel fees	$3,000
Car rental fees	2,000
Airline ticket fees	5,000

Will Alan be pleased? Why or why not?

PROBLEMS

15. (LO 5) The Shearer Wind Finder Company sells weathervanes for $18 each. Variable manufacturing costs are $8, and variable selling, general, and administrative costs are $3 per unit. Fixed costs, which are incurred uniformly throughout the year, are $840,000.
    Required:
    a.   Calculate the breakeven point in units and dollars.
    b.   How many units must be sold to earn $80,000 in pretax profits?
    c.   Assume a tax rate of 35%. How many units have to be sold to yield an after-tax profit of $140,000?
    d.   If labour costs are 35% of variable manufacturing costs and 20% of total fixed costs, by how much would an 8% decrease in labour costs have an effect?

16. (LO 5) Robin McLeod Enterprises makes two types of travel bags: hanging bags and case-type bags. The firm sells these in the ratio of one hanging bag to two case-type bags. Selling prices are $54 and $38, respectively, and variable costs are $22 and $15, respectively. Fixed costs are $860,000. The firm is in the 35% tax bracket.
    Required:
    Calculate the number of each type of bag necessary to achieve each of the following:
    a.   Breakeven point
    b. $200,00 of pretax profit
    c. $200,000 of after-tax profit
    d.   Pretax profit of 20% of revenue
    e.   After-tax profit of 1.9% of revenue

17. (LO 2, 6) The Judith Poë Corporation produces children's golf clubs. The company has received a large order for 10,000 golf clubs from a retail establishment that is willing to pay $26 each. This sale will have no impact on present sales.

    Ray Piano, the sales manager, noted that the unit cost of goods sold, based on present production of 50,000 units, was $26.60. No marketing or administrative costs will be incurred with this order. This offer was $0.60 below the present cost as shown below.

Judith Poë Corporation
Income Statement
For the Year Ended December 31

Sales	$1,850,000
Cost of goods sold	1,330,000
Gross profit	$ 520,000
Marketing and administrative expenses	250,000
Income before taxes	$ 270,000

Required:
    a.   What advice would you give the company on accepting the order given the following facts:
        i.   Poë will save $0.30 per unit because the chain will be attaching its own brand-name labels.
        ii.   Of the total cost of goods sold, the variable cost of goods is $1,006,400 and variable marketing and administrative costs are $146,000. The remainder of the cost of good sold is fixed.
    b.   Based on the information in part (a):
        i.   Calculate the breakeven point in units for the current year.
        ii.   Calculate the margin of safety under the present sales level.

18. (LO 2, 6) Boudreaux Company makes small, flat-bottomed boats called pirogues. The president, Bayou Boudreaux, enlists your help in predicting the effects of some changes she is contemplating and gives you the following information:

Variable costs to produce each pirogue	
Direct materials	$ 90
Direct labour	100
Variable factory overhead	20
Average variable selling cost per pirogue	30
Average variable general and administrative cost per pirogue	10
Annual fixed production overhead	$660,000
Annual fixed selling expenses	190,000
Annual fixed general and administrative expenses	300,000

PROBLEMS

Bayou advises you that each pirogue sells for $400 and that demand for the current year is 14,400 pirogues or $5,760,000 of sales.

The following are some of the changes Bayou is considering:
1. The sales staff believe that demand will increase 15% if price is reduced 10%.
2. The engineering design staff believe that spending $30 on each pirogue to strengthen the hull will cause demand to increase 20% because consumers will believe the pirogue to be superior to any other product on the market.
3. The sales manager believes that increasing advertising by $25,000 will increase demand by 20%.

Required:
a. Calculate the breakeven point in units and dollars.
b. Calculate the margin of safety in units, dollars, and percentage.
c. Calculate the effects on profit and dollar breakeven point of the independent proposition (ignore tax implications). For each proposition, advise the president about the proposal.

19. (LO 2, 3, 5, 6) You are considering acquiring one of two local firms (VPI and TECH) that manufacture slip rings. VPI employs a considerable amount of labour in its manufacturing processes, and its salespeople all work on commission. TECH employs the latest technology in its manufacturing operations, and its salespeople are all salaried.

You have obtained the following financial information concerning the two firms:

	VPI		TECH	
	2010	2011	2010	2011
Sales	$100,000	$160,000	$100,000	$140,000
Expenses including taxes	88,000	137,200	88,000	111,200
Net income	$ 12,000	$ 22,800	$ 12,000	$ 28,800

After examining cost data, you determine that the fixed costs for VPI are $10,000, while the fixed costs for TECH are $50,000. The tax rate for both firms is 40%.

Required:
a. Determine breakeven sales for each of the firms in 2010 and 2011.
b. Determine the relative operating leverage for each firm in 2010 and 2011.
c. Suppose you could acquire either firm for $200,000 and you want an after-tax return of 12% on your investment. Determine what sales level for each firm would allow you to reach your goal.
d. Assuming the demand for slip rings fluctuates widely, comment on the relative positions of the firms.
e. Prepare a profit–volume graph for each firm.

20. (LO 2, 6) Gilda Serrao Ltd. has decided to introduce a new product, which can be manufactured by either a capital-intensive method or a labour-intensive method. The manufacturing method will not affect the quality of the product. The estimated manufacturing costs by the two methods are as follows.

	Capital-Intensive	Labour-Intensive
Raw materials	$5.00	$5.60
Direct labour	(0.5 h @ $12/h) $6.00	(0.8 h @ $9/h) $7.20
Variable overhead	(0.5 h @ $6/h) $3.00	(0.8 h @ $6/h) $4.80
Directly traceable incremental fixed manufacturing costs	$2,440,000	$1,320,000

Gilda's market research department has recommended an introductory unit sales price of $30. The incremental selling expenses are estimated to be $500,000 annually plus $2 for each unit sold regardless of manufacturing method.

Required:
a. Calculate the estimated breakeven point in annual unit sales of the new product if Gilda Serrao Ltd. uses the:
   i. capital-intensive manufacturing method
   ii. labour-intensive manufacturing method
b. Determine the annual unit sales volume at which Gilda Serrao Ltd. would be indifferent between the two manufacturing methods.

PROBLEMS

c.   Serrao's management must decide which manufacturing method to employ. One factor it must consider is operating leverage.
   i.   Explain operating leverage and the relationship between operating leverage and business risk.
   ii. Explain the circumstances under which Gilda Serrao Ltd. should employ each of the two manufacturing methods.
d.   Identify the business factors other than operating leverage that Gilda Serrao Ltd. must consider before selecting the capital-intensive or labour-intensive manufacturing method.

(IMA adapted)

21. (LO 1, 7, 8) Rochelle Inc. produces and sells custom parts for powerboats. The company uses a costing system based on actual costs. Selected accounting and production information for the current year is as follows:

Net income (under absorption costing)	$ 400,000
Sales	3,400,000
Fixed manufacturing overhead	600,000
Fixed selling and administrative costs (all these costs are fixed)	400,000
Net income (under variable costing)	310,000
Units produced	2,000
Units sold	?

Rochelle Inc. had no work in process inventory at either the beginning or the end of the current year. The company also did not have any finished goods inventory at the beginning of the fiscal year.

Required:
a.   Calculate the units sold.
b.   Calculate the total contribution margin under variable costing.
c.   Calculate the gross margin under absorption costing.
d.   Calculate the cost per unit sold under variable costing.
e.   Calculate the cost per unit sold under absorption costing.

Problem 21 is extracted from *Management Accounting 1 Examination*, published by the Certified General Accountants Association of Canada (© CGA-Canada 2003). Reprinted with permission.

22. (LO 1, 2, 7, 8) Anne Cowan, vice-president of Abscorp Ltd., is not happy. Sales have been rising steadily, but profits have been falling. In September, Abscorp had record sales, but the lowest profits ever. Below are the results for the months of July, August, and September.

ABSCORP LTD.
Comparative Monthly Income Statements ($000s)

	July	August	September
Sales (@ $25)	$1,750	$1,875	$2,000
Less cost of goods sold:			
Opening inventory	80	320	400
Costs applied to production:			
Variable manufacturing (@ $9)	765	720	540
Fixed manufacturing overhead	595	560	420
Cost of goods manufactured	1,360	1,280	960
Goods available for sale	1,440	1,600	1,360
Less ending inventory	320	400	80
Cost of goods sold	1,120	1,200	1,280
Underapplied/(overapplied) fixed overhead	(35)	–	140
Adjusted cost of goods sold	1,085	1,200	1,420
Gross margin	665	675	580
Less selling and administrative expenses	620	650	680
Net income (loss)	$ 45	$ –25	$ (100)

PROBLEMS

You have been asked to explain to the vice-president that the problem is more apparent than real, by reinterpreting the results in a variable costing format. You have obtained the following information to assist you in this task:

	July units	August units	September units
Production	85,000	80,000	60,000
Sales	70,000	75,000	80,000

Additional information about the company's operations is as follows:
- 5,000 units of finished goods were in opening inventory on July 1.
- Fixed manufacturing overhead costs totalled $1,680,000 per quarter and were incurred evenly throughout the quarter. The fixed manufacturing overhead cost is applied to units of production on the basis of a planned production volume of 80,000 units per month.
- Variable selling and administrative expenses are $6 per unit sold. The remainder of the selling and administrative expenses on the comparative monthly income statements is fixed.
- The company uses a FIFO cost flow assumption. Work in process inventories are nominal and can be ignored.

Required:
a. Compute the monthly breakeven point under variable costing.
b. i. Calculate the variable costing net income for each month.
   ii. Prepare a numerical reconciliation of the variable costing and absorption costing net incomes for each month.
   iii. Explain why profits have not been more closely correlated with changes in sales volume.

Problem 22 is extracted from *Management Accounting 1 Examination*, published by the Certified General Accountants Association of Canada (© CGA-Canada 2000). Reprinted with permission.

23. (LO 8) David Roost Corporation is a manufacturer of a synthetic element. David Roost, the president of the company, has been eager to get the operating results for the fiscal year just completed. He was surprised when the income statement revealed that income before taxes had dropped to $885,000 from $900,000 even though sales volume had increased by 100,000 kg. This drop in net income had occurred even though Roost had implemented the following changes during the past 12 months to improve the profitability of the company.
   - Due to a 10% increase in production costs, the sales price of the company's product was increased by 12%. This action took place on December 1.
   - The managers of the selling and administrative departments were given strict instructions to spend no more in year 2 than in year 1.

Roost's accounting department prepared and distributed to top management the comparative income statements presented below. The accounting staff also prepared related financial information that is presented in the schedule following the income statements to assist management in evaluating the company's performance. Roost uses the FIFO inventory method for finished goods.

David Roost Corporation
Statements of Operating Income
For the Years Ended November 30, Years 1 and 2
($000 omitted)

	Year 1		Year 2	
Sales revenue		$9,000		$11,200
Cost of goods sold	$7,200		$8,320	
Manufacturing overhead variance	(600)		495	
Adjusted cost of goods sold		6,600		8,815
Gross margin		$2,400		$ 2,385
Selling and administrative expenses		1,500		1,500
Income before taxes		$ 900		$ 885

PROBLEMS

David Roost Corporation
Selected Operating and Financial Data

	Year 1	Year 2
Sales volume (in units)	900,000 kg	1,000,000 kg
Beginning inventory (in units)	300,000 kg	600,000 kg
Sales price	$ 10/kg	$ 11.20/kg
Material cost	1.50/kg	1.65/kg
Direct labour cost	2.50/kg	2.75/kg
Variable overhead cost	1.00/kg	1.10/kg
Fixed overhead cost	3.00/kg	3.30/kg
Fixed overhead costs	3,000,000	3,300,000
Selling and administrative (all fixed)	1,500,000	1,500,000

Required:

a. Explain to David Roost why the company's net income decreased in the current fiscal year despite the sales price and sales volume increases.

b. A member of Roost's accounting department has suggested that the company adopt variable (direct) costing for internal reporting purposes.

  i. Prepare an operating income statement before taxes for year 2 for Roost Corporation using the variable (direct) costing method.

  ii. Present a numerical reconciliation of the difference in income before taxes using the absorption costing method as currently employed by Roost and the variable (direct) costing method as proposed.

c. Identify and discuss the advantages and disadvantages of using the variable (direct) costing method for internal reporting purposes.

(IMA adapted)

24. (LO 7, 8) Ida Copelavici Corporation Ltd. (ICC) prepares external financial statements using absorption costing and internal financial statements using variable costing. You have the following information regarding the operations of ICC for the past two years:

	Year 1	Year 2
Sales in units (@ $35 per unit)	25,000	35,000
Production in units	30,000	30,000
Variable production costs per unit	$20.00	$20.00
Fixed production costs	$120,000	$120,000
Fixed marketing costs	$50,000	$50,000
Beginning inventory	0	?

Required:

a. Prepare absorption costing income statements for the two years ended December 31. Include a column for totals for the two years.

b. Prepare variable costing income statements for the two years ended December 31. Include a column for totals for the two years.

c. Prepare reconciliation for the year-to-year differences in net income under the two methods.

Problem 24 is extracted from *Management Accounting 1 Examination*, published by the Certified General Accountants Association of Canada (© CGA-Canada 2002). Reprinted with permission.

25. (LO 7) The following information concerns the first four years of operation at Basic Black Ltd.:

Cost per unit:	
Direct materials	$ 4.50
Direct labour	2.00
Variable production costs	0.60
Fixed production costs ($200,000 ÷ 400,000 units expected volume)	0.50
Total	$ 7.60
Selling price per unit	$ 11.00
Other expenses:	
Variable selling expense per unit	$ 0.60
Other fixed expenses	$200,000

PROBLEMS

Production and sales data in units:

Year	1	2	3	4
Production	360,000	400,000	420,000	400,000
Sales	300,000	410,000	420,000	450,000

Required:
Prepare income statements under absorption costing and variable costing methods for each of the four years. Charge any variances to Cost of Goods Sold.

26. (LO 7) Golf-Go Equipment Company produces and sells electric golf carts. The company uses a costing system based on actual costs. Selected accounting and production information for the current fiscal year follows:

Net income (under absorption costing)	$ 400,000
Sales	$3,400,000
Fixed manufacturing overhead cost incurred	$ 600,000
Variable selling and administrative costs	$ 400,000
Fixed selling and administrative costs	$ 500,000
Net income (under variable costing)	$ 310,000
Units produced	2,000
Units sold	?

Golf-Go had no Work in Process Inventory at either the beginning or end of the fiscal year. The company also did not have any Finished Goods Inventory at the beginning of the fiscal year.

Required:
Compute each of the following:
a. Number of units sold
b. Cost of one unit under variable costing
c. Cost of one unit under absorption costing
d. Total contribution margin under variable costing
e. Gross margin under absorption costing

27. (LO 7, 8) Jay Leno Ltd. has been recording inventory on an absorption costing basis. There are plans to convert to a variable costing basis for internal reporting purposes. To get an impression of the overall impact of the change, the management team would like to see the effect on the company's income figures since its inception three years ago. Data for the last three years follow:

	Yr 1	Yr 2	Yr 3
Absorption costing income	$80,000	$110,000	$200,000
Fixed manufacturing costs	$50,000	$54,000	$70,000
Units produced	5,000	6,000	7,000
Units sold	4,000	5,000	7,000

Required:
Calculate the variable costing income for each of the three years. Assume the fixed manufacturing overhead application rate is based on actual units produced. If necessary, use a FIFO cost flow assumption.

28. (LO 7, 8) The following information was taken from the cost records of Reed Incorporated for the current year. The company had no units in Finished Goods Inventory at the beginning of the year, and no units in Work in Process Inventory at either the beginning or end of the year. Reed uses variable costing.

	Variable Costs	Fixed Costs
Direct materials	$3 per unit	
Direct labour	5 per unit	
Manufacturing overhead	2 per unit	$200,000
Selling and administrative expenses	2 per unit	350,000

The product contribution margin in the current year was $8 per unit, and net income was $200,000.

Required:
a. What was the company's sales price per unit?
b. How many units were sold?
c. What were total revenues?
d. Prepare a variable costing income statement for the current year.

29. (LO 8) As a member of the board of directors of MJ Company, you are reviewing the following income statement for the year ended December 31, the company's first year of operations. During this first year, MJ was able to sell all 100,000 units that it produced. However, it had a maximum production capacity of 400,000 units.

MJ Company
Income Statement (Absorption Costing)
Year ended December 31

Sales (100,000 @ $50.00)		$5,000,000
Cost of goods sold:		
Variable (100,000 @ $10.00)	$1,000,000	
Fixed	4,000,000	5,000,000
Gross profit		0
General and administrative expenses (all fixed)		500,000
Net loss		$ (500,000)

You and the other members of the board of directors are concerned about this loss. One of the consultants who helped start up the company proposes that she take over as president and be paid a bonus based on 50% of any profits the company makes while she is president. The board of directors agrees to these terms.

The new president decides that production should be increased in year 2 to 300,000 units. Sales for year 2 remain at the same level as for year 1, that is, 100,000 units. At the end of the year, MJ's income statement, prepared on the same basis as the year before, shows income before the president's bonus of $2,166,667. The president receives a bonus in accordance with the agreement.

Required:

a. Prepare, in good form, the income statement of MJ for the year ended December 31, which shows a net income after the president's bonus. Ignore income taxes.

b. Explain fully why you have concerns about the profits and the bonus paid to the president in year 2.

c. Under variable costing, indicate what the net income (loss) would be for each of the two years.

d. At what sales level, compared to production, would the president be indifferent to the product costing approach used to determine her bonus? Explain fully.

e. At what sales level, compared to production, would the president prefer variable costing to absorption costing? Explain fully.

CASES

1. Contractor Equipment Ltd. is a Halifax company that invents and manufactures innovative equipment for contractors. You, as the company CEO, need to decide what price to charge for a compact self-cleaning cement mixer. For some reason or reasons, two of your vice presidents have different opinions.

Sandy Rinaldo, the VP of marketing, wants to charge $3,000 per unit; she and her sales employees would be able to sell all that could be manufactured each year.

The VP controller wants a higher price, though he realizes that a higher price will lead to fewer sales. He is arguing for $4,000 as this will better cover costs and leave a larger profit. Both VPs recognize that there is a downward-sloping demand curve. With normal goods, customers will tend to buy more product at a low price and less of it at a higher price.

You are not sure whom to believe. You hire a market research firm to contact potential clients to gauge the sales levels for the new cement mixer that the company is most likely to achieve at different prices. Expected sales for different prices, based on this market research, are shown in Exhibit 3-1.

Regarding capital expenditure, it would cost $15 million to make between 7,000 and 25,000 units a year. That equipment would have a life of about 15 years and no salvage value. Other fixed costs would be $12 million a year. Variable costs would be $2,000 per unit.

Required:

Using the case approach, recommend a price to charge for new cement mixers and resolve the differences between the two vice presidents.

CASES

Price Per Unit	Units Demanded
$2,500	25,000
3,000	23,000
3,500	21,000
4,000	19,000
4,500	17,000
5,000	15,000
5,500	13,000
6,000	11,000
6,500	9,000
7,000	7,000

EXHIBIT 3-1

Expected Sales at Various Per Unit Prices

2. Headmaster Electronics Worldwide (HEW) makes a wide range of electronics parts for original equipment manufactures located in all areas of the world. To meet this world-wide demand, it has 32 plants in Asia and North America.

HEW's approach to its divisional income statements is as shown in Exhibit 3-1. These divisional statements are important, for divisional managers who are remunerated based on "income before income taxes."

At the beginning of last year, HEW acquired an independent firm, Signal Direct Limited, from the original founder, Oliver Rockport. Mr. Rockport was retained as the general manager. Signal Direct used the absorption format, as noted in Exhibit 3-2.

Mr. Rockport is demanding a share of the bonus pool since he has met and exceeded the budgeted "income before income taxes." He is also arguing that his method of reporting is superior to HEW's. The CEO, Laura Bush, has asked you as the management accountant to help her resolve the confusion.

On examining the financial statements of Signal Direct, you realize that it sold only 75% of the units it produced; the surplus 25% has been placed in inventory. Sales and production were much better matched for all of HEW's divisions.
Required:
Using the case approach, address the CEO's concerns.

```
Sales
Variable cost of goods sold
Product contribution margin
Variable selling expenses
Total contribution margin
Fixed expenses
        Manufacturing
        Selling and administration
        Total fixed expenses
Income before income taxes
```

EXHIBIT 3-1

Income Statement—HEW Format

```
Sales
Cost of goods sold
Gross margin
Operating expenes
        Selling and administration
Income before income taxes
```

EXHIBIT 3-2

Income Statement—Absorption Format

3. At Yun Incorporated, a new ERP system was introduced last year. Many changes were made to implement the ERP system. Not all of these changes are fully understood by users, and modifications are expected. Compared to last year, this year (the first year with the ERP system), sales are down, profits are level, and inventories are up for most manufacturing divisions. The VP and general manager for the manufacturing group, who directs 12 plants

through Yun's plant managers, is very concerned. As your boss, he has contacted you, the newly appointed controller for the manufacturing group. Before you arrived, there was no group controller; the corporate controller was responsible for the accounting at all levels.

To address the VP's concerns, first you examine the format of the operating statement (see Exhibit 3-1). During a telephone call with the corporate controller, Hillary McCain, you mention the VP's concerns. McCain tells you to determine whether the operating statements are being produced using absorption costing or variable costing. She thinks that the default method with the ERP system is absorption costing.

Plant managers are evaluated based on income before income taxes. As revenues are based on market prices, over which plant mangers have no control, they seek to minimize the cost of goods sold. Operating expenses are largely fixed.

Required:

With the case approach, address the VP's concerns.

EXHIBIT 3-1

Operating Statement Format

Sales
Cost of goods sold
Gross margin
Operating expenes
      Selling and administration
Income before income taxes

ETHICS

1. The president of a large automotive firm is speaking at a conference and has been asked to specify the breakeven point for his firm in either units or sales dollars. The president of the firm replies that this is not possible because of the many variables that have to be taken into consideration in determining a breakeven point. The questioner replies that the president is being evasive and expresses doubt that the shareholders of the firm are being adequately served by a management team that does not even know the firm's breakeven point. You are in the audience and the person next to you asks you to answer the following:
   a. What are some of the variables that the president of the firm has in mind?
   b. How could the person who asked the question have reached the stated conclusion about the management team of the firm?

2. Rumsfield Chemical Company's new president has learned that, for the past four years, the company has been dumping its industrial waste into the local river and falsifying reports to authorities about the levels of suspected cancer-causing materials in that waste. His plant manager says that there is no proof that the waste causes cancer, and there are only a few fishing towns within a hundred kilometres downstream. If the company has to treat the substance to neutralize its potentially injurious effects and then transport it to a legal dump-site, the company's variable and fixed costs will rise to a level that might make the firm uncompetitive. If the company loses its competitive advantage, 10,000 local employees could become unemployed, and the town's economy could collapse.
   a. What kinds of variable and fixed costs can you think of that would increase (or decrease) if the waste were treated rather than dumped? How would these costs affect product contribution margin?
   b. What ethical conflicts does the president face?
   c. What rationalizations can you detect that have been devised by plant employees?
   d. What options and suggestions can you offer the president?

3. Assume that, as a service to your community, you have agreed to serve on a community board that is investigating the possibility of opening a daycare centre and preschool for area children. You are the financial expert on the board. Details follow:
   • The Community Club plans to open a childcare centre that will operate five days a week, 50 weeks each year, and charge $25 per week for each child. It has been determined that $20,000 must be spent to upgrade the facilities in the club building to meet provincial standards. These facilities have an estimated life of five years.

- Supplies for each child are estimated to cost $0.50 per day, and food is estimated to cost $0.75 per day. Each year $1,000 must be spent on new equipment for the centre. For every 10 children, one paraprofessional must be included on the staff. Annual salaries for professionals and paraprofessionals are $9,000 and $4,000 respectively.
- Due to space limitations in the facility, only 60 children can be accepted. This would require a staff of three professionals and six paraprofessionals.

Required:

a. Prepare a schedule showing the first year's cash financial results of operating the centre with 20, 40, and 60 children.

b. Discuss some of the problems (including ethical ones) of employing financial analysis in this type of problem.

4. Lily Simon is a sales representative for a heavy construction equipment manufacturer. She is compensated by a moderate fixed salary plus an 8% bonus on sales. Simon is aware that some of the higher-priced items earn the company a lower contribution margin and some of the lower-priced items earn the company a higher contribution margin. She learned this information from the variable costing financial statements produced by the company for management-level employees. One of Simon's best friends is a manager at the company.

Simon has recently started pushing sales of the high-priced items (to the exclusion of lower-priced items) by generously entertaining receptive customers and offering them gifts through the company's promotion budget. She feels that management has not given her adequate raises in the 20 years she has been with the company, and now she is too old to find a better job. As Simon's best friend and as a manager of the company, you are being asked to contemplate the following:

a. Are Simon's actions legal?

b. What are the ethical issues involved in the case from Simon's standpoint?

c. Are there ethical issues in the case from company management's standpoint?

d. What do you believe Simon should do? Why?

5. In Japan, the decision to stop production of a product or to close down a plant has different cost consequences than in Canada or the United States. One principal difference is that Japanese managers are much less likely to fire workers who are displaced by an event such as a plant closing; Japanese managers simply try to move the displaced workers to active plants. However, this concept of permanent or lifetime employment can be awkward to manage when economic times become difficult and prudent financial management suggests that activities, including employment, be scaled back to cut costs. Several years ago, one Japanese company found the following unique solution.

Nissan Motor Co., as a sign that its severe slump may have been worsening, took the unusual step of lending some of its idle factory workers to a rival auto maker. Nissan said it would assign 250 of its production employees to work for six months at factories run by Isuzu Motors Ltd., a 37% owned affiliate of General Motors Corp. Nissan's spokesman, Koji Okuda, called the move an attempt to deal with the company's sharp drop in auto output in Japan. In May of that year, Nissan's Japanese auto production fell 26% from a year earlier. "Demand is low," Mr. Okuda said. "We have to adjust our operations."

As an economic journalist of a large international publication, you have been asked to contemplate the following issues.

a. What specific types of costs might Nissan have considered relevant in its decision to lend employees to Isuzu?

b. Why would Isuzu be interested in hiring, on a temporary basis, workers of Nissan?

c. What were the likely impacts of this arrangement on the quality of the output at Isuzu? the quality of output at Nissan?

6. Men often receive reports of positive PSA (prostate specific antibody) when, in actuality, these results are negative. Newspaper accounts detail an industry utilizing overworked, undersupervised, and poorly paid technicians to perform these tests. Some labs allow workers to analyze up to four times as many tests per year as experts recommend for accuracy. Workers may be paid $10 to analyze a smear when patients are charged $35.

Required:

a. Discuss the cost–volume–profit relationships that exist in this case.

b. Discuss the ethics of the laboratories' owners who allow technicians to be paid piecework for such analysis work.

c. Discuss the ethics of the workers who rush through the test analyses.

SOLUTIONS TO SELF-TEST QUESTIONS

1. b. Selling price = $100,000 ÷ 2,000 = $50.00 per unit
   Contribution margin is $50 − ($15 + $5) = $30
   Breakeven is ($35,000 + $20,000 + $5,000) ÷ $30 = 2,000 units

2. c. Income before taxes = $90,000 ÷ 0.6 = $150,000
   ($45,000 + $150,000) ÷ ($32 − $12) = 9,750 bottles

3. c. The term "unit" is important here.

4. c. Operating leverage is 1.48 computed as follows:
   Operating leverage = Contribution margin ÷ Profit before taxes
   = $650,000 ÷ $440,000= 1.48

5. c. 89,000 ÷ [(750,000 − 150,000 − 100,000 − 60,000 − 6,000) ÷ 50,000] = 10,254 units

6. c. [(50,000 + 89,000)] ÷ [(750,000 − 150,000 − 100,000 − 60,000 − 6,000) ÷ 50,000]
   = 16,014

7. d. Contribution margin per unit: $40 − $14 = $26
   Total contribution margin at 2,400 units = $26 × 2,400 = $62,400
   Additional sales needed: ($62,400 × 0.4) $24,960 ÷ 26 = 960 units × $40 = $38,400

8. c. Contribution margin of X = $9 − $7 = $2;
   Contribution margin of Y = $6 − $3 = $3
   $117,000 ÷ [(3 × $2) + (1 × $3)] = 13,000
   X = 13,000 × 3 = 39,000;
   Y = 13,000 × 1 = 13,000

9. b. {$1,552,000 − [($1,552,000 ÷ 160) × $95]} − $201,500 = $429,000

10. b. $7.50 × 4,500 units = $33,750
    $5.00 × 6,750 units = $33,750
    It is a fixed cost.

11. c. Contribution margin per boxed set:
    [4 ($21 − $21 ÷ 1.5)] + [6 ($10 − $10 ÷ 1.6)] = $50.50

12. a. [$100 − ($20 + $30 + $15) − ($100 × 0.10)] ÷ $100 = 25%

13. b.

14. b. Selling price − [$10 + $15 + (0.45 × $15)] = 0.22 of selling price
    Selling price − $31.75 = 0.22 of selling price
    0.78 of selling price = $31.75
    Selling price $40.71

15. d. Selling price − Variable costs = Fixed costs
    Selling price − $31.75 = $8.25
    Selling price = $40.00

16. d. Fixed costs = ($25,000 + $2,000) × 40% = $10,800
    Contribution margin $30,000 − [($25,000 + $2,000) × 60%] = $13,800
    Contribution margin ratio = $13,800 $30,000 = 0.46
    Breakeven in sales = $10,800 ÷ 0.46 = $23,478

17. b.

18. a. (70,000 − 60,000) × ($630,000 ÷ 70,000) = $90,000

19. d. (70,000 − 60,000) × ($945,000 ÷ 70,000) = $135,000

20. c. [$1,400,000 − [($945,000 − $135,000)] − ($98,000 + $140,000)] = $352,000

21. c. $1,400,000 − $945,000 − $238,000 + $90,000 = $307,000
    or $352,000 − ($135,000 − $90,000) = $307,000

ENDNOTES

1. Kevin D. Thompson, "Planning for Profit," *Black Enterprise*, pp. 93–94. Copyright April 1993, The Earl Graves Publishing Co. Inc., 130 Fifth Avenue, New York, NY 10011.

2. Frank Kuhn, "Use Excel Spreadsheet Formulas to Determine Your Company's Breakeven Point," *Inside Microsoft Excel*, February 2004, p. 10.

3. Frank Kuhn, "Use Excel Spreadsheet Formulas to Determine Your Company's Breakeven Point," *Inside Microsoft Excel*, February 2004, p. 10.

4. Eric Bellman and Stephen Power, "As Tata Soars, So Do Its Risks," *Wall Street Journal*, December 27, 2007; Agence France Presse, "Asia Carmakers Eye Wider Horizons at Geneva Auto Show," March 4, 2008; Nirmal John, "Tata's Nano May Be Just a Click Away," *DNA Daily News & Analysis*, February 23, 2008; "Learning from Tata's Nano: The Breakthrough Innovations of the $2,500 Nano Car Carry a Lot of Important Lessons for Western Executives," BusinessWeek.com, February 28, 2008.

5. Kishore Singh, "Luxury Cruise on Kerala Backwaters," *Business Standard*, October 8, 2004.

6. Mercedes B. Suleik, "Capital View: Financial Literacy for Directors," *Business World*, September 2007.

7. *Relevant range* is the range of activity over which a variable cost will remain constant per unit and a fixed cost will remain constant in total.

8. Robert Spaller, "Leveraging Contribution Margin to Gain a Competitive Advantage," *Journal of Bank Cost and Management Accounting*, May 2006.

9. Mike Spector, "The Prix Fixe Is In," *Wall Street Journal*, October 7, 2006.

10. David Smagalia, "Japanese Experiences With B2C E-Commerce," *MIT Sloan Management Review*, Spring 2004.

11. Tony Van Alpen, "Auto Imports Jump 68% in 2007," *Toronto Star*, January 9, 2008, B3. Lionel Perror, Retuers News Agency, *Toronto Star*, July 5, 2008, B2. Canadians Importing Record Number of U.S. Autos.

12. Chris Sorenson, "WestJet Aiming to Bulk Up: Targets Market Share," *Financial Post*, February 15, 2007, pg. FP4.

13. Once the constant percentage contribution margin in a multiproduct firm is determined, all situations regarding income points can be treated the same as they were earlier in the chapter—remembering that the answers reflect the bag assumption.

14. Robin Cooper and Robert S. Kaplan, "How Cost Accounting Distorts Product Costs," *Management Accounting*, April 1998, p. 27.

15. Matt Hamblen, *Computerworld*, August 21, 2000, p. 48.

16. Simon Houpt, "Seeing the Lights Go Out Off-Broadway," *Globe and Mail*, July 3, 2006, pg. R1.

17. Ian McKinnon and Carol Howes, "BP Amoco Outsources Accounting," *Financial Post*, January 12, 2000, C11.

18. Simon Avery, "BCE Profit Rises on Growth in New Services," *Globe and Mail*, August 5, 2004.

19. Catherine McLean, "Investors Punish Rogers Despite Big Boost in Payout," *Globe and Mail*, January 8, 2008, B2.

20. Bruce Stanley (Hong Kong) and Daniel Michaels (Toulouse), "Singapore Air Aims High for A380—Carrier to Pamper Premium Passengers on Giant Jetliner's First Flight," *Wall Street Journal Asia*, October 24, 2007.

21. Direct costing is, however, a misnomer for variable costing. All variable manufacturing costs, whether direct or indirect, are considered product costs under variable costing.

22. Relevant costing is covered in Chapter 9 and budgeting is discussed in Chapter 6.

23. Robert S. Kaplan, "One Cost System Isn't Enough," *Harvard Business Review*, January–February 1988, p. 61.

24. The income statement approach can readily be adapted to a computerized spreadsheet format, which can be used to obtain results quickly for many different combinations of the CVP factors.

Chapter 4

Overhead and Job Costing

LEARNING OBJECTIVES

After completing this chapter, you should be able to answer the following questions:

1 How
are predetermined overhead rates developed and how does the selection of a capacity measure affect predetermined overhead rates?

2 Why
are separate predetermined overhead rates generally more useful than combined rates?

3 How
is underapplied or overapplied overhead accounted for at year-end and why are these accounting techniques appropriate?

4 What
are the purposes of the documents used in a job order cost system, and what production situations are appropriate for a job order product costing system and why?

5 How
are service department costs allocated to revenue-producing departments using the direct and step methods? (Appendix)

www.mys.ca

Myster Mover Ltd.

Myster Mover's mission is to provide high-quality personalized service at great rates. The company is a full-service moving company. "We recognize that the quality of our service is a reflection of ourselves both as individuals and as a team," says the president. The company has a reputation for excellence built on friendly and reliable service, which it ensures by hiring only the best employees.

By experience, the company knows that customers require consistent personal attention to the fine details of their shipments. It offers competitive rates on loads, from single pallets (skids) to truckloads. The company offers a range of innovative services that provide customers the advantages of choice. It is committed to providing a level of quality and service that consistently exceeds customers' expectations and competitors' performance. Its personalized approach to moving reflects the person behind each move. Because every customer is different, no two household moves are ever the same. When customers have a concern, the company adopts that concern as its own and begins to work toward a moving solution that's right for the client.

To maintain profitability the company must understand what its costs are and how those costs behave under various conditions. Overhead is a cost that must be monitored very carefully. Understanding overhead costs is essential to operating a business. Transportation rates and delivery schedules for long-distance moves (over 125 kilometres) are determined based on the weight of the shipment and the distance from origin to destination. Local moves (under 125 kilometres) are usually charged on an hourly rate.

The company guarantees that it will not employ subcontractors or day labourers. All movers are experienced employees of the company. The company ensures that its employees are qualified, trained packers who will handle the client's belongings with care and expertise.

The company's philosophy is, "The best way to see if something works is to try it—to not be afraid to change things. Some people may find it hard to operate that way."

Until recently, for most companies, direct materials and direct labour were the largest costs of producing a product or providing a service. Overhead was merely another cost, a necessary one but not exceptionally significant. Today most business people are concerned about overhead costs. In manufacturing operations, automation and product variety have caused overhead costs to increase tremendously, while direct labour cost has declined to less than 10% in many companies. In service businesses, overhead costs for marketing, distribution, bonding, and storage continue to rise.

To determine the profitability of various products, managers must understand the factors that drive the overhead costs related to those products. Such information is also needed to ensure that managers can better control overhead costs. Understanding the activities that cause costs to be incurred may help managers make better decisions about product pricing and company strategies.

For a company in the trucking business, it is important to understand how overhead impacts the increase in the number of long-haul versus short-haul jobs. Long-haul jobs require more prorated provincial licence plate fees, more time spent at weight-check stations, and (possibly) more costs to add truck amenities that make the drivers more comfortable.

Once trucking companies know the specific factors that generate overhead costs, they can choose to accept or decline additional long-haul business (a strategic business decision). If they choose to accept more long-haul business and to incur more overhead costs, the additional overhead should be assigned to the business that generated those overhead costs so that an appropriate selling price can be set. Spreading the additional overhead costs across short- and long-haul runs will make the short-haul runs seem less profitable than they actually are and the long-haul runs more profitable than they actually are. Thus, finding the best method to assign overhead to services rendered or units produced is critical.

SOURCE: Adapted from Susan Stellin, "The Movers Are Here," *New York Times,* July 29, 2007.

LEARNING OBJECTIVE **1**

How are predetermined overhead rates developed and how does the selection of a capacity measure affect predetermined overhead rates?

actual cost system
a method of accumulating product or service costs that uses actual direct materials, actual direct labour, and actual overhead costs

CAPACITY MEASURES AND SETTING OVERHEAD RATES

The three elements of production cost are direct materials, direct labour, and overhead. Accountants can use an actual or a normal cost system to accumulate product cost[1] (see Exhibit 4-1). In an **actual cost system**, all cost elements are actual costs. Actual direct materials and direct labour costs are accumulated in Work in Process Inventory (WIP) as they are incurred. Actual overhead costs are accumulated separately from materials and labour and are assigned to WIP at the end of a period. Actual cost systems are less than desirable because they require that all overhead cost information be known before any cost assignment can be made to products or services. Waiting for the information reduces management's ability to make timely operating decisions.

EXHIBIT 4-1
Actual Versus Normal
Cost System

	Actual Cost System	**Normal Cost System**
Direct Materials	Actual cost	Actual cost
Direct Labour	Actual cost	Actual cost
Overhead	Actual cost assigned	Predetermined rate used to assign cost

normal cost system
a method of accumulating product or service costs that uses actual direct materials and direct labour cost, but assigns overhead costs to Work in Process through the use of a predetermined overhead rate

predetermined overhead rate
an estimated constant charge (rate) per unit of activity used to assign overhead costs to production or services

Many companies choose to employ a **normal cost system**, which accumulates actual direct materials and labour costs but uses a predetermined overhead rate (or rates) to assign overhead cost to WIP Inventory. A **predetermined overhead rate** (or OH application rate) is an estimated, average constant charge per unit of activity for a group of related overhead amounts. It is calculated by dividing total estimated annual overhead cost in each group by a related estimated measure of volume or activity of the cost driver. The formula for a predetermined overhead rate is:

$$\text{Predetermined OH rate} = \frac{\text{Total estimated overhead costs}}{\text{Estimated level of related volume or activity}}$$

The time frame over which to estimate the overhead cost and level of activity is typically one year. However, a longer period would be appropriate for, say, a ship-builder or a company that constructs roads, bridges, and office towers.

Fixed overhead costs are incurred in lump sums rather than on a per-service or per-unit basis, which makes assigning these costs to services or units of product a complex task. Applying predetermined overhead rates is more useful than attempting to assign actual costs; generally, it also provides more meaningful information. To illustrate how a predetermined OH rate is calculated, assume that a company has total estimated overhead costs for the year of $1,550,000. Company accountants should determine which of these overhead costs are created by the same cost driver and separate the costs into **cost pools**. Assume that the cost driver of one overhead cost pool of $650,000 is the total number of truck kilometres. Estimated truck kilometres for the current year are 250,000. The predetermined OH rate for mileage related costs is $2.60 per kilometre ($650,000 ÷ 250,000). The remaining $900,000 of overhead costs should be divided into related cost pools, and appropriate cost drivers should be used to establish predetermined rates. There may be hundreds of cost drivers in a business, so to separate costs into that many cost pools would be excessively cumbersome and expensive. Thus, a limited number of drivers should be used to provide a manageable number of cost pools.

cost pool
a grouping of all costs associated with the same activity or cost driver

There are three primary reasons for using predetermined OH rates rather than actual overhead costs for product costing. First, a predetermined overhead rate allows overhead to be assigned to the goods produced or services rendered during the period rather than at the end of the period. If actual overhead costs are assigned, all overhead costs must be known before any assignment can be made. Total overhead costs cannot be determined until all overhead cost transactions of the period have occurred. Thus, the use of a predetermined rate increases the availability of timely information for use in planning, controlling, and decision making.

A second reason to use predetermined OH rates is that they can compensate for fluctuations in actual overhead costs that have nothing to do with activity levels. Overhead may vary on a monthly basis because of seasonal or calendar factors. For instance, factory utility costs may be higher during the summer, due to the need for air conditioning, than at other times of the year. If production were constant each month and actual overhead were assigned to production, the increase in utilities would cause product cost per unit to be greater during the summer months than in other months.

Assume that a company has overhead costs of $220,000 per month, excluding utilities. Utility costs for two months (March and July) are $20,000 and $30,000, respectively. This company makes a single product and defines activity as units of production. Production each month is 20,000 units. The actual overhead cost per unit is calculated as follows:

	March	**July**
$\dfrac{\text{Actual Overhead}}{\text{Actual Units Produced}}$	$\dfrac{\$240,000}{20,000} = \$12$ per unit	$\dfrac{\$250,000}{20,000} = \$12.50$ per unit

While the above example does not show an extreme per-unit difference, it does illustrate the intended point. Using units as an activity basis is only acceptable if the company is manufacturing a single product. Realistically, the product did cost more to make during July. However, that cost differential has nothing to do with the product itself; rather, it has to do with a noncontrollable weather factor: heat. When prices are set on the basis of cost, should an item that is produced in July be priced higher than the same item produced in March to cover the additional cost?

The $0.50 cost differential between these two months is related solely to the $10,000 difference in the numerators, not to any difference in the product itself.

Third, predetermined overhead rates can overcome the problem of fluctuations in activity levels that have no impact on actual fixed overhead costs. Activity levels may vary because of seasons or monthly calendar differences, including holiday periods. Even if total overhead costs were equal each period, changes in activity would cause a per-unit change in cost because of the fixed cost element of overhead.

Suppose that Carlton Movers Ltd. has $357,000 of actual fixed overhead cost in both January and February and defines activity as kilometres driven. The company drives 17,500 and 17,000 kilometres in January and February, respectively. Actual fixed overhead per kilometre increases by $0.60 from January to February:

	January	February
Actual fixed overhead ÷ Actual kilometres	$357,000 ÷ 17,500 = $20.40 per km	$357,000 ÷ 17,000 = $21 per km

Fixed overhead cost per unit changes inversely with changes in activity levels. It is important to realize that this type of fluctuation occurs only in relation to fixed overhead costs. Total variable overhead costs rise in direct proportion to increases in production levels, but the per-unit variable cost does not change.

Since variable and fixed overhead costs behave differently, separate predetermined overhead rates should be developed for the variable and fixed elements of overhead cost. Remember that variable costs increase in total with changes in activity and remain constant on a per-unit basis. Fixed costs, on the other hand, remain constant in total with increases in activity but vary inversely on a per-unit basis with activity changes. Additionally, since costs are caused or driven by different factors, separate predetermined rates should be developed for the various cost pools of an organization.

A fourth reason for using predetermined rates is that it makes the accountant's job significantly easier, because new overhead costs per unit of activity do not have to be calculated each month.

In order to apply overhead properly it is necessary to examine costs at different levels of activity. Using the various cost formulas developed through the use of the scattergraph, high–low, or regression analysis methods that were discussed in Chapter 2, managers can estimate overhead costs at various activity levels. These estimated overhead costs can be presented in a series of financial plans that detail the individual cost factors comprising total cost and then present those costs at the different levels of activity. Costs are treated as either variable or fixed, meaning that mixed costs are separated into their variable and fixed components.

LEARNING OBJECTIVE 2

Why are separate predetermined overhead rates generally more useful than combined rates?

DEVELOPING AND USING PREDETERMINED OVERHEAD RATES

With the detailed information about overhead, companies can compute separate overhead rates for variable and fixed overhead costs.

Variable Overhead Rate

Variable overhead (VOH) is that amount of overhead which changes proportionately in total with some measure of volume or activity. It includes indirect materials, variable indirect labour costs, and the variable portion of any mixed cost. A predetermined overhead rate should be computed for each variable overhead cost pool that is caused by a different cost driver. The information needed for these computations can be taken from any level of activity that is within the relevant range. Total cost for each cost pool is then divided by the level of activity on which the estimate was based. Variable overhead will be applied to production using the related activity base.

Since VOH is assumed to be constant per unit at all activity levels within the relevant range, the activity level chosen to estimate total variable cost is unimportant. For example, at Bartiromo Ltd., a small moving company run by students on the weekends, the total kilometres per year amount to 25,000. At this level of activity the company estimates that $2,500 of cost will be incurred for indirect materials. These estimates give a predetermined variable overhead rate for indirect materials of $0.10 per kilometre ($2,500 ÷ 25,000 kilometres). Correspondingly, if indirect materials cost is truly variable, the company will have estimated a total cost of $3,600 for 36,000 kilometres, or the same $0.10 per kilometre.

The activity base or cost driver selected should be one that provides a logical relationship between the driver and the overhead cost incurrence. The cost driver that generally first comes to mind is volume. However, unless a company makes only one type of output, volume is not really a feasible activity measure for an overhead cost. If multiple products or services are produced, overhead costs will be incurred because of numerous factors, including the differing nature of the items, product variety, and product complexity.

Virtually all cost assignment involves averaging. If heterogeneous products are produced, or heterogeneous services are performed, some common denominator or set of common denominators must be used that is homogeneous to all products and services so that the averaging process used to assign overhead will be meaningful.

The concept of homogeneity underlies all cost allocation. Some measure of activity that is common to all costs in a given cost pool must be determined in order to allocate overhead to heterogeneous products and services. The volume measures used most often and appropriately include direct labour hours, direct labour dollars, machine hours, production orders, engineering change orders, or some product-related physical measure such as litres. Direct labour hours and direct labour dollars have long been the most commonly used measures of activity in a labour-intensive operation.

As technology and the manufacturing environment change, companies need to recognize that they may have to adjust their cost information systems. Using a less-than-appropriate allocation base and a minimal number of cost pools can result in poor managerial information. The failure of traditional, labour-based, single/double pool systems to accurately assign costs is becoming more apparent as companies automate, increase the number and variety of product lines, and incur higher overhead costs than ever before.

For example, using direct labour to allocate overhead costs in highly automated plants results in extremely large overhead rates because the costs are applied over an ever-decreasing number of labour hours (or dollars). When automated plants allocate overhead on the basis of labour, managers are often concerned about the high rates per labour hour. Often they conclude that the way to reduce overhead is to reduce labour. This conclusion is erroneous. The overhead charge is high because labour is low; further reducing labour will simply increase the overhead rate! In highly automated plants, if only one activity base is to be used for overhead allocations, machine hours will be a more appropriate base than either direct labour hours or direct labour dollars.

Many companies are looking at multiple cost pools and new activity measures for overhead allocation, including number or time of machine setups, number of different parts, material handling time, and quantity of product defects.[2] Regardless of how many cost pools are created or which activity base is chosen, the method of

The company pictured uses minimal operator involvement. In such a situation it is highly unlikely that direct labour is an appropriate basis on which to assign overhead costs to products.

overhead application is the same. The predetermined overhead rate is used in a normal costing system to apply or assign overhead to WIP Inventory based on the actual quantity of the activity base used. At this time, for simplicity, separate cost pools for variable and fixed overhead will be assumed, as will a single activity measure to allocate each.

To illustrate the calculation of predetermined variable overhead, rate information for the Jack Abbott Manufacturing Corporation is given in Exhibit 4-2. The company uses machine hours to compute its predetermined variable overhead rate,

EXHIBIT 4-2

The Jack Abbott Manufacturing Corporation Predetermined Variable Overhead Rate Calculation

---

1. Estimate total machine hours (MHs) for planned output for 2010   100,000 MHs

2. Estimate total cost of each component at a selected level of 2010 activity:

	Total Estimated Cost at 100,000 MHs
Estimated variable indirect labour	$ 40,000
Estimated indirect materials	20,000
Estimated variable utilities and variable portion of other mixed costs	260,000
Total estimated variable overhead cost	$320,000

3. Divide the total estimated variable overhead cost by the selected level of activity (MHs) to find the total predetermined variable overhead rate:

Total estimated variable overhead cost at 100,000 machine hours ÷ 100,000 machine hours

   = $320,000 ÷ 100,000 machine hours
   = $3.20 per MH

Note: The above computation produces the necessary information for product costing purposes, but it does not provide the detail needed by managers. For example, to plan or control variable overhead costs, managers need the individual costs per unit of activity shown below:

Estimated variable indirect labour	$ 40,000 ÷ 100,000 = $ 0.40
Estimated indirect materials	20,000 ÷ 100,000 = $ 0.20
Estimated variable utilities and variable portion of other mixed costs	260,000 ÷ 100,000 = $ 2.60

because the company is highly automated and most variable overhead costs are created through machinery use. Computation of the predetermined rate is made in 2009, using estimated variable overhead and estimated machine hours for 2010. Predetermined overhead calculations are always made in advance of the year of application. As machine hours are used in 2010, charges will be made to WIP Inventory to record overhead cost using the predetermined rate. The process of making this assignment is shown in Exhibit 4-3 on page 180.

Fixed Overhead Rate

Fixed overhead (FOH) is that portion of total overhead that remains constant in total with changes in activity within the relevant range. Fixed overhead includes manufacturing supervisors' salaries, straight-line depreciation on factory buildings and equipment, and the fixed portion of mixed manufacturing costs. Estimates must be made for all fixed overhead costs; these estimates are then assigned to appropriate cost pools to make up the numerator of the predetermined overhead rate calculations.

Since fixed overhead is constant in total, it varies inversely on a per-unit basis with changes in activity; therefore, a different unit cost will result at every different level of activity. Thus, a particular level of activity must be specified in order to calculate the predetermined rate per measurement unit. This level of activity is usually stated as the **expected activity** for the firm for the upcoming period. Expected activity is a short-run concept representing the anticipated level of activity for the upcoming year. If actual results are close to expected results (both dollar and volume), this capacity measure should result in product costs that most closely reflect actual historical costs.

expected activity
a short-run concept representing the anticipated level of activity for the upcoming year

Companies may choose to use some activity level other than expected activity to compute their predetermined fixed overhead rates. Alternative measurement bases include theoretical, practical, or normal capacity. It is appropriate to think of these levels in terms of any relevant measure of activity. For example, the capacity of the purchasing department could be measured by the number of purchase orders that could be processed.

The estimated absolute maximum potential activity that could occur during a specified time frame is called **theoretical capacity**. This measure assumes that all production factors are operating perfectly; as such, it disregards realities such as machinery breakdowns and reduced or halted plant operation on holidays. Because of the unrealistic assumptions, theoretical capacity is generally considered an unacceptable basis for overhead application. Reducing theoretical capacity by ongoing, regular operating interruptions (such as holidays, downtime, and start-up time) provides the **practical capacity** that could be achieved during regular working hours. This measure is a more reasonable basis of activity measurement than theoretical capacity, but it is still not probable if the goal is to consistently attain practical capacity.

theoretical capacity
some estimated absolute maximum potential activity that could occur during a specific time frame

practical capacity
the activity level that could be achieved during normal working hours giving consideration to ongoing, regular operating interruptions, such as holidays, downtime, and start-up time

Sometimes managers wish to give consideration to historical and estimated future production levels and to cyclical and seasonal fluctuations. Therefore, they may use a **normal capacity** measure that encompasses the long-run (5 to 10 years) average activity of the firm. This measurement represents a reasonably attainable level of activity, but it still will not provide costs that are most similar to actual costs. Distortions of cost could arise if activity levels varied significantly within the long-run period.

normal capacity
the long-run (5 to 10 years) average activity of the firm that gives effect to historical and estimated future production levels and to cyclical and seasonal fluctuations

To continue the Jack Abbott Manufacturing Corporation example, information on the company's estimated machine-related fixed overhead costs is given in

Exhibit 4-3. Total estimated fixed overhead for this cost pool for fiscal 2009 is $178,000; expected activity is 100,000 machine hours. Using these estimates, the predetermined fixed overhead rate is calculated as $1.78 per machine hour.

EXHIBIT 4-3

The Jack Abbott Manufacturing Corporation Predetermined Fixed Overhead Rate Calculation

Estimated machine-related fixed overhead costs for fiscal 2010:	
Straight-line depreciation on machines	$ 62,000
Machine lease payments	13,000
Machine insurance	16,000
Machine maintenance workers' salaries	53,000
Fixed portion of utilities	34,000
Total estimated fixed costs	$178,000

Total estimated machine-related fixed overhead ÷ 100,000 machine hours

$178,000 ÷ 100,000 = $1.78 per MH

OVERHEAD APPLICATION

Once the variable and fixed predetermined overhead rates are calculated, they are used throughout the following year to apply overhead to WIP. Overhead may be applied as production occurs, when goods or services are transferred out of WIP Inventory, or at the end of each month. **Applied overhead** is the amount of overhead assigned to WIP as a result of incurring the activity that was used to develop the application rate. Application is made using the predetermined rates and the actual level of activity.

Jack Abbott Manufacturing Corporation maintains a variable overhead account as well as a fixed overhead account. When overhead is incurred, the overhead account is debited and cash or a receivable is credited. These entries, for actual overhead incurred, are as follows:

applied overhead
the amount of overhead assigned to WIP Inventory as a result of incurring the activity that was used to develop the application rate; computed by multiplying the quantity of actual activity by the predetermined rate

Variable Manufacturing Overhead	8,800	
Accounts Payable/Cash		8,800
To record overhead incurred		
Fixed Manufacturing Overhead	5,990	
Accounts Payable/Cash		5,990
To record overhead incurred		

To illustrate the application process, assume that during January 2010 the Jack Abbott Manufacturing Corporation's machines run 3,000 hours. Using the calculation from Exhibit 4-2 on page 178, variable overhead is applied at the rate of $3.20 per machine hour. Thus, variable machine-related overhead for the month is $9,600 (3,000 × $3.20).

Using the fixed OH rate computed in Exhibit 4-3, $5,340 (3,000 × $1.78) of fixed machine-related overhead is applied to WIP Inventory. When overhead is applied to work in process, Work in Process Inventory is debited and the appropriate overhead account is credited. Thus the journal entries to apply January machine-related overhead for the corporation are:

Work in Process Inventory	9,600	
Variable Overhead		9,600
To apply machine-related variable overhead for January.		
Work in Process Inventory	5,340	
Fixed Overhead		5,340
To apply machine-related fixed overhead for January.		

At this point the overheard accounts appear as follows:

Variable Manufacturing Overhead		Fixed Manufacturing Overhead	
Actual Overhead Costs	Applied Overhead Costs	Actual Overhead Costs	Applied Overhead Costs
8,800	9,600	5,990	5,340

Under- and Overapplied Overhead

While companies may be able to estimate future overhead costs and expected activity with some degree of accuracy, there is simply a human inability to precisely project future events. Thus, actual overhead incurred during a period will rarely, if ever, equal applied overhead. This inequality of amounts represents under- or over-applied overhead. When the amount of overhead applied to Work in Process is less than actual overhead, the overhead is said to be **underapplied**. The opposite situation (applying more overhead to Work in Process than was actually incurred) is referred to as **overapplied overhead**.

Choice of capacity level has its impact on the amount of fixed manufacturing overhead applied to products. Assignment of Direct Material, Direct Labour, and Variable Overhead is virtually unaffected by the choice. Use of theoretical or practical capacity would typically result in underapplied overhead at the end of the year.

It is important to note that the incurrence of actual manufacturing overhead costs does not affect the process of overhead application. Actual manufacturing overhead costs may be recorded in the accounts on a daily, weekly, or monthly basis. Those overhead costs are created because activity takes place in the production area of the company. The application of predetermined overhead is based on the predetermined overhead rate multiplied by the actual quantity of the cost driver. Thus, applied overhead is the amount of overhead assigned to Work in Process Inventory as a result of incurring the activity that was used to develop the application rate.

Applied overhead is only indirectly related to the amount of actual overhead cost incurred by the company. Overhead is applied to Work in Process as a representation of actual costs incurred, while applied overhead is directly related to the amount of actual activity incurred. This direct relationship exists because application is based on the predetermined estimated rate multiplied by the actual activity.

The manufacturing overhead accounts used for recording actual and applied overhead amounts are temporary accounts. The amount of under- or overapplied overhead must be closed at the end of the period because expected activity was used to develop the predetermined rate. Since expected activity refers to a one-year time frame, disposition of the balance of under- or overapplied overhead should take place at year-end.

underapplied overhead
an occurrence that results when the overhead applied to Work in Process Inventory is less than actual overhead

overapplied overhead
an occurrence that results when the overhead applied to Work in Process is greater than actual overhead

DISPOSITION OF UNDER- AND OVERAPPLIED OVERHEAD

LEARNING OBJECTIVE 3

How is underapplied or overapplied overhead accounted for at year-end and why are these accounting techniques appropriate?

In a typical costing system, as actual overhead costs are incurred they are debited to the variable and fixed overhead general ledger accounts and credited to the various sources of overhead costs. Applied overhead is debited to Work in Process using the predetermined rates and credited to the variable and fixed overhead general ledger accounts. Applied overhead is added to actual direct materials and actual direct labour costs in the development of the amount of cost of goods manufactured.

The end-of-period balance in each overhead general ledger account represents underapplied (debit) or overapplied (credit) overhead.

Normally, a firm waits until the end of the year to account for any differences between incurred and applied overhead. In our example the firm uses both a fixed manufacturing overhead account and a variable manufacturing overhead account. At month end the overhead accounts are as shown below:

Variable Manufacturing Overhead		Fixed Manufacturing Overhead	
8,800	9,600	5,990	5,340

The amount of variable manufacturing overhead incurred was $8,800, which is evidenced by the debit to the variable manufacturing overhead account. The amount of variable overhead applied was $9,600, based on the predetermined rate. The amount applied was $800 greater than what was incurred. This means that the estimated amount of overhead charged to the manufacturing process was greater than the amount incurred.

The amount of the fixed manufacturing overhead incurred was $5,990, but the amount applied was only $5,340. Since the amount applied is $650 less than the amount incurred, fixed manufacturing overhead is underapplied by $650. Therefore the amount of fixed overhead charged to the manufacturing process was less than what was incurred.

Disposition of underapplied or overapplied manufacturing overhead depends on the materiality (significance) of the amount involved. If the amount of the difference is immaterial (small), it is closed to Cost of Goods Sold or Cost of Services Rendered in a services firm. When overapplied overhead is closed (credit balance), it causes the balance in Cost of Goods Sold (or Cost of Services Rendered) to decrease because too much overhead was applied to production during the period. Alternatively, closing underapplied overhead (debit balance) causes Cost of Goods Sold (or Cost of Services Rendered) to increase because not enough overhead was applied to production during the period.

In this case these amounts are considered immaterial (small); thus the journal entries to close these balances is as follows:

Variable Manufacturing Overhead	800	
Cost of Goods Sold		800
To close overapplied variable manufacturing overhead to cost of goods sold.		
Cost of Goods Sold	650	
Fixed Manufacturing Overhead		650
To close underapplied fixed manufacturing overhead to cost of goods sold.		

It is important to understand the nature of these entries. Since too much variable overhead has been charged to the manufacturing process, the entry credits Cost of Goods Sold for $800. By this entry, the overcharge of $800 is taken out of Cost of Goods Sold. The Variable Manufacturing Overhead account now has a zero balance and is ready for the next period's entries.

In the case of Fixed Manufacturing Overhead—it was underapplied. The above entry shows that the $650, which had not been charged to Work in Process Inventory, but which had been incurred, is now added to Cost of Goods Sold.

Fixed Manufacturing Overhead is also closed to a zero balance. As a result of these entries, Cost of Goods Sold now has a balance of $19,850. The ledger accounts after these entries are posted appear as follows:

Variable Manufacturing Overhead

8,800	9,600
800	
9,600	

Fixed Manufacturing Overhead

5,990	5,340
	650
	5,990

Cost of Goods Sold

	20,000	800
	650	
	20,650	
Balance	19,850	

Allocating Significant Over- and Underapplied Manufacturing Overhead

If the amount of underapplied or overapplied manufacturing overhead is significant (large), it should be allocated among the accounts containing applied overhead (Work in Process Inventory, Finished Goods Inventory, and Cost of Goods Sold or Cost of Services Rendered). Allocation to the accounts is based on the relative ending account balances. A significant amount of underapplied or overapplied manufacturing overhead means that the balances in these accounts are quite different from what they would have been had actual overhead costs been assigned to production. The underapplied or overapplied amount is allocated among the affected accounts so that their balances conform more closely to actual costs as required for external reporting by GAAP.

Exhibit 4-4 on page 184 uses assumed amounts to illustrate the technique of apportioning overapplied variable manufacturing overhead among the necessary accounts. Had the amount been underapplied, the accounts debited and credited in the journal entry would have been reversed. The computations would also not have differed if the overhead had been fixed rather than variable.

Managers feel that the use of predetermined overhead rates for fixed overhead allocation is a dilemma because when the economy turns down and production declines from the estimated numbers that were used to set the predetermined overhead, units are being charged with capacity charges over which they have no control. They feel that the cost of the units will be increased because fixed costs will be spread over fewer numbers of items that are being produced. The CICA recognizes that underapplied fixed overhead that occurs in these periods should be shown as a lump sum on the income statement as opposed to being allocated to cost of goods sold or to prorated to work in process, finished goods, and cost of goods sold. Section 3031.13 of the *CICA Handbook* states the following:

> The allocation of fixed production overheads to the costs of conversion is based on the normal capacity of the production facilities. Normal capacity is the production expected to be achieved on average over a number of periods or seasons under normal circumstances . . .
> Unallocated "fixed" overhead is recognized as an expense in the period in which they are incurred. In periods of abnormally high production, the amount of fixed overhead allocated to each unit of production is decreased so that inventories are not measured above cost.

EXHIBIT 4-4

Apportioning Overapplied
Overhead

Variable Manufacturing Overhead Balance	
Actual	$293,600
Applied	377,800
Overapplied	$ 84,200

Variable Manufacturing Overhead			
Actual	293,600	Applied	377,800
		Balance	84,200

Steps to follow:

1. Calculate the ratio of the balances of each of the affected accounts to their total amount.

	VOH Balance	Proportion	Percentage
Work in Process	$ 234,000	$234,000 ÷ $1,560,000	15%
Finished Goods	390,000	$390,000 ÷ 1,560,000	25%
Cost of Goods Sold	936,000	$936,000 ÷ 1,560,000	60%
Total	$1,560,000		100%

2. Multiply percentages times overapplied variable overhead amount to determine the amount of adjustment needed:

	%	×	Overapplied VOH	= Adjustment Amount
Work in Process	15%	×	$84,200	$12,630
Finished Goods	25%	×	$84,200	21,050
Cost of Goods Sold	60%	×	$84,200	50,520

3. Prepare journal entry to close variable manufacturing overhead account and assign adjustment amount to appropriate accounts:

Variable Overhead	84,200	
Work in Process		12,630
Finished Goods		21,050
Cost of Goods Sold		50,520

With regard to variable overhead, the CICA states that "variable production overheads are allocated to each unit of production on the basis of the actual use of the production facilities."

Using predetermined overhead rates (if based on valid cost drivers) provides a rational and systematic manner of assigning overhead costs to products for external financial statement preparation. Separate variable and fixed overhead rates and accounts developed using separate cost pools provide more refined information for planning, controlling, and decision making. Despite this, companies may (and commonly do) choose to use combined overhead rates rather than separate ones for variable and fixed overhead.

COMBINED OVERHEAD RATES

Companies may use a single overhead application rate rather than separate rates for the numerous variable and fixed overhead cost pools. The single rate can be related to a particular cost pool (such as machine related overhead) or to overhead costs in general. Combined overhead rates are traditional in businesses for three reasons: clerical ease, cost savings, and no requirement to separate overhead costs by cost behaviour.

The calculation of a combined predetermined overhead rate requires specification of an expected activity level because of the behaviour of fixed costs. All variable and fixed overhead costs at the expected activity level are estimated and totalled.

The summation is divided by the expected activity level to derive the single overhead application rate.

Assume that the Jack Abbott Manufacturing Corporation (from Exhibits 4-2 and 4-3) decides to use a combined predetermined overhead rate for machine-related overhead costs. The company designates 100,000 machine hours as its expected activity level. Abbott's combined predetermined machine-related overhead rate is calculated as follows:

Total estimated machine-related variable overhead at	
100,000 MH (from Exhibit 4-2)	$320,000
Total estimated machine-related FOH	
(from Exhibit 4-3 and the same at	
any number of machine hours within	
the relevant range)	178,000
Total estimated machine-related OH cost	$498,000
Divided by expected activity in machine hours	÷100,000
Predetermined overhead rate per machine hour	$4.98

For each machine hour used in 2010, Abbott's Work in Process account will be charged with $4.98 of overhead. (This single rate is equal to the sum of the variable and fixed rates calculated earlier on page 180.) Thus, when Abbott uses 3,000 machine hours in January, it will apply overhead as follows:

Work in Process Inventory	14,940	
Machine-Related Overhead		14,940
To apply machine-related overhead for January		

While this particular entry provides the same total application to WIP Inventory as did the variable and fixed entries, Abbott's managers have eliminated an important source of information about overhead costs.

Assume that the total machine use during 2010 was 95,000 hours and that the actual overhead costs were exactly as estimated: Variable—$3.20 per machine hour and $178,000 in total for fixed.

Total actual overhead costs would be $482,000 ($304,000 + $178,000)
Total applied overhead would be $473,100 ($4.98 x 95,000).

Using separate rates, the applied overhead would have been

Variable	$304,000 ($3.20 × 95,000)
Fixed	$169,100 ($1.78 × 95,000)

The $8,900 ($482,000 − $473,100) of underapplied overhead is specifically caused by fixed overhead, not by variable overhead—a fact not observable from the combined rate.

As the degree of aggregation increases from simply combining related cost pools to combining all manufacturing overhead, information may become more and more distorted.

USING PLANTWIDE VS DEPARTMENTAL OVERHEAD RATES

Gordon Company Ltd.'s information is used to provide a simple example of the differing results obtained between using a departmental and a plantwide overhead rate. The company has two departments: Assembly and Finishing. Assembly work is performed by robots, and a large portion of this department's overhead cost consists of depreciation and electricity charges. Finishing work is performed manually by skilled labourers, and most charges in this department are for labour, fringe benefits, indirect materials, and supplies.

Gordon Company makes two products: A and B.

	Assembly Department	**Finishing Department**
Product A	5 machine hours	1 direct labour hour
Product B	2 machine hours	3 direct labour hours

Exhibit 4-5 provides information about estimated overhead costs and activity measures and shows the computations of departmental and plantwide overhead rates. Product overhead application amounts for A and B are also given.

Note the significant difference in the overhead applied to each product using departmental versus plantwide rates. If departmental rates are used, product cost

EXHIBIT 4-5

Gordon Company Ltd.
Departmental Versus Plantwide
Overhead Rates

	Assembly	**Finishing**
Estimated annual overhead	$300,200	$99,800
Estimated annual direct labour hours (DLH)	5,000	20,000
Estimated annual machine hours (MH)	38,000	2,000

Departmental overhead rates:
Assembly (automated) $300,200 ÷ 38,000 = $7.90 per MH
Finishing (manual) $ 99,800 ÷ 20,000 = $4.99 per DLH

Total plantwide overhead $300,200 + $99,800 = $400,000
Plantwide overhead rate (using MH) $400,000 ÷ 40,000 = $10.00
Plantwide overhead rate (using DLH) $400,000 ÷ 25,000 = $16.00

	Overhead Assigned			
	To Product A		**To Product B**	
Using departmental rates:				
Assembly	5 × $7.90	$39.50	2 × $7.90 =	$15.80
Finishing	1 × $4.99	4.99	3 × $4.99 =	14.97
Total		$44.49		$30.77
Using plantwide rate:				
based on MH	5 × $10.00	$50.00	2($10.00) =	$20.00
based on DLH	1 × $16.00	$16.00	3($16.00) =	$48.00

more clearly reflects the different amounts and types of machine/labour work performed on the two products. If a plantwide rate is used, essentially each product only absorbs overhead from a single department—from Assembly if machine hours are used and from Finishing if direct labour hours are used. Use of either of these plantwide rates ignores the dissimilarity of work performed in the two departments.

Use of plantwide overhead rates rather than departmental rates may also contribute to problems in product pricing. While selling prices must be reflective of market conditions, management typically uses cost as a starting point for setting prices. If plantwide rates distort the true cost of a product, selling prices may be set too low or too high, causing management to make incorrect decisions.

Assume in the case of Gordon Company that direct materials and direct labour costs for Product A are $5 and $35, respectively. Adding the various overhead amounts to these prime costs gives the total product cost under each method. Exhibit 4-6 shows these product costs and the profit or loss that would be indicated if Product A has a normal market selling price of $105.00.

	Departmental Rates	Plantwide Rate (MH)	Plantwide Rate (DLH)
Direct materials	$ 5.00	$ 5.00	$ 5.00
Direct labour	35.00	35.00	35.00
Overhead	44.49	50.00	16.00
Total cost	$ 84.49	$ 90.00	$ 56.00
Selling price	$105.00	$105.00	$105.00
Gross profit	$ 20.51	$ 15.00	$ 49.00
Rate of profit	19.5%	14.3%	46.7%

EXHIBIT 4-6

Gordon Company Total Product Costs and Profits

Use of the product costs developed from plantwide rates could cause Gordon's management to make erroneous decisions about Product A. If the cost figure developed from a plantwide direct labour hour basis is used, management may think that Product A is significantly more successful than it actually is. Such a decision could cause resources to be diverted from other products. If the cost which contains overhead based on the plantwide machine hour allocation is used, management may believe that Product A should not be produced, since it appears not to be generating a very substantial gross profit. In either instance, assuming that machine hours and direct labour hours are the best possible allocation bases for the Assembly and Finishing Departments, respectively, the only cost that gives management the necessary information on which to make resource allocation and product development/elimination decisions is the one produced by using the departmental overhead rates.

While clerical cost savings may result from the use of a combined rate, the ultimate costs of poor information are significantly greater than the savings that are generated. Combined rates result in a lack of detail that hinders managers' ability to plan operations, control costs, and make decisions. Additionally, cause–effect relationships between costs and activities are blurred when combined rates are used. This factor may contribute to an inability to reduce costs or improve productivity.

Even retail stores incur overhead costs. In contrast, open-air markets allow merchants to eliminate the many fixed overhead costs associated with capital facilities—depreciation, utilities, property taxes, and so forth.

Since most companies produce a wide variety of products or perform a wide variety of services, different activity measures are normally necessary in different departments of the same company and for different types of overhead costs. Machine hours may be the most appropriate activity base in a department that is highly automated. Direct labour hours may be the best basis for assigning most overhead costs in a labour-intensive department. In the quality control area, the number of defects may provide the best allocation base. Separate departmental and cost-pool activity bases are generally thought to be superior to a combined, plantwide base, because they allow cost accumulation and cost application to be more homogeneous. Different rates will provide better information for planning, control, performance evaluation, and decision making. The following News Note discusses the need for complete information in order to make good decisions.

GENERAL NEWS NOTE

Distorted Information Leads to Distorted Decisions

"Not everything that counts can be counted and not everything that can be counted counts," read a sign in Einstein's office.

Armed with so-called dashboard displays on their PCs, CEOs can effortlessly summon up a cornucopia of performance indicators. Call up this week's sales by product line; throw in profit by region, cost per widget produced, and change in inventory levels. Compare it all with last week, with the same week last year, and with forecasts and goals. And there you have it: a comprehensive guide to the organization's performance and what you need to do to improve it.

If only it were that easy. The fact is, this sort of data worship can provide a distorted, misleading view of what's going on, and it can lead to flat-out bad decisions. Part of the problem is that some of the most important inputs aren't easily quantifiable. Things that are hard to quantify tend to get left out of the decision-making process. This isn't a new problem. Managers have always had a misplaced confidence in numbers. But the ability to do more and more with the data in an increasingly high-tech fashion is making things worse. Indeed, the availability of slick new data-crunching tools, and the hype they're receiving, has lead executives to rely on them more.

Sometimes the data that go into a dashboard are incomplete or biased in subtle but significant ways that can lead a manager astray. Even when the data are complete, there are plenty of ways to misinterpret it. None of this is to say that dashboards are the enemy here. Indeed, CEOs probably get into more trouble when they fail to bring enough data into the decision-making process.

SOURCE: David H. Freedman, "What's Next: The Dashboard Dilemma. Do You Manage by the Numbers? Be Careful If You Do: Your Data May Be Playing Tricks on You," *Inc.*, November 2006, p. 59.

To compute the cost of products, it is necessary to decide on (1) the product costing system, and (2) the valuation method to be used. The costing system valuation method specifies how the costs will be measured. Companies must have both a cost system and a valuation method. These activities are necessary for strategic success.

When it comes to moving companies, for instance, because the cost of a move is typically based on the total weight of the items moved, the distance they will travel, and many other variables, the cost of each move will be different. The other variables that must be considered are whether any items require special handling, whether the movers have to climb stairs, and the price of fuel, among other factors.[3]

The rest of this chapter introduces and discusses the job order costing system that would be used by Myster Mover and other companies that produce customized products and provide customized services.

JOB ORDER COSTING SYSTEM

Product costing is concerned with (1) cost identification, (2) cost management, and (3) product cost assignment. In a **job order costing system**, costs are accumulated individually by **job**—defined as a single unit[4]—or a group of like units identifiable as being produced to distinct customer specifications.

> There are thousands of printers throughout the world, from Helsinki to Auckland, from Vladivostok to Cape Town, from Beirut to Hong Kong. No two print jobs are identical, no two print shops are the same, and the needs of no two print customers are exact counterparts.
>
> The basic economic problem of printers is pricing their conversion service for hundreds of different jobs using technology that is [constantly] shifting. Printers try to predict the cost of a job in order to mark it up for pricing. . . . Many hours of effort are devoted to job cost predictions.[5]

Becky Douthat, vice president of National Business Forms, says that current sales and growth will come primarily from more specialized products.

> Plain vanilla traditional product orders are down. Customized invoices and statements can make a big difference in the impression and end-users' customers have of the firm and serve as effective marketing tools. Emphasize that those documents are all about the company, and they should want to look nice and appealing.[6]

Building a specialized product to order is not what could be called mass manufacturing! But, like making any other product, it requires converting raw materials to a finished product through the use of direct labour and manufacturing overhead. Since each order is substantially different from any other order, it would be very difficult to develop a set of costs for this process. A method of costing called job order costing is used to record the conversion process.

The following News Note describes how customization has increased the use of job costing.

Customization and Job Costing

Remember when the ultimate in personalizing a gift was adding a monogram? Today, inscribing initials on luggage or towels seems quaintly old-fashioned compared to what's available on the Web. Thanks to improvements in software that displays customized goods online, guides users through the selection process, and automates production, individualizing a gift has gotten far more sophisticated—and, dare we say, trendy—this holiday season. Go really crazy and send in a photo—you can have the child's freckle pattern replicated on the actual doll. "There are 42,000 combinations of dolls available without doing anything special," says Gary Lindsey, vice-president for marketing with ETOYS ....

Customization—which requires painstaking, detailed labour—used to be the privilege of the rich. But thanks to the Internet, shoppers can instantly purchase custom-made goods online, creating the necessary volume that retailers need to justify the costs and make such products affordable to all consumers.

SHOPPERS DRUG MART, for example, has been acquiring data on the purchasing habits of its customers through its Optimum Rewards card. It recently started sending out customized offers to clients, based on what it knows. For example, clients who buy diapers regularly will receive a Shoppers offer for HUGGIES.

GENERAL NEWS NOTE

BREAKING NEWS

GENERAL NEWS NOTE

Job order costing is useful for companies like DELL COMPUTER CORPORATION, which concentrates on direct selling to customers on the Internet. The company configures computers to meet each customer's needs. The use of job order costing allows the costs and profits of each job to be known.

Not only is customization available on the Web, we see, even with the proliferation of off-the-rack clothing and shirt sales galore, there is obviously still a thriving market for custom-sewn cotton shirts.

Forget about the facial scrub, paraffin pedicures, and the yoga mat. These may be standard issue for the modern male metrosexual but there remains one thing that separates a gentleman from the trendy crowd—a bespoke shirt.

A handmade shirt will cost you anywhere from $250 to $1,000 depending on the detail and the fabric. A bespoke shirt has at least 33 separate features, including a customized 12-part collar, sleeves cut on the straight grain to avoid twisting, a split yoke, and lock-stitched buttons sewn in a "H" rather than "X" formation. If there are any checks or stripes, they'll be perfectly matched. The bespoke shirt's most distinguishing characteristic is a perfect fit.

Think you've got the right clubs in your golf bag? COBRA GOLF wants to make sure. Cobra fitting specialists measure how fast and how far a player hits the ball with a driver and takes into account other metrics of ability and performance. The end result? A set of clubs custom-made for you at Cobra's manufacturing facility. The cost is about $1,500, including the bag. A custom-fitting session is part art and part science. "We have our Cobra Speed Monitor measure ball speed, launch angle, and average distance" "That's very helpful, but you also need to get a feel for the player that you're fitting—where they miss shots most often, typical ball flight, and shot dispersion. These aspects all factor into getting the best clubs into a player's bag."

Companies that are job or project oriented, such as those in construction-related fields, need to track costs by project, and a system such as XBRL GL framework may be an important tool in running these companies efficiently. Job-oriented industries are different from retail, process/repetitive manufacturing and distribution in that costs are tracked more directly to a specific job rather than repeatedly spread over many homogeneous products. Construction projects in particular typically have long life cycles, and multiple parties, such as subcontractors, are involved in different activities within the job or project. This determines the need to keep appropriate track of events and resources as the project progresses toward completion. Job costing is crucial for construction companies, and the capability to track multiple jobs with the related phases and cost codes is a key feature in this respect.

SOURCES: "Web Retailing Gets Really Personal," by Amey Stone, *Business Week*, November 2004; Thomas Lee, "I Want It My Way," *St. Louis Post–Dispatch*, April 18, 2003; Susan Heinrich, "Direct Marketing Gets Xerox Makeover," *Financial Post*, November 15, 2004; Cheryl Caswell, "Not Just Off the Cuff; Fourth-Generation Tailor Finds There's Still a Market for Custom-Made Clothing," *Charleston Daily Mail*, November 26, 2001; Deirdre McMurdy, "Bespoke Shirts a Cuff Above," *Financial Post*, September 16, 2006, FWZ; Monica Gagnier, "A Set of Clubs Made Just for You," *Business Week*, May 29, 2007; G. Garbellotto, "XBRL GL by Industry: Construction and Job Costing," *Strategic Financial*, September 2007, p. 59.

Each job in a job costing system is treated as a unique "cost entity" or cost object. Job costing is used in situations where products consume different amount of inputs and where accurate cost information for each product or job is essential.[7]

Costs of different jobs are maintained in separate subsidiary ledger accounts and are not added together or commingled in the ledger accounts. The logic of separating costs for individual jobs is shown by the following example. During March, Dan Ondrack, an artist, made drawings and three small to-scale clay models, each for a different customer. When completed, one of the models will be 33 metres high, the second one will be 12 metres, and the third will be 27 metres. To total all of Ondrack's business costs for March and to divide them by the three projects would produce a meaningless average cost for each project. This type of average cost per job would be equally meaningless in any entity that manufactures products or provides services geared to unique customer specifications. Since job results are heterogeneous and distinctive in nature, the costs of those jobs are, logically, not averageable.

Exhibit 4-7 provides the Work in Process control and subsidiary ledger accounts for Ondrack's job order product costing system. Note that the ending balance of the Work in Process Control account is the sum of the three subsidiary ledger accounts.

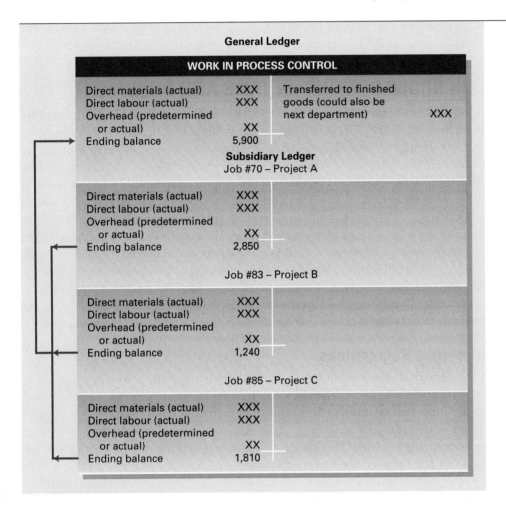

EXHIBIT 4-7

Separate Subsidiary Ledger Accounts for Jobs

The usual production costs of direct materials, direct labour, and manufacturing overhead are accumulated for each job. The typical job order inventory accounts use actual direct materials and actual direct labour cost combined with predetermined overhead rates multiplied by some actual cost driver (such as direct labour hours, cost or quantity of materials used, or number of materials requisitions). This method is called normal costing and is used because actual direct material and actual direct labour costs are fairly easy to identify and can be associated with a particular job.[8]

Overhead costs are not usually traceable to specific jobs and must be allocated to production. For example, Ondrack's electricity cost during March is related to all jobs worked on during that month. It would be difficult, if not impossible, to accurately determine which jobs created the need for what amount of electricity. To help ensure the proper recording of costs, the amounts appearing in the subsidiary ledger accounts are periodically compared and reconciled to the Work in Process Inventory control account in the general ledger.

The output of a given job can be a single unit or multiple similar or dissimilar units. For example, Ondrack's output is a clay model of each customer's contracted-for project. If a job's output is a single product, the total costs accumulated for the job are assigned to the individual unit. When multiple outputs result, a unit cost may only be computed if the units are similar. In such a case, the total accumulated job cost is averaged over the number of units produced to determine a cost per unit. If the output consisted of dissimilar units (for instance, if all Ondrack's three projects were for the same customer), no cost per unit could be determined, although it is still possible to know the total cost of the job.

These basic facts about the nature of a job order costing system provide the necessary foundation to account for individual jobs.

JOB ORDER COSTING: DETAILS AND DOCUMENTS

A job can be categorized by its stage of existence in its production life cycle. There are three basic stages of production: (1) agreed-upon but not yet started, (2) jobs in process, and (3) completed jobs. These stages of processing reflect the related inventory accounts of Raw Materials, Work in Process, and Finished Goods. The Finished Goods from one job, however, could become the raw materials for another job in the same or different company. Since job order costing is used by companies making products according to user specifications, unique raw materials may be required. Raw materials are often not acquired until a job is agreed upon. The materials acquired, although often separately distinguishable and related to specific jobs, are accounted for in a single general ledger control account (Raw Materials Inventory) with subsidiary ledger backup. The materials may, however, be designated in the storeroom (and possibly in the subsidiary records) as being "held for use in Job XX." Such designations should keep the materials from being used on a job other than the one for which they were acquired.

Materials Requisitions

materials requisition form
a source document that indicates the types and quantities of materials to be placed into production or used in performing a service; causes materials and their costs to be released from the raw materials warehouse and sent to Work in Process Inventory

When materials are needed for a job, a materials requisition form is prepared so that the materials can be released from the warehouse and sent to the production area. A **materials requisition form** (shown in Exhibit 4-8) is a source document that indicates the types and quantities of materials to be placed into production or used in performing a service. The form provides a way to track responsibility for materials cost and links materials to specific jobs.

Materials requisitions release warehouse personnel from further responsibility for the issued materials and assign responsibility to the department that issued the requisition. As materials are issued, their costs are released from Raw Materials Inventory

EXHIBIT 4-8
Materials Requisition Form

Date_____	Requisition # 629
Job Number_____	Department_____
Authorized by_____	Issued by_____
Received by_____	Inspected by_____

Item No.	Part No.	Description	Unit of Measure	Quantity Required	Quantity Issued	Unit Cost	Total Cost

and, if the materials are direct to the job, are sent to Work in Process Inventory. If the Raw Materials Inventory account also contains indirect materials, those costs are assigned to Overhead when the indirect materials are issued. The journal entry will be

Work in Process Inventory (Direct Materials)	XXX	
Manufacturing Overhead (Indirect Materials)	XXX	
Raw Material Inventory		XXX

To put direct and indirect materials into production.

Completed materials requisition forms are important documents in the audit trail of company records because they provide the ability to verify the flow of materials from the warehouse to the department and job that received the materials. Such documents are usually prenumbered and come in multicopy sets so that completed copies can be maintained in the warehouse and the department, and with each job.

When direct materials are first issued to production, a job moves from the first stage of its production life cycle into the second—jobs in process. In this state, it is necessary to begin the process of cost accumulation using the primary accounting document in a job order system—the job order cost sheet (also called a job cost record).

Job Order Cost Sheet

The source document that provides virtually all financial information about a particular job is the **job order cost sheet**, as shown in Exhibit 4-9. The set of all job order cost sheets for uncompleted jobs composes the Work in Process Inventory subsidiary ledger. Job order cost sheets are equivalent to the tickets that garages use to accumulate costs and bill customers for repair work, the hospital records that accumulate medical charges per patient, or the fee sheets used at college registration. The total costs contained in all job order cost sheets for uncompleted jobs should reconcile to the Work in Process Inventory control account balance in the general ledger, as shown in Exhibit 4-7.

job order cost sheet
a source document that provides virtually all the financial information about a particular job; the set of all job order cost sheets for uncompleted jobs composes the Work in Process Inventory subsidiary ledger

The top portion of a job order cost sheet includes a job number, a description of the task, customer identification, various scheduling information, delivery instructions, and contract price. The remainder of the form details actual costs for materials and labour and applied overhead costs. The form might also include estimated cost information.

Exhibit 4-9 illustrates a job order cost sheet for Exhibits International, Inc. The company has been contracted to produce signs for the Calgary Museum of Natural History. Direct materials and direct labour costs are assigned to jobs, and the amounts are indicated on the job order cost sheet as work on the job is performed. Direct materials information is gathered from the materials requisition forms, while direct labour information is found on employee time sheets or employee labour tickets. (Employee time sheets are discussed in the next section.)

At Exhibits International, overhead is applied to production using two predetermined overhead rates. Companies should use whatever overhead application bases best reflect the drivers of the costs. Multiple overhead cost pools provide more accurate information than single cost pools. The first rate is based on the number of materials requisitions, and the second is based on direct labour hours. Exhibits International's management has found that these two activity bases better reflect the incurrence of costs than would a single base. Using the number of materials requisitions reflects management's determination that numerous parts create substantially more of some types of overhead support costs, such as warehousing and purchasing. Direct labour hours provides a reasonable allocation base for overhead costs such as electricity, indirect labour, and indirect materials.

EXHIBIT 4-9
Job Order Cost Sheet

Job Number: __186__

Customer Name and Address
Calgary Museum of Natural History
3497 Azores Blvd.
Calgary, AB

Description of Job:
Signs as per attached illustrations

Contract Agreement Date:	3/25/09
Scheduled Starting Date:	4/5/09
Agreed Completion Date:	3/1/10
Actual Completion Date:	
Delivery Instructions:	Crate and deliver to museum

Contract Price: __$182,521__

Department A—Art

Direct Materials (Est. $10,900)			Direct Labour (Est. $3,969)			Overhead based on # of Requisitions (@ $15)			# of DLH (@ $8)		
Date	Source	Amount	Date	Source	Amount	Date	Source	Amount	Date	Source	Amount
4/5	MR# 630	$ 35	4/9	wk ended	$368	4/30	2 MRs	$30	4/30	45 DLH	$360
4/21	MR# 637	125	4/23	wk ended	981						

Department B—Moulding
(same format as above but with different OH rates)

Department C—Welding
(same format as above but with different OH rates)

SUMMARY

	Art Dept. Actual	Estimated (Budget)	Moulding Dept. Actual	Estimated (Budget)	Welding Dept. Actual	Estimated (Budget)
Direct Materials	$11,034	$10,900	$23,176	$24,500	$22,639	$17,640
Direct Labour	3,890	3,969	22,985	24,118	3,421	3,310
Overhead (Req.)	193	180	4,987	4,804	2,995	2,940
Overhead (DLH)	1,029	1,056	3,952	3,783	1,347	1,460
Totals	$16,146	$16,105	$55,100	$57,205	$30,402	$25,350

Final Costs:		Actual	Estimated (Budgeted)
	Art Dept.	$ 16,146	$16,105
	Molding Dept.	55,100	57,205
	Welding Dept.	30,402	25,350
	Total	$101,648	$98,660

Employee Time Sheets

An **employee time sheet** or **time ticket** (Exhibit 4-10) indicates, for each employee, what jobs were worked on during the day and the amount of time employees worked on them. These time sheets are most reliable if the employee fills them out as the day progresses. As work arrives at an employee station, it is accompanied by a tag specifying its job order number. The times that work was started and stopped are noted on the time sheet.[9] These time sheets should be collected and reviewed by supervisors to ensure that the information is as accurate as possible.

employee time sheet (time ticket)
a source document that indicates, for each employee, what jobs were worked on during the day and for what amounts of time

EXHIBIT 4-10
Employee Time Sheet

For Week Ending _____
Department _____
Employee Name _____
Employee I.D. Number _____

| Type of Work | | Job | Start | Stop | Day (circle) | Total |
Code	Description	Number	Time	Time		Hours
					M T W Th F S	
					M T W Th F S	
					M T W Th F S	
					M T W Th F S	
					M T W Th F S	
					M T W Th F S	

_____   _____
Employee Signature   Supervisor Signature (for overtime)

In today's highly automated factories, employee time sheets may not be extremely useful or necessary documents. However, machine time can be tracked in the same way as human labour through the use of machine clocks or counters. As jobs are transferred from one machine to another, the clock or counter can be reset to mark the start and stop times. Machine times can then be equated to employee–operator time. Another convenient way to track employee time is through bar coding. Using bar coding also provides the ability to trace machine depreciation to specific products by using a time-related depreciation measure (such as depreciation per hour of use).

Transferring employee time sheet (or an alternative source document) information to the job order cost sheet requires a knowledge of employee labour rates. Wage rates are found in the employees' personnel files. The employee time spent on the job is multiplied by the employee's wage rate. The amounts are summed to find total direct labour cost for the period, and the summation is recorded on the cost sheet. Since most payroll systems are now automated, computers may be programmed to automatically charge employee time to specific jobs. This process would allow detailed information to be readily available. Time sheet information is also used for payroll preparation. All indirect labour costs are charged to manufacturing overhead. The journal entry to record the information follows:

Work in Process Inventory (Direct Labour)	XXX	
Manufacturing Overhead (Indirect Labour)	XXX	
Wages Payable		XXX

To record direct and indirect labour.

Time sheets are filed and retained because they are basic documents that can be referenced to satisfy various future information needs. If total actual labour costs for the job differ significantly from the original estimate, the manager responsible for labour cost control can be asked to clarify the reasons underlying the situation.

In addition, if a job is being billed at cost plus a specified profit margin (a **cost-plus job**), the number of hours worked may be checked by the buyer. This situation is quite common and especially important when dealing with government contracts. Hours not worked directly on the contracted job cannot be arbitrarily or incorrectly charged to the cost-plus job without the potential for detection.

Lastly, time sheets provide information on overtime hours. Under the *Employment Standards Act*, overtime must be paid at a time-and-a-half rate to all nonmanagement employees.

The following News Note addresses a problem related to labour costs. The important thing to remember is to keep good records on all costs, including those related to employees.

cost-plus job
a job being billed at cost plus a specified profit margin

GENERAL NEWS NOTE

Uncompensated Overtime

We are not a nation of clock-punchers. Most of us do not leap up with alacrity and head for the exits at precisely 5 p.m. Some employees leave at a designated time, but most, at least on some days, leave later—sometimes a lot later.

Many people work well beyond their designated hours as a matter of course without expectation of extra pay. Employees are expected, at least implicitly, to finish all urgent tasks before leaving the office. A class action brought against CIBC across Canada is claiming overtime for all employees who have worked more than eight hours in any given day, retroactively.

The CIBC lawsuit likely will just drive overtime underground, with more employers prescribing policies and more employees taking work home. It will make the Canadian economy more like the uncompetitive French one, which places strict limits on hours worked. Rather than dramatically increasing their wage loads by paying overtime, employers will hire fewer employees and contract out more work.

"We believe unpaid overtime is widespread in many industries in this country," Louis Sokolov of SACK GOLDBLATT MITCHELL told a Toronto newspaper. No doubt it happens more than it should. If you're a team player, you don't claim for the extra time you spent preparing documents or faxing them late to concerned parties. For example, articling students and associates are also frequently expected to work 14- and even 16-hour days for no extra pay: "Unpaid overtime appears to be widespread in the financial services industry, affecting some of the lowest paid and most vulnerable employees," says Louis Sokolov. "Because of a lack of effective enforcement of federal labour laws, class actions like this one can be an effective means to compel employers to comply with the law."

The BANK OF NOVA SCOTIA also has a claim. It's statement of claim alleges that class members are assigned heavier workloads than can be completed within their standard working hours. They are required or permitted to work overtime to meet the demands of their jobs, and the Bank of Nova Scotia has failed to pay for the overtime work in direct contravention of the Canada Labour Code under which they are regulated.

Uncompensated overtime also affects the distribution of indirect overhead costs. When uncompensated overtime is not recorded, overhead that is applied on a direct labour basis is applied for only 35 or 40 hours. This results in an underallocation of overhead to jobs on which professionals work during their uncompensated overtime hours.

CANADIAN NATIONAL RAILWAY is also facing an overtime class action lawsuit, which alleges that the company misclassifies first-line supervisors as management employees in order to escape its obligations to pay overtime under the Canada Labour Code. It also alleges that CN first-line supervisors are routinely required to work hundreds of hours of overtime annually, for which they are not paid.

Buzz Hargrove, president of the CANADIAN AUTO WORKERS, says that forced overtime is one of the most common complaints of non-unionized employees who approach his union for help in organizing against their employers.

SOURCES: Howard Levitt, "CIBC Suit to Set Standard: Overtime Is a Given for Most Workers," *Financial Post,* June 13, 2007; Kate MacNamara, "Unpaid Overtime More Widespread Than Just the Banks," *Calgary Herald,* June 28, 2007; Richard Berk, "Uncompensated Overtime," *Management Accounting,* August 1991, pp. 31–32. Published by the Institute of Management Accountants, Montvale, N.J.; Craig Sebastiano, "CN Faces Overtime Suit," *Benefits Canada,* March 25, 2008; Craig Sebastiano, "Unpaid Overtime Class Action Launched Against Scotiabank," *Benefits Canada,* December 11, 2007; Virginia Galt, "Lawsuit Has Employers Working Overtime," *Globe and Mail,* June 8, 2007.

Overhead

Actual overhead incurred during production is included in an overhead control account. If actual overhead is applied to jobs, the cost accountant will wait until the end of the period and divide actual overhead incurred by some related measure of activity or cost driver. Actual overhead would be applied to jobs by multiplying the actual overhead rate by the actual measure of activity associated with each job.

More commonly, overhead is applied to job order cost sheets by using one or more annualized predetermined overhead application rates. Overhead is assigned to jobs by multiplying the predetermined rate by the actual measure of the activity base that was incurred during the period and was associated with each job. Basically, when predetermined rates are used, overhead is applied at the end of the period or at completion of production, whichever is earlier. Overhead is applied at the end of each period so that the Work in Process Inventory account contains costs for all three product elements (direct materials, direct labour, and overhead). When jobs are completed during a period, overhead is applied to Work in Process Inventory so that a complete product cost can be transferred to Finished Goods Inventory. The journal entry to apply overhead is as follows:

Work in Process Inventory	XXX	
Manufacturing Overhead		XXX
To apply overhead to work in process.		

Completion of Production

When a job is completed, its total cost is transferred to the Finished Goods Inventory account.

Finished Goods Inventory	XXX	
Work in Process Inventory		XXX
To transfer completed goods to finished goods inventory.		

Job cost sheets for completed jobs are removed from the WIP subsidiary ledger and are transferred to a Finished Goods file. They serve as a subsidiary ledger for that account. When goods are sold, the cost shown on the job order cost sheet is transferred to Cost of Goods Sold.

Cost of Goods Sold	XXX	
Finished Goods Inventory		XXX
To record sale of goods.		

Job cost sheets for sold jobs are kept in a company's permanent files. A completed job cost sheet provides management with a historical summary of total costs and if appropriate, the cost per finished unit for a given job. The cost per unit may be helpful for planning and control purposes as well as for bidding on future contracts. If a job was exceptionally profitable, management might decide to pursue additional similar jobs. If a job was unprofitable, the job cost sheet may provide indications of areas in which cost control was lax. Such indications are more readily determinable if the job cost sheet presents the original estimated cost information.

Job order cost sheets are extremely valuable to managers for both current period performance evaluation and future planning functions. These cost sheets indicate where costs were controlled and where they were not. A potential cause of noncontrolled costs is overengaging in nonvalue-added activities.

The News Note below discusses how technology can improve efficiency and profitability.

GENERAL NEWS NOTE

Impact of Technology

The ability of Johnson [president of HIS LIFE WOODWORKS] to visualize and develop designs for large custom projects helps the company get business, but that custom emphasis creates problems because all of the details have to be tracked.

"Custom woodworks is a progressive experience. The customer is never done making up his/her mind. There's so much freedom to add, change and remove things."

His Life Woodworks uses BusinessMaster, an operations management program that is designed to improve purchasing, order entry, inventory control, production scheduling, job costing, etc.

"Implementing the system and getting controls in place showed us how low we were pricing our goods, and why we weren't making any money." Ultimately, you know which jobs you'll lose money on, and you can make the difficult choice to turn them down, Brim [the vice-president] says. "Now we have valid information to decide whether we want to do that kind of work anymore."

SOURCE: Adapted from Karl D. Forth, "Breaking Down Barriers to Growth," *Chartwell Communications, Inc.*, Vol. 74, Issue 4, March 2002, pp. 40–46.

In any job order product costing system, the individual job is the focal point. One important reason to trace product costs to individual jobs is that the cost of a product or service may be a major determinant of sales price. This relationship is especially true in job order environments because of the product service's lack of similarity to other items and, thus, the absence of a "market leader" to set the sales price. In order to increase sales, companies that do business internationally are adapting their products to a cost that meets the pockets of their customers. This is discussed in the following International News Note.

What Business Is Doing to Meet the Needs of Developing Countries?

Michael Dell was in Shanghai to unveil the first product to emerge from the PC maker's new Chinese product rollout. A lot of brainpower went into the design of the Dell EC280, a compact, energy-efficient computer that packs considerable processing power. The DELL Chinese design team decided they needed to create something that would appeal to consumers who have never bought computers before and who live in less affluent parts of the country, where electricity—both its cost and its availability—is a bigger issue than in wealthy coastal cities like Beijing, Shanghai, and Shenzhen. Dell wanted to design something optimized for users and the environments that the computers are going into. Market research showed that most PCs have more features than most Chinese need. For instance, most computers have several slots to allow add-ons, but the Chinese generally need only one.

Because many urban Chinese live in modest apartments, the Dell EC280 is much smaller than an ordinary desktop. Also, it consumes only 65 watts compared to an ordinary PC's 250 watts. And because it consumes far less power, it requires only one fan, which makes it much quieter.

PROCTER & GAMBLE, to ensure satisfactory profit margins, in developing countries uses what it calls "reverse engineering." Instead of creating an item and then assigning a price to it—as in most developed markets—P&G first considers what consumers can afford. From there, it adjusts the features and manufacturing processes to meet various pricing targets.

Every day, Martina Perez Diaz spends five hours sewing 70 pairs of black loafers by hand for a wage of 120 pesos, or about $11. When she wants to wash her hair, she walks to her local *tiendita* ("small shop") to buy a single-use packet of P&G's Head & Shoulders. The price? Two pesos, or about 19 cents. "That I usually can afford," she says.

Shoppers like Ms. Diaz factor heavily into P&G's plan to conquer more of the globe. The consumer-products giant has a goal of increasing total sales by 5 to 7% annually over the next three years. As part of that mission, it is looking to tap roughly 1 billion additional consumers—most of them very poor women in developing countries.

P&G emphasizes to its employees that products developed for high-frequency markets must "delight, not dilute." Quality, executives say, is still critical. "You cannot trick a low-income consumer, because they can't afford to buy products that don't work," says a company spokesperson. If a product doesn't perform, "they won't ever buy you again, and they'll tell everyone they know about it, too."

SOURCES: Bruce Einhorn, "Dell's New PC for the China Masses," *Business Week,* March 21, 2007; Ellen Byron, "Emerging Ambitions—P&G's Global Target: Shelves of Tiny Stores—It Woos Poor Women Buying Single Portions," *Wall Street Journal,* July 16, 2007.

The following section presents a comprehensive job order costing illustration using Exhibits International, Inc., the company introduced earlier.

JOB ORDER COST ILLUSTRATION

Exhibits International, Inc. normally sets selling prices at cost plus 85%. The sales price ($182,521) of the signs are established by multiplying the total estimated (budgeted) cost information shown in Exhibit 4-9 ($98,660) by 185%. This sales price was agreed to by the Calgary Museum of Natural History in a contract dated March 25, 2009. Exhibits International's managers scheduled the job to begin on April 5 and be completed by March 1 of the following year. The job is assigned the number 186 for identification purposes.

The journal entries on page 200 illustrate the flow of costs for the Art Department of Exhibits International, Inc. during April 2009. Several jobs were worked on in the Art Department during that month, including Job #186. Although costs would be accounted for individually for each job worked on during the month, only the details for Job #186 are shown.

In entries 1, 2, and 4 (following), Work in Process Inventory—Art Dept. has been debited twice to highlight the costs associated with Job #186 versus those associated with other jobs. In practice, the Work in Process control account for a given department would be debited only once for total costs assigned to it. The details for posting to the individual job cost records would be presented in the journal entry explanations.

1. During April 2009, materials requisition forms #628–641 indicated that $4,995 of raw materials were issued from the warehouse to the Art Department. This amount included $160 of direct materials used on Job #186 (issued on April 5 and 21) and $4,245 of direct materials used on other jobs. The remaining $590 of raw materials issued during April were indirect materials.

Work in Process Inventory—Art Dept. (Job #186)	160	
Work in Process Inventory—Art Dept. (other jobs)	4,245	
Manufacturing Overhead—Art Dept. (indirect materials)	590	
Raw Materials Inventory		4,995
To record direct and indirect materials issued per requisitions during April.		

2. The April time sheets and payroll summaries of the Art Department were used to trace direct and indirect labour to that department. Total labour cost for the Art Department for April was $15,075. Job #186 required $1,349 of direct labour cost during the two biweekly pay periods of April 9 ($368) and April 23 ($981). The remaining jobs in process required $12,576 of direct labour costs. Indirect labour costs for April totalled $1,150.

Work in Process Inventory—Art Dept. (Job #186)	1,349	
Work in Process Inventory—Art Dept. (other jobs)	12,576	
Manufacturing Overhead—Art Dept. (indirect labour)	1,150	
Salaries and Wages Payable		15,075
To record salaries and wages associated with the Art Dept. during April.		

3. In addition to indirect materials and indirect labour, the Art Department incurred other overhead costs during April. Repairs and maintenance costs were paid in cash. Overhead costs were also incurred for supplies, etc.; these costs have been credited to "Various other accounts." The following entry summarizes the accumulation of these other actual overhead costs for April.

Manufacturing Overhead—Art Dept.	846	
Accumulated Depreciation		285
Prepaid Insurance		50
Utilities Payable		325
Cash		110
Various other accounts		76
To record actual overhead costs of the Art Dept. during April exclusive of indirect materials and indirect labour.		

4. Exhibits International, Inc., prepares financial statements at the end of each month. To do so, Work in Process Inventory must include all production costs—direct materials, direct labour, and overhead. Exhibits International allocates overhead to the Art Department Work in Process Inventory based on

two predetermined overhead rates: $15 per materials requisition and $8 per direct labour hour. In April, materials for Job #186 required two materials requisitions, and the artists had worked a total of 45 hours. The other jobs worked on during the month received total applied overhead of $1,493 (19 requisitions × $15 and 151 DLH × $8).

Work in Process Inventory—Art Dept. (Job #186)	390	
Work in Process Inventory—Art Dept. (other jobs)	1,493	
Manufacturing Overhead—Art Dept.		1,883
To apply overhead to the Art Dept. Work in Process for		
April using predetermined application rates.		

Notice that the amount of overhead actually incurred during April in the Art Department ($590 + $1,150 + $846 = $2,586) is not equal to the amount of overhead applied to that department's Work in Process Inventory ($1,883). This $703 difference is the underapplied overhead for the month. Because the predetermined rates are based on annual estimates, differences in actual and applied overhead will accumulate during the year. Under- or overapplied overhead will be closed at year-end, as shown earlier in the Chapter, to either Cost of Goods Sold (if the under- or overapplied amount is immaterial) or to WIP, FG, and CGS (if significant).

The preceding summarizations indicate the types of entries that each department at Exhibits International Inc., would make. Direct materials and direct labour data are posted to each job order cost sheet on a continuous basis (usually daily); entries are posted to the general ledger control accounts at less frequent intervals (usually monthly).

Similar entries for the other signs are made throughout the production process. Exhibit 4-9 shows the completed cost sheet for Job #186 for Exhibits International. Note that direct materials requisitions, direct labour cost, and applied overhead shown earlier in items 1, 2, and 4 are posted on the job cost sheet. Other entries are not detailed.

Job #186 will be worked on by all departments, sometimes concurrently. When the job is completed, its costs are transferred to Finished Goods Inventory. The journal entries related to completion and sale are as follows:

Finished Goods Inventory—Job #186	101,648	
Work in Process Inventory—Art Dept.		16,146
Work in Process Inventory—Moulding		55,100
Work in Process Inventory—Welding		30,402
To record transfer of completed job to finished		
goods inventory.		
Cost of Goods Sold—Job #186*	101,648	
Finished Goods Inventory—Job #186		101,648
To record the sale.		

* Under- or overapplied overhead has been disregarded for this illustration.

Accounts Receivable—Calgary Museum	182,521	
Sales		182,521
To record sale on credit.		

The completed job cost sheet can be used by managers in all departments to determine how well costs were controlled. Although the Art Department experienced higher direct materials cost than estimated, direct labour in that department was under the estimated amount. In the Moulding Department, actual direct materials and direct labour costs were slightly below the estimated amount. The welding department experienced a rather substantial unfavourable difference in materials costs. Overall, costs were controlled relatively well on this job, since total costs were only 3% above the estimate.

Managers are interested in controlling costs on each job as well as by department for each time period. Actual direct materials, direct labour, and manufacturing overhead costs are accumulated in departmental accounts and are periodically compared to estimates so that managers can respond to significant deviations. Transactions must be recorded in a consistent, complete, and accurate manner to have information on actual costs available for periodic comparisons. Managers may stress different types of cost control in different types of businesses. This is true for Signature Special Event Services, whose owner, Tom Brown, says, "We do job costing on every job we do, and I personally review those for a number of reasons. We want to see if our pre-bid matches up with what our actual costs are, so we know if we're really making money on a job, which helps us when we're bidding in the future."[10]

The Exhibits International Inc. example assumed the use of predetermined overhead rates. Attempting to use actual overhead costs for determination of job cost is difficult because of the delayed timing of overhead information and differences in periodical activity levels. The delay in information may be critical when a job is being provided for a customer on a cost-plus basis. Atypical variations in periodic activity could cause management to make incorrect assumptions about the cost per job. A manager might mistakenly determine that a particular job's cost was significantly higher or lower than it would have been in a period of normal activity. In a cost-plus contract, incorrect assumptions about costs could result in overcharging some customers while undercharging others. Such problems are overcome by using predetermined overhead rates. The following News Note discusses some of the deficiencies in quoting and costing jobs.

GENERAL NEWS NOTE

What Does This Job Really Cost?

Quoting profitably depends on knowing costs. Poor costing can actually create most losses. Costing rates are most often computed by taking actual hourly pay rates and adding an hourly amount for overhead. The overhead amount is computed by dividing total shop overhead by labour hours. Rates computed in this manner are often significantly understated. Hours used in the calculation of an overhead rate may be too high. Rather than total labour hours, they should reflect only the portion of employee time that is actually charged to orders, to ensure that all overhead relating to operations is recovered in costing. The use of direct labour as a basis for applying overhead can be a significant deficiency. Traditional job costing systems rely on reporting of labour time.

Another type of misallocation of cost occurs in shops that use a single rate. Operations in shops are diverse; they also vary significantly in their costs. Additionally, the amounts of time that orders spend in each operation differ depending on their requirements. Using a shopwide rate creates misleading results as to order profitability. An overhead-intensive order, for example, may be significantly underpriced.

The use of rates encourages managers to look at costs as if they were entirely variable. For example, if the hours for a disassembly operation cease, the related costs are assumed to discontinue as well. Unfortunately, it is not that simple. Many costs are fixed and do continue. These include costs of factory administration, occupancy, and idled manufacturing capacity.

SOURCE: Adapted from William H. Wiersema, "What Does This Job Really Cost?" *Electrical Apparatus,* June 2007. Copyright 2008, Barks Publications Inc., Chicago, Ill.

Myster Mover uses job costing to cost each of its moves. For moves that require packaging materials, the company costs the number of boxes required. Since not every move requires only two movers, the cost of direct labour will be different for each move. Overhead is applied to each job based on the number of hours for packing and unpacking and the time involved in the move on a per-person basis. If the move is a long-distance one, the overhead might be applied based on the number of kilometres driven as opposed to the number of hours involved.

JOB ORDER COSTING TO ASSIST MANAGEMENT

Job order costing is useful to managers in planning, controlling, decision making, and evaluating performance. Knowing the costs of individual jobs will allow managers to better estimate future job costs and establish realistic selling prices.

The major difference in job costing for a service organization and a manufacturing firm is that a service organization uses an insignificant amount of direct materials on each job. In such cases, direct materials may be treated (for the sake of convenience) as part of overhead rather than being accounted for separately. The accountant in the service company may only need to trace direct labour to jobs and allocate all other production costs to overhead. Allocations of these costs may be accomplished most effectively by using a predetermined rate per direct labour hour or, if wage rates are approximately equal throughout the firm, per direct labour dollar. Other alternative cost drivers may also be used as possible overhead allocation bases.

Whether the entity is a manufacturer or a service organization that tailors its output to customer specifications, company management will find that job order costing techniques will help in the managerial function.

The following examples demonstrate the usefulness to managers of job order costing.

Wainwright & Trumbley

Wainwright & Trumbley is a large brokerage firm with a diversified set of clients and types of jobs. Ms. Wainwright, the firm's managing partner, wanted to know which clients were the most profitable and which were the least profitable. To determine this information, she requested a breakdown of profits per job measured on both a percentage and an absolute dollar basis.

Ms. Wainwright found that the firm did not maintain records of costs per client job. Costs had been accumulated only by type—travel, entertainment, and so forth. Mr. Mumford, a partner in the firm, was certain that the largest profits came from the firm's largest accounts. A careful job cost analysis was performed. It was found that the largest accounts contributed the most revenue to the firm but also the smallest percentage and absolute dollars of incremental profits. Until Ms. Wainwright requested this information, no one had totalled all the costs spent on obtaining each client and on the communications, entertainment, and other costs associated with maintaining each client.

When a company has a large number of jobs that vary in size, time, or effort, it may be difficult to know which jobs are responsible for disproportionately large amounts of costs. Job order costing can help determine which jobs are truly profitable and can help managers better monitor costs. As a result of the cost analysis, Ms. Wainwright changed the firm's strategy: it began focusing on smaller clients located closer to the head office. These efforts caused profits to increase substantially because significantly fewer costs were incurred for travel and entertainment. A job order cost system was implemented to track the per-period and total costs associated with each client. Unprofitable accounts were dropped, and account managers felt more responsible for monitoring and controlling costs related to their particular accounts.

It is important for a service-type business to determine which types of clients are most profitable to it. Obtaining clients who will generate below-average profit margins, at the expense of clients who would generate above-average profit margins, wastes company resources and is highly inefficient. Of course, if the more profitable clients are unavailable regardless of the effort expended, any revenues generated above variable costs will help cover fixed costs.

Seawind Company

The Seawind Company manufactures three types of boats built to customer specifications.[11] Before job order costing was instituted, the owner (Ronnie Trump) had no means of determining the costs associated with the production of each type of boat. When a customer provided boat specifications and asked what the selling price would be, Ronnie merely estimated costs in what he felt was a reasonable manner. In fact, during the construction process, Ronnie did not assign any costs to Work in Process Inventory; all production costs were sent to the Finished Goods Inventory account.

After implementing a job order costing system, Seawind Company had better control over its inventory, better inventory valuations for financial statements, and better information with which to prevent part stockouts (not having parts in inventory) and production stoppages. The job order costing system provided Mr. Trump with information on what work was currently in process and at what cost. From this information, Ronnie was better able to judge whether additional work could be accepted and when current work would be completed. Since job order costing assigns costs to Work in Process Inventory, balance sheet figures were more accurate. As materials were used in the production system, the use of materials requisitions to transfer goods from Raw Materials Inventory to Work in Process produced inventory records that were more current and reflective of raw materials quantities on hand. Finally, the use of a job order product costing system gave Mr. Trump an informed means by which to estimate costs and more adequately price future jobs.

One other thing with job costing—when you catch what looks like a problem or potential problem, you actually have to get off your butt and do something about it. If you wait for a problem to correct itself or just somehow quietly go away next week, Mr. Murphy and his law will ensure that the little problem becomes a much bigger problem.[12]

Job Order Product Costing in High-Tech Environments

Seawind Company and Wainwright & Trumbley represent the kinds of businesses usually linked with job order product costing systems—that is, they are businesses with limited volume, high direct labour involvement, and the need for frequent cost information. Although it is unusual to link job order costing with "high-tech" manufacturing concepts, the two are not incompatible.

Automated production and its influence on manufacturing and cost accounting are discussed at length later in the text. This section of the present chapter is included to illustrate that a cost accounting system must reflect the manufacturing environment in which it is being used. No single system can be designed for use in all companies. A specific product costing system is selected based on its "fit" with the product and the production process. It is the production situation that dictates the type of costing system to be used and that may provide the impetus for change in that system.

Companies manufacturing customized goods have often scheduled production in batches that emphasize smoothing the work flow, specializing the workforce, and minimizing the average unit cost of setups.[13]

When they batch production, job shops often face long lead times and significant inventory buildup. Many job shops are increasingly heading toward automation. The reasons why generally centre on competitiveness and quality. This is evident in the following News Note.

Book Manufacturer's Job Management Solution Improves Workflow by 33%

GENERAL NEWS NOTE

WEBCOM LIMITED is a Toronto-based independently owned book manufacturing company that first went into business in 1975. Its more than 300 employees produce about 50 million books each year. Under one roof the company houses core services as well as the manufacturing process, a set-up that requires smooth flow of information which was not backed up by Webcom's aging IT infrastructure. Many areas of the business required manual input resulting in communication breakdown and inefficiencies leading to extra expenses and impacted customer service.

One of the key manual tasks was order entry. With each sales representative having a slightly different way of recording the information, thus leaving it open for interpretation, it could take the estimating department days, sometimes a week to calculate job cost estimates for customers. The longer Webcom's customers had to wait for a quote the longer they had to find someone else to take their business to.

The company saw the potential of an upgraded IT system, one that would allow for more of the processes to be automated, and with the help of IDEACA and use of Microsoft Business Solutions—Navisions, Webcom started on a three-year path of upgrading to a more collaborative system that would allow for smoother flow of information and uninterrupted workflow throughout the manufacturing processes. The result was an award-winning business management application called Production Order Estimating Management (POEM).

Thanks to POEM, Webcom's business processes, from order entry to job cost to manufacturing, are now fully automatic. More than 80 percent of all quotations can now be produced within minutes. Automation has resulted in 33 percent improvement in workflow. Mark Delvecchio, IT and ERP Business Manager at Webcom, believes it is due to the company's decision to automate that Webcom, one of the few independently owned book manufacturing companies in Canada, is still around.

SOURCE: Adapted from Microsoft Customer Solution, Manufacturing Industry Case Study. "Book Manufacturing Job Management Solution Improves Workflow by 33 Percent," Feb. 2006. Found at: http://www.ideaca.com.

ERP Helps Control Costs

The term ERP (enterprise resource planning) originally referred to how a large organization planned to use organization-wide resources. In the past, ERP systems were used in larger, more industrial types of companies. Today, however, the term can be applied to any type of company in any industry. ERP systems can now be found in almost any type of organization, large or small.

Integration is extremely important to an ERP. ERP's main goal is to integrate data and processes from all areas of an organization and unify them for easy access and work flow. ERPs usually accomplish integration by creating a single database that employs multiple software modules that provide different areas of an organization with various business functions.

Enterprise systems appear to be a dream come true. These commercial software packages promise the seamless integration of all the information flowing through a company—financial and accounting information, human resource information, supply chain information, customer information. For managers who have struggled, at great expense and with great frustration, with incompatible information systems and inconsistent operating practices, the promise of an off-the-shelf solution to the problem of business integration is enticing.

A good enterprise system is a technological tour de force. At its core is a single comprehensive database. The database collects data from and feeds data into modular applications supporting virtually all of a company's business activities—across functions, across business units, across the world. When new information is entered in one place, related information is automatically updated.

Autodesk, a leading maker of computer-aided design software, used to take an average of two weeks to deliver an order to a customer. Now, having installed an Enterprise System, it ships 98% of its orders within 24 hours.[14]

SITE ANALYSIS

Myster Mover Ltd.

"Low overhead" are words to live by. Since overheads are now such a high proportion of most companies' costs, it is essential to keep them as low as possible because "customers have no allegiance to anything but low prices."

Knowing how overhead costs behave, being able to estimate costs at various levels of activity, and assigning overhead to services (and products) are essential techniques in successful business planning and control. Direct attachment of costs to services and products should be the rule to the extent feasible and possible. By directly attaching as many costs as possible, companies will be minimizing the role of direct labour as a basis for assigning costs, thus making the costs that are developed more accurate and appropriate. The concepts covered in this chapter are important to all disciplines so that managers can make more effective and efficient resource allocations and can understand what profits are being generated by what services (and products).

Two primary overhead costs for many companies are training and employee fringe benefits. At Myster Mover, each new employee receives several hours of training. As to fringe benefits, the company provides employees with a generous and comprehensive package that includes health care, career counselling, and product discounts. Giving employees a stake in the outcome of the business helps imbue them with a sense of loyalty and corporate culture.

Since the company cannot control the cost of direct materials and direct labour, they must control overhead costs. At Myster Mover control does not mean making certain that all overhead costs are as low as they can be. Control means making certain that the dollars spent for overhead costs are in some way contributing to business profitability. And this often means spending more to improve the well-being of the employees, who in turn contribute to the successful operations of the moving company.

APPENDIX 4A

Allocation of Service Department Costs

Organizations incur costs for two basic types of activities: those that generate revenue (products and services) and those that do not. Organizational support areas consist of **service departments** and **administrative departments**. Service departments (such as central purchasing and central computing) provide one or more specific functional tasks for other internal units; administrative departments (including top management personnel and organization headquarters) perform management activities that benefit the entire organization. Costs of service and administrative departments are referred to collectively as "service department costs," since company administration provides service to the rest of the company.

Managers understand that the selling prices charged for the organization's goods or services must cover both the costs of revenue-generating activities and the costs of support activities before profits can be achieved. Non–revenue-producing activities are conducted merely to support revenue-producing activities. Thus, service department costs are, in essence, simply another form of overhead that must be allocated to revenue-generating departments and, finally, to units of product or service.

To make managers of revenue-producing areas more aware that their activities are responsible for covering all organizational costs, service department costs are often allocated or charged to user departments. A rational and systematic allocation base for service department costs should reflect the management accountant's consideration of four criteria: (1) the benefits received by the revenue-producing department from the service department; (2) a causal relationship between factors in the revenue-producing department and costs incurred in the service department; (3) the fairness or equity of the allocations between or among revenue-producing departments; and (4) the ability of revenue-producing departments to bear the allocated costs.

Benefits received and causal relationships are the two criteria used most often to decide on allocation bases. These two criteria are reasonably objective and produce rational allocations. Fairness is a valid theoretical basis for allocation, but it is difficult to implement since everyone does not have the same perception of what is fair or equitable. The ability-to-bear criterion is not normally used to allocate service department costs to revenue-producing departments because it often results in unrealistic or profit-detrimental actions. For example, managers might employ financial and logistical manipulations in an attempt to minimize the basis on which costs are to be allocated to their departments.

Applying the two primary criteria (benefits and causes) to the allocation of service department costs can help specify some acceptable allocation bases. It is essential that the allocation base selected be valid because an improper base will always yield improper information regardless of how complex or precise the allocation process appears to be.

Methods of Service Department Cost Allocation

When service department costs are going to be allocated to revenue-producing areas, the basic cost pools are comprised of all revenue-producing and service departments and their direct costs. These costs can be gathered and specified in terms of cost behaviour (variable and fixed) or in total. Intermediate pools are then

sidebar
LEARNING OBJECTIVE 5

How are service department costs allocated to revenue-producing departments using the direct and step methods? (Appendix)

service departments
organizational units that provide one or more specific functional tasks for other internal units

administrative departments
organizational units that perform management activities that benefit the entire organization

NEL   Chapter 4   Overhead and Job Costing   **207**

developed in the allocation process. There may be one or more layers of intermediate pools; however, the last layer will consist of only revenue-producing departments. The number of layers and the costs shown in the intermediate pools depend on the type of allocation method selected. The costs of the intermediate pools are then distributed to final cost objects (such as products, programs, or functional areas).

There are two basic methods of allocating the pooled costs of the service departments to revenue-producing departments: the direct method and the step method.[15] The **direct method** of allocation is the easiest method. Service department costs are assigned directly to the revenue-producing areas using one specific basis for each department. There are no intermediate cost allocations. For example, Personnel Department costs might be assigned to production departments based on the number of people in each production department.

The **step method** of cost allocation assigns indirect costs to cost objects after considering the interrelationships of the cost objects. A specific base is also utilized in this method, but the step method employs a ranking for the quantity of services provided by each service department to other areas. This **"benefits-provided" ranking** lists service departments in an order that begins with the one providing the most service to all other corporate areas (both non-revenue and revenue-producing). The ranking ends with the service department that provides the least service to all but the revenue-producing areas. After the ranking is developed, service department costs are allocated down the list until all costs have been assigned to the revenue-producing areas. This ranking sequence is recommended because the step method partially recognizes the reciprocal relationships among the service departments. For example, since Personnel provides services for all areas of the company, Personnel might be the first department listed in the ranking; all other areas would then receive a proportionate allocation of the Personnel Department's costs.

direct method (of service department allocation)
uses a specific base to assign service department costs directly to revenue-producing departments

step method (of service department allocation)
assigns service department costs to cost objects using a specific base after considering the interrelationships of the service departments and the revenue-producing departments

"benefits-provided" ranking
a listing of service departments in an order that begins with the one providing the most service to all other organizational areas; the ranking ends with the service department that provides the least service to all but the revenue-producing areas

Illustration of Service Department Cost Allocation

Amy Nijmeh Enterprises has two production divisions (Black Cat Sportswear and Magic Products) and three service departments (Administration, Personnel, and Public Relations). Estimated costs are as follows:

Administration	$ 600,000
Personnel	280,000
Public Relations	320,000
Black Cat Sportswear	940,000
Magic Products	1,125,000

The service departments above are listed in the order of their ranking. Selected potential allocation bases are presented below.

	Number of Employee Hours	Number of Employees	Assets Employed ($)
Administration	9,400	4	$380,000
Personnel	16,240	3	140,000
Public Relations	4,160	2	90,000
Black Cat Sportswear	11,250	5	400,000
Magic Products	16,875	6	600,000

Amy Nijmeh's management thinks that administration costs should be allocated on the basis of employee hours, personnel costs on the basis of number of employees, and public relations costs on the basis of dollars of assets employed.

Use of the direct method of service department allocation produces the total budgeted costs for Black Cat Sportswear and Magic Products shown in Exhibit 4-11.

Administration Costs	Base	% of Total Base	Amount to Allocate	Amount Allocated
(employee hours)				
Black Cat Sportswear	11,250	40	$600,000	$240,000
Magic Products	16,875	60	600,000	360,000
Totals	28,125	100		$600,000
Personnel Costs				
(# of employees)				
Black Cat Sportswear	5	46	$280,000	$128,800
Magic Products	6	54	280,000	151,200
Totals	11	100		$280,000
Public Relations Costs				
Assets employed ($)				
Black Cat Sportswear	$ 400,000	40	$320,000	$128,000
Magic Products	600,000	60	320,000	192,000
Totals	$1,000,000	100		$320,000
Grand total of allocated departmental costs:				
Black Cat Sportswear				$ 496,800
Magic Products				703,200
Total allocated				$1,200,000

EXHIBIT 4-11

Amy Nijmeh Enterprises, Direct Method Allocation of Service Department Costs

To apply the step method of allocation, the "benefits provided" ranking specified by Amy Nijmeh Enterprises is used. Departments are first listed in the order designated by Nijmeh and costs are assigned using an appropriate, specified allocation base to the departments receiving service. Once costs have been assigned from a department, no additional costs are charged back to that department. Step allocation of Amy Nijmeh Enterprises service costs is shown in Exhibit 4-12.

Administration Costs	Base	% of Total Base	Amount to Allocate	Amount Allocated
(employee hours)				
Personnel	6,240	16	$600,000	$ 96,000
Public Relations	4,160	11	600,000	66,000
Black Cat Sportswear	11,250	29	600,000	174,000
Magic Products	16,875	44	600,000	264,000
Totals	38,525	100		$ 600,000
Personnel Costs				
(# of employees)				
Public Relations	2	15	$376,000	$ 56,400
Black Cat Sportswear	5	39	376,000	146,640
Magic Products	6	46	376,000	172,960
Totals	13	100		$376,000
Public Relations Costs				
($s of assets employed)				
Black Cat Sportswear	$ 400,000	40	$442,400	$176,960
Magic Products	600,000	60	442,400	265,440
Totals	$1,000,000	200		$442,400
Grand total of allocated departmental costs:				
Black Cat Sportswear				$ 497,600
Magic Products				702,400
Total allocated				$1,200,000

EXHIBIT 4-12

Amy Nijmeh Enterprises, Step Method Allocation of Service Department Costs

For simplicity, cost behaviour in all departments has been ignored. A more appropriate allocation process would specify different bases in each department for the variable and fixed costs. Costs would then be assigned in a manner more reflective of their behaviour. Such differentiation would not change the process of allocation but would change the results for each of the two methods (direct and step). Separation of variable and fixed costs would, however, provide better allocations. Again, use of the computer would now make this process more practical than it has been in the past.

CHAPTER SUMMARY

1 **How are predetermined overhead rates developed and how does the selection of a capacity measure affect predetermined overhead rates?**

Accountants can calculate predetermined overhead rates by dividing estimated overhead costs by a selected level of activity. Such rates assign overhead cost to goods or services based on the actual quantity of activity used to produce the goods or services. The use of predetermined rates eliminates the delays and distortions that occur when actual manufacturing overhead is applied.

Since unit variable costs remain constant over the relevant range of activity, total variable overhead can be divided by any level of activity to compute the predetermined rate. The predetermined fixed overhead rate is computed as estimated fixed overhead at a specific level of activity divided by that level of activity. Most companies select the expected annual capacity level as the activity measure.

Companies must choose a cost measurement method. Actual costing assigns the actual costs of direct materials, direct labour, and/or overhead to products (or services). Normal costing uses actual direct materials and direct labour costs, but uses predetermined rates to assign overhead to products and services.

2 **Why are separate predetermined overhead rates generally more useful than combined rates?**

While some companies use a combined predetermined overhead rate to determine product costs, use of separate rates according to cost behaviour and multiple rates for different cost pools will yield costs that better reflect the resources sacrificed to perform a service or to produce a product. Since variable costs remain constant per unit over the relevant range of activity, total variable overhead can be divided by any level of activity to compute the predetermined rate. To calculate a fixed overhead rate, however, a specific level of activity must be chosen; most companies select the expected annual capacity level. Estimated fixed overhead is then divided by the chosen level of activity to obtain the predetermined rate.

Separate rates computed according to cost behaviour yield costs that best reflect the resources sacrificed to make a product or perform a service.

3 **How is underapplied or overapplied manufacturing overhead accounted for at year-end and why are these accounting techniques appropriate?**

Using predetermined rates normally results in either underapplied or overapplied overhead at year-end. If the total amount of underapplied or overapplied overhead is small, it is closed to Cost of Goods Sold or Cost of Services Rendered. If the amount is large, it is allocated to Work in Process Inventory, Finished Goods Inventory, and Cost of Goods Sold/Services Rendered.

4 **What are the purposes of the documents used in a job order cost system and what production situations are appropriate for a job order product costing system?**

Job order costing is used in companies that make a limited quantity of products or provide a limited number of services uniquely tailored to customer specifications. Job order costing is especially appropriate and useful for many service businesses, such as accounting, advertising, legal, and architectural firms. In contrast to manufacturers, many service companies often do not attempt to trace direct materials to jobs but consider them part of overhead cost. A job order costing system considers the "job" as the cost object for which costs are accumulated. A job can consist of one or more units of output. Job costs are accumulated on a job order cost sheet.

In an actual job order costing system, direct material and direct labour are traced specifically (during the period and for each department) to the individual jobs in process. Direct materials are traced through materials requisition forms; direct labour is traced through employee time sheets.

In an actual or normal job order costing system, actual overhead is assigned to jobs. More commonly, however, a normal costing system is used where overhead is applied using one or more predetermined overhead rates multiplied by the actual activity bases(s) incurred. Overhead is applied to Work in Process Inventory at the end of the month or when the job is complete, whichever is earlier.

Job order costing assists management in planning, controlling, decision making, and evaluating performance. It allows managers to trace costs specifically associated with current jobs to better estimate costs for future jobs.

5 **How are service department costs allocated to revenue-producing departments using the direct and step methods? (Appendix)**

When service department costs are allocated to revenue-producing areas, the basic cost pools are the direct costs of each revenue-producing and service department. These costs can be gathered and specified in terms of cost behaviour (variable and fixed) or in total. The service department cost pools are allocated to the revenue producing departments.

Two basic methods of allocating the pooled costs of the service department are the direct method and the step method. The direct method assigns service department costs directly to the revenue-producing areas with one specific allocation basis. The step method assigns service-department costs to revenue-producing departments in a multiple-step process. The relationships are listed in a benefits-provided ranking that begins with the service department providing service to the most organizational areas (both non–revenue-producing and revenue-producing) and ends with the department that provides service primarily to revenue-producing areas. After the ranking is developed, a specific allocation base for each department is indicated. Service department costs are allocated down the list until all costs have been assigned to the revenue-producing areas.

Key Terms

Actual cost system (p. 174)
Administrative department (p. 207)
Applied overhead (p. 180)
"Benefits-provided" ranking (p. 208)
Cost-plus job (p. 196)
Cost pool (p. 175)
Direct method (of service
   department allocation) (p. 208)
Expected activity (p. 179)
Employee time sheet (time ticket)
   (p. 195)
Job (p. 189)
Job order cost sheet (p. 193)

Job order costing system (p. 189)
Materials requisition form (p. 192)
Normal capacity (p. 179)
Normal cost system (p. 174)
Overapplied overhead (p. 181)
Practical capacity (p. 179)
Predetermined overhead rate (p. 174)
Service department (p. 207)
Step method (of service department
   cost allocation) (p. 208)
Theoretical capacity (p. 179)
Underapplied overhead (p. 181)

POINTS TO REMEMBER

Predetermined overhead rate

Predetermined OH rate = Total estimated manufacturing overhead ÷ Estimated level of activity (Should be separated into variable and fixed rates and by related cost pools)

Underapplied and Overapplied Manufacturing Overhead

Variable/Fixed Manufacturing Overhead	XXX	
Various accounts		XXX
Actual overhead is debited to the Overhead General Ledger account and credited to the Sources of the overhead costs.		

Work in Process Inventory*	YYY	
Variable/Fixed Manufacturing Overhead		YYY
Applied overhead is debited to WIP Inventory and credited to the Overhead General Ledger Account.		

*Can be debited directly to Cost of Services Rendered (CSR) in a service company.

A debit balance in Variable or Fixed Manufacturing Overhead at the end of the period is underapplied overhead; a credit balance is overapplied overhead. An immaterial underapplied or overapplied balance in the OH account is closed at the end of the period to CGS or CSR; a material amount is prorated to WIP Inventory, FG Inventory, and CGS or CSR.

Service Department Cost Allocation

Direct method:
1. Determine rational and systematic allocation base for each service department.
2. Assign costs from each service department directly to revenue-producing areas using specified allocation bases.

Step method:

1. Determine rational and systematic allocation base for each service department.
2. List service departments in order from the one that provides the most service to all other areas (both revenue- and non–revenue-producing) to the one that only provides service to revenue-producing areas (benefits-providing ranking).
3. Beginning with the first service department listed, allocate the costs from that department to all remaining departments; repeat the process until only revenue-producing departments remain.

Basic Journal Entries in a Job Order Costing System

Raw Material Inventory	XXX	
Accounts Payable		XXX
To record the purchase of raw materials.		

Work in Process Inventory—Dept. (Job #)	XXX	
Manufacturing Overhead	XXX	
Raw Material Inventory		XXX
To record the issuance of direct and indirect materials requisitioned for a specific job.		

Work in Process Inventory—Dept. (Job #)	XXX	
Manufacturing Overhead	XXX	
Wages Payable		XXX
To record direct and indirect labour payroll for production employees.		

Manufacturing Overhead	XXX	
Various Accounts		XXX
To record the incurrence of actual overhead costs (Account titles to be credited must be specified in an actual journal entry.)		

Work in Process Inventory—Dept. (Job #)	XXX	
Manufacturing Overhead		XXX
To apply overhead to a specific job. (This may be actual overhead or overhead applied using a predetermined rate. Predetermined overhead is applied at job completion or end of period, whichever is earlier.)		

Finished Goods Inventory (Job #)	XXX	
Work in Process Inventory		XXX
To record the transfer of completed goods from Work in Process to Finished Goods.		

Cost of Goods Sold	XXX	
Finished Goods Inventory		XXX
To record the cost of goods sold.		

Accounts Receivable	XXX	
Sales		XXX
To record the sale of goods on account.		

DEMONSTRATION PROBLEMS

Problem 1

The Forrester Company's predetermined total overhead rate for product costing purposes is $23 per unit. Of this amount, $18.00 is the variable portion. Cost information for two levels of activity is as follows:

Overhead Components	800 units	1,200 units
Indirect materials	$6,400	$9,600
Indirect labour	5,600	8,400
Handling	2,600	3,800
Maintenance	2,000	3,000
Utilities	2,000	2,800
Supervision	4,000	4,000

Required:

a. Determine the fixed and variable values for each of the preceding components of overhead and determine the total overhead cost formula.
b. What is the company's expected volume level if the predetermined rate is based on expected capacity?
c. Determine the expected overhead costs at the expected activity level.
d. Forrester Company's management decides to revise its expected activity level to be 100 units greater than the present level. Determine the new total predetermined overhead rate for product costing purposes.

Problem 2

Clear Springs Ltd. is a newly formed firm that builds towers for equipment used in radio, television, and communications transmission. Each tower is custom engineered based on the site conditions and height requirements. The towers are built in sections in the firm's factory and then hauled by rail or truck to the site where they are assembled.

Organizationally, the firm is comprised of two departments: Construction and Assembly. The Construction Department is responsible for engineering and manufacturing each tower; the Assembly Department assembles and erects the towers.

In its first year of operations, Clear Springs obtained contracts for the construction of three towers:

> Tower One: a 1,500 metre tower for pubic television in Edmonton, Alberta
> Tower Two: a 300 metre radio tower in St. John's, Newfoundland
> Tower Three: a 500 metre radio tower in Winnipeg, Manitoba

The firm uses a job order costing system based on normal costs. Overhead is applied in the Construction Department at the predetermined rate of $40 per tonne of metal processed. In the Assembly Department, overhead is applied at the predetermined rate of $100 per metre of tower that is erected.

For the year, significant transactions are summarized as follows:

1. Raw materials (metal) were purchased on account: 2,000 tonnes at $100 per tonne.
2. Materials were requisitioned for use in the three towers (all materials used are regarded as direct materials): Tower One—1,300 tonnes; Tower Two—200 tonnes; and Tower Three—300 tonnes. All of the materials were issued to the Construction Department.
3. The time sheets and payroll summaries indicated the following direct labour costs:

	Construction Department	% Complete	Assembly Department	% Complete
Tower One	$200,000	100%	$300,000	100%
Tower Two	25,000	100%	$ 40,000	50%
Tower Three	30,000	40%	$ 0	0%

4. Indirect manufacturing costs were incurred in each department as follows:

	Construction Department	Assembly Department
Labour	$20,000	$ 40,000
Utilities	10,000	5,000
Depreciation	40,000	110,000

5. Manufacturing overhead was applied based on the predetermined overhead rates in effect in each department.

6.   Tower One was completed and sold at a price equal to cost plus $40,000.
7.   Any under-or overapplied overhead is assigned to Cost of Goods Sold.

Required:

a.   Record the journal entries for items 1 through 7.
b.   As of the end of the year, determine the total cost assigned to Tower Two and Tower Three.

Problem 3 (Appendix)

World Bank has three revenue-generating areas: chequing accounts, savings accounts, and loans. The bank also has three service areas: administration, personnel, and accounting. The direct costs per month and the interdepartmental service structure are shown below in a benefits-providing ranking:

		% of Service Used By					
Department	**Direct Costs**	**Admin**	**Pers.**	**Acctg.**	**Chequing**	**Saving**	**Loans**
Administration	$60,000	—	10	10	40	20	20
Personnel	40,000	10	—	10	20	40	20
Accounting	60,000	10	10	—	20	20	40
Chequing accts	60,000						
Savings accts	50,000						
Loans	100,000						

Required:

a.   Compute the total cost for each revenue-generating area using the direct method,
b.   Compute the total cost for each revenue generating area using the step method,

Solutions to Demonstration Problems

Problem 1

a.

	(b) Value		(a) Value	
Indirect Material	(9,600 − 6,400) ÷ 400	$ 8.00	9,600 − (8 × 1,200)	$ 0
Indirect Labour	(8,400 − 5,600) ÷ 400	7.00	8,400 − (7 × 1,200)	0
Handling	(3,800 − 2,600) ÷ 400	3.00	3,800 − (3 × 1,200)	200
Maintenance	(3,000 − 2,000) ÷ 400	2.50	3,000 − (250 × 1,200)	0
Utilities	(2,800 − 2,000) ÷ 400	2.00	2,800 − (2 × 1,200)	400
Supervision	(4,000 − 4,000) ÷ 400	0.00	4,000 − (0 × 1,200)	4,000
		$22.50		$4,600

$y = 4,600 + \$22.50x$

b.   Fixed rate = $23.00 − $18.00 = $5.00
Fixed overhead rate of $5.00 = $4,600 ÷ Expected activity
Expected capacity = $4,600 ÷ $5.00 = 920

c.

	Variable	Fixed	Total
Indirect Materials	$ 7,360	$ 0	$ 7,360
Indirect Labour	6,440	0	6,440
Handling	2,760	200	2,960
Maintenance	2,300	0	2,300
Utilities	1,840	400	2,240
Supervision	0	4,000	4,000
Totals	$20,700	$4,600	$25,300

d.   New level: 920 units + 100 units = $1,020 units
New fixed overhead rate = $4,600 ÷ 1,020 = $4.51
New total predetermined overhead rate = $22.50 + $4.51 = $27.01

Problem 2

a. 1 Raw Materials 200,000
         Accounts Payable   200,000
         To record purchase of materials.

    2 WIP—Construction (Tower One) 130,000
       WIP—Construction (Tower Two) 20,000
       WIP—Construction (Tower Three) 30,000
         Raw Materials   180,000
         To record requisition and issuance of materials.

    3 WIP—Construction (Tower One) 200,000
       WIP—Construction (Tower Two) 25,000
       WIP—Construction (Tower Three) 30,000
       WIP—Assembly (Tower One) 300,000
       WIP—Assembly (Tower Two) 40,000
         Wages Payable   595,000
         To record direct labour costs.

    4 Manufacturing Overhead—Construction 70,000
       Manufacturing Overhead—Assembly 155,000
         Wage Payable   60,000
         Utilities Payable   15,000
         Accumulated Depreciation   350,000
         To record indirect manufacturing costs.

    5 WIP—Construction (Tower One) 52,000
       WIP—Construction (Tower Two)   8,000
       WIP—Construction (Tower Three) 12,000
         Manufacturing Overhead—Construction   72,000
         To record application of Construction Dept. manufacturing
         Overhead.

       WIP—Assembly (Tower One) 150,000
       WIP—Assembly (Tower Two) 15,000
         Manufacturing Overhead—Assembly   165,000
         To record application of Assembly Dept. manufacturing
         Overhead.

    6 Finished Goods 832,000
         WIP—Construction (Tower One)   382,000
         WIP—Assembly (Tower One)   450,000
         To record completion of Tower One.

       Cost of Goods Sold 832,000
         Finished Goods   832,000
         To record cost of tower sold.

       Accounts Receivable 1,232,000
         Sales   1,232,000
         To record sale of Tower One.

    7 Manufacturing Overhead—Construction   2,000
       Manufacturing Overhead—Assembly 10,000
         Cost of Goods Sold   12,000
         To close overhead to cost of goods sold.

b.

	Tower Two	Tower Three
Direct Materials—Construction	$ 20,000	$30,000
Direct Labour—Construction	25,000	30,000
Manufacturing Overhead—Construction	8,000	12,000
Direct Materials—Assembly	0	0
Direct Labour—Assembly	40,000	0
Manufacturing Overhead—Assembly	15,000	0
Totals	$108,000	$72,000

Problem 3 (Appendix)

a.

	Chequing	Savings	Loans
Administration	40/80	20/80	20/80
Personnel	20/80	40/80	20/80
Accounting	20/80	20/80	40/80

	Direct	Chequing	Savings	Loans
Administration	$ 60,000	$ 30,000	$ 15,000	$ 15,000
Personnel	40,000	10,000	20,000	10,000
Accounting	60,000	15,000	15,000	30,000
	$160,000	$ 55,000	$ 50,000	$ 55,000
Direct Costs		60,000	50,000	100,000
Total Costs		$115,000	$100,000	$155,000

b.

	Personnel	Accounting	Chequing	Savings	Loans
Admin	10/100	10/100	40/100	20/100	20/100
Personnel		10/90	20/90	40/90	20/90
Accounting			20/80	20/80	40/80

	Personnel	Accounting	Chequing	Savings	Loans
Admin ($60,000)	$6,000	$6,000	$ 24,000	$ 12,000	$ 12,000
Pers. ($40,000 + $6,000)		5,111	10,222	20,445	10,222
Acctg. ($60,000 + $11,111)			17,788	17,788	35,555
			$ 52,000	$ 50,223	$ 57,777
Direct Costs			60,000	50,000	100,000
Total Costs			$112,000	$100,223	$157,777

End-of-Chapter Materials

SELF-TEST QUESTIONS

(SOLUTIONS APPEAR AT THE END OF THE CHAPTER.)

Questions 1 through 3 are based on the following information: Legal Eagles Ltd. has two departments, criminal law and civil law. Support staff, such as word processing personnel, serve both departments. The following information is for the support staff and the two departments:

	Support Staff Hours Charged to Department	Payroll Cost of Department
Criminal Law	12,000	$500,000
Civil Law	6,000	$200,000
Support Staff		$300,000

1. How much of the support staff cost should be allocated (on the basis of support staff hours) to the criminal department?
   a. $200,000
   b. $214,286
   c. $333,333
   d. $466,667

SELF-TEST QUESTIONS

2. How much of the support staff cost should be allocated (on the basis of payroll cost of departments) to the civil department?
   a. $85,714   c. $228,571
   b. $142,857   d. $333,333

3. Of the $300,000, the support staff fixed costs are $180,000 and are allocated on the basis of department payroll, and the remainder are variable costs and are allocated on the basis of hours charged to the department. What is the cost allocation to the civil department?
   a. $58,096   c. $185,714
   b. $91,429   d. $208,571

(Self-Test Questions 1 to 3 are adapted by the authors from *Management Accounting Examination* published by the Certified General Accountants Association of Canada © CGA-Canada, March 2003, used by permission.)

4. Alpha Co. has the following estimated costs for next year.

Direct materials	$ 6,000
Direct labour	20,000
Rent on factory building	15,000
Sales salaries	25,000
Depreciation on factory equipment	8,000
Indirect labour	12,000
Production supervisor's salary	15,000

Alpha estimates that 20,000 direct labour hours will be worked during the year. If manufacturing overhead is applied on the basis of direct labour hours, what will be the overhead rate per hour?
   a. $2.50   c. $3.75
   b. $3.50   d. $5.05

5. On September 30, the fixed manufacturing overhead account of Atla Ltd. showed a debit balance of $6,000 after fixed manufacturing overhead had been applied for the month. If the actual total manufacturing overhead cost incurred in September was $108,600 and the production was 8,550 units, what was the rate for applying fixed manufacturing overhead cost?
   a. $12.00 per unit   c. $13.00 per unit
   b. $12.80 per unit   d. $13.40 per unit

(Self-Test Questions 4 and 5 are adapted by the authors from *Management Accounting Examination* published by the Certified General Accountants Association of Canada © CGA-Canada, #4, March 2000 and March 2005, used by permission)

6. Which of the following statements is normally true about a company that produces less than its planned volume for the year?
   a. The company will underapply overhead.
   b. The company will overapply overhead.
   c. The company will not necessarily over- or underapply overhead.
   d. None of the above.

7. A company estimates that 27,000 direct labour hours will be worked during the year. Manufacturing overhead is applied on the basis of direct labour hours.

Direct materials	$ 4,500
Direct labour	27,000
Rent on factory building	12,500
Sales salaries	31,000
Depreciation on factory equipment	5,000
Indirect labour	13,500
Production supervisor's salary	16,000

What will the overhead rate of allocation be considering the following estimated costs for next year?
   a. $1.15   c. $2.24
   b. $1.74   d. $2.89

(Self-Test Question 7 is adapted by the authors from Management Accounting examinations published by the Certified General Accountants Association of Canada © CGA-Canada, March 2005, used by permission)

8. In job costing, the basic document to accumulate the cost of each order is the:
   a. Invoice
   b. Job cost sheet
   c. Tequisition sheet
   d. Purchase order

9. Knowing the cost of individual jobs will allow managers to:
   a. Better estimate future job costs
   b. Tailor output to customer specifications
   c. Charge the customer more
   d. Predetermine the overhead rate to charge

10. John Black Corp. would most likely use a job order costing system for the manufacturing of:
    a. Grass seed
    b. Paper
    c. Chocolates
    d. Computer programs

11. The use of indirect materials for a job would usually be reflected in the general ledger as:
    a. Raw Materials
    b. Work in Process
    c. Manufacturing Overhead
    d. Finished Goods

12. When direct materials that have been previously issued for a particular job are returned to the warehouse, the following journal entry is made:
    a. Work in Process
          Raw Materials Inventory
    b. Raw Materials Inventory
          Work in Process
    c. Purchases Returns
          Work in Process
    d. Raw Materials Inventory
          Manufacturing Overhead

13. Ida Copelovici Ltd. manufactures flutes to customer specifications. The following data pertain to the Rebecca job for April:

Direct materials used	$4,200
Direct labour rate per hour	$8.00
Applied manufacturing overhead rate per machine hour	$15.00
Machine hours used	200
Direct labour hours worked	300

What is the total cost recorded for the Rebecca job for the month of April?
    a. $ 8,800
    b. $ 9,600
    c. $11,100
    d. $10,300

QUESTIONS

1. Why are direct labour hours losing favour as an activity base in some manufacturing companies? Would direct labour still be a valid basis for applying overhead in service companies? Discuss the reasoning behind your answer.

2. Why would the question of whether overhead was assigned using actual rate or predetermined rates make a difference in costing a product?

3. List three reasons to use predetermined overhead rates rather than actual costs to apply indirect costs to products. Why would these reasons be of importance to managers? To marketers? To accountants?

4. Why must a particular level of activity be specified to calculate a predetermined fixed overhead rate? Why is such specificity not required to calculate a predetermined variable overhead rate?

5. A company might use one of four different measures of capacity to compute its predetermined fixed overhead rate. What are these four capacity measures, and what differences exist between them? Under what conditions would each provide the best product cost information?

6. Why is it necessary to separate mixed costs into their variable and fixed cost elements for product costing purposes?

7. How does fixed cost per unit change as production increases?

8. How would overhead that was materially underapplied at the end of a year be treated? How might this underapplication affect product costs and annual profits?

9. Why do some companies use multiple cost pools, rather than a single cost pool, to allocate overhead costs?

10. In the context of job order product costing, what is a job?

11. If the costs in all of the subsidiary ledgers for all work that has been started but not yet completed were summed, the total would equal the balance in which control account? Why?

12. When materials are used in the production process, their costs are charged to one of two accounts, What are the two account and how is it determined which account should be charged?

13. If job order product costing is in use, what is the primary document for attaching the costs associated with individual jobs? What information is shown on this document?

14. What is the primary source document for determining how much of an employee's time should be charged to a specific job? When should this document be prepared?

15. Once a job is completed, in which account are the costs associated with the job found? What constitutes the support for the information in this control account?

16. The sum of all costs on the job cost sheets for all the products that are sold during a period would equal the balance in which account? Would this account balance typically be determined using a perpetual or a periodic inventory system? Why?

17. Why would a change from a labour-intensive production system to a machine-driven production system likely necessitate changes in the job order costing system?

18. What is the primary difference between job order costing for a manufacturing firm and job order costing for a service organization? Why does this difference arise?

19. What types of service organizations are likely to use job order costing?

20. (Appendix) Why are service department costs often allocated to revenue-producing departments?

21. (Appendix) How does service department costs allocation create a feeling of cost responsibility among revenue-producing area managers?

22. (Appendix) What similarities and differences exist between the direct and step methods of allocating service department costs?

23. (Appendix) Why is a "benefits provided" ranking used in the step method of allocation?

EXERCISES

1. (LO 1) The IT department at Hong Kong Corporation was set up with the intent that the facilities would be used by production department A approximately 60% of the time and by production department B approximately 40% of the time.

   The IT department's budgeted costs for February are:

Variable	$245 per processing hour
Fixed	$258,000 per month

   The IT Department's actual results for February were:

Department A usage	630 processing hours
Department B usage	315 processing hours
Total costs of the IT department for the month	$489,525

   Based on the above results, management allocated the costs of the IT department as follows: $489,525 ÷ 945 hours = $518.016 per hour

Costs charged to department A	630 hours × $518.016/hour = $326,350
Costs charged to department B	315 hours × $518.016/hour = $163,175

   Required:
   a. As the manager of department A, what objections would you have to the method of cost allocation used?
   b. How should the costs have been allocated?

2. (LO 2) Benji Tal Enterprises prepared the following data:

   Machine Hours

	10,000	11,000	12,000	13,000
Factory Costs				
Variable	$40,000	$44,000	$48,000	$52,000
Fixed	15,000	15,000	15,000	15,000

   Benji has set 11,000 machine hours as the expected annual capacity. It takes two machine hours to produce each product. The company plans to operate at one-twelfth of the expected annual capacity each month.

   Required:
   a. Calculate separate variable and fixed rates using (1) machine hours and (2) units of products.
   b. Calculate the combined overhead rate using (1) machine hours and (2) units of products.

3. (LO 2) Use the information from Exercise 2. In April the company produced 442 units. During the month, Benji Tal incurred $3,360 of variable overhead and $1,310 of fixed overhead and used 884 actual machine hours.

   Required:
   a. What amount of fixed factory overhead should be applied to production in April?
   b. What amount of variable factory overhead should be applied to production in April?
   c. Calculate the over- or underapplied variable and fixed overhead for April.

4. (LO 2) Nova Scotia Upholstery has two departments: Framing and Covering. Framing is highly automated, and machine hours are used as the factory overhead allocation activity in that department. Covering is labour-intensive, so it uses direct labour hours as the activity base. Corporate plans follow:

   Machine Hours (MHS)

Framing Overhead	3,000	4,000	5,000	6,000
Variable	$ 6,600	$ 8,800	$11,000	$13,200
Fixed	4,200	4,200	4,200	4,200
Total	$10,800	$13,000	$15,200	$17,400

   Direct Labour Hours (DLHs)

Covering Overhead	9,000	15,000	18,000	12,000
Variable	$45,000	$60,000	$75,000	$90,000
Fixed	3,000	3,000	3,000	3,000
Total	$48,000	$63,000	$78,000	$93,000

EXERCISES

The firm produces one style of sofa, which can be covered in a variety of fabrics. Each sofa requires one hour of machine time and three hours of direct labour. Next year, Nova Scotia Upholstery plans to produce 6,000 sofas, which is 1,000 more than normal capacity.

Required:
a. What are the a and b values for the cost formula for each department?
b. Predict next year's factory overhead for each department.
c. Using normal capacity, calculate the predetermined total factory overhead per sofa. Using expected capacity, calculate the predetermined total factory overhead per sofa.
d. Management wants to earn a gross margin of 50% on cost. Which of the two capacity measures used in part c would you select to determine total cost per sofa, and why?

5. (LO 2, 3). Pat Bollen Products Ltd. applies overhead at a combined rate for fixed and variable overhead at 175% of direct labour cost. During the first three months of the current year, actual costs were incurred as follows:

	Direct Labour Cost	Actual Overhead
January	$360,000	$640,000
February	330,000	570,400
March	340,000	600,000

Required:
a. What amount of overhead was applied to production in each of the above months?
b. What was the under- or overapplied overhead for each month and in total for the quarter?

6. (LO 3) Stan Fink Inc., makes potato mashers. Management has decided to apply overhead to products using a predetermined rate. To determine the rates, management estimated the following data:

Variable factory overhead at 10,000 direct labour hours	$43,500
Variable factory overhead at 13,000 direct labour hours	65,250
Fixed factory overhead at all levels between 10,000 and 18,000 direct labour hours	40,500

Practical capacity is 18,000 direct labour hours; expected capacity is two-thirds of practical capacity.

Required:
a. What is Stan Fink, Inc.'s predetermined variable overhead rate?
b. What is the most common activity measure used to calculate a predetermined overhead rate? Using this measure, calculate the predetermined fixed overhead rate.
c. Use your answers to (a) and (b). If the firm incurred 11,500 direct labour hours during the period, how much total overhead could be applied? If actual overhead during the period were $90,000, what would be the annual amount of under- or overapplied overhead?

7. (LO 1, 3) Brooke Corporation opened for business on January 1. Paul Martin, the newly hired controller, was asked to establish a predetermined overhead rate to use in applying overhead to the various jobs. After consulting with various individuals in the accounting department, he came up with the following estimated data:

Supervision	$ 50,000
Indirect labour	115,000
Inspection	70,000
Maintenance	35,000
Indirect material	25,000
Heat, light, power	20,000
Depreciation	35,000
Miscellaneous manufacturing overhead	10,000
Total manufacturing overhead	$360,000
Direct labour hours	144,000

EXERCISES

At the end of the fiscal year, the first year of operations, the following results were recorded:

Supervision	$ 51,000
Indirect labour	99,000
Inspection	73,000
Maintenance	39,000
Indirect material	20,000
Heat, light, power	18,000
Depreciation	35,000
Miscellaneous manufacturing overhead	3,000
Total manufacturing overhead	$338,000
Direct labour hours	121,500

Required:

a. Compute the predetermined overhead rate.
b. Determine the over- or underapplied overhead for the year.
c. Explain the causes for over- or underapplied overhead.

8. (LO 1, 3) Letterman Glassworks had the following information in its Work in Process Inventory account for June:

Work in Process Inventory

Beginning Balance	5,000	Transferred Out	167,500
Materials added	75,000		
Labour (10,000 DLH)	45,000		
Applied Overhead	60,000		
Ending Balance	17,500		

All workers are paid the same rate per hour. Manufacturing overhead is applied to Work in Process Inventory on the basis of direct labour hours. The only work left in process at the end of the month had a total of 1,430 direct labour hours accumulated to date.

Required:

a. What is the total predetermined overhead rate per direct labour hour?
b. What amounts of material, labour, and overhead are included in the ending Work in Process Inventory balance?
c. If actual total overhead for June is $61,350, what is the amount of underapplied or overapplied overhead?

9. (LO 1, 3) Ambrus Paper Supply Company manufactures recycled paper. The company has decided to use predetermined manufacturing overhead rates to apply manufacturing overhead to its products. To set such rates, the company has gathered the following estimated data:

Variable manufacturing overhead at 12,000 machine hours	$72,000
Variable manufacturing overhead at 14,000 machine hours	84,000
Fixed manufacturing overhead at all levels between	
12,000 and 20,000 machine hours	72,000

Practical capacity is 20,000 machine hours; expected capacity is 75% of practical capacity.

Required:

a. What is the company's predetermined variable manufacturing overhead rate?
b. Compute the company's fixed manufacturing overhead rate based on expected capacity. Using practical capacity, compute the company's predetermined fixed manufacturing overhead rate.
c. If the company incurred a total of 13,500 machine hours during a period, what would be the total amount of applied manufacturing overhead, assuming fixed manufacturing overhead was applied based on expected capacity? practical capacity?
d. If actual manufacturing overhead during the period was $155,000, what was the amount of underapplied or overapplied manufacturing overhead, assuming fixed

EXERCISES

manufacturing overhead was applied based on expected capacity? practical
capacity? (Use your answers to parts (a) and (b).)

e.   Based on your answers to parts (c) and (d), explain why most firms use expected
capacity as the manufacturing overhead allocation base. What is the benefit of
using practical capacity?

10. (LO 3) Michael Baldwin is the newly hired manager of the production department at
the Genoa City Company. The company allocates manufacturing overhead on a predetermined basis using direct labour cost as a base.

The accounting department has prepared the following analysis of actual results
compared to estimated figures.

	Estimated	Actual
Sales (units)	20,000	18,000
Production (units)	20,000	19,000
Direct materials	$ 50,000	$ 46,400
Direct labour	36,000	45,750
Supplies	2,000	1,400
Building depreciation	2,000	2,000
Salaries		
Manager	13,000	15,000
Assistant Manager	10,000	10,750
Total manufacturing cost	$113,000	$121,300

Additional information:
There were no beginning or ending inventories of work in process.

Required:
If the company prorates any under- or overapplied manufacturing overhead to the
inventory accounts and to cost of goods sold, how much manufacturing overhead will
be allocated to cost of goods sold? What is the impact of this allocation on the cost of
goods sold?

11. (LO 3) Nijmeh Technologies has determined that a single overhead application rate
no longer results in a reasonable allocation of overhead to its diverse products.
Accordingly, the company has restructured its overhead application. It has
established six cost pools and identified appropriate cost drivers. The new cost
pools, allocation bases, and rates are as follows:

Cost Pool	Application Rate
Setup costs	$37 per setup
Machine costs	15 per machine hour
Labour-related costs	7 per direct labour hour
Material handling costs	1 per kilogram of material received
Quality costs	80 per customer return
Other costs	4 per machine hour

During the year, the company experienced the following volume for each cost
application base:

Setups	300
Machine hours	9,000
Direct labour hours	8,000
Kilograms of material received	100,000
Customer returns	250

Required:
a.   Determine the amount of overhead applied.
b.   Assume that the company incurred $362,000 in actual overhead costs. Compute
the company's underapplied or overapplied overhead.
c.   Why are more firms adopting multiple application rates to apply overhead?

EXERCISES

12. (LO 3) Ray Davidson Chemical Products Company produces two products, A and B. The company's expected manufacturing overhead costs for the coming year are as follows:

Overhead Items	Amounts
Utilities	$ 300,000
Setup	250,000
Materials handling	800,000
Total	$1,350,000

The company's expected production and related statistics follow:

	Product A	Product B
Machine hours	35,000	15,000
Direct labour hours	20,000	25,000
Direct materials (kilograms)	75,000	125,000
Number of units produced	10,000	5,000

Additional data:

a. One direct labour hour costs $10
b. 200,000 kilograms of material were purchased for $360,000

Required:

a. Determine the total cost for each product and the cost per unit under the following assumptions:
   i. overhead is applied based on direct labour hours
   ii. overhead is applied based on machine hours
b. Explain why your answers to parts (i) and (ii) differ.

13. (LO 3) Information for David Didona Manufacturing Ltd. at May 1 is given below:

Inventories:

Raw materials (all direct)	$2,500
Work in process	1,040
Finished goods	1,890

Transactions in May:
1. Purchased $22,400 of direct materials on account.
2. Transferred $18,800 of direct materials into production.
3. Production wages totalled $6,500, of which direct labour accounted for $5,000.
4. Salary in May for the production supervisor was $3,000.
5. Total utility cost was $520, of which $410 was variable and $110 was fixed.
6. Transferred $1,300 of indirect material from factory supplies into production.
7. Depreciation on manufacturing assets for May was $22,500.
8. Expiration of prepaid insurance on manufacturing assets was $1,600.

Other information:

a. David Didona Manufacturing Ltd. transfers actual overhead costs during each month to the work in process inventory account. It uses separate accounts to record the incurrence of fixed and variable overhead.
b. During May, goods with a value of $52,450 were completed and transferred to finished goods.
c. During May, finished goods with a value of $51,315 were sold on account for $74,670.

Required:

Using T-accounts, show the flow of costs into and out of the Manufacturing Overhead and Cost of Goods Sold accounts for the month of May. Also compute the value of each of the raw materials, work in process, and finished goods inventories at the end of May. Be sure to use separate accounts as necessary.

14. (LO 3) Rose Reed Research Services Company has an overapplied overhead balance of $31,000 at the end of the year. Selected account balances at year-end are:

Work in Process Inventory	$ 27,000
Finished Goods Inventory	60,000
Cost of Goods Sold	213,000

EXERCISES

Required:
a. Prepare the necessary journal entries to close the overapplied overhead balance assuming that:
   i. the amount is material.
   ii. the amount is immaterial.
b. Which approach is the better choice, and why?

15. (LO 3) Gaetane Labelle Maraj Company has an overapplied overhead balance the end of the current year of $27,975. The amounts of overhead contained in other selected account balances at year-end are:

Work in Process	$ 45,000
Finished Goods	84,000
Cost of Goods Sold	171,000

Required:
a. Prepare the necessary journal entries to close the overapplied overhead balance under two alternative approaches.
b. Which approach is the better choice, and why?

16. (LO 3) Connie Reed Company's books reflected the following balances:

	Jan. 1	Dec. 31
Raw Materials	$18,000	$11,000
Work in Process	8,700	11,000
Finished Goods	38,000	22,500

During the year, $54,000 of direct materials were added to manufacturing and $36,000 of direct labour (6,000 hours at $6.00 per hour). Total machine hours run during the year were 75,000. The firm charges a fixed overhead rate of $0.60 per machine hour and a variable overhead rate of $0.04 per machine hour. Actual overhead costs were $47,500.

Required:
a. Prepare a schedule of cost of goods manufactured.
b. Calculate Cost of Goods Sold before closing over- or underapplied overhead.
c. By what amount would the closing of over- or underapplied overhead affect cost of goods sold? (Hint: Without knowing the amount of overhead contained in each account balance, you must use the relationships of the totals to allocate under- or overapplied OH.)

17. (LO4) The following is a list of different types of firms.
A firm that:
a. manufactures jet airplanes to customer specifications.
b. manufactures household paints.
c. produces three types of soft drinks.
d. is an automobile repair shop.
e. is a corporate law firm.
f. manufactures hair spray and hand lotion.
g. is a hospital.
h. cans salmon and tuna.
i. provides lawn care services.
j. is a commercial freight company.
k. cleans and dries grain and seeds for commercial growers.

Required:
Select those companies, based on the type of production process and the nature of the product or service, that would use a costing system based on job order costing (JOC).

18. (LO 4) Wayne Cowan specializes in painting custom murals in office lobbies and other commercial sites. The firm uses a job order costing system. During July, the company worked on jobs for the following companies:

	Shearer	Reed	Yun
Direct labour hours	80	250	500
Direct materials, cost	1,560	6,200	12,600

Cowan is able to trace direct materials to each job since most costs associated with materials are related to paint or and other supplies. The firm's accountant has set the annual production overhead application rate at $30 per direct labour hour. The normal labour cost is $25 per hour.

Required:

a.   Determine the total cost for each of the accounts for each of the jobs.

b.   Is the firm using an actual costing system or a normal costing system? Explain.

19. (LO 4) The Stratychuk Auto Shop uses a job order costing system based on normal costs. Overhead is applied at the rate of 80% of direct labour costs. Jobs in process at the end of November are as shown:

	Job No. 313	Job No. 318	Job No. 340
Direct materials	$5,000	$7,000	$9,400
Direct labour	12,000	*b*	*c*
Overhead	*a*	10,000	*d*
Total	*e*	*f*	27,400

Required:

Find the values for *a* through *f*.

20. (LO 4) The Calgary Blacksmith Shop is a small firm whose specialty is the production of custom metal products. The firm employs a job order costing system based on normal cost. Overhead is applied to production at the rate of $12 per direct labour hour. During August, the firm finished Job No. 129, a batch of metal steps for mobile homes. The total direct material and direct labour costs assigned to Job No. 129 were $14,000 and $18,000, respectively. The firm's direct labour rate is $9 per hour.

Required:

a.   Compute the total cost of Job No. 129.

b.   Record the journal entry to transfer the job to Finished Goods Inventory.

c.   Compute the sales price of Job No. 129 if the job is priced to yield a gross margin equal to 40% of the sales price.

21. (LO 4) The Heather Hattery uses a perpetual inventory system. The firm maintains one inventory account for various materials that are used to make hats as well as the supplies that are used to lubricate and maintain its production machinery. For the month of August, the firm had the following transactions that affected its materials inventory account:

- Purchased felt material on account, $80,000
- Issued felt for hat production, $38,000
- Issued lubricants for machinery maintenance, $2,000

Required:

Record journal entries for the above three transactions.

22. (LO 4) Dixie Reed Industries is a newly formed firm that manufactures various items of equipment used in the bakery business. For its first month of operations, it recorded the following activity:

- $800,000 of direct materials was purchased on account.
- Of the total direct materials purchased, $650,000 was used in production operations.
- 16,000 direct labour hours at a rate of $12 per hour were incurred.
- The following manufacturing overhead costs were incurred during the period: indirect labour, $400,000; utilities, $300,000; rent $200,000; and depreciation, $300,000. All costs, except depreciation, were paid in cash.

The firm employs a job order costing system based on actual costs.

Required:

a.   Prepare the journal entries to record the previous transactions.

b.   Prepare the journal entry that would be recorded at the end of its first month to charge production for the overhead costs.

c.   Assuming no products were completed during the period, compute the ending balances in the Raw Material Inventory and Work in Process Inventory accounts.

23. (LO 4) You are provided with the inventory general ledger accounts for the past year of William Wong Corporation. You know that indirect labour for the year was 20% of direct labour and that factory supervision costs were 60% of other manufacturing costs.

EXERCISES

Raw Materials Inventory		
30,000	35,000	
40,000	4,000	
31,000		

	Work in Process		
	50,000	76,000	
(1)	35,000		
(2)	40,000		
(3)	22,000		
	71,000		

	Finished Goods		
	40,000	90,000	
(4)	76,000		
	26,000		

	Manufacturing Overhead		
(5)	4,000	22,000	
(6)	8,000		
(7)	6,000		
(8)	10,000		
	6,000		

Required:

a. Explain to your new assistant what the numbered entries (1 to 8) in the ledger accounts pertain to.

b. What was the amount of the cost of goods sold for the year?

24. (LO 4) Malcolm Winters Heavy Industries is a new firm, which began operations on January 1. The company manufactures various items of equipment used in handling products made of concrete. For its first month of operations, it recorded the following activity:
   - Purchased direct materials on account, $400,000
   - Used $325,000 of the purchased materials in production operations
   - Incurred direct labour costs: 8,000 hours at $12 per hour
   - Incurred manufacturing overhead costs: indirect labour, $200,000; utilities, $150,000; rent, $100,000; depreciation, $150,000

The firm employs a job order costing system based on actual costs.

Required:

a. Prepare the journal entries to record the transactions.

b. Prepare the journal entry that would be recorded at the end of January 2008 to charge production for the overhead costs.

c. Assuming no products were completed during the period, compute the ending balances in the Raw Materials Inventory and Work in Process Inventory accounts.

25. (LO 4) J.R. Uing Landscaping, Inc. employs a job order costing system based on actual costs. Overhead cost is assigned to jobs based on the hours J.R. works on each job (overhead is assigned weekly). J.R. is the only employee. During the first week in May, J.R. performed work for three homeowners: Ali, Hyatt, and Bartlett. The following transactions occurred during the week:
   - Trees were purchased for Ali, $500
   - Brick pavers were purchased for Hyatt for $2,000
   - Materials for a sprinkler system were purchased for Bartlett, $1,800
   - Overhead expenses were incurred as follows: fuel, $40; depreciation, $200; utilities, $60; insurance, $100; repairs/maintenance, $200

J.R. worked the following hours and was paid $25 per hour for his labour:
   - 20 hours installing the sprinkler system for Bartlett
   - 10 hours planting the trees for Ali
   - 30 hours installing the brick pavers for Hyatt

All three jobs were completed during the first week of May.

Required:

a. Record the journal entries for each of the transactions.

b. Determine the total cost assigned to each job.

c. If J.R. prices each job at 180% of cost, determine the price charged for each landscaping job.

26. (LO 4) Forrester Creations Ltd. produces high-fashion gowns. The company uses a job order costing system. The company has no beginning or ending inventory in work in process or finished goods. Manufacturing overhead is applied at the rate of $4.50 per

EXERCISES

direct labour hour. All over- or underapplied overhead is closed to cost of goods sold. Actual results for the fiscal year are:

Direct labour hours	225,000
Direct labour	$ 600,000
Indirect labour	120,000
Opening raw materials inventory	50,000
Ending raw materials inventory	250,000
Purchases of raw materials	500,000
Light, heat, and power	210,000
Indirect raw materials	37,500
Miscellaneous manufacturing overhead	240,000
Cost of goods sold	1,912,500

Required:

a. What amount of manufacturing overhead was applied to production during 2008?
b. What amount of manufacturing overhead was actually incurred during the year?
c. Was the manufacturing overhead under- or overapplied during the current year? If so, by how much?
d. What is the amount of cost of goods sold?

27. (LO 4) The Welland Bridge Company constructs bridges for the large 400-series highways. In its first year of operations, the firm worked on three bridges. Each bridge is built on-site and treated as a separate job. Overhead is applied to jobs based on the number of tonnes of direct material consumed. On average, direct materials cost $50 per tonne. Some relevant information on the jobs follows:

	Bridge 1	Bridge 2	Bridge 3	Total
Direct materials	$ 45,000	$ 54,000	$135,000	$234,000
Direct labour	180,000	213,000	599,000	992,000
Manufacturing overhead				439,920

Required:

a. Compute the overhead rate per tonne of direct materials.
b. Compute the amount of overhead assigned to each bridge.
c. Compute the total costs assigned to each bridge for the first year.
d. Assuming Bridge 3 is the only one that was finished during the year, compute the year-end balance in Work in Process Inventory.

28. (LO 4) The following two jobs were in process on June 1, at David Rosenberg Ltd. The company uses a job order costing system.

	Job No. 43	Job No. 59
Direct (raw) materials	$1,000	$900
Direct labour	1,200	200
Manufacturing overhead applied	1,800	300

There was no opening finished goods inventory at the beginning of the month. During the month of June, Jobs No. 60 to 75 inclusive were put into process.

Direct material issued amounted to $13,000, direct labour cost incurred during the month amounted to $20,000, and actual manufacturing overhead recorded during the month amounted to $28,000. Manufacturing overhead is applied based on direct labour dollars.

The only job in process at the end of June was Job No. 75, and the costs incurred for this job were $1,150 of raw materials and $1,000 of direct labour. In addition, Job No. 73, which was 100% complete, was still on hand as of June 30. Total costs allocated to this job were $3,300.

Required:

Prepare journal entries to record:

i. cost of goods manufactured
ii. cost of goods sold
iii. closing of any over- or underapplied manufacturing overhead to cost of goods sold

29. (LO 5) Gina Roma operates a restaurant and catering business. She wants to allocate administrative cost to the two revenue-producing areas. Administrative costs for the period were $43,650. Gina believes that direct labour hours of each department are the

proper basis for allocation. Direct labour hours incurred by each department are as follows: administrative, 5,100; restaurant, 21,000; and catering, 12,000.

Required:

What amount of administrative cost should be allocated to the restaurant and catering areas?

30. (LO 5) Lauren Fenmore Ltd. allocates its service department costs to its producing departments using the direct method. Information for September of this year is as follows:

Services provided to other departments	Personnel	Maintenance
Personnel		10%
Maintenance	15%	
Fabricating	45%	60%
Finishing	40%	30%
Service department costs	$68,000	$50,000

Required:

a. What amount of personnel and maintenance costs should be assigned to fabricating for September?

b. What amount of personnel and maintenance costs should be assigned to Finishing for September?

PROBLEMS

1. (LO 1) Lawrence Chung Enterprises makes only one product. It has a theoretical capacity of 50,000 units annually. Practical capacity is 80% of theoretical capacity, and normal capacity is 80% of practical capacity. The firm is expecting to produce 36,000 units next year. The company president, Lawrence Chung, has estimated the following manufacturing overhead costs for the coming year:

Indirect materials	$2.00 per unit
Indirect labour	$144,000 plus $2.50 per unit
Utilities for the plant	$6,000 plus $0.04 per unit
Repairs and maintenance for the plant	$20,000 plus $0.34 per unit
Material handling costs	$16,000 plus $0.12 per unit
Depreciation on plant assets	$0.06 per unit
Rent on plant building	$50,000 per year
Insurance on plant building	$12,000 per year

Required:

a. Determine the cost formula for total manufacturing overhead.

b. Assume that Chung produces 35,000 units during the year and that actual costs are exactly as estimated. Calculate the over- or underapplied overhead for each possible measurement base. Chung uses separate overhead rates for fixed and variable overhead.

c. Which information determined in part (b) would be the most beneficial to management, and why?

2. (LO 1) Ida Copelovici Manufacturing Ltd. is composed of a cutting department and an assembly department. The cutting department is staffed by only one person, Greys Anatomy, who runs 15 machines. The assembly department is highly labour-intensive, with 20 direct labourers and three machines. All products manufactured by Copelovici pass through both departments. Product KL85 uses the following quantities of machine time and direct labour hours.

	Cutting	Assembly
Machine hours	9.00	0.12
Direct labour hours	0.03	3.00

Copelovici Manufacturing Ltd. has estimated the following total manufacturing overhead costs and activity levels for each department for the year.

PROBLEMS

	Cutting	Assembly
Planned machine hours	72,000	14,280
Planned direct labour hours	5,200	40,000
Planned manufacturing overhead	$862,200	$432,000

Required:

a. Copelovici Manufacturing Ltd.'s accountant, Joe Kirnen, uses a plantwide rate based on machine hours for manufacturing overhead application. What rate will be used?

b. How much manufacturing overhead is assigned to each unit of Product KL85 under the method currently in use?

c. The company's auditors inform management that the method being used to apply manufacturing overhead is inappropriate. They indicate that machine hours should be used as an application base in cutting and direct labour hours should be used in assembly. Using these bases, determine the departmental rates for the fiscal year.

d. Using the information from part (c), how much manufacturing overhead would be assigned to each unit of Product KL85 if departmental rates were used?

3. (LO 2, 3) Baruch Hoffman, marketing manager for International Hydraulic Systems, has become increasingly discontented over his firm's competitive position in the market for custom hydraulic systems. Recently, he discovered that his bids for relatively simple custom projects have not been competitive with those of other firms in the industry; however, his bids on more complex projects have almost always been acceptable. An example of two recent bids follows:

	Bid #1341	Bid #1372
Direct materials	$18,000	$27,000
Direct labour	12,000	18,000
Manufacturing overhead*	21,000	21,000
Total cost	$51,000	$66,000
Markup (40% of costs)	20,400	26,400
Bid price	$71,400	$92,400

*Applied at the rate of $30 per machine hour

In attempting to find a solution to the competitive pricing problem, Baruch Hoffman sends the information on the two bids to the company's new cost accountant, Georgia Dennis. Mrs. Dennis is somewhat surprised at the relative amounts of manufacturing overhead costs assigned to the two projects. She believes that Project #1372 was much more complex to manufacture and should bear a greater share of the overhead cost. As a result, she decides to investigate whether the use of a single manufacturing overhead rate is appropriate. With the aid of production managers and engineers, she determines that it is possible to separate the overall application rate into several rates based on different application bases and cost pools. A summary of the proposed new cost pools, application bases, and application rates follows:

Cost Pool	Application Base	Application Rate
Setup costs	Number of setups	$120
Material handling	Number of parts	9
Quality costs	Number of inspections	60
Machine costs	Number of machine hours	10
Other costs	Dollars of direct labour	20% of DL cost

Mrs. Dennis then wants to examine how the new application rates will affect the bid prices on the two projects. She gathers the following additional information:

	Bid #1341	Bid #1372
Number of setups	10	70
Number of parts	400	1,200
Number of quality inspections	5	15

Required:

Mrs. Dennis calls you in for a conference and asks that you provide her with the following information:

a. Determine the amount of overhead cost assigned to each of the two projects using the new application rates.

b.   Determine the new bid price for each project.

c.   Which manufacturing overhead costs were distorted most in the allocations that used the single overhead application rate?

4.   (LO 2, 3) Sharon Newman Manufacturing's predetermined total overhead rate is $6.70, of which $6.30 is variable. Costs at two production levels are:

Overhead Items	8,000 MH	10,000 MH
Indirect materials	$12,800	$16,000
Indirect labour	27,000	33,000
Maintenance	3,700	4,500
Utilities	4,000	5,000
All other	6,700	8,300

Required:

a.   Determine the variable and fixed values for each item and give the total overhead formula.

b.   What is Newman's expected activity if the predetermined rate given is based on expected activity?

c.   Determine the expected overhead costs at the expected activity.

d.   If the firm raises its expected activity by 3,000 machine hours from that found in part (b), calculate a new predetermined overhead rate.

e.   Draft a memo to management to explain why the rate has changed.

5.   (LO 2, 3) Andrew Bell Company uses the formula $= a + bX$ to predict and analyze overhead costs. In the previous year, Bell used $1,750 per month for the (a) factor and $0.35 for the (b) factor in applying overhead. Bell has used direct labour hours in the past but is wondering whether overhead behaviour is more closely associated with machine hours. The following data have been generated for consideration:

Month	Machine Hours	Overhead Costs
1	425	$2,525
2	460	2,961
3	410	2,454
4	480	2,649
5	502	2,705
6	418	2,496

Required:

a.   Determine the fixed and variable values using machine hours.

b.   For April of the coming year, Bell expects 3,150 direct labour hours and 492 machine hours. Predict overhead costs using (1) direct labour hours and (2) machine hours.

c.   If April's actual fixed overhead costs are $1,525 and actual variable overhead costs are $1,200, which activity base appears better?

d.   Discuss criteria in choosing the best activity base for Bell Company.

6.   (LO 2, 3) The Ann Cowan Company's predetermined total overhead rate for product costing purposes is $23.00 per unit. Of this amount, $18.00 is the variable portion. Cost information for two levels of activity is as follows:

Overhead components	800 units	1,200 units
Indirect materials	$6,400	$9,600
Indirect labour	5,600	8,400
Handling	2,600	3,800
Maintenance	2,000	3,000
Utilities	2,000	2,800
Supervision	4,000	4,000

Required:

a.   Determine the fixed and variable values for each of the preceding components of overhead and determine the total overhead cost formula.

b.   What is the company's expected volume level if the predetermined rate is based on expected capacity?

c.   Determine the expected overhead costs at the expected activity level.

d.   Ann Cowan Company management decides to revise its expected activity level to be 100 units greater than the present level. Determine the new total predetermined overhead rate for product costing purposes.

PROBLEMS

7. (LO 3) After preparing for your managerial accounting exam, you confidently turn to your roommate and declare, "I think I've finally figured out how product costs flow through the various accounts and how they are reflected on income statements and balance sheets."

On hearing this wonderful news, your roommate responds, "Hey, if you really want to test your understanding of product costing, try working a problem my old prof gave me."

After rummaging for 15 minutes through various files, folders, and shelves, your roommate slaps a sheet of paper in front of you and explains that the sheet contains information pertaining to one year of operations for the Peterson Manufacturing Company. Applied manufacturing overhead is 60% of direct labour cost. The sheet contains the following information:

Beginning inventory, direct material	$ 20,000
Ending inventory, direct material	40,000
Direct material used	400,000
Sales	900,000
Beginning Work in Process Inventory	100,000
Ending Work in Process Inventory	160,000
Cost of products completed during the year	800,000
Actual manufacturing overhead costs incurred	190,000
Selling and administrative expenses	140,000
Beginning Finished Goods Inventory	200,000
Ending Finished Goods Inventory	170,000
Beginning balance—Property, Plant and Equipment	450,000
Ending balance—Property, Plant and Equipment	480,000

Required:

Compute the following:

a. Cost of direct materials purchased
b. Cost of direct labour
c. Applied manufacturing overhead
d. Cost of Goods Sold before closing underapplied or overapplied manufacturing overhead
e. Net income or net loss before closing underapplied or overapplied manufacturing overhead

8. (LO 1, 2, 3) Last night, the sprinkler system at Plant A was accidentally set off. The ensuing deluge destroyed most of the cost records in Plant A for the month just completed (May). The plant manager has come to you in a panic—he has to complete his report for head office by the end of today. He wants you to give him the numbers that he needs for his report. He can provide you with some fragments of information that he has been able to salvage:

Raw Materials				Work in Process		
Beginning	25,000			Beginning	15,000	
Ending	55,000					

Finished Goods				Cost of Goods Sold		
		Withdrawals in May	400,000			
Ending	50,000					

Manufacturing Overheads*				Accrued Wages Payable		
Beginning	0				Beginning	10,000
					Ending	20,000

*(Variable and fixed combined)

Other information:

a. Total direct materials requisitions for the month were $180,000.
b. A total of 10,000 direct labour hours were worked during the month at an average wage of $15 per hour.
c. Overhead is applied to production at $10 per direct labour hour.

PROBLEMS

d. On May 31, there was one job, #XL235, left in Work in Process. It included $4,000 of direct materials; 20 direct labour hours had been worked on this job to date (the job was started on May 30).

e. Actual manufacturing overhead expenses for May were $95,000.

Required:

Compute the following:

i. Material purchases during May.
ii. Cost of Work in Process Inventory at the end of May.
iii. Amount paid to labour force in May.
iv. Cost of goods sold in May.
v. Over/underapplied overhead in May.
vi. Cost of goods transferred from Work in Process to Finished Goods in May.
vii. Cost of Finished Goods Inventory at the beginning of May.

Extract from *Management Accounting Examination*, published by the Certified General Accountants Association of Canada (© CGA-Canada). Reprinted with permission.

9. (LO 1, 2, 3) Evelyn Thomasos, the chief accountant, is looking at the following situations:

	Case 1	Case 2	Case 3
Sales	$9,300	$?	$112,000
Direct materials used	1,200	?	18,200
Direct labour	?	4,900	?
Prime cost	3,700	?	?
Conversion cost	4,800	8,200	49,300
Manufacturing overhead	?	?	17,200
Cost of goods manufactured	6,200	14,000	?
Beginning work in process	500	900	5,600
Ending work in process	?	1,200	4,200
Beginning finished goods	?	1,900	7,600
Ending finished goods	1,200	?	?
Cost of goods sold	?	12,200	72,200
Gross profit	3,500	?	?
Operating expenses	?	3,500	18,000
Net income (loss)	2,200	4,000	?

Required:

For each of the above cases, compute the missing figures.

10. (LO 2, 3) Southwest Manufacturing's predetermined total factory overhead rate is $6.70 per machine hour, of which $6.30 is variable. Costs at two production levels are as follows:

Factory Overhead Items	8,000 MH	10,000 MH
Indirect material	$12,800	$16,000
Indirect labour	27,000	33,000
Maintenance	3,700	4,500
Utilities	4,000	5,000
All other	6,700	8,300

a. Determine the variable and fixed values for each item, and give the total factory overhead formula.

b. What is Southwest's expected capacity level if the predetermined rate given as based on expected capacity?

c. Determine the expected factory overhead costs at the expected activity level.

d. Assuming the firm raises its expected capacity level by 2,375 machine hours over that found in part b, calculate a new predetermined total factory overhead rate.

e. Draft a memo to management to explain why the rate has changed.

11. (LO 4) The Kitowsky Publishing Company recorded the following transactions for October:

a. Purchased materials on account, $900,000.

b. Issued materials into production, $700,000. Of the total materials issued, $500,000 could be traced directly to specific jobs.

c. Manufacturing labour costs in the amount of $650,000 were incurred. Only $500,000 of this amount could be attributed to specific jobs.

PROBLEMS

    d.   Overhead was applied to jobs on the basis of 110% of direct labour cost.

    e.   Job #807 costing $250,000 was completed.

    f.   Job #807 was sold on account for $400,000.

Required:

Record all necessary journal entries to account for the previous transactions.

12. (LO 2, 3) Saleem Kassam Didona Enterprises makes only one product. It has a theoretical capacity of 50,000 units annually. Practical capacity is 80% of theoretical capacity, and normal capacity is 80% of practical capacity. The firm is expecting to produce 36,000 units next year. The company president, Barbara Didona, has planned for the following factory overhead costs for the coming year:

- Indirect materials: $2.00 per unit
- Indirect labour: $144,000 plus $2.50 per unit
- Utilities for the plant: $6,000 plus 5.04 per unit
- Repairs and maintenance for the plant: $20,000 plus 5.34 per unit
- Material handling costs: $16,000 plus $.12 per unit
- Depreciation on plant assets: $.06 per unit
- Rent on plant building: $50,000 per year
- Insurance on plant building: $12,000 per year

Required:

    a.   Determine the cost formula for total factory overhead.

    b.   Assume that Kassam produces 35,000 units during the year and that actual costs are exactly as estimated. Calculate the overapplied or underapplied overhead for each possible capacity base.

    c.   Which information determined in part b would be the most beneficial to management, and why?

13. (LO 4) Technotronix Inc. custom manufactures robots that are used in repetitive production tasks. At the beginning of the current year, three jobs were in process. The costs assigned to the jobs as of January 1, are as follows:

	Job No. 114J	Job No. 117N	Job No. 128P
Direct materials	$200,000	$1,400,000	$100,000
Direct labour	150,000	800,000	60,000
Overhead	100,000	600,000	42,000
Total	$450,000	$2,800,000	$202,000

During the course of the year, two more jobs were started, 133I and 134P, and the following transactions occurred:

    i.   Purchases of materials $1,200,000

    ii. Direct materials were issued to production:

        Job 114J $ 212,000

        Job 117N   158,000

        Job 128P   410,000

        Job 133I   160,000

        Job 134P   125,000

    iii. Indirect materials were issued to production $ 111,900

    iv. Labour costs were incurred as follows:

        Job 114J $ 175,000

        Job 117N   302,000

        Job 128P   450,000

        Job 133I   205,000

        Job 134P   110,000

        Indirect labour   300,000

    v.   Other overhead costs were incurred $ 500,000

    vi. Actual overhead costs were applied to jobs on the basis of machine hours. The machine hours consumed on each job were:

        Job 114J   1,200

        Job 117N   1,800

        Job 128P   3,400

        Job 133I   900

        Job 134P   700

Required:
a. Prepare the journal entries to record the previous events.
b. Assume that Jobs 114J and 117N were completed during the year. Prepare the journal entries to record the completion of these jobs.
c. Assume Job 117N was sold during the year for $3,000,000. Prepare the necessary journal entries to record the sale.

14. (LO 4) The Jerry Dykopf Safety Company manufactures metal shields for various pieces of power equipment to protect machine operators. The shields are created in a two-step process. First, materials are cut and formed in the Stamping Department. This department is very machine-intensive and highly automated. Overhead in this department is applied based on machine time ($12 per machine hour). The second department, the Finishing Department, welds materials received from the Stamping Department and then applies either a paint or galvanized finish. The Finishing Department is very labour-intensive, and consequently overhead is applied based on direct labour hours ($8 per direct labour hour).

During June Dykopf worked on three separate jobs. Information on the three jobs follows:

	Department	
	Stamping	**Finishing**
Job # 8721		
Direct labour hours	1,600	2,000
Machine hours	4,000	800
Direct labour cost	$ 16,000	$18,000
Direct materials cost	88,000	4,000
Job # 8722		
Direct labour hours	3,600	5,000
Machine hours	9,000	1,200
Direct labour cost	$ 36,000	$45,000
Direct materials cost	190,000	9,000
Job # 8723		
Direct labour hours	400	1,300
Machine hours	2,000	300
Direct labour cost	$ 4,000	$11,700
Direct materials cost	28,000	1,000

Jerry Dykopf Safety Company employs a job order product costing system based on normal cost. Actual overhead costs in the Stamping and Finishing Departments for the month were, respectively, $200,000 and $65,000.

Required:
a. Determine the total amount of overhead to be applied to each of the three jobs.
b. Calculate the total cost of each job.
c. Calculate the difference between the overhead applied to each department and the overhead incurred in each department.

15. (LO 4) Ridge Maroni Ltd., a small manufacturer of swimwear, uses a job order costing system. The corporate policy is to close all over- and underapplied overhead to Cost of Goods Sold. The company had the following inventory balances:

	Opening Balance **January 1**	**Ending Balance** **December 31**
Raw material inventory	$54,000	$39,000
Work in process	82,500	?
Finished goods	90,000	?

The actual data for the year included:
1. Overhead was applied at a rate of $4.50 per direct labour hour.
2. Purchases of materials and supplies totalled $219,000. Both are accumulated in the Raw Materials Inventory account.
3. Of the total materials requisitions, 90% were for direct materials and 10% were for supplies.

PROBLEMS

4. Direct labour hours were 33,000 for a total cost of $264,000.
5. Work in process at December 31 consisted of units with the following costs:

Direct materials	$15,000
Direct labour (7,500 hours)	60,000

6. At year-end, the manufacturing overhead account had a debit balance of $750.
7. Sales for the year were $744,000, with gross profit equal to 25% of sales before adjusting for under- or overapplied overhead.

Required:

a. Calculate each of the following:
   i. Direct materials used.
   ii. Work in process inventory, December 31.
   iii. Cost of goods manufactured.
   iv. Finished goods inventory, December 31.
   v. Actual manufacturing overhead incurred.
b. There are two ways of dealing with over- or underapplied overhead. Explain each.

16. (LO 5) Eva Novotney Corporation allocates its service department costs to its producing departments using the direct method. For September, the Personnel Department incurred $69,000 of costs and the Maintenance Department incurred $50,000 of costs. Other information for the month follows:

**Percentage of Services Provided
to Other Departments**

	Personnel	Maintenance
Personnel		50%
Maintenance	10%	
Fabricating	30%	30%
Finishing	60%	20%

Required:

a. What amount of Personnel and Maintenance costs should be assigned to Fabricating for September?
b. What amount of Personnel and Maintenance costs should be assigned to Finishing for September?
c. Why would the step method of allocating service department costs be preferred for this company?

17. (LO5) Adventura Hospital has 5 departments: 3 are classified as service departments (S) and 2 are classified as producing departments (P). All service centre costs are allocated to the producing departments. The percentage distribution of actual services during a recent period is as follows:

To	S1	S2	S3	P1	P2
From					
S1	0%	20%	20%	30%	30%
S2	20%	0%	30%	40%	10%
S3	15%	15%	0%	35%	35%

The operating costs of the service departments are as follows:

S1	$10,000
S2	20,000
S3	5,000

The overhead costs of the producing departments are as follows:

P1	$20,000
P2	30,000

Required:

Using the direct method of service department cost allocation, prepare a schedule showing the total overhead in each of the two producing departments.

(Problem 17 is adapted by the authors from Management Accounting examinations published by the Certified General Accountants Association of Canada © CGA-Canada, March 2005, used by permission)

CASES

1. Black's main business is publishing books and magazines. Marlena Evans is the production manager of the Moncton plant, which manufactures paper used in all of Black's publications. The Moncton plant has no sales staff and only limited contact with outside customers since most of the sales are made to other divisions of Black. As a consequence, the Moncton plant is evaluated by merely comparing its expected costs to its actual costs to determine how well costs were controlled.

The accounting reports that Evans receives are produced by the financial accounting system, with little information to help her perform her job. Consequently, the entire accounting process is perceived as a negative motivational device that does not reflect how hard or effectively she works as a production manager. In discussions with Hope Brady, controller of the Moncton plant, Evans said, "I think the cost reports are misleading. I know I have better production over a number of operating periods, but the cost reports still say I have excessive costs. I know how to get a good-quality product out. Over the years, I have even cut raw materials used to do it. The cost reports do not show any of this; they are always negative, no matter what I do. There is no way you can win with accounting or the people at headquarters who use these reports."

Brady gave Evans little consolation when she stated that the accounting system and the cost reports generated by headquarters are just part of the corporate game and almost impossible for an individual to change: "Though these reports are used to evaluate your division and your performance, you should not worry too much. You have not been fired! Besides, these cost reports have been used by Black for the last 15 years."

From discussion with the operations people at other Black divisions, Evans knows that the turnover of production managers has been high, even though relatively few have been fired. A typical comment has been: "The accountants may be quick with numbers, but they do not know anything about production. I wound up completely ignoring cost reports. No matter what they say about not firing people, negative cost reports mean negative evaluations. I am better off working for another company."

A copy of the most recent cost report for the Moncton plant is shown in Exhibit 4-1.
Required:
As a consulting management accountant hired by Evans, explain what needs to be done with the cost reports. Use the case approach for your answer.

EXHIBIT 4-1
Monthly Cost Report, November (000s)

	Expected Cost	Actual Cost	Excess Cost
Raw materials	$ 400	$ 437	$ 37
Direct labour	560	540	(20)
Overhead	100	134	34
Total	$1,060	$1,111	$ 51
(ICMA adapted)			

2. Moss Manufacturing has just completed a major change in its quality control (QC) process. Previously, products were reviewed by QC inspectors at the end of each major process, and the company's 10 QC inspectors were charged as direct labour to the operations or job. In an effort to improve efficiency and quality, the company purchased a computerized video QC system for $250,000. The system consists of a minicomputer, 15 video cameras, other peripheral hardware, and software.

The new system uses cameras stationed by QC engineers at key points in the production process. Each time an operation changes or there is a new operation, the cameras are moved, and a new master picture is loaded into the computer by a QC engineer. The camera takes pictures of the units in process, and the computer compares them with the picture of a "good" unit. Any differences are sent to a QC engineer, who removes the bad units and discusses the flaws with the production supervisors. The new system has replaced the 10 QC inspectors with two QC engineers.

CASES

The operating costs of the new QC system, including the salaries of the two QC engineers, have been included in overhead in calculating the company's overhead rate. The computations of the overhead rate before and after automation are shown in Exhibit 4-1.

"Three hundred percent" lamented the president. "How can we be competitive with such a high overhead rate?"

Required:
Using the case approach, eliminate the president's confusion.

EXHIBIT 4-1
Overhead Rate Calculation

	Before	After
Estimated overhead	$1,900,000	$2,100,000
Estimated direct labour costs	1,000,000	700,000
Estimated overhead rate	1.9	3.0

3. Your brother-in-law became a contractor by accident. He had been trained as a carpenter at a pulp mill in northern Quebec. He received his carpenter certificate or ticket about 20 years ago and was happily employed at the pulp mill until it closed two years ago. With the mill being the only large employer, the town literally died. There were no jobs in town for the massive number of displaced pulp mill workers. This forced your brother-in-law to leave town to seek employment in Montreal.

He arrived in Montreal in the early winter. There were few jobs for carpenters as the winter is the slow season for construction, the main employer of carpenters. He remained without work for more than a month. Then he met a family who happened to need their home renovated. They asked if he was willing to do the renovation and how much he would charge. A deal was struck. Subsequently, by word of mouth he was recommended for other renovation projects. After a few months of doing renovations, be stopped looking for a carpenter job as he was now a renovator.

Your brother-in-law had a simple way doing business. He was asked to quote on a relatively large number of renovation projects. He estimated the costs of materials, any outside labour he had to hire, $30 for every hour he expected to work on the renovation project, plus a contingency of 10% to cover unexpected costs and general office supplies. At the end of the project, he collected the money owing by the customer and paid for materials and all outside labour. The amount that is left after all payments is the amount he has earned for his labour. He expects that he earns a higher actual hourly wage (what is left to a project divided by the number of hours he works on the project) on some projects and less on others, but he is unsure. He hopes that, once the contingency is included, his actual hourly rate does not vary much from the quoted rate ($30 per hour).

Knowing his actual hourly rate has become important. At first he had few projects and lots of extra time. Now he has so many projects to choose from that he wants to understand what types of projects are the most profitable in order to choose those that maximize his profits.

Your brother-in-law asks you how to solve the problem.

Required:
Using the case approach, assist your brother-in-law in solving his problem.

ETHICS

1. Assigning overhead costs to products is necessary to more accurately estimate the cost of producing a product or performing a service. One product that takes on an exceptional number of additional charges for overhead is an aspirin dose (two units) in a cosmetics hospital. Following is an estimate of why a patient is charged $7 for a dose of aspirin. Some costs are referred to as "shared and shifted costs"; others are called overhead. In all cases, this simply means that these costs are not covered by revenue dollars elsewhere and so must be covered for the hospital to do all of the things a hospital charges for—including administering aspirin.

Peterborough Cosmetics Hospital Product Costing Sheet

	Unit	Unit Cost	Total Units	Total Cost
Raw Material				
Aspirin	each	$ 0.006	2	$0.012
Direct Labour				
Physician	hour	60.000	0.0084	0.500
Pharmacist	hour	30.000	0.0200	0.600
Nurse	hour	20.000	0.0056	0.112
Indirect Labour				
Orderly	hour	12.000	0.0167	0.200
Recordkeeping	hour	12.000	0.0167	0.200
Supplies				
Cup	each	0.020	1	0.020
Shared and Shifted Costs				
Unreimbursed Medical Costs		0.200	1	0.200
Indigent Care		0.223	1	0.223
Uncollectible Receivables		0.084	1	0.084
Malpractice Insurance*		0.034	2	0.068
Excess Bed Capacity		0.169	1	0.169
Other Operating Costs		0.056	1	0.056
Other Administrative Costs		0.112	1	0.112
Excess Time Elements		0.074	1	0.074
Product Cost				$2.630
Hospital Overhead Costs @ 32.98%				0.867
Full Cost (Including Overhead)				$3.497
Profit (@ 100%)				3.497
Price (Per Dose)				$6.994

*Note that the dose is charged twice for malpractice insurance—once for each aspirin!
SOURCE: Based on David W. McFadden, "The Legacy of the $7 Aspirin," *Management Accounting*, April 1990, p. 39. Adapted with permission of the Institute of Management Accountants, Montvale, N.J., USA. Web site: www.imanet.org.

Required:

a. Discuss the reasons why such cost shifting is necessary.

b. What other kinds of costs might be included in the additional overhead charge at the rate of 32.98%?

c. Discuss the ethical implications of shifting costs—such as those for uncollectible receivables and excess bed capacity—to a patient receiving a dose of aspirin.

d. Are you willing to accept the way the hospital estimates its $7 charge for a dose of aspirin, knowing what costs are considered in developing such a charge if you are a customer or the hospital administrator? Discuss the reasons behind your answers.

2. In March, the Aviation Administration began investigating allegations that some maintenance supervisors for one of the large airlines had been signing off on maintenance work that actually was not performed on individual aircraft.

a. Why could an individual airplane be considered a "job" for an airline company?

b. One of the maintenance tasks that was allegedly not completed was the washing of a cabin head air exchanger. Assume the following facts. Some of the airline's mechanics were on strike. The task is considered routine; the plane was only one year old and in excellent condition. The plane was scheduled to depart the airport in 30 minutes on a fully booked flight; washing the exchange filter would have taken a minimum of one hour. The airline is currently having problems with on-time departures and arrivals. The plane arrived safely at its destination. Discuss the possible perceptions and thoughts of the maintenance supervisor at the time that this maintenance should have been performed.

c. Discuss the perceptions and thoughts of the passengers at the terminal if the maintenance had been performed.

d. Discuss the ethical issues involved.

3. Dr. Lelia Sulyma is a plastic surgeon who treats both paying and nonpaying patients. In the past month, several very wealthy patients have been in for tummy tucks, face lifts,

and liposuction. One patient, on whom Dr. Sulyma has worked countless hours for over a year, is a young boy who was in a motorcycle accident; the child is a pro bono case.

Required:

a. Discuss the practical aspects of shifting some appropriately assigned overhead costs from the child's case to the wealthy patients.

b. Discuss the ethical aspects of shifting some appropriately assigned overhead costs from the child's case to the wealthy patients.

c. By accepting nonpaying patients who require such extensive treatment, Dr. Sulyma is not making a reasonable income from her profession. She is considering closing her practice and working only in a private for-profit hospital. Do you have any suggestions on how she might be able to continue serving both charity and wealthy patients and still earn a reasonable income?

4. Tom Savin has recently been hired as a cost accountant by the Offset Press Company, a privately held company that produces a line of offset printing presses and lithograph machines. During his first few months on the job, Savin has discovered that Offset has been underapplying factory overhead to the Work in Process account, while overstating expenses through the general and administrative accounts. This practice has been going on since the start of the company six years ago. The effect in each year has been favourable, having a material impact on the company's tax position. No internal audit function exists at Offset, and the external auditors have not yet discovered the underapplied factory overhead.

Prior to the sixth-year audit, Savin had pointed out the practice and its effect to Mary Brown, the corporate controller, and had asked her to let him make the necessary adjustments. Brown directed him not to make adjustments but to wait until the external auditors had completed their work and see what they uncovered.

The sixth-year audit has now been completed, and the external auditors have once more failed to discover the underapplication of factory overhead. Savin again asks Brown if he could make the required adjustments and once again is told not to make them. Savin, however, believes that the adjustments should be made and that the external auditors should be informed of the situation.

Since there are no established policies at Offset Press Company for resolving ethical conflicts, Savin is considering following one of three alternative courses of action:

• Follow Brown's directive and do nothing further.
• Attempt to convince Brown to make the proper adjustments, and advise the external auditors of her actions.
• Tell the Audit Committee of the Board of Directors about the problem and give them the appropriate accounting data.

Required:

a. For each of the three alternative courses of action that Tom Savin is considering, explain whether the action is appropriate. (Refer to the Code of Ethics for Society of Management Accountants.)

b. Without prejudice to your answer in part (a), assume that Tom Savin again approaches Mary Brown to make the necessary adjustments and is unsuccessful. Describe the steps that Tom Savin should take in proceeding to resolve this situation.

(CMA adapted)

SOLUTIONS TO SELF-TEST QUESTIONS

1. a: $300,000 \times [12,000 \div (\$12,000 + \$6,000)] = \$200,000$

2. a: $300,000 \times [\$200,000 \div (\$500,000 + \$200,000)] = \$85,714$

3. b: $180,000 \times [\$200,000 \div (\$200,000 + \$500,000)]$ $51,429

 $120,000 \times [6,000 \div (12,000 + 6,000)]$ 40,000
 \$91,429

4. a: $[(\$15,000 + \$8,000 + \$12,000 + \$15,000) \div 20,000] = \$2.50$

5. a: $(\$108,600 - \$6,000) \div 8,550 = \$12.00$

SOLUTIONS TO SELF-TEST QUESTIONS

6. a.
7. b: ($12,500 + $5,000 + $13,500 + $16,000) ÷ 27,000 = $1.74
8. b.
9. a.
10. d.
11. a.
12. b.
13. b. [($15.00 × 200) + ($8.00 × 300) + $4,200] = $9,600

ENDNOTES

1. Another alternative exists. This type of system is called a "standard cost system" and is covered in chapter 7.

2. Use of such nontraditional activity measures to allocate overhead and the resultant activity-based costs is discussed in Chapter 8.

3. Susan Stellin, "The Movers Are Here. Have You Done Your Homework?" *New York Times,* July 29, 2007.

4. To eliminate the need for repetition, units should be read to mean either products or services, since job order product costing is applicable to both manufacturing and service companies. For the same reason, *produced* can mean *manufactured or performed.*

5. Roger V. Dickeson, "We Need Better Tools," *Printing Impressions,* Philadelphia, September 2001, pp. 116–17.

6. Janet R. Gross, "Stick With Tradition," *Business Forms, Labels & Systems*, May 20, 2004.

7. *Pharmaceutical Care: Cost Estimation and Cost Management*, February 16, 1998.

8. Although actual overhead may be assigned to jobs, such an approach would be less common because total overhead would not be known until the period was over, causing an unwarranted delay in overhead assignment.

9. One alternative to a time sheet prepared for the day is an individual time ticket for each job. These forms could be handed out by supervisors to employees as employees are assigned new jobs. Another alternative is to have supervisors maintain a record of which employees worked on what jobs for what period of time. This alternative is extremely difficult to implement, however, if a supervisor is overseeing a large number of employees or when the employees are dispersed through a large section of the plant.

10. Natasha Garber, "Opportunity Rocks," *Special Events Magazine*, October 1, 2004, p. 66.

11. This example is based on an article by Leonard A. Robinson and Loudell Ellis Robinson, "Steering a Boat Maker Through Cost Shoals," *Management Accounting,* January 1983, pp. 60–66.

12. Frank Greer, "Job Costing Basics," *Painting & Wallcovering Contractor*, St. Louis, March/April 2004, Vol. 55, Iss. 2, p. 16.

13. The algebraic or reciprocal approach to service department cost allocation considers all interrelationships of departments and reflects these in simultaneous equations. This technique is covered in any standard cost accounting text.

14. TECH-FAQ (Copyright 2007); Thomas H. Davenport, "Putting the Enterprise into the Enterprise System," *Harvard Business Review,* July–August 1998.

15. James Ashton and Frank Cook, Jr, "Time to Reform Job Shop Manufacturing," *Harvard Business Review.* March–April, 1989, pg. 107.

Chapter 5

Process Costing

LEARNING OBJECTIVES

After completing this chapter, you should be able to answer the following questions:

1 **What**
production situations are appropriate for a process costing system and why?

2 **How**
is a cost of production report prepared under the weighted average method of process costing?

3 **How**
are equivalent units of production, unit costs, and inventory values computed using the FIFO method of process costing?

4 **How**
is a cost of production report prepared under the FIFO method of process costing?

5 **What**
is the effect of multidepartmental processing on the computation of equivalent units of production? (Weighted Average Method)

6 **How**
do normal and abnormal losses of units differ and how is each treated in the calculation of equivalent units of production?

ON SITE

www.ganong.com

Ganong Bros. Ltd.

The name "GANONG" whets appetites across Canada and around the world wherever these fine chocolates are available. Ganong candies and chocolates have enlivened many a Christmas morning and special occasion since 1873, when two brothers embarked on an experiment in candy making in St. Stephen, New Brunswick. The company was launched when brothers James and Gilbert Ganong opened a general merchandise store that also made fresh candy. Deciding that the candy business had more potential than grocery or general merchandise retail, they changed focus.

The business grew. The brothers offered sweet-toothed customers hard candies, such as the cinnamon and chocolate Chicken Bones and, of course, chocolate. Ganong Original Chicken Bones are still made today as they were when Ganong invented them back in 1885.

The company, whose New Brunswick factory is located at 1 Chocolate Drive in the town of St. Stephen, claims to have created the chocolate bar and the heart-shaped Valentines chocolate box. It also says it sold the first lollipop in Canada.

The business has faced its share of obstacles. Five years ago, New Brunswick's Lantic Sugar refinery closed and Ganong had to look for an alternative source for the millions of kilograms of liquid sugar the company consumes annually.

Buying from Lantic's Montreal factory was going to cost more money, but by shipping raw sugar instead of liquid sugar, Ganong was able to limit the cost increase. The company now liquefies sugar at its factory.

The company introduced the wrapped chocolate bar in 1906 and had invented the milk chocolate bar by 1910. Ganong also invented a worldwide phenomenon—the wrapped chocolate cream bar.

It was Arthur D. Ganong, president from 1917 to 1957, and his head of manufacturing, George Ensor, who actually came up with the idea of wrapping snack-sized portions of chocolate in cellophane. The two men enjoyed spending warm spring days fishing, and they soon discovered that warm weather wreaked havoc on the unwrapped chocolate pieces they had stashed in their pockets. They began wrapping the chocolate soon after, but it took a while before they realized that they could make some money from the idea. "It finally dawned on them that, if this was a convenience food for them, why wouldn't it be a convenience food for others?" says the current president, David Ganong.

Although the actual name of the first chocolate bar to hit the shelves in 1910 is debated within the company, Mr. Ganong says he knows it was chocolate on the outside with a sweet centre.

Boxed chocolates represent only about a quarter of his company's business, says Mr. Ganong, just the fourth president—all of whom have been family members—since the firm's formation in 1873.

The rest is divided among three other categories: the fast-developing business of fruit snacks; bagged candies, such as jujubes and peppermints; and bulk candy products and chocolate bars, such as Chicken Bones, Ganong's signature hard candy with a chocolate centre.

No one makes Chicken Bones like Ganong. "We do take the extra time and cost to put a layer of clear, hard candy around the outside of it after all the colour and flavour is inside," Mr. Ganong said. "It gives it this really wonderful shine that a Ganong Chicken Bone has. The appearance, because of the hard candy on the outside, is really spectacular."

There is also substance, beyond the looks. "The chocolate centre of a Ganong Chicken Bone is a special, rich, bitter flavour that blends perfectly with the cinnamon candy jacket," he said.

Tradition. Quality. Innovation. They are Ganong hallmarks and part of its heritage. It's what sets Ganong apart. Among the thousands of privately owned companies in Canada, Ganong has a certain distinction. Its name is synonymous with fine chocolate, and it's also recognized as a good business.

The *National Post* said in 1999 that Ganong is one of "Canada's 50 Best Managed Private Companies." The *Post* says that's because of "the high importance placed on hiring, training, and motivating staff. The second link is timing: beating the competition to the punch on both the creative and delivery fronts."

"Ganong Bros. has been a part of our province's [New Brunswick's] business community for over a century, and through the decades it has evolved to meet the needs of the marketplace," New Brunswick Business Minister Peter Mesheau said. "We're proud of this company's commitment to the community of St. Stephen and to the province of New Brunswick. Manufacturers like Ganong are absolutely vital to the provincial economy. They account for a significant portion of our province's foreign exports, which totalled $8.5 billion in 2003 alone."

Therein lies the key to Ganong's continued success as one of the country's preeminent candy and chocolate makers. Take tradition mixed with the never-ending pursuit of quality, add good, talented people, and beat the competition with the best product. It works every time.

SOURCES: Sharda Prashad, "The Sweet Smell of Succes," *Toronto Star*, November 27, 2005, A19. Reprinted with permission Torstar Syndication Services. *National Post*, December 15, 1999; Gordon Pitts, "Ganong Boss Aims for Sweet Spot," *Globe and Mail*, March 3, 2003, Pg. B4; Chuck Brown, "Make No Bones About These Chicken Bones," *New Brunswick Telegraph Journal*, November 25, 2002; "Federal and Provincial Investments Improve Ganong's International Competitiveness," *Business New Brunswick*, July 13, 2004; Ganong Bros. website www.ganong.com (reprinted by permission of Ganong). Gordon Pitts, Shaken by chocolate woes, Ganong goes outside for help; *The Globe and Mail*, Saturday July 19, 2008, page B3.

We have seen that to compute the cost of products, it is necessary to decide on (1) the product costing system, and (2) the valuation method to be used. The costing system defines the cost object and the method of assigning costs to production. In this chapter the process costing system is studied.

LEARNING OBJECTIVE 1

What production situations are appropriate for a process costing system and why?

Introduction to Process Costing

Process costing, unlike job order costing, is used in companies that mass produce similar products. Job order costing is appropriate for companies making products or providing services in limited quantities that conform to customer specifications.

In contrast, the mass production of candy and chocolate is totally unlike the job order production process discussed in the previous chapter. Because the process itself differs, so must the method of accounting for that process. Ganong Bros., like many other chocolate producers, would use **process costing** to determine the product cost of its candy and chocolates. Process costing is used by manufacturers that make large quantities of homogeneous products in a continuous mass production environment to accumulate and assign costs to units of production.

process costing
a method of accumulating and assigning costs to units of production in companies that make large quantities of homogeneous products

Process costing is used for mass produced homogeneous items.

Process costing deals mainly with products that are regular in specification and are made continuously. The fundamental idea, as with job order costing, is to allocate costs of material, labour, and overhead inputs to the output designations of the system.

The key assumption in the design of process costing systems is that all units of output passing through a particular process during a specified time period are alike in all economic respects. When all products are not homogeneous, the accountant must allocate the costs of the process among two or more products. This gives rise to what is referred to as joint processing costs, a topic that will be covered in Chapter 9.[1]

There are two methods of calculating the product unit cost in a process costing system—Weighted Average and FIFO. The major difference between these two methods is in the treatment of the Beginning Work in Process Inventory. This difference has an impact on the calculation of the product unit cost. Once this cost has been determined, it is used to value the department's ending Work in Process Inventory and the cost of the units transferred out of the department.

In some ways, the cost accumulation in a process costing system is similar to job order product costing procedures. In a **process costing system**, as in a job order system, costs are accumulated by cost component in each production department. As units are transferred from one department to the next, unit costs are also transferred, so that a total cost is accumulated by the end of the production. In a job order system, accumulated departmental costs are assigned to specific jobs, which may be single units or batches of units. In contrast, in a process costing system, accumulated departmental costs are assigned to all the units that flowed through the department during the period. The valuation method chosen affects which costs are included in the inventory accounts.

process costing system
a product costing system used by companies that produce large amounts of homogeneous products through a continuous production flow

Two other differences between job order and process costing are (1) the quantity of production for which costs are being accumulated at any one time and (2) the cost object to which the costs are assigned. For example, an entrepreneur who bakes cakes and cookies for specific orders would use a job order product costing system. The costs of the direct materials, direct labour, and overhead associated with production of each baking job would be gathered and assigned to the individual jobs. The cost per cookie could be determined if all the cookies baked for the job were similar.

In contrast, bakeries such as Weston Bakeries Ltd., which makes more than two million cookies a week, would not use a job order system because volume is simply too great and the cookies are reasonably homogeneous. At Weston Bakeries Ltd., direct materials, direct labour, and overhead costs could be gathered during the period for each department and each product. Because a variety of cookies are produced in any department during a period, costs must be accumulated by and assigned to each type of cookie worked on during the period. Production does not have to be complete for costs to be assigned in a process costing system.

As shown in Exhibit 5-1, the costs of inventory components are accumulated in the accounts as the inventory flows through the production process. At the end of production, the accumulated costs must be assigned to all the units produced to determine the cost per unit for purposes of inventory measurement and calculation of cost of goods sold.

EXHIBIT 5-1

Flow of Costs though Production

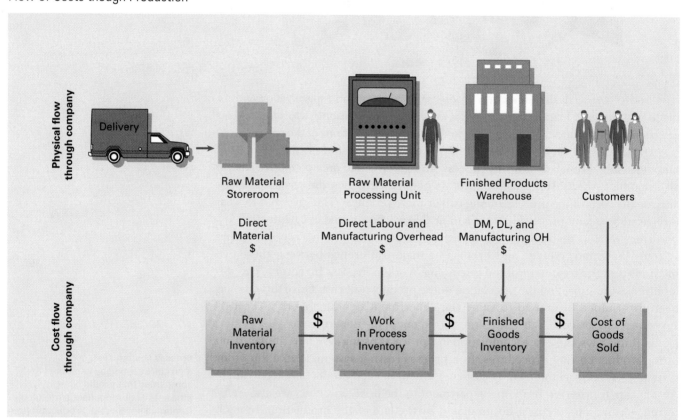

Exhibit 5-2 presents the source documents and records used to make initial cost assignments to production departments during a period. As goods are transferred from one department to the next, the related departmental costs are also transferred. The three products in the exhibit are started in Department One. Then Products A and B and their related production costs are transferred to Department Two. Additional costs in Department Two will attach to these products before they are sent to Finished Goods Inventory. Product C, however, does not have to go through Department Two, and thus its cost will consist only of materials, labour, and overhead costs from Department One.

EXHIBIT 5-2

Cost Flows and Cost
Assignments

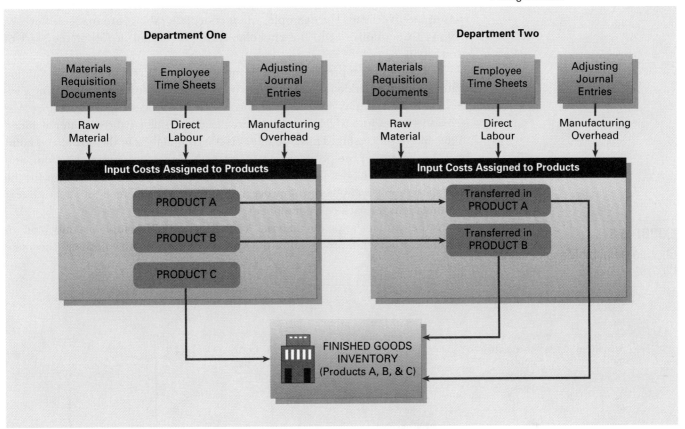

As in job order costing, the direct material and direct labour components of product cost present relatively few problems for cost accumulation and assignment. Direct material cost can be measured from the materials requisition slips and raw material invoice prices; direct labour cost can be determined from the employee time sheets and wage rates for the period. These costs are assigned at the end of the period (usually weekly, biweekly, or monthly) from the departments to the units produced. Although direct material and direct labour are easily traced to production, overhead must be allocated to units.

Either an actual overhead amount or a predetermined rate may be used to assign overhead to products. If actual overhead is relatively constant each period and production volume is relatively steady over time, then using actual overhead costs provides a fairly stable production cost. If such conditions do not exist, application of actual overhead will yield fluctuating product costs, and a predetermined overhead rate (or rates) should be used.

Accumulating Costs by Separate Cost Components

Cost assignment in any process costing environment using actual costs is an averaging process. In general, and in the simplest of situations, a product's unit cost results from dividing a period's departmental production costs by that period's departmental quantity of production. However, in most situations, cost components are added at different points in the production process, and thus separate accumulations must be made for each cost component.

For a production operation to begin, some direct material must be introduced. Without any direct material, there would be no need for labour or overhead to be incurred. The material added at the start of production is 100% complete throughout the process regardless of the percentage of completion of labour and overhead. For example, when chocolate rabbits are made at Barbara Didona Chocoholics Ltd., the chocolate must be added in full at the start of production.

Most production processes require more than one direct material. Additional materials may be added at any point or may be added continuously during processing. Materials may even be added at the end of processing. For instance, the individual boxes into which the rabbits are placed for sale are direct material added at the end of processing. Thus, the rabbit is 0% complete as to the box at any point prior to the end of the production process, although other material, labour, and overhead may have been incurred. Exhibit 5-3 provides the production flow for the chocolate rabbit manufacturing process and illustrates the need for separate cost accumulations for each cost component.

As the exhibit shows, the material "chocolate" is 100% complete at any point in the rabbit production process after the start of production; no additional chocolate

EXHIBIT 5-3

Chocolate Rabbit Manufacturing Process

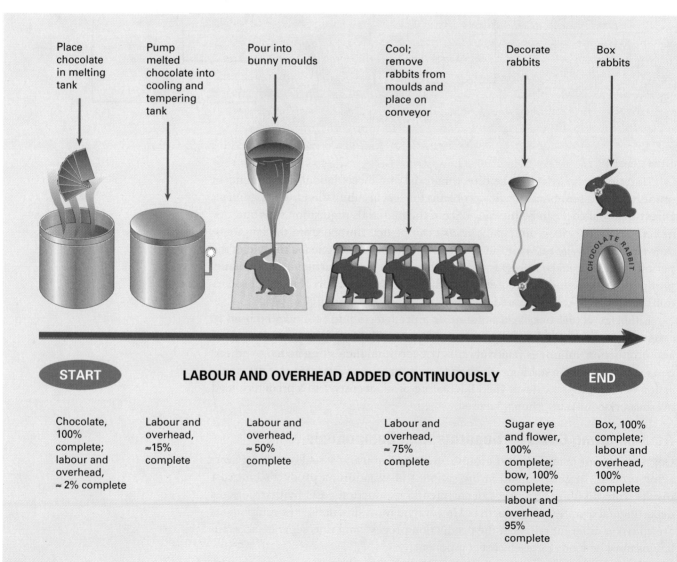

is added later. When labour and overhead reach the 95% completion point, a sugar eye, flower, and bow are added. Before the 95% point, the eyes, flowers, and bows are 0% complete; after this point, these materials are 100% complete. Last, the rabbits are boxed and are 100% complete. Thus, at the end of a period, rabbits could be anywhere in the production process. If, for example, the rabbits were 75% complete as to labour and overhead, they would be 100% complete as to chocolate, and 0% complete as to eyes, flowers, bows, and boxes.

When different components of a product are at different stages of completion, separate cost accumulations are necessary for each cost component. But a single cost accumulation can be made for multiple cost components that are at the same degree of completion. For example, separate cost accumulations would need to be made for the chocolate and the boxes. However, because the sugar eyes, flowers, and bows are added at the same point, these can be viewed as one ingredient (decorations) and a single cost accumulation can be made for this. Additionally, because direct labour and overhead are incurred at the same rate in the chocolate bunny–making process, these two components may be combined and one cost accumulation can be made for "conversion" as a single category.

The present authors agree that the assumption that all conversion costs are incurred uniformly in proportion to the degree of product completion is difficult to justify on theoretical grounds. It has been observed that the conversion costs sequence usually consists of a number of standard operations or a standard number of hours, days, weeks, or months for mixing, heating, cooling, again, curing, and so forth. Thus, the degree of completion for conversion costs depends on what proportion of the total effort that is needed to complete one unit or one batch has been devoted to units still in process. Many others, without presenting a solution to the problem, have taken a conceptual approach, maintaining that standard cost systems (covered in Chapter 7) are most often used when identical units are produced on a continuous basis. They suggest that the use of standard costs eliminates the need to compute the cost per equivalent unit. The equivalent unit is the standard cost. Additionally, the costs transferred out are equal to the number of units completed times the standard cost per equivalent unit. Others affirm that in process cost accounting, the problem of determining unit costs is resolved by using equivalent units. Some researchers feel that the level of Work in Process units must be estimated by qualified technical staff. They transfer the problem to "qualified technical personnel." But who are these "qualified technical personnel"? It is likely that the researchers are referring to engineering, process control, or production control technicians. The problem with this approach is that, though technical personnel might well be qualified to calculate the physical completion rate, they are less likely to be qualified to calculate the completion level in terms of costs. The completion level that must be used to calculate the equivalent units of production is the cost completion rate. Unit cost is not calculated on the basis of physical units; rather, it is calculated on the basis of cost equivalent unit performance— that is, on the basis of charges or doses of cost needed to complete a given unit.[2]

In a process costing environment, costs are accumulated by department and then by cost component for a single time period. Additionally, because most companies manufacture more than one type of product, costs must also be accumulated by product. For example, the candy company would accumulate the costs of producing peanut butter 175-gram rabbits separately from the costs of producing white chocolate 500-gram rabbits.

Calculating Equivalent Units of Production

After production costs have been accumulated by department and by cost component, they need to be assigned to the units produced during the period of cost accumulation. If all units were 100% complete at the end of each accounting period, units could simply be counted to obtain the denominator for cost assignment. But in most production processes, an inventory of partially completed units called Work in Process Inventory (WIP) exists at the end of each period. Any partially completed ending inventory of the current period becomes the partially completed beginning inventory of the next period. Process costing assigns costs to both fully and partially completed units by converting partially completed units to equivalent whole units or equivalent units of production.

How much of a totally finished good is represented by a unit in process? The answer is provided by the finishing level percentage of the unit in process. By using the completion level percentage, it is possible to make a comparison between the units in process and these same units considered as being fully completed. Consequently, the number of equivalent units of production corresponds to the number of units in Work in Process as converted into completed units, through the use of a defined completion rate. With the cost of raw materials, which are introduced entirely at the beginning of the production process, the completion level is 100%. However, when raw materials and other resources are combined in the course of the production process, the completion level should be estimated. Note that the completion level must have meaning in economic terms and not merely in physical terms. The completion level must represent how much a unit in Work in Process has received of the cost load needed to start and finish the units completely.[3]

Equivalent units of production (EUP) approximate the number of whole units of output that could have been produced during a period from the actual effort expended during that period. Using EUP is necessary because using only completed units to determine unit cost would not clearly reflect all the work accomplished during a period. For instance, if 45 partially completed units were determined to be two-thirds complete, these partially completed units would be counted as 30 whole units (45 × 2/3). To calculate equivalent units of production for a period, it is necessary to multiply the number of actual units being produced by their percentage of completion at the end of the period.

For example, assume that Department One had no beginning Work in Process inventory. During January, Department One produced 100,000 complete units and 10,000 units that were 20% complete. These incomplete units are in ending Work in Process Inventory. The period's equivalent units of production are 102,000 [(100,000 × 100%) + (10,000 × 20%)]. This quantity is used to calculate the departmental equivalent unit product costs.

Use of equivalent units of production requires recognition of two factors related to inventory. First, units in beginning Work in Process Inventory were started last period but will be completed during the current period. This two-period production sequence means that some costs for these units were incurred in the prior period and additional costs will be incurred in the current period. Second, partially completed units in the ending Work in Process Inventory were started in the current period, however these will not be completed until the next period. Thus, ending Work in Process Inventory includes all costs incurred as a result of this period's production efforts. However, to finish the units, additional costs will need to be incurred in the next period.

Qualified production personnel should inspect ending work in process units to determine what proportion of work was completed during the current period. The mathematical complement to this proportion represents the amount of work to be performed next period. Physical inspection at the end of last period provided the information about the work to be performed on the beginning inventory in the current period.

equivalent units of production
an approximation of the number of whole units of output that could have been produced during a period from the actual effort expended during that period

In a continuous processing system qualified production personnel need to perform a physical inspection. Process costing is the appropriate cost system to use in most food production environments.

INTRODUCING WEIGHTED AVERAGE AND FIFO PROCESS COSTING

One purpose of any costing system is to determine product costs for financial statements. When goods are transferred from Work in Process Inventory of one department to another department or to Finished Goods Inventory, a cost must be assigned to those goods. In addition, at the end of any period, a cost amount must be assigned to goods that are only partially complete and still remain in Work in Process Inventory.

As stated earlier, the alternative methods of accounting for cost flows in process costing are the **weighted average method** and the **FIFO** (first-in, first-out) **method**.

These methods relate to the way in which physical cost flows are accounted for in the production process. The weighted average method computes a single average cost per unit based on the combined beginning inventory and current period production. The FIFO method separates the prior period production and its cost (Beginning Work in Process Inventory) from the current period production and its cost so that a current period cost per unit can be calculated. Both methods result in approximately the same unit cost unless a large cost change has occurred between periods.

EUP Calculations and Cost Assignment

Exhibit 5-4 outlines the six steps necessary to determine the costs assignable to units completed and to units still in process (Ending WIP) at the end of the period in a process costing system. Each of these steps is discussed briefly, and then a complete example is provided.

Step One. Calculate the total physical units for which the department is responsible, or the **total units to account for**. This amount is equal to the total number of whole or partial units worked on in the department during the current period—beginning WIP inventory units plus units started.

weighted average method
a method of process costing that computes an average cost per equivalent unit of production; combines beginning inventory units with current production and beginning inventory costs with current costs to compute that average

FIFO method
a method of process costing that computes an average cost per equivalent unit of production using only current production and current cost information; units and costs in beginning inventory are accounted for separately

total units to account for
total whole or partial physical units for which the department is responsible during the current period; beginning WIP inventory units plus units started

EXHIBIT 5-4

Steps in Process Costing

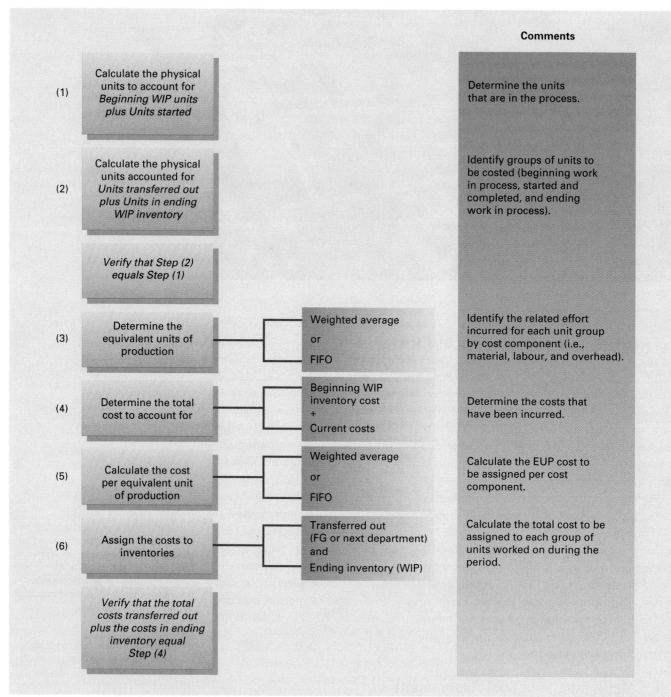

Step Two. Determine what happened to the units to account for during the period. This step also requires the use of physical units that may fit into one of two categories: (1) completed and transferred out or (2) partially completed and remaining in Ending Work in Process Inventory.[4]

At this point, verify that the total units for which the department was accountable are equal to the total units that were actually accounted for. If these amounts are not equal, any additional computations will be incorrect.

Step Three. Use one of the process costing methods (weighted average cost or FIFO) to determine the equivalent units of production for each cost component. If all materials are at the same degree of completion, a single materials computation can be made. If multiple materials are used and are placed into production at different points, multiple EUP calculations may be necessary for each of the various materials. If overhead is applied to production using direct labour as a base or if these two factors (labour and overhead) are always at the same degree of completion, a single EUP schedule can be made for conversion. If neither condition exists, separate EUP calculations must be prepared for labour and overhead.[5]

Step Four. Find the **total cost to account for**, which includes the balance in Work in Process Inventory at the beginning of the period plus all current costs for direct material, direct labour, and overhead.

Step Five. Compute the cost per equivalent unit for each cost component using either the weighted average or the FIFO equivalent units of production calculated in Step Three.

Step Six. Use the costs computed in Step Five to assign costs from the production process to the units completed and transferred out of the production process and to the units remaining in ending Work in Process Inventory. After this cost assignment is made, verify that the total costs assigned equal the total costs accountable for from Step Four.

Barbara Didona Chocoholics Ltd. (BD) is used to demonstrate the steps involved in the computation of equivalent units of production and cost assignment for both process costing methods. BD uses the same manufacturing process in making solid chocolate greeting cards as it uses in making chocolate bunnies. The production process consists of two departments: Moulding and Packaging. Chocolate is purchased from a vendor and is the only direct material. For purposes of simplicity, any decoration on the cards is minimal and is considered part of overhead. Since the chocolate is added at the start of processing, Work in Process Inventory is 100% complete as to direct material as soon as processing has begun. Labour and overhead are assumed to be added at the same rate throughout the production process. Exhibit 5-5 presents information for June regarding BD's production inventories and costs for the Moulding Department.

total cost to account for
the balance in Work in Process Inventory at the beginning of the period plus all current costs for direct material, direct labour, and overhead

	Units
Beginning WIP inventory	
(100% complete as to direct material; 30% complete as to conversion)	12,000
Cards started during current period	115,500
Cards completed and transferred to the next department	120,700
Ending WIP inventory	
(100% complete as to direct material; 80% complete as to conversion)	6,800
Cost of beginning WIP inventory:	
Direct material	$ 45,000.00
Direct labour and overhead	4,678.60
Total Cost of Beginning WIP Inventory	$ 49,678.60
Current period costs:	
Direct material	$334,950.00
Direct labour and overhead	202,191.00
Total Current Costs	$537,141.00

EXHIBIT 5-5

Barbara Didona Chocoholics Ltd. Production and Cost Information

Department One—Moulding for the Month of June

Although quantities are given for both cards transferred out of and cards remaining in ending Work in Process Inventory, it is not essential to provide both of these figures. The number of chocolate greeting cards remaining in process at June 30 can be calculated as the total cards to account for minus the cards completed and transferred out during the period. Alternatively, the number of cards transferred out can be computed as the total cards to account for minus the cards in ending Work in Process Inventory.

Weighted Average Method

The weighted average method of computing equivalent units of production adds the units in beginning Work in Process Inventory to the new units started during the current period to determine the potential quantity of production for the period. The work performed during the period does not necessarily always result in complete whole units. The weighted average method is *not* concerned about what quantity of work was performed in the prior period on the units in beginning WIP inventory. This method focuses only on units that are *completed* in the current period and units that remain in ending inventory. Thus, this method includes the units and costs of the beginning Work in Process Inventory in the calculation of the unit cost.

The BD information in Exhibit 5-5 is used to illustrate each step listed in Exhibit 5-4 for the Moulding Department.

Step One: Calculate the total units to account for

Units in beginning WIP Inventory	12,000
Units started during current period	115,500
Total units to account for	127,500

Step Two: Calculate the total units accounted for

Units completed and transferred out	120,700
Units in ending WIP Inventory	6,800
Total units accounted for	127,500

The units detailed in Step Two indicate the categories (those transferred out and those in ending WIP Inventory) to which costs will be assigned in the final step. The number of units accounted for in Step Two equals the number of units to account for in Step One.

Completed units are either (1) beginning WIP inventory units that have been completed during the current period, or (2) units started and completed during the period. They could be both. The number of **units started and completed** (S&C) equals the total units completed during the period minus the units in beginning WIP inventory.

units started and completed
the total units completed during the period minus the units in beginning inventory; alternatively, units started minus units in ending inventory

At BD, all raw material for the cards is added at the start of the process, and conversion takes place continuously during the process. Exhibit 5-6 shows a schematic of what happened in the first department (Moulding) during the month

EXHIBIT 5-6

Flow of Product in
Department One—Moulding

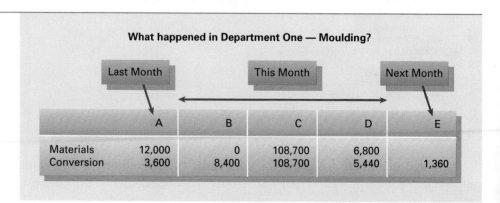

What happened in Department One — Moulding?

	Last Month		This Month		Next Month
	A	B	C	D	E
Materials	12,000	0	108,700	6,800	
Conversion	3,600	8,400	108,700	5,440	1,360

of June. "A" represents the work completed in May; "B," "C," and "D" represent the amount of work completed during June. "E" represents the work that will be done in the month of July to complete the units started in June.

The units for conversion for A, B, D, and E are arrived at as follows:

A: 12,000 × 30% complete as to conversion   = 3,600
B: 12,000 × 70% completion of units in A   = 8,400
D: 6,800 × 80% complete as to conversion   = 5,440
E: 6,800 × 20% to be completed next period = 1,360

Step Three: Determine the equivalent units of production

At the end of the period, the units in beginning Work in Process Inventory and the units that were started and completed this period are 100% complete as to all cost components. The units in ending Work in Process Inventory are complete as to direct material, but only 80% complete as to labour and overhead. Since labour and overhead are at the same degree of completion, a single EUP conversion calculation can be made for both of these cost components.

The weighted average computations for equivalent units of production are as follows:

	Direct Material EUP	Conversion (Direct Labour and Overhead) EUP
BWIP (Whole units × % complete) (A)	12,000 × 100% = 12,000	12,000 × 30% = 3,600
BWIP completion (B)		12,000 × 70% = 8,400
Units started and completed in June (Whole units × % complete) (C)	108,700 × 100% = 108,700	108,700 × 100% = 108,700
EWIP (Whole units × % complete) Units started in June (D)	6,800 × 100% = 6,800	6,800 × 80% = 5,440
Equivalent Units of Production	127,500	126,140

Note that the lines labelled A, B, and C above [BWIP (12,000) and Units started and completed (108,700)] are equal to the total units completed and transferred out (120,700) as shown in Step Two.

Only when all product components are placed into production at the same time and at the same rate will material, labour, and overhead all be at equal percentages of completion. Generally, the cost components are at different degrees of completion and as such the completion percentage must be separately determined *for each cost component*. If the percentages of completion differ, separate EUP calculations must be made for each cost component.

The weighted average method does not distinguish between units in beginning Work in Process Inventory and units entering production during the period. In Step Three, the weighted average method includes the number of whole units in beginning Work in Process Inventory and the number of units started and completed during the period. By doing so, the weighted average method treats beginning Work in Process Inventory units as though they were started and completed in the current period.

Step Four: Determine the total cost to account for

The total cost to account for equals beginning WIP inventory cost plus the additional current period costs. Note that information is provided in Exhibit 5-5 on the cost for each element of production—direct material, direct labour, and overhead. For Barbara Didona Chocoholics Ltd., the total cost to account for is $586,819.60.

	Direct Material	Conversion	Total
Beginning WIP cost	$ 45,000.00	$ 4,678.60	$ 49,678.60
Current period costs	334,950.00	202,191.00	537,141.00
Total cost to account for	$379,950.00	$206,869.60	$586,819.60

Total cost will be assigned in Step Six to the goods transferred out to the next department and to ending Work in Process Inventory in relation to the whole units or equivalent whole units contained in each category.

Step Five: Calculate the cost per equivalent unit of production

A cost per equivalent unit of production must be computed for each cost component for which a separate calculation of EUP is made. The weighted average method does not distinguish between units in beginning Work in Process Inventory and units started during the period, nor does it differentiate between beginning Work in Process Inventory costs and current period costs. The costs of beginning Work in Process Inventory and of the current period are summed for each cost component and averaged over that component's weighted average equivalent units of production. The calculation of unit cost for each cost component at the end of the period is as follows:

Cost per equivalent unit =
[(Beginning Work in Process Inventory cost + Current period cost)
÷ Total weighted average equivalent units of production]

Under the weighted average method, costs from two different periods are totalled to form the numerator of the unit cost equation, and units from two different periods are used in the denominator. This computation allows total costs to be divided by total units, which produces an average component cost per unit. The weighted average calculations for cost per EUP for material and conversion are as follows:

	Direct Material	Conversion	Total
Beginning WIP inventory costs	$ 45,000.00	$ 4,678.60	$ 49,678.60
Current period costs	334,950.00	202,191.00	537,141.00
Cost to account for (Step Four)	$379,950.00	$206,869.60	$586,819.60
Divided by EUP (Step Three)	÷ 127,500	÷ 126,140	
Cost per EUP	$ 2.98	$ 1.64	$ 4.62

The unit costs for the two product cost components (direct material and conversion) are summed to find the total production cost for all whole units completed during June. For Barbara Didona Chocoholics Ltd., this cost is $4.62.

Step Six: Assign costs to inventories

This step assigns total production costs to units of product. Cost assignment in a department involves determining the cost of (1) goods completed and transferred out during the period and (2) the units in ending Work in Process Inventory.

Under the weighted average method, the cost of goods transferred out is found by multiplying the total number of units transferred out by the total cost per EUP (from Step Five). Because this method is based on an averaging technique that combines prior and current period work, the period in which the transferred-out units were started is not important. All units and all costs have been commingled. The total cost transferred out for BD for June is ($4.62 × 120,700) or $557,634.

Ending Work in Process Inventory cost is calculated based on the equivalent units of production for each cost component. The equivalent units of production are multiplied by the component cost per unit computed in Step Five. The cost of ending Work in Process Inventory under the weighted average method is as follows:

Ending Work in Process Inventory:
Direct material (6,800 × 100% × $2.98) $20,264.00
Conversion (6,800 × 80% × $1.64)   8,921.60
Total cost of ending Work in Process Inventory $29,185.60

The quantities that result from multiplying whole units by the percentage of completion are equal to the equivalent units of production.

The total costs assigned to transferred-out units and units in ending Work in Process Inventory must equal the total cost to account for. For Barbara Didona Chocoholics Ltd., total cost to account for (Step Four) was $586,819.60, which equals transferred-out cost ($557,634) plus ending work in process cost ($29,185.60).

The steps just discussed can be combined into a **cost of production report.** This document details all manufacturing quantities and costs, shows the computation of cost per EUP, and indicates the cost assignment to goods produced during the period. Exhibit 5-7 shows the cost of production report for Barbara Didona Chocoholics Ltd. under the weighted average process costing method.

cost of production report
a document used in a process costing system; details all manufacturing quantities and costs, shows the computation of cost per equivalent unit of production (EUP), and indicates the cost assignment to goods produced during the period

LEARNING OBJECTIVE 2

How is a cost of production report prepared under the weighted average method of process costing?

EXHIBIT 5-7

Cost of Production Report for the Month Ended June 30 (Weighted Average Method)

Production Data	Equivalent Units of Production		
	Whole Units	**DM**	**Conversion**
BWIP	12,000[1]	12,000	3,600
Units started	115,500		
To account for	127,500		
BWIP completed	12,000	0	8,400
S&C	108,700	108,700	108,700
Units completed	120,700		
EWIP	6,800[2]	6,800	5,440
Accounted for	127,500	127,500	126,140

Cost Data			
	Total	**DM**	**Conversion**
BWIP cost	$ 49,678.60	$ 45,000.00	$ 4,678.60
Current period costs	537,141.00	334,950.00	202,191.00
Total cost to account for	$586,819.60	$379,950.00	$206,869.60
Divided by EUP		÷ 127,500	÷ 126,140
Cost per EUP	$ 4.62	$ 2.98	$ 1.64

Cost Assignment		
Transferred out (120,700 × $4.62)		$557,634.00
Ending Work in Process inventory:		
Direct material		
(6,800 × 100% × $2.98)	$ 20,264.00	
Conversion (6,800 × 80% × $1.64)	8,921.60	29,185.60
Total cost accounted for		$586,819.60

[1] Fully complete as to direct material; 30% as to conversion.
[2] Fully complete as to direct material; 80% as to conversion.

PROCESS COSTING USING FIFO VALUATION

LEARNING OBJECTIVE 3

How are equivalent units of production, unit costs, and inventory values computed using the FIFO method of process costing?

FIFO Method

As mentioned previously, the FIFO method of determining EUP more realistically reflects the way in which most goods actually physically flow through the production system. The FIFO method does not commingle units and costs of different periods, which allows this method to focus specifically on the work performed during the current period. Equivalent units and costs of beginning Work in Process Inventory are withheld from the computation of the average unit current period cost.

Steps One and Two

Steps One and Two are the same for the FIFO method as for the weighted average method because these two steps involve the use of physical units. Therefore, based on the data from Exhibit 5-5, the total units to account for and accounted for are 127,500. (The calculations are shown on page 254.)

Step Three: Determine the Equivalent Units of Production

Under FIFO, as mentioned, the work performed in the prior period is not commingled with work of the current period. The EUP schedule for FIFO (based on Exhibit 5-6) is as follows:

	Direct Material EUP	**Conversion EUP**
BWIP (Whole units × % not completed in prior period) (B)	12,000 × 0% = 0	12,000 × 70% = 8,400
Units started and completed this period (Whole units × % complete) (C)	108,700 × 100% = 108,700	108,700 × 100% = 108,700
EWIP (Whole units × % complete) (D)	6,800 × 100% = 6,800	6,800 × 80% = 5,440
EUP	115,500	122,540

Under FIFO, only the work performed on the beginning Work in Process Inventory *during the current period* is shown in the EUP schedule. This work equals the whole units in beginning Work in Process Inventory multiplied by a percentage equal to 1 minus the percentage of work done in the prior period. In the Barbara Didona Chocoholics Ltd. example, no additional direct material is needed in June to complete the 12,000 units in beginning WIP inventory because all direct material is added at the start of the process. The beginning WIP inventory is only 30% complete as to conversion; therefore, the company needs to complete the other 70% conversion on the 12,000 beginning WIP inventory during June—or the equivalent of 8,400 units.

The remaining figures in the FIFO EUP schedule are the same as those for the weighted average method. The only difference between the weighted average and FIFO EUP computations is that under the FIFO method, the work performed in the prior period on beginning Work in Process Inventory is not included in the current period EUP. This difference is equal to the number of units in beginning Work in Process Inventory multiplied by the percentage of work performed in the prior period. A reconciliation of EUPs determined by the two methods follows.

	Direct Material	**Conversion**
FIFO EUP	115,500	122,540
Plus the EUP in BWIP (Work done in the prior period: 100% Direct Material; 30% Conversion)	12,000	3,600
Weighted Average EUP (Shown in Exhibit 5-7)	127,500	126,140

Step Four: Determine the Total Cost to Account For

This step is the same as under the weighted average method. The total cost to account for is $586,819.60.

Step Five: Calculate the Cost Per Equivalent Unit of Production

Because cost determination is made on the basis of equivalent units of production, different results will be obtained for the weighted average and FIFO methods. The calculations for cost per equivalent unit reflect the difference in quantity that each method uses for beginning WIP inventory. The EUP calculation for FIFO ignores work performed on beginning Work in Process Inventory during the prior period; therefore, the FIFO cost computation per EUP also ignores prior period costs and uses only costs incurred in the current period. The FIFO cost per EUP calculation is as follows:

$$\text{Cost per equivalent unit} = \frac{\text{Current period cost}}{\text{FIFO equivalent units of production}}$$

Calculations for Barbara Didona Chocoholics Ltd. are:

	Direct Material	Conversion	Total
Current period costs	$334,950.00	$202,191.00	$537,141.00
Divided by EUP (Step Three)	÷ 115,500	÷ 122,540	
Cost per EUP	$ 2.90	$ 1.65	$ 4.55

The production cost for each whole unit produced during June under the FIFO method is $4.55. It is useful to recognize the difference between the two total cost computations. The weighted average total cost of $4.62 is the average total cost of each unit completed during June, *regardless of when production was begun.* The FIFO total cost of $4.55 is the total cost of each unit that was *both started and completed* during the current period. The $0.07 difference results from the difference in the treatment of beginning Work in Process Inventory costs.

Step Six: Assign Costs to Inventories

This step assigns total production costs to units of product. Cost assignment in a department involves determining the cost of (1) goods completed and transferred out during the period and (2) units in ending Work in Process inventory. The FIFO method assumes that the units in beginning WIP inventory are completed first during the current period, and thus they are the first units transferred out. The remaining units transferred out during the period were both started and completed in the current period. As shown in the cost of production report in Exhibit 5-8 the two-step computation needed to determine the cost of goods transferred out distinctly presents this FIFO logic.

The first part of the cost assignment for units transferred out relates to the units that were in beginning inventory. These units had the cost of material and some conversion costs attached to them at the start of the period. These prior period costs were not included in the cost per EUP calculations in Step Five. The costs to finish these units were incurred in the current period. To determine the total cost of producing the units in beginning WIP inventory, the cost of the beginning WIP inventory is added to the current period costs that were needed to complete the units. The second part of the cost assignment for units transferred out relates to the units started and completed in the current period. The cost of these units is computed using current period costs.

This cost assignment process for Barbara Didona Chocoholics Ltd., which had beginning June WIP inventory of 12,000 units and 120,700 cards transferred out during the month, is as follows:

Transferred out:
(1) Beginning inventory (prior period costs)* $ 49,678.60
        Completion of beginning Work in Process Inventory
            Direct material (12,000 × 0% × $2.90)   0
            Conversion (12,000 × 70% × $1.65)   13,860.00
        Total cost of beginning Work in Process Inventory
        transferred out $ 63,538.60
(2) Units started and completed (108,700 × $4.55)   494,585.00
        Total cost of units transferred out $558,123.60

*From initial information in Exhibit 5-5.

Beginning WIP inventory of chocolate greeting cards was 100% complete as to direct material at the beginning of June; thus, no additional cost for material was added during the month. Conversion at the start of the month was only 30% complete, so 70% of the conversion work (direct labour and overhead), is performed during June at current period costs. The units started and completed are costed at the total current period FIFO cost of $4.55, because these units were fully manufactured during the current period.

The method of calculating the cost of ending Work in Process Inventory is the same under both the FIFO and weighted average methods. Although the number of equivalent units is the same under both methods, cost per unit differs. Ending Work in Process Inventory cost under FIFO is as follows:

Ending Work in Process Inventory:
    Direct material (6,800 × 100% × $2.90) $19,720.00
    Conversion (6,800 × 80% × $1.65)   8,976.00
    Total cost of ending Work in Process Inventory $28,696.00

The total cost of the units transferred out ($558,123.60) plus the cost of the ending Work in Process Inventory units ($28,696.00) equals the total cost to be accounted for ($586,819.60).

The steps discussed earlier are shown in the cost of production report (Exhibit 5-8).

Cost assignment is easier for the weighted average method than for the FIFO method. However, simplicity is not the only consideration in choosing a cost flow method. The FIFO method reflects the actual physical flow of goods through production. Furthermore, when period costs do fluctuate, the FIFO method gives managers better information with which to control costs and on which to base decisions because it does not combine costs of different periods. In addition, the FIFO method focuses on current period costs, and managerial performance is usually evaluated on the basis of costs incurred only in the current period.

LEARNING OBJECTIVE 4

How is a cost of production report prepared under the FIFO method of process costing?

Process Costing in a Multidepartmental Setting

LEARNING OBJECTIVE 5

What is the effect of multidepartmental processing on the computation of equivalent units of production?

Most companies have multiple, rather than single, department processing facilities. In a multidepartmental processing environment, goods are transferred from a predecessor department to a successor department. For example, the production of chocolate greeting cards at Barbara Didona Chocoholics Ltd. was said to occur in two departments: Moulding and Packaging.

Manufacturing costs always follow the physical flow of goods. The costs of completed units of predecessor departments are treated as input material costs in successor departments. Such a sequential treatment requires the use of an additional cost component element called "transferred in" or "prior department cost." This element always has a percentage of completion factor of 100%, since the goods

Production Data	Equivalent Units of Production		
	Whole Units	**DM**	**Conversion**
BWIP	12,000[1]	12,000	3,600
Units started	115,500		
To account for	127,500		
BWIP completed	12,000	0	8,400
Started and completed	108,700	108,700	108,700
Units completed	120,700		
EWIP	6,800[2]	6,800	5,440
Accounted for	127,500	115,500	122,540

Cost Data

	Total	**DM**	**Conversion**
BWIP cost	$ 49,678.60		
Current period costs	537,141.00	$334,950.00	$202,191.00
Total cost to account for	$586,819.60	$334,950.00	$202,191.00
Divided by EUP		÷ 115,500	÷ 122,540
Cost per EUP	$ 4.55	$ 2.90	$ 1.65

Cost Assignment

Transferred out		
Beginning Work in Process Inventory costs	$ 49,678.60	
Cost to complete:		
Conversion (8,400 × $1.65)	13,860.00	
Total cost of BWIP transferred	$ 63,538.60	
Started and completed (108,700 × $4.55)	494,585.00	$558,123.60
Ending Work in Process Inventory:		
Direct material (6,800 × 100% × $2.90)	$ 19,720.00	
Conversion (6,800 × 80% × $1.65)	8,976.00	28,696.00
Total cost accounted for		$586,819.60

[1] Fully complete as to direct material, 30% as to conversion. The quantities under EUP for this line are not included in the final EUP summation.
[2] Fully complete as to direct material, 80% as to conversion.

EXHIBIT 5-8

Cost of Production Report (FIFO Method)

would not have been transferred out of the predecessor department if they had not been fully complete. The transferred-in element is handled the same as any other cost element in the calculations of EUP and cost per EUP.

A successor department may add additional raw material to the units that have been transferred in or may simply provide additional labour, with the corresponding incurrence of overhead. Anything added in the successor department requires its own cost element column for calculating equivalent units of production and cost per equivalent unit (unless the additional elements have the same degree of completion, in which case they can be combined).

Exhibit 5-9 provides a cost of production report for the Packaging Department at Barbara Didona Chocoholics Ltd. Weighted average unit costs from Exhibit 5-7 are used for the units transferred in from the previous department. In this department, chocolate greeting cards are placed in cellophane-fronted cardboard boxes and sealed for customer delivery. The beginning Work in Process Inventory is assumed to be 100% complete as to transferred-in units and cost, 0% complete as to packaging, and 90% complete as to conversion. The ending Work in Process Inventory is assumed to be 100% complete as to transferred-in units and cost, 0% complete as to packaging, and 75% complete as to conversion in this department. The Packaging Department uses the weighted average process costing method.

EXHIBIT 5-9

Multidepartmental Setting—
Packaging Department
(Weighted Average Method)

Production Data		Equivalent Units of Production		
	Whole Units	**Transferred in**	**DM**	**Conversion**
BWIP	9,300[1]	9,300	0	8,370
Units transferred in	120,700			
To account for	130,000			
BWIP completed	9,300	0	9,300	930
S&C	113,100	113,100	113,100	113,100
Units completed	122,400			
EWIP	7,600[2]	7,600	0	5,700
Accounted for	130,000	130,000	122,400	128,100

Cost Data				
	Total	**Transferred in**	**DM**	**Conversion**
BWIP cost	$ 44,930.30	$ 41,666	$ 0	$ 3,264.30
Current period costs	642,329.70	557,634	36,720	47,975.70
Total cost to account for	$687,260.00	$599,300	$36,720	$51,240.00
Divided by EUP		÷130,000	÷122,400	÷ 128,100
Cost per EUP	$ 5.31	$ 4.61	$ 0.30	$ 0.40

Cost Assignment			
Transferred out (122,400 × $5.31)			$ 649,944
Ending Work in Process Inventory:			
Transferred in (7,600 × $4.61)		$35,036	
Conversion (7,600 × 0.75 × $0.40)		2,280	37,316
Total cost accounted for			$ 687,260

[1] Fully complete as to transferred-in; 0% as to direct material; 90% as to conversion.
[2] Fully complete as to transferred-in; 0% as to direct material; 75% as to conversion.

Recording Information in the Accounts

Summary journal entries and T-accounts for Barbara Didona Chocoholics Ltd. for June are given in Exhibit 5-10. For these entries, the following assumptions are made: sales for June were 121,000 chocolate greeting cards; all sales were on account at $10 per unit; a perpetual weighted average inventory system is in use. Assume that Barbara Didona Chocoholics Ltd. began June with no Finished Goods Inventory.

SPOILED AND LOST UNITS

LEARNING OBJECTIVE 6

How do normal and abnormal losses of units differ and how is each treated in the calculation of equivalent units of production?

spoilage (*spoiled unit, defective unit*) unit of product with imperfections that cannot be corrected in an economical way

Our earlier examples assumed that there was perfect production—what went in came out of the system. However, in most production processes, some **spoilage** occurs, in which units are **spoiled** or **defective** and are not up to specification.

Loss of units occurs as a result of evaporation or leakage. For example, at Tom Anderson's Chocolate Kitchen, approximately 5% of the original weight is lost in the first department, as a result of shrinkage.

All scrap is not created equal. Some scrap is the result of employee errors, for instance, while other scrap is inherent in the design process. Companies have a variety of ways of accounting for scrap, which generally will recognize these distinctions.

Scrap that is necessary is just as costly as the scrap caused by someone's procedural error. Perhaps the engineers designed too loose a tolerance, or the company couldn't afford the 'really good' equipment. By calling scrap "necessary," a company hides the

1.	Work in Process Inventory—Moulding	334,950.00	
	Raw Material Inventory		334,950.00
	To record issuance of direct material (chocolate) to production (Exhibit 5-5).		
2.	Work in Process Inventory—Moulding	202,191.00	
	Various accounts		202,191.00
	To record labour and overhead costs into production (Exhibit 5-5).		
3.	Work in Process Inventory—Packaging	557,634.00	
	Work in Process Inventory—Moulding		557,634.00
	To transfer greeting cards from the Moulding Department to the Packaging Department (Exhibit 5-8).		
4.	Work in Process Inventory—Packaging	36,720.00	
	Raw Material Inventory		36,720.00
	To record issuance of direct material (boxes) to production (Exhibit 5-9).		
5.	Work in Process Inventory—Packaging	47,975.70	
	Various accounts		47,975.70
	To record labour and overhead costs into production (Exhibit 5-9).		
6.	Finished Goods Inventory	649,944.00	
	Work in Process Inventory—Packaging		649,944.00
	To transfer cost of completed units to finished goods (Exhibit 5-9).		
7.	Cost of Goods Sold	642,510.00	
	Finished Goods Inventory		642,510.00
	To transfer cost of goods sold from finished goods to cost of goods sold (121,000 × $5.31) (cost information from Exhibit 5-9 and sales information from supplementary data above).		
8.	Accounts Receivable	1,210,000.00	
	Sales		1,210,000.00
	To record June sales on account (121,000 × $10; information from supplementary data above).		

EXHIBIT 5-10

Process Costing Journal Entries and T-Accounts

Work in Process Inventory—Moulding

Beginning balance		49,678.60	Transferred out (3)	557,634.00
Direct material	(1)	334,950.00		
Conversion	(2)	202,191.00		
Ending balance		29,185.60		

Work in Process Inventory—Packaging

Beginning balance		44,930.30	To finished goods (6)	649,944.00
Transferred in	(3)	557,634.00		
Direct Material	(4)	36,720.00		
Conversion	(5)	47,975.70		
Ending balance		37,316.00		

Finished Goods Inventory

Beginning balance		0	Cost of Goods Sold (7)	642,510.00
From WIP Inventory— Packaging	(6)	649,944.00		
Ending balance		7,434.00		

Cost of Goods Sold

June Cost of Goods Sold	(7)	642,510.00	

(Numbers in parentheses indicate the related journal entry.)

EXHIBIT 5-11

Barbara Didona Chocoholics Ltd. T-Accounts

opportunity to make more money now and in the future. This "necessary scrap" exists because no one has thought of a process improvement to make it not necessary.[6]

Types of Lost Units

Losses in the manufacturing process can be due to either **normal spoilage** or **abnormal spoilage**. Normal losses are those that are expected to occur during the production process, while abnormal losses generally arise because of human or machine error during the production process. At Tom Anderson's Chocolate Kitchen, the weight loss that occurs during the melting process does so uniformly throughout the process.

Accounting for Lost Units

How lost units are accounted for depends on whether the loss is considered normal or abnormal. The two ways of treating normal losses are either to charge the losses to overhead or (more commonly) to include them as part of the cost of good units resulting from the process. Thus, the cost of a loss is included in Work in Process and Finished Goods Inventories and becomes an expense only when the good units are sold. This treatment has been considered appropriate because normal losses have been viewed as unavoidable costs in the production of good units.

The costs of normal **continuous losses** are calculated using the **method of neglect**. Using this method, the spoiled units are excluded in the equivalent units schedule; thus, a smaller number of equivalent units of production (EUP) results. When the cost of production is divided by a smaller EUP, the cost per equivalent unit is higher. The cost of the spoiled units is spread over the remaining units in Work in Process Inventory and over the good units transferred to the next department or to Finished Goods Inventory.

Illustrations of Lost Units
Normal Loss Charged to Good Output

At Tom Anderson's Chocolate Kitchen, in Department One—Melting, where the chocolate is melted, shrinkage normally occurs. Management considers any decrease of 5% or less of the kilograms of chocolate placed into production to be normal. This example assumes the FIFO method of calculating equivalent units. The June data for Tom Anderson's Chocolate Kitchen follows:

Kilograms:		
Beginning WIP Inventory (40% complete)	4,000	
Started during month	30,000	
Completed and transferred out	26,400	
Ending WIP Inventory (70% complete)	6,400	
Lost kilograms (normal)	1,200	
Costs:		
Beginning WIP inventory:		
Material	$10,000	
Conversion	1,420	$11,420
Current period:		
Material	$68,500	
Conversion	17,094	85,594
Total costs		$97,014

As shown in Exhibit 5-12, the melting department is accountable for 34,000 kilograms of chocolate: 4,000 kilograms in beginning Work in Process Inventory plus 30,000 kilograms introduced into the department during June. Before the 1,200 lost units are considered, 32,800 kilograms are accounted for (26,400 transferred out and 6,400 units in ending Work in Process Inventory).

EXHIBIT 5-12

Cost of Production Report—
Normal Spoilage (FIFO)

Production Data	Equivalent Units of Production		
	Whole Units	**Material**	**Conversion**
Beginning WIP inventory (100%; 40%)	4,000		
Kilograms started	30,000		
Kilograms to account for	34,000		
Beginning WIP Inventory completed			
(0%; 60%)	4,000	0	2,400
Kilograms started and completed	22,400	22,400	22,400
Total kilograms completed	26,400		
Ending WIP Inventory (100%; 70%)	6,400	6,400	4,480
Normal shrinkage	1,200		
Kilograms accounted for	34,000	28,800	29,280

Cost Data			
	Total	**Material**	**Conversion**
Beginning WIP Inventory costs	$11,420		
Current costs	85,594	$68,500	$17,094
Total costs	$97,014	$68,500	$17,094
Divided by EUP		÷ 28,800	÷ 29,280
Cost per FIFO EUP	$2.9618	$2.3785	$0.5838

Cost Assignment

Transferred Out:

Beginning WIP Inventory	$11,420.00		
Cost to complete: Conversion (2,400 × $0.5838)	1,401.12		
Total cost of beginning WIP inventory	$12,821.12		
Started and completed (22,400 × $2.9618)	66,344.32		
Total cost of kilograms transferred out		$79,165.44	
Ending WIP Inventory:			
Material (6,400 × $2.378)	$15,219.20		
Conversion (4,480 × $0.5838)	2,615.42	17,834.62	
Total costs accounted for		$97,000.06*	

*Due to rounding

The following journal entries would have been made in this department.

Work in Process Inventory	85,594.00	
Raw Materials Inventory		68,500
Wages Payable (and/or other appropriate accounts)		17,094
To record current period costs.		

Finished Goods Inventory	79,165.44	
Work in Process Inventory		79,165.44
To record cost transferred from the department.		

Spoilage—Abnormal and Normal Spoilage

Assume, in our previous example, that management considers spoilage in excess of 3% of the kilograms placed into production—rather than 5%—to be abnormal. Since 30,000 kilograms were started in June, the maximum allowable normal shrinkage is 900 kilograms (30,000 × 3%). Because the total reduction in units in June was 1,200 kilograms, 300 kilograms are considered abnormal spoilage. Exhibit 5-13 presents the cost of production report for this new information.

Minimizing Spoilage

This chapter has assumed that there is no nonconforming production, but in reality, most businesses do produce some spoiled or defective units. Managers should always be alert for ways to minimize spoilage in a production process. The control aspect of quality implementation requires knowledge of the answers to three specific questions.

EXHIBIT 5-13

Cost of Production Report—
Abnormal and Normal Spoilage

Production Data	Equivalent Units of Production		
	Whole Units	**Material**	**Conversion**
Beginning WIP Inventory (100%; 40%)	4,000		
Kilograms started	30,000		
Kilograms to account for	34,000		
Beginning WIP Inventory completed (0%; 60%)	4,000	0	2,400
Kilograms started and completed	22,400	22,400	22,400
Total kilograms completed	26,400		
Ending WIP Inventory (100%; 70%)	6,400	6,400	4,480
Normal shrinkage	900		
Abnormal shrinkage (100%; 100%)	300	300	300
Kilograms accounted for	34,000	29,100	29,580

Cost Data			
	Total	**Material**	**Conversion**
Beginning WIP Inventory costs	$11,420		
Current costs	85,594	$68,500	$ 17,094
Total costs	$97,014	$68,500	$ 17,094
Divided by EUP		÷ 29,100	÷ 29,580
Cost per FIFO EUP	$2.9318	$2.3539	$0.57789

Cost Assignment

Transferred out:

From Beginning WIP Inventory	$11,420.00	
Cost to complete: Conversion (2,400 × $0.5779)	1,386.96	
Total cost of beginning inventory	$12,806.96	
Started and completed (22,400 × $2.9318)	65,672.32	
Total cost of kilograms transferred out		$78,479.28
Ending WIP Inventory:		
Material (6,400 × $2.3539)	$15,064.96	
Conversion (4,480 × $0.5779)	2,588.99	17,653.95
Abnormal loss (300 × $2.9318)		879.54
Total costs accounted for		$97,012.77*

*Due to rounding

The following journal entries would have been made in this department when both normal and abnormal spoilage exist.

Work in Process Inventory	85,594.00	
Raw Materials Inventory		68,500.00
Wages Payable (and/or other appropriate accounts)		17,094.00
To record current period costs. (from page 264)		
Finished Goods Inventory	78,479.28	
Work in Process Inventory		78,479.28
To record cost transferred from the department.		
Loss from Abnormal Spoilage	879.54	
Work in Process Inventory		879.54
To remove the cost of abnormal spoilage from Work in Process Inventory.		

Our illustrations have used FIFO process costing. If the weighted average method were used, the difference would appear only in the treatment of beginning inventory and its cost.

1. What does the spoilage actually cost?
2. Why does the spoilage occur?
3. How can the spoilage be controlled?

   Many companies find it difficult, if not impossible, to answer the question of what spoilage (or lack of quality) costs. One cause of this difficulty is a traditional method of handling spoilage in process costing situations: spoiled units are simply excluded from the calculation of equivalent units of production. The total cost of producing both good and spoiled units is assigned solely to the good units, raising the cost of those units. Because the spoiled units are excluded from the extensions in the calculation of equivalent units, the costs of those units are effectively buried and hidden in magnitude from managers. In a job order costing environment, an estimate of spoilage cost is often added to total budgeted overhead when the predetermined overhead rate is calculated. When this occurs, spoilage cost is again hidden and ignored.

In service organizations, the cost of spoilage may be even more difficult to determine because spoilage, from a customer's viewpoint, is poor service; the customer simply may not do business with the organization again. Such a cost is not processed by the accounting system. Thus, in all instances, a potentially significant dollar amount of loss from nonconformance to requirements is unavailable for investigation as to its planning, controlling, and decision-making ramifications.

As to the second question, managers may be able to pinpoint the reasons for spoilage or poor service but those managers may have a mindset that condones lack of control. First, the managers may believe that a particular cause creates only a minimal amount of spoilage; because of this attitude, they settle for an **accepted quality level** with some tolerance for error. These error tolerances are built into the system and they become justifications for problems. Production is graded on a curve that allows for a less-than-perfect result.

accepted quality level
a predetermined level of acceptability

Incorporating error tolerances into the production system and combining such tolerances with the use of the method of neglect results in a situation in which managers do not have the information necessary to determine how much spoilage is costing the company. Therefore, although they believe that the quantity and cost of spoiled goods are minimal, the managers do not have historical or even estimated accounting amounts on which to base such a conclusion. If managers were aware of the spoilage cost, they could make more informed decisions about whether to ignore the problem causing the spoilage or try to correct its causes.

Just about every manufacturing company has some problems related to scrap. In these competitive times, the issue holds significance for companies because excessive scrap (or waste or spoilage or anything else you may call it) leads to costs that are higher than they need to be. By keeping track of scrap, cost managers can detect when scrap exceeds standards that are considered normal or acceptable. Moreover, cost managers want to continuously review the current standards to make sure the allowances for scrap are realistic. Excessively liberal allowances can sometimes be cut back; other times, processes can be changed to reduce the standard allowances.[7]

In other instances, managers may believe that spoilage is uncontrollable. In some cases, this belief is accurate. For example, when a conventional printing press converts from one job to the next, some paper and ink is wasted in the make-ready process. The amount is not large, and process analysis has proven that the cost of attempting to correct this production defect would be significantly greater than the savings resulting from the correction. But in most production situations and almost every service situation, the cause of spoiled goods or poor service is controllable. It is necessary only to determine the cause and institute corrective action.

Spoilage has often been controlled through a process of inspecting goods or, in the case of service organizations, surveying customers. Now, companies are deciding that if quality is built into a process to prevent defects, there will be less need for inspections or surveys, because spoilage and poor service will be minimized. The goal is, then, to maintain quality through process control rather than output inspection and observation.

Many companies are now implementing quality programs to minimize defects or poor service. These companies often employ statistical process control (SPC) techniques to analyze their processes for situations that are out of control and creating spoilage. SPC techniques are based on the theory that a process varies naturally over time from normal, random causes but that some variations occur that fall outside the limits of the natural variations. These uncommon or special-cause variations are typically the points at which the process produces errors, which may be defective goods or poor service. Often, these variations can be and have been eliminated by the installation of computer-integrated manufacturing systems, which have internal controls to evaluate tolerances and sense production problems.

HOW HAVE COMPANIES IMPROVED WITH THE INSTALLATION OF AN ERP SYSTEM?

Organizations today are constantly in search for ways to achieve better business performance and sustain competitive advantages through the effective deployment of resources and business processes. To improve business performance, organizations require an efficient planning control system that synchronizes planning of all processes across the organization. The key to competitiveness lies in a solid information system infrastructure seamlessly aligned with core business processes developed for the delivery of high-quality products and services to customers within the optimal time and with few errors. These demands have prompted more firms to shift from developing in-house information systems to purchasing application software such as ERP systems, in order to generate synergies and enhance operating efficiency.

Adhunik Group of Industries, a manufacturer of iron and steel products used in automobiles, construction, and engineering, has installed SAP ERP. "The most important benefit that we have achieved after deploying SAP ERP is that we have succeeded in eliminating wrong dispatches," says Rajat Subhra Datta, general manager (IT).

The company maintains an inventory of 40,000 items. These include spares but exclude raw materials. Most of the company's products are manufactured in batches. Each batch has a unique hit number and is identified by grade. Adhunik has 300 types of grades. The company sometimes used to load the wrong hit numbers onto trucks for dispatch to the wrong customer.

Before, there were no mechanisms to physically verify that the correct materials had been dispatched. "We have automobile customers that use our products in critical areas of manufacturing," says Datta. "If the customers received the wrong hit number, it had to be shipped back to our factory [so that] the correct hit number could be sent to the customer. This was affecting our profit margins." In 2005, Adhunik Group's top managers felt that they needed ERP to optimize production costs, squeeze out more revenue, improve quality, enhance customer satisfaction, and increase the company's competitiveness.

While enhancing overall efficiency across the organization, the centralized system ensures that information across the business is available to management, not just as raw data, but also in the form of detailed reports. Through these reports, management gains a clear view of revenues and costs as well as the performance of the business.

SAP ERP has helped the company's top managers immensely in their efforts to oversee inventories and procurement. Today the company is in a better position to synchronize manufacturing and logistics so as to deliver complete orders on time. ERP has led to better monitoring and tighter control. Product cost analysis has been streamlined. Before SAP was installed, the company had no system to analyze product costs and found it difficult to even measure those costs, since all estimates were based in inaccurate calculations. The company is now able to obtain more realistic product costs simply and automatically. This new system has helped the finance department drastically reduce the time it spends maintaining and checking financial records.

IBM's Storage Systems Division has reduced the time it needs to reprice its products from 5 days to 5 minutes, the time it needs to ship a replacement part from 22 days to 3 days, and the time it needs to complete a credit check from 20 minutes to 3 seconds. Fujitsu Microelectronics has reduced its cycle time for filing orders from 18 days to a day and a half and has cut the time it requires to close its financial books from 8 days to 4 days.

Cost–benefit analysis can be used to compare the overall effectiveness of an ERP system with the investment it requires. An ERP system's costs vary with firm size, type of software, required IT infrastructure, and project size. In terms of effectiveness, reduced inventory costs and shorter production and delivery cycles can be reasonably attributed to ERP systems. With regard to profitability, however, no adequate mechanism is available for measuring sales growth and customer satisfaction.[8]

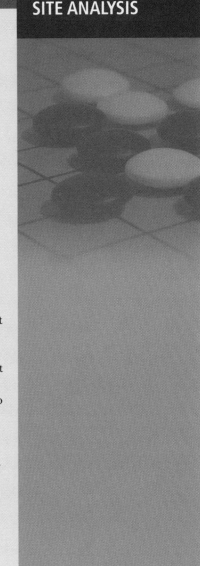

SITE ANALYSIS

Ganong Bros. Ltd.

Finding and being successful in new markets has led Ganong Bros. Ltd. to form strategic partnerships with companies such as Kerr Bros., or to use the Sunkist label. Decisions like these must first be passed by the company's board of directors, with members from outside industries such as financial institutions, food production, and even beer manufacturing and marketing.

Mr. Ganong says a board of directors has been around since his grandfather's day, and he wholeheartedly endorses it. "A management team in any business can get carried away by its own ideas— and they may not necessarily be the best ideas," he says. "We've used [the board of directors] as a way to generate very, very good ideas over the years."

He acknowledges that the industry is changing. Technological changes, for example, have transformed the industry. But the biggest change has come on the heels of a string of consolidations in the grocery, drug, and major retail areas. "The old days of shipping large quantities to retailers and giving them discounts have really disappeared. They want what they want—when they want it," Mr. Ganong says. In fact, in cases such as Wal-Mart, a late or incomplete shipment can mean a financial penalty or fine. "That's the way the world is. We could grumble about it if we thought it was unfair, but that's the way our customers are operating their businesses today."

"The Ganong Bros. Ltd. candy factory is experiencing a dramatic employee shortage that is slowing down business," a company executive says. Dave Pigott, the company COO, adds that the business is turning down customers and orders because it can't get enough workers to keep up with demand.

"What happens is there is work that we can't take on without disappointing customers, which we don't want to do," he explains. "So we have to turn down orders, which means that work is going elsewhere, which means to other countries, because there aren't that many chocolate factories left. Ganong is coming up with new and competitive ways to attract workers."

Ganong, Canada's last family-owned chocolate maker with distribution and sales across the country, celebrated 130 years of sweet success in 2003. The historic, family-owned company celebrated throughout 2003, and created a new relationship by raising money for the Canadian Breast Cancer Research Foundation as part of its marketing initiatives. The company pledged and delivered $130,000 in its 130th year.

SITE ANALYSIS

Ganong has reached an agreement with Archibald Candy (Canada) Company of Toronto, to supply Laura Secord stores with a broad range of the Canadian retailer's fine chocolate and confectionery needs. The supply agreement was negotiated over several months and represents a significant portion of Laura Secord's annual requirements. David Ganong says that "putting this agreement together required a large effort by both organizations." The contract continues even though Archibald has sold Laura Secord.

Ganong has received an investment by both the federal and provincial governments to expand operations and purchase new equipment to produce and supply Laura Secord with quality chocolates and confectionery items. As a result, the company has created 40 new jobs at the St. Stephen facility.

"Continuing to maintain a globally competitive, efficient company here in St. Stephen and competing against other international companies of this world is a significant challenge," Ganong says. "These are international giants with strong research and development capabilities, high levels of technology and a lot of muscle in the marketplace. To compete in this market, our goal at Ganong has been to grow strategically, with contracts such as Laura Secord, to ensure our long-term cost competitiveness. Clearly, the loan (partially forgivable) will undoubtedly offer more unique opportunities for the family of Ganong products as the company continues to grow."

All four company leaders have been family members, but Mr. Ganong is not certain that trend will continue. Though eldest daughter Bryana is manager of industrial affairs and product public affairs and son Nicholas is in charge of mechanical chocolate dipping, he says that leadership will pass to the person best-suited for the job. In 1977 when David Ganong, at age 34, took over the president's job at his family's chocolate company he was unprepared and Ganong Bros. Ltd. suffered while he was learning the ropes. Ganong is determined not to make the same mistake with regard to his own succession. Mr. Ganong says "The Company needs someone younger; it needs some new ideas; it needs some new energy."

The board has appointed Doug Ettinger to succeed David Ganong as president and CEO. Mr. Ettinger took the reins of the company on Tuesday, July 22, 2008. He will be only the 5th president in the 135-year company history and the first one not to be a family member.

Every month, Mr. Ganong receives at least one unsolicited buyout offer for the company, but he doesn't return the calls. He says he's not interested in selling.

Since 1873 the Ganong family and friends have put their heart and soul into the chocolate confectioner's art. The special skills in making quality confectionery have been passed down from father to son throughout the generations in the small town of St. Stephen, New Brunswick.

Today, the love of chocolate and devotion to excellence leads Mr. Ganong, a fourth-generation chocolate maker, to preserve and perpetuate this rich heritage. The result is a joy. At Ganong, you'll discover many old-fashioned varieties that haven't been made in half a century, together with exquisite masterpieces of the confectioner's art.

Mr. Ganong says his company has been forced to slash costs, including cutting management and rank-and-file jobs, and invest in better equipment. The Company has benefited from its ability to perform contract production for other brands. Contract and private label volumes have risen to more than half of total production.

Ganong Bros.'s Global Export business provides high-quality products suitable for many markets throughout the world. The company ships to numerous countries outside North America. Products such as Ganong Fruitfull have had great success internationally.

The firm's manufacturing processes are efficient yet offer some flexibility for adaptation to local market requirements. Based on their experience in many markets, they offer modifications in formulation and packaging on volume purchases.

Ganong Bros. is committed to the further development of exports and has put in place the appropriate resources to ensure that market opportunities are adequately explored. It has an interest in forging strategic partnerships in various parts of the world.

The company is recognized as one of Canada's best-managed private companies and continues to be one of New Brunswick's strongest and most reputable. The Company employs more than 340 people, up 40 from a year ago. It rebounded to double-digit growth last year (2007) and should be able to do it again this year.

SOURCES: Canadian Press, "Worker Shortage Costs Candy Maker Customers," *Toronto Star*, September 28, 2007, B5. Reprinted with permission of The Canadian Press; Terrence Belford and Kira Vermond, "A Day of Fishing Led to Chocolate Bar's Invention," *National Post*, December 15, 1999, E2; Canadian Press, "Ganong Bros. Limited Celebrates 130 Sweet Years!" January 28, 2003; Canadian Press, "Ganong Strikes a Sweet Deal to Supply Laura Secord Candy," January 19, 2004; "Federal and Provincial Investments Improve Ganong's International Competitiveness," News Release, *Business New Brunswick*, July 13, 2004; Sharda Prashad, "The Sweet Smell of Success," *Toronto Star*, November 27, 2005, A19; Ganong website, found at: http//www.ganongbros.ca; Gordon Pitts, Shaken by chocolate woes, Ganong goes outside for help; *The Globe and Mail*, Saturday July 19, 2008, page B3.

CHAPTER SUMMARY

To be strategically successful, organizations frequently need to have a cost accounting system or a systematic way of recording and valuing costs. A cost accounting system should be compatible with the manufacturing environment in which it is used.

What production situations are appropriate for a process costing system and why?
Process costing is used in manufacturing companies producing large quantities of homogeneous products that are manufactured on a continuous basis. It is an averaging method used to assign manufacturing costs to units of production.

Either the weighted average method or the FIFO method can be used to compute equivalent units of production and assign costs in a process costing system. The difference between the two methods lies solely in the way work performed in the prior period on the beginning Work in Process Inventory is treated.

How is a cost of production report prepared under the weighted average method of process costing?
To prepare a cost of production report under the weighted average method of process costing, it is necessary first to calculate the total units to account for. Second, calculate the total units accounted for. Third, determine the equivalent units of production. Under the weighted average method, work on beginning inventory is combined with current period work in the calculation of the units. Fourth, determine the total cost to account for. In this step, the cost of the beginning inventory and the cost of the current period are added to obtain the total costs, which are averaged over all units. Fifth, calculate the cost per equivalent unit. Sixth, assign the costs to the inventory balances. These steps are discussed on pages 254 to 257. The sample report is shown on page 257.

How are equivalent units of production, unit costs, and inventory values computed using the FIFO method of process costing?
Under the FIFO method, work performed in the last period on beginning Work in Process Inventory is not commingled with current period work, nor are costs of beginning Work in Process Inventory added to current period costs to derive unit production cost. With FIFO, current period costs are divided by current period production to generate a unit production cost related entirely to work performed in the current period. The steps are discussed on pages 257 to 260.

How is a cost of production report prepared under the FIFO method of process costing?
The FIFO method reflects the actual physical flow of goods through production.

The six steps that need to be followed to prepare the cost of production report are described on pages 257 to 260. A sample report is shown on page 261.

5   **What is the effect of multidepartmental processing on the computation of equivalent units of production?**

In multidepartmental process environments, costs must be tracked as the goods move through departments and from one department to the next. The tracking takes place through the use of a transferred-in cost component for EUP and cost per EUP computation. Other cost components include direct material, direct labour, and overhead. If different materials have different degrees of completion, each material is considered a separate cost component. If overhead is applied on a direct labour basis or is incurred at the same rate as direct labour, labour and overhead may be combined as a single cost component and referred to as conversion cost.

6   **How do normal and abnormal losses of units differ and how is each treated in the calculation of equivalent units of production?**

Management typically specifies a certain level of shrinkage/spoilage that will be tolerated as normal. If lost units exceed that expectation, the excess is considered abnormal. Normal losses are treated as product costs and abnormal losses are treated as period costs.

Accounting for spoiled units is essential when total quality does not exist. The traditional methods of accounting for spoilage often "bury" the cost of poor quality by spreading that cost over good output. An attempt should be made to isolate the cost of spoilage. Managers who are aware of spoilage costs can make better decisions as to whether to ignore the causes of spoilage or to try to correct them. Impediments to such awareness include using the method of neglect and burying the cost of spoilage in predetermined overhead rates rather than accounting for the spoilage separately. Managers may rationalize the existence of these impediments because they believe that a particular cause only creates an insignificant amount of spoilage; thus, tolerances for error are built into the system.

Key Terms

Abnormal spoilage (p. 264)
Accepted quality level (p. 267)
Continuous loss (p. 264)
Cost of production report (p. 257)
Defective unit (see *spoilage*) (p. 262)
Equivalent units of production
(p. 250)
FIFO method (p. 251)
Method of neglect (p. 264)

Normal spoilage (p. 264)
Process costing (p. 245)
Process costing system (p. 245)
Spoilage (p. 262)
Spoiled unit (see *spoilage*) (p. 262)
Total cost to account for (p. 253)
Total units to account for (p. 251)
Units started and completed (p. 254)
Weighted average method (p. 251)

Points to Remember

Steps in Process Costing Computations

1. Compute the total units to account for (in physical units):
   Beginning inventory in whole (physical) units
   + Units started (or transferred in) during period

2. Compute units accounted for (in physical units):
   Units completed and transferred out
   + Ending inventory in whole (physical) units
3. Compute equivalent units of production per cost component:
   a. Weighted average
      Beginning inventory in whole (physical) units
      + Units started and completed*
      + (Ending inventory × Percentage complete)
   b. FIFO
      (Beginning inventory × Percentage not complete at start of period)
      + Units started and completed*
      + (Ending inventory × Percentage complete)

      * Units started and completed = Units transferred – Units in beginning inventory.
4. Compute total cost to account for:
   Cost in beginning inventory
   + Cost of current period
5. Compute cost per equivalent unit per cost component:
   a. Weighted average
      Cost of component in beginning inventory
      + Cost of component for current period
      = Total cost of component
      ÷ EUP for component
   b. FIFO
      Cost of component for current period
      ÷ EUP for component
6. Assign costs to inventories:
   a. Weighted average
      1. Transferred out
         Whole units transferred × (Total cost per EUP for all components)
      2. Ending inventory
         Sum of EUP for each component × Cost per EUP for each component
   b. FIFO
      1. Transferred out:
         Beginning inventory cost
         + (Beginning inventory × Percentage not complete at beginning of
            period for each component × Cost per EUP for each component)
         + (Units started and completed × Total cost per EUP for all components)
      2. Ending inventory:
         Sum of (EUP for each component × Cost per EUP for each component)

Spoilage

Normal Loss Treatment
All good production (both fully and partially completed) absorbs the cost of the lost units through higher per-unit costs.

Abnormal Loss Treatment
The cost of lost units is assigned as a period loss.

DEMONSTRATION PROBLEMS

Problem 1

Sandra Chowfen manufactures several smoked food items, including smoked salmon. The firm has two departments: the Smoking Department is highly labour-intensive and the Packaging Department is highly automated. Salmon production occurs during four months of the year. Costs in the Smoking Department are accumulated in three cost pools: direct material, direct labour, and overhead. The following production and cost data relate to the November production of smoked salmon.

Production Data:

Beginning Work In Process Inventory	15,000 kilograms
(This inventory is 100% complete as to material, and 35% complete as to conversion.)	
Started this period	250,000 kilograms
Ending Work In Process Inventory	8,000 kilograms
(This inventory is 100% complete as to material, and 40% complete as to conversion.)	

Cost Data:

	Material	Conversion Cost
Beginning inventory	$ 34,000	$ 14,601
Costs incurred in November	787,500	508,415

Required:

a. Use the weighted average method to determine the cost of the smoked salmon transferred to WIP Inventory Packaging and the cost of the packages of smoked salmon in the Smoking Department's EWIP for November.
b. Repeat part (a) using the FIFO method.

Problem 2

Amanda Lang produces pipes. Spoilage occurs continually throughout the process. Spoilage of 1% or fewer of the metres of raw material placed into production is considered normal. The following information is available for May:

Opening inventory (60% complete as to material; 70% complete as to conversion)	8,000 m
Started during May	180,000 m
Ending inventory (40% complete as to material; 20% complete as to conversion)	4,000 m
Spoiled	1,400 m

Required:

a. How many metres are transferred out?
b. What are the FIFO equivalent units of production for material? for conversion?

Solutions to Demonstration Problems

Problem 1

a. Weighted average method:

Step 1: Calculate total units to account for:

Beginning inventory	15,000
Units started during current period	250,000
Units to account for	265,000

Step 2: Calculate the total units accounted for:

Units completed and transferred out	257,000
Units in ending WIP inventory	8,000
Units accounted for	265,000

Step 3: Determine the equivalent units of production:

	Material	Conversion Cost
BI (whole units)	15,000	15,000
Units started and completed	242,000	242,000
EWIP (whole units × 100%; 40% Complete as to conversion)	8,000	3,200
EUP	265,000	260,200

Step 4: Determine the total cost to account for:

	Material	Conversion Cost
BI cost	$ 34,000	$ 14,601
Current period cost	787,500	508,415
Total cost to account for	$821,500	$523,016

Total all cost pools = $821,500 + $523,016 = $1,344,516

Step 5: Calculate the cost per equivalent unit of production:

	Material	Conversion Cost
Total cost	$821,500	$523,016
Divided by EUP	÷265,000	÷260,200
Cost per EUP	$ 3.10	$ 2.01

Total cost per EUP = $3.10 + $2.01 = $5.11

Step 6: Assign costs to inventories and goods transferred out:

Cost of goods transferred (257,000 × $5.11)		$1,313,270
Cost of ending inventory:		
Material (8,000 × $3.10)	$24,800	
Conversion (3,200 × $2.01)	6,432	31.232
Total cost accounted for		$1,344,516

b. **FIFO method:**

Step 1: Calculate total units to account for:

Beginning inventory	15,000
Units started during current period	250,000
Units to account for	265,000

Step 2: Calculate the total units accounted for:

Units completed and transferred out	257,000
Units in ending WIP Inventory	8,000
Units accounted for	265,000

Step 3: Determine the equivalent units of production:

	Material	Conversion Cost
BI (EUP not completed in October)	0	9,750
Units started and completed	242,000	242,000
EI (whole units × % complete)	8,000	3,200
EUP	250,000	254,950

Step 4: Determine the total cost to account for:

	Material	Conversion Cost
BWIP cost	$ 34,000	$ 14,601
Current period cost	787,500	508,415
Total cost to account for	$821,500	$523,016

Total all cost pools = $821,500 + $523,016 = $1,344,516

Step 5: Calculate the cost per equivalent unit of production:

	Material	Conversion Cost
Total cost	$787,500	$508,415
Divided by EUP	÷250,000	÷254,950
Cost per EUP	$ 3.15	$ 1.99

Total cost per EUP = $3.15 + $1.99 = $5.14

Step 6: Assign costs to inventories and goods transferred out:

Cost of goods transferred out:		
Beginning WIP Inventory cost ($34,000 + $14,601)		$ 48,601.00
Costs to complete beginning WIP:		
Material (0 × $3.15)		0.00
Conversion (9,750 × $1.99)		19,402.50
Total cost of beginning WIP Inventory		$ 68,003.50
Started and completed (242,000 × $5.14)		1,243,880.00
Total cost of goods transferred out		$1,311,883.50
Cost of Ending WIP Inventory:		
Material (8,000 × $3.15)	$25,200	
Conversion (3,200 × $1.99)	6,368	
Total cost of ending WIP Inventory		31,568.00
Total cost accounted for		$1,343,451.50

Problem 2

All spoilage is normal because the 1400 metres is less than 0.01 x 180,000.
a and b

	Units	Material	Conversion
Opening inventory (60%; 70%)	8,000		
Metres started	180,000		
Total to account for	188,000		
Opening inventory completed	8,000	3,200	2,400
Metres started and completed	174,600	174,600	174,600
Total transferred	182,600		
Ending inventory (40%; 20%)	4,000	1,600	800
Normal Spoilage	1,400	0	0
Metres accounted for (FIFO EUP)	188,000	179,400	177,800

End-of-Chapter Materials

SELF-TEST QUESTIONS

(SOLUTIONS APPEAR AT THE END OF THE CHAPTER.)

Use the information below to answer Questions 1 to 3.

The following is information about Gilda Serao Ltd., a chemical producer, for the month of June:

Work in process, beginning inventory	50,000 units
Transferred-in units: 100% complete	
Direct materials: 0% complete	
Conversion costs: 80% complete	
Transferred in during June	200,000 units
Completed and transferred	
out during June	210,000 units
Work in process, ending inventory	? units
Transferred-in units: 100% complete	
Direct materials: 0% complete	
Conversion costs: 40% complete	

1. How many units are in ending Work in Process Inventory?
   a. 0 units   c. 20,000 units
   b. 16,000 units   d. 40,000 units

2. Under FIFO, what are the equivalent units of production for the month of June with respect to materials?
   a. 186,000 equivalent units
   b. 200,000 equivalent units
   c. 210,000 equivalent units
   d. 250,000 equivalent units

3. Under FIFO, what are the equivalent units of production for the month of June with respect to conversion costs?
   a. 186,000 equivalent units
   b. 200,000 equivalent units
   c. 210,000 equivalent units
   d. 250,000 equivalent units

   Extract from *Management Accounting 1 Examination*, published by the Certified General Accountants Association of Canada (© CGA-Canada 2003). Reprinted with permission.

4. Ashley Co.'s beginning Work in Process Inventory consisted of 11,000 units, 100% complete as to materials costs and 30% complete as to conversion costs. The total cost of the beginning inventory was $22,400. During the month, 45,000 units were transferred out. The equivalent unit cost for production during the month was computed to be $1.20 for materials and $3.40 for conversion costs under the weighted average method. What was the total cost of the units completed and transferred out?
   a. $182,500
   b. $184,600
   c. $204,980
   d. $207,000

5. Activity in the Fay Estrin Company's assembly department for the month of March was as follows:

		Percent Complete	
	Number of Units	Materials	Conversion Costs
Work in Process Inventory, March 1	6,000	60%	45%
Started into production during March	65,000		
Work in Process Inventory, March 31	4,000	35%	20%

   What are the equivalent units of production for conversion costs for March, using the weighted average method?
   a. 67,800 units
   b. 69,000 units
   c. 69,600 units
   d. 71,000 units

   Self-Test Questions 4 and 5 are extracted from *Management Accounting Examination*, published by the Certified General Accountants Association of Canada (© CGA-Canada 2002). Reprinted with permission.

Use the following information to answer Questions 6 to 8.

The following information pertains to production activities in the refining department of Brittany Hodges Corporation. All units in work in process (WIP) were costed using the FIFO cost flow assumption.

Refining Department	Units	Percentage of Completion	Conversion Costs
WIP, February 1	25,000	80%	$ 22,000
Units started and cost incurred during February	135,000		$143,000
Units completed and transferred to the mixing department	100,000	50%	
WIP, February 28	?		?

6. What were the conversion costs per equivalent unit of production last period and this period, respectively?
   a. $1.10 and $1.30
   b. $1.10 and $1.45
   c. $1.30 and $1.30
   d. $1.30 and $1.43

7. What was the conversion cost in the Work in Process Inventory account at February 28?
   a. $39,000   c. $42,500
   b. $36,600   d. $45,000

SELF-TEST QUESTIONS

8. What was the per unit conversion cost of the units started last period and completed this period?
   a. $0.86   c. $1.25
   b. $1.14   d. $1.30

Use the following information to answer Questions 9 to 10.

Finishing Department had 5,000 incomplete units in beginning Work in Process Inventory. The units were 100% complete for materials and 70% complete for conversion costs. During the period 15,000 units were started into the process. The ending Work in Process Inventory contains 2,000 units that are 50% complete for materials and 30% complete for conversion costs. The FIFO method is used.

9. How many units were transferred out during the period?
   a. 12,000   c. 18,000
   b. 13,000   d. 20,000

10. How many units were started and completed during the period?
    a. 12,000   c. 18,000
    b. 13,000   d. 20,000

11. In a cost-of-production report, the total costs accounted for are equal to the cost of units completed and transferred out plus the cost of which of the following?
    a. Beginning Work in Process
    b. Units started and finished
    c. Units completed but still on hand
    d. Ending work in process

    (Self Test questions 9, 10 and 11 are adapted by the authors from *Management Accounting Examination* published by the Certified General Accountants Association of Canada © CGA-Canada, December 2004, used by permission)

12. Pat Bollin Ltd. uses the weighted average method units process costing system. Information for Department C for the month of January is as follows:

	Materials	Conversion
Work in Process, opening	$4,000	$3,000
Current cost added	$20,000	$16,000
Equivalent units	100,000 units	95,000 units
Unit costs	$0.24	$0.20
Goods completed	90,000 units	
Work in Process, ending	10,000 units	

Materials are all added at the beginning of the process. The ending Work in Process is 50% complete with respect to conversion costs. How would the total "costs accounted for" be distributed between costs completed and transferred out, and ending Work in Process?

	Costs Completed and Transferred Out	Ending Work in Process
a.	$39,600	$3,400
b.	$39,600	$4,400
c.	$43,000	$ 0
d.	$44,000	$3,400

(Self Test question 12 is adapted by the authors from *Management Accounting Examination* published by the Certified General Accountants Association of Canada © CGA-Canada, March 2005, used by permission)

13. Normal spoilage is defined as follows:
    a. Spoilage that results from normal operations
    b. Waste which is uncontrollable and is a result of a special production run
    c. Spoilage that arises under inefficient operations
    d. Controllable spoilage.

14. Which of the following is an inventoriable cost?

	Abnormal Spoilage	Normal Spoilage
a.	No	No
b.	No	Yes
c.	Yes	No
d.	Yes	Yes

15. In a process costing system, the cost of abnormal spoilage should be:
    a. Allocated between units transferred out and ending inventory
    b. Included in the cost of units transferred out
    c. Treated as a loss in the period in which it is incurred.
    d. None of the above

16. Reed Corporation incurred normal spoilage of $10,000 and abnormal spoilage of $12,000 during the month of September. How much of the spoilage cost should be written off as a period cost for the month of September?
    a. $22,000
    b. $12,000
    c. $10,000
    d. $0

QUESTIONS

1. Describe the characteristics of a production environment in which process costing would likely be found.

2. How are job order and process costing similar? How do they differ?

3. What is meant by the term *equivalent units of production*? Why are equivalent units of production needed in process costing but not in job order costing?

4. What are the six steps involved in assigning product costs in a process costing environment? In your answer, indicate in which steps physical units are used and in which steps equivalent units are used.

5. What is the purpose of a cost of production report? Discuss the information provided to managers by this document.

QUESTIONS

6. Under what circumstances will a department have a cost component called *transferred in*? What degree of completion will the units in this component have?

7. A company has two sequential processing departments. On the cost of production reports, will the cost per unit transferred out of the first department always be equal to the cost per unit transferred in to the second department? Why or why not?

8. At the end of a period, a department's total production costs are assigned to two groups of products. What are the two groups and where do their costs appear on the financial statements?

9. How are units started and completed calculated?

10. In computing the cost per equivalent unit of production, is one equivalent unit computation sufficient for all of the cost categories (direct materials, direct labour, and overhead)? Explain.

11. Doug Hyatt Ltd. uses a process costing system that has three sequential processing departments (Cutting, Stitching, and Finishing, respectively). What journal entry would identify the cost of goods manufactured?

12. In a firm that uses a process costing system as a tool both to evaluate periodic cost control and to assign costs to products, would weighted average or FIFO more likely be used? Explain.

13. Does the weighted average or FIFO method provide the better picture of the actual amount of work accomplished in a period? Explain.

14. In an inflationary environment (costs are rising from period to period), which process costing method, FIFO or weighted average, would assign the higher cost to the ending Work in Process in a department? (Assume that production is stable from period to period.) Explain.

15. Why does the transferred-out cost under the weighted average method include only one computation but the FIFO method includes multiple computations?

16. Describe a circumstance (or circumstances) in which the FIFO and weighted average costs per equivalent unit of production would be identical or nearly identical.

17. How are the FIFO and weighted average methods similar and how do they differ?

18. Why should companies design process accounting systems to capture costs of spoilage?

19. What is meant by the method of neglect? How does the use of this method affect the cost of good production?

20. Why is the cost of spoilage so difficult to determine in a service provider?

EXERCISES

1. (LO 2) Judith Poë Ltd. produces a chemical compound in which all material is added at the beginning of the production cycle. At May 1, there were 36,000 litres in opening inventory. During May, the company started 920,000 litres of raw material into production and completed 945,000 litres.

   The beginning inventory was 60% complete as to conversion. The ending Work in Process Inventory was 30% complete as to conversion. The company uses the weighted average method.
   Required:
   a. Determine the total number of litres to account for.
   b. Determine the equivalent units of production for direct material.
   c. Determine the equivalent units of production for conversion.

2. (LO 2) Kevin Fisher Corp. uses a weighted average process costing system. All material is added at the start of the process; labour and overhead costs are incurred evenly throughout the production process. The company's records for September contained the following information:

Beginning Work in Process Inventory	32,000 kilograms
Started during September	800,000 kilograms
Transferred to finished goods	808,000 kilograms

EXERCISES

As of September 1, the beginning inventory was 60% complete as to labour and overhead. On September 30, the ending inventory was 35% complete as to labour and overhead.

Required:

a. Determine the total number of kilograms to account for.
b. Determine the equivalent units of production for direct material.
c. Determine the equivalent units of production for conversion.

3. (LO 2) The Gilda Company produces tubes of tanning gel in a continuous flow production process. The company uses weighted average process costing to assign production costs to products. All of the gel materials are added at the beginning of the process in Department One; the plastic tubes are added in Department Two. Direct labour and overhead costs are incurred evenly throughout the process. Information on the physical unit activity and costs for April is as follows:

	Kilograms of Gel
Beginning Work in Process Inventory	42,000
Transferred out this period	150,000
Ending Work in Process Inventory	30,000

	Direct Material Cost	Conversion Cost
Beginning Work in Process Inventory	$ 6,420	$ 7,056
Incurred this period	15,180	34,944

The April beginning and ending Work in Process Inventories are, respectively, 75% and 60% complete as to conversion.

Required:

a. Determine the equivalent units of production for direct material and conversion for April.
b. Determine the cost per equivalent unit of production for direct material and conversion for April.
c. Determine the cost of the kilograms of gel transferred out and the kilograms of gel remaining in ending Work in Process Inventory.

4. (LO 2) The following are individual situations.

a.	Units started in production	280,000
	Units transferred out	200,000
	Beginning Work in Process Inventory (60% complete)	40,000
	Ending Work in Process Inventory (75% complete)	120,000
b.	Units started in production	240,000
	Units transferred out	?
	Beginning Work in Process Inventory (25% complete)	40,000
	Ending Work in Process Inventory (60% complete)	60,000
c.	Units started in production	135,000
	Units transferred out	130,000
	Beginning Work in Process Inventory (30% complete)	15,000
	Ending Work in Process Inventory (90% complete)	?
d.	Units started in production	?
	Units transferred out	180,000
	Beginning Work in Process Inventory (20% complete)	10,000
	Ending Work in Process Inventory (70% complete)	20,000

Required:

For each of the above situations, determine the equivalent units of production using the weighted average method.

5. (LO 2) Esther Deutsch Corporation uses a weighted average process costing system to account for its production costs. All materials are added at the start of the process while labour and overhead costs are incurred evenly throughout the production process. The company's records for the month of September contained the following information:

Opening inventory	8,000 litres
Started during September	200,000 litres
Transferred to finished goods	202,000 litres

As of December 1, the beginning inventory was 40% complete as to conversion. On December 31, the ending inventory was 60% complete as to conversion.

EXERCISES

Required:
a.   Determine the total number of units to account for.
b.   Determine the equivalent units of production for direct materials.
c.   Determine the equivalent units of production for direct labour and manufacturing overhead.

6.   (LO 2) On March 1, BUG-B-GONE had 12,000 litres of bug spray in work in process in Department A—the first stage of its production cycle. Costs attached to these litres were $37,160 for materials and $24,620 for conversion. Materials are added at the beginning of the process, and labour and overhead are applied evenly throughout the process. Conversion was 70% complete on March 1.

During March, 58,000 litres were started, $172,840 of material costs were incurred, and $141,780 of conversion costs were incurred. On March 31, Department A had 8,000 litres in ending work in process that were 25% complete as to conversion. The company uses the weighted average method of process costing.

Required:
a.   How much cost should be assigned to the litres transferred out during March?
b.   How much cost should be assigned to the litres in March ending Work in Process Inventory?

7.   (LO 2) Nicholas Sperry Ltd. manufactures a special type of fast-drying paint. You are attempting to verify the balances at the end of the year, which are recorded on the books of Nicholas Sperry Ltd. as follows. (A physical count revealed that the ending physical units are correct.)

	Units	Cost
Work in Process (50% complete as to conversion costs)	450,000	$ 991,440
Finished goods	300,000	1,514,700

Materials are added at the beginning of the manufacturing process. Overhead is applied at 50% of direct labour costs. There was no beginning finished goods inventory.

Additional information:

Costs	Units	Materials	Conversion
Beginning WIP (50% complete)	300,000	$ 300,000	$ 472,500
Units started	1,500,000		
Material costs		1,950,000	
Conversion costs			2,992,500
Units completed	1,350,000		

Required:
Using the weighted average method, compute the following:
a.   Equivalent units of production
b.   Unit costs of production of materials, and conversion
c.   Costs of the Finished Goods Ending Inventory and Ending Work in Process Inventory

Extracted from *Management Accounting Examination*, published by the Certified General Accountants Association of Canada (© CGA-Canada 2001). Reprinted with permission.

8.   (LO 2) The Judy Pereira Company produces ice cream and employs a process costing system based on the weighted average method to assign costs to production. Various materials are added at discrete stages in the production process while direct labour and factory overhead are incurred evenly throughout the process. For the first week in May, the company experienced the following results:

Litres of ice cream in opening inventory	4,000
Litres of ice cream completed	30,000
Litres of ice cream completed	24,000

For the same week, the relevant costs were as follows:

	Conversion
Opening inventory	$ 3,800
Costs this period	14,500

EXERCISES

Also for this week, the beginning inventory was 25% complete as to conversion. The ending inventory was 60% complete as to conversion.

Required:
a. Compute equivalent units of production for conversion.
b. For conversion, compute the cost per equivalent unit of production.
c. For conversion, determine the cost of the ending inventory and the cost transferred to finished goods.

9. (LO 2) The Shearer Pellet Company manufactures alfalfa pellets used as animal feed. Alfalfa is processed in a two-department sequential process. The first process, dehydration, removes moisture from raw alfalfa; the second process, pelletizing, compresses the alfalfa into pellets. The following transactions occurred at Shearer Pellet in January. Journalize each transaction.
a. Alfalfa costing $200,000 was removed from Raw Material Inventory and entered into processing in the Dehydration Department.
b. The Dehydration Department paid labour costs of $240,000; of this amount, $160,000 was considered direct.
c. Other overhead costs amounting to $140,000 were incurred in the Dehydration Department. (Note: credit Accounts Payable.)
d. Goods costing $660,000 were transferred from the Dehydration Department to the Pelletizing Department.
e. Labour costs of $162,000 were incurred in the Pelletizing Department; $124,000 of this amount was considered direct.
f. Other overhead costs incurred in the Pelletizing Department amounted to $226,000. (Note: credit Accounts Payable.)
g. Goods costing $980,000 were transferred from the Pelletizing Department to Finished Goods Inventory.
h. Goods costing $900,000 were sold for $1,460,000 cash.

Required:
Prepare journal entries for each of parts (a) to (h).

10. (LO 3) Repeat Exercise 5, assuming that Esther Deutsch Corporation uses the FIFO method of process costing.
Required:
a. Determine the total number of units to account for.
b. Determine the equivalent units of production for direct materials.
c. Determine the equivalent units of production for direct labour and overhead.
d. Is the FIFO number of equivalent units different for each of the cost categories under the weighted average equivalent units? If so, why? Explain.

11. (LO 3) The following information has been extracted from Department One of Paula Freedman Ltd.'s cost records for the month of October. The information pertains to direct materials used in this department. The company utilizes the FIFO process costing system.

Opening inventory (20% complete as to direct materials)	100,000 kilos
Ending inventory (70% complete as to direct materials)	80,000 kilos
Direct material costs incurred in October	$ 93,600
Direct material costs transferred out	$ 90,400
Cost per equivalent unit for October	$ 0.10

Required:
a. Equivalent units of production for direct materials in October.
b. Cost per equivalent unit for direct materials in September.
c. Cost of direct materials assigned to the ending WIP Inventory in October.

12. (LO 3) Answer parts (a), (b), and (c) of Exercise 1 assuming that Judith Poë Ltd. uses the FIFO method of process costing.

13. (LO 3) For each of the situations given in Exercise 4, determine the equivalent units of production using the FIFO method of process costing.

14. (LO 2, 3) Jaylee Leno Company had 70,000 units in beginning Work in Process Inventory in Department 1 that were 90% complete as to material and 60% complete as to conversion. During July, 360,000 units were started in Department 1, and 395,000 units were

EXERCISES

completed and transferred to Department 2. Ending Work in Process Inventory in Department 1 on July 31 was 80% complete as to material and 45% complete as to conversion.

Required:

a. What are the equivalent units of production under the weighted average method?

b. What are the equivalent units of production under the FIFO method?

c. Reconcile the equivalent units of production calculated in parts (a) and (b).

15. (LO 3, 4) Answer parts (a) and (b) of Exercise 6, assuming that BUG-B-GONE uses the FIFO method of process costing.

16. (LO 2, 5) Nickel Kidman produces fruit drinks in a three-department production process (Steaming, Mixing, and Packaging). Limited information on the inventory accounts for March follows:

WIP Inventory—Steaming				WIP Inventory—Mixing		
Beg.	90,000			Beg.	300,000	
DM	270,000	?		Trans In	?	
DL	60,000			DM	?	600,000
OH	75,000			DL	?	
Ending	54,000			OH	?	
				Ending	210,000	

WIP Inventory—Packaging				Finished Goods Inventory		
Beg.	270,000			Beg.	495,000	
Trans In	?			CGM	?	1,440,000
DM	300,000			Ending	?	
DL	600,000	?				
OH	180,000					
Ending	330,000					

Required:

a. What was the cost of goods transferred from the Steaming Department to the Mixing Department in March?

b. What was the sum of direct material, direct labour, and overhead costs in the Mixing Department for March?

c. What was the cost of goods manufactured for March?

17. (LO 3, 4, 5) Kathryn Heigel Inc. produces calendars in a two-process, two-department operation. In the Printing Department, materials are printed and cut. In the Assembly Department, the materials received from Printing are assembled into individual calendars and bound. Each department maintains its own Work in Process Inventory account. In Assembly, conversion costs are incurred evenly throughout the process; direct material is added at the end of the process. For the current month, the following production and cost information is available:

Beginning inventory:		
(30% complete as to conversion)		20,000 calendars
Transferred-in cost	$25,000	
Conversion cost	1,114	
Transferred in during the month:		
Current period costs:		
Transferred-in	$80,000	
Direct Material	10,500	
Conversion	14,960	
Ending Work in Process Inventory:		
(80% complete as to conversion)		30,000 calendars

Required:

a. For the Assembly Department, using the weighted average method, compute the:

   i. Equivalent units of production for each cost component

   ii. Cost per equivalent unit for each cost component

   iii. Cost transferred to Finished Goods Inventory

   iv. Cost of ending Work in Process Inventory

b. Compute all of the above, assuming that the company uses the FIFO costing method.

EXERCISES

18. (LO 3, 6) Dan Segal Corporation manufactures T-shirts on a mass-production basis. Spoilage occurs throughout the process. Normal spoilage is considered to be 0.4% or less of the materials placed into production. The following data are available for March:

Beginning Work in Process Inventory (20% complete as to material; 30% complete as to conversion)	8,000 units
Started during March	180,000 units
Ending Work in Process Inventory (70% complete as to material; 80% complete as to conversion)	4,000 units
Spoiled	1,400 units

Required:
a.   How many units were transferred out?
b.   How much normal spoilage occurred?
c.   How much abnormal spoilage occurred?
d.   What are the FIFO equivalent units of production for materials? for conversion costs?
e.   Explain how costs associated with the normal spoilage are handled.
f.   Explain how costs associated with the abnormal spoilage are handled.

19. (LO 2, 6) The Regina Co. Ltd. uses a weighted average process costing system in accounting for a product that passes through two departments—A and B. In Department B, material is added only to those units that pass inspection. Inspection takes place when the product is 95% complete. A spoilage rate of 4% of finished product is considered normal.

On October 1, 3,000 units were in process in Department B and were estimated to be 40% complete. At the end of September, $25,000 of Department A costs and $13,000 of Department B costs had been assigned to these units.

During the month of October, 20,000 units were received from Department A. A total of 17,000 units were transferred to Finished Goods. At the end of October, 5,000 units were still in process and were estimated to be 70% complete.

Excerpts from Department B's cost of production report for October showed the following:

Finished units (17,000 × $22.00)		$374,000
Ending inventory:		
(5,000 @ $9.00)	$45,000	
(3,500 @ $11.00)	38,500	83,500

Required:
What costs were charged to Department B during October?

PROBLEMS

1. (LO 2) The following is partial information for the month of March for Brad Carlton Company, a two-department manufacturer that uses process costing:

Department B

Work in process, beginning	12,000 units (2/3 converted)
Cost of beginning work in process:	
Transferred in from Department A	$9,500
Materials	$0
Conversion	$11,200
Units completed and transferred out during March	44,000 units
Units transferred in during March from Department A	?
Ending work in process	16,000 units (3/8 converted)
Material costs added during March	$13,200
Conversion costs added during March	$63,000

Other information:
  i.   Material is introduced at the beginning of the process in Department A, and additional material is added at the very end of the process in Department B.
  ii.   Conversion costs are incurred uniformly throughout both processes.

PROBLEMS

iii. As the process in Department A is completed, goods are immediately transferred to Department B; as goods are completed in Department B, they are transferred to finished goods.

iv. Unit costs of production in Department A in March were:

Materials	$0.55
Conversion	0.40
	$0.95

v. The company uses the weighted average method.

Required:

a. Compute the cost of goods transferred out of Department B in March.

b. Compute the cost of the March ending Work in Process Inventory in Department B.

Extract from *Management Accounting Examination*, published by the Certified General Accountants Association of Canada (© CGA-Canada 1992). Reprinted with permission.

2. (LO 2) Creative Cake Bakery Ltd. produces sheet cakes in mass quantities and uses a process costing system to account for its costs. The bakery production line is set up in one department. Batter is mixed first, with all necessary ingredients added at the start of production. The batter is poured into pans, baked, and cooled. The cake is then iced with a mixture of confectioners' sugar and water. The last step in the process is to let the icing harden. The cake is then moved to a display case. Icing is added when the cakes are at the 85% stage of completion.

Production and cost data for April follow. Beginning inventory consisted of 20 cakes, which were 80% complete as to labour and production overhead. The batter associated with beginning inventory had a cost of $66.10, and related conversion costs totalled $40.66. A total of 430 cakes were started during April, and 440 were completed. The ending inventory was 90% complete as to labour and production overhead. Costs for the month were: batter, $1,324.40; icing, $166.50; and conversion cost, $857.34.

Required:

a. Determine the equivalent units of production for each cost component for April for Creative Cake Bakery using the weighted average method.

b. Calculate the cost per unit for each cost component for the bakery for April using the weighted average method.

c. Determine the appropriate valuation for April's ending Work in Process Inventory and the units transferred to finished goods for sale.

d. The bakery sells its cakes for $12.50 each. During April, 427 cakes were sold. What was the total gross profit margin on the sale of the cakes?

3. (LO 2) Gloria Abbott Company produces a preservative used for canned food products. The company employs a weighted average process costing system. All material is introduced at the start of the process. Labour and overhead are at the same degree of completion throughout the process. The following information pertains to the company's October operations.

Unit Data

Beginning work in process (70% complete)	12,000 litres
Started this period	24,000 litres
Ending work in process (40% complete)	17,000 litres

Cost Data	Direct Material	Conversion
Beginning work in process	$ 9,500	$14,700
Incurred this period	35,600	73,080

Required:

a. Determine the total number of units to account for.

b. Compute the equivalent units of production for both material and conversion.

c. Compute the total cost to account for and total cost for both material and conversion.

d. Compute the cost per equivalent unit for material and conversion.

e. Compute the cost assigned to the goods transferred to Finished Goods Inventory and the cost of ending Work in Process Inventory.

4. (LO 2) You are the production supervisor at Jen and Berry's. The company produces ice cream in one-litre containers and uses a weighted average process costing system to assign costs to production. All dairy ingredients are added at the beginning of the production process and pecans are added when the ice cream is 90% complete. The ice

PROBLEMS

cream is put into containers in the second production department. Direct labour and overhead are incurred evenly throughout the process. For May, the company recorded the following results:

BWIP (40% complete)	12,000
Litres started	90,000
EWIP (80% complete)	5,000

For the same period, total costs (beginning and current) were as follows:

Dairy ingredients	$107,100
Pecans	29,100
Conversion costs	88,880

Required:

a. Compute equivalent units of production for the dairy ingredients, pecans, and conversion.
b. Compute the cost per equivalent unit of production for each cost component.
c. Determine the cost transferred to the second production process and the cost of ending Work in Process Inventory.

5. (LO 2) Chip & Dale makes chipmunk and squirrel food. In the Mixing Department, all material is added at the beginning of the process. Labour and overhead are incurred evenly throughout the process. Unit and cost information for a recent period follows:

Beginning inventory (40% complete)	1,500 bags
Units started	56,000 bags
Ending inventory (80% complete)	800 bags

	Direct Material	Conversion
Beginning Work in Process Inventory	$ 2,440	$ 3,587
Current period costs	112,560	68,088

Required:

Prepare a cost of production report for Chip & Dale, assuming that the company employs a weighted average process costing system.

6. (LO 2, 3) The Rogue Tobacco Company produces cans of smokeless tobacco (chewing tobacco). The company employs a process costing system to assign production costs to the units produced. For the second week in June, the firm had a beginning inventory of 20,000 cans that were 20% complete as to materials and 50% complete as to conversion costs. During the week an additional 100,000 cans were started in production. At the end of the week, 25,000 cans remained in the Work in Process Inventory, and were 70% complete as to materials and 30% complete as to conversion costs.

Required:

For the second week in June:

a. Compute the total units to account for.
b. Determine how many units were started and completed.
c. Determine the equivalent units of production for each cost component based on the FIFO method.
d. Determine the equivalent units of production for each cost component based on the weighted average method.
e. Reconcile your answers in parts (c) and (d).

7. (LO 2) Ambrus Kecskés Inc. manufactures tubular steel products in a three-process operation. December information on the first process, Milling, follows:

Tonnes in process, December 1	12,000
Tonnes started in production	90,000
Tonnes in process, December 31	10,000

All material is added at the start of the process. Work in Process Inventory on December 1 was 40% complete as to labour and overhead. Work in Process Inventory on December 31 was 30% complete as to labour and overhead. A summary of costs follows:

	Beginning Inventory	December
Material	$82,980	$630,000
Labour	27,290	540,000
Manufacturing overhead	23,320	357,490

Required:

Prepare a cost of production report for the Milling Department for December, assuming that Ambrus Kecskés Inc. uses a weighted average process costing system.

8. (LO 3) The Sutherland Brewery Company employs a process costing system (based on the FIFO method) in its beer production plants. In the company's small Ontario plant, beer is packaged in 16 litre kegs. Materials are added at the beginning of the process, and conversion costs are incurred evenly throughout the process. Unit information for a recent period follows:

Opening inventory	900 kegs (40% complete)
Units started	4,000 kegs
Ending inventory	1,000 kegs (80% complete)

The following costs were incurred for the same period:

	Direct Materials	Conversion Costs
Opening inventory	$1,900	$ 1,000
Current period costs	7,200	11,718

Required:

a. Determine the total units to account for.
b. Determine the equivalent units of production.
c. Determine the cost per equivalent unit.
d. Determine the cost of the ending inventory and the cost of goods completed and transferred out.
e. Prepare the journal entry for the transfer of goods from Work in Process to Finished Goods.

9. (LO 3) The Apple Sugar Company employs a process costing system based on the FIFO method. For the month January, the following information was extracted from the company's record for direct labour costs:

Opening inventory (400 complete as to labour)	10,000 kilos
Ending inventory (80% complete as to labour)	20,000 kilos
Direct labour cost in opening inventory	$900
Total direct labour costs incurred	$20,000
Cost per equivalent unit for direct labour	$0.10

Required:

a. Total equivalent units (kilos) for direct labour in January.
b. The cost of direct labour in goods completed and transferred out.
c. The cost of direct labour in the ending WIP Inventory.

10. (LO 2, 5) Alison Ground Automotive Ltd. manufactures car bumpers in a continuous two-department process. For August, company records indicate the following production results in the Machining and Finishing departments:

	Machining	Finishing
Units in beginning Work in Process Inventory	500	350
Units started or transferred in	40,000	?
Units in ending Work in Process Inventory	2,000	600

All materials are added at the beginning of production in Machining and at the end of production in Finishing. The company is highly automated and there is no separate labour category in either department. The conversion rates of completion for units in process at August 1 and 31 follow:

Machining:	August 1 (40%);	August 31 (80%)
Finishing:	August 1 (30%);	August 31 (60%)

Cost records indicate the following for the month:

	Machining		Finishing	
	Beginning	Current	Beginning	Current
Transferred in	N/A	N/A	$11,235	$?
Material	$11,140	$794,000	0	133,875
Conversion	5,105	618,450	4,533	246,432

PROBLEMS

Required:
Prepare a cost of production report for each department for August assuming that both departments use the weighted average costing method.

11. (LO 2, 3, 4) David Letterman Company produces gourmet canned cat food. The company employs a process costing system to assign production costs to the units produced. For the second week in July, the firm had a beginning inventory of 20,000 cans that were 20% complete as to material and 50% complete as to conversion. During the week, an additional 100,000 cans were started in production. At the end of the week, 25,000 cans were still in process; these cans were 70% complete as to material and 80% complete as to conversion. Cost information follows:

	Direct Material	Conversion
Beginning Work in Process Inventory	$ 785	$ 915
Current period	15,190	8,400

Required:
a. Compute the total units to account for.
b. Determine the number of units started and completed.
c. Determine the total cost to account for.
d. Determine the equivalent units of production for each cost component based on the weighted average method.
e. Determine the cost per equivalent unit of production for each cost component based on the weighted average method.
f. Assign costs to goods transferred out and goods in ending work in process, using your answers in part (e).
g. Determine the equivalent units of production for each cost component, based on the FIFO method.
h. Based on the FIFO method, determine the cost per equivalent unit of production for each cost component.
i. Assign costs to goods transferred out and to goods in ending work in process, using your answers in part (h).

12. (LO 2, 3, 4) The Howard Price Paint Co. uses a process costing system. You have been given the following selected information for July.

	Physical Units	% Complete
Beginning work in process	6,000	60%
Units started	24,000	
Ending work in process	10,000	40%

The total cost of the beginning work in process was $37,000, of which $7,000 represented direct labour costs. Overhead is applied on the basis of direct labour costs.

During July, the company added $69,400 of direct materials, $50,500 of direct labour, and $60,600 of overhead to work in process.

All direct materials are added at the beginning of the process, and the conversion costs are incurred uniformly through the process.

Required:
a. Calculate the overhead rate.
b. Calculate the direct materials, the direct labour, and the overhead components of the beginning work in process.
c. Calculate the number of equivalent units that would be used to establish the weighted average costs for direct materials, direct labour, and overhead.
d. Calculate the number of equivalent units that would be used to establish the FIFO costs for direct materials, direct labour, and overhead.
e. Assuming weighted average, calculate the cost of goods completed and transferred out.
f. Assuming FIFO, calculate the cost of ending Work in Process Inventory for direct materials, direct labour, and overhead. Show each component separately.

Extract from *Management Accounting Examination*, published by the Certified General Accountants Association of Canada (© CGA-Canada 1999). Reprinted with permission.

PROBLEMS

13. (LO 2, 3, 4) Jia Chen Corp. manufactures chemical additives for industrial applications. As the new cost accountant for Jia Chen Corp., you have been assigned the task of completing the production cost report for the most recent period. Jia Chen Corp. uses the FIFO method of process costing.

The following information pertains to the most recent period:

Beginning WIP inventory:	16,000 units, 75% complete as to materials, 70% complete as to conversion costs
Units started into production this period:	27,000 units
Units completed and transferred out:	33,000 units
Ending WIP inventory:	10,000 units, 60% complete as to materials, 50% complete as to conversion costs
Costs in beginning inventory:	$32,000 materials; $64,000 conversion costs
Current period costs:	$252,000 materials; $440,000 conversion costs

Required:
a. Prepare a complete production report for the period using the FIFO method, which the company has in place at the present time.
b. The company is considering the use of the weighted average method and would like to see what the difference would be. Prepare a complete production report for the period using the weighted average method.

(For both parts, round the cost per equivalent unit to three decimal places, and round the costs in the cost report to the nearest dollar.)

Extract from *Management Accounting Examination*, published by the Certified General Accountants Association of Canada (© CGA-Canada 2003). Reprinted with permission.

14. (LO 2, 3, 4) The Soda Factory uses a process costing system. All material is added at the start of the production process; overhead is applied on a machine hour basis and thus is not related to direct labour. Summary information for April on units and costs in the Blending Department follows:

Beginning inventory (40% complete as to conversion)	3,000,000 litres
Units started	15,000,000 litres
Ending Work in Process Inventory (60% complete as to conversion)	2,300,000 litres
Beginning Work in Process Inventory costs:	
Material	$ 390,000
Conversion	558,500
Current period costs:	
Material	$ 3,750,000
Conversion	15,627,800

Required:
a. Determine the equivalent units of production for each cost component based on the weighted average method.
b. Determine the cost per equivalent unit of production for each cost component based on the weighted average method.
c. Assign costs to goods transferred out and ending work in process using your answers to part (b).
d. Determine the equivalent units of production for each cost component based on the FIFO method.
e. Determine the cost per equivalent unit of production for each cost component based on the FIFO method.
f. Assign costs to goods transferred out and ending work in process using your answers to part (e).
g. What is the cost per equivalent unit for each cost component of the beginning inventory? Given this information, what questions would you, as plant manager, be asking and of whom?

PROBLEMS

15. (LO 3, 4) Assume that Chip & Dale (from Problem 5) uses a FIFO process costing system.
    Required:
    a. Prepare a cost of production report for the Mixing Department.
    b. As the manager reviewing the cost of production report, what oddity would you notice about the beginning Work in Process Inventory cost per equivalent unit for conversion costs? What might explain this oddity?

16. (LO 3, 4) Douglas Hunter Industries, Inc., manufactures outdoor patio lights that are sold to major department stores under private labels. At the beginning of March, the company had 4,000 lights in beginning Work in Process Inventory, which were 90% complete as to material and 75% complete as to conversion. During the month, 22,000 units were started; at the end of March, 5,000 remained in process. The ending Work in Process Inventory was 60% complete as to material and 40% complete as to conversion.

    Actual cost data for the month were as follows:

	Material	Conversion	Total
Beginning inventory	$ 82,200	$ 31,000	$113,200
Current costs	397,800	245,000	642,800
Total costs	$480,000	$276,000	$756,000

    Required:
    a. Prepare equivalent units of production schedules under the weighted average and FIFO methods.
    b. Prepare cost of production reports under the weighted average and FIFO methods.
    c. Discuss the differences in the two reports prepared for part (b). Which would provide better information to departmental managers? Why?

17. (LO 3, 4) Stephen Harper, a baker of European breads and pastries, uses a process costing system. You are provided with the following selected information about its best selling item for the month of November.

	Physical Units	% Complete
Opening work in process	10,000	60%
Units completed	60,000	
Ending work in process	20,000	40%

    The opening Work in Process Inventory consisted of the following:

Transferred-in costs	$10,875
Direct materials	1,750
Conversion	2,800

    Costs added during November were:

Transferred-in costs	$69,125
Direct materials	15,750
Conversion	46,400

    When the process is 15% complete, 40% of the direct materials are added, with the remainder being added when the process is 50% complete. Conversion costs are incurred uniformly throughout processing.

    Required:
    a. What was the cost of the units completed and transferred out to the next department during November:
       i. under the weighted average method?
       ii. under the FIFO method?
    b. What was the weighted average cost of the ending WIP inventory for November?
    c. Will using the FIFO method result in a higher or lower cost per unit of ending WIP inventory for November? Why is there a difference between the FIFO and weighted average methods? Do not calculate the amount.

    Problem 17 was adapted by the authors from *Management Accounting Examination*, published by the Certified General Accountants Association of Canada © CGA-Canada, 1998. Used by permission.

18. (LO 2, 3, 4) Rochelle Gordon Ltd. manufactures a high-quality brick that is used in residential and commercial construction. The firm is small but highly automated and typically produces about 300,000 bricks per month. A brick is formed in a continuous production operation. In the initial step, a tightly controlled mixture of soils and water is forced into a brick mould that ravels on a continuous conveyor belt. No other materials

PROBLEMS

are required to produce a brick. The conveyor belt moves at a snail's pace, and each brick spends two to three days on the conveyor belt before it emerges at the end of the factory as a finished brick. Approximately the last thirty-six hours on the conveyor belt are spent inside a gigantic oven that removes a substantial portion of the moisture from the product. The actual time each brick spends on the conveyor depends on temperature and humidity conditions inside and outside of the plant building. The speed of the conveyor is controlled and monitored by a computer. The firm uses a process costing system based on actual costs to assign production costs to output. Costs are accumulated in three cost pools: materials, direct labour, and overhead. The following are cost and production data for the month of November.

Opening Work in Process Inventory	25,000 bricks
(100% complete as to materials, 60% complete as to conversion cost)	
Started this period	305,000 bricks
Ending Work in Process Inventory	
(100% complete as to materials, 50% complete as to conversion cost)	30,000 bricks

Costs	Materials	Conversion Costs
Opening inventory	$ 1,330	$ 1,287
Costs incurred in November	12,200	33,180

Required:

a. Using the six steps discussed in the text, determine the cost of bricks in ending WIP and the cost of bricks transferred to Finished Goods Inventory for November. Assume the company uses the weighted average method.

b. Repeat part (a), assuming the company uses the FIFO method.

19. (LO 2, 3, 4) In a single-process production system, Amy Nijmeh Corporation produces wax lips for Halloween. For September, the company's accounting records reflected the following:

Opening Work in Process Inventory (100% complete as to Material A; 0% complete as to Material B; 60% complete as to conversion)	10,000 units
Started during the month	80,000 units
Ending Work in Process Inventory (100% complete as to Material A; 0% complete as to Material B; 40% complete as to conversion)	15,000 units

Cost Data	Beginning Inventory	September
Material A	$1,900	$ 8,000
Material B	0	37,500
Conversion	2,725	16,550

Required:

a. For September, prepare a cost of production report, assuming the company uses the weighted average method.

b. Prepare a cost of production report for September, assuming the company uses the FIFO method.

c. Explain to your plant manager how the weighted average method helps disguise the apparently poor cost control in August.

20. (LO 3, 4, 5) Use the information in Problem 10 to prepare a cost of production report assuming that Alison Ground Automotive Ltd. uses a FIFO process costing system. Regardless of the amount calculated as the cost transferred out of Machining, assume that $1,364,055 was the amount transferred in to Finishing for the period.

21. (LO 2, 3, 4, 5) James Znajda Ltd., a company that manufactures quality paint sold at premium prices. Production begins with the blending of various chemicals, which are added at the beginning of the process, and ends with the canning of the paint. Canning occurs when the mixture reaches the 90% stage of completion. The litre cans are then transferred to the Shipping Department for crating and shipment. Labour and overhead are added continuously throughout the process. Manufacturing overhead is applied on the basis of direct hours at the rate of $3.00 per hour.

PROBLEMS

Prior to May, when a change in the process was implemented, work in process inventories were insignificant. The change in the process enables greater production but results in material amounts of work in process for the first time. The company has always used the weighted average method to determine equivalent production and unit costs. Now, production management is considering changing from the weighted average method to the first-in, first-out method (FIFO).

The following data relate to actual production during the month of May.

Costs for May	Dollars
Work in process inventory, May (4,000 litres 25% complete)	
Direct materials—chemicals	$45,600
Direct labour ($10 per hour)	6,250
Manufacturing overhead	1,875

Costs for May	
May costs added	
Direct materials—chemicals	$228,400
Direct materials—cans	7,000
Direct labour ($10 per hour)	35,000
Manufacturing overhead	10,500

Units for May	Litres
Work in process inventory, May 1 (25% complete)	4,000
Sent to Shipping Department	20,000
Started in May	21,000
Work in process inventory May 31 (80% complete)	5,000

Required:

a. Prepare a schedule of equivalent units for each cost element for the month of May using the:
   i. weighted average method
   ii. first-in, first-out method

b. Calculate the cost (to the nearest cent) per equivalent unit for each cost element for the month of May using the:
   i. weighted average method
   ii. first-in, first-out method

c. Discuss the advantages and disadvantages of using the weighted average method versus the first-in, first-out method, and explain under what circumstances each method should be used.

(Adapted by authors, #7 IMA, 1991)

22. (LO 2, 6) Catherine Chancellor Ltd. uses a weighted average process costing system in accounting for its product, which moves through two manufacturing departments.

In Department 2, material is not added until the product is 95% complete. Inspection takes place when the product is 80% complete and it is expected that 3% of the units inspected will be defective.

Information for Department 2 for the month of October was as follows:

	Units	Dollars
Beginning inventory, 40% complete:	1,000	
Department 1 costs		$ 5,700
Department 2 costs		980
Received from Department 1	10,000	60,300
Department 2 costs:		
Materials		5,760
Conversion costs		25,000
Transferred to Finished Goods	9,600	
Ending inventory, 90% complete	1,050	

Required:

Prepare a cost of production report for Department 2 for the month of October.

(Problem 22 was adapted by the authors from *Management Accounting Examinations,* published by the Certified General Accountants Association of Canada © CGA-Canada, 1997, used by permission.)

CASES

1. Customer Lawn Fertilizer is a new business. The founder based the business on the premise that lawn owners vary greatly in what they expect a fertilizer to accomplish and what they will tolerate it to do to the environment. At the extreme are those customers who will use any fertilizer (even ones considered harmful to the environment) and a great deal of water to get lush, green grass. At the other extreme are customers who use fertilizers that are environmentally benign and that require no water. Fertilizers can be chemically composed to consist of attributes for growth, greenness, pest destruction, weed destruction, draught resistant, and so on.

   The company sells 32 different varieties of fertilizer. Each particular type has attributes to meet the needs of a certain type of customer. When the founder started the business six years ago, he had 12 varieties and he offered to custom-make fertilizers from the 50-plus chemicals he stocked. By year 3 he had the 32 different varieties of fertilizers, named for their ingredients. The 32 seem sufficient as they have met all customer requirements during the last two years.

   As well as the 32 varieties of fertilizers, the founder has a strong understanding of the demand for each variety. This knowledge allows the founder to prepare large amounts of fertilizer of each type in advance to make optimal use of production facilities. Inventory is stored in the 32 different varieties until needed. When a particular type of inventory declines to a trigger point, more of that inventory is produced.

   Production facilities include an assembly line with stations for adding the ingredients, mixing the ingredients, bagging and weighting, and marking the bags for ingredients. The different fertilizers vary in cost because of the ingredients. These ingredient costs are known and are used to set prices. The different fertilizers also vary as to production costs, which are not known.

   The founder has asked a management accountant to comment on how costs are accumulated and make suggestions for improvements.
   Required:
   As the management accountant, adhere to the owner's requests, using the case approach.

2. You started a consulting business with a university friend and two friends from corporate finance just seven years after your first job in corporate finance. You had entered that first job right out of MBA school, and from the beginning you had recognized that you excelled in corporate finance. You worked long hours, and you saw opportunities to improve the efficiency and effectiveness of the corporate finance unit. Your particular advantage was your understanding of both corporate finance and information technology—for example, enterprise resource planning systems and business intelligence systems. Recognizing your motivation and special skills, your boss at that first job gave you opportunities to improve the corporate finance processes. Promotion after promotion came your way.

   By joining the Financial Executives Institute of Canada (FEIC), you met CFOs from many firms who gave you feedback on your innovations and who encouraged you to continue in your innovations. Before long, you were being asked to speak at FEIC luncheons and related conferences. Many senior CFOs were asking you for advice, and you received a large number of job offers, despite being very happy with your first job. Eventually, you accepted the CFO job at a medium-sized Canadian bank; you were not yet 30 when you accepted the offer.

   The bank was a challenge. The job required you to successfully implement a number of significant changes within your first four years. You met those conditions one year early. During those three years, you started teaching corporate finance at a university and wrote a book on leading-edge corporate finance practices. More and more job offers came. You realized that your main interest was improving corporate finance practices rather than being a CFO.

   It excited you to improve corporate finance units. Many organizations needed what you could offer, and you did not want to join just one firm. You wanted to help many firms, write books, and teach at the university level. The solution seemed to be to form a consulting firm.

CASES

The firm consisted of a senior partner (you, with 60% of the shares), two partners (your two friends, each with 20% of the shares), and 18 consultants. You, the other two partners, and each of the consultants have a charge-out rate based on market value to clients. The hourly charge-out rates are usually two times actual hourly pay to cover overhead and profits.

The consulting business model is to sell corporate finance assignments to clients. These assignments are similar in that they all deal with corporate finance processes, but they also differ by the specific aspect of corporate finance. When an assignment is sold to a client, the agreement or contract specifies the work to be done and the costs, which include work by consultants plus any expenses incurred such as travel and report preparation. The contract also specifies that clients will be charged for actual work performed and expenses incurred as long as the total costs do not exceed the amount specified in the contract.

Your consulting firm will begin business next week, and you have just remembered that you need some way to cost the consulting assignments. You vaguely remember that costing systems were covered in your MBA program's management accounting course.
Required:
Using the case approach, recommend a costing system.

3. Rexdale Machine Shop produces custom machinery. The company was started by Gus Prem, a tool-and-die maker with a small shop that did machinery repairs. Gus's son Vijay trained as a mechanical engineer. After working for four years at an automotive manufacturer's engineering department, Vijay joined his father's business to expand it into custom machinery. His father's skilled tradespeople can make machinery as well repair it. Repairs often require that parts be made; custom machinery requires that more parts be made. Vijay, an engineer, is able to design machinery and parts. Three engineers have been hired to design machinery and parts.

Many companies need special-purpose machinery. Often manual processes are automated with special-purpose machinery. Existing machinery can be replaced with digital machinery for improvements in efficiency and effectiveness as well to reduce maintenance costs. There is a constant demand for custom machinery, especially when Vajay and one of the engineers provide ideas to clients.

Each item of custom machinery is unique; often a client orders multiple custom machines. The custom machinery manufacturing business has been very successful in the first four months. In addition, this new thrust into custom machinery has exposed the company to more clients and thereby stimulated the company's repair business. Six more tradespeople have been hired.

Gus isn't sure whether the expansion is such a good idea. There are more employees and more sales. However, he does not know whether the custom machinery is profitable or whether the new repair work is profitable. In the past, he has gauged profitability based on total revenues less total expenses incurred.

You have been asked to help Gus determine where profits are being made. How should Gus ensure that he knows what business is profitable and what business is not?
Required:
Using the case approach, address Gus's concerns about the profitability of the various parts of the business.

ETHICS

1. McDonald's announced plans to install kitchen "McRobots." These automatons are supposed to put the "fast" back in fast food. They will cook and shake fries and then dump them in bins for scooping. They will also prepare drinks for customers.
Required:
   a. Do you foresee a fully automated McDonald's in the near future? Why or why not?
   b. Do you think computers would be better at the drive-through windows than humans? Why or why not?
   c. Do you think the use of computers will reduce the number of "rejects" (hamburgers that have been kept hot for more than 30 minutes) at McDonald's? Why or why not?

2. One of the more hotly contested political issues in recent years was whether the minimum wage should be increased (or should be increased again). Proponents of an increase in the minimum wage argue that such an increase is necessary for low-paid employees to maintain a decent standard of living. Opponents suggest that an increase in the cost of labour would cause firms to fire employees to control labour cost increases—thereby harming the very group that was intended to be the beneficiary of the wage increase.

Required:

Analyze the likely effects of an increase in the minimum wage from the perspective of:

a. its likely effects on quality

b. ethical issues

3. Empowering workers has been an increasingly popular idea to reduce costs and raise productivity; an effort to "white-collarize" factories has been adopted by about 40% of manufacturers. In a process environment, workers are empowered to stop production lines if defects or variations are noticed. Direct labour costs are reduced and overhead costs rise. But are all workers ready for empowerment? Apparently not—some workers find it extremely stressful.

Required:

a. As an employee, would you want to be empowered, and thus responsible for activities such as multitasking (being able to operate a variety of equipment), machine maintenance, quality, and team member discipline? Why or why not?

b. As a manager, would you want your employees to be empowered? Why or why not?

c. What impacts might employee empowerment have on a process environment?

4. FulRange Inc. produces complex printed circuits for stereo amplifiers. The circuits are sold primarily to major component manufacturers, and any production overruns are sold to small manufacturers at a substantial discount. The small manufacturer segment appears very profitable because the basic operating budget assigns all fixed expenses to units made for the major manufacturers, the only predictable market.

A common product defect that occurs in production is a "drift" caused by failure to maintain precise heat levels during the production process. Rejects from the 100% testing program can be reworked to acceptable levels if the defect is drift. However, in a recent analysis of customer complaints, George Wilson, the Management Accountant, and the quality control engineer have ascertained that normal rework does not bring the circuits up to standard. Sampling shows that about one-half of the reworked circuits will fail after extended, high-volume amplifier operation. The incidence of failure in the reworked circuits is projected to be about 10% over one to five years' operation.

Unfortunately, there is no way to determine which reworked circuits will fail, because testing will not detect this problem. The rework process could be changed to correct the problem, but the cost/benefit analysis for the suggested change in the rework process indicates that it is not practical. FulRange's marketing analyst has indicated that this problem will have a significant impact on the company's reputation and customer satisfaction if it is not corrected. Consequently, the board of directors would interpret this problem as having serious negative implications for the company's profitability.

Wilson has included the circuit failure and rework problem in his report for the upcoming quarterly meeting of the board of directors. Due to the potentially adverse economic impact, Wilson has followed a longstanding practice of highlighting this information.

After reviewing the reports to be presented, the plant manager and her staff were upset and indicated to the controller that he should control his people better. "We can't upset the board with this kind of material. Tell Wilson to tone that down. Maybe we can get it by this meeting and have some time to work on it. People who buy those cheap systems and play them that loud shouldn't expect them to last forever."

The controller called Wilson into his office and said, "George, you'll have to bury this one. The probable failure of reworks can be referred to briefly in the oral presentation, but it should not be mentioned or highlighted in the advance material mailed to the board."

Wilson feels strongly that the board will be misinformed on a potentially serious loss of income if he follows the controller's orders. Wilson discussed the problem with the quality control engineer, who simply remarked, "That's your problem, George."

Required:

a. Discuss the ethical considerations that George Wilson, a Management Accountant, should recognize in deciding how to proceed in this matter.

b. Explain what ethical responsibilities should be accepted in this situation by
   i. The controller
   ii. The quality control engineer
   iii. The plant manager and her staff

c. What should George Wilson do in this situation? Explain your answer. (Refer to the Society of Management Accountants Code of Ethics.)

(IMA adapted)

SOLUTIONS TO SELF-TEST QUESTIONS

1. d. $(50,000 + 200,000) - 210,000 = 40,000$

2. c. $50,000 + 160,000 + 0 = 210,000$

3. a. $[50,000 \times (100\% - 80\%)] + 160,000 + (40,000 \times 40\%) = 186,000$

4. d. $(\$1.20 + \$3.40) \times 45,000 = \$207,000$

5. a.

To account for:		Equivalent units of production:	
Opening inventory	6,000	Transferred out	67,000
Plus: started	65,000	Plus: ending inventory	
Less: ending inventory	4,000	(4,000 × 0.2)	800
Transferred out	67,000		67,800

6. a. Conversion cost per unit last period – $[\$22,000 \div (25,000 \times 0.8)]$ $\$1.10$
   Conversion cost per unit this period – $(\$143,000 \div 110,000^*)$ $\$1.30$

   Calculation of equivalent units

   Production Report:

WIP, February 1	25,000	units
Started	135,000	units
Less: transferred out	100,000	units
WIP, February 28	60,000	units @ 50% completion

   Equivalent units (EU) of production:

EUP in WIP, February 28	30,000	units
Plus: completed and transferred out	100,000	units
Less: EUP in WIP, February 1 @ 80%	20,000	units
	110,000	units

7. a. $\$143,000 \div 110,000 \times 30,000 = \$39,000$

8. b. $[(\$1.10 \times 0.8) + (\$1.30 \times 0.2)] = \$1.14$
   or $[\$22,000 + (25,000 \times 0.2) \times \$1.30] \div 25,000 = \$1.14$

9. c.

10. b.

11. d.

12. a. Ending Inventory $(10,000 \times \$0.24) + (10,000 \times 0.50 \times \$0.20) = \$3,400$
    Transferred out $(\$4,000 + \$20,000 + \$3,000 + \$16,000) - \$3,400 = \$39,600$.

13. a.

14. b.

15. c. Abnormal spoilage is not expected to occur under normal operating conditions, and because it is unusual it is treated as a loss in the period in which it happens.

16. b. The amount of the normal spoilage should be charged as a period cost.

ENDNOTES

1. Volker Thormählen, "Bull GmbH, Suitability of Oracle Applications for Standard and Activity Based Costing," *Oracle-IC94*, p. 9-134.

2. Reinaldo Guerreiro, Edgard Cornachione, and Armando Catelli, "Equivalent Units of Production: A New Look at an Old Issue," *Managerial Auditing Journal* 21, no. 3 (2006): 303.

3. Ibid.

4. A third category (spoilage/breakage) does exist. It is assumed at this point that such happenings do not occur. Accounting for spoilage in process costing situations will be covered in Appendix 4A of this chapter.

5. As discussed in Chapter 4, overhead may be applied to products using a variety of traditional allocation bases (direct labour hours or machine hours) or a variety of nontraditional allocation bases (such as number of machine set-ups, kilograms of material moved, and/or number of materials requisitions). The number of equivalent unit computations that need to be made results from the number of different cost pools and overhead allocation bases established in a department or company. If there are multiple cost pools and allocation bases, a separate computation will need to be made for each cost pool that is at a different level of completion. Additionally, some highly automated manufacturers may not account for direct labour cost separately (because it is too insignificant); thus, only a single conversion cost category would exist.

6. "Scrap, Drop, Spoilage and Off-Fall: What's in a Name?" *Cost Management Update*, February 2001.

7. Ibid.

8. Chien Shih-Wen and Tsaur Shu-Ming, "Investigating the Success of ERP Systems: Case Studies in Three Taiwanese High-Tech Industries," *Computers in Industry*, March 23, 2007; Asia Africa Intelligence Wire, "Financial Express: Getting a Clear Picture," *Financial Express*, December 23, 2007; Thomas H. Davenport, "Putting the Enterprise into the Enterprise System," *Harvard Business Review*, July–August 1998.

Chapter 6

The Budgeting Process

LEARNING OBJECTIVES

After reading this chapter, you should be able to answer the following questions:

1 What
is the importance of the budgeting process?

2 What
is the difference between strategic and tactical planning and how do these relate to the budgeting process?

3 What
are the benefits and disadvantages of imposed budgets and participatory budgets?

4 What
is a flexible budget?

5 What
complicates the budgeting process in a multinational environment?

6 What
is the starting point of a master budget and how do the components relate to one another?

7 How
does traditional budgeting differ from zero-based budgeting?

8 What
are future perspectives for budgeting?

ON SITE

www.sickkids.ca

The Hospital for Sick Children

THE HOSPITAL FOR SICK CHILDREN in Toronto, affectionately and more commonly known as "Sick Kids," is both the largest children's hospital in Canada and a world-leading pediatric academic health science centre. Sick Kids provides leading-edge health care for children, teaches the next generation of medical leaders, and produces medical research that has changed the lives of millions.

Trainees and researchers come from all five continents of the world to learn and work at the hospital. Some stay for good, and others return to their country of origin to put into practice the training that they have acquired. Parents are very happy with the quality of care that Sick Kids provides: the hospital consistently scores top marks in parental approval for the quality of care provided in Ontario provincial hospital surveys.

In terms of patient care, 14,000 in-patients and 309,000 emergency and outpatients are seen annually. This includes a significant number of patients from other Canadian provinces and other countries. Sick Kids is a hospital of last resort: the sickest patients from other centres are transferred to Sick Kids to give children access to the very best possible care, and so the best possible chance for a positive outcome.

The organization is very complex. Approximately 60 different departments, with specialists in their own fields, interact with one another to provide the best health care possible. Cooperation is essential: all patients need not just care from their specialist clinical physicians, but also expert and timely diagnostic information from the pediatric experts in Laboratory Medicine and Diagnostic Imaging; expert data provision from Information Services and Health Records; and high-quality support work from departments such as Medical Engineering, Facilities, and Housekeeping. More than 5,000 employees make sure that these services are available on a 24/7/365 basis.

The activities of the hospital are funded in different ways. Health care costs, running at about $400 million per year, are funded mainly by the Ontario Ministry of Health and Long-Term Care. Research activities, which cost around $102 million per year, are funded by a wide variety of governmental, charitable, and private funding agencies. The single biggest contributor is the Hospital for Sick Children Foundation, which contributes on an annual basis $62 million of this total through donations.

Health care funding and budgeting is a complex issue, not helped in Canada by the fact that there is remarkably little information on how much individual health services actually cost. Hospitals such as Sick Kids are given a fixed amount of money every year and are expected to provide appropriate services with it. Budgeting for these services is largely based on past costs. Some attempts are made to forecast activity, but as the Ontario government does not fund on this basis, activity measures are not exhaustively pursued. Nevertheless, activity can make or break hospital budgets: as hospitals have little control over the number of patients that are referred to them, and as hospitals such as Sick Kids have a policy of never turning patients away, there is an ever-present tension between funding and the ability of the hospital to provide the services needed by the patients. In acute situations, this tension has led to Sick Kids' being forced to refer elsewhere patients requiring intensive care.

Breakdowns of this global funding at the patient level have been attempted through a "top-down" approach (i.e., taking the total budget of a hospital as allocated to its individual departments, and attempting to suballocate portions of it to specific patients through weighted averages and through specific tracking of high-cost resources). However, the complexity and time-consuming nature of this task has meant that no hospital in Ontario has yet managed to produce effective patient-specific budgeting.

SOURCES: www.sickkids.ca; Interview with Brian Mackie, former Financial Operations Director Information and Diagnostic Services, The Hospital for Sick Children.

The annual budget is the financial plan to implement the organization's strategy for the next year. When that organization's environment is relatively stable, budgeting factors are fairly predictable and the budgeting process is less challenging than when environmental factors are highly uncertain. For many organizations, some of the underlying budget assumptions are extremely unpredictable, such as, in our discussion of the Hospital for Sick Children, the number of patients that come to the hospital for care. These are factors that can significantly affect the budget and require an ongoing monitoring process as the year progresses.

Regardless of the type of endeavour in which you engage, it is necessary at some point to visualize the future, imagine what results you want to achieve, and determine the activities and resources required to achieve those results.

This chapter covers the behavioural aspects of budgeting and how the budget relates to the management planning process, as well as the quantitative aspects of the process and the preparation of a master budget.

PURPOSES OF BUDGETING

Planning is the cornerstone of effective management, strategic development, and implementation. One vital part of good planning is budgeting. During the planning process, managers attempt to agree on company goals and objectives and how to achieve them. Typically, goals are stated in abstract terms, while objectives are quantifiable for a period of time. Achievement of goals and objectives requires undertaking complex activities and providing diverse resources that, in turn, typically demand a formalized planning or budgeting process.

Planning should include qualitative narratives of goals, objectives, and means of accomplishment. However, if plans were limited to qualitative narratives, the process of comparing actual results to expectations would only allow generalizations, and trying to measure how well the organization met its specified objectives would be impossible. Therefore, management translates qualitative narratives into a quantitative format, or **budget**, which expresses an organization's commitment to planned activities and resource acquisition and use. A budget is more than a mere forecast. A forecast is a prediction of what could happen. In contrast, a budget involves a commitment to make an agreed-upon outcome happen.

budget
the quantitative expression of an organization's commitment to planned activities and resource acquisition and use

Budgeting is the process of devising a financial plan for future operations. Budgeting is a management task, not an accounting task. The accounting function simply assembles the information provided into a known and consistent format. Budgeting is an important part of an organization's planning and controlling processes.

A good budget is more than just a process of collecting and consolidating numbers; it's a map that can guide your company to competitive advantage. It's all about allocating resources to achieve your company's strategy and objectives, and providing a forum for making decisions related to those allocations. It ties all the pieces together, providing the goals and benchmarks against which to measure performance.[1]

Budgets can be used to indicate direction and priorities; measure individual, divisional, and corporate performance; encourage achievement and continuous improvement efforts; and identify areas of concern. The process itself can be performed in a variety of ways: top-down, bottom-up, or a combination of the two. The basics of the budgeting process are illustrated in the flow diagram in Exhibit 6-1 on page 302; the individual steps are discussed in this chapter.

Like any other planning activity, budgeting helps managers focus on one direction chosen from many future alternatives. Management generally defines the chosen path using some accounting measure of financial performance, such as net income, earnings per share, or sales level in dollars or units. Budgeting is the tool that managers use to successfully plan and manage operations and programs.[2] Such accounting-based measures provide specific quantitative criteria against which future performance (also recorded in accounting terms) can be compared. Budgets, then, are a type of standard, and variances from budget can be computed.

Budgeting can also help identify potential problems in achieving specified goals and objectives. For example, assume that a particular company has fiscal objectives of generating $55 million in revenues and $2.5 million of net income for the year. The budget might indicate that, based on current prices and expenses, such objectives cannot be attained. Managers could then brainstorm to find ways to increase revenues or reduce costs so that these objectives can be reached. By quantifying potential difficulties and making them visible, budgets can help stimulate managers to think of ways to overcome those difficulties.

A well-prepared budget as a means of implementing strategy can be an effective device to communicate objectives, constraints, and expectations to people throughout an organization. Such communication helps everyone understand exactly what is to be accomplished, how those accomplishments are to be achieved, and how resources are to be allocated. Decisions about resource allocations are made, in part, through a process of obtaining information, justifying requests, and negotiating compromises. Allowing managers to participate in the budgeting process motivates them and instills a feeling of teamwork. Employee participation is needed to effectively integrate necessary information from various sources as well as to obtain individual managerial commitment to the resulting budget.

The budget indicates the resource constraints under which managers must operate for the upcoming budget period. Thus, the budget becomes the basis for controlling activities and resource usage. Periodic budget-to-actual comparisons allow managers to determine how well they are doing and to assess how well they understand their operations.

While budgets are typically expressed in financial terms, the budgeting and planning processes are concerned with all organizational resources—raw materials inventory, supplies, personnel, and facilities. These processes can be viewed from a long-term or a short-term perspective.

budgeting
the process of determining a financial plan for future operations

LEARNING OBJECTIVE 1

What is the importance of the budgeting process?

EXHIBIT 6-1

The Budgeting Process

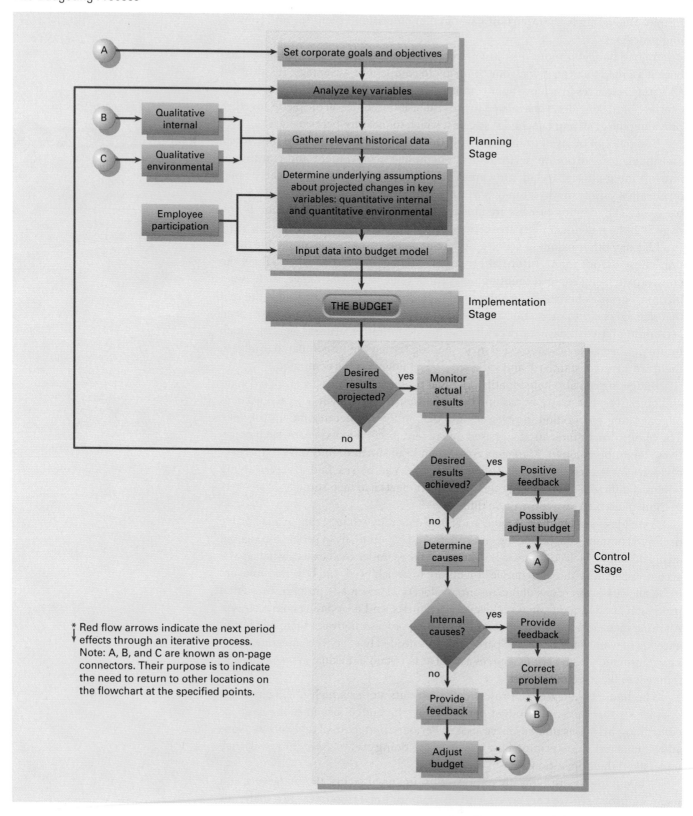

Strategic and Tactical Planning

When managers plan on a long-term basis (5 to 10 years), they are engaged in **strategic planning**. This process is generally performed only by top-level management with the assistance of several key staff members. The result of the process is a statement of long-range goals for the organization and of the strategies and policies that will help in the achievement of those goals.

Strategic planning is not concerned with day-to-day operations, although the strategic plan will be the foundation on which short-term planning is based. Managers engaging in strategic planning should identify **key variables**, or critical factors believed potentially to be direct causes of the achievement or nonachievement of organizational goals and objectives. Key variables can be internal or external. Exhibit 6-2 provides the results of one study about the external factors considered to be the most critical in determining the strategic plans of manufacturing companies. One conclusion from the survey was that a "firm's long-term success is dependent on the integration of the forces in its environment into its own planning process so that the firm *influences* its own destiny instead of constantly *reacting* to environmental forces."[3] Internal key variables are under the control of management, while external key variables are normally uncontrollable.

After key variables have been identified, information related to them can be gathered. Much of this information will be historical and qualitative but provide a useful starting point for tactical planning activities.

The process of determining the specific objectives and means by which strategic plans will be achieved is called **tactical** (or operational) **planning**. Although some tactical plans, such as corporate policy statements, exist for the long term and address repetitive situations, most tactical plans are short-term (1 to 18 months). Such short-term tactical plans are considered "single-use" plans and are developed to address a given set of circumstances or for a specific time frame.

LEARNING OBJECTIVE 2

What is the difference between strategic and tactical planning and how do these relate to the budgeting process?

strategic planning
the process of developing a statement of long-range (5 to 10 years) goals for the organization and defining the strategies and policies that will help the organization achieve those goals

key variable
a critical factor believed to be a direct cause of the achievement or nonachievement of organizational goals and objectives; can be internal or external

tactical planning
the process of determining the specific objectives and means by which strategic plans will be achieved; are short-term (1 to 18 months), single-use plans that have been developed to address a given set of circumstances or for a specific time frame

---

Organizational Characteristics

- Market share
- Quality of products
- Discretionary cash flow/gross capital investment

Market and Consumer Behaviour

- Market segmentation
- Market size
- New market development
- Buyer loyalty

Industry Structure

- Rate of technological change in products or processes
- Degrees of product differentiation
- Industry price/cost structure
- Economies of scale

Supplier

- Major changes in availability of raw materials

Social, Economic, and Political

- GNP trend
- Interest rates
- Energy availability
- Government-established and legally enforceable regulations

EXHIBIT 6-2

External Factors to Include in Strategic Plans

SOURCE: Republished with permission of the Institute of Management Accounting from James F. Brown, Jr., "How U.S. Firms Conduct Strategic Planning," *Management Accounting,* February 1986.

LEARNING OBJECTIVE 3

What are the benefits and disadvantages of imposed budgets and participatory budgets?

The annual budget is an example of a single-use tactical plan. Although a budget's focus is on a 12-month period, intermediate (quarterly and monthly) plans should also be included for the budget to work effectively.

A well-prepared budget "translates the strategic plans of the organization and [the company's] implementation programs into period-oriented operational guides to company activities."[4] Exhibit 6-3 illustrates the relationships among strategic planning, tactical planning, and budgeting.

EXHIBIT 6-3

Relationships Among Planning Processes

Who?	What?	How?	Why?
Top management	Strategic planning	Statement of organizational mission, goals, and strategies, long-range (5 to 10 years)	Establish a long-range vision of the organization and provide a sense of unity and commitment to specified purposes
Top and mid-management	Tactical planning	Statement of organizational objectives and operational plans, short-range (12 to 18 months)	Provide direction for the achievement of strategic plans; state strategic plans in terms that can be acted on; furnish a basis against which results can be measured
Top, mid-, and operational management	Budgeting	Quantitative and monetary statements that coordinate company activities for periods of 12 months or less	Allocate resources effectively and efficiently; indicate a commitment to objectives; provide a monetary control device

Both strategic and tactical planning require that information regarding the economy, environment, technological developments, and available resources be incorporated into the setting of goals and objectives.

Once management has evaluated the operating environment and relevant product life cycles and has decided on the organization's strategic plan, budgeting activity should begin for future periods. The budgeting process requires carefully integrating a complex set of facts and projections with human relationships and attitudes. Therefore, no single system of budgeting is right for all organizations. However, it is recognized that there are basically two ways by which budgets can be derived: from the top down (**imposed budgets**) or from the bottom up (**participatory budgets**).

As noted in Exhibit 6-4, imposed budgeting works well when the firm is new, small, or in a financial crisis. Senior management takes charge and literally imposes its will and budget on subordinates. Imposed budgets are not usually expansionary or insightful, but they control costs, which is usually important for the company. However, if senior managers dictate the budget, subordinates are alienated from "ownership" of the budget and are unlikely to implement it successfully.

An alternative to an imposed budget is a participatory budget (see Exhibit 6-5). With this type, the manager prepares the budget for his or her unit of responsibility. The senior managers then review the budget and offer suggestions, but they do not impose their own budget. The degree to which managers are allowed to participate in budget development usually depends on two factors: the confidence that senior managers have in the manager, and favourable economic circumstances. Participatory budgeting motivates managers to be expansionary and

imposed budget
a budget that is prepared by senior management with little or no input from operating personnel, who are simply informed of the budget goals and constraints

participatory budget
a budget that has been developed through a process of joint decision making by senior management and operating personnel

EXHIBIT 6-4
Imposed Budgets

Best Times to Use:
- In start-up organizations
- In extremely small businesses
- In times of economic crisis
- When operating managers lack budgetary skills or perspective
- When organizational units require precise coordination of efforts

Advantages of Imposed Budgets:
- Increase probability that the organization's strategic plans will be incorporated in planned activities
- Enhance coordination among divisional plans and objectives
- Use senior management's knowledge of overall resource availability
- Reduce the possibility of input from inexperienced or uninformed lower-level employees
- Reduce the time frame for the budgeting process

Disadvantages of Imposed Budgets:
- May result in dissatisfaction, defensiveness, and low morale among individuals who must work under the budget
- Reduce the feeling of teamwork
- May limit the acceptance of the stated goals and objectives
- Limit the communication process between employees and management
- May create a view of the budget as a punitive device
- May result in unachievable budgets for international divisions if local operating and political environments are not adequately considered
- May stifle the initiative of lower-level managers

insightful. Jack Welch provides a prime example of this in his book, *Jack: Straight from the Gut:*

> You know the drill. There's a business team in the field, working for a month on a presentation at headquarters, trying to develop the case for the minimum number they think they could "sell." The headquarters team comes to the same meeting armed to squeeze out the maximum. The field team comes with all kinds of charts on the weak economy, the tough competition, and says, "We can produce 10." The [senior] management comes in that morning wanting 20.
>
> The presentation usually takes place in a windowless room. No customers are present. You know what happens. After mountains of PowerPoint and hours of give-and-take, the budget is set at 15. It's an enervating exercise in minimalization. The field team flies back, high-fiving one another. They didn't have to give all they had to headquarters. [Senior] management thinks it had a great day, ratcheting the objectives to new heights.
>
> Why is this game played? Over the years, people everywhere have learned that if you made your number, you got a pat on the back or better, and if you missed your budget, you'd get a stick in the eye or worse. Everyone plays by these rules.[5]

The budgeting scenario Welch describes creates a far bigger problem than just wasted effort: it provides an incentive for deception. Budgeting as traditionally practised could more appropriately be called "liars' poker."[6] Each side tries to get the other side to get to each other's point. Management tries to up the ante while the other side tries to lower the ante.

EXHIBIT 6-5
Participatory Budgets

Best Times to Use:
- In well-established organizations
- In extremely large businesses
- In times of economic affluence
- When operating managers have strong budgetary skills and perspectives
- When organizational units are quite autonomous

Advantages of Participatory Budgets:
- Provide information from persons most familiar with the needs and constraints of organizational units
- Integrate knowledge that is diffused among various levels of management
- Lead to better morale and higher motivation
- Provide a means to develop fiscal responsibility and the budgetary skills of employees
- Develop a high degree of acceptance of and commitment to organizational goals and objectives by operating management
- Are generally more realistic
- Allow organizational units to coordinate with one another
- Allow subordinate managers to develop operational plans that conform to organizational goals and objectives
- Include specific resource requirements
- Blend overview of senior management with operating details
- Provide a social contract that expresses expectations of senior management and subordinates

Disadvantages of Participatory Budgets:
- Require significantly more time than imposed budgets
- Create a level of dissatisfaction with the process similar to that occurring under imposed budgets when the effects of managerial participation are negated by top-management changes
- Create an unachievable budget when managers are ambivalent or unqualified to participate
- May cause lower-level managers to introduce slack into the budget
- May support "empire building" by subordinates
- May start the process earlier in the year when there is more uncertainty about the future year

budget slack
the intentional underestimation of revenues and/or overestimation of expenses

Managers may introduce **budget slack** (the intentional underestimation of revenues and/or overestimation of expenses) into the budgeting process. Slack, if it exists, is usually built into the budget during the participation process; it is not often found in imposed budgets. Having slack in the budget allows subordinate managers to achieve their objectives with less effort than if there were no slack. Budget slack creates problems because of the significant interaction of budgeting factors. If sales are understated, for example, problems can arise in the production, purchasing, and personnel areas. To reduce the possibility of slack, management may want to consider having the budget activities rather than costs. This will be discussed in Chapter 8.

Since the functions of employees are affected by the budget and these individuals must work under the budget guidelines, input from the operating level is often invaluable in the planning process. Although there is no concrete evidence as to how well participatory budgeting works in all circumstances, such participation by operating managers also seems to create a higher commitment to the budget's success. To the extent that participation reduces the precarious aspect of projections by providing managers with a greater quantity and quality of information, it results in more accurate budgets.

The budgeting process, as mentioned, represents a continuum with imposed budgets on one end and participatory budgets on the other. Currently, most business budgets are prepared through a coordinated effort that includes input from managers and revision by senior management. In this manner, plans of managers at all levels can be considered. Senior management first sets strategic objectives for lower-level management, then lower-level managers suggest and justify their operations' performance targets. Upper-level managers combine all component budgets, evaluate the overall results, and provide feedback on any needed changes to the lower-level managers.

Regardless of whether the process is top-down or bottom-up, management must review the completed budget before approving and implementing it. This process is necessary to determine (1) if the underlying assumptions on which the budget is based are reasonable and (2) if the budgeted results are acceptable and realistic. The budget may indicate that the results expected from the planned activities do not achieve the desired objectives. In this case, planned activities should be reconsidered and revised. The revision should guide the company toward the desired outcomes expressed during planning for the intermediate term.

THE BUDGETING PROCESS

The budget is normally prepared on an annual basis and detailed first by quarters and then by months within those quarters. At a minimum, budget preparation should begin two to three months before the period to be covered, but management must keep two things in mind: (1) participatory budget development will take longer than an imposed budget process; and (2) the larger and more complex the company is, the longer the budgeting process will take.

The speed of change in today's economy has generated a trend toward adopting continuous budgeting as part of the planning process.

Some companies use a continuous (or rolling) budget, an ongoing 12-month budget that adds a new budget month (12 months into the future) as each current month expires. **Continuous budgets** make the planning process less sporadic and disruptive. Rather than "going into the budgeting period" at a specific point in time, managers are continuously involved in planning and budgeting. Continuous budgets also provide a longer-range focus so that no surprises occur at year-end. This is illustrated in the News Note on page 308.

continuous budget
an ongoing 12-month budget that adds a new budget month (12 months into the future) as each current month expires

Another method being adopted by companies is the use of Web-based budgeting systems, which allow companies to react to changes in the economy and other elements at a much faster pace. PerkinElmer, a manufacturer of scientific equipment, recently found that it was becoming increasingly difficult to prepare budgets. The company revamped its budgeting process in three ways—(1) moved to two semi-annual budgets rather than one annual budget; (2) linked its incentive compensation program to the budgeting process; and (3) migrated its budgeting and planning process to a Web-based business.

PerkinElmer company is pleased with its new direction in budgeting, however Rob Friel, the CFO Research Services, says that divining the future will never be a perfect science. "We require the business units to come back to us and tell us what would happen if the revenues move up or down either 5% or 10% and what they would do about it. We debate the contingency action that they would do ahead of time, so when we see the market change, we don't have to then say, 'Okay, now what are we going to do?'"[7]

Using Continuous Budgeting

THE HON COMPANY, the largest maker of mid-priced office furniture in the United States and Canada, has overcome obstacles of change through the use of a continuous three-month budget cycle. The budget has become the integral planning and control device for achieving two strategic objectives: ongoing new product and service development, and rapid continuous improvement. The budget also serves as an important vehicle for ensuring that the corporate culture is unified in its understanding of—and commitment to—strategic objectives.

Managers at the Hon Company communicate and coordinate operating plans through a process called continuous quarterly budgeting. All departments work together to produce an updated four-quarter budget at the beginning of each quarter. Thus, a budget prepared for the third quarter of the year includes plans for the third and fourth quarters of the year and for the first two quarters of the next year. Each quarterly budget requires the next four quarters to be completely re-budgeted. By having a detailed quarterly budget that is up-to-date and comprehensive, managers and employees in all areas are prepared to deal with rapid change.

SOURCE: Ralph Ortina, Steve Hoeger, and John Schaub, "Continuous Budgeting at the Hon Company," *Management Accounting*, January 1996.

In the illustration shown in Exhibit 6-6, management is working within the present one-month component of a full 12-month annual budget at any point in time.

Electronic spreadsheets such as Microsoft's Excel have dramatically improved the budgeting process. Spreadsheets make it possible to quickly and inexpensively examine "what if" scenarios and to link interrelated budgets so that relationships can be understood. They also make continuous budgeting easy to implement.

EXHIBIT 6-6

Continuous Budget

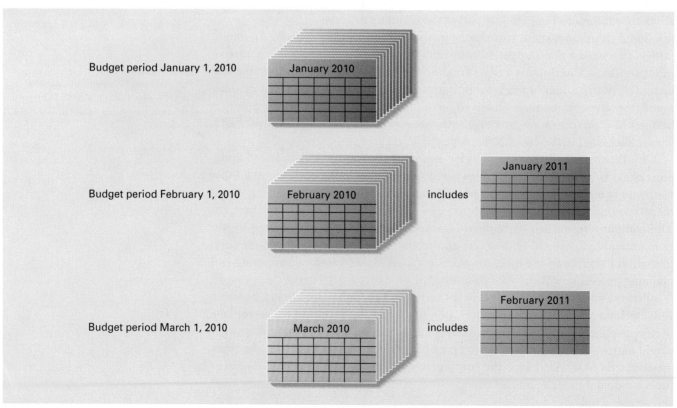

Nevertheless, according to Microsoft, spreadsheets have some shortcomings. For example:
- They are not designed to process the large amounts of information inherent in budgeting.
- They are cumbersome to change when there are revisions.
- They offer poor security.
- They are prone to error and thus suffer from a lack of accuracy.

To address these shortcomings, Microsoft and other vendors have developed budgeting software that can be built into the organization's accounting or ERP system. Instead of preparing the budget outside with spreadsheets and then importing it into the accounting or ERP system, these software applications prepare the budget *inside* the system. Built-in budgeting systems have some clear advantages over spreadsheets. For example, with respect to Microsoft's Forecaster:
- They speed up the budgeting cycle.
- They increase numerical accuracy.
- They quickly and accurately change numbers.
- They involve more affected mangers.
- They allow users to be more efficient and productive.
- They make possible active control over results.
- They enable real-time views of the organization's budgetary performance.

They allow quick and cost effective budget implementation.[8]

A good budget requires a substantial amount of time and effort from the persons engaged in preparing it. This process can be improved by the availability of an organizational **budget manual**, a detailed set of documents that provides information and guidelines about the budgetary process. The manual should include the following:

budget manual
a detailed set of documents that provides information and guidelines about the budgetary process

1. Statements of the budgeting purpose and its desired results
2. A listing of specific budgetary activities to be performed
3. A calendar of scheduled budgetary activities
4. Sample budget forms
5. Original, revised, and approved budgets

The *statements of budgeting purpose and desired results* communicate the reasons behind the process and should flow from general statements to specific details. An example of a general statement of budgeting purpose is: "The cash budget provides a basis for planning, reviewing, and controlling cash flows from and for various activities; this budget is essential to the preparation of a pro forma Cash Flow Statement." Specific statements regarding the cash budget could include references to minimum desired cash balances and periods of high cash needs. These needs are taken into consideration when the cash budget portion of the master budget is prepared.

Budgetary activities should be listed by job rather than by a person's name because the responsibility for actions should be delegated to whomever is holding each specific job when the manual is implemented. This section should indicate who has the final authority for revising and approving the budget. Budget approval may be delegated to a budget committee or to one or several members of senior management.

The *budget calendar* coordinates the budgetary process and should include a timetable for all budgetary activities. The budget timetable is unique to each organization. The larger the organization, the more time will be needed to gather information, coordinate the information, identify weak points in the process or the budget itself, and take corrective action. The calendar should also indicate control points for the upcoming periods, when budget-to-actual comparisons will be made, and when and how feedback will be provided to managers responsible for operations.

Sample forms provide a means for consistent presentation of budget information by all individuals, making summarizations of information easier, quicker, and more effective. The sample forms should be understandable and could include standardized worksheets that allow managers to update historical information to arrive at budgetary figures. This section of the manual may also provide standard cost tables for items on which the organization has specific guidelines or policies. For example, in estimating employee fringe benefit costs, the company's rule of thumb may be 30% of base salary. Similarly, a company policy may set the daily meal allowance for salespersons at $50; therefore in estimating meal expenses for the future period, the sales manager would simply multiply total estimated travel days by $50.

The last section of the manual should include the original and revised budgets. It is helpful for future planning to understand how the revision process works and why changes were made. The final approved budget is known as the master budget. It is composed of many individual budgets and serves as a control document for budget-to-actual comparisons.

Implementation and Control

After a budget is prepared and accepted, it is implemented. Budget implementation means that the budget is now considered a standard against which performance can be measured. Managers operating under budget guidelines should be provided with copies of all appropriate budgets. These managers should also be informed that their performance will be evaluated by comparing actual results to budgeted amounts. Such evaluations should generally be made by budget category for specific periods of time.

Once the budget is implemented, the control phase begins. Control includes making actual-to-budget comparisons, determining variances, providing feedback to managers, investigating the causes of the variances, and taking any necessary corrective action. This control process indicates the cyclical nature of budgeting (see Exhibit 6-7). Feedback (both positive and negative) is essential to the control process and must be provided in a timely manner to be useful.

EXHIBIT 6-7

Nature of the Budgeting Process

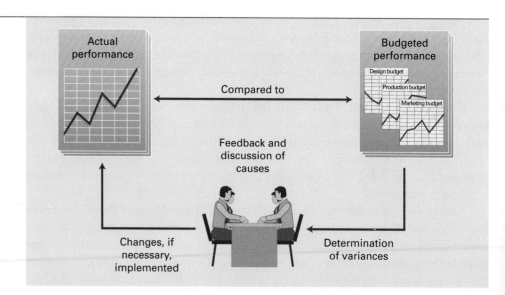

The problems with fixed budget targets at the individual level seem to translate to the organizational level as well. The approved budget becomes the basis on which senior management makes commitments.

PREPARING FLEXIBLE BUDGETS

A **flexible budget** is a series of financial plans detailing the individual cost factors that comprise total cost and presenting those costs at different levels of activity. Thus, a flexible budget is simply a formula that permits the budgeted manufacturing costs to be determined for any activity level within the relative range of activity for which the behavioural classification of costs is valid. Using a flexible budget allows the performance at one activity level to be compared with the same activity level, rather than comparing the activity with a different, static budget activity. Basically a flexible budget is a series of mini-budgets for different levels of activity.

The flexible budget technique is primarily used to determine budgeted overhead. Overhead is an aggregate that includes fixed and variable components, as opposed to the direct material and direct labour components. Although the manufacturing overhead area provides the basic need and justification for flexible budgets, the technique can be applied to include all cost and revenue items.

In summary, the flexible budget can be expressed in the form of the following equation:

$$y = a + bx$$

where:

y = total cost

x = volume

a = the fixed cost component

b = the variable cost rate

As was seen in Chapter 2, the above equation is simply the formula for a straight line.

The activity levels shown on a flexible budget usually cover management's contemplated range of activity for the upcoming period. If all activity levels are within the relevant range, costs at each successive level should equal the amount of the previous level plus a uniform dollar increment for each variable cost factor. The increment is the variable cost per unit of activity multiplied by the quantity of additional activity.

At Basic Black Ltd., the following static budget has been developed for the cutting department for the month of November, when expected production is 4,000 units.

Direct material	$ 8,000
Direct labour	9,200
Manufacturing overhead:	
Indirect material	1,000
Indirect labour	800
Utilities	400
Depreciation	6,400
Total	$25,800

Analysis of the earlier costs has shown that indirect labour of $600, utilities of $200, and depreciation of $6,400 are fixed and are incurred on a monthly basis regardless of the level of production. Using the above information, we can prepare a flexible budget for Basic Black Ltd. for the following production levels: 3,500 units, 4,000 units, and 4,500 units.

LEARNING OBJECTIVE 4

What is a flexible budget and how are budget variances computed and used to analyze differences between budgeted and actual revenues?

flexible budget
a budget that is a series of financial plans detailing the individual cost factors that comprise total cost

Units	3,500	4,000	4,500
Direct material	$ 7,000	$ 8,000	$ 9,000
Direct labour	8,050	9,200	10,350
Manufacturing overhead:			
Indirect material	875	1,000	1,125
Indirect labour	775	800	825
Utilities	375	400	425
Depreciation	6,400	6,400	6,400
Total	$23,475	$25,800	$28,125

Variable costs = $4.65 [$2.00 + $2.30 + $0.25 + $0.05 + $0.05]

Fixed costs = $7,200 [$600 + $200 + $6,400]

Formula = $7,200 + $4.65x

static budget
incorporates anticipated value about volume, prices, and costs that are conceived before the period in question begins

Thus far we have looked only at a fixed plan, called a **static budget**, in which anticipated costs and expenses are based on a single estimated sales or production volume. As noted earlier, a flexible budget, in which costs and expenses are determined for a range of output levels, would permit comparisons to actual events and allow revision of the budget estimates in the light of changes in sales or production volume. Managers are then able to make valid budget-to-actual cost comparisons to determine if total variable costs were properly controlled.

The use of flexible budgets for planning and control of overhead costs requires that overhead items be classified by their behaviour patterns. Direct material and direct labour are always considered to be variable; however the classification of manufacturing overhead cost is more difficult. The flexible budget shows the manufacturing overhead costs that are expected at several different possible production volumes during the budgetary period. Thus, the cost behaviour patterns expressed in the budget formula can be used for planning purposes.

Budgets allow formal comparisons of expected and actual costs. But budgets can be properly prepared only when the reasons for periodic cost changes are understood, and cost control can be achieved only with an understanding of why costs may differ from budgeted amounts.

Costs may change from previous periods or differ from budget expectations for many reasons. Some costs change because of their underlying behaviour. Total variable cost increases or decreases with increases or decreases in activity level. If the current-period activity level differs from a prior period's activity level or the budgeted activity level, total actual variable cost will differ from the prior period or the budget. A flexible budget can compensate for such differences by providing expected variable costs at the actual activity level.

The flexible budget requires the segregation of fixed and variable costs. The budget amount at any rate of activity can be determined by taking fixed costs, which by definition do not vary in total dollar amount within the relevant range with changes in the volume of activity, and adding to that number the total variable costs for that selected activity. The total variable costs are calculated by multiplying the variable overhead rate times the activity level.

What Factors Might Cause Costs to Differ?

1. *Cost changes due to inflation/deflation.* Fluctuations in the value of the dollar are called general price level changes. When the general price level changes, the amount of goods and services that can be purchased with a dollar also changes. General price level changes affect almost all costs approximately equally and in the same direction, if all other factors are constant.

2. *Cost changes due to technology advances.* As a general rule, if the technology of producing a good or service advances, the cost of that good or service declines. The result of this type of change is referred to as a specific price level change.
3. *Cost changes due to supply and demand.* The relationship of the availability of goods and services to the demand for these items affects costs. If the supply of a good is low and demand is high relative to the past, the cost of the goods or services increases. On the other hand, if demand for a good falls but supply remains constant, the cost of the good will fall. Like cost changes related to technology, changes related to supply and demand also cause specific price level changes that may move in the same or the opposite direction as the general price level changes.
4. *Cost changes due to tax or regulatory adjustments.* As taxes or regulations increase, costs will increase. Companies must pass their increased costs on to the next consumer in the supply chain.
5. *Cost changes due to quantity of competition.* The number of competitors can also create a specific price level change. As the number of suppliers of a good or service increases, the competitive environment causes the cost of that good or service to fall. A change in the quantity of suppliers is not the same as a change in the quantity of supply. If the supply of an item is large, one normally expects the price to be low, but if there is only one supplier, the price can remain high because of supplier control. Thus, in the airline industry, airfares could be expected to increase as more airlines declare bankruptcy and, thus, reduce the number of suppliers.
6. *Cost changes due to seasonality or other timing factors.* Certain goods and services cost more at certain times of the year because of use or demand. For example, it is generally less expensive to travel on the airlines at "nonpeak" times, such as on weekends or during January after the holiday rush.
7. *Cost changes due to quantity purchased.* Firms are normally given quantity discounts, up to some maximum level, when purchases are made in bulk. Therefore, the cost per unit may change because quantities are purchased in different lot sizes than previous periods or other than as projected. Companies using one airline for all their business travel may be able to negotiate substantial discounts because of the volume of purchases.

Budget Revisions

Exhibit 6-8 indicates some possible problems and causes of poor actual-to-budget performance. This exhibit is not intended to be a comprehensive list, and some factors may work together in performance problems. Once the causes of the performance deviations are known, management may wish to consider budget revisions.

Arrangements cannot usually be made rapidly enough to revise the current month's budget. However, under certain circumstances and if it so desires, management may decide to revise future months' budgets. If actual performance is substantially less than what was expected, the budget may or may not be adjusted depending on the causes of the variances. If the causes are beyond the organization's control (such as with airlines after September 11, 2001), management may decide to revise budget estimates upward to reflect costs more realistically. If the causes are internal (sales staff simply is not selling the product), management may leave the budget in its original form so that the lack of operational control is visible in the comparisons.

If actual performance is substantially better than expected, budget alterations may be made. However, sometimes when positive results occur, management may decide not to alter the budget so that the positive performance is highlighted.

EXHIBIT 6-8

Problems and Causes of Poor Performance

Problem	Possible Causes (or lack of consideration given to)
Sales significantly less than expected	Weakening economic conditions that reduced company product sales volume or necessitated a lower selling price
Direct materials cost significantly higher than expected	Inflation rate that caused direct materials cost to increase; use of higher quality materials
Compensation cost higher than expected	Changes in labour contract rates or increases in minimum wage law
Overhead cost higher than expected	Increased fringe benefit costs, insurance costs, or utility rates
Severe cash-flow difficulties	Declining collection patterns, increases in interest rates and costs, or weakened money supply
Selling expenses higher than expected	Advertising rates increased or media changes made (substituted TV spots for print advertising)
Interest cost higher than expected	Inflation, tightened money supply
Production not able to keep up with demand	Shortages of critical direct material or supplies

Regardless of whether the budget is revised, managers should commend those responsible and communicate the effects of such performance to related departments. For example, if the salesforce has been very effective and has sold significantly higher quantities of product than expected (at the expected selling price), the production and purchasing areas will need to be notified to increase the number of units manufactured and materials bought.

Performance Evaluation

One important reason that management must decide whether to revise is that the budget is often used to evaluate performance. When external circumstances do not turn out as expected, management must communicate to those people being evaluated how or if budget revisions will affect their performance evaluations. Although revised budgets may provide more accurate information, they also create a fluctuating measure against which people may be uncertain of their performance. Thus, if revised budgets are prepared, senior management may want to compare performance to both the original and the revised budgets and then use multiple evaluation tools to judge the quality as well as the quantity of performance.

The possibility that operating managers may attempt to introduce budgetary slack into their budgets was mentioned earlier in the chapter. One way in which senior management can try to reduce slack is to evaluate actual performance against budgeted performance through a bonus system. Operating managers would be rewarded with large bonuses for budgeting relatively high performance levels and achieving those levels. If performance is set at a low or minimal level, achievement of that performance is either not rewarded or only minimally rewarded.

In addition to including budget slack in the process, managers may play other budget games, although managerial game playing sometimes reflects a lack of skills and know-how rather than devious intentions. It is one thing to be able to identify the games managers play and quite another to be able to do something about them. Some of these games are discussed in Exhibit 6-9.

EXHIBIT 6-9
Budget Games

1. *The Dictator Game*
   This game is simply imposed budgeting. The budget is developed by senior management and is handed down to lower levels with no room for discussion.
2. *The Father-Knows-Best Game*
   In this game, input is requested from lower-level managers but either is not used or is changed with no reasons provided. This game allows people to believe at first that they are important to the process, but they recognize in the end that they are not.
3. *The Do-What-You-Want (and Fail) Game*
   In this game, lower-level managers submit their own budgets, which are then used for performance evaluation purposes. Unfortunately, individual managers are not informed of the "big picture" and then at year-end fail to measure up because their budget figures were (a) too high and unachievable to begin with or (b) too low and not acceptable to begin with.
4. *The It's-Not-in-the-Budget Game*
   In this game, a manager submits a worthwhile project that is turned down because money is unavailable. Then, when the manager's performance level is low, he or she may be criticized for not justifying the project convincingly.
5. *The Cut-Everything-10% Game*
   This game is a favourite of all organizations. Rather than allowing managers to decide to cut certain expenditures and have the opportunity to justify why others need to be raised, the mandate is simply handed down. Managers get to figure out how to pay with what remains. A problem with this game, if played too often by senior management, is that lower-level managers simply increase their budget requests by 10% and, therefore, are not disturbed by the reduction.
6. *The End-of-Year (or Spend-It-or-Lose-It) Game*
   Lower-level managers, recognizing that the end of the period is near, evaluate the remaining budget dollars per category and spend everything that is left. In this way, they can justify budget increases next year, because "I used everything I was budgeted for this year, and you know costs will increase."
   (The opposite of this game is played by senior managers. Budget dollars that were not spent this period are lost, regardless of the reasons. This is a tough game when played with personnel budgets—a person not replaced is a position lost.)
7. *The It-Wasn't-My-Fault Game*
   The object of this game is for a manager to try to shift the blame for failure to meet the budget on someone or something else. This game probably allows for the most creativity. (Hint: The "economy" is always a good target because it's hard to prove or disprove.)
8. *The Accounting Change Game*
   This game requires a high degree of understanding of accounting rules but can work wonders on income statements. Unfortunately, you are only allowed one play for any given accounting change.
9. *The Sell-It-No-Matter-What Game*
   Managers who play this game are probably headed for a transfer and wanting to make a final name for themselves. They should be aware of CVP relationships; if the contribution margin is high and fixed costs are low, then increased volume will pad the bottom line substantially. But if the sales were accomplished using high-pressure techniques or by reducing quality, watch out for returns next period.
10. *The Build-a-Kingdom Game*
    This game allows managers to use budgets to create their own kingdoms. The larger the budget that can be obtained, the more "possessions" (equipment, personnel, etc.) the kingdom has. This game provides many opportunities to win friends by helping others maintain or increase their budget requests while extracting promises from those who help you maintain or increase your kingdom. However, these relationships can only work for a limited period of time before the kingdoms are in competition for the same budget dollars, and then war occurs.

These games exist because of human nature. If managers (either top-level or subordinate) are playing one or more of these games in the budgeting process, performance evaluations will become very ineffective, since many of the numbers become more sham, than real, projections. Company management often expects that good budgets will result simply because participating is allowed and encouraged. Good budgets result only from having responsible individuals involved in the process and from creating an atmosphere of sound interpersonal relationships. In other words, good budgeting relies heavily on trust among the parties involved.

If budgets are to be used in effectively evaluating performance, they should be challenging but achievable. The advantages of using achievable budget targets include the following:[9]

1. Managers' commitment to achieving the budget targets is increased because the managers will have little reason not to be able to meet the targets.
2. Managers' confidence remains high; achievement of the target is perceived as successful performance.
3. Organizational control costs decrease because there is less necessity to apply the management by exception principle when targets are achieved.
4. The risk of managers engaging in harmful short-term "income-management" practices (such as delaying maintenance or shifting sales between years) is reduced.
5. Effective managers are allowed greater operating flexibility because they may be able to accumulate some additional resources on the basis of good performance.
6. The corporation is somewhat protected against the costs of optimistic projections, such as overproduction and warehousing.
7. The predictability of corporate earnings is increased because the probability of target achievement is high.

The degree of "achievability" needed in budgets to obtain the previous seven benefits depends, of course, on the organization's stage of life, its environmental considerations (past performance, need for sales, types of products, and product life cycles), and its management personnel and their motivation levels.

Budgets are not the "be-all and end-all" managerial accounting technique. Budgets, if used properly, can provide significant benefits; if used improperly, they can cause serious organizational problems.

The News Note on page 317 discusses how The Jim Pattison Group attains success in its budgeting efforts.

LEARNING OBJECTIVE 5

What complicates the budgeting process in a multinational environment?

BUDGETING IN AN INTERNATIONAL BUSINESS

Similar to many other business practices, the budgeting process and budget uses are unique to individual businesses. The budgeting process in a small, closely held company may be informal and, potentially, imposed on lower-level managers by senior management. As the organization becomes more complex, so does the budgeting process. Lower-level managerial participation in the budgeting process may be more important. When an organization reaches multinational status, participatory budgeting is not simply desired; it becomes necessary for the effort to be effective.

In a multinational environment, an organization faces an almost unlimited number of external variables that can affect the planning process, for example, the effects of foreign currency exchange rates, interest rates, inflation, inventory transfer price implications, and so forth. The risk may necessitate the preparation of separate budgets for each international market served in addition to a coordinated corporatewide budget. Budget preparation must incorporate a thorough understanding of local market conditions, including all known external forces and estimates of potential economic and market changes. Thus, each foreign operation's budget should also be supported by a comprehensive list of assumptions explaining how budget figures were derived. The News Note on page 318 describes how Bayer AG, a multinational company, solved its budgeting problems.

Budgeting at The Jim Pattison Group

It's February 10 and over the next two weeks, senior executives from across THE JIM PATTISON GROUP will be in Vancouver for quarterly meetings. They come from almost two dozen companies, which are organized in eight divisions. Pattison's deal with division managers is typically straightforward. He will virtually ignore their existence for 361 days of the year. In return, they will show up every three months with detailed presentations that pinpoint the performance of every aspect of their operations. Ideally the presentations will be slick and entertaining, perhaps sprinkled with video clips and advanced-user PowerPoint features. Less optionally, they will portray excellent results.

This morning's presentation is by the auto group. It's an 8 o'clock meeting, so the executives in charge of Pattison's dealerships, lease operations, and auto malls know to start trickling in at 6:15, a half-hour behind Pattison and his secretary of 41 years. As expected the meeting begins at 7.

Each quarterly has a distinct function. In May, head office looks at an updated forecast of what the year in progress will bring. August affords some time for blue-skying and includes a social aspect. November is when budgets are finalized for the year to come. And February's round, the only one convened at head office, rather than on the divisions' home turfs, concentrates on the year just passed. Always the reports proceed in a prescribed manner with special attention paid to precise metrics that allow the corporate office to make easy comparisons across the division and over time. When the meetings have wrapped up, Pattison will voluntarily put his own hide on the line before a gathering of his advisory board of directors.

Another one of Pattison's sayings is that it's always fun if you're making money and a veteran of many quarterlies attests that the atmosphere can be very light hearted when times are good. And (it is) excruciatingly intense when they are not.

Once the senior executives have made their presentations and prior to Jimmy Pattison's turn to speak, he gives the group a fifteen-minute break. He is back at the table in nine minutes waiting on everyone. His half-hour address has two rationales. The first is of the Big Three and the potential of China—that managers had better be thinking about if they aren't already. The second is to underline his belief in the importance of people. During the presentations, he asked virtually every presenter if there were any problems "on the people side." He concludes his benediction with a query: "Have we at corporate office provided the support you need to do your job?"

Within minutes, the auto group executives have departed. So long to head office until the next quarterly [meeting].

SOURCE: Jim Sutherland, "Jimmy Has the Last Laugh," *The Globe and Mail*, April 2004. Reprinted by permission of the author.

Budgets are not only developed differently in different types of companies, but they are also used differently. In small organizations, the budget may be used simply as a basis against which actual results are compared and not as a control or managerial performance evaluation mechanism. As the business expands, the need for budgeting as a control and coordination tool arises because of interactions among multiple departments or organizational units. Managerial and employee performance may then be gauged against the budget and resulting comparisons may be used in a reward system.

In many circumstances, it is difficult to determine the underlying causes of budget variations because of the effects of noncontrollable factors such as competitive manoeuvres, economic conditions, and government regulations. In an international organization, the supporting list of assumptions is critical if the budget is to be used for control and evaluation purposes. Managers and employees should not be faulted for failing to achieve budget targets if the underlying causes reflect

The budgeting process differs among organizations and cultures. Budgets in Japanese firms are more flexible and short-run oriented than budgets in Western firms. The underlying rationale is that employees can better focus on near-term targets to ascertain that they comply with the organization's highly inflexible vision and strategic plan.

unforeseen, noncontrollable factors such as newly introduced governmental policies relating to import or export restrictions, exchange rate fluctuations, or market disturbances created by economic adjustments in a foreign country. Managers should, however, be held accountable for not taking advantage of new opportunities created by these same factors.

GENERAL NEWS NOTE

How Bayer Changed Its System

Budgeting can be a cumbersome and tedious process. In fact, a large percentage of the people responsible for budgeting planning probably wish they could wave a magic wand, say the magic word, and pull an accurate, comprehensive budget out of a hat.

At the pharmaceutical division of BAYER CORPORATION, they don't have a magic wand—they have a wizard. The Planning Wizard is a Web-based tool that allows managers at the company's more than 600 centres to create yearly budget plans with speed, accuracy, and efficiency.

The system allows seamless communications between all the facilities and Bayer AG's corporate headquarters in Leverkusen, Germany. As a replacement to the previous budgeting system—a paper-based system that used Excel spreadsheets and required manual input by the managers—it not only helps reduce costs and maximize profits, but it has been embraced by managers as an easy-to-use system.

The Planning Wizard has effectively integrated cost centre budgeting with capital and headcount planning (a particularly crucial element for Bayer). Cost centre managers were provided with an effective desktop tool that allows access from multiple sites, provides transparency to information with a user-friendly front end, and enables line management to plan for and manage their cost centres.

Today, the pharmaceutical division has one of the industry's first Web-enabled planning applications to streamline the planning process and empower its cost centre managers to take control of budgeting, capital, and headcount planning through the use of the Planning Wizard.

Not quite magic out of a hat, but pretty impressive.

SOURCE: Roland Hoelscher, "Bayer's Unique Planning System Cures Budgeting Headaches," *Afp Exchange*, January/February 2002.

THE MASTER BUDGET

From an accounting standpoint, the budgeting process culminates in the preparation of a **master budget**, which is a comprehensive set of an organization's budgetary schedules and pro forma (projected) financial statements. The master budget comprises both operating and financial budgets. **Operating budgets** are expressed in both units and dollars. When an operating budget is related to revenues, the units are those expected to be sold, and the dollars reflect selling prices. When an operating budget relates to expense items, the units are those expected to be used and the dollars reflect costs.

Monetary details from the operating budgets are aggregated in **financial budgets**, which reflect the funds to be generated or consumed during the budget period. Financial budgets include the company's cash and capital budgets as well as its pro forma financial statements. These budgets are the ultimate focal points for the firm's senior management.

The master budget is prepared for a specific period and is static rather than flexible. It is static in that it is based on a single, most probable level of output demand. Expressing the budget on a single level of output is necessary to facilitate the many time-consuming financial arrangements that must be made before beginning operations for the budget period. Such arrangements include hiring an adequate number of people, obtaining needed production and/or storage space, obtaining suppliers, and confirming prices, delivery schedules, and quality of resources.

The output level of sales or service quantities selected for use in the preparation of the master budget affects all organizational components. It is essential that all the components interact in a coordinated manner. Exhibit 6-10 indicates the budgetary interrelationships among the primary departments of a manufacturing organization. A budget developed by one department is commonly an essential ingredient in developing another department's budget.

Exhibit 6-11 presents an overview of the master budget preparation sequence and component budgets. It indicates the department responsible for each budget's preparation, and illustrates how the budgets relate to one another. The process begins with Sales Department estimates of the types, quantities, and timing of demand for products and services. This information is needed by both Production and Accounts Receivable. Production managers combine sales estimates with information from Purchasing, Human Resources, Operations, and Capital Facilities to determine the types, quantities, and timing of products to be produced and transferred to finished goods. Accounts Receivable uses sales estimates, in conjunction with estimated collection patterns, to determine the amounts and timing of cash receipts. Cash receipts information is necessary for the treasurer to manage the organization's flow of funds properly. All areas create cash disbursements that must be matched with cash receipts so that cash is available when it is needed.

Note that certain information must flow back into a department in which it began. For example, the Sales Department must receive finished goods information to know if goods are in inventory (or can be produced to order) before selling products. The treasurer must continually receive input information on cash receipts and disbursements as well as provide output information to various organizational units on the availability of funds so that proper funds management can be maintained.

Assuming that senior management is engaging in participatory budgeting, each department in the budgetary process either prepares its own budget or provides information for inclusion in a budget.

master budget
the comprehensive set of all budgetary schedules and the pro forma financial statements of an organization

operating budget
a budget that is expressed in both units and dollars

financial budget
a budget that reflects the funds to be generated or used during the budget period; includes the cash and capital budgets and the projected or pro forma financial statements

LEARNING OBJECTIVE 6

What is the starting point of a master budget and how do the components relate to one another?

EXHIBIT 6-10

The Budgetary Process in a
Manufacturing Organization

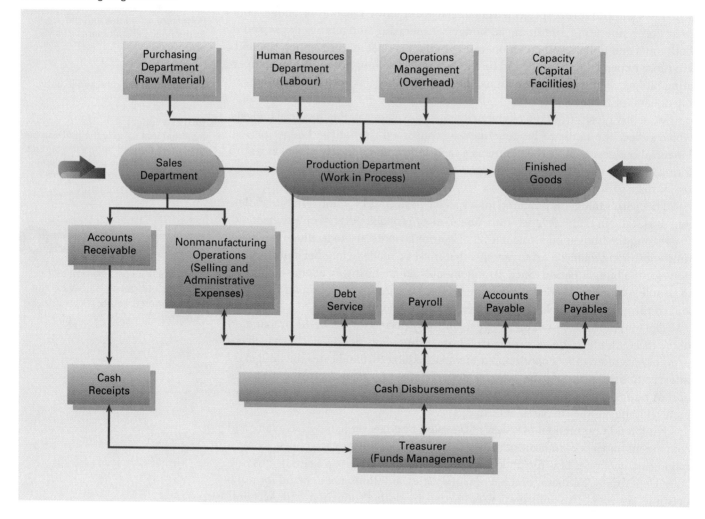

While the flow of information is visible in Exhibit 6-11, the quantitative and monetary implications are not. The remainder of the chapter reflects these implications through the preparation of a master budget.

THE MASTER BUDGET ILLUSTRATED

Triton Enterprises Inc. is used to illustrate the process of preparing a master budget for fiscal 2008. The company produces metal shut-off valves for use in the natural gas industry. The master budget is prepared for the entire year and then subdivided into quarterly and monthly periods. Triton Enterprises Inc.'s Marketing Division has estimated total sales for the year at 2,000,000 valves. While annual sales are detailed on a monthly basis, the Triton Enterprises Inc. illustration focuses only on the first-quarter budgets. The process of developing the master budget is the same regardless of whether the time frame is one year or one quarter.

The December 31, balance sheet presented in Exhibit 6-12 provides account balances needed to prepare the master budget. The December 31 balances are really projections rather than actual figures because the budget process for next

EXHIBIT 6-11
The Master Budget:
An Overview

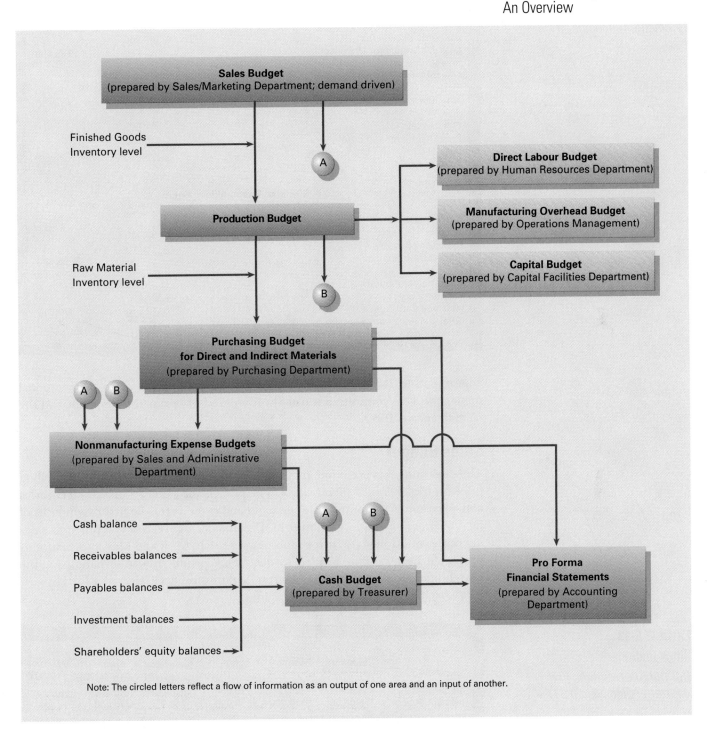

Note: The circled letters reflect a flow of information as an output of one area and an input of another.

year must begin significantly before December 31 of the current year. A company's budgetary time schedule depends on many factors, including its size and its degree of forecasting sophistication. Triton Enterprises Inc. starts its budgeting process in November when the sales forecast is received by either management or the *budget committee*. The **budget committee** reviews and approves, or makes

budget committee
a group, usually composed of senior management and the chief financial officer, that reviews and approves or makes adjustments to the master budget and/or the budgets submitted from operational managers

EXHIBIT 6-12

Triton Enterprises Inc. Balance Sheet

(projected) December 31

Assets		
Current Assets		
Cash		$ 5,090
Accounts Receivable	$ 168,000	
Less Allowance for Uncollectible Accounts	(2,400)	165,600
Inventories		
Direct Material (87,580 grams)	$ 17,516	
Finished Goods (15,400 units @ $1.26)	19,404	36,920
Total Current Assets		$207,610
Plant Assets		
Property, Plant, and Equipment	$ 540,000	
Less Accumulated Depreciation	(180,000)	360,000
Total Assets		$567,610
Liabilities and Shareholders' Equity		
Current Liabilities		
Accounts Payable	$ 80,000	
Dividends Payable (due 1/15)	15,000	
Total Current Liabilities		$ 95,000
Shareholders' Equity		
Common Stock	$ 300,000	
Retained Earnings	172,610	472,610
Total Liabilities and Shareholders' Equity		$567,610

adjustments to, the master budget and/or the budgets submitted from operational managers. This committee is usually composed of senior management and the chief financial officer.

Sales Budget

The sales budget is prepared in terms of both units and sales dollars. The selling price set for 2008 is $2.00 per valve. The price is the same for all sales territories and all customers. Monthly sales demand and revenue for the first five months of next year are shown in Exhibit 6-13. Dollar sales figures are computed as sales quantities multiplied by the product selling price. April and May information is presented because it is needed to determine production information for the March budget. The "Total for Quarter" column reflects sales only for January, February, and March.

EXHIBIT 6-13

Sales Budget

(for the three months and quarter ending March 31)

	January	February	March	Total for Quarter	April	May
Sales in units	220,000	205,000	195,000	620,000	180,000	195,000
Sales in dollars	$440,000	$410,000	$390,000	$1,240,000	$360,000	$390,000

Production Budget

The production budget follows naturally from the sales budget and uses information regarding the type, quantity, and timing of units to be sold. Sales information is combined with information on beginning and ending inventories so that managers can schedule the necessary production.

Ending inventory policy (as to quantity of units) is generally specified by company management. Desired ending inventory is normally a function of the quantity and timing of demand in the upcoming period together with the firm's production capacity and speed. Before making a decision about how much inventory to keep on hand, managers should consider the high costs of stockpiling inventory. Management may stipulate that ending inventory be a given percentage of the next period's projected sales. Other alternatives include maintaining a constant amount of inventory, building up inventory levels for future high-demand periods, and keeping inventory levels near zero under a just-in-time system. The decision about ending inventory levels affects whether a firm has constant production with varying inventory levels or variable production with constant inventory levels. As indicated in the following quote, the size of the inventory is also directly related to cash flow.

> Mismanagement of your company's inventory can create a financial hemorrhage that may cripple the business for life. Excessive inventory purchases, slow-moving inventory, and the inability to reorder in a timely fashion can all wreak havoc on your cash flow. Remember that inventory is "cash" sitting on your shelves without earning any interest. Actually, it may be one of your firm's largest expenditures, depending on the type of business and industry you are in.[10]

Demand for valves varies throughout the year, and Triton Enterprises Inc. carries very little inventory. Production time is short, so company management has a policy that Finished Goods Inventory need be only 7% of the next month's sales. Based on the ending inventory policy and the sales information from Exhibit 6-13, the production budget shown in Exhibit 6-14 is prepared.

EXHIBIT 6-14
Production Budget
(for the three months and quarter ending March 31)

	January	February	March	Total
Sales in units (from Exhibit 6-13)	220,000	205,000	195,000	620,000
+ Desired ending inventory	14,350	13,650	12,600	12,600
Total needed	234,350	218,650	207,600	632,600
− Beginning inventory	(15,400)[1]	(14,350)	(13,650)	(15,400)
Units to be produced	218,950	204,300	193,950	617,200

[1]From Exhibit 6-12
Note: April's production would be 180,000 + 13,650 − 12,600 = 181,050

The beginning inventory balance shown for January is the number of units on hand at December 31. This inventory figure is 15,400 units (from Exhibit 6-12), which represents 7% of January's estimated 220,000 units of sales. March's ending inventory balance is 7% of April's estimated 180,000 units of sales (from Exhibit 6-13). Triton Enterprises Inc. has no Work in Process Inventory because all units placed into production are fully completed each period.[11]

Direct Materials Purchases Budget

Direct materials are essential to production and must be purchased each period in sufficient quantities to meet production needs and to conform with the company's ending inventory policies. Triton Enterprises Inc.'s management has established that direct materials will be 10% of the following month's production needs. This inventory level is slightly higher than that of the finished goods because the lead time to acquire direct materials is somewhat longer and more uncertain than the production time to complete finished goods.

The direct materials purchases budget is first stated in whole units of finished products. It is subsequently converted to individual direct material component requirements. Production of each valve requires four grams of metal alloy. The quantity of material used in the valve gate and its cost are insignificant, so that item is treated as indirect material. Unit material cost has been estimated by the purchasing agent to be $0.20 per gram. The whole-unit and component purchases budgets for each month of the first quarter are shown in Exhibit 6-15. The beginning inventory for January is 10% of January production.

EXHIBIT 6-15

Materials Purchases Budget

(for the three months ending March 31)

	January	February	March
Units to be produced (from Exhibit 6-14)	218,950	204,300	193,950
+ Ending Inventory units (10% of next month's production)	20,430	19,395	18,105[1]
= Total whole unit quantities needed	239,380	223,695	212,055
− Beginning inventory units (10% of current production)	(21,895)[2]	(20,430)	(19,395)
= Purchases required in whole unit quantities	217,485	203,265	192,660
× Grams per unit	× 4	× 4	× 4
Total grams to be purchased	869,940	813,060	770,640
× Price per gram	× $0.20	× $0.20	× $0.20
Total cost of alloy	$ 173,988	$162,612	$154,128

[1]10% of April's production (from Exhibit 6-14)

[2]Beginning inventory of Direct Material was 87,580 grams, or enough for 21,895 units (from Exhibit 6-12).

Given expected production, the Engineering and Human Resources Departments can work together to determine the necessary labour requirements for the factory, salesforce, and office staff. Labour requirements are stated in total number of people, and number of specific types of people (skilled labourers, salespeople, clerical personnel), as well as production hours required of factory employees. Labour costs are computed based on items such as union labour contracts, minimum wage laws, fringe benefit costs, payroll taxes, and bonus arrangements. The various personnel amounts are shown, as appropriate, in either the direct labour budget, the manufacturing overhead budget, or the selling and administrative costs budget.

Direct Labour Budget

The management of Triton Enterprises Inc. has reviewed the staffing requirements and has developed the direct labour cost estimates shown in Exhibit 6-16 for the first quarter. Manufacturing direct labour costs are based on the standard hours of labour needed to produce the number of units shown in the production budget. The average wage rate shown in the exhibit includes both the basic direct labour

EXHIBIT 6-16

Direct Labour Budget

(for the three months ending March 31)

	January	February	March	Total
Units to be produced	218,950	204,300	193,950	617,200
× Standard hours per unit	× 0.022	× 0.022	× 0.022	× 0.022
Total hours allowed	4,816.90	4,494.60	4,266.90	13,578.40
× Average wage rate (including fringe benefits)	× $10	× 10	× $10	× $10
Direct labour cost (rounded)	$ 48,169	$ 44,946	$ 42,669	$ 135,784

payroll rate and the payroll taxes and fringe benefits related to direct labour. Taxes and fringe benefits usually add between 25% and 30% to the base labour cost. All compensation is paid in the month in which it is incurred.

Overhead Budget

Overhead is another production cost that must be estimated by management. Exhibit 6-17 presents Triton Enterprises Inc.'s monthly cost of each overhead item for the first quarter. The company has determined that machine hours are the best predictor of overhead costs.

	Fixed Cost	Value of Variable Cost per Unit	January	February	March	Total
Estimated Machine Hours (x) (given)			220	200	190	610
Manufacturing Overhead Items:	(a)	(b)				
Non-cash item						
Depreciation	$14,000	$10.00	$16,200	$16,000	$15,900	$ 48,100
Cash items						
Indirect materials	—	$ 0.10	$ 22	$ 20	$ 19	$ 61
Indirect labour	$ 7,000	0.50	7,110	7,100	7,095	21,305
Utilities	3,000	1.60	3,352	3,320	3,304	9,976
Property taxes	5,000	—	5,000	5,000	5,000	15,000
Insurance	6,500	—	6,500	6,500	6,500	19,500
Maintenance	2,600	5.80	3,876	3,760	3,702	11,338
Total cash items	$24,100	$ 8.00	$25,860	$25,700	$25,620	$ 77,180
Total Cost (y)	$38,100	$18.00	$42,060	$41,700	$41,520	$125,280

EXHIBIT 6-17
Manufacturing Overhead Budget
(for the three months and quarter ending March 31)

In estimating overhead, all costs must be specified and mixed costs must be separated into their (a) fixed and (b) variable elements. Each overhead amount shown is calculated by use of the $y = a + bx$ formula for a mixed cost,[12] in which x is the number of units of activity (in this case, machine hours). For example, February maintenance cost is the fixed amount of $2,600 plus the variable portion ($5.80 $\times$ 200 estimated machine hours), or $2,600 + $1,160 = $3,760. Both the total cost and the cost net of depreciation are shown in the budget. The cost net of depreciation is the amount that is expected to be paid in cash during the month and will, therefore, affect the cash budget.

Selling and Administrative (S&A) Budget

Selling, general, and administrative expenses for each month can be predicted in the same manner as overhead costs. Exhibit 6-18 presents the selling and administrative budget. Note that sales figures rather than production levels are used as the measure of activity in preparing this budget. Triton's salesforce consists of a manager with a monthly salary of $5,000 and four salespeople who receive $500 per month plus a 20% commission on sales. Administrative staff salaries total $18,000 per month.

Capital Budget

The budgets included in the master budget focus on the short-term or upcoming fiscal period. Managers, however, must also consider long-term needs in the area of

EXHIBIT 6-18

Selling and Administrative
Budget

*(for the three months and quarter
ending March 31)*

	Value of		January	February	March	Total
Predicted Unit Sales (from Exhibit 6-13)			220,000	205,000	195,000	620,000
	Fixed Cost (a)	**Variable Cost per Unit** (b)				
S&A Items:						
Non-cash item						
Depreciation	$ 3,800	——	$ 3,800	$ 3,800	$ 3,800	$ 11,400
Cash items						
Supplies	$ 350	$0.04	$ 9,150	$ 8,550	$ 8,150	$ 25,850
Utilities	200	—	200	200	200	600
Miscellaneous	500	—	500	500	500	1,500
Salaries:						
Sales manager	5,000	—	5,000	5,000	5,000	15,000
Salespeople	2,000	0.20	46,000	43,000	41,000	130,000
Administrative	18,000	—	18,000	18,000	18,000	54,000
Total cash items	$26,050	$0.24	$78,850	$75,250	$72,850	$226,950
Total Cost (y)	$29,850	$0.24	$82,650	$79,050	$76,650	$238,350

capital budgeting
a process for evaluating proposed
long-range projects or courses of
future activity for the purpose of
allocating limited resources to
desirable projects

plant and equipment purchases. The process of assessing such needs and budgeting for the expenditures is called **capital budgeting**, which is covered in Chapter 14. The capital budget is prepared separately from the master budget, but since expenditures are involved, capital budgeting does affect the master budgeting process. Sometimes the timing of current-year planned capital purchases is dependent on the extent to which actual revenues conform to budgetary revenues.

Corporate financial professionals should recognize that capital asset decisions are the most irrevocable long-range activities because they (1) involve significant corporate funding, (2) are the least flexible in terms of changing the strategic direction of the business, (3) are the least flexible for conversion into more liquid assets, (4) may geographically impact the long-term raw material supply capability as well as the long-term customer access of the business, and (5) involve decisions about assets that are unique to the company. Since the unique features of capital assets represent the source of a company's product individuality and position in the marketplace, capital decisions must support the company's strategic plans.[13]

As shown in Exhibit 6-19, the managers of Triton Enterprises Inc. have decided that only one capital purchase will be made in the first quarter. The company is planning to acquire a network of state-of-the-art computers to better control shop-floor activities. This network will cost $240,000 and will be purchased and placed into service at the beginning of January 2008. The company will pay for this acquisition at the end of February. Depreciation on this computer network is included in the overhead calculation in Exhibit 6-17. No other equipment will be sold or scrapped when the network is purchased.

EXHIBIT 6-19

Capital Budget

*(for the three months and quarter
ending March 31)*

	January	February	March	Total
Acquisitions:				
Computer network	$240,000	$ 0	$0	$240,000
Cash payments:				
Computer network	$ 0	$240,000	$0	$240,000

Readjusted Budgeting and Analysis

GENERAL NEWS NOTE

A recent study found that almost 50% of executives report that finance unit employees are tied up in transactional activities such as processing accounts and tax transactions. Only 25% are focused on the more important service of supporting management decisions. A major problem with finance employees is that they are making Excel do what it was never meant to do: function as a multi-user system. Excel does not have the functionality needed by growing organizations, which require more complex applications. These organizations need not depend on Excel; many other firms are producing software for budgeting, analysis, and decision support.

Peter Fraser, director of finance for the ONTARIO COLLEGE OF ART AND DESIGN (OCAD) recently introduced a new budgeting and forecasting software system to support changes caused by growth. In particular, the software is used to establish decentralized budgeting. Fraser contends that the technology is not the biggest challenge; rather, the challenge resides in getting faculty members to upgrade their system skills and financial skills.

Similarly, Mark Cross, the planning manager at UNION ENERGY, has acquired a new budgeting and analysis system to replace Excel, which the finance department had to control. The new system functions as an internal management reporting tool, allowing everyone to report on their key performance indicators (KPIs).

SOURCE: Robert Colman, "Readjusted Budgeting and Analysis," *CMA Management*, March 2006, pp. 16–17.

Cash Budget

After all the preceding budgets have been developed, a cash budget can be constructed. The cash budget may be the most important schedule prepared during the budgeting process because without cash a company cannot survive.

The following model can be used to summarize cash receipts and disbursements in a manner that helps managers devise appropriate financing measures to meet company needs.

Cash Budget Model

Beginning cash balance
+ Cash receipts from collections
= Cash available for disbursements exclusive of financing
− Cash needed for disbursements
= Cash excess or deficiency (a)
− Minimum desired cash balance
= Cash (needed) or available for investment or repayment

Financing methods:
± Borrow money (repay loans)
± Issue (reacquire) capital stock
± Sell (acquire) investments or plant assets
± Receive (pay) interest or dividends
  Total impact (+ or −) of planned financing (b)
= Ending cash balance (c) = (a) Cash excess (or deficiency) ± (b) Total impact of planned financing

Cash budgets can be used to predict seasonal variances in any potential cash flow. Such predictions can indicate a need for short-term borrowing and a potential schedule of repayments. The cash budget may also show the possibility of surplus cash, which can be used for funds management, such as for investment. Cash budgets can be used to measure the performance of the accounts receivable and accounts payable departments by comparing actual to scheduled collections, payments, and discounts taken.

Cash Receipts and Accounts Receivable

Once sales revenues have been determined, managers translate that information into expected cash receipts through the use of an expected collection pattern. This pattern considers the actual collection patterns experienced in recent past

Budgeting for cash collections at a movie theatre is less complicated than at many organizations. Ticket revenue is predominantly cash, with multi-tiered pricing for adults, children, students, and seniors. Thus, there are no cash discounts for prompt payment and no uncollectible accounts.

periods and management's judgment about changes that could disturb current collection patterns. For example, changes that could weaken current collection patterns include recessionary conditions, increases in interest rates, or less strict credit-granting practices.

In specifying collection patterns, managers should recognize that different types of customers pay in different ways. Any sizable, unique category of clientele should be segregated. It is essential for companies to know their customers' payment patterns.

Triton Enterprises Inc. has two types of customers: 40% of the customers pay cash and receive a 2% discount; 60% of the customers purchase products on credit and have the following collection pattern—30% in the month of sale, 69% in the month following the sale, and 1% of credit sales are uncollectible. The collection pattern of Triton Enterprises Inc. is illustrated in Exhibit 6-20.

Using the sales budget, information on December sales, and the collection pattern, management can estimate cash receipts from sales during the following three months. The December sales amounted to $400,000. Management must have this sales information because collections for credit sales extend over two months, meaning that some collections from the December sales will occur in January. Projected monthly collections for the first quarter are shown in Exhibit 6-21. The individual calculations relate to the alternative collection patterns and corresponding percentages presented in Exhibit 6-20.

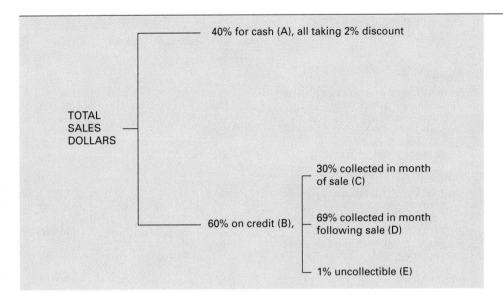

EXHIBIT 6-20
Collection Pattern for Sales

In January, the collections relating to December sales can be reconciled to the December 31 balance sheet (Exhibit 6-12), which indicated an Accounts Receivable balance of $168,000. This amount appears in the collection schedule as follows:

January collections of December sales	$165,600
January estimate of December uncollectible accounts	2,400
December 31 Accounts Receivable balance	$168,000

The remaining monthly amounts are computed in the same manner. Note that the collection in the month after the sale is 69% of the original credit sale, and uncollectible accounts are 1% of the original credit sales, not of the remaining balance.

Once the schedule of cash collections is prepared, the balances of the Accounts Receivable and Allowance for Uncollectible Accounts can be projected. The T-accounts for Triton Enterprises Inc. are shown next and will be used in preparing the pro forma first-quarter financial statements. Note that the Allowance account balance indicates that Triton Enterprises Inc. has not written off any accounts receivable since December. The company may still believe that some of these accounts are collectible.

Accounts Receivable			
Dec. 31, Bal. (Ex. 6-12)	168,000	January collections (Ex 6-21)	417,280
January Sales (Ex. 6-13)	440,000	January discounts (Ex. 6-21)	3,520
February Sales (Ex. 6-13)	410,000	February collections (Ex. 6-21)	416,680
March Sales (Ex. 6-13)	390,000	February discounts (Ex. 6-21)	3,280
		March collections (Ex. 6-21)	392,820
		March discounts (Ex. 6-21)	3,120
March 31 Balance	171,300		

Allowance for Uncollectible Accounts			
		Dec. 31, Balance (Ex. 6-12)	2,400
		January estimate (Ex. 6-21)	2,640
		February estimate (Ex. 6-21)	2,460
		March estimate (Ex. 6-21)	2,340
		March 31 Balance	9,840

EXHIBIT 6-21

Cash Collections

(for the three months and quarter ending March 31)

	January	February	March	Total
January				
Previous month's credit sales collected ($400,000 × 60% × 69%)	$165,600			$ 165,600
Current month's cash sales ($440,000 × 40%)[1]	172,480 N			172,480
Current month's credit sales collected ($440,000 × 60% × 30%)	79,200			79,200
February				
Previous month's credit sales collected ($440,000 × 60% × 69%)		$182,160		182,160
Current month's cash sales ($410,000 × 40%)[1]		160,720 N		160,720
Current month's credit sales collected ($410,000 × 60% × 30%)		73,800		73,800
March				
Previous month's credit sales collected ($410,000 × 60% × 69%)			$169,740	169,740
Current month's cash sales ($390,000 × 40%)[1]			152,880 N	152,880
Current month's credit sales collected ($390,000 × 60% × 30%)			70,200	70,200
Totals	$417,280	$416,680	$392,820	$1,226,780

[1]The result multiplied by 98% yields the amount collected; the result multiplied by 2% yields the amount of the discount. "N" stands for "Net of discount."
Total discount = $9,920 [January $440,000 × 40% × 2% = $3,520; February $410,000 × 40% × 2% = $3,280; March $390,000 × 40% × 2% = $3,120]
Total amount uncollectible = $7,440 [January $440,000 × 60% × 1% = $2,640; February $410,000 × 60% × 1% = $2,460; March $390,000 × 60% × 1% = $2,340

Cash Disbursements and Accounts Payable

Using the purchases information from Exhibit 6-15, management can prepare an estimated cash disbursements schedule for Accounts Payable. All purchases of direct material are made on account by Triton Enterprises Inc. The company pays for 40% of each month's purchases in the month of purchase, taking a 2% cash discount. The remaining 60% of each month's purchases are paid for in the month following the month of purchase; no discount is available for these payments.

Exhibit 6-22 presents the cash disbursements information related to purchases for the first quarter. The December 31 Accounts Payable balance of $80,000 reflected in Exhibit 6-12 represents the 60% remaining payment required for December purchases. This amount is also shown in Exhibit 6-22 as the first amount paid. (All amounts in this exhibit have been rounded to whole dollars.)

The Accounts Payable activity is summarized in the following T-account. The March 31 balance represents 60% of March purchases that will be paid during April.

Accounts Payable			
		Dec. 31, Balance (Ex. 6-12)	80,000
January payments (Ex. 6-22)	148,203	January purchases (Ex. 6-15)	173,988
January discounts taken (Ex. 6-22)	1,392		
February payments (Ex. 6-22)	168,137	February purchases (Ex. 6-15)	162,612
February discounts taken (Ex. 6-22)	1,301		
March payments (Ex. 6-22)	157,985	March purchases (Ex. 6-15)	154,128
March discounts taken (Ex. 6-22)	1,233		
		March 31 Balance	92,477

EXHIBIT 6-22

Cash Disbursements-Accounts Payable

(for the three months ending March 31)

	January	February	March	Discount
Payment for purchases of:				
December (from Exhibit 6-12)	$ 80,000			
January (from Exhibit 6-15)				
$173,988(40%)(98%)	68,203 N			$1,392
$173,988(60%)		$104,393		
February (from Exhibit 6-15)				
$162,612(40%)(98%)		63,744 N		1,301
$162,612(60%)			$ 97,567	
March (from Exhibit 6-15)				
$154,128(40%)(98%)			60,418 N	1,233
Total disbursements for Accounts Payable	$148,203	$168,137	$157,985	$3,926[1]

[1]Discounts taken: January [($173,988 × 0.40) × 0.02]; February [($162,612 × 0.40) × 0.02]; March [($154,128 × 0.40) × 0.02]

Note: "N" stands for "Net of discount." The total amount of gross purchases being paid for in the month of purchase is the sum of the net of discount payment plus the amount shown on the same line in the discount column.

Using the cash budget model, the company uses the cash receipts and disbursements information to prepare the cash budget shown in Exhibit 6-23. The company has established $5,000 as its desired minimum cash balance. The primary reason for maintaining a minimum cash balance is the uncertainty associated with the budgeting process. If management had perfect certainty about cash inflows and outflows, there would be no need for this cash "cushion."

All borrowings by Triton Enterprises Inc. are assumed to take place in increments of $100 at the beginning of a month. All repayments and investments are made in

EXHIBIT 6-23

Cash Budget

(for the three months and quarter ending March 31)

	January	February	March	Total
Beginning cash balance (Exhibit 6-12)	$ 5,090	$ 5,088	$ 5,002	$ 5,090
Cash collections (Exhibit 6-21)	417,280	416,680	392,820	1,226,780
Cash available exclusive of financing	$ 422,370	$ 421,768	$397,822	$1,231,870
Disbursements:				
Accounts payable (Exhibit 6-22)	$ 148,203	$ 168,137	$157,985	$ 474,325
Direct labour (Exhibit 6-16)	48,169	44,946	42,669	135,784
Overhead (Exhibit 6-17)[1]	25,860	25,700	25,620	77,180
S&A expenses (Exhibit 6-18)[1]	78,850	75,250	72,850	226,950
Total planned disbursements	$ 301,082	$ 314,033	$299,124	$ 914,239
Cash excess or (inadequacy)	$ 121,288	$ 107,735	$ 98,698	$ 317,631
Minimum cash balance desired	5,000	5,000	5,000	5,000
Cash available or (needed)	$ 116,288	$ 102,735	$ 93,698	$ 312,631
Financing:				
Borrow (repay)	$ 0	$ 35,800	$ (35,800)	$ 0
Issue (reacquire) stock	0	0	0	0
Liquidate (acquire) investments	(101,200)	101,200	(57,600)	(57,600)
Sell (pay for) plant assets (Exhibit 6-19)	0	(240,000)	0	(240,000)
Receive (pay) interest or dividends[2]	(15,000)	267	(239)	(14,972)
Total impact of planned financing	$(116,200)	$(102,733)	$ (93,639)	$ (312,572)
Ending cash balance	$ 5,088	$ 5,002	$ 5,059	$ 5,059

[1]These amounts are the net of depreciation figures.

[2]Dividends payable on the December 31, balance sheet were shown as being payable on January 15. Interest on investments is calculated assuming a 6% rate, and interest on borrowings is calculated assuming an 8% rate. Borrowings are made at the beginning of the month, and repayments or investments are made at the end of the month. For February, interest owed is $239 ($35,800 × 0.08 × 1/12) and interest received is $506 ($101,200 × 0.06 × 1/12). In March, interest owed is $239 ($35,800 × 0.08 × 1/12).

$100 amounts and are assumed to occur at the end of a month. These assumptions are simplistic, since management would not actually borrow until the need for funds arose and would repay as quickly as possible so as to minimize interest expenditures. Interest on any company investments is assumed to be added to the company's bank account at the end of each month.

Exhibit 6-23 indicates that Triton Enterprises Inc. has $121,288 in excess cash available in January. This excess not only meets the specified $5,000 minimum balance and the dividend payment requirement from the December balance sheet, but also gives the firm an opportunity to invest $101,200. In February, Triton Enterprises Inc. expects to have enough cash to meet its desired minimum cash balance but not enough to pay for the computer network purchased in January. The January investment must be liquidated and an additional $35,800 borrowed. Since the machine does not have to be paid for until the end of the month, the investment can continue to draw interest until that time. The borrowing has been assumed, however, to occur at the beginning of the month for consistency with the previously specified plan. Thus, Triton Enterprises Inc. earns interest on the investment but must pay interest on the borrowings for February. In March, there is enough cash available to meet budgeted disbursements, pay off the February borrowings, and make a $57,600 investment. Calculations of interest on borrowings and investments are shown at the bottom of Exhibit 6-23. Any changes in interest rates will affect any future budget-to-actual comparisons.

Several things should be specially noted involving the total column in Exhibit 6-23. First, the beginning cash balance is not the total of the three months, but is the balance at January 1. Second, the monthly and quarterly minimum cash balance is $5,000, not $15,000. Last, the ending cash balance should be the same as what appears in the final month of the quarter. These figures (beginning, minimum, and ending cash balances), cash available exclusive of financing, cash excess or inadequacy, and cash available or needed are the only ones that are not summed across from the three-month information; all other figures are totals. These figures can be updated monthly; a spreadsheet program is very useful for this function.

Budgeted Financial Statements

The final step in the budgeting process is the development of budgeted or pro forma financial statements for the period. These statements reflect the results that will be achieved if the estimates and assumptions used for all previous budgets actually occur. Such statements allow management to determine whether the predicted results are acceptable for the period. If the predicted results are not acceptable, management has the opportunity to change and adjust items before the beginning of the period.

For example, if expected net income is not considered a reasonable amount, management may discuss raising selling prices or finding ways to decrease costs. Any specific changes considered by management may have related effects that must be included in the revised projections. For example, if selling prices are raised, volume may decrease. Alternatively, reductions in costs from using a lesser grade of materials could increase spoilage during production or the lower-quality product could cause a decline in demand. Computer spreadsheet programs are used to quickly and easily make the recalculations necessary from such changes in assumptions.

Cost of Goods Manufactured Statement

Before an income statement can be drafted, management must prepare a cost of goods manufactured statement, which is necessary to determine the cost of goods sold. Using information from previous budgets, Triton Enterprises Inc.'s accountant has prepared the budgeted cost of goods manufactured statement shown in Exhibit 6-24. Since there were no beginning or ending work in process inventories, cost of goods manufactured is equal to the manufacturing costs of the period.

Cost of direct material used:	
Beginning balance of direct material (Exhibit 6-12)	$ 17,516
Purchases (net of $3,926 of discounts taken) (from	
Accounts Payable)[1]	486,802
Total direct material available	$504,318
Ending balance of direct material (Note A)	(14,484)
Cost of direct material used	$489,834
Direct labour (Exhibit 6-16)	135,784
Manufacturing overhead (Exhibit 6-17)	125,280
Total costs to be accounted for	$750,898
Plus: Beginning work in process	0
	$750,898
Less: Ending work in process	0
Cost of goods manufactured	$750,898

Note A

Ending balance (Exhibit 6-15) in units	18,105
Grams of alloy per unit	× 4
Total grams needed	72,420
Price per gram	× $0.20
Ending balance	$14,484

[1] Total Purchases = $490,728 (Exhibit 6-15) [$173,988 + $162,612 + $154,128] minus Discounts $3,926 (Exhibit 6-22) = Net Purchases of $486,802.

EXHIBIT 6-24

Pro Forma Cost of Goods Manufactured Statement *(for the first quarter)*

Income Statement

The projected income statement for Triton Enterprises Inc. for the first quarter is presented in Exhibit 6-25. This statement uses much of the information previously developed in determining the revenues and expenses for the period.

Balance Sheet

Upon completion of the income statement, Triton Enterprises Inc.'s accountant can prepare a pro forma March 31 balance sheet (Exhibit 6-26). The letters in parentheses after some of the items in Exhibit 6-26 refer to the calculations shown at the bottom of the exhibit.

Cash Flow Statement

The information found on the income statement, balance sheet, and cash budget is used in preparing a cash flow statement (CFS). This statement is a principal internal, as well as external, report. The CFS explains the change in the cash balance by reflecting the company's inflows and outflows of cash. Such knowledge is useful in judging the company's ability to handle fixed cash outflow commitments,

EXHIBIT 6-25

Pro Forma Income Statement
(for the first quarter)

Sales (Exhibit 6-13)		$1,240,000
Less: Sales discounts (from Accounts Receivable, p. 329)		(9,920)
Net sales		$1,230,080
Cost of goods sold:		
Finished goods—Dec. 31, 2007 (Exhibit 6-12)	$ 19,404	
Cost of goods manufactured (Exhibit 6-24)	750,898	
Cost of goods available for sale	$770,302	
Finished goods—March 31, 2008 (Note A)	(15,876)	(754,426)
Gross margin		$ 475,654
Expenses:		
Bad debts expense (Note B)	$ 7,440	
S&A expenses (Exhibit 6-18)	238,350	
Interest expense/income (net) (Exhibit 6-23)[1]	(28)	(245,762)
Income before income taxes		$ 229,892
Income taxes (assumed rate of 30%)		(68,968)
Net income (profit)		$ 160,924

[1]Interest Expense (net) [Feb. $239 + March $239 – Interest Income Feb. $506]

Note A

Beginning finished goods (Exhibit 6-12)		15,400
Production (Exhibit 6-14)		617,200
Units available for sale		632,600
Sales (Exhibit 6-13)		(620,000)
Ending finished goods (Exhibit 6-14)		12,600
Costs per unit:		
Direct material[1] (Exhibit 6-12)	$ 0.80	
Conversion (assumed) (Exhibit 6-12)	0.46	× $1.26
Cost of ending inventory		$ 15,876

Note B

Total sales	$1,240,000
× % credit sales	× 0.60
= Credit sales	$ 744,000
× % estimated uncollectible	× 0.01
= Estimated bad debts (from Exhibit 6-21)	$ 7,440

[1][($17,516 ÷ 87,580 grams) × 4 grams per unit]

adapt to adverse changes in business conditions, and undertake new commitments. Further, because the cash flow statement identifies the relationships between net income and net cash flow from operations, it assists managers in judging the quality of the company's earnings.

While the cash budget is essential to current cash management, the budgeted CFS gives managers a more global view of cash flows by rearranging them into three distinct major activities: operating, investing, and financing. Such a rearrangement permits management to judge whether the specific anticipated flows are consistent with the company's strategic plans. In addition, the CFS incorporates a schedule or narrative about significant noncash transactions, such as an exchange of shares for land, which are ignored in the cash budget.

Under Section 1540 of the *CICA Handbook*, it is acceptable for external reporting to present the operating section of the cash flow statement on either a direct or an indirect basis. The direct basis uses pure cash flow information—cash collections and cash disbursements for operating activities. The indirect basis begins the operating section with net income and makes reconciling adjustments to derive cash flow from operations. Exhibit 6-27 provides a cash flow statement for Triton Enterprises Inc. using the information from the cash budget in Exhibit 6-23. Indirect presentation of the operating section uses the information from the income

EXHIBIT 6-26

Pro Forma Balance Sheet
(March 31)

Assets

Current Assets		
Cash (Exhibit 6-23)		$ 5,059
Investments (Exhibit 6-23)		57,600
Accounts Receivable (p. 329)	$171,300	
Less Allowance for Uncollectibles (a)	(9,840)	161,460
Inventory		
Direct Materials (Exhibit 6-24, Note A)	$ 14,484	
Finished Goods (Exhibit 6-25, Note A)	15,876	30,360
Total Current Assets		$254,479
Plant Assets		
Property, Plant, and Equipment (b)	$780,000	
Less Accumulated Depreciation (c)	(239,500)	540,500
Total Assets		$794,979

Liabilities and Shareholders' Equity

Current Liabilities		
Accounts Payable (p. 330)		$ 92,477
Income Taxes Payable (Exhibit 6-25)		68,968
Total Current Liabilities		$161,445
Shareholders' Equity		
Common Stock	$300,000	
Retained Earnings (d)	333,534	633,534
Total Liabilities and Shareholders' Equity		$794,979

(a)	Beginning balance (Exhibit 6-12)	$ 2,400
	Additional allowance (Note B; Exhibit 6-25)	7,440
	Total	$ 9,840
(b)	Beginning balance (Exhibit 6-12)	$540,000
	Purchased network computer system (Exhibit 6-19)	240,000
	Ending balance	$780,000
(c)	Beginning balance (Exhibit 6-12)	$180,000
	Factory depreciation (Exhibit 6-17)	48,100
	S&A depreciation (Exhibit 6-18)	11,400
	Ending balance	$239,500
(d)	Beginning balance (Exhibit 6-12)	$172,610
	Net income (profit) (Exhibit 6-25)	160,924
	Ending balance	$333,534

statement in Exhibit 6-25 and the balance sheets in Exhibits 6-12 and 6-26. This method appears at the bottom of Exhibit 6-27.

Both cash flows from operations and net income are necessary for long-run success in business. It appears that Triton Enterprises Inc. is performing well on both counts.

ZERO-BASED BUDGETING

Traditional budgeting is often limited in its usefulness as a control tool because poor budgeting techniques are often used. One such technique involves beginning with the prior year's funding levels and treating these as given and essential to operations. Decisions are then made about whether and by what percentage to incrementally raise existing **appropriations**, which represent maximum allowable expenditures. Such an approach has often resulted in what is known as the "creeping commitment syndrome," in which activities are funded without systematic annual regard for priorities or alternative means for accomplishing objectives.

LEARNING OBJECTIVE   7

How does traditional budgeting differ from zero-based budgeting?

appropriation
a maximum allowable expenditure for a budget item

EXHIBIT 6-27

Pro Forma Cash Flow Statement
(for the first quarter)

Operating Activities:			
Cash collections:			
From sales		$1,226,780	
From interest		28	$1,226,808
Cash payments:			
For manufacturing costs:			
Direct material	$474,325		
Direct labour	135,784		
Overhead	77,180	$ 687,289	
For nonmanufacturing costs:			
Salaries	$199,000		
Supplies	25,850		
Other S&A expenses	2,100	226,950	
			(914,239)
Net cash inflow from operating activities			$ 312,569
Investing Activities:			
Purchase of plant asset		$ (240,000)	
Net cash outflow from investing activities			(240,000)
Financing Activities:			
Short-term investment		$ (57,600)	
Issuance of short-term note payable		35,800	
Repayment of short-term note payable		(35,800)	
Payment of dividends (owed at Dec. 31)		(15,000)	
Net cash outflow from financing activities			(72,600)
Net decrease in cash			$ (31)
Alternative (Indirect) Basis			
Operating Activities:			
Net income			$ 160,924
+ Depreciation ($48,100 + $11,400)[1]			59,500
+ Decrease in Accounts Receivable			
($165,600 – $161,460)		$ 4,140	
+ Decrease in Inventory ($36,920 – $30,360)		6,560	
+ Increase in Accounts Payable ($92,477 – $80,000)		12,477	
+ Increase in Taxes Payable		68,968	92,145
Net cash inflow from operating activities			$ 312,569

[1]Exhibits 6-17 and 6-18

zero-based budgeting
a comprehensive budgeting process that systematically considers the priorities and alternatives for current and proposed activities in relation to organizational objectives

To help eliminate the creeping commitment syndrome, **zero-based budgeting (ZBB)** was developed by Texas Instruments in overhead expenditures. ZBB is a comprehensive budgeting process that systematically considers the priorities and alternatives for current and proposed activities relative to organizational objectives. Annual justification of activities is required so that managers must rethink priorities within the context of agreed-upon objectives. Specifying that each operation be evaluated from a zero-cost base would be unrealistic and extreme, but ZBB does require that managers reevaluate all activities at the start of the budgeting process to make decisions about which activities should be continued, eliminated, or funded at a lower level. Differences between traditional budgeting and zero-based budgeting are shown in Exhibit 6-28.

Zero-based budgeting is applicable to the overhead areas in all organizations. ZBB does not, however, provide measures of efficiency, and it is difficult to implement because of the significant amount of effort necessary to investigate the causes of prior costs and justify the purposes of budgeted costs.

The ZBB process is based on organizational goals and objectives and involves three steps: (1) converting activities into decision packages, (2) ranking each decision package, and (3) allocating resources based on priorities. A decision package contains information about the activity: objectives and benefits, consequences of not funding, and necessary costs and staffing requirements. The decision packages are ranked and prioritized on the basis of need, costs, and benefits.

Traditional Budgeting	Zero-Based Budgeting
Starts with last year's funding appropriation	Starts with a minimal (or zero) figure for funding
Focuses on money	Focuses on goals and objectives
Does not systematically consider alternatives to current operations	Directly examines alternative approaches to achieving similar results
Produces a single level of appropriation for an activity	Produces alternative levels of funding based on availability of funds and desired results

EXHIBIT 6-28
Differences Between Traditional Budgeting and Zero-Based Budgeting

Zero-based budgeting is a rigorous exercise that demands considerable time and effort, as well as wholehearted commitment by the organization's personnel to make it work. An organization lacking the time, effort, and commitment needed should not attempt ZBB. An organization that can supply these three ingredients can use ZBB to become more effective in planning for and controlling overhead costs. One of the major benefits of ZBB is that, in using it, managers focus on identifying nonvalue-added activities and work to reduce items that are unnecessary or ineffective expenses.

An organization considering ZBB should assess whether the benefits are worth the costs. Management may consider "zero-basing" certain segments of the company on a rotating basis over a period of years as an alternative to applying the approach to the entire firm annually.

THE IMPACT OF ENTERPRISE RESOURCE PLANNING SYSTEMS ON BUDGETING

This chapter is premised on the assumption that budgets are generally prepared for a year in advance and then divided into monthly budgets. Consequently, budgeting is developed to provide guidance to decision making during the year when financial reporting is not available. Then, at the end of each month, when the income statement is available, actual performance is compared to the expected performance in the budget to ascertain operational success.

A major assumption underlying budgeting is that the environment is relatively stable and that a budget for the month or year represents an agreement between the manager and the manager's superior. There is sufficient certainty in the environment that the manager can forecast what will likely happen in terms of customers and competitors, and comfortably commit to a level of performance.

Also, budgeting is premised on the assumption that feedback is not instantaneous. It takes time to process the information and to explain what has happened in financial terms. In the past the delay has been that financial performance is reported a few days or weeks after the end of the month. The result is that decision making is done in advance of the information on those decisions. Budgets help this situation by providing guidance for that decision making.

Budgeting has been a standard and acceptable management practice for U.S. manufacturing and retail firms since General Motors and DuPont introduced budgeting in the 1920s. The Hudson's Bay Company was using a form of budgeting before 1700. In recent years, despite the general and long-term acceptance of budgeting as an integral part of management, a movement has developed among many major firms to discontinue budgeting. The Beyond Budgeting Round Table (BBRT), a group of mostly large European firms, was formed in 1998 to discuss best practices to replace traditional budgeting.[14] Some of the BBRT's members at the time included Anheuser Busch, Barclays Bank, Cadbury Schweppes, Mars Confectionery, Siemens, Standard Life, and Texas Instruments. The BBRT is seriously focused on eliminating or at least significantly changing the way budgeting is practised.

The BBRT has gathered information to make the case that budgeting—for example, as discussed in this chapter—is failing users:

- Few firms are satisfied with their budgeting processes. The BBRT cites surveys where 88%[15] and 66%[16] of chief financial officers were dissatisfied with their budgeting and planning processes.
- Far too much time is devoted to budgeting and too little time is spent on strategy. The BBRT cites research showing that 78% of the companies do not change their budgets with the fiscal cycle,[17] 60% of the organizations do not link their strategy to budgeting,[18] and 85% of management teams devote less than one hour per week to discussing strategy.
- Fixed assets are a small part of the market values of many firms. The BBRT notes that intangible assets such as brands and systems for dealing with customers and suppliers are often more valuable. Thus, budgeting for fixed assets and other balance sheet items becomes less important as the value of the company is contained in off balance sheet intangible assets.
- Budgeting is very expensive and often adds little value. The BBRT cites a study showing costs in terms of person years, which indicated that budgeting consumes a large part of the time of managers, especially senior managers.[19]

"The corporate planning and budgeting ritual is already the bane of managers everywhere. It's a cancer and it's in every blue-chip organization," states Mr. Hope, co-author of *Beyond Budgeting*. He is behind a movement that would scrap the annual budgeting process and replace it with a more adaptive, continuing process.

"In companies such as Enron, the rot began with fixed targets, extended to the hyped guidance for investment analysis, and ended with outright cheating to make the numbers add up," he says.

He makes the following recommendations:

- Replace annual budgets with constant rolling forecasts
- Get rid of the fixed numerical target
- Adopt a new vision that moves away from command-and-control direction from the top and "empowers" people to take ownership of processes and work to serve strategy and customers, not numbers

Mr. Hope argues that with his model, managers do not lose control, "in fact, they get more control—they get control over what's happening next." The average company, he says, spends four to five months on the annual planning of the budget, and the cost is onerous—Ford Motor Co. spends an estimated US$12 billion a year to do the numbers.[20]

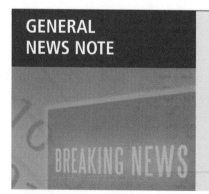

GENERAL NEWS NOTE

Companies Abandon Traditional Budgets to Boost Shareholder Value

The annual budget may be going the way of the dinosaur as companies introduce new and more accurate financial models capable of linking budgeting to overall corporate strategy, according to results of a recent global ACCENTURE/CRANFIELD SCHOOL OF MANAGEMENT study. The research also points to a correlation between companies modifying their budget processes and stock price performance.

"Companies are able to reduce their budget cycle time 30% to 40% by adopting approaches to the budget process that are more in concert with their overall strategic planning," says Herman Heynes, partner at Accenture's Financial and Performance

Management practice and author of the study. The study, entitled "Driving Value Through Strategic Planning and Budgeting," concludes that among these new approaches are rolling budgets, and in some instances, elimination of budgets entirely.

"Our study indicates that the budget process is obsolete given today's economy, resulting in documents that are time consuming to produce, of little predictive value, subject to gamesmanship and, quite frankly, out of date by the time they're implemented," Heynes adds. "We found that companies are beginning to radically modify their budget processes and are thinking actively about approaches beyond budgeting."

Based on the findings of the study, corporations are moving away from preparing annual budgets towards reducing costs, improving forecasting, and better managing investor expectations in order to reduce the risk of missed earnings targets and analyst downgrades. Emerging technology is providing corporations with the tools to modify their budget processes.

"Three themes clearly emerged in the study," says Professor Andy Neely, director of the Centre of Business Performance at Cranfield School of Management. "First companies can no longer justify the time and effort they invest in the budgeting process; second, budgets have to be much more responsive, enabling nearly real-time tracking; and third, management must understand that budgets cannot serve as both control and motivational devices. Companies that understand this and act on it are poised to enhance their credibility and performance."

For more information visit www.accenture.com.

SOURCE: Professor Andy Neely, Cranfield School of Management; Michael R. Sutcliff, Accenture and Herman R. Heyns, Accenture. *CMA Management*, February 2002, p. 9. Reprinted by permission of Accenture.

GENERAL NEWS NOTE

BREAKING NEWS

After demonstrating the marginal benefit of budgeting in many organizations, the BBRT indicates some of the management innovations over the last few decades that have been put forth to address these shortcomings. Budgeting innovations include, for example, zero-based budgeting, activity-based budgeting, faster, cheaper, rolling budgets, and the balanced scorecard.

After reviewing the problems with traditional budgeting and examining what many of its member organizations have been doing to replace traditional budgeting, the BBRT made a recommendation that traditional budgeting be replaced with an alternative that includes the use of an enterprise resource planning system (ERP) that allows all parts of the organization to be tied together via information.

In fact, to stay financially viable, corporations must bridge the gap between the quickening pace of business operations and the much slower rate of the traditional financial planning and budgeting process. To accomplish this, they should tightly integrate their business planning and budgeting applications into a single solution while extending collaboration capabilities beyond the walls of the finance department. Going one step further, companies should consider integrating this single solution with other ERP systems, including customer relationship management (CRM), supplier relationship management (SRM), and human capital management (HCM). In sum, the results of this integration—between planning and budgeting applications and between these applications and other ERP applications—can radically enhance a company's ability to respond intelligently and quickly to dynamic market conditions.[21]

The BBRT says that the IT system should be derived from and thus support business strategy, not the IT specialists. The operations should be managed in terms of activities rather than in terms of finances. With the activity and information orientation, the organization should be measured against its strategy—not in financial terms, but in operational terms from multiple perspectives with a balanced scorecard (which is discussed in Chapter 12). Using the balanced scorecard, performance should be benchmarked (discussed in Chapters 10 and 12) against peers internally and externally.

If the balanced scorecard and benchmarking are used to measure operational or physical performance, budgeting is not needed as the ERP systems can be used frequently to forecast the expected financial results to the end of the next month, quarter, or year. These rolling forecasts can be interpreted within the framework of a shareholder value model such as economic value added (EVA), which is discussed in Chapter 12.

The BBRT-recommended replacement for budgeting is really the management of the organization in physical terms with standards or expectations that, if achieved, will yield the desired financial performance. This alternative is achievable if information is sufficiently extensive to manage in physical terms and if the organization periodically or frequently forecasts the performance.

Pressures on costs and pricing make lean, efficient operations necessary for survival. Ironically research has found that the traditional budgeting practice is the root cause of many organizations' current problems. These businesses need to replace their budgeting process with management tools that offer continuous planning and adaptive control. In the example that Jack Welch used in his book, one can see that the budgeting process is simply a negotiating game. In fact, the budget becomes the goal.

Some argue that traditional budgets are necessary to keep costs in check because they are a company's primary tool for authorizing spending. However, practice shows that the budgeting process has the opposite effect. Although it may set a ceiling on expenses, a budget typically also sets a floor. Managers spend up to the authorized levels to avoid having to go through the approval process to make sure that their budget is not cut in the following year.[22]

CONCLUDING COMMENTS

What's the point of budgeting? In uncertain times like the present, when economic conditions can change from month to month and resources need to be juggled to seize opportunities or avoid approaching threats on the fly, a growing number of companies are convinced that the traditional annual numbers fest is a barrier rather than an aid to good management.[23]

A report released in the summer of 2004 by the Chartered Institute of Management Accountants (CIMA) and the Institute of Chartered Accountants in England and Wales (ICAEW) said, "The budget is dead. Long live the budget." The report notes that no one is really in love with budgeting—there are still many disadvantages. Principal among these are the way budgets can stifle creativity, entrepreneurial spirit, or a risk-taking culture; make businesses abandon projects because the money has been spent for the year; or make a company too inward-focused, concentrating on details of the budget rather than on competitiveness and agility—"gaming" to keep control of enough resources or capture more.[24]

Many have asked the question: "Should budgeting, as most companies practise it, be abolished"? In effect, should the old-fashioned, slow-to-respond, fixed performance contract be replaced by a more flexible form of budgeting—along with other types of goals and measures that track the performance of the company relative to its peers and world-class benchmarks? It certainly seems to make sense—but only to a point. A company's financial tool kit will always have room for the traditional budget. True, the use of a new, more dynamic form of budgeting—such as the rolling forecast—is now needed to support a more responsive overall corporate strategy development. However, the traditional budget will continue to play a role.[25]

The budgeting process should be understood as just the first phase of the rest of the life of the firm. To foster this attitude, some companies conduct their budget-planning process on a rolling basis, updating and extending the plan regularly (perhaps semiannually). Some set their short-term plans not according to the annual financial reporting calendar but according to the full sweep of their company's normal business cycle; this is common practice among Japanese firms like Toyota and deserves to be adopted more widely in other parts of the world. Rolling plans of two to three years' duration keep managers' eyes on a more distant horizon, and that has real implications for their investment decisions.[26]

Understanding the reasons for not meeting a budget can be useful in controlling future operations within the budget period, evaluating performance, and budgeting more accurately in the future. Finally, management should be aware that forecasted sales and profits may not materialize and factors beyond the business's control may create problems. In such instances, it is essential that management has made a contingency plan.

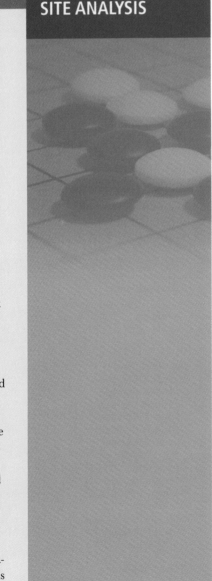

SITE ANALYSIS

The Hospital for Sick Children

At The Hospital for Sick Children, a new approach is being taken to address the conflict between funding and activity that plagues hospitals. Rather than try to define costs using a top-down averaging approach, a structurally sound bottom-up approach similar to activity-based costing is being piloted in five departments. It is based on a German methodology, *Grenzplankostenrechnung* (or GPK for short), that has been used in Europe for over 40 years but is virtually unheard of in North America.

As in ABC, direct costs are broken down to a level where they can be associated with a specific, measurable activity. Overhead costs are allocated to the activity where appropriate, or excluded and reported entirely separately in those cases where the cost cannot be fairly associated with the activity. A direct and indirect cost per activity is generated, and can be used for planning, budgeting, and management purposes. Overhead is managed and budgeted separately.

One of the big differences with GPK is that the activity-based cost breakdowns are built directly into the General Ledger (GL)—in ABC, they are usually kept in a separate system, and consequently are often not monitored as closely as the cost breakdowns in the General Ledger. The building of this activity-based structure caused an exponential increase in the number of cost centres being used and monitored in the GL, but at the same time it also caused an exponential increase in the understanding of the relationship between activity and cost at the hospital. (See Exhibit 6-29.)

In the Health Records department, for example, the departmental budget is around $5 million. The department has over 100 staff dedicated to maintaining a "complete, accurate and timely health record for patient care, planning, outcome management, and research purposes." Despite multiple activities and processes going on within the department, only four cost centres were being used. Consequently, the costs of specific activities were obscured by the costs of other activities accounted for within the same cost centre. The department's cost centres were restructured, with 15 new cost centres being created and specific costs and activity measures collected for each new cost centre.

The implications of this approach were immediately clear. For example, within the old Admitting cost centre, emergency registrations were mixed in with outpatient registrations as well as some sundry activities that were not directly related to patient registrations

SITE ANALYSIS

at all. After implementing the GPK cost centre restructuring, the new financial reports showed that outpatient registrations (at approximately $6 per registration), are much cheaper than emergency registrations (at approximately $9 per registration). Much less work is involved in outpatient registrations. Not only can this information be used for management purposes (the department now manages to GPK cost per activity measures, before reviewing global financial measures), but it can also be used as the basis for future budgets. For example, the department now knows exactly how much an additional 1,000 patients of any type will cost to register, and it will in future be able to split these costs into their direct/indirect components.

With this sort of detailed, structured, and activity-based information available across the hospital, not only will budgeting be much easier, but relating funding to patient services will be much easier too. This should lead to smoothing the funding negotiation process with the Ontario Ministry of Health and Long-Term Care.

SOURCES: Brian Mackie, former Financial Operations Director Information and Diagnostic Services, The Hospital for Sick Children; Kip R. Krumwiede, "Rewards and Realities of German Cost Accounting," *Strategic Finance*, April 2005, pp. 26–34; Carl S. Smith, "Going for GPK," *Strategic Finance*, April 2005, pp. 36–39; Paul Sharman and Kurt Vikas, "Lessons From German Cost Accounting," *Strategic Finance*, December 2004, pp. 28–35, www.imanet.org/ima/pdf/12sharman.pdf; Paul Sharman, "Bring On German Cost Accounting," *Strategic Finance*, December 2003, pp. 1–9, http://www.imanet.org/ima/docs/2000/1975.pdf; Paul Sharman, "The Case for Management Accounting," *Strategic Finance*, October 2003, pp. 1–5, www.imanet.org/ima/docs/1900/1857.pdf.

EXHIBIT 6-29

Restructuring of Cost Centres in the Department of Health Records at the Hospital for Sick Children, using GPK Methodology

Old Cost Centre	New (GPK) Cost Centre	Activity Measure
Admitting	Emergency Registrations	No. of emergency registrations
Admitting	Clinic Registration	No. of clinic registrations
Admitting	Admitting Support	Overhead cc—no direct activity measure
Admin & Clerical	Chart Retrieval – Stat	No. of charts pulled—Stat
Admin & Clerical	Chart Retrieval – Clinic	No. of charts pulled for clinic
Admin & Clerical	Chart Pick Up/Delivery	No. of charts picked up/delivered
Admin & Clerical	Loose Report Management	No. of inches of loose reports filed
Admin & Clerical	KidCHART	No. of pages scanned
Admin & Clerical	Inpatient Discharges	No. of inpatient discharges
Admin & Clerical	Admin & Clerical Support	Overhead cc—no direct activity measure
Management Admin	Ambulatory Coding	No. of charts abstracted—ambulatory
Management Admin	Inpatient Coding	No. of charts abstracted—inpatient
Management Admin	Release of Information	No. of release-of-information requests completed
Management Admin	Chart Deficiency Management	No. of charts processed
Management Admin	Research Support	No. of research charts signed out
Management Admin	Management & Admin Support	Overhead cc—no direct activity measure
Management Admin	IS Support	Overhead cc—no direct activity measure
Transcription	Transcription	No. of lines transcribed

CHAPTER SUMMARY

Traditional budgeting is now ingrained in most organizations' fabric and covers all areas of organizational activity. Thus, budgeting serves an important integrative function within the organization and provides a most important benchmark for ex-post performance evaluation with reference to the original target. It is convenient, but by no means complete, to categorize the critics of traditional practice and their suggestions into two groups: one advocating maintaining and improving the budgeting process and the other advocating abandoning it.[27]

In the last few years, critics have charged that planning and budgeting systems are rife with politics and game playing; generate only incremental changes vis-à-vis prior period plans and budgets; are not responsible to rapidly changing environments; impose a vertical command-and-control structure, centralize decision making, and stifle initiative; focus on cost reductions rather than value creations; and are too costly for the few benefits they produce. Among the proposals for improvement, smaller changes tweak the process slightly, such as updating plans more frequently by using rolling budgets.[28]

An organization is an open system that must successfully adapt to its environment to survive and prosper. The firm's adaptation process and business strategy are influenced by its operating environment, which includes market structure, government regulation, and supply-and-demand relationships. New global markets are providing sales opportunities but these markets are also creating pricing and quality pressures for domestic firms.

What is the importance of the budgeting process?

Planning is the process of setting goals and objectives and translating them into activities and resources required for their accomplishment within a specified time horizon. Budgeting is the quantification of a company's financial plans and activities. Budgets facilitate communication, coordination, and teamwork. A budget is the primary basis and justification for financial operations in a firm. Implementing and administering a budget are parts of the coordination and control functions. A well-prepared budget provides the following benefits:

a. Detailed path for managers to follow to achieve organizational goals
b. Improved planning and decision making
c. Allocation of resources among departments
d. Better understanding of key business variables
e. Recognition of departmental interrelationships
f. A means of employee participation and influence
g. A means to determine troublesome or hard-to-control cost areas
h. A means of responding more rapidly to changing economic conditions
i. A means by which managerial performance can be judged

What is the difference between strategic and tactical planning and how do these relate to the budgeting process?

Strategic planning is not concerned with day-to-day operations, although the strategic plan will be the foundation on which short-term planning is based. Managers engaging in strategic planning should identify key variables, or critical factors believed potentially to be direct causes of the achievement or nonachievement of organization goals and objectives. Tactical (or operational) planning is the process of determining the specific objectives and means by which strategic plans will be achieved. Although some tactical plans, such as corporate policy statements, exist for the long term and address repetitive situations, most tactical plans are short-term (1 to 18 months).

3 **What are the benefits and disadvantages of imposed budgets and participatory budgets?**

No single system of budgeting is right for all organizations. There are basically two ways by which budgets can be derived: from the top down (imposed budgets) or from the bottom up (participatory budgets). In either case senior management is responsible for assuring that the budget is attainable and acceptable. A participatory budget is one that has been developed through a process of joint decision making by senior management and operating personnel and ensures buy-in by all involved. Imposed budgets cause dissatisfaction, stifle the initiative of lower-level managers, and result in limited acceptance of the stated goals and objectives of lower-level managers. A full list of the advantages and disadvantages of both types of budgets is covered on pages 305 and 306.

4 **What is a flexible budget?**

A flexible budget is a series of financial plans detailing the individual cost factors that comprise total cost and presenting those costs at different levels of activity. A flexible budget is simply a formula that permits the budgeted manufacturing costs to be determined for any activity level within the relative range of activity for which the behavioural classification of costs is valid.

5 **What complicates the budgeting process in a multinational environment?**

As an organization becomes more complex, so does the budgeting process. When an organization reaches multinational status, participatory budgeting is not simply desired, it becomes necessary for the effort to be effective. In a multinational environment, an organization faces an almost unlimited number of external variables that can affect the planning process, for example, the effects of foreign currency exchange rates, interest rates, inflation, inventory transfer price implications, and so forth. Budget preparation must incorporate a thorough understanding of local market conditions, including all known external forces and estimates of potential economic and market changes.

6 **What is the starting point of a master budget and how do the components relate to one another?**

A master budget is a comprehensive set of projections (pro forma financial statements and their supporting schedules) for a specific budget period. It is composed of operating and financial budgets and is usually detailed by quarters and months.

Because of its fundamental importance in the budgeting process for implementing strategy, demand must be predicted as accurately and with as many details as possible. Sales forecasts must indicate type and quantity of products to be sold, geographic locations of the sales, types of buyers, and points in time at which the sales are to be made. Such detail is necessary because different products require different production and distribution facilities; different customers have different credit terms and payment schedules; and different seasons or months may necessitate different shipping schedules or methods.

Sales demand is the proper starting point for the master budget. Once sales demand is determined, managers forecast revenues, production costs, and cash flows for the firm's activities for the upcoming period. These expectations reflect the firm's input and output of resources and are used in preparing the master budget.

Various organizational departments interact with each other and the budget for one department may form the basis of or have an effect on the budgets in other departments. The production department's production budget is predicated on sales demand provided by the sales department. The production budget then influences the purchasing department's budget as well as the treasurer's budgeting of cash flows and accounts payable management. Sales also affect cash flows and the selling and administrative expense budget.

After the master budget and all of its pro forma financial statements have been developed, they can and should be used for a variety of purposes. They help managers determine if their plans will provide the desired results, in terms of both net income and cash flow. Inadequate results should cause a re-evaluation of the objectives that have been set, and appropriate changes should be made.

How does traditional budgeting differ from zero-based budgeting?

Traditional budgeting is based on the prior year's activities and decisions are made in the budgeting process about whether and by what percentage to incrementally raise existing appropriations. Zero-based budgeting is a comprehensive budgeting process that systematically considers the priorities and alternatives for current programs and proposed activities relative to organizational objectives. It requires annual justification for those programs and activities, and requires that managers rethink priorities. It is a rigorous exercise that demands considerable time and effort. Zero-based budgeting does not, however, provide measures of efficiency, and it is difficult to implement because of the significant amount of effort necessary to investigate the causes of prior costs and justify the purposes of budgeted costs.

What are future perspectives for budgeting?

In recent years, despite the general and long-term acceptance of budgeting as an integral part of management, a movement has developed among many major firms to discontinue budgeting. Today's businesses need to use planning and budgeting processes as a strategic tool in maintaining a long-term competitive advantage. Budgets have to be aligned to strategies and effective strategic planning and management processes have to be introduced. A company's main goal in a planning and budgeting system is to devise a seamless, faster system of top-down planning and budgeting that links performance to strategic vision.[29] The Beyond Budgeting Round Table (BBRT) recommended that traditional budgeting be replaced with an alternative that includes the use of an enterprise resource planning system (ERP) that allows all parts of the organization to be tied together via information.

Clearly, creating a budget is under attack. In addition to promoting gamesmanship among managers, key criticisms include the lack of linkage with firm strategy, and high cost and inefficiency. While the debate will continue to rage in both corporate boardrooms and academic circles, the reality is that the annual budget is not going to disappear anytime soon.[30]

Key Terms

Appropriation (p. 335)	**Imposed budget** (p. 304)
Budget (p. 300)	**Key variable** (p. 303)
Budget committee (p. 321)	**Master budget** (p. 319)
Budgeting (p. 301)	**Operating budget** (p. 319)
Budget manual (p. 309)	**Participatory budget** (p. 304)
Budget slack (p. 306)	**Static budget** (p. 312)
Capital budgeting (p. 326)	**Strategic planning** (p. 303)
Continuous budget (p. 307)	**Tactical planning** (p. 303)
Financial budget (p. 319)	**Zero-based budgeting** (p. 336)
Flexible budget (p. 311)	

Points to Remember

Budget Manual

Should include
1. Statements of the budgetary purpose and its desired results
2. A listing of specific budgetary activities to be performed
3. A calendar of scheduled budgetary activities
4. Sample budgetary forms
5. Original, revised, and approved budgets

Sales Budget

    Units of sales
$\times$ Selling price per unit
= Dollars of sales

Production Budget

    Units of sales
+ Units desired in ending inventory
− Units in beginning inventory
= Units to be produced

Direct Materials Purchases Budget

    Units to be produced
+ Ending inventory in units
= Total whole unit quantities needed
− Beginning inventory in units
= Purchases required in whole unit quantities
$\times$ Appropriate quantity measure of input material
= Quantity of input material needed
$\times$ Price per unit measure of input quantity
= Cost of purchases

Direct Labour Budget

    Direct labour hours required for production
$\times$ Wages per hour
= Cost of direct labour compensation

Overhead Budget

    Predicted activity base
$\times$ VOH rate per unit of activity
= Total variable overhead cost
+ Fixed overhead cost
= Total overhead cost

Selling and Administrative Budget

    Predicted sales dollars (or other variable measure)
$\times$ Variable selling and administrative rate per dollar (or other variable measure)
= Total variable selling and administrative cost
+ Fixed selling and administrative cost
= Total selling and administrative cost

Schedule of Cash Collections (for sales on account)

Dollars of credit sales for month
× Percent collection for month of sale
= Credit to Accounts Receivable for month's sales
− Sales discounts allowed and taken
= Receipts for current month's sales
+ Current month's cash receipts for prior months' sales
= Cash receipts for current month

Schedule of Cash Payments (for purchases on account)

Total cost of purchases
× Percent payment for current purchases
= Debit to Accounts Payable for month's purchases
− Purchase discounts taken
= Cash payments for current month's purchases
+ Current month's payments for prior months' purchases
= Cash payments for Accounts Payable for current month

Cash Budget

Beginning cash balance
+ Cash receipts
= Cash available for disbursements
− Cash needed for disbursements:
    Cash payments for Accounts Payable for month
    Cost of compensation
    Total cost of overhead less depreciation
    Total selling general and administrative cost less depreciation
= Cash excess or deficiency
− Minimum desired cash balance
= Cash needed or available for investment or financing

= Cash excess or deficiency
+ Various financing amounts
= Ending cash balance

DEMONSTRATION PROBLEM

The balance sheet of Linda Geraldine Cosmetics Ltd. at April 30, 2008, includes the following:

Cash	$ 25,000 debit
Accounts Receivable	100,800 debit
Allowance for Uncollectible Accounts	2,240 credit
Merchandise Inventory	21,000 debit

John Snow, the company CEO, has designated $25,000 as the firm's monthly minimum cash balance. Other information about the firm follows:

- Revenues of $280,000 and $336,000 are expected for May and June, respectively. All goods are sold on account.
- The collection pattern for Accounts Receivable is 55% in the month of sale, 44% in the month following the sale, and 1% uncollectible.

- Cost of Goods Sold approximates 60% of sales revenue.
- Management's desired ending balance of Merchandise Inventory is 10% of that month's budgeted sales.
- All Accounts Payable are for inventory and are paid in the month of purchase.
- Other monthly expenses are $37,800, which includes $2,800 of depreciation but does not include bad debt expense.
- Borrowings or investments can only be made in $5,000 amounts. Interest will be paid at the rate of 10% per year; interest will be earned at the rate of 8% per year.

Required:

a.   Forecast the May cash collections.
b.   Forecast the May and June cost of purchases.
c.   Prepare the cash budget for May including the effects of financing (borrowing or investing).

Solution to Demonstration Problem

a.
	May Collections
From April ($100,800 − $2,240)	$ 98,560
From May ($280,000 × 0.55)	154,000
Total	$252,560

b.
	May	**June**
Sales	$280,000	$336,000
Cost of goods (60%)	$168,000	$201,600
Add: Desired ending inventory balance	16,800	20,160
Total purchases	$184,800	$221,760
Less: Beginning inventory balance	(21,000)	(16,800)
Cost of purchases	$163,800	$204,960

c.
	May Cash Budget		
Beginning cash balance		$ 25,000	
May collections		252,560	
Total cash available before financing		$277,560	
Disbursements:			
Purchases of merchandise	$163,800		
Other monthly expenses ($37,800 − $2,800)	35,000		
Total disbursements		(198,800)	
Cash excess (a)		$ 78,760	
Less: Minimum cash balance desired		(25,000)	$ 25,000
Cash available		$ 53,760	
Financing: Acquire investment (b)		(50,000)	3,760
Ending cash balance (c); (c = a − b)			$ 28,760

End-of-Chapter Materials

SELF-TEST QUESTIONS

(SOLUTIONS APPEAR AT THE END OF THE CHAPTER.)

1. Orion Corporation is preparing a cash budget for the six months beginning January 1, 2008. Shown below is the company's historical collection pattern:
   - 65% collected in month of sale
   - 20% collected in the first month after sale
   - 10% collected in the second month after sale
   - 4% collected in the third month after sale
   - 1% uncollectible

   Budgeted credit sales for the period are as follows:

   January, $160,000; February, $185,000; March, $190,000; April, $170,000.

   The estimated total cash collections during April from accounts receivable would be:
   a. $154,900   d. $173,400
   b. $167,000   e. $176,200
   c. $171,666

Use the following information to answer Questions 2 and 3.

Phyllis Abbott Ltd. manufactures an animated rabbit with moving parts and a built-in voice box. Projected sales in units for the next five months are as follows:

Month	Projected Sales in Units
January	30,000
February	36,000
March	33,000
April	40,000
May	29,000

Each rabbit requires basic materials that Abbott purchases from a single supplier at $3.50 per rabbit. Voice boxes are purchased from another supplier for $1.00 each. Assembly labour cost is $2.00 per rabbit and variable overhead cost is $0.50 per rabbit.

Fixed manufacturing overhead applicable to rabbit production is $12,000 per month. Abbott's policy is to manufacture 1.5 times the coming month's projected sales every **other** month (i.e., odd-numbered months) starting with January for February sales, and to manufacture 0.5 times the coming month's projected sales in alternate months. This allows Abbott to allocate limited manufacturing resources to other products as needed during the even-numbered months.

2. The unit production budget for animated rabbits for January is:
   a. 45,000 units   d. 14,500 units
   b. 16,500 units   e. 60,000 units
   c. 54,000 units

3. The dollar production budget for animated rabbits for February is:
   a. $327,000   d. $127,500
   b. $390,000   e. $432,000
   c. $113,500

4. Which one of the following is the last schedule to be prepared in the normal budget preparation process?
   a. Cash budget
   b. Cost of goods sold budget
   c. Direct labour budget
   d. Manufacturing overhead budget
   e. Selling expense budget

   (Self-Test Questions 1–4 are IMA adapted.)

5. Losell Co. has budgeted sales of 42,000 units for the upcoming three months, from January 1 to March 31. The company has 22,000 units of finished goods on hand in opening inventory and would like to have 24,000 units on hand at March 31. It requires three litres of raw material to produce one litre of finished goods. Opening inventory is 90,000 litres of raw materials and the target ending inventory is 110,000 litres. How many litres must Losell purchase in the period from January 1 to March 31?
   a. 44,000 litres   c. 152,000 litres
   b. 132,000 litres   d. 200,000 litres

6. The total master budget variance for Jag Corp. for the month of November was $7,000 U. The total flexible budget variance was $3,000 U. The actual results for the month showed net operating income of $3,000. What amount of operating income (loss) would the flexible budget have shown for November?
   a. $(4,000)   c. $6,000
   b. $4,000   d. $(10,000)

7. The following data were collected by Bold 'N' Beauty Co. for the month of May:

   Master budget data:

Sales	9,000 units @ $30
Variable costs	$23 per unit
Total fixed costs	$18,800

   Actual results:

Sales	9,600 units @$29
Variable costs	$24 per unit
Total fixed costs	$18,200

   Self-Test Questions 5 and 7 are an extract from *Management Accounting 1 Examination*, published by the Certified General Accountants Association of Canada (© CGA-Canada 2003). Reprinted with permission.

What was the May variance from the master budget operating income?

a. $14,400 F   c. $29,800 U
b. $14,400 U   d. $44,200 F

Use the following information to answer Questions 8 and 9.

Sally Spectra Co. makes and sells T-shirts. Each T-shirt requires three metres of Material A. Budgeted production for the next three months is as follows:

August	14,000 units
September	15,500 units
October	11,900 units

The company wants to maintain monthly ending inventories of Material A equal to 20% of the following month's production needs. On July 31, 2,000 metres of Material A were on hand. The cost of Material A is $0.80 per metre. The company wishes to prepare a direct materials budget for the last quarter.

8. What is the total cost of Material A that should be purchased in August?

a. $34,320
b. $39,440
c. $42,900
d. $49,300

9. What is the desired ending inventory of Material A for the month of September?

a. 3,100 metres
b. 7,140 metres
c. 8,400 metres
d. 9,300 metres

Self-Test Questions 8 and 9 are an extract from *Management Accounting 1 Examination*, published by the Certified General Accountants Association of Canada (© CGA-Canada 2000). Reprinted with permission.

10. Zero-based budgeting is used for:

a. Production costs
b. Engineering costs
c. Overhead costs
d. Future costs

QUESTIONS

1. Why is budgeting important? Briefly describe the basic budgeting process. Which steps do you consider to be the most critical?

2. When are imposed budgets appropriate? Why?

3. Why do most organizations use participatory budgets? Discuss the disadvantages of using such budgets.

4. Define *budget slack*. Why does it occur, and what might be done to reduce or eliminate it?

5. What does the sales price variance measure? What does the sales volume variance measure? Collectively, what do the sales price and sales volume variances explain?

6. Why should cost variances be based on actual volume of sales rather than budgeted volume of sales?

7. What is a continuous budget? Why would a company use a continuous budget?

8. Why is it important to put organizational plans in written form? List the sections of a budget manual and briefly explain the role of each section.

9. Why is the master budget said to be a static budget? Why is it necessary for the master budget to be static?

10. What is a flexible budget? When using a flexible budget, how does fixed cost per unit change as production increases within the relevant range? variable cost per unit?

11. Why is the sales budget the first of the operating budgets prepared?

12. Explain the purposes of the production budget. How is this budget influenced by the firm's inventory policies?

13. What are the primary inputs in the determination of the purchases budget?

14. What source documents would likely be used to compile a direct labour budget?

15. Explain the importance of the cash budget. How are cash collections from sales determined? What part do cash collections play in the budgeting process?

16. How do a firm's credit terms for credit sales affect the pattern for cash collections? Why would a firm give a discount for early payment? Why would a firm wish to maintain a minimum cash balance?

17. Give some examples of items included in the financing section of a cash flow statement and their cash flow effects.

18. Why would it be desirable to prepare the master budget using a spreadsheet program and link the individual budgets?

19. What is zero-based budgeting? Why do you think it began in the governmental sector rather than in the business sector?

20. What is the name of the group that is pursuing the elimination of budgets, or seriously trying to change the way in which budgeting is practised? What are some examples of how budgeting has failed its users?

EXERCISES

1. (LO 1, 3, 4, 7) Match the numbered item on the right with the lettered term on the left.

a. Budget committee
b. Budgeting
c. Imposed budget
d. Budget
e. Participatory budget
f. Appropriation
g. Zero-based budgeting

1. Developed through joint decision making by senior managers and operating personnel
2. A quantitative expression of commitment to planned activities and resource acquisition and use
3. Prepared by senior managers with little or no input from operating personnel
4. Reviews, adjusts, and approves the master budget and/or budgets submitted by operational managers
5. Developing a quantitative plan in financial terms to satisfy company goals and objectives
6. Systematically (re)considers current or proposed activities in light of priorities and alternatives for achievement of organizational goals and objectives
7. Maximum allowable expenditure for an item in the budget

2. (LO 3) Senior management has asked for your assistance in trying to determine the advantages of imposed and participatory budgets and has suggested a number of goals it would like to achieve in whatever type of budget it might choose. Indicate whether each of the following is an advantage of an imposed budget (AI), an advantage of a participatory budget (AP), or neither (N).
a. Develops fiscal responsibility and budgetary skills of operating personnel
b. Blends overview of senior management with operating details
c. Reduces budgeting to entering data into a computer program
d. Increases chances that strategic plans will be incorporated into planned activities
e. Allows operating managers to take over the budgeting process completely
f. Incorporates senior management's knowledge of overall resource availability
g. Produces more realistic budgets
h. Improves morale and motivation
i. Encourages operating managers to establish long-run company goals
j. Incorporates inputs from persons most familiar with the needs and constraints of organizational units

EXERCISES

3. (LO 4) Kitchen Care Inc. (KCI) is a manufacturer of toaster-ovens. To improve control over operations, the president of KCI wants to install a flexible budgeting system, rather than only the single master budget being used presently. The following data is available for KCI's expected costs for production levels of 90,000, 100,000 and 110,000 units.

    Variable costs:

Manufacturing	$6.00/unit
Administrative	3.00/unit
Selling	1.00/unit

    Fixed costs:

Manufacturing	$ 150,000
Administrative	80,000

    Required:
    a. Prepare a flexible budget for each of the 90,000, 100,000, and 110,000 unit possible production levels.
    b. If KCI sells the toaster-ovens for $15.00 each, calculate the number of units it will have to sell to make a profit of $250,000. Ignore income taxes.

    Extract from *Management Accounting Examination*, published by the Certified General Accountants Association of Canada (© CGA-Canada 2002). Reprinted with permission.

4. (LO 4) Seinfeld does wedding photography on weekends. He had been charging $225 for a complete album, and his costs averaged $78 each. He believed he could book 30 weddings in 2011, and on that basis he prepared the following budget:

Revenue (30 × $225)	$6,750
Costs (30 × $78)	2,340
Projected profits	$4,410

    In 2011, Seinfeld was contemplating his results and was disappointed that his profits were only $4,256. He asks for your help in understanding the shortfall. Review of his journal shows that his fee averaged $218 per wedding and that his costs averaged $85. Seinfeld photographed 32 weddings in 2011.

    Required:
    Explain to Seinfeld why he made less than he budgeted.

5. (LO 4) Monk Ltd.'s predetermined total manufacturing overhead rate for product costing purposes is $23 per unit. Of this amount, $18 is the variable portion. Cost information for two levels of activity follows:

Overhead Components	800 Units	1,200 Units
Indirect materials	$4,000	$6,000
Indirect labour	5,600	8,400
Handling	2,600	3,800
Maintenance	800	1,200
Utilities	2,000	2,800
Supervision	4,000	4,000

    Required:
    a. Determine the fixed and variable values for each of the preceding components of manufacturing overhead and determine the total manufacturing overhead cost formula.
    b. What is the company's planned volume level if the predetermined rate is based on expected capacity?
    c. Determine the budgeted factory overhead costs at the expected capacity level.
    d. Monk Ltd.'s management decides to raise its expected capacity level 80 units over the present level. Determine the new total predetermined manufacturing overhead rate for product costing purposes.

6. (LO 4) Judith Poë Training Ltd. delivers two-day statistical process control seminars for manufacturing workers. The fee for each program amounts to $4,000. Last year Judith presented 30 seminars, and she budgeted a 20% increase in programs for the current year. At the end of the current year, she is disappointed that her actual revenue is only $136,500. She presented 39 programs during the year. She is puzzled by this and wants answers to the following:

    Required:
    a. What was her expected revenue for the current year?
    b. Why was the budgeted revenue not achieved?

EXERCISES

7. (LO 6) Vicki Gabereau Company has budgeted its third-quarter unit sales for 2011 as follows:

July	8,000
August	10,000
September	11,000

The company desires an ending inventory equal to 8% of budgeted sales of the following month. October's sales are expected to be 12,000 units.

Required:

As manager of production, prepare a third-quarter production budget by month and in total.

8. (LO 6) Alison Ground Electronics has projected quarterly sales of electric motors for the year 2011 as follows:

First quarter	200,000
Second quarter	150,000
Third quarter	250,000
Fourth quarter	180,000

The firm expects to begin fiscal 2008 with 80,000 motors. Desired ending balances are to be 40% of the subsequent quarter's sales. Sales in the first quarter of 2011 are expected to be 220,000 motors.

Required:

a. Prepare a production budget by quarter and in total for the year 2008.

b. Explain how the firm might benefit by reducing the level of finished goods inventories carried.

9. (LO 6) Shearer Fins Ltd. expects to sell 15,200 pairs of swim fins during June. Two kilograms of rubber are required to make each pair. The company's June 1 opening inventory includes 3,300 pairs of fins and 10,200 kilograms of rubber. The company wishes to end June with 7,200 pairs of fins and 16,000 kilograms of rubber. Because fins can be made very quickly from heated rubber, the firm does not maintain any work-in-process inventory.

Required:

How much rubber should Shearer Fins Ltd. budget to buy for June?

10. (LO 7) Lawrence Chung Metals Ltd. expects to sell 74,000 units of its major product in April 2011. Each unit requires two kilograms of material A and five kilograms of material B. Material A costs $4.80 per kilogram, and material B costs $2.10 per kilogram. Expected beginning and ending inventories are as follows:

	April 1	April 30
Finished goods (units)	4,000	6,300
Material A (kilograms)	4,000	4,900
Material B (kilograms)	6,100	6,000

Required:

a. How many kilograms of material A does Lawrence Chung Metals Ltd. plan to purchase in April? What is the expected cost of those purchases?

b. How many kilograms of material B does Lawrence Chung Metals Ltd. plan to purchase in April? What is the expected cost of those purchases?

c. Briefly describe how improved raw materials inventory management could reduce the level of raw materials inventories carried.

11. (LO 6) Rochelle Gordon Inc. wants to estimate the cost of manufacturing overhead in the master budget. Overhead is a mixed cost with the following flexible budget formula: $y = \$320,000 + \$14.25x$, where x represents machine hours. The fixed overhead includes $35,000 of depreciation.

Required:

a. Calculate the overhead cost assuming Rochelle Gordon Inc. plans to incur 12,000 machine hours for the coming year.

b. Determine how much cash will be spent for overhead if the company incurs the 12,000 machine hours.

12. (LO 6) Forrest Creations Ltd. is experiencing difficulty in estimating cash collections for the second quarter of 2011 and has asked you, its consultant, for help. Inspection of records and documents reveals the following sales information:

February	March	April	May	June
$252,000	$232,000	$248,000	$292,000	$272,000

Analysis of past collection patterns has helped management to develop the following information:

- 30% of each month's sales are for cash, with no discount.
- Of the credit sales, 50% are collected in the month of sale; all customers paying during this time are given a 2% discount.
- 40% of credit sales are collected in the month following the sale.
- 10% of credit sales are collected in the second month after the sale. Bad debts are negligible and should be ignored.
- Forrest Creations Ltd.'s Accounts Receivable balance at April 1 is estimated at $98,840.

Required:

a. Prepare a schedule of cash received from sales for each month in the second quarter (April to June 2011).

b. Calculate the Accounts Receivable balance at the end of the second quarter.

13. (LO 6) Joanne Steinman Consulting Ltd.'s records revealed an Accounts Receivable balance of $194,000 at June 1. Analysis shows that $140,000 of this balance remains from May billings. June billings are expected to be $210,000. The company's pattern of collections is 30% in the month of billing for services, 40% in the month following the service, 29% in the second month following the service, and 1% uncollectible. No write-off of bad debts has been made for April or May billings.

Required:

a. What were the April billings?

b. What amount of the May billings is expected to be uncollectible?

c. What are the projected cash collections in June?

d. Prepare a brief report to Joanne Steinman's managers describing how they might change their credit policies to collect credit sales sooner.

e. What types of information should be gathered before making a decision to change a credit policy?

14. (LO 6) Wilf Blitzer Inc. expects sales of $400,000, $300,000, and $360,000 for January, February, and March, respectively. Blitzer has determined the following collection profile from its sales, all of which are on account:

Collections from:

Current month's sales	22%
Prior month's sales	60%
Second month after sale	14%
Uncollectible accounts	4%

A bank loan is due in March, so Blitzer's managers want you, their accountant, to be sure that they have done a good job of predicting collections.

Required:

a. How much cash can Blitzer expect to collect in March?

b. Write a brief report to Blitzer's managers describing actions they might take to reduce the level of uncollectible accounts.

15. (LO 6) Dan Ondrack Tennis Ltd. is trying to budget the November cash payments for Accounts Payable. Management believes that, of a given month's purchases, 40% are paid in the month of purchase, and a 2% discount is given on one-half of what is paid in that month. The remaining 60% are paid in the following month. Expected unit purchases for October and November are 91,200 and 68,300, respectively. The cost per unit is $3.80. As Ondrack's consultant, you have been asked to provide the following answers.

Required:

a. What are expected cash payments for purchases on account in November?

b. If Ondrack expects a temporary cash shortage in November, what actions might managers take with respect to its creditors to address the cash shortage?

EXERCISES

16. (LO 6) Rose Reed Factory Ltd. manufactures two products—chairs and stools. Each chair requires three metres of upholstery and four kilograms of steel. Each stool requires two metres of upholstery and five kilograms of steel. Upholstery costs $2 per metre and steel costs $0.25 per kilogram.

Inventories at January 1 are expected to be:

Chairs	Stools	Upholstery	Steel
25 units	15 units	75 metres	150 kilograms

Inventories of raw materials should not be allowed to fall below the figures given as at January 1. Inventories of finished furniture at the beginning of each month should be sufficient to cover 25% of the anticipated sales for that month. Upholstery is ordered in units of 100 metres and steel in units of 50 kilograms.

Half of the materials purchased are paid for in the month of purchase and the other half in the following month.

The sales budget for the first three months of fiscal 2008 is:

	January	February	March
Chairs	100 units	120 units	80 units
Stools	60 units	80 units	60 units

Required:

Calculate the cash disbursements in February related to purchases of steel. Show all your supporting calculations.

Extract from *Management Accounting 1 Examination*, published by the Certified General Accountants Association of Canada (© CGA-Canada 1999). Reprinted with permission.

17. (LO 6) Bold Enterprises Ltd. expects to begin fiscal 2011 with a cash balance of $10,000. Cash collections from sales on account are expected to be $468,600. The firm wants to maintain a minimum cash balance of $4,000. It will have notes payable of $45,600, and the interest on the notes will be $4,200. Cash disbursements are projected as follows:

Purchase of computer system	14,800
Payments on account for operating costs and purchases	90,000
Direct labour payments	100,000
Overhead payments	127,000
Selling and administrative payments	93,000

Required:

As assistant to Bold Enterprises' financial vice-president, you have been asked to prepare the 2011 cash budget in good form.

18. (LO 6) The controller of Newman Enterprises wishes to improve the company's control system by preparing a month-by-month cash budget. The following information relates to the month of July.

June 30 cash balance	$45,000
Dividends to be declared on July 15*	12,000
Cash expenditures to be paid in July for operating expenses	36,800
Amortization expense in July	4,500
Cash collections to be received in July	89,000
Merchandise purchases to be paid in cash in July	56,200
Equipment to be purchased for cash in July	20,500

*Dividends are payable to shareholders of record on declaration date, 30 days after declaration.

Newman Enterprises wishes to maintain a minimum cash balance of $25,000.

Required:

a. Prepare a cash budget for the month ended July 31 and indicate how much, if anything, Newman Enterprises will need to borrow to meet its minimum cash requirement.

b. Explain how cash budgeting can reduce the cost of short-term borrowing.

Extract from *Management Accounting 1 Examination*, published by the Certified General Accountants Association of Canada (© CGA-Canada 2003). Reprinted with permission.

EXERCISES

19. (LO 6) Maria Bartiromo Supplies Ltd. is trying to complete preparation of its master budget. The firm provides you, its management accountant, with the following expected data:

Work in Process Inventory—January 1	$ 9,200
Work in Process Inventory—December 31	3,300
Direct Material Inventory—January 1	2,300
Direct Material Inventory—December 31	5,200
Purchases of direct material—from purchases budget	287,700
Direct labour—from human resources compensation budget	106,700
Manufacturing overhead—from manufacturing overhead budget	115,500

Required:

Prepare a pro forma cost of goods manufactured statement.

20. (LO 7) Describe some alternative procedures to budgeting where control is exercised but the inherent bureaucracy of traditional budgeting is eliminated.

PROBLEMS

1. (LO 3) Match the numbered possible causes on the right with the lettered problems on the left in assessing poor performance (more than one numbered cause may be appropriately matched with a problem, and a cause can be used more than once).

a.	Compensation cost higher than expected	1.	Shortage in supply of direct materials was greater than expected
b.	Sales volume less than expected	2.	Increased rate for fringe benefits, insurance, or utilities
c.	Severe cash flow difficulties	3.	Increase in labour contract rates or minimum wage law
d.	Overhead cost higher than expected		
e.	Production cannot keep up with demand	4.	Recessionary economic conditions
		5.	Inflation
f.	Selling expense higher than expected	6.	Declining collection patterns
		7.	Operations are at a maximum capacity
g.	Direct materials cost higher than expected	8.	Advertising rates increased
h.	Interest cost higher than expected		

2. (LO 3) Match the numbered descriptions on the right with the lettered names of budget games on the left.

	Name of Game		**Description**
a.	It-Wasn't-My-Fault	1.	Trying to increase the bottom line without regard to reducing customer satisfaction and subsequent sales returns
b.	It's-Not-in-the-Budget		
c.	The Accounting Change		
d.	Build-a-Kingdom		
e.	Sell-It-No-Matter-What	2.	Imposed budgeting with no room for discussion
f.	The Dictator		
g.	Father-Knows-Best	3.	Mandated across-the-board cuts without opportunity to justify selected increases and decreases
h.	Cut-Everything-10-Percent		
i.	Spend-It-or-Lose-It		
j.	Do-What-You-Want	4.	Inputs by operating personnel are encouraged but subsequently ignored
		5.	Worthwhile projects are rejected, and manager is later blamed for low performance because the project was not adequately justified
		6.	Changing accounting methods to influence calculated net income
		7.	Shifting blame for failure to achieve budget to someone else or something else

PROBLEMS

8. Pushing for larger budgets to gain power
9. Withholding support information; allowing a subordinate manager to undertake budgetary projects that are probably destined to fail
10. Spending everything left at end of period in a budget so that next period's budget will not be reduced

3. (LO 3) An effective budget converts the objectives and goals of management into data. The budget often serves as a blueprint that represents management's plan for operating the business.

The budget frequently is the basis for control. Management performance can be evaluated by comparing actual results with the budget. Thus, creating the budget is essential for the successful operation of an organization.

Finding the resources to implement the budget (i.e., the process of getting from a starting point to the ultimate goal) requires the extensive use of human resources. The manner in which the people involved perceive their roles in the budget operation is important to the successful use of the budget as an effective management tool for planning, communicating, and controlling.

Required:
a. Discuss the behavioural implications on budgetary planning and budgetary control when a company's management employs:
   i. an imposed budgetary approach
   ii. a participative budgetary approach
b. Communication plays an important part in the budget operation whether an imposed or participatory budgetary approach is used.
   i. Describe the differences between the communication flows in these two budgetary approaches.
   ii. Discuss the behavioural implications on the communication process for each of these budgetary approaches.

(IMA 1983 Question 8)

4. (LO 4) Dixie Reed Ltd. employs flexible budgeting techniques to evaluate the performance of several of its activities. The selling expense flexible budgets for three representative monthly activity levels are shown below:

Representative Monthly Flexible Budgets for Selling Expenses

Activity Measures:			
Unit sales volume	400,000	425,000	450,000
Dollar sales volume	$10,000,000	$10,625,000	$11,250,000
Number of orders	4,000	4,250	4,500
Number of salespersons	75	75	75
Monthly Expenses:			
Advertising and promotion	$ 1,200,000	$ 1,200,000	$ 1,200,000
Administrative salaries	57,000	57,000	57,000
Sales salaries	75,000	75,000	75,000
Sales commissions	200,000	212,500	225,000
Salesperson travel	170,000	175,000	180,000
Sales office expenses	490,000	498,750	507,500
Shipping expenses	675,000	712,500	750,000
Total selling expenses	$ 2,867,000	$ 2,930,750	$ 2,004,500

The following assumptions were used to develop the selling expense flexible budgets.
• The average size of Dixie Reed's salesforce during the year was planned to be 75 people.
• Salespersons are paid a monthly salary plus commission on gross dollar sales.
• The travel cost is best characterized as a step variable cost. The fixed portion is related to the number of salespersons while the variable portion tends to fluctuate with gross dollar sales.

PROBLEMS

- Sales office expenses are a mixed cost with the variable portion related to the number of orders processed.
- Shipping expenses are a mixed cost with the variable portion related to the number of units sold.

A salesforce of 80 persons generated a total of 4,300 orders resulting in a sales volume of 420,000 units during November. The gross dollar sales amounted to $10.9 million. The selling expenses incurred for November were as follows:

Advertising and promotion	$1,350,000
Administrative salaries	57,000
Sales salaries	80,000
Sales commissions	218,000
Salesperson travel	185,000
Sales office expense	497,200
Shipping expense	730,000
Total	$3,117,200

Required:
a. Explain why flexible budgeting is a useful management tool.
b. Explain why the selling expense flexible budgets presented on page 357 would not be appropriate for evaluating Dixie Reed Ltd.'s November selling expenses, and indicate how the flexible budget would have to be revised.
c. Prepare a selling expense report for November that Dixie Reed Ltd. can use to evaluate its control over selling expenses. The report should have a line for each selling expense item showing the appropriate budgeted amount, the actual selling expense, and the monthly dollar variation.

(IMA 4–29 Page 257 December 1982 #2)

5. (LO 6) During November, the following forecasted sales figures were presented to the management of Mark Haines Manufacturing Ltd.

	January	February	March	Total	April
Sales in units	36,000	32,000	30,000	98,000	28,000

The following are estimates of finished units and direct material in kilograms at various times:

	December 31	January 31	February 28	March 31
Finished units	9,000	8,000	7,500	7,000
Direct material M	6,750	6,000	5,625	5,250
Direct material N	4,500	4,000	3,750	3,500
Direct material O	9,000	8,000	7,500	7,000

The production process requires three kilograms of material M, two kilograms of material N, and four kilograms of material O. You have just been hired as chief accountant and have been assigned to address the following company needs:

Required:
a. Prepare a monthly production and purchases budget for the first quarter (January–March).
b. The company is considering the installation of new production equipment before the fiscal year. Such equipment would largely replace the current labour-intensive production system. Write a memo to corporate management explaining why new production equipment could affect the production and purchases budgets.
c. If new production equipment is installed, who should be consulted to determine the new material requirements per unit?

6. (LO 6) Lilly Simon Reliable Tools Ltd. makes two products: saws and hammers. Estimated production needs for a unit of each product follow:

	Saws	Hammers
Steel (in kilograms)	2	4
Wood (in board feet)	0.5	0.2
Direct labour (in hours)	2	4
Machine hours	0.5	3

Overhead is applied to production at the rate of $16 per machine hour.

The estimated sales by product for 2008 are:

	Saws	Hammers
Sales (in units)	40,000	15,000

The estimated beginning and required ending inventories for 2008 are:

	Beginning	**Ending**
Steel (kilograms)	1,000	700
Wood (board feet)	400	300
Saws (units)	400	320
Hammers (units)	600	450

Lilly Simon, company president, has been preoccupied with astrology interests and has asked you, her company accountant, to assist her by addressing the following:

Required:
a.   Prepare the following budgets: production, purchases, direct labour hours (only), and overhead.
b.   What evidence exists to support the argument that this company uses modern methods to manage inventories of material and products?

7.   (LO 6) Lloyd Robertson Mercantile Ltd. expects its June Cost of Goods Sold to be $420,000. Included in this amount is $24,000 of fixed overhead. Total variable cost approximates 70% of sales. Lloyd Robertson's gross margin percentage averages 35% of sales, and net income averages 15% of sales. Depreciation is $7,000 per month. All other expenses and purchases are paid 60% in the month incurred and 40% in the following month. Lloyd Robertson purchases only enough goods to satisfy sales of any given month.

Required:
a.   Estimate Lloyd Robertson's expected June sales.
b.   Estimate Lloyd Robertson's expected variable selling and administrative costs for June.
c.   How much are Lloyd Robertson's total expected fixed costs for June?
d.   Lloyd Robertson Mercantile Ltd. normally collects 75% of its sales in the month of sale and 25% in the following month. Estimate cash collections and cash payments in June related only to June transactions.

8.   (LO 6) Ashley Abbott Furniture Co. makes bookcases. Sales quantities, sales dollars, and cash collections for the first quarter of 2011 are as follows:

	January	**February**	**March**	**Total**
Quantity (units)	6,400	5,200	7,400	19,000
Revenue	$73,600	$59,800	$85,100	$218,500
Collections	76,200	61,300	81,100	218,600

The December 31, 2010, estimated balance sheet contains the following balances: Cash, $18,320; Direct Material Inventory, $8,230; Finished Goods Inventory, $23,200; and Accounts Payable, $5,800. The Direct Material Inventory balance represents 2,000 kilograms of scrap iron and 3,200 bookcase bases. Finished Goods Inventory consists of 4,220 bookcases.

Each bookcase requires two kilograms of scrap iron, which costs $2 per kilogram. Bookcase bases are purchased from a local lumber mill at a cost of $1.80 per unit. Beginning in 2008, management asked that the ending balance of Direct Material Inventory be equal to 25% of the following month's production requirements. Management also stated that the ending balance of Finished Goods Inventory should be equal to 20% of the next month's sales. Sales for April and May are expected to be 8,000 bookcases per month.

The payment pattern for purchases is 75% in the month of purchase with a 1% discount. The remainder is paid in the next month with no discount.

Direct labour is budgeted at $0.70 per bookcase and out-of-pocket plant overhead runs $24,000 per month plus $1.30 per bookcase. Total monthly out-of-pocket period costs run $13,600 plus 10% of sales revenue. All out-of-pocket costs are paid in the month of incurrence, with the exception of material purchases, as discussed above.

Management requires a minimum cash balance of $15,000. The company has a policy of borrowing funds in multiples of $1,000 at the beginning of a month and repaying

PROBLEMS

borrowed funds in multiples of $1,000 plus interest at the end of a month at the rate of 12% per year.

The president, Ashley Abbott, has asked you, a newly hired staff accountant, to prepare the following items.

Required:

a. Monthly production budget for the first quarter of 2011
b. Monthly direct material purchases budget for the first quarter of 2011
c. Monthly schedule of cash payments for purchases for the first quarter of 2011
d. Combined payments schedule for manufacturing overhead and period costs on a monthly basis for the first quarter of 2011
e. Cash budget for each month and in total for the first quarter of 2011
f. Assume that you, as the new staff accountant, will be assigned to work on the materials purchasing budget. With whom are you likely to confirm the credit policies of the firm's vendors? Explain.

9. (LO 6) Margaret Connor Wholesale Appliances Ltd.'s April 30, balance sheet follows:

Assets		Liabilities and Shareholders' Equity	
Cash	$ 40,000	Accounts payable	$272,000
Accounts receivable (net of		Total liabilities	$272,000
$3,800 allowance for bad debts)	144,400		
Inventory	108,000		
Plant assets (net of $40,000		**Shareholders' Equity**	
of accumulated depreciation)	320,000	Common stock $120,000	
		Retained earnings 220,400	340,400
		Total liabilities and	
Total assets	$612,400	shareholders' equity	$612,400

Other information about the company follows:
• The company wants a minimum cash balance of $40,000.
• Revenues of $360,000 and $480,000 are expected for May and June 2008, respectively.
• The collection pattern is 60% in the month of sale, 38% in the next month, and 2% uncollectible.
• Cost of goods sold is 75% of sales.
• Purchases each month are 60% of the current month's sales and 40% of the following month's sales. All purchases are paid for in the month following the purchase.
• Other monthly expenses total $48,000. This amount includes $2,000 of depreciation but does not include bad debts expense.

Required:

a. May cash collections
b. May 31 inventory balance
c. May 31 retained earnings balance
d. May cash budget, including the amount available for investment or to be borrowed during May
e. Why would the firm want to maintain a minimum cash balance of $40,000? Who would set such a policy?

10. (LO 6) Jay Leno Jokes-for-Blokes is a wholesale distributor of joke books and humorous magazines. The company is preparing its budget for the first three months of the next year. At the end of that year, the following balances are estimated:

Accounts Receivable	$188,280
Inventory	52,875
Accounts Payable*	41,700
Other Payables	7,120

*For inventory purchases

Management has agreed on the following guidelines in preparing the budget:
Collections
• Credit sales are billed on the last day of each month.
• Cash customers and credit customers who pay by the 10th of the month after billing are allowed a 1% discount.

- 10% of sales are for cash. Of the credit sales, 10% are received within the discount period; another 40% are received during the rest of the month after billing; 40% are received in the second month after billing; and 10% are received in the third month after billing.

Payments

- 40% of purchases are paid for in the month of purchase. The rest are paid in the next month.
- Of the operating expenses incurred, 60% are paid in the month incurred and the remainder is paid in the next month.

Other Operating Statistics

- All sales are made at 200% of cost.
- Desired ending inventory is set at 75% of the following month's Cost of Goods Sold.
- Actual and projected sales are estimated at

October	$122,000
November	128,000
December	133,000
January	141,000
February	139,000
March	124,000
April	127,000

Selling and administrative expenses run 10% of sales plus $6,000 monthly. Included in the monthly selling and administrative expenses is $1,500 of depreciation.

Required:

a. Determine total monthly cash receipts for the first quarter.
b. Determine monthly purchases for the first quarter.
c. Determine monthly cash disbursements for the first quarter.

11. (LO 6) Baldwin's Fresh Fruit Stand purchases and retails fresh fruits and vegetables. Company estimates reveal the following for the first three fiscal months:

	Purchases	Sales
June	$66,000	$102,000
July	58,000	92,000
August	79,600	116,000

Management expects that May purchases and sales will be $80,000 and $120,000, respectively. The company usually pays 60% of any month's purchases in the month of purchase and takes an average 2% discount. The remaining amount is paid in the following month with no discount. Other monthly payments for expenses run $24,000 plus 12% of sales. Depreciation is $4,000 per month. The company wishes to maintain a minimum cash balance of $28,000 and expects to start May with $36,000 cash.

All retail sales are on credit. Overall, experience indicates the following expected collection pattern for sales: 25% in the month of sale, 60% in the month after the sale, and 15% in the second month after the sale. The company has no debt other than what is currently owed for purchases on account.

Required:

a. Calculate the July 31 balances for Accounts Receivable and Accounts Payable.
b. Calculate the cash collections expected in August.
c. Calculate the expected total cash disbursements in August.
d. Present a cash budget for August. Assume management wants no more cash on hand at August 31 than the minimum cash balance desired.
e. Prepare an income statement for August. Assume an average gross margin percentage of 40%. Ignore income taxes.
f. Explain how and why inventory management must be different for perishable commodities than for nonperishable commodities.

12. (LO 6) City Hospital provides a wide range of health services in its community. City Hospital's board of directors has authorized the following capital expenditures.

Inter-aortic balloon pump	$1,100,000
CT scanner	700,000
X-ray equipment	600,000
Laboratory equipment	1,400,000
	$3,800,000

PROBLEMS

The expenditures are planned for October 1, 2011, and the board wishes to know the amount of borrowing, if any, necessary on that date. Brian Mackie, Hospital Controller, has gathered the following information to be used in preparing an analysis of future cash flows.

- Billings, made in the month of service, for the first six months of 2011 are listed below.

Month	Actual Amount
January	$4,400,000
February	4,400,000
March	4,500,000
April	4,500,000
May	5,000,000
June	5,000,000

90% of City's billings are made to third parties such as Liberty Medical, provincial governments, and private insurance companies. The remaining 10% of the billings are made directly to patients. Historical patterns of billing collections are presented below.

	Third-Party Billings	Direct Patient Billings
Month of service	20%	10%
Month following service	50	40
Second month following service	20	40
Uncollectible	10	10

Estimated billings for the last six months of 2011 are listed next. The same billing and collection patterns that have been experienced during the first six months of 2011 are expected to continue during the last six months of the year.

Month	Estimated Amount
July	$4,500,000
August	5,000,000
September	5,500,000
October	5,700,000
November	5,800,000
December	5,500,000

- The purchases that have been made during the past three months and the planned purchases for the last six months of 2011 are presented in the following schedule.

Month	Estimated Amount
April	$1,100,000
May	1,200,000
June	1,200,000
July	1,250,000
August	1,500,000
September	1,850,000
October	1,950,000
November	2,250,000
December	1,750,000

All purchases are made on account, and accounts payable are remitted in the month following the purchase.

- Salaries for each month during the remainder of 2011 are expected to be $1,500,000 per month plus 20% of that month's billings. Salaries are paid in the month of service.
- City Hospital's monthly depreciation charges are $125,000.
- City Hospital incurs interest expense of $150,000 per month and makes interest payments of $450,000 on the last day of each calendar quarter.
- Endowment fund income is expected to continue to total $175,000 per month.
- City Hospital has a cash balance of $300,000 on July 1, 2011, and has a policy of maintaining end-of-month cash balance of 10% of the current month's purchases.
- City Hospital employs a calendar year reporting period.

Required:

Brian Mackie, the Hospital Controller, asks that you:

a. Prepare a pro forma schedule of cash receipts by month for the third quarter of 2011.

PROBLEMS

b.   Prepare a pro forma schedule of cash disbursements by month for the third quarter of 2011.

(IMA June 1984 #4)

13. (LO 6) The projected January 31, 2011, balance sheet for Lawrence Rubber Co. follows (all dollar amounts are in thousands):

Assets

Cash	$ 16,000
Accounts Receivable (net of allowance for uncollectible accounts of $4,000)	76,000
Inventory	32,000
Property, Plant, and Equipment (net)	70,000
Total Assets	$194,000

Liabilities and Shareholders' Equity

Accounts Payable	$165,000
Common Stock	100,000
Retained Earnings (deficit)	(71,000)
Total Liabilities and Shareholders' Equity	$194,000

Additional information:

* Sales are budgeted as follows:

February	$220,000
March	240,000

* Collections are expected to be 60% in the month of sale, 38% in the next month, and 2% uncollectible.
* The company's gross margin is projected at 25% of sales. Purchases each month are 75% of the next month's projected sales, and these are paid in full in the following month.
* Other expenses for each month, paid in cash, are expected to be $31,000. Monthly depreciation is $10,000.

Required:

a.   Prepare a pro forma income statement for February.

b.   Prepare a pro forma balance sheet for February.

c.   Describe any special problems this company may encounter because of its weak balance sheet. As a management accountant, recommend actions that the firm might take to improve the balance sheet.

14. (LO 6) The Josh Lyman Co. is a new company. The information below pertains to the operations of Lyman for the three months from January to March (that is, the first quarter, Q1) of 2011.

Expenses for Quarter 1

Depreciation	$40,000
Manufacturing overhead	10,000
Income taxes	15,000
Payroll	30,000
Selling costs (Commission: 2% of sales)	8,000
Administrative costs	10,000

Costs are assumed to be incurred evenly throughout the year with the exception of the following:

* Depreciation is taken on new assets starting in the quarter subsequent to the quarter in which the item was purchased.
* Income taxes are payable in half-yearly installments, on the first day of each six-month period, based on last year's actual tax expense of $30,000.

Other information:

i.   Sales (made evenly throughout the quarter)

Q1, actual	$400,000
Q2, forecast	400,000
Q3, forecast	800,000

  Collection from sales is as follows: 50% in the quarter of the sale; 45% in the quarter following; 5% uncollectible.

PROBLEMS

    ii. Purchases (made evenly throughout the quarter)

        Q1, actual $200,000

        Q2   ?

        Note that merchandise purchased during a quarter would equal inventory to meet the current quarter's sales demands plus 25% of the next quarter's forecasted sales. The gross margin ratio is constant at 60%.

        Cash payments for purchases are as follows: 50% in the quarter of purchase; 50% in the quarter thereafter.

    iii. The company purchased capital equipment in the amount of $100,000 in February 2011. The estimated useful life of this equipment is 10 years; estimated scrap value is $0. Dividends of $20,000 are declared on the last day of each quarter, to be paid at the end of the following month. Cash in the bank at the end of Q1 equals $25,000.

Required:

a. Prepare a cash budget for Lyman for Q2 of 2011. Show all your supporting calculations.

b. List three advantages of budgeting.

Extract from *Management Accounting Examination*, published by the Certified General Accountants Association of Canada (© CGA-Canada 2000). Reprinted with permission.

15. (LO 6) Reed Associates Ltd. makes an environmentally friendly artificial fireplace log. You have been asked to prepare the company's 2008 master budget and have been provided with the following:

    a. The following projected December 31, 2010, balances are:

Assets

Cash		$ 4,330
Accounts Receivable		8,450
Direct Material Inventory (2,046 kilograms)		409
Finished Goods Inventory (1,200 logs)		2,808
Plant and Equipment	$220,000	
Less: Accumulated Depreciation	(57,700)	162,300
Total Assets		$178,297

Liabilities and Shareholders' Equity

Accounts Payable	$ 1,109	
Note Payable	20,000	
Total Liabilities		$ 21,109
Common Stock	$100,000	
Retained Earnings	57,188	157,188
Total Liabilities and Shareholders' Equity		$178,297

    b. Each log requires the following standards for direct material and labour:

      3.3 kilograms of material mix at $0.20 (0.3 kilograms is discarded as waste) $0.66

      2 minutes of labour time; direct labour averages $14.40 per hour   0.48

      Each finished log requires three minutes of machine time. Variable overhead is applied at the rate of $12 per hour of machine time. Annual fixed production overhead of $42,000 is applied based on an expected annual production capacity of 70,000 logs. The total fixed manufacturing overhead comprises the following:

Salaries	$26,000
Insurance	1,800
Fixed portion of utilities	5,300
Depreciation	8,900

      Fixed overhead is incurred evenly throughout the year.

    c. Expected sales in units for the first five months of 2008 are:

January	6,000
February	9,000
March	6,500
April	5,900
May	5,100

Reed Associates grants no discounts, and all sales are on credit at $6 per log. The company's collection pattern is 80% in the month of sale, 15% in the month following the sale, and 5% in the second month following the sale. The Accounts Receivable balance in the balance sheet represents amounts remaining due from November sales of $33,000 and December sales of $34,000.

d. Reed Associates completes all production each day. The desired ending balance of Direct Material Inventory is 10% of the amount needed to satisfy the next month's production for finished goods. The desired ending balance in Finished Goods Inventory is 20% of the next month's sales.

e. Purchases are paid 70% in the month of purchase and 30% in the month following the purchase. No discounts are taken. The note payable has a 12% interest rate, and the interest is paid at the end of each month. The $20,000 balance of the principal on the note is due on March 31, 2011.

f. Reed Associates' minimum desired cash balance is $4,000. The firm may borrow at the beginning of a month and repay at the end of the month in $500 increments. Interest on these short-term loans, if any, is payable monthly at a 14% rate. Investments and investment liquidations are made only in $500 amounts at the end of a month. Investments earn 12% per year, collected monthly at month's end.

g. Period (selling and administrative) expenses, paid as incurred, run $9,000 per month plus 1% of revenue. Direct labour and overhead are paid as incurred.

h. The company accrues income taxes at a 40% rate. A quarterly tax installment will be paid on April 15, 2011.

Required:
Prepare master budget schedules on a monthly basis for the first quarter of 2011 and pro forma financial statements at the end of the first quarter. (Round all numbers in the schedules and pro forma statements to the nearest whole dollar.)

16. (LO 6). Lexicon Services Inc. provides word-processing services to local public schools and public accounting firms, and charges clients $25 per billable hour of word-processing production. Because of the nature of its clientele, the company has a cyclical business and has instituted a fiscal year from April 1 to March 31, where the least activity occurs during the first quarter of the fiscal year and the most activity is in the fourth quarter. The budget for the year ending March 31, 2011, was completed in January 2010 and is presented below.

Lexicon Services Inc.
Annual Budget
For the Year Ending March 31, 2011

	First Quarter	Second Quarter	Third Quarter	Fourth Quarter	Full Year
Revenues	$168,750	$225,000	$337,500	$393,750	$1,125,000
Expenses:					
Administrative salaries	$ 50,000	$ 50,000	$ 50,000	$ 50,000	$ 200,000
Wages	108,000	108,000	108,000	108,000	432,000
Benefits	20,800	20,800	20,800	20,800	83,200
Temporary help	–	–	67,500	101,250	168,750
Depreciation—equipment	5,000	5,000	5,000	5,000	20,000
Equipment rental	–	–	2,000	3,000	5,000
Rent and utilities	6,000	6,000	6,000	6,000	24,000
Supplies	7,350	9,600	14,100	16,350	47,400
Advertising	4,500	4,500	4,500	4,500	18,000
Other costs	1,000	1,000	1,000	1,000	4,000
Total expenses	$202,650	$204,900	$278,900	$315,900	$1,002,350
Earnings before tax	$(39,900)	$ 20,100	$ 58,600	$ 77,850	$ 122,650
Tax expense	(13,560)	(8,040)	(23,440)	(31,140)	(49,060)
Net earnings	$(20,340)	$ 12,060	$ 35,160	$ 46,710	$ 73,590

PROBLEMS

Rochelle Gordon, Lexicon's controller, prepared this budget based on the historical sales growth and cycles. Some of the assumptions used by Gordon follow.

- The sales pattern by quarter for the projected total of 45,000 billable hours is 15%, 20%, 30%, and 35% in each of the respective quarters. Each word-processing employee produces 450 hours per quarter.
- Lexicon maintains 20 full-time word processors or 80% of the average word-processing employees needed for the expected annual volume. All other billable hours are covered with temporary employees who are hired from an agency.
- The administrative staff for all other functions includes five full-time employees earning a combined $200,000 for the year.
- Word-processing equipment owned by Lexicon includes 20 word-processing stations. Equipment rental is for additional workstations at a cost of $200 per quarter for each station.

Recently, Lexicon implemented an aggressive advertising campaign to expand its market. As a result of this promotion, there has been a one-third increase in sales for the first quarter of the fiscal year ending March 31, 2011, and this additional business is expected to have the same cyclical sales pattern as Lexicon's other clients.

Required:

a. Assuming the one-third increase in sales experienced in the first quarter continues for the rest of the fiscal year, discuss at least two ways that this will affect operations in each of the following functional areas at Lexicon Services Inc. other than affecting the number of personnel required. No calculations are necessary.
   i. Word-processing production
   ii. Financial management and accounting
   iii. Marketing
   iv. Human Resources
b. Rochelle Gordon has suggested that Lexicon Services Inc. implement a continuous (rolling) budgeting process.
   i. Define the concept of continuous budgeting.
   ii. Discuss how Lexicon could benefit from the implementation of a continuous budgeting process.

(IMA 1993 Question 5)

17. (LO 6). Bushie Company Ltd. is a manufacturer of leather goods operating from several regional divisions treated individually as profit centres. A master operating plan based on divisional projections for each fiscal year is prepared at corporate headquarters. Several years ago, Bushie implemented an incentive plan to reward the performance of key personnel. The main features of the incentive plan, presented below, were designed to avoid "managed" earnings and recognize careful planning.

- The performance of each division's manager and other key personnel is measured against the division's annual operating plan. The plan is to be prepared by the division manager but is subject to revision during the corporate budgeting process.
- Acceptable performance is defined as 90% to 110% of the division's budgeted operating income. For every percentage point achieved above 90%, 1% of the division's operating income is placed in the division's bonus fund. The maximum bonus fund contribution is 20% of operating income for achieving 110% of the budgeted operating income.
- The compensation committee of the board of directors has the authority to increase the bonus funds calculated above by 25%. The board uses the following criteria to make its judgment: nonquantifiable achievements, uncontrollable external influences, and major expenses made this year to benefit the division in future periods.

PROBLEMS

Bushie's sales declined during the recent recession, and its performance has not rebounded as well as the industry as a whole. Bushie's Income Statement for the year ended November 30, 2010, is presented as follows:

Bushie Company Ltd.
Income Statement
For the Year Ended November 30, 2010
(in thousands)

Net sales		$16,800
Expenses		
Cost of goods sold	$12,600	
Selling expense	1,560	
Administrative expense	1,800	
Interest expense	280	
Total expenses		16,240
Income before Income taxes		$ 560
Income taxes		224
Net income		$ 336

Bushie's turnover of average assets of four times and return on average assets before interest and taxes of 20% are both well below the industry average. In addition, the company's return on sales before interest and taxes was 5% in fiscal 2010 compared to the industry average of 9%.

Richard Cheney, president of Bushie, is unhappy with this performance and wants to improve these ratios to be more comparable to the industry averages. While preparing the master budget, Cheney established the following goals for fiscal 2011 even though the divisional projections did not support all of these targets.

Return on sales before interest and taxes	8%
Turnover of average assets	5 times
Return on average assets before interest and taxes	30%

When establishing these goals, Cheney issued the following operational directives for fiscal 2011, which he believes will improve profitability:

- Increase unit sales 5%.
- Increase selling prices 10%.
- Increase advertising by $300,000 while holding all other selling and administrative expenses at fiscal 2010 levels.
- Increase production capacity by increasing the average investment in inventory and equipment by $600,000 while holding all other assets at fiscal 2010 levels.
- Finance the additional assets at an annual interest rate of 10% and hold all other interest expense at fiscal 2010 levels.
- Improve the marketability of products carried, which will increase the unit cost of goods sold by 7%.

Bushie's 2011 effective *income* tax rate is expected to be 40%, the same as in fiscal 2010.

These operating goals and directives have just been presented at a meeting of the divisional managers and controllers. Connie Rice, controller of the Atlantic Division, has several reservations about Cheney's plan and had the following conversation with Colin Powell, controller of the Gulf Coast Division.

Rice: "These directives have little resemblance to the numbers I submitted for Atlantic. Although I didn't mention anything at the meeting, I think the ratio improvements are unrealistic, don't you?"

Powell: "It'll be a reach for us to follow Cheney's plan and achieve these targets. But, if it really does improve profits, our bonuses will be better."

Rice: "I don't think Cheney cares about our bonuses. All he's looking for is better corporate performance; he made no mention of the effect these directives will have on divisional performance."

Powell: "Well, I'm going to support Cheney's targets."

PROBLEMS

Rice: "Not me. I think I can convince my management team at Atlantic that it will be better for us to follow the original plan that we submitted to headquarters for two or three months in order to prove my point."

Required:

a. i.   Evaluate at least three strengths and at least three weaknesses of Bushie Company Ltd.'s incentive plan in terms of its effectiveness in achieving the desired behaviour of avoiding "managed" earnings and preparing careful plans.

   ii.   Describe the likely behavioural impact that Richard Cheney's operational directives and goals will have on the divisional management teams.

b.   Assuming that Richard Cheney's operational directives are carried out and his projected increase in unit sales is achieved, you are asked to:

   i.   Prepare a pro forma income statement for Bushie Company Ltd. for the fiscal year ending November 30, 2011.

   ii.   Determine whether the goals for ratio improvement will be achieved.

(IMA adapted)

18. (LO 6). The Independent Underwriters Insurance Co. (IUI) established a Systems Department two years ago to implement and operate its own data processing systems. IUI believed that its own system would be more cost effective than the service bureau it had been using.

IUI's three departments—Claims, Records, and Finance—have different requirements with respect to hardware and other capacity-related resources and operating resources. The system was designed to recognize these differing needs. In addition, the system was designed to meet IUI's long-term capacity needs. The excess capacity designed into the system would be sold to outside users until needed by IUI. The estimated resource requirements used to design and implement the system are shown in the following schedule.

	Hardware and Other Capacity-Related Resources	Operating Resources
Records	30%	60%
Claims	50	20
Finance	15	15
Expansion (outside use)	5	5
Total	100%	100%

IUI currently sells the equivalent of its expansion capacity to a few outside clients.

At the time the system became operational, management decided to redistribute total expenses of the Systems Department to the user departments based upon actual computer time used. The actual costs for the first quarter of the current fiscal year were distributed to the user departments as follows:

Department	Percentage Utilization	Amount
Records	60%	$330,000
Claims	20	110,000
Finance	15	82,500
Outside	5	27,500
Total	100%	$550,000

The three user departments have complained about the cost distribution method since the Systems Department was established. The Records Department's monthly costs have been as much as three times the costs experienced with the service bureau. The Finance Department is concerned about the costs distributed to the outside user category because these allocated costs form the basis for the fees billed to the outside clients.

Sean Brady, IUI's controller, decided to review the distribution method by which the Systems Department's costs have been allocated for the past two years. The additional information he gathered for his review is reported in the three tables presented below.

Table 1
Systems Department Costs and Activity Levels

| | Annual Budget | | First Quarter | | | |
| | | | Budget | | Actual | |
	Hours	Dollars	Hours	Dollars	Hours	Dollars
Hardware and other capacity-related costs	–	$600,000	–	$150,000	–	$155,000
Software development	18,750	562,500	4,725	141,750	4,250	130,000
Operations:						
Computer related	3,750	750,000	945	189,000	920	187,000
Input/output related	30,000	300,000	7,560	75,600	7,900	78,000
		$2,212,500		$556,350		$550,000

Table 2
Historical Utilization by Users

| | Hardware and Other Capacity Needs | Software Development | | Operations | | | |
| | | | | Computer | | Input/Output | |
		Range	Average	Range	Average	Range	Average
Records	30%	0–30%	12%	55–65%	60%	10–30%	20%
Claims	50	15–60	35	10–25	20	60–80	70
Finance	15	25–75	45	10–25	15	3–10	6
Outside	5	0–25	8	3–8	5	3–10	4
	100%		100%		100%		100%

Table 3
Utilization of Systems Department's Services In Hours
First Quarter

| | Software Development | Operations | |
		Computer-Related	Input/Output
Records	425	552	1,580
Claims	1,700	184	5,530
Finance	1,700	138	395
Outside	425	46	395
Total	4,250	920	7,900

Brady has concluded that the method of cost distribution should be changed to reflect more directly the actual benefits received by the departments. He believes that the hardware- and capacity-related costs should be allocated to the user departments in proportion to the planned, long-term needs. Any difference between actual and budgeted hardware costs would not be allocated to the departments but remain with the Systems Department.

The remaining costs for software development and operations would be charged to the user departments based upon actual hours used. A predetermined hourly rate based upon the annual budget data would be used. The hourly rates that would be used for the current fiscal year are as follows:

Function	Hourly Rate
Software development operations	$ 30
Computer related	200
Input/output related	10

Brady plans to use first-quarter activity and cost data to illustrate his recommendations. The recommendations will be presented to the Systems Department and the user departments for their comments and reactions. He then expects to present his recommendations to management for approval.

Required:

a. Calculate the amount of data processing costs that would be included in the Claims Department's first-quarter budget according to the method Sean Brady has recommended.

b. Prepare a schedule to show how the actual first-quarter costs of the Systems Department would be charged to the users if Sean Brady's recommended method was adopted.

c. Explain whether Sean Brady's recommended system for charging costs to the user departments will:

   i.   Improve cost control in the Systems Department.

   ii. Improve planning and cost control in the user departments.

   iii. Be a more equitable basis for charging costs to user departments.

(IMA June 1983 #5)

19. (LO 6). The Spudas Agency, a division of General Service Industries, offers consulting services to clients for a fee. The corporate management at General Service is pleased with the performance of the Spudas Agency for the first nine months of the current year and has recommended that the division manager of the Spudas Agency, Karina TenVeldhuis, submit a revised forecast for the remaining quarter, as the division has exceeded the annual year-to-date plan by 20% of operating income. An unexpected increase in billed hour volume over the original plan is the main reason for this gain in income. The original operating budget for the first three quarters for the Spudas Agency is as follows:

2010–2011 Operating Budgets

	1st Quarter	2nd Quarter	3rd Quarter	Total
Revenue:				
Consulting fees				
Management consulting	$315,000	$315,000	$315,000	$ 945,000
IT consulting	421,875	421,875	421,875	1,265,625
Total	$736,875	$736,875	$736,875	$2,210,625
Other revenue	10,000	10,000	10,000	30,000
Total	$746,875	$746,875	$746,875	$2,240,625
Expenses:				
Consultant salaries	$386,750	$386,750	$386,750	$1,160,250
Travel and entertainment	45,625	45,625	45,625	136,875
General and administration	100,000	100,000	100,000	300,000
Depreciation	40,000	40,000	40,000	120,000
Corporate allocation	50,000	50,000	50,000	150,000
Total	$622,375	$622,375	$622,375	$1,867,125
Operating income	$124,500	$124,500	$124,500	$ 373,500

When comparing the actuals for the first three quarters against the original plan, TenVeldhuis analyzed the variances. Her revised forecast for the fourth quarter will reflect the following information:

• The division currently has 25 consultants on staff—10 for management consulting and 15 for IT consulting—and has hired 3 additional management consultants to start work at the beginning of the fourth quarter in order to meet the increased client demand.

• The hourly billing rate for consulting revenues is acceptable in the market and will remain at $90 per hour for each management consultant and $75 per hour for each IT consultant. However, owing to the favourable increase in billing hour volume, the hours for each consultant will be increased by 50 hours per quarter. New employees are as capable as current employees and will be billed at the current rates.

• The budgeted annual salaries and actual annual salaries, paid monthly, are the same at $50,000 for a management consultant and 8% less for an IT consultant. Corporate management has approved a merit increase of 10% at the beginning of the fourth quarter for all 25 existing consultants, while the new consultants will be compensated at the planned rate.

- The planned salary expense includes a provision for employee fringe benefits amounting to 30% of the annual salaries; however, the improvement of some corporatewide employee programs will increase the fringe benefit allocation to 40%.
- The original plan assumes a fixed hourly rate for travel and other related expenses for each billing hour of consulting. These expenses are not reimbursed by the client, and the previously determined hourly rate has proven to be adequate to cover these costs.
- Other revenues are derived from temporary rentals and interest income and remain unchanged for the fourth quarter.
- Administrative expenses have been favourable at 7% below the plan; this 7% savings on fourth-quarter expenses will be reflected in the revised plan.
- Depreciation for office equipment and microcomputers will stay constant at the projected straight-line rate.
- Because of the favourable experience for the first three quarters and the division's increased ability to absorb costs, the corporate management at General Service Industries has increased the corporate expense allocation by 50%.

Required:

a. Prepare a revised operating budget for the fourth quarter for the Spudas Agency, which TenVeldhuis will present to General Service Industries. Be sure to furnish supporting calculations for all revised revenue and expense amounts.

b. Discuss the reasons why an organization would prepare a revised forecast.

(CMA adapted)

20. (LO 6) You, as a new business school graduate, were hired six months ago by the Ontario division of Athens and McGill as the manager of maintenance and renovations. Athens and McGill is a major office property owner. You are responsible for numerous maintenance and renovation activities for the 26 buildings owned by Athens and McGill in Toronto and Ottawa. These renovations have had cost control problems. The following is a monthly record of actual costs versus budget for renovations:

Month	Actual Costs	Budgeted Costs
July	$1,541,157	$1,200,000
August	1,623,559	1,200,000
September	1,487,991	1,200,000
October	1,308,528	1,200,000
November	1,731,703	1,200,000
December	1,457,206	1,200,000

You are concerned about the unfavourable variances that have occurred each month. You investigated the variances by examining the process by which renovations are handled at the individual building level. Each building has a building manager who initiates renovations and hires contractors. Competitive bids are not sought when hiring contractors. Generally, the office building managers hire the contractors they prefer. (For example, one office building manager hires his son.) You, as the manager of maintenance and renovations, have approved all building manager-recommended renovation projects and the selected contractors, just as the previous manager of maintenance and renovations did.

Once the contractor has been selected, a payment schedule is put together along with the work schedule. The contractors are paid according to this schedule. In your investigation, you have found that the contractors are paid according to the schedule, even when the work has not been completed according to the schedule. Overpayment occurs if the work is not completed on time.

Required:

Identify and discuss why the unfavourable variances are occurring and make recommendations to eliminate the unfavourable variances.

21. (LO 6). Katsya Corporation, a rapidly expanding crossbow distributor to retail outlets, is in the process of formulating plans for 2011. Lisa Katsya, the director of marketing, has completed her 2011 forecast and is confident that sales estimates will be met or exceeded. The following sales figures show the growth expected and will provide the planning basis for other corporate departments.

PROBLEMS

Month	Forecasted Sales	Month	Forecasted Sales
January	$1,800,000	July	$3,000,000
February	2,000,000	August	3,000,000
March	1,800,000	September	3,200,000
April	2,200,000	October	3,200,000
May	2,500,000	November	3,000,000
June	2,800,000	December	3,400,000

Sandie Rinoldo, the assistant controller, has been given the responsibility for formulating the cash flow projection, a critical element during a period of rapid expansion. The following information will be used in preparing the cash analysis:

- Katsya Corporation has experienced an excellent record in accounts receivable collections and expects this trend to continue. The company collects 60% of billings in the month after the sale and 40% in the second month after the sale. Uncollectible accounts are insignificant and should not be considered in the analysis.
- The purchase of crossbows is Katsya's largest expenditure; the cost of these items equals 50% of sales. The company receives 60% of the crossbows one month prior to sale and 40% during the month of sale.
- Prior experience shows that 80% of accounts payable are paid by Katsya one month after receipt of the purchased crossbows, and the remaining 20% are paid the second month after receipt.
- Hourly wages, including fringe benefits, are a function of sales volume and are equal to 20% of the current month's sales. These wages are paid in the month incurred.
- Administrative expenses are projected to be $2,640,000 for 2011. All of these expenses are incurred uniformly throughout the year except the property taxes. Property taxes are paid in four equal installments in the last month of each quarter. The composition of the expenses is:

Salaries	$ 480,000
Promotion	660,000
Property taxes	240,000
Insurance	360,000
Utilities	300,000
Depreciation	600,000
Total	$2,640,000

- Income tax payments are made by Katsya in the first month of each quarter based on income for the prior quarter. Katsya's income tax rate is 40%. Katsya's net income for the first quarter of 2011 is projected to be $612,000.
- Katsya has a corporate policy of maintaining an end-of-month cash balance of $100,000. Cash is invested or borrowed monthly, as necessary, to maintain this balance.
- Katsya uses a calendar year reporting period.

Required:

a. Prepare a pro forma schedule of cash receipts and disbursements for Katsya Corporation, by month, for the second quarter of 2011. Be sure that all receipts, disbursements, and borrowing/investing amounts are presented on a monthly basis. Ignore the interest expense and/or interest income associated with the borrowing/investing activities.

b. Discuss why cash budgeting is particularly important for a rapidly expanding company such as Katsya Corporation.

c. Do monthly cash budgets ignore the pattern of cash flows within the month? Explain.

(CMA adapted)

22. (LO 6). Quinn Management Education Inc. (QME) is a nonprofit organization that sponsors a wide variety of management seminars throughout western Canada. In addition, it is heavily involved in research into improved methods of teaching and motivating college administrators. The seminar activity is largely supported by fees and the research program by membership dues.

QME operates on a calendar year basis and is in the process of finalizing the budget for 2011. The following information has been taken from approved plans, which are still tentative at this time:

Seminar Program

Revenue—The scheduled number of programs should produce $12,000,000 of revenue for the year. Each program is budgeted to produce the same amount of revenue as the others. The revenue is collected during the month the program is offered. The programs are scheduled during the basic academic year and are not held during June, July, August, or December. In each of the first five months of the year 12% of the revenue is generated, and the remainder is distributed evenly during September, October, and November.

Direct expenses—The seminar expenses are made up of three types:
- Instructors' fees are paid at the rate of 70% of seminar revenue in the month following the seminar. The instructors are considered independent contractors and are not eligible for QME employee benefits.
- Facilities fees total $5,600,000 for the year. Fees are the same for all programs and are paid in the months the programs are given.
- Annual promotional costs of $1,000,000 are spent equally in all months except June and July, when there is no promotional effort.

Research Program

Research grants—The research program has a large number of projects nearing completion. The other main research activity this year includes feasibility studies for new projects to be started in 2011. The total grant expense of $3,000,000 for 2011 is expected to be paid out at the rate of $500,000 per month during the first six months of the year.

Salaries and Other QME Expenses

Office lease—Annual amount of $240,000 paid monthly at the beginning of each month.

General administrative expenses—$1,500,000 annually or $125,000 per month; these are paid in cash as incurred.

Depreciation expense—$240,000 per year.

General QME promotion—Annual cost of $600,000, paid monthly.

Salaries and benefits—

Number of Employees	Annual Cash Salary	Total Annual Salaries
1	$50,000	$ 50,000
3	40,000	120,000
4	30,000	120,000
15	25,000	375,000
5	15,000	75,000
22	10,000	220,000
50		$960,000

Employee benefits amount to $240,000, or 25% of annual salaries. Except for the pension contribution, the benefits are paid as salaries are paid. The annual pension payment of $24,000, based on 2.5% of total annual salaries, is due on April 15, 2011.

Other Information

Membership income—QME has 100,000 members, and each pays an annual fee of $100. The fee for the calendar year is invoiced in late June. The collection schedule is as follows: July, 60%; August, 30%; September, 5%; and October, 5%.

Capital expenditures—The capital expenditures program calls for a total of $510,000 in cash payments to be spread evenly over the first five months of 2011.

Cash and temporary investments—At January 1, 2011, these are estimated at $750,000.

Required:
a. Budget of the annual cash receipts and disbursements for 2011.
b. Cash budget for QME Inc. for January 2011.

(CMA adapted)

PROBLEMS

23. (LO 6) London Corporation manufactures and sells extended keyboard units to be used with microcomputers. Elizabeth Windsor, budget analyst, coordinated the preparation of the annual budget for the year ending August 31, 2011. The budget was based on the prior year's sales and production activity. The pro forma statements of income, cost of goods manufactured, and cost of goods sold schedule are as follows:

London Corporation
Pro Forma Statement of Income
For the Year Ended August 31, 2011
($000 omitted)

Net sales		$ 25,550
Cost of goods sold		(16,565)
Gross profit		$ 8,985
Operating expenses		
Marketing	$3,200	
Selling and administrative	2,000	(5,200)
Income from operations before income taxes		$ 3,785

London Corporation
Pro Forma Cost of Goods Manufactured Statement
For the Year Ended August 31, 2011
($000 omitted)

Direct material:		
Direct materials inventory, September 1, 2010	$ 1,200	
Plus: Purchases of direct material	11,400	
Direct materials available for use	$12,600	
Less: Direct materials inventory, August 31, 2011	1,480	
Direct materials used		$11,120
Direct labour		980
Manufacturing overhead		
Indirect materials	$ 1,112	
General manufacturing overhead	2,800	3,912
Cost of goods manufactured		$16,012

London Corporation
Pro Forma Cost of Goods Sold Schedule
For the Year Ended August 31, 2011
($000 omitted)

Finished goods inventory, September 1, 2010	$ 930
Plus: Cost of goods manufactured	16,012
Goods available for sale	$16,942
Less: Finished goods inventory, August 31, 2011	377
Cost of goods sold	$16,565

On December 10, 2010, Elizabeth Windsor met with Philip Mountbatten, vice-president of finance, to discuss the first quarter's results (the period September 1 to November 30, 2010). After their discussion, Mountbatten directed Windsor to reflect the following changes to the budget assumptions in revised pro forma statements.

• The estimated production in units for the fiscal year should be revised from 140,000 to 145,000 units, with the balance of production being scheduled in equal segments over the last months of the year. The actual first quarter's production was 25,000 units.
• The planned inventory for finished goods of 3,300 units at the end of the fiscal year remains unchanged and will be valued at the average manufacturing cost for the year. The finished goods inventory of 9,300 units on September 1, 2010, had dropped to 9,000 units by November 30, 2010.
• Due to a new labour agreement, the labour rate will increase 8% effective June 1, 2011, the beginning of the fourth quarter, instead of the previously anticipated effective date of September 1, 2011, the beginning of the next fiscal year. The assumptions remain unchanged for direct material inventory at 16,000 units for

PROBLEMS

beginning inventory and 18,500 units for ending inventory. Direct material inventory is valued on a first-in, first-out basis. One unit of direct material is needed for each keyboard produced. During the first quarter, direct material for 27,500 units of output was purchased for $2,200,000. Although direct material will be purchased evenly for the last nine months, the cost of the direct material will increase by 5% on March 1, 2011, the beginning of the third quarter.

- Indirect material costs will continue to be projected at 10% of the cost of direct material consumed.
- One-half of general manufacturing overhead and all of the marketing and general and administrative expenses are considered fixed.

Required:

a. Based on the revised data presented, calculate London Corporation's projected sales for the year ending August 31, 2011, in (1) number of units to be sold and (2) dollar volume of net sales.

b. Prepare the pro forma schedule of cost of goods sold for the year ending August 31, 2011.

c. In light of the fact that management is aware that certain changes (price change for materials and rate increase for labour) are forthcoming, what actions might management take to exploit the changes?

d. For each budgetary change mentioned, identify the source or sources of information Philip Mountbatten might have used to become aware of the change.

(CMA adapted)

24. (LO 6) Your Canadian-based consumer electronics firm, CanadaExcel, is in the process of establishing a video camera assembly plant in Malaysia. The manager of the Malaysian plant is to have responsibility for the following: sourcing materials (about 60% of materials will be acquired from outside the company and the other 40% will be acquired from internal plants located in Canada and Mexico); hiring, training, and supervising workers; controlling operating costs; meeting a production schedule that is based on projected sales; and maintaining production quality. Completed units will be shipped to internal marketing divisions located in North America.

Required:

Place yourself in the position of the controller of CanadaExcel. It is your job to incorporate the operating plans for the Malaysian assembly plant into the company's formal budget. Describe, in general terms, what information you would need to acquire to develop the budget for the Malaysian operation and where you would expect to acquire such information. Further, describe any significant decisions that you would be responsible for making in compiling the budget. What problems and concerns might you have in getting the required information on the Malaysian operations? How might you handle these problems and concerns?

CASES

1. Manuel Torres is a trained carpenter and the owner of Cottage Renovators, which operates in the Lake District, just north of your home city. Most of the company's business involves cottage renovations in the area. The cold and snow in this northern community make outdoors activities difficult, so the renovation work is seasonal. The firm is small but growing rapidly.

All work is done between April and November. Manuel gets contracts to renovate cottages; renovations take an average time of two months from signing the contract to completion. After the contract is signed, Manuel orders materials, hires employees, carries out the renovations, and receives payment, except for a 10% holdback.

Employees must be paid biweekly. Suppliers must be paid within 30 days because those are the requirements of the credit card Manuel uses for acquiring materials. Most renovation customers pay 10% up front and 80% on completion, with a 10% holdback payable in 60 days. Paying employees and suppliers has always been a challenge, as most of the cash from contracts comes after payments are due to employees and suppliers.

The renovation business has been good, as indicated by the company's profitability. The very favourable income statement for the most recent year is an example of that profitability. Cash flow is a problem as expenditures must be made before all cash for a contract is received. There are substantial growth opportunities, but Manuel is reluctant to expand because it will cause problems with regard to making payments to employees and suppliers.

Manuel will expand if he can arrange a bank line of credit or bank loan to meet temporary cash shortages. His bank manager would be happy to provide the required line of credit provided that Manuel can show him each month a 12-month estimate of revenues, expenses, net income, and cash flow.

Manuel has asked you how to meet the bank manager's request.
Required:
Using the case approach, advise Manuel on how to meet the bank manager's requirement.

2. Your mother always wanted to run her own tea shop, but she did not have the money to start a business. She had to be content with working in a tea shop. Now she has the money. She was the beneficiary of the life insurance from your father's unexpected death in London last year, when a cyclist going against a red light knocked him into flow of taxis going the other direction. The insurance provided $100,000.

Your mother has planned the Tea Shop in the way she had always imagined "her" tea shop would look. She contends that the insurance settlement is "free" money; for some strange reason you had thought it to be part of your inheritance.

One day, about a month before the shop is to open, you ask your mother if the tea shop will generate enough profit to pay its bills. She says, "I hope it will, because the $100,000 is almost gone." After further discussion, you realize that your mother's plans have not included any assessment of the tea shop's expected profitability. You are alarmed, but offer to calculate the profitability for her.

Here are the details on what she expects from the tea shop. She has rented space in a tourist area of the central business district. The 500 square metres of retail space cost $2,000 per month; that cost includes all utilities and property taxes. To renovate the space she has spent $40,000 on leasehold improvements and $20,000 on equipment. Both capital outlays are expected to be written off over 10 years, which equals the lease term plus the exercise of the option for a second 5 years.

Sales consist of two parts: restaurant (tea and food) and retail (tea products and ancillary products). Your mother expects sales to equal $15,000 per month, 60% from restaurant and 40% from retail. The gross profit margins are 50 and 40% respectively.

Besides the cost of goods sold, the cost of employees is expected to average $5,000 a month. This includes a competitive salary for your mother plus wages for three part-time employees. Supplies, cash register, and miscellaneous expenses are expected to be $1,000 per month. Inventory is expected to be 50% of monthly sales.
Required:
Using the case approach, calculate the profitability of the Tea Shop for your mother.

3. A young woman wants to open a knitting store, the Knitting Nook, in a suburban middle-class area that is currently without a knitting shop. She chooses a small, open-concept store in an old part of town, away from the box stores. Her inventory includes various wools (alpaca and sheep), synthetic yarns, and combination yarns from all over the world. The rent and utilities cost $1,200 per week. Her starting costs include display shelves, a computer system connected to a cash register, a website with a mail-order system, and inventory. The total to start up the business is $350,000: $50,000 for inventory and $300,000 for leasehold improvements. The leasehold improvements will be written off over 10 years, which is the life of the lease.

The average number of people walking by per day is 400, while about 900 cars drive by. These traffic flows were studied to determine the number of customer sales. Most customers who enter the store are current or future knitters and purchase products during their visit. Sunday and Monday the store is open from 12 to 4 p.m.; Tuesday,

Wednesday, Friday, and Saturday, from 10 to 6 p.m.; and Thursday, from 10 to 8 p.m. Thursdays and Saturdays are the busiest days, with an average of 20 purchases per hour. On the other days, sales are expected to be 15 purchases per hour.

She hires six part-time staff to run the store and give knitting lessons. They are paid $15 an hour plus 15% benefits. Each works an average of 15 hours a week, with the owner filling in the rest of the hours. The owner is paid $25 per hour (15% benefits) for 40 hours per week. Purchases vary from $10 to $100, with the average being $55. The cost of goods sold is expected to be 40%. Miscellaneous and other expenses are expected to be $2,000 per week.

The young women's parents will invest in the business if it is profitable.

Required:

As the young women's parents, use the case approach to determine profitability. Be supportive.

ETHICS

1. As a budget analyst for a diversified financial services company, you are responsible for reviewing all unit budgets in the corporate office. This responsibility includes examining the four unit budgets in the treasurer's division. Your reviews of unit budgets are to ensure that proper assumptions are being followed for salary and other increases, that approved strategies are being followed, and that the unit budgets and consolidations are numerically correct. In one unit you see that money has been budgeted for the acquisition of the remaining shares of an 80% owned subsidiary. The budget details indicate that $8 a share will be offered for all outstanding shares. Currently, the shares are selling for $5.50 each. Having quickly noticed that you can make money with no risk, you immediately buy 10,000 shares.

   Did you do anything wrong? Justify your response.

2. The owner of the company where you work as the controller is in the process of selling the business to an international venture capital firm. As part of its due diligence, the buyer has sent a consultant to examine the budget for the following year and to discuss its underlying assumptions. The budget is the basis for setting the price for the sale. It was you who developed the budget, but your boss, the CEO and owner, inflated sales and consequently profits in order to obtain more money from the sale.

   What should you do? Justify your response.

3. Your firm rewards branch managers with bonuses tied to the extent to which their financial performance exceeds budgeted profits. To prevent branch managers from developing undemanding budgets that can easily be exceeded, you as the budget officer review each budget for reasonable assumptions. One branch manager is extremely unwilling to accept any revisions to his budgeting. He argues loudly that you are being unfair to him. The conflict is extreme, and he will not agree to any changes. You are about to give in to him, thereby allowing him to have an easy budget that he is most likely to exceed for a substantial bonus. However, that would be unfair to the other branch managers.

   What should you do? Justify your response.

SOLUTIONS TO SELF-TEST QUESTIONS

1.	d.	From April	$110,500
		From March	38,000
		From February	18,500
		From January	6,400
		Total	$173,400

2. c. $36,000 \times 1.5 = 54,000$

3. d. Production = (16,500 × Variable cost) + $12,000
= (16,500 × $7.00) + $12,000 = $127,500

4. a.

5. c. [(42,000 – 22,000 + 24,000) × 3] – 90,000 + 110,000 = 152,000

6. c. $3,000 + $3,000 = $6,000

7. b. {[9,000 × ($30 – $23)] – $18,800} – {[9,600 × ($29 – $24)] – $18,200} = $14,400 U

8. b. Purchases in August:

For August production (14,000 × 3)	42,000 metres
Plus: required ending inventory (15,500 × 3 × 0.2)	9,300
Less: opening inventory	(2,000)
Purchases	49,300 metres
Times: cost per metre	× $0.80
Purchases	$39,440

9. b. Desired ending inventory in September: 11,900 × 3 × 0.2 = 7,140 metres

10. c. Overhead costs

ENDNOTES

1. Kathryn Jehle, "Budgeting as a Competitive Advantage," *Strategic Finance,* October 1999, pp. 54–57.

2. Diane Contino, "Budget Training: It's Overdue," *Nursing Management,* Chicago, August 2001.

3. James F. Brown, Jr., "How U.S. Firms Conduct Strategic Planning," *Management Accounting,* February 1986, p. 55.

4. Neil C. Churchill, "Budget Choice: Planning vs. Control," *Harvard Business Review,* July–August 1984, p. 151.

5. Jack Welch with John A. Byrne, *Jack: Straight From the Gut,* New York: Warner Books, 2001, pp. 386–387, Copyright © 2001 by John F. Welch, Jr. Foundation.

6. Steve Player, "How Does Your Budgeting System Impact Ethical Behaviour?" *Cost Management,* May–June 2004.

7. "Web-Budgeting Systems Help PerkinElmer and Raycom React Faster," *IOMA's Report on Financial Analysis, Planning, and Reporting,* June 2003.

8. T. Leahy, "Control: The End of the Spreadsheet Budgeter," http://www.frxsoftware.com.

9. Kenneth A. Merchant, "How Challenging Should Profit Budget Targets Be?" *Management Accounting,* November 1990, pp. 46–48.

10. Leslie N. Masonson, ed., *Cash Management Performance Report,* Boston: Warren, Gorham & Lamont, January 1991, p. 1.

11. Most manufacturing entities do not produce only whole units during the period. Normally, partially completed beginning and ending in-process inventories exist. Consideration of partially completed inventories is covered in Chapter 4.

12. This concept was discussed in Chapter 2.

13. Henry R. Migliore and Douglas E. McCracken, "Tie Your Capital Budget to Your Strategic Plan," *Strategic Finance,* June 2001.

14. Jeremy Hope and Robin Fraser, *Beyond Budgeting, White Paper,* Beyond Budgeting Round Table, CAM-I Europe, May 2001.

15. Russ Banham, "Revolution in Planning," *CEO Magazine,* August 1999.

16. Cathy Lazere, "Altogether Now," *CFO Magazine,* February 1998.

17. "Corporate Strategic Planning Suffers from Inefficiencies," *Hackett Benchmarking PR Newswire*, October 25, 1999.

18. Robert S. Kaplan and David P. Norton, *The Strategy Focused Organization,* Boston Harvard Business School Press, 2001, p. 274.

19. Benchmarking Solutions, http://www.thgi.com/ppfax.htm

20. Gordon Pitts, "The Root of All Corporate Evil? The Budget," *The Globe and Mail*, September 20, 2003, p. 135.

21. Jim Gahagan, "Reaching for Financial Success," *Strategic Finance*, November 2004.

22. Fraser, Hope, Player, "Becoming Lean, Adaptive and Ethical: How to Move Beyond Budgeting," *Business Performance Management*, November 2003.

23. Simon Caulkin, *The Observer*, April 13, 2003, p. 17.

24. Robert Colman, "Better Budgeting," *CMA Management*, October 2004.

25. "Should Your Company Do Away With Its Budget Process?" *IOMA's Report on Financial Analysis, Planning & Reporting*, August 2003, Vol. 3.

26. Robert A. Howell, "Turn Your Budgeting Process Upside Down," *Top-Line Growth*, July–August 2004.

27. Peter Clarke, "The Budgeting Process," *Accountancy Ireland*, October 2004, Vol. 36.

28. Stephen Hansen, David T. Otley, and Wim A. Van der Stede, *Journal of Management Accounting Research*, 2003, Vol. 15, p. 95.

29. *Driving Value Through Strategic Planning and Budgeting*, A Research Report from Cranfield School of Management and Accenture, in association with Cranfield University School of Management.

30. Michael Senyshen, "Spreadsheet Superheroes," *CGA Magazine*, September–October 2002, pp. 24–30.

Chapter 7

Introduction to a Standard Cost System

LEARNING OBJECTIVES

After reading this chapter, you should be able to answer the following questions:

1 Why
are standard cost systems used?

2 How
are standards for material and labour set?

3 How
are material, labour, and overhead variances calculated?

4 How
can variances be used for control and performance evaluation purposes?

5 How
do organizational evolution and desired level of attainability affect standard setting?

6 How
are standard setting and standard usage changing in modern business?

7 How
are budget variances computed and used to analyze differences between budgeted and actual revenue? budgeted costs and actual costs?

8 What
journal entries are needed in a standard cost system? (Appendix 7A)

9 What
use do standard costs have in a process costing system? (Appendix 7B)

www.brightpearlseafood.com

Bright Pearl Seafood Restaurant Inc.

BRIGHT PEARL SEAFOOD RESTAURANT INC., a large restaurant specializing in Chinese cuisine, operates in downtown Toronto, serving thousands of customers per week. The company's mission statement expresses a philosophy of producing and serving very high-quality products, and it has been a winner of many awards for both service and food quality.

This restaurant is right on Spadina Avenue beside Kensington Market, in the historic Hsin Kuang-Yellow Building, a Chinatown landmark. During the day the restaurant serves dim sum, the Chinese version of brunch. Dim sum means "light the heart" or "touch the heart." Bright Pearl serves between 80 and 100 different dim sum dishes in the traditional way—servers quietly glide through the buzzing crowd with rolling steam carts, from which the guests can pick out what they like or are adventurous enough to try out.

In the evening the steam carts are put away and guests enjoy a classic sit-down dinner of delicious Chinese delicacies. Bright Pearl's signature dishes include Peking duck, fresh lobster, and sizzling prawns and scallops.

Production is enhanced because Bright Pearl's workforce is highly trained. Additionally, the workers are provided with tools and resources to perform effectively. Workers strive to eliminate downtime, reduce scrap, and maintain consistently high production quality.

The company operates in an area of strong competition and thus differentiates its products by focusing on providing high levels of product and service quality to its customers. This quality focus provides the underlying rationale for the company's emphasis on employee training.

Preparing dishes at the restaurant is a standardized process; each order needs to be identical to the last. Because of the substantial level of competition, price is set by the competitors and Bright Pearl must exercise extreme cost control efforts. Thus, material and labour specifications must be available and adhered to for each product so that the company can meet customer expectations and remain profitable. Standard costing allows company management to understand the quality expected and the costs that will be incurred in the preparation of each dish, and, more important, what impacts deviations from these standards will have on costs and profits.

SOURCE: Interview with Stephen Chan, Bright Pearl Seafood Restaurant, Inc. 346–368 Spadina Avenue, Toronto, ON; http://www.brightpearlseafood.com; http://www.yummytoronto.com.

*T*he major goal at Bright Pearl Seafood Restaurant is to deliver outstanding customer service. To help attain this goal and have strategic success, the company establishes production standards that allow management to determine causes of variations, take corrective action, and monitor and reward performance. Performance can be evaluated by comparing actual results against a predetermined measure or criterion. Thus, standards (or benchmarks) must exist to ensure product quality and consistency and thereby to implement strategy. Without the actual-to-standard comparison, employees and management cannot know whether expectations are met or whether problems exist. Such lack of knowledge makes managerial control impossible.

Almost all organizations develop and use some type of standards. For example, charities set a standard for the amount of annual contributions to be raised, sales managers set standards against which employee business expenses are compared, and hotels have standard lengths of time for cleaning a guest room.

Canada Post (a Crown corporation) has commissioned a scientific study into the amount of exertion involved in walking, as part of a drive to update time standards that dictate how hard the country's letter carriers have to work. It is hoped that the results can be incorporated in standards that already set out in minute detail how much mail carriers have to deliver in their 480-minute day. "From the time the letter carrier begins his day to the time the carrier delivers his last piece of mail, everything is measured. Even taking elastics off bundles [of mail]—there are time values for that." Carriers are expected, for instance, to cover each foot of their route in an average of 0.0037 minutes. And no room is left for error in determining the length (distance) between segments on the delivery route, with management and union representatives using a wheel to jointly measure the distance.[1]

Because different production methods and information objectives exist in organizations, no single standard cost system is appropriate for all situations. Thus, many forms of standard cost systems are in use. Some systems use standard prices but not standard quantities; other systems (especially in service entities) use labour, but not material, standards. Traditional standard cost systems require price and quantity standards for both material and labour.

This chapter discusses a traditional standard cost system using standards for the three product cost components: direct material (DM), direct labour (DL), and manufacturing overhead (OH). The chapter examples assume the use of only one material and one labour category in production activities. The chapter provides information on why standard cost systems are used, how material and labour standards are developed, how deviations (or variances) from standard are calculated, and what information can be gained from detailed variance analysis. Innovative trends in the use of standard costing systems are also discussed. Journal entries used in a standard cost system are presented in Appendix 5A.

LEARNING OBJECTIVE 1

Why are standard cost systems used?

STANDARD COST SYSTEMS

Standard product costing methods were developed in the mid-twentieth century to help managers in mass production companies make decisions. Since their introduction they have been widely used by companies around the world for various purposes, including cost control, inventory valuation, budgeting, and cost reduction. Standard costing gained popularity among managers because it allowed them to employ management by exception—an approach that investigates only the most significant deviations from predetermined levels of performance. This approach allocates energies to those areas that would benefit most from managers' attention.

One assumption of standard costing is that all overheads need to be assigned to the product and that these overheads generally relate to the amount of labour required to make the product. This leads to a distortion of product costs—that is, some products seem to cost more than they really do, while others seem to cost less. These costs mislead people and cause them to make wrong decisions relating to pricing, profitability, make/outsource (buy), and so forth.[2]

Standards can be used with either job order or process costing systems to provide important information for managerial planning, controlling, and decision making. Standard costing assists in setting budgets and evaluating managerial performance.

standards
benchmarks or norms against which actual results may be compared

Standard cost systems are usually process cost systems in which accountants use set standards instead of attempting to compute an actual cost per unit for each period. The major advantage of a standard cost system is that it highlights and allows management to manage by exception; that is, it allows management to concentrate on the areas where there are inefficiencies.[3]

A report in *Cost Management Update* states that a large percentage of companies are using standard costing. A **standard costing system** of some kind is used by 64.7% of all the survey respondents. Standard costing is favoured among all types of manufacturing firms. Of the 61 nonmanufacturing firms, roughly a third (34.4%) use standard costs, reflecting the difficulty in developing standards for unique services provided to customers. Of the firms using standard costing, about 16% report using activity-based costing (this topic is discussed in Chapter 8) to develop or update cost standards.

standard costing system
a product costing method using unit norms for production costs

Standard costing, according to various authors, is inconsistent with today's manufacturing environment. Many have predicted that shorter product life cycles, advanced manufacturing technologies, decreasing emphasis on labour in the production process, and global competition may lead to the demise of standard costing.[4]

The challenges faced by nonmanufacturing firms using **standard costs** are as varied as the types of firms represented. Allocating overhead was cited as the number one challenge in developing standards.[5]

standard cost
a budgeted or estimated cost to manufacture a single unit of product or perform a single service

Under a standard cost system, the values in the Work in Process account and the Finished Goods account are used to determine inventory values. These values are needed in the determination of the company's financial position and its periodic profit. But these figures, particularly on a unit basis, are also important in pricing, bidding, and other managerial decisions. Such decisions must often be made before production is complete, and thus the value of the predetermined or standard cost is substantial.[6]

In planning, standards are used to coordinate activities more quickly and easily than otherwise would be possible. For example, if Bright Pearl Seafood Restaurant

These patrons have enjoyed a delicious ten-course meal at Bright Pearl Seafood Restaurant.

variance
any difference between actual and standard costs or quantities

plans to produce 20,000 spring rolls in March, management can project materials, labour, and overhead costs by reviewing the standard costs established for each of these cost elements.

Standards can also be used for motivation and control. One requirement for control is that managers be aware of differences between the actual activities and resource consumption and the expected activities and resource consumption. A standard cost system helps companies recognize **variances**—or deviations between actual and standard costs or quantities—and correct problems resulting from excess costs or usage. Actual cost systems do not provide these benefits.

Standard costs are predetermined costs that, presumably, represent what costs should have been as opposed to historical costs that represent what costs were. Proponents of standard cost systems view the standard costs as the true cost of activity or production, whereas actual costs generally represent the true cost plus losses due to inefficiency, faulty operations, and inadequate control.

To be theoretically sound, standard costs must reflect "should be" costs and this favours regular updating. This also poses something of a paradox, for if costs change often, the instability suggests that no standard exists. People who are bothered by this paradox have a static conception of a standard. The dynamic conception seems better to fit the theory that standard costs represent a measure of what should be done under the circumstances that prevail. On the other hand, in the extreme case, cost changes could be so frequent that the standard costs in effect become actual costs.[7]

When the variances are significant, this is a signal for investigation. Managers, having discovered the cause, can exert influence to correct it. Suppose Bright Pearl's actual cost for raw materials for the 20,000 spring rolls was $1,000 less than expected. Management would investigate this difference to determine its cause. Several possibilities exist: the price paid for the wrappers and the filling was less than expected, or new technology or employee cross-training and team efforts made production more efficient by generating less scrap and, thus, lowered cost.

Note that the explanations for the $1,000 difference suggest that there are two possible underlying causes of the variance: raw material cost, and quantity of raw material used. These causes can exist separately or together. To evaluate performance properly, managers need to be able to determine which part of the total variance relates to which cause.

The availability of standards speeds up and improves decision making because managers have a predetermined, rigorous set of expectations upon which to base decisions, such as accepting an order at a specified price. Performance evaluation is also improved through comparing actual and standard costs of operations and highlighting significant differences.

DEVELOPMENT OF A STANDARD COST SYSTEM

Although initiated by manufacturing companies, standard cost systems are also applicable to service entities. Regardless of the type of organization, it is critical that the standards development process is handled in a knowledgeable and thorough manner.

The estimated cost to manufacture a single unit of product or to perform a single service is the standard cost. Standards are traditionally established for each component (material, labour, and overhead) of product cost. Developing a standard cost involves judgment and practicality in identifying the types of material and labour to be used and their related quantities and prices. Developing standards for overhead requires that costs have been appropriately classified according to cost behaviour, valid allocation bases have been chosen, and a reasonable level of activity has been specified.

A primary objective in manufacturing a product or performing a service is to minimize unit cost while achieving certain quality specifications. Almost all products can be manufactured with a variety of inputs (material, labour, and overhead) that would generate the same basic output. This is true even after output quality has been specified. Input choices ultimately affect the standards that are set.

Quantity and price standards can be developed once management has established the design and manufacturing process that will produce the desired output quality and has determined which input resources will be used. Standards should be developed by representatives from the following areas: management accounting, product design, industrial engineering, human resources, data processing, purchasing, and production management. It is especially important in the process of standard setting to involve managers and, to some extent, employees whose performance will be compared with the standards. Involvement helps assure credibility of the standards and helps motivate personnel to operate as closely as possible to the standards. Information from suppliers can also be useful, especially in the area of setting material price standards.

MATERIAL STANDARDS

LEARNING OBJECTIVE 2

How are standards for material and labour set?

In developing material standards, the specific direct material components used to manufacture the product or to perform the service must be identified and listed. Three things must be known about the materials: what inputs are needed, what the quality of those inputs must be, and what quantities of inputs of the specified quality are needed.

Determination of what inputs are needed is a design (recipe) specification. For example, to make a spring roll, Bright Pearl must have wrappers, pork, prawns, spring onions, ginger, bean sprouts, and carrots. Many cost-benefit trade-offs are involved in making quality decisions, so managers should consult material experts, accountants, and marketing personnel to determine which choices are most appropriate. Generally, as the grade of raw material rises, so does the cost. Decisions about material input components usually attempt to balance the interrelationships of cost, quality, quantity, and selling price.

Given the quality selected for each necessary component, physical quantity estimates can be made in terms of weight, size, volume, or other measures. These estimates can be based on results of engineering tests, opinions of people using the materials, and/or historical data. Information about direct material components, their specifications (including quality), and their quantities are listed on a **bill of materials**.

bill of materials
a document that contains information about product material components, their specifications (including quality), and the quantities needed for production

Each spring roll has been manufactured according to specifications.

Even companies that do not have formal standard cost systems are likely to develop a bill of materials for each of their products simply as a guide for production activity.

The example of Bright Pearl Seafood Restaurant illustrates that cost accounting can be used in businesses other than large manufacturing concerns.

We will use the firm of D&B Didona Clothing Ltd. (DBD) to illustrate the use of standard costing in a manufacturing operation. This firm, located in western Canada, specializes in the production of men's shirts.

Exhibit 7-1 illustrates a bill of materials for a six-button men's shirt produced by DBD. Company management has chosen to view the thread used in production as an indirect material and part of variable overhead. Thus, thread is not shown on the bill of materials.

EXHIBIT 7-1

Bill of Materials

Product: Six-button-front shirt
Product Number: Stock Keeping Unit (SKU) 312

Revision Date: 3/1/10
Standard Job Size: 400

Component ID#	Quantity Required	Description of Component	Comments
F-4	1.2 square metres	White cotton fabric	Highest quality
B-3	6 buttons	Bone buttons	Multicolour; imprinted with DBD logo
L-1	1 label	Label	Imprinted with DBD logo

After the standard quantities of material components have been developed, prices are determined for each component. The purchasing agent is most likely to have the expertise to estimate standard prices. Prices should reflect factors such as desired quality, reliability and physical proximity of the supplier, and quantity and purchase discounts allowed. If purchasing agents are involved in setting reasonable price standards for materials, these individuals are more likely to be able to explain causes of any future variations from the standards.

When all quantity and price information has been gathered, component quantities are multiplied by unit prices to yield the total cost of each component. These totals are summed to determine the total standard material cost of one unit of product.

LABOUR STANDARDS

The procedures for developing labour standards are similar to those used for material standards. Each worker operation—such as bending, reaching, lifting, moving materials, cutting and sewing fabric, attaching sundry items (such as snaps and patches), and packaging—should be identified. When operations and movements are specified, activities such as setup must be considered because they are performed during the production process. All unnecessary movements by workers and of materials as well as any rework activities should be disregarded when time standards are set and should be minimized or eliminated as nonvalue-added activities.

Each production operation must be converted to quantitative information to be a usable standard. Time and motion studies, discussed in the News Note on page 387, may be performed by the company.[8] Alternatively, times developed from industrial engineering studies or from historical data may be used.[9] Historical data, however, may incorporate past inefficiencies or may not consider recently added technologically advanced machinery or recently received worker training.

The Beginning of Time and Motion Studies

Frederick Winslow Taylor was born in 1856 to a prominent Philadelphia family. Taylor nevertheless went to work in a steel factory, first as a machinist and then as a foreman. There he began to develop his ideas about ways to reorganize factory work to increase efficiency, minimize waste, and encourage labourers to work harder.

As a foreman, Taylor was upset when employees slacked off, and he became obsessed with finding ways to speed up their work. Beginning in 1882, Taylor and his associates began time-and-motion studies. They would break down complex manufacturing tasks into smaller motions and time these as they were performed by workers considered efficient. Using the results as a norm, and factoring in time for delays and rest, Taylor came up with a set of instructions for work to be efficiently performed. Workers were expected to meet the standard rate, with bonuses paid for faster work and penalties given for slower.

Eventually, BETHLEHEM STEEL and other business owners hired Taylor to improve efficiency in their own shops. Shovel makers used his name as a seal of approval in their advertising. His theories laid the groundwork for the creation of the assembly line and were exported to Germany and the Soviet Union. Later, Taylor's disciples suggested that his management principles could be applied to non-industrial bureaucracies, such as government and schools.

Not everyone was happy with Taylor's ideas, however. For much of his career, Taylor was virulently opposed by workers' groups, unions, and muckraking journalists, who contended that his management system dehumanized workers.

SOURCE: Scott Heller, "Taking Taylor's Measure: Book Weighs Cultural Impact of Efficiency Expert's Ideas," *Chronicle of Higher Education,* July 21, 1993, A12. This is excerpted from the condensed version. Copyright 1993, *Chronicle of Higher Education.* Reprinted with permission of Scott Heller and the *Chronicle of Higher Education.*

We can see in the following News Note how Dell keeps on top of its time and motion studies.

Dell Does It Again

At DELL, an order that hits the factory floor at 9 A.M. is typically stacked in the back of a truck motoring down a highway by 1 P.M.

Inside Dell, the world's largest computer maker, executives study the assembly process with the intensity of Alfred Kinsey and his researchers. They wheel in video equipment to examine a work team's every movement, looking for any extraneous bends or wasted twists. Eliminating even a single screw from a product represents a saving of roughly four seconds per machine built—the time they've calculated it takes an employee, on average, to use the pneumatic screwdriver dangling above his or her head.

Computer software clocks the assembly-line performance of workers, whether they're putting together PCs or the servers and storage equipment that Dell sells to large companies. The most able are declared "master builders" and then videotaped so that others may watch and learn. The weak are told that it takes a special set of talents to cut it on the Dell factory floor—and shown the door.

SOURCE: Adapted from Gary Rivlin, "Who's Afraid of China?" *New York Times,* December 19, 2004, p. 244.

After labour tasks have been analyzed, an **operations flow document** can be prepared that lists all necessary activities and the time allowed for each. All activities should be analyzed as to their ability to add value to the product or service. Any nonvalue-added activities that are included in the operations flow document should

operations flow document
a listing of all tasks necessary to make a unit of product or perform a service and the time allowed for each operation

be targeted for reduction or elimination. Exhibit 7-2 presents a simplified operations flow document that reflects the manufacturing process for a six-button shirt at DBD. This document shows 5.5 minutes of move time that is nonvalue-added.

EXHIBIT 7-2

Operations Flow Document

Product: Six-button-front shirt Product Number: Stock Keeping Unit (SKU) #312				Revision Date: 3/1/10 Standard Job Size: 400
Operation ID#	**Department**	**Standard Labour Minutes per Shirt**	**Description of Task**	
27	Cutting	8.5	Align fabric for cutting (actual machine time, 6 minutes)	
29	Cutting	6.5	Cut fabric (actual machine time, 4 minutes)	
		5.5	Move to Sewing Department	
33	Sewing	7.0	Stitch fabric pieces together (actual machine time, 5.5 minutes)	
35	Sewing	3.5	Attach buttons (actual machine time, 2.0 minutes)	
37	Sewing	1.5	Attach label (actual machine time, 0.5 minutes)	

Labour rate standards should reflect the wages and fringe benefits paid to employees who perform the various production tasks. All personnel doing the same job in a given department may be paid the same wage rate. Alternatively, if employees within a department performing the same or similar tasks are paid different wage rates, a weighted average rate must be computed and used as the standard. The average rate is computed as the total wage cost per hour divided by the number of workers. At some companies, to promote a team rather than an individualistic perspective, company workers receive a bonus if the entire facility meets its production and quality targets. This bonus would not be considered in determining standard cost variances for direct labour.

As the composition of a labour team changes, the time needed to make a product may also change. For instance, workers who have been doing a job longer may be paid more and be able to do the job more quickly than those who were just hired. Often trade-offs must be made between rates and times for labour just as trade-offs are made between price and quality for material.

OVERHEAD STANDARDS

Management may use either a single predetermined plantwide rate or multiple departmental rates as the amount of the overhead standard cost. Additionally, the rate or rates may have separate variable and fixed components or be a combined rate.

The Cutting and Sewing departments at DBD rely heavily on direct labour. The predetermined variable manufacturing overhead rate for these two departments is $7 per direct labour hour. The two departments work a total of 27 (15 + 12) minutes on each shirt, so the total variable manufacturing overhead applied per shirt is $3.15 [(27 ÷ 60) × $7]. The fixed overhead rate for these two departments is $6 per machine hour. According to the operations flow document in Exhibit 7-2, the departments have a total of 18 (6 + 4 + 5.5 + 2 + 0.5) minutes of machine time. Thus, a total of $1.80 [(18 ÷ 60) × $6] of fixed manufacturing overhead will be applied to each shirt in these two departments. The costs associated with the 5.5 minutes of move time are considered part of manufacturing overhead and the overhead costs caused by move time are included in the predetermined manufacturing overhead rates.

After the bill of materials, operations flow document, and standard overhead costs have been developed, a **standard cost card** is prepared. The total standard material cost, along with other total costs, for one six-button-front shirt produced by DBD is shown in Exhibit 7-3. This document is shown as Exhibit 7-3 and summarizes all the standard quantities and costs needed to complete one six-button-front SKU #312 shirt.

standard cost card
a document that summarizes the direct materials and direct labour standard quantities and prices needed to complete one unit of product as well as the overhead allocation bases and rates

EXHIBIT 7-3
Standard Cost Card

Product: One size fits all, six-button-front shirt					SKU Number: 312

Direct Material

Departments

ID#	Unit Cost	Total Quantity	Cutting Cost	Sewing Cost	Total Cost
F-4	$3.50 per sq. metre	1.2 sq. metres	$4.20		$4.20
B-3	$0.15 each	6 per shirt		$0.90	0.90
L-1	$0.08 each	1 per shirt		0.08	0.08
Direct Material Totals			$4.20	$0.98	$5.18

Direct Labour

ID#	Average Wage per Minute	Total Minutes	Cutting Cost	Sewing Cost	Total Cost
27	$0.16	8.5	$1.36		$1.36
29	0.16	6.5	1.04		1.04
33	0.20	7.0		$1.40	1.40
35	0.24	3.5		0.84	0.84
37	0.14	1.5		0.21	0.21
Direct Labour Totals		27.0	$2.40	$2.45	$4.85

Production Overhead

Type of Overhead	Cost Driver	Standard Time Allowed	Standard Departmental Rate	Total Cost
Variable	Direct Labour Time	27 minutes	$7.00 per DLH	$3.15
Fixed	Machine Time	18 minutes	$6.00 per MH	1.80
Overhead Total				$4.95

Total Cost = $5.18 + $4.85 + $4.95 = $14.98

Standard costs and quantities are used during the period to assign costs to inventory accounts. In an actual or normal cost system, actual material and labour costs are charged to Work in Process Inventory as production occurs. In most standard cost systems, standard rather than actual costs of production are charged to Work in Process Inventory.[10] Any difference between actual and standard costs is a variance.

Because they are common input measures, direct labour hours and machine hours are used as cost drivers and referred to in the models that follow. Alternative cost drivers, such as setup time, metres of material moved, or number of defective units produced, may be more appropriately related to cost incurrence. Using these measures does not change the manner in which the calculations are made.

VARIANCE COMPUTATIONS

The most basic variance computation is the total difference between actual cost incurred and standard cost allowed for the period's output. This variance can be diagrammed as follows:

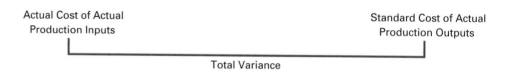

A total variance can be computed for each production cost element; however, total variances do not provide useful information for determining why cost differences occurred. To help managers in their control function, total variances for materials and labour are subdivided into price and quantity elements.

price variance
the difference between what was paid and what should have been paid for inputs during the period

A **price variance** reflects the difference between what was paid and what should have been paid for inputs during the period. A **quantity variance** provides a monetary measure of the difference between the quantity of actual inputs and the standard quantity of inputs allowed for the actual output of the period. Quantity variances focus on the efficiency of results—the relationship of inputs to outputs. Quantity can be measured as metres of material, hours of direct labour time, number of setups, or any other specified and reasonable indicator of output.

quantity variance
the difference between the quantity of actual inputs and the standard quantity of inputs for the actual output of the period multiplied by a standard price or rate

The diagram used to calculate a total variance can be expanded to provide a general model indicating the subvariances:

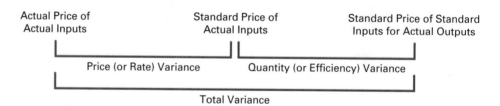

standard quantity allowed
a measure of quantity that translates the actual output achieved into the standard input quantity that should have been used to achieve that output

The middle column is a planned (budget) column and indicates what costs should have been incurred for actual inputs. The far-right column uses a measure of output known as the **standard quantity allowed**, which translates actual output into the standard quantity of input that *should have been used* to achieve the actual level of output. This measurement is computed as the standard quantity allowed multiplied by the standard price of the input resources.

A simplified diagram using the abbreviated notations is shown in Exhibit 7-4. This model progresses from the *actual* price of *actual* input on the left to the *standard* price of *standard* input allowed on the right. The middle measure of input is a hybrid of *actual* quantity and *standard* price. The price variance portion of the total variance is measured as the actual input quantity multiplied by the difference between the actual and standard prices:

$$\text{Price variance} = \text{AQ} \, (\text{AP} - \text{SP})$$

The quantity variance is determined as the standard price multiplied by the difference between the *actual* quantity used and the standard quantity allowed for the *actual* output:

$$\text{Quantity variance} = \text{SP} \, (\text{AQ} - \text{SQ})$$

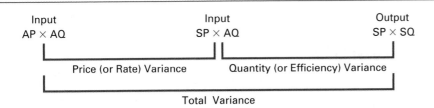

EXHIBIT 7-4

Simplified Variance Model

where AP = Actual material price or actual labour rate
AQ = Actual quantity of material or actual labour hours
SP = Standard material price or standard labour rate
SQ = Standard quantity of material or standard labour hours

Production of the Six-Button-Front Shirt #312 in the Cutting Department of DBD is used to illustrate variance computations. The standard costs in this department are taken from the standard cost card in Exhibit 7-3 on page 389, and are repeated at the top of Exhibit 7-5. Also shown in Exhibit 7-5 are the actual quantity and cost data for the week of June 12–16, 2010. This information is used in computing

EXHIBIT 7-5

Cutting Department's Information for One Six-Button-Front Shirt

Standards for One Six-Button-Front Shirt SKU #312

1.2 square metres of white cotton fabric at $3.50 per square metre	$4.20
15 minutes of labour at $9.60 per hour ($0.16 per minute)	2.40
Applied variable manufacturing overhead (based on 15 minutes of direct labour time at $7 per DLH)	1.75
Applied fixed manufacturing overhead (based on 10 minutes of machine time at $6 per machine hour (MH)*	1.00
Total standard Cutting Department cost per shirt	$9.35

Actual Data for June 12–16, 2010

Number of shirts produced	2,200
Square metres of cotton fabric used	2,730
Square metres of cotton fabric purchased	3,000
Direct labour hours incurred	500
Machine hours used	350
Actual price per square metre of cotton fabric used	$ 4.15
Average direct labour rate per hour	10.00
Total variable manufacturing overhead cost	3,360.00
Total fixed manufacturing overhead	2,875.00

Standard Quantities Allowed

Direct Material:
Standard quantity allowed for cloth = 2,200 shirts × 1.2 square metres per shirt
= 2,640 square metres

Direct Labour:
Standard quantity allowed for direct labour hours = 2,200 shirts × 15 minutes per shirt
= 33,000 minutes or 550 hours.

Variable Manufacturing Overhead:
Applied on the basis of direct labour hours = 2,200 shirts × 15 minutes per shirt
= 33,000 minutes or 550 hours

Fixed Manufacturing Overhead:
Standard quantity allowed for machine hours = 2,200 shirts × 10 minutes per shirt
= 22,000 minutes or 366 2/3 hours

*The $6 rate per machine hour is based on total expected fixed overhead of $124,800 for the year and an expected 20,800 machine hours related to the production of these shirts. This product is expected to be produced evenly at the rate of 2,496 shirts per week for 50 weeks of the year or 124,800 shirts for the year.

the material, labour, and overhead variances for the week. Variance computations must indicate whether the variance is favourable (F) or unfavourable (U).

Material Variances

Using the model and inserting information concerning material quantities and prices provides the following computations. (Note that the standard quantity for cloth is taken from Exhibit 7-5.)

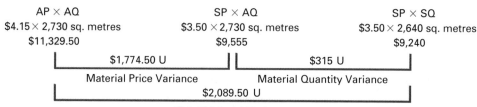

The subvariances for materials are known as the material price and material quantity variances. A **material price variance** exists if the amount is either above or below the standard price for the quantity of materials purchased. If this amount is less than standard the variance is considered favourable (F). If the amount spent is greater than standard it is considered an unfavourable variance (U). For DBD, the actual price paid for cotton fabric was $4.15 per square metre, while the standard price was $3.50, giving an unfavourable material price variance of $1,774.50. This variance can also be calculated as [2,730 ($4.15 − $3.50) = $1,774.50]. The sign of the unfavourable variance is positive because the actual price is more than the standard price.[11]

It has been suggested that the use of purchase price variances will lead to an increase in order quantities in order to obtain lower prices. The result will be excess inventory, increased carrying costs, and the purchasing of low-quality materials because quality and delivery are ignored.[12]

The **material quantity variance** (MQV) indicates the cost saved (F) or expended (U) because of the difference between the actual quantity of material used and the standard quantity of material allowed for the goods produced or services rendered during the period. The company has been more efficient than expected if the actual quantity used is less than the standard quantity allowed. If a greater quantity has been used than allowed, the company has been less efficient. DBD used 90 more square metres of cotton fabric than the standard allowed for the actual production of 2,200 shirts. This inefficient usage resulted in an unfavourable material quantity variance [$3.50 × (2,730 − 2,640) = $3.50 × (90) = $315].

The total material variance of $2,089.50 U can be calculated by taking the difference between the total actual cost of inputs ($11,329.50) and the total standard cost of the outputs ($9,240). The total variance also represents the summation of the individual material price and quantity subvariances: ($1,774.50 U + $315 U = $2,089.50 U).

Point of Purchase Material Variance Model

A total variance for a cost component generally equals the sum of the price and quantity subvariances. An exception to this rule occurs when the quantity of material purchased is not the same as the quantity of material placed into production. In such cases, the general model is altered slightly to provide information more rapidly for management control purposes.

Because the material price variance relates to the purchasing (not production) function, the altered model calculates the material price variance at the point of

material price variance
the amount of money spent below (F for favourable) or above (U for unfavourable) the standard price for the quantity of materials purchased

material quantity variance
the cost saved (F) or expended (U) because of the difference between the actual quantity of material used and the standard quantity of material allowed for the goods produced or services rendered during the period

purchase and bases that calculation on the quantity of materials *purchased* rather than the quantity of materials *used*. This variation in the model allows the material price variance to be isolated or pinpointed as close to the variance source and as quickly as possible. The material quantity variance is still computed on the basis of the actual quantity of materials used in production.

Assume that DBD had purchased 3,000 square metres of cotton fabric for production of SKU #312 shirts; however, as shown in Exhibit 7-5, the Company had only used 2,730 square metres during the week of June 12–16, 2010. The point of purchase material price variance (Material Purchase Price Variance) is calculated as shown below.

$$\text{AP} \times \text{AQ} \qquad\qquad\qquad \text{SP} \times \text{AQ}$$
$$\$4.15 \times 3{,}000 \qquad\qquad \$3.50 \times 3{,}000$$
$$\$12{,}450 \qquad\qquad\qquad \$10{,}500$$

$$\$1{,}950 \text{ U}$$
Material Price Variance

This change in the general model is shown below, with subscripts to indicate actual quantity purchased (p) and used (u).

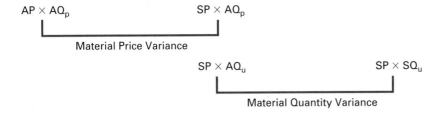

$$\text{AP} \times \text{AQ}_p \qquad\qquad \text{SP} \times \text{AQ}_p$$

Material Price Variance

$$\text{SP} \times \text{AQ}_u \qquad\qquad \text{SP} \times \text{SQ}_u$$

Material Quantity Variance

The material quantity variance is still calculated as presented earlier because the actual quantity of cotton fabric used in production is determined by the amount used and not by the amount purchased. Thus, the MQV would remain at $315 U. A point-of-purchase variance computation results in the material price and quantity variances being computed from different bases. For this reason, the above variances should not be summed; thus, no total material variance can be determined in this case.

Basing Price Variance on Purchases Rather Than Usage

Traditionally, the material price variance computation has been more commonly based on purchases rather than on usage. This choice allows management to calculate the variance as near as possible to the time of cost incurrence. Although a point-of-purchase calculation allows managers to see the impact of buying decisions more rapidly, such information may not be highly relevant in a just-in-time environment. Buying materials that are not needed currently requires that the materials be stored and moved—both nonvalue-added activities. Any price savings from such purchases should be measured against the additional costs of such a purchase.

Additionally, a point-of-purchase price variance may reduce a manager's ability to recognize a relationship between a favourable material price variance and an unfavourable material usage variance. If a favourable price variance results from the purchase of lower quality materials, the effects of that purchase are not known until the materials are actually used.

Labour Variances

The price and usage elements of the total labour variance are called the labour rate and labour efficiency variances. The model for computing these variances and computations for DBD follow. The standard quantity is taken from Exhibit 7-5 on page 391 for direct labour hours.

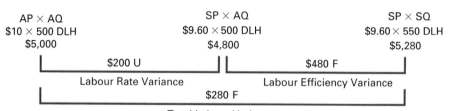

AP × AQ	SP × AQ	SP × SQ
$10 × 500 DLH	$9.60 × 500 DLH	$9.60 × 550 DLH
$5,000	$4,800	$5,280

$200 U — Labour Rate Variance
$480 F — Labour Efficiency Variance
$280 F — Total Labour Variance

labour rate variance
the difference between the total actual direct labour wages for the period and the standard rate for all hours actually worked during the period

labour efficiency variance
the difference between the number of actual direct labour hours worked and the standard hours allowed for the actual output multiplied by standard labour rate per hour

The **labour rate variance** (LRV) shows the difference between the actual rate or actual weighted average rate paid to the direct labour workers for the period and the standard rate for all hours actually worked during the period. The labour rate variance is computed as [500 × ($10 − $9.60)] = $200 U.

The **labour efficiency variance** (LEV) compares the number of actual direct labour hours worked with the standard hours allowed for the actual number of shirts produced. The difference is multiplied by the standard labour rate to establish a dollar value for the efficiency (F) or inefficiency (U) of the direct labour workers. The labour efficiency variance can also be calculated as [$9.60 × (500 − 550)] = −$480 F. The sign of the favourable variance is negative because the actual number of hours worked is *fewer than* the standard hours allowed to make the actual number of shirts.

The total labour variance ($280 F) can be determined by subtracting the total standard labour cost for the actual production ($5,280) from the total actual labour cost ($5,000). Alternatively, the total labour variance can be found by adding the labour rate and efficiency variances [$200 U + (−$480 F)].

The following News Note provides a slightly different perspective on efficiency variances. It suggests that the efficiency variance is truly composed of two elements—quality problems and efficiency problems—that should be accounted for separately.

GENERAL NEWS NOTE

Separating Quality Problems from Efficiency Problems

Historically, efficiency variances have been computed by multiplying excess inputs by the standard price. In recent years, this approach has been criticized for motivating managers to ignore quality concerns to avoid unfavourable efficiency variances. In other words, there is an incentive to produce a low-quality product by minimizing the amount of material used or the time spent in production.

An approach could be taken that separates the efficiency variance from the quality variance. Inputs consisting of conversion time or material used in defective units would be captured in the quality variance.

Separating the two variances allows production decision makers to evaluate the trade-offs between efficiency and quality. They can minimize production time to gain a favourable efficiency variance but this probably will increase the number of defective units and result in an unfavourable quality variance. Likewise, trying to minimize the number of defective units may result in investing more time and more material and therefore having an unfavourable efficiency variance.

SOURCE: Carole Cheatham, "Updating Standard Cost Systems," *Journal of Accountancy*, December 1990, pp. 59–60.

As the News Note points out, a company may achieve reductions in labour time and, thus, have favourable efficiency variances by producing defective or poor-quality units. For example, assume that workers who are earning $15 per hour can produce one unit of product in two hours. During a period, 1,500 units are made in 2,610 hours. The standard quantity of time allowed for production is 3,000 hours. The labour efficiency variance is AR(AH − SH) = $15 (2,610 − 3,000), or $5,850 F. However, 80 of the 1,500 units were defective and nonsaleable. The favourable efficiency variance of $5,850 fails to include the impact of those nonquality units. A quality variance can be computed as follows: 80 defective units × 2 hours per unit × $15 per hour or $2,400 U. Subtracting this unfavourable quality variance from the $5,850 favourable efficiency variance provides a net true efficiency variance for the production of 1,420 good units, or $3,450 F. This restated efficiency variance can be shown as follows:

1,420 (1,500 − 80) good units × 2 hours per unit = 2,840 standard hours allowed (SHA)
2,840 (1,420 × 2) SHA − 2,610 actual hours = 230 hours less than standard (F)
230 hours × $15 standard cost per hour = $3,450 (F) efficiency variance

Manufacturing Overhead Variances

The use of separate variable and fixed manufacturing overhead application rates and accounts allows the computation of separate variances for each type of overhead. These separate computations provide managers with the greatest detail as well as the greatest flexibility for control and performance evaluation purposes. Also, because of increased use of nonsimilar bases for various overhead allocations, each different cost pool for variable and fixed manufacturing overhead may require separate price and usage (quantity) computations. In the Cutting Department of DBD, variable and fixed manufacturing overhead calculations are based, respectively, on direct labour hours and machine hours.

As with material and labour, total variable and total fixed manufacturing overhead variances can be subdivided into specific price and quantity subvariances for each type of overhead. The overhead subvariances are referred to as follows:

Variable overhead price element ⟶ Variable overhead spending variance

Variable overhead quantity element ⟶ Variable overhead efficiency variance

Fixed overhead price element ⟶ Fixed overhead spending variance

Fixed overhead quantity element ⟶ Fixed overhead volume variance

Variable Overhead

The total variable overhead (VOH) variance is the difference between actual variable manufacturing overhead costs incurred for the period and standard variable manufacturing overhead cost applied to the period's actual production or service output. The difference at year-end is the total variable manufacturing overhead variance, which is also the amount of underapplied or overapplied variable manufacturing overhead. The following diagram illustrates the computation of the total variable overhead variance.

Actual Variable Overhead Cost   Variable Overhead Cost Applied to Production*

Total Variable Overhead (VOH) Variance

*based on standard hours allowed

The following variable manufacturing overhead variance computations use the June 12–16, 2010, data for the Cutting Department of DBD Ltd. The actual variable manufacturing overhead cost for the week was $3,360 for 500 direct labour hours or $6.72 per direct labour hour; 550 standard direct labour hours were allowed for that week's production. The variable manufacturing overhead for each direct labour hour was expected to cost the company $7. The variable overhead variances for the Cutting Department are computed as shown below.

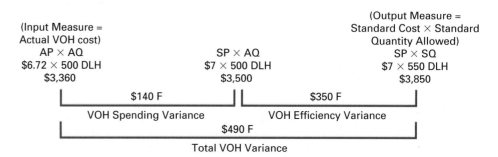

variable overhead spending variance the difference between actual variable overhead and budgeted (planned) variable overhead based on actual input

variable overhead efficiency variance the difference between budgeted (planned) variable overhead at actual input activity and budgeted variable overhead at standard input activity allowed

The **variable overhead spending** (or budget) **variance** is the difference between actual variable manufacturing overhead and budgeted (planned) variable manufacturing overhead based on actual input. The **variable overhead efficiency variance** is the difference between budgeted (planned) variable manufacturing overhead at the actual input activity and budgeted (planned) variable manufacturing overhead at standard input (such as DLHs) allowed. This variance quantifies the effect of using more or less actual input than the standard allowed. When actual input exceeds standard input allowed, operations appear inefficient. Excess input also means that more variable overhead is needed to support the additional input.

Fixed Overhead

The total fixed manufacturing overhead (FOH) variance is the difference between actual FOH cost incurred and standard FOH cost allowed for the period's actual production. The following model shows the computation of the total fixed overhead variance.

*based on standard hours allowed for production achieved.

The total fixed manufacturing overhead variance is subdivided into its price and quantity elements by the insertion of budgeted (planned) fixed overhead as a middle column into the model.

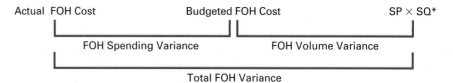

*based on standard hours allowed for production achieved.

In the model, the left column is simply labelled "actual FOH cost" and is not computed as a price times quantity measure because fixed overhead is generally acquired in lump-sum amounts rather than on a per-unit input basis. The **fixed overhead spending** (or budget) **variance** is the difference between actual and planned fixed overhead. The fixed overhead **volume variance** is the difference between budgeted and standard fixed overhead bases on production achieved. The volume variance occurs by producing at a level different from that used to set the predetermined overhead rate.

Fixed overhead is a constant amount throughout the relevant range; thus, *the middle column is a constant figure regardless of the actual quantity of input or the standard quantity of input allowed.* This concept is a key element in computing FOH variances. The budgeted amount of fixed overhead is equal to the standard FOH rate times the estimated capacity measure used to compute the standard rate.

The Cutting Department of D & B Didona Clothing Ltd. had estimated that 2,496 shirts would be produced each week, amounting to a total of 416 hours of machine time ($2,496 \times 10$ minutes = 24,960 minutes; 24,960 minutes $\div$ 60 minutes = 416 hours). Based on the production plan, the weekly fixed manufacturing overhead budget for the department is $2,496 (416 hours $\times$ $6).[13]

The standard fixed overhead equals the FOH application rate ($6.00) times the standard input allowed for the production achieved. In regard to fixed manufacturing overhead, the standard input allowed for the production achieved measures capacity utilization for the period. The standard input for DBD's Cutting Department is 10 minutes of machine time per shirt. Since 2,200 shirts were produced, the standard machine time allowed is 366 2/3 hours, as shown at the bottom of Exhibit 7-5.

Inserting the data for the Cutting Department into the model gives the following:

fixed overhead spending variance
the difference between actual and budgeted (planned) fixed overhead

volume variance
the difference between budget (planned) capacity and standard hours allowed for production attained (basically a measure of utilization of the plant facilities)

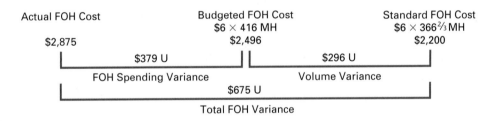

The week's actual fixed overhead cost is $2,875, while the planned amount is $2,496. The $379 unfavourable difference is the FOH spending variance, which could be related to a variety of causes such as increased rent payments or increased insurance premiums for machinery and equipment.

The FOH application rate is $6 per machine hour. This rate exists because the company expected a total of $124,800 in fixed overhead costs for the year and chose an expected annual capacity level of 20,800 machine hours. Each shirt requires 10 minutes of machine time, so the company can make six shirts in an hour. Therefore, expected capacity of shirts for the year is 124,800 shirts (20,800 hours $\times$ 6 shirts per hour) over a 50-week work-year. Had any capacity level other than 20,800 machine hours been chosen, the fixed overhead rate would have been different, even though the total amount of budgeted fixed overhead ($124,800) would have been the same. *If any level of capacity is experienced other than that which was used in determining the application rate, a volume variance will occur.* For example, if DBD had chosen a yearly amount of 110,000 shirts (2,200 shirts per week) as the denominator level of activity for setting the predetermined FOH rate, there would be no volume variance for the week of June 12–16. If any number of shirts less than 2,200 had been chosen as the denominator level of activity, the volume variance would have been favourable.

The difference between the $2,496 budgeted FOH and the $2,200 standard FOH gives the $296 unfavourable volume variance for the week. This variance is also equal to the difference of 296 shirts (2,496 − 2,200) that the company expected to make but did not produce multiplied by the $1 standard fixed overhead rate per shirt.[14] The variance is unfavourable because fewer shirts were produced this week than budgeted. The $675 unfavourable total fixed manufacturing overhead variance is the underapplied balance in the fixed manufacturing overhead account for the week.

variance analysis
the process of categorizing the nature (favourable or unfavourable) of the differences between standard and actual costs and seeking the reasons for those differences

COST CONTROL AND VARIANCE RESPONSIBILITY

Cost control focuses on the variances between actual costs incurred for a period and the standard costs that should have been incurred based on actual output. To exercise any type of effective control, managers first must be provided with detailed information on the various cost components. Second, a well-designed system of cost control and variance analysis should capture variances as early as possible.

Variance analysis is the process of categorizing the nature—favourable (standard is greater than actual) or unfavourable (actual is greater than standard)—of the differences between standard and actual costs and seeking the reasons for those differences. It is important to recognize the fact that a favourable variance does not mean "good" and an unfavourable variance does not mean "bad." Given this fact, it is important to analyze all variances in order to understand what circumstances gave rise to them.

The cost control and variance analysis system should help managers determine who or what is responsible for the variance and who is best able to explain it. When variances reflect poor performance, an early measurement system may allow operational performance to be improved. The longer the reporting of a variance is delayed, the more difficult it becomes to determine its cause.

Material price and labour rate variances are not as controllable at the production or service level as are material quantity and labour efficiency variances. Price and rate standards are more dependent on outside forces, such as market competition and wage contracts, than are usage standards.

Material Variances

Material price variances are normally determined at the point of purchase. Although not always able to control prices, purchasing agents, if given adequate lead time and resources, should be able to influence prices. This influence is exerted through knowing what suppliers are available and choosing suppliers that provide the appropriate material in the most reasonable time span at the most reasonable cost. The purchasing agent can also influence material prices by purchasing in quantities that provide price discounts or by engaging in contractual arrangements such as long-term purchase contracts.

The purchasing agent is usually the person who is best able to explain why a material price variance occurs. Also, as part of the team that originally set the material price standard, the purchasing agent is usually the individual responsible for material price variances.

Material quantity variances can be determined when materials are issued or used. Such variances are considered the responsibility of the person in charge of the job or department. Materials are ordinarily requisitioned based on the number of actual units to be produced times the standard quantity per unit. When additional materials are taken out of inventory, material requisition slips of a different colour may be filled out. These colour-coded excess requisition slips allow control to occur as work is underway rather than at the end of the period or when production is completed. Monitoring requisition slips for significant excess material withdrawals alerts managers to seek causes for the excesses and, if possible, take timely corrective action.

Some production settings, such as chemical and petroleum processing, involve a continuous flow of material. In these cases, it may not be practical or reasonable to isolate quantity variances when materials are placed into production. The material quantity variance is more feasibly measured when production is complete and the total quantity of production is known. Measuring usage for relatively short time periods and reporting quantity variances after production is complete can still assist management in controlling operations. Labour efficiency variances are also more appropriately measured at the end of production in these types of manufacturing operations.

There are exceptions to the normal assignment of responsibility for material price and quantity variances. Assume that the manager in the Cutting Department at DBD asks the purchasing agent to acquire, without adequate lead time, additional quantities of cotton fabric. She makes this request because the marketing manager has just told her that the demand for Six-Button-Front Style #312 shirts has unexpectedly increased. Making a spur-of-the-moment acquisition of this kind could result in paying a price higher than standard. Price variances resulting from these types of causes should be assigned to production or marketing/merchandising—for inadequate predictions—not to purchasing.

In contrast, if the purchasing agent acquires inferior-quality cotton fabric that results in excess consumption and an unfavourable quantity variance. This quantity variance should be assigned to purchasing rather than to production. Such situations are likely to be identified from continuous, rather than end-of-period, reporting.

Labour Variances

Labour rate and labour efficiency variances are commonly identified as part of the payroll process and assigned to the person in charge of the production or service area. The labour rate variance is often caused by inappropriate hiring and thus the responsibility should be shared by both the Human Resources (HR) area and the Production department. This assignment assumes that the manager has the ability to influence the type of labour personnel used. In many cases, however, it is very difficult to focus blame on any one individual. For instance, the Cutting Department manager could use skilled or unskilled workers to align, mark, and cut material. Using highly skilled, highly paid individuals for lower-level jobs could cause an unfavourable labour rate variance, accompanied by a favourable labour efficiency variance. Thus, as with material variances, correlations may exist between labour variances.

Sometimes a common factor may cause multiple variances. For instance, in manufacturing, the purchase of inferior-quality materials could result in a favourable material price variance, an unfavourable material quantity variance, and an unfavourable labour efficiency variance. The efficiency variance could reflect increased production time, since many units were rejected as substandard because of the inferior materials. In another common situation, the use of lower-paid, less-skilled workers results in a favourable rate variance but causes excessive material usage and decreased labour efficiency.

The probability of detecting relationships among variances is improved, but not assured, by timely variance reporting. The accounting and reporting process should highlight interrelationships of variances, and managers should be aware of the possibility of such relationships when reviewing variance reports.

Overhead Variances

The difference between actual and applied overhead is the amount of underapplied and overapplied overhead or the total overhead variance that must be explained. Control purposes differ for variable and fixed overhead because of the types of costs that make up the two categories and the ability of managers to influence those costs. This is borne out by the example at Howmet Castings' Whitehall casting facility, discussed in the News Note below.

GENERAL NEWS NOTE

Challenges With Standard Costing

Tom McDonald, information systems manager and assistant controller at HOWMET CASTINGS' Whitehall, Michigan, casting facility, finds the biggest challenge he faces with standard costing is handling fixed and semi-fixed costs. Volume changes will result in different fixed costs per unit because, by definition, these costs (in total) do not change with different volumes (at least within a certain range of production). There's a danger management will mistakenly think its fixed costs have decreased due to higher volumes and underprice its parts, even when future volumes are lower.

To determine volume for standard fixed cost allocation, Whitehall's cost managers look at the various operations or capital equipment required, and use 80% of total capacity (to allow for normal downtime for maintenance and as a buffer for unforeseen breakdowns). Accounting textbooks might refer to this as "practical capacity." Using practical capacity in developing fixed cost allocation rates results in cost standards that include only the cost of capacity actually used in production. Whitehall partially tracks the cost of unused capacity through efficiency percentages.

SOURCE: Kip R. Krumwiede, "Tips From the Trenches on Standard Costing," *Cost Management Update*, IMA, Issue 106, April 2000.

Variable Overhead

Variable overhead (VOH) costs are incurred on a continual basis as work is performed and are directly related to that work. Because of this direct relationship to activity, control of VOH costs is similar to control of material and labour. Companies control variable overhead by (1) keeping actual costs in line with planned costs for the actual level of activity and (2) getting the planned output yield from the overhead resources placed into production.

Variable overhead spending variances are commonly caused by price differences—paying average actual prices that are higher or lower than the standard prices allowed. Such fluctuations often occur because price changes have not been reflected in the standard rate. For instance, average indirect labour wage rates, supply costs, or utility rates may have increased or decreased since the standard VOH rate was computed. In such instances, the standard rate should be adjusted.

If managers have no control over prices charged by external parties, they should not be held accountable for variances arising because of such price changes. In contrast, if managers could influence prices—for example through long-term purchase arrangements—such options should be investigated as to their long-term costs and benefits before a decision is made to change the standard. Waste or spoilage of resources, such as indirect materials, is another possible cause of the VOH spending variance.

The VOH efficiency variance reflects the managerial control implemented or needed in regard to the yield of output as related to input. VOH represents a variety of resources that, like direct material and direct labour, bear a known and measurable relationship to the activity base used to represent production activity. These resources are managed by monitoring and measuring their actual use in conformity with standard usage, promptly investigating any variances, and adjusting resource usage when necessary. Control of the variable overhead resource elements can only be achieved if the variance from standard for each VOH component is analyzed rather than attempting to analyze and control variable overhead in total. The cost and usage of each component of VOH could react independently of the others.

If variable manufacturing overhead is applied on the basis of direct labour hours, the signs (favourable or unfavourable) of the variable overhead and direct labour efficiency variances will be the same, because the actual and standard hours compared in the two calculations are the same. However, when alternative overhead application bases are used, the signs of these two variances may no longer be related to each other. Use of any alternative base, including those provided under activity-based costing,[15] does not affect the implementation of a standard cost system.

Fixed Overhead

Control of fixed manufacturing overhead is distinctly different from control of variable manufacturing overhead because fixed overhead may not be directly related to current activity. Since many types of fixed manufacturing costs must be committed to in lump-sum amounts before current period activity takes place, managers may have only limited ability to control FOH costs in the short run. Once managers commit to a fixed cost, it becomes unchangeable for some period of time *regardless of whether actual work takes place*. Thus, control of many fixed overhead costs must occur at the *time of commitment* rather than at the *time of production activity*.

Fixed Overhead Spending Variance

The FOH spending variance normally represents a variance in the costs of fixed overhead components, although this variance can also reflect mismanagement of resources. Control over the FOH spending variance often must take place on a transaction-by-transaction basis when managers arrange for facilities. Many fixed overhead costs are basically uncontrollable in the short run. For example, depreciation expense is based on the equipment's historical cost, salvage value, and expected life. Utility costs, which are partially fixed, are often set by rate commissions and are influenced by the size and type of the physical plant. Even a "turn-off-the-lights" program can reduce utility costs only by a limited amount. Repairs and maintenance, which are also partially fixed, can be controlled to some extent, but are highly affected by the type of operation involved. Salaries are contractual obligations that were set at the time of employment or salary review.

The information provided by a total FOH spending variance amount would not be specific enough to allow management to decide whether corrective action was possible or desirable. Individual cost variances for each component need to be reviewed. Such a review will help managers determine the actual causes of and responsibility for the several components of the total fixed overhead spending variance.

Volume Variance

In addition to controlling spending, utilizing capacity is another important aspect of managerial control. Capacity utilization is reflected in the volume variance because that computation is directly affected by the capacity level chosen to calculate the predetermined or standard fixed overhead application rate. Although utilization is controllable to some degree, the volume variance is the variance over which managers have the least influence and control, especially in the short run. But it is important that managers exercise what ability they do have to influence and control capacity utilization.

An unfavourable volume variance indicates less-than-expected utilization of capacity. If available capacity is currently being used at a level below or above that which was anticipated, managers should recognize that condition, investigate the reasons for it, and initiate appropriate action as needed. The degree of capacity utilization should always be viewed in relation to inventory and sales. If capacity is overutilized (a favourable volume variance) and inventory is stockpiling, managers should decrease capacity utilization. A favourable volume variance could, however, be due to increased sales demand with no stockpiling of inventory—in which case no adjustments should be made to reduce utilization.

If capacity is underutilized (an unfavourable volume variance) and sales are back-ordered or going unfilled, managers should try to increase capacity utilization. However, managers must understand that underutilization of capacity is not always undesirable. In a manufacturing company, it is more appropriate for managers not to produce goods that would simply end up in inventory stockpiles. Unneeded inventory production, although it serves to utilize capacity, generates substantially more costs for material, labour, and overhead, including storage and handling costs. The positive impact that such unneeded production will have on the fixed overhead volume variance is outweighed by the unnecessary costs of accumulating excess inventory.

Managers can sometimes influence capacity utilization by modifying work schedules, taking measures to relieve production constraints, eliminating nonvalue-added activities, and carefully monitoring the movement of resources through the production or service process. Such actions should be taken during the period rather than after the period has ended. Efforts made after work is completed may improve next period's operations but will have no impact on current work.

Expected annual capacity—rather than practical or theoretical capacity—is often selected as the denominator level of activity by which to compute the predetermined fixed manufacturing overhead application rate. Use of this base does, however, ignore an important management concern—that of unused capacity. Having but not using capacity creates additional nonvalue-added organizational costs. The only way these costs can be highlighted is through the selection of practical or theoretical capacity to compute the fixed manufacturing overhead application rate.

Rather than using the traditional fixed overhead computations, companies may want to compute fixed overhead variances in a manner that could provide additional information. This innovative process is described in Exhibit 7-6 below using DBD's production of the Six-Button-Front Shirt #312. In this example, the fixed manufacturing overhead rate is computed on the basis of practical capacity rather than expected annual capacity. This computation allows managers to focus on the cost of unused capacity so that it can be accounted for and, therefore, analyzed and controlled.[16]

Total fixed manufacturing overhead costs (from Exhibit 7-5)	$124,800
Total practical annual capacity of the factory in Machine Hours (MH)	25,000
Total expected annual capacity of the factory in MH (from Exhibit 7-5)	20,800

Predetermined fixed manufacturing overhead rate based on practical capacity
= $124,800 ÷ 25,000 = ≈ $4.99 per MH

Practical capacity	25,000	MH
Expected annual capacity	20,800	MH
Unused capacity	4,200	MH
Multiplied by the cost per MH	×$4.99	
Cost of unused capacity	$20,958	

If 20,000 MH are the standard hours allowed for actual production, the company would have a capacity utilization variance of $3,992 U [(20,800 − 20,000) × $4.99].

If 21,000 MH are the standard hours allowed for actual production, the company would have a capacity utilization variance of $998 F [(20,800 − 21,000) × $4.99].

EXHIBIT 7-6
Calculating a Capacity Utilization Variance

CONVERSION COST AS AN ELEMENT IN STANDARD COSTING

Conversion cost consists of both direct labour and manufacturing overhead. The traditional view separates the elements of product cost into three categories: direct material, direct labour, and overhead. This practice is appropriate in labour-intensive production settings; however, in more highly automated factories, direct labour cost generally represents an extremely small part of total product cost. In such circumstances, one worker may oversee a large number of machines and may deal more with troubleshooting machine malfunctions than converting raw materials into finished products. These new conditions mean that workers' wages are more closely associated with indirect labour than direct labour.

Many companies have responded to having large overhead costs and small direct labour costs by adapting their standard cost systems to provide for only two elements of product cost: direct material and conversion. In these situations, conversion costs are likely to be separated into their variable and fixed components. Conversion costs are also likely to be separated into direct and indirect categories based on their ability to be traced to a machine rather than to a product. Overhead may be applied by use of a variety of cost drivers, including machine hours, cost of materials, number of production runs, number of machine setups, and throughput time.

Variance analysis for conversion cost in automated plants normally focuses on the following: (1) spending variances for overhead costs, (2) efficiency variances for machinery and production costs rather than labour costs, and (3) the traditional volume variance for production. In an automated system, managers are likely to be able to better control not only the spending and efficiency variances but also the volume variance. Variance analysis under a conversion cost approach is illustrated in Exhibit 7-7. Regardless of the method by which they are computed, variances that are significant in amount must be analyzed so that they can assist managers in gaining production efficiencies and in controlling costs.

EXHIBIT 7-7
Variances Under a
Conversion Cost Approach

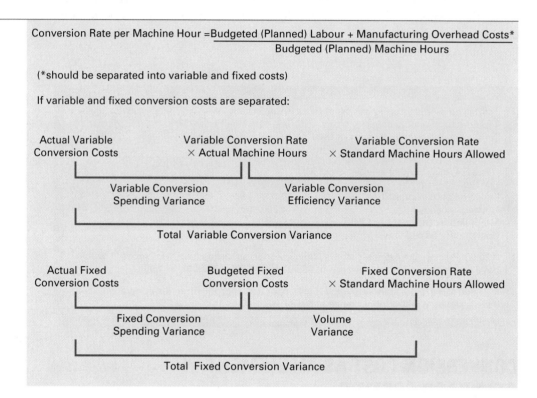

Conversion Rate per Machine Hour = (Budgeted (Planned) Labour + Manufacturing Overhead Costs*) / Budgeted (Planned) Machine Hours

(*should be separated into variable and fixed costs)

If variable and fixed conversion costs are separated:

| Actual Variable Conversion Costs | Variable Conversion Rate × Actual Machine Hours | Variable Conversion Rate × Standard Machine Hours Allowed |

Variable Conversion Spending Variance | Variable Conversion Efficiency Variance

Total Variable Conversion Variance

| Actual Fixed Conversion Costs | Budgeted Fixed Conversion Costs | Fixed Conversion Rate × Standard Machine Hours Allowed |

Fixed Conversion Spending Variance | Volume Variance

Total Fixed Conversion Variance

LEARNING OBJECTIVE 5

How do organizational evolution and desired level of attainability affect standard setting?

CONSIDERATIONS IN ESTABLISHING STANDARDS

When standards are established, appropriateness and attainability should be considered. Appropriateness, in relation to a standard, refers to the basis on which the standards are developed and how long they are expected to last. Attainability refers to the degree of difficulty or rigour that should be incurred in achieving the standard.

Appropriateness

Although standards are developed from past and current information, they should reflect technical and environmental factors expected for the period in which the standards are to be applied. Factors such as material quality, normal ordering quantities, employee wage rates (including expectations of increases in the minimum wage), degree of plant automation, facility layout, and mix of employee skills should be considered. Management should not think that standards, once set, will remain useful forever. Standards must evolve over an organization's life to reflect its changing methods and processes. Current operating performance cannot be compared against out-of-date standards because to do so would generate variances that would be illogical for planning, controlling, decision making, or evaluating performance.

When standard costing systems are used, standards must be modified at specific points in the production process. Companies that do so at levels that are difficult to achieve may face resistance from employees. This is a potential obstacle, one that may discourage manufacturers from modifying standards to address environmental changes.[17]

To illustrate this point, suppose that Bright Pearl Seafood Restaurant had set labour time standards before initiating the modular, cross-functional teams that caused labour times to decline drastically, in part because of the elimination of many nonvalue-added labour movements. If these standards were not changed after the reorganization, consistently favourable labour efficiency variances would result. Managers should recognize that these efficiency variances would not be relevant to evaluating worker performance, determining inventory valuation, or making product pricing decisions. Rather, the new time reductions would make the standards obsolete and worthless. The following News Note provides further insight into the rationale for not using historical information.

Don't Carry Your Mistakes Forward

GENERAL NEWS NOTE

Using historical information for standards is seldom specific enough and never provides targets. If you have operated inefficiently and spent too much in the past, you simply build all those costs and problems and deficiencies into the system. That kind of cost accounting is really an obstacle to improving productivity because it accepts and rewards inefficiency. If you are going to improve, you need to know how much you should be spending, not just how much you've spent in the past. That means going over every product, looking at every part, examining every process and operation, breaking each down into its individual components and then coming up with standard costs for everything you do.

SOURCE: Jack Stack, *The Great Game of Business*, New York: Currency Doubleday, 1992, p. 101.

In some Japanese firms, standards are changed quite frequently. For example, at Citizen Watch Company, Ltd., standards are changed every three months to accommodate the effects of continuous improvement (CI) efforts. The standard is adjusted the month after the CI change is implemented. For instance, suppose a worker who had been standing on the right side of a production line to perform a task found that he could reduce the time to perform that task by 15 seconds if he stood on the left side of the line. This change is implemented in March, however, the standard is not adjusted until April. The delay in changing the standard is made so that the worker will have time to get used to the new procedure. By April, company management expects no labour time variance to occur from the new standard.

Citizen measures its success in meeting standards using an "achievement ratio," which is expected to be 100%, that is, no variance. If a 1% unfavourable variance occurs, a review of the process is triggered. Such a low tolerance for nonconformance is not unusual in Japanese firms and indicates how tightly Japanese production processes are controlled.[18]

Attainability

Standards provide a target level of performance and can be set at various levels of rigour. The level of rigour reflected in the standard affects motivation, and one reason for using standards is to motivate employees. Standards can be classified by their degree of rigour, ranging from easy to difficult. The classifications are similar to the levels of capacity discussed in Chapter 4: expected, practical, and theoretical.

Expected standards are set at a level that reflects what is actually expected to occur in the future period. Such standards anticipate future waste and inefficiencies and allow for them. As such, expected standards are not of significant value for motivation, control, or performance evaluation. Any variances from expected standards should be minimal and managers should take care that expected standards are not set to be too easy to achieve.

expected standard
a standard that reflects what is actually expected to occur in a future period

practical standards
standards that can be reached or slightly exceeded approximately 60% to 70% of the time with reasonable effort by workers

theoretical standards
standards that allow for no inefficiencies of any type; encompass the highest level of rigour and do not allow for normal operating delays or human limitations such as fatigue, boredom, or misunderstanding

management by exception
a technique in which managers set upper and lower limits of tolerance for deviations and investigate only deviations that fall outside those tolerance ranges

Standards that can be reached or slightly exceeded approximately 60% to 70% of the time with reasonable effort by workers are called **practical standards**. These standards allow for normal, unavoidable time problems or delays such as machine downtime and worker breaks. Practical standards represent an attainable challenge and have traditionally been thought to be the most effective at inducing the best worker performance and at determining how effectively and efficiently workers are performing their tasks. Both favourable and unfavourable variances result from the use of moderately rigorous standards such as these.

Standards that allow for no inefficiencies of any type are called **theoretical standards**. Theoretical standards encompass the highest level of rigour and do not allow for normal operating delays or human limitations such as fatigue, boredom, or misunderstanding. Traditionally, theoretical standards were not used because they resulted in discouraged and resentful workers who ultimately ignored the standards. Variances from theoretical standards were always unfavourable and these variances were not considered useful for constructive cost control or performance evaluation. Even in a plant that is entirely automated, there is still the possibility of human or machine failure. This traditional perspective has, however, begun to change, as the next section explains.

Depending on the type of standard in effect, the acceptable ranges used to apply the management by exception principle differ. **Management by exception** allows managers to set upper and lower limits of tolerance for deviations and investigate only deviations that fall outside those tolerance ranges. This difference is especially notable for deviations on the unfavourable side. If a company uses expected standards, the ranges of acceptable variances should be extremely small, since actual cost should closely conform to the standard. In contrast, a company using theoretical standards would expect variances to fall within very wide ranges of acceptability because of the level of rigour of the standards. The News Note below, about a study of manufacturing company controllers, provides some reasons why managers are using more formalized methods of judging when to investigate variances than those used in the past.

GENERAL NEWS NOTE

When to Investigate Variances

Variance investigation policies for materials and labour at large companies are moving away from pure judgment and toward the use of structured or formalized exception procedures.

One explanation is that the results are being driven by manufacturing innovations that lead to shorter production runs and shorter product life cycles. In such an environment, monthly variance reports may be so untimely as to be virtually useless. In a flexible manufacturing environment, production runs can be extremely short—only days or perhaps even hours. To provide timely feedback in an environment where the nature of operations and the products being produced change rapidly, more accounts and greater reporting frequency are required.

Another explanation relates to the increasing globalization of markets rather than to the characteristics or individual operating policies of the firm. When competing internationally, companies face more competitors, are less likely to be the lowest-cost producers, and face more uncertainties than in domestic markets. By reducing production cost surprises, intensified management accounting (in the frequency of reports and the details of variance composition) can compensate for these additional uncertainties.

SOURCE: Bruce R. Gaumnitz and Felix P. Kollaritsch, "Manufacturing Variances: Current Practice and Trends," *Journal of Cost Management*, Spring 1991, pp. 63–64. Reprinted with permission from *Journal of Cost Management*, © 1991, by RIA, 395 Hudson Street, New York, NY, 10014.

Variances large enough to fall outside the ranges of acceptability generally indicate trouble. The variances themselves, though, do not reveal the cause of the trouble or the person or group responsible. To determine causes of variances, managers must investigate problems through observation, inspection, and inquiry. Such investigations involve the time and effort of people at the operating level as well as accounting personnel. Operations personnel should be alert in spotting variances as they occur and should record the reasons for the variances to the extent that those causes can be determined. For example, operating personnel can readily detect and report causes such as machine downtime or material spoilage.

How well a company determines the causes of variances is often proportional to how much time, effort, and money is spent in gathering information about variances during the period. Managers must be willing and able to accumulate variance information regularly and consistently to evaluate the evidence, isolate the causes, and if possible influence performance to improve the process. If variances are ignored when they occur, it is often impossible or extremely costly to determine the relevant data and to take corrective action at a later time.

CHANGES IN THE USE OF STANDARDS

LEARNING OBJECTIVE 6

How are standard setting and standard usage changing in modern business?

Sometimes, in using variances from standards for control and performance evaluation purposes, accountants (and to a certain extent businesspeople in general) believe that an incorrect measurement is employed. For example, the chapter stated that material standards often include a factor for waste and labour standards are commonly set at the expected level of attainment, even though this level allows for downtime and human error. The practice of using standards that are not aimed at the highest possible theoretical level of attainment is now being questioned in a business environment concerned with world-class operations, especially continuous improvement.

Use of Theoretical Standards for Quality Improvement

Japanese influence on North American management philosophy and production techniques has been substantial in the recent past. **Just-in-time** (JIT) production systems and **total quality management** (TQM) concepts were both imported to this country as a result of an upsurge in Japanese productivity. These two world-class concepts are notable departures from the traditional view that ideals should not be used in standards development and application. Rather than including waste and inefficiency in the standards and then accepting additional waste and spoilage deviations under a management by exception principle, both JIT and TQM begin from the premises of zero defects, zero inefficiency, and zero downtime. Under such a system, theoretical standards become expected standards, with either no or only a minimal acceptable level of deviation from standards.

just-in-time
a philosophy about when to do something; the *when* is "as needed" and the *something* is a production, purchasing, or delivery activity

total quality management
a philosophy for organizational management and organizational change that seeks ever-increasing quality

Although workers may, at first, resent the introduction of standards set at a "perfection" level, it is in their and management's best long-run interest to have such standards. When a standard permits a deviation from the ideal, managers are allowing for inefficient resource utilization. Setting standards at the tightest possible theoretical level is intended to produce the most useful information for managerial purposes as well as the highest-quality products and services at the lowest possible cost. If no inefficiencies are built into or tolerated in the system, deviations from standards should be minimized and overall organizational performance improved.

If theoretical standards are to be implemented, management must be prepared to go through a four-step "migration" process. First, teams should be established to determine where current problems lie and identify the causes of those problems. Second, if the causes relate to equipment, facility, or workers, management must be ready to invest in plant and equipment items, equipment rearrangements, or worker training so that the standards are amenable to the operations. Training is essential if workers are to perform at the high levels of efficiency demanded by theoretical standards. If the causes are related to external sources, such as poor-quality material, management must be willing to change suppliers or pay higher prices for higher-quality input. Third, because workers have now often been assigned the responsibility for quality, they must also be given the authority to react to problems, as discussed in the following News Note. "The key to quality initiatives is for employees to move beyond their natural resistance-to-change mode to a highly focused, strategic, and empowered mind-set. This shift unlocks employees' energy and creativity, and leads them to ask, 'How can I do my job even better today?'"[19] Fourth, requiring people to work at their maximum potential demands recognition, meaning that management must provide rewards for achievement.

GENERAL NEWS NOTE

Empowering Employees Is an Ethical Business Practice

Making employees more involved in and responsible for their work activities increases the value of those individuals not only to the organization, but also to themselves and to society as a whole. The organizational benefits gained from empowerment are that employees have a sense of ownership of and work harder toward goals they have set for themselves. Thus, employee involvement automatically promotes a higher degree of effort on the part of the workforce. We avoid the basis of the Marxist critique of capitalism: the exploitation and subsequent alienation and rebellion of the worker. Problems will be solved more quickly and, therefore, the cost of errors will be reduced.

Providing training to employees for improving skills and/or decision making results in a person who is a more valuable and productive member of the company and society. Additionally, empowered employees are less likely to become bored and should experience more job satisfaction. Lastly, empowering employees provides a valuable means by which people's "timeless quest to express themselves and establish their individuality be furthered in the face of a world that is becoming more complex and more dependent on technology." The pinnacle of Maslow's hierarchy of needs is achieved as well: self-actualization.

SOURCE: Cecily Raiborn and Dinah Payne, "TQM: Just What the Ethicist Ordered," *Journal of Business Ethics*, 15 (1996): 969. Reprinted with kind permission from Springer Science and Business Media.

Whether setting standards at the theoretical level will become the norm of North American companies cannot be determined at this time. However, the authors believe that the level of attainability for standards will move away from the expected and closer to the ideal. This conclusion reflects the current business environment in which companies most often must meet competitors head-to-head; if a company's competitor uses the highest possible standards as product norms, that company must also use such standards to compete on quality and to meet cost and, thus, profit margin objectives. Higher standards for efficiency automatically mean lower costs because of the elimination of nonvalue-added activities such as waste, idle time, and rework.

Long-Term Versus Short-Term Standards

Standards have traditionally been set after prices and quantities for the various cost elements were comprehensively investigated. These standards were almost always retained for at least one year and, sometimes, for many years. The current business environment—including outsourcing, supplier contractual relationships, technology advancements, competitive niches, and enhanced product design and time-to-market considerations—changes so rapidly that a standard may no longer be useful for management control purposes throughout an entire year. Company management needs to consider whether to ignore rapid changes in the environment or to incorporate those changes into the standards during a year in which significant changes occur.

Ignoring the changes is a simplistic approach that allows the same type of cost to be recorded at the same amount all year. Thus, for example, any material purchased during the year is recorded at the same standard cost regardless of when the purchase was made. This approach, although simplifying recordkeeping, eliminates any opportunity to adequately control costs or evaluate performance. Additionally, such an approach could create large differences between standard and actual costs, making standard costs unacceptable for external reporting.

Changing the standards to reflect price or quantity changes makes some aspects of management control and performance evaluation more effective and others more difficult. For instance, financial plans prepared under the original standards must be adjusted before appropriate actual comparisons can be made against them. Changing the standards also creates a problem for recordkeeping and inventory measurement. At what standard cost should a product be recorded—the standard in effect when that product was made, or the standard in effect when the financial statements are prepared? If standards are changed, they are more closely related to actual costs but many of the benefits discussed earlier in the chapter might be compromised.

Management may consider combining these two choices in the accounting system. Plans prepared by use of original and new standards can be compared; any variances reflect changes in the business environment. These variances can be designated as: uncontrollable, such as changes in the market price of raw materials; internally initiated, such as changes in standard labour time resulting from employee training or equipment rearrangement; or internally controllable, such as excess usage of material or labour time caused by the purchase of inferior materials.

SALES PRICE AND SALES VOLUME VARIANCES

LEARNING OBJECTIVE 7

How are budget variances computed and used to analyze differences between budgeted and actual revenue? budgeted costs and actual costs?

When actual-to-budget comparisons are made, managers are held accountable for the revenues (if any) and the costs in the operating areas over which they have authority and responsibility. Actual performance should be compared against budgeted performance to determine variances from expectations. In making such comparisons, however, management needs to be certain that it is considering results from a proper perspective.

For an operating area in which revenues are being generated (for example, sales for the Lexus Division of Toyota Motor Corporation), comparisons should first be made on the revenue level to determine how closely projected revenues are being met. As discussed earlier, a total variance from standard can have both a price and a quantity element. Thus, revenue variance calculations should be made for both of these elements.

Calculating the difference between actual and budgeted selling prices and multiplying this number by the actual number of units sold will provide the **sales price variance**. This variance indicates the portion of the total variance that is related to a

sales price variance
the difference between actual and budgeted selling prices multiplied by the actual number of units sold

sales volume variance
the difference between actual and budgeted volumes multiplied by the budgeted selling price

change in selling price. A variance is also created by the difference between actual and budgeted sales volumes; multiplying this difference by the budgeted selling price yields the **sales volume variance**. The sales variance model is as follows:[20]

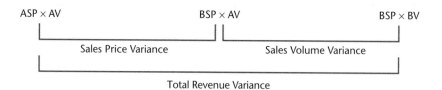

where ASP = Actual selling price
       AV = Actual volume
       BSP = Budgeted selling price
       BV = Budgeted volume

To illustrate these computations, assume that the Tool Division of Howard Price Ltd. has budgeted sales of 10,000 units per month at a selling price of $35 for the current fiscal year. Thus, monthly budgeted sales are $350,000. Actual January sales were $306,000, creating a total unfavourable revenue variance of $44,000. To make a valid comparison, it is also necessary to know that the $306,000 of revenue was composed of a sales volume of 10,200 units sold at $30. Thus, the following variance calculations can be made:

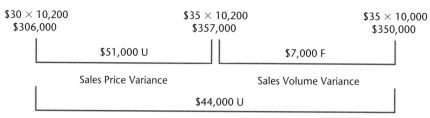

Company managers should be pleased with the increased volume but displeased with the reduced selling price. Discussions with the responsible division managers might indicate that the games were sold at a promotional discount for the first month to get individuals interested.

Analyzing Cost Variances

After revenue variances have been explained, managers can focus on analyzing cost variances. It is important that costs be analyzed in relation to the *actual* volume of sales rather than the *budgeted* volume of sales. Such analysis requires the use of flexible budgets and flexible budget formulas (i.e., looking at costs and revenues at different sales and production levels).

For example, assume that Howard Price Ltd.'s Tool Division has a flexible budget formula for selling expenses of $12,000 per month plus 5% of sales dollars. Then the original selling expense budget estimate for January would have been $18,500 {$1,000 + [0.05 × (10,000 × $35)]}. However, since the Tool Division achieved an actual sales level of $306,000, the division should only expect selling expenses of $16,300 {$1,000 + [0.05 × (10,200 × $30)]}. If actual selling expense were $18,500, the division did not perform up to expectations; it should recognize a $2,200 unfavourable variance for selling expenses. Comparing actual expenses to budgeted expenses that were calculated at a different level of sales will not provide valid information on how well costs were controlled during a period.

In addition to determining whether costs were controlled, managers need to analyze the ways in which money was spent. Donald A. Curtis, a senior partner at the international public accounting firm of Deloitte & Touche, emphasizes, "Just because a budget was not overspent doesn't mean it was well spent."[21] Spending analysis should focus on individual line items, not just totals, and on spending within categories. Oftentimes, money is spent simply because it is available for spending—not because there was a need for spending.

As with any variance computation, the reason for making income statement actual-to-budget comparisons is to determine why the actual results differed from those that were planned. To determine the underlying reasons for variances requires that comparisons be made as early as possible. Delaying variance computations until the end of a period may impede a manager's ability to detect and, therefore, control variance causes. Providing useful variance computations requires that an effective and prompt variance reporting system be maintained.

Management should also consider the effects that current changes in conditions may have on future operations and on the types and extent of future budgetary variances. Will increased sales today mean reduced sales in later periods? Could a current selling price reduction spur product demand sufficiently to increase revenues to total projected levels? Does the increased cost of a raw material make the use of an alternative, higher-quality material more cost beneficial? These are some of the possible questions that management needs to consider when making actual-to-budget comparisons.

The Future of Standard Costing

Critics of standard costing question the relevance of traditional variance analysis for cost control and performance appraisal in today's manufacturing and competitive environment. As we see in the News Note below, the companies that have implemented lean accounting do not feel that standard costing works today. Nevertheless, standard costing systems continue to be widely used. This is because standard costing systems provide cost information for many other purposes besides cost control. Standard costs and variance analysis would still be required for other purposes even if they were abandoned for cost control.

Does Standard Costing Work In Today's Business Environment?

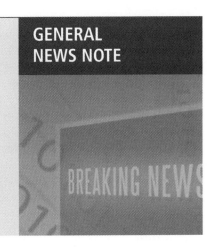

GENERAL NEWS NOTE

Standard costs are based on past operations. These costs include the past utilization of labour, the excess capacity of machines, and market adjustments that affect overhead. Standard cost accounting establishes a cost of labour per standard hour, a machine cost per standard hour, and a cost of overhead per standard hour. The standard hour is based on the earned or value-added hours from the product produced and on the production time required for each product. These total hours are divided into the total cost of labour to determine the cost of labour per standard hour. This same computation is performed for machine and overhead costs.

For example, the standard cost of labour includes overtime when labour doesn't complete its required production in the planned amount of time. Standard cost includes excess capacity owing to faulty forecasts, underutilized production lines, failed automation projects, and so on—put simply, it includes a complete history of the plant's inefficiencies.

"Traditional accounting was designed to support mass production", says Mike Kuhn, CPA, partner with VRAKAS/BLUHM. Traditional cost accounting reports were developed to present an accurate view of the company to outsiders. Their purpose wasn't to help managers run their operations better.

When standard costing was developed in the early 1900s, most companies' cost structures consisted of 60% direct labour, 30% materials, and 10% overhead. Companies typically allocated overhead costs to products in the same proportion as direct labour. "Overhead was so insignificant that even if the allocation was incorrect, it wasn't a big deal," Orest J. Flume, a retired vice-president of finance, adds. Today, the percentage of direct labour in most manufacturing processes is somewhere between 5% and 15%, says David Arnsdorf, president of the ALASKA MANUFACTURERS' ASSOCIATION. Therefore, he does not feel that it is not a good measure of allocation.

In lean manufacturing operations, standard costing does not work—as some nonfinancial measures (including lead times, scrap rates, and on-time deliveries) show significant improvements yet aren't captured well.

There is a better newer way of looking at the numbers. For starters, rather than categorizing costs by department, they can be organized by value stream. A value stream includes everything done to create value for a customer that can reasonably be associated with a product or product line, says Brian Maskell, president of BMA INC.

According to Mike Kuhn, "many of the accounting assumptions contradict lean manufacturing." As a result, a growing number of companies are implementing the "lean accounting" concept to better capture the performance of their operations.

SOURCE: John Lenz, "Justification for Future Competitiveness," *Manufacturing Engineering,* December 2006, p. 91; Karen M. Kroll, "The Lowdown on Lean Accounting," *Journal of Accountancy,* July 1, 2004, Volume 198, Issue 1.

Traditional companies use standard costing as their primary method of maintaining control of production costs. To achieve this, they must track the so-called "actual" costs at each stage in the production. This leads to the development of complicated shop-floor data collection systems and the generation of huge quantities of wasteful and confusing transactions. This kind of data collection system is the opposite of lean thinking.

Standard costing does not provide the information required to support and motivate lean manufacturing. Waste is concealed within the standard cost itself. Instead of the accounting systems' revealing waste, they hide the waste. The waste is tied up in the overhead allocations and is very difficult to unravel. An emphasis on reducing the standard cost will often lead to making changes in the process that do not reduce the true cost of the product and often increase it.[22]

Many Japanese companies are saying good-bye to standard costing. Japanese companies that have used standard cost systems seem to be moving beyond them. Japanese companies put much more emphasis on measuring the nonfinancial aspects of factory performance.

For example, Daihatsu's market-driven philosophy helps to explain why standard cost systems are not used as widely in Japan as they are in North America. Standard costs reflect an engineering mindset and technology-driven management. The goal is to minimize variances between budgeted and actual costs—to perform as closely as possible to best available practice. Market-driven management, on the other hand, emphasizes doing what it takes to achieve a desired performance level under market conditions. How efficiently a company *should* be able to build a product is less important to the Japanese than how efficiently it *must* be able to build it for maximum marketplace success.[23]

For those organizations that have implemented activity-based systems, standard costing still has an important role to play in controlling the costs of unit level activities. Unit level activities can be defined as those activities that are performed each time a unit of product or service is produced.[24]

The following News Note discusses the future of standard costing in Japan.

Does Standard Costing Work in Japan?

INTERNATIONAL NEWS NOTE

One reason why standard costing is falling out of favour in Japan is the shortening of product life cycles owing to stronger competition and small-lot production. When the life cycles of products become short, even if the standard cost of each product is established by using the detailed scientific analysis, the benefits that derive from such standards are very small compared to the costs incurred to establish such standards and the short time available to apply those standards. Under such situations, companies may be reluctant to establish standard cost systems. When product life cycles are short and new products are planned and developed one after another, cost reductions at the planning and design stage become much more important than cost reductions during manufacturing, which is when standard costing is most often used.

At the planning and design stage, Japanese companies apply a unique cost management technique called *genkja kikaku*. This is an effective tool for reducing costs (i.e., rather than controlling them) during design and planning. It is best suited to factories that make various products in low volumes and where robotics have been introduced. It allows for flexibility as well as high quality and service in addition to cost reductions. It differs from standard costing in that it is a market-oriented tool.

Although there is no doubt that standard costing helps get the largest output through the smallest input, the use of *genkja kikaku* helps achieve, very effectively, not only cost reduction goals but also other goals such as improving quality, flexibility, and service.

It seems that production efficiency is still important for most North American companies. In contrast, Japanese companies more often resort to market-oriented tools for managing costs. Standard costing is often a key factor when individual employees are being evaluated.

SOURCE: Anura De Zoysa and Siriyama Kanthi Herath, "Standard Costing in Japanese firms," *Industrial Management and Data Systems* 107, no. 2 (2007): 271–87.

Standard Costs and Enterprise Resource Planning Systems

Although expensive to implement and operate, enterprise resource planning (ERP) systems provide a much higher level of accuracy than traditional approaches to gathering cost information. With most manufacturing processes being automated and operated with little direct labour, ERP systems have the advantage of keeping an accurate record of numerous overhead cost pools at all levels in an organization. In addition, as a manufacturing facility can be used for an increasing variety of products, ERP systems are able to allocate common costs to a large number of different products. The greater capacity of ERP systems to accurately allocate costs means that ERP systems are important for developing accurate standards. Standard costs can be prepared with, for example, the sub-module mySAP.com Financials.

ERP systems address one of the major problems with standard costing, and that is the complexity of the value creation chain. Complexity characterizes a value creation chain when there are multiple products and many manufacturing and testing activities. Complexity similarly exists with service organizations that have many different services and many different customers. ERP systems are able to deal with the complexity facing standard costs by allocating costs based on actual activities. This will be discussed in Chapter 13.

ERP systems—by using common charts of accounts, standard practices, and standard data definitions—are able to provide comparable data among the various parts of an organization. This standardization imposes standards across an organization. By reporting in an equivalent fashion, separate units can be compared and standards can be established based on the organizational units with superior performance. In a typical pre-ERP organization, each department or unit is a separate "fiefdom" with a tendency to resist openness. With ERP systems, openness cannot be easily avoided, and it is more difficult for inferior performers to say, "We are different and therefore we cannot be compared."

The following News Note is an example of how an ERP system (rather than standard costing) is used at one large firm.

GENERAL NEWS NOTE

How ERP Systems Help

Although quite expensive to implement, enterprise resource planning (ERP) systems can provide a much higher level of standard costing sophistication than traditional information systems. Alan McKnight, a controller with OVERHEAD DOOR CORP. (which makes garage doors and Genie openers), reports that with most of the manufacturing process now automated, there's little direct labour content in each garage door. The company is moving in the direction of defining cost pools at the department and cell level, which would not have been possible before the ERP system. At the same time, the company is reorganizing its manufacturing facilities along geographic lines rather than product lines. Since each plan will produce more than one type of product, it will be harder to assign overhead costs. Using activity-based methods enabled by the ERP system will allow Overhead Door to reasonably cost its various products and maintain good standards.

"To be successful with standard costing," advises McKnight, "you must have buy-in from operations." For instance, the biggest challenge with standard costing at Overhead Door Corp. was getting the operations people to accurately report labour and scrap. Prior to the new system, production workers often forgot to enter scrapped materials because they would get picked up at inventory time. The company had to estimate cost of sales each month based on what it sold, along with physical inventories twice a year. This method was inadequate for accurate costing as well as production control.

With the ERP implementation initiative, operations managers began to insist that scrapped materials be reported accurately into the system. McKnight said that the company is now getting much better reporting of both scrap and labour. He attributes the better reporting to the big part operations people played in implementing the ERP system. ERP was the vehicle through which the company increased discipline in production reporting from operations personnel.

SOURCE: Kip R. Krumwiede, "Tips From the Trenches on Standard Costing," *Cost Management Update*, April 2000, Issue No. 106.

Bright Pearl Seafood Restaurant Inc.

It only takes a short conversation with managing director Stephen Chan at Bright Pearl Seafood Restaurant Inc. to understand the organization's success. He continuously emphasizes his company's dedication to two things: a quality product and an empowered workforce. Without the first, Bright Pearl could not retain its clients; without the second, the company could never produce its high-quality products. Bright Pearl's product simply has to be better; it can't compete solely on the basis of cost.

The institution of the modular team concept was a radical step for such a small organization. It required substantial training so that employees could perform multiple tasks and perform them well. Employee empowerment provided a benefit not originally considered: it took the matter of worker productivity out of the hands of company management and placed it in the work teams. "The teams are self-disciplining. If a team member is not performing up to par, the other team members either get that person 'on board' or make the comfort level such that that person would prefer not to continue." Thus, labour efficiency variances are negligible.

Bright Pearl's primary concern these days is not about standard cost variances. Costs are under control; productivity is high; workers are achieving bonuses based on team activity goals; and, best of all, employee morale is high in a work environment typically viewed as tedious. The concern of company management is an ability to remain profitable in the face of potential additional increases in costs such as labour and utilities that will affect Bright Pearl. The company knows that customers are willing to pay for a quality product and the company has "tightened its belt" to be competitive. But if costs are increased, will customers be willing to pay a higher price for their product? Chan hopes so—for the sake of the workers that his company has so carefully trained to be concerned about customer satisfaction through product quality.

Bright Pearl has hosted many wonderful events with distinguished guests in attendance, including Mike Harris, the former Premier of Ontario; Mel Lastman, the former mayor of Toronto; Hazel McCallion, the long-time mayor of Mississauga; Adrienne Clarkson, the former Governor General of Canada; and Zhou Xingbao, Consul General of the People's Republic of China.

According to Stephen Chan, Bright Pearl's managing director, "You don't have to be a VIP to be treated like one." He adds that "every event, every celebration, every guest is important to us. We do everything we can to please our guests. We'll customize a spectacular menu, arrange a wide variety of entertainment, supply audiovisual equipment, and decorate the space."

There is an old Chinese proverb: "Enjoy yourself! It's later than you think." So don't wait another day to experience the culinary delights at Bright Pearl Seafood Restaurant.

SOURCE: Interview with Stephen Chan, Managing Director, Bright Pearl Seafood Restaurant Inc.; http://www.brightpearlseafood.com.

APPENDIX 7A

Standard Cost System Journal Entries

Journal entries for the information contained in the chapter related to DBD's Cutting Department are given in Exhibit 7-8. The material price variance in this exhibit is accounted for based on the secondary information that 3,000 square metres of cotton fabric were purchased (from Exhibit 7-5). Note that unfavourable variances have debit balances and favourable variances have credit balances. Unfavourable variances represent excess costs, while favourable variances represent cost savings. Since standard costs are shown in Work in Process Inventory (a debit-balanced account), it is reasonable that excess costs are also debits.

Although standard cost systems are useful for internal reporting, such costs are not acceptable for external reporting unless they are substantially equivalent to those that would have resulted from using an actual cost system.[25] If standards are achievable and updated periodically, this equivalency should exist. Using standards for financial statements should provide fairly conservative inventory valuations because the effects of excess prices and/or inefficient operations are minimized.

EXHIBIT 7-8

Journal Entries for Cutting Department, Week of June 12–16

Raw Material Inventory	10,500	
Material Price Variance	1,950	
Accounts Payable		12,450
To record the purchase of 3,000 square metres of cotton fabric at $4.15 per square metre. (From Exhibit 7-5 on page 391.)		
Work in Process Inventory Cutting Dept.	9,240	
Material Quantity Variance	315	
Raw Material Inventory		9,555
To record the issuance and usage of 2,730 square metres of cotton fabric for 2,200 shirts. (From Exhibit 7-5)		
Work in Process Inventory—Cutting Dept.	5,280	
Labour Rate Variance	200	
Labour Efficiency Variance		480
Wages Payable		5,000
To record the usage of 500 direct labour hours at a wage rate of $10 per DLH. (From Exhibit 7-5)		
Variable Manufacturing Overhead—Cutting Dept.	3,360	
Various accounts		3,360
To record actual variable overhead costs. (From Exhibit 7-5.)		
Fixed Manufacturing Overhead—Cutting Dept.	2,875	
Various accounts		2,875
To record actual fixed overhead costs. (From Exhibit 7-5.)		
Work in Process Inventory—Cutting Dept.	6,050	
Variable Manufacturing Overhead—Cutting Dept.		3,850
Fixed Manufacturing Overhead—Cutting Dept.		2,200
To apply variable overhead at $7 per DLH and fixed overhead at $6 per MH for actual production of 2,200 shirts. (From Exhibit 7-5) (VOH = 550 hours × $7 = $3,850; FOH = 366 2/3 hours × $6 = $2,200.)		
Variable Manufacturing Overhead—Cutting Dept.	490	
VOH Spending Variance—Cutting Dept.		140
VOH Efficiency Variance—Cutting Dept.		350
To close the variable overhead account. (From page 396.)		
FOH Spending Variance—Cutting Dept.	379	
FOH Volume Variance—Cutting Dept.	296	
Fixed Manufacturing Overhead—Cutting Dept.		675
To close the Fixed Manufacturing Overhead account. (From page 397.)		

If actual costs are used in financial statements, the standard cost information shown in the accounting records must be adjusted at year-end to approximate actual cost information. The nature of the year-end adjusting entries depends on whether the variance amounts are significant or not.

All manufacturing variances (material, labour, and overhead) are considered together in determining the appropriate year-end disposition. If the combined impact of these variances is considered insignificant, standard costs are approximately the same as actual costs, and the variances are closed to Cost of Goods Sold (or Cost of Services Rendered in a service organization). Unfavourable variances are closed by being credited; favourable variances are closed by being debited. In a manufacturing company, although all production of the period has not yet been sold, this treatment of insignificant variances is justified on the basis of the immateriality of the amounts involved.

If it is assumed that the variances shown in Exhibit 7-8 are insignificant, the following journal entry for material and labour is made:

Labour Efficiency Variance	480	
Cost of Goods Sold	1,985	
Material Price Variance		1,950
Material Quantity Variance		315
Labour Rate Variance		200
To close insignificant material and labour		
variances to Cost of Goods Sold.		

As well the year-end disposition of overhead variances (Exhibit 7-8) which are considered insignificant follow.

VOH Spending Variance	140	
VOH Efficiency Variance	350	
Cost of Goods Sold		490
To close insignificant VOH manufacturing		
variances to Cost of Goods Sold.		

Cost of Goods Sold	675	
FOH Spending Variance		379
FOH Volume Variance		296
To close insignificant FOH manufacturing		
variances to Cost of Goods Sold.		

In contrast, if the total variance amount is significant, the overhead variances are prorated at year-end to ending inventories (Work In Process and Finished Goods) and Cost of Goods Sold in proportion to the relative size of those account balances. This proration disposes of the variances and presents the financial statements in a way that approximates the use of actual costing. The disposition of significant variances is similar to the disposition of large amounts of underapplied or overapplied overhead shown in Chapter 4. The material price variance based on purchases is prorated among Raw Material Inventory, Work in Process Inventory, Finished Goods Inventory, and Cost of Goods Sold or Cost of Services Rendered. All other variances occur as part of the conversion process and are prorated only to the Work in Process Inventory, Finished Goods Inventory, and Cost of Goods Sold or Cost of Services Rendered accounts.

APPENDIX 7B

Process Costing With Standard Costs

LEARNING OBJECTIVE 9

What use do standard costs have in a process costing system?

All examples in the chapter use actual historical costs to assign values to products under either the weighted average method or FIFO method. Companies may prefer to use standard rather than actual costs for inventory measurement purposes. The use of standard costs simplifies process costing and allows variances to be measured during the period. Actual costing requires that a new production cost be computed each production period. Standard costing eliminates such recomputations, although standards do need to be reviewed (and possibly revised) at least once a year to keep the amounts current.

There are still some operations that are heavily labour-oriented. The following is an example. At Motivatit Seafood, removing the shells and meats from oysters, crabs, and crawfish must be done very gently and dexterously for machines to handle completely. Although half-shelled oysters move down an assembly line, human hands seem to do the real work. And at what pace? The best shuckers can repeat the rhythmic hammering, prying, and tossing motion at the rate of almost 500 oysters per hour, thereby setting a high standard against which to measure actual production activity.[26]

Calculations of equivalent units of production for standard process costing are identical to those for FIFO process costing. Unlike the weighted average method, both standard costing and FIFO emphasize the measurement and control of current production and current period costs. The commingling of units and costs that occurs when the weighted average method is used reduces the emphasis on current effort that standard costing is intended to represent and measure.

In a standard cost process costing system, actual costs of the current period are recorded and are compared with the standard costs of the equivalent units of production. If actual costs are less than standard, there is a favourable variance; unfavourable variances arise if actual costs are greater than the standard. Units are transferred out of a department at the standard cost of each production element.

CHAPTER SUMMARY

A standard cost is a budget (or plan) for one unit of product or service output and provides a norm against which actual cost can be compared. In a traditional standard cost system, standards are computed for prices and quantities of each product component.

1 **Why are standard cost systems used?**
Standard costing systems highlight and allow management to manage by exception; that is, they allow management to concentrate on the areas where there are inefficiencies. They assist in setting budgets and evaluating managerial performance. The availability of standards speeds up and improves decision making because managers have a predetermined, rigorous set of expectations upon which to base decisions, such as accepting an order at a specified price. Performance evaluation is also improved through comparing actual and standard costs of operations and highlighting significant differences.

2 **How are standards for material and labour set?**
Standards should be developed by a team comprising professional staff and managers as well as employees whose performance will be evaluated by those standards. A standard cost card is used to accumulate and record specific information about the

components, processes, quantities, and costs that form the standard for a product. The material and labour sections of the standard cost card are derived from the bill of materials, and the operations flow document, respectively.

How are material, labour, and overhead variances calculated?
The most basic variance computation is the total difference between actual cost incurred and standard cost allowed for the period's output. Each total variance is separated into subvariances relating to price and quantity or rate and efficiency elements.

A price variance reflects the difference between what was paid and what should have been paid for inputs during the period. A quantity variance provides a monetary measure of the difference between the quantity of actual inputs and the standard quantity of inputs allowed for the actual output of the period.

Material variances are subdivided into price and quantity variances, while labour is subdivided into rate and efficiency variances. Variable overhead variances are subdivided into spending and efficiency variances while fixed overhead variances are subdivided into spending and volume variances.

How can variances be used for control and performance evaluation purposes?
Variance analysis provides a basis for management planning, control, and performance evaluation. Using standard costs, managers can forecast what costs should be at various levels of activity and compare those forecasts with actual results. When large variances are observed, the causes should be determined and, if possible, corrective action should be taken. For this reason, variances should be recorded as early and as often in the production/service process as is feasible.

How do organizational evolution and desired level of attainability affect standard setting?
Standards should be appropriate and attainable. They should reflect current relevant technical and operational expectations. The level of rigour chosen for the standards should be based on realistic expectations and motivational effects on employees. The practical level has typically been thought to have the best motivational impact; however, some Japanese firms use theoretical standards to indicate their goals of minimum cost and zero defects. Standards are often important in implementing strategies where cost and quality must be controlled.

When standards are established, appropriateness and attainability should be considered. Appropriateness, in relation to a standard, refers to the basis on which the standards are developed and how long they are expected to last. Attainability refers to the degree of difficulty or rigour that should be incurred in achieving the standard.

Management should not think that standards, once set, will remain useful forever. Standards must evolve over an organization's life to reflect its changing methods and processes.

How are standard setting and standard usage changing in modern business?
Some companies are changing the way in which standards are set and used. Traditionally, standards have included some level of waste and spoilage and, regarding fixed overhead, have been based on expected activity levels. These standards were commonly held constant for a year or longer. Recently, many firms have discovered that their standards have not been useful in implementing process, quality, or cost improvements. Thus managers are revising standards to reflect technology advances, process improvements and global market competitiveness.

7 How are budget variances computed and used to analyze differences between budgeted and actual revenues?

Actual operating results should be compared against budget figures to measure how effectively and efficiently organizational goals were met. Sales price and sales volume variances should be calculated before expense comparisons are made. Expense comparisons should be made based on the actual level of sales volume achieved rather than on budgeted volume. Regardless of whether variances are unfavourable or favourable, feedback to operating personnel is an important part of the budgeting process. Additionally, managers should recognize that budget games may be played and should strive to create a climate of mutual trust and respect to minimize or eliminate this counterproductive behaviour.

8 What journal entries are needed in a standard cost system? (Appendix 7A)

Journal entries are made in a similar fashion to normal entries with the only addition being the breaking out of the variances. Unfavourable variances represent excess costs, while favourable variances represent cost savings.

9 What use do standard costs have in a process costing system? (Appendix 7B)

The use of standard costs simplifies process costing and allows variances to be measured during the period. In a standard cost process costing system, actual costs of the current period are recorded and are compared with the standard costs of the equivalent units of production. If actual costs are less than standard, there is a favourable variance; unfavourable variances arise if actual costs are greater than standard.

Key Terms

Bill of materials (p. 385)
Expected standard (p. 405)
Fixed overhead spending variance (p. 397)
Just-in-time (p. 407)
Labour efficiency variance (p. 394)
Labour rate variance (p. 394)
Management by exception (p. 406)
Material price variance (p. 392)
Material quantity variance (p. 392)
Operations flow document (p. 387)
Practical standards (p. 406)
Price variance (p. 390)
Quantity variance (p. 390)
Sales price variance (p. 409)

Sales volume variance (p. 410)
Standard cost (p. 383)
Standard cost card (p. 389)
Standard costing system (p. 383)
Standard quantity allowed (p. 390)
Standards (p. 383)
Theoretical standards (p. 406)
Total quality management (p. 407)
Variable overhead efficiency variance (p. 396)
Variable overhead spending variance (p. 396)
Variance (p. 384)
Variance analysis (p. 398)
Volume variance (p. 397)

Points to Remember

Variances in Formula Format:

Material price variance = AQ(AP − SP)
Material quantity variance = SP(AQ − SQ)
Labour rate variance = AQ(AP − SP)
Labour efficiency variance = SP(AQ − SQ)
Variable overhead spending variance = Actual VOH − (SR × AQ)
Variable overhead efficiency variance = SR(AQ − SQ)
Fixed overhead spending variance = Actual FOH − Budgeted FOH
Fixed overhead volume variance = Budgeted FOH − (SR × SQ)

Variances in Diagram Format:

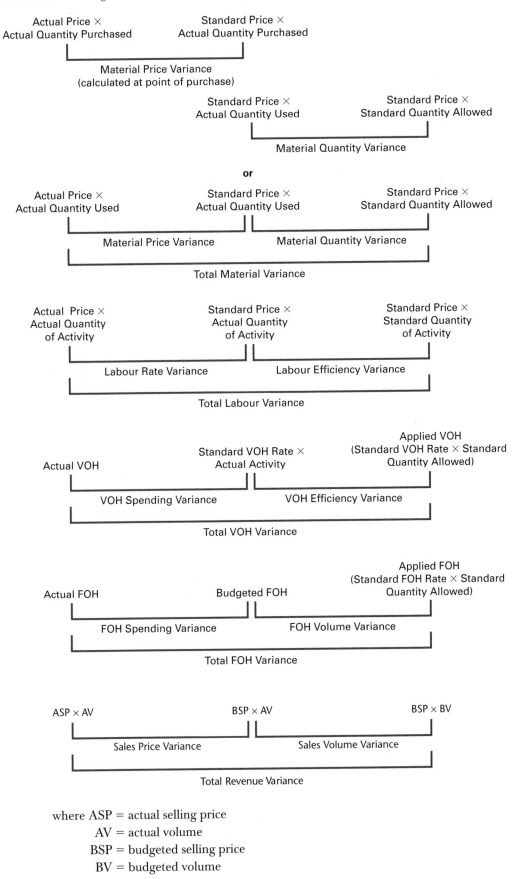

Actual Price ×
Actual Quantity Purchased

Standard Price ×
Actual Quantity Purchased

Material Price Variance
(calculated at point of purchase)

Standard Price ×
Actual Quantity Used

Standard Price ×
Standard Quantity Allowed

Material Quantity Variance

or

Actual Price ×
Actual Quantity Used

Standard Price ×
Actual Quantity Used

Standard Price ×
Standard Quantity Allowed

Material Price Variance

Material Quantity Variance

Total Material Variance

Actual Price ×
Actual Quantity
of Activity

Standard Price ×
Actual Quantity
of Activity

Standard Price ×
Standard Quantity
of Activity

Labour Rate Variance

Labour Efficiency Variance

Total Labour Variance

Actual VOH

Standard VOH Rate ×
Actual Activity

Applied VOH
(Standard VOH Rate × Standard
Quantity Allowed)

VOH Spending Variance

VOH Efficiency Variance

Total VOH Variance

Actual FOH

Budgeted FOH

Applied FOH
(Standard FOH Rate × Standard
Quantity Allowed)

FOH Spending Variance

FOH Volume Variance

Total FOH Variance

ASP × AV

BSP × AV

BSP × BV

Sales Price Variance

Sales Volume Variance

Total Revenue Variance

where ASP = actual selling price
AV = actual volume
BSP = budgeted selling price
BV = budgeted volume

DEMONSTRATION PROBLEMS

Problem 1

Forrest Ltd. manufactures a line of swimsuits for women under the Ambrosia label. The standard variable costs of producing one swimsuit are as follows:

	Standard Quantity or Hours	Standard Price or Rate	Standard Cost
Direct materials	?	$8 per metre	$?
Direct labour	?	?	?
Variable overhead	?	$3 per direct labour hour	?
Total standard cost per suit			$63.00

In June 1,500 swimsuits were produced and all were sold. Selected information for June production follows:

	Materials Used	Direct Labour	Variable Overhead
Total standard cost for June's production	$?	$24,000	$ 4,800
Actual costs incurred	65,000	?	4,860
Materials quantity variance	1,200 U		

During June, 1,700 actual direct labour hours were incurred, and the difference between standard and actual cost per swimsuit produced was $0.42 U.

Required:

a. Total standard cost of the materials required for June production
b. Standard direct materials required per swimsuit
c. Total materials price variance
d. Standard direct labour rate per hour
e. Total actual direct labour cost incurred
f. Labour rate variance
g. Labour efficiency variance
h. Variable overhead efficiency variance
i. Variable overhead spending variance
j. Standard variable cost for one swimsuit

Problem 2

Bush Company applies fixed and variable overhead on the basis of machine hours. Below are Bush Company's results for the month just past:

Machine hours used to set the predetermined overhead rate	40,000
Variable overhead per machine hour	$ 2.80
Actual variable overhead cost incurred	117,000
Actual fixed overhead cost incurred	302,100
Variable overhead cost applied to production	117,600
Variable overhead efficiency variance (unfavourable)	8,400
Fixed overhead budget variance (unfavourable)	2,100

Required:

a. Compute the following:
   i. Budgeted fixed overhead
   ii. Fixed portion of the predetermined overhead rate
   iii. Standard hours allowed for units produced
   iv. Fixed overhead volume variance
   v. Fixed overhead cost applied to production

    vi.   Variable overhead spending variance

    vii.   Actual machine hours worked

    viii.   Underapplied or (overapplied) overhead

b.   Why is it important to separate the spending variance from the efficiency variance in variable overhead variance analysis?

c.   How would you interpret the volume variance in fixed overhead variance analysis?

Extract from *Management Accounting Examination*, published by the Certified General Accountants Association of Canada (© CGA-Canada 2000). Reprinted with permission.

Problem 3

Amanda Lang Ltd. budgeted (estimated) sales of 20,000 units at a selling price of $10.00 per unit and a contribution margin of $3.00 per unit. The company actually sold 18,500 units at $10.50 per unit. Cost variances were $2,500 unfavourable variable costs and $1,000 favourable fixed costs.

Required:

Determine the following:

a.   Sales variance, by calculating the quantity sold variance and the selling price variance.

b.   Net income variance.

Solutions to Demonstration Problems

Problem 1

a.   Total standard cost for swimsuits produced during June:

1,500 × $63		$94,500
Less: Standard costs of labour and overhead		
Direct labour	$24,000	
Variable overhead	4,800	28,800
Standard cost of materials used during June		$65,700

b.

Standard cost of materials used during June:	$65,700
Number of swimsuits produced	1,500
Standard materials cost per swimsuit	
($65,700 ÷ 1,500)	43.80
Standard metres of direct materials per swimsuit	
($43.80 ÷ $8)	5.475 metres

c.

Actual cost of materials used:	$65,000
Standard costs of materials used	65,700
Total material usage price variance	$ 700 F
Total materials variance:	
Materials usage price variance (from above)	$ 700 F
Materials quantity variance	1,200 U
	$ 500 U

d.

Standard variable overhead cost for June	$ 4,800
Standard variable overhead rate per direct labour hour	$ 3
Standard direct labour hours for June (4,800 ÷ 3)	1,600
Standard direct labour rate per hour (24,000 ÷ 1,600)	$ 15

or

Standard labour cost per unit	$24,000 ÷ 1,500 = $16
Standard variable overhead per unit	$63 − ($43.80 + $16) = $3.20
Standard labour hours per unit	$3.20 ÷ $3 = $1.0667
Standard labour rate per hour	$16 ÷ 1.0667 = $15

e. Actual cost per swimsuit produced ($63.00 + $0.42) $ 63.42
    Number of swimsuits produced   ×   1,500
    Total actual costs of production $95,130.00

        Less: Actual cost of materials $65,000
               Actual cost of variable overhead   4,860   69,860.00
        Actual cost of direct labour $25,270.00

f. Labour rate variance   (AH × AR) − (AH × SR)
                                         $25,270 − (1,700 × $15)
                                         $25,270 − $25,500
                                         $230 F

g. Efficiency variance   (AH × SR) − (SH × SR)
                                         (1,700 × $15) − $24,000
                                         $1,500 U

h. Variable overhead efficiency variance   (SH × SR) − (AH × SR)
                                             $4,800 − (1,700 × $3)
                                             $300 U

i. Variable overhead spending variance   (AH × SR) − (AH × AR)
                                             $5,100 − $4,860
                                             $240 F

j.

	Standard Quantity or Hours	Standard Price or Rate	Standard Cost
Direct materials	5.475 metres	$ 8 per metre	$43.80
Direct labour	1.067 hours	$15 per hour	16.00
Variable overhead	1.067 hours	$ 3 per hour	3.20
Total standard cost per swimsuit			$63.00

Problem 2

a.

i.   Budgeted fixed overhead:
     Fixed overhead budgeted variance = $2,100
     $2,100 = Actual fixed overhead − Budgeted fixed overhead
     $2,100 = $302,100 − Budgeted fixed overhead
     Budgeted fixed overhead = $300,000

ii. Fixed portion of predetermined overhead rate:
     Budgeted fixed overhead ÷ Machine hours to set predetermined rate
     = $300,000 ÷ 40,000 hours = $7.50 per hour

iii. Standard hours allowed for production:
     = Applied variable overhead ÷ Variable overhead rate per hour
     = $117,600 ÷ $2.80
     = 42,000 hours

iv. Volume variance = Budgeted fixed overhead − SH_A × SFOHR
                      = $300,000 − (42,000 h × $7.50)
                      = $300,000 − $315,000
                      = $15,000 F

v. Fixed overhead applied:
= Predetermined fixed overhead $\times SH_A$
= $7.50 \times 42,000\ h$
= $315,000

vi. Variable overhead spending variance
Variable overhead controllable variance =
Variable overhead efficiency variance + Variable overhead spending variance
∴ Actual VOH incurred − VOH applied to production =
$117,000 − $117,600 = $600 F
$600 F = $8,400 + Variable overhead spending variance
Variable overhead spending variance = $9,000 F

vii. Actual machine hours worked:
Variable Overhead Spending Variance = Actual variable overhead − (AH $\times$ Standard variable overhead rate per hour)
$9,000 F = $117,000 − (AH $\times$ $2.80)
$126,000 = AH $\times$ $2.80
Actual hours = 45,000 hours

viii. Underapplied or overapplied overhead:

Variable overhead spending variance	$ 9,000	F
Variable overhead efficiency variance	8,400	U
Fixed overhead budget variance	2,100	U
Fixed overhead volume variance	15,000	F
Total	$13,500	F

Overhead overapplied by $13,500

b. It is important to separate the spending variance from the efficiency variance because each measures a different aspect of the overall variable overhead variance, and each has a different cause. The spending variance measures whether the inputs were acquired at an appropriate cost or price, and the efficiency variance measures whether the inputs were used efficiently in production. In order to correct an unfavourable variance, it is necessary to identify its cause(s). Also, when evaluating performance, it is important to recognize that the two variances may often be the responsibility of two different individuals.

c. The volume variance in fixed overhead variance analysis assigns a dollar value to the "cost" of operating at less than the planned activity level, or the "benefit" of operating at greater than the planned activity level.

Problem 3

a. Quantity sold variance:

(18,500 − 20,000) x $3 = 1,500 x $3)	$4,500 U

Selling price variance:

($10.50 − $10.00) x 18,500 = $0.50 x 18,500	9,250 F
Sales variance	$4,750 F

b.

Sales variance	$4,750 F
Variable cost variances	2,500 U
Fixed cost variances	1,000 F
Net income variance	$3,250 F

End-of-Chapter Materials

SELF-TEST QUESTIONS

(SOLUTIONS APPEAR AT THE END OF THE CHAPTER.)

1. You are provided with the following selected information for Spectra Ltd.

Capacity machine hours	20,000
Budgeted machine hours	15,000
Actual machine hours	15,000
Standard machine hours allowed for actual production	18,000

   Which of the following variances does Spectra Ltd. have?
   a. An unfavourable volume variance
   b. A favourable volume variance
   c. No volume variance
   d. A favourable variable overhead spending variance

2. Restless Style Ltd. produces and sells Lipgloss. In the production of this product, the standard direct labour amounts to 5 hours at $20.00 per hour. During February, 5,000 units were produced using 26,000 direct labour hours at $21.00 per hour. What was the direct labour efficiency variance?
   a. $46,000 U
   b. $21,000 U
   c. $20,000 U
   d. $20,000 F

3. For the month of April, the manufacturing overhead volume variance at Chancellor Ltd. was $6,660 favourable. The organization uses a fixed overhead rate of $3.70 per direct labour hour.

   What does this mean for the standard direct labour hours allowed for April's output?
   a. They exceeded actual hours by 1,800 hours.
   b. They exceeded capacity activity by 1,800 hours.
   c. They fell short of capacity activity by 1,800 hours.
   d. They fell short of actual hours by 1,800 hours.

4. Squawk Box Ltd. makes and sells a single product and uses a standard cost system. During May, the company's management accountant, Mark Haines, budgeted $320,000 in manufacturing overhead cost at a capacity activity of 20,000 machine hours. At standard, each unit of finished product requires 4 machine hours. The following costs and activities were recorded during May:

Total actual manufacturing overhead cost incurred	$335,500
Units of product completed	4,700 units
Actual machine hours worked	21,000 machine hours

What was the amount of overhead cost that Squawk Box Ltd. applied to work in process for May?
   a. $300,800   c. $335,500
   b. $315,370   d. $336,000

5. When a direct labour efficiency variance is prorated to inventories and cost of goods sold, the accounts affected include (more than one answer may be correct):
   a. Raw Materials Inventory
   b. Work in Process
   c. Finished Goods
   d. Accrued Payroll

Self-Test Questions 4 and 5 are extracted from *Management Accounting Examination*, published by the Certified General Accountants Association of Canada (© CGA-Canada 1999 and 2000). Reprinted with permission.

6. Variable overhead is applied on the basis of standard direct labour hours. If, for a given period, the direct labour efficiency variance is unfavourable, the variable overhead efficiency variance will be:
   a. Favourable
   b. Unfavourable
   c. Zero
   d. The same as the labour efficiency variance
   e. Indeterminable since it is not related to the labour efficiency variance.

Use the following list of variances for the Baruch Hoffman Company to answer Self-Test Questions 7 to 10.

Direct materials price variance	$ 7,000 U
Direct materials quantity variance	5,000 U
Direct labour price variance	4,160 F
Direct labour efficiency variance	4,000 U
Variable overhead spending variance	960 U
Variable overhead efficiency variance	2,000 U
Fixed overhead budget variance	2,000 U
Fixed overhead production volume variance	10,000 F

Additional information:

Actual units produced	10,000
Planned units of production	8,000
Standard labour hours for actual output	5,000
Standard material units for actual output	100,000
Actual direct labour costs	99,840
Actual price paid for direct materials	132,000

Variable overhead is applied at the rate of $10.00 per direct labour hour. The materials purchase price was $0.028 higher than the standard price of $0.50 per unit.

7. What was the actual number of units of direct materials purchased?
   a. 100,000   c. 178,570
   b. 114,000   d. 250,000

8. How many actual direct labour hours were worked?
    a. 4,808
    b. 4,992
    c. 5,000
    d. 5,200

9. By how much was the actual amount of fixed overhead incurred more than or less than planned?
    a. Actual fixed overhead incurred was $2,000 less than budget.
    b. Actual fixed overhead incurred was $2,000 more than budget.
    c. Actual fixed overhead incurred was $8,000 less than budget.
    d. Actual fixed overhead incurred was $8,000 more than budget.

10. What was the standard cost for one unit of output, assuming that variable costing was used?
    a. $20.00   c. $25.00
    b. $21.00   d. $30.00

Self-Test Question 7–10 are extracted from Management Accounting Examination, published by the Certified General Accountants Association of Canada (© CGA-Canada 2002). Reprinted with permission.

Use the following information to answer parts (11) and (12):

David Chow Corp. reported the following results for the period:

	Labour	Material	Variable Overhead
Rate:			
Actual	$21.00/hr	$4.50/kg	$1.05/hr
Standard	$20.00/hr	$5.00/kg	$1.00/hr
Quantity per unit of output:			
Actual	20 minutes	1.9 kg	20 minutes
Standard	30 minutes	2.0 kg	30 minutes

11. Assuming that all overhead is variable, what is the total variance per unit of output produced?
    a. $2.50 U
    b. $3.00 F
    c. $4.30 U
    d. $4.60 F

12. Assume that all overhead costs of $50,000 are fixed and that normal production volume is 20,000 units. What is the standard cost of 1 unit?
    a. $20.50
    b. $22.50
    c. $30.50
    d. $31.00

Self-Test Questions 11 and 12 are extracted from *Management Accounting Examination,* published by the Certified General Accountants Association of Canada © CGA-Canada June 2005.

Use the following information to answer parts (13) and (14):

Redel Inc. has the following results for the current period:

	Budget	Actual
Fixed overhead	$156,000	$160,000
Units produced	6,500 units	6,000 units
Direct labour hours (DLH)	13,000 hours	12,500 hours

Fixed overhead is applied at $12 per DLH. Variable overhead is applied at $27.50 per DLH. The standard per unit is 2 DLH. Actual variable overhead was $310,600.

13. Which of the following amounts represents the fixed overhead budget variance?
    a. $ 4,000 U
    b. $ 6,000 F
    b. $10,000 U
    d. $16,000 F

14. Which of the following amounts represents the variable overhead variance?
    a. $13,750 U
    b. $19,400 F
    c. $33,150 F
    d. $46,900 F

March 2005 MA 1, CGA b and c

Self-Test Questions 13 and 14 are extracted from *Management Accounting Examination,* published by the Certified General Accountants Association of Canada © CGA-Canada March 2005.

15. Sales volume variance is
    a. Flexible budget amounts − Static budgeted amounts
    b. Actual operating income − Flexible budget operating income
    c. Actual unit price − Budget unit price x Actual units
    d. Budgeted unit price × Difference between actual inputs and budgeted inputs for the actual activity level achieved

16. Actual and budgeted information about the sales of a product are presented below for June:

	Actual	Budget
Units	8,000	10,000
Sales revenue	$92,000	$105,000

The sales price variance for June was:
    a. $ 8,000 favourable
    b. $10,000 favourable
    c. $10,500 unfavourable
    d. $ 8,500 unfavourable

QUESTIONS

1. Why is a standard costing system regarded as both a planning and a control tool?

2. What is a variance and what does it measure?

3. Why are standards necessary for each cost component of a product or service?

4. Why is a predetermined overhead rate considered a standard?

5. Why is the computation of the material price variance frequently based on the quantity of material purchased, rather than the quantity used, during the period?

6. What is variance analysis and why is it conducted by managers?

7. Why is a "conversion cost" category emerging in some companies to replace the traditional cost categories of direct labour and manufacturing overhead?

8. If the material price variance is computed on the basis of quantity of material purchased (point of purchase) rather than used, can a total material variance be computed? Explain your answer.

9. As the manufacturing vice-president of Geraldo Controls, you have noticed that one manufacturing plant experienced several large unfavourable material quantity variances during the prior quarter. Before starting your probe of the matter, list some possible reasons for this type of variance.

10. Your manufacturing operations this period have shown a large favourable labour rate variance. Why might this have occurred? Would you expect your labour efficiency variance to be favourable or unfavourable? Why?

11. You are the supervisor of the Harvey Mail Service. Service quality in the organization is not measured relative to direct labour time. Additionally, there is a consistently large favourable efficiency variance. Provide one positive and one negative analysis of this variance.

12. "Overhead standards should be set using the most available measurement in the production or service area, such as direct labour hours." Discuss the validity of this statement.

13. What is meant by "standard quantity allowed" when this term is used in relation to direct material? to direct labour? to overhead? Provide an example for each cost element.

14. Is fixed manufacturing overhead controlled by management on a per-unit basis? Explain your answer.

15. Of what importance is capacity utilization to managers? When managers control utilization, are they always controlling costs? Explain.

16. For the following variances, indicate (i) when each variance should be calculated and (ii) to whom responsibility for the variance should be assigned and why.
    a. Material price variance
    b. Material quantity variance
    c. Labour rate variance
    d. Labour efficiency variance
    e. Variable overhead spending variance
    f. Volume variance

17. In a standard cost system, is standard cost or actual cost charged to Work in Process Inventory for direct material and direct labour? Explain. How are actual costs reflected in a standard cost system?

18. What is a sales variance? What information does it provide management?

19. If the sales variance is favourable, must the net income variance also be favourable?

20. How do ERP systems affect the standard setting process within an organization?

21. How do ERP systems make organizations more transparent?

22. (Appendix 7A) If the variances incurred in a given period are not significant in amount, how are they typically closed out at the end of the period? Why is this disposition acceptable?

EXERCISES

1. (LO 1, 2, 3, 4, 5) Match each item in the right-hand column with a term in the left-hand column.

   a. Operations flow document
   b. Practical standard
   c. Standard
   d. Theoretical standard
   e. Labour rate variance
   f. Overhead spending variance
   g. Volume variance
   h. Standard cost card
   i. Variance analysis
   j. Bill of materials

   1. A standard that allows for no human or mechanical error
   2. The difference between budgeted (estimated) and applied fixed overhead
   3. A listing of tasks required to make a product
   4. A document specifying the materials required for a product
   5. The process of identifying causes of variances
   6. A norm for a cost or a quantity
   7. The difference between the actual and budgeted (estimated) overhead
   8. The standard of performance that has reasonable probability of attainment
   9. The difference between standard and actual labour wages
   10. The document listing the standard cost of all inputs for a product

2. (LO 3) You are the purchasing agent for the Zoo Company, which makes statues of endangered animals. Wildlife and environmental groups sell the statues at fundraisers. In June, you bought 105,600 kg of material at an average price of $2.40/kg. That month, 99,400 kg of material was used to produce 225 statues. The material standard for each statue is 420 kg of material at a standard cost of $2.25/kg.
   Required:
   a. Calculate the material price variance, based on quantity purchased.
   b. Calculate the material quantity variance.
   c. What potential reasons might you have for the price variance?

3. (LO 3) Judy Pereira Company Ltd. has experienced the following costs and quantities related to direct material during August:
Actual quantity purchased	136,500 litres
Actual quantity used	130,500 litres
Standard quantity allowed	132,900 litres
Actual unit price per litre	$14.50
Standard unit price per litre	$13.90

   Required:
   a. Compute the material price variance based on (1) quantity purchased and (2) quantity used.
   b. Compute the material quantity variance.
   c. Why can a material price variance be computed on two different bases, but a labour rate variance cannot?

4. (LO 3) Calley Toons incurred the following direct material costs in November for printing:
Actual unit purchase price	$0.165 per sheet
Standard unit price	$0.168 per sheet
Quantity purchased in November	100,000 sheets
Quantity used in November	90,000 sheets
Standard quantity allowed for good production	89,800 sheets
Standard unit price	$0.168 per sheet

   Required:
   a. Materials purchase price variance.
   b. Materials quantity variance.

EXERCISES

5. (LO 3) John Stewart's Canvas Shop experienced the following costs related to direct materials during August:

Actual quantity purchased	45,500 kg
Actual quantity used	43,500 kg
Standard quantity allowed	44,300 kg
Actual unit price	$22.00
Standard unit price	$22.50

Required:

The company president has requested that you determine the material price variances and the material quantity variance. (Compute the material price variance based on (a) quantity purchased and (b) quantity used.)

6. (LO 3) Micksteamy's Raincoats experienced the following costs related to direct materials during August:

Actual quantity purchased	37,500 kilos
Actual quantity used	40,000 kilos
Standard quantity allowed	35,000 kilos
Standard unit price	$17.50
Actual unit price	$19

Required:

Determine

a. material purchase price variance
b. material quantity variance.

7. (LO 3) The Alison Krentel Print Shop incurred the following direct material costs in November for high-volume routine printing jobs:

Sheets of paper purchased in November	500,000
Sheets of paper used in November	390,000
Standard quantity allowed for good production	397,000
Actual unit purchase price per sheet	$0.035
Standard unit price per sheet	$0.032

Required:

a. Calculate the material price variances based on the quantity purchased and the material quantity variance.
b. Does this company employ standards based on theoretical performance? Explain
c. As the vice-president of manufacturing, would you want to move to a more rigorous standard than the one presently used? Why?

8. (LO 3) You have just received the following information related to your company's purchases and usage of paper during October. The company runs high-volume calendar printing jobs.

Sheets of paper purchased in October	1,000,000
Sheets of paper used in October	780,000
Standard quantity allowed for good production	794,000
Actual unit purchase price per sheet	$0.037
Standard unit price per sheet	$0.039

Required:

a. Calculate the material price variance based on the quantity purchased and the material quantity variance.
b. You have asked the vice-president of manufacturing to explain the difference between theoretical, practical, and expected standards. How might she explain these differences?
c. How would using theoretical standards change the variance information calculated in part (a)? (No specific numerical calculations are necessary.)

9. (LO: 3) Jane Shearer Ltd. makes school uniforms. During February the business experienced the following direct labour costs:

Efficiency variance (unfavourable)	$8,690
Actual direct labour rate per hour	$3.75
Standard direct labour rate per hour	$3.95
Standard hours allowed for production	10,000

EXERCISES

Required:
a. Actual hours worked during February
b. Total payroll
c. Labour rate variance

10. (LO 3) David Ho-A-Yun Automotive uses a standard cost system and experienced the following results related to direct labour in December:

Actual hours worked	41,250
Standard hours allowed for production	40,500
Actual direct labour rate	$7.25
Standard direct labour rate	$6.75

Required:
a. Total actual payroll
b. Labour rate variance
c. Labour efficiency variance

11. (LO 3) Bre Van De Kamp Fabrics uses a standard cost system. The company experienced the following results related to direct labour in December:

Actual hours worked	27,500
Standard hours allowed for production	27,000
Actual direct labour rate	$7.25
Standard direct labour rate	$6.75

Required:
a. Total actual payroll
b. Labour rate variance
c. Labour efficiency variance

12. (LO 3) Thomasas Towels uses a standard cost system. The company experienced the following results related to direct labour in December:

Actual hours worked	13,750
Standard hours allowed for production	13,500
Actual direct labour rate	$7.25
Standard direct labour rate	$6.75

Required:
a. Total payroll
b. Labour rate variance
c. Labour efficiency variance

13. (LO 3) Esther Deutsch Quilts makes a one-design queen-size quilt and uses a standard costing system. During February, the following direct labour hours and costs were incurred:

Standard hours	5,400
Actual hours	5,100
Standard wage rate per hour	$11.75
Actual wage rate per hour	$12.00

Required:
a. Determine total actual labour cost, standard labour cost, and the labour rate and efficiency variances.
b. Write a memo to Esther Deutsch about the possible causes of the rate and efficiency variances.

14. (LO 3) Hooked-On-Rugs make a one-design residential four-by-six metre rug. The firm uses a standard costing system. During February, the firm experienced the following direct labour hours and costs:

Standard hours	1,350
Actual hours	1,275
Standard wage rate per hour	$12.00
Actual wage rate per hour	$12.10

Required:
a. Total actual labour cost
b. Standard labour cost
c. Labour rate and efficiency variance

EXERCISES

15. (LO 3) Jack Abbott Insurance Ltd.'s information about direct labour for September is as follows:

Efficiency variance	$17,380 U
Actual direct labour rate per hour	$7.50
Standard direct labour rate per hour	$7.90
Standard hours allowed	20,000

Required:
   a. Calculate the actual hours worked during September.
   b. Calculate the total payroll.
   c. Calculate the labour rate variance.
   d. Given the above information, Mr. Jack Abbott has asked your human resources firm, HR Sources, for some suggestions to better motivate his employees. Prepare a short memo providing some feedback to him.

16. (LO 3) Connie Reed Cabinets builds 1.2-by-1.8 metre bookcases. Each bookcase requires 7 direct labour hours. The average standard hourly wage of workers is $9. During October, Connie Reed Cabinets built 1,200 bookcases. Direct labour time was 8,000 hours, and gross pay was $74,800.

Required:
   a. Compute the labour variances.
   b. Provide an explanation of the direct labour variances that is consistent with the results.

17. (LO 3) Rose Reed Ornaments Ltd. builds kitchen cabinets in uniform sets. Each set requires a standard quantity of 23.5 direct labour hours. The average standard hourly wage of the crew of cabinetmakers is $16.50. During October, the company built 150 sets. Production required 3,400 hours, and direct labour paid out amounted to $58,650.

Required:
Rose Reed, the president, has asked you to prepare an analysis of direct labour for her.

18. (LO 3) Wild River Ltd., a manufacturing company, has the following standard costs for one unit of production:

Direct materials (5 kg at $6.00)	$ 30.00
Direct labour (3 hr at $15.00)	45.00
Manufacturing overhead:	
Variable (3 direct labour hours at $6.00)	18.00
Fixed (3 direct labour hours at $12.00)	36.00
Total standard cost	$ 129.00

Actual results for the last quarter were:

Production volume	3,000 units
Direct materials (18,000 kg at $6.30)	$113,400
Direct labour (8,900 hours at $15.60)	138,840
Manufacturing overhead:	
Variable	51,000
Fixed	93,000

Required:
Calculate the variances for direct material, direct labour, and variable overhead for the last quarter for Wild River.

(Exercise 18 is adapted by the authors from *Management Accounting examinations* published by the Certified General Accountants Association of Canada © CGA-Canada, March 2005, used by permission)

19. (LO 3, 4) Celine Corp. produces engraved wood plaques; each plaque requires 15 minutes of machine time. During April, 1,800 units were manufactured. The company's predetermined variable overhead rate per machine hour is $14. In April, $6,200 of variable overhead costs were incurred and machine time was clocked at 410 hours.

Required:
   a. What is the total applied variable overhead for the month?
   b. Calculate the variable overhead variances.
   c. This is the sixth month in a row in which there has been a significant favourable variable overhead efficiency variance. Provide the company's management accountant with an appropriate explanation as to why so few machine hours are being used relative to the standard.

EXERCISES

20. (LO 3, 4) Better Manufacturing Company employs a standard costing system. In the company's Halifax plant, manufacturing overhead is applied to production based on machine hours. The following information is from the Halifax plant's records pertaining to October:

Standard machine hours for the month	2,100
Actual machine hours for the month	2,200
Standard variable manufacturing overhead rate per machine hour	$ 12
Standard fixed manufacturing overhead rate per machine hour	10
Total budgeted monthly fixed manufacturing overhead	20,000
Actual fixed manufacturing overhead	21,000
Actual variable manufacturing overhead	25,850

Required:
a. Total actual overhead cost
b. Total applied overhead
c. Variable overhead variances
d. Fixed overhead variances

21. (LO 3, 4) Joanne Steinman Manufacturing Ltd. employs a standard costing system. In the company's Montreal plant, manufacturing overhead is applied to production on the basis of machine hours. The following information from the Montreal plant pertains to October:

Standard machine hours for month	4,200
Actual machine hours for month	4,400
Standard variable manufacturing overhead rate per machine hour	$ 12
Standard fixed manufacturing overhead rate per machine hour	10
Total budgeted monthly fixed manufacturing overhead	40,000
Actual fixed manufacturing overhead	45,000
Actual variable manufacturing overhead	47,500

Required:
a. Total actual overhead cost
b. Total applied overhead
c. Variable overhead variances
d. Fixed overhead variances

22. (LO 3, 4) Mike Delfino Office Ltd. manufactures a table-top office filing system. The company uses a standard cost system and applies manufacturing overhead to production using direct labour hours. For the current year, budgeted fixed manufacturing overhead was $160,000; budgeted direct labour hours were 20,000; and the standard variable manufacturing overhead rate was set at $12 per direct labour hour. The standard direct labour time per unit is 0.5 hours. The following data pertain to the current year:

Number of units produced	41,000
Actual direct labour hours	21,000
Actual variable manufacturing overhead cost	$257,250
Actual fixed manufacturing overhead cost	$172,000

Required:
a. Compute the amount of total applied manufacturing overhead.
b. Compute the total actual cost of manufacturing overhead.
c. Calculate the variable manufacturing overhead variances.
d. Calculate the fixed manufacturing overhead variances.

23. (LO 3, 4) Ray Davidson Concrete Ltd. manufactures industrial pipe. The company uses a standard cost system and applies variable manufacturing overhead to production using kilograms of product moved. The standard variable manufacturing overhead rate is set at $9 per kilogram moved. The standard weight per unit is 0.75 kg. For the current year, budgeted fixed manufacturing overhead is $480,000; fixed manufacturing overhead is applied to production using direct labour hours. The standard time per unit is 0.5 direct labour hours. Budgeted direct labour hours for the current year were 60,000. The following data pertains to the current year:

Number of units produced	82,000
Actual weight of units (kilograms)	62,300
Actual direct labour hours	42,000
Actual variable overhead cost	$582,000
Actual fixed overhead cost	$476,000

EXERCISES

Required:

a.   The company CEO, Judith Poë, has asked you to determine the amount of total applied overhead, variable overhead variances, and fixed overhead variances.

b.   What explanations might you offer Ms. Poë for the variances calculated in part (a)?

24.   (LO 3, 4) The Harrison Co. Ltd. manufactures one product, for which it has developed the following standard cost:

Materials, 5 L @ $20/L	$100
Direct labour, 2 h @ $12/h	24
Variable overhead	16
Fixed overhead	50
	$190

Normal activity of 2,400 direct labour hours was used as a denominator in arriving at the fixed overhead rate. Variable costs are allocated based on direct labour hours. There were no inventories on January 1. During January, the following actually occurred:

i.   6,000 L of material was purchased for $119,700.

ii.   1,000 units were transferred to finished goods inventory.

iii.   5,100 L of material was issued to production.

iv.   The direct labour payroll was $24,304 for 1,960 hours.

v.   Actual overhead costs totalled $16,001 variable and $58,000 fixed.

vi.   800 units were sold on account at a unit price of $250.

vii.   Selling and administrative expenses totalled $25,000.

Required:

a.   Compute two variances for each element of manufacturing costs.

b.   Compute the Cost of Goods Sold assuming all variances are prorated.

25.   (LO 7) West Wing Company has budgeted sales of 200,000 units at a selling price of $40 per unit. The company president, Jeb Bartlett, asked you why budgeted revenue had not been achieved. Investigation revealed the following:

Actual sales volume	206,000
Actual average sales price	$38

Required:

Analyze the facts given and provide an explanation for the president.

26.   (LO 7) As sales manager of Cliff Taylor Dairies, you have been asked by the company owner why sales of milk are below budget. A review of the budget reveals that revenue was expected to be $42,000, based on expected sales of 420,000 litres at $0.10 per litre. Inspection of the records shows that 430,000 litres were actually sold at $0.09 per litre.

Required:

Analyze sales and explain what happened.

27.   (LO 7) David Rosenberg Training Ltd. delivers two-day statistical process control seminars for manufacturing workers. The fee for each program amounts to $4,000. Last year Rosenberg presented 30 seminars, and he budgeted a 20% increase in programs for the current year. At the end of the current year, he is disappointed that his actual revenue is only $136,500. He presented 39 programs during the year and is puzzled by this and wants answers to the following:

Required:

a.   What was the expected revenue for the current year?

b.   Why was the budgeted revenue not achieved?

28.   (LO 8) The following information pertains to the operations of Sulyma Plastics for the current fiscal year. The company manufactures exquisite pink yard flamingos.

Purchase of material (at standard cost)	$600,000
Standard cost of material issued to production	552,000
Direct labour (at standard cost)	288,000
Material price variance	3,700 U
Material quantity variance	9,100 F
Direct labour rate variance	2,100 F
Direct labour efficiency variance	3,900 U

Required:

a.   Record the journal entry for purchasing direct material on account.

b.   Record the journal entry for issuing direct material into production.

c.   Record the journal entry to accrue direct labour costs.

d.   Record the year-end journal entry to close the variance accounts, assuming the variances are not material in amount.

29. (LO 8) The following information pertains to the operations of David Seed Ltd., a maker of roof coatings.

Purchase of materials (at standard cost)	$200,000
Standard cost of materials issued to production	184,000
Direct labour (at standard cost)	96,000
Material price variance	3700 F
Material quantity variance	9,100 U
Direct labour rate variance	2,100 U
Direct labour efficiency variance	3,900 F

Required:

a.   Record the journal entry to purchase the direct materials on account.

b.   Record the journal entry for issuing direct materials into production.

c.   Record the journal entry to accrue direct labour costs.

d.   Record the year-end journal entry to close the variance accounts.

(Assume that the variances are not material in amount.)

PROBLEMS

1.   (LO 3) Assume in all cases that the material price variance is calculated on the basis of quantity purchased rather than quantity used.

	Case 1	Case 2	Case 3	Case 4
Units produced	500	9,000	g	1,760
Standard litres per unit	a	d	12.5	10.6
Standard price per litre	$0.90	e	$1.30	j
Standard litres allowed	10,000	36,000	h	k
Actual litres purchased	b	34,900	4,900	20,000
Actual litres used	9,800	36,450	4,895	18,450
Actual price per litre	$0.92	$5.04	i	$2.55
Material price variance	$214 U	$1,396 U	$490 F	l
Material quantity variance	c	f	$26 U	$515F

Required:
For each of the independent cases, supply the missing amounts.

2.   (LO 3) Dalton McGuinty Ltd. manufactures electrical supply boxes. The company uses a standard costing system. Its standard quantities and costs for one electrical supply box follow:

Direct materials	3 square metres at $1.10 per square metre
Direct labour	6 minutes at $14 per hour

In May, 60,000 boxes were produced. The company's purchasing agent bought 195,000 square metres of material in May at $1.11 per square metre. The May factory payroll amounted to $87,420 of direct labour cost for 6,200 hours. In May, 179,000 square metres of direct materials were placed into production.

Required:
Calculate the material and labour variances. (Base the material price variance on the quantity purchased.)

3.   (LO 3) Peter Mansbridge Corporation has a union contract provision that guarantees a minimum wage of $1,000 per month to each direct labour employee. Currently, 100 employees are covered by this provision. All direct labour employees are paid $10.00 per hour.

The direct labour amount for the current fiscal year was based on an annual rate of 200,000 direct labour hours at $10 per hour, or a total of $2,000,000 per year. Because of the contract provision, $100,000 (100 × $1,000 per month) was treated as a fixed monthly cost. Each monthly plan was calculated using the following formula: $100,000 + $7.00 per direct labour hour.

PROBLEMS

Figures for the first three months of the fiscal year are:

	January	February	March
Direct labour hours worked	22,000	32,000	42,000
Direct labour costs planned	?	?	?
Direct labour costs incurred	$220,000	$320,000	$420,000
Variance	?	?	?

These figures are a source of concern because they show unfavourable variances when production is high, and favourable variances during slow months. The manager of the factory is certain that this trend does not reflect reality.

Required:

a. Calculate the variance for each of the months of January, February, and March. What is the explanation for the variances relative to the company's budget cost formula?

b. Explain the error in logic in this variance calculation and, using a formula for direct labour costs more appropriate to the actual cost behaviour, recalculate the variances for January, February, and March.

Extract from *Management Accounting Examination*, published by the Certified General Accountants Association of Canada (© CGA-Canada 2003). Reprinted with permission.

4. (LO 3) Rick Santelli's Jewellery makes pendants using a variety of stock moulds. One-eighth of a kilogram of direct material and 15 minutes of direct labour are required to produce a pendant. Direct material costs of $6.20/kg are standard, and the standard direct labour rate is $12/h.

During April, 32,000 pendants were made, and the company experienced a $744 favourable material quantity variance. The purchasing agent had purchased 800 kg of material in excess of what the company used, incurring a favourable price variance of $1,235. Total direct labour hours worked were 8,200, and a total unfavourable labour variance of $1,700 was incurred.

Required:

a. Standard quantity of material allowed
b. Actual quantity of material used
c. Actual quantity of material purchased
d. Actual price of material purchased
e. Standard hours allowed for production
f. Labour efficiency variance
g. Labour rate variance
h. Actual labour rate paid

5. (LO 3) Anne Cowan Co. manufactures electrical supply boxes and accounts for production using a standard cost system. Standard quantities and costs for one electrical supply box follow:

Direct material	2 square metres @ $2.10 per square metre
Direct labour	10 minutes @ $13.20 per hour

In May, 39,600 boxes were produced. You, as the company's purchasing agent, bought 115,000 square metres of material in May at $1.70 per square metre. The May manufacturing payroll reflected $93,500 of direct labour for 6,900 hours. In May, 88,500 square metres of direct material was placed in production.

Required:

a. Calculate the material variances, basing the price variance on quantity purchased.
b. Calculate the labour variances.
c. Prepare a memo to Christopher Cowan, the controller, addressing the probable cause of the price variance and how that price affected the other variances.

6. (LO 3) Terry Hatcher's Brooches Ltd. manufactures brooches using a variety of stock moulds. One-eighth of a kilogram of direct material and 15 minutes of direct labour are required to produce a brooch. Direct material cost $5.20 per kilogram at standard, and the standard direct labour rate is $12.00 per hour.

During April, 32,000 brooches were made, and the company experienced a $130 unfavourable material quantity variance. The purchasing agent had purchased 800 kilograms of material more than the company used, incurring a favourable price variance of

PROBLEMS

$965. Total direct labour hours worked were 8,200, and a total unfavourable labour variance of $1,580 was incurred.

Required:

Determine the following:

a. Standard quantity of material allowed
b. Actual quantity of material used
c. Actual quantity of material purchased
d. Actual price of material purchased
e. Standard hours allowed for production
f. Labour efficiency variance
g. Labour rate variance
h. Actual labour rate paid

7. (LO 3) Information for each independent case follows:

	Case 1	Case 2	Case 3	Case 4
Units produced	600	d	320	1,250
Standard hours per unit	2	0.6	g	j
Standard hours allowed	a	600	480	k
Standard rate per hour	$6	e	$5.50	$8
Actual hours worked	1,230	580	h	5,100
Actual labour cost	b	f	$1,656.80	$30,600
Labour rate variance	$246 U	$290 U	$15.20 F	l
Labour efficiency variance	c	$80 F	i	$600 U

Required:

Supply the missing amounts.

8. (LO 3) The following information pertains to independent cases:

	Case 1	Case 2	Case 3	Case 4
Units produced	600	d	310	215
Standard hours per unit	2	0.3	g	j
Standard hours allowed	a	1,200	930	k
Standard rate per hour	$5	e	$9.50	$8
Actual hours worked	1,230	1,170	h	450
Actual labour cost	b	f	$3,230	$3,645
Labour rate variance	$62 U	$117 U	$475 F	I
Labour efficiency variance	c	$360 F	i	$ 160 U

Required:

Supply the missing amounts.

9. (LO 3) Sue Thomas Corp. produces evening handbags. In June, company president Ms. Sue Thomas received the following information:

Standard metres of material allowed per handbag	1.5
Standard labour time allowed per handbag	3 hours
Month's production	300 handbags
Actual hours worked	880
Actual cost of material purchased and used ($14.90 per metre)	$7,152
Material quantity variance	$450 U
Labour rate variance	$2,640 U
Standard labour rate per hour	$9

Ms. Sue Thomas is puzzled by the information and its method of presentation.

Required:

a. Material price and labour efficiency variances
b. Standard prime (material and labour) cost to produce one handbag
c. Prepare a memo to Ms. Sue Thomas explain the variances and the potential causes of the variances.

10. (LO 3) Sandra Chowfen Ltd. was founded several years ago by two designers who had developed several popular lines of living room, dining room, and bedroom furniture for other companies. The designers believed that their design for dinette sets could be standardized and would sell well. They formed their own company and soon had all the orders they could complete in their small plant in Moncton, New Brunswick.

PROBLEMS

From the beginning, the firm was successful. The owners bought a computer and software that produced financial statements, which an employee prepared. The owners thought that the information they needed was contained in these statements.

Recently, however, the employees have been requesting raises. The owners wonder how to evaluate the employees' requests. At the suggestion of Lawrence Chung, CA, the firm's external accountant, the owners have hired a consultant to implement a standard cost system. The consultant believes that the calculation of variances will aid management in setting responsibility for labour's performance.

The supervisors believe that under normal conditions, a dinette set can be assembled with 5 hours of direct labour costing $20/hour. During the month, the actual direct labour wages paid to employees amounted to $127,600 for 5,800 hours of work. The factory produced 1,200 dinette sets during the month.

Required:
Prepare variance computations for management's consideration.

11. (LO 3, 4) Zoe Busiek Industries Ltd. makes a very popular 36-inch window shade. Standard time and costs per stock window shade follow:

Machine time (hours)	0.20
Variable overhead rate per machine hour	$8.50
Fixed overhead rate per machine hour	$6.50

During the year, the following operating statistics were compiled:

Total fixed manufacturing overhead applied to production	$715,000
Actual variable manufacturing overhead	937,400
Actual fixed manufacturing overhead	709,000
Volume variance	17,000 F
Variable manufacturing overhead spending variance	10,900 U

Required:
a. For fixed manufacturing overhead, calculate the following:
   i.   Standard machine hours allowed
   ii. Number of window shades produced
   iii. Budgeted fixed overhead
   iv. Expected annual capacity in machine hours
   v.   Fixed manufacturing overhead spending variance
   vi. Fixed manufacturing overhead total variance
b. For variable manufacturing overhead, calculate the following:
   i.   Total applied variable manufacturing overhead
   ii. Total variable manufacturing overhead variance
   iii. Actual machine hours incurred
   iv. Variable manufacturing overhead efficiency variance
c. Assume that you are the president of Zoe Busiek Industries and you are curious about the causes of the variable manufacturing overhead spending variance. Whom would you call to explain the variance? Defend your answer.

12. (LO 3, 4) Chris Matthews Ltd. makes an adjustable window screen. Standard time and costs per screen follow:

Machine time (hours)	0.20
VOH rate per machine hour	$8.50
FOH rate per machine hour	$6.50

At the end of May, papers on the desk of the company's accountant, Ms. Linda Nazareth, were partially ruined by a driving rain blowing through the screened windows. The following operating statistics were still legible on the accountant's report to management:

Total fixed overhead applied to production	$715,000
Actual variable overhead	937,400
Actual fixed overhead	709,000
Volume variance	13,000 F
Variable overhead spending variance	10,900 U

PROBLEMS

Ms. Linda Nazareth is on vacation. Because you recently took a management accounting course paid for by Chris Matthews Ltd., you have been asked to provide the following information:

Required:
a. Standard machine hours allowed
b. Number of screens produced
c. Budgeted fixed overhead
d. Expected annual capacity in machine hours
e. Fixed manufacturing overhead spending variance
f. Fixed manufacturing overhead total variance
g. For variable overhead:
   i. Total applied variable overhead
   ii. Total variable overhead variance
   iii. Actual machine hours incurred
   iv. Variable overhead efficiency variance
   v. Actual variable overhead rate per machine hour
h. Tim Russert, the president of Chris Matthews Ltd., is curious about the possible causes of the variable overhead spending variance. Whom would you suggest that he call (other than the vacationing accountant) to explain the variance? Defend your answer.

13. (LO 3, 5) Baldwin and Williams is a small law firm. Variable and fixed overhead are applied to legal cases as follows:
   • Variable overhead: Applied on a basis of per page of documentation generated during the month at the rate of $0.22 per page
   • Fixed overhead: Applied on a basis of monthly billable hours generated at the rate of $15 per hour; this rate was derived with the expectation of 1,600 billable hours per month.

   During July, the lawyers at Baldwin and Williams worked on a variety of cases: 198,000 pages of documentation were generated during July; total billable hours were 1,450. Actual variable and fixed overhead amounts for July were $48,650 and $25,000, respectively.

   Required:
   a. What is the budgeted annual fixed overhead for Baldwin and Williams?
   b. Determine the variable and fixed overhead variances for the month of July.
   c. Explain the variable overhead efficiency variance. In a law firm, what bases other than pages of documentation might be more useful to allocate variable overhead? Could a standard ever be set for these bases so that an efficiency variance could be calculated?

14. (LO 3, 4) Lily Simon Ltd. uses a standard costing system for planning and control purposes. For August, the firm expected to produce 4,000 units of product. At that level of production, expected manufacturing overhead costs are:

Variable	$ 9,600
Fixed	24,000

At standard, 2 machine hours are required to produce a single unit of product. Actual results for August follow:

Units produced	4,200
Machine hours worked	8,600
Actual variable manufacturing overhead	$ 9,460
Actual fixed manufacturing overhead	$24,900

Required:
a. Calculate standard hours allowed for actual output.
b. Calculate all overhead variances.
c. For the next year, the firm is considering automating its current manual production process. In its standard costing system, which standards would likely be affected by such a change? Explain. What individuals would likely be consulted to assist in revising the standards?

PROBLEMS

15. (LO 3) You have been given the following information about the production of Gamma Co., and are asked to provide the plant manager with information for a meeting with the vice-president of operations.

Standard Cost Card

Direct materials (DM) (6 kg @ $3 per kg)	$18.00
Direct labour (DL) (0.8 h @ $5 per h)	4.00
Variable overhead (VOH) (0.8 h @ $3 per h)	2.40
Fixed overhead (FOH) (0.8 h @ $7 per h)	5.60
	$30.00

The following is a production report for the last period of operations:

Costs	Variances Total Standard Cost	Price/ Rate	Spending/ Budget	Quantity/ Efficiency	Volume
DM	$405,000	$6,900 F		$9,000 U	
DL	90,000	4,850 U		7,000 U	
VOH	54,000		$1,300 F	?	
FOH	126,000		500		$14,000 U

Required:

a. How many units were produced last period?
b. How many kilograms of raw material were purchased and used during the period?
c. What was the actual cost per kilogram of raw material?
d. How many actual direct labour hours were worked during the period?
e. What was the actual rate paid per direct labour hour?
f. What was the actual variable overhead cost incurred during the period?
g. What is the total fixed cost in the company's budget?
h. What were the denominator hours for the last period?

Extract from *Management Accounting Examination*, published by the Certified General Accountants Association of Canada (© CGA-Canada 2000). Reprinted with permission.

16. (LO 3) Under a contract with the provincial government, ChemLabs Inc. analyzes the chemical and bacterial composition of well water in various municipalities in the interior of British Columbia. The contract price is $25.20 per test performed. The normal volume is 10,000 tests per month. Each test requires two testing kits. The standard price of each is $3.80. Direct labour time to perform the test is 10 minutes at $22.80 per hour. Overhead is allocated on the basis of direct labour hours. At normal volume, the overhead costs are as follows:

Variable overhead costs:		
Indirect labour	$18,000	
Utilities	4,000	
Labour-related costs	15,000	
Laboratory maintenance	11,000	$ 48,000
Fixed overhead costs:		
Supervisor	$30,000	
Amortization	28,000	
Base utilities	9,000	
Insurance	2,000	69,000
Total overhead		$117,000

During May, 9,000 tests were performed. The records show the following actual costs and production data:

	Activity	Actual Cost
Number of test kits purchased	19,000	$70,300
Number of test kits used	18,500	
Direct labour	1,623 h	$37,646
Total overhead costs: Variable		$45,200
Fixed		$68,500

Test kits are kept in inventory at standard cost. At the end of May, no tests were in process.

PROBLEMS

Required:

a.   Prepare a standard cost card for a water test.

b.   Calculate the direct materials price and quantity variances and the direct labour rate and efficiency variances for May, indicating whether they are favourable or unfavourable.

c.   Calculate the laboratory variable overhead variances for the month, indicating whether they are favourable or unfavourable.

(CMA adapted)

17.   (LO 3, 4) The David Faber Company Ltd. manufactures plastic and aluminum products. During the winter, substantially all production capacity is devoted to lawn sprinklers. Because a variety of products are made throughout the year, factory volume is measured by machine hours rather than units of product.

The company has developed the following standards for the production of a lawn sprinkler:

Direct materials:		
Aluminum	0.2 kg @ $0.40 per kg	$0.08
Plastic	1.0 kg @ $0.38 per kg	0.38
Direct labour	0.3 h @ $4.00 per h	1.20
Manufacturing overhead:*		
Variable	0.5 hours @ $1.60 per machine hour	0.80
Fixed	0.5 hours @ $2.20 per machine hour	1.10

*Based on an expected annual capacity of 48,000 machine hours.

During February 2008, 8,500 sprinklers were manufactured, and the following costs were incurred and charged to production:

Materials requisitioned for production:		
Aluminum	1,900 kg @ $0.40 per kg	$ 760
Plastic		
Regular grade	6,000 kg @ $0.38 per kg	2,280
Low grade*	3,500 kg @ $0.38 per kg	1,330
Direct labour:		
Regular time	2,300 h @ $4.00 per h	9,200
Overtime	400 h @ $6.00 per h	2,400
Manufacturing overhead:		
Variable	4,340 machine hours	6,400
Fixed	4,340 machine hours	9,230
Total costs charged to production		$31,600

*Because of plastic shortages, the company was forced to purchase lower-grade plastic than called for in the standards. This increased the number of sprinklers rejected on inspection.

Material price variations are not charged to production but to a material price variance account at the time the invoice is entered. All materials are carried in inventory at standard prices. Material purchases for February were

Aluminum	1,800 kg @ $0.48 per kg	$ 864
Plastic		
Regular grade	3,000 kg @ $0.50 per kg	1,500
Low grade*	6,000 kg @ $0.29 per kg	1,740

*Because of plastic shortages, the company was forced to purchase lower-grade plastic than called for in the standards. This increased the number of sprinklers rejected on inspection.

Required:

a.   What is the total difference between standard and actual cost for production in February?

b.   Compute the material and labour variances.

c.   Compute the variable and fixed overhead variances.

d.   The standard material quantities already include an allowance for acceptable material scrap loss. In this situation, what is the likely cause of the material quantity variance?

e.   Prepare a memo to the company president about your variance computations.

(CMA adapted)

PROBLEMS

18. (LO 3, 5) Jim Cramer Ltd. manufactures picnic table kits that are sold in various large discount department stores. The standard cost card indicates that the following costs are incurred to produce a single picnic table kit:

60 board feet of pine lumber	$54
2 pipe frame units	18
1 package of fasteners	8
0.5 hours of direct labour at $14 per hour	7
Variable manufacturing overhead at $20 per machine hour	4
Fixed manufacturing overhead at $15 per machine hour*	3
Total	$94

*Based on budgeted annual FOH of $30,000 and expected annual capacity of 2,000 hours.

During the current year, the firm had the following actual data related to the production of 11,000 picnic table kits:

Purchase and Usage of Materials:

Lumber	690,000 board feet at $0.85 per board foot
Pipe frame units	22,250 units at $9.10 per unit
Packages of fasteners	11,120 packages at $6.90 per package
Direct Labour Used	5,600 hours at $14.20 per hour
Manufacturing Overhead Costs	
Actual machine hours recorded	2,000
Actual variable manufacturing overhead incurred	$38,000
Actual fixed manufacturing overhead incurred	$32,300

Required:
a. Calculate material, labour, and overhead variances
b. Provide a possible explanation for each variance computed.

19. (LO 3, 4) Richard Li Ltd. uses a standard costing system in its pipe manufacturing facility in Montreal. The company is automated and direct labour costs are relatively low, so a conversion cost pool is used rather than separate cost pools for direct labour and overhead. For the year, standards were set as follows:

Variable conversion cost rate	$14 per machine hour
Fixed conversion cost rate*	$20 per machine hour

*Based on 5,000 expected machine hours.

At standard, one machine hour is required to produce 50 metres of pipe. In the current year, the company produced 300,000 metres of pipe, worked 5,800 machine hours, and incurred the following costs:

Variable conversion costs	$ 75,400
Fixed conversion costs	$102,500

Required:
a. Compute the variable conversion cost and fixed conversion cost variances for the year.
b. Why is an annual computation of variances not useful to managers?

20. (LO 2, 5, 6) Margaret Bianco Associates (MBA) is a rapidly expanding company involved in the mass reproduction of instructional materials. Margaret Bianco, owner and manager of MBA, has made a concentrated effort to provide a quality product at a fair price with delivery on the promised due date. Expanding sales have been attributed to this philosophy. Bianco is finding it increasingly difficult to supervise the operations of MBA personally and would like to institute an organizational structure that would facilitate management control.

The loss of personal control over the operations of MBA caused Bianco to look for a method of efficiently evaluating performance. Lawrence Chung, a new cost accountant, proposed the use of a standard costing system. Variances for material, labour, and manufacturing overhead could then be calculated and reported directly to Bianco.
Required:
a. Assume that MBA plans to implement a standard costing system and establish standards for materials, labour, and manufacturing overhead. Identify and discuss for each of these cost components:
   i. Who should be involved in setting the standards
   ii. The factors that should be considered in establishing the standards
b. Describe the basis for assignment of responsibility under a standard costing system.

(IMA adapted)

PROBLEMS

21. (LO 5) The following two issues arise with the use of standard costing and variance analysis: (1) which standard to use to measure performance, and (2) when to investigate variances from the standard.

    Required:

    Identify and briefly describe two types of standards that may be used.

    Problem 21 is extracted from *Management Accounting Examination,* published by the Certified General Accountants Association of Canada © CGA-Canada June 2005.

22. (LO 7) Deluxe Spa Products Ltd. employs a budgeting system to aid in organizational planning and control. At the end of the period, actual results are compared against budgeted amounts. The company's actual and budgeted data for the current year appear below:

	Budgeted	**Actual**
Unit sales		
Product A	24,000	20,000
Product B	16,000	30,000
Dollar sales		
Product A	$96,000	$85,000
Product B	48,000	75,000
Cost of sales (all variable)		
Product A	$48,000	$50,000
Product B	32,000	60,000

    Required:

    a. Compute the budgeted gross margin for each product.
    b. Compute the actual gross margin for each product.
    c. Compute the sales variances for each product.
    d. Why do the sales volume and price variances not explain the entire difference between budgeted and actual gross margin for both products?

23. (LO 7) Wayne Greatsky Sporting Goods manufactures two products: pucks and shoulder pads. For the current year, the firm budgeted the following:

	Pucks	**Shoulder Pads**
Sales	$800,000	$1,200,000
Unit sales price	40	30

    At the end of the year, managers were informed of the following:

    i. Actual sales of pucks were 21,000 units. The price variance for pucks was $63,000 unfavourable.
    ii. Actual sales of shoulder pads generated revenue of $1,120,000 and a volume variance of $240,000 unfavourable.

    Required:

    a. Compute the budgeted sales volume for each product.
    b. Compute the volume variance for the year for pucks.
    c. Compute the price variance for the year for shoulder pads.
    d. Summarize the difference between budgeted and actual sales for the year.

24. (LO 7) Kevin O'Reilly manages the marketing department at Festive Figurines Limited. He is evaluated based on his ability to meet budgeted revenues. For May, his revenue budget was as follows:

	Price Per Unit	**Unit Sales**
Daniel Boone	$240	1,600
Funny Bunny	130	2,150
Barbie Doll	160	4,200

    The actual sales generated by the marketing department in May were as follows:

	Price Per Unit	**Total Sales Dollars**
Daniel Boone	$230	$391,000
Funny Bunny	140	282,800
Barbie Doll	150	622,500

Required:
a. For May, compute the sales price variance for Festive Figurines for each product.
b. For May, compute the sales volume variance for Festive Figurines.
c. Assuming that the variances you computed in parts (a) and (b) are controllable by Kevin O'Reilly, discuss what actions he may have taken to cause actual results to deviate from budgeted results.

CASES

1. The Evergreen Shovels Division makes hand shovels for the Canadian market. It is an autonomous division of Tool Man Corporation. Evergreen shovels are used and valued by professional and hobby gardeners. All major retailers carry Evergreen shovels. The shovel seems not to have changed in decades. However, Evergreen constantly innovates with the product in terms of wood components, steel components, tempering of the steel blade, balance of the shovel, and all other design aspects. Evergreen also constantly innovates with its process for making its shovels.

   Tool Man Corporation has 12 shovel divisions in various markets around the world. These divisions are managed as a group, which is headed by a vice president named Jason Tim.

   Jason evaluates the 12 divisions on their ability to meet their budgets. For September, Evergreen has met its sales and profit targets, as shown in Exhibit 7-1. Normally, meeting the profit target is all that is demanded of divisional managers. However, for September, Evergreen's sales were 500 units less than the 8,500 expected. As there was no change in inventory during September, Jason is not sure what the shortfall in sales means.
   Required:
   Jason Tim has asked you to analyze Evergreen's September performance. Use the case approach to respond.

EXHIBIT 7-1

Divisional Operating Statement, September

	Actual	Budget
Sales	$85,000,000	$85,000,000
Variable costs		
Direct labour	19,000,000	17,000,000
Direct material	16,000,000	17,000,000
Variable mfg. overhead	8,000,000	8,500,000
Variable marketing costs	8,000,000	8,500,000
	51,000,000	51,000,000
Contribution before fixed costs	34,000,000	34,000,000
Fixed costs		
Manufacturing	10,300,000	10,000,000
Marketing	6,600,000	7,000,000
Administration	5,100,000	5,000,000
	22,000,000	22,000,000
Contribution after fixed costs	$12,000,000	$12,000,000

2. Ready Sports has two divisions, Retail and Manufacturing. The Retail Division has 14 outlets across Canada that sell and install specialty, high-performance custom mufflers and exhaust systems. The custom muffler and exhaust systems are produced by the Manufacturing Division, which has a single plant in Winnipeg. No inventories are maintained; all exhaust systems are customized within a day or two.

   The owner has delegated the management of sales to a vice president of sales and the management of the Manufacturing Division to a vice president of manufacturing. All products sold by the stores are made by the Manufacturing Division. As all sales are for custom systems, there is no Work in Process Inventory at the end of period; thus sales equal manufacturing output. The owner places great importance on the divisions meeting their budget commitments.

The last year was not very good for the Retail Division: its sales were 90% of budget or expected. The owner was not happy. When he met with the two vice presidents and the controller, he praised the manufacturing VP for keeping the costs of manufacturing below budget. See Exhibit 7-1 for the Manufacturing Division's performance. The owner realized that sales in the automotive parts market, in which Ready Sports competes, had declined 20%. Nevertheless, he insisted that the VP of the Retail Division should have tried harder to achieve the budget.

Required:
As the controller, assess the owner's judgment as to his assessment of the two divisions.

	Actual	Budget
Variable costs		
Direct labour	$ 490,000	$ 500,000
Direct material	580,000	600,000
Variable mfg. overhead	280,000	300,000
Variable marketing costs	200,000	200,000
	$1,550,000	$1,600,000
Fixed costs		
Manufacturing	210,000	205,000
Administration	150,000	155,000
	260,000	260,000
Total costs	$1,810,000	1,860,000

EXHIBIT 7-1
Ready Sports Manufacturing Operating Statement

3. Sam Chiu Company employs a standard costing system using absorption costing. The standards for manufacturing overhead are established at the beginning of each year by estimating the total variable and fixed manufacturing overhead costs for the year and then dividing the costs by the estimated activity base. Chiu has a fairly automated manufacturing operation, and the variable overhead closely follows machine hour use. Thus, machine hours are used to apply both variable and fixed manufacturing overhead.

The standard manufacturing overhead application rates shown below are based on an estimated manufacturing overhead for the coming year of $4,080,000, of which $1,440,000 is variable and $2,640,000 is fixed. These costs are expected to be incurred uniformly throughout the year. The total machine hours (MH) for the expected annual output, also expected to be uniform throughout the year, are estimated at 120,000.

Standard Manufacturing Overhead Application Rates
Variable per MH	$12
Fixed per MH	22
Total per MH	$34

Chiu has reduced production over the past three months because orders have been less than expected. In fact, manufacturing activity for the current month is 80% of what was expected. This reduced level of demand for Chiu's products is expected to continue for at least the next three months.

Linda Ondrack, cost accountant, has prepared some preliminary figures on manufacturing overhead for the current month at the request of Sandra Chowfen, vice president of production. These amounts are presented in Exhibit 7-1.

Ondrack and Chowfen have the following conversation about this analysis.

Chowfen: I just don't understand these numbers. I have tried to control my costs with the production cutback. I figured that my budget for one month should be about $340,000, which would give me a $33,000 favourable variance, yet you show that I have a $35,000 unfavourable variance.

Ondrack: Well, you may have done a pretty good job in controlling your costs. You really cannot take one-twelfth of your annual estimated costs to get the

CASES

monthly budget to compare to your actual costs. A detailed variance analysis of manufacturing overhead would shed more light on your performance. The largest component is probably your fixed manufacturing overhead volume variance.

Chowfen: Can you do that detailed variance analysis for me? What do I have to do to reduce or eliminate that fixed manufacturing overhead volume variance?

Ondrack: Sure we can do the detailed variance analysis. I would have done it for you, but we just got these figures together now. The fixed manufacturing overhead volume variance is not that important. I'm not sure that you really can or want to reduce it under our present economic situation.

Required:

As Ondrack, advise Chowfen on the variance analysis and what can be done to improve performance. Use the case approach.

EXHIBIT 7-1

Manufacturing Overhead: Preliminary Figures for the Month

Actual machine hours for the month		8,050
Standard machine hours allowed for actual output produced		8,000
Total applied manufacturing overhead		$272,000
Actual manufacturing overhead:		
Variable	$ 95,800	
Fixed	211,200	307,000
Total manufacturing overhead variance		$ 35,000 U

ETHICS

1. In today's business world, some customers treat suppliers almost like employees. Supplier representatives work in customers' factories, attend production meetings, place orders for parts, and have access to a variety of data, including sales forecasts. This environment was developed to instill harmony and create efficiencies within both customers and suppliers.

   For example, at Honeywell's Golden Valley plant, the company reduced inventory levels to those that can be measured in days rather than weeks or months, cut purchasing agents by one-fourth, and has received numerous suggestions as to part standardization so that products can retain their quality levels, but be made for less. (Note: This discussion was adapted from a January 13, 1995, *Wall Street Journal* article entitled "Strange Bedfellows: Some Companies Let Suppliers Work On Site and Even Place Orders.")

   Required:
   a. Discuss risks that customers bear when they allow suppliers to have access to critical inside information.
   b. What types of costs would customers expect to save by having representatives of suppliers on-site? Explain.
   c. How would responsibility for purchase price variances change when vendors are allowed to submit their own purchase orders?

2. Mera O'Brien was hired a month ago at the Montreal Division of the Peerless Manufacturing Company. O'Brien supervises plant production and is paid $6,500 per month. In addition, her contract calls for a percentage bonus based on cost control. The company president has defined cost control as "the ability to obtain favourable cost variances from the standards provided."

   After one month, O'Brien realized that the standards that were used at the Montreal Division were outdated. Since the last revision of standards, the Montreal Division had undergone some significant plant layout changes and installed some automated equipment, both of which reduced labour time considerably. However, by the time she realized the errors in the standards, she had received her first month's bonus cheque of $5,000.

Required:

a. Since the setting of the standards and the definition of her bonus arrangement were not her doing, O'Brien does not feel compelled to discuss the errors in the standards with the company president. Besides, O'Brien wants to buy a new Porsche. Discuss the ethics of her not discussing the errors in the standards and/or the problems with the definition of cost control with the company president.

b. Assume instead that O'Brien has an elderly mother who has just been placed in a nursing home. The older O'Brien is quite ill and has no income. The younger O'Brien lives in an efficiency apartment and drives a six-year-old car so that she can send the majority of her earnings to the nursing home to provide for her mother. Discuss the ethics of her not discussing the errors in the standards and/or the problems with the definition of cost control with the company president.

c. Assume again the facts in part (b). Also assume that the company president plans to review and revise, if necessary, all production standards at the Montreal Division next year. Discuss what may occur if O'Brien does not inform the president of the problems with the standards at the current time. Discuss what may occur if O'Brien informs the president of all the facts, both professional and personal. Can you suggest a way in which she may keep a bonus and still have the standards revised? (Consider the fact that standard costs have implications for sales prices.)

3. James Znajda Corporation needs to hire four factory workers who can run robotic equipment and route products through processing. All factory space is on a single floor. Labour standards have been set for product manufacturing. At this time, the company has had 10 experienced people apply for the available jobs. One of the applicants is David Sima. David is paralyzed and uses a wheelchair. He has several years' experience using the robotic equipment, but for him to use the equipment, the controls must be placed on a special panel and lowered. Willie Roberts, the human resources director, has interviewed David and has decided against hiring him because Willie does not believe David can work "up to the current labour standard."

Required:

a. How, if at all, would hiring a person with a physical disability affect labour variances (both rate and hours) if the standards had been set based on workers without physical disabilities? Provide a rationale for your answer.

b. If a supervisor has decided to hire a worker with a physical disability, how (if at all) should that worker's performance evaluations be affected? Provide a rationale for your answer.

c. What are the ethical implications of hiring people with physical disabilities in preference to those without physical disabilities? What are the ethical implications of hiring the people without physical disabilities in preference to those with physical disabilities?

d. Do you believe that the hiring of individuals with physical disabilities could come under the umbrella concept of "workplace diversity"? Why or why not?

4. Governments have instituted academic standards in English, history, math, and science. These standards specify what students should learn in what grades.

Required:

a. Assume that you have been asked to chair your province's committee to develop the math standard for Grade 6. What issues would you consider in setting the standard? (This question does not ask you to address the specific items that you believe the students should know, but rather the fundamental concepts that need to be considered before establishing the standard.)

b. Once the standard has been set, what circumstances might cause you to consider changing the standard? Why?

c. Should there be national, rather than provincial, standards for education? Discuss the rationale for your answer, including potential obstacles and how they might be overcome.

SOLUTIONS TO SELF-TEST QUESTIONS

1. b. Standard hours for production attained – Budgeted machine hours = $3,000 F.

2. c.

Actual hours of input, at the standard rate ($26,000 \times \$20$)	$520,000
Standard hours allowed for output, at the standard rate	
$[(5,000 \times 5) \times \$20]$	500,000
Unfavourable direct labour efficiency variance	$ 20,000

3. b. Fixed overhead volume variance = $6,660 applied at $3.70 per direct labour hour
$6,660 ÷ $3.70 = 1,800 direct labour hours

   Since the output required more hours at standard than expected, the output was greater than expected. Thus, the volume variance is favourable.

4. a. Fixed overhead application rate $320,000 ÷ 20,000 = $16.00 per machine per hour

   4,700 units of output at 4 machine hours each requires $4,700 \times 4$ = 18,800 machine hours at standard; $18,800 \times \$16$ = $300,800

5. b. and c. Proration adds to Work in Process and to Finished Goods.

6. b. Overhead is based on the direct labour hours and if this is unfavourable then the variable overhead efficiency will also be unfavourable.

7. d. $132,000 ÷ ($0.50 + $0.028) = 250,000

8. d. $5,000 \times SR = \$99,840 + \$4,160 - \$4,000$
SR = $20.00
AH = ($99,840 + $4,160) ÷ $20 = 5,200

9. b. Overspending is measured by the fixed overhead budget variance only

10. a.

Material	$(100,000 ÷ 10,000) \times \$0.50$	$ 5.00
Direct labour	$(5,000 ÷ 10,000) \times \$20$	10.00
Overhead	$(5,000 ÷ 10,000) \times \$10$	5.00
		$20.00

11. d. $[(\$20 \times 0.50) + (\$5 \times 2) + (\$1 \times 0.50)] - [(\$21 \times 1/3) + (\$4.50 \times 1.9)$
$+ (\$1.05 \times 1/3)] = \$4.60$ F

12. b.

VC = $[(\$20.00 \times 0.50) + (\$5.00 \times 2)]$	$20.00
FC = $50,000 ÷ 20,000	2.50
	$22.50

13. a. $160,000 − $156,000 = $4,000 U

14. b. $(6,000 \times 2)(\$27.50) - \$310,600 = \$19,400$ F

15. a.

16. a.

ENDNOTES

1. Tom Blackwell, "Union Fears New Study on Physical Exertion: How Much Mail Can a Mail Carrier Carry?" *National Post*, March 7, 2005.

2. Brian Maskell, "Solving the Standard Cost Problem," *Cost Management*, Boston. January–February 2006, p. 27; Anura De Zoysa and Siriyama Kanthi Herath, "Standard Costing in Japanese firms," *Industrial Management and Data Systems* 107, no. 2 (2007): 271–87.

3. Volker Thormählen, "Bull GmbH, Suitability of Oracle Applications for Standard and Activity Based Costing," *Oracle-IC94*, p. 9–134.

4. Maliah Sulaiman, Nik Nazli Nik Ahmad, and Norhayati Mohd Alwi, "Is Standard Costing Obsolete?" Malaysia. *Managerial Auditing Journal* 20, no. 2 (2005): 109–24.

5. Kip R. Krumwiede, "Results of 1999 Cost Management Survey: The Use of Standard Costing and Other Costing Practices," *Cost Management Update*, December 1999–January 2000.

ENDNOTES

6. Volker Thormählen, "Bull GmbH, Suitability of Oracle Applications for Standard and Activity Based Costing," *Oracle-IC94*, p. 9–134.

7. Ibid.

8. In performing internal time and motion studies, observers need to be aware that employees may engage in slowdown tactics when they are being clocked. The purpose of such tactics is to have a relatively long time set as the standard, so that the employees will appear more efficient when actual results are measured.

9. An employee time sheet indicates what jobs were worked on and for what period of time. Time sheets can also be prepared for machines by use of machine clocks or counters. Bar coding is another way to track work flow through an organization.

10. The standard cost of each cost element (direct material, direct labour, variable overhead, and fixed overhead) is said to be applied to the goods produced. This terminology is the same as that used when overhead is applied to inventory based on a predetermined rate.

11. The material price and quantity variances will have to be calculated for buttons and labels as well. These calculations will not be shown in the chapter.

12. De Zoysa and Herath, "Standard Costing in Japanese Firms."

13. Each hour of machine time is expected to cost $6 (Exhibit 7-5).

14. $6 per hour ÷ 6 shirts per hour.

15. Activity-based costing is discussed in Chapter 8.

16. This discussion is based on the work of Robert S. Kaplan in "Flexible Budgeting in an Activity-Based Costing Framework," *Accounting Horizons*, June 1994, pp. 104–109.

17. Ibid.

18. Robin Cooper, *When Lean Enterprises Collide: Competing Through Confrontation*, Boston: Harvard Business School Press, 1995, pp. 247–48.

19. Sara Moulton, Ed Oakley, and Chuck Kremer, "How to Assure Your Quality Initiative Really Pays Off," *Management Accounting*, January 1993, p. 26.

20. These computations assume the company sells a single product. If the company sells multiple products, another variance will exist called the sales mix variance. This variance explains the change in budgeted revenue caused by selling a mix of products different from the expected. Sales mix is discussed in Chapter 3 on cost–volume–profit analysis. Sales mix variance computations require information on the estimated percentage of total expected sales for each product.

21. Thomas A. Stewart, "Why Budgets Are Bad For Business," *Fortune*, June 4, 1990.

22. Bruce Baggaley and Brian Maskell, "Value Stream Management for Lean Companies, Part II," *Journal of Cost Management*, May–June 2003, p. 24.

23. Toshiro Hiromoto, "Another Hidden Edge—Japanese Management Accounting," *Harvard Business Review*, Reprint 88406.

24. Cohn Drury, "Standard Costing: A Technique at Variance With Modern Management?" *Management Accounting*, November 1999, pp. 56–58.

25. Actual product costs should not include extraordinary charges for such items as waste, spoilage, and inefficiency. Such costs should be written off as period expenses.

26. Bruce Brumberg and Karen Alexrod, "Tastes of Louisiana," *New Orleans Times–Picayune*, September 1, 1996, El, E5.

Chapter 8

Activity-Based Management and Costing

LEARNING OBJECTIVES

After reading this chapter, you should be able to answer the following questions:

1 How
can reasonably accurate product and service cost information be developed?

2 What
are the differences among value-added, nonvalue-added, and business value-added activities?

3 What
might cause decreased manufacturing cycle efficiency?

4 How
would the cost drivers in an activity-based costing system be developed?

5 What
distinguishes activity-based costing from conventional overhead allocation methods?

6 When
is the use of activity-based costing appropriate?

7 What
are the benefits and limitations of using activity-based costing?

ON SITE

www.purolator.com
Purolator Courier Limited

Courier companies are an important part of many business models. For example, Dell depends on courier companies to deliver custom PCs to customers. This important business is also competitive, and thus costs must be understood. Because Purolator understands its costs, the company is successful and profitable.

Purolator is Canada's largest courier company, with 12,500 employees, of whom more than 3,500 are couriers. It is owned 94% by Canada Post Corporation. Total revenues were $1.3 billion in 2006. Purolator is big, with 123 operation locations, 20 regional sales offices, 3,143 courier vehicles, and 15 dedicated chartered aircraft. On an average day it picks up and delivers 1.1 million packages.

Purolator was not always as profitable. In 2000, it was losing money. To make things worse, it suffered from a weak information system. Underdeveloped management information meant that the root causes of the lack of profitability were poorly understood. Because the information system could not provide the answers, the company conducted an activity-based costing study to seek the causes of the profitability problem. This special, one-off ABC study found that a small but significant number of unprofitable customers were hurting profitability. Once these customers were charged prices that covered costs plus profits, the profit problem disappeared.

Over the following two years, Purolator developed its own ABC system, called PROFS. With the better information, Purolator has been profitable every year since introducing ABC, which aligns *what* Purolator does and *how* Purolator does it with *who* Purolator does it for. The "what it does" question is answered by identifying activities, of which there are 170 at Purolator—pickup, depot sort, and so forth. The "how Purolator does it" question is answered by identifying the cost drivers, such as time per stop, number of pieces, and the like. The "who Purolator does it for" question is answered by identifying the multitude of customers and the products and services they buy.

ABC has shifted Purolator's focus from reducing costs to generating profits.

SOURCES: Janet Pierce, "The ABCs of Purolator Profitability," CMA/CAM-I Summit on Process, Performance, and Cost Management, October 23–24, 2007. Found at http://www.cam-i.org/associations/ 3733/files/CMA%20B3%202007%20Janet%20Pierce%20CMA%20CAM-I% 20Presentation-ABC%27s% 20of%20Purolator%20Profitability. (Feb. 4, 2008); Purolator Corporate Information. Found at: http://www. purolator.com/media/corporate/ faq.html; Purolator Annual Review 2006. Found at: http://www.purolator. com/media/corporate/annual.html.

*L*ike many other companies, Purolator has numerous, complex processes that generate a wide variety of services. Overhead allocations in such organizations are best made using multiple predetermined overhead rates rather than a single one. These rates should be developed and based on the underlying drivers of the overhead costs.

As global competitiveness increases, companies will need to understand the causes of costs, work harder to control costs, and be acutely aware of product line profitability.

Over the course of the past two decades, a management tool called **activity-based costing (ABC)** has become one of the more widely embraced of new management methods. Although its core lies in cost accounting, it has attracted the attention of business managers in general, and it has been the subject of articles in the Harvard Business Review, Fortune, and elsewhere in the business press. And not only is it a major theme in business, but it also has been adopted in parts of government.[1]

ABC falls under the umbrella heading of activity-based management (ABM). The simple difference between ABC and ABM has been defined as follows: ABC is about gathering cost information. ABM shows you how to do something about it.[2] This chapter defines ABM and ABC, illustrates the process of analyzing organizational activities and cost drivers, and shows how the analysis results can be used to allocate overhead costs to products and services more appropriately. The chapter also discusses the conditions under which ABC systems provide better information than traditional overhead allocations.

In recent years, the challenge in allocated indirect resources has increased greatly, for several reasons. First, indirect cost as a fraction of total cost has increased (e.g., automation, the substitution of machines [indirect] for direct labourers [easily traced]). Second, there is increasing proliferation of product models and types, where complex production scheduling, parts inventories, etc., add to indirect costs (e.g., automobile models and options). Third, the reliability of the "base" that has traditionally been used to allocate direct costs is decreasing. The design of an ABC system rests on identifying the relationship between an indirect resource and the "activity" that consumes it. Once that is done, the product or service cost is simply the sum of the cost of activities that were incurred to make that product or service.[3]

activity-based costing
an accounting information system that identifies the various activities performed in an organization and collects costs on the basis of the underlying nature and extent of those activities

THE ABC SYSTEM

Imagine that you and three friends go to a restaurant. You order a cheeseburger and they each order an expensive prime rib. When the waiter brings the bill they say, 'Let's split the total amount evenly.' How would you feel? That is how many products and service lines 'feel' when the accountants take a large amount of indirect and support overhead expenses and allocate them to costs without any logic.[4]

A well-designed activity-based costing (ABC) system has three strategic objectives. The first is to report accurate costs that can be used to identify the source of firm profits. The second is to identify the cost of activities so that more efficient ways to perform them or produce their outputs can be identified. The final one is to identify the future need for resources so that they can be acquired more efficiently. ABC is strategically important because it allows accurate costs to be calculated. Good decisions require the accurate understanding of costs.

ABC systems necessarily model the way resources are consumed, not how they are acquired. That is, the systems relate the amount of resources consumed by activities to the outputs of those activities, not to the amount of resources acquired in the period. It is this property that allows ABC systems to report the same cost for products from period to period (assuming no change in the quantity of resources consumed and the price paid for them) even when the volume of production changes. This objective is achieved by removing the cost of unused capacity from the cost of the resources driven to the activities and then subsequently to outputs in the ABC model.[5]

DEVELOPING PRODUCT/SERVICE COST INFORMATION

Product or service costs are developed to (1) have information for financial and regulatory reporting; (2) help management make product pricing and product line expansion/contraction decisions; and (3) allow management to monitor and control operations. In many organizations, the first purpose has often overridden the other purposes for two reasons. First, external parties (such as the Securities Commissions, CICA and Canada Revenue Agency (CRA), and other regulatory agencies) have established rules about what should be included in or excluded from determining product cost; there have been no mandates, however, about how product costs should be determined for internal management purposes. Second, it is often easier to use the same product costing system for all three purposes. Using the mandated definitions may diminish the resulting costs' internal usefulness as summarized by the following quote: "Today's management accounting information, driven by the procedures and cycles of the organization's financial reporting system, is too late, too aggregated, and too distorted to be relevant for managers' planning and control decisions."[6]

Although it is impossible to determine exact product costs, managers should develop the best possible cost estimates. The best estimate occurs when the majority of production or service costs can be traced directly to the resulting products or services. Direct tracing requires the use of valid measures of resource consumption called cost drivers. Direct material and direct labour costs have always been traced easily to products because, by definition, these costs must be physically and conveniently traceable to cost objects.

LEARNING OBJECTIVE 1

How can reasonably accurate product and service cost information be developed?

To get from one point to another, the easiest route is the most direct one. Determining product cost is also easiest if costs incurred can be traced directly to related products.

Allocating costs to products is similar to wandering aimlessly through a mall—the costs may finally get to the right place, but oftentimes it's quicker to stop at the most convenient location.

If the best estimate results when the largest numbers of costs are traced directly, then the best estimate will also be obtained when the fewest costs are assigned arbitrarily. However, because overhead cannot be directly traced to individual products or services, it must be attached to products or services using a valid cost predictor (or driver) or an arbitrary method. In the past, manufacturing overhead was often attached to products using direct labour hours. Although this base may not have been the most accurate measure of resource consumption, it was generally considered a reasonable, rather than an arbitrary, allocation method.

The modern manufacturing environment is more machine-intensive, with low direct labour and high overhead costs. Attempts to use direct labour as the overhead allocation base in such an environment can lead to significant product cost distortions. Most overhead costs in these environments are machine-related: depreciation on high-cost machinery; utilities to run that machinery; and repair and maintenance to keep that machinery operating. As illustrated in Exhibit 8-1, overhead allocation rates based on direct labour can be very high and will assign primarily machine-related overhead costs to products that use high amounts of direct labour rather than to the products that are truly creating the costs to be incurred—those products that use the machine technology. The exhibit illustrates the difference in the amounts of overhead that would be applied under each of the methods. As a result, a more sophisticated method of overhead cost allocation is needed.

EXHIBIT 8-1

Cost Distortions in a Machine-Intensive Environment

Overhead costs per month, primarily machine-related	$600,000
Total direct labour hours (DLH)	800
Overhead rate per DLH ($600,000 ÷ 800)	$750
Total machine hours (MH)	2,400
Overhead rate per MH ($600,000 ÷ 2,400)	$250

Product A (10,000 units per month)		Product B (10,000 units per month)	
Total DLH	600	Total DLH	200
OH assigned using DLH (600 × $750)	$450,000	OH assigned using DLH (200 × $750)	$150,000
OH per unit ($450,000 ÷ 10,000)	$45	OH per unit ($150,000 ÷ 10,000)	$15
Total MH	400	Total MH	2,000
OH assigned using MH (400 × $250)	$100,000	OH assigned using MH (2,000 × $250)	$500,000
OH per unit ($100,000 ÷ 10,000)	$10	OH per unit ($500,000 ÷ 10,000)	$50

Machine time is often a useful overhead allocation base in the modern manufacturing environment. But even machine hours may not be adequate as the sole allocation base for overhead costs. If overhead is created by factors such as product variety, product complexity, or other cost drivers, multiple allocation bases will result in more accurate estimates of product or service cost. Because companies now have the technology to collect, process, analyze, and use a much greater quantity of information than in the past, it is possible to obtain greater accuracy in product costing by using multiple cost pools to accumulate and to rationally allocate, rather than arbitrarily assign, overhead costs.

ACTIVITY ANALYSIS

The development of product or service cost may be designated as an accounting function, but this task concerns all managers. Costs should be computed in a systematic and rational manner so that they are as accurate as possible and may be relied on for planning, controlling, and decision-making purposes. For example, product costs affect decisions on corporate strategy (Is it profitable to be in a particular market?), marketing (What is the relationship between product cost and product price?), production (Should a component be made or purchased?), and finance (Should money be invested in additional plant assets to manufacture this product?).

ABC, however, traces costs to the products that cause them, providing a much more accurate picture. Indirect costs are driven first to the activities and processes that occur in an organization, and then to the actual services themselves. ABC thus allocates these indirect costs more accurately and allows staff to manage activities rather than to just manage dollars.[7]

Ideally, it would not matter how much it cost to make a product or perform a service if enough customers were willing to buy that item at a price that would cover a company's costs and provide a reasonable profit margin. In reality, there are two problems with this concept. First, customers usually only purchase items that provide acceptable value for the price being charged. Second, prices are often set by competitive market forces rather than by specific companies. Thus, management should be concerned about whether customers perceive selling price and value to be equal. This concern is normally addressed by ascertaining that the product meets customer quality and service expectations. Additionally, management must decide whether the company can make a reasonable profit, given external prices and internal costs. If the market price is considered a given, then cost becomes the controlling variable in profitability.

Activity-Based Management

Managers can use **activity-based management (ABM)** to help enhance customer value and organizational profits by increasing organizational efficiency and effectiveness and producing more accurate costs. ABM concepts overlap with numerous other disciplines, as shown in Exhibit 8-2.

activity-based management
a discipline that focuses on how the activities performed during the production/performance process can improve the value received by a customer and the profit achieved by providing this value

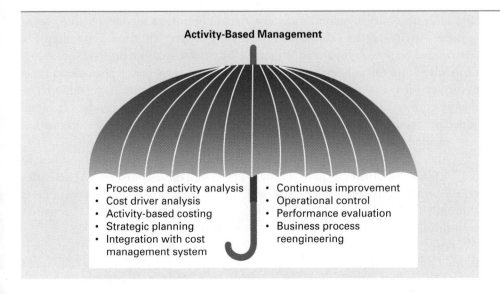

Activity-Based Management

- Process and activity analysis
- Cost driver analysis
- Activity-based costing
- Strategic planning
- Integration with cost management system
- Continuous improvement
- Operational control
- Performance evaluation
- Business process reengineering

EXHIBIT 8-2

The Activity-Based Management Umbrella

Depending on one's perspective, ABM could be viewed as part of a total quality management or business process reengineering effort. Alternatively, total quality management and business process reengineering could result from implementing activity-based management. But, most important, activity-based management should be integrated with management's strategic planning and with the organization's cost management system. Without this integration factor, activity-based management is like a book on a shelf. The book is brought down off the shelf when needed (e.g., for a process improvement project). Once the project is complete, the book can be placed back on the shelf next to the other books (improvement tools).[8] Integration into the planning process and the cost management system indicates that all the concepts under the ABM umbrella are viewed as integral parts of the organization's customer focus and long-range fiscal success.

The use of activity-based management first requires an analysis of an organization's activities. An **activity** is any repetitive action, movement, or work sequence performed to fulfill a business function. Each activity should be able to be described with a verb and a noun. For example, *lift material, open door,* and *insert document* are all activities.

The activities performed in making or doing something can be detailed on a flowchart or grid called a **process map**. These maps should include all activities performed to accomplish a specific task or process, not just the obvious ones. For example, "Walk from the front desk with a change drawer" and "Break open rolls of coins" would not be on a typical list of Steps in Cash Register Operation. However, these activities must be performed each time a new clerk opens a register. Many activities that require significant time are not viewed as true parts of the process. By detailing all activities, process maps allow duplication, waste, and unnecessary work to be identified. These maps can also be used as **benchmarking** guides to assist all departments or divisions in an organization to adopt the best possible practices. Detail from a process map is included in the **value chart** shown in Exhibit 8-3. Some process maps are called value charts because they indicate the time spent in each activity from the beginning to end of a process and assess the value of each activity.

Value-Added and Nonvalue-Added Activities

Activities may be value-added, nonvalue-added, or business value-added. A **value-added (VA) activity** increases the worth of a product or service to customers and is one for which customers are willing to pay. VA activities are functions absolutely necessary to manufacture a product or perform a service. The time spent in these activities is the **value-added processing** (or **service**) **time**. For example, a telecommunications company in Winnipeg, Manitoba, makes a product that recognizes whether a call is being made by human voice or by data transmission (as is necessary for fax, Internet, and other modem telecommunications traffic). The manufacturing time needed to incorporate this ability into the product is value-added processing time and the time spent in making the voice/data determination is value-added service time for customers.

Other activities simply increase the time spent on a product or service but do not increase its worth to the customer. These **nonvalue-added (NVA) activities** create unnecessary additional costs, which, if eliminated, would decrease costs without affecting the product's or service's market value or quality. NVA activities exist throughout an organization and, in general, are extremely expensive.

Processing or service time may be nonvalue-added if activities are being performed simply to keep people and machines busy. Also, any processing time spent in unnecessarily packaging a product is nonvalue-added. For example, packaging

activity
a repetitive action, movement, or work sequence performed to fulfill a business function

process map
a flowchart or diagram that indicates every step in making a product or providing a service

benchmarking
process of studying the best practices of comparable organizations or their units and then using the insights gained to improve the organization's own performance and to set appropriate performance expectations

value chart
a visual representation of the value-added and nonvalue-added activities and the time spent in all of these activities from the beginning to the end of a process

LEARNING OBJECTIVE 2
What are the differences among value-added, nonvalue-added, and business value-added activities?

value-added activity
an activity that increases the worth of a product or service to the customer and for which the customer is willing to pay

value-added processing time
the time it takes to perform the functions necessary to manufacture a product

value-added service time
the time it takes to perform all necessary service functions for a customer

nonvalue-added activity
an activity that increases the time spent on a product or service but does not increase its value or worth to the customer

EXHIBIT 8-3
Value Chart

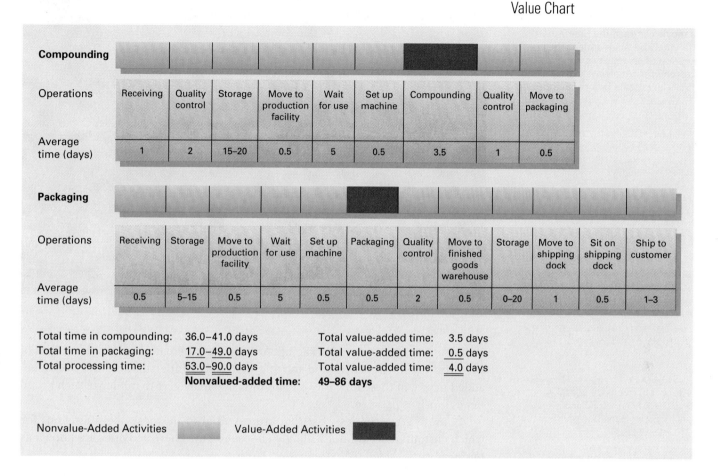

Compounding									
Operations	Receiving	Quality control	Storage	Move to production facility	Wait for use	Set up machine	Compounding	Quality control	Move to packaging
Average time (days)	1	2	15–20	0.5	5	0.5	3.5	1	0.5

Packaging												
Operations	Receiving	Storage	Move to production facility	Wait for use	Set up machine	Packaging	Quality control	Move to finished goods warehouse	Storage	Move to shipping dock	Sit on shipping dock	Ship to customer
Average time (days)	0.5	5–15	0.5	5	0.5	0.5	2	0.5	0–20	1	0.5	1–3

Total time in compounding: 36.0–41.0 days   Total value-added time: 3.5 days
Total time in packaging: 17.0–49.0 days   Total value-added time: 0.5 days
Total processing time: 53.0–90.0 days   Total value-added time: 4.0 days
                             Nonvalued-added time: 49–86 days

Nonvalue-Added Activities ▭   Value-Added Activities ▪

a man's dress shirt into a cellophane package would most likely be viewed as nonvalue-added, although packaging medicines for health and safety reasons would be perceived as value-added by customers. Many companies are focusing attention on minimizing or eliminating packaging to help reduce time and cost as well as to be environmentally conscious.

Nonvalue-added activities also include moving and waiting. Moving products or components from one place to another constitutes **transfer time**; storage time and time spent waiting at the production operation for processing are referred to as **idle** (or wait) **time**. Although this time is nonvalue-added, few companies can eliminate all transfer or idle time.

Performing quality assurance activities results in **inspection time**. In most instances, quality control inspections are considered nonvalue-added if the concept of total quality management is adopted. Under a TQM system, the goal is zero defects by both people and machines. If this goal is being met or being strived for, inspections are simply a matter of looking for a needle in a haystack. A company, such as Motorola, with a 6 sigma achievement (incurring only 3.4 defects per million units) does not need to spend time inspecting: there is no cost–benefit justification. Alternatively, customers purchasing food or pharmaceuticals or buying seats on an airplane may view quality control inspections as very value-added.

The value chart in Exhibit 8-3 illustrates the manufacturing activities of Elyssa Corporation. Only four days of value-added production time are needed in the entire sequence; even within this sequence, as mentioned earlier, the company may

transfer time
the time it takes to move products or components from one place to another (move time)

idle time
storage time and time spent waiting at a production operation for processing

inspection time
the time taken to perform quality control

Chatting over a drink or lunch appears to be a good example of a nonvalue-added activity. However, if these individuals are lawyers discussing a movie contract, the time would definitely be value-added. The perception of an activity's value to a customer is not always the same as fact—investigate before categorizing.

question the time spent in packaging. Additionally, there is an excessive amount of time consumed in storing and moving materials. Understanding the nonvalue-added nature of these functions should motivate managers to minimize such activities as much as possible.

Some NVA activities exist that are essential to business operations but for which customers would not willingly choose to pay. These activities are known as **business value-added (BVA) activities**. For instance, publicly held companies must have an audit at the end of their fiscal year. Customers know that this activity must occur and that it creates costs. However, because the audit adds no direct value to companies' products or services, customers would prefer not to have to pay for this activity.

The News Note "Activity-Based Costing at UPS" describes how UPS adopted activity-based costing. This note indicates that, regardless of the terminology used, there is a high degree of importance to analyzing activities.

business value-added activity
an activity that is necessary for the operation of a business but for which a customer would not want to pay

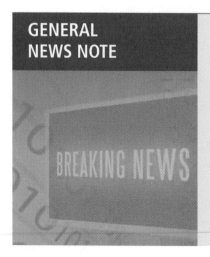

GENERAL NEWS NOTE

Activity-Based Costing at UPS

UNITED PARCEL SERVICE (UPS) adopted activity-based costing to manage its work activities, which were extremely complex with a wide variety of service options, operating conditions, and support activities. The focus was to identify the key activities within a function or process, measure the cost associated with the activities, and assign costs to products, customers, and processes based on the use of the activities. The UPS system was based on traditional ABC in that it took detailed functional costs and mapped them to products based on the activities that were driven by the products. Collaboratively, finance and accounting, engineering, IT, and operations produced a series of ABC models.

The company adopted this system when markets and technology were changing. Transportation needs were moving toward time-definite, feature-based services:
- JIT was used to reduce inventory.
- The economy was moving from manufacturing to more of a service base.
- An information-driven business environment was developing.

At the same time, providing information about the package became a major priority and increased downstream activities.

Consequently, UPS developed new business strategies, which focused on meeting customer needs. It also extended activity-based costing techniques to measure invested capital. It has been observed that in today's competitive marketplace, companies will not survive without a firm understanding of cost. Detailed knowledge of cost to serve by product and customer became a priority. UPS's ABC system is unique in that it leverages a database of work measurement and package movement detail to improve on the company's understanding of activity cost drivers. The market drove the need to better understand specific segments of the business. A focus on "average" cost was no longer satisfactory.

SOURCE: United States Department of the Treasury. www.treas.gov/offices/domestic-finance/ups/pdf.

ABC as Accounting Data Translator

ABC does not replace a company's general ledger. Rather, ABC is a means of translating general ledger information into usable management accounting information (see Exhibit 8-4). The framework transforms financial accounting information into information to support decision making.

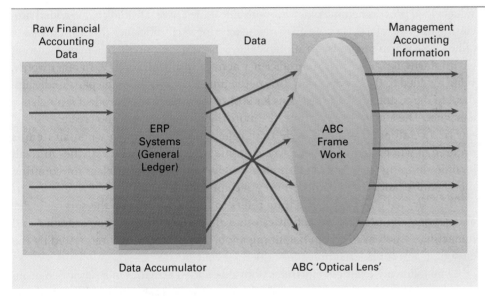

EXHIBIT 8-4

ABC as an Accounting Data Translator

SOURCE: Pieter Buys and Kevin Green, "Strategic Costing Techniques—Activity-Based Costing," Figure 2, *Accounting SA,* November 2006, pp. 36–39.

General ledgers focus on financial transactions, whereas ABC focuses on activities, or work. To provide information for decision making, ABC must be able to convert financial transactions into work activities. Consider the following example, in which the general ledger has captured financial transactions for a unit of the controller's division that conducts management activities.

General Ledger—Management Accounting Unit

Expense Items	Actuals
Salaries	$110,000
Wages	72,000
Office supplies	10,000
Rentals	10,000
Facilities	32,000
Total	$234,000

When they translate the general ledger expenses into actual work or activities, managers are better able to understand costs. Below, the $234,000 of transaction costs are shown by activity.

Activity Costs–Management Accounting Unit

Activity	Activity Costs
Budgeting	$ 70,000
Cost analyses	40,000
Variance analyses	100,000
Miscellaneous	24,000
Total	$234,000

When both general ledger expenses and activity costs are used, managers are more informed. They know where monies were spent and which activities (work) required costs or resources. But only part of the advantage of ABC is that it translates general ledger expenses into activities. ABC reaches its full potential when it is used to manage activities as well as to understand costs. Then it is called activity-based management.

cycle time
the time from when a customer places an order to the time that the product or service is delivered or, using a full life-cycle approach, the time from the conceptualization of a product or service to the time the product or service is delivered to the market/customer

manufacturing cycle efficiency
value-added production time divided by total cycle time; provides a measure of processing efficiency

Cycle Efficiency

In a manufacturing environment, the total **cycle time** reflects the time from the receipt of an order to completion (or delivery) of a product. Thus, total cycle time is equal to value-added processing time plus total nonvalue-added time. Dividing value-added processing time by total cycle time gives **manufacturing cycle efficiency (MCE)**, a measure of how well a firm's manufacturing capabilities use time resources. In a manufacturing environment, typically, cycle time efficiency at most companies is 10%. In other words, value is added to the product only 10% of the time from receipt of the parts until shipment to the customer. Waste accounts for 90% of the cycle time. A product is much like a magnet. The longer the cycle time, the more the product attracts and creates cost.[9]

In a retail environment, cycle time refers to the time from when an item is ordered to when that item is sold to a customer. Nonvalue-added activities in retail include shipping time from the supplier, receiving department delays for counting merchandise, and storage time between receipt and sale.

In a service company, cycle time refers to the time between the service order and service completion. All activities other than actual service performance and nonactivity (such as delays in beginning a job, unless specifically requested by the customer) are considered nonvalue-added *for that job*.

The following example illustrates nonvalue-added activities in a service environment. On Monday at 9:00 A.M., the telephone company is asked to install a telephone line for a customer. The job is scheduled for Tuesday at 3:30 P.M. Upon arriving at the customer's house, the service technician spends 20 minutes installing the telephone jack, 5 minutes writing an invoice, and 5 minutes chatting with the homeowner. The total cycle time is 31 hours (9:00 A.M. Monday to 4:00 P.M. Tuesday) or 1,860 minutes—of which only 20 to 25 minutes is value-added time for that particular job! (The 5 minutes spent writing the invoice could be perceived as value-added because, if a problem occurs, the invoice shows that the work was performed by a telephone company employee.) Thus, the service cycle efficiency is a mere 1.3% (25 minutes ÷ 1,860 minutes). Alternatively, if the customer did not want the line installed on Monday and asked for a delay until 3:30 P.M. on Tuesday, the total cycle time is 30 minutes and the cycle efficiency is 66 or 83% (depending on the classification of the invoice-writing time).

Nonvalue-added activities can be attributed to systemic, physical, and human factors. For example, a system may require that products be manufactured in large batches to minimize machinery setup costs or that service jobs be taken in order of importance. A building's layout does not always provide for the most efficient transfer of products, especially in multistorey buildings in which receiving and shipping are on the ground floor and storage and production are on other floors. People may be responsible for NVA activities because of improper skills, improper training, or a need to be sociable (as when workers discuss weekend sports events on Monday morning). Attempts to reduce nonvalue-added activities should focus on those activities that create the most unnecessary costs.

In a perfect environment, the manufacturing or service cycle efficiency would be 100% because all NVA time would be eliminated. Such an environment will never exist, but companies are moving toward higher cycle efficiencies. One means by which companies can move toward such an optimized environment is through the use of just-in-time (JIT) inventory, where inventory is manufactured or purchased only as it is needed or in time to be sold or used. JIT eliminates a significant portion of the idle time consumed in storage and transfer processes.

Dell has implemented JIT practices on its manufacturing floor, sequencing all production activities in such a way that in-process material continually moves toward the completed product. At Dell's Metric 12 facility, this process, commonly known as flow manufacturing, is complemented by a high level of automation. Hydraulic tools and conveyers lift in-process material between production areas, cutting the number of times a human touches the product by 50%. This significantly reduces the opportunity for damage and the need for product rework. Dell also reduces the need for rework and the chance for faulty parts through its stringent quality control process. Dell has neither the time nor workforce (nor desire) to inspect incoming parts. Instead, it relies on regular on-site audits of suppliers as well as quick diagnostic tests during the assembly process. These JIT practices have allowed Dell to shrink the cycle time for its PCs from order to shipment. Impressive, but Dell's JIT job is not done. Efforts are being made to consolidate production part inventories into a single supplier logistics centre that will be managed by a third party. Having a single facility will allow Dell to deal with a single truck with multiple parts in it. It will also reduce suppliers' costs.[10]

Preparing process maps or constructing value charts for each product or service would be quite time-consuming. A few such charts, however, can quickly indicate where a company is losing time through NVA activities. A cost estimate of that time can be made by totalling costs such as depreciation on storage facilities, wages for warehouse employees, and an interest charge on working capital funds that are tied up in inventory. Often organizations find that it is not profitable to supply small orders to customers. When this occurs there are a number of ways with the use of good information to ensure that small orders are profitable.[11] Profitability can be improved by charging extra service fees, refusing orders under a certain quantity, providing incentives for larger orders, and offering special services with larger orders. Good management accounting information contributes to profitable orders.

Cost Drivers

As companies engage in activities, resources are consumed and costs are incurred. All activities have one or more related cost drivers, which are factors that have direct cause-and-effect relationships to costs. For example, cost drivers for a purchasing area include the number of purchase orders, supplier contacts, and shipments received. Some cost drivers in a die-casting operation might include the sizes of dies, thicknesses of dies, number of dies to be cast per batch, and percent of changes in previously designed dies.

LEARNING OBJECTIVE 4

How would the cost drivers in an activity-based costing system be developed?

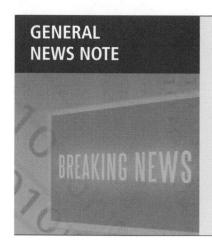

How Do Pieces Impact Costs?

PUROLATOR USES ABC to determine its costs. Each item shipped by Purolator is called a "piece." As a piece is shipped to its destination, it generates depot and hub-sorting costs.

Sorting costs include labour (sorters). At the depot or "hub," where workers sort the pieces, costs vary with the effort required. Is the piece a letter or a parcel? Is a signature required? Is it a dangerous or fragile parcel? And so on. Other cost factors at a depot include the volume (i.e., number) of pieces, their weight, the amount of time it takes to sort a piece, and the amount of paperwork required.

SOURCE: Janet Pierce, "The ABCs of Purolator Profitability," CMA/CAM-I Summit on Process, Performance, and Cost Management, October 23–24, 2007. Found at: http://www.cam-i.org/associations/3733/files/CMA%20B3%202007%20Janet%20Pierce%20CMA%20CAM-I% 20Presentation-ABC%27s%20of%20Purolator%20Profitability. (Feb. 4, 2008).

The number of cost drivers that can be identified is probably not the number that should be used for overhead allocation purposes. The more cost drivers and cost pools are used, the greater is the degree of accuracy of reported product costs. But the benefits provided by increased cost accuracy need to be greater than the cost of defining, accumulating, and maintaining the data.

Management should select a reasonable number of important cost drivers and be certain that the cost of measuring them is not excessive. For instance, finding and using eight cost drivers might increase organizational costs by 1% but provide enough data to reduce total costs by 10%—a net cost reduction of 9%. Adding another eight drivers to the system might reduce costs another 10% but may increase costs by 14%. Companies should use cost–benefit analysis to determine where significant cost improvements are possible. Additionally, cost drivers that are selected for use should be easy to understand, directly related to the activity being performed, and appropriate for performance measurement.

As compared to traditional cost accounting methodology, ABC provides the ability to more directly observe where, how, and why costs are incurred. ABC accomplishes this by focusing on the actual activities directly associated with providing a product.

With traditional costing, departmental expenses are typically allocated directly to products, based on direct labour hours spent or some other high-level allocation base.

With ABC, costs are first traced to the activities associated with them. Only then are they assigned to products. Inserting activities between time spent by employees and the products they deliver provides a subtle, but very important advantage.

In other words, unlike traditional costing methodology, ABC has been designed "from the ground up" to explain why costs are incurred, not just to quantify them. This is a crucial difference![12]

ACTIVITY-BASED COSTING

Gathering costs into related cost pools, recognizing that various activity and cost levels exist, and using multiple cost drivers to assign costs to products and services are the three underlying elements of activity-based costing (ABC). ABC is an accounting information system that identifies organizational activities and collects costs by considering the underlying nature and extent of those activities. Activity-based costing attaches costs to products and services based on the activities used to make, perform, distribute, or support products and services. The relationship between ABM and ABC can be seen in Exhibit 8-5.

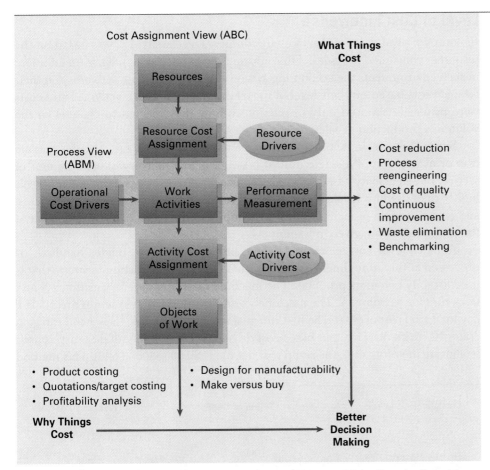

Cost Assignment View (ABC)

Process View (ABM)

What Things Cost

- Cost reduction
- Process reengineering
- Cost of quality
- Continuous improvement
- Waste elimination
- Benchmarking

- Product costing
- Quotations/target costing
- Profitability analysis

- Design for manufacturability
- Make versus buy

Why Things Cost

Better Decision Making

EXHIBIT 8-5

Relationship Between AMB and ABC

SOURCE: *60 Minute ABC Book for Operations Management* (Hard) by White, Timothy. Copyright 1997 by Consortium for Advanced Manufacturing-IN. Reproduced with permission of Consortium for Advanced Manufacturing-IN in the format Textbook via Copyright Clearance Center.

Overhead has traditionally been accumulated into one or two cost pools (total overhead or variable and fixed overhead), either by department or plantwide. Furthermore, one or two drivers (direct labour hours or machine hours) have typically been used to assign costs to products. Activity-based costing focuses on resource-consuming activities as indicated in Exhibit 8-6. The ABC method of collecting cost information allows a more detailed perspective of how costs can be controlled. For example, expediting orders, correcting errors, issuing credits, and amending orders (a total of $240,000 or 40% of the department's costs) are probably nonvalue-added activities and candidates for elimination or reduction. These costs are buried in the traditional resource classifications.

Traditional Focus on Resources		ABM Focus on Activities	
Salaries	$460,000	Take orders	$300,000
Space	50,000	Expedite orders	70,000
Depreciation	50,000	Correct errors	60,000
Supplies	30,000	Issue credits	80,000
Other	10,000	Amend orders	30,000
	$600,000	Answer queries	20,000
		Supervise employees	40,000
			$600,000

EXHIBIT 8-6

Traditional Versus ABM Focus on Sales Order Department Activities

SOURCE: Tom Pryor, "Making New Things Familiar and Familiar Things New," *Journal of Cost Management*, Winter 1997, p. 39. Reprinted by permission of Research Institute of America Group.

Level of Cost Incurrence

In complex production or service environments, reclassifying costs based on the resources consumed provides better information for decision making. In addition, in such environments the accounting system should accumulate activities and their related costs based on their level of incurrence. Traditionally, activities and costs were primarily assessed only in relation to how they reacted to changes in the volume of production or sales.

unit-level cost
a cost created by the production or acquisition of a single unit of production or the delivery of a single unit of service

Some costs are, in fact, strictly variable **unit-level costs** created by the production or acquisition of a single unit of product or the delivery of a single unit of service. But an activity-based system recognizes that costs may vary at activity levels higher than the unit level. These higher levels include batch, product or process, and organizational or facility levels.[13] Examples of the kinds of costs that occur at the various levels are given in Exhibit 8-7.

batch-level cost
a cost that is created by a group of similar things made, handled, or processed at a single time

A **batch-level cost** is created when similar things are made, handled, or processed at the same time. Assume that a company has a casting machine that is used for only two of its products. The machine casts thin dies for customer X and thick dies for customer Y. The machine's setup cost is $150; two setups are made a day for a total cost of $300. The first run generates 500 thin dies; the second run generates 100 thick dies. If a unit-based cost driver (such as number of dies cast) is used to allocate the setup cost, the setup cost per die is $0.50 ($300 ÷ 600). This method

EXHIBIT 8-7
Levels of Costs

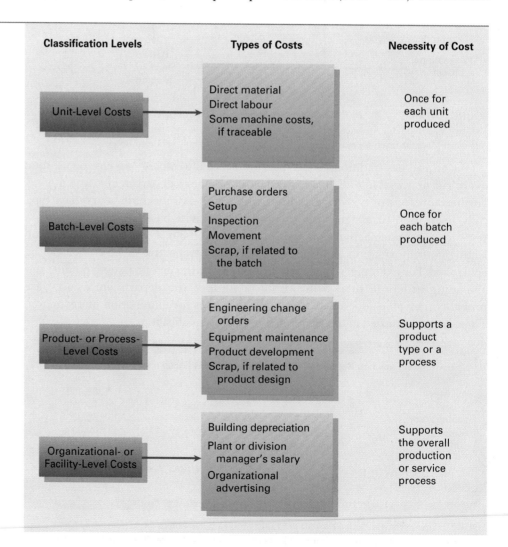

would assign the majority of the setup cost to the thin dies (500 × $0.50 = $250). However, setup is a batch-level cost, so $150 should be spread over the 500 thin dies for a cost of $0.30 per piece, and $150 should be spread over 100 thick dies for a cost of $1.50 per piece. A batch-level perspective shows the commonality of the cost to units within the batch and indicates more clearly the relationship between the activity (setup) and the driver (different casting runs).

A cost incurred in support of different products or processes is a **product-** or **process-level cost**. These costs are created by activities such as developing products, processing engineering change orders, or maintaining production specifications. The costs of these activities can be assigned to individual products, but the costs are independent (i.e., fixed) regardless of the number of batches or the number of units of each product produced.[14] Product- or process-level costs vary with increases in the number of products or processes that need to be sustained in an organization.

product-level (or process-level) cost
a cost created by the need to implement or support a specific product

To illustrate a product- or process-level cost, assume that a company's billing department revised five forms during May. Of these forms, four related to casting customers (Group One) and one was related to aluminum wheel customers (Group Two). None of the form changes related to catalytic-converter customers (Group Three). Each form revision costs $3,000 to issue. During May, the company billed 2,000 Group One customers, 3,000 Group Two customers, and 10,000 Group Three customers. If form-revision cost is treated as a unit-level cost, the total $15,000 cost would be spread over the 15,000 forms produced for a cost of $1 per unit. However, this method inappropriately assigns $10,000 of form-revision cost to Group Three, which had no form revisions for the month! Treating form-revision cost as a product- or process-level cost results in the assignment of $12,000 and $3,000 of cost, respectively, to Group One and Group Two customers. These cost amounts would be assigned not only to bills issued in the current month, but also to all Group One and Group Two customer bills produced during the entire time that the revisions are in effect, because the costs benefit all current and future issuances.

Organizational- or **facility-level costs** are incurred to support and sustain a business unit such as a department, division, or headquarters. If the unit has an identifiable output, costs may be attachable to that output in a reasonable allocation process. But if the costs incurred at this level are common to many different activities, products, or services, these costs can only be assigned arbitrarily. For instance, the salary of the organization's executive officers, cost of the annual corporate audit, and cost of shareholder meetings are companywide organizational costs. Although these costs appear to be fixed, as the organization grows, additional costs will be incurred: more executives will be added; audit costs will become more expensive; and shareholder meetings will require larger space and greater costs.

organizational-level cost (or facility-level cost)
a cost incurred to support ongoing operations, which in turn provide available facilities

Thus, batch-level, product/process-level, and organizational/facility-level costs are all variable, but they vary with causes other than changes in production or service volume. Accounting traditionally assumed that costs that did not vary with unit-level changes in activity were fixed rather than variable. This assumption is too narrowly conceived. In contrast, activity-based systems often refer to fixed costs as being long-term variable costs. Essentially, **long-term variable costs** are step fixed costs and, rather than ignoring the steps, ABC acknowledges their existence. Professor Robert Kaplan of Harvard University refers to the Rule of One: any time there is more than one unit of a resource, that resource is variable and the appropriate cost driver simply needs to be identified. Knowledge of the driver may help to eliminate the source of a potential cost change.

long-term variable cost
a cost that has traditionally been viewed as fixed but that will actually react to some significant change in activity; also referred to as a step fixed cost

For this reason, more accurate estimates of product or service cost can be made if costs at the unit, batch, and product/process activity levels are accumulated separately.

If organizational/facility-level costs are related to a particular product or service, the costs should be assigned to that product or service.

In contrast, organizational- and facility-level costs may not be product- or service-related. If these costs cannot be associated with specific products or services, they should be subtracted in total from net product margin. An activity-based costing system will not normally try to assign organizational-level costs to products because the allocation base would be too arbitrary.

Exhibit 8-8 indicates how cost accumulation at the various levels can be used to determine a total unit product cost. Each product's total unit cost is multiplied by

EXHIBIT 8-8

Determining Product Profitability and Company Profits

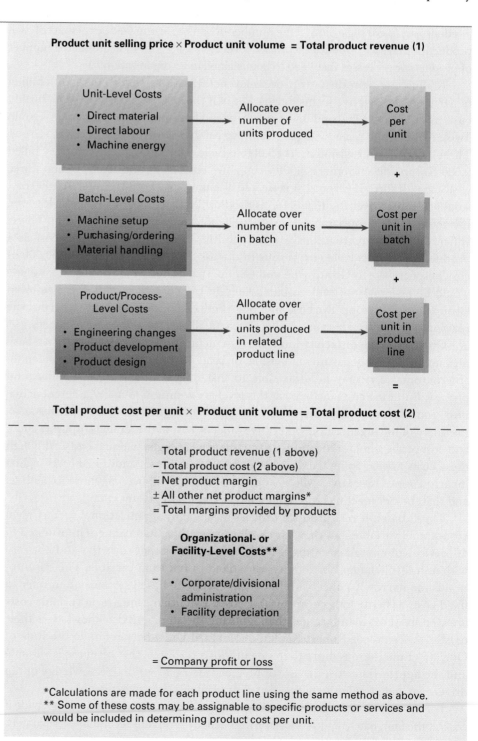

the number of units sold, and that product's cost of goods sold is subtracted from its total product revenue, yielding a net product margin. After these computations are performed for each product line, the product-line profits are summed to determine net product revenues. The unassigned organizational-level costs are subtracted to find the company profit or loss. In this model, the traditional distinction between product and period costs is not visible because the emphasis is on analyzing product profitability for internal management decision making rather than for financial statement presentation.

Two-Step Allocation

After initial recording, costs are accumulated in activity centre cost pools. An **activity centre** is any segment of the production or service process for which management wants separate information about the costs of the activities performed. In defining these centres, management should consider the following issues: geographical proximity of equipment; defined centres of managerial responsibility; magnitude of product costs; and a need to maintain a manageable number of activity centres. Costs having the same driver are accumulated in pools reflecting the appropriate level of cost incurrence (unit, batch, or product/process). If a relationship exists between a cost pool and a cost driver, then reducing or eliminating that cost driver should also reduce or eliminate the related cost.

In the past, most companies accumulated overhead using a vertical or functional approach. For example, all sales department costs were grouped together and separated from costs incurred in other parts of the organization. But production and service activities are horizontal by nature. A product or service flows through an organization, affecting numerous departments along the way. Gathering costs in pools reflecting the same cost drivers allows managers to better recognize these organizational cross-functional activities and focus on their cost impacts. Exhibit 8-9 provides

activity centre
a segment of the production or service process for which management wants a separate report of the costs of activities performed

---

EXHIBIT 8-9
Horizontal Work Activities

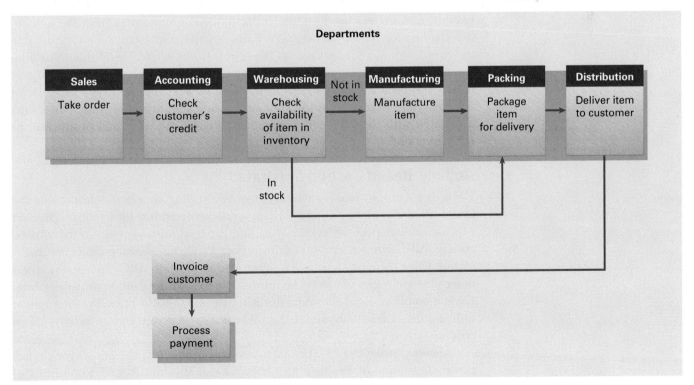

an example of the horizontal nature of organizational work; in this case, all activities have occurred because the sales department received an order from a customer.

After accumulation, costs are allocated out of the activity centre cost pools and assigned to products and services by use of an activity cost driver. An **activity cost driver** measures the demands placed on activities as well as the resources consumed by products and services; thus, an activity driver often indicates an activity's output. Exhibit 8-10 provides some common activity cost drivers.

activity cost driver
a measure of the demands placed on activities and, thus, the resources consumed by products and services; often indicates an activity's output

EXHIBIT 8-10
Activity Drivers

Activity Centre	Activity Cost Drivers
Accounting	Reports requested; dollars expended
Personnel	Job change actions; hiring actions; training hours; counselling hours
Data processing	Reports requested; transactions processed; programming hours; program change requests
Production engineering	Hours spent in each shop; job specification changes requested; product change notices processed
Quality control	Hours spent in each shop; defects discovered; samples analyzed
Plant services	Preventive maintenance cycles; hours spent in each shop; repair maintenance actions
Material services	Dollar value of requisitions; number of transactions processed; number of personnel in direct support
Utilities	Direct usage (metered to shop); space occupied
Production shops	Fixed per-job charge; setups made; direct labour; machine hours; number of moves; material applied

SOURCE: Republished with permission of the Institute of Management Accounting, from "Completing the Picture," Michael D. Woods, *Management Accounting*, December 1992; permission conveyed through Copyright Clearance Center, Inc.

The process of cost assignment is the same as the overhead application process illustrated in Chapter 4. Exhibit 8-11 illustrates this two-step process of tracing costs to products and services in an ABC system. As indicated in the exhibit, cost drivers used for the collection stage may differ from the activity drivers used for the allocation stage. Some activity centre costs are not traceable to lower levels of activity. Costs at the lowest (unit) activity level should be allocated to products using volume- or unit-based drivers. Costs incurred at higher (batch and product/process) levels may also be allocated to products by use of volume-related drivers, but the volume measure should include only those units associated with the batch or the product/process—not the total production or service volume.

Activity-Based Costing Illustrated

To be of maximum value, a management accounting system should provide the information a company needs to make strategic decisions, for example, product price, customer profitability analysis, and process improvement. Activity-based costing (ABC) can generate such information. While traditional product cost information tells a company how well it performed in the past, ABC can help managers determine strategies to use in the future. The following example provides a brief illustration of overhead allocation using both a traditional overhead costing system utilizing direct labour hours as the plantwide cost driver and an activity-based costing system.

Abbott Cosmetics Ltd. manufactures three products. The company manufactures 5,000 units of Product A, 2,000 units of Product B, and 1,000 units of

EXHIBIT 8-11

Tracing Costs in an Activity-
Based Costing System

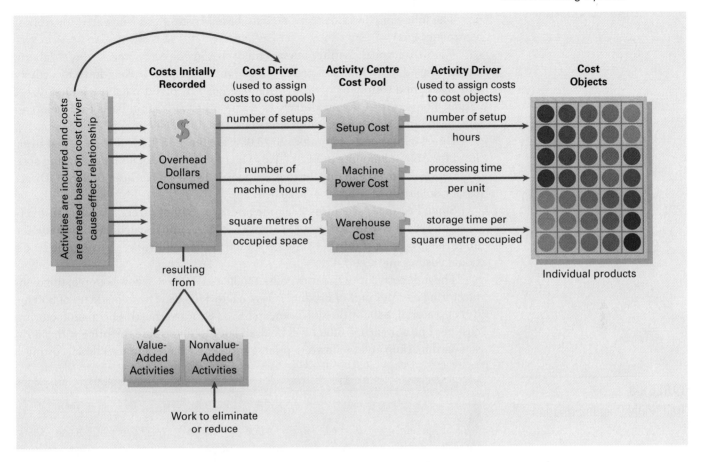

Product C. Table 8-1 shows the breakdown of costs for the company. Note that overhead represents 44.8% of the total production costs. The number of runs, orders, units per order, and direct labour hours for each product is shown in Table 8-2.

TABLE 8-1

Manufacturing Cost Proportions

Direct material	$ 900,000	30.7%
Direct labour	720,000	24.5
Overhead	1,315,340	44.8%
Total	$2,935,340[1]	100,0%

[1]See information in Table 8-3.

TABLE 8-2

Annual Production Information

	Products		
	A	B	C
Number of units manufactured	5000	2,000	1,000
Number of runs	10	40	50
Number of orders	1	4	5
Number of units per order	5,000	500	200
Number of direct labour hours per unit	2	8	10
Total direct labour hours	10,000	16,000	10,000

The products vary significantly in production factors. This product variation will be used to illustrate the inability of traditional costing to capture costs accurately. On the basis of the information shown in Table 8-2, calculations for both traditional and activity-based costing were done.

The following describes how activity-based costing was calculated for Abbott Cosmetics Ltd.

With traditional costing, management assigns direct material, direct labour, and overhead to each unit of production. Overhead is not broken down by activity but is assigned simply by dividing total overhead by direct machine hours, direct labour hours, direct labour dollars, or some other allocation basis to develop an overhead rate. Abbott assigned overhead using a direct labour application base.

Direct labour costs amount to $720,000, as shown in Table 8-1. Note that overhead for Abbott amounts to $1,315,340, which is 44.8% of total manufacturing cost. Therefore, the overhead rate for the company is 182.7% (Overhead dollars ÷ Direct labour dollars or $1,315,340 ÷ $720,000).

Since Product A requires 2 labour hours, or $40 of direct labour cost, overhead of $73.08 is assigned to it ($40 × 182.7%). A similar calculation is made for all three products. Table 8-3 shows the distribution of overhead using the traditional costing method.

The unit costs for each product are totalled in Table 8-3. For example, the manufacturing cost per unit of Product A is equal to $163.08. This is made up of $50 for direct material, $40 for direct labour, and $73.08 for overhead. The manufacturing cost per unit for each product will be used later to determine the price with a 40% standard markup and to illustrate pricing problems inherent in traditional costing.

TABLE 8-3
Traditional Cost Information

	A	B	C	Total
	5,000	2000	1,000	8,000
Units		**Cost per Unit**		**Total Cost**
Direct material	$ 50.00	$200.00	$250.00	$ 900,000[1]
Direct labour ($20 per hour)	40.00	160.00	200.00	720,000[2]
Overhead (182.7% of DL$)	73.08	292.32	365.40	1,315,440[3]
Manufacturing cost per unit	$163.08	$652.32	$815.40	$2,935,440[4]

[1][($50 × 5,000) + ($200 × 2,000) + ($250 × 1,000)]
[2][($40 × 5,000) + ($160 × 2,000) + ($200 × 1,000)]
[3][($73.08 × 5,000) + ($292.32 × 2,000) + ($365.40 × 1,000)]
[4][($163.08 × 5,000) + ($652.32 × 2,000) + ($815.40 × 1,000)]

ABC requires an investigation of each department to determine (a) how much time personnel actually spend on each product and (b) what factor drives costs in that department. At Abbott, extensive interviews and record analysis showed that activities for engineering, materials handling, setup, quality assurance, and packing/shipping could be evaluated using ABC criteria. Table 8-4 shows the results of the investigation and cost calculations for each product by department or process.

Departmental Analysis

Engineering Department—Engineering cost is driven by the number of orders for each product. For instance, one customer places one order annually for Product A, which has an engineering cost of $21,210 per order. Because there is only one order per year, the total engineering cost for Product A is $21,210. On the other end of the

TABLE 8-4

Activity-Based Cost Information

	Products			
	A	**B**	**C**	**Total**
Engineering/order	$ 21,210	$ 21,210	$ 21,210	
× Number of orders	1	4	5	
Total Engineering Costs	$ 21,210	$ 84,840	$106,050	$ 212,100
Materials handling	$ 26.25	$ 26.25	$ 26.25	
× Number of units	5,000	2,000	1,000	
Total Materials Handling	$ 131,250	$ 52,500	$ 26,250	$ 210,000
Setup	$ 1,590	$ 1,590	$ 1,590	
× Number of runs	10	40	50	
Total Setup Costs	$ 15,900	$ 63,600	$ 79,500	$ 159,000
Quality assurance	$ 9.75	$ 9.75	$ 9.75	
× Number of units	5,000	2,000	1,000	
Total Quality Assurance	$ 48,750	$ 19,500	$ 9,750	$ 78,000
Packing/shipping	$ 46.875	$ 46.875	$ 46.875	
× Number of units	5,000	2,000	1,000	
Total Packing/Shipping	$ 234,375	$ 93,750	$ 46,875	$ 375,000
Other Overhead	$ 93,780	$ 93,780	$ 93,780	$ 281,340
Total Overhead	$ 545,265[1]	$407,970[2]	$362,205[3]	$1,315,440

[1]($21,210 + $131,250 + $15,900 + $48,750 + $234,375 + $93,780)
[2]($84,840 + $52,500 + $63,600 + $19,500 + $93,750 + $93,780)
[3]($106,050 + $26,250 + $79,500 + $9,750 + $46,875 + $93,780)

spectrum is Product C with an engineering cost of $106,050 for 5 orders per year, or $21,210 per order.

Materials Handling Department—The cost driver for materials handling is the number of units produced. An analysis of records for the materials handling department shows that the cost to provide parts to assembly ranges from $26,250 for Product C to $131,250 for Product A. The difference is due primarily to the greater number of units for Product A, which increases materials delivery costs.

Setup—A special team from engineering, maintenance, and production recalibrates the assembly line during production changeover (adequate records were available to separate these individuals' time on this task from other activities). Setup costs vary according to production runs. Each production run (the cost driver) requires a setup. One Product A setup, for example, costs $1,590; total setup cost, with 10 runs annually, is $15,900.

Quality Assurance Department—Each unit of production requires a quality assurance inspection. Total quality assurance for Product A is $48,750 ($9.75 per unit × 5,000 units).

Packing/Shipping—This varies from $234,375 for Product A to $46,875 for Product C.

Other Overhead—The ABC investigation revealed that the remaining processes were difficult to separate by activity. Since the product line itself was the most significant cost driver, all other activities were lumped together under "other overhead" and the cost was distributed evenly between products at the rate of $93,780 per product. This is a poor practice, but it is used here to expain the difference between the traditional method and the ABC method. A better practice is to leave the other costs unallocated. It is important to note here that under traditional costing, $1,315,440 was distributed in this fashion; however, using ABC, this non-activity-based distribution was reduced to $281,340 or 22.3% of total overhead. In other words, ABC divided 77.7% of total overhead more realistically among the five products.

In general, the value of ABC as a better overhead allocation technique is based on the percentage of overhead that is allocated by activities or cost drivers. The higher the percentage of "other overhead" not allocated by assigned activities, the more the allocation will reflect what would have been calculated using traditional methods.

Calculating Unit Costs Using ABC

The next step is a mathematical calculation of all overhead activity cost to a per-unit level.

Some of the activities identified in Table 8-4—materials handling, quality assurance, packing/shipping costs, and other overhead—are already calculated by unit. However, engineering and setup costs require further computation.

For example, the engineering cost and the setup cost per unit for Product B is calculated as shown next.

Product B Engineering Cost

$21,210.00	Engineering cost per order
× 4	Number of orders (cost driver)
$84,840.00	
÷ 2,000	Number of units produced
$ 42.42	Engineering cost per unit produced

Product B Setup Cost

$ 1,590.00	Setup cost per run
× 40	Number of runs (cost driver)
$63,600.00	
÷ 2,000	Number of units produced
$ 31.80	Setup cost per unit produced

Other Overhead—The remaining overhead is assigned by dividing the amount by the number of units of each product. For instance, dividing $93,780 by 2,000 units yields a per-unit "Other Overhead" of $46.89 for Product B (see Table 8-5).

TABLE 8-5

ABC Information per Product Unit

			Product		
		A	B	C	Total
Units		5,000	2,000	1,000	8,000
			Per Unit Cost		Total Cost
1. Direct Material		$ 50.00	$ 200.00	$250.00	$ 900,000
2. Direct Labour ($20 per hour)		40.00	160.00	200.00	720,000
3. Engineering		4.24*	42.42	106.05	212,100
4. Materials Handling		26.25	26.25	26.25	210,000
5. Setup		3.18	31.80	79.50	159,000
6. Quality Assurance		9.75	9.75	9.75	78,000
7. Packing/Shipping		46.88*	46.88	46.88	375,000
8. Other Overhead		18.76*	46.89	93.78	281,340
9. ABC Cost per Unit		$199.06	$ 563.99	$812.21	$2,935,440
10. Traditional Cost per Unit		163.08	652.32	815.40	2,935,440
11. Difference		$ 36	$ −88.33	$ −3.19	$ 0

*rounded

Comparison to Traditional Costing

For comparison purposes, row 10 of Table 8-5 shows the traditional accounting unit costs given in Table 8-3 ("Manufacturing cost per unit"). The per unit differences between traditional costing and ABC are shown in line 11. The total production cost (cost to produce all products) is the same for the two costing methods. The difference is in the cost assigned to each product, or in the division of overhead among products. For instance, Abbott Company's Product A costs $163.08 using traditional costing and $199.06 using ABC. This is a vivid example of product cross-subsidization.

The effect of ABC versus traditional costing is shown by comparing the cost and cost-based selling price differences between the two approaches. Prices for each product are calculated based on an across-the-board 40% markup of costs as shown in Table 8-6. The respective costs are simply multiplied by 1.4 (140%). For example, under traditional costing at Abbott, the price of Product A is $228.31, and under ABC, it is $278.68.

TABLE 8-6
Price and Markup Analysis at 40% Markup

Product A Cost		Product B Cost		Product C Cost	
Traditional	ABC	Traditional	ABC	Traditional	ABC
$163.08	$199.06	$652.32	$563.99	$815.40	$812.21

Product A Price		Product B Price		Product C Price	
$228.31	$278.68	$913.25	$789.59	$1,141.56	$1,137.09
15%[1]	ABC Markup	61.9%[2]	ABC Markup	40.5%[3]	ABC Markup

[1][($228.31 − $199.06) ÷ $199.06]
[2][($913.25 − $563.99) ÷ $563.99]
[3][($1,141.56 − $812.21) ÷ $812.21]

In the bottom row is the calculated markup based on the activity-based cost and traditional price. We call this important calculation the revised ABC markup (Table 8-6). At Abbott, for Product A, the ABC markup is 15%.

Because activity-based cost accounting generates more accurate costs than traditional costing, prices based on ABC are more likely to reflect the desired markup for each individual product. Although in many industries the competitive market forces significantly influence pricing decisions, the product cost is usually an integral part of pricing decision criteria. With traditional costing, the costs that Abbott assigns for Product A are 22.1% lower [($199.06 − $163.08) ÷ $163.08] and for Product B they are 13.5% higher [($563.99 − $652.32) ÷ $652.32] than with ABC. Since traditional pricing is based on a 40% markup of traditionally calculated costs, the prices are also lower or higher by the same percentage. Abbott thinks it has a 40% markup for each of its products. Based on ABC costs for Product A, the price markup is about 15% [($228.31 − $199.06) ÷ $199.06], or 25% less than expected. Product B has a markup using ABC of 61.9% [($913.25 − $563.99) ÷ $563.99].

Abbott should be concerned that market forces will influence sales. If competitors are properly pricing their products (i.e., based on accurate costs), Abbott's products will be either over- or underpriced. Sales of the two underpriced products will probably increase, whereas the sales of the overpriced products will decrease. Over time, the product mix will change, with the company selling more of the lower-margin products (based on ABC costs), to the point of filling the available capacity with lower-margin products. The magnitude of change will depend on the markets, competitive actions, and price elasticity of the products. Abbott's revenue, profit, and profit margin will deteriorate, while total number of units sold may actually increase. At some future time, management will look at the results and ask, "What happened?"

A forward-looking attribute of ABC is that it yields better information for setting appropriate prices and determining the cost and profit impact of different product mixes. With traditional costing, a company may inappropriately assume that a particular product is contributing more profit than it actually is.

This example reflects a company operating with 45% overhead (Table 8-3, $1,315,440 ÷ $2,935,440). One should analyze the relationship between overhead level and the impact of ABC. The yardstick to measure this is the actual markup for each product ("ABC Markup" in Table 8-6). The closer the ABC markup is to the desired gross profit margin, the better.

In this scenario, if Abbott Corporation (45% overhead) uses traditional costing for pricing decisions, it could experience major changes in product demand and unexpected negative impacts on profitability.

These calculations show the impact of only a few changes in a relatively narrow product mix. Many companies deal with more products and make such decisions numerous times each year. In our example, Product A, the underpriced and least profitable product, is more likely to increase in demand. Prices lower than competitors' create higher demand. The reverse is true for overpriced products. This demonstrates another effect of inaccurate costing and consequent pricing, that is, the probable increase in sales volume of less profitable products and decrease in sales of more profitable products.

Although even a 5% cost difference is significant when used as a basis for pricing decisions, we will use a 10% difference to postulate when it might be beneficial to implement ABC costing. This is because even ABC includes some "arbitrary" allocation of overhead that is not allocated by assigned activities or cost drivers. Therefore, with overhead costs of about 15% or more of total cost, it appears that the more accurate costing with ABC would be beneficial. At overhead cost levels of less than 15% of total costs, a cost–benefit analysis would be appropriate to further investigate the implementation benefits of the specific situation.

In a study of 10 British firms of varying size, the average implementation cost was found to be approximately $30,000, with the implementation time varying from 20 to 52 weeks (implementation cost was correlated to implementation time). Six of these firms reported no increase in operating costs of the ABC system after implementation, with seven reporting improved management information after the ABC implementation. Therefore, a company near (or below) the 15% overhead point should consider the expected increase in cost recovery through improved pricing and the estimated cost to implementation.[15]

LEARNING OBJECTIVE 6

When is the use of activity-based costing appropriate?

DETERMINING WHETHER ABC IS APPROPRIATE

Not every accounting system that uses direct labour or machine hours as the cost driver provides inadequate or inaccurate cost information. Activity-based costing is a useful tool, but it is not necessarily appropriate for all companies. There are two primary assumptions that underlie ABC: (1) the costs in each cost pool are driven by homogeneous activities, and (2) the costs in each cost pool are strictly proportional to the activity.[16] If these assumptions are true, then ABC will be advantageous under the following conditions:
• There is significant product/service variety or complexity.
• There is a lack of commonality in the creation and use of overhead.

- There are problems with current cost allocations.
- There has been significant change in the environment in which the organization operates.

Exhibit 8-12 illustrates a comparison of the traditional versus ABC overhead allocation.

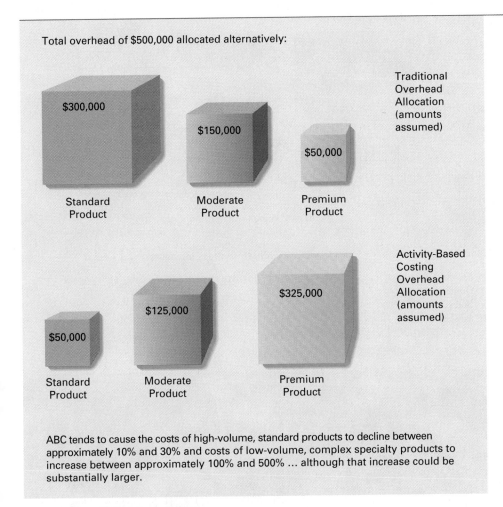

EXHIBIT 8-12

Traditional Versus ABC Overhead Allocations

Product/Service Variety or Complexity

Two factors commonly associated with a need to consider activity-based costing are product/service variety and complexity. **Product variety** refers to the number of different types of products made. **Service variety** refers to the number of different types of services provided. The items may be variations of the same product line (such as Hallmark's different types of greeting cards or the local bank's different types of chequing accounts), or they may be in numerous product families (such as Procter & Gamble's detergents, diapers, fabric softeners, and shampoos). In either case, product/service additions cause numerous overhead costs to increase. Exhibit 8-13 illustrates the potential for increased overhead with an increase in product variety. In addition, the changes in overhead costs resulting from increased product variety show that seemingly fixed costs (such as warehousing, purchasing, and quality control) are in fact long-term variable costs.

In the quest for product variety, many companies are striving for **mass customization** of products. This production method refers to the use of a flexible

product variety
the number of different types of products produced

service variety
the number of different types of services provided

mass customization
the relatively low-cost mass production of products to the unique specifications of individual customers; requires the use of flexible manufacturing systems

EXHIBIT 8-13
Product Variety Creates Overhead Costs

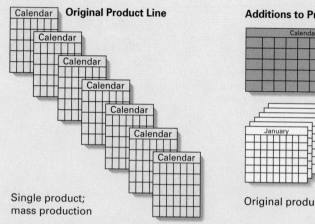

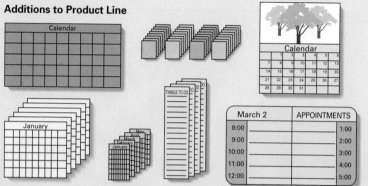

Original Product Line

Single product; mass production

Additions to Product Line

Original product made in mass quantities; each additional product made in extremely limited quantities.

With which product set would the company have more?

- Inventory carrying costs?
- Purchasing costs?
- Scheduling costs?
- Setup and change-over costs?
- Expediting costs?
- Quality control costs?
- Scrap costs?
- Rework costs?

To which products do these increased costs relate?

Which product line would bear the majority of the costs?

Production overhead at P&G is significant—costs are created not only because of multiple varieties of the same type of product (detergent, diapers, etc.) but because of numerous product lines. In such a situation, using a single cost pool and driver would be efficient but highly ineffective for product cost determination.

product complexity
the number of components in a product or the number of processes or operations through which a product flows

manufacturing system to mass produce, relatively inexpensively, unique products for individual customers.

Product complexity refers to the number of components in a product or the number of processes or operations through which a product flows. Management can minimize product complexity by redesigning products and processes to standardize them and reduce the number of different components, tools, and processes required. Pareto analysis generally reveals that 20% of the components are used in 80% of the products. This is often referred to as the 20:80 rule. If this is the case, then companies need to consider two other factors. First, are the remaining compo-

German Cost Accounting at Work

In 2004, the HOSPITAL FOR SICK CHILDREN (Sick Kids) implemented *Grenzplankostenrechnung* or GPK. This technique has been used in Europe for over 40 years, but it is virtually unheard of in North America.

GPK proposes, among other things, that the activities identified within an ABC framework should each be given their own cost centre. The cost centres are set up within an organization's general ledger, and activity measures are tracked alongside activity-specific financial accounting information. Periodic reporting can then take place at a very detailed level, but it can be rolled up to an organizationally consolidated level.

In this way, ABC becomes integrated within an organization's financial accounting system; activity management and financial management coincide. IT integration issues are avoided, and the cost centre structure gives a solid framework within which to address the perceived "complexity" of ABC.

SOURCE: Brian Mackie, former Financial Operations Director, The Hospital for Sick Children, Toronto, ON, January 2005.

---

nents used in key products? If so, could equal quality be achieved by using the more common parts? If not, can the products be sold for a premium price to cover the costs associated with the use of low-volume components? Second, are the nonstandard parts used in products purchased by important customers who are willing to pay a premium price for the products? If so, the benefits from the complexity may be worth the cost. However, would customers be equally satisfied if more common parts were used and the product price were reduced? Parts complexity is acceptable only if it is value-added from the customer's point of view.

Process complexity may develop over time, or it may exist because of a lack of sufficient planning in product development. Processes are complex when they create difficulties for the people attempting to perform production operations (physical straining, awkwardness of motions, or wasted motions) or for the people using manufacturing machinery (multiple and/or detailed setups, lengthy transfer time between machine processes, or recalibration of instruments). Process complexity reflects numerous nonvalue-added activities that cause time delays and cost increases.

A company can employ simultaneous engineering to reduce both product and process complexity. **Simultaneous** (or **concurrent**) **engineering** refers to involving all the primary functional areas and personnel that contribute to a product's origination and production from the beginning of a project. Multifunctional teams are used to design the product by considering customer expectations, vendor capabilities, parts commonality, and production process compatibility. Such an integrated design effort is referred to as a design-for-manufacturability approach. Simultaneous engineering helps companies shorten the time to market for new products and minimize complexity and cost.

Even when simultaneous engineering is used in process development, processes may develop complexity over time. One way to overcome this type of complexity is **business process reengineering (BPR)** or process innovation and redesign. BPR's goal is to find and implement radical changes in how things are made or how tasks are performed to achieve substantial cost, service, or time reductions. Emphasizing continuous improvement, BPR ignores the way it is and looks instead for the way it should be. BPR may redesign old processes or design new ones to eliminate complexity.

Process redesign takes a current process, improves its effectiveness, and can bring about improvements that range from 300% to 1000%. This technique is the right choice for about 70% of the business processes. [In contrast, new process design]

simultaneous engineering (or concurrent engineering) an integrated approach in which all primary functions and personnel contributing to a product's origination and production are involved continuously from the beginning of a project

business process reengineering process innovation and redesign aimed at finding and implementing radical changes in how things are made or how tasks are performed to achieve substantial cost, service, or time reductions

completely ignores the present process and organizational structure. This technique takes advantage of the latest mechanization, automation, and information techniques available. New process design can lead to improvements that range from 700% to 2000%. New process design costs more and takes more time to implement than process redesign. It also has the highest degree of risk . . . and is very disruptive to the organization.[17]

Many traditional cost systems were not designed to account for information such as how many different parts are used in a product, so management may not be able to identify products made with low-volume or unique components. Activity-based costing systems are more flexible and gather such details, thereby providing important information about relationships among activities and cost drivers. Armed with these data, people can focus reengineering efforts on the primary causes of process complexity and those that create the highest level of waste.

Lack of Commonality in Overhead Costs

Certain products, services, or types of customers create substantially more overhead costs than others. Although some of these additional overhead costs may be caused by product variety or process complexity, others may be related to support services. For example, some products require substantially more advertising than others; some use higher cost distribution channels; and some necessitate the use of high-technology machinery. In addition, some companies' output volumes differ significantly among their products and services. Each of these differences creates additional overhead costs. If only one or two overhead pools are used, overhead related to specific products will be spread over all products. The result will be increased costs for products that are not responsible for the increased overhead.

Problems in Current Cost Allocations

If a company has undergone one or more significant changes in its products, processes, or customer base, then managers and accountants need to investigate whether the existing cost system still provides a reasonable estimate of product or service cost. Many companies that have automated their production processes have experienced large reductions in labour cost and large increases in overhead. In such companies, using direct labour as an overhead allocation base tends to charge products made by automated equipment with insufficient overhead and products made with high proportions of direct labour with too much overhead.

Traditional cost allocations also tend to assign product costs (direct material, direct labour, and manufacturing overhead) to products and expense the majority of period costs when incurred. ABC recognizes that some period costs may be distinctly and reasonably associated with specific products and therefore should be traced and allocated to those products. This recognition changes the traditional view of product versus period cost.

Changes in Business Environment

A change in the competitive environment in which a company operates may also require better cost information. Increased competition may occur for several reasons: (1) other companies have recognized the profit potential of a particular product or service, (2) the product or service has become cost-feasible to make or perform, or (3) an industry has been deregulated. If many new companies are competing for old business, the best estimate of product or service cost must be available to management so that profit margins and prices can be reasonably set.

Changes in management strategy can also signal a need for a new cost system. For example, if management wants to begin new operations, the cost system must be capable of providing information on how costs will change. The traditional variable versus fixed cost classifications may not allow the effective development of such information. The use of ABC offers a different perspective about how the planned operational changes will affect activities and costs through its analysis of costs as short-term versus long-term variables as well as its emphasis on the use of cost drivers.

Many companies are currently engaging in continuous improvement efforts that recognize the need to eliminate nonvalue-added activities so as to reduce lead time, make products or perform services with zero defects, reduce product costs on an ongoing basis, and simplify products and processes. Activity-based costing, by promoting an understanding of cost drivers, allows the NVA activities to be identified and their causes eliminated or reduced—thereby enhancing operational performance.

The choice to implement activity-based costing should mean that management is willing to accept the new information and use it to plan, control, and evaluate operating activities. If this is the case, then management must have some ability to set prices relative to cost changes; accept alternative business strategies—such as eliminating or expanding product or service offerings—if the new costs should so indicate; and reduce waste where necessary, including downsizing or job restructuring. If management is powerless to institute changes for whatever reason (for example, centralized control or industry regulation), then the ABC-generated information is nothing more than an exercise in futility—and probably a fairly costly one.

Regardless of why there is a need for change in their costing systems, companies at least now have the technological capability to implement ABC systems. Introduction of the personal computer, bar coding, generic software packages, and other advanced technologies means that significantly more information can be readily and cost effectively supplied. In the past, ABC implementation would have been prohibitively expensive or technologically impossible for most companies.

This can be seen at Reichhold, Inc. Over the past 10 years, Reichhold, Inc. has transformed itself from a product line-focused, divisional-structured company into a customer-focused, team-based organization. Reichhold has been implementing activity-based costing to analyze the cost implications of the changes occurring in production as a result of the shift to specialty products. The implementation has been bottom-up with local teams leading the process.

The company formed an ABC steering committee, which included a member of the senior management team, a business team leader, a member of the corporate manufacturing team, and several members of the financial team. The committee is responsible for overseeing ABC implementation in the United States and Canada. The company conducted pilot projects at several sites, one of which was at Weston, Ontario.

The most important contribution of ABC at the company has been the comprehensive and accurate analysis of the profitability of the company's different products. This was achieved by moving costs out of the traditional cost centres toward the activities and product lines.[18]

ABC and the Service Sector

It may appear that ABC is designed specifically for the manufacturing sector, but in reality it applies equally well to the service sector. Even within the manufacturing sector, the activities of purchasing, materials handling, and setup are in fact services supporting the manufacturing function. Within the pure service sector, the same decisions that management has in manufacturing are made by managers in service-oriented businesses. Managers need to make decisions on proper resource allocation, product offering mix and diversity, and most important, which of the many clients are profitable and worth servicing and which of them are not.

ABC is a natural fit for the banking industry because there are easily identifiable cost drivers that can be measured and priced per event. As an example, most demand deposit accounts are priced and measured based on monthly activity and usage. A business is charged a certain cost for each cheque that is written and for each item that is deposited into the business chequing account. Similarly, the concept can be applied to commercial lending transaction activities, from the initial

GENERAL NEWS NOTE

German Cost Accounting Has ABC Attributes

The German cost accounting system called *Grenzplankostenrechnung* or GPK has a similar functionality to ABC systems. GPK developed from government-standardized financial accounting with the intention to have a cost centre for each activity. Consequently, German companies using GPK tend to have a relatively larger number of cost centres than most companies in Canada do in order to establish a robust cause-and-effect relationship between resources consumed and an appropriate cost driver.

For a cost centre to be defined:
- costs must be separable—they must be specific to the output being produced in the cost centre.
- the output produced must be repetitive.
- the output must be the responsibility of an individual manager. A cost centre may have only one manger, but one manager may manage more than one cost centre.
- cost centre size should be manageable.
- cost/technology/resource type/work performed must be similar.
- cost assignment drivers must be quantifiable and able to be planned. The centre must be either primary or support. Support for a primary cost centre is one that performs work directly contributing to the manufacturer of the product or performance of the service for a customer (e.g., packing for shipment).

In GPK, cost centres have tended to be designed so that each centre revolves around a single activity where each department has only one cost driver, such as number of tests performed by the quality-test cost centre. In essence, activity-specific cost centres accomplish the same thing as ABC attempts to do in organizations where cost centres are defined by organizational/responsibility grouping. With GPK, a single manager may be responsible for multiple cost centres, but in ABC a manager will manage a cost centre that produces multiple activities. In ABC the cost centre expenses have to be distributed to activities. What this accomplishes in GPK but not in ABC is to create activity/cost centre entities within the cost accounting/management system and therefore the budgeting and reporting systems.

Advances in German cost accounting software make it feasible to leave cost centres consolidated and to have multiple subordinate cost pools, each with an individual assignment driver. When subordinate cost pools and drivers are used, it is necessary to analyze cost by resource output/driver type within the cost centre, almost as if there were a number of separate cost centres within the cost centre. Here the architecture begins to resemble a typical ABC system, although the premise for arriving at the solution is one that starts from cost centres.

GPK and ABC are complementary. However, GPK is concerned with manufacturing overhead, including fixed costs in operations and support departments in order to improve product and service cost/profitability analysis. When GPK has been expanded to customer-service cost centre performance including sales, order processing, distribution, and customer service, it has been called *Prozesskostenrechnung* (PK). The application of PK allows managers to know customer profitability in detail. GPK and PK are an integrated decision-support, budgeting, planning, and control system.

SOURCE: Paul A. Sharman, "Bring on German Cost Accounting," *Strategic Finance*, December 2003, pp. 30–38.

loan review and setup to the myriad advance requests, accounting maintenance requests, and payment applications.

Some key benefits of the ABC approach are that it changes the way an organization thinks about its costing system and revitalizes the bank's penetration strategies and processes. ABC also forces a company to consider its activities, to seek efficiencies, and to consolidate tasks in providing services and conducting business. Considering this action for the banking industry immediately shows that this is a win–win scenario in all circumstances. The customer benefits from a higher level of customer service, and the bank benefits from a streamlined, more cost-effective approach to providing services.[19]

A recent study showed that understanding how resources are consumed can help group practices control costs. The Academy of Orthopaedic Surgeons study used an activity-based costing system to measure how resources are consumed in providing medical services. They measured resource consumption by assigning costs to each process according to how much time is spent on related work activities. The study found that an ABC business process model critically tracks how resources are consumed in providing medical services.[20]

One difference between service organizations and manufacturing organizations is that there tends to be a much higher use of time-related or duration cost drivers as opposed to transaction-based cost drivers such as the number of setups or inspections. In a manufacturing process, many costs are related to units or batches passing through certain activities, while in a service-oriented business, costs accumulated based on time will depend on the particular case; for instance, the time for a mechanic to repair a car will depend on the particular problem with that car, or the time for a dentist to do a root canal will depend on the particulars of the patient's case and is not standard to each patient.[21]

ABC Compared to Process Costing and Job-Order Costing

This chapter has discussed ABC, which is a technique for allocating overhead. Chapters 4 and 5 discussed process costing and job-order costing. Differences between ABC and process costing and job-order costing can be emphasized by applying the same data to each technique. After this application, the uses and advantages of each will be better understood, particularly in comparative terms.

Consider a company that makes wooden bedroom furniture. For about five years the sales have been constant at about 18,000 sets of furniture annually; in 2009, its sales were again flat. The president decided in 2009 to establish a superior line of solid wood bedroom furniture to supplement the sales of the standard line of bedroom furniture, which used veneers and chipboard rather than solid wood for the wood components. The superior line was sold at $800 per set compared to $400 per set for the standard line. Both prices were competitive in their respective markets. The president decided to evaluate the profitability of each product line for 2010 using the process costing method, which had been used when the company only produced the standard line of furniture. The income statement for 2010 is shown in Exhibit 8-14.

Exhibit 8-15 shows the application of process costing. The primary purpose of process costing is to determine unit costs, where all units are deemed to be homogeneous. The total of the cost of goods sold, $6,665,000 is divided by the number of sets, 20,000 (on the assumption that each set is the same as the next) to equal $333.25. Thus, the gross profit for each standard set is $66.75, while the gross profit for each superior set is $466.75. The president was elated with these results. However, she realized that the two furniture sets are not homogeneous and thus the

EXHIBIT 8-14

Bedroom Sets Inc., Income Statement

Year Ended December 2010	
Revenue	$8,800,000
Cost of Goods Sold:	
Direct materials	2,380,000
Direct labour	1,100,000
Factory overhead	3,185,000
	6,665,000
Gross Profit	2,135,000
General and Administrative	
Selling and advertising	600,000
Administrative	600,000
	1,200,000
Income (before taxes)	$ 935,000

SOURCE: This example was based on D. Perkins, S. Stovall, and N.J. Fessler, "Caprock Cycle Company," *Journal of Accounting Case Research* Vol. 8, no. 2 (2005): 16–26.

EXHIBIT 8-15

Process Costing Solution

	Standard Set		Superior Set		Company
	Per Set	Total	Per Set	Total	Total
Sales	$400.00	7,200,000	$800.00	1,600,000	$8,800,000
Production costs*	333.25	5,998,500	333.25	666,500	(6,665,000)
Gross profit	$ 66.75	1,201,500	$466.75	933,500	$2,135,000

*Determination of costs per set = Total production costs/total sets produced
= $6,665,000/20,000 sets
= $333.25

averaging technique inherent in process costing creates the potential for significant costing inequities.

In recognizing the possible erroneous profit for the different sets, the president decided to apply job-order costing. First she gathered information on how the cost of goods sold were related to the two different sets of bedroom furniture. With the help of the management accountant, she developed product costs according to the job-order method. This took three months and she is comfortable with their accuracy. The direct cost information is provided in Exhibit 8-16. Manufacturing overhead is applied to products based on direct labour hours incurred. Direct labour hours is a handy but not necessarily an accurate driver.

EXHIBIT 8-16

Cost of Goods Sold Per Set

	Standard Set	Superior Set
Direct materials	$110	$200
Direct labour	4 hours of unskilled labour at $10 per hour	9.5 hours of skilled labour at $20 per hour

From Exhibit 8-17, it can be seen that the gross profit for the standard set of bedroom furniture is $110 with job-order costing compared to $66.75 when process costing was employed. For the superior set, the gross profit went from $466.75 per set with process costing to a profit of $77.50 per set with job-order costing. This was a major surprise for the president. Without any change in the actual costs, gross profit changed by changing the costing method.

| | Standard Set | | Superior Set | | Company |
	Per Set	Total	Per Set	Total	Total
Sales	$ 400	7,200,000	$800.00	1,600,000	$8,800,000
Direct materials	110		200.00		
Direct labour	40		190.00		
Overhead*	140		332.50		
Total costs	(290)	(5,220,000)	(722.50)	(1,445,000)	(6,665,000)
Gross profit	$ 110	1,980,000	$ 77.50	155,000	$2,135,000

*Determination of overhead cost per direct labour hour:
 = $3,185,000/(4 × 18,000 + 9.5 × 2000)
 = $3,150,000/91,000
 = $35/direct labour hour

EXHIBIT 8-17
Job-Order Costing Solution

Compared to the process costing information, the job-order cost system better reflects product cost differences involving material and labour because it recognizes that the two sets of bedroom furniture could differ as to labour and material costs. However, it also assumes that the overhead costs are related to the amount of direct labour incurred. This may or may not be the case, as the president surmised.

The president thought that if the costing system made a difference in the calculation of the gross margin earned on a bedroom set, then it would be best to employ activity-based costing (ABC) for more accurately allocating the significant manufacturing overhead. In preparing for implementing ABC, she considered the flow of activities that comprise manufacturing overhead: purchasing and receiving; design; cutting and assembly; sanding and finishing; inspection; and packaging and shipment.

Purchasing and receiving: The basic materials used in the manufacture of bedroom sets are woods, metal frames, glues, wood finishes, and hardware. The wood for the standard set includes various veneers and chipboard. Only solid woods are used with the superior sets. The company's accounting system releases purchase orders via the Internet as needed, and the company receives materials on a just-in-time basis. This cost pool is for all costs associated with administration and physical movement of parts around the manufacturing facility. Since more parts require more purchasing, receiving, and material handling, these costs should be assigned based on the number of parts in each product. The numbers of parts in the standard set and the superior set are 20 and 35, respectively.

Design: The design for the standard bedroom set is standard. Customers who purchase the superior bedroom set use the company's CAD (computer-assisted design) program to custom design their bedroom sets. The costs in this category consist primarily of salaries for the technicians who assist customers in designing their customized superior sets. These costs should be assigned equally to each superior set.

Cutting and assembly: For the standard set, workers cut the 4-foot-by-8-foot sheets of chipboard and veneer into components. Then, with glue and hardware, these components are assembled into bedroom sets. For the superior set, solid wood boards are selected based on grain pattern, cut to length, glued together, and then planed to the appropriate thickness. Then there is a cutting step to make the components, which are then assembled into bedroom sets (with glue and hardware). This cost pool consists of overhead costs incurred to support the activities of cutting and assembly. These labour-supporting costs—such as utilities, equipment depreciation, and building depreciation—should be assigned based on the number of labour hours spent on each set.

Sanding and finishing: The assembled sets are sanded to remove rough spots. Wood finishing compounds are applied to the finished sets. Only one coat is applied to the standard sets, while two coats are applied to the superior sets. The customers choose the finish for the superior sets, while there is no selection for the standard sets. As with cutting and assembly, these costs should be assigned based on the number of labour hours spent on each.

Inspection: All sets are visually inspected to ensure that quality expectations are met. Defects are corrected before allowing sets to proceed. As they are driven by the number of sets inspected, these costs should be assigned based on the number of sets.

Packaging and shipment: Workers pack each set in boxes to be loaded on a truck for shipment. Each superior set incurs twice the labour and materials as a standard set. Thus, these costs should be allocated on the number of equivalent units, with each superior set being considered as two standard sets.

The costs for the pools are specified in Exhibit 8-18.

EXHIBIT 8-18

Activity-Based Cost Pools

Activities	Costs
Purchasing and receiving	$ 400,000
Design	85,000
Cutting and assembly	900,000
Sanding and finishing	800,000
Inspection	400,000
Packaging and shipment	600,000
	$3,185,000

Based on the activities that contribute to the manufacturing overhead costs of $3,185,000, Exhibit 8-19 lists the major activities. The exhibit also indicates the appropriate cost driver for allocating activity costs to the furniture sets.

EXHIBIT 8-19

Summary of Cost Drivers

Activity/ Product	Purchasing and Receiving	Design	Cutting and Assembly	Sanding and Finishing	Inspection	Packaging and Shipment
Standard	Per part	N/A	Per labour hour	Per labour hour	Per set	Per set
Superior	Per part	Per set	Per labour hour	Per labour hour	Per set	Per set

With this information on the activities and activity cost pools, it is possible to allocate the manufacturing overhead with ABC. Exhibit 8-20 shows the cost driver requirements for each cost pool.

EXHIBIT 8-20

Driver Demand for Each Cost Pool

	Standard		Superior		Totals	
Cost Pools	Cost Driver Units	% of Total Demand	Cost Driver Units	% of Total Demand	Cost Drivers	%
Purchasing and receiving	360,000	83.7	70,000	16.3	430,000	100.0
Design	N/A	N/A	2,000	100.0	2,000	100.0
Cutting and assembly	72,000	79.1	19,000	20.9	91,000	100.0
Sanding and finishing	72,000	79.1	19,000	20.9	91,000	100.0
Inspection	18,000	90.0	2,000	10.0	20,000	100.0
Packing and shipment	18,000	81.8	4,000	18.2	22,000	100.0

In Exhibit 8-21 the cost per set for each cost driver is calculated. Exhibit 8-22 shows the gross profit per set when ABC is used to allocate manufacturing overhead.

EXHIBIT 8-21

Driver Demand for Each Cost Pool

Cost Pools	Cost Driver Total*	Total Cost Pool**	Cost Per Driver Unit($)	Standard # Drivers Per Set	Standard Cost Per Set($)	Superior # Drivers Per Set	Superior Cost Per Set($)
Purchasing and receiving	430,000	400,000	0.9302	20	18.60	35	32.56
Design	2,000	85,000	42.50	0	0	1	42.50
Cutting and assembly	91,000	900,000	9.89	4	39.56	9.5	93.96
Sanding and finishing	91,000	800,000	8.79	4	35.16	9.5	83.51
Inspection	20,000	400,000	20.00	1	20.00	1	20.00
Packaging and shipment	22,000	600,000	27.27	1	27.27	2	54.54

*From Exhibit 8-21
**From Exhibit 8-18

EXHIBIT 8-22

Activity-Based Costing Solution

	Standard Per Set	Standard Total	Superior Per Set	Superior Total	Company Total
Sales	400.00	7,200,000	800.00	1,600,000	8,800,000
Cost of Goods Sold:					
Direct materials	110.00	1,980,000	200.00	400,000	2,380,000
Direct labour	40.00	720,000	190.00	380,000	1,100,000
Purchasing and receiving	18.60	334,884	32.56	65,116	400,000
Design	0	0	42.50	85,000	85,000
Cutting and assembly	39.56	712,080	93.96	187,920	900,000
Sanding and finishing	35.16	632,980	83.51	167,020	800,000
Inspection	20.00	360,000	20.00	40,000	400,000
Packaging and shipment	27.27	490,909	54.54	109,091	600,000
	290.59	5,230,853	717.07	1,434,147	6,665,000
Gross Profit	109.41	1,969,147	82.93	165,853	2,135,000

Note that materials and direct labour are allocated directly as they are direct costs and attach obviously to the sets.

In summary, the gross profits for the two sets of bedroom furniture changed with the method of costing, as shown below:

Gross Profit Per Set

	Standard	Superior
Process costing	$ 66.75	$466.75
Job-order costing	110.00	77.50
Activity-based costing	109.41	82.93

The president was shocked at the change in gross margin with the change to ABC, which is a more accurate method for allocating manufacturing overhead. With process costing, the company was showing a gross profit of $466.75 per superior bedroom set. Job-order costing reduced this profit to $77.50 per set, and, with more accuracy, ABC increased the gross margin slightly to $82.93 per set. Alternatively, the gross profit per standard set increased with the change in costing method.

The president recognized that ABC is a means of allocating all overhead and not merely manufacturing overhead. Exhibit 8-14 showed that the company had $1,200,000 in overhead for general and administrative expenses. The allocation of general and administrative overhead to the two bedroom sets would provide a fuller understanding of their relative profitability. As noted in Exhibit 8-23, $1.2 million goes to general and administrative expenses, evenly incurred by the selling and advertising unit and the administrative unit.

EXHIBIT 8-23

Full Activity-Based Costing Solution

	Standard		Superior		Company
	Per Set	Total	Per Set	Total	Total
Sales	400.00	7,200,000	800.00	1,600,000	8,800,000
Cost of Goods Sold:	290.59	5,230,853	717.07	1,434,147	6,665,000
Gross Profit	109.41	1,969,147	82.93	165,853	2,135,000
General and Administrative					
Selling and advertising	20.00	360,000	120.00	240,000	600,000
Administration	26.67	480,000	60.00	120,000	600,000
	46.67	840,000	180.00	360,000	1,200,000
Net Income	62.74	1,129,147	(97.07)	(194,147)	935,000

To understand how these expenses are incurred, the president asked the selling and advertising manager about what drives those costs. The manager estimated that about 40% of the expenses were for the superior set, while 60% were for the standard set. Similarly, the administrative managers estimated that 20% of their costs were attributable to the superior set and the remaining 80% related to the standard set. The president realized that she was getting estimates rather than more accurately traced costs with appropriate drivers. Nevertheless, these estimates were deemed to be sufficient for identifying profit concerns. Consequently, the president allocated the general and administrative costs to each set, as shown in Exhibit 8-23.

The net income for the standard sets is $62.74 each, while it is a loss of $97.07 each for the superior sets. This costing is fairly accurate. The direct costs for materials and labour are allocated directly, which is accurate. The overhead (manufacturing, selling and advertising, administration) is allocated with ABC, which is also fairly accurate. The conclusion that the company is losing money on each sale of superior furniture sets is very definite: money is being lost. This information should be used to make the production of superior furniture profitable. The information raises some questions:

- Can the price be increased?
- Can the materials be acquired at a lower cost?
- Can less expensive labour be used?
- Can processes be improved so that less labour is required?
- Can the processes be improved so that less overhead is needed?

In summarizing, it should be noted that process and job-order costing are systems for allocating costs. ABC is an option for allocating overhead, and an alternative to the traditional method for allocating with volume drivers such as labour and machine hours. Thus, ABC works in conjunction with process and job-order costing, and not as an alternative to them.

OPERATIONAL AND STRATEGIC PLANNING AND CONTROL USING ABC

Activity-based management and costing provide many benefits for production and service organizations. The list of companies using activity-based costing is large and impressive. These companies are using ABC to make both operational and strategic decisions, such as more effectively controlling costs; adjusting product, process, or marketing strategy; influencing behaviour; and evaluating performance.

LEARNING OBJECTIVE   7

What are the benefits and limitations of using activity-based costing?

To control costs, managers must understand where costs are being incurred and for what purpose. This understanding is provided by more appropriate tracing of overhead costs to products and services. Viewing fixed costs as long-term variable costs provides useful information for assessing the cost–benefit relationship of obtaining more customers or providing more goods and services. Additionally, differentiating between value-added and nonvalue-added activities helps managers visualize what needs to be done to control these costs, implement cost reduction activities, and plan resource utilization.

Traditional accounting systems concentrate on controlling cost incurrence, while ABC focuses on controlling the cause of the cost incurrence. Concentrating on the causes of costs makes cost reduction efforts more successful because they can be directed at specific cost drivers. It is critical, however, to understand that simply reducing cost drivers or activities will not cause a decline in total costs unless excess resources are eliminated or reassigned to value-adding areas.

Managers who better understand the underlying cost of making a product or performing a service can obtain new insight into product or service profitability. This improved information can result in management decisions about expanding or contracting product variety, raising or reducing prices, and entering or leaving a market. For example, managers may decide to raise selling prices of low-volume specialty output. Or they may decide to discontinue such production because that output consumes disproportionately more resources than does high-volume output.

ABC information can even affect decisions about plant and equipment investments and highlight the benefits that can be obtained if high-technology processes are implemented. Installing computerized equipment may reduce nonvalue-added production activities and increase efficiency. Activity-based costing helps managers understand the effects of the various activities that are needed in the changing business environment (especially relative to technology) and provides flexibility in designing systems that are able to cope with this environment. Although activity-based costing only indirectly changes the cost accumulation process, it directly changes the cost assignment process, making it more realistic regarding how and why costs are incurred.

ABC is a system for accurately allocating indirect or overhead costs. ABM is a system for improving performance by integrating ABC with the organization's strategy. Strategy and ABC work together.

Problems With ABC

Despite the definite advantage to ABC of accurate costs compared to traditional overhead allocation methods, many companies do not implement ABC. And, of the companies that do implement ABC, many soon discontinue it. This lack of sustainability is unexpected given the superiority of ABC. *Why would a company discontinue using a superior technique?* The answer to this question would probably explain why many companies do not adopt ABC in the first place. Paul Sharman, a Toronto resident and the president of Focused Management Inc., has found the following reasons why ABC implementation failed:[22]

- Software was not IT integrated. Accountants and operating managers want cost accounting to be part of their integrated general ledger, monthly reporting, analysis, performance measurement, and the associated network of operational systems. Small start-up companies developed ABC systems, generally in the late 1980s, as PC-based modelling tools. To this day they have not been integrated enterprisewide.

- ABC, and ABM, applications are generally not integrated into organization measurement and management systems. Central to managers' going about their business is accountability for their actions. Accountability is accomplished by having managers develop a plan, act upon the plan, and then monitor their performance. As ABC was largely deployed as a retrospective modelling analysis of prior-period results (often too late to be of any relevance), managers were not required to use ABC logic as part of the planning process. Successful applications of ABC use it to do planning.

- Most applications have been implemented poorly. The most daunting problem has been the lack of agreement as to what ABC is and how it should deployed. No institution took responsibility for developing standards for the development and deployment of ABC early in the process. Every consultant, software company, and author took it upon himself or herself to become the definitive source, yet the most successful were the ones with the best connections, not necessarily the greatest experience or competence. It has become quite common to see the presidents of ABC software companies making presentations on the subject to define what they perceive to be appropriate practices for ABC, and yet none of them have any management accounting experience. Writings are awash with advice on how to do and how not to do ABC. There is little consistency. Certainly, there has not been a serious process for the development, exposure, and creation of consensus toward what represents good practice.

Sharman adds that the frustrating part of ABC's lack of sustainability is that it remains a good and valid analytical technique. The technique needs to be incorporated into future management practices, but in such a way as to overcome the causes of its previous lack of longevity.

These problems with the implementation and application of ABC are not with the technique itself, but come from one major source: inadequate systems. The Hospital for Sick Children (Sick Kids) in Toronto was able to avoid these problems by introducing ABC with a variation of the German cost accounting methodology *Grenzplankostenrechnung*, or GPK.

CRITICISMS OF AND CONCLUSIONS ABOUT ABC

No currently existing accounting technique or system can provide management with exact cost information for every product or with all the information needed to make consistently perfect decisions. Activity-based costing, although it can provide better information than a traditional overhead allocation process, is not a panacea for all managerial difficulties. The following points should be noted as some of this method's shortcomings.

First, implementing ABC requires a significant investment in time and cost. If implementation is to be successful, substantial support is needed throughout the organization. An environment for change must be created, and this requires overcoming a variety of individual, organizational, and environmental barriers. Individual barriers are typically related to fear of (1) the unknown or a shift in the status quo, (2) a possible loss of status, or (3) the need to learn new skills.

Organizational barriers may be related to territorial, hierarchical, or corporate-culture issues. Environmental barriers are often built by employee groups including unions, regulatory agencies, or other stakeholders.

To overcome barriers, managers must recognize that those barriers exist, investigate their causes, and communicate information about ABC to all concerned parties. It is essential that top management be involved with and support the implementation process. Lack of commitment or involvement by top management will make achieving meaningful progress very slow and difficult. Additionally, employees and managers must be educated in some nontraditional techniques, including new terminology, concepts, and performance measurements. Such an educational process cannot occur overnight. Assuming that top management supports the changes in the internal accounting system and employees are educated about the system, additional time will be required to analyze the activities taking place in the activity centres, trace costs to those activities, and determine the appropriate cost drivers.

Another shortcoming of ABC is that it does not conform specifically with generally accepted accounting principles (see Exhibit 8-24). ABC would suggest that some traditionally designated period costs (such as research and development costs and some service department costs) be allocated to products, and that some traditionally designated product costs (such as factory building depreciation) not be allocated to products. Because of the differing perspectives, many companies implemented ABC as a supplemental system for internal reporting while continuing to use a more traditional system to account for product and period costs, allocate indirect costs, and prepare external financial statements. It is possible that, as ABC systems become more widely used, either the differences between GAAP and ABC cost accumulation will narrow or companies will become more adept at making the appropriate adjustments at the end of a period to bring internal information into compliance with GAAP's external reporting requirements. In either event, the need for two costing systems would be eliminated.

Inventoriable Indirect Cost	GAAP	ABC
Marketing, selling, advertising, and distribution costs	E	I
Interest	E	I, E
Research and experimental costs	E	I, E
General and administrative costs	E	I
Costs of strikes	P	E
Rework labour, scrap, and spoilage	P	I
Insurance	P	I, E
Distribution and warehousing	E	I

I = inventoriable; E = expensed; P = practice varies

EXHIBIT 8-24

Differences in Inventoriable Indirect Costs Under GAAP and ABC

SOURCE: Extracted from Richard B. Troxel, "The Relationship Between Activity-Based Costing and Generally Accepted Accounting Principles," *Handbook of Cost Management: 1998 Edition.* Boston: Warren, Gorham & Lamont/RIA Group, p. C5–10. Reprinted from *Handbook of Cost Management,* © 1998, by RIA, 395 Hudson Street, New York, NY, 10014.

As indicated by the following quote, another criticism that has been levelled at activity-based costing is that it does not promote total quality management and continuous improvement:

> Activity-based prescriptions for improved competitiveness usually entail steps that lead to selling more or doing less of what should not be sold or done in the first place. Indeed, activity-based cost information does nothing to change old remote-control,

top-down management behaviour. Simply because improved cost information becomes available, a company does not change its commitment to mass produce output at high speed, to control costs by encouraging people to manipulate processes, and to persuade customers to buy output the company has produced to cover its costs. North American businesses will not become long-term global competitors until they change the way managers think. No cost information, not even activity-based cost management information, will do that.[23]

Companies attempting to implement ABC as a cure-all for product failures, volume declines, or financial losses will quickly recognize that the statement above is true. However, companies can implement ABC and its related management techniques in support of and in conjunction with TQM, BPR, JIT, and any other world-class methodology. The customers of these companies will be provided with the best variety, price, quality, service, and cycle time of which they are capable. Not coincidentally, they should find their businesses booming. Activity-based costing and activity-based management can effectively support continuous improvement, short lead times, and flexible manufacturing by helping managers to do the following:

- Identify and monitor significant technology costs
- Trace many technology costs directly to products
- Promote achievement of market share through use of target costing (discussed in Chapter 10)
- Identify the cost drivers that create or influence cost
- Identify activities that do not contribute to perceived customer value (i.e., nonvalue-added activities or waste)
- Understand the impact of new technologies on all elements of performance
- Translate company goals into activity goals
- Analyze the performance of activities across business functions
- Analyze performance problems
- Promote standards of excellence

Activity-based costing, in and of itself, does not change the amount of overhead costs incurred, but it distributes those costs in a more equitable manner. ABC does not change the cost accumulation process, but it makes that process more realistic through a reflection of how and why costs are incurred. Finally, activity-based costing does not eliminate the need for assigning indirect overhead costs to products and services, but it uses a more appropriate means of doing so than has been possible under traditional methods. In summary, ABC is an improved cost accounting tool that helps managers know how the score is kept so that they can play the game more competitively.

Activity-based costing (ABC) is a cost management method that addresses shortcomings inherent in traditional costing methods, for the handling of indirect costs (or overhead). ABC focuses on understanding the cause-and-effect relationship between resource consumption and cost expenditure, so that overhead can be traced directly to the cost object—i.e., product, process, or customer—as opposed to being arbitrarily allocated. The ability to accurately trace overhead has gained importance as overhead costs continue to rise sharply for many manufacturers.[24]

ABC and ERP

ERP systems include modules or subsystems for ABC. An ERP system is developed from the underlying activities that an organization undertakes in pursuing its value creation chain or its part of another organization's value creation chain. Activities are coded and costs are assigned to activities. Products and services are also coded, which allows their costs to be accurately calculated.

Direct costs such as material and direct labour are readily assigned with the ABC modules of ERP systems. Overhead or fixed costs are more difficult to assign. ERP systems develop cost pools at various organizational levels, to whose products and services cost drivers are subsequently assigned with consistency and accuracy.

With ERP systems, the ABC system is fully integrated with all other subsystems such as process costing, financial statements, and fixed assets. The fixed asset costs or depreciation costs are automatically recorded in cost pools and then those costs are allocated to activities and then to products and services. Similarly, those allocated costs are transferred to inventory and/or cost of goods sold, and to the financial statements, which can be produced upon demand.

Purolator Courier Limited

ABC has succeeded at Purolator. Yet the company's ABC system would still benefit from some refining. The shortcomings of PUROLATOR'S present ABC model include these:

- Variable costs are the sole focus.
- Not all costs are considered with customer pricing decisions.
- Fixed network costs are being unfairly allocated to certain customers, leading to bad decisions.
- More fixed costs need to be allocated (e.g., the costs of information technology, human resource management, marketing, and sales).
- The model needs to be improved so that better short- and long-term decisions can be made.
- A decision support system (i.e., business intelligence) is needed.

Future ABC refinements being considered include the following:

- Use ABC to drive cost improvements.
- Continue to use ABC to determine sales prices, and expand use to drive cost reductions.
- Use best practices from depots to set company-wide benchmark costs for sorting, pick-up, and delivery costs.
- Implement SAP Event Manager so that customers can view the exact locations of their packages.
- Reward profitability rather than sales.
- Monitor more meaningful metrics, such as profitability per piece (rather than revenue per shipment) and customer profitability (rather than customer variable margin).

SOURCE: Janet Pierce, "The ABCs of Purolator Profitability," CMA/CAM-I Summit on Process, Performance, and Cost Management, October 23–24, 2007. Found at: http://www.cam-i.org/associations/ 3733/files/CMA%20B3%202007%20Janet%20Pierce%20CMA%20CAM-I% 20Presentation-ABC% 27s%20of%20Purolator%20Profitability. (Feb. 4, 2008).

CHAPTER SUMMARY

1 **How can reasonably accurate product and service cost information be developed?**

Activity-based costing (ABC) is a technique for allocating overhead. ABC has been identified as the most accurate costing method for modern manufacturing environments and as being crucial for strategic success. It allocates indirect or overhead costs based on the actual consumption of the resources by each activity and provides direction for improving the operational performance of systems. Activity-based costing is a costing system that allocates indirect or overhead costs to products or cost objects based on the level of activity. It adopts a two-stage process to allocate costs to products. First, costs are accumulated in relatively homogeneous activity cost pools. Second, these costs are traced to products or cost objects according to the level of activity. Activity-based management involves using activity-based costing to manage and improve the business.

2 **What are the differences among value-added, nonvalue-added, and business value-added activities?**

In a highly competitive business environment, companies need to reduce costs to make profits. One way to reduce costs without reducing quality is to decrease the number of nonvalue-added organizational activities. Value is added to products only during production (manufacturing company), performance (service company), or display (retail company). Most other activities, such as inspecting, moving, storing, and waiting, are nonvalue-added.

Activity-based management views organizational processes as value-added and nonvalue-added activities. Process mapping can be used to determine all the activities that take place in the production of a product or the performance of a service. Each activity is designated as value-added or nonvalue-added on a value chart. Management should strive to minimize or eliminate nonvalue-added activities because they create unnecessary costs and longer lead times without providing extra worth for customers.

A third category of activities, known as business value-added activities, also exists. Although customers would not want to pay for these activities, they are currently necessary to conduct business operations.

3 **What might cause decreased manufacturing cycle efficiency?**

Cycle efficiency will decrease when value-added processing time decreases and/or total nonvalue-added time increases. Product and process variety and complexity often cause a business's costs to increase because of unobserved increases in nonvalue-added activities. Simultaneous engineering and business process reengineering can help firms to accelerate the time to market of new products as well as reduce design or process complexity and the related costs (both direct and indirect) of these new products and of the processes by which they are made.

4 **How would the cost drivers in an activity-based costing system be developed?**

Activity-based management is also concerned with finding and selecting an appropriate number of activity cost pools and then identifying the cost drivers that best represent the firm's activities and are the underlying causes of costs. The activities chosen by management are those judged to reflect the major and most significant company processes. These activities normally overlap several functional areas and are said to occur horizontally across the firm's departmental lines. Cost drivers can also be used to evaluate the efficiency and effectiveness of the firm's activities.

Costs incurred in one area often result from activities in other areas—for instance, poor product quality or defects may be related to engineering design. Activity-based management highlights and provides feedback about relationships between and among functional areas as well as suggests areas that might benefit from process improvements or waste elimination. ABM allows and encourages the use of non-financial measures, such as lead time, as indicators of activity and performance.

5 **What distinguishes activity-based costing from conventional overhead allocation methods?**

Traditional or conventional costing systems often accumulate costs in one cost pool (or very few cost pools) and allocate those costs to products using one cost driver (generally related to direct labour or machine hours). Activity-based costing accumulates costs for activity centres in multiple cost pools at a variety of levels (unit, batch, product/process, and organizational/facility). ABC then allocates these costs to output using appropriate cost drivers (both volume-related and non-volume-related).

6 When is the use of activity-based costing appropriate?
ABC should be used when there are many products being made, or services provided, that draw upon resources differentially.

7 What are the benefits and limitations of using activity-based costing?
Costs are assigned more accurately, and managers can focus on controlling activities that create costs rather than trying to control the resulting costs themselves. Activity-based costing provides a more accurate way to assign overhead costs to products than what has been used traditionally.

Key Terms

Activity (p. 456)
Activity-based costing (p. 452)
Activity-based management (p. 455)
Activity centre (p. 467)
Activity cost driver (p. 468)
Batch-level cost (p. 464)
Benchmarking (p. 456)
Business process reengineering (p. 477)
Business value-added activity (p. 458)
Concurrent engineering (p. 477)
Cycle time (p. 460)
Facility-level cost (p. 465)
Idle time (p. 457)
Inspection time (p. 457)
Long-term variable cost (p. 465)
Manufacturing cycle efficiency (p. 460)
Mass customization (p. 475)

Nonvalue-added activity (p. 456)
Organizational-level cost (p. 465)
Process-level cost (p. 465)
Process map (p. 456)
Product complexity (p. 476)
Product-level cost (p. 465)
Product variety (p. 475)
Service variety (p. 475)
Simultaneous engineering (p. 477)
Transfer time (p. 457)
Unit-level cost (p. 464)
Value-added activity (p. 456)
Value-added processing time (p. 456)
Value-added service time (p. 456)
Value chart (p. 456)

Points to Remember

Manufacturing Cycle Efficiency (MCE)

$$MCE = \text{Value-added processing time} \div \text{Total cycle time}$$

1. Determine the activity centres of the organization.
2. Determine activities and the efforts needed to conduct those activities—the cost drivers.
3. Determine the resources the organization consumes in conducting its activities and the level at which those resources are consumed (unit, batch, product/process, organizational/facility).
4. Allocate the resources to the activity centres based on the cost drivers.
5. Allocate unit-, batch-, and product/process-level costs to products and services based on activities and activity cost drivers involved.
6. Treat organizational/facility-level costs as nonattachable to products.

DEMONSTRATION PROBLEM

Casper Manufacturing Co. uses a traditional approach to overhead allocation. The company produces two types of products: a regular (Model R) and a programmable (Model P) thermostat. In fiscal 2007, the company incurred $300,000 of manufacturing overhead and produced 40,000 units of Model R and 20,000 units of Model P. The predetermined manufacturing overhead rate used was $10 per direct labour hour. Based on this rate, the unit cost of each model in fiscal 2007 was as follows:

	Model R	Model P
Direct material	$ 6	$10
Direct labour	5	5
Manufacturing overhead	5	5
Total	$16	$20

The market is becoming more competitive, so the firm is considering the use of activity-based costing in fiscal 2008. Analysis of the fiscal 2007 data revealed that the $300,000 of overhead could be assigned to three activities as follows:

	Setups	Materials Handling	Equipment Operations	Total
Fiscal 2007 overhead	$20,000	$60,000	$220,000	$300,000

Management determined that the following activity drivers were appropriate for each overhead category:

	Activity Driver	2007 Activity Volume
Setups	Number of setups	160 setups
Materials handling	Kilograms of material	120,000 kilograms
Equipment operations	Machine hours	40,000 MH

Activity drivers and units produced in fiscal 2007 for each product were

	Model R	Model P
Number of units	40,000	20,000
Number of setups	100	60
Kilograms of materials handled	60,000	60,000
Machine hours	14,000	26,000

Required:

a. In fiscal 2007, the company used the traditional allocation based on direct labour hours. How much total manufacturing overhead was allocated to Model R units and to Model P units?

b. For fiscal 2007, how much total manufacturing overhead would have been allocated to each model if ABC had been used? Calculate a unit cost for Model R and Model P.

c. Casper Manufacturing has a policy of setting selling prices with unit costs in mind. What direction do you think the prices of Model R and Model P will take if the company begins using activity-based costing? Why?

Solution to Demonstration Problem

a. Model R: 40,000 units × $5 $200,000
   Model P: 20,000 units × $5   100,000
   Total allocated overhead $300,000

b. Cost per setup: $20,000 ÷ 160 = $125
   Cost per kilogram: $60,000 ÷ 120,000 = $0.50
   Cost per machine hour: $220,000 ÷ 40,000 = $5.50

	Model R			Model P	
100 setups × $125	$ 12,500		60 setups × $125	$ 7,500	
60,000 kilograms × $0.50	30,000		60,000 kilograms × $0.50	30,000	
14,000 MH × $5.50	77,000		26,000 MH × $5.50	143,000	
Assignable manufacturing OH	$119,500		Assignable manufacturing OH	$180,500	
Divided by units	÷ 40,000		Divided by units	÷ 20,000	
Manufacturing OH per unit	= $2.99		Manufacturing OH per unit	= $9.03	

	Model R	Model P
Direct material	$ 6.00	$10.00
Direct labour	5.00	5.00
Manufacturing overhead	2.99	9.03
Total activity-based product cost	$13.99	$24.03

c. Because the cost of Model R is $13.99 under ABC and $16 under traditional costing, the price of Model R should be reduced; this pricing decision will probably make Model R more competitive and increase its sales volume. In contrast, because the cost of Model P is $20 based on the traditional approach and $24.03 using ABC, Model P's price should be raised. ABC provides more accurate costing information so that management's abilities to plan, control, solve problems, and evaluate choices should be enhanced.

End-of-Chapter Materials

SELF-TEST QUESTIONS

(SOLUTIONS APPEAR AT THE END OF THE CHAPTER.)

1. An accounting system that collects financial and operating data on the basis of the underlying nature and extent of the cost drivers is:
    a. Activity-based costing
    b. Variable costing
    c. Weighted average costing
    d. FIFO costing

    (IMA adapted)

2. Cost drivers are:
    a. Activities that cause costs to increase as the activity increases
    b. Accounting techniques used to control costs
    c. Accounting measurements used to evaluate whether performance is proceeding according to plan
    d. A mechanical basis—such as machine hours, computer time, size of equipment, or size of the factory—used to assign costs to activities

    (IMA adapted)

3. What is the normal effect on the numbers of cost pools and allocation bases when an activity-based cost (ABC) system replaces a traditional cost system?

	Cost Pools	Allocation Bases
a.	No effect	No effect
b.	Increase	No effect
c.	No effect	Increase
d.	Increase	Increase

    (Material from the *Uniform CPA Examination Questions and Unofficial Answers*, Copyright © 1994 by the American Institute of Certified Public Accountants, Inc., is adapted with permission.)

4. Which of the following statements about activity-based costing is not true?
    a. Activity-based costing is useful for allocating marketing and distribution costs.
    b. Activity-based costing is more likely to result in major differences from traditional cost systems if the firm manufactures only one product rather than multiple products.
    c. In activity-based costing, cost drivers are what cause costs to be incurred.
    d. Activity-based costing differs from traditional costing systems in that products are not cross-subsidized.

    (IMA adapted)

Questions 5 and 6 are based on the following information.

Spectra Fashions Inc. is preparing its annual profit plan. As part of its analysis of the profitability of individual products, the controller estimates the amount of overhead that should be allocated to the individual product lines from the information given as follows:

	Ladies' Umbrellas	Men's Umbrellas
Units produced	25	25
Material moves per product line	5	15
Direct labour hours per unit	200	200
Budgeted materials handling costs	$50,000	

5. Under a costing system that allocates overhead on the basis of direct labour hours, the materials handling costs allocated to one ladies' umbrella would be:
   a. $1,000
   b. $500
   c. $2,000
   d. $5,000

   (IMA adapted)

6. Under activity-based costing (ABC), the materials handling costs allocated to one ladies' umbrella would be:
   a. $1,000
   b. $500
   c. $1,500
   d. $2,500

   (IMA adapted)

7. Which of the following kinds of properties should you consider when you evaluate an activity-based management system as a cost management tool?
   a. Behavioural, cultural, and technical properties
   b. Behavioural, ethical, and financial properties
   c. Cultural, ethical, and financial properties
   d. Financial, ethical, and technical properties

8. Which of the following statements best describes activity-based management?
   a. It is an approach developed in response to the competitive pressures of today's global market.
   b. It does not use activity-based costing to improve a business.
   c. It is designed to set the goals and objectives of an organization.
   d. It focuses on functional areas and products.

Use the following information to answer Questions 9 and 10.

Fine Cutlery Inc. is a manufacturer of quality carving knives. The company has always used a plantwide allocation rate for allocating manufacturing overhead to its products, but the plant manager believes that it is time to change to a better method of cost allocation. The accounting department has established the following relationships between production activities and manufacturing overhead costs.

Activity	Cost Driver	Allocation Rate
Materials handling	Number of parts	$4 per part
Assembly	Labour hours	$40 per hour
Inspection	Time spent by item at inspection station	$6 per minute

The previous plantwide allocation rate method was based on direct manufacturing labour hours, and if that method is used, the allocation rate is $400 per labour hour.

9. Assume that a batch of 1,000 carving knives requires 2,000 parts, 20 direct manufacturing labour hours, and 30 minutes of inspection time. What are the indirect manufacturing costs per carving knife to produce a batch of 1,000 carving knives, assuming the previous plantwide allocation rate method is used?
   a. $8.00
   b. $9.80
   c. $800.00
   d. $980.00

10. Assume that a batch of 100 carving knives requires 200 parts, 12 direct manufacturing labour hours, and 5 minutes of inspection time. What are the indirect manufacturing costs per carving knife to produce a batch of 1,000 carving knives, assuming the activity-based method of allocation is used?
    a. $4.80
    b. $8.00
    c. $13.10
    d. $48.00

Self-Test Questions 7–10 are extracted from *Management Accounting Examination*, published by the Certified General Accountants Association of Canada (© CGA-Canada 2001). Reprinted with permission.

QUESTIONS

1. Why does management need product cost information?

2. Why is it not possible to develop totally accurate product or service costs?

3. Define value-added activity and nonvalue-added activity. Compare these types of activities and give examples of each. Why is the concept of value-added activities a customer-oriented notion?

4. What is a business value-added activity? Why is it not always possible to eliminate this type of activity? Give an example, other than the one in the text, of a business value-added activity that it would not be possible to eliminate.

5. Define cycle efficiency and explain how it is calculated in a manufacturing environment and in a service environment.

6. What is a cost driver and how is it used?

7. Does conventional cost accounting use cost drivers? If so, explain how. If not, explain why.

8. Why is ABM considered a process view and ABC considered a cost assignment view of an organization?

9. What are the four levels of cost drivers? Which level is the focus in traditional costing systems?

10. Briefly describe the cost accumulation and assignment process in an ABC system.

11. Why do the more traditional methods of overhead assignment overload standard products with overhead costs, and how does ABC improve overhead assignments?

12. What organizational characteristics of a company might indicate that ABC could provide improved information to the company's managers?

13. Explain why product or service variety creates substantial overhead costs.

14. How can (a) simultaneous engineering and (b) business process reengineering help reduce process complexity?

15. Why can control in an activity-based management system be more effective than control in a conventional system?

16. Why is ABC often adopted as a stand-alone control system rather than as the main product costing system?

17. Can some firms expect to benefit more than others from adopting ABC? Why or why not?

18. What are the shortcomings of activity-based costing as an accounting system methodology? How might these be overcome?

19. Are ABC systems part of ERP systems?

20. How are activities included in both ERP systems and ABC systems?

EXERCISES

1. (LO 1, 2, 3) Match each item in the right-hand column with a term in the left-hand column.

a.	Activity-based costing	1. Something that increases the worth of a product to a customer
b.	Value chart	
c.	Process map	2. A measure of the demands placed on an activity
d.	Activity driver	
e.	Manufacturing cycle efficiency	3. A measure of processing efficiency
f.	Long-term variable cost	4. Something that increases the time and cost of production but not the worth of a product to a customer
g.	Value-added activity	
h.	Business process reengineering	
i.	Nonvalue-added activity	5. A cost created by a group of things processed at a single time
j.	Batch-level cost	
		6. Process innovation and redesign
		7. A cost that has traditionally been viewed as fixed
		8. A flowchart indicating all steps in producing a product or performing a service
		9. A representation of the value-added and nonvalue-added activities and the time spent in these activities from the beginning to the end of a process
		10. A system that collects costs according to the nature and extent of activities

EXERCISES

2. (LO 1, 2, 3) Match each item in the right-hand column with a term in the left-hand column.

<table>
<tr><td>a.</td><td>Activity centre</td><td>1.</td><td>A process that involves all design and production personnel from the beginning of a project</td></tr>
<tr><td>b.</td><td>Pareto principle</td><td></td><td></td></tr>
<tr><td>c.</td><td>Product complexity</td><td></td><td></td></tr>
<tr><td>d.</td><td>Transfer time</td><td>2.</td><td>A methodology that focuses on activities to improve the value delivered to customers</td></tr>
<tr><td>e.</td><td>Activity-based management</td><td></td><td></td></tr>
<tr><td>f.</td><td>Simultaneous engineering</td><td></td><td></td></tr>
<tr><td>g.</td><td>Mass customization</td><td>3.</td><td>The number of components, operations, or processes needed to make a product</td></tr>
<tr><td>h.</td><td>Activity</td><td></td><td></td></tr>
<tr><td>i.</td><td>Idle time</td><td></td><td></td></tr>
<tr><td>j.</td><td>Product variety</td><td>4.</td><td>The relatively low-cost bulk production of products to customer specifications</td></tr>
<tr><td></td><td></td><td>5.</td><td>The time spent in storage or waiting for processing</td></tr>
<tr><td></td><td></td><td>6.</td><td>The time spent moving products or components from one place to another</td></tr>
<tr><td></td><td></td><td>7.</td><td>A repetitive action performed to fulfill a business function</td></tr>
<tr><td></td><td></td><td>8.</td><td>A part of the organization for which management wants separate reporting</td></tr>
<tr><td></td><td></td><td>9.</td><td>The different types of products produced in an organization</td></tr>
<tr><td></td><td></td><td>10.</td><td>A fundamental principle often referred to as the 20:80 rule</td></tr>
</table>

3. (LO 2) Baldwin and Williams opened a legal practice ten months ago. Williams, in a discussion with Lawrence Chung, an accountant, listed all the different tasks she performs during a week. Chung suggested that she list her activities as well as her partner's activities for a typical week. This list follows:

Activity	Time (hours)
Take depositions	10.4
Do legal research for cases	14.2
Make calls concerning legal cases	6.6
Travel to/from court	7.8
Litigate cases	11.9
Write correspondence	9.9
Eat lunch with clients	6.8
Eat dinner at office while watching the soaps	2.5
Contemplate litigation strategies	10.7
Play golf	3.2
Write wills for clients	4.9
Assign tasks to the firm's secretary	6.7
Fill out time sheets for client work	10.1

Required:
a. List the value-added activities and explain why they are value-added.
b. List the nonvalue-added activities and explain why they are nonvalue-added.
c. Why might it be more difficult for a small, start-up law firm to reduce the nonvalue-added activities listed in your answer to part (b) than it might be for a large, well-established law firm?

4. (LO 2) Soprano Construction Company constructs beachfront vacation homes. Mr. Soprano, the CEO, has developed the following information about the average length of time it takes to complete one home:

Operation	Average Number of Days
Receive materials	1
Store materials	6
Move materials to job site	2
Measure and cut materials	7
Set up and move scaffolding	5
Wait for crew who are completing a previous job	6
Frame structure	4
Cut and frame doors and windows	3
Build gas fireplace	4
Attach siding and seal joints	5
Construct inside of home	9
Inspect home (by municipal inspectors)	1

Required:

a.   What are the value-added activities and their total time?

b.   What are the nonvalue-added activities and their total time?

c.   How did you classify the inspection time? Why? Could this have been classified in another manner? Explain.

5. (LO 2) Spectra Ltd. is investigating the costs of schedule changes in its factory. The following is a list of the activities, estimated times, and average costs required for a single schedule change.

Activity	Estimated Time	Average Cost
Review impact of orders	30 min–2 h	$ 300
Reschedule orders	15 min–24 h	800
Reschedule production orders	15 min–1 h	75
Contact production supervisor; stop production and change over; generate paperwork to return materials	5 min–2 h	45
Return excess inventory and allocate new materials	20 min–6 h	1,500
Generate new production paperwork; change routings; change bill of materials	15 min–4 h	500
Change purchasing schedule	10 min–8 h	2,100
Collect paperwork from the floor	15 min	75
Review new line schedule	15 min–30 min	100
Account for overtime premiums	3 h–10 h	1,000
Total		$6,495

Required:

a.   Which of the previous activities, if any, are value-added?

b.   What is the cost driver in this situation?

c.   How can the cost driver be controlled and the activities eliminated?

6. (LO 2) You are planning a weekend trip to Vancouver. You will be travelling by plane and will need a hotel room when you arrive. These two reservations will be made by you through 1-800 numbers. Because you are planning to stay in the city, you will take the airport shuttle service to and from your hotel and will not need a car.

Required:

a.   Describe the process of preparing for this trip by listing the activities in which you would engage.

b.   Indicate which of the above listed activities are value-added and which are nonvalue-added.

c.   How might you reduce or eliminate the time spent in nonvalue-added activities?

7. (LO 2) The College of Business has recently selected you as its representative on a committee to improve the preregistration process at your university.

Required:

a.   Describe the activities that make up the current preregistration process.

b.   Estimate the time required for the various activities listed in part (a).

c.   What activities do you perceive as not adding value and why?

d.   How would you improve the preregistration process?

8. (LO 2) Jack Sheriton is the front desk clerk at the Salem Inn. Jack performs the following functions when a guest checks into the hotel:

Function	Time (minutes)
Greet guest and ask for name	1.0
Find reservation in computer system	1.0
Ask guest to fill in card with personal information: name, address, credit card number	0.5
Wait for guest to fill in card	3.0
Answer and talk on phone to another guest	2.5
Ask guest what type of room he/she prefers and listen to response	1.5
Check computer system for this preferred room type	1.5
Obtain plastic key card and program it	0.5
Put key card in paper sleeve and write guest room number on it	1.0
Ask guest if he/she needs help with luggage	0.5
Get bellhop if help is needed	2.0
Wish guest a pleasant stay	0.5

Required:
a. Indicate whether each activity is value-added or nonvalue-added.
b. Calculate the cycle time and service cycle efficiency of this process.
c. Make recommendations to increase the service cycle efficiency.

9. (LO 2, 3) The following functions are performed in making chowder at Brady's Chowder Shoppe.

Function	Time (minutes)
Receiving ingredients	45
Moving ingredients to stockroom	15
Storing ingredients in stockroom	7,200
Moving ingredients from stockroom	15
Mixing ingredients	50
Cooking ingredients	185
Bottling ingredients	90
Moving bottled chowder to warehouse	20
Storing bottled chowder in warehouse	10,080
Moving bottled chowder from warehouse to trucks	30

Required:
a. Indicate whether each activity is value-added or nonvalue-added.
b. Calculate the cycle time and manufacturing cycle efficiency of this process.
c. Make some recommendations to Sean Brady (the owner) that would improve the company's manufacturing cycle efficiency.

10. (LO 4) The following is a list of overhead cost pools at Williams Cosmetics Inc.
a. Equipment maintenance
b. Factory utilities
c. Factory depreciation
d. Machinery rent
e. Quality inspection labour
f. Computer operations
g. Materials handling
h. Setup
i. Engineering changes
j. Advertising
k. Freight for materials
l. Scheduling meetings
m. Obtaining purchase order quotes
n. Filing purchase orders
o. Checking on overdue purchase orders

Required:
Identify a cost driver for each and explain why it is appropriate.

EXERCISES

11. (LO 4) The following activities take place at the local pizza delivery shop.
    a. Pizza oven electricity
    b. Delivery vehicle repairs, maintenance, and insurance
    c. Building insurance
    d. Plastic cups for side orders of anchovies and jalapenos
    e. Property taxes
    f. Gasoline for delivery vehicles
    Required:
    Determine the cost drivers for the above activities.

12. (LO 4) Katie's Kopies is a self-service photocopy outlet that has 25 photocopiers for customer use. A manager is always on duty to handle complaints or problems and monitor the machines.
    a. Store manager's salary
    b. Electricity expense
    c. Depreciation on the photocopiers
    d. Property taxes on the building
    e. Order costs for purchasing paper and toner
    f. Cost of paper
    g. Cost of toner
    h. Cost of labour to place paper and toner in machines
    i. Repairs expense
    j. Insurance expense on photocopiers
    k. Advertising and promotion expense
    Required:
    Determine whether each of the above costs for Katie's Kopies is a unit-level (U), batch-level (B), product/process-level (P), or organizational-level (O) cost.

13. (LO 4) Classify each of the following costs as being incurred at a unit level (U), batch level (B), product/process level (P), or organizational/facility level (O).
    a. Cost of printing books at a publishing house
    b. Cost of preparing payroll cheques
    c. Cost of supplies used in research and development on an existing product
    d. Salary of the vice-president of marketing
    e. Cost of developing an engineering change order
    f. Depreciation on the camera at the drivers' licence office in the Ministry of Transportation
    g. Salary of guard for five-storey headquarters building
    h. Cost of paper and cover for a passport

14. (LO 5) Triton Ltd. is concerned about the profit generated by its regular paperback dictionaries. Kate Roberts, the CEO, is considering producing only the top-quality, hand-sewn dictionaries with gold-edged pages. Triton currently uses production hours to assign its $500,000 of production overhead to both types of dictionaries. Some additional data follow.

	Regular	Hand-Sewn
Direct costs	$2,500,000	$1,200,000
Number produced	1,000,000	700,000
Production hours	85,000	15,000
Square metres of space occupied	1,500	2,500
Inspection hours	5,000	25,000

The $500,000 of production overhead comprises $100,000 of utilities, $100,000 of factory/storage rent, and $300,000 of quality control inspectors' salaries.
Required:
a. How much production overhead is currently being assigned to the regular and to the hand-sewn dictionaries?
b. Determine the production overhead cost that should be assigned to each type of dictionary, using the activity driver appropriate for each type of overhead cost.
c. Should Triton Publishing stop producing the regular dictionaries? Explain.

15. (LO 4) As the manager of the five-employee Purchasing Department at Vancouver Ltd., you have decided to implement an activity-based product costing system. Annual departmental costs are $710,250 per year. Finding the best supplier takes the majority of the department's effort and creates the majority of the department's costs.

Activity	Allocation Measure	Number of of People	Cost
Find best supplier	Number of telephone calls	3	$450,000
Issue purchase orders	Number of purchase orders	1	150,000
Review receiving reports	Number of receiving reports	1	110,250

During the year, the Purchasing Department makes 150,000 telephone calls, issues 10,000 purchase orders, and reviews 7,000 receiving reports. Many purchase orders are received in a single shipment.

One product manufactured by the company required the following activities in the Purchasing Department over the year: 118 telephone calls, 37 purchase orders, and 28 receiving reports.

Required:

a. What amount of Purchasing Department cost should be assigned to the manufacturing of this product?

b. If 200 units of the product are manufactured during the year, what is the Purchasing Department's cost per unit?

c. This analysis has caused you to investigate the need for such complexity in this product. After engaging in discussions with Vancouver Ltd.'s engineering design personnel and some of the company's best suppliers, it has been agreed that the number of parts in this product can be reduced and that suppliers will monitor parts supply levels on an ongoing basis. If the same type of analysis is performed for other products, you estimate that departmental costs, on average, will decrease by 25%. You have also estimated that, under the new circumstances, making 200 units of this product next year will only require 20 telephone calls, 15 purchase orders, and 8 receipts. What would be the Purchasing Department's new cost per unit for this product next year?

16. (LO 4) For the past 20 years, Williams Investigations Corp. has maintained an internal Research and Development (R&D) Department that provides services to in-house manufacturing departments. Costs of operating this department have been rising dramatically. You have suggested instituting an activity-based costing system to control costs and to charge service users for product and process development. The principal departmental expense is professional salaries. Activities in this department fall into three major categories. These categories, estimated related professional salary costs, and suggested allocation bases follow.

Activity	Salary Cost	Allocation Base
Evaluation of market opportunities	$ 600,000	Hours of professional time
Product development	1,800,000	Number of products developed
Process design	2,400,000	Number of engineering changes

In the fiscal year, the R&D Department worked 15,000 hours evaluating market opportunities, worked on the development of 100 new products, and responded to 500 engineering-process change requests.

Required:

a. Determine the allocation rate for each activity in the R&D Department.

b. How can the rates developed in part (a) be used for evaluating output relative to costs incurred in the R&D Department?

c. How much cost would be charged to a manufacturing department that had consumed 1,000 hours of market research time, received help in developing 14 new products, and requested 75 engineering process changes?

d. What alternative does the firm have to maintaining an internal R&D department? What potential benefits and problems might arise if the company pursued this alternative?

EXERCISES

17. (LO 4) Nicholas Sperry-Rand Plastics makes large plastic water bottles and plastic composite control panels for aircraft. Plastic bottles are relatively simple to produce and are made in large quantities. The control panels are more complicated to produce because they must be customized to individual plane types. Nicholas Sperry-Rand sells 200,000 plastic bottles annually and 5,000 control panels. A variety of information follows related to the annual production and sale of these products.

	Plastic Bottles	Control Panels
Revenues	$6,000,000	$13,000,000
Direct labour hours	2,000	53,000
Machine hours	120,000	86,250
Direct material	1,360,000	1,200,000

Labour is paid at $14 per hour. Production overhead consists of $9,500,000 of supervisors' salaries, labour fringe benefits, design and engineering, and other human-related costs and $2,500,000 of machine-related costs. Administrative costs total $1,200,000 and are allocated to individual product lines.

Required:
a. Calculate the profit or loss on each product if total overhead (production and administrative) is assigned according to direct labour hours.
b. Calculate the profit or loss on each product if total overhead (production and administrative) is assigned according to machine hours.
c. Calculate the profit or loss on each product if human-related overhead is assigned according to direct labour hours, machine-related overhead is assigned according to machine hours, and administrative overhead is assigned according to dollars of revenue.
d. Calculate the profit or loss on each product if overhead is assigned as in part (c) except that administrative overhead is deducted from total company income rather than being allocated to the individual product lines.
e. Does your answer in part (a), (b), (c), or (d) provide the best representation of the profit contributed by each product? Explain.

18. (LO 6) Under what circumstances can activity-based management have a negative impact on an organization? Explain briefly, and include an example.

Extract from *Management Accounting 2 Examination*, published by the Certified General Accountants Association of Canada (© CGA-Canada 1999). Reprinted with permission.

19. (LO 6) A company manufactures two types of windows: aluminum and PVC. The actual cost accounting system is very simple. Direct costs are traced to products, and a mark-up of 40% is added to establish the sale price. Aluminum windows are usually customized, whereas PVC windows are standard. The indirect costs are not separated as to aluminum and PVC production.

The controller of the company has been asked to implement an activity-based costing and management (ABCM) system in the company. He has some training in ABCM, but nobody else in the firm has been exposed to this new costing approach.

The preliminary analysis performed with activity-based costing has shown that aluminum windows are much more expensive to manufacture than expected. In fact, their unit cost is so high that at the current price, the company is losing money with this type of window. The controller wonders why this is the case and how ABCM information can be used by the company to improve profitability.

Required:
a. Explain why, with ABCM, aluminum windows would cost more than expected.
b. Briefly describe the types of decisions the company could make with the ABCM information.
c. Identify *five* major steps of activity-based analysis that could be performed to review the manufacturing process.

Extract from *Management Accounting 2 Examination*, published by the Certified General Accountants Association of Canada (© CGA-Canada 2002). Reprinted with permission.

20. (LO 7) Explain the similarities and differences among ABC, process costing, and job-order costing.

PROBLEMS

1. (LO 2) You are the new controller of David Faber Ltd., a small job shop that manufactures special-order desk nameplate stands. As you review the records, you find that all of the orders are shipped late, the average process time for any order is three weeks, and the time actually spent in production operations is two days. The president of the company has called you to discuss missed delivery dates.
   Required:
   Prepare a report for the executive officers in which you address
   a. Possible causes of the problem
   b. How a value chart could be used to address the problem

2. (LO 2, 3) Linda Goldberg has just been elected mayor of Ottawa. She is highly concerned about deficit spending by her city. As a manager of the city's road construction workers, you have been asked to evaluate their performance in an effort to reduce costs. You noted the following activities after spending some time observing the workers.

Activity	Time (hours)
Driving to the work location	1
Blocking off the road	2
Setting up the road stripper	3
Drinking coffee	13
Stripping the road	10
Setting up the asphalt layer machine	7
Talking to each other	4
Laying asphalt on the road	5
Unblocking the road	3
Loading equipment and leaving the area	2

   Required:
   a. What are the value-added activities and times?
   b. What are the nonvalue-added activities and times?
   c. Calculate the cycle efficiency. Discuss the result. What suggestions can you offer the mayor regarding the road construction operations?

3. (LO 2) As company president, you asked Josh Lyman, the management accountant, to determine the cost of the nonvalue-added activities for each production run of the product as shown in the value chart in Exhibit 8-3. He gathered the following information:

Annual salary for receiving clerks	$28,000
Annual salary for quality control personnel	40,000
Annual salary for material/product handlers (movers)	19,000
Annual salary for setup personnel	26,000

   Each unit requires one square metre of storage space in a 100,000-square-metre storage building. Depreciation per year on the building is $125,000, and property taxes and insurance total $35,000. Assume a 365-day year for plant assets and a 240-day year for personnel. Where a range of time is indicated, assume an average. Waiting time (all time other than production and storage time) is estimated at $50 per lot per day. Each day of delay in shipping time is estimated to cost $50 per unit per day. The average production lot size is 500 units.
   Required:
   Determine the total cost of nonvalue-added activities per unit.

4. (LO 4, 5) Catherine Seguin Corp. makes grey metal five-drawer desks, and occasionally takes custom orders. The company's overhead costs for a month in which no custom desks are produced are as follows:

PROBLEMS

Purchasing department for raw materials and supplies (10 purchase orders per month)	$ 5,000
Setting up machines for production runs (4 times per month after maintenance checks)	1,240
Utilities (based on 3,200 machine hours)	160
Supervisors (2)	8,000
Machine and building depreciation (fixed)	5,500
Quality control and inspections (performed on random selection of desks each day; one quality control worker)	2,500
Total overhead costs	$22,400

Factory operations are highly automated and overhead is allocated to products based on machine hours. This allocation process has resulted in a manufacturing overhead allocation rate of $7 per machine hour ($22,400 ÷ 3,200 MH).

In June, six orders were filled for custom desks. Selling prices were based on charges for actual direct materials, actual direct labour, and the $7 per machine hour for an estimated 200 hours of machine time. During that month, the following costs were incurred for 3,200 hours of machine time.

Purchasing department for raw materials and supplies (22 purchase orders)	$ 6,200
Setting up machines for production runs (18 times)	1,640
Utilities (based on 3,200 machine hours)	160
Supervisors (2)	8,000
Machine and building depreciation (fixed)	5,500
Quality control and inspections	2,980
Engineering design and specification costs	3,000
Total overhead costs	$27,480

Required:

a. How much of the purchasing cost is variable and how much is fixed? What types of purchasing costs would fit into each of these categories?

b. Why might the number of machine setups have increased from four to 18 when only six custom orders were received?

c. Why might the cost of quality control and inspections have increased?

d. Why did the engineering design and specification costs included during June not appear in the original overhead cost listing?

e. If Catherine Seguin Corp. were to adopt activity-based costing, what would you suggest as the cost drivers for each of the overhead cost items?

f. Do you think the custom orders should have been priced using an overhead rate of $7 per machine hour? Explain the reasoning behind your answer.

5. (LO 4, 5) Brash Manufacturing Ltd. has recently finished an analysis of its manufacturing labour-related costs. As vice-president of finance, you are concerned about controlling these costs. The following summary presents the major categories of labour costs identified by Brash's Accounting Department.

Category	Amount
Base wages	$63,000,000
Healthcare benefits	10,500,000
Payroll taxes	5,040,000
Overtime	8,700,000
Training	1,875,000
Retirement benefits	6,900,000
Workplace Safety and Insurance Board (WSIB)	1,200,000

Your assistant has identified the following potential cost drivers for labour-related costs as well as their annual volume levels.

PROBLEMS

Potential Activity Driver	Annual Volume Level
Average number of factory employees	2,100
Number of new hires	300
Number of regular labour hours worked	3,150,000
Number of overtime hours worked	288,000
Volume of production in units	12,000,000
Number of production process changes	600
Number of production schedule changes	375
Total factory wages	$71,700,000

Required:

a. Use the appropriate activity driver to determine the per unit cost for each labour cost pool category.

b. Based on your judgment and your calculations in part (a), which activity driver should receive the most attention from company managers in their efforts to control labour-related costs? How much of the total labour-related cost is attributable to this activity driver?

c. In the contemporary environment, many firms are asking their employees to work record levels of overtime. What activity driver does this practice suggest is a major contributor to labour-related costs? Explain.

6. (LO 4, 5) The budgeted manufacturing overhead costs of West Wing Ltd. for the year are as follows.

Type of Cost	Cost Amount
Electric power	$ 600,000
Work cells	3,600,000
Materials handling	1,200,000
Quality control inspections	1,200,000
Product runs (machine setups)	600,000
Total budgeted overhead costs	$7,200,000

For the last five years, the cost accounting department has been charging overhead production costs based on machine hours. The estimated capacity for the fiscal year is 1,200,000 machine hours.

You have recently attended a seminar on activity-based costing and believe that implementation of ABC might give the company an edge in pricing over its competitors. At your request, the production manager has provided the following data regarding expected activity for the cost drivers of the preceding budgeted overhead costs for the fiscal year.

Type of Cost	Activity Drivers
Electric power	120,000 kilowatt hours
Work cells	720,000 square metres
Materials handling	240,000 material moves
Quality control inspections	120,000 inspections
Product runs (machine setups)	60,000 product runs

You have just received an order for 5,000 doors from a local construction company. The head of cost accounting has prepared the following cost estimate for producing the 5,000 doors.

Direct material cost	$120,000
Direct labour cost	$360,000
Machine hours	12,000
Direct labour hours	18,000
Electric power (kilowatt hours)	1,200
Work cells (square metres)	9,600
Number of materials handling moves	120
Number of quality control inspections	60
Number of product runs (setups)	30

Required:

a. What is the predetermined overhead rate if the traditional measure of machine hours is used?

b. What is the manufacturing cost per door under the present cost accounting system?

PROBLEMS

c.   What is the manufacturing cost per door under the proposed ABC method?

d.   If the prior two costing systems will result in different cost estimates, which cost accounting system is preferable as a pricing policy and why?

(Source: Reprinted by permission of Institute of Management Accountants, Montvale, N.J., USA, www.imanet.org.)

7. (LO 4; 5, 6) Edmonton Cosmetic Hospital is under increasing pressure for the charges it assesses its patients. Except for an explicit consideration of direct costs for surgery, medication, and other treatments, the current pricing system is an ad hoc one based on pricing norms for the geographical area. As the hospital controller, you have suggested that pricing would be less arbitrary if there were a tighter relationship between costs and patient charges. As a first step, you have determined that most costs can be assigned to one of the following three cost pools.

Cost Pool	Amount	Activity Driver	Quantity
Professional salaries	$900,000	Professional hours	30,000 hours
Building costs	450,000	Square metres used	15,000 square metres
Risk management	320,000	Patients served	1,000 patients

Hospital services are classified into three broad categories. The services and their volume measures follow.

Service	Professional Hours	Square Metres	Number of Patients
Surgery	6,000	1,200	200
Inpatient care	20,000	12,000	500
Outpatient care	4,000	1,800	300

Required:

a.   Determine the allocation rate for each cost pool.

b.   Allocate costs among the three hospital services using the allocation rates derived in part (a).

c.   What bases might be used as activity cost drivers to allocate the costs of the services among the patients served by the hospital? Defend your selections.

8. (LO 4, 5, 6) Poë Chemical Products has a total of $1,551,000 in overhead costs. The company's products and related statistics follow.

	Product A	Product B
Direct material (in kilograms)	93,000	127,000
Direct labour hours	20,000	25,000
Machine hours	35,000	15,000
Number of setups	200	500
Number of units produced	10,000	5,000

Additional data:

One direct labour hour costs $12, and the 220,000 kilograms of material were purchased for $363,000.

Required:

a.   Assume that Poë Chemical Products uses direct labour hours to apply overhead to products. Determine the total cost for each product and the cost per unit.

b.   Assume that Poë Chemical Products uses machine hours to apply overhead to products. Determine the total cost for each product and the cost per unit.

c.   Determine the total cost for each product and the cost per unit, assuming that Poë Chemical Products uses the following activity centres, cost amounts, and activity drivers to apply overhead to products.

Cost Pool	Cost Driver	Cost	Volume
Utilities	Number of machine hours	$500,000	50,000
Setup	Number of setups	105,000	700
Materials handling	Kilograms of material	946,000	220,000

9. (LO 4, 5, 7) Glow By Jabot Ltd. has identified activity centres to which overhead costs are assigned. The cost pool amounts for these centres and their selected cost drivers for fiscal 2007 are as follows.

PROBLEMS

Cost Pool	Cost	Cost Driver	Volume
Utilities	$487,500	Machine hours	65,000
Scheduling and setup	273,000	Setups	780
Materials handling	640,000	Kilograms of material	1,600,000
Building depreciation	457,600	Square metres occupied	35,200

The company's products and other operating statistics follow.

	Product A	Product B	Product C
Direct material and labour costs	$40,000	$65,000	$90,000
Kilograms of materials used	500,000	300,000	800,000
Machine hours	35,000	10,000	20,000
Number of setups	130	380	270
Square metres occupied	12,000	8,300	14,900
Number of units produced	63,000	10,000	40,000
Direct labour hours	32,000	18,000	50,000

Required:

a. Determine total unit product cost. Apply overhead to products with activity-based costing using the appropriate cost drivers for each type of cost.

b. Before installing an ABC system, Glow By Jabot Ltd. allocated manufacturing overhead to products using direct labour hours. Determine the pre-ABC total unit product cost.

c. The company operates in a fairly noncompetitive market and product prices are set at 20% over cost. Determine the selling price for each product using the product costs determined (1) in part (a) and (2) in part (b).

d. Explain how ABC improves product cost information and, thus, determination of selling prices for Glow By Jabot Ltd.

10. (LO 4, 5, 6, 7) Count D. Cash, CMA, was not entirely convinced that his fees for different types of services were based on accurate costs. His son, Petty, who was home for the summer, had just received an A in a managerial accounting course where he learned about ABC. Petty suggested applying ABC to find more accurate costs for his father's accounting and auditing, tax, and management services. They identified the following activity centres, costs and quantities, and cost drivers.

Activity Centre	Cost	Quantity	Cost Driver
Planning and review	$ 65,240	93,200	Billable time (hours)
Information Technology	72,000	7,200	Computational time (hours)
Personnel	56,160	52	Number of people
Library	21,948	186	Books and periodicals purchased
Programming	56,160	4,160	Programming time (hours)
Building	87,000	15,000	Square metres
Administration	150,000	500	Number of clients
Total	$508,508		

Petty also compiled the following statistics for each of the services provided to clients during the past year.

	Accounting & Auditing	Tax	Management
Direct costs	$1,952,000	$1,610,000	$732,000
Hours of billable time	48,800	32,200	12,200
Hours of computational time	4,320	2,400	480
Number of people	30	16	6
New purchases for the library	51	99	36
Hours of programming time	1,200	520	2,440
Square metres occupied	8,800	4,875	1,325
Number of clients	170	280	50

Required:

a. Assign each of the activity costs to the three services.

b. Determine the total cost of each class of service.

PROBLEMS

c. Prior to this year, Count D. Cash applied overhead based only on professional labour hours (billable time). The overhead rate was found simply by dividing total budgeted overhead by total budgeted professional hours. Using the original information, (1) what overhead rate would Count D. Cash have used for the current year, and (2) how much overhead would have been assigned to each service area?

d. Assuming Count D. Cash bases his service prices on the cost of rendering the services, in general how would the relative prices of services differ between parts (b) and (c)?

11. (LO 4, 5, 6, 7) Cricket Components Ltd. makes three products: fax stands, organizers, and printer stands. In fiscal 2010, the company incurred $1,000,000 of manufacturing overhead costs and produced 100,000 fax stands, 10,000 organizers, and 30,000 printer stands. Using the company's overhead application rate of $10 per direct labour hour, the per unit product cost was as follows:

	Fax Stands	Organizers	Printer Stands
Direct material	$ 4.00	$15.00	$ 8.00
Direct labour	6.00	18.30	9.00
Manufacturing overhead	4.00	30.00	10.00
Total	$14.00	$63.30	$27.00

In the past few years, Cricket Components' profitability has been lagging and its overseas competition has been increasing. The company is considering implementing an activity-based costing system for 2011. In analyzing the fiscal 2010 data, you determined that the $1,000,000 of manufacturing overhead could be assigned to four basic activities: quality control, setup, materials handling, and equipment operation. Data from fiscal 2010 on the costs associated with each of the four activities follow.

	Quality Control	Setup	Materials Handling	Equipment Operation
Cost	$50,000	$50,000	$150,000	$750,000
Activity driver	Number of units produced	Number of setups	Kilograms of material used	Number of machine hours
Volume of driver	140,000	500	1,000,000	500,000

Volume measures for fiscal 2010 for each product and each activity driver were as follows:

	Fax Stands	Organizers	Printer Stands
Number of units	100,000	10,000	30,000
Number of setups	100	200	200
Kilograms of material	200,000	500,000	300,000
Number of machine hours	100,000	200,000	200,000

Required:

a. For fiscal 2010, determine the total amount of overhead allocated to each product group using the current overhead application method.

b. For fiscal 2010, determine the total overhead allocated to each product group using the activity-based costing allocation measures. Compute the cost per unit for each product group.

c. If the company sets prices based on product costs, how would the sales prices using activity-based costing differ from those using the traditional overhead allocation?

12. (LO 1, 4, 6, 7) For the past five years, Judy has been running a consulting practice in which she provides two major services: general management consulting, and executive training seminars. Judy is not quite sure that she is charging appropriate fees for the different services she provides. She recently read an article about activity-based costing (ABC) that convinced her she could employ ABC to improve the accuracy of her costing. She has approached you to help determine whether the application of ABC would be possible. She has provided you with the following selected information concerning her consulting practice during the previous year:

PROBLEMS

Overhead Activity	Cost Pool	Quantities	Cost Driver
Planning and review	$ 300,000	60,000 hours	Billable hours
Research	48,000	200 journals	Journals purchased
General administration	600,000	300 clients	Number of clients
Building and equipment	84,000	1,200 square metres	Square metres
Clerical	85,000	17 professionals	Professional staff
	$1,117,000		

In addition, Judy provided you with the following statistics for each of the two types of services provided to clients during the year.

Overhead Activity	Management Consulting	Executive Training
Direct labour costs	$900,000	$450,000
Billable hours	45,000	15,000
Research—Journals purchased	140	60
Number of clients	120	180
Square metres	800	400
Professional staff	10	7

Required:

a. In the past, Judy divided the total overhead costs by the total billable hours to determine an average rate. To this amount she would then add the direct labour costs per hour and double that total amount to establish her average hourly charge-out rate. What was Judy's average hourly charge-out rate using this method?

b. Using ABC, what would Judy's charge-out rate be? Note that Judy will continue to add the overhead to the direct labour costs per hour on a service basis and then double this amount to set an average hourly charge-out rate.

c. After reviewing the ABC methodology described in part (b), identify one significant flaw in how overhead costs will be allocated by Judy in the ABC system. Discuss how this flaw would affect the average hourly charge-out rates (i.e., increase or decrease the rates) for management consulting and executive training. You do not have to calculate the new rates to answer this part of the question.

d. Identify and discuss three ways in which ABC leads to more accurate product costs.

e. Identify and discuss two limitations of ABC.

13. (LO 1, 7) Last year, the accounts receivable department at Canada Hydro spent $22,500,000 to collect receivables from more than 2 million customers throughout the country. In order to better understand the nature and cost of activities of the accounts receivable department, Canada Hydro's top management has decided to perform an activity-based analysis to gather the information that will help improve the processes and make them more cost-efficient.

Required:

a. Describe the steps that Canada Hydro should follow to gather the information.

b. Identify the factors that Canada Hydro's top management should consider before carrying out an activity-based analysis of the accounts receivable department.

14. (LO 1, 7) Kiddy Company manufactures bicycles. It recently received a request to manufacture 10 units of a mountain bike at a price lower than it normally accepts. Bruce, the sales manager, indicated that if the order were accepted at that price, the company could expect additional orders from the same client. Bruce believes that if Kiddy could offer this price in the market generally, sales of this bike would increase by 30%. Melany, president of Kiddy, is skeptical about accepting the order. The company has a policy of not accepting any order that does not provide a markup of 20% on full manufacturing costs. The price offered is $575 per bike.

The controller, Sanjay, has recently researched the possibility of using activity-based multiple overhead rates instead of the single rate currently in use. He has promised more accurate product costing, and Melany is curious about how this approach would affect product costing and pricing of the mountain bike.

The plantwide overhead rate is based on an expected volume of 15,000 direct labour hours and the following budgeted overhead:

PROBLEMS

Machine operating costs	$ 75,000
Rework labour	45,000
Inspection	25,000
Scrap costs	35,000
General manufacturing overhead	120,000
Total	$300,000

Expected activity for selected cost drivers for the current year is:

Machine hours	25,000
Units reworked	600
Inspection hours	500
Units scrapped	140
Direct labour hours	15,000

Estimated data for the production of one mountain bike are:

Direct materials	$160
Direct labour (7.5 hours per unit)	$180
Number of machine hours	6
Number of units reworked	0.25
Number of inspection hours	0.10
Number of units scrapped	0.05

Required:

a. Using the existing single-rate method to assign overhead on a plantwide basis, determine whether or not Kiddy should accept the order for the 10 mountain bikes. Explain your decision.

b. Using activity-based costing to assign overhead, determine whether or not Kiddy should accept the order for 10 mountain bikes. Explain your decision.

15. (LO 1, 6, 7) Mars Company has four categories of overhead: purchasing and receiving materials, machine operating costs, materials handling, and shipping. The costs expected for these categories for the coming year are as follows:

Purchasing and receiving materials	$200,000
Machine operating costs	450,000
Materials handling	80,000
Shipping	170,000
Total	$900,000

The plant currently applies overhead using machine hours and expected annual capacity. Expected capacity is 150,000 machine hours. Robert, the financial controller, has been asked to submit a bid on Job #287, on which he has assembled the following data:

Direct materials per unit	$0.35
Direct labour per unit	$0.85
Applied overhead	?
Number of units produced	6,000
Number of purchases and receipts	2
Number of machine hours	1,500
Number of material moves	300
Number of kilometres to ship to the customer	2,300

Robert has been told that Arrow Company, a major competitor, is using activity-based costing and will bid on Job #287 with a price of $2.95 per unit. Before submitting his bid, Robert wants to assess the effects of this alternative costing approach. He estimates that 850,000 units will be produced next year, 2,500 purchases and receipts will be made, 400,000 moves will be performed plantwide, and the delivery of finished goods will be 300,000 kilometres. The bid price policy is full manufacturing cost plus 25%.

Required:

a. Calculate the bid price per unit of Job #287 using machine hours to assign overhead.

b. Using an activity-based approach, determine whether Mars or Arrow will produce the most competitive bid and obtain the contract. Show all your calculations.

Problems 12–15 are adapted by the authors from *Management Accounting Examinations*, published by the Certified General Accountants Association of Canada © CGA-Canada, 1999 (#12 and 15) and 2000 (#13 and 14), used by permission.

PROBLEMS

16. (LO 5, 6) The Canadian Motorcycle Company (CMC) produces two models of motor-cycles: Faster and Slower. The company has five categories of overhead costs: purchasing, receiving, machine operating costs, handling, and shipping. Each category represents the following percentages of total overhead costs, which amount to $4,200,000.

Purchasing	25.0%
Receiving	12.5%
Machine operating	37.5%
Handling	10.0%
Shipping	15.0%

Current capacity is 200,000 machine hours, and the current production uses 100% of available hours. The sales mix is 45% Faster and 55% Slower. Overhead costs are applied to each model based on machine hours.

Production costs for each model of motorcycle and other relevant information are as follows:

	Faster	Slower
Directs materials per unit	$8,000	$6,500
Direct labour per unit	$1,750	$1,850
Applied overhead	?	?
Number of units produced	450	550
Number of purchases	5	4
Number of shipments received	3	3
Percentage of machine hours consumed by each product	50%	50%
Number of moves in handling	75	100
Number of kilometres to ship to customers	4,000	4,250

Required:

a. CMC determines prices by adding 40% to the cost of direct materials and direct labour. Is this pricing policy appropriate? Show all calculations to support your answer.

b. Use an activity-based approach to determine whether CMC can make a profit if it sells the Faster model for $15,000. Show all supporting calculations. Round all answers to the nearest dollar.

Extract from *Management Accounting 2 Examination*, published by the Certified General Accountants Association of Canada (© CGA-Canada 2002). Reprinted with permission.

17. (LO 5, 6) ProDriver Inc. (PDI) recently started operations to obtain a share of the growing market for golf. PDI manufactures two models of specialty drivers: the Thunderbolt model and the Earthquake model. The company was formed as a partnership by two professional engineers and a professional golfer, none of whom had any accounting background. The business has been very successful, and to cope with the increased level of activity, the partners have hired a CGA as their controller. One of the first improvements that the controller wants to make is to update the costing system by changing from a single overhead application rate using direct labour hours to activity-based costing. The controller has identified the following three activities as cost drivers, along with the related cost pools:

Model	Number of Material Requisitions	Number of Product Inspections	Number of Orders Shipped
Thunderbolt	46	23	167
Earthquake	62	31	129
Costs per pool	$54,000	$8,200	$103,000

Required:

a. Using activity-based costing, prepare a schedule that shows the allocation of the costs of each cost pool to each model. Show your calculations.

b. Identify *three* conditions that should be present in PDI in order for the implementation of activity-based costing to be successful.

Extract from *Management Accounting 1 Examination*, published by the Certified General Accountants Association of Canada (© CGA-Canada 2002). Reprinted with permission.

18. (LO 5, 6, 7) Kimberleigh & Associates (K&A) is a small national firm of public accountants specializing in forensic and fraud-related accounting. Its clients include criminal lawyers, police forces, government departments, business partners, and shareholders. K&A has 50 professionals consisting of three managing partners, seven partners, and 40 associates.

PROBLEMS

K&A employs a job costing system and defines a job as either a client or a case. The system consists of a single direct cost category and a single indirect/overhead cost pool. The direct cost category consists of only chargeable/billable professional labour that is traced directly to clients on a per hour basis. The remaining nonchargeable/ nonbillable professional labour that is not traced to clients includes idle time and time for professional development. It is added to the single indirect/overhead cost pool. Also included in the single indirect/overhead cost pool are general support costs such as secretarial costs, fringe benefits to professional labour, telephones/fax machines, computer time, photocopying, travel, entertainment, and office rent.

The indirect/overhead cost pool is charged to clients using a budgeted rate that is set at the beginning of the year as the ratio of budgeted total indirect/overhead cost to budgeted total chargeable professional-labour hours. Exhibit 8-1 provides budgeted and actual information for 2010.

	Budgeted	Actual
Professional labour compensation	$8.0 million	$8.2 million
General support costs*	$5.2 million	$6.0 million
Professional labour hours available	96,000	96,000
Professional labour hours billed to clients	72,000	67,200

*Excludes nonchargeable professional labour cost

EXHIBIT 8-1
Budgeted and Actual Information for 2010

K&A regularly loses some contracts because it submits bids that are too high. Other contract bids are sometimes too low, resulting in client complaints after the fact when a higher final invoice is submitted for payment. Some clients even demand to see details that make up the invoice.

In response to these problems, an internal committee consisting of one managing partner and three associates has evaluated K&A's job costing and pricing system and has made the following recommendations:

i.   An attempt should be made to trace more of the so-called general support costs to individual clients.
ii. The number of indirect cost pools for the remaining indirect costs (general support costs) should be increased
iii. In all cases, clients should pay for only budgeted or predetermined amounts, including the number of chargeable professional hours and the rates for both direct and indirect costs.
iv. The profit component of clients' work should be negotiated and should compare favourably with that of the competition.
v.   Both direct and indirect costs should be controlled.

At present, the managing partners have no formal system in place for evaluating the performance of the associates. They consider the associates as fellow professionals and expect them to behave as such. Complaints from clients are handled only casually without any serious investigations. There is also no incentive system besides the competitive salaries and promotion to partner status. Promotion to the position of partner requires a minimum of 10 years of "superior" performance. Superior performance is subjectively determined by the partners, whose decision must be unanimous.

Required:
a.   Refer to the information in Exhibit 8-1 for 2010. Determine the cost of a client's job that was estimated to require 40 chargeable professional-labour hours but instead required 45 hours, using: (1) K&A's present job costing system, and (2) only recommendation 3 of the internal committee.
b.   Identify and explain *one* analytical technique that K&A may find useful in implementing recommendation 2 of the internal committee.

19. (LO 5, 6) Refer to Question 18.
    Required:
    Evaluate the management control system at K&A. Limit your evaluation to *only* the following issues:

PROBLEMS

a. Strengths and weaknesses of: (1) K&A's management control system in the use of a single direct cost category and a single indirect cost pool for the costing of a client's job, (2) *each* of the five recommendations of the internal committee.

b. Recommendations and explanation of specific key success factors that K&A's managing partners can use to control the activities of its professionals and improve the profitability of its operations

Problems 18 and 19 are extracted from *Management Accounting 2 Examination*, published by the Certified General Accountants Association of Canada (© CGA-Canada 1998). Reprinted with permission.

20. (LO 4) Ranbi moonlights as a deejay in addition to doing his regular daytime job. His customers are local residents giving private parties. The activities involved and the time required for each activity are as follows:

Activity	Time in Hours
Discuss the types of guests with the customer	0.5
Prepare the list of songs to be played	1.0
Travel to and from party (average)	1.0
Set up and take down equipment	1.5
Play music at party	Depends on customer

Ranbi believes that his time should be priced at $25.00 per hour to make the business economically viable. Ranbi charges $0.50 per kilometre (one way only) from the city centre to the customer as a travelling charge, and also hires an assistant who is paid an additional $10.00 per hour for the time at the party (and nothing during the travelling or set-up and take-down time).

Required:

a. How much should Ranbi charge a customer who lives 10 kilometres from the city centre and gives a party for 7 hours?

b. A customer requires special lighting that will cost Ranbi $50 to rent and will increase the set-up and take-down time by 2 hours. How much should Ranbi charge this customer if she lives 10 kilometres from the city centre and gives a party for 8 hours?

Extract from *Management Accounting 1 Examination*, published by the Certified General Accountants Association of Canada (© CGA-Canada 2002). Reprinted with permission.

21. (LO 4–7) Tony Soprano has just purchased a 100,000-cubic-metre commercial cold-storage warehouse as rental property. The previous owner had charged customers a flat monthly rate of $0.04 per kilogram of goods stored. The reason the warehouse was on the market was because its owner had become dissatisfied with its profitability. Despite the fact that the warehouse remained relatively full, revenues had not kept pace with operating costs. Tony asks his accountant, Stephie Demara, about using activity-based costing to better understand the causes of operational costs and to possibly revise the pricing formula. Ms. Demara determines that most costs of the warehouse can be associated with one of four activities. Those activities and their related costs, volume measures, and volume levels for the fiscal year follow.

Activity	Monthly Cost	Volume Measure	Monthly Volume
Send/receive goods	$6,000	Weight in kilograms	500,000
Store goods	4,000	Volume in cubic metres	80,000
Move goods	5,000	Volume in square metres	5,000
Identify goods	2,000	Number of packages	500

Required:

a. Based on the activity cost and volume data, determine the amount of cost assigned to the following customers, whose goods were all received on the first day of last month.

Customer	Weight of Order	Cubic Metres	Square Metres	Number of Packages
Lori Eisen	40,000	3,000	300	5
Paula Pressberger	40,000	2,000	200	20
Christina Kim	40,000	1,000	1,000	80

b. Determine the price to be charged to each customer under the previous owner's pricing plan.

PROBLEMS

c. Determine the new price, assuming Tony would add a 40% markup to the cost determined in part (a).

d. How well did the previous owner's pricing plan capture the costs incurred to provide the warehouse services? Explain.

SOURCE: Adapted from Harold P. Roth and Linda T. Sims, "Costing for Warehousing and Distribution," *Management Accounting*, August 1991, pp. 42–45. Adapted with permission of the Institute of Management Accountants, Montvale, N.J., USA, www.imanet.org.

22. (LO 4–7) The following production and cost analysis for each product made by Roth and Borthick Company is for the year 2007.

Cost Component	Product A	Product B	Both Products	Cost
Units produced	10,000	10,000	20,000	
Raw materials used (units)				
Material X	50,000	50,000	100,000	$ 800,000
Material Y		100,000	100,000	$1,200,000
Labour used (hours)				
Department 1				$ 681,000
Direct labour ($375,000)	20,000	5,000	25,000	
Indirect labour				
Inspection	2,500	2,500	5,000	
Machine operations	5,000	10,000	15,000	
Setups	200	200	400	
Department 2				$ 462,000
Direct labour ($200,000)	5,000	5,000	10,000	
Indirect labour				
Inspection	2,500	5,000	7,500	
Machine operations	1,000	4,000	5,000	
Setups	200	400	600	
Machine hours used				
Department 1	5,000	10,000	15,000	$ 400,000
Department 2	5,000	20,000	25,000	$ 800,000
Power used (kwh)				$ 400,000
Department 1			1,500,000	
Department 2			8,500,000	
Other activity data				
Building occupancy				$1,000,000
Square metres occupied				
Purchasing			10,000	
Power			40,000	
Department 1			200,000	
Department 2			250,000	
Purchasing				$ 100,000
Number of purchase orders				
Material X			200	
Material Y			300	

Faye Harold, the management accountant, has just returned from a seminar on activity-based costing. To apply the concepts she has learned, she decides to analyze the costs incurred for Products A and B from an activity basis. In doing so, she specifies the following first and second allocation processes.

First Stage: Allocations to Departments

Cost Pool	Cost Object	Activity Allocation Base
Building occupancy	Departments	Square metres occupied
Purchasing	Materials	Number of purchase orders
Power	Departments	Kilowatt hours

PROBLEMS

Second Stage: Allocations to Products

Cost Pool	Cost Object	Activity Allocation Base
Departments		
Indirect labour	Products	Hours worked
Power	Products	Machine hours
Machinery-related	Products	Machine hours
Building occupancy	Products	Machine hours
Materials		
Purchasing	Products	Units of material

Required:

a. Determine the total overhead for Roth and Borthick Company.

b. Determine the plantwide overhead rate for the company, assuming the use of direct labour hours.

c. Determine the cost per unit for Product A and for Product B using the overhead application rate found in part (b).

d. Using activity-based costing, determine the cost allocations to departments (first-stage allocations). Allocate in the following order: building occupancy, purchasing, and power.

e. Using the allocations found in part (d), determine the overhead cost allocations to products (second-stage allocations).

f. Determine the cost per unit for Product A and Product B using the overhead allocations found in part (e).

SOURCE: Adapted from Harold P. Roth and A. Faye Borthick, "Getting Closer to Real Product Costs," *Management Accounting*, May 1989, pp. 28–33. Adapted with permission of the Institute of Management Accountants, Montvale, N.J., U.S.A., www.imanet.org.

23. (LO 4–7) Alison Baird CarryAll Company produces briefcases from leather, fabric, and synthetic materials in a single production department. The basic product is a standard briefcase made from leather and lined with fabric. CarryAll has a good market reputation because its standard briefcase is of high quality and has been produced for many years.

Last year, Alison Baird CarryAll decided to expand its product line and produce briefcases for special orders. These briefcases differ from the standard in that they vary in size, contain both leather and synthetic materials, and are imprinted with the buyer's logo. Synthetic materials are used to hold down the materials cost. To reduce labour cost per unit, most of the cutting and stitching on the specialty briefcases is done by automated machines that are used sparingly in the production of the standard briefcases. Because of these changes in the design and production of the specialty briefcases, Alison Baird CarryAll believed that they would cost less to produce than the standard briefcases. However, because they are specialty items, they were priced at $32, slightly higher than the standard briefcases, which are priced at $30.

After reviewing last month's results of operations, Alison Baird CarryAll's president became concerned about the profitability of the two product lines. The standard briefcase showed a loss while the specialty briefcases showed a greater profit margin than expected. The president is considering dropping the standard briefcase and focusing entirely on specialty items. The cost data for last month's operations follow.

	Standard		Specialty	
Units produced		10,000		2,500
Direct material				
Leather	1.0 square metres	$15.00	0.5 square metres	$ 7.50
Fabric	1.0 square metres	5.00	1.0 square metres	5.00
Synthetic		....	0.5 square metres	5.00
Total material		$20.00		$17.50
Direct labour	0.5 hours @ $12	6.00	0.25 hours @ $12	3.00
Manufacturing overhead	0.5 hours @ $8.98	4.49	0.25 hours @ $8.98	2.25
Cost per unit		$30.49		$22.75

Manufacturing overhead is applied using direct labour hours. The rate of $8.98 per DLH was calculated by dividing $50,500 of total overhead for the month by 5,625 direct labour hours.

PROBLEMS

Assume that the following costs and activity drivers have been identified. The purchasing department cost is $6,000, primarily created by the number of purchase orders processed. During the month, the purchasing department prepared 20 purchase orders for leather, 30 for fabric, and 50 for synthetic material.

Receiving and inspecting materials cost is $7,500. This cost is driven by the number of deliveries. During the month, 30 deliveries were made for leather, 40 for fabric, and 80 for synthetic material.

The cost of setting up the production line to produce the different types of briefcases is $10,000. A setup for production of the standard briefcases requires one hour, while setup for the specialty briefcases requires two hours. Standard briefcases are produced in batches of 200; specialty briefcases are produced in batches of 25. During the last month, there were 50 setups for the standard items and 100 setups for the specialty items.

The cost of inspecting finished goods is $8,000. All briefcases are inspected to ensure that quality standards are met. The inspection of standard briefcases takes very little time because the employees identify and correct quality problems as they do the hand-cutting and stitching. Inspection personnel indicated that, during the month, they spent 150 hours inspecting standard briefcases and 250 hours inspecting specialty cases.

Equipment-related costs are $6,000 for repairs, depreciation, and utilities. These costs are assigned to products using machine hours. A standard briefcase requires 0.5 hours of machine time, and a specialty briefcase requires 2 hours.

Plant-related costs are $13,000 for items such as property taxes, insurance, and administration. These costs are assigned to products using machine hours.

Required:

a.   Using activity-based costing concepts, what overhead costs are assigned to the two product lines?

b.   What is the unit cost of each type of product using activity-based costing concepts?

c.   Re-evaluate the president's concern about the profitability of the two product lines.

(IMA adapted)

24. (LO 4–7) Jenny Horton Corporation manufactures several types of printed circuit boards, two of which account for the majority of the company's sales. The first, a television (TV) circuit board, has been an industry standard for several years. The market for this type of board is competitive and, therefore, price sensitive. Horton plans to sell 65,000 of the TV circuit boards in fiscal 2010 for $150 per unit. The second high-volume product, a personal computer (PC) circuit board, is a recent addition to Horton's product line. The PC board incorporates the latest technology and can be sold at a premium price; the 2010 plans include the sale of 40,000 PC boards at $300 per unit.

Horton's management group is meeting to discuss how to spend sales and promotion dollars in fiscal 2010. You, the sales manager, believe that the market share for the TV board could be expanded by concentrating Horton's promotional efforts in this area. In response to this suggestion, the production manager said, "Why don't you go after a bigger market for the PC board? The cost sheets that I get show that the contribution from the PC board is more than double the contribution from the TV board. I know we get a premium price for the PC board; selling it should help overall profitability."

The following cost and time data apply to the TV and PC boards.

	TV Board	PC Board
Direct material	$80	$140
Direct labour	1.5 hours	4 hours
Machine time	0.5 hours	1.5 hours

Variable manufacturing overhead is applied using direct labour hours. For 2010, variable manufacturing overhead is budgeted at $1,120,000 and 280,000 direct labour hours are budgeted. FOH is applied based on machine hours incurred. Hourly rates for machine time and direct labour are $10 and $14, respectively. Horton applies a materials handling charge at 10% of material cost; this charge is not included in variable manufacturing overhead. Total expenditures for materials are budgeted at $10,800,000.

Van Amberg, Horton's controller, believes that before making a decision about allocating promotional dollars to individual products it might be worthwhile to look at these products on the basis of their production activities. Van Amberg has

PROBLEMS

prepared the following schedule to help the management group understand
activity-based costing.

Budgeted Cost	Cost Driver	Annual Activity for Cost Driver	
Material overhead:			
Procurement	$ 400,000	Number of parts	4,000,000 parts
Production scheduling	220,000	Number of boards	110,000 boards
Packaging and shipping	440,000	Number of boards	110,000 boards
	$1,060,000		
Variable overhead:			
Machine setup	$ 446,000	Number of setups	278,750 setups
Hazardous waste disposal	48,000	Kilograms of waste	16,000 kilograms
Quality control inspections	560,000	Number of inspections	160,000 inspections
General supplies	66,000	Number of boards	110,000 boards
	$1,120,000		
Manufacturing:			
Machine insertion	$1,200,000	Number of parts	3,000,000 parts
Manual insertion	4,000,000	Number of parts	1,000,000 parts
Wave soldering	132,000	Number of boards	110,000 boards
	$5,332,000		

Required Per Unit	TV Board	PC Board
Parts	25	55
Machine insertions	24	35
Manual insertions	1	20
Machine setups	2	3
Hazardous waste	0.02 kg	0.35 kg
Inspections	1	2

"This information," Van Amberg explained, "can be used to calculate an activity-based
cost for each TV and PC board. The only cost that remains the same for the current
and the ABC cost methods is direct material cost. Cost drivers replace direct labour,
machine time, and overhead costs in the current costs."

Required:

a. Using the current costing system, calculate the total gross profit (sales minus cost
of goods sold) expected in fiscal 2010 for the:
   i.   TV board
   ii. PC board
b. On the basis of activity-based costs, calculate the total gross profit expected in
fiscal 2010 for the:
   i.   TV board
   ii. PC board
c. Explain how the comparison of the results of the two costing methods may
impact the decisions made by Horton Corporation's management group.
d. Identify three general advantages that are associated with activity-based costing.

(CMA)

25. (LO 4–7) Halifax Valley Architects Inc. provides a range of engineering and architectural
consulting services through its three branch offices in Halifax, Saint John, and Moncton.
The company allocates resources and bonuses to the three branches based on the net
income reported for the period. The following presents the results from the year 2010
(dollars are in thousands).

	Halifax	Saint John	Moncton	Total
Sales	$1,500	$1,419	$1,067	$ 3,986
Direct material	(281)	(421)	(185)	(887)
Direct labour	(382)	(317)	(317)	(1,016)
Overhead	(710)	(589)	(589)	(1,888)
Net income	$ 127	$ 92	$ (24)	$ 195

Overhead is accumulated in one overhead pool and allocated to the branches. This
pool includes rent, depreciation, taxes, etc., regardless of which office incurred the

PROBLEMS

expense. This method of accumulating costs forces the offices to absorb a portion of the overhead incurred by other offices. For 2010, the overhead rate was $1.859 for every direct labour dollar incurred by an office.

Management is concerned with the results of the 2010 performance reports. During a review of overhead, it became apparent that many items of overhead were not correlated with direct labour dollars. Management decided that applying overhead based on activity-based costing and direct tracing where possible should provide a more accurate picture of branch profitability.

An analysis of the overhead revealed that the following amounts could be traced directly to the office that incurred the overhead (dollars are in thousands).

	Halifax	Saint John	Moncton	Total
Direct overhead	$180	$270	$177	$627

Activity pools and activity drivers were determined from the accounting records and staff surveys as follows.

Activity Pools		Activity Driver	Halifax	Saint John	Moncton
General admin.	$ 409,000	Direct labour cost	$ 382,413	$ 317,086	$317,188
Project costing	48,000	Number of time sheet entries	6,000	3,800	3,500
Accounts payable/ receiving	139,000	Number of vendor invoices	1,020	850	400
Accounts receivable	47,000	Number of client invoices	588	444	96
Payroll/mail sort & delivery	30,000	Number of employees	23	26	18
Personnel recruiting	38,000	Number of new hires	8	4	7
Employee insurance processing	14,000	Insurance claims filed	230	260	180
Proposals	139,000	Number of proposals	200	250	60
Sales meetings/ sales aids	202,000	Contracted sales	1,824,439	1,399,617	571,208
Shipping	24,000	Number of projects	99	124	30
Ordering	48,000	Number of purchase orders	135	110	80
Duplicating costs	46,000	Number of copies	162,500	146,250	65,000
Blueprinting	77,000	Number of blueprints	39,000	31,200	16,000
	$1,261,000				

Required:

a. What overhead costs should be assigned to each branch based on activity-based costing concepts?
b. What is the contribution of each branch before subtracting the results obtained in part (a)?
c. What is the profitability of each branch office using activity-based costing?
d. Evaluate the concerns of management regarding the traditional costing technique currently used.

(IMA)

CASES

1. The fusion of the telephone, the PC, and the Internet provided an opportunity for Robert Jason. He developed a product—PassPortal, a combination cellphone and music player—and a company to design, assemble, and sell it. Robert started the company—Pass Portal—while he was still a student. He perfected his device and sold it successfully. Later, he added other features, including Internet access, messaging, photography, and karaoke.

The product is very complicated. It is also a cutting-edge portable music device, one that enables owners to listen to their favourite music at any time and to use that same music for karaoke. Younger customers use it only for listening; only older customers also use it for karaoke.

At the assembly plant in Halifax where PassPortals are made, costs are classified as follows:
- Components, materials
- Materials handling, labour, and manufacturing overhead
- Basic unit assembly, labour, and manufacturing overhead
- Music subunit assembly, labour, and manufacturing overhead
- Karaoke subunit assembly, labour, and manufacturing overhead
- Packaging, labour, materials, and manufacturing overhead

Currently, there is only one product. Next year, three products will be made: the original one, a simple or basic product, and a deluxe product. The three products require different manufacturing resources.

PassPortal operates in a highly competitive market in which products must constantly be improved. That is why PassPortal has a strong R&D department, which adds considerably to nonmanufacturing overhead. Other nonmanufacturing overhead includes selling and administrative costs.

Robert has just celebrated the 10th anniversary of PassPortal. There were many financial challenges during the first decade, but now the urgency to stay liquid has dissipated. Robert now wants to put in place a better management accounting system. As a first step, he wants accurate product costs for the current product and for the future products.
Required:
Using the case approach, provide Robert with the requested assistance.

2. Montreal-based Morel Industries is a highly successful global manufacturer of consumer products with numerous plants. It produces branded products, specializing in three market segments: juvenile products (e.g., infant car seats); home furnishings (e.g., a wide variety of ready-to-assemble furniture); and recreational/leisure items (e.g., bicycles). Last year, 72% of Morel's sales were made in the United States, 5% in Canada, and 23% in Europe and elsewhere. It employs around 4,700 people in 15 countries. Morel also has eight offices in China, headquartered in Shanghai, to oversee the sourcing, engineering, and logistics of the company's Asian supply chain.

Morel uses the following four sales and distribution arrangements: salaried Morel employees; individual agents, who carry Morel's products on either an exclusive or a nonexclusive basis; individual specialized agents, who sell products, including Morel's, exclusively to one customer, such as a major discount chain; and sales agencies, which employ their own sales forces.

Morel has two main customers, Wal-Mart and Kmart. These two accounted for 47.3% of Morel's total revenue last year. By providing a high-quality, industry-leading level of service, Morel has developed successful relationships with major retailers. It has achieved high levels of customer satisfaction by fostering especially close associations between its sales representatives and its clients. For example, Morel has a permanent, full-service account team dedicated to Wal-Mart. This sales team is located near Wal-Mart's headquarters in Bentonville, Arkansas. Similarly, Morel has assigned sales teams exclusively to Kmart and Toys "R" Us. The teams ensure that Morel meets these major retailers' demanding inventory and supply requirements and that any problems are addressed quickly. The sales teams also provide product and market analysis to help these major companies with product specifications and designs.

Morel has been highly successful in a competitive world market. It has taken a global approach to organizing and coordinating its many brands and plants with a large number of suppliers and customers. Morel is managed as a group of plants fed by a centralized supply chain; in turn its products are fed into a centralized distribution system.

Senior management has focused on supply chains and distribution, leaving the plants to be managed independently. Each plant has a simple accounting system that is not designed to track costs by product—only by direct materials and direct labour. Manufacturing overhead is allocated arbitrarily, based on direct labour. Many different products are made at each plant. The products vary by direct materials and direct labour as well as by overhead.

Senior managers have identified the inability to track costs accurately as a problem to be solved. They want accurate product costs. You have been hired as a consultant to resolve this problem.

Required

Using the case approach, provide senior management with advice on product costing.

3. Paige Slocter has been in the top 10 of Re-Max Real Estate salespeople worldwide for most of the past 20 years. She sells more than 400 houses a year in Edmonton. As a part-time job separate from her real estate business, she works as a high-priced coach for real estate agents all over North America. She also claims to work no more than 40 hours a week.

The essence of her real estate sales business is to list the houses of vendors and then show these listings to prospective buyers. There are three major activities: list the property, show property, and finalize the sale of the property.

Ms. Slocter is the main salesperson and the one who attracts listings by guaranteeing to sell the property within six months; indeed, she promises that if she does not, she will buy it herself. Specifically, the seller (vendor) is guaranteed that the property will be sold for at least 97% of list (as determined by Paige), or Paige will buy it for 95% of list. The commission on house sales is 6%.

When Paige acquires a property, there are often additional expenses to do with getting the property in good condition for sale. These expenses include cleaning, yard work, and minor repairs and renovations. That is too much work for Paige to do herself, so she delegates most of the work to seven subordinates, who are paid by the hour.

Sales have increased in recent years, but profits have stayed flat. The accounting records are simple. The format for the operating statement is total revenue less total expenses. There is no understanding of which properties are profitable and which are not.

Paige has asked you to suggest a method that will allow her to know where her profits and losses are coming from.

Required:

Using the case approach, advise Paige on a method for ascertaining the sources of profits and losses.

ETHICS

1. You are the vice president of operations with a Montreal-based diversified manufacturing and assembly firm. One of your subordinates was promoted from manager to director. She had been an outstanding manager with responsibility for a small number of employees, whom she supervised directly. Because of her excellent performance as a manager, she was promoted to director. Your boss, the vice president, wondered about the promotion, but you were adamant. The new job included more subordinates, but these subordinates were at different locations. It also required selling the unit's services to outside customers.

After six months, you realize that the new director is not performing adequately in her new position. You meet with her and offer help, which she accepts. The next six-month review indicates the same results: she is unable to perform to the level required by the job, and now she realizes that the director's job is not appropriate for her.

What should you do as the employer? Elaborate.

2. As the controller, you have just applied ABM to assess the controller's division. This has been a very demanding exercise, and now you are proceeding with the large number of organizational changes that accompany ABM. As the division will now be managed based on activities rather than functions, there is a surplus of managers. The division will no longer require three management levels; two will be enough. You fully accept these organizational changes.

You worked in the division for eight years before becoming controller two years ago. The managers are your friends, and two of them mentored you. You are very reluctant to eliminate about half their jobs, so you have asked the HR director to announce the organizational changes and the reduction in managers. She will also meet with the redundant managers to explain their terminations.

Is there anything left for you to do? Elaborate.

ETHICS

3. You have been asked to analyze and update costing and pricing practices at your division, the manufacturer of paints. You use ABC for this analysis. The division's product line has changed over time from general paints to specialized paints. Though some large orders have been received, most business is now generated by products designed and produced in small lots to meet detailed and specific environmental requirements.

The division has experienced major overhead growth, including costs in customer service, production scheduling, inventory control, and laboratory work.

You find the current method for allocating overhead—direct labour hours—to be misleading. ABC is much more accurate. However, ABC is pointing toward a revision of overhead cost allocations: more overhead is to be allocated to the specialized paints and less to the general paints. As a result, the specialized paints are now less profitable than once believed, and the general paints are now more profitable.

After reviewing these results, your boss, the vice-president of the division, has asked you not to implement ABC. He explains that it was his idea to pursue speciality paints, which he believes are more profitable than general paints.

What should you do? Elaborate.

SOLUTIONS TO SELF-TEST QUESTIONS

1. a. ABC identifies the causal relationship between the incurrence of costs and activities. It determines the cost driver for each activity and applies the cost to products on the basis of resources consumed.

2. a. A cost driver is a measure of activity, such as direct labour hours, machine hours, etc. It is a basis used to assign costs to cost objects.

3. d. In an ABC system, cost allocation is more precise than in a traditional system because activities rather than functions or department are defined as cost objects.

4. b. ABC determines the activities associated with the incurrence of costs and then accumulates a cost pool for each activity using the appropriate activity base. If a company produces only one product, then all costs are assigned to the one product. It does not matter which method is used.

5. a. $50,000 is allocated over 10,000 hours (25 × 200 hours) + (25 × 200 hours). Overhead cost per hour is $5 ($50,000 ÷ 10,000 hours), and the per unit overhead cost of ladies' umbrellas is $1,000 ($5 × 200 direct labour hours).

6. b. ABC allocates overhead on the basis of some causal relationship between the incurrence of cost and activities. Because the moves for umbrellas constitute 25% (5 ÷ 20) of total moves, the umbrellas should absorb 25% of the total materials handling costs, or $12,500 (25% × $50,000). The remaining $37,500 is allocated to men's umbrellas. The cost per ladies' umbrella is $500 ($12,500 ÷ 25).

7. a.

8. a.

9. a. 20 × $400 = $8,000 per batch. $8,000 ÷ 1,000 = $8.00 per unit.

10. c. Materials handling: $4 × 200 = $800

    Assembly $40 × 12 = $480

    Inspection $6 × 5 = $30

    $1,310 ÷ 100 = $13.10 per unit.

ENDNOTES

1. Anne Fortin, Hamid Haffaf, and Chantal Viger, "The Measurement of Success of Activity-Based Costing and Its Determinants: A Study Within Canadian Federal Government Organizations," *Accounting Perspectives* 3 (2007): 231–62.

2. Daniel J. McConville, "Start With ABC," *Industry Week*, September 6, 1993, p. 31.

ENDNOTES

3. Frederick W. Lindahl, *Human Resource Planning, Activity-Based Costing Implementation and Adaptation*, Human Resource Planning Society, 1996.

4. "Strong Advocate of Activity-Based Management Explains It All to You," *Cost Management Update*, December 2001–January 2002.

5. Robin Cooper and Regine Slagmulder, "Activity-Based Budgeting, Part 1," *Strategic Finance*, September 2000, pp. 85–86.

6. H. Thomas Johnson and Robert S. Kaplan, *Relevance Lost*, Boston: Harvard Business School Press, 1987, p. 1.

7. Joseph P. Naughton–Travers, "Activity-Based Costing: The New Management Tool," *Behavioral Health Management*, March–April 2001.

8. James Reeve, "Projects, Models and Systems—Where Is ABM Headed," *Journal of Cost Management*, Summer 1996, p. 7.

9. Tom E. Pryor, "Activity Accounting: Key to Waste Reduction," *Accounting Systems Journal*, Fall 1989, p. 34.

10. Tim Minahan, *Purchasing*, September 4, 1997, p. 47.

11. D. Kuchta and M. Troska, "Activity-Based Costing and Customer Profitability," *Cost Management*, May–June 2007, pp. 18–25.

12. Michael J. Kohl and Thomas Pagano, "Learn the ABC Basics," *Credit Union Management*, September 2000.

13. Robin Cooper, "Cost Classification in Unit-Based and Activity-Based Manufacturing Cost Systems," *Journal of Cost Management*, Fall 1990.

14. Robin Cooper, "Cost Classification in Unit-Based and Activity-Based Manufacturing Cost Systems," *Journal of Cost Management*, Fall 1990, p. 6.

15. Robert J. Vokurka and Rhonda R. Lummus, "At What Overhead Level Does Activity-Based Costing Pay Off?" *Production and Inventory Management Journal*, first quarter 2001.

16. Harold P. Roth and A. Faye Borthick, "Are You Distorting Costs by Violating ABC Assumptions?" *Management Accounting*, November 1991, p. 39.

17. H. James Harrington, "Process Breakthrough: Business Process Improvement," *Journal of Cost Management*, Fall 1993, pp. 36, 38.

18. Edward Blocher, Betty Wong, and Christopher T. McKittrick, "Making Bottom Up ABC Work at Reichhold Inc.," *Strategic Finance*, April 2002.

19. Mehmet C. Kocakulah and Douglas Dickmann, "Implementing Activity-Based Costing (ABC) to Measure Commercial Loan Profitability," *Journal of Bank Cost and Management Accounting* 14, no. 2 (2001): pp. 3–15.

20. Thomas L. Zeller, Gary Seigel, Gail Kacinuba, and Amy H-L Lau, *Healthcare Financial Management*, September 1999, pp. 46–50.

21. Hilary Becker, Carleton University, 2001.

22. Paul A. Sharman, "The Case for Management Accounting," *Strategic Finance*, October 2003, pp. 43–47.

23. H. Thomas Johnson, "It's Time to Stop Overselling Activity-Based Concepts," *Management Accounting*, September 1992, pp. 31, 33.

24. Kim L. Needy, Bopaya Bidanda, and Mehmet Gulsen, "A Model to Develop, Assess and Validate an Activity-Based Costing System for Small Manufacturers," *Engineering Management Journal*, March 2000.

Chapter 9

Relevant Costing

LEARNING OBJECTIVES

After reading this chapter, you should be able to answer the following questions:

1 What
constitutes relevance in a decision-making situation?

2 Why
is an opportunity cost relevant in decision making but a sunk cost (such as a joint cost) is not?

3 What
are the relevant costs in equipment replacement decisions?

4 What
are the relevant costs and qualitative factors that exist in a make-or-outsource (buy) decision?

5 How
can management best utilize a scarce resource?

6 How
does relevant costing relate to sales mix, sales pricing decisions, compensation changes, advertising budget and special order pricing decisions?

7 How
is product margin used to determine whether a product line should be retained, expanded, or eliminated?

www.gillette.com

The Gillette Company

Founded in 1901, the **GILLETTE COMPANY** is the world leader in male grooming, a category that includes blades, razors, and shaving preparations, and in selected female grooming products, such as wet shaving products and hair epilation devices. In addition, the company holds the number one position worldwide in alkaline batteries and in manual and power toothbrushes. Gillette's manufacturing operations are conducted at 32 facilities in 14 countries, and products are distributed through wholesalers, retailers, and agents in over 200 countries and territories.

In 1905, Gillette opened a sales office in London and a factory in Paris, which were the beginning of today's global company. That year, King C. Gillette's portrait and signature debuted on razor blade packaging and quickly became the worldwide symbol of Gillette quality.

Of the world's annual 20 billion razor blade sales, 33% are made by Gillette, even though most nondomestic markets have local manufacturers of double-edged blades. In 2004, blades and razors accounted for $4.3 billion of Gillette's total sales of $10.5 billion.

A key driver of Gillette's success has been a steady stream of new products. For every 15 product candidates that Gillette identifies, only one actually makes it into development. And, of those, only one-third advance from development to eventually reach the market. The others are dropped or "shelved" because manufacturing costs are higher than the company would like. This is the major reason that Gillette has outpaced its competition for decades: the company has the ability to reduce manufacturing costs consistently while improving quality.

In 1998, the company introduced the biggest shaving innovation in decades, the triple-bladed Mach3. Backed by an unprecedented advertising campaign, the Mach3 system quickly became a worldwide success. The Gillette Company, on November 7, 2002, introduced Sensor 3, the only disposable razor with three independently spring-mounted Sensor® blades that adjust to the curves and contours of the skin. Gillette Sensor 3 provides overall the best shave of any disposable razor. "Sensor 3 represents a significant breakthrough in disposable razor performance," said Peter K. Hoffman, president, Gillette Grooming Products. "It is one more example of our unwavering commitment to deliver the best shave possible for users of all types of wet shaving products."

"As the undisputed leader in men's grooming, Gillette is committed to innovation and to developing products and programmes that will provide men with a superior shaving performance," said Prakash Nedungadi, regional business director for the Middle East and Africa. Gillette has redefined the standards of male grooming in the UAE with the introduction of the first Gillette Perfect Shave program to provide men with the complete shaving experience. It consists of three essential steps—pre-shave preparation with Gillette Series Shave Gel, shave Gillette MACH3 Turbo razor, and post-shave Gillette Series After-Shave Gel. Gillette's Perfect Shave program is the most recent of "firsts from the organization that has been driven by the conviction that 'there is a better way to shave and we will find it.' The new Gillette Perfect Shave concept fulfills that promise and will harness Gillette's strength in the blades and razors business to grow the personal care franchise."

Gillette continues to be a leader in the field. It is stepping up its efforts to win the hearts and chins of shavers in Japan, which has been one of the toughest markets in the world to crack. The stakes are high: Japan is the world's second largest economy after the United States. The Boston razor giant, number one in Western Europe, Russia, China, and the United States, has been a distant second in Japan to Schick, its Bristol, CT, rival. But since launching Fusion last year, Gillette's share in Japan has jumped to 33% from 21%, nicking away at Schick's grip on the razor market, according to market research firm ACNielsen Japan. It was Gillette's largest increase ever in Japan, after nearly a decade of stagnant or single-digit growth in the country.

Japan is the only place in the world where the new razor is marketed as "Fusion 5+1" (the number of blades). Local research showed that the Japanese notion of Fusion by itself did not resonate. Gillette took a direct stab at Schick by labelling its bright-orange packages with "Superior versus four blade products."

SOURCES: Gillette Company 2003 Annual Report; Rita Koselka, "It's My Favourite Statistic," *Forbes*, September 12, 1994, pp. 172, 176; The Gillette Company, Annual Report, December 2004, p. 83; William H. Miller, "Gillette's Secret to Sharpness and The Gillette Advantage," *Industry Week*, January 3, 1994, pp. 26, 28; Business Editors, "The Gillette Company Celebrates Its Centennial in 2001," *Business Wire*, New York, September 4, 2001; Newstream.com Multimedia News for the 21st Century Newsroom, Found at: http://www.newstream.com/ is/story; Strategy, Found at: http://www.strategy.com, "Gillette Launches Its Perfect Shave Program in UAE," January 5, 2005; Jenn Abelson, "Looking to Clean Up in Japan—Gillette Makes Inroads with a New Ad Strategy," *Boston Globe*, June 24, 2007, A1.

*G*illette has made numerous decisions about which products it will sell, the pricing of the products, and which product lines to eliminate. In addition, while the company would prefer universality in its products, it occasionally must adapt to a particular foreign market, since only approximately 71% of its sales come from the North American market. For instance, in some foreign markets, razors are selling well even though a razor could cost almost a month's pay. Many customers cannot afford to purchase replacement blades so the company has altered its packaging to make them affordable. In a business where even tenths of pennies are important, many such decisions must be based solely on monetary factors. The company commonly assesses the viability of its decisions using **relevant costs**, which are those costs that are pertinent to or logically associated with a specific problem or decision, and which differ between alternatives.

relevant cost
a cost that is pertinent to or logically associated with a specific problem or decision and that differs between alternatives

Gillette's business choices reflect a common type of decision: how to competently allocate available but limited organizational resources so that company goals and objectives are achieved.

Wal-Mart's three-year push to get suppliers to tag cases and pallets of products with radio frequency identification (RFID) chips has been a long slog. Pacific Coast is benefiting from Wal-Mart's in-store RFID efforts. Data generated show which stores aren't doing a good job keeping products on shelves.[1]

Procter & Gamble was one of the first 100 suppliers to comply with Wal-Mart's requirement that products be tagged with RFID chips. This has improved the accuracy of its deliveries to the retailer, especially during time-sensitive promotions. "Ensuring that the right product is at the right place at the right time is priceless," says a company spokesman. "P&G's overall investment in RFID technology, which was multiple millions of dollars, has been recovered. It's been a fruitful collaboration between ourselves and Wal-Mart."[2]

RFID is a technology that can revolutionize business but also erode privacy. It uses a computer chip the size of a grain of rice to store data, which is transmitted wirelessly by a tiny antenna to a receiver. The chips, embedded in tags, now track pallets in warehouses and let drivers pass toll booths without stopping, but their potential is almost limitless.[3]

Using its technology expertise and working with experts in the field, SAP has developed an RFID offering that is seamlessly integrated with key SAP solutions. SAP RFID technology provides complete process support for capturing and handling RFID data, streamlining and automating supply chain processes, and integrating RFID information into enterprise systems. SAP can use RFID technology to adapt to changing conditions and events—and then drive rapid responses through supply chain management and executive systems. As well, many gains can be made in production and logistics processes. For example, companies can reduce the time it takes to process orders, and less inventory can be maintained. The ability to seamlessly track reusable assets such as containers and returnable packaging in the transport and delivery processes ensures greater process security while lowering operating costs, improving asset management, and enhancing service performance.[4]

Gillette was one of eight suppliers to participate in a pilot with Wal-Mart, with the result that most of the cases of razors, shaving cream, and toothpaste it ships to Wal-Mart are tagged at its distribution centre in Romeoville, Illinois. But because Gillette thinks the benefits will be greater the earlier in the process it can tag goods, the company has also launched a pilot to "tag at source" at its packaging facility in Fort Devens, Massachusetts, where it puts electronic product code (EPC) tags on cases of Venus razors.

Like a licence plate on a car, the EPC uniquely identifies a case or pallet. It uses five key pieces of information: the company code; product code; serial number, which uniquely identifies the item; a header that defines different types of tags, such as those in the consumer products industry; and a filter value that allows a company to read only pallet-level tags, ignoring case-level tags or vice versa.

By tagging at the point of packaging, Gillette can reduce the labour costs associated with manually scanning each case and curb errors. Workers currently key five entries onto a keyboard and do three bar code scans for each pallet, according to Jamshed Dubash, director of auto-ID technology at Gillette. He says a business process analysis showed that the company will annually save 25% in operational costs once all cases are being tagged at the packaging point rather than at the distribution centre.[5]

A recent study by Accenture forecasts that there will be cheaper labour costs of up to 65% in receiving, 25% in stocking and cycle counting, and 100% in physical counting, all because of the automatic capture of inventory data. Theft reduction of almost 1% of sales will occur as the tags set off alarms when foul play is afoot.[6]

If you use an Esso Speedpass or Shell Easypay key fob to buy gas, you may already be an RFID addict. Just wave the plastic tab at the gas pump and your fill-up and payment are authorized, freeing you from having to dig around for your credit card.[7]

RFID tags are being used by New York Presbyterian Hospital/Weill Cornell to improve patient care in its cardiac surgery department. "A lot of times we were unable to determine what was happening to our inventory," says Martin Dagata, "So it was a matter of money. But there's also a patient safety aspect to what we are doing. The RFID system secures our inventory. If anything goes missing, I know exactly who took it *out of the cabinet. The hospital has also been able to cut its inventory because the system offers a digital view into what supplies it currently has. The hospital has been able to save $230,000 in inventory carrying value.[8]*

Accounting information can improve but not perfect management's understanding of the consequences of resource allocation decisions. To the extent that this information can reduce management's uncertainty about the economic facts, outcomes, and relationships involved in various courses of action, the information is valuable for decision-making purposes and necessary for conducting business.

As discussed in Chapter 3, many decisions are made on the basis of incremental analysis. Such analysis encompasses the concept of relevant costing, which allows managers to focus on pertinent facts and disregard extraneous information. This chapter illustrates the use of relevant costing in decisions about making or outsourcing (buying) a product or part, allocating scarce resources, and determining the appropriate sales or production mix. Although these decisions are often viewed by managers as short-run, each decision also has significant long-run implications that must be considered.

LEARNING OBJECTIVE 1

What constitutes relevance in a decision-making situation?

THE CONCEPTS OF RELEVANCE AND RELEVANT COSTING

Managers routinely make decisions concerning alternatives that have been identified as feasible solutions to problems or feasible methods for the attainment of objectives. In doing so, they must weigh the relevant costs and benefits associated with each course of action and then determine which is the best. Relevant costs are those costs that are pertinent to or logically associated with a specific problem or decision and that differ between alternatives.

Information is relevant when it logically relates to a decision about a future endeavour. Costs provide information, and different costs can be used for many different purposes. No single cost can be relevant in all decisions or to all managers. The challenge is to get specific information.

Accountants can assist managers in determining which costs are relevant to the objectives and decisions at hand. The challenge is to get the most specific information. To the extent possible and practical, **relevant costing** allows managers to focus on pertinent facts and disregard extraneous information by comparing the differential, incremental revenues and costs of alternative decisions. *Differential* refers to the different costs between or among the choices. *Incremental* means the additional or extra amount associated with some action. Thus, **incremental revenue** is the additional revenue resulting from a contemplated sale or provision of service. An **incremental cost** is the additional cost of producing or selling a contemplated additional quantity of output.

Success in strategic development and implementation requires that managers, in making decisions, are completely clear on what costs are relevant. They must be able to separate the relevant from the irrelevant to be effective in decision making.

Decision making is facilitated by an organization's having an ERP system. ERP systems with their rigorous handling of the recording and allocating of costs provide more accurate costs. Similarly, the greater accuracy with recording revenues allows for more accurate revenue data. This greater accuracy means that relevance can be more precisely considered in an ERP environment.

relevant costing
a process that allows managers to focus on pertinent facts and disregard extraneous information by comparing, to the extent possible and practical, the differential, incremental revenues and incremental costs of alternative decisions

incremental revenue
the additional revenue resulting from a contemplated sale of a quantity of output

incremental cost
the additional cost of producing or selling a contemplated quantity of output

Differential and, therefore, incremental costs are relevant costs. These costs may be variable or fixed. Two general rules for short-run decision making are that (1) most variable costs are relevant and (2) most fixed costs are not. The reasoning behind this rule is that, as sales or production volumes change, variable costs change but fixed costs do not. There are, however, some exceptions that must be acknowledged in the decision-making process.

For example, the direct material cost of a product is a relevant incremental variable cost in a decision to make each additional unit. In contrast, the fixed cost of the available production machinery would not be relevant to the production of each additional unit. However, the cost of buying new machinery is an incremental fixed cost relevant to the decision to produce a new product line or expand an existing one beyond the current relevant range.

Some relevant costs, such as sales commissions and the prime costs of production (direct material and direct labour), are easily identified and quantified. These factors are integral parts of the accounting system. Other factors (such as opportunity costs) may be relevant and quantifiable but are not recorded in the accounting system. An **opportunity cost** represents the benefits forgone when one course of action is chosen over another. For example, by choosing to attend university, a student incurs an opportunity cost of the forgone earnings that could have been made by working at a paying job instead. Such factors cannot be overlooked simply because they may be more difficult to obtain or may require the use of estimates.

A **sunk cost** is one that has already been incurred and cannot be changed regardless of the alternative selected. A sunk cost is not a relevant cost since it is a cost that will not be incurred in the future; it has already been incurred.

The difference between the incremental revenue and incremental cost of a particular alternative is the positive or negative incremental benefit of that course of action. When evaluating alternative courses of action, managers should select the alternative that provides the highest incremental benefit to the company. Such a comparison may superficially appear simple but often is not, because relevance is a concept that is inherently individual. For example, an investment proposal might provide a high rate of return for a company but might also create a future potential environmental hazard. One unit manager might view the potential hazard as very relevant, while another manager might minimize the relevance of that possibility. In some instances, all alternatives result in incremental losses, and managers must choose the one that creates the smallest incremental loss.

One alternative course of action often considered is defensive avoidance, or the "change nothing for the moment" option. Although other alternatives have certain incremental revenues and costs associated with them, the "change nothing" alternative represents current conditions. It may serve as a baseline against which all other alternatives can be measured. However, even the "change nothing" alternative may involve the risk of loss of competitive advantage. If a firm chooses this alternative while its competitors upgrade processes, that firm may incur the ultimate incremental loss—losing its market. Also, the opportunity costs associated with the status quo may result in less benefit than another alternative.

The "change nothing" alternative should be chosen only when it is perceived to be the best decision choice. Often, however, this alternative is selected only because it is easier than making changes.

At other times, the selection of "change nothing" is made because decision makers, lacking information, perceive uncertainty to be so great that they consider the risk of making a change to be greater than the risk of continuing the current course of action. When this condition exists, the results achieved from the "change nothing" alternative (current results) are thought to be more advantageous than the potential incremental benefit of any other alternative.

Wonder Bread's bright white wrapper dotted with blue, red, and yellow balloons remained unchanged for more than 40 years—the problem was that the bread stayed bright white, too. In filing for bankruptcy court protection from creditors in September 2004, Interstate Bakeries Corp. blamed low-carbohydrate diets for Wonder's woes. In reality, the low-carb trend only hastened a steady decline as different owners squeezed Wonder to boost profits while competitors passed it by, joining the trend toward more healthful foods like multigrain breads. "Wonder is no longer wonderful," declared Tony Oszlanyi, baking consultant and a retired operations chief for former Wonder owner Continental Baking Co.[9]

In some situations, such as those involving government regulations or mandates, a "change nothing" alternative does not truly exist. For example, if a company were polluting river water and a governmental regulatory agency issued an injunction against that company, it would be forced to correct the pollution problem (assuming it wished to continue in business). The company could, of course, delay installation of the pollution control devices at the risk of fines or closure, creating additional incremental cost effects that would have to be considered. Managers in this situation must make decisions using a "now-versus-later" attitude and may determine that now is better regardless of the cost.

More global financial service companies are jumping on the offshoring bandwagon in a bid to cut costs and keep shareholders happy. "Offshoring" refers to the practice of moving jobs to lower cost countries such as India and China. Cost saving was the reason cited for offshoring by 79% of the executives surveyed. Indeed, 74% of financial services companies did save costs, the survey found.

As stories circulate about the cultural barriers that North American companies face when outsourcing IT to locations in India, offshore service providers are moving some operations back to North America. Some Indian service providers— once considered the darlings of the outsourcing industry—today face challenges that are causing North American clients to question the benefits of sending all their work overseas. Also, with the value of the U.S. dollar dropping in relation to the Indian rupee, some offshore providers are being compelled to raise prices, which negates the cost savings that North American companies expect when offshoring IT work to India. While it is less expensive than operating solely in North America, the cost of doing business in India has become more onerous, largely because the demand for talent there is now so high that workers want more money, which has increased staff turnover. As a result, many Indian service providers are now setting up service centres in Eastern Europe and Mexico.[10]

Since a comprehensive evaluation of all alternative courses of action is part of rational management behaviour, the chosen course should be the one that will make the business and its stakeholders better off in the future. This means that managers must provide some mechanism for including all nonmonetary or inherently non-quantifiable considerations in the decision process. They can do that by attempting to quantify items or simply by making instinctive value judgments about nonmonetary benefits and costs.

To illustrate this point, consider the factors that should be evaluated when a labour-intensive company analyzes the labour savings that would result from replacing employees with robots or, as discussed in the News Note on page 531, from changing locales or suppliers.

For example, LogiCan Technologies Inc. transformed a manufacturing platform into a robotized customization operation that is an outsource manufacturer for high-tech customers around the world. The company produces and can deliver

Where Is It Cheaper?

At the CHICKASAW NATIONAL RECREATION AREA, the live reptiles and birds of prey that are on exhibit need food. Staff at Chickasaw spent time and money raising their own feeder mice to feed to the snakes and owls. As part of the Interior Department's effort to spend budget dollars as efficiently as possible, Chickasaw asked this question: "Do we really need to be in the business of raising our own feeder mice or is there a cheaper way to get them?"

Chickasaw calculated what it costs to raise its own feeder mice and compared that with the cost of buying feeder mice from private vendors. It found that vendors could provide the feeder mice Chickasaw needed at a lower cost.

Today, Chickasaw saves $15,000 per year by buying feeder mice from a private vendor. Chickasaw now has more money to spend on core priorities, such as nature trails, that more directly benefit its visitors.

LEVI STRAUSS & CO., whose jeans are an all-American symbol, said it was closing six U.S. plants and eliminating 3,600 jobs, or 22% of its workforce, as it moves away from the business of actually making the clothes it sells. "There is no question that we must move away from owned-and-operated plants in the United States to remain competitive in our industry," said Philip Marineau, chief executive officer. Contracting to outside manufacturers will enable the company to have a more flexible cost structure, protect its profit margins, and invest more in product development, marketing, and retailing, Mr. Marineau said.

We can see much the same thing happening at HORNBY'S HOGWARTS EXPRESS, a company that produces model train sets. The company has now outsourced all production to China. The chief executive said the decision to outsource all production to China meant that the group could sell products with "substantially better detail and authenticity" for the same cost. Hornby's site near Hong Kong employs 1,100 people for the same amount it cost to employ 500 people in the United Kingdom "If we had not moved to China we may not have been in business now; our profits and market share were in decline," he said.

RIS, which was in the midst of setting up its first offshore office, had about 360 staff and hoped to employ about 20 or 30 in Bucharest by the end of 2003. It's all about cost and global competition. A software developer in India or Romania might cost half to one-eighth of what a Canadian-equivalent developer does. For a software or IT outsourcing company, most of its costs are labour, so the offshore savings can't be ignored. Now more than ever before it's easier and cheaper to just hire full-time employees halfway around the world in a place like Bangalore, India.

GENERAL MOTORS CORP planned to boost significantly the amount of "white-collar" and design work it hands to Canadian firms as part of its efforts to implement sweeping cost-cutting measures. Most of the US $3.5-million GM moved out of the US in 2003 went to one Canadian supplier. Industry watchers say the reason GM is likely willing to risk potentially unpopular moves is because of a compelling need to cut costs in an industry characterized by high vehicle incentives and thin profit margins.

SOURCES: http://www.whitehouse.gov/results/difference/chickasaw.html; Clifford and Kripalani, with Dawley in London, "Different Countries, Adjoining Cubicles," *Business Week,* New York, August 28, 2000; Joost Akkermans, "Royal Philips Poised to Shed 1,600 Workers," Bloomberg News, *Toronto Star,* March 14, 2003; "Levi Shuts Factories, Shifts Focus," *Globe and Mail,* April 9, 2002, B12; "Harry Puts Hornby on Track; Scale of Success: Outsourcing Production to China Good Move," *Birmingham Post,* Birmingham, U.K., February 5, 2002; Scott Adams, *Financial Post,* June 16, 2003; Chris Sorenson, "GM to Assign 'White-Collar' Work to Canada," March 25, 2004, *National Post,* FP6.

anywhere, within 72 hours, dozens of high-tech items ranging from switches for industrial equipment to health monitors, heat tractors, modems, radio frequency products, and radios for NATO. A company spokesperson said, "The reason we can compete with the world is robotics, not by sewing seatbelts. Our labour component is less than 20% of the product cost so we can compete with the world. That's what we're proving can be done."[11]

Company managers need to weigh potential future cost reductions and increases in productivity against possible short- and long-range negative public reaction toward the company because of the layoffs. Although public reactions are difficult to measure and quantify and may not be immediately noticeable, such reactions should still be factored into the decision. In addition, there may be very relevant but highly non-quantifiable costs resulting from ethical considerations, such as the moral obligations the firm has toward the displaced workers. Such costs must be estimated in a reasonable manner if the decision to replace workers is to be based on a truly valid analysis.

The need for specificity in information depends on how important that information is relative to management objectives. If all other factors are equal, more precise information is given greater weight in the decision-making process. However, if information is important but qualitative and imprecise, management should find a way to estimate the impact such information may have on known monetary details and company profits.

Information can be based on past or present data but is relevant only if it relates to a future choice and creates a differential effect in regard to alternative choices. All managerial decisions are made to affect future events, so the information on which decisions are based should reflect future conditions. The future may be the short run (two hours from now or next month) or the long run (five years or more from now).[12]

Future costs are the only costs that can be avoided, and the longer into the future a decision's time horizon extends, the more costs are **avoidable**, controllable, and relevant. *Only information that has a bearing on future events is relevant in decision making.* But people too often forget this basic truth and try to make decisions using inappropriate data.

SUNK COSTS AND JOINT PROCESSES

One common error is trying to use a previously incurred, historical cost to make a current decision. Current costs (such as replacement or budgeted costs) are assumed to be accurate or reasonably accurate at the current time. As such, these costs represent relevant information and should be considered in the decision-making process. In contrast, historical costs incurred in the past to acquire an asset or a resource—called sunk costs—are not recoverable and cannot be changed, regardless of what current circumstances exist or what future course of action is taken. A current or future selling price may be present for an asset, but that is the result of current or future conditions and is not a recouping of a historical cost. The following discussion illustrates why sunk costs are not relevant costs.

Like Gillette, almost every company makes and sells a wide variety of products. Companies often must engage in multiple production processes to produce their products; for instance, Gillette could not manufacture its razors and Oral-B toothbrushes in the same manufacturing operation. However, it is possible for a single process to generate several different outputs simultaneously, as when Tyson Foods processes chickens to produce whole birds, parts, and "nuggets." Industries that produce multiple products from a single process include refineries, lumber mills, food, chemical, and cosmetics manufacturers. A single process in which one product cannot be manufactured without others being produced is known as a **joint process**.

In joint cost settings there exists a fundamental nonseparability of the costs of any process that generates two or more split products. Such circumstances invite product-linked allocations that achieve economies of scope. The most frequently encountered model, net realizable value (NRV),[13] allocates according to maximized profit at the point of product sales.[14]

A company undertakes a joint production process to generate outputs known as **joint products**. Each type of joint product has substantial revenue-generating ability. In contrast, **by-products** and **scrap** are incidental outputs of a joint process. Both are saleable, but their sales values alone would not be enough for management

avoidable costs are costs which can be traced directing to a segment and would disappear if that segment was estimated.

joint process a process in which one product cannot be manufactured without others being produced

joint products two or more products that have relatively significant sales values and are not separately identifiable as individual products until the split-off point

by-products products that have minor sales value as compared with the sales value of the major products and are not separately identifiable as individual products until they have become split off

scrap inputs that do not become part of the outputs but have very minor values

to justify undertaking the joint process. By-products are viewed as having a higher sales value than scrap. A final output from a joint process is waste. **Waste** is a residual output that has no sales value. A normal amount of waste is considered a production cost that cannot be avoided.

A corn processing plant will be used to illustrate the types of outputs resulting from a joint process. Outputs may include corn on the cob and whole-kernel corn (joint products), partial corn kernels (by-products) used for cornmeal, inferior kernels (scrap) for sale to producers of animal food, and cobs (waste) that are discarded. Exhibit 9-1 shows the outputs of such a joint process.

waste
inputs that do not become part of the output

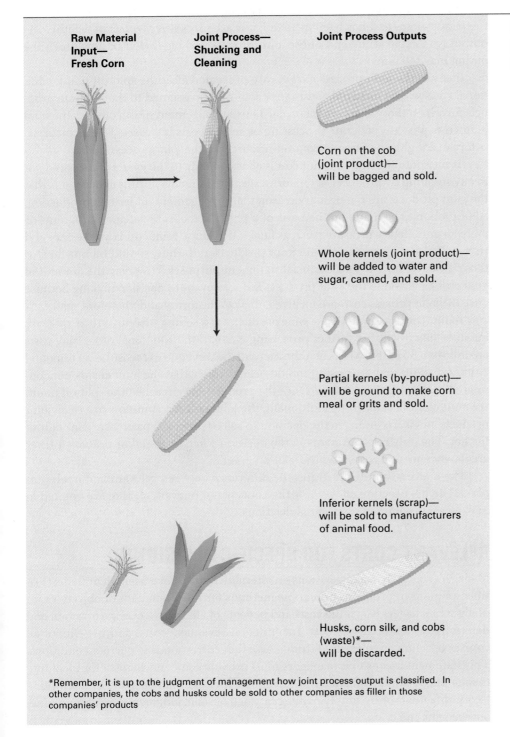

EXHIBIT 9-1

Illustration of Joint Process Output

The point at which the outputs of a joint process are first identifiable as individual products is called the **split-off point**. A joint process may have one or more split-off points, depending on the number and types of output produced. Output may be sold at the split-off point, if a market exists for products in that condition. Alternatively, some or all of the products may be processed further after exiting the joint process.

The costs incurred for materials, labour, and overhead during a joint process (up to the split-off point) are referred to as the **joint cost** of the production process. For companies to engage in a joint process, total revenues from sales of all resulting products should exceed the total costs of those products. The joint process results in a "basket" of products, and managers must be aware that some output from the joint process may require additional processing to make it saleable. However, after the joint process cost has been incurred, it is a sunk cost *regardless* of whether the output is saleable at the end of the joint process and *regardless* of how much the output may sell for.

If any of the joint process *outputs* are processed after the split-off point, additional costs will be incurred. Costs after split-off are assigned to the separate products for which those costs are incurred. Thus, management must consider the total joint costs plus any separate processing or selling costs it expects will be incurred before making the decision to commit resources to the joint process.

At the split-off point, the joint cost is allocated only to the joint products and not to any resulting by-products, scrap, or waste. The rationale for this allocation is that the joint products are the primary reason that management undertook production. Allocation may be made on the basis of a physical measure (such as kilograms or units) or a monetary measure (such as final sales value). Joint cost is a necessary and reasonable cost of producing the joint products and, thus, should be attached to those products for external financial statement purposes. However, the amount of joint cost allocated to the joint products is not relevant to decision making because once the joint process costs are incurred, they are historical and, therefore, sunk.

To illustrate, assume that a joint product has a selling price of $10 at split-off, but its selling price after further processing is $16. If the additional processing costs are less than $6 ($16 − $10), then the incremental revenue exceeds the incremental costs and additional processing should occur. Notice that the joint cost is not considered in this decision process. Once the products have reached the split-off point, the joint cost is a sunk cost. Additionally, the joint cost is a common cost of all joint products and is irrelevant to the decision to sell or process a particular joint output further. The only relevant items in the decision whether to sell or process further are the incremental costs after the split-off point.

The above example illustrates the difference between relevant and irrelevant costs. The next section shows how the concepts of relevant costing are applied in making some common managerial decisions.

RELEVANT COSTS FOR SPECIFIC DECISIONS

Managers routinely make decisions on alternatives that have been identified as feasible solutions to problems or feasible methods for the attainment of objectives. In doing so, managers weigh the costs and benefits of alternative courses of action and determine which course is best. Incremental revenues, costs, and benefits of all courses of action are measured from a base that corresponds to current conditions. This statement means that managers must provide some mechanism for including the inherently nonquantifiable considerations. Inclusion can be made by attempting to quantify items or by simply making instinctive value judgments about nonmonetary benefits and costs.

When evaluating alternative courses of action, managers should select the alternative that provides the highest incremental benefit to the company. In some instances, all alternatives result in incremental losses, and managers must choose the one that creates the smallest incremental loss.

When Kraft received some bad earnings news, the company reviewed its existing locations and corporate policies and had to make some very firm decisions. The following News Note discusses what happened at Kraft Foods.

Making Changes at Kraft

What happened at KRAFT FOODS is a good example of evaluating different courses of action and making changes. In the second quarter of 2004, Kraft reported a 25.5% drop in earnings, the latest in a string of disappointing results. Therefore Kraft Foods announced that it would eliminate 6,000 jobs and close 20 plants worldwide by the end of 2006. Several factors are behind Kraft's problems. Its familiar cheese brands—including Cracker Barrel, Velveeta, and Cheez Whiz—still account for almost one-fifth of its sales and prices for raw ingredients are increasing. It is expected that these raw ingredients will raise Kraft's costs by $650 million to $700 million. What's more, Kraft's labels, like many big-name brands, have lost sales to lower-cost store brands, and the food industry has been a target of lawsuits by consumer advocates protesting the marketing of what they contend are unhealthful products, especially to children.

Roger Deromedi, Kraft's chief executive officer, says that Kraft, as part of its recovery plan, is making significant changes both to its product line and its marketing budget, increasing its outlays for advertising and marketing. It is giving special emphasis to price gap management (narrowing the difference in price between Kraft's products and those of its competitors). Deromedi also hinted recently that some of the low-performing brands would be cut loose, though he did not name names. "We need to focus on categories we can drive forward and really win with," he said recently. Consequently, Kraft is offering a more healthful line and being more selective in where it sells products.

Rising grain and dairy prices are taking a growing slice out of household incomes as food giants such as Kraft Foods Inc. hike their prices to cover higher input costs. Kraft, which operates in 145 countries, said it had offset higher raw food prices by passing the increases on to consumers.

Kraft Foods Inc.'s Canadian unit plans to sell several of its brands (including Aylmer vegetables and Primo pasta) to buyout firms (including Sun Capital Partners Inc. and EG Capital LLC) in order to focus on faster growing lines. The transaction will involve selling four factories in Ontario (one of them in Toronto) and another in Quebec. These asset sales are the slower growth lines. Their sale is part of a three-year plan to reduce annual costs by U.S.$400 million. CEO Roger Deromedi also plans to introduce healthier products and to increase marketing for cheeses, crackers, and Maxwell House coffee.

SOURCES: Adapted from Jo Napolitano, "After Setbacks, Kraft Seeks a Bright Spot," *New York Times*, August 11, 2004; Chris Barritt, "Kraft Canada Unloads Brands," *Toronto Star*, December 28, 2005; Alia McMullen, "Rising Food Costs Make Prices Hard to Swallow, BMO Says," *Financial Post*, July 29, 2008 page F1.

Equipment Replacement Decisions

Many business decision situations relate to assets. After an asset or resource is acquired, managers may find that the product produced or service performed by that asset is no longer marketable or that the asset is no longer adequate for the intended purposes, does not perform to expectations, or is not technologically current.

Decisions must then be made whether to keep or dispose of the old asset and, if disposed, whether to replace it. Commercial printer Transcontinental Inc. is cutting 135 jobs and booking a fourth-quarter charge as it ramps up productivity improvement measures and invests millions in new equipment. The Montreal-based company is buying three Goss presses and advanced finishing equipment for $53 million. The three presses will replace seven older machines. In a news release, the company said the presses "will significantly improve productivity, flexibility and overall product quality."[15] Although asset acquisition decisions are covered in depth in Web Chapter 14, the following illustration provides an excellent starting point to introduce the concept of using relevant cost information for making asset replacement decisions.

Assume that Spiros Zervos purchases a computer system for $3,200 on December 28, from a company that is going out of business on December 31. Spiros expects the computer to last for his three years at law school and, after that time, to have no salvage value. This computer will be referred to as the "old" computer. One week later, on January 4, Spiros notices an advertisement for a similar computer for $2,300 at one of the major electronics discount stores. This computer also has an estimated life of three years and no salvage value. This "new" computer will perform as well as the "old" computer and, in addition, has a larger hard drive memory for faster processing time. The new computer will save $300 per year in operating, maintenance, and repair costs over the old computer. Upon investigation, Spiros discovers that he can sell his week-old computer for only $2,200—the "going out of business" price had not been such a bargain, and he is unable to return it to the store since it no longer exists.

What should Spiros do? Keep the old or buy the new?

Data on the old and new computers are shown in Exhibit 9-2.

EXHIBIT 9-2

Decision-Making Information for Spiros Zervos

	Old Computer (Purchased on December 28)	New Computer (Available on January 4)
Cost	$3,200	$2,300
Annual operating cost	1,200	900
Salvage value	0	0
Current resale value	2,200	Not applicable
Life in years	3	3

Spiros has two options: (1) use the old computer or (2) sell the old computer and buy the new one. Exhibit 9-3 presents the relevant costs Spiros should consider in making his asset replacement decision. As shown in the computations in Exhibit 9-3, the $3,200 purchase price of the old computer does not affect the decision process. This $3,200 was "gone forever" when Spiros bought the computer. However, if he sells the old computer, he will effectively be able to reduce the net cash outlay for the new computer to $100 because he will have $2,200 more than he has currently. Using either computer, Spiros will spend money over the next three years for operating costs, but he will spend $900 less using the new computer ($300 savings per year × 3 years).

Alternative 1: Use old computer		
Operating cost over life of old computer ($1,200 × 3 years)		$3,600
Alternative 2: Sell old computer and buy new		
Cost of new computer	$2,300	
Resale value of old computer	2,200	
Effective net outlay for new computer	$ 100	
Operating cost over life of new computer ($900 × 3 years)	2,700	
Total cost of new computer		2,800
Benefit from purchasing new computer		$ 800

EXHIBIT 9-3

Relevant Costs Related to Spiros' Alternatives

The $1,000 difference between the $3,200 original cost and the $2,200 resale value is either a current period loss or, if he keeps the computer, future period depreciation. Thus, the $1,000 loss or its equivalent in depreciation charges is the same in magnitude whether Spiros disposes of the old computer and buys the new one or retains the old computer and uses it. This $1,000 cannot be avoided under either alternative; it will be either a loss or an expense. Since the amount is the same under both alternatives, it is not relevant to the decision process.

The relevant factors in deciding whether to purchase the new computer are:
a. the cost of the new computer ($2,300)
b. the current resale value of the old computer ($2,200)
c. the annual savings of the new computer ($300) and the number of years (three) that the savings would be enjoyed

The common tendency is initially to believe that Spiros should not purchase the new computer because he will incur a $1,000 loss on an asset that he has only had for seven days. Even if Spiros received only $1,500 from its sale, the choice would have remained the same. In this case, he would save a total of $100 by buying the new computer and abandoning the old, as shown in the following computation:

Operating cost of old computer		$3,600
Cost of new computer:		
Purchase price ($2,300 – $1,500)	$ 800	
Operating cost	2,700	3,500
Savings by purchasing new computer		$ 100

Spiros must resign himself to accept the past as a fact and make new choices given his set of future alternatives.

Another avenue one may look at is investing in new technology to ensure profitability.

Don't let Wal-Mart fool you. Retailing is and has always been an inefficient business. Retailers, particularly those that operate large chains, have to predict the desires of fickle customers, buy and allocate complex sets of merchandise, set the right prices, and offer the right promotions for each individual item. Often there are gaps, often wide ones, between supply and demand, which leave stores holding too much of what customers don't want and too little of what they do.

Wal-Mart ensures that its shelves are full of inventory that customers want to purchase.

Wal-Mart has been cutting inventory to reduce costs and remove "clutter" from its stores. In May 2006, the company announced that first-quarter inventory levels had risen 2.7% over a year earlier. Thus it had easily achieved its goal, which was to grow inventory at half the rate of sales. The retailer had missed that target in recent quarters. Many suppliers say that Wal-Mart asked them to cut back on shipments in the first quarter, and some blamed those cutbacks for luke-warm sales and profits. Wal-Mart CFO Tom Schoewe says that inventory improvements probably won't be as dramatic in the coming quarters.[16] Not making the right decision can be deadly, especially for those that sell merchandise with a short shelf life—whether Christmas cards, computers, or apparel.

Yield-management applications have already brought precision pricing and capacity management to the airline and hotel industries. But until recently, merchandising optimization has been beyond the capabilities of retailers.

There is a solution: a sophisticated new set of software tools has emerged, which promises to revolutionize the entire merchandising chain from buying to stocking to pricing. These merchandising optimization systems, as they're called, determine the right quantity, placements, and price of items to maximize retailers' returns. Early users are already reporting promising results with gains in gross margins in the range of 5% to 15%.[17]

Zellers was struggling with inventory and supply-chain issues. Sometimes the discount retailer had too much product on hand, sometimes too little, and sometimes no product at all. Perhaps most frustrating, it was losing sales from empty shelves while good inventory stood by collecting dust in the back room. Something had to change if survival was in its future. As late as 1999, the retailer was using pen and paper to keep track of stockroom inventory across its chain of 300 stores. Something had to be done. Click on 2004, and Zellers is winning accolades for its inventory and supply-chain management system known internally as LIDS (listed inventory database system) installed in stores over the last three years.[18]

RFID gives any object its own programmable digital identity that can be read wirelessly. About the size of a grain of rice, an RFID tag emits a radio signal that can be picked up by a handheld or stationary reader or even a computer network. Retailers and manufacturers have started using it to better track their products from the factory line to store shelves.

The following News Note shows how RFID chips help track individual items and reduce the cost of labour.

RFID and Manufacturing

GENERAL NEWS NOTE

RFID is likely to add more value in manufacturing environments with complex flows, less value where flows are simple. Well-defined flows in a process industry, such as sugar, limit the value of RFID. In a make-to-order setting, on the other hand, RFID tags linked to each job can improve the ease and accuracy of data gathering. This enables the manufacturer to make schedule adjustments based on the actual state of the job shop.

Item-level RFID can help improve manufacturing for highly customized, high-value items. For instance, Vauxhall Motors uses it to increase accuracy when building customized Astra models. Here, an RFID tag containing assembly details is attached to each vehicle. The system has increased quality and decreased labour costs associated with customization.

The gains from RFID can be more significant in manufacturing environments such as pharmaceuticals, where the tracking and maintenance of compliance records is required. IBM is launching a system that tracks medications through the supply chain until they reach consumers; the goal is to help the pharmaceutical industry combat drug counterfeiting. The system employs the same RFID tags as are already being used to track packages of drugs, especially drugs that attract counterfeiters. Purdue Pharma, for example, has been using RFIDs since 2004 to track OxyContin, a pain reliever. IBM's system helps drug manufacturers create electronic certificates of authenticity for medications—down to the individual bottle—as they move from manufacturers and distributors to pharmacies and hospitals.

The gains are also more substantial in certain food processing activities. For example, Wells Dairy, an ice cream supplier to Wal-Mart, has reduced quality control costs by tagging each two-bucket case of ice cream.

Canadian Linen and Uniforms Service's Company looks like they are working for NASA. The company was early to introduce RFID technology to its laundering process. The company's equipment reads the RFID chip sewn into the label of garments to monitor laundering services. The radio chip is like a transponder with a digital number that is quickly read by its computers. The chip keeps track of how many times the garment has been laundered, whether it's been repaired and what kind of repairs have been made, when it needs to be returned and when it should be taken out of rotation. At the end of the laundering process the RFID chip, label and serial number are used to accurately sort garments according to wearer and company.

Companies like Wal-Mart that cross-dock supplies from multiple suppliers into their distribution centres can improve efficiency by using case- or pallet-level RFIDs. These benefits show up in the time and labour requirements for the cross-docking operations. RFID can also help track crates, forklifts, and trucks during the shipping process. Asset-level RFID can be used to match assets to shipments and improve loading and unloading schedules.

SOURCES: Susan Hall, "IBM Launches Medication-Tracking System," *USA Today*, August 9, 2007; Sunil Chopra and ManMohan S. Sodhi, "Looking for the Bang from the RFID Buck," *Supply Chain Management Review*, May/June 2007, pg. 34–41; Mary Teresa Bitti, "The Future of Laundry Is Here," *Financial Post*, August 2, 2008.

It will probably take a few more years for RFID to catch on. Today's price per chip is from 25 to 45 cents. Other companies are working on new methodology that will cost a penny a tag.[19] "'RFID technology and applications are revolutionizing supply-chain management and are enabling companies to obtain an enormous amount of data in a short period of time,' said Paul Peercy, dean of UW's College of Engineering. 'It's only in its infancy state, but it's going to affect nearly all industries.'"[20]

Relevant costing techniques are also appropriate in make-or-outsource (buy) decisions.

LEARNING OBJECTIVE **4**

What are the relevant costs and qualitative factors that exist in a make-or-outsource (buy) decision?

outsource
use a source external to the company to provide a service or manufacture a needed product or component

make-or-outsource (buy) decision
a decision that compares the cost of internally manufacturing a product component with the cost of purchasing it from outside suppliers or from another division at a specified price and, thus, attempts to assess the best uses of available facilities

RELEVANT COSTS IN MAKE-OR-OUTSOURCE (BUY) DECISIONS

A constant concern in manufacturing is whether components of the right quality will be available at the right time and at the right price, and so companies often ensure a component's availability by manufacturing it themselves. For some companies, the decision for in-house production may have been made because the company is interested in embarking on a vertical integration path, in which one division or subsidiary can serve as a supplier to the others within the same company. Other companies prefer to **outsource**, or purchase some or all components from external parties.

The decision to buy externally can lead to cost savings in internal manufacturing when a company can take advantage of the expertise, economies of scale, and smoother production schedules of external suppliers. The management accountant's role in the decision is to provide an accurate analysis of the relevant cost of the make-or-outsource (buy) decision; these costs can then be used in make-or-outsource (buy) decisions. The allocation and assignment of manufacturing overhead to an internally manufactured product may make its cost appear larger than the price of other similar products in the marketplace. Even so, a decision to outsource (buy) may turn out to be suboptimal because previously allocated and assigned overheads are still being incurred by the company. For example, if a product is discontinued, the overhead previously assigned to or recovered against that product will be assigned to or recovered by the remaining products. One or more of these remaining products may now appear expensive and be discontinued and an equivalent product may be bought externally. Also, all costs can vary in the long term, and thus there is a need to identify the cost of the additional resources required from outsourcing (buy), such as goods receiving and inspection, material handling, production scheduling, and accounts payable.[21]

Toyota, for example, makes only about 25% of its parts.[22] Dell buys circuit boards, disk drives, and other modules—designed specifically for Dell—from outside manufacturers and assembles the computers in its own warehouses.[23] For all components, a **make-or-outsource (buy) decision** must be made in which the company evaluates all of its costs and options for either making or procuring the component from another firm.

The car industry can save time and hundreds of millions of dollars of investment in factories by outsourcing some parts of the production of vehicles. The car makers can also be more flexible by outsourcing and not taking on large fixed costs.

Many European auto makers are handing production of niche models to companies like Magna Steyr, a unit of Aurora, Ontario-based Magna International Inc. It is the largest of the niche producers. Visitors to Magna Steyr AG's research and development centre in Austria have to register with a guard at the gate and be escorted past a camera and through two sets of security doors. The procedures are designed to prevent the company's clients—DaimlerChrysler AG, Bayerische Motoren Werke AG, and General Motors Corp.—from seeing what new models Magna Steyr is working on for their competitors.

Munich-based BMW contracted production of its new X3 sport-utility vehicle to Magna Steyr to avoid having to build a plant, saving two years in bringing the vehicle to market, spokesman Marc Hassinger said. BMW laid out the parameters for making the vehicle and has BMW engineers at Magna Steyr's plant monitoring production and quality.

The manufacturing of the Porsche Boxster and the Chrysler Crossfire are also being outsourced to other companies.[24]

This type of outsourcing (make-or-buy) decision should be made only after proper analysis. Like any organizational decision, outsourcing requires effective evaluation of the potential advantages and disadvantages. Exhibit 9-4 presents the top 10 reasons companies outsource.

EXHIBIT 9-4

Top 10 Reasons Companies Outsource

1. Reduce and control operating costs.
2. Improve company focus.
3. Gain access to world-class capabilities.
4. Free internal resources for other purposes.
5. Resources are not available internally.
6. Accelerate re-engineering benefits.
7. Function difficult to manage/out of control.
8. Make capital funds available.
9. Share risks.
10. Cash infusion.

SOURCE: Survey of Current and Potential Outsourcing End-Users, The Outsourcing Institute Membership, 1998.

Managers should compare the cost of internally manufacturing a product component with the cost of purchasing it from an outside supplier (or from another division). The company should also assess the best uses of the available facilities. Consideration of the in-house production option implies that the company has the available capacity for that purpose.

Companies who outsource some of their production or business processes may appear to cut costs and maximize profitability, however every outsourcing decision requires effective management. Relevant information for an outsourcing (buy) decision includes both quantitative and qualitative factors, some of which are presented in Exhibit 9-5. Many of the quantitative factors (such as incremental production costs per unit and the purchase price quoted by the supplier) are known with a high degree of certainty. Other factors, such as the opportunity cost associated with production facilities, must be estimated. The qualitative factors should be evaluated by more than one individual so that personal biases do not cloud valid business judgments.

Exhibit 9-6 provides information about a motor for a ladies' electric shaver that is produced by Copelovici Ltd., a company that produces a variety of health and beauty aids. The total cost to manufacture one motor is $5. The company can outsource the production of the motors to Chancellor Manufacturing Ltd. for $4.75 per unit. Ida Copelovici (the president and CEO) and Bradley Carlton (Copelovici's accountant) are trying to determine whether the company should make the motors or outsource their production to an outside supplier.

EXHIBIT 9-5

Make-or-Outsource (Buy)
Factors To Consider

Relevant Quantitative Factors

Incremental production costs for each unit
Unit cost of purchasing from outside supplier (price less any discounts available plus
   shipping)
Availability of production capacity to manufacture components
Opportunity costs of using facilities for production rather than for other purposes
Availability of storage space for units and raw materials

Relevant Qualitative Factors

Relative net advantage given uncertainty of estimates (costs, risks, and so forth)
Reliability of source(s) of supply
Ability to assure quality when units are purchased from outside
Nature of the work to be subcontracted (such as the importance of the part to the
   whole product)
Number of available suppliers
Impact on customers and markets
Future bargaining position with supplier(s)
Perceptions regarding possible future price changes
Perceptions about current product prices (Is the price appropriate or—as may be the
   case with international suppliers—is product dumping involved?)
Strategic and competitive importance of component to long-run organizational success

EXHIBIT 9-6

Make-or-Outsource (Buy) Cost
Information

	Present Manufacturing Cost per Motor	Relevant Cost per Motor to Manufacture
Direct materials	$1.60	$1.60
Direct labour	2.00	2.00
Variable manufacturing overhead	0.80	0.80
Fixed manufacturing overhead[1]	0.60	0.20
Total unit cost	$5.00	$4.60
Quoted price from Chancellor Manufacturing Ltd.		$4.75

[1] Of the $0.60 fixed manufacturing overhead, only $0.20 is directly linked to production of the motors. This amount is related to the production supervisor's salary and could be avoided (not incurred) if the firm chose not to produce shaver motors. The remaining $0.40 of fixed manufacturing overhead is an allocated indirect (common) cost that would continue even if shaver motor production ceased.

Relevant costs are those costs that are pertinent and avoidable, regardless of whether they are variable or fixed. In a make-or-outsource (buy) decision, variable costs of production are relevant. Fixed production costs may be relevant if they can be avoided by discontinuing production. Production of each shaver motor requires a cost outlay of $4.40 for materials, labour, and variable overhead. In addition, $0.20 of the fixed overhead is considered a relevant product cost because it specifically relates to the manufacture of the motors. This $0.20 is an incremental cost, since it could be avoided if shaver motors were not produced. The remaining $0.40 of fixed overhead is not relevant to the decision of whether to make or buy the motors. This $0.40 is a common cost that cannot be associated with shaver motor production and is incurred because of general production activity. Because this portion of the fixed cost would continue under either alternative, it is not relevant.

The relevant cost for the "make" alternative is $4.60—the cost that would be avoided if the product were not made. This amount should be compared with the $4.75 price quoted by the supplier under the "outsource" alternative. The $4.60 is the incremental cost of production, and the $4.75 is the incremental cost of outsourcing the manufacturing of the motor. Based solely on the quantitative information, management should choose to manufacture the motors rather than outsource them, since the company will save $0.15 on each motor produced rather than purchased.

The opportunity cost associated with the facilities being used by production may also be relevant in a make-or-outsource (buy) alternative. Copelovici's management must determine whether an alternative purpose exists for the facilities now being used to manufacture the motors. If a more profitable alternative is available, management should consider diverting the capacity to this alternative use.

For example, assume that Copelovici Ltd. has an opportunity to rent the building now used to produce motors to an outside tenant for $176,000 per year. Copelovici presently produces 800,000 motors annually. Thus, it incurs an opportunity cost of $0.22 per unit ($176,000 ÷ 800,000 motors) by using the facilities rather than renting them. There are two ways to treat this opportunity cost. Both methods point to the same selection decision.

First, the $0.22 per unit can be treated as a reduction in the outsourcing cost because the facilities can be rented only if the component is outsourced. Second, $0.22 per unit can be added to the production cost, since the company is giving up this amount by choosing to make the component. (This treatment is more consistent with the definition of an opportunity cost.) The giving up of inflows is as much a cost as the incurrence of an outflow. Exhibit 9-7 shows these two treatments on a per unit and a total cost basis. Under either format, the comparison indicates that there is a $0.07 per unit advantage to outsourcing rather than producing.

EXHIBIT 9-7

Opportunity Cost in a Make-or-Outsource (Buy) Decision Copelovici Ltd.

Per Unit	I Make	Outsource	or	II Make	Outsource
Direct production costs	$4.60			$4.60	
Opportunity cost (revenue forgone)		(0.22)		0.22	
Outsource cost		$4.75			$4.75
Cost per motor	$4.60	$4.53		$4.82	$4.75

In Total	Make	Buy	Difference in Favour of Purchasing
Revenue from renting facility	$ 0	$ 176,000	$ 176,000
Direct cost for 800,000 motors	(3,680,000)[1]	(3,800,000)[2]	$(120,000)
Net (cost) or revenue	$(3,680,000)	$(3,624,000)	$ 56,000[3]

[1] $4.60 × 800,000
[2] $4.75 × 800,000
[3] The $56,000 represents the net purchase benefit of $0.07 per unit multiplied by the 800,000 units to be purchased during the year.

Copelovici Ltd.'s accountant should inform management that, based on the information shown in Exhibit 9-7, it is more economical to outsource the manufacturing of the motors to Chancellor Manufacturing Ltd. for $4.75 than to manufacture the motors. Such information is the typical starting point of the decision process—determining whether an alternative satisfies the quantitative considerations associated with a problem. If it does, managers then use judgment to assess the qualitative aspects of the decision.

Assume that Copelovici's purchasing agent recently read in the *Globe and Mail* that Chancellor Manufacturing Ltd. was in poor financial condition and was likely to file for bankruptcy. In this case, Copelovici's management would probably decide to continue producing the motors rather than outsourcing their manufacturing to Chancellor. Even though quantitative analysis supports the outsourcing of the units, qualitative judgment suggests that this would not be a wise course of action, since the stability of the supplying source is questionable. If Copelovici stops motor production and rents out its facilities and Chancellor Manufacturing Ltd. goes bankrupt, Copelovici could be faced with high start-up costs to revitalize its motor production process. This was essentially the situation faced by Stoneyfield Farm, a yogurt company that subcontracted its yogurt production and, one day, found its supplier bankrupt—creating an inability to fill customer orders. It took Stoneyfield two years to acquire the necessary production capacity and regain market strength.

These additional considerations also indicate that there are many potential long-run effects of a theoretically short-run decision. Control over product quality and on-time delivery are two other important factors in decisions to buy from suppliers. Outsourcing may appear on the surface to be the best answer to cost control; however, if contract manufacturers do not produce properly, it may be less expensive to acquire internal resources.

Outsourcing has dramatic long-term consequences. It involves an ongoing relationship with considerable complexity and business risk. Future business environments may bear little resemblance to those of today, possibly nullifying the benefits of outsourcing.

Outsourcing is not right for all organizations, nor is it a cure-all or a quick-fix solution to a long-term challenge, but it is a potentially beneficial strategy when used in the right situation.[25]

Some companies have taken a more long-range perspective of certain make-or-outsource (buy) decisions. Gillette, for instance, took a very long-run perspective when it decided to manufacture razor blades internally rather than outsource the production to outside suppliers. The company believed that there was a competitive advantage to be obtained by determining how to shape and strengthen the blade on internally designed laser welding equipment. This choice was apparently the right one: total razor and blade sales for Gillette have increased both in North America and worldwide.

Another example is that of IBM, which developed magneto-resistive (MR) disk-drive recording heads. MR heads can increase a disk drive's data-storage capacity by a factor of 10, but achieving that increase is not an easy feat. A drive maker cannot simply outsource these heads and then plug them into a conventionally designed product. The disk and dozens of other elements must be modified as the heads are incorporated. MR technology isn't understood well enough for engineers to specify to a supplier which attributes of the head are most critical. Also, engineers don't yet understand how changes in design affect manufacturability or how subtle changes in manufacturing methods affect performance. So IBM has to build these devices in-house.[26]

Canadian Kettlebells is a small manufacturer of weights. The owner, Chris Gattey, went into business when he found that a 12 kg kettlebell from a California-based distributor cost $200, which he thought was too expensive. He located a foundry in Vancouver to produce the kettlebells and began shipping product, but to his annoyance he found that the price kept rising with subsequent orders. Also, the foundry was not completing the kettlebells properly and he was having to finish and paint them himself.

He received an e-mail from a company in China offering to make the kettlebells. He went to China, interviewed the company, and made arrangements for it to produce the kettlebells. The Chinese were able to make them for less than half the price of the Canadian ones; furthermore, they came finished and ready to deliver. Mr. Gattey was able to drop his prices by 30% and to build in enough margin to allow him to wholesale to others who need a margin for retailing. Since linking up with the Chinese manufacturer, his sales have increased by 80%.

Bonnie Rich, CEO of the Canada/China Business Investment Group, says that the Chinese always work based on relationships, even for small things: "You either have to have someone in China with the relationship or you have to create the relationship yourself." Mr. Gattey is proof that the savings can be great. His Chinese experience has been very positive.[27]

Make-or-outsource (buy) decisions are not confined to manufacturing entities. Many service organizations must make the same kinds of choices. For example, Rose Patten, executive vice-president of human resources and head of Bank of Montreal's office of strategic management, researched for almost a year before deciding to outsource the human resource processing function to Exult—an arrangement she describes as a partnership rather than "a hand-off." As part of the selection process, Ms. Patten met executives at some of Exult's other client companies, including Bank of America. If Exult performs as promised—among other things, it has guaranteed that the outsourcing arrangement will cost BMO roughly 20% less than it would otherwise have spent in-house—the bank will recommend the company to other prospective clients. Ms Patten said that the outsourcing arrangement allows BMO to concentrate its human resources strategy on four key areas: "talent management, performance alignment and compensation, equity and employment, and learning and development."[28]

Outsourcing to a third-party document services provider can afford companies the flexibility to customize the right number of up-to-the minute documents without sacrificing quality. "Companies can forget about storage and shipping costs. By tapping into the Kinko's high-speed, high-bandwidth digital network, your documents are produced on-demand, on your site, around the corner, or around the world," Gary Kusin, (Kinko's president and CEO) states. "Kinko's outsourcing is perfect for larger corporations looking to trim costs as well as companies with offices in multiple cities to ensure that all employees have access to the same documents."

Doctors must investigate the relative merits of having blood drawn and tested in their offices or having this work done in separate lab facilities; considerations include cost, quality of results, and convenience to patients. These examples simply indicate that the term "make" in "make-or-outsource" does not necessarily mean converting a raw material to a finished component; it can also mean providing an in-house service.

The News Note below discusses how the workplace has changed in Japan and what business needs Japanese companies outsource.

The New Workplace: Outsourcing in Japan

INTERNATIONAL NEWS NOTE

Growth. Change. Challenge. Today Japanese companies are increasingly making the same strategic decisions as the United States and Europe—they are using outsourcing for their business solutions and to meet their business needs faster, cheaper, and smarter.

Japanese businesses are under increasing pressure from new domestic and international competitors. There is a flourishing market for IT outsourcing and in design and production, but the pressure on management to reduce costs for all areas of business operations is increasing dramatically. "Outsourcing is being driven by a strong need and desire among companies to improve performance after a nine-year-long slump, especially cash flow, and to handle people decently while doing it," says a spokesperson for PRICEWATERHOUSECOOPERS JAPAN. But Malcolm Norquoy (COMPUTER SCIENCES CORP.) notes that traditional Japanese outsourcing is not interpreted quite the same as outsourcing elsewhere in the world. "Historically Japanese organizations in all industries and markets have aligned themselves with usually one Japanese provider," he says. But this picture has begun to change and Japan is moving towards a more traditional outsourcing model.

In recent years, outsourcing services have started to expand dramatically in Japan, observes Norquoy. For example, Japanese IT providers have purchased complementary companies from around the world as well as creating global subsidiaries such as Hitachi Data Systems, Amdahl, and ICL. Additionally, technology and consulting companies have started to expand, including IBM, CSC, SAP, PWC, and others.

Today the outsourcing picture is made up mostly of large companies in the banking and insurance industries.

SOURCE: The Outsourcing Institute, http://www.outsourcing.com.

Outsourcing has become a critical component of companies looking to direct business strategies to allow their key talent to focus on running the core business. Today, technology is enabling more business processes to be automated and more companies are interested in outsourcing non-essential business functions.[29]

Make-or-outsource (buy) decisions consider the opportunity costs associated with utilized facilities because those facilities are in limited supply. If capacity is occupied in one way, it cannot be used at the same time for another purpose. Limited capacity is only one type of scarce resource that managers need to consider when making decisions.

LEARNING OBJECTIVE 5

How can management best utilize a scarce resource?

scarce resources
resources that are available only in limited quantity; they create constraints on producing goods or providing services and may include money, machine hours, skilled labour hours, raw materials, and production capacity

SCARCE RESOURCE DECISIONS

Managers are frequently confronted with the short-run problem of making the best use of **scarce resources** that are essential to production activity but are available only in limited quantity. Scarce resources create constraints on producing goods or providing services.[30] These resources may include money, machine hours, skilled labour hours, raw materials, and production capacity. In the long run, management may desire and be able to obtain a greater abundance of a scarce resource, for example, by purchasing additional machines to increase availability of machine hours. However, in the short run, management must make the best current use of the scarce resources it has.

Determining the best use of a scarce resource requires that specific company objectives be recognized. If management's objective is to maximize company contribution margin and profits, the best use of a scarce resource is for the production and sale of the product that has the highest contribution margin per unit of the scarce resource. This strategy assumes that the company is faced with only one scarce resource.

Exhibit 9-8 presents information on the two products made by Reed Ltd. on its plastic moulding machines. Reed Ltd. has only 4,000 machine hours available per month to make plastic housings for either hair dryers or hot rollers or some combination of both of these. Demand is unlimited for both products.

EXHIBIT 9-8

Reed Ltd. Product Information

Scarce Resource—Machine Hours

		Hair Dryers		Hot Rollers
Selling price per unit (a)		$ 30		$ 24
Variable production cost per unit:				
Direct material	$ 6		$ 5	
Direct labour	8		4	
Variable overhead	6		2	
Total variable cost per unit (b)		(20)		(11)
Unit contribution margin [(c) = (a) − (b)]		$ 10		$ 13
Units of output per machine hour (d)		80		40
Contribution margin per machine hour [(c) × (d)]		$800		$520

Note that a hair dryer's $30 unit selling price minus its $20 unit variable cost provides a contribution margin of $10 per unit. The hot rollers' contribution margin per unit is $13 ($24 − $11). Fixed overhead totals $320,000 and is allocated to products on a machine hour basis for purposes of inventory valuation. Fixed overhead, however, does not change with production levels within the relevant range and, therefore, is not a relevant cost for a decision on scarce resource mix.

Since fixed overhead per unit is not relevant in the present case, unit contribution margin rather than unit gross margin is the appropriate measure of profitability of the two products. Unit contribution margin is multiplied by the number of units of output per unit of the scarce resource (in this case, machine hours) to obtain the contribution margin per unit of scarce resource. The last line in Exhibit 9-8 shows contribution margin per machine hour of $800 ($10 × 80) for hair dryers compared with $520 ($13 × 40) for hot rollers. Hair dryers are the more profitable item for Reed Ltd. to produce.

At first, it would appear that hot rollers would be more profitable, since their $13 unit contribution margin is higher than the $10 unit contribution margin for hair dryers. However, since one hour of machine time produces twice as many hair dryers as hot rollers, a greater amount of contribution margin per hour of scarce resource is generated by the production of hair dryers. If Reed Ltd. wanted to achieve the highest possible profit, it would dedicate all machine time to the production of hair dryers. If all units produced were sold, this strategy would provide a total contribution margin of $3,200,000 per month ($800 per hour × 4,000 available hours).

When one limiting factor is involved, the outcome of a scarce resource decision will always indicate that a single type of product should be manufactured and sold. Most situations, though, involve several limiting factors that compete with one another. One method used to solve problems that have several limiting factors is linear programming. Analysts use this method to find the optimal allocation of scarce resources when there is one objective and multiple restrictions on achieving that objective.[31]

Managers must be concerned about the quantitative effects of scarcity of resources, but they must also remember that not all factors involved in the decision alternatives can be readily quantified. Company management must consider qualitative aspects of the problem in addition to quantitative ones. For example, to achieve the maximum possible profit, Reed Ltd. would have to produce only hair dryers during the time available on its plastic moulding machines. Before choosing such a strategy, managers would need to assess the potential damage to the company's reputation and image from limiting its market assortment of products by providing one product to the exclusion of another. Concentrating on a single product might also create market saturation and cause future sales to decline.

Other situations can also make providing multiple products desirable: the products may be complementary (silver serving sets and silver polish), one product may not be usable without the other (razors and razor blades), or one product may be the key to high revenue generation in future periods. To illustrate the latter possibility, consider Mattel Inc., the producer of Barbie dolls. Would it be reasonable for Mattel to produce only Barbie dolls and none of the related accessories (clothes, dream house, car, camper, and so forth)? While the sale of Barbie dolls is profitable, the income flow from the total group of Barbie products is enormous.

For all of the above reasons, management may decide that some less profitable products are necessary components in the company's product mix. Production mix translates into sales mix on the revenue side. The next section addresses the issue of sales mix.

How does relevant costing relate to sales mix, sales pricing decisions, compensation changes, advertising budget and special order pricing decisions?

sales mix
the relative combination of quantities of sales of the various products that make up the total sales of a company

SALES MIX AND SALES PRICING DECISIONS

Management continuously strives to satisfy a variety of company goals such as maximization of company profit, improvement of relative market share, and generation of customer goodwill and loyalty. These goals are achieved through selling products or performing services. Regardless of whether the company is a retailer, manufacturer, or service organization, **sales mix** refers to "the relative combination of quantities of sales of the various products that make up the total sales of a company."[32] One way a company can achieve its goals is to manage its sales mix effectively.

Dell Computer is introducing complementary items to its core PC line to increase overall profits. In addition to printers and scanners, Dell is adding a micro-portable projector. "Nick Eades, Marketing Director at Dell Computer Corporation, says projectors are a logical complement to a notebook computer for presenters. 'Our goal with this product is to deliver the practicality and features our customers want at a great value. We've created a projector that not only addresses the needs of a broad spectrum of customers, but stands on its own as a strong entry into the market.'"[33]

With U.S.$100 plus oil prices and most of their fat already trimmed, the world's airlines are looking for new ways to drive up sales without driving up ticket prices. For that, they need to find other ways to make money. Selling things on board has become extremely important to them. Toronto-based Guestlogix is a leading provider of wireless handheld devices to the airline that allows passengers to purchase items on their flights using credit cards. Customers will no longer need to hunt for cash to pay for on-board refreshments, etc. WestJet is betting big that the devices will help it drive up its ancillary revenues. Guestlogix Inc. is striking deals to allow passengers to purchase everything from train tickets to passes for Broadway shows to flowers. Passengers can now even rent a car before landing.[34]

On-board retail items can earn margins up to 10 times the margins of ticket fares. Guestlogix provides the devices and support systems free of charge and earns between 2% and 4% on each transaction.

Some important factors affecting the appropriate sales mix of a company are product selling prices, salesforce compensation, and advertising expenditures. A change in one or all of these factors may cause a company's sales mix to shift.

Sales Price Changes and Relative Profitability of Products

Managers must continuously monitor the selling price of company products, in relation to each other as well as to competitors' prices. This process may provide information that causes management to change one or more selling prices. Ann Cowan Corporation is an established manufacturing company that produces three types of

Each of Cowan Corporation's scales yields a different contribution margin.

Basic	**Deluxe**	**Talking**

bathroom scales. Its complete line includes basic, deluxe, and talking scales. If Cowan Corporation found that the talking scale sold better at the beginning of the year (after the holidays) than at other times, it might increase the sales price of this scale during this period. Factors that might influence price changes include fluctuations in demand, production distribution costs, economic conditions, and competition. Any shift in the selling price of one product in a multiproduct firm will normally cause a change in the sales mix of that firm because of the economic law of demand elasticity with respect to price.[35] The data presented in Exhibit 9-9 are used to illustrate the effects on sales mix relating to this line.

EXHIBIT 9-9
Ann Cowan Corporation—
Product Information

	Basic Scale	Deluxe Scale	Talking Scale
Unit selling price	$100.00	$130.00	$150.00
Variable unit costs:			
Direct material	$ 15.00	$ 20.00	$ 36.00
Direct labour	10.00	15.00	31.00
Variable manufacturing overhead	3.00	7.00	17.00
Total variable production cost	$ 28.00	$ 42.00	$ 84.00
Variable selling expense[1]	10.00	13.00	15.00
Total variable cost	(38.00)	(55.00)	(99.00)
Contribution margin per unit	$ 62.00	$ 75.00	$ 51.00

[1]The only variable selling expense is a sales commission, which is always 10% of unit selling price.

However in the following two examples we can see that products' sales mix can cause profits and margins to suffer.

We can see the effect of sales mix in the results of the Christmas season for the Cost Plus furniture store chain. The company has revised its fourth-quarter same-store sales estimates downward, from a 2.5% increase to a 1.5% decrease. It has cut fourth-quarter earnings expectations from $1.32 per share to $1.06. The reason cited is a larger than anticipated shift in sales mix to lower-margin consumables and additional markdowns of seasonal inventories remaining after the holidays."[36]

At Office Depot's North American retail segment, although operating profit climbed 7% in the third quarter, gross margin remained flat as a percentage of sales during the three-month period as this was offset by the increased sales mix of lower-margin technology sales.[37]

Cowan's management has set profit maximization as the primary corporate goal. This strategy does not necessarily mean selling as many units as possible of the product with the highest selling price and as few as possible of the products with lower selling prices. The product with the highest selling price per unit does not necessarily yield the highest contribution margin per unit or per unit of scarce resource. In Cowan Corporation's case, the talking scale yields the lowest unit contribution margin of the three products. The talking scale also requires more direct labour and machine time. Costs are high for direct labour and variable manufacturing overhead. Even making the simplistic assumption that no resources are scarce, it is more profit-beneficial to sell the deluxe scale than either the basic or talking scales, since a deluxe scale provides the highest unit contribution margin of the three products. Even a basic scale is more profitable than a talking scale because, although the basic scale has the lowest unit selling price, its unit contribution margin is greater than that of the talking scale.

If profit maximization is the company's goal, a product's sales volume and unit contribution margin should be considered. Total company contribution margin is equal to the combined contribution margins provided by all the products' sales. Exhibit 9-10 indicates the respective total contribution margins of Cowan Corporation's three types of bathroom scales. Although the basic scale does not have the highest unit contribution margin, it does generate the largest total product line contribution margin because of its sales volume. To maximize profits, Cowan's management must maximize total contribution margin rather than per unit contribution margin.

EXHIBIT 9-10

Relationship Between Contribution Margin and Sales Volume

	Unit Contribution Margin (From Exhibit 9-9)	Current Sales Volume in Units	Total
Basic scale	$62	20,000	$1,240,000
Deluxe scale	75	13,000	975,000
Talking scale	51	8,000	408,000
Total contribution margin of product sales mix			$2,623,000

The sales volume of a product or service is almost always intricately related to its selling price. When selling price is increased and demand is elastic with respect to price, demand for that product decreases.[38] Thus, if Cowan's management, in an attempt to increase profits, decides to raise the price of the basic scale to $120, there should be some decline in demand. Assume that consultation with marketing research personnel indicates that such a price increase would cause demand for the product to drop from 20,000 to 12,000 scales per period. Exhibit 9-11 shows the effect of this pricing decision on total contribution margin.

EXHIBIT 9-11

Relationship Between Sales Price and Demand

	Unit Contribution Margin	New Sales Volume in Units	Total
Basic scale	$80.00[1]	12,000	$ 960,000
Deluxe scale	$75.00	13,000	975,000
Talking scale	$51.00	8,000	408,000
Total contribution margin of product sales mix			$2,343,000

[1]Calculated as:

New selling price	$120
Total variable production cost (from Exhibit 9-9)	(28)
Total variable selling expense (10% of selling price)	(12)
Contribution margin	$ 80

Even though the contribution margin per unit of the basic scale increased from $62 to $80, the total dollar contribution margin generated by sales of the product has declined because of the decrease in sales volume. This example assumes that customers did not switch their purchases from the basic scale to other Cowan Corporation bathroom scales when the price of the basic scale was raised. Price increases normally cause customers to switch from a company's high-priced products to its lower-priced products or to a competitors' product. In this instance, switching within the company was ignored because the basic scale was the company's lowest-priced scale. It is *unlikely* that customers would stop buying the basic scale because of a $20 price increase and begin buying the deluxe scale (which costs even more)—but that situation could occur. Customers might believe that the difference in quality between the basic and deluxe scales is worth the extra $10 (rather than the $30 previously) and make such a purchasing switch.

In making decisions to raise or lower prices, the relevant quantitative factors include (1) prospective or new contribution margin per unit of product, (2) both short-term and long-term changes in product demand and production volume caused by the price increase or decrease, and (3) best use of any scarce resources. Some relevant qualitative factors involved in decisions regarding price changes are (1) influence on customer goodwill, (2) customer product loyalty, and (3) competitors' reactions to the firm's new pricing structure.[39]

When deciding to change the prices of current products or to introduce new products that will compete with current products that may affect their sales volumes, managers need to be certain that their assumptions about consumer behaviour are rational. Comparisons are typically made against a "base case" scenario, which estimates how consumers will behave if no changes are made. Often companies implicitly assume that the base case is simply a continuation of the status quo, but this assumption ignores market trends and competitor behaviour. Using the wrong base case is typical of product launches in which the new product will likely erode the market for the company's existing product line.[40] Failure to diversify as product demand for current products and services wanes can be costly. The following example illustrates this point.

Mattel is building on its best-selling Barbie doll, adding pets and houses to the "What's Her Face" line of write-on, wipe-off dolls, and new baby dolls called Shining Stars that include materials to name and register them with the International Star Registry. Still, double-digit international Barbie sales and strong sales in other girls' products pushed the division to an overall sales gain of 3%. In late 2002, the company introduced a line of women's accessories, including china and stationery sets designed with colours and patterns from vintage Barbie dresses and featuring more subtle Barbie images.[41] Barbie is big at Mattel. The doll and all her paraphernalia account for practically one-third of the toy company's sales. Mattel is now capitalizing on its core brands, particularly with licensing deals. For example, the company persuaded REM Eyewear to develop a line of Barbie eyewear for little girls.[42]

Compensation Changes

Many companies compensate their salespeople by paying a fixed commission rate on gross sales dollars. This approach motivates salespeople to sell the highest priced products rather than try to achieve profit maximization for the firm. They will be motivated to sell the talking scale, rather than the basic or deluxe scales. Emphasizing sales of the talking scale will not help the company achieve its profit maximization objective, however, since this scale provides the lowest unit contribution margin.

The starting point for a change in the compensation structure is knowledge of the product contribution margin, which is selling price minus total variable production costs. The per unit product contribution margins of Cowan Corporation's line of scales are as follows:

	Selling Price	Total Variable Production Cost*	Product Contribution Margin
Basic scale	$100	$28	$72
Deluxe scale	130	42	88
Talking scale	150	84	66

* The variable production costs are the same as those in Exhibit 9-9. The product contribution margin above does not include the variable selling expenses.

Cowan Corporation is considering a new policy of paying salespeople a commission of 15% on product contribution margin rather than 10% on sales price. This policy should motivate sales personnel to sell more of the product that produces the highest commission for them, which, in turn, will shift the original sales mix toward sales of products that have a greater contribution to the company.

Exhibit 9-12 compares Cowan Corporation's total contribution margin based on the original sales mix and commission structure shown in Exhibit 9-9 with total contribution margin under the new assumed sales mix and salesperson commission structure. The new commission policy is beneficial for the company because it shifts the sales mix from the high-priced, low-contribution margin talking scale toward the low-priced but more profitable basic and deluxe scales. The product contribution margins are shown below.

EXHIBIT 9-12

Impact of Change in Commission Structure

Old Policy—Commissions equal 10% of selling price (from Exhibit 9-9)

	Product Contribution Margin Before Commission	Commission	Contribution Margin After Commission	Total Old Volume	Contribution Margin
Basic scale	$72	(0.1 × $100) $10	$62	20,000	$1,240,000
Deluxe scale	88	(0.1 × $130) 13	75	13,000	975,000
Talking scale	66	(0.1 × $150) 15	51	8,000	408,000
Total contribution margin for product sales					$2,623,000

New Policy—Commissions equal 15% of product contribution margin per unit

	Product Contribution Margin Before Commission	Commission	Contribution Margin After Commission	Total New Volume	Contribution Margin
Basic scale	$72	(0.15 × $72) $10.80	$61.20	22,000	$1,346,400
Deluxe scale	88	(0.15 × $88) $13.20	74.80	21,500	1,608,200
Talking scale	66	(0.15 × $66) $ 9.90	56.10	2,500	140,250
Total contribution margin for product sales					$3,094,850

Fixed costs are not considered in setting sales commissions. All sales and production volumes of the respective products are assumed to be within the relevant range of activity for the company. Thus, regardless of a shift in activity levels, total fixed costs will remain constant.

For morale purposes, the sales personnel must be shown that the new commissions are expected to slightly exceed the total commissions under the original plan. These computations are shown in Exhibit 9-13. In this instance, the total volume is assumed to increase by 5,000 units because there will be a shift to more sales of the deluxe and basic scales by the salespersons.

Sales personnel should be made aware that attempts to increase sales of the basic and deluxe scales should be easier than attempts to increase sales of the talking scale, and such efforts will result in even higher total commissions and higher company income. The relationships should be stressed so that the sales personnel will work more effectively at accomplishing the company profit objective and thus achieve **goal congruence**.

Advertising Budget Changes

Another factor that may cause shifts in the sales mix involves either increasing the total company advertising budget or reallocating the budget among the products that the company sells. This discussion uses the original sales mix data for the line

goal congruence
a condition that exists when the personal and organizational goals of decision makers throughout the firm are consistent and mutually supportive

EXHIBIT 9-13

Total Effect of Changing Sales Commissions

Original Plan

Product	Commission	Volume	Total Commission
Basic scale	$10.00	20,000	$200,000
Deluxe scale	13.00	13,000	169,000
Talking scale	15.00	8,000	120,000
Total			$489,000

New Plan

Product	Commission[1]	Volume	Total Commission
Basic scale	$10.80	22,000	$237,600
Deluxe scale	13.20	21,500	283,800
Talking scale	9.90	2,500	24,750
Total			$546,150

[1]From Exhibit 9-12

of scales of Cowan Corporation (Exhibit 9-9) and examines a proposed increase in the company's total advertising budget.

Cowan Corporation's advertising manager, Michael Baldwin, has proposed doubling the advertising budget from $30,000 to $60,000 per year. Baldwin thinks the increased advertising will result in the following additional unit sales during the coming year: basic, 200 scales; deluxe, 500 scales; and talking, 100 scales.

If the company spends the additional $30,000 for advertising, will the additional 800 units of sales raise profits? The original fixed costs as well as the contribution margin generated by the old sales level are irrelevant to the decision. The relevant items are the increased sales revenue, increased variable costs, and increased fixed cost—the incremental effects of the change. The difference between incremental revenues and incremental variable costs is the incremental contribution margin. The incremental contribution margin minus the incremental fixed cost is the incremental benefit (**or** loss) resulting from the decision.[43]

Exhibit 9-14 shows how the increased advertising expenditures are expected to affect contribution margin. The $55,000 of additional contribution margin far exceeds the $30,000 incremental cost for advertising, so Cowan Corporation should definitely increase its advertising budget by $30,000.

EXHIBIT 9-14

Incremental Analysis of Increasing Advertising Cost

	Basic	Deluxe	Talking	Total
Increase in volume	200	500	100	800
Contribution margin per unit	$ 62	$ 75	$ 51	
Incremental contribution margin	$12,400	$37,500	$5,100	$55,000
Less: Incremental fixed cost of advertising				30,000
Incremental benefit of increased advertising expenditure				$25,000

Increasing advertising may cause changes in the sales mix or the number of units sold. Companies could also target their advertising at specific products and change the sales and the mix. Sales can also be affected by opportunities that allow companies to obtain business at a sales price that differs from the normal price.

special order pricing
determining a sales price to charge
for manufacturing or service jobs
that are outside the company's
normal production or service realm

Special Order Pricing

In **special order pricing**, management must determine a sales price to charge for manufacturing or service jobs that are outside the company's normal production or service realm. Special order situations include jobs that require a bid, are taken during slack periods, or are manufactured to a particular buyer's specifications. Typically, the sales price quoted on a special order job should be high enough to cover the variable costs of the job and any incremental (additional) fixed costs caused by the job, and to generate a profit. Special order pricing requires knowledge of the relevant costs associated with the specific problem or decision at hand.

Cowan Corporation has been given the opportunity to bid on a special order for 1,000 deluxe scales. Company management wants to obtain the order as long as the additional business will provide a satisfactory contribution to profit. The company has machine and labour hours that are not currently being used (idle capacity), and raw materials can be obtained from the supplier. Also, Cowan Corporation has no immediate opportunity to use its current excess capacity in any other way, so opportunity cost is not a factor.

The information necessary to determine a bid price on the deluxe scale is presented in Exhibit 9-9 on page 549 Direct material, direct labour, and variable manufacturing overhead costs are relevant to setting the bid price because these variable production costs will be incurred for each additional deluxe scale manufactured. Although all variable costs are normally relevant to a special pricing decision, the variable selling expense is irrelevant in this instance because no sales commission will be paid on this sale.

Fixed production overhead and fixed selling and administrative expenses are not expected to increase because of this sale, so these expenses are not included in the pricing decision.

Using the available cost information (shown in Exhibit 9-9, on page 549), the relevant cost used to determine the bid price for the scale is $42 (direct material, direct labour, and variable manufacturing overhead). This cost is the minimum special order price at which the company should sell a deluxe scale. If the existing fixed costs have been covered by regular sales, any price set higher than $42 will provide the company with some profit.

In setting the bid price, management must decide how much profit it would consider to be reasonable on the special order. As another example, since Cowan Corporation's usual selling price for a deluxe scale is $130, each sale provides a normal contribution margin of $75 or approximately 58%. Setting the bid price for the special order at $66.36 would cover the variable production costs of $42 and provide a normal 37% contribution margin. This computation illustrates a simplistic cost-plus approach to pricing but ignores both product demand and market competition. Cowan Corporation's bid price should also reflect the latter considerations. In addition, company management should consider the effect that the special order will have on all other company activities (purchasing, receiving, warehousing, and so forth) and whether these activities will create additional, unforeseen costs.

There are situations in which a company will depart from its typical price-setting routine. For example, a company may "low-ball" bid some jobs. A low-ball bid may only cover variable costs or it may be below such costs. The rationale behind making low-ball bids is to obtain the job in order to introduce company products or services to a particular market segment.

Special pricing of this nature may provide work for a period of time but cannot be continued for the long run. To remain in business, a company must set product or service selling prices to cover total variable costs, to cover an appropriate amount of fixed, selling, or administrative costs, and to provide a reasonable profit margin. An exception to this general rule, however, may occur when a company produces related or complementary products, as can be seen in the following discussion.

Imagine a future where your computer hardware and software are free and you only pay for the services you use. The computer itself will be a thin, bare-boned display and keyboard, all the software will sit in a central server, and you carry cutting-edge technology such as smartphones, Bluetooth devices, and high-speed roaming in your pocket. That's the vision that Scott McNealy, chairman and CEO of Sun Microsystems Inc., painted at a keynote speech at Oracle Open World in San Francisco at the end of 2004. "The telecoms do it, they give you a phone for free for signing up a two-year contract with them, and you only pay for the services you use and a low-cost monthly subscription. That's the future of personal computing."[44]

At first Gillette gave away a razor and sold the blades. Adobe Systems was one of the first to realize that this model made sense in the digital world as well: Adobe gave away its basic Acrobat Reader software to better sell its high-margin creative tools, such as Acrobat Distiller. Adobe is now the second-largest North American PC-software company, with annual revenues exceeding $1.2 billion. Other companies quickly followed suit, including Oracle, which gives away its development tools to promote sales of its database software, and Sun Microsystems, which supplies Java for free and sells workstations and the Sun operation system.[45]

Special pricing concessions may also be justified when orders are of an unusual nature (because of the quantity, method of delivery, or packaging) or because the products are being tailor-made to customer specifications. Further, special pricing can be used when producing goods for a one-time job, such as an overseas order that will not affect domestic sales.

When setting a special order price, management must consider the qualitative issues as well as the quantitative ones. For instance, will a low bid price cause this customer (or others) to feel that a precedent has been established for future prices? Will the contribution margin on a bid set low enough to acquire the job earn an amount sufficient to justify the additional burdens placed on management or employees by this activity? How, if at all, will special order sales affect the company's normal sales? If the job is taking place during a period of low business activity (off-season or recession), is management willing to take the business at a lower contribution or profit margin simply to keep a trained workforce employed?

RELEVANT COSTS IN PRODUCT LINE DECISIONS

LEARNING OBJECTIVE 7

How is product margin used to determine whether a product line should be retained, expanded, or eliminated?

To facilitate performance evaluations, operating results in multiproduct environments are often presented in terms of separate product lines. In reviewing these disaggregated statements, managers must distinguish relevant from irrelevant information for each product line. If all costs (variable and fixed) are allocated to product lines, a product line or segment may be perceived to be operating at a loss when actually it is not. Such perceptions may be caused by the commingling of relevant and irrelevant information on the statements.

Exhibit 9-15 presents basic earnings information for the Men's Products Division of James Znajda Ltd., which manufactures three product lines: Canadian Woods Shaving Creme, Jamaican Gold Aftershave, and Prairie Cologne. The format of the information in the top half of the exhibit makes it appear that the shaving creme and aftershave lines are operating at a net loss ($16,500 and $5,250, respectively). Managers reviewing such results might reason that Znajda's Men's Products Division would be $21,750 ($16,500 + $5,250) more profitable if both of these products were

EXHIBIT 9-15
Product Line Income Statements

	Shaving Creme	Aftershave	Cologne	Total
Sales	$150,000	$ 85,000	$380,000	$615,000
Total direct variable expenses	(87,500)	(55,250)	(228,000)	(370,750)
Total contribution margin	$ 62,500	$ 29,750	$152,000	$244,250
Total fixed expenses[1]	(79,000)	(35,000)	(77,000)	(191,000)
Net income (loss)	$(16,500)	$ (5,250)	$ 75,000	$ 53,250

[1] Fixed expenses:

(a) Traceable fixed expenses[2]	$50,000	$32,000	$48,000	$130,000
(b) Nontraceable fixed expenses	9,000	1,000	6,000	16,000
(c) Allocated common costs	20,000	2,000	23,000	45,000
Total	$79,000	$35,000	$77,000	$191,000

[2] This cost will no longer exist if the product is dropped.

eliminated. This conclusion may be premature, however, because of the mixture of relevant and irrelevant information in the income statement presentation. This problem results from the fact that all fixed expenses have been allocated to the individual product lines.

Fixed cost allocations are traditionally based on one or more measures that are presumed to provide an "equitable" division of costs. These measures might include the number of square metres of the manufacturing plant occupied by each product line, number of machine hours incurred for production of each product line, or number of employees directly associated with each product line. Regardless of the allocation base, allocations may force fixed costs into specific product line operating results even though the costs may not have actually been caused by the making or selling of that product line. This inequity results from the fact that most cost allocation schemes currently used by managers are arbitrary.

The detail in Exhibit 9-15 separates the Men's Products Division's fixed expenses into three categories: (1) those that could be avoided by elimination of the product line; (2) those that are directly associated with the product line but are unavoidable; and (3) those that are incurred for the division as a whole (common costs) and allocated to the individual product lines. The latter two categories are irrelevant to the question of whether to eliminate a product line.

An unavoidable cost will be shifted to another product line if the product line with which it is associated is eliminated. For example, the division has several senior employees who work in the shaving creme area. If that product line were eliminated, those employees would be transferred to the aftershave or cologne areas. Similarly, depreciation on factory equipment used to manufacture a specific product is an irrelevant cost in product line decisions. If the equipment were kept in service and used to produce other products, its depreciation expense would be unavoidable. However, if the equipment were sold, the selling price would be relevant because it would increase the marginal benefit of a decision to discontinue the product line.

As to common costs, they will be incurred regardless of which product lines are retained. One example of a common cost is the insurance premium on a manufacturing facility that houses all product lines.

If Znajda eliminated both shaving creme and aftershave, its total profit would decline by $10,250 [$12,500 + ($2,250)]. This amount represents the combined lost **product margin** of the two product lines as shown in Exhibit 9-16.

product margin
the excess of a product's revenues over both its direct variable expenses and any avoidable fixed expenses related to the product; the amount remaining to cover unavoidable direct fixed expenses and common costs and then to provide profits

EXHIBIT 9-16

Product Line Income Statements

	Shaving Creme	Aftershave	Cologne	Total
Sales	$150,000	$ 85,000	$ 380,000	$ 615,000
Total direct variable cost	(87,500)	(55,250)	(228,000)	(370,750)
Product contribution margin	$ 62,500	$ 29,750	$ 152,000	$ 244,250
(1) Traceable fixed cost	(50,000)	(32,000)	(48,000)	(130,000)
Product margin	$ 12,500	$ (2,250)	$ 104,000	$ 114,250
(2) Nontraceable direct fixed cost (see Exhibit 9-15)				(16,000)
Product line operating results				$ 98,250
(3) Allocated common cost				(45,000)
Profit before tax				$ 53,250

Product margin represents the excess of revenues over direct variable costs and avoidable fixed costs. It is the amount remaining to cover unavoidable direct fixed costs and common costs and then to provide profits.[46] The product margin is the appropriate figure on which to base a decision to continue or eliminate a product, since that figure measures the product's ability to help cover indirect and unavoidable costs.

For the Men's Products Division, the decrease in total before-tax profit from eliminating both shaving creme and aftershave can be shown in the following alternative computations:

Current before-tax profit	$ 53,250
Increase in income due to elimination of aftershave product line (product margin)	2,250
Decrease in income due to elimination of shaving creme product line (product margin)	(12,500)
New before-tax income	$ 43,000

or

Product contribution margin of cologne line	$152,000
Minus avoidable fixed expenses of cologne line	(48,000)
Product margin of the cologne line	$104,000
Minus all remaining expenses shown on Exhibit 9-16 ($16,000 + $45,000)	(61,000)
Before-tax profit with one product line	$ 43,000

Based on the quantitative information in Exhibit 9-16, the Men's Products Division should eliminate only the aftershave line. That product line is generating a negative product margin and thus is not even covering its own costs. If that product line were eliminated, total divisional income would increase by $2,250, the amount of the negative product margin.

Before making decisions to discontinue a product line or sell off a segment, management should also carefully consider what it would take to turn that product line or division around. Some product lines (and even segments or divisions of companies) must be abandoned through either discontinuance or sale.

The News Note that follows discusses some actions taken by companies to improve their financial situation.

Product Line Decisions

North Americans are spending more at restaurants and less at supermarkets. Now KRAFT FOODS, the world's second largest food company, is paying the price. Packaged-food companies, which aim their products at ordinary shoppers, are beginning to see slower growth because consumers are choosing the convenience of eating at restaurants or relying on take-out—all the while making fewer trips down grocery aisles. The packaged-food industry is also feeling pressure from higher oil prices. Manufacturers like Kraft transport their products mainly by truck to distribution centres and supermarkets and use petroleum in their plastic packaging. Kraft has struggled with these challenges more than its rivals. It has been criticized for failing to develop new products that would excite consumers and would allow the

company to charge higher prices. Kraft announced recently that it would be closing plants and deleting 10% of its brand portfolios.

In January 2008, TALBOTS INC. announced that it would be closing its 78 children's and men's apparel stores to focus on its core customers: middle-aged women. The move would affect 800 employees. "These kids' and men's stores really weren't complementary to the overall focus of the company," said a company spokesperson, "which is the 35-year-old-plus female customers. The kids' and men's stores were either neutral or loss-making overall to the rest of the company."

KODAK CANADA shut down its Toronto manufacturing plant in 2005, eliminating 360 jobs and capacity as the market swings away from traditional film to digital pictures. "It is a function of the industry shift and the rising popularity of digital photography and the need for Kodak to balance its capacity and requirements on the traditional side of the business," (Kodak president) Ducy said.

In 1989, DELL COMPUTER CORP. became the first computer producer to sell at "superstore" outlets; in July 1994, it was "the first to pull out as it abandoned its unprofitable retail efforts." Dell Computer has decided to go retail once again, only using a different model than it did earlier. Michael Dell is back in charge of the troubled computer company he founded 23 years ago. He's already shaken things up. But can he bring back the magic?

In recent months the company has stepped beyond Internet and telephone sales—the famous Dell direct model. Michael Dell spent a day with P&G's marketing guys, who know a thing or two about how to sell consumer products to different customers around the globe. "We were doing everything wrong," Dell recalls. Still, nothing approaches Dell's radical decision to move back into retail sales. Dell has placed its products in 10,000 outlets, including Wal-Mart, Staples, as well as in chains in Japan, China, Russia, and Britain. Wal-Mart has put Dell in the mass market, where lower priced PCs are the biggest sellers. Staples for its part, is a good place to reach small businesses and people with home offices.

Dell says that in the near future, the company intends to have two or three retail partners in each of the 20 countries with the highest GDP. The reason? The consumer market, now just 15% of Dell's $60 billion in sales, has the potential to expand more quickly than its corporate and government market.

To jump-start consumer sales, Dell has designed a series of new machines that beg a second look. The XPS M1330, which debuted in July 2007, is an ultra-thin laptop. Its crisp, minimalist design, energy-efficient 13.3-inch screen, snazzy colours, and powerful processors have created such a demand that Dell can't keep up with orders.

The importance of how a computer looks has made retail stores more important than ever for Dell and other manufacturers. People want to see the computer, touch it, and operate it next to other machines.

Rethinking retail was a matter of necessity. Mr. Dell notes that a lot has changed since the company tried and abruptly exited retail sales in 1994. The shift in the consumer market toward notebooks, which customers want to try before buying, is part of it. So is Dell's need to do better in foreign markets, where people are less comfortable buying computers by phone or over the Internet. "We're going after those new customers with retail partners," Mr. Dell says.

On the other hand, we see many companies looking at individual product line profits. UNILEVER has an enormous portfolio of some 1,800 brands, which it believes to be three-quarters too many. Its next strategic move will be to reduce the stable of brands, enabling the company to focus on the core brands. From its A list and B list, it is looking to cut a number of B-list items. All nonprofitable brands have quietly been dropped, such as the complementary range to Pears soap, or sold off, such as the Harmony brand.

Canadian retailers, if they're lucky, manage to turn a slim and unpredictable profit on merchandise sales from year to year. As a result many companies are turning to financial services. These services have fast become the industry's saving grace. THE BRICK GROUP WAREHOUSE lays out a model that relies on its "financial services" division for between 41% and 53% of earnings before profit sharing, income taxes, and extraordinary items between 2002 and 2004. More than 50% of purchases made at The Brick are done with a Brick Card. This is true as well for CANADIAN TIRE (31%). Sales of extended warranties provide a great deal of increased revenue for most companies. IKEA, the home furnishings retailer, won permission to run its own diesel-powered freight trains between Sweden and Germany, becoming the first private European company to operate a cross-border train. Ikea, which sells furniture at low cost in large warehouses outside city centres, is turning to trains to lower distribution costs. The company aims for 40% of its European shipments to be made by train, replacing 50 daily truckloads, Sweden's railroad operator said on its Website.

SOURCES: Melanie Warner, "Kraft Plans to Cut Jobs and Plants," *New York Times*, January 31, 2005; Mark Jewell, "Talbots Will Close 78 Kids' and Men's Stores to Focus on Its Women Customers: About 800 Job Cuts Planned," *St. Louis Post-Dispatch*, January 5, 2008, A30. Christopher Helman, "Michael Dell Is Back in Charge," *Forbes*, December 10, 2007; <author?> "Trying to Refocus at Dell," *New York Times*, September 9, 2007; "Dude, You're Getting a Dell . . . At Best Buy," CMP TechWeb, December 6, 2007. Steve Erwin and John Valorzi, "Kodak Canada Closing Toronto Factory," *Toronto Star*, December 10, 2004; Jack Kaskey, "Dupont Sheds Jobs in Push to Save US $900 M a Year: Focus on Profitable Lines," *National Post*, April 13, 2004; "Gateway Computer Closes Canadian Stores; 220 Laid Off," *Sault Star*, March 31, 2001, C5; Scott McCartney, "Dell Computer Plans to Quit Retail Field and Refocus on Its Mail Order Business," *Wall Street Journal*, July 12, 1994, A2; Rasha Mourtadaa, "Dude, Touch My Dell," *Canadian Business*, November 25, 2002; Imogen Matthews, "Unilever: Making It Happen in the Mass Market, *European Cosmetic Markets*, August 1, 1999; Ian Karleff, "Brick Trust Investors Banking on Warranties," *Financial Post*, June 2, 2004; Philip Lagerkranseer, "Ikea Starts Its Own Railway in Europe," *Financial Post*, January 8, 2002.

PRODUCT EXPANSION OR EXTENSION

The other decision relative to product lines is expansion or extension. Expansion refers to the introduction of totally new products. We see that Gillette constantly strives to bring a steady stream of new products to market; it is the key driver of Gillette's success. Gillette launched the first twin-blade shaving system, the Trac II, in 1971. In 1989, the Sensor shaving system debuted, with its automatically adjusting twin blades. "Building on the tremendous success of the MACH3 franchise, we're powering up the world's best shave and providing a superior shaving experience, said Peter K. Hoffman, president blades and razors, Gillette Company. "We expect this new system to substantially fuel the value of the blade and razor category, in the same way that MACH3Turbo has driven growth over the past two years."

In addition to its revolutionary powered razor, Gillette M3Power includes other innovations that contribute to a superior shaving performance. Hundreds of men confirm that M3Power is the new gold standard in shaving performance.[47]

Incremental costs of expansions and extensions (other than the variable costs of the product) include market research, product and packaging development, product introduction, and advertising. Extensions have often been viewed as fairly low-cost endeavours especially if a company has excess capacity. However, sometimes unanticipated incremental costs of expansions and extensions (other than the variable costs of the product) become necessary; these costs include market research, product and packaging development, product introduction, and advertising.

The following News Note shows how some companies have expanded their product lines to meet consumer tastes while others have made changes to adapt their business to meet the new economic times.

Changes to Product Lines

At the dawn of China's great consumer boom in the 1990s, Western companies had only the crudest understanding of what Chinese consumers wanted. They often took existing Western products and force-fit onto them the little they knew about Chinese tastes. Lately, though, Western companies have begun copying what successful native Chinese companies have done all along. They're utterly reinventing their fare to reflect a much deeper understanding of how Chinese shoppers view food and other goods.

You can still get crispy chicken and mashed potatoes at the 1,100 KFC outlets in China. But some of the chain's best-selling items here probably never passed through Colonel Harland Sanders' lips—like soup made from spinach, egg, and tomato. It's the same at a Beijing McDonald's, whose menu features red-bean sundaes, or in Chinese homes, where couch potatoes, watching TV chomp on Frito-Lay chips flavoured with lemon.

Peerless Clothing Inc. is a maker of men's suits in Montreal, but within two years at least one-third of its workforce will be moved overseas—and those jobs aren't coming back. Canada's clothing and textile sectors provide textbook cases of how companies react when governments radically and rapidly dismantle trade barriers. This move has caused factory closings and layoffs, but it has also forced companies to reinvent themselves to survive.

In the case of Peerless, it meant moving jobs offshore. But for Grand National Apparel in Toronto, it accelerated a switch to importing clothes—taking advantage of the cheap foreign goods—instead of manufacturing them in Canada. Jeff Otis, president, said "It's hard to keep making clothes in Canada when dress pants made in Canada and sold at $80 in stores could be retailed for $50 instead if they were made in Bangladesh.

SOURCES: Geoffrey A. Fowler and Ramin Setoodeh, "Outsiders Adapt to China's Tastes," *Wall Street Journal*, August 5, 2004; Steven Chase, "Apparel Firms Dealing With New Realities," *Globe and Mail*, April 16, 2004.

Extension refers to the introduction of "offshoots" of current products because the company decides that the market needs to be more highly segmented. The segmentation might focus on price, size, operating costs, or aesthetics issues; alternatively, extensions may be necessary to meet competitive pressures. The following News Note illustrates an example of this.

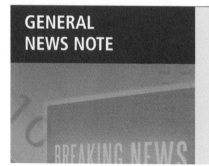

GENERAL NEWS NOTE

Longo Brothers Fruit Markets Inc. Expands With an E-Grocer

The Mississauga-based Longo's, which was looking for an online expansion opportunity, is acquiring Grocery Gateway Inc. Longo Brothers Fruit Markets Inc. praised Grocery Gateway as a "natural fit" that would complement its chain of stores in the Greater Toronto Area.

Grocery Gateway, the online grocer, has branched out into a wide assortment of goods, including wine (through a partnership with the Liquor Control Board of Ontario), hardware items (supplied by Home Depot), and office supplies (through Staples/Business Depot).

Longo Brothers will radically alter the online grocer's supply chain in a bid to put it in the black, selling a 280,000-square-foot distribution centre and sourcing perishables and canned goods from its own network of grocery stores.

SOURCES: Adapted from Hollie Shaw, "Longo To Buy Online Grocer," *Financial Post*, August 25, 2004; Rick Westhead, "Grocery Gateway Lost Millions," *Toronto Star*, August 26, 2004; Marina Strauss, "Longo to Acquire Grocery Gateway," *Globe and Mail*, August 25, 2004.

GENERAL NEWS NOTE

One can see that over the years, Gillette has added to its product lineup such leading brands as Right Guard deodorants, Foamy shave cream, Braun electric shavers, Oral-B manual toothbrushes, and Braun Oral-B power toothbrushes.[48]

Matt Wolh, Gillette's general manager for new male products and shave care, insists that the company will defend its growth and continue to pick up momentum because it understands customers better and has a long-term plan tailored to the market. When Gillette launched its Phantom razor (a black-and-silver version of the Fusion) in Japan in the summer of 2007, it was the first time the company's ads featured local athletes and celebrities such as famous DJ Chris Peppler and breast stroke gold medalist Kosuke Kitajima. And the razor wasn't called Phantom, as it is in the rest of the world, because it didn't translate well. For Japan, it was renamed Air.[49]

It is important to note that many of Gillette's products are extensions of existing products.

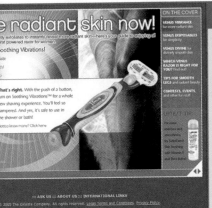

SITE ANALYSIS

The Gillette Company

Gillette's chairman and CEO, James M. Kilts, believes in rapid cycle time—getting there first with the highest quality. Company profit margins increased as customers began using expensive "shaving systems" rather than cheap disposable razors.

Whether deciding to introduce a new product, cut or raise a price in a market, or discontinue a product line, Gillette's management must understand the incremental costs and benefits of each alternative. Recognizing how the benefit of cutting fractions of a cent off a variable production cost is compounded focuses management's attention on controlling costs when large volumes of that product are sold.

Over the years, Gillette has had great success applying a trade-up strategy to its blades and razors. Periodically, Gillette comes out with a new razor with added features. Then it uses marketing campaigns to convince consumers they should replace their old razors with the new higher-priced product.

Gillette has announced its strategy to go after a bigger cut of the women's shaving market. In the spring of 2005 the company rolled out a battery-powered Venus Vibrance shaver that sends vibrations to the skin to raise the hair for a closer shave. It also added Venus disposables. Since Venus's introduction, women have traded up to more expensive razors. These new products bring superior technology and performance to the women's shaving category. The company expects this brand to add $100–$150 million in sales.

SITE ANALYSIS

In 2007, P&G launched Pure Divine, a body wash for women under the Gillette brand. This is meant to be the first of many crossovers in the pipeline.

What sort of man does Procter & Gamble think worthy of being the face of the Gillette razor, a $16 billion brand? What sort of man deserves to endorse the five-blade shaving surface technology with the precision inner blade?

It seems that the new faces of the "Gillette Champions Program"—Roger Federer, Thierry Henry, and Tiger Woods—not only had to achieve "the best a man can get" on the sports field but also had to have super, squeaky-clean private lives, as smooth as a power glide blade. According to P&G, the men were selected "not only for their accomplishments but also for their behaviour away from the game."

Once upon a time, razors with multiple blades were a joke. The first broadcast of *Saturday Night Live* included a mock commercial for the "Triple Track," a three-bladed razor, featuring this slogan: "Because you'll believe anything." But that was 30 years ago. Three-blade razors are now as common as contoured toothbrushes and deodorant body spray. Schick's four-blade Quattro has been selling well for more than two years. The Gillette five-blade Fusion had early testers saying they liked it. "It was unbelievable how close a shave I experienced," one of the testers said.

In 2005, Gillette extended its rich history of innovation with the unveiling of its newest shaving system: Gillette Fusion™ and Gillette Fusion™ Power, revolutionary new wet shaving systems for men and the world's first razors to feature advanced technology on the front and back of the blade cartridge. Both shaving systems outperform the world's leading razors, MACH3Turbo and M3Power respectively, by incorporating breakthrough innovations that provide a dramatic increase in shaving closeness and comfort. This five-bladed razor has a trimmer on the back of the cartridge aimed at the 50 percent of men who have mustaches and beards. Fusion™ is Gillette's latest product geared at maintaining the company's leading share of the world's razor and blade market.

After reading patent filings, analysts say that Gillette may be working on blades with chemical strips that heat up when placed under hot water. There is also talk of ceramic-coated blades that don't wear out but need to be replaced when dropped.

Gillette's $54 billion sale to Procter & Gamble (P&G) in 2005 was the largest consumer products takeover to date and makes P&G the world's biggest consumer goods company, with combined annual revenues of more than $63 billion. One of the major attractions of Gillette was the opportunity to add a masculine dimension to P&G's overwhelmingly female-based portfolio. Women have historically accounted for about 80% of P&G's customers. The purchase of Gillette, a company that primarily serves men, gives both companies the opportunity to tap into each other's expertise. The imminent launch of Pure Divine, a body wash for women under the Gillette brand, is likely to be the first of many crossovers.

Using ERP software, Gillette has linked five business units that had operated as a cluster of independent companies with different fiscal year ends. Previously, razor blades and toothbrushes were delivered to the same customer in different trucks using different invoices. With SAP software, Gillette standardized much of its business transaction processing and consolidated its products into two divisions—one for batteries, shampoos, and razors, the other for toothbrushes, coffee makers, and stationery. The ERP implementation also resulted in a restructuring of operations whereby Gillette cut its labour force by 11% and closed 14 factories, 12 warehouses, and 30 offices, for a total annual savings of $200 million.

SOURCES: Theresa Howard, "Gillette Hopes to Power Shaver Sales to Women With Vibrance," *USA Today*, December 16, 2004; Naomi Aoki, "Gillette Hopes to Create a Buzz with Vibrating Women's Razor," *Boston Globe*, December 1, 2004; Claire Davies, "Gillette and the Road to Perfect Retail," *Supply Chain Europe*, May 2004; Naomi Aoki, "For Gillette CEO, It Was A $29 M Year," *Boston Globe*, March 31, 2005; Robin Goldwyn Blumenthal, "Procter & Gamble's Not New Look A Beauty!," *Barron's*, August 22, 2005; Europe Information, Consumer Goods: Conditional Go-Ahead for Gillette/Procter &

SITE ANALYSIS

CHAPTER SUMMARY

Management's task is to allocate its finite stock of resources effectively and efficiently to accomplish its chosen set of corporate goals and objectives. Managers should explain how requested information will be used so that accountants can make certain that relevant information is provided in an appropriate form. Thus, managers will have a reliable quantitative basis on which to analyze problems, compare viable solutions, and choose the best course of action. Managers use relevant cost information to determine the incremental benefits of alternatives. One option often available is to "change nothing." This option may, however, be strategically risky if competitors gain advantage by upgrading their processes. After rigorous analysis of the quantifiable factors associated with each alternative, a manager must assess the merits and potential risks of the qualitative factors involved so that the best possible course of action is chosen.

Relevant information may be quantitative or qualitative. Variable costs are generally relevant to a decision; they are irrelevant only when they cannot be avoided under any possible alternative or when they do not differ between (or among) alternatives. Direct avoidable fixed costs are also relevant to decision making. Sometimes costs seem relevant when they actually are not. Examples of such irrelevant costs include sunk costs, and arbitrarily allocated common costs.

Quantitative analysis is short-range in perspective. Additional qualitative factors should be reviewed by management in each case. Some of these qualitative factors may have long-range planning and policy implications. Others may be short-range in nature. Managers must decide the relevance of individual factors based on experience, judgment, knowledge of economic theory, and logic.

1 **What constitutes relevance in a decision-making situation?**
For information to be relevant, it must (1) relate to the decision at hand, (2) be important to the decision and (3) have a bearing on a future endeavour. Relevant costing compares the incremental or additional revenues and/or costs associated with alternative decisions.

2 **Why is an opportunity cost relevant in decision making but a sunk cost (such as a joint cost) is not?**
In a further processing decision about products at split-off, ignore the total or allocated joint cost. The only relevant items are the incremental revenues and costs of processing further.

Direct avoidable fixed costs are also relevant to decision making. Sometimes costs seem relevant when they actually are not. An example of an irrelevant cost is a sunk cost, which has already been incurred and cannot be changed regardless of the alternative selected; it is not a relevant cost since it will not be incurred in the future. An opportunity cost may be relevant but is not recorded in the accounting records. It represents the benefits forgone when one course of action is chosen over another.

3 What are the relevant costs in equipment replacement decisions?

The relevant factors to be considered in equipment replacement decisions include the cost of the new asset, the current resale value of the old asset and the annual savings of the new asset, and the number of years that the savings would be enjoyed. The cost of the old asset is a sunk cost and is not considered.

4 What are the relevant costs and qualitative factors that exist in a make-or-outsource (buy) decision?

In a make-or outsource (buy) decision, management should include the opportunity costs associated with the make alternative as the outsourcing alternative may provide an opportunity to make plant assets and personnel available for other purposes. It is important to recognize any opportunity costs if they exist.

5 How can management best utilize a scarce resource?

In a decision involving a single scarce resource, if the objective is to maximize company contribution margin and profits, then production and sales should be focused toward the product with the highest contribution margin per unit of scarce resource.

6 How does relevant costing relate to sales mix, sales pricing decisions, compensation changes, advertising budget and special order pricing decisions?

Changes in selling prices and advertising normally affect a company's sales volume and sales mix, thus changing the company's total contribution margin. Tying sales commissions to contribution margin will motivate salespeople to sell the products that are most beneficial to the company's profit picture. Special orders and their pricing should be considered using variable costs as a starting point.

7 How is product margin used to determine whether a product line should be retained, expanded, or eliminated?

In a product line decision, product lines should be evaluated on their product margins rather than on their income amounts. Product margin includes any relevant direct costs, but excludes any allocated common costs of the entity.

Key Terms

Avoidable costs (p. 532)
By-products (p. 532)
Goal congruence (p. 552)
Incremental cost (p. 528)
Incremental revenue (p. 528)
Joint cost (p. 534)
Joint process (p. 532)
Joint products (p. 532)
Make-or-outsource (buy) decision (p. 540)
Opportunity cost (p. 529)

Outsource (p. 540)
Product margin (p. 556)
Relevant cost (p. 526)
Relevant costing (p. 528)
Sales mix (p. 548)
Scarce resources (p. 546)
Scrap (p. 532)
Special order pricing (p. 554)
Split-off point (p. 534)
Sunk cost (p. 529)
Waste (p. 533)

Points to Remember

General rule of decision making: choose the alternative that yields the greatest incremental benefit (or the smallest incremental loss).

> Incremental (additional) revenues
> – Incremental (additional) costs
> = Incremental benefit (positive or negative)

Relevant Costs

> Direct materials and direct labour
> Variable production overhead
> Variable selling expenses related to each alternative (may be greater or less than under the "change nothing" alternative)
> Avoidable fixed production overhead
> Avoidable fixed selling/administrative costs (if any)
> Opportunity cost of choosing some other alternative (can be viewed as either increasing one alternative's cost or reducing the cost of the other)

Single Scarce Resource

1. Determine the scarce resource.
2. Determine the production per unit of the scarce resource.
3. Determine the contribution margin (CM) per unit of the scarce resource.
4. Multiply units of production times CM per unit of the scarce resource to obtain total CM provided by the scarce resource. Production and sale of the product with the highest CM per unit of scarce resource will maximize profits.

> **Product Lines**
> Sales
> – Direct variable expenses
> = Contribution margin
> – Avoidable fixed expenses
> = Product margin*

* The decision to retain or eliminate a product line should be based on this line item.

DEMONSTRATION PROBLEMS

Problem 1

Mountifield Home Products is a firm that manufactures several types of high-quality home appliances. One of the company's product lines consists of electric coffeepots. The company produces three different models of coffeepots. Mountifield is presently considering a proposal from a supplier who wishes to supply the company with glass carafes for the coffeepots. The company currently produces all of the carafes it requires. Because customers have differing preferences, Mountifield now offers two alternative carafes for each coffeepot model (therefore, the company currently produces a total of six different types of carafes). The supplier has indicated it would produce three different types of carafes for each coffeepot model, thus expanding the variety of carafes that could be offered to the customer. This supplier would charge Mountifield $2.60 per carafe.

Mountifield produces its carafes along with all the other coffeepot components in its factory in Victoria, British Columbia. For the coming year, Mountifield has projected the costs of carafe production as follows (based on a projected volume of 100,000 units):

Direct materials	$ 75,000
Direct labour	65,000
Variable overhead	55,000
Fixed overhead	
Depreciation on equipment[1]	50,000
Property taxes on production space and equipment[2]	15,000
Factory supervision[3]	34,970
Total production costs	$294,970

[1]The equipment used to produce the carafes has no alternative use and no material market value.

[2]The space occupied by carafe production activities will remain idle if the company purchases rather than makes the carafes.

[3]The factory supervision cost reflects the salary of a production supervisor who oversees carafe production. This individual would be dismissed from the firm if carafe production ceased.

Required:

a. Determine the net advantage or disadvantage of purchasing rather than producing the carafes that are required for the coming year.

b. Determine the level of coffeepot production at which Mountifield would be indifferent between buying and producing the carafes. If the volume of production were expected to increase in the future, would the firm be more likely to make or outsource (buy)?

c. For this part only, assume that the space presently occupied by carafe production could be leased to another firm for $45,000 per year. How would this affect the make-or-outsource (buy) decision?

d. What other factors should the company take into account in determining whether it should make or outsource (buy) the carafes?

e. Assume that Mountifield Home Products is currently experiencing a $25,000 loss from operations. The company has an opportunity to sell an additional 10,000 carafes to a foreign distributor. Mountifield has the capacity to produce the additional carafes and no opportunity costs are associated with the order. What is the minimum price per carafe that the company should charge for the special order? What price should the company charge if it wants to achieve a $5,000 net income?

Problem 2

Alberta Products Ltd. produces a line of dolls in three different qualities: economy, standard, and deluxe. The selling price, average variable cost, and market demand (in units) for each type of doll are shown below:

	Price	Average Variable Cost	Market Demand
Economy	$ 25.00	$12.00	100,000
Standard	40.00	21.00	80,000
Deluxe	100.00	72.00	50,000

Mr. Montreal, the production manager, and Mr. Nova Scotia, the sales manager, have determined that three possible production and sales plans are feasible for the coming year.

	Plan #1 Units	Plan #2 Units	Plan #3 Units
Economy	90,000	110,000	100,000
Standard	60,000	75,000	85,000
Deluxe	30,000	50,000	35,000
Fixed production and marketing costs	$1,500,000	$3,000,000	$2,000,000

In addition to the costs shown above, committed fixed costs related to this product line are $1,400,000, regardless of the level of production and sales.

Required:

a. Determine the most profitable alternative for the company from the three plans given.

b. The president, Mr. British Columbia, after reviewing the results of part (a), suggests that gross margin per product should be calculated to see whether each of the products is covering its fixed costs. Respond briefly, but fully, to the president's suggestion.

Solutions to Demonstration Problems

Problem 1

a. Relevant costs to make 100,000 carafes:

Direct materials ($0.75 per unit)	$ 75,000
Direct labour ($0.65 per unit)	65,000
Variable overhead ($0.55 per unit)	55,000
Factory supervision	34,970
Total	$229,970
Cost to outsource (buy) 100,000 × $2.60	(260,000)
Net advantage of in-house production	$ 30,030

Note that the only fixed cost that is relevant to the decision is the cost of factory supervision. The other fixed costs would be unaffected by the decision.

b. The total relevant cost to make the carafes can be expressed as $34,970 + $1.95X$, where X represents production volume. The item $34,970 is the relevant fixed cost and the item $1.95X$ represents the total relevant variable costs. The total relevant cost to outsource (buy) the required carafes can be expressed as $2.60X$, where X represents production volume.

When the production cost equation is set equal to the purchase cost equation, the point of indifference can be found:

$2.60X = $1.95X + $34,970$

$0.65X = $34,970$

$X = 53,800$ units

As production volume goes up, so does the benefit of in-house production, because the average cost per unit will continually decline (due to the fixed cost element) and total cost rises only at a rate of $1.95 per unit rather than $2.60 per unit.

c. Referring to the solution to part (a), the net advantage of in-house production is $30,030. The possibility of renting the production space for $45,000 per year increases the cost of in-house production because an opportunity cost of $45,000 is incurred. Consequently, the balance shifts to favour the outsourcing of the carafes:

Original advantage of producing in-house	$ 30,030
Additional opportunity cost (lost rent)	(45,000)
Net cost of producing the carafes (or net advantage of outsourcing)	$(14,970)

d. Among the additional factors that might be considered are the quality of the carafes produced relative to the quality of the carafes outsourced, supplier reliability, number of competing suppliers, effect of the additional variety of carafes on customer demand, likelihood of supplier price increases in the future, and alternative (cost-reducing or income-generating) uses of the space currently utilized to produce carafes.

e. The minimum selling price per unit would be the $1.95 variable cost per unit. The price that would allow the company to make $5,000 would be $4.95 [($25,000 + $5,000) ÷ 10,000] = $3.00; $3.00 + $1.95 = $4.95.

Problem 2

a.

Production of	Plan #1	Plan #2	Plan #3
Economy	$ 1,170,000[1]	$ 1,300,000[4]	$ 1,300,000[7]
Standard	1,140,000[2]	1,425,000[5]	1,520,000[8]
Deluxe	840,000[3]	1,400,000[6]	980,000[9]
Total CM	$ 3,150,000	$ 4,125,000	$ 3,800,000
Less: Fixed Production & Mfg. Cost	$ 1,500,000	$ 3,000,000	$ 2,000,000
Committed Fixed Cost	1,400,000	1,400,000	1,400,000
Total Fixed Cost	$ 2,900,000	$ 4,400,000	$ 3,400,000
Net Income	$ 250,000	$ (275,000)	$ 400,000

[1] 90,000 × $13   [4] 100,000 × $13   [7] 100,000 × $13
[2] 60,000 × $19   [5] 75,000 × $19   [8] 80,000 × $19
[3] 30,000 × $28   [6] 50,000 × $28   [9] 35,000 × $28

The most profitable alternative is Plan 3.

b.   The problem with the president's suggestion is that it assumes that fixed costs can be attributed specifically to each of the three models. The information implies that the fixed costs are common to the line and thus not separable unless one uses an arbitrary application base. The relevant metric here would be to see whether each product has a positive contribution margin (which each has) and further, if information were given, whether there were any production constraints that would affect the relative contribution margin per constraining factor for each of the products.

End-of-Chapter Materials

SELF-TEST QUESTIONS

(SOLUTIONS APPEAR AT THE END OF THE CHAPTER.)

1. In an equipment replacement decision, which of the following is considered a relevant cost?
    a.   Annual depreciation of the old equipment
    b.   Write-off of the book value of the old equipment
    c.   Book value of the old equipment
    d.   Annual depreciation of the new equipment
    e.   None of the above

2. Why are joint costs irrelevant to the decision of whether to sell or process further?
    a.   Joint costs are full costs.
    b.   Joint costs do not change, regardless of the decision.
    c.   Joint costs can be allocated to the products.
    d.   Joint costs are used to process the products further.

    Extract from *Management Accounting 2 Examination*, published by the Certified General Accountants Association of Canada (© CGA-Canada 2003). Reprinted with permission.

3. If a firm is operating at full capacity, what costs must a minimum special order price cover?
    a.   Variable and incremental fixed manufacturing costs associated with the special order plus forgone contribution margin on regular units not produced
    b.   Variable and fixed manufacturing costs associated with the special order
    c.   Variable manufacturing costs associated with the special order
    d.   Variable and incremental fixed manufacturing costs associated with the special order

Use the following information to answer Questions 4 and 5.

The following are Desmond Teelucksing Inc.'s costs for making and selling an item at a volume of 10,000 units per month (the company's normal capacity):

Costs and Expenses

Manufacturing:

Direct materials	$10,000
Direct labour	20,000
Variable manufacturing overhead	5,000
Fixed manufacturing overhead	4,000

Selling and administrative:

Variable	20,000
Fixed	8,000

Current sales are 750 units per month. An order for 100 units has been received from a customer in a foreign market. The order would not affect current sales volume or price, nor would it require an increase to production beyond normal capacity. The variable selling and administrative expenses would be incurred for this special order as well as for all other sales.

4. By how much will the company's profits be increased if it prices the 100 units at $8 each?
    a. $150   c. $310
    b. $250   d. $350

5. Assume that at year-end, the company has some defective units. These units cannot be repaired and will have to be sold at a reduced price for scrap. The sale of these defective units will have no effect on the company's current sales. What should the minimum unit price be?
    a. $0.50   b. $1.00
    c. $2.00   d. $5.90

6. Which of the following factors would a firm not need to consider when evaluating the replacement of old equipment?
   a. Installation costs of the new equipment
   b. Costs for repairs made on the old equipment last year
   c. The current market value of the equipment to be replaced
   d. Changes in direct labour costs attributable to the new equipment

Self-Test Questions 5 and 6: Extract from *Management Accounting Examination*, published by the Certified General Accountants Association of Canada (© CGA-Canada 2000). Reprinted with permission.

7. What is the definition of opportunity cost?
   a. The benefit forgone when an action is taken
   b. A past cost that differs between alternatives
   c. A future cost that differs between alternatives
   d. A cost that cannot be changed regardless of the alternative selected

Extract from *Management Accounting 2 Examination*, published by the Certified General Accountants Association of Canada (© CGA-Canada 2000). Reprinted with permission.

8. Ebberes Corp. manufactures its own component parts. The following costs were incurred in the manufacture of 20,000 units of Part #33:

Direct materials	$ 6
Direct labour	30
Variable manufacturing overhead	12
Unitized fixed manufacturing overhead	16
	$64

   Tchyco Co. has offered to sell 20,000 units of Part #33 to Ebberes for $60 per unit. If Ebberes accepts the offer, $9 per unit of the fixed manufacturing overhead could be eliminated and the released facilities could be used to save relevant costs in the manufacture of Part #46. In order for Ebberes to realize an overall saving of $25,000, what amount of relevant costs would have to be saved by using the released facilities in the manufacture of Part #46?
   a. $ 80,000
   b. $ 85,000
   c. $125,000
   d. $140,000

Extract from *Management Accounting 1 Examination*, published by the Certified General Accountants Association of Canada (© CGA-Canada 2003). Reprinted with permission.

9. A retail store is planning to expand its business by adding a new product line. Since the resources available are limited, only one new line can be acquired. If the store decides to add Product Line 1, it cannot add Product Line 2. If the store adds Product Line 1, what are the profits that it could have made on Product Line 2 called?
   a. Differential costs
   b. Opportunity costs
   c. Sunk costs
   d. Variable costs

Extract from *Management Accounting 1 Examination*, published by the Certified General Accountants Association of Canada (© CGA-Canada 2000). Reprinted with permission.

10. Newman Enterprises Ltd. is considering closing down Phyllis Shampoo, one of its divisions. The division presently has a contribution margin of $500,000. Overhead allocated to the division is $1,250,000, of which $125,000 cannot be eliminated. If this division were discontinued, by what amount would Newman's pretax income increase?
    a. $125,000   c. $625,000
    b. $500,000   d. $750,000

Use the following information to answer parts (11), (12), and (13).

A company manufactures two products. The following table includes information about these products:

	A	B	Total
Sales	$100	$300	$400
Variable costs	40	100	140
Contribution margin	60	200	260
Fixed costs—direct	20	30	50
Fixed costs allocated[1]	50	100	150
Income (loss)	$ (10)	$ 70	$ 60

[1]The allocation is based on units of sales: 100 units for product A and 200 units for product B.

11. If product A were eliminated, what would the company's total income be?
    a. $20   b. $60
    c. $70   d. $80

12. If product A were eliminated and the unit sales of product B increased by 50%, what would the company's total income be?
    a. $ 90   b. $115
    c. $120   d. $180

13. Product A could be eliminated and replaced with a new product, C, which would have direct fixed costs of $40. Product C would sell for $5 per unit and have unit variable costs of $1 and expected sales of 40 units. What would the company's income be?
    a. $100   b. $120
    c. $140   d. $190

(Self-Test question 11-13 is adapted by the authors from Management Accounting examinations published by the Certified General Accountants Association of Canada © CGA-Canada, September 2004, used by permission)

Use the following information to answer parts (14) and (15).

Alpha Inc. is a manufacturer of plastic equipment. Some of the components used in the final products are manufactured internally while others are purchased from external suppliers. The following unit costs are for the production of 30,000 units of component A21:

Unit Cost:	
Direct materials per unit	$3.78
Direct labour at $18.75 per hour	$0.94
Manufacturing overhead costs at $24/machine hour	$1.20

Variable overhead represents 25% of the overhead costs.

SELF-TEST QUESTIONS

14. Assume that Alpha Inc. has excess capacity on the assembly line. Sigma Inc. has made an offer to supply Alpha with all the units of A21 that will be needed during the coming year. The component supplied by Sigma is equivalent to component A21 except that it will require 2 more minutes on an automatic soldering machine on the assembly line. What is the maximum price per unit that Alpha should pay to acquire the component from Sigma?

    a. $4.82
    b. $5.02
    c. $5.12
    d. $5.72

15. Assume that Alpha Inc. is operating at full capacity. Omega Inc. has offered to supply Alpha with a component that is similar to A21 at a price of $4.85 per unit. The capacity could be used to manufacture 5,000 units of a product with a contribution margin of $8 per unit. Which of the following options represents the best decision and the related increase in income for Alpha?

    a. Buy component from Omega and increase income by $45,100
    b. Buy component from Omega and increase income by $72,100
    c. Manufacture 30,000 units of A2l and increase income of $45,100
    d. Manufacture 30,000 units of A2l and increase income of $72,100

    (Self-Test question 15 is adapted by the authors from Management Accounting examinations published by the Certified General Accountants Association of Canada © CGA-Canada, December 2004, used by permission)

16. HeartHeathy Ltd. produces two models of treadmills: standard and deluxe. The manufacturing capacity of the specialized machinery needed to produce the treadmill rollers is 12,000 hours per year. The two models have the following production data:

	Standard	Deluxe
Machine time per unit	2 hours	4 hours
Contribution margin per unit	$10	$15
Maximum sales volume per year	5,000 units	4,000 units

    How many units should the company produce of the standard and deluxe models, respectively?

    a. 1,000 units; 4,000 units
    b. 1,000 units; 5,000 units
    c. 5,000 units; 500 units
    d. 6,000 units; 0 units

    (Self-Test question 16 is adapted by the authors from Management Accounting examinations published by the Certified General Accountants Association of Canada © CGA-Canada, June 2005, used by permission)

17. Produce Ltd. has approached Farmers' Supply Co. with a proposal to build a greenhouse supply warehouse. Farmers' Supply would provide a building to store supplies and would handle all record keeping. Farmers' Supply has a storage barn that is not currently in use. Shelving would be required for stacking the product, and a special concrete pad would be added for delivery truck access. The existing Farmers' Supply accountant would assume the additional accounting duties and would receive an additional $5,000 per annum. Farmers' Supply would be paid a fee based on the volume of product stored. Which of the following items is *not* a relevant consideration in deciding whether to establish a greenhouse supply warehouse?

    a. Book value of storage barn
    b. Cost of special concrete pad
    c. Farmers' Supply accountant's raise
    d. Projected volume of product for storage

18. Ming Tam Inc. has received an offer from an outside supplier to supply Ming Tam's annual needs of 10,000 component parts used in the manufacture of one of its products. Information on making versus outsourcing (buy) is as follows:

Cost to Make (per unit)	Cost to Outsource (Buy) (per unit)
Direct materials	$10.00
Direct labour	8.00
Variable manufacturing overhead	2.00
Allocated overhead	3.00
Production supervisor's salary	7.00
Outside supplier price	$24

    The production supervisor will be transferred to another department if the production of the component part is discontinued. Which of the following is the appropriate decision and related cost?

    a. Produce internally, based on a positive margin of $10,000
    b. Purchase (outsource) externally, based on a positive margin of $30,000
    c. Produce internally, based on a positive margin of $40,000
    d. Purchase (outsource) externally, based on a positive margin of $60,000

    (Self-Test question 18 is adapted by the authors from Management Accounting examinations published by the Certified General Accountants Association of Canada © CGA-Canada, June 2005, used by permission)

QUESTIONS

1. What three characteristics must a cost possess to be relevant to a decision? Why are these characteristics important?

2. What is meant by the term *incremental* as it applies to costs and revenues?

3. On November 13, Bill paid Jim $25 for a concert ticket that Jim had originally purchased for $50. On December 15, Ted offered Bill $30 for the ticket. Which of the costs mentioned are relevant in Bill's decision regarding whether to sell the ticket to Ted or attend the concert? What opportunity cost will Bill incur if he decides to attend the concert? Explain.

4. What category of costs is often relevant in decision making, but is probably never directly recorded in a company's accounting records? Explain. Are future variable costs always relevant costs? Discuss the rationale for your answer.

5. What term is used to describe historical costs? Are such costs relevant in making decisions? Explain.

6. What is the "change nothing" alternative? Why is it not always a feasible alternative?

7. In an asset replacement decision, which of the following costs would typically be relevant?
   a. The purchase cost of the new machine
   b. The purchase cost of the old machine
   c. The cost of electricity to run the old machine
   d. The cost of electricity to run the new machine
   e. The annual depreciation expense on the old machine

8. What are joint products, and what is the split-off point? Once joint products have reached the split-off point, are joint costs relevant? Are joint costs relevant before joint products reach the split-off point? Explain.

9. In a make-or-outsource (buy) decision, could some of the fixed costs associated with the "make" option be relevant? Explain.

10. What are some qualitative factors that should be considered in make-or-outsource (buy) decisions?

11. In production decisions that involve the allocation of a single scarce production resource among multiple products, which of the following is relevant? Explain the reasons for your answers.
    a. Sales demand for each product
    b. Sales price of each product
    c. Fixed production costs
    d. Variable selling costs for each product
    e. Variable production costs for each product

12. Evaluate the merit of the following statement: "In the long run, the only binding constraint on a firm's output is capital; in the short run, nearly any resource can be a binding constraint."

13. Why does the compensation structure for marketing personnel have a direct effect on the sales mix?

14. In allocating a scarce production resource in a multiproduct corporation whose goal is to maximize the total corporate contribution margin, why would management not simply produce the product that generates the highest contribution margin per unit?

15. In a multiproduct company, what is meant by the term *sales mix*? What factors are most likely to be manipulated in managerial attempts to change a company's sales mix?

16. How are special prices set and when are they used?

17. "In a special order decision, to avoid losing money on the order, the minimum selling price a company should charge is the sum of all the incremental costs of production and sales." Is this a true statement? Discuss the rationale for your answer.

18. In considering a special order that will enable a company to make use of currently idle capacity, which costs are likely to be relevant? Which costs are likely to be irrelevant?

19. Why are some direct fixed costs irrelevant to the decision to eliminate a product line?

20. What is product margin and how is it related to the decision to keep or eliminate a product line?

21. In the short run, which of the following must be non-negative in order to retain a product line?
    a. product line contribution margin
    b. product line segment margin
    c. product line net income.
    Why?

EXERCISES

1. (LO 2; Process further) The Pana Canada Petro-Chemical Company uses a production process that generates joint products. The joint costs associated with the process are $30,000.

Product ID	Units of Output	Selling Price at Split-Off	Additional Processing Costs	Final Selling Price
AA	10,000	$1.00	$0.75	$1.50
BB	20,000	$0.50	$1.00	$3.00
CC	500	$0.75	$0.10	$0.90

Required:
a. Compute the incremental revenue and incremental costs associated with further processing of each joint product.
b. Compute the incremental profit generated from further processing of each joint product. Which of the joint products should be processed beyond the split-off point?

2. (LO 2) A certain joint process yields two joint products, A and B. The joint cost for June is $32,000. The sales value of the output at split-off is $86,000 for product A and $27,000 for product B. Management is trying to decide whether to process its products further. If the products are processed beyond split-off, the final sales value will be $100,000 for product A and $38,000 for product B. The additional costs of processing are expected to be $16,000 for A and $4,000 for B.
Required:
a. Should management process the products further? Show computations.
b. Are any revenues and/or costs not relevant to the decision? If so, what are they and why are they not relevant?

3. (LO 2) Because of an increasing demand for Brady Company's Chow-Chow bottles, the company overproduced the product in both 2009 and 2010. In 2011, another company began to produce a much improved product that made Brady Company's product obsolete. In 2011, after the inventory was counted, Brady had $50,604 worth of Chow-Chow bottles on hand. After considering many alternatives, it was determined that the company could sell the product for scrap for $6,850 or recycle it into another product. It will cost $12,500 to rework the product, and it will sell for $20,500. On top of this additional cost, salespeople will receive 3% of the selling price.
Required:
What should Brady Company do with the inventory of Chow-Chow bottles?

4. (LO 3) Managers at Harry's Mutt & Cutt are trying to decide whether they should keep their old dog grooming equipment or invest in new energy-efficient equipment. Some data on both groups of equipment are:

	Old Equipment	New Equipment
Remaining life	5 years	5 years
Original cost	$12,000	$21,000
Accumulated depreciation	$ 4,000	$ 0
Annual cash operating costs	$ 7,000	$ 3,000
Current salvage value	$ 2,000	$21,000
Salvage value in 5 years	$ 0	$ 0

EXERCISES

Required:
a. Identify any sunk costs listed above.
b. Identify any irrelevant (nondifferential) future costs.
c. Identify all relevant costs to the equipment replacement decision.
d. What are the opportunity costs associated with the alternative of keeping the old machine?
e. What is the incremental cost to purchase the new machine?

5. (LO 3) Two years ago, Roses R Us Flower Shop purchased a two-tonne delivery truck. Because of increases in fuel prices and the other high costs of operating the truck, the company is considering replacing the truck with a smaller, more efficient pickup. Data on the existing and proposed truck follow:

	Old Truck	Proposed Truck
Remaining life	3 years	3 years
Original cost	$20,000	$10,000
Market value now	$ 5,000	$10,000
Salvage value in 3 years	$ 0	$ 0
Annual cash operating costs	$ 6,000	$ 4,500
Annual depreciation	$ 4,000	$ 3,333

Required:
a. What is the incremental cost of the proposed truck?
b. What are the incremental savings in annual operating costs?
c. What should the company do? Support your decision with calculations.

6. (LO 3) Reed Corporation Ltd. makes specialized metal engine stampings for one of the major automobile manufacturers. Reed is considering the replacement of one of the stamping machines presently used in the production of this product. The new machine would have a useful life equal to the remaining useful life of the current machine. However, the controller, Rose Reed, is hesitant because the stamping machine is a specialized piece of equipment and, due to the limited second-hand market for such a machine, the current one could be sold for only $150,000, resulting in a loss on disposal of $250,000.

The following data is available on all aspects of the two alternatives:

	Current Machine	New Machine
Useful life remaining in years	7	7
Current age in years	8	0
Original cost	$750,000	$500,000
Book value	$400,000	
Salvage value at end of useful life	$ 0	$ 0
Disposal value now	$150,000	
Disposal value in 7 years	$ 0	$ 0
Annual cash operating costs	$ 36,000	$ 20,000

Required:
Ignoring income taxes and time value of money, prepare a quantitative analysis of the best course of action for Reed Corporation, in respect of the two alternatives.

Extract from *Management Accounting 1 Examination*, published by the Certified General Accountants Association of Canada (© CGA-Canada 2003). Reprinted with permission.

7. (LO 4) The Kevin Fisher Shoe Company manufactures various types of shoes for sports and recreational use. Several types of shoes require a built-in air pump. The company presently makes all of the air pumps it requires for production, however, management is evaluating an offer from the Gloria Air Supply Company to provide air pumps at a cost of $5 each. Fisher's management has estimated that the variable production costs of the air pump amount to $3 per unit. The firm also estimates that it could avoid $50,000 per year in fixed costs if it outsourced rather than produced the air pumps.

Required:
a. If Fisher requires 20,000 pumps per year, should it make them or outsource (buy) them from Gloria Air Supply Company?

EXERCISES

b. If Fisher requires 30,000 pumps per year, should it make them or outsource (buy) them?

c. Assuming all other factors are equal, at what level of production would Fisher be indifferent between making and outsourcing (buying) the pumps? Show computations.

8. (LO 4) T.J. Holestrum Company has been purchasing a component part from another company since it began operations five years ago. Holestrum now has a steady demand for its product and feels it has the capacity to produce the component part itself. Last year Holstrum purchased 120,000 units at a cost of $1.10 per unit and feels it will purchase 10% more this year at the same price. If Holestrum produces this part, its costs will be:

Direct material	$0.45
Direct labour	$0.30
Variable overhead	$0.20
Avoidable fixed manufacturing overhead	$33,000

Required:
Should the T.J. Holestrum Company outsource (buy) this part or produce it in-house?

9. (LO 4) The David Didona Corporation needs 100 rock crushers to use in its gravel production plant. An outside supplier has offered to sell the company the required crushers at a price of $4,000 per rock crusher. If the company does not manufacture the rock crushers, it can manufacture gravel grinders. The manufacture of gravel grinders would produce $6,000 of additional contribution margin. Costs for Didona Corporation to manufacture 100 rock crushers follow:

Direct material	$130,000
Direct labour	150,000
Variable overhead	72,000
Fixed overhead ($70,000 allocated and $50,000 direct)	120,000

Required:
a. Identify the relevant out-of-pocket costs to produce the rock crushers.
b. Identify any other relevant costs.
c. Should Didona Corporation make the rock crushers or outsource them?

10. (LO 5) Lawrence Chung's Accounting Emporium provides two types of services—tax and financial accounting. All company personnel can perform either service equally well. In efforts to market its services, Lawrence Chung relies heavily on radio and billboard advertising. Information on Lawrence Chung's project operations for the current year are as follows:

	Taxes	Financial Accounting
Revenue per billable hour	$ 30	$ 25
Variable cost of professional labour	20	15
Material costs per billable hour	1	2
Allocated fixed costs per year	100,000	200,000
Projected billable hours for the year	12,000	8,000

Required:
a. What is Lawrence Chung's project profit or (loss) for the current year?
b. If $1 spent on advertising could increase either tax services revenue by $20 or financial accounting services revenue by $20, on which service should the advertising dollar be spent?
c. If $1 spent on advertising could increase tax services billable time by one hour or financial accounting services billable time by one hour, on which service should the advertising dollar be spent?

11. (LO 5) Because of a labour strike in the plant of its major competitor, Joe Kernen Tool Co. has found itself operating at peak capacity. The firm makes two electronic woodworking tools: sanders and drills. At this time the company can sell as many of either product as it can make. The firm's machines can only be run 90,000 hours per month. Data on each product follow:

EXERCISES

	Sanders	Drills
Sales	$45	$28
Variable costs	30	19
Contribution margin	$15	$ 9
Machine hours required per unit	8	6

Fixed costs are $110,000 per month.

Required:

a. How many of each product should the company make? Explain your answer.

b. How much profit would the company expect to earn based on your recommendation in part (a)?

12. (LO 6) Among many products made by the Baldwin Toy Company is a plastic tricycle. The company's projections for this product:

Projected volume in units	100 000
Sales price per unit	$ 62
Variable production costs per unit	$ 42
Variable selling costs per unit	$ 8
Total fixed production costs	$500,000
Total fixed selling and administration costs	$200,000

Required:

a. Compute the projected profit to be earned on tricycle sales.

b. Corporate management estimates that unit volume could be increased by 15% if the sales price were decreased by $4. How would such a change affect the profit level projected in part (a)?

c. Rather than cutting the sales price, management is considering holding the sales price at the projected level and increasing advertising by $200,000. Such a change would increase expected volume by 20%. How would the level of profit under this alternative compare with the profit projected in part (a)?

13. (LO 6) Lauren Fenmore Hound Pound Ltd. provides two types of services to dog owners: grooming and training. All company personnel can perform either service equally well. To expand sales and market share, Fenmore relies heavily on radio and billboard advertising. For the current year advertising expense is expected to be very limited. Information on projected operations for next year follows:

	Grooming	Training
Projected billable hours	10,000	8,000
Revenue per billable hour	$15	$25
Variable cost of labour	$5	$10
Material cost per billable hour	$1	$2
Allocated fixed costs per year	$100,000	$90,000

Required:

a. What is Fenmore's projected profit or loss?

b. If $1 spent on advertising could increase either grooming revenue or training revenue by $20, on which service should the advertising dollar be spent?

c. If $1 spent on advertising could increase grooming billable time or training billable time by one hour, on which service should the advertising dollar be spent?

14. (LO 6) Nukoko, a cellular phone manufacturer, has the following production and sales data:

Direct labour costs	$4,675,000 per year
Raw materials costs	$5,425,000 per year
Overhead expenses (portion of fixed overhead is 52%)	$7,200,000 per year
Variable selling and administrative expenses	$6.35 per cellular phone
Fixed selling and administrative expenses	$4.85 per cellular phone
Sales price	$75 per cellular phone
Number of cellular phones produced and sold	360,000 per year

The company wants to increase its profit and has two possible options:

Option A: Acquire higher-quality raw materials at a 33% higher cost. The selling price would increase by $3.50 per cellular phone and annual sales would increase to 385,000 cellular phones.

Option B: Decrease the average sales price to $70 per cellular phone. Sales volume would increase by 25%.

Required:

a.   Determine the effect of Option B on net income

b.   Determine which option the company should select.

(Exercise 14 is adapted by the authors from Management Accounting examinations published by the Certified General Accountants Association of Canada © CGA-Canada, March 2005, used by permission)

15. (LO 6) Katie Couric Company produces a plastic courtroom set that includes a judge's bench, witness stand, jury box, and 25 people. The set is sold to exclusive toy stores for $200. Plant capacity is 20,000 sets per year. Production costs are as follows:

Direct materials costs per set	$20
Direct labour cost per set	30
Variable overhead cost per set	40
Variable selling cost per set	10
Fixed overhead cost per year	$1,100,000

A prominent Montreal store, which has not previously purchased from Katie Couric Company, has approached the marketing manager about buying 5,000 sets for $170 each. No selling expenses would be incurred on this offer, but the Montreal store wants the set to include five plastic briefcases. This request means that Katie Couric Company will incur an additional $2 cost per set. The company is currently selling 18,000 courtroom sets, so therefore the acceptance of this order would require that the company to reject some of its current business.

Required:

a.   What is the current operating income of Katie Couric Company?

b.   If the company accepted this offer, what would its operating income be? Should the company accept the offer?

c.   If Katie Couric Company were currently selling only 10,000 sets per year and wanted to earn $150,000 of income for the year, what selling price would the company have to quote the Montreal store?

16. (LO 6) The manufacturing capacity of the Wolfe Blitzer Ltd. plant is 60,000 units of product per year. A summary of operations for the year ended December 31, 2009, is as follows:

Sales (36,000 units at $75 per unit)		$ 2,700,000
Variable manufacturing costs	$1,440,000	
Variable selling costs	180,000	(1,620,000)
Contribution margin		$ 1,080,000
Fixed costs		(990 000)
Operating income		$ 90,000

An offshore distributor has offered to buy 20,000 units at $60 per unit during 2010. Assume all costs (including variable selling expenses) will be at the 2009 level during fiscal 2010.

Required:

If Wolfe Blitzer Ltd. accepts this offer and also sells as many units to regular customers as it did in 2009, what would be the total operating income for 2010? (Normal variable selling costs will be incurred on this order and all other transactions.)

17. (LO 6) Tim Russert Ltd. has been approached by a volume buyer with an offer to purchase 50,000 toy pianos at $21.50 per unit. Delivery must be made within 30 days and variable selling costs will be $1 per unit. The productive capacity of Russert is 320,000 pianos per month and 10,000 pianos are currently on hand. At the regular price, sales of 300,000 pianos are expected for this month. The sales manager believes that 40% of sales lost during this month could be recovered later in the year. Price and cost data of regular sales are as follows:

Selling price		$33
Variable costs		
Production	$18	
Selling	6	24
Contribution		$ 9

EXERCISES

Required:

    a.   Determine whether Tim Russert Ltd. should accept or reject this special order.

    b.   To breakeven on this order, what price would have to be charged?

    c.   What other factors should be considered before accepting the order?

18. (LO 6) At the start of your employment with Deluxe Spa Products Inc., you are given the following income statements for the months of September and October.

	September	October
Sales revenue	$ 100,000	$ 120,000
Costs	140,000	150,000
Net loss	$(40,000)	$(30,000)

You are able to obtain the following additional information:

    i.   Each dollar of variable cost is made up of 40% direct materials, 35% direct labour, and 25% variable manufacturing overhead.

    ii. Total fixed costs amount to $90,000.

    iii. The selling price of each unit is $5.00.

    iv. The capacity of the plant is 40,000 units per month.

A new customer is willing to purchase 20,000 units at $3.50 per unit. During October, Deluxe Spa Products received confirmed orders from its regular customers for November sales of 25,000 units at $5.00 per unit. Direct labour costs on the special order would be reduced by 5%, but additional insurance and administrative costs will result in an increase of $10,000 if the special order is accepted.

Required:

Should this special order be accepted? Support your answer with full calculations.

19. (LO 6) Kate Roberts Ltd. makes miniature holiday wax figurines, which are sold in gift shops. The selling price is $1.25 each. Roberts' costs are as follows:

Variable production cost per unit	$0.45
Fixed production cost per unit	0.15

Roberts pays her salespeople a 10% commission on all sales. Other period expenses are all fixed in total at $20,000 per year. Fenmores, a large department store, has asked Roberts to bid on providing 1,000 figurines for the holiday season. Kate Roberts Ltd. has sufficient unused capacity to fill the order and has already done sufficient business to be profitable for the year prior to the bid request.

Required:

    a.   What is the lowest bid price that would not result in a loss on this special order?

    b.   What price should Roberts bid to make a 10% profit on the order?

    c.   Accepting this order will increase fixed expenses by $200. What price should Roberts bid for the 1,000 figurines in order to earn 5% profit on the order?

20. (LO 6). Rene Chu Ltd. makes specialty decorative candles to be sold in her chain of gift shops. The selling price is $12.50 each. The costs are as follows:

Variable production cost per unit	$4.50
Fixed production cost per unit (based on actual cost and actual production)	1.50

Chu pays the salespeople a 10% commission on all sales. Period expenses are fixed in total at $200,000 per year. Recently a request from a large department store was received asking that the firm bid on providing 1,000 candles during the Holiday season. Chu has sufficient unused capacity to fill the order. The company had already passed the breakeven point of sales for the current year prior to the bid request.

Required:

    a.   What is the minimum selling price that would result in no loss on this order?

    b.   Due to a special requirement of the department store, Chu expects the additional candles will increase fixed production expense by $20,000. What price would Chu have to bid in order that the firm would earn a 5% profit over total costs on the order? Explain.

    c.   Define the term "opportunity cost" and briefly explain how it may be relevant in a decision such as Chu's (that is, whether to accept a special order).

Extract from *Management Accounting 1 Examination*, published by the Certified General Accountants Association of Canada (© CGA-Canada 2003). Reprinted with permission.

EXERCISES

21. (LO 7) The management at Erika Kane Company is currently contemplating the elimination of one of its products, Pimples, because this product is now showing a loss. An annual income statement follows:

Erika Kane Company
Income Statement
For Year Ended August 31, 2011
(In Thousands)

| | **Product** | | | |
	Wimples	**Pimples**	**Bimples**	**Total**
Sales	$ 2,200	$1,400	$ 1,800	$ 5,400
Variable cost of sales	(1,400)	(800)	(1,080)	(3,280)
Production contribution margin	$ 800	$ 600	$ 720	$ 2,120
Traceable fixed and variable				
marketing costs	$ 630	$ 525	$ 520	$ 1,675
Allocated fixed costs	90	80	105	275
Total fixed costs	$ 720	$ 605	$ 625	$ 1,950
Operating profit	$ 80	$ (5)	$ 95	$ 170

Required:

a. Should the management at Erika Kane Company management discontinue sales of Pimples? Support your answer with appropriate schedules.

b. How would the net income of the company be affected by the decision?

22. (LO 7) The new controller of Books 'R' Us wants to launch a profitability review of the various product lines offered by the store. She is examining the product-line financial statement shown below:

Books 'R' Us
Product-Line Financial Statement
Three months ended March 31, 2011
(in thousands)

	Total	**Books**	**Supplies**	**General Merchandise**
Sales revenue	$400	$200	$80	$ 120
Cost of goods sold				
(assume all variable)	300	160	45	95
Gross margin	100	40	35	25
Less fixed costs:				
Rent	18	6	6	6
Salaries of sales staff	40	16	10	14
Marketing and administrative	36	12	12	12
Operating profit (loss)	$ 6	$ 6	$ 7	$ (7)

The company's accountant has informed the controller that if the general merchandise department were eliminated, the following would be relevant:

1. All of the sales staff in the general merchandise department could be terminated.
2. The rent is for a single building; there is no other use for the space if the general merchandise department is discontinued.
3. Marketing and administrative costs would be reduced by $6,000.
4. The sales of other product lines would be unaffected by the discontinuance of the general merchandise department.

Required:

a. Prepare an analysis showing whether it would be in the best interests of Books 'R' Us to eliminate the general merchandise department.

b. Prepare an analysis showing whether it would be in the best interest of Books 'R' Us to eliminate the general merchandise department if the resulting vacated space could be used to increase the sales of books (which would have the same contribution margin ratio) by 40%. The sales staff now in general merchandise would staff the larger book department and the marketing and administrative costs would only decrease by $2,000.

(Exercise 22 is adapted by the authors from Management Accounting examinations published by the Certified General Accountants Association of Canada © CGA-Canada, March 2005, used by permission)

PROBLEMS

1. (LO 2) Shearer, Inc., produces two final products, C and D, from a joint process. Process 1 yields 400 units of intermediate product A and 600 units of intermediate product B. For this yield, a cost of $15,000 is incurred in process 1. The 400 units of product A are then sent to process 2. Joint costs of $16,000 are incurred in process 2 to produce 800 units of product C and 1,200 units of product D. The final sales price for products C and D are, respectively, $10 and $20.
   Required:
   Assuming the 400 units of intermediate product A could have been sold for $18,000, should this intermediate product have been processed further? Explain your answer.

2. (LO 2) Esther Valentine Textiles Ltd. produces three products (pre-cut fabrics for hats, shirts, and pants) from a joint process. Rather than sell the products at the split-off point, the company can complete each product. Information related to these products is shown below:

	Hats	Shirts	Pants	Total
Number of units produced	5,000	8,000	3,000	16,000
Joint cost allocated	$ 56,250	$?	$?	$180,000
Sales value at split-off point	?	129,000	40,000	300,000
Additional costs of processing further	13,000	10,000	39,000	62,000
Sales value after all processing	150,000	134,000	105,000	389,000

   Required:
   a. As a management accountant, describe the process you may have used to determine the additional costs of processing further.
   b. What sales value for hats at the split-off point would make the firm indifferent between completing the hats and selling pre-cut fabric for hats?
   c. What amount of joint cost allocated to pre-cut shirts would make it economically infeasible to produce them?
   d. What is the effect on the corporate profit of completing the pants rather than selling pre-cut fabric for pants?

3. (LO 2) The joint process at Losell Co. Ltd. produces three separate products. The current estimated average cost of one batch of joint inputs is $1,000. Each of the products—Aferon, Beteron, and Ceteron—can either be sold at the split-off point or processed further and then sold. After the joint process, each product is independently processed. The management of Losell Co. Ltd. has gathered the following information:

	Total	Variable Costs	Fixed But Avoidable With Shutdown of Process	Fixed, Not Avoidable With Shutdown of Process
Cost of joint process	$1,000	$600	$250	$150
Cost of separate process:				
Aferon	40	30	8	2
Beteron	60	40	15	5
Ceteron	20	15	3	2

   At the split-off point, Aferon can be sold for $450 or processed further at an incremental cost of $40 and then sold for $520.

   At the split-off point, Beteron can be sold for $300 or processed further at an incremental cost of $60 and then sold for $350.

PROBLEMS

At the split-off point, Ceteron can be sold for $250 or processed further at an incremental cost of $20 and then sold for $265.

Required:

a.   Advise the management of Losell whether it should sell the products at split-off, sell them in their fully processed form, discontinue production, or employ some other course of action.

b.   There is an opportunity for Losell to modify the units that result from the separate process for Ceteron at an incremental cost of $140. This product (to be called Deteron) would be sold at a price of $400. Should Losell produce Deteron rather than Ceteron?

Extract from *Management Accounting Examination*, published by the Certified General Accountants Association of Canada (© CGA-Canada 1995). Reprinted with permission.

4.   (LO 3) Obama Inc. has operations in all of the provinces. Obama is in the business of growing soybeans and processing the beans into two products: soybean oil and soybean meal. These products are then sold for various commercial uses. The manager of each of the provincial divisions has his performance evaluated based (in large part) on annual profits. These managers typically receive an annual bonus equal to 0.5% of corporate profits.

The manager of the Nova Scotia operations is Guiliani. Guiliani is sixty-three years old and has been with Obama for thirty-nine years. He would like to sell the existing bean crusher and purchase a new, technologically superior one. To evaluate the feasibility of such a move, Guiliani's controller has prepared the following information. This information has created a tremendous dilemma for Guiliani.

Expected remaining life of the old crusher	5 years
Expected life of the new crusher	5 years
Incremental cost of the new crusher	$2,000,000
Expected effect of the new crusher on net profit for the next five years:	
Year 1: Decrease in operating costs	$ 600,000
Loss on disposal of old crusher	1,500,000
Net decrease in profit	($900,000)
Year 2; Net increase in profit	400,000
Year 3: Net increase in profit	500,000
Year 4: Net increase in profit	510,000
Year 5: Net increase in profit	600,000

Required:

a.   What is the source of Guiliani's dilemma?

b.   Is the expected book loss on the disposal of the old equipment relevant to Guiliani's decision?

c.   Is Guiliani's age likely to be an important factor in his decision? Why or why not?

d.   What should Guiliani do? Explain in detail.

5.   (LO 3) The Funky Chicken Conglomerate offers products and services to various restaurants under a franchising arrangement. For operating purposes, The Funky Chicken has three autonomous divisions: Steamed, Fried, and Barbecued. For the current year, the Steamed Division has projected its net income at $1.2 million.

One of the Steamed Division's most important operations involves a water boiler that is used to steam the chickens. The division's management has recently asked its controller to prepare a comparative financial analysis of a new steam-generating technology with the existing boiler. The following information was presented by the controller to division management:

	Old Boiler	New Technology
Remaining life	8 years	8 years
Original cost	$3,000,000	$2,000,000
Market value now	200,000	—
Operating costs	400,000	50,000
Salvage value in 8 years	0	0
Accumulated depreciation	1,000,000	—

After allowing the Steamed Division manager to examine the previous information for a few moments, the division controller said, "As the financial information clearly indicates, we must invest in the new technology."

Required:

a.   Identify the costs that are relevant to the Steamed Division's equipment replacement decision.

b.   Do you agree with the controller's conclusions? Provide your own computations based only on relevant costs.

6.   (LO 3) For two years, Judy Pereira Corporation has operated a successful business making miniature fibreglass boats. It must decide whether to refurbish the moulds it uses or replace them. The moulds were purchased two years ago for $600,000. They have an expected useful life of three more years, a terminal disposal value of $0 at the end of that time, a current disposal value of $90,000, and a book value of $360,000. Below are expected costs under the two alternatives:

	Refurbish	Replace
Capital cost	$300,000	$750,000
Variable manufacturing cost per hull	$12.00	$9
Expected production and sales of boats per year	60,000	60,000
Selling price per boat	$25	$25

The expected useful life of the old moulds after refurbishing is three years. The refurbishment would not affect the terminal disposal value. The expected useful life of the replacement moulds is three years with $0 disposal value at the end of that time. If the old mould is refurbished, the additional $300,000 would be depreciated over the remaining three years of life. The new equipment would be depreciated using the straight-line basis.

Required:

a.   Should Pereira refurbish or replace the moulds? Show all calculations and explain.

b.   The capital expenditure to replace the moulds is $750,000 but the demand is not known for certain. For what annual sales/production quantity would Pereira prefer to (i) replace the moulds, (ii) refurbish the moulds? Briefly explain.

7.   (LO 4) The New Sulyma Lighting Company manufactures various types of household light fixtures. Most of the light fixtures require 60-watt light bulbs. Historically, the company has produced its own light bulbs. The costs to produce a bulb (based on capacity operation of 3,000,000 bulbs per year) are as follows:

Direct materials	$0.10
Direct labour	0.05
Variable manufacturing overhead	0.01
Fixed manufacturing overhead	0.03
Total	$0.19

→Avoidable

The fixed manufacturing overhead includes $60,000 of depreciation on equipment for which there is no alternative use and no external market value. The balance of the fixed → Unavoidable manufacturing overhead pertains to the salary of the production supervisor. The production supervisor of the light bulb operation has a lifetime employment contract; she also has skills that could be used to displace another manager (the part-time supervisor of electrical cord production), who draws a salary of $15,000 per year but is due to retire from the company.

The M. Connor Electric Company has recently approached New Sulyma with an offer to supply all the light bulbs New Sulyma requires at a price of $0.18 per bulb. Anticipated sales demand for the coming year will be 2,000,000 bulbs.

Required:

a.   Identify the relevant costs in this make-or-outsource (buy) decision.

b.   What is the total annual advantage or disadvantage (in dollars) of outsourcing (buying), rather than making, the bulbs?

PROBLEMS

c. What qualitative factors should be taken into account in this make-or-outsource (buy) decision?

d. As a management accountant, how would you obtain information about the employment contracts of factory managers?

e. As the human resources manager, how might you respond to a suggestion by the accounting staff to fire the supervisor of electrical cord production?

8. (LO 4) Mimi Lockhart Ltd. uses 1,000 units of component IMC2 every month in order to manufacture one of its products. The unit costs incurred to manufacture the component are the following:

Direct materials	$ 65.00
Direct labour	48.00
Manufacturing overhead	126.50
Total	$239.50

Manufacturing Overhead costs include variable material handling costs of $6.50, which are applied to products on the basis of direct material costs. The rest of the overhead costs are applied on the basis of direct labour dollars and consist of 50% variable costs and 50% fixed costs.

A vendor has offered to supply the IMC2 component at a price of $200 per unit.

Required:

a. Should Lockhart outsource the manufacturing of the component to an outside vendor if its capacity remains idle?

b. Should Lockhart outsource the manufacturing of the component to an outside vendor if it can use its facilities to manufacture another product? What information will Lockhart need to use to make an accurate decision? Show your calculations. Support your answer with values where appropriate.

c. What are the qualitative factors that Lockhart will have to consider when making this decision?

Extract from *Management Accounting 1 Examination*, published by the Certified General Accountants Association of Canada (© CGA-Canada 2000). Reprinted with permission.

9. (LO 4). Powersport is an energy drink that is well known among sports federations and athletes. Since it came out on the market three years ago, sales have increased continuously. The company believes it will sell 200,000 cases next year. A case contains twelve 375-mL bottles of Powersport and is sold for $18 per case to vendors at sporting events, which sell the bottles for $3 each.

Based on the production of 200,000 cases, the production costs are:

Labour	$2.75 per case
Raw materials	$3.75 per case
Variable and fixed manufacturing overhead	$3.00 per case
Total fixed manufacturing overhead	$400,000

The company received an offer last month from Lawrence Chung Ltd., a manufacturer that makes containers out of recycled materials, to make the bottles for $0.15 each. This proposition would enable Powersport to decrease its cost of labour and raw materials by 20%. The company's variable manufacturing overhead would decrease to $0.60 per case.

Required:

a. Should Powersport accept the proposition? Show all calculations.

b. Calculate the maximum price that Powersport should pay for a case of bottles.

c. The estimated sales are now 300,000 cases instead of 200,000 cases, but Powersport cannot produce more than 250,000 cases without having to purchase a new machine to make the bottles. The new machine can be bought for $150,000 and has a useful life of 10 years. Variable overhead costs would increase by 20%. Should Powersport accept the proposition in part (a)? Show all calculations.

Extract from *Management Accounting 2 Examination*, published by the Certified General Accountants Association of Canada (© CGA-Canada 2003). Reprinted with permission.

PROBLEMS

10. (LO 4) Gaetane Labelle Maraj Inc. (GLM) produces top-quality motors for high-speed boats and all the components needed in the production process. Component SPE is the most important part of the motor. A vendor who specializes in manufacturing a similar component has offered to supply GLM with 100,000 units at a price of $62.50 per unit. GLM has computed the following cost information pertaining to component SPE (based on a volume of 100,000 units):

Direct materials	$ 2,800,000
Direct labour	2,100,000
Variable manufacturing overhead	1,200,000
Fixed manufacturing overhead:	
Depreciation on equipment[1]	190,000
Property taxes on production facility	
space and equipment[2]	110,000
Factory supervision[3]	80,000
Total production costs	$ 6,480,000

[1]The equipment used to produce component SPE has no alternative use and no material market value.

[2]The space used for activities related to the production of component SPE will remain idle if the company purchases component SPE instead of producing it.

[3]The factory supervision costs include the salaries of two supervisors for the production of SPE. These two people would be laid off if the firm decides to purchase component SPE.

Required:

a. Determine whether GLM should make or outsource (buy) component SPE.

b. Determine the level at which GLM would be indifferent between outsourcing (buying) and making component SPE.

c. Assume that the space presently used for the production of component SPE could be leased to another firm for $100,000 per year. How would this affect the make-or-outsource (buy) decision?

d. Identify three qualitative factors that the company should consider in its make-or-outsource (buy) decision.

(Problem 10 is adapted by the authors from Management Accounting examinations published by the Certified General Accountants Association of Canada © CGA-Canada, March 2005, used by permission)

11. (LO 4) David Faber Inc. is a wholesale distributor supplying moderately priced sporting equipment to large chain stores. About 60% of Faber's products are outsourced (purchased) from other companies, while the rest are manufactured by Faber. The company's Plastics Department currently manufactures moulded fishing tackle boxes. Faber manufactures and sells 8,000 tackle boxes annually, making full use of its direct labour capacity at available workstations. Following are the selling price and costs associated with Faber's tackle boxes:

Selling price per box		$86.00
Costs per box:		
Moulded plastic	$ 8.00	
Hinges, latches, handle	9.00	
Direct labour ($15 per hour)	18.75	
Manufacturing overhead	12.50	
Selling and administrative costs	17.00	65.25
Profit per box		$20.75

Faber believes that the company could sell 12,000 tackle boxes if it had sufficient manufacturing capacity. The company has looked into the possibility of outsourcing (purchasing) the tackle boxes for distribution. Mark Haines Products, a steady supplier of high-quality products, would be able to provide up to 9,000 tackle boxes per year at a price of $68 per box delivered to Faber's facility.

PROBLEMS

Joe Kernen, Faber's product manager, has suggested that the company could make better use of its Plastics Department by manufacturing skateboards. A market report indicates an expanding skateboard market and a need for additional suppliers. Kernen believes that Faber could sell 17,500 skateboards per year at $45 per skateboard. Manufacturing cost estimates follow:

Selling price per skateboard		$45 00
Costs per skateboard:		
Moulded plastic	$5.50	
Wheels, hardware	7.00	
Direct labour ($15 per hour)	7.50	
Manufacturing overhead	5 00	
Selling and administrative costs	9.00	34.00
Profit per skateboard		$11.00

In the Plastics Department, Faber uses direct labour as the application base for manufacturing overhead. This year, the Plastics Department has been allocated $50,000 of factorywide fixed manufacturing overhead. Every unit of product that Faber sells, whether outsourced or manufactured, is allocated $6 of fixed overhead cost for distribution; this amount is included in the selling and administrative cost. Total selling and administrative costs for the purchased tackle boxes would be $10 per unit.

Required:

Using the data presented, determine which products David Faber, Inc., should manufacture and which it should outsource. Support your answer with appropriate calculations.

(IMA adapted)

12. (LO 4). Marlene Lovinsky Company purchases sails and produces sailboats. It currently produces 1,200 sailboats per year, operating at normal capacity, which is about 80% of full capacity. Marlene Lovinsky Company presently outsources the manufacture of the sails and pays $260 each. The company is considering using the excess capacity to manufacture the sails in-house instead. The manufacturing cost per sail would be $100 for materials, $80 for direct labour, and $100 for manufacturing overhead. The $100 manufacturing overhead is based on an annual fixed manufacturing overhead amount of $72,000 that is allocated using normal capacity.

The president of Marlene Lovinsky Company has come to you for advice. "It would cost me $280 to make the sails," she says, "but only $260 to outsource the manufacturing of the sails. Should I continue outsourcing them or have I missed something?"

Required:

a. Prepare a per unit analysis of differential costs. Briefly explain whether Marlene Lovinsky Company should make or outsource (buy) the sails.

b. If Marlene Lovinsky Company suddenly finds an opportunity to rent out the unused capacity of its factory for $80,000 per year, would your answer to part (a) change? Briefly explain.

c. Identify three qualitative factors that should be considered by Marlene Lovinsky Company in this make-versus-outsource (buy) decision.

Extract from *Management Accounting Examination*, published by the Certified General Accountants Association of Canada (© CGA-Canada 2002). Reprinted with permission.

13. (LO 4) Gomes Active Wear Corporation is a large clothing manufacturer. Profitability has gone down in the past few years, and after a bitter internal struggle, Gamon Gomes has been appointed the new CEO. Gomes' opinion is that the company can increase profitability by discontinuing the Distribution Department and hiring a trucking firm to transport the company's products to retail outlets. As a management accountant, you have been given the task of determining whether he is correct. The following information (given in thousands) is available for the preceding fiscal year:

PROBLEMS

	Manufacturing	Packaging	Distribution	Total
Salaries and wages	$4,000	$ 500	$1,950	$ 6,450
Material	2,000	750	0	2,750
Office supplies	500	350	350	1,200
Occupancy costs	420	300	300	1,020
Selling and administrative expense	650	310	450	1,410
Depreciation	200	75	90	365
Total	$7,770	$2,285	$3,140	$13,195

Additional information:

- After a detailed review of personnel, management decides it can transfer the distribution supervisor (who earns a salary of $35,000), an assistant distribution supervisor (who earns a salary of $25,000), and six part-time labourers (who earn average wages of $15,000) to the Packaging Department to prepare goods for shipment.
- Owing to more stringent requirements imposed by trucking companies, an additional $100,000 will have to be spent annually for packaging materials.
- The space of the Distribution Department will be required by the Packaging Department for storage of goods prior to shipment.
- The cost of office supplies for the Packaging Department is expected to increase by $50,000.
- Insurance costs included in selling and administrative expenses are expected to decline by $50,000. Other administrative costs are expected to increase, because of the addition of three part-time staff members in Accounts Payable at an annual rate of $12,000 per employee and two additional part-time people in the Payroll Department at an annual salary of $15,000 each. In addition, management will need to add four part-time clerical positions at an annual rate of $10,000 each.
- A trucking company has offered to provide shipping for $2.5 million annually.
- None of the equipment that is presently in use in the Distribution Department has alternative applications or any external market value.

Required:

a. Prepare a statement setting forth in comparative form the costs of product distribution under the present arrangement and under the proposed change in operations. Determine the net savings or cost of accepting the proposal.

b. Assuming the company is functionally organized (that is, Manufacturing, Packaging, Distribution, and Marketing currently all have separate managements), what concerns might these managers have in the restructuring that Gamon Gomes should address?

(IMA adapted)

14. (LO 5) Jan Spears Ltd. manufactures four different products. Because the quality of the products is high, the demand for the products exceeds the units Jan Spears Ltd. can produce.

Based on the inquiries made by current and potential customers, you have estimated the following for the coming year:

Product	Estimated Demand in Units	Selling Price Per Unit	Direct Materials Cost Per Unit	Direct Labour Cost Per Unit
A	8,000	$ 50	$ 5	$ 5
B	24,000	60	10	9
C	20,000	150	25	30
D	30,000	100	15	20

The following information is also available:

- The direct labour rate is $15 per hour and the factory has a capacity of 80,000 hours. For the next year, Jan Spears Ltd. is unable to expand this capacity.
- Jan Spears Ltd. is unwilling to increase its selling prices.

- Apart from direct materials and direct labour, there are no other variable expenses except for variable manufacturing overhead. The variable manufacturing overhead is 50% of direct labour cost.
- Fixed manufacturing overhead is estimated to be $1,000,000 for the coming year. Fixed marketing and administrative expenses are estimated to be $750,000 for the coming year.

Required:

Which products and how many of each should Jan Spears Ltd. produce in the coming year in order to maximize its operating income?

Extract from *Management Accounting 1 Examination,* published by the Certified General Accountants Association of Canada (© CGA-Canada 1999). Reprinted with permission.

15. (LO 5) The Marta Stewart Bakery produces three types of cakes: birthday, wedding, and special occasion. The cakes are made from scratch and baked in a special cake oven. During the holiday season (roughly November 15 through January 15), total demand for the cakes exceeds the capacity of the cake oven. The cake oven is available for baking 690 hours per month, but because of the size of the cakes, it can bake only one cake at a time. Management must determine how to ration the oven time among the three types of cakes. Information on costs, sales prices, and product demand is as follows:

	Birthday Cakes	Wedding Cakes	Special Occasion Cakes
Required minutes of oven time per cake	10	80	18
Sales price	$ 25	$100	$40
Variable costs:			
Direct material	5	30	10
Direct labour	5	15	8
Variable manufacturing overhead	2	5	4
Variable selling	3	12	5
Fixed costs (monthly):			
Manufacturing	$1,200		
Selling and administrative	800		

Required:

a. If demand is essentially unlimited for all three types of cakes during the holiday season, which cake or cakes should Marta Stewart bake during the holiday season? Why?

b. Based on your answer in part (a), how many cakes of each type will be produced? What is the projected level of monthly profit for the holiday season?

c. If you were the marketing manager for Marta Stewart, how would your marketing efforts differ between the holiday season and the rest of the year?

16. (LO 6) Catherine Chancellor Manufacturing, Inc. is presently operating at 50% of practical capacity producing about 50,000 units annually of a patented electronic component. Chancellor recently received an offer from a company in Yokohama, Japan, to purchase 30,000 components at $6.00 per unit, FOB Chancellor's plant. Chancellor has not previously sold components in Japan. Budgeted production costs for 50,000 and 80,000 units of output follow:

Units	50,000	80,000
Costs:		
Direct material	$ 75,000	$120,000
Direct labour	75,000	120,000
Manufacturing overhead	200,000	260,000
Total costs	$350,000	$500,000
Cost per unit	$7.00	$6.25

The sales manager, Jack Abbott, thinks the order should be accepted, even if it results in a loss of $1.00 per unit, because he feels that the sale may build up future markets. The production manager does not wish to have the order accepted primarily because the order would show a loss of $0.25 per unit when computed on the new average unit cost.

PROBLEMS

The treasurer, Jill Abbott, has made a quick computation indicating that accepting the order will actually increase gross margin.

Required:

a. Explain what apparently caused the drop in cost from $7.00 per unit to $6.25 per unit when budgeted production increases from 50,000 to 80,000 units.

b. i. Explain whether (either or both) the production manager and the treasurer are reasoning correctly.

 ii. Explain why the conclusions of the production manager and the treasurer differ.

c. Explain why each of the following may affect the decision to accept or reject the special order:

 i. The likelihood of repeat special sales and/or all sales to be made at $6.00 per unit

 ii. Whether the sales are made to customers operating in two separate, isolated markets or whether the sales are made to customers competing in the same market

(IMA adapted)

17. (LO 6) One year ago, Victor Newman gave up his position as the movie critic and sportswriter of the local paper and purchased the rights (under a five-year contract) to several concession stands at a local municipal football stadium. After analyzing the results of his first year of operations, Newman is somewhat disappointed. His two main products are "dogs" and "burgers," and he had expected to sell about the same number of each product over the course of the year. However, his sales mix was approximately two-thirds dogs and one-third burgers. Newman feels that this combination is less profitable than a balanced mix of dogs and burgers. He is now trying to determine how to improve profitability for the coming year and is considering strategies to improve the sales mix. His first year operations are summarized below:

Dogs:

Sales	(100,000 @ $1.50)	$150,000	
Less:	Direct materials	(40,000)	
	Direct labour	(15,000)	
	Fixed costs	(45,000)	
Net profit			$50,000

Burgers:

Sales	(50,000 @ $2.50)	$125,000	
Less:	Direct materials	(55,000)	
	Direct labour	(10,000)	
	Fixed costs	(15,000)	
Net profit			45,000
Total profit			$95,000

If Newman takes no action to improve profitability, he expects sales and expenses in the second year to mirror the first-year results. Newman is considering two alternative strategies to boost profitability.

Strategy 1:   Add point-of-sale advertising to boost burger sales. The estimated cost per year for such advertising would be $29,000. Newman estimates the advertising would decrease dog sales by 6,000 units and increase burger sales by 22,000 units.

Strategy 2:   Provide a sales commission to his employees. The commission would be paid at a rate of 10% of the product contribution margin (sales less variable production costs) generated on all sales. Newman estimates this strategy would increase dog sales by 10% and burger sales by 25%.

Required:

a. Determine what Newman should do: take no action, adopt Strategy 1, or adopt Strategy 2. (Show your supporting calculations.)

b. Assuming Newman decides to implement either of the new strategies, what behavioural concerns should he be prepared to address? Explain.

PROBLEMS

18. (LO 6) Jenny Fong's company makes and sells "Huggable Brown"—her famous stuffed puppy for young children. The puppies are sold to department stores for $50. The capacity of the plant is 20,000 Huggables per year. Costs to make and sell each stuffed animal are as follows:

Direct materials	$ 5.50
Direct labour	7.00
Variable manufacturing overhead	10.00
Fixed manufacturing overhead	12.00
Variable selling expenses	3.00

An Australian import/export company has approached Jenny about buying 2,000 Huggables. Fong Company is currently making and selling 20,000 Huggables per year. The Australian firm wants its own label attached to each stuffed animal, which will raise costs by $0.50 each. No selling expenses would be incurred on this order. Jenny Fong feels that she must make an extra $1 on each stuffed animal to accept the order.

Required:
a. What is the opportunity cost per unit of selling to the Australian firm?
b. What is the minimum selling price that Jenny should set?
c. Predict how much more operating profit Jenny will have if she accepts this order at the price specified in part (b).
d. Prove your answer to part (c) by providing operating profits with and without the new order.

19. (LO 6) Mark Haines Ltd. manufacturers and sells a single product. The company has the capacity to produce and sell 30,000 units per year. Costs and revenues associated with this level of operations are given below:

	Per Unit
Direct materials	$15
Direct labour	8
Variable manufacturing overhead	3
Variable selling	4
Fixed manufacturing overhead	9
Fixed selling	6
Total	$45

The selling price is $50 per unit.

Haines expects to sell only 25,000 units next year through regular channels. J. Kernen Ltd., a large discount chain, has offered to buy 5,000 units if Haines will lower its price by 16%. As this is a direct sale, there would be no sales commission, reducing variable selling expenses by 75%. However, the purchaser would require a slight modification to the product, necessitating Haines to buy a special piece of equipment for $10,000.

Required:
a. What would be the effect on cash flows next year if Haines accepted the offer from J. Kernen Ltd.?
b. Bartiromo Ltd., a different firm, wishes to make a one-time purchase of 5,000 units. (The regular production and sales for Mark Haines Ltd. are expected to be 25,000 units). Bartiromo would pay on a "manufacturing cost plus" basis and also pay Haines $1.80 per unit above its full cost of production. Bartiromo would pick up the units in its own trucks, so there would be no selling costs. If Haines accepts the offer, what would be the effect on profits?
c. Assume that Haines can sell 30,000 units without Bartiromo's order. On the basis of financial/quantitative analysis only, should Haines accept Bartiromo's order?

Extract from *Management Accounting 1 Examination*, published by the Certified General Accountants Association of Canada (© CGA-Canada 2000). Reprinted with permission.

PROBLEMS

20. (LO 7) Forrester Creations Ltd. is presently considering the elimination of one of its existing products (product C) because decreased sales have resulted in the product's generating a loss. The following information is available for the most recent operating year:

	A	B	C
Units produced and sold	1,000	1,500	1,000
Sales price per unit	$2.00	$4.00	$2.10
Cost of goods:			
Material per unit	0.80	2.00	1.05
Labour per unit	0.30	0.75	0.80
Manufacturing overhead per unit	0.35	0.45	0.35
Selling and administrative expenses per unit	0.15	0.30	0.20

The following information is also available:
i. If product C were eliminated, the sales of products A and B would remain the same.
ii. Variable manufacturing overhead is charged as follows: product A, $0.25 per unit; product B, $0.35 per unit; product C, $0.20 per unit.
iii. Variable selling and administrative expenses are charged as follows: product A, $0.10 per unit; product B, $0.20 per unit; product C, $0.15 per unit.

Required:
Prepare a schedule to help Forrester Creations Ltd.'s management decide whether to eliminate product C. What is your choice, and what are your reasons for this choice?

21. (LO 3, 7) You have been presented with the following income statements for three products that Esther Deutsch Ltd. produces. The production costs for all three products are similar. The fixed selling and administrative expenses are allocated on the basis of square metres occupied by the production of each product.

	A	B	C	D
Unit sales	5,000	250,000	62,500	317,500
Revenues	$46,250	$ 50,000	$28,750	$125,000
Cost of goods sold:				
Variable	$14,250	$ 17,500	$ 7,500	$ 39,250
Fixed	15,210	14,450	8,340	38,000
	$29,460	$ 31,950	$15,840	$ 77,250
Gross margin	$16,790	$ 18,050	$12,910	$ 47,750
Selling and administrative expenses:				
Variable	$13,500	$ 10,000	$ 4,000	$ 27,500
Fixed	10,290	5,050	3,910	19,250
Income before taxes	$(7,000)	$ 3,000	$ 5,000	$ 1,000

The president of the company is concerned about the loss incurred on product A and has been presented with two alternative courses of action. You have been requested to advise her on whether to:
a. Maintain the status quo
b. Go with Alternative I, or
c. Go with Alternative II.

The following are Alternatives I and II.

Alternative I: Purchase new machinery to manufacture product A, which would result in an immediate cash outlay of $100,000 and increase the fixed costs allocated to product A by $4,800 per year. This new machinery would result in the total variable expenses of product A being reduced to 55% of total revenues. No additional fixed costs would be allocated to products B and C.

Alternative II: Stop manufacturing product A. Product C's sales would increase by 50%. The present machinery devoted to product A would be sold and after disposition costs the company would not have a gain or loss on disposal. This would reduce the fixed costs allocated to product A by $4,290. The remaining fixed costs allocated to product A include $5,000 rent expense paid per year to a leasing company. This space could be sublet to an outside party for $6,000 per year.

PROBLEMS

Required:

As a management accountant advise the president which of the alternatives is best for the company.

22. (LO 7) The projected quarterly operating expenses at normal volume levels for the Western Division of McCain Company are given below. These quarterly expense patterns are expected to hold for the next few years.

Variable production (50% of sales)	$800,000
Variable selling (18.75% of sales)	300,000
Direct fixed	600,000
Allocated fixed	250,000

The direct fixed costs represent the salary of the division manager, $200,000; depreciation on the equipment, $300,000; and the quarterly rental payment on leased facilities, $100,000. The division manager has a contract that guarantees her a job at her present salary for the next five years. The lease on the facilities can be cancelled, without penalty, six months after notifying the owner of the facility. The $300,000 of quarterly depreciation applies to equipment that has no alternative use or tangible market value.

Required:

a. Assuming next quarter's projected sales are $1,600,000, develop an income statement that identifies the Western Division's projected segment margin and net income or less for next quarter.

b. What is the minimum acceptable level of sales for the upcoming quarter for the Western Division to be retained?

c. For a quarter commencing more that six months from the present time (but less than five years from now), what is the minimum acceptable level of sales that must be achieved in order to keep the division operating? (As indicated earlier, assume that total variable costs will be equal to 68.75% of sales revenue)

23. (LO 7) Newman Enterprises Ltd. began operations 15 years ago as a manufacturer of athletic shoes. It later added a successful line of athletic socks, and then introduced a line of athletic sportswear that has become its most profitable product line. Over the years, competition from Asia Corporation has forced Newman to reduce the prices of its athletic shoes to the point where this product line now consistently has a negative segment margin. Typical monthly statistics for the three product lines are shown in the chart below.

	Sportswear		Athletic Shoes		Athletic Socks	
Sales	$600,000	100%	$350,000	100%	$180,000	100%
Variable costs	258,000	43	262,500	75	90,000	50
Contribution margin	$342,000	57%	$ 87,500	25%	$ 90,000	50%
Traceable fixed costs	132,000	22	105,000	30	77,400	43
Segment margin	$210,000	35%	$ (17,500)	(5%)	$ 12,600	7%

Newman is considering discontinuing the manufacture and sale of athletic shoes. All costs traceable to the product line would be eliminated if the product line were discontinued. Management estimates that the sale of athletic socks would decline 20% from this decision because both products are sold to the same customers. Sportswear is sold to different customers, and sales of that product are not anticipated to decline as a result of the decision.

Required:

a. i. Prepare a schedule of operating data for Newman Enterprises Ltd. assuming that the athletic shoe line is discontinued.

    ii. What is the net effect on Newman's segment margin?

    iii. Would you recommend that Newman discontinue the athletic shoe product line?

b. Assume that Newman Enterprises Ltd. believes that a concentrated advertising effort of $10,000 for sportswear would increase sales of sportswear by 10% if the athletic shoe line were discontinued.

    i. What is the net effect on Newman's segment margin?

    ii. Would this affect your decision in part (a)iii?

(IMA December 1995 Question 2)

PROBLEMS

24. (LO 7) The Rochelle Gordon Paper Company produces three types of consumer products: sticky note pads, tablets, and custom stationery. The firm has become increasingly concerned about the profitability of the custom stationery line.

A segmented income statement for the most recent quarter follows:

	Sticky Notes	Tablets	Custom Stationery
Sales	$800,000	$400,000	$1,000,000
Variable costs:			
Production	(200,000)	(150,000)	(550,000)
Selling	(150,000)	(100,000)	(200,000)
Fixed costs:			
Production	(160,000)	(80,000)	(300,000)
Selling	(200,000)	(60,000)	(180,000)
Net income	$ 90,000	$ 10,000	$ (230,000)

Because of the significance of the loss on custom stationery products, the company is considering the elimination of that product line. Of the fixed production costs, $400,000 are allocated to the product lines based on relative sales value; likewise, $250,000 of fixed selling expenses are allocated to the product lines based on relative sales value. All of the other fixed costs charged to each product line are direct and would be eliminated if the product line were dropped.

Required:

Recast the income statements in a format more meaningful for deciding whether the custom stationery product line should be eliminated. Based on the new income statements, determine whether any product line should be eliminated and discuss the rationale for your conclusion.

CASES

1. Spectra Classic Clothing is a retail organization that sells upscale clothing to professional women in central Canada. Each year store managers, in consultation with their supervisors, establish financial goals. Actual performance is captured by a monthly reporting system.

District A has three stores. This district has historically been a very poor performer. Consequently, its supervisor has been searching for ways to improve the performance of her three stores. For May, the district supervisor has set performance goals with the managers of stores 1 and 2. Each of these managers will receive bonuses if certain performance measures are exceeded. The manager of store 3 has decided not to participate in the bonus scheme. The manager of store 1 will receive a bonus based on sales in excess of budgeted sales of $570,000, while the manager of store 2 will receive a bonus based on net income in excess of budgeted net income. The company's net income goal for each store is 12% of sales. The budgeted sales for store 2 are $530,000. Other pertinent data for May follow:

- At store 1, sales were 40% of total District A sales, while sales at store 2 were 35% of total District A sales. The cost of goods sold at both stores was 42% of sales.
- Variable selling expenses (sales commissions) were 6% of sales for all stores and districts.
- Variable administrative expenses were 2.5% of sales for all stores and districts.
- The maintenance cost includes janitorial and repair services and is a direct cost for each store. The store manager has complete control over this outlay; however, this cost should not be below 1% of sales.
- Advertising is considered a direct cost for each store and is completely under the control of the store manager. Store 1 spent two-thirds of District A's total outlay for advertising, which was 10 times more than store 2 spent on advertising.
- The rent expense at store 1 is 40% of District A's total, while store 2 incurs 30% of District A's total.
- District A expenses are allocated to the stores based on sales.

CASES

Required:

As a consultant hired by the corporate office to advise the district supervisor, assess the performance measurement systems of the stores. Use the case approach.

(CMA adapted)

2. Ping Zhang Products Ltd. makes three products from three different material inputs. The president realizes that a machine on the production line is due for replacement. The machine can be produced in-house or outsourced (purchased) from another firm for $1,010,000. The following is the income statement for last year:

Sales	$ 6,210,000
Cost of goods sold	(5,047,500)
Selling and administrative expense	(270,000)
Operating profit	$ 892,500

Additional information:

- Plant capacity is 162,500 machine hours.
- The material inputs (X, Y, and Z) for products A, B, and C are as follows:

Input (in units)

Product	X	Y	Z
A	7	2	5
B	4	6	3
C	5	3	2

- Variable overhead is based on machine hours used and is applied at the rate of $12 per hour. Machine hours used for product A are 3.75 hours; for product B, 5 hours; and for product C, 1.875 hours.
- Per unit costs for material inputs are as follows:

Input	Current Cost	Replacement Cost
X	$5	$6
Y	7	7
Z	3	5

- The requirements for the new machine in terms of materials are part X, 2,000 units; part Y, 2,000 units; and part Z, 1,000 units. In addition, the company will need to purchase materials totalling $150,000 to produce the machine.
- Sales for last year were as follows: product A, 10,000 units; product B, 15,000 units; and product C, 5,000 units.
- Fixed production costs of $450,000 are allocated based on units produced.
- Direct labour hours for product A are 3 hours; for product B, 4 hours; and for product C, 2.5 hours.
- Selling and administrative expenses, fixed and variable, are allocated based on units sold. Fixed selling and administrative expenses are $150,000.
- The selling price for product A is $186; for product B, $248; and for product C, $126.
- If Ping Zhang builds the machine rather than buys it, construction will use 30% of the machine hour capacity. If building the machine and producing the three existing products exceeds total capacity, production of the product with the lowest contribution margin will be reduced.
- Constructing the machine will require 10,000 direct labour hours.
- Ping Zhang expects unit sales and contribution margins to remain constant throughout the year.

Required:

Should Ping Zhang Products Ltd. outsource (purchase) the new machine or produce it in-house? As the management accountant, advise the president. Use the case approach.

CASES

3. You are a member of an independent consulting firm that specializes in the restaurant industry. Unlike many consulting firms that are extensions of audit firms, your firm has serious and in-depth expertise with the restaurant industry. The following is a typical assignment.

Family is a chain of Italian casual dinning restaurants which are located in Quebec. The restaurants are at the top end of the casual dining segment; guests are offered many of the benefits of fine dining without the formality. The menu is limited to a set number of entrées to ensure a high level of execution and service. Menu items such as steaks, ribs, roast beef, chicken, seafood, and salads are complemented by a wide assortment of alcoholic and other beverages.

The chain is only six years old, and already there are 50 outlets. The owners had planned to expand the number of outlets to 90 in Quebec and Ontario over the next two years and then expand across Canada and into the United States. However, recent performance has been disappointing.

All 50 restaurants are basically the same. Sales have exceeded expectations, but profits are much less than expected. There is some variability in sales among the 50 restaurants. There is a scheduling model that assigns employees based on sales, with more sales requiring more employees in order to maintain service quality. The planning, budgeting, and financial reporting systems are completely adequate. Employees are remunerated with basic wages plus incentives tied to sales. These incentives account for about 20% of the average employee's remuneration, and thus employees are keen to maximize sales.

In your consulting assignment, the main question facing you is this: What is going wrong with the restaurants? You suspect operational problems, thus you and your associates study a random sample of 5 of the 50 restaurants. All 5 are very similar, with the restaurant described in Exhibit 9-1 being representative.

Required:

Using the case approach, identify and solve the profit problems facing the model restaurant.

EXHIBIT 9-1

Current Operating Statement (000s)

	Budget	Actual
Sales	$1,500	$1,700
Variable cost of sales		
Direct materials	$ 250	$ 360
Direct labour	450	576
Variable overhead	200	260
	$ 900	$1,196
Contribution margin	$ 600	$ 504
Fixed costs		
Other labour	$ 75	$ 76
Rent	100	99
Utilities	75	77
Miscellaneous	25	24
Subtotal	$ 275	$ 276
Net Income	$ 325	$ 228
Number of meals	30,000	30,000
Average price per meal	$50.00	$56.67

ETHICS

1. Sunk costs are said to be irrelevant to decision making. However, sunk costs may have behavioural effects. For example, if a manager knows that she will be charged with a loss resulting from a decision to scrap obsolete inventory that she purchased, the manager may decide to do nothing even though the cost of the inventory is a sunk cost.
   Required:
   a. Is the manager, by doing nothing, behaving in an ethical manner? Why or why not?
   b. By making managers responsible for such losses, is the company behaving in an ethical manner? Why or why not?

2. Aspinall Computers Ltd. manufactures computers and all their components. The purchasing agent recently informed the company owner, Patrick Aspinall, that another company has offered to supply keyboards for Aspinall's computers at prices below the variable costs at which Aspinall can make them. Incredulous, Mr. Aspinall hired an industrial consultant to explain how the supplier could offer the keyboards at less than Aspinall's variable costs.

   The consultant explained that she suspected that the supplier was purchasing from countries that use lower-paid individuals to work in its factories. These people are poverty stricken and will take such work at substandard wages. The purchasing agent and the plant manager feel that Aspinall should buy the keyboards from the supplier, as "no one can blame us for the supplier's hiring practices, and no one will even be able to show that we knew of those practices."
   Required:
   a. What are the ethical issues involved in this case?
   b. What are the advantages and disadvantages of buying from this competitor supplier?
   c. What do you think Mr. Aspinall should do, and why?

SOLUTIONS TO SELF-TEST QUESTIONS

1. e.

2. b.

3. a.

4. b. $100 \times (\$8 - \$1 - \$2 - \$0.50 - \$2) = \$250$

5. c.   The future variable selling expense of \$2.00 per unit is relevant. The other costs are either fixed or sunk.

6. b.

7. a.

8. b. $20,000 \times \{\$60 - [\$64 - (\$16 - \$9)]\} + \$25,000 = \$85,000$ or
        $[20,000 \times (60 + 7)] - (20,000 \times 64 + 25,000) = \$85,000$

9. b.

10. c.

Overhead that can be eliminated (\$1,250,000 − \$125,000)	\$1,125,000
Less: Contribution margin	500,000
	\$ 625,000

11. a. $(\$60 - \$40) = \$20$

12. c. $(\$60 - \$40) = \$20 + (\$200 \times 50\%) = \$120$

13. c. $(5 - 1)\ 40 = \$160 - 40 = 120 + 20 = \$140$

14. a.   Savings = $\$3.78 + \$0.94 + (0.25 \times \$1.20) = \$5.02$
        Additional variable overhead = $[0.25 \times (\$24 \div 60 \times 2)] = \$0.20$
        Maximum price: Net savings are $\$5.02 - \$0.20 = \$4.82$

SOLUTIONS TO SELF-TEST QUESTIONS

15. c.   Savings = $3.78 + $0.94 + (0.25 × $1.20) = $5.02 × 30,000 units = $150,600
Cost of buying from Omega: 30,000 units × $4.85 = $145,500
Additional contribution margin: 5,000 units × $8 = $40,000
Increase in income = $150,600 − $145,500 + $40,000 = $45,100

16. c.

	Standard	**Deluxe**
CM per unit	$10	$15
CM per hour	$10 ÷ 2 = $5	$15 ÷ 4 = $3.75

   Therefore maximum production of standard = 5,000 units
Number of units of deluxe = [12,000 − (5,000 × 2)] 4 = 500 units

17. a.

18. c.   10,000 [$24 − ($10 + $8 + $2)] = $40,000

ENDNOTES

1. Mary Hayes Weler, "Supplier Likes What IT's Getting from Wal-Mart's RFID Push," *Information Week*, September 17, 2007, p. 40.

2. Marc Songini, "Procter & Gamble: Wal-Mart RFID Effort Effective," *Computerworld*, February 26, 2007, p. 14.

3. Ryan J. Foley/Associated Press, "Bar codes could go the way of the dodo with RFID; Tiny chip transmits data by antenna," *Globe and Mail*, September 1, 2005, B11.

4. "RFID Technology in the Automotive Industry," SAP 50 075 241, May 2007. ©SAP.

5. Carol Sliwa, "Gillette Saves Costs With RFID," *Computerworld*, January 5, 2005; *Techworld*, www.techworld.com.

6. David Ticoll, "Prepare For a Bar Code Revolution," *Globe and Mail*, July 17, 2003.

7. Ibid.

8. "Keeping Up with Supplies," *Health Data Management*, January 1, 2008. ©2008 Health Data Management and Source Media, Inc.

9. Jim Kirk and John Schmeltzer, "Old Brands Feel Squeeze Over Time," *Chicago Tribune*, October 3, 2004.

10. "Offshore Finance Will Boom by 2008, Poll Says," *Report on Business Globe and Mail*, Staff. September 15, 2005, pg. B8. Reprinted with permission from The Globe and Mail; Denise Dubie, "Outsourcing Moves Closer to Home," December 3, 2007, http://www.networkworld.com.

11. Diane Francis, "Research and Development 'Myth in Canada,'" *Financial Post*, January 8, 2005, FP6.

12. Short-run decisions typically focus on a measure of accounting income that excludes some past costs, such as depreciation on old assets. Long-range decision analysis commonly uses cash flow as its decision criterion; this topic is covered in Web Chapter 14.

13. This topic will be discussed in more advanced courses in management accounting.

14. P.M. Trenchard and R. Dixon, "The Clinical Allocation of Joint Blood Product Costs," *Management Accounting Research*, June 2003, pp. 165–76.

15. Bertrand Marotte, "Transcontinental Invests in New Presses," *Globe and Mail*, November 17, 2004.

16. Emily Kaiser, "New Upscale Merchandise Pays Off," *Toronto Star*, May 17, 2006.

17. Scott Friend and Patricia Walker, "Welcome to the New World of Merchandising," *Harvard Business Review*, Reprint R0110K.

18. Erik Heinrich, "Zellers Tocks Up On the Right Gear," *Toronto Star*, October 21, 2004.

19. "Zap! And Lost Bag is Found," *Toronto Star*, January 10, 2005.

20. Ryan J. Foley/Associated Press, "Bar Codes Could Go the Way of the Dodo with RFID; Tiny Chip Transmits Data by Antenna," *Globe and Mail*, September 1, 2005, B11.

ENDNOTES

21. John A. Brierley, Christopher J. Cowton, and Colin Drury, "The Application of Costs in Make-or-Buy Decisions: An Analysis," *International Journal of Management,* Vol. 23, no. 4 (2006).

22. Alex Taylor III, "The Auto Industry Meets the New Economy," *Fortune,* September 5, 1994, p. 56.

23. Shawn Tully, "You'll Never Guess Who Really Makes . . . ," *Fortune,* October 3, 1994, p. 124.

24. Bret Okeson, "Where Out Is In: European Automakers are Handling Production of Niche-Market Models to Companies Like Magna-Steyr," *National Post,* February 5, 2004.

25. "Outsourcing Information Systems," *Management Accounting Guideline 23,* Society of Management Accountants, Canada, 1994.

26. Clayton M. Christensen, *Business Week,* August 28, 2000, pp. 180–81.

27. Nathan VanderKlippe, "Little Guy Gets Leg Up from China," *Financial Post,* January 7, 2008.

28. Virginia Galt, "Take Our Business, Take Our People," *Globe and Mail,* May 19, 2003.

29. "Variable-Cost Document Outsourcing: Uncovering Alternative BPO Opportunities," Outsourcing.com

30. For additional information on the theory of constraints and linear programming, see Web Chapter 10.

31. Linear programming is discussed in a later chapter.

32. Institute of Management Accountants (formerly National Association of Accountants), *Statement on Management Accounting Number 2: Management Accounting Terminology* (Montvale, N.J.: National Association of Accountants, June 1, 1983), p. 94.

33. M2 Communications Ltd., "Dell Introduces New Micro-Portable Projector; Light, Bright, Affordable Projector Complements Dell's Notebook Computers," June 27, 2002.

34. Scott Deveau, "Guestlogix Helps Airlines Lift Top Line," *Financial Post,* January 7, 2008. Scott Deveau, "Guestlogix Near Deal to Service WestJet: In-Flight Purchases," *Financial Post,* July 18, 2008, FP3.

35. The law of demand elasticity indicates how closely price and demand are related. Product demand is highly elastic if a small price reduction generates a large demand increase. If demand is less elastic, large price reductions are needed to bring about moderate sales volume increases.

36. James Temple, "Holiday Sales Results are Nothing to Celebrate," *Contra Costa Times,* January 7, 2005.

37. Malester, "Office Depot N.A. Sales Rise 3%," *Twice,* October 25, 2004.

38. Such a decline in demand generally does not occur when the product in question has no close substitute or is not a major expenditure in consumers' budgets.

39. Patrick Barwise, Paul R. Marsh, and Robin Wensley, "Must Finance and Strategy Clash?" *Harvard Business Review,* September–October 1989, p. 86.

40. In regard to this last item, consider what occurs when one airline raises or lowers its fares between cities. It typically does not take very long for all the other airlines flying that route to adjust their fares accordingly Thus, competitive advantage often exists only for a short time. Another example of this is seen in the following news item. "On March 10, 2002, Delta announced that it would no longer pay commissions to travel agents for booking flights. As a result, Air Canada stated that it will eliminate base commissions to travel agents for all tickets sold in Canada." (Keith McArthur, *Globe and Mail,* March 23, 2002, B3.)

41. Abigail Goldman, *Los Angeles Times,* February 28, 2002, C1.

42. Hoover's Company In-depth records, Mattel, Inc., October 27, 2004.

43. This same type of incremental analysis is shown in Chapter 3 in relation to CVP computation.

ENDNOTES

44. Scott McNealy, "The Future Will Be Free," keynote address to Oracle Open World, San Francisco, December 14, 2004, http://it.asia1.com.sg/newsdaily.

45. Richard Martin, "Business Strategy: The Razor's Edge," *Industry Standard,* August 6, 2001.

46. It is assumed here that all common costs are fixed costs; this is not always the case. Some common costs are variable, such as costs of processing purchase orders and computer time-sharing expenses for payroll or other corporate functions.

47. Dow Jones & Reuters, "Gillette Powers Up the World's Best Shave with New M3 Power," *Business Wire*, January 15, 2004.

48. James M. Kilts, "The Gillette Company Celebrates Its Centennial in 2001," *Business Wire,* September 4, 2001.

49. Jenn Abelson, "Looking to Clean Up in Japan," *Boston Globe*, June 24, 2007.

Chapter 10

Controlling Costs

LEARNING OBJECTIVES

After reading this chapter, you should be able to answer the following questions:

1 **Why**
is cost consciousness of great importance to all members of the organization?

2 **How**
does a company determine from whom, how much, and when to order inventory?

3 **What**
is outsourcing and when should it be used?

4 **What**
is JIT, and how does it affect costs?

5 **What**
is life cycle costing?

6 **What**
are target costing and value engineering, and in which life cycle stage are these tools used?

7 **What**
is process-based management?

ON SITE

www.aircanada.ca and www.westjet.ca

Controlling Costs in the Skies

In the 1980s the cost structure of the Canadian airline industry allowed a full-service airline such as **AIR CANADA** to survive and prosper. In the 1990s cost pressures made it possible for Air Canada to acquire its major competitors, Ward Air and Canadian Airlines. However, this was only a short-term solution as the cost structure of the international airline industry was changing, with new low-cost entrants such as Southwest Airlines in the United States. Air Canada's business model had to change if it was to survive.

WESTJET started flying in 1996 with a low-cost business model designed after that of Southwest Airlines.

Back in 2001, Air Canada was a high-cost airline. Tae Oum, director of the Centre for Transportation Studies at the University of British Columbia, prepared a report for the federal government that examined Air Canada's cost competitiveness and productivity. The report concluded that Air Canada was 25% less productive than the top nine U.S. carriers, despite having an advantage in labour costs because of the lower Canadian dollar.

At the time the connection between productivity and earning power was evident when comparing Air Canada with WestJet. Air Canada operated with roughly 136 employees per aircraft, as opposed to WestJet's 64 employees per aircraft. WestJet had a highly efficient workforce, motivated through profit sharing to reduce costs and increase profitability. Job descriptions were less rigid at WestJet, where, after landing, both pilots and cabin crew cleaned the cabin. This cooperation contributed to a faster turnaround at the gate, and more flying time meant more revenue. The result was that Air Canada and just about every other airline lost money in September 2001, whereas WestJet was profitable. In October 2001, WestJet's market valuation was close to $1 billion, much more than the market value of Air Canada.

On April 1, 2003, Air Canada formally filed for protection from its creditors in order to reduce its cost structure, to be a "lean, more efficient, low-cost airline." The need to cut costs was not a surprise. The Office of Financial Institutions, which oversees pensions at federally regulated companies, ordered Air Canada to pay $135 million into its underfunded pension plans immediately; Air Canada management was livid. It is difficult to understand Air Canada's position, however, as there was a legal and moral obligation to meet pension requirements, and pursuing the wrong strategy and business model was the fault of Air Canada management.

After 18 months, Air Canada emerged from bankruptcy, but it was no simple restructuring. Usually, a company such as Air Canada uses the *Companies' Creditors Arrangement Act* to clean up its balance sheet by settling debts at cents per dollar. Former shareholders were virtually wiped out. Air Canada provided creditors with cents on the dollar, while giving them about 87% of the common shares. In addition, under pressure from the two judges assigned by the court, Air Canada and its unions cut its $3 billion annual unionized labour bill by $1.1 billion.

In recent years, Air Canada and WestJet have shared 95% of the Canadian domestic market in relative harmony. However, since October 2006, Porter Airlines has been challenging Air Canada and WestJet from its base at the Toronto City Centre Airport. With its convenient location, just a short ferry ride from downtown Toronto, Porter is serving a growing list of popular destinations. Porter is the most promising new airline this country has seen in years. Judging from their tactics, it seems that Porter's two big rivals are determined to take a familiar approach to eliminating competition: predatory pricing. Specifically, Air Canada and WestJet have targeted the new competitor with below-cost fares that are impossible for their rival to sustain. This tactic is a large part of the reason why Canada has a long history of inadequate airline competition. For customers, fare wars may seem wonderful at the time. In the long term, though, every time Air Canada (and now WestJet) eliminates a new rival, ticket prices rise and service diminishes.

SOURCES: Frances Fiorino, "Bleak Vistas for Air Canada," *Aviation Week & Space Technology*, November 12, 2001, p. 15; Peter Verburg, "Prepare for Takeoff," *Canadian Business*, December 25, 2000, pp. 94–99; Peter Verburg, "Turbulent Times," *Canadian Business*, October 29, 2001, pp. 72–77; Guy Dixon, "Air Canada Talks Fail in Anger," *Globe and Mail*, April 2, 2003, B1; Keith McArthur, "Don't Blow It," *Report on Business*, February 2004, pp. 55–58; Keith McArthur and Brent Jang, "How Air Canada Got Back on a New Flight Path," *Globe and Mail*, August 28, 2004, B4–B5; Jason Kirby, "Upstart Porter Takes On Air Canada, WestJet," *Maclean's*, June 4, 2007.

*A*ny business wanting to succeed must not only generate reasonable levels of revenues but also control the costs that generate those revenues. For airlines, there is often limited control over fares—a competitor's price on a given route must usually be matched or the organization can lose market share. It is imperative for the organization's survival to determine ways to get a handle on costs. Organizational management quickly recognizes the interaction among cost control, efficiency, and profitability.

Previous chapters presented various ways to control costs. For example, control of direct materials and direct labour costs is typically linked to the development and implementation of job and processing costing systems. Outsourcing is another way to reduce costs. ABC identifies nonvalue-adding costs that can be eliminated. Future chapters discuss other cost-reducing techniques. Budgeting was discussed in Chapter 6. Variance analysis or the comparison of actual costs to expectations (see Chapter 7) is another technique for controlling costs.

This chapter focuses on seven topics related to cost control. First, the importance of cost control consciousness is discussed. The desire among members of an organization to reduce costs on an ongoing basis is necessary for the effective use of all cost control techniques. Second, this chapter discusses economic order quantity (EOQ), a technique for reducing the cost of carrying inventory. Third and fourth, the effects of outsourcing and just-in-time are discussed as further approaches for reducing inventory and other costs. Fifth, the life cycle of products and services is discussed as to the different opportunities for reducing costs. Sixth, target costing and value engineering are discussed as methods for controlling costs. Seventh, process-based management (PBM) is discussed as a means of controlling groups of activities.

COST CONTROL

Cost control is an integral part of the overall organizational decision support system. A **cost control system** should provide information to managers for planning and for determining the efficiency of activities. As indicated in Exhibit 10-1, effective control can be exercised at three points: before, during, and after an event.

Managers alone cannot control costs. They must motivate and direct subordinates to want to control costs. An organization comprises a group of individuals whose attitudes and efforts should be considered in determining how an organization's costs may be controlled. Cost control is a continuous process that requires the support of all employees at all times. Good control encompasses not only the functions shown in Exhibit 10-1, but also the ideas about cost consciousness shown in

LEARNING OBJECTIVE   1

Why is cost consciousness of great importance to all members of the organization?

cost control system
a logical structure of formal and informal activities designed to influence costs and to enable management to analyze and evaluate how well expenditures were managed during a period

Control Point	Reason	Cost Control Methods
Before an event	Preventive; reflects planning	Budgets: standards; policies concerning approval for deviations; expressions of quantitative and qualitative objectives
During an event	Corrective; ensures that the event is being pursued according to plans; allows managers to correct problems as they occur	Periodic monitoring of ongoing activities; comparison of activities and costs against budgets and standards; avoidance of excessive expenditures
After an event	Diagnostic; guides future actions	Feedback; variance analysis; responsibility reports

EXHIBIT 10-1

Functions of an Effective Cost Control System

Exhibit 10-2. **Cost consciousness** refers to an organization-wide employee attitude toward the topics of cost understanding, cost containment, cost avoidance, and cost reduction. Each of these topics is important at a different stage of the control system.

cost consciousness
an organizationwide employee attitude toward cost understanding, cost containment, cost avoidance, and cost reduction

Cost Understanding

Control requires that a set of expectations exists. Cost control is first exercised when an expectation for that cost is prepared, which can be done only when the reasons for periodic cost changes are understood. Expectations can be compared with

EXHIBIT 10-2

Cost Control System

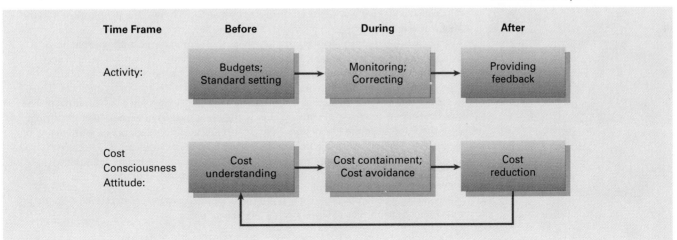

actual costs. Knowing that variations occurred is important, but cost control can be achieved only if managers understand why costs differed from expected amounts.

Cost Differences Related to Cost Behaviour

cost behaviour
the manner in which a cost responds to a change in a related level of activity

work-out
a management activity designed to take unnecessary work out of the system

Costs may change from previous periods or differ from expectations for many reasons. Some costs change because of their underlying **cost behaviour**. A total variable or mixed cost increases or decreases with increases or decreases in activity level. If the current period's activity level differs from a prior period's activity level or from the expected activity level, total actual variable or mixed cost will differ from that of the prior period or the total expected cost. For example, Air Canada's food costs (on meal-hour flights) will vary almost in direct proportion with the

GENERAL NEWS NOTE

Cost Management at General Electric

GENERAL ELECTRIC (GE) developed a technique called "work-out" for reducing costs. A **work-out** means just what the words imply: "taking unnecessary work out of the system." These work-outs consist of groups of 40 to 100 employees meeting for two to three days to share their views on the business and bureaucracy that increases costs without creating value for customers.

A work-out starts with a presentation by the manager, for the division or unit wanting cost savings, who might issue a challenge or outline a broad agenda for changing processes to reduce costs, and then leave. Without the boss present and with a neutral facilitator, employees are asked to list problems, debate solutions, and be prepared to sell their ideas when the boss returns.

GE insists that its managers make on-the-spot decisions on each proposal. Each manager with a work-out is expected to give a yes-or-no decision on at least 75% of the cost-saving suggestions. If the manager is unable to make it on-the-spot, there is an agreed-upon date for a decision. Decisions cannot be avoided. As employees see their proposals implemented, the work-outs become a "true bureaucracy buster."

Jack Welch, retired chairman and CEO of GE, provides an example of a work-out:

A union production worker was in the middle of a presentation on how to improve the manufacturing of refrigerator doors. He was describing a part of the process that occurred on the second floor of the assembly line.

Suddenly, the chief steward of the plant [union] jumped up to interrupt him.

"That's [not true]," he said. "You don't know what [you are] talking about. You've never been up there."

He grabbed a magic marker and began scribbling on the easel in the front of the room. Before you knew it, he had taken over the presentation and had the answer. His solution was accepted immediately.

Welch adds that work-outs confirm what we already knew: "the people closest to the work know it best."

The work-outs are successful except where there are internal and external barriers that prevent necessary changes. For example, improvement to the processing of accounts receivable could not be done solely by the accounting department. Other functional departments such as the sales organization plus the customers had to be involved. Thus, to be truly effective in managing and reducing costs all barriers have to be removed. The internal barriers have to be removed among the functions: engineering, manufacturing, sales, etc. Moreover, the distinctions between domestic and foreign operations have to be eliminated. Barriers are also eliminated between GE and its suppliers and between GE and its customers. By eliminating these barriers, GE became a boundaryless company where all functions as well as suppliers and customers became part of one single process.

SOURCE: From *Jack: Straight from the Gut* by Jack Welch. Copyright © 2001 by John F. Welch, Jr. Foundation. By permission of Grand Central Publishing.

number of passengers. Total expected costs for Air Canada will be total meals multiplied by expected cost per meal.

In addition to the reactions of variable costs to changes in activity levels, the following three factors can cause costs to differ from those of prior periods or from expected costs for the current period. In considering these factors, remember that an external price becomes an internal cost when a good or service is acquired.

Cost Differences Related to Quantity Purchased

A simple reason for an actual per-unit cost differing from expected is that the quantity purchased was different from what was expected. Firms are normally given quantity discounts, up to some maximum level, when bulk purchases are made. Therefore, a cost per unit may change when quantities are purchased in lot sizes different from those of previous periods or those projected. Involvement in group purchasing arrangements can make quantity discounts easier to obtain.

Cost Differences Related to Inflation/Deflation

Fluctuations in the value of money are called general price level changes. When the general price level changes, the prices of goods and services also change. General price level changes affect almost all prices approximately equally and in the same direction, if all other factors are constant. An estimated cost of $150,000 might become an actual cost of $154,500 with an annual inflation rate of 3%.

Some companies include price-escalation clauses in sales contracts to cover the inflation occurring from order to delivery. Such escalators are especially prevalent in industries having production activities that require substantial time. For instance, according to Statistics Canada the consumer price index, often used as a base for negotiating wage and salary contracts, increased 1.9% in the 12 months preceding October 2007.[1]

Cost Differences Related to Supply/Supplier Cost Adjustments

The relationship of the availability of a good or service to the demand for that item affects its selling price. If supply of an item is low but demand is high, the selling price of the item increases. The higher price often stimulates greater production, which, in turn, increases supply. In contrast, if demand falls but supply remains constant, the price falls. This lowered price should motivate lower production, which lowers supply. Therefore, price is consistently and circularly influenced by the relationship of supply to demand. Price changes for independent items are specific price level changes, and these may move in the same or the opposite direction as a general price level change.

Specific price level changes may also be caused by advances in technology. As a general rule, as suppliers advance the technology of producing a good or performing a service, its cost to producing firms declines. Assuming competitive market conditions, such cost declines are often passed along to consumers of that product or service in the form of lower selling prices. To demonstrate the basic interaction of increasing technology and decreasing selling prices and costs, consider the greeting cards that play songs when they are opened. Those cards contain more computer processing power than existed in the entire world before 1950.[2]

Of course, when companies incur additional production or performance costs, they typically pass such increases on to their customers as part of specific price level changes. Such costs may be within or outside the company's control. A cost factor that is within an organization's control is the necessity to upgrade computer systems to remain competitive. Sometimes, cost increases are caused by external factors. Though climbing oil prices affect most industries, few are hit as hard as the airline industry. A $1 per barrel change in jet fuel prices has an impact of about $25 million on Air Canada's earnings before interest, taxes, depreciation, amortization, and rent. For WestJet, the impact on earnings is about $5 million.[3]

The quantity of suppliers of a product or service can also affect selling prices. As the number of suppliers increases in a competitive environment, prices tend to fall. Likewise, a reduction in the number of suppliers will, all else remaining equal, cause prices to increase. A change in the number of suppliers is not the same as a change in the quantity of supply. If the supply of an item is large, one normally expects a low price; however, if there is only one supplier (or one primary supplier), the price can remain high because of supplier control. For example, with the demise in 2001 of Canada 3000, many air travellers were fearful that Air Canada would be more likely to increase air fares on transborder destinations where Canada 3000 was no longer flying.

In some cases, all other factors are not equal, and the quantity of suppliers may not affect the selling price of a good or service. Firms may unethically conspire to engage in **price fixing** or setting an item's price at a specified level. Buyers must purchase the good or service at the specified price because no suppliers are offering the item at a lower price. Price fixing may be vertical or horizontal.

Vertical price fixing (also known as resale price maintenance) involves agreements by businesses and their distributors to control the prices at which products may be sold to consumers. All vertical price fixing is illegal. Companies may set suggested retail selling prices for items, but any attempts to prohibit retailers from selling below those prices are considered anticompetitive activities.

In **horizontal price fixing,** competitors attempt to regulate prices by agreeing on either a selling price or the quantity of goods that may be produced or offered for sale. Airlines, oil and credit card companies, and banks have all been accused of horizontal price fixing.

Although the preceding reasons indicate why costs change, they do not indicate what managers can do to contain the costs. Minimizing the upward trends means controlling costs. The next section discusses some concepts of cost containment.

Cost Containment

To the extent possible, managers should attempt to practise **cost containment** through minimizing period-by-period increases in per-unit variable and total fixed costs. Cost containment is generally not possible for increases resulting from inflation, tax and regulatory changes, and supply and demand adjustments because these forces occur outside the organizational structure.

However, costs that rise because of reduced competition, seasonality, and quantities purchased are subject to cost containment activities. A company should look for ways to cap upward changes in these costs. For example, purchasing agents should be aware of alternative suppliers for needed goods and services and determine which of those suppliers can provide needed items in the quantity, quality, and time desired. Comparing costs and finding new sources of supply can increase buying power and contain or reduce costs.

If bids are used to select suppliers, the purchasing agent should remember that a bid is merely the first step in negotiating. Although a low bid may eliminate some competition from consideration, additional negotiations between the purchasing agent and the remaining suppliers may result in a purchase cost lower than the bid amount, or concessions such as faster and more reliable delivery may be obtained. Purchasing agents must remember that the supplier offering the lowest bid amount

price fixing
a practice by which firms conspire to set a product's price at a specified level

vertical price fixing
collusion between producing businesses and their distributors to control the prices at which their products may be sold to consumers

horizontal price fixing
the practice by which competitors attempt to regulate prices through an agreement or conspiracy

cost containment
the process of attempting, to the extent possible, to minimize period-by-period increases in per-unit variable and total fixed costs

Higher Wages Mean Higher Profits: The Costco Way

In developing business models it is frequently considered necessary to reduce employee wages and salaries to be competitive. Often this means outsourcing to countries with lower labour costs. However, there is a factor that should not be overlooked: productivity of labour should not be considered constant as labour wages and salaries are reduced. In other words, higher-cost labour could be more productive, thereby decreasing labour costs per unit of output compared to low-cost labour.

Evidence that paying employees more money and attracting more productive employees will reduce costs comes from a comparison of COSTCO with WAL-MART's Sam's Clubs, the warehouse unit that competes directly with Costco. The evidence below shows that by paying employees generously to motivate and retain good workers, one-fifth of whom are unionized, Costco gets lower turnover and higher productivity. By selling a mix of higher-margin products to more affluent customers, Costco actually keeps its labour costs lower than Wal-Mart's as a percentage of sales, and its 68,000 hourly employees in the United States sell more per square foot. In other words, the 102,000 Sam's employees in the United States generated some $35 billion in sales in 2003, while Costco did $34 billion with one-third fewer employees. Moreover, Costco in the United States achieved $13,647 in operating profit per hourly employee in 2003, versus $11,039 at Sam's. During the past five years, Costco's operating income grew at an average of 10.1% per year, a slightly faster rate than Sam's 9.8%.

In conclusion, in developing a business model the concern should be with maximizing the cost effectiveness of labour rather than merely with minimizing wages and salaries.

	Costco	Wal-Mart's Sam's Club
Average hourly wage	$15.97	$11.52
Annual health costs per worker	$5,735	$3,500
Covered by health plan	82%	47%
Annual retirement costs per worker	$1,330	$747
Covered by retirement plans	91%	64%
Employee turnover	6% a year	21% a year
Labour and overhead costs	9.8% of sales	17% of sales
Sales per square foot	$795	$516
Profits per employee	$13,647	$11,039
Five year annual operating-income growth	10.1%	9.8%

SOURCE: Stanley Holmes and Wendy Zeller, "The Costco Way," *Business Week*, April 12, 2004, pp. 76–77; www.reclaimdemocracy.org/articles_2004/costco_employee_benefits_walmart.html, http://www.usatoday.com/money/industries/retail/2004-09-23-costco_x.htm.

Airlines are acutely aware of the need to control costs including meal costs. Air Canada tends to limit meals to longer flights. WestJet provides free snacks and beverages and a "buy-on-board" service for long haul flights. WestJet also encourages guests to "brown bag" it.

is not necessarily the best supplier to choose. Additionally, reduced costs can often be obtained when long-term or single-source contracts are signed with suppliers.

Companies should be aware of the suppliers available for needed goods and services. New suppliers should be investigated to determine whether they can provide needed items in the quantity, quality, and time desired. Comparing costs and finding new sources of supply can increase buying power and reduce costs. Buying in bulk is not a new or unique idea, but it is often not applied on an extended basis for related companies or enterprises. In a corporation, one division can take the responsibility for obtaining a supplier contract for items (such as computer disks) that are necessary to all divisions. The savings resulting from buying a combined quantity appropriate for all divisions could offset the additional costs of shipping the disks to the divisions.

An organization may circumvent seasonal cost changes by postponing or advancing purchases of goods and services. However, such purchasing changes should not mean buying irresponsibly or incurring excessive carrying costs. As discussed later in this chapter, the concepts of economic order quantities, safety stock levels, materials requirements planning, and the just-in-time philosophy should be considered in making purchases.

Cost Avoidance and Reduction

Cost containment can prove very effective if it can be implemented. In some instances, cost containment may not be possible but cost avoidance may be. **Cost avoidance** means finding acceptable alternatives to high-cost items and not spending money for unnecessary goods or services. Avoiding one cost may require that an alternative, lower cost be incurred. For example, WestJet does not provide meals to travellers, in order to offer bargain-basement fares. This lack of meals is not a burden to travellers as the flights are all relatively short.

Closely related to cost avoidance, **cost reduction** means lowering current costs. Management at many companies believes that cost reduction automatically means labour reduction. For example, Air Canada sees its bankruptcy as a means of reducing labour costs. If Air Canada is to provide jobs, employees must take lower wages and salaries. The following quote provides a more appropriate viewpoint:

> Cutting staff to cut costs is putting the cart before the horse. The only way to bring costs down is to restructure the work. This will then result in reducing the number of people needed to do the job, and far more drastically than even the most radical staff cutbacks could possibly accomplish. Indeed, a cost crunch should always be used as an opportunity to re-think and to re-design operations.[4]

Sometimes cutting costs by cutting people merely creates other problems. The people who are cut may have been performing a value-added activity, and by eliminating them, a company may reduce its ability to perform necessary and important tasks. To reduce costs, unnecessary or nonvalue-adding activities should be eliminated and the efficiency of value-adding activities should be improved through automation or improved procedures.

Organizations are beginning to view their personnel needs from a strategic staffing perspective. This outlook requires departments to analyze their personnel needs by considering long-term objectives and determining a specific combination of permanent and temporary or highly skilled and less-skilled employees that offers the best opportunity to meet those needs. Contract employees are used if there are time limits to the demand for a skill. If an organization's workload fluctuates substantially, temporary employees (temps) can be hired for peak periods. Temps are also being hired to work on special projects, provide expertise in a specific area, or fill in until

cost avoidance
a process of finding acceptable alternatives to high-cost items and not spending money for unnecessary goods or services

cost reduction
a process of lowering current costs, especially those in excess of necessary costs

the right full-time employee can be found for a particular position. Temps may cost more per hour than full-time workers, but total cost may be reduced because organizations do not have to pay for benefits. Using temporary employees provides a flexible staffing "cushion" that helps insulate the jobs of permanent, core employees. Nevertheless companies should be sensitive to the needs of employees when making decisions to replace permanent employees with temporary employees. Temporary positions do not meet the needs of those who prefer permanent positions.

A starting point for determining appropriate cost-reduction practices is to focus on the activities that are creating costs. As discussed in Chapter 8 on activity-based management, reducing or eliminating nonvalue-added activities will cause the associated costs to be reduced or eliminated. Carrier Corporation, the world's largest producer of air conditioning and heating products, has instituted an effective activity-based costing and management system that is used, in part, to highlight areas that increase product costs and need to be cut. Carrier uses that system to "quantify the benefits of redesigning plant layouts, using common parts, outsourcing, strengthening supplier and customer relationships, and developing alternative product designs."[5]

Organizations may also reduce costs by outsourcing specific activities or services rather than maintaining internal departments. Information technology, internal audit, legal, travel, and accounting are all prime candidates for outsourcing. As indicated in Chapter 1, however, companies must make certain that they are not outsourcing core competencies or competitive advantage activities. Both cost savings and higher quality can be advantages of outsourcing.

Implementing Cost Control

Managers may adopt the five-step method of implementing cost control shown in Exhibit 10-3. First, the types of costs incurred by an organization must be understood. Are the costs under consideration fixed or variable, product or period? What

EXHIBIT 10-3
Implementing Cost Control

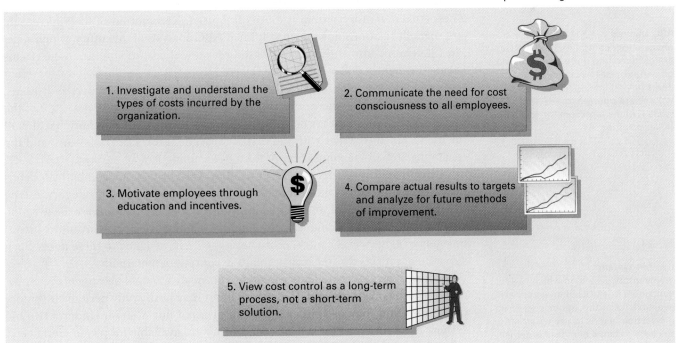

1. Investigate and understand the types of costs incurred by the organization.

2. Communicate the need for cost consciousness to all employees.

3. Motivate employees through education and incentives.

4. Compare actual results to targets and analyze for future methods of improvement.

5. View cost control as a long-term process, not a short-term solution.

cost drivers affect those costs? Has management committed to incurring the costs for the long term or the short term? Second, the need for cost consciousness must be communicated to all employees for the control process to be effective. Employees must be aware of which costs need to be better controlled and why cost control is important to both the company and the employees themselves. Third, employees must be educated in cost control techniques, encouraged to provide ideas on how to control costs, and motivated by some type of incentive to embrace the concepts. The incentives may range from simple verbal recognition to monetary rewards to time off with pay. Managers must also be flexible enough to allow for changes from the current method of operation. Fourth, reports must be generated indicating actual results, estimate-to-actual comparisons, and variances. These reports must be evaluated by management as to why costs were or were not controlled in the past. Such analysis may provide insightful information about cost drivers so that the activities causing costs may be better controlled in the future. And fifth, the cost control system should be viewed as a long-run process, not a short-run solution.

Following these five steps will provide an atmosphere conducive to controlling costs to the fullest extent possible as well as deriving the greatest benefit from the costs that are incurred. Expected future costs should be compared to expected benefits before cost incurrence takes place. Alternatively, future costs may be controlled based on information learned about past costs. Cost control should not cease at the end of a fiscal period or because costs were reduced or controlled during the current period.

LEARNING OBJECTIVE 2

How does a company determine from whom, how much, and when to order inventory?

ABC analysis
an inventory control method that separates items into three groups based on annual cost-to-volume usage; items having the highest dollar volume are referred to as A items, while C items represent the lowest dollar volume

two-bin system
an inventory system in which two containers or stacks of inventory are available for production needs; when production begins to use materials in the second bin, a purchase order is placed to refill the first bin

MANAGING INVENTORY

To control costs, management needs to control its inventory outlays in a way that maximizes attention paid to the most important inventory items and minimizes attention paid to the least important items. Unit cost is commonly a factor in the degree of control that is maintained over an inventory item. As the unit cost increases, internal controls, such as access to inventory, are typically tightened, and a perpetual inventory system is more often used. Recognition of the appropriate cost–benefit relationships may result in an **ABC analysis** of inventory, which separates inventory into three groups based on annual cost-to-volume usage. Items having the highest dollar volume are referred to as A items, while C items represent the lowest dollar volume. All other inventory items are designated as B items. Exhibit 10-4 provides the results of a typical ABC inventory analysis: 20% of the inventory items account for 80% of the total inventory cost;[6] an additional 30% of the items, taken together with the first 20%, account for 90% of the cost; and the remaining 50% of the items account for the remaining 10% of the cost.

Once inventory items are categorized as A, B, or C, management can determine the best inventory control method for the items within each category. A-type inventory should require a perpetual inventory system. Such items are likely candidates for purchasing techniques that minimize the funds tied up in inventory investment. The highest-level control procedures should be assigned to these items. Such a treatment reflects the financial accounting concept of materiality.

Controls on C-type inventory items are normally minimal because of the immateriality of the inventory cost. C-category items may justify only periodic inventory procedures and may use either a two-bin or a red-line system. Under a **two-bin system**, two containers (or stacks) of inventory are available for production needs. When it is necessary to begin using materials from the second bin, a purchase order

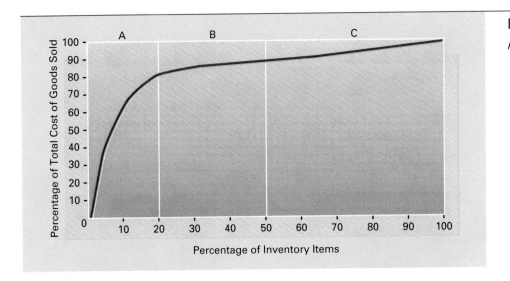

EXHIBIT 10-4
ABC Inventory Analysis

is placed to refill the first bin. Having the additional container or stack of inventory on hand is considered reasonable because the dollar amount of investment for C-category items is insignificant. In a **red-line system**, a red line is painted on the inventory container at a designated reorder point. Both the two-bin and red-line systems require that estimates of production needs and receipt times from suppliers be fairly accurate.

For B-type items, the inventory system (perpetual or periodic) and the level of internal control depend on management judgment. Such judgment will be based on how crucial the item is to the production process, how quickly suppliers respond to orders, and whether the estimated benefits of increased controls are greater than the costs. Advances in technology, such as computers and bar coding, have made it easier and more cost beneficial to institute additional controls over inventory.

Costs Associated with Inventory

Most organizations engaging in a **conversion** process use both intangible and tangible inputs. For example, direct labour and other types of services are nonphysical and are supplied and consumed simultaneously. In contrast, raw materials are tangible and may be stockpiled for later use. Similarly, outputs of a manufacturing process may be stored until sold. The potential for physical items to be placed in or withdrawn from storage creates opportunities for managers to improve organizational effectiveness and efficiency relative to the quantities in which such items are purchased, produced, and stored.

Good inventory management relies largely on cost-minimizing strategies. As indicated in Exhibit 10-5, there are three basic costs associated with inventory: (1) purchasing or production, (2) ordering or setup, and (3) carrying or not carrying goods in stock.

The **purchasing cost** of inventory is the quoted purchase price, minus any discounts allowed, plus shipping cost and insurance charges while the items are in transit. In a manufacturing company, **production cost** includes costs associated with buying direct materials, paying for direct labour, incurring traceable overhead, and absorbing allocated fixed overhead. Purchasing or production cost is recorded in Merchandise Inventory, Raw Materials Inventory, Work in Process Inventory, or Finished Goods Inventory.

red-line system
an inventory system in which a single container (or stack) of inventory is available for production needs, and a red line is painted on the inventory container (or the wall, for a stack) at a point deemed to be the reorder point

conversion
the transformation of organizational inputs into outputs

purchasing cost
the quoted purchase price minus any discounts allowed plus shipping charges

production cost
in a manufacturing company, includes costs associated with buying direct materials, paying for direct labour, incurring traceable overhead, and absorbing allocated fixed overhead

EXHIBIT 10-5

Categories of Inventory Costs

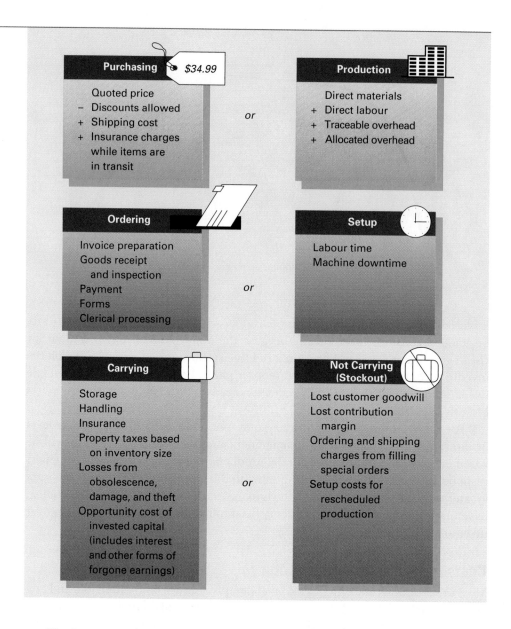

Purchasing $34.99

    Quoted price
− Discounts allowed
+ Shipping cost
+ Insurance charges
    while items are
    in transit

or

Production

    Direct materials
+ Direct labour
+ Traceable overhead
+ Allocated overhead

Ordering

Invoice preparation
Goods receipt
   and inspection
Payment
Forms
Clerical processing

or

Setup

Labour time
Machine downtime

Carrying

Storage
Handling
Insurance
Property taxes based
   on inventory size
Losses from
   obsolescence,
   damage, and theft
Opportunity cost of
   invested capital
   (includes interest
   and other forms of
   forgone earnings)

or

Not Carrying (Stockout)

Lost customer goodwill
Lost contribution
   margin
Ordering and shipping
   charges from filling
   special orders
Setup costs for
   rescheduled
   production

ordering costs
the variable costs associated with preparing, receiving, and paying for an order

setup costs
the direct and indirect labour costs of getting equipment ready for a new production run

carrying costs
the (variable) costs of carrying one unit of inventory in stock for one year; consist of storage, handling, insurance charges, property taxes based on inventory size, possible losses from obsolescence or the like, and opportunity cost

The incremental, variable costs associated with preparing, receiving, and paying for an order are **ordering costs**. These costs include the cost of forms and a variety of clerical costs. Ordering costs are traditionally expensed as incurred. Under an activity-based costing system, however, these costs can be traced to the items ordered as an additional direct cost. Retailers incur ordering costs for all of their merchandise inventory. Manufacturers incur ordering costs for raw material purchases. If a manufacturer produces rather than orders a part, direct and indirect **setup costs** (rather than ordering costs) are incurred as equipment is readied for each new production run.

Inventory **carrying costs** consist of storage, handling, insurance charges, and property taxes based on inventory size. Because inventory is one of many organizational investments, it should be expected to earn a rate of return similar to other investments.[7] Carrying cost should include an opportunity cost for the amount invested in inventory. One additional opportunity cost that is often ignored is any possible loss that might result from inventory obsolescence or damage. Carrying costs can be estimated by use of information from various estimates, special studies, or other analytical techniques. Estimates of annual carrying cost in the range of 20% to 30% of inventory value are not unusual.

Although excess inventory generates costs, so can a fully depleted inventory. When a company does not have inventory available upon customer request, a stockout occurs. Stockout cost is not easily determinable or recordable. It is an opportunity cost that includes lost customer goodwill, lost contribution margin from not being able to fill a sale, and the ordering and shipping charges incurred from filling special orders.

All of the costs associated with inventory should be considered when purchasing decisions are made—and purchases should be made in reasonable quantities. The economic order quantity model is one technique that is often used to determine reasonable quantity. It is discussed later in this chapter.

Suppliers and Quantities

When buying inventory, a purchasing manager needs to make essentially three decisions—from whom, how much, and when. Each of these decisions depends in part on the relationship an organization has with its suppliers. In the past, the buyer–supplier relationship was generally viewed as adversarial; however, many companies are now viewing this relationship as a more cooperative, integrated partnership. Suppliers are stakeholders.

Which Supplier?

Traditionally, deciding from whom to buy was based primarily on price. A company found several firms that could provide the desired item and chose the firm offering the lowest price. However, the lowest-cost supplier in the short run is not necessarily the best supplier for the long run. The partnership approach views purchase cost in relation to quality and reliability, while taking a long-run perspective on the management of relationships with suppliers. Purchases are made from suppliers offering the most appropriate quality at the best overall price—and delivering in the most reliable manner—to prevent the necessity of having to return unfit goods, the creation of nonvalue-added paperwork, production delays, or the need to seek alternative suppliers.

Moving from the adversarial to the partnership view of buyer–supplier relations takes time, effort, and trust on the part of both entities. To accommodate such a partnership, changes must be made relative to contract agreements, quality, delivery, and conditions to communicate information openly.

In the traditional system, buyers would order large quantities of goods to obtain quantity discounts or to maximize usage of truck or other shipping container volumes. In contrast, in buyer–supplier partnership arrangements, order size is often considerably reduced and frequency of delivery increased. Long-term supplier contracts are negotiated, and then delivery reliability is monitored. Generally, suppliers missing a certain number of scheduled deliveries by more than a specified number of hours are dismissed. To comply with the need for frequent deliveries, it is desirable for vendors to be located close to the company, which helps to minimize both delivery time and shipping cost. Alternatively, overnight delivery services can be used. These services have recognized the critical nature of prompt delivery and have risen in importance in the business world. Managers of both buying and supplying companies are becoming well-versed in analyzing the cost–benefit relationship involved in using such services.

To build truly productive relationships, purchasing firms should help suppliers improve their processes to achieve reduced costs. Purchasing firms should also solicit information from suppliers about cost reduction possibilities related to new or existing products. Such an interchange of information and ideas requires that the partnership be built on a foundation of trust.

What Quantity?

After the supplier is selected, the firm must decide how many units to buy at a time. The objective is to buy in the most economical quantity possible, which requires consideration of the ordering and carrying costs of inventory. One tool used in this decision process is the **economic order quantity** (EOQ) model. The EOQ model provides an estimate of the number of units per order that would achieve the optimal balance between ordering and carrying costs. The EOQ formula is

economic order quantity
an estimate of the least costly number of units per order that would provide the optimal balance between ordering and carrying costs

$$EOQ = \sqrt{(2QO \div C)}$$

where EOQ = economic order quantity in units
   Q = estimated quantity in units used per year
   O = estimated cost of placing one order
   C = estimated cost to carry one unit in stock for one year

The EOQ formula does not include purchasing cost, since that amount relates to "from whom to buy" rather than "how many to buy." Purchasing cost does not affect ordering and carrying costs, except to the extent that opportunity cost is calculated on the basis of cost.

In a manufacturing company, managers are concerned with "how many units to produce" in addition to "how many units (of a raw material) to buy." The EOQ formula can be modified to provide the appropriate number of units to manufacture in an economic production run. The economic production run quantity minimizes the total costs of setting up a production run and carrying a unit in stock for one year. In the economic production run formula, the terms of the EOQ equation are defined as manufacturing costs rather than purchasing costs:

$$\text{Economic production run} = \sqrt{(2QS \div C)}$$

where Q = estimated quantity in units produced per year
   S = estimated cost of setting up a production run
   C = estimated cost of carrying one unit in stock for one year

Assume that WPI purchases pulpwood for its production. The purchasing manager has found several suppliers who can continuously provide tonnes of the proper quality of pulpwood at a cost of $400 per tonne. Exhibit 10-6 provides information for use in calculating economic order quantity. The exhibit uses an estimate to show the total costs of purchasing 4,200 tonnes per year in various order sizes.

EXHIBIT 10-6

Yearly Purchasing Cost for Tonnes of Pulpwood

Quantity needed per year (Q) = 4,200 tonnes
Cost of ordering (O) = $30 per order
Cost of carrying (C) = $10 per tonne

Size of order (tonnes)	50	100	150	200	300
Number of orders	84	42	28	21	140
Average inventory (tonnes)	25	50	75	100	150
Annual ordering cost	$2,520	$1,260	$ 840	$ 630	$ 420
Annual carrying cost	250	500	750	1,000	1,500
Total annual cost	$2,770	$1,760	$1,590	$1,630	$1,920

The EOQ model assumes that orders are filled exactly when needed, so when the order arrives, the inventory on hand is zero units. The average inventory size is half of the order size. The frequency with which orders must be placed depends on how many units are ordered each time. The total number of orders equals the total annual quantity of units needed divided by the size of the order.

Based on total costs, Exhibit 10-6 indicates that WPI's most economical order size is between 150 and 200 tonnes. The formula yields a value of 159 tonnes for the economic order quantity:

$$EOQ = \sqrt{(2QO \div C)}$$
$$= \sqrt{(2(4{,}200)(\$30) \div \$10)}$$
$$= 159 \text{ tonnes (rounded)}$$

The total annual cost to place and carry orders of 159 tonnes is $1,587, calculated as follows:

Number of orders (4,200 ÷ 159)	26.4	(rounded)
Average inventory (159 ÷ 2)	79.5	
Cost of ordering (26.4 × $30)	$ 792.0	
Cost of carrying (79.5 × $10)	$ 795.0	(rounded)
Total cost	$1,587.0	

Note again that this total cost does not include the $400 purchase cost per tonne.

Exhibit 10-7 shows graphically the costs relationships from the table in Exhibit 10-6.

The EOQ formula contains estimated values and may produce answers that are unrealistic. For example, it is not feasible to place an order that includes fractions of

EXHIBIT 10-7

Graphic Solution to Economic Order Size

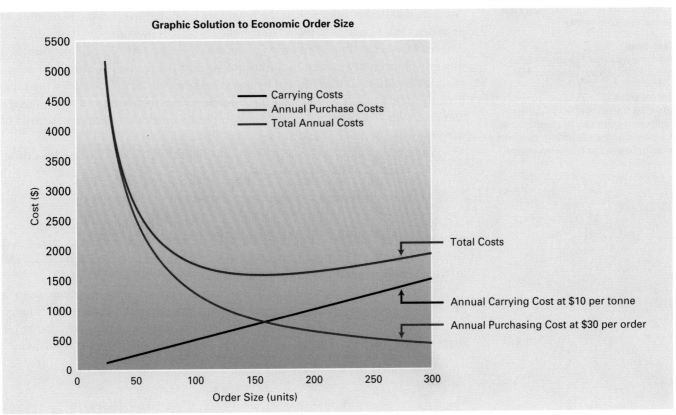

a tonne. And, WPI's supplier may only sell pulpwood in 10-tonne quantities. In that case, WPI will need to order 150 or 160 tonnes at a time. In most instances, small errors in estimating costs or rounding results do not have major effects on total cost. If the cost of ordering quantities close to the EOQ level is not significantly different from the cost of ordering at the EOQ level, some leeway is available in choosing the order size. Other factors, such as cash availability and storage space constraints, should also be considered.

As order size increases, the number of orders and the total annual ordering costs decline. At the same time, the total annual cost of carrying inventory increases because more units are being held in stock at any given point. Conversely, smaller orders reduce carrying costs but increase annual ordering costs.

Companies are currently decreasing their order costs dramatically by using techniques such as electronic data interchange and open purchase ordering. A single purchase order, which expires at a set or determinable future date, is prepared to authorize a supplier to provide a large quantity of one or more specified items. The goods will then be requisitioned in smaller quantities as needed by the buyer over the extended future period.

Another development in this area involves carrying costs, which are increasing. Companies are using higher estimates of these costs in part because of a greater awareness of the high cost of nonvalue-added activities, such as move time and storage time for units that were purchased but not needed. As carrying costs rise, the economic order quantity falls. For example, if WPI's ordering and carrying costs were reversed and estimated at $10 and $30, respectively, the EOQ would be 53 tonnes of pulpwood.

When to Order?

order point
the inventory level that triggers the placement of an order

lead time
the time from the placement of an order to the arrival of the goods

safety stock
the quantity of inventory kept on hand by a company to compensate for potential fluctuations in usage or unusual delays in receiving orders

Although the EOQ model indicates how many units to order, managers are also concerned with the **order point**—the inventory level that triggers the placement of an order. Order point is based on usage, the amount of inventory used or sold each day; **lead time**, the time from order placement to order arrival; and **safety stock**, a quantity of inventory carried for protection against stockouts. The size of the safety stock for a particular item should be based on how crucial the item is to the business, the item's purchase cost, and the amount of uncertainty related to both usage and lead time. The optimal safety stock is the quantity that balances the cost of carrying with the cost of not carrying safety stock units.

When companies can project a constant figure for both usage and lead time, the order point is calculated as follows:

$$\text{Order point} = (\text{Daily usage} \times \text{Lead time}) + \text{Safety stock}$$

Assume that WPI uses 15 tonnes of pulpwood per day and the company's supplier can deliver pulpwood in three days. If no safety stock is carried, pulpwood should be reordered when 45 tonnes (15×3) are in inventory, and the order should arrive precisely when the inventory reaches zero.

However, companies often experience excess usage or excess lead time. In such cases, safety stock provides an inventory cushion. Although WPI's average daily usage is 15 tonnes of pulpwood, the company occasionally uses a greater quantity, but never more than 19 tonnes in one day. A simple way to estimate safety stock is as follows:

$$\begin{aligned} \text{Safety stock} &= (\text{Maximum usage} - \text{Normal usage}) \times \text{Lead time} \\ &= (19 - 15) \times 3 \text{ tonnes} \\ &= 12 \text{ tonnes} \end{aligned}$$

Using this estimate, WPI would reorder pulpwood when 57 tonnes (45 original order point + 12 safety stock) were on hand.

Problems with the EOQ Model

Mathematical determination of economic order quantity and optimal quantity of safety stock will help a company control its investment in inventory. However, such models are only as valid as the estimates used in the formulas. For example, projecting costs such as lost customer goodwill may be extremely difficult. In some cases, the degree of inaccuracy may not be important; in other cases, however, it may be crucial.

The basic EOQ model determines what quantity of inventory to order. But there are at least three major problems associated with this model. First, identifying all the relevant inventory costs, especially carrying costs, is very difficult. Second, the model does not provide any direction for managers attempting to control the individual types of ordering and carrying costs. By considering only trade-offs between total ordering and total carrying costs, the EOQ model fails to lead managers to consider inventory management alternatives that might simultaneously reduce cost in both categories. Third, relationships among inventory items are ignored. For example, WPI might require 8 tonnes of pulpwood for each standard production run. If the EOQs for tonnes of pulpwood and the chemicals needed for each production run are computed independently, this interrelationship could be overlooked. WPI might find that, at a time when 96 tonnes of pulpwood are on hand (enough for 12 production runs), there are only enough chemicals on hand for three production runs.

The most significant shortcoming of EOQ is the assumption that there is some optimal level of inventory. That assumption is contrary to the just-in-time approach to inventory, which assumes the optimal level of inventory to be no inventory. More will be said about just-in-time later in this chapter.

OUTSOURCING

In the present business environment, **outsourcing** is an integral part of strategy. Virtually any process or activity in the value creation chain required to generate a product or service can be outsourced. For example, marketing and sales, accounting, engineering, manufacturing, customer service, and product distribution have all been outsourced. In the accounting domain, the payroll function is increasingly being outsourced, as is the financial accounting function and all aspects of information technology. By outsourcing processes and activities, organizations can concentrate their resources on strategically important functions. The outsourcing decisions should be made only after proper analysis. Managers should, with the assistance of management accounting, compare the cost of manufacturing a product component internally with the cost of purchasing it from outside suppliers (or from another division at a specific transfer price.)

outsourcing
the contracting with outside manufacturers or vendors for necessary goods or services rather than producing the goods or performing services in-house

Relevant management accounting information for an insource/outsource decision includes both quantitative and qualitative factors, some of which are shown in Exhibit 10-8. Many of the quantitative factors—such as incremental production cost per unit and the purchase price quoted by the supplier—are known with a high degree of certainty. Other quantitative factors—such the opportunity cost associated with production facilities—must be estimated. The qualitative

EXHIBIT 10-8

Relevant Considerations in
Insource/Outsource Decision

Relevant Quantitative Factors

- Incremental product costs for each unit
- Unit cost of purchasing from outside supplier (price less any discounts available plus shipping, etc.)
- Availability of production capacity to manufacture components
- Opportunity costs of using facilities for production rather than for other purposes
- Availability of storage space for units and raw materials

Relevant Qualitative Factors

- Relevant net advantage given uncertainty of estimates (costs, risks, etc.)
- Reliability of source(s) of supply
- Ability to assure quality when units are purchased from outside
- Nature of the work to be subcontracted (such as the importance of the part to the whole)
- Availability of suppliers
- Impact on customers and supplier(s)
- Perceptions regarding future price changes
- Perceptions about current product price—is the price appropriate or, as with an international supplier, is product dumping involved?
- Strategic and competitive importance to long-run organizational success

factors should be evaluated by more than one employee so that personal bias does not cloud valid business judgment.

These additional considerations indicate that there are many potential long-run effects of what are often regarded as short-run decisions. Managers should take a long-range perspective for insource/outsource decisions; they need to recognize that when an activity is outsourced, some degree of control is lost. Thus, the organization's management should carefully evaluate the viability of activities to be outsourced. With nonmonetary considerations, corporate management may make a decision not to outsource, even though the costs would be less. The activity or function may be considered too critical to the organization's long-term viability (e.g., product research and development); the organization may be pursuing a core competency relative to this function; or issues such as product/-service quality, time of delivery, flexibility of use, or reliability of supply cannot be resolved to the company's satisfaction. In such instances, the company's management may want to re-evaluate its activities relative to this function to determine how to perform the function at a lower cost than quoted by an outside organization.

If outsourcing is chosen, the organization should, with the aid of management accounting information, prepare a comprehensive list of criteria for selecting suppliers or vendors, and these criteria must be communicated to the potential suppliers. Although monetary considerations are important, corporate management generally recognizes that some nonmonetary needs, such as those mentioned above, are even more critical.

After a supplier has been selected, there must be regular monitoring and evaluation of performance. Again, financial accounting information may be important and is easily assessed (e.g., the invoices received from the supplier are not for the amount originally quoted per unit of product or service). However, other performance criteria must also be evaluated with management accounting, such as whether the supplier shipped defective parts or whether goods were late.

In making outsourcing decisions, a company should first define its primary reasons for outsourcing. By outsourcing noncore competencies, an organization can focus more intensely on developing its core competencies and devote additional resources to those skills or expertise that represent potential sources of competitive advantage. The International News Note provides a list of hidden costs with outsourcing.

INTERNATIONAL NEWS NOTE

Controlling the Hidden Costs of Outsourcing

Puranam and Srikanth surveyed 62 senior executives from the 100 largest financial services firms in the United States and Europe. They also conducted about 100 interviews with outsourcing clients and vendors. The findings from this survey revealed hidden costs of outsourcing, and some techniques for minimizing those costs.

Questions to Ask Before Outsourcing	Recommended Actions
Contracting	
Is it difficult to measure the performance of the process?	Conduct careful due diligence on vendors.
Are company-specific skills necessary to adequately perform this function?	Prepare for constant monitoring and contract management efforts.
Is the function so specialized that only one or two vendors can perform it with the necessary competence?	Consider setting up a "captive" (i.e., owned) unit.
Transition	
Are existing work manuals and operating procedures out of date?	Prepare to invest in codifying knowledge of business processes.
Is the performance of the process affected greatly when there is employee turnover?	Motivate employees who currently deliver the process to share knowledge with those who will take it on (e.g., through exit bonuses).
Does it take a long time to train employees to executive the process effectively?	Do not authorize the transition to the vendor unit until you are sure that knowledge capture and transfer is complete.
Interaction	
Do the personnel executing this process have to be in constant touch with the personnel executing other, linked processes?	Prepare to invest in re-engineering the process to make interactions with other processes as structured as possible.
Will changes to this process lead to many changes in several of the linked processes?	Build formal communication channels between client and vendor organizations to smooth coordination; use appropriate IT.
Is performing this process time-sensitive to performing other, related processes?	Encourage periodic face-to-face meetings to foster informal communication, develop relationships, and build a common understanding of how the processes are linked.

SOURCE: Phanish Puranam and Kannan Srikanth, "Seven Myths About Outsourcing," *Wall Street Journal*, June 16–17, 2007, R6. Reprinted with permission of *The Wall Street Journal*.

JUST-IN-TIME SYSTEMS

Just-in-time (JIT) is a philosophy about when to do something. The *when* is "as needed" and the *something* is a production, purchasing, or delivery activity. The basic elements of the JIT philosophy are outlined in Exhibit 10-9. JIT tends to be used in larger organizations rather than small organizations because it works best when there are extensive repetitive operations. Small organizations tend to have one-off activities that cannot use JIT. In addition, regardless of the type of organization (retail, service, or manufacturing) in which it exists, a just-in-time system has three primary goals:

- Eliminate any production process or operation that does not add value to the product/service
- Continuously improve production/performance efficiency
- Reduce the total cost of production/performance while increasing quality

EXHIBIT 10-9

Elements of JIT Philosophy

- Inventory is a liability, not an asset; eliminate it to the extent possible.*
- Storage space is directly related to inventories; eliminate it in response to the elimination of inventories.
- Long lead times cause inventory buildup; keep lead times as short as possible by using frequent deliveries.
- Creative thinking doesn't cost anything; use it to find ways to reduce costs before making expenditures for additional resources.
- Quality is essential at all times; work to eliminate defects and scrap.
- Suppliers are essential to operations; establish and cultivate good relationships with them, including the use of long-term contracts.
- Employees often have the best knowledge of ways to improve operations; listen to them.
- Employees generally have more talents than are being used; train them to be multiskilled and increase their productivity.
- Ways to improve operations are always available; constantly look for them, being certain to make fundamental changes rather than superficial ones.

*This paradoxical statement, that inventory is a liability, reflects the attitude that if a company is holding inventory for which there is no immediate demand or use, the company is unnecessarily incurring the carrying costs described in Exhibit 10-5. The statement also implies that there are creative ways of avoiding the costs of not carrying inventory, as described in Exhibit 10-5.

JIT manufacturing system
acquires components and produces inventory units only as they are needed, minimizes product defects, and reduces lead/setup times for acquisition and production

For example, a company using a **JIT manufacturing system** attempts to acquire components and to produce inventory units only as they are needed, to minimize product defects, and to reduce lead/setup times for acquisition and production.

Production was traditionally dictated by the need to smooth operating activity over time, which allowed a company to maintain a steady workforce and generate continuous machine use. However, smooth production often tends to build in buffer stocks of inventory and components. This process creates a just-in-case rather than a just-in-time scenario. It leads to work in process and finished goods inventories. Some of these inventories may never be needed.

push system
a production system in which work centres may purchase or produce inventory that is not currently needed because of lead time or economic order (production) quantity requirements; the excess inventory is stored until it is needed

In traditional systems, the various types of inventory—raw material, components, supplies, and work in process—were generally maintained at high enough levels to cover up for inefficiencies in acquisition or production. The traditional philosophy is that the level representing inventory should be kept high enough to address any problems without disrupting production. This technique is intended to solve the original problems, but it creates a new one. By covering up the problems, the excess inventory adds to the difficulty of making corrections. In other words, traditional or **push systems** result in excess inventories—with inherent storage and obsolescence costs—that create unnecessary or nonvalue-adding costs. In contrast, the JIT manufacturing philosophy is to lower the inventory level, expose the problems, and eliminate those problems to the extent possible.

Just-in-time manufacturing has many names, including zero inventory production system (ZIPS), material as needed (MAN), and **kanban** (the Japanese word for *card*). The JIT system originated in Japan from the use of cards to control the flow of materials between work centres. In a JIT system, products are not produced until customers have demanded them; no manufacturing activity occurs unless the resulting product is needed by the next work centre in the production line. These factors make JIT a pull, rather than a push, system of production control.

In a **pull system** of production, parts are delivered or manufactured only as they are needed by the work centre for which they are intended. There are no storage areas to which unneeded work can be "pushed." Exhibit 10-10 illustrates a pull system of production. Exhibit 10-11 shows a push system of production.

Because JIT is a pull system, it depends on accurate market data, since a tight linkage is required between sales and production volume. Forecasted sales demand is the controlling production force. Once demand is estimated, the production schedule is set for an extended period (such as a month), and schedule changes

kanban
the Japanese word for *card*; another name for just-in-time manufacturing, which originated in Japan from the use of cards to control the flow of materials or units between work centres

pull system
a production system in which parts are delivered or manufactured only as they are needed

---

EXHIBIT 10-10
Pull System of Production Control

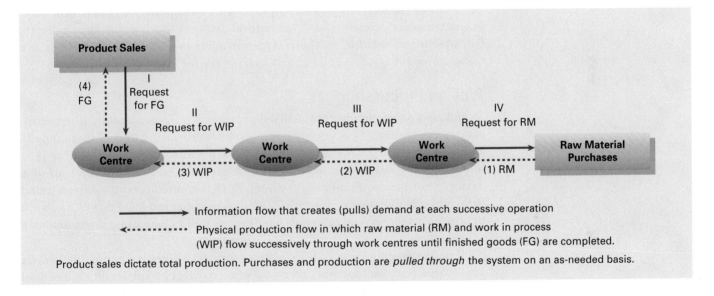

Information flow that creates (pulls) demand at each successive operation

Physical production flow in which raw material (RM) and work in process (WIP) flow successively through work centres until finished goods (FG) are completed.

Product sales dictate total production. Purchases and production are *pulled through* the system on an as-needed basis.

should be minimal. Level scheduling creates a constant rate of use for component materials, labour, equipment, materials handling, maintenance, and support functions. Additionally, high-quality production processes are mandatory so that defects can be avoided. Slack time in the schedule is not treated as idle time. If workers are not needed for production activities, time is used for employee training, machine maintenance, and workplace organization.

JIT cannot be implemented overnight; Toyota took more than 20 years to develop its system and realize significant benefits from it. Although JIT techniques are becoming better known and can be more quickly and easily implemented, the most impressive benefits are normally reached only after the system has been operational for five to ten years. Any company that aims to achieve the JIT goals must change the majority of its organizational functions. It must investigate the partnership-type purchasing arrangements discussed earlier in the chapter. It must also address product design, product processing,

---

EXHIBIT 10-11

Push System of Production
Control

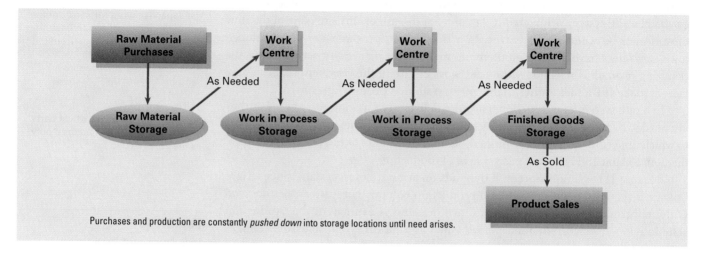

Purchases and production are constantly *pushed down* into storage locations until need arises.

plant layout considerations, and employee empowerment. No matter how carefully a company prepares, however, natural disasters—such as the December 16, 2007, record snowfall in southern Ontario—made inoperable the infrastructure essential for JIT.

Product Processing

In making processing improvements, one primary JIT consideration is to reduce machine setup time. Reducing setup time allows processing to shift more rapidly among different types of units, and makes the manufacturing process more flexible. An organization may need to incur some costs to reduce setup time—for example, for new equipment or training. Such increased costs have been found to be more than recovered by the savings derived from reducing downtime, work in process inventory, and materials handling, as well as increasing safety and ease of operation.

Another essential part of JIT product processing is implementing the highest quality standards and focusing on a goal of zero defects. High quality is essential because inferior quality causes additional costs for downtime, rework, scrap, warranty work, and lost customer goodwill. Under JIT systems, quality is determined on a continual basis rather than at quality control checkpoints. Organizations using JIT systems achieve continuous quality first by ensuring vendor product quality and then by ensuring quality in the conversion processes.

Quality in manufacturing can be partially obtained through the use of modern production equipment, which often relies on computerized technology to schedule, control, and monitor production processes. Some elements of the production system may be designed to be self-checking. In the most integrated systems, sophisticated computer programs monitor each process in the production stream and develop statistical data on the reliability of both components and processes. The data are then available for use in programs that design new products and processes, and in evaluating the reliability of components obtained from each internal and external supplier. In the event that defective products are made, they should be promptly discovered and the problem that created them identified and corrected.

Often, the traditional cost accounting system "buries" quality control costs and costs of scrap in the standard cost of production. For instance, adding excess materials or labour time into the standard quantities creates a buried cost of quality. Such costs are often 10 to 30% of total production cost. Consider a company making a $10 product that has quality inspection and scrap costs of 10%, or $1 per unit. If that company's annual cost of goods sold is $10,000,000, its quality inspection and scrap costs are $1,000,000! When quality is controlled on an ongoing basis, costs of obtaining high quality may be significantly reduced. It is less costly in many manufacturing situations to avoid mistakes than to correct them.

Plant Layout

In an effective JIT system, the physical plant is arranged in a way that is conducive to the flow of goods and the organization of workers. Equipment is placed in a rational arrangement based on the materials flow. Such a layout reduces materials handling costs and the lead time required to get work in process from one point to another. Streamlined design allows people to see problems—such as excess inventory, product defects, equipment malfunctions, and out-of-place tools—more easily.

One way to minimize cycle time through the plant is to establish linear or U-shaped groupings of workers or machines, commonly referred to as manufacturing cells. A U-shaped manufacturing cell is depicted in Exhibit 10-12. These cells improve materials handling and flow, increase machine utilization rates, maximize communication among workers, and result in better quality control.

EXHIBIT 10-12

Depiction of a Manufacturing Cell

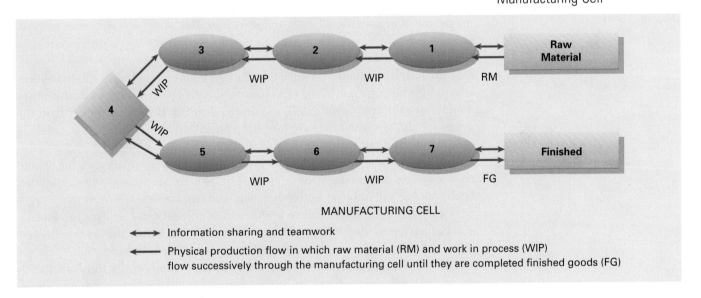

MANUFACTURING CELL

⟷ Information sharing and teamwork

⟵ Physical production flow in which raw material (RM) and work in process (WIP) flow successively through the manufacturing cell until they are completed finished goods (FG)

Manufacturing cells create an opportunity for workers to be cross-trained and thereby broaden their skills and deepen their workplace involvement. Training workers to be multiskilled is valid even in nonmanufacturing companies. For instance, USAA, a San Antonio, Texas, insurance and financial services company, consolidated its departments and trained its salespeople to handle every aspect of processing insurance policies after installing a huge network of automated equipment. The cost of training in such situations can be substantial, and workers often resent change. In the long run, however, employers have a more viable workforce, and workers seem to be more satisfied with their jobs. Additionally, companies may

Having workers in linear groups means that there is less opportunity for backlogs to accumulate. Additionally, components or partially completed units do not have to be gathered in batches and moved to distant workstations within the plant.

find that workers, when they know more about the process as a whole, are better able to provide helpful suggestions about process improvement.

Employee Empowerment

An underlying feature of a just-in-time system and its emphasis on cross-training is the concept of employee **empowerment**. Employees can only be empowered if they have the abilities, tools, and training to perform tasks. They must be involved in organizational planning. Also, employees must trust management and be trusted by management. Given these factors, employees will be able to commit themselves to the pursuit of organizational goals and objectives. But before any employee empowerment can take place, the organization must be willing to invest resources in people and training activities.

Any business should recognize that the first condition of hiring and placement is to put the right people in the right jobs. Employees placed in jobs for which they do not have the appropriate skills are destined to fail. If workers do not have the necessary abilities when they are hired, the organization is responsible for making certain that they can acquire these abilities through training.

Training should not be limited to giving people basic competencies but should be an ongoing process designed to increase employees' knowledge and capabilities. Such training will improve both job quality and employee self-esteem. Employees who learn more are better able to perform their current tasks, analyze those tasks, and suggest methods for improvements. They are also better able to acquire new skills, and participate to a greater degree in organizational planning.

The organization must provide employees with the necessary tools—including equipment, information, and authority—to perform their jobs in a manner consistent with organizational objectives. Employees who use improperly maintained or ineffective equipment, who do not have the necessary problem-solving tools and information to investigate and correct problems, or who cannot effect solutions to identified problems are not empowered in their jobs.

At a minimum, involvement in organizational planning requires that employees be told of, and agree with, the business's basic strategy. However, true empowerment means that the company has flattened the organizational structure and pushed decision-making authority and responsibility down to the lowest reasonable level. Flatter structures are more flexible, allowing decisions to be made rapidly in response to need. When such structures exist, feedback must be provided to employees about their involvement and the impact of their decisions.

empowerment
all practices that are designed to give workers the training, authority, and responsibility they need to manage their own jobs and make decisions about their work

For empowerment to work effectively in an organization, there must be an atmosphere of trust among all employees at all levels. This element of empowerment is crucial and often difficult to obtain, because many organizations currently operate in an atmosphere of mistrust between managers and subordinates.[8] This mistrust creates a wide variety of fears: fear of making mistakes, fear of retaliation (including job loss), fear of being viewed as a troublemaker, fear of taking risks, fear of speaking out, and, very importantly, fear of change. Employees' fears can be eliminated only through development of mutual trust, which will allow the fears and their underlying causes to be confronted, analyzed, and resolved.

Overall, the just-in-time philosophy is more than a cost-cutting endeavour. JIT requires good human resource management and a dedication to teamwork. It is important to note that just-in-time systems may not be appropriate for all types of companies. Companies whose raw materials or components are crucial to processing activities may be unable to afford the potential stockout cost of maintaining minimal inventories.

Finally, when there are unexpected occurrences, such as a rail strike, companies using a just-in-time system may face business closure or limited production for some time—even if they have arranged for alternative means of transport. We are currently seeing circumstances surrounding international conflict leading to long delays for motorists at the Canada–United States border. This makes JIT problematic (for example, for the automotive industry) because without predictable lead times, JIT cannot be effective.

The Two Most Important Relationships for JIT

Each organization tends to have a set of upstream suppliers and a set of downstream customers in its value creation chains. It is at the upstream and downstream interfaces of these relationships that real opportunities for improvement exist. By building improved cooperation, communication, and integration, these entities can treat each other as extensions of themselves. In so doing, they can enjoy gains in quality, output, and cost efficiency. Nonvalue-added activities can be reduced or eliminated and performance of value-added activities can be enhanced. Shared expertise and problem solving can be very beneficial. Products and services can be provided faster and with fewer defects, and activities can be performed more effectively and reliably with fewer deficiencies and less redundancy.

Consider the following opportunities for improvement between entities:
- Improved communication of requirements and specifications
- Greater clarity in requests for products or services
- Improved feedback regarding unsatisfactory products or services
- Improvements in planning, controlling, and problem solving
- Shared managerial and technical expertise, supervision, and training

All of the above can also be said for individuals and groups within an organization. Within the organization or work centre, employees have both an upstream supplier and a downstream customer who form the context within which work is accomplished. When employees see their internal suppliers and customers as extensions of themselves and work to exploit the opportunities just indicated, teamwork is significantly enhanced.

Backflush Costing

Accounting in a JIT system focuses on the plant's output to the customer.[9] Because each area depends on the previous area, any problems will quickly stop the production process. Daily accounting for the individual costs of production is no longer necessary; all costs should be at standard, since variations are observed and corrected almost immediately.

Further, since costs are more easily traced to their related output in a JIT system, fewer costs are arbitrarily allocated to products. Costs are incurred in specified cells on a per-hour or per-unit basis. Energy costs are direct to production in a comprehensive JIT system because there should be a minimum of downtime by machines or unplanned idle time for workers. Virtually the only costs still being allocated are costs associated with the structure (building depreciation, rent, taxes, and insurance) and machinery depreciation. By using more cost drivers, activity-based costing allocates manufacturing overhead costs to products more accurately than traditional cost accounting, which uses many fewer cost drivers.

backflush costing
a costing system that focuses on output and works backward through the system to allocate costs to cost of goods sold and inventory

Backflush costing is a streamlined cost accounting method that speeds up, simplifies, and reduces accounting effort in an environment that minimizes inventory balances, requires few allocations, uses standard costs, and has minimal variances from standard. During the period, this costing method records purchases of raw material and accumulates actual conversion costs. Then, either at completion of production or upon the sale of goods, an entry is made to allocate the total costs incurred to Cost of Goods Sold and to Finished Goods Inventory, using standard production costs.

Implementation of a just-in-time system can result in significant cost reductions and productivity improvements. But even within a single organization, not all inventories need to be managed according to a just-in-time philosophy. The costs and benefits of any inventory control system must be evaluated before management installs the system.

Exhibit 10-13 provides information on a product of the Bernard Company. This information is used to illustrate the journal entries for backflush costing. The company

EXHIBIT 10-13
Backflush Costing

Bernard Company's standard production cost per unit:

Raw material	$ 75
Conversion	184
Total cost	$259

No beginning inventories exist.

(1) Purchased $1,530,000 of raw material in June:

Raw and In Process Inventory	1,530,000	
Accounts Payable		1,530,000

Purchased material at standard cost under a long-term agreement with supplier.

(2) Incurred $3,687,000 of conversion costs in June:

Conversion Costs	3,687,000	
Various accounts		3,687,000

Record conversion costs. Various accounts include wages payable for direct and indirect labour, accumulated depreciation, supplies, etc.

(3) Completed 20,000 units of production in June:

Finished Goods (20,000 × $259)	5,180,000	
Raw and In Process Inventory (20,000 × $75)		1,500,000
Conversion Costs (20,000 × $184)		3,680,000

(4) Sold 19,800 units on account in June for $420:

(a) Cost of Goods Sold (19,800 × $259)	5,128,200	
Finished Goods		5,128,200
(b) Accounts Receivable (19,800 × $420)	8,316,000	
Sales		8,316,000

Ending Inventories:

Raw and In Process ($1,530,000 – $1,500,000)	$30,000
Finished Goods ($5,180,000 – $5,128,200)	51,800

In addition, there are underapplied conversion costs of $7,000 ($3,687,000 – $3,680,000).

has a long-term contract with its supplier for raw material at $75 per unit, so there is no material price variance. Bernard's JIT inventory system has minimum inventories that remain constant from period to period. Beginning inventories for June are assumed to be zero.

Three alternatives are possible to the entries in Exhibit 10-13. First, if Bernard's production time was extremely short, the company might not journalize raw mate-

Data Mining, a New Technique for Understanding Cost

INTERNATIONAL NEWS NOTE

Management accounting traditionally provided management with information for decision making by conducting variance analyses. IT advances beginning in the 1990s have significantly transformed how data are processed for management decision making.

New ERP systems have fuelled rapid growth in electronic transactional data. The extensive databases provided by ERP systems are excellent candidates for data mining, which involves searching for valuable information in large volumes of data in order to extract potentially useful information. The tools it uses include pattern recognition and various statistical and mathematical techniques.

Data mining differs from variance analysis in a number of ways. For one thing, it focuses on machine-driven model building whereas variance analysis emphasizes a prior set of manual procedures. For another, data mining builds models whereas variance analysis is supervised by a management accountant with preconceived ideas about what to examine. With variance analysis, relevant associations may be overlooked. In contrast, data mining builds dependency hypotheses and thus can identify patterns and make accurate predictions to improve profitability. For example, for sales:

> Take Wal-Mart, for instance, and its accurate prediction about the demand for umbrellas in rain drenched portions of California [in the winter of 2005]. Through the analysis of historical sales data from stores in the region, national weather service predictions and the study of satellite weather patterns, the retailer accurately predicted not only the needed umbrella inventory, but the style and colour most desired by its customers . . . Wal-Mart's capabilities in data mining [are] able to determine the best location for umbrellas in a specific store for purposes of enhancing sales.

Another example of data mining comes from a study of default rates on car loans:

> The performance of 6,996 auto loans from January 1998 to March 2003 was examined. The findings suggest that just as insurance companies base rates on the make and model of the car being insured, banks should consider dropping their "house rates" for auto loans and adjust interest rates according the type of car being financed, i.e.,
> - Loans for European and Japanese cars had a lower average default rate (2.9 percent) than loans for American cars (4.7 percent).
> - Loans for Saturns had defaults 22 times higher than the defaults of Toyotas.
> - Loans for Mazdas were six times more likely to be in default than loans for Toyotas.

More and more business applications are being found for data mining. Banks, hotels, retailers, and hospital services are all finding uses for it. Data mining has the potential to provide management accountants with more cost insights.

SOURCES: Sumit Agarwal, Brent W. Ambrose, and Souphala Chomsisengphet, "Automobile Loans and Information Asymmetry," in Brent Ambrose and Sumit Agarwal, *Household Credit Usage: Personal Debt and Mortgages* (New York: Palgrave Macmillan, 2007); Michael J.A. Berry and Gordon Linoff, *Data Mining Techniques: For Marketing, Sales, and Customer Support* (New York: Wiley, 1997); Marty Jerome, "Study Claims That Car Loans Should Be Adjusted for Make," *Business Week*, August 13, 2007; Kevin Fickenscher, "The New Frontier of Data Mining," *Health Management Technology*, October 2005, pp. 26–30; Amir Hormozi and Stacy Giles, "Data Mining: A Competitive Weapon for Banking and Retail Industries," *Information Systems Management*, Spring 2004, pp. 62–71; Sang Lee and Keng Siau, "A Review of Data Mining Techniques," *Industrial Management and Data Systems* 1 (2001); Vincent Magnini, Earl Honeycutt, Jr., and Sharon Hodge, "Data Mining for Hotel Firms: Use and Limitations," *Cornell Hotel and Restaurant Administration Quarterly*, April 2003, pp. 94–105.

rials purchases until completion of production. In that case, entries (1) and (3) from Exhibit 10-13 could be combined as follows:

Raw and In Process Inventory	30,000	
Finished Goods	5,180,000	
Accounts Payable		1,530,000
Conversion Costs		3,680,000

If goods were immediately shipped to customers on completion, Bernard could use a second alternative, in which entries (3) and (4a) from Exhibit 10-13 could be combined in the following manner to complete and sell the goods:

Finished Goods	51,800	
Cost of Goods Sold	5,128,200	
Raw and In Process Inventory		1,500,000
Conversion Costs		3,680,000

The third alternative reflects the ultimate JIT system, in which only one entry is made to replace entries (1), (3), and (4a) in Exhibit 10-13. For Bernard, this entry would be:

Raw and In Process Inventory (minimal overpurchases)	30,000	
Finished Goods (minimal overproduction)	51,800	
Cost of Goods Sold	5,128,200	
Accounts Payable		1,530,000
Conversion Costs		3,680,000

Note that in all cases, entry (2) is not affected. All conversion costs must be recorded as incurred, or accrued at the end of a period, because of their effect on a variety of accounts.

LEARNING OBJECTIVE 5

What is life cycle costing?

LIFE CYCLE COSTING

The product life cycle is a significant consideration in executing an organization's planning and control functions regarding product costs and other costs. The stage a product has reached in its life cycle significantly affects sales volume, price, and costs. Both revenues and costs for a given product change as it advances through the development, introduction, growth, maturity, and harvest stages.

Total revenues are nonexistent during the development stage and commence during introduction. They typically rise during growth, level off in maturity, and decline during harvest. In contrast, costs are characteristically high during development and introduction and tend to stabilize as production becomes routine. Rigorous product development and design efforts are usually worthwhile because 80% to 90% of a product's life cycle cost is determined by decisions made before production begins.

Products and services, like people, go through a series of life cycle stages. It is not easy to determine how old a product must be before it moves from one stage to another. Some products, such as the hula hoop, come and go fairly quickly; others, such as Barbie and Ken dolls, have changed minimally and managed to remain popular products. Still other products, such as bell-bottoms and miniskirts, have been revitalized and have come back with renewed vigour. Services, too, change over time. For instance, 30 years ago personal financial planning and home health care services

Fashion trends seem to run through the product life cycle over and over again. However, changes do occur relative to colours, patterns, and fabric usage.

were in their infancy, and long-distance bus service was beginning to decline in importance. Today, long-term care insurance is making its debut. It is difficult, if not impossible, to predict what services will be available in 2015.

The stages of the product life cycle are development, introduction, growth, maturity, and harvest; relative sales levels for these stages are shown in Exhibit 10-14. Organizations must be aware of the life cycle stage at which each of their products has arrived, because the stage may have a tremendous impact on costs, sales, and pricing strategies.

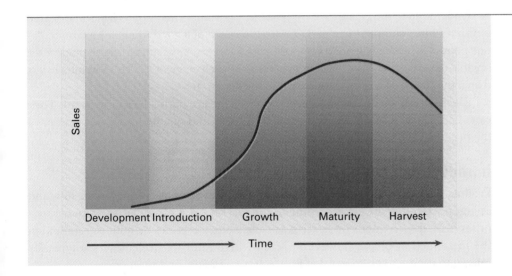

EXHIBIT 10-14
Product Life Cycle

Development Stage

If products are designed properly, they should require few engineering changes after being released to production. Each time an engineering change is made, one or more of the following activities occur, creating additional costs: the operations flow document must be reprinted, workers must relearn tasks, machine dies or setups must be changed, and parts currently ordered or in stock may be made obsolete. As indicated in Exhibit 10-15, if cost and time to market are not to be affected significantly, any design changes must be made early in the process.

EXHIBIT 10-15

Design Change Effects on Cost
and Time to Market

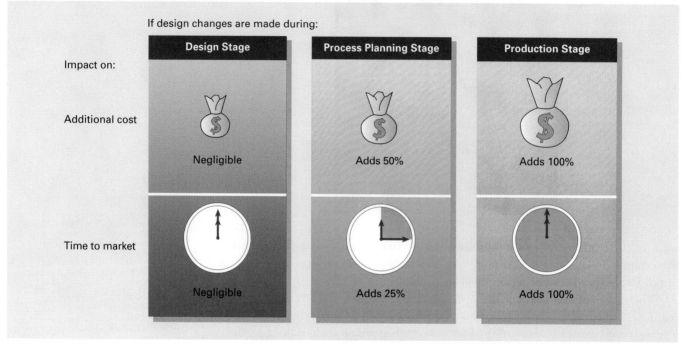

SOURCE: Reprinted from the 1992 issue of *BusinessWeek/Reinventing America* by special permission. Copyright (1992) by The McGraw-Hill Companies.

Products need to be designed to use the smallest number of parts, and parts should be standardized to the greatest extent possible. Consumers may appreciate some degree of variety, but a company can end up with too much of a good thing; for example, "at one point, Nissan had 300 different ashtrays in its cars."[10] Changes can be made after original design, but any cost savings generated by such changes will be substantially less than if the changes had been made early in the design/ development process.

Decisions made during the development stage are particularly important. They can affect product sales, design, production costs, and quality for the remainder of the product's life cycle.

Introduction Stage

Product introduction is essentially a startup phase. Sales are usually quite low, and selling prices often are set according to the market price of similar substitute goods or services, if such goods or services are available. Costs can be quite substantial in the introduction phase, however. Costs incurred during this phase are typically related to product design, market research, advertising, and promotion.

Growth, Maturity, and Harvest Stages

The growth stage begins when the product first breaks even. During the growth stage, the product has been accepted by the market, and profits begin to rise. Product quality also may improve during this stage because competitors may have improved on original production designs. Prices are fairly stable during this period because many substitutes exist or because consumers have become attached to the product and are willing to pay a particular price for it rather than buy a substitute.

In the maturity stage, sales begin to stabilize or slowly decline, and firms often compete on the basis of selling price. Costs are often at their lowest level during this period, so profits may be high. Some products, like Kool-Aid and Jell-O, seem to remain at this stage forever.

The harvest (decline) stage reflects waning sales. During the harvest stage, prices are often cut dramatically to stimulate business. As the name implies, management usually attempts to generate as much short-term profit and cash flow as possible at this stage.

Cost and Price Changes Over Life

Customers are concerned with obtaining a high-quality product or service for a price they perceive to be reasonable. Product prices change, however, over the product life cycle. Producers of goods and providers of services should be concerned with maximizing profits over a product's or a service's life cycle because, to be profitable, the product or service must generate revenues in excess of its total (not single period-by-period) costs.

Because each stage of the product life cycle influences sales and costs differently, each requires its own expected cost focus. Then, as activities take place and plans are implemented, a monitoring system needs to be in place to capture sales and costs and compare them to an appropriately prepared expectation for each particular life cycle stage. Such a comparison provides feedback so that managers will have the information by which to direct activities to achieve desired results throughout each stage of the product life cycle.

Reducing time to market is merely one of many ways a company can reduce costs; other ways are listed in Exhibit 10-16. Getting products to market quickly and profitably requires a compromise between the advantages associated with speed of product innovation and superior product design. Rapid time to market may mean that a firm incurs costs associated with design flaws (such as the costs of future changes) that could have been avoided if more time had been allowed for the product's development. Also, if a flawed product is marketed, some costs will likely be incurred for returns, warranty work, or customer skepticism regarding the firm's reputation for product quality.

EXHIBIT 10-16

Actions to Substantially Reduce Product Costs and Improve Performance

- Develop new production processes.
- Capture learning curve and experience effects.
- Increase capacity utilization.
- Focus factory arrangements to reduce coordination costs.
- Design for manufacturability to reduce assembly time, training costs, warranty costs, and required number of spare parts.
- Design for logistical support.
- Design for reliability.
- Design for maintainability.
- Adopt advanced manufacturing technologies to reduce inventory levels, production floor space, defects, rework, and quality costs.

SOURCE: Adapted from Gerald I. Susman, "Product Life Cycle Management," *Journal of Cost Management*, Summer 1989, pp. 8–22. Reprinted by permission of Research Institute of America Group.

Another aspect of an organization's operating environment is supplier relations. Many companies that have formed long-term alliances with suppliers have found such relationships to be effective cost control mechanisms. For example, by involving suppliers early in the design and development stage of new products, a better design for manufacturability will be achieved and the likelihood of meeting target costs will be improved.

What are target costing and value engineering, and in which life cycle stage are these tools used?

target costing
a process of determining an allowable cost for a product or component that is inferred from projecting a market price for the product and subtracting a required profit margin

TARGET COSTING

Target costing, shown on the right-hand side of Exhibit 10-17, is a process of determining an allowable cost for a product or component that is inferred from projecting a market price for the product and subtracting a required profit margin. This method originated in Japan. As market price is the starting point in target costing, and market price equates to a customer's valuation of the value creation chain output, target costing is a customer-driven analysis. By subtracting the required profit margin from the estimated market price, the allowance for the total cost for research and development, product design, manufacturing, marketing, distribution, and customer service is determined.

In developing products to market, Western manufacturers have traditionally confined their approach to the following sequence: a product is designed, its costs are determined, and a selling price is set, based to some extent on the costs involved. If the market will not bear the resulting selling price, either the company does not make as much profit as it had hoped or it attempts to lower production costs. This process is illustrated on the left-hand side of Exhibit 10-17.

Let us consider a target costing example. Suppose a car assembler decides to introduce a sub-compact car to compete with the existing sub-compacts of the other automotive assemblers, domestic and imports. After careful consideration of the market and existing sub-compacts, a spot in the lineup and features are chosen that suggest a wholesale price of $14,000 to dealers. With the expected profit margin on sales of, say, 18%, this means all costs need to be $11,480 per unit ($14,000 × (1.00 − 0.18)). Thus, over the planned lifetime of the car, the total costs need to be $11,480 per unit. These total costs include all costs for research and development, product design, manufacturing, marketing, distribution, and customer service. To succeed in meeting the requirements of expected customers and the financial performance requirements of the organization, the proposed sub-compact needs to be produced for the target cost of $11,480. The profit margin is expected to be $2,520 ($14,000 − $11,480 or 0.18 × $14,000).

The implied maximum, or target cost, is compared with the expected product cost. If the target cost is less than the expected cost, the organization has several alternatives. First, the product design or production process can be changed to reduce costs. Preparation of cost tables helps in determining how such adjustments can be made. These tables are databases that provide information about how using different input resources, manufacturing processes, and design specifications would affect product costs. Second, a less-than-desired profit margin can be accepted. Third, the organization can decide that it does not want to enter this particular product market at the current time because it cannot generate the profit margin it desires.

To reduce estimated costs, both production processes and production components can be examined. For those components that are produced in-house, outsourcing may be considered if the components can be purchased at a lower cost. For those parts that are purchased from vendors, negotiation with vendors may lead to price concessions; alternatively, vendors may collaborate in redesigning the product so that the cost of components or conversion processes can be reduced.

The degree to which target costing techniques are used is affected by the type of product being manufactured. As product cost and complexity increase and as the production stage of the life cycle is shortened because of changing consumer preferences, target costing becomes more important, because proper design can generate greater potential savings.

Value Engineering

value engineering
a tool used to manage the relationship between product design, product price, and target cost

Value engineering works in tandem with a target costing system. For value engineering to be applied, the total value (price) of the finished product must be

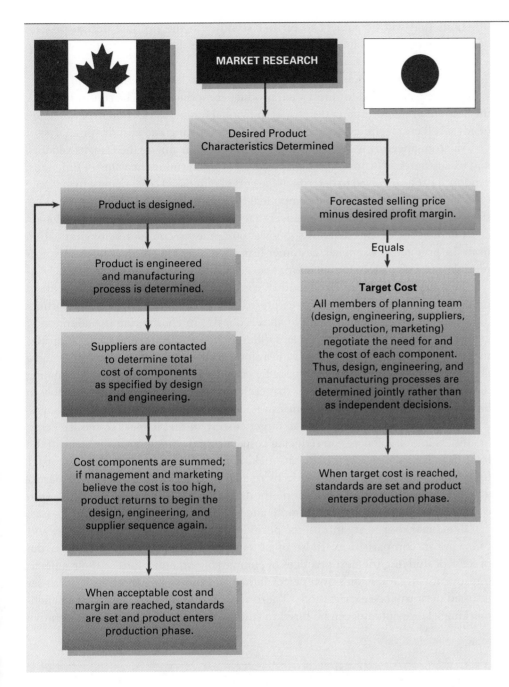

EXHIBIT 10-17
Developing Product Costs

decomposed into the various functions of the product. Product functions are the product/service design features that deliver value to the customer. Collectively, the values of the individual functions equal the value of the product. To illustrate, the value of an automobile can be decomposed into values for the following functions: basic transportation, air conditioning, power steering, power brakes, power seats, safety equipment, towing capacity, warranty terms, fuel economy, sound system, etc.

Once the customer value associated with each function has been determined, the cost of each function is estimated. The cost of each function consists of the costs of buying or making the component parts, plus the costs of assembly and installation. With estimates of both the value and cost of each function in hand, managers can identify those functions that have poor value-to-cost relationships. It is these functions that will be subject to further scrutiny in the product design process because the object of value engineering is to improve the value-to-cost relationship so that the target profit can be realized.

By pushing the cost analysis down to the function level, the design and conversion processes required for individual product components can be scrutinized. For the accountant, determining the cost of individual functions can require application of advanced cost techniques such as activity-based costing and cost driver analysis.

Value engineering leads to exchanges of information among the firm, its vendors, and its customers. Customer input is necessary to determine the value of functions; vendors must be involved to determine the cost of purchased components, to generate ideas on alternative product and component designs, and to identify engineering constraints. Functions that cannot be delivered to the customer at an acceptable value-to-cost relationship, despite all efforts to lower cost, may be considered for elimination from the product. For supplier/customer firms that have long-term relationships, it is possible to develop more formal information systems that combine information.

The **survival triplet** in Exhibit 10-18 consists of three dimensions that define a product: cost/price (internal cost structure/external selling price), quality (conformity to specifications), and functionality (what it does).[11] In considering the adoption of generic strategies—cost leadership and differentiation—the survival triplet indicates that only products with acceptable values along each of the three dimensions stand a chance of continuing. The survival range for each dimension is defined by determining the minimum and maximum values that each dimension can have for the product to be successful. To survive, the company must operate competitively within those ranges.

Kaizan costing is comparable to target costing in that it seeks to reduce costs, but differs in that it focuses on reducing costs during the manufacturing stage of the total. A Japanese word, *kaizan* means making improvements to a process in order to reduce costs. Kaizan costing works by regular meetings by those involved, particularly front-line workers, to discuss methods for reducing costs. Frequently, kaizan costing is tied to profit sharing for motivational reasons.

Benchmarking is organizations' periodic examination of their activities and processes in comparison to those of other organizations. Benchmarking is the process of studying the best practices of comparable organizations or their units to improve the organization's own performance and then using those insights to set justified performance expectations. There are two other ways to undertake benchmarking: (1) consultants can be hired to study your organization and comparative

survival triplet
the cost/price, quality, and functionality that products need to demonstrate in order to survive and prosper

kaizan costing
a technique used to reduce costs during the manufacturing stage of the total life cycle of a product

benchmarking
process of studying the best practices of comparable organizations or their units to improve the organization's own performance and then using those insights to set justified performance expectations

EXHIBIT 10-18
The Survival Triplet

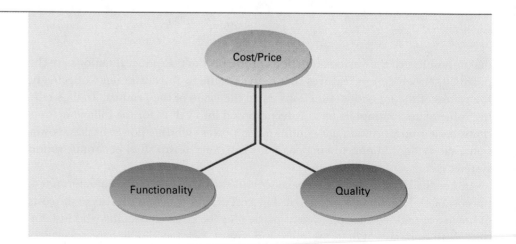

organizations, and (2) employees of an organization can develop their own informal networks for comparing specific activities and processes.

PROCESS-BASED MANAGEMENT

Organizations create value through their activities, which are linked together as processes. As groups of activities, processes accomplish specific objectives within the organization's strategy. Two examples of processes are "deliver products from the organization's factory to customers' warehouses" and "receive materials from suppliers."

Process-based management is about managing processes to accomplish objectives. A process-based organization is one that is managed with the explicit recognition that business processes are undertaken to meet or exceed stakeholders' needs, with the customer the predominant stakeholder at all times.[12]

Process-based management includes:

- promoting a process-based culture;
- managing end-to-end business processes to continuously improve the cost, quality, flexibility, and timing of products and services to customers;
- understanding and meeting customer expectations;
- integrating diverse initiatives into a process-oriented approach; and
- linking incentives and compensation to process performance.[13]

Many techniques have been used over the past few decades to improve quality via improved processes.[14] Examples include total quality management (TQM), business process re-engineering (BPR), activity-based management (ABM), lean manufacturing, International Standards Organization (ISO) certification, and Sigma Six. These techniques, however, tend to be limited in that they examine only some of the processes within an organization. Process-based management is more comprehensive.

Process-based management is largely a philosophy in that it seeks to change an organization's mindset about customer value. U.S.-based Southwest Airlines is one organization that uses process-based management. A crucial component of Southwest's business model is aircraft turnaround times. The process of turnaround involves all employees, including pilots, helping with the activities that need to be completed before the aircraft can proceed with the next load of passengers. This airline turns around an aircraft in 25 minutes, which is only possible because it has taken an integrated processes/systems view. In Canada, WestJet has successfully copied Southwest (see On Site at the beginning of the chapter).

Process-based management differs from functional management. Functions include accounting, sales, and manufacturing. Functional management occurs when functions are managed separately from one another. The result is functional "silos" and a reduced ability to create value for customers, since processes usually cut across functions. To manage processes successfully, organizations must be developed and structured in the context of an organization-wide management system. Functions must be subordinated to processes. Exhibit 10-19 contrasts process management with functional management.

Process-based management brings together what appear to be unrelated activities, functions, processes, and business lines and enables them all to focus together on achieving the organization's strategy and on adding value for customers. Process-based management requires a relentless desire to improve services to customers, which can only happen when processes are redesigned end to end.

Improvements to services require a well-rounded approach. Processes must be aligned with customer needs and expectations if process management is to work.

LEARNING OBJECTIVE 7

What is process-based management?

process-based management
involves managing processes in order to accomplish objectives

EXHIBIT 10-19

Workflows in Functional Process-Based Organizations

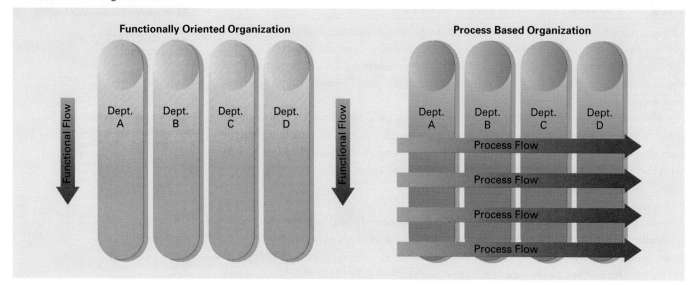

SOURCE: Dennis C. Daly, Patrick L. Dowdle, Robert T. McCarty, and Jerry W. Stevens, *Process Based Management: A Foundation for Business Excellence* (Burleson, TX: CAM-I, 2004).

Customers' exposure to processes should appear seamless and transparent. Positive overtures to customers encourage them to trust the organization and develop an ongoing relationship with it.

The implementation of an ERP system provides an opportunity to shift management away from functions and toward processes.[15] Usually by the time an ERP is proposed, the organization has developed a silo structure. An ERP system consists of process-oriented state-of-the-art modules, which usually require changes to existing processes. Creating processes that reflect the intricacies of an integrated business can only make an ERP system more effective.

GENERAL NEWS NOTE

The Four Cs of Customer-Focused Solutions

Using process-based management to get around silos can be difficult, as most organizations are not set up to deliver customer solutions. Specific changes to organizational structures, incentives, and relationships are needed for an organization to go from selling commoditized products to selling solutions. Difficulties arise, because while knowledge and expertise may exist, those silos are reluctant to release either.

A study of senior executives found that organizations that succeed with process management have been able to increase customer value by engaging in four sets of activities:

Coordination. They establish structural methods and processes that enable employees to improve their focus on customers by harmonizing information and activities across silos.

Cooperation. They encourage employees from all parts of the organization to work together to increase value to customers.

Capability development. They guarantee that enough employees in the organization have the skills to deliver customer-focused solutions, and they specify clearly marked career paths for employees with those skills.

Connection. They develop relationships with outside partners in order to increase the value of solutions in a cost-effective way.

SOURCE: Ranjay Gulati, "Silo Busting: How to Execute on the Promise of Customer Focus," *Harvard Business Review*, May 2007, pp. 98–108.

Airlines

The airline industry's business model is changing from full-service (what AIR CANADA pursued until bankruptcy) to the low-cost model of Southwest. Air Canada should have been more aware of and proactive toward the changes occurring in the marketplace—bankruptcy, as a technique to lower costs, was too late and too drastic. Look at the before- and after-bankruptcy situations at Air Canada: it now has less debt, lower operating revenue, and lower labour costs, but it also has fewer employees and planes.

	Before	After
Debt	$13 billion	$5 billion
Number of full-time equivalent employees	39,996	32,986
Number of planes in operation	232	193
Operating revenue	$9.8 billion	$9.1 billion
Domestic market share	82%	59%
Annual labour bill	$3 billion	$1.9 billion

Air Canada is leaner and its new business model is more capable of competing with WestJet, which is modelled after United States-based Southwest Airlines, the most consistently profitable airline ever. Its management insists that WestJet's extraordinary performance is due to its corporate culture. "The entire environment is conducive to bringing out the best in people . . . [it is] the culture that creates the passion to succeed." Management admits that there is one thing that could spoil WestJet—unionized employees. In contrast to this anti-union attitude at WestJet, Southwest is unionized, and that has not impeded its success. Southwest has been successful because it invested in relationships, not only with front-line employees, but with its unions and supervisors. It makes you think, the most successful and best managed airline—Southwest—is not troubled by its unions. Union relationships need to be managed just like those with other stakeholders.

SOURCES: Peter Verburg, "Prepare for Takeoff," *Canadian Business*, December 25, 2000, pp. 94–99; Jody Hoffer Gittell, "Investing in Relationships," *Harvard Business Review*, June 2001, pp. 28; Keith McArthur, "Don't Blow It," *Report on Business*, February 2004, pp. 55–58; and Keith McArthur and Brent Jang, "How Air Canada Got Back on a New Flight Path," *Globe and Mail*, August 28, 2004, B4–B5.

CHAPTER SUMMARY

1 **Why is cost consciousness of great importance to all members of the organization?**
Cost control is essential to an organization's long-run success. Effective cost control encompasses efforts before, during, and after a cost is incurred. Regardless of the type of cost involved, managers and other employees must exercise attitudes of cost consciousness to provide the best base for cost control. Cost consciousness reflects employees' predisposition toward cost understanding, cost containment, cost avoidance, and cost reduction.

2 **How does a company determine from whom, how much, and when to order inventory?**
Another type of cost control is the careful management of inventory. There are a number of available techniques. Classifying inventory into ABC categories allows management to establish controls over inventory items that are related to the cost and volume of inventory items. A-category items require good inventory controls

and usually are accounted for using a perpetual inventory system. In contrast, the two-bin and red-line systems are acceptable for C-category inventory items because of the limited financial investment that they involve.

Costs associated with inventory can be significant for any company, and sound business practices seek to limit the amounts of those costs. Inventory costs include the costs of purchasing, ordering, carrying, and not carrying inventory. The economic order quantity (EOQ) model determines the purchase order size that minimizes, in total, the costs of ordering and carrying inventory. (This model can also be adapted to find the most economical production run.)

3 **What is outsourcing and when should it be used?**
Outsourcing is contracting with outside suppliers for goods and services that could be produced in-house. Outsourcing is used to reduce costs and improve functionality, but not with core activities.

4 **What is JIT, and how does it affect costs?**
A pull system of production control, such as just-in-time (JIT) manufacturing, involves the purchase or production of inventory only as needs arise. Storage is eliminated except for a minimal level of safety stock.

The JIT philosophy can be applied to some extent in any company having inventories. JIT requires that purchases be made in small quantities and that deliveries be frequent. Production lot sizes are minimized so that many different products can be made on a daily basis. Products are designed for quality, and component parts are standardized to the extent possible. Machine setup time is reduced so that production runs can easily be shifted between products. To eliminate the need for or buildup of buffer inventories between operations, plant layout emphasizes manufacturing cells, and the operating capabilities of all factory equipment are considered.

5 **What is life cycle costing?**
The product life cycle—development, introduction, growth, maturity, and harvest—provides opportunities to control costs. The costs are planned or estimated for each stage. More control can be exercised in the development stage than at any other stage.

6 **What are target costing and value engineering, and in which life cycle stage are these tools used?**
Other tools for sharing information during the design of new products or services include target costing and value engineering. These tools facilitate cost management across the value creation chain in the life cycle design stage. Other types of information often shared within a value creation chain are data on product cost, quality, technology, and research.

7 **What is process-based management?**
Process-based management is concerned with managing processes, comprised of activities, to accomplish objectives. A process-based organization is managed with the explicit recognition that business processes are undertaken to meet or exceed stakeholders' needs, with the customer being the predominant stakeholder.

Key Terms

ABC analysis (p. 608)
Backflush costing (p. 624)
Benchmarking (p. 632)
Carrying costs (p. 610)
Conversion (p. 609)

Cost avoidance (p. 606)
Cost behaviour (p. 602)
Cost consciousness (p. 601)
Cost containment (p. 604)
Cost control system (p. 601)

Cost reduction (p. 606)
Economic order quantity (p. 612)
Empowerment (p. 622)
Horizontal price fixing (p. 604)
JIT manufacturing system (p. 618)
Kaizan costing (p. 632)
Kanban (p. 619)
Lead time (p. 614)
Ordering costs (p. 610)
Order point (p. 614)
Outsourcing (p. 615)
Price fixing (p. 604)
Process-based management (p. 633)

Production cost (p. 609)
Pull system (p. 619)
Purchasing cost (p. 609)
Push system (p. 618)
Red-line system (p. 609)
Safety stock (p. 614)
Setup costs (p. 610)
Survival triplet (p. 632)
Target costing (p. 630)
Two-bin system (p. 608)
Value engineering (p. 630)
Vertical price fixing (p. 604)
Work-out (p. 602)

Points to Remember

Economic Order Quantity

$$EOQ = \sqrt{(2QO \div C)}$$

where EOQ = economic order quantity in units
       Q = estimated quantity in units used per year
       O = estimated cost of placing one order
       C = estimated cost to carry one unit in stock for one year

Economic Production Run

$$EPR = \sqrt{(2QS \div C)}$$

where ERP = economic production run
       Q = estimated quantity in units produced per year
       S = estimated cost of setting up a production run
       C = estimated cost of carrying one unit in stock for one year

Order Point

Order point = (Daily usage × Lead time) + Safety time

DEMONSTRATION PROBLEM

Monica Pickles owns a large office supply store in the university section of London, Ontario. She wonders how many legal-sized writing pads to order at a time, when to place an order, and how many legal pads she should maintain as a safety stock. Upon analysis, she determines the following information:

Annual sales in units	10,400
Number of days the store is open	260
Average lead time in days to receive an order	3
Cost per order	$ 4
Cost of carrying one unit for one year	$0.10
Maximum lead time in days	5
Maximum daily sales in units	50

Required:

a. What is the EOQ?
b. Assuming no safety stock, what is the reorder point?
c. Assuming according to the question, the lead time varies, what will be the safety stock?
d. Assuming according to the question, the daily consumption varies, what will be the safety stock?
e. Using the information calculated in parts (c) and (d), determine a conservative order point.
f. Determine the total order cost using EOQ.
f. Determine the total carrying cost using EOQ.

Solution to Demonstration Problem

a. $EOQ = \sqrt{[(2 \times 10,400 \times \$4.00) \div \$.10]} = 912$
b. Daily usage $= 10,400 \div 260 = 40$ per day
   Order point $= 40 \times 3 = \underline{\underline{120}}$
c. Safety stock for extra lead time $= 40 \times 2 = 80$
d. Safety stock for extra, maximum sales $(50 - 40) \times 5 = 50$
e. Non-safety stock order point   120
   Safety stock for extra lead time   80
   Safety stock for extra sales   <u>50</u>
                250
f. Total ordering cost $=$ Cost per order $\times$ Number of orders
   Number of orders $= 10,400 \div 912 = 11.4$ orders
   Total ordering cost $= \$4 \times 11.4 = \$45.60$
g. Total carrying cost $=$ Average inventory $\times$ Carrying cost per unit
   Average inventory $=$ (EOQ $\div$ 2) $+$ Safety stock $= [(912 \div 2) + 20] = 476$
   Total carrying cost $= 476 \times \$.10 = \$47.60$

End-of-Chapter Materials

SELF-TEST QUESTIONS

(SOLUTIONS APPEAR AT THE END OF THE CHAPTER.)

1. General Electric's technique for reducing costs is called a:
   a. pull system
   b. push system
   c. survival triplet
   d. work-out

2. Which of the following is least likely to be outsourced when controlling costs?
   a. Core activity
   b. Noncore activity
   c. Payroll
   d. Human resources

3. Which is not a step in constraining costs?
   a. Investigate and understand the types of costs incurred by the organization
   b. Reduce the available funding
   c. Communicate the need for cost consciousness to all employees
   d. Compare actual results to targets and analyze for future methods of improvement

4. Which is not a life cycle stage?
   a. Development
   b. Introduction
   c. Exit
   d. Harvest

5. Which is not related to target costing?
   a. Assets
   b. Price
   c. Cost
   d. Profit margin

6. Value engineering is concerned with:
   a. Actual input and actual output
   b. Planned output and actual input
   c. Actual output and planned output
   d. Product design and product price

7. C-category inventory items may justify the use of a:
   a. Just-in-time system
   b. Saving system
   c. Costing system
   d. Two-bin system

8. An EOQ model indicates:
   a. What quantity
   b. The order point
   c. Lead time
   d. Safety stock

9. How many bins does a red-line system have?
   a. 1
   b. 2
   c. 3
   d. 4

10. Backflush costing records product costs:
   a. Before production
   b. With LIFO
   c. After production
   d. With FIFO

QUESTIONS

1. In cost control, at what points in time can control over an activity be exerted? Why are these points of cost control important?

2. Explain the meaning and significance of cost consciousness.

3. Why is on-the-job training an important component in the process of instilling cost consciousness within an organization?

4. What factors may cause costs to change from one period to another? Which of these are subject to cost containment and which are not? What creates the difference in controllability?

5. What options does a company have when its costs change because of higher prices from suppliers or because of increased costs of complying with government regulations?

6. Compare and contrast general and specific price level changes.

7. In an ABC analysis of inventory, what are the characteristics of the items that would be placed in each category?

8. List four costs included in each of the following categories: ordering inventory, carrying inventory, and not carrying inventory. How does incurring costs in one of these categories affect the costs in the other categories?

9. Describe some major considerations in deciding from whom to buy. How have the considerations changed over time?

10. In buyer–supplier relationships, why is it desirable for the supplier to be located geographically close to the buyer?

11. Assuming that all costs in the EOQ formula could be determined with absolute precision, discuss some reasons that a company might not buy at the economic order quantity amount.

12. Why is it said that JIT views inventory as a liability rather than as an asset?

13. What are the primary goals of the JIT philosophy, and how does JIT attempt to achieve these goals?

14. What is empowerment, and why does it frequently accompany the adoption of JIT?

15. "Philosophically, JIT is aimed at minimizing time, space, and energy." Discuss what you think was meant by the person making this statement.

16. Why are decisions that are made during the development stage of a product so important?

17. Give three examples of industries in which time to market is critical. Give three examples of industries in which time to market is almost irrelevant. Discuss the reasons for importance or lack thereof in each industry.

18. Why is a product life cycle stage such an important consideration in managing production costs?

19. How do target costing and value engineering facilitate the exchange of information between firms in the same value creation chain?

20. As a decision-making structure, cross-functional teams are used extensively in business today. What advantages might be gained by organizing a cross-functional team to design a new product rather than delegating the entire design responsibility to the in-house engineering department?

21. Which stakeholder is the most important in process-based management?

EXERCISES

1. (LO 1) Below are various actions taken by management teams to control costs. For each item listed, indicate whether the action indicates an application of cost understanding, cost containment, cost avoidance, or cost reduction.
   a. A company cancelled its contract with an external firm that it used for training in computerized manufacturing methods. At the same time, the firm created an in-house training department. Even though the in-house training will be more expensive, management believes the extra cost to be justified because of the flexibility in scheduling training sessions.
   b. A municipality, faced with a 13% increase in health insurance premiums, raised the deductible on its coverage, and was able to keep health insurance costs at the prior year's level.
   c. Anticipating a rise in raw material prices, a manufacturing organization used forward contracts to acquire a year's supply of materials at the current prices.
   d. Because beef by-product costs had been rising over the past year, a dog food manufacturer increased the proportion of pork by-products relative to the content of beef by-products in the mix of its dog food.
   e. Because a small foreign country offered a 10-year income tax holiday for new businesses, a Canadian leather-goods manufacturer relocated its production facilities to that country.
   f. Because it had suffered large losses caused by currency fluctuations, a Canadian importer instituted a practice of hedging its currency translation risk.
   g. After the new union contract was signed, wage rates for highly skilled workers rose by 18%. As a result, a tool-and-die maker elected to automate three of its higher-volume production processes. This decision resulted in a cost savings of $1,400,000 over a period of five years.

2. (LO 1) You have just been appointed director of Youth Hotline, a not-for-profit organization that operates a phone bank for individuals experiencing emotional difficulties. The phones are staffed by qualified social workers and psychologists who are paid on an hourly basis. In your first week at Youth Hotline, you took the following actions:
   a. Increased the funding appropriation for advertising of the Hotline
   b. Exchanged the more expensive pushbutton, cream-coloured designer telephones for regular, pushbutton desk telephones
   c. Eliminated the call-forwarding feature installed on all telephones since Youth Hotline will now be staffed 24 hours a day
   d. Eliminated two paid clerical positions and replaced these individuals with volunteers
   e. Ordered blank notepads for the counsellors to keep by their phones; the old notepads (stock now depleted) had the Youth Hotline logo and address printed on them
   f. Negotiated a new contract with the telephone company. Youth Hotline will now pay a flat rate of $100 per month, regardless of the number of telephones installed by the Hotline. The previous contract charged the organization $10 for every telephone. At the time that contract was signed, Youth Hotline only had ten telephones. However, with the increased staff, you plan to install at least five additional telephones

   Required:
   Indicate whether each of the actions represents cost understanding, cost containment, cost avoidance, or cost reduction. Some actions may have more than one implication; if they do, indicate the reason.

3. (LO 2, 3, 4) A business publication to which you subscribe has recently included a crossword puzzle listing the items on the right below. Your roommate has provided you with the terms listed on the left below, and has challenged you to match the numbered items on the right to the lettered items on the left:

EXERCISES

a. Push system
b. ABC analysis
c. Outsourcing
d. Lead time
e. Two-bin system
f. Pull system
g. Setup cost
h. Kanban
i. Manufacturing cell

1. The process of contracting with external parties to provide inputs or services
2. Time from placing an order to receiving the goods
3. U-shaped grouping of workers or machines
4. Segregates inventory into three groups based on cost and volume
5. Inventory is acquired/produced no sooner than it is needed/sold
6. Inventory is produced and stored before it is sold
7. Direct and indirect labour costs of getting equipment ready for a production run
8. When it is necessary to begin using materials from the second bin, a purchase order is issued to refill the first bin
9. A system using cards to control the flow of material or units between work centres

4. (LO 2) Following is a list of techniques used to control inventories.
   a. Perpetual inventory system
   b. Daily inventory counts
   c. Monthly inventory counts
   d. Annual inventory count
   e. Limited access to storage areas
   f. Open-access display areas
   g. Red-line system
   h. Two-bin system
   i. Specific identification inventory method
   j. Weighted-average cost flow
   k. Rigorous, in-depth demand estimation (EOQ, lead time, order point, safety stock)

   Required:
   Management of the company for which you are working as an intern has asked you to indicate whether each of the items just listed would most likely be used for A-, B-, or C-type inventory items. More than one type of inventory item may be indicated for a given technique.

5. (LO 2) The president of a company for which you are consulting has requested that you help personnel managing inventory to classify each of the following items as a cost of ordering (O), carrying (C), or not carrying (N) inventory. Use N/A for items not fitting any of the categories.
   a. Contribution margin lost on a sale because of a stockout
   b. Spoilage of products in storage
   c. Opportunity cost of capital invested in inventory
   d. Inventory storage cost
   e. Wages of staff in purchasing agent's office
   f. Long-distance calls to vendor to get prices
   g. Property tax on inventory
   h. Freight-out on sales of inventory
   i. Purchase order forms, receiving report forms, disbursement voucher forms
   j. Insurance on warehouse and its inventory contents
   k. Extra freight on rush orders necessitated by stockouts
   l. Freight-in on special purchases/orders
   m. Postage to send purchase orders
   n. Handling costs for products on hand
   o. Purchase price of products

EXERCISES

6. (LO 2) Your best friend knows that you have taken a course in managerial accounting. He has a new business and has asked you to determine the carrying costs for an item costing $12, given the following per-unit cost information:

Shipping cost	$0.04
Storage cost	0.15
Handling cost	0.05
Production labour cost	0.95
Insurance	0.06
Import taxes (per unit)	0.29

7. (LO 2) In a job interview, you are given the following information as part of a qualifying test for the job. Rows (a) through (e) below represent five independent situations, each with a missing item of data.

	EOQ	(Q) Quantity Used Per Year	(O) Ordering Cost	(C) Carrying Cost
a.	?	8,100	$1	$2
b.	40	?	$2	$4
c.	100	1,000	$15	?
d.	20	400	$5	?
e.	30	150	?	$3

Required:
Provide the missing numbers.

8. (LO 2) Archer Toy Company manufactures its Little Red Wagon. Among the parts needed to manufacture each wagon are two axles and four wheels. These parts are purchased from external vendors. The annual ordering costs, carrying costs, and demand for each follow:

Component	Ordering Cost	Carrying Cost	Demand
Axles	$20	$0.50	2,000
Wheels	$36	$3.00	4,000

Required:
a. Compute the EOQ for each component.
b. Compute the average inventory level for each component assuming that no safety stock is carried.
c. Write a memo to management discussing any problems you perceive in managing the inventories of these two components. Also, suggest solutions to any problems you identify.

9. (LO 2) Jean Lefleur is a British Columbia salmon farmer. His fish eat approximately 7,300 kilograms of feed per year. On the average, 18 days go by from the time he places an order until the feed is delivered. It costs Jean $0.75 to place each order and $0.48 per kilogram for the annual carrying cost.
Required:
a. What is Jean's EOQ?
b. Assuming he holds no safety stock, calculate Jean's order point.
c. Assuming the lead time varies by three days, calculate a safety stock.
d. Assuming the average daily consumption per fish varies 10%, calculate a safety stock.
e. Using the information calculated in parts (c) and (d), determine a conservative order point.

10. (LO 3) A company that produces 50,000 bicycles each year is considering the purchase of wheels from an outside vendor. This outsourcing would enable the company to increase its production by 15%. The company would pay the vendor $60 for two wheels, whereas it now costs $52 to produce the two wheels. Variable manufacturing costs are $28 per bicycle where the company produces the wheels in-house, but would decrease to $25 per bicycle if the wheels were outsourced. Other unit variable costs would remain at $80. The company sells all the bicycles for $280 each.
Required:
What would be the increase or decrease in net income for this outsourcing project?

EXERCISES

11. (LO 6) Answer both parts.
    a. How does kaizen costing differ from traditional cost reduction in standard costing systems?
    b. Explain *two* problems that can arise when firms use target costing.

12. (LO 6) Define target costing in regard to the product life cycle.

13. (LO 6) Identify which of the following statements represents the *main* objective of kaizen costing and explain the statement.
    a. Kaizen costing accumulates all costs that are associated with a short- or long-term project.
    b. Kaizen costing simplifies the computation of costs in a just-in-time environment.
    c. Kaizen costing reduces costs and improves quality through continuous improvement.
    d. Kaizen costing evaluates the amount of costs related to the quality of a product.

14. (LO 6) Kaizen costs are generally used during which period of the life cycle of a product?

    Exercises 10 and 12–14 are an extract from *Management Accounting 2 Examination*, published by the Certified General Accountants Association of Canada (© CGA-Canada 2003). Reprinted with permission.

15. (LO 6) Describe in detail the objective of kaizen costing.

    Extract from *Management Accounting 2 Examination*, published by the Certified General Accountants Association of Canada (© CGA-Canada 2002). Reprinted with permission.

16. (LO 1) Which of the following topics in accounting integrates the subjects of management accounting, information systems, and strategy? Explain your choice.
    a. Contribution margin analysis
    b. Relevant cost analysis
    c. Activity-based analysis
    d. Management control

    Extract from *Management Accounting 2 Examination*, published by the Certified General Accountants Association of Canada (© CGA-Canada 1998). Reprinted with permission.

17. (LO 2) In an effort to minimize its carrying costs, Holbrook Manufacturing decided to reduce its safety stock of raw materials by 75%. What is the effect of this decision on Holbrook's economic order quantity (EOQ)?

    Extract from *Management Accounting 1 Examination*, published by the Certified General Accountants Association of Canada (© CGA-Canada 1999). Reprinted with permission.

18. (LO 4) In a JIT production system, what would be the ideal ratio of manufacturing time to processing time? Explain

    Extract from *Management Accounting 1 Examination*, published by the Certified General Accountants Association of Canada (© CGA-Canada 2000). Reprinted with permission.

19. (LO 6) When identifying benchmarking partners, which of the following is not a critical factor for consideration? Explain your answer.
    a. Sizes of the partners
    b. Locations of the partners
    c. Number of partners
    d. Degree of trust among partners

    Extract from *Management Accounting 2 Examination*, published by the Certified General Accountants Association of Canada (© CGA-Canada 2000). Reprinted with permission.

20. (LO 6) What is the process of comparing the performance of one organization to other organizations and/or ideal performance standards? Explain your answer.
    a. Nonfinancial performance measurement
    b. Value-for-money auditing
    c. Benchmarking
    d. Opportunism

    Exercises 11 and 20 are an extract from *Management Accounting 2 Examination*, published by the Certified General Accountants Association of Canada (© CGA-Canada 1999). Reprinted with permission.

21. (LO 7) Describe the process at your local fast-food restaurant to serve customers.

PROBLEMS

1. (LO 1) Temporary or part-time employees are sometimes hired to:
   a.   Draw house plans for construction companies
   b.   Make desserts for restaurants
   c.   Perform legal research for law firms
   d.   Prepare tax returns for CA firms
   e.   Sell clothing in department stores during the Christmas season
   f.   Serve as security guards
   g.   Tailor men's suits for department stores
   h.   Teach evening courses at universities
   i.   Work as medical doctors in the emergency rooms of hospitals
   j.   Write articles for monthly magazines

   Required:
   For each job listed, suggest potential advantages and disadvantages of using temporary or part-time employees from the perspective of the employer.

2. (LO 2) The following 20 items, along with unit costs and volumes of sales last year, are part of an ABC analysis of Andy's Diving Goods:

Items		Unit Cost	Volume Sold
Fins (pair):	Men's	$ 3.00	320
	Women's	2.50	210
	Children's	1.80	66
Masks:	Men's	4.00	280
	Women's	3.40	172
	Children's	2.80	40
Weight belts:	Men's	1.80	63
	Women's	1.70	46
	Children's	1.20	12
Snorkels		1.20	420
Air tanks		36.00	42
Meters and connections		42.00	36
Wet suits:	Men's	60.00	170
	Women's	52.00	102
	Children's	42.00	12
Weights:	Large	2.00	160
	Medium	1.50	180
	Small	1.25	64
Underwater watches		25.00	32
Ear plugs		0.25	120

   Required:
   a.   Rearrange the items in descending order of magnitude according to the result of multiplying cost times volume. Use these headings: Items; Unit Cost; Volume Sold; and Cost × Volume.
   b.   Classify the items in three groups: A-items (to include 20% of the total volume sold); B-items (to include the next 30% of the total value sold); and C-items (to include the final 50% of the value sold).
   c.   Recommend a technique to control each group (i.e., you should recommend three techniques in total, one for each group).

3. (LO 2) BetterMetalWorks has been evaluating its policies with respect to control of the costs of sheet metal, one of the firm's major component materials. The firm's controller has gathered the following financial data, which may be pertinent to controlling costs associated with the sheet metal:

Ordering Costs

Annual salary of purchasing department manager	$72,500
Depreciation of equipment in purchasing department	$45,300
Cost per order for purchasing department supplies	$0.95
Typical phone expense per order placed	$3.20
Monthly expense for heat and light in purchasing department	$900

Carrying Costs

Annual depreciation on material storage building	$35,000
Annual inventory insurance premium (per dollar of inventory value)	$0.15
Annual property tax on material storage building	$3,700
Obsolescence cost, per dollar of average annual inventory	$0.12
Annual salary of security officer assigned to the material storage building	$38,000

Required:

a. Which of the ordering costs would BetterMetalWorks' controller take into account in using the EOQ model? Explain.

b. Which of the carrying costs would BetterMetalWorks' controller take into account in using the EOQ model? Explain.

4. (LO 2) Fortress Construction Company's requirement for cement amounts to 80,000 bags per year. Cement costs $4 a bag; carrying cost is $6 per unit per year; and processing a purchase order costs $24. The lead time is 30 days.

Required:

a. Find the EOQ.

b. Calculate the total cost of ordering and carrying inventory for a period of one year.

c. Determine the order point.

d. How does total inventory cost change if the firm orders in a lot size of 4,000 units rather than the EOQ?

e. Why might the company prefer to order in a lot size of 4,000 units rather than the EOQ?

5. (LO 2) Each of the following independent cases has a missing amount.

	Case A	Case B	Case C	Case D	Case E
Order point	400	*b*	120	300	500
Daily usage	20	30	*c*	15	*e*
Lead time (days)	12	10	7	*d*	5
Safety stock	*a*	60	50	30	60

Required:

Supply the missing amounts for the lettered spaces.

6. (LO 4) Items (a) through (i) describe features of just-in-time systems. The descriptions labelled D, U, and T also relate to JIT systems. Indicate by letter which of the three categories applies to each item. More than one category may apply to an item.

D—desired intermediate result of using JIT

U—ultimate goal of JIT

T—technique associated with JIT

a. Reducing setup costs

b. Reducing total cost of producing and carrying inventory

c. Pulling purchases and production through the system based on sales demand

d. Designing products to minimize design changes after production starts

e. Monitoring quality on a continuous basis

f. Using manufacturing cells

g. Minimizing inventory stored

h. Using backflush costing

i. Having workers and machines continuously monitor quality during processing

7. (LO 4) The next table gives symbols for areas where changes occur as a result of the implementation of JIT. Categorize items (a) through (q) in the list that follows the table by associating the appropriate symbol with each item.

PROBLEMS

Symbol	Area of Change Related to Use of JIT
PSR&D	Purchasing, Supplier Relationships, and Distribution
PD	Product Design
PP	Production Processing
PL	Plant Layout
JP	JIT Philosophy
AI	Accounting Implications of JIT

a. Management recognizes that employees often know best how to improve operations.
b. Careful design minimizes the number of subsequent changes.
c. The ideal is one vendor for each part or raw material.
d. Setup time is reduced.
e. Layout is intended to minimize production time.
f Long-term contracts are negotiated.
g. Physical arrangement is conducive to a worker's handling a greater number of tasks.
h. Inventory is viewed as a liability.
i. A single conversion account combines direct labour and overhead.
j. Fewer costs need to be arbitrarily allocated.
k. Workers and machines monitor quality during processing.
l. U-shaped groupings of workers and machines are used.
m. Many setup tasks are performed while machines are running.
n. Layout makes the use of visual controls more effective.
o. The plan is to use the fewest parts (reduce product complexity).
p. Creative thinking doesn't cost anything.
q. As many parts as possible are standardized.

8. (LO 2) The company by which you are employed as a cost accountant requires 150,000 litres of a special chemical per year and operates 300 days per year. The cost of placing an order is $60 while the annual carrying costs are $5 per litre. Use of the chemical is mainly steady, but on rare occasions it can increase by 10% for a day. The delivery time from the supplier is 10 days.

Required:
a. Compute the economic order quantity.
b. Compute the safety stock.
c. Compute the reorder point.
d. Compute the safety stock and reorder point assuming the delivery time takes an additional two days.

9. (LO 2) The XYZ Manufacturing Company requires 250,000 kilograms of a semi-precious metal for its manufacturing operations as an input. It operates 300 days per year. The cost of placing an order is $750 while the annual carrying costs are $9 per kilogram. Use of the semi-precious metal is steady, but on rare occasions it can increase by 100 kilograms a day. The delivery time from the supplier is seven days.

Required:
a. Compute the economic order quantity.
b. Compute the safety stock.
c. Compute the reorder point.
d. Compute the safety stock and reorder point assuming the delivery time takes an additional three days.

Problems 8 and 9 are an extract from *Management Accounting 1 Examination*, published by the Certified General Accountants Association of Canada (© CGA-Canada 1998). Reprinted with permission.

10. (LO 2) Penturn Limited is a St. John's-based technology firm. Due to the company's distance from the mainland, it is sometimes more economical to make certain products rather than outsourcing them. Consequently, Penturn decided to produce Part N232 internally. A secondary decision is to determine what batch size to employ in producing N232.

Part N232 is a precision product. The basic material at standard will be 481,000 kilograms at a cost of $8,177,000. Production will take three direct labour hours per unit at a total cost

PROBLEMS

of $3,330,000. Variable overhead costs excluding the cost of setting up a production run are $480,000 for a year. It costs $24,000 to set up a production run for Part N232.

Each unit of N232 costs $47 per year to store and 37,000 units will be needed for a year.
Required:
a.   Determine the optimal production run for Part N232.
b.   What is the total cost of Part N232, at standard, including storage?

11.   (LO 3) The Grand River Bank is considering outsourcing the processing of its accounts payable function. As a regional bank, Grand River has centralized its accounts payable function. There are seven accounts payable clerks and one supervisor. You as the controller have received the following information on the accounts payable process from the assistant controller.

Accounts payable clerk, average annual salary	$27,000
Accounts payable supervisor	$41,700
Supplies	$3,400
Computer costs	$22,500
Controller's salary	$110,000
Benefits	18% of salaries
Annual cost of 1,000 square feet of space, utilities	$120,000
Number of accounts payable processed per year	24,000

You have been quoted a price of $18 per account payable by a firm specializing in processing accounts payable. In looking over the above information, you recognize that about 5% of your time is devoted to the accounts payable function, and in the future that 5% will merely be spread over your other activities. You will use the space now occupied by the accounts payable function for larger offices for existing accounting employees. Your salary is 80,000 per year.
Required:
Should the accounts payable function be outsourced? What are some other concerns with outsourcing?

12.   (LO 3) The Dap Appliance Stores has had its own delivery trucks. However, its board of directors has asked you, the controller, to consider outsourcing the delivery of appliances.

A local delivery firm has quoted a cost of $40 per appliance and agreed to follow existing delivery practices (i.e., delivery within one week and within three hours of the time promised). Existing costs for delivering 90,000 appliances include:

30 drivers and helpers, with benefits	$1,062,000
Fuel and repairs	450,000
Cost of trucks, gross book value	900,000
Delivery supervisor salary with benefits	50,000
Delivery scheduler salary, with benefits	38,000
Savings on facilities	700,000
Savings on overhead	950,000

Required:
Should the delivery of the appliances be outsourced? What are some of the concerns with outsourcing?

13.   (LO 3) Centrix Manufacturing is always considering opportunities to reduce production costs. At present, the company has its own salesforce. Remee Marketing has offered to market and sell Centrix's industrial products for a commission of 12% of the cost of goods manufactured. You, as the management accountant, are considering the offer. One of the analysts has gathered the following information, based on the current budget.

Sales	$900,000
Cost of goods manufactured	540,000
Sales and marketing employee costs, with benefits	47,000
Facilities, utilities for selling and marketing	15,000
Other selling and marketing costs	21,000
Vice-president, marketing and sales, with benefits	150,000

Upon closer investigation of her contract, you realize that you cannot terminate the vice-president of marketing and sales. Nevertheless, you can assign her to the administration of the contract with Remee, which will take about 10% of her time. The remainder of her

PROBLEMS

time will be used to develop new business opportunities. Consequently, you realize that there will be no immediate savings related to the VP's $150,000 salary.

Required:

Should the marketing and selling be outsourced? What are some of the concerns with this arrangement?

14. (LO 3) The Municipality of Four Rivers is considering contracting out its telephone centre. Telephone activities have grown steadily over the years, and the present arrangement is inadequate for the telephone volume. There are two alternatives: expand the present telephone services, or outsource the telephone operation to a company specializing in telephone centres. If the telephone operation is outsourced, most of the current employees would lose their jobs because they do not wish to relocate to the new telephone centre location. Regardless of where the call centre is located, customers will call a toll-free number. Moreover, if the telephone centre were outsourced, more multilingual operators would be available. The following annual costs have been identified.

Cost of Present Telephone Centre

Labour costs, benefits	$320,000
Space rent	40,000
Telephone costs	70,000
Miscellaneous	30,000

If the telephone centre were outsourced, office equipment would be sold to the new telephone operator for $15,000. The equipment originally cost $85,000 and the book value is currently, $20,000. The municipality would no longer need to rent space for the telephone operations. Existing telephone centre employees have the opportunity to transfer to the outsourcer, in which case their salaries would be paid by the outsourcer. The outsourcer is asking for $500,000 per year.

Required:

Should the telephone operation be outsourced? What are some of the concerns with this arrangement?

15. (LO 4) The question facing Centrix Manufacturing is whether to use just-in-time with its Lovell manufacturing plant or to remain with a push process. There are many factors to consider, but in the end, the decision must be economically viable. The controller has asked you to evaluate the costs and benefits of a change in plant layout. You meet with the production and marketing managers and then you compile the following estimates:
- Total sales will increase by 25% to $6,000,000 due to a decrease in product cycle time required under the new plant layout. The average contribution margin (sales dollars minus variable costs) is 35% of sales.
- The costs of carrying inventory will decrease by 30% because of an expected decrease in work-in-process inventory. Currently, the annual average carrying value of work-in-process inventory is $300,000. The annual inventory financing cost is 10%.
- The transition to JIT manufacturing will cost $300,000 for moving and reinstallation equipment.

Required:

Should just-in-time be implemented/? What are your concerns with JIT?

16. (LO 4) Dap Appliance Stores is considering just-in-time for its appliance business. There will be major changes to its operations.
- Sales will increase by $1,000,000 because of a decrease in the time it takes to bring appliances from the manufacturers. The average contribution margin (sales dollars minus variable costs) is 28%.
- Inventory-related costs will decrease by 25% because of an expected decrease in inventory being carried in the retail outlets and warehouse. Presently, the annual average cost of carrying inventory is $400,000, and the annual cost of inventory financing is 10%.
- Facility changing and computerization will cost $300,000.

Required:

Should just-in-time be implemented/? What are your concerns with JIT?

17. (LO 5) New environmental requirements have caused Jamborg Appliances Company to be responsible for the eventual recycling or destruction of its environmentally harmful appliances. This new law will lead to a cost of $50 per appliance, plus a fixed cost of

PROBLEMS

$1 million to establish the disposal operation. With these new costs, Jamborg needs to consider the next 10 years, which is the estimated life of the appliances. In view of its downward demand curve, it could charge $700 or $800 per unit.

	$700 Appliance	$800 Appliance
Anticipated units sold	30,000	20,000
Price per unit	$700	$800
Variable costs per unit	$350	$400
Disposal fee per unit	$50	$50

The fixed costs will be the same for both the 20,000 level of production and the 30,000 level of production, $5 million, plus the additional $1 million for the disposal operation.

Required:

For the remaining years of this product, which price would you select? Justify your decision.

18. (LO 5) There is generally a downward demand curve facing all products. In a practical sense, this means that if a lower price is charged, more product can be sold. In the research and development stage when the costs of the entire life cycle can be planned, it is important to determine the price in order to optimize profitability. Kosmos Tractors is in the research and development stage for a small tractor for developing countries. The 55 horsepower tractor can be sold for $3,000 with anticipated 10-year lifetime sales of 100,000 or at $4,000 for anticipated 10-year lifetime sales of 50,000.

	$3,000 Tractor	$4,000 Tractor
Anticipated units sold	100,000	50,000
Price per unit	$3,000	$4,000
Variable costs per unit	$1,700	$1,900
Fixed costs	$40 million	$37.5 million

Required:

What price would you recommend? Why?

19. (LO 6) Kosmos Tractors manufactures farm tractors, farm equipment, and construction equipment for a worldwide market. Kosmos needs a full product line in each of its equipment categories, in order to allow customers to stay with the same equipment as their requirements increase or decrease. Marketing has determined that there is an adequate market for a 140 horsepower four-wheel-drive tractor that would be designed and sourced in Canada but assembled in seven other Kosmos plants around the world. The sales price before sales taxes and transportation costs to customers would be $27,000. Kosmos expects to earn (before income taxes) a net margin of 18% on sales. Parts, components, and assembly include:

Engine	$2,200
Transmission	900
Wheels and tires	900
Frame	800
Ancillary power takeoff, etc.	300
Miscellaneous parts	900
Direct labour	2,500
Manufacturing overhead	1,300
Depreciation	1,000
Share of this year's R&D	2,000
Painting	1,000
Warranty	4,000
Marketing and selling	2,500

Required:

With the target price of $27,000 and the other costs, determine if it is economically viable to produce the new tractor. What should the target cost be?

20. (LO 6) You own a fast-food restaurant in a small town in Northern Ontario. Because of the limited population size, the major fast-food restaurants have refused to locate in your town.

PROBLEMS

You have observed the crew members who work five-hour shifts performing the following activities: serving customers, preparing food, delivering food, cleaning, and stocking. You have also measured how long crew members take to do their assigned activities.

Activity	Actual Time Requirements
Serve customers	30 seconds per order
Prepare food	30 seconds per order
Deliver food	5 seconds per order
Clean	20 minutes per shift
Stock	15 minutes per shift

The actual time required for an activity does not necessarily mean that it has been done satisfactorily. During the observations, three crew members worked in the preparation area, where two computer monitors displayed orders entered with registers A and B. A maximum of six orders were displayed on a screen, which limited the number of customers being served. For most of the day this is not a problem, however, during peak periods this capacity limited the speed of serving customers and led to many customers' waiting to order or leaving without ordering. This was unnecessary as there was a second unused line with two monitors to the left of the first set of monitors. The second line could double capacity.

The manager does not schedule crew members based on the day's expected orders, which are predictable, and so there are sometimes inappropriate numbers of employees working. This overstaffing results in a recording of more employee time than it should take for the activities accomplished. Consequently, the standard for preparing food should be 15 seconds and not the actual time of 30 seconds.

The manager has the opportunity to schedule crew members appropriately for peak periods and to explicitly direct their activities. This is a particular problem with cleaning, which gets less time than is required although "clean" is only vaguely defined. A consultant reviewed your fast-food restaurant's cleanliness and deemed it insufficient. She noted that there were trays and food packaging on unoccupied tables, the seating areas and floors were dirty, the garbage containers were full, and the restrooms were filthy.

Required:

How can you be more effective in using employee resources? Please explain why you believe each of your suggestions would be effective and add value.

21. (LO 2, 4) John Holster, controller for ProCorp Inc., has been examining all phases of ProCorp's manufacturing operations in order to reduce costs and improve efficiency. The reason for urgency is that the company's salesforce has been complaining about lost sales caused by product stockouts, and the production people are unhappy about downtime caused by shortages of raw material. Holster believes that the company may be losing as much as $220,000 in revenue as a result of these problems.

ProCorp manufactures only one product: boomerangs (trademarked "Boomers"). The single raw material used in making Boomers is plastic, with each Boomer requiring 0.5 kilograms of red plastic. ProCorp expects to manufacture 300,000 Boomers this year with a steady demand through the entire year. The ordering costs for clerical processing are $30 per order of plastic. There is a three-day delay between placement of an order and receipt of the inventory. The carrying costs for storage, handling, insurance, and interest are $0.72 per Boomer unit per year.

Required:

a. Discuss the general benefits of a well-managed inventory policy.

b. By using the economic order quantity formula, ProCorp Inc. determined that the optimal economic order quantity is 2,500 kilograms of plastic, which will produce 5,000 units.

   i.   Discuss how an increase in each of the following components will affect the economic order quantity: annual sales demand; ordering costs; and carrying costs for storage, handling, insurance, and interest.

   ii. Determine the number of times ProCorp will order plastic during the year.

c. ProCorp Inc., while reviewing its safety stock policy, has determined that an appropriate safety stock is 1,250 kilograms of plastic, which will produce 2,500 units.

   i.   Describe the factors that affect an appropriate safety stock level.

  ii. List the effects of maintaining an appropriate safety stock level on ProCorp's short-term and long-term profitability.

  iii. Identify the effect that a well-implemented just-in-time inventory procedure will have on safety stock level, and explain why it will have this effect.

(CMA adapted)

22. (LO 4) The management at Megafilters Inc. has been discussing the possible implementation of a just-in-time (JIT) production system at its Manitoba plant, where oil filters and air filters for heavy construction equipment and large, off-road vehicles are manufactured. The Metal Stamping Department at the Manitoba plant has already instituted a JIT system for controlling raw materials inventory, but the remainder of the plant is still discussing how to proceed with the implementation of this concept. Some of the other department managers have grown increasingly cautious about the JIT process after hearing about the problems that have arisen in the Metal Stamping Department.

Robert Goertz, manager of the Manitoba plant, is a strong proponent of the JIT production system and recently made the following statement at a meeting of all departmental managers. "Just-in-time is often referred to as a management philosophy of doing business rather than a technique for improving efficiency on the plant floor. We will all have to make many changes in the way we think about our employees, our suppliers, and our customers if we are going to be successful in using just-in-time procedures. Rather than dwelling on some of the negative things you have heard from the Metal Stamping Department, I want each of you to prepare a list of things we can do to make a smooth transition to the just-in-time philosophy of management for the rest of the plant."

Required:

a. The just-in-time management philosophy emphasizes objectives for the general improvement of a production system. Describe several important objectives of this philosophy.

b. Discuss several actions that Megafilters Inc., can take to ease the transition to a just-in-time production system at the Manitoba plant.

c. For the JIT production system to be successful, Megafilters Inc. must establish appropriate relationships with its vendors, employees, and customers. Describe each of these three relationships.

(CMA adapted)

23. (LO 4) AgriCorp is a manufacturer of farm equipment that is sold by a network of distributors throughout Canada. A majority of the distributors are also repair centres for AgriCorp equipment and depend on AgriCorp's Service Division to provide a timely supply of spare parts.

In an effort to reduce the inventory costs incurred by the Service Division, Richard Bachman, division manager, implemented a just-in-time inventory program on June 1, 2010, the beginning of the company's fiscal year. Because JIT has been in place for a year, Bachman has asked the division controller, Janice Grady, to determine the effect the program has had on the Service Division's financial performance. Grady has been able to document the following results of JIT implementation:

a. The Service Division's average inventory declined from $550,000 to $150,000.

b. Projected annual insurance costs of $80,000 declined 60% because of the lower average inventory.

c. A leased 8,000-square-metre warehouse, previously used for raw material storage, was not used at all during the year. The division paid $11,200 annual rent for the warehouse and was able to sublet three-quarters of the building to several tenants at $2.50 per square metre, while the balance of the space remained idle.

d. Two warehouse employees whose services were no longer needed were transferred on June 1, 2010, to the Purchasing Department to assist in the coordination of the JIT program. The annual salary expense for these two employees totalled $38,000 and continued to be charged to the indirect labour portion of fixed overhead.

e. Despite the use of overtime to manufacture 7,500 spare parts, lost sales caused by stockouts totalled 3,800 spare parts. The overtime premium incurred amounted to $5.60 per part manufactured. The use of overtime to fill spare parts orders was immaterial prior to June 1, 2010.

PROBLEMS

Prior to the decision to implement the JIT inventory program, AgriCorp's Service Division had completed its 2010–2011 expected financial performance. The division's pro forma income statement, without any adjustments for JIT inventory, is presented next. AgriCorp's borrowing rate related to inventory is 9% after income taxes. All AgriCorp pro forma income statements are prepared using an effective tax rate of 40%.

Agricorp Service Division
Pro Forma Income Statement
for the Year Ending May 31, 2011

Sales (280,000 spare parts)		$ 6,160,000
Cost of goods sold		
Variable	$2,660,000	
Fixed	1,120,000	(3,780,000)
Gross profit		$ 2,380,000
Selling and administrative expense		
Variable	$ 700,000	
Fixed	555,000	(1,255,000)
Operating income		$ 1,125,000
Other income		75,000
Income before interest and taxes		$ 1,200,000
Interest expense		(150,000)
Income before income taxes		$ 1,050,000
Income taxes		(420,000)
Net income		$ 630,000

Required:

a. Calculate the after-tax cash savings (loss) for AgriCorp's Service Division that resulted during the 2010–2011 fiscal year from the adoption of the JIT program.

b. Identify and explain the factors, other than financial, that should be considered before a company implements a JIT program.

(CMA adapted)

24. (LO 1) Peter Babic, president of the Newmarket Company (NMC), sat dejectedly in his chair after reviewing the year 2011 first-quarter financial report on one of the organization's core products: a standard, five-speed transmission (Product Number 2122) used in the heavy equipment industry in the manufacture of earth-moving equipment. Some of the information in the report follows:

Market Report, Product Number 2122, Quarter 1, 2011

Sales data:	
Total sales (dollars) Quarter 1, 2011	$4,657,500
Total sales (units) Quarter 1, 2011	3,450
Total sales (dollars) Quarter 1, 2010	$6,405,000
Total sales (units) Quarter 1, 2010	4,200
Market data:	
Industry unit sales, Quarter 1, 2011	40,000
Industry unit sales, Quarter 1, 2010	32,000
Industry average sales price, Quarter 1, 2011	$1,310
Industry average sales price, Quarter 1, 2010	$1,640
Profit data:	
NMC average gross profit per unit, Quarter 1, 2011	$45
NMC average profit per unit, Quarter 1, 2010	$160
Industry average profit per unit, Quarter 1, 2011	$75
Industry average profit per unit, Quarter 1, 2010	$140

NMC's strategy for this transmission is to compete on the basis of price. NMC's transmission offers no features that allow it to be differentiated from those of major competitors and NMC's level of quality is similar to the average of the industry.

Also on Mr. Babic's desk was a report from his business intelligence unit. Mr. Babic underlined some key pieces of information in the report. The underlined items follow:

PROBLEMS

1. Commodity transmission components (nuts, bolts, etc.), which all major transmission producers acquire from specialty vendors, decreased in price by approximately 5% from January 2010 to January 2011.
2. Two major competitors moved their major assembly operations to China from the United States in early 2010. These competitors are believed to have the lowest unit production cost in the industry.
3. A third major competitor ceased manufacturing major gear components and began outsourcing these parts from a Mexican firm in mid-2010. This firm increased its market share in 2010 from 10% to 14% after a major decrease in sales price.
4. NMC's production operations did not change in any material respect from 2010 to 2011.
5. NMC manufactures approximately 83% of the components used in the heavy industrial transmission. The industry norm is to make 57% of the components.
6. For the balance of 2011, industry experts agree that quarterly demand for the heavy industrial transmission will be even higher than the levels posted for the first quarter of 2011.

Required:

a. Examine the information as Mr. Babic does. Analyze the data that are given to identify as specifically as possible the problems that have led to NMC's loss of profit and market share in the heavy industrial transmission market.
b. Based on your analysis in part (a), and the information given to Mr. Babic, suggest specific alternatives that Mr. Babic should consider to make his firm more competitive in the heavy industrial transmission market. Use concepts presented in the chapter as the basis of your recommendations.

CASES

1. You and two colleagues have formed a partnership to develop a chain of retail stores that will offer customers an entirely new experience in purchasing beds and related furnishings. Beds Everywhere expects to focus exclusively on these and will provide a high level of service throughout the purchase and delivery experience. Specifically, all sales will be delivered to customers in two to five days. It is expected that this focus will lead to a number of competitive advantages, which the company believes will make its performance sustainable and provide the platform for future growth.

   You and your colleagues have acquired a cash register and inventory recording system with a relational database. It will record all inventory and sales transactions. It will also order automatically all inventory items from suppliers via product codes when inventory is needed for a sale or when minimal inventory levels are reached. In effect, Beds Everywhere has acquired a specialized enterprise resource planning (ERP) system.

   There will be about 2,000 inventory items, which will be supplied by about 100 vendors or suppliers. The suppliers and product codes have been identified. About three-quarters of the items can be obtained in less than two days; the rest will require two to three weeks for delivery. The latter items are smaller in both volume and dollar value.

   One of your colleagues is responsible for establishing the inventory system, including ordering and levels to be maintained. From her university management accounting course, she recalls the economic order quantity (EOQ) formula: EOQ equals the square root of two times the estimated quantity in units used per year times the estimated cost of placing one order divided by the estimated cost to carry one unit in stock for one year. This model minimizes the costs of ordering and carrying inventory.

   That colleague has begun to develop the EOQ for each of the 2,000 products. After 400 items, she recognizes that the amount of inventory she plans to hold will exceed the available space. She explains the problem to you and your other colleague.

   Required:

   As a partner in Beds Everywhere, resolve the inventory problem. Use the case approach.

CASES

2. Budward is a regional department store chain that operates through 10 highly integrated stores in southern Ontario. It has a distribution centre through which all inventory passes on the way to stores. Budward, like many retailers, has recently suffered a decline in profits. Your task is to recommend cost changes to improve profitability. As a first step, you review and analyze the operating statements in Exhibits 10-1 and 10-2.

EXHIBIT 10-1

Operating Statements, 2007 to 2010 ($000's)

	2007	2008	2009	2010
Revenue	280,000	300,000	321,000	342,000
Cost of goods sold				
—Beginning inventory	50,000	56,000	60,000	80,000
—Purchases	174,000	184,000	219,000	242,000
—Ending inventory	(56,000)	(60,000)	(80,000)	100,000)
	168,000	180,000	199,000	222,000
Gross margin	112,000	120,000	122,000	120,000
Overhead				
—Store	34,000	36,000	42,000	50,000
—Region	22,000	24,000	26,000	28,000
—Head office	14,000	15,000	17,000	20,000
	70,000	75,000	85,000	98,000
Net income	42,000	45,000	37,000	22,000

EXHIBIT 10-2

Net Income by Department, 2010 ($000's)

	Bed & Bath	Electronics	Furniture	Kitchens
Revenue	47,880	44,460	41,040	37,620
COGS				
Beg. Invent.	9,000	13,000	8,000	11,000
Purchases	27,000	41,000	24,000	33,000
End. Invent.	(10,000)	(17,000)	(9,000)	(16,000)
	26,000	37,000	23,000	28,000
Gross margin	21,880	7,460	18,040	9,620
Sales staff	3,000	5,000	3,000	4,000
Occupancy	1,680	1,560	1,440	1,320
IT	560	520	480	440
Amortization	420	390	360	330
Supplies	280	260	240	220
Management	200	400	200	300
	6,140	8,130	5,720	6,610
Net income	15,740	(670)	12,320	3,010

	Appliances	Women	Men	Babies & Kids
Revenue	34,200	68,400	41,040	27,360
COGS				
Beg. Invent.	7,000	19,000	8,000	5,000
Purchases	21,000	57,000	24,000	15,000
End. Invent.	(8,000)	(25,000)	(9,000)	(6,000)
	20,000	51,000	23,000	14,000
Gross margin	14,200	17,400	18,040	13,360
Sales staff	2,000	7,000	2,000	1,000
Occupancy	1,200	2,400	1,440	960
IT	400	800	480	320
Amortization	300	600	360	240
Supplies	200	400	240	160
Management	200	300	200	200
	4,300	11,500	4,720	2,880
Net income	9,900	5,900	13,320	10,480

CASES

Then, in your discussion with your boss, the controller, you ask whether Budward is concerned about its inventory practices. He tells you that inventories have grown to unexpectedly high levels in general, but he does not know exactly why. He then adds that Budward is often out of inventory that is in high demand—but often has surpluses in unpopular inventory, to the extent that some of it has become obsolete. You also ask how well the company has been doing at meeting its budget. Your boss says that the company has been doing well with sales and prices but that some costs have been greater than expected.

The distribution centre is integral to Budward's success. All of the consumer products sold by the chain are first delivered to its distribution centre, then distributed from there to individual stores. Budward buyers utilize independent or unintegrated systems and processes to generate purchase orders. These purchase orders are submitted to suppliers via the Internet. The suppliers fill the orders with available inventory and then deliver through specified transportation networks.

After analyzing the available data and questioning buyers and suppliers, you identify a number of inefficiencies in the present operations of the distribution centre:

- The suppliers have a limited idea of future demand requirements at Budward.
- Budward buyers lack suppliers' category/market insights that would lead to better forecasts and orders.
- Budward buyers and suppliers forecast their needs independently.
- Past supply chain outages have driven both suppliers and Budward buyers to build buffer stocks to accommodate surprises. In addition, Budward buyers have built additional safety stock based on outdated past or historical supply and demand variability in order to preserve service levels.
- When demand and supply outages occur, relationships become adversarial.

Required:
Resolve the inventory problem. In responding to your boss, use the case approach.

3. You and your partner started a clothing store Clothes R Us immediately after graduating from business school. At first the store sold fashionable women's clothing, with great success. Your partner had, unexpectedly, an outstanding ability to determine what would sell. Within two years, sales had increased many fold more than had ever been hoped, and the space occupied by the store had to expand three times.

After three years' success with women's clothing, you and your partner expanded into men's clothing. Success continued. Your partner was again outstanding, this time with purchasing men's clothing. Expansion was necessary every year or two, and now, 10 years after graduating, you and your partner have the largest clothing store in Toronto with the following product areas: men's casual, men's professional, women's casual, women's professional, youth female casual, and youth male casual. To minimize costs, only sales are tracked by area; in other words, costs are not tracked by area. There is a manager for each area, and all of them provide your partner with advice on what clothes to buy rather than on how to manage their areas.

Sales are good, and as marketing majors you and your partner are pleased with yourselves. However, profitability started to level off about two years ago despite sales growth. You and your partner have not discussed the weak profitability. Exhibit 10-1 shows the operating statements for the business for the last two years.

	2010	2009
Sales		
Men's casual	60,000	50,000
Men's profession	90,000	75,000
Women's casual	120,000	100,000
Women's professional	180,000	150,000
Youth female casual	90,000	75,000
Youth male casual	60,000	50,000
Total	600,000	500,000
Cost of good sold	360,000	275,000
Gross margin	240,000	225,000
Store costs	190,000	175,000
Net margin	50,000	50,000

EXHIBIT 10-1
Operating Statement for the year ending December 31 ($000s)

Part of the success of the business has been a result of sales-based employee compensation. Employees are motivated to sell clothes. On average, 30% of an employee's compensation comes from sales-based commissions and 70% from wages.

You and your partner want to improve profitability. You undertake a study of the gross margins (which you roughly equate with the contribution margins) for the past year for each of the areas. The results of your study are as follows:

Men's casual	50%
Men's professional	50
Women's casual	30
Women's professional	30
Youth female casual	50
Youth male casual	50
Total	40%

Required:

Using the case approach, assess profitability. Explain the issue or issues to your partner and recommend ways to improve profitability.

4. Canadian Automobiles Company (CAC) is a century-old company that assembles seven different lines of cars and light trucks. It has 12 divisions, including the Assembly Division and the Grand Prairie plant.

Competition has been severe since the 1970s, when the Japanese car companies entered the North American market. This competition intensified after the Koreans entered the North American market in the 1990s.

When CAC started business in the early 1900s, it was obliged not only to assemble cars but also to make virtually all parts. For the first few decades, CAC even made its own steel and windshield glass. Making the parts was necessary until suppliers were established, first in some generic products such as tires and batteries, then more recently for nearly all parts. CAC has gone from a manufacturer of cars and light trucks to almost entirely an assembler.

The relatively few parts that CAC still makes are unique to the company's cars and trucks. CAC's Grand Prairie plant still makes platforms for the Assembly Division, which assembles all of the parts into cars and trucks. The entire production of the Grand Prairie plant is sold to the Assembly Division at a transfer obtained by marking up variable costs by 65%. However, the general manager of the Grand Prairie plant is not content with the transfer price as it yields an ROI less than that earned by the Assembly Division. He is asking for a transfer price that will allow him to earn at least a 25% ROI, which is the minimum needed for him to qualify for incentive pay.

There have been no external sources for these platforms, at least not until recently, when Autopartna International made an offer to provide all platforms to the Assembly Division. Autopartna is a Canadian parts manufacturer with divisions all over the world. It has been a leader in using advanced flexible technology in manufacturing a wide range of automobile parts. Autopartna has offered to provide the platforms to the Assembly Division at prices that average a 5% discount from the present transfer prices.

The general manager of the Assembly Division wants to accept Autopartna's offer. However, the general manager of the Grand Prairie plant wants the offer rejected—and she, as noted, also wants a higher transfer price. The CEO of CAC has called on you, as the CFO of CAC, to resolve the dispute.

You review the current budgets for both divisions. These divisions seem able to meet their budgets. You realize that if the outsourcing of the platforms were accepted, only $40 million of the Grand Prairie plant's fixed costs would be avoidable.

Required:

As the chief financial officer of the parent company, CAC, address the concerns of the two general managers. Use the case approach.

CAC Assembly Division
Operating Budget (000,000)
For the Year Ending December 31

Revenue:	$2,600
Variable costs:	
Manufacturing	1,210
Administration	340
	1,550
Fixed expenses:	
Manufacturing	230
Administration	310
Research and development	120
	660
Operating income	$ 390
Working capital	$ 100
Net fixed assets	1,130
Investment	$1,230
ROI (390/1,230)	0.32

Grand Prairie Division
Operating Budget (000,000)
For the Year Ending December 31

Revenue:	$330
Variable costs:	
Manufacturing	140
Administration	60
	200
Fixed expenses:	
Manufacturing	40
Administration	20
Research and development	20
	80
Operating income	$ 50
Working capital	$ 60
Net fixed assets	175
Investment	$235
ROI (50/235)	0.21

5. John's Furniture House is a national volume retailer of upholstered and wooden household furniture. It has a strong market following with a 30% share of the total Canadian household furniture market. Most of the furniture is purchased in the central part of Canada and sold in all parts of Canada under the manufacturer's name. Inventory is purchased in advance and shipped to the central warehouse of John's Furniture. Later, the inventory is shipped to regional warehouses, then to the individual stores for sale to customers. The regional warehouses connect with the stores through the central warehouse computer with direct order communication lines and, thus, orders can be quickly processed. In recent years, furniture manufacturers have been able to provide more frequent but smaller-sized orders because of technological innovations.

John's Furniture details its monthly sales budget one year in advance. The budget is used as the basis for planning purchasing activities. The company makes purchases to meet budgeted sales and to ensure adequate inventory in all regional warehouses. The rigidity of the inventory requirements has benefited the company through favourable prices on central purchasing to the extent of 2% on sales. Yet the fears of excess inventories and the difficulties of adjusting after the commencement of the fiscal

CASES

year have encouraged the purchase of only those products that, based on past performance, are sure to sell. Sales personnel perceive this rigidity as a reason for losing opportunities to meet changes in market demand.

A recent study indicated that only about 25% of the space in the central warehouse is being used. The space utilization rates average about 50% for the regional warehouses.

The costs of handling inventory from manufacturer, to central warehouse, to regional warehouse, to stores average 7.2% of gross sales even after deducting the 2% savings from central purchasing, and these costs have increased in recent years. In addition, these costs are allocated to the stores based on sales volume. The store managers tend to believe that the allocations are unfair because comparable charges for competitors average about 3.5%.

You recently joined John's Furniture as the controller. As your first special assignment, the president has asked you to suggest ways to reduce the costs of handling inventory, which currently stands at 7.2% of sales.

Required:

As the new controller, use the case approach to address the president's request to reduce the costs of handling inventory.

ETHICS

1. You work for a major retailer as a management accountant. You are responsible for cost accounting, in particular, the implementation of ABC. Recently, a friend of yours failed in an attempt to get a job in your employer's warehouse. He claims that the jobs are going to friends of the warehouse manager. Specifically, he claims that all seven warehouse employees hired in the past year were in the same military reserve unit as that in which the warehouse manager serves as a sergeant. Your friend has documented the names and ranks of those seven newly hired warehouse employees.

   What should you do? Elaborate.

2. The controller has asked you, the financial analyst, to assess the economic viability of outsourcing parts of the HR function. As part of this assignment, you will be judged on your interpersonal skills—that is, your ability to earn the respect and cooperation of those employees with whom you work. You find that there is very convincing economic evidence for outsourcing payroll, reference checking, and benefits administration.

   The HR director is not pleased with your work. She is threatening to complain to the controller that your have poor interpersonal skills if you persist in recommending the outsourcing of payroll and benefits administration. Two of her managers will collaborate with her on what you believe to be bogus claims.

   What should you do? Elaborate.

3. After four years with a well-established manufacturer of residential furniture, Mary recently joined an information technology company that develops customized applications for a variety of clients from both the public and the private sectors. The difference in culture between the two organizations was more pronounced than Mary expected. Over the years, the manufacturing company had developed a comprehensive set of rules and procedures that left little or no discretion to employees. On the other hand, the policies of the information technology company were more general, and the behaviour of the employees was constrained only by their personal ethics.

   While reviewing billing for an important project with the Canada Revenue Agency (CRA), Mary wondered whether some programmers were billing more hours then they were actually working. Occasionally she had noticed that two of them were talking and drinking coffee for fairly long periods of time while they were supposed to be working on the project. Mary did not know what to do. She could either bring her concerns to the attention of her manager or talk to the programmers themselves.

   What should Mary do? Please elaborate.

Extract from *Management Accounting 2 Examination*, published by the Certified General Accountants Association of Canada (© CGA-Canada 2002). Reprinted with permission.

SOLUTIONS TO SELF-TEST QUESTIONS

1. d, 2. a, 3. b, 4. c, 5. a, 6. d, 7. d, 8. a, 9. a, 10. c

ENDNOTES

1. www.statcan.ca/english/Subjects/Cpi/cpi-en.htm

2. John Huey, "Waking Up to the New Economy," *Fortune,* June 27, 1994, p. 37.

3. Jonathan Ratner, "WestJet and Air Canada: How Oil Prices Will Impact Upcoming Earnings," Trading Desk, *National Post,* July 25, 2007.

4. Peter Drucker, "Permanent Cost Cutting," *The Wall Street Journal,* January 11, 1999, A8.

5. Dan W. Swenson, "Managing Costs Through Complexity Reduction at Carrier Corporation," *Management Accounting,* April 1998, pp. 20–21.

6. This is often called the 20/80 inventory rule (i.e., 20% of the inventory items account for 80% of the inventory costs).

7. The rate of return should be the weighted average cost of capital, which is discussed in Chapter 11.

8. Pam Withers, "Finders–Keepers: The Six Secrets of Attracting and Retaining Great Employees," *CMA Magazine,* October 2001, pp. 24–26.

9. A company may wish to measure the output of each manufacturing cell or work centre rather than total output. Although this practice may reveal problems in a given area, it does not correlate with JIT philosophy, which emphasizes a team approach, plantwide attitude, and total cost picture.

10. Jacob M. Schlesinger, Michael Williams, and Craig Forman, "Japan Inc., Wracked by Recession, Takes Stock of Its Methods," *Wall Street Journal,* September 29, 1993, A4.

11. Robin Cooper and Regine Slagmulder, *Target Costing and Value Engineering,* Montvale, NJ: The IMA Foundation for Applied Research, Inc., 1997, pp. 5–6.

12. Dennis Daly and Tom Freeman, *The Road to Excellence: Becoming a Process-Based Company* (Bedford, TX: CAM-I, 1997).

13. Dennis Daly, Patrick Dowdle, Robert McCarty, and Jerry Stevens, *Process-Based Management: A Foundation for Business Excellence* (Burleson, TX: CAM-I, 2004).

14. Todd Scaletta, "Beyond Process Improvement: The Pathway to Process-Based Management," *CMA Management,* June–July 2006, pp. 22–25.

15. Dan Snider, "Alignment: Do Your Processes Really Line Up?" *CMA Management,* June–July 2006, pp. 26–31.

Chapter 11

Responsibility Accounting and Transfer Pricing in Decentralized Organizations

LEARNING OBJECTIVES

After reading this chapter, you should be able to answer the following questions:

1 When
are decentralized operations appropriate?

2 How
does responsibility accounting relate to decentralization?

3 What
are the differences among the four types of responsibility centres?

4 What
is suboptimization and what are its effects?

5 How and why
are transfer prices for products used in organizations?

6 What
are the differences among the various definitions of product cost for transfer pricing?

7 How and why
are transfer prices for services used in organizations?

8 How
are transfer prices set in a multinational setting?

ON SITE

Multiversity

Multiversities are sprawling conglomerates. Often called research universities, they are the basis of a country's research, innovation, enterprise, and ideas. Multiversities have become the dominant institutional form for universities in Anglo-American countries. They offer undergraduate liberal education; professional education at both the undergraduate and graduate levels; and various graduate programs up to doctorate. Most important, multiversities are strongly committed to research.

Multiversities are controlled in two ways. Overall control is exercised by the board of governors. Most governors, who serve without pay, are highly respected business and community leaders. Academic control is exercised by the senate, on which are represented the multiversity's various stakeholders, with faculty members (i.e., professors) dominating.

The president reports to both the board of governors and the senate. In this reporting relationship, the president must juggle budgets against academic concerns. The president is responsible for the entire multiversity as well as for the time-consuming task of fundraising.

The multiversity is divided into relatively autonomous faculties such as business, arts, sciences, medicine, engineering, and education. One expert on universities recently spoke of faculties within multiversities as "a series of individual faculty entrepreneurs held together by a common grievance over parking."

Typically, the following people (among others) report directly to the president:
- vice president academic
- vice president student affairs
- vice president research
- vice president finance and administration
- director of information technology
- director of marketing and public relations

After the president, the vice president academic is the most powerful person on campus. The deans of the various faculties report to the vice president academic. Thus all students, all faculty, and most administrative personnel come under the vice president academic. Most multiversities have the following faculties:
- arts
- business
- education
- engineering
- environmental studies
- fine arts
- graduate studies
- law
- medicine and health

- professional studies
- science

Though they do not pursue profits, multiversities are accountable to various stakeholders—students, professors, the provincial government, the board of governors, and others. A multiversity's long-term plan (usually 10 years) is approved by the board of governors after extensive consultations with stakeholders.

The board of governors also approves the one-year budget. Revenue comes from two sources: (1) student tuition and fees, and (2) government grants. Both are based on enrollment. Donations are a third source of revenue, but for Canadian universities this is a much smaller component than the other two.

Faculties have revenues and expenses, which are required to balance. All other parts of the multiversity are cost centres. Thus, a faculty's revenue is based on number of students. Each faculty must use this money to pay for professors, administrators, and the like. To achieve breakeven, faculties prepare annual budgets, which must be approved by the board of governors. Each faculty receives a monthly report comparing actual revenue and expenses to budgeted amounts.

SOURCE: George Fallis, *Multiversities, Ideas, and Democracy* (Toronto: University of Toronto Press, 2007).

*M*any large organizations expand over the years until their structures are so cumbersome that they hinder, rather than help, achievement of organizational goals and objectives. In such cases, top managers often decide to change those structures so the organizations can more effectively use their resources and their employees' talents. Each organization's structure evolves as its goals, technology, and employees change. For many organizations, the progression goes from highly centralized to highly decentralized. The degree of centralization reflects a chain of command, authority and responsibility relationships, and decision-making capabilities. The structure affects the management accounting practices used by the organization. This chapter discusses the extent to which top managers delegate authority to subordinate managers and the reporting systems and management accounting practices that can be used to communicate managerial responsibility. In addition, since many decentralized organizations exchange goods and services internally, the concept of transfer pricing among organizational units is discussed.

LEARNING OBJECTIVE 1

When are decentralized operations appropriate?

centralization
an organizational structure in which top management makes most decisions and controls most activities of the organizational units from the organization's central headquarters

decentralization
the downward delegation by top management of authority and decision making to the individuals who are closest to internal processes and customers

DECENTRALIZATION

The degree to which authority is retained by top management (**centralization**) or released from top management and passed to lower managerial levels (**decentralization**) can be viewed in terms of a continuum. In a completely centralized firm, a single individual, usually the company owner or president, performs all decision making and retains full authority and responsibility for that organization's activities. In contrast, a purely decentralized organization has virtually no central authority, and each subunit acts as a totally independent entity. Either of these extremes represents a clearly undesirable arrangement. In the totally centralized company, the single individual may not have enough expertise or information to make decisions in all areas. In the totally decentralized firm, subunits may act in ways that are not consistent with the goals of the total organization. Factors associated with pure centralization and pure decentralization are presented in Exhibit 11-1. Most businesses—regardless of national domicile—fall somewhere between the extremes at a point dictated by practical necessity or by management design.

EXHIBIT 11-1

Continuum of Authority in
Organizational Structures

Factor	Continuum	
	Pure Centralization	**Pure Decentralization**
Age of firm	Young ⟶	Mature
Size of firm	Small ⟶	Large
Stage of product development	Stable ⟶	Growing
Growth rate of firm	Slow ⟶	Rapid
Expected impact of incorrect decisions on profits	High ⟶	Low
Top management's confidence in subordinates	Low ⟶	High
Historical degree of control in firm	Tight ⟶	Moderate or loose
Use of technology	Low ⟶	High
Rate of change in the firm's market	Slow ⟶	Rapid

While almost every organization is decentralized to some degree, quantifying the extent of decentralization may not be possible. Some subunits may have more autonomy than others. In addition to top management philosophy, decentralization depends on the type of organizational unit. For example, a unit, segment, or division that operates in a turbulent environment and that must respond quickly to new and unanticipated problems is likely to be a prime candidate for decentralization.

Top management must also consider the subunit managers' personalities and perceived abilities. Managers in decentralized environments must be goal-oriented, assertive, decisive, and creative. While these employee traits are always desirable, they are essential for decentralized company managers. In decentralized companies, managers must also be willing to accept the authority delegated by top management and to be judged based on the outcomes of the decisions that they make. Some subunit managers may be either reluctant or unable to accept this authority or responsibility. Therefore, a company may allow some units to be highly decentralized, while others are only minimally decentralized. Since managerial behaviours change and managers are replaced, supervisors should periodically reassess their decisions about a unit's extent of decentralization.

Decentralization does not necessarily mean that a unit manager has the authority to make all decisions concerning that unit. Top management selectively determines what types of authority to delegate and what types to withhold. For example, many large, diversified companies want decentralization with centralized reporting and control. They achieve this goal in part by establishing coordinated accounting methods and by retaining certain functions at headquarters. Treasury and legal work is often provided by headquarters, sometimes through freestanding service centres whose output is charged to the various decentralized units. In addition, purchasing is frequently consolidated for efficiency, effectiveness, and coordination. A multiversity would likely centralize security and parking but not research programs.

Like any management technique, decentralization has advantages and disadvantages. These pros and cons are summarized in Exhibit 11-2 and are discussed in the following sections.

Increasingly, with information technology such as ERP systems, decentralization and centralization are possible at the same time. Front-line employees can be delegated authority to make decisions while senior management can maintain detailed responsibility with modern information technology. This situation is common and explains the elimination of many management positions between senior management and the front line.

EXHIBIT 11-2

Advantages and Disadvantages
of Decentralization

Advantages

- Helps top management recognize and develop managerial talent
- Allows managerial performance to be comparatively evaluated
- Often leads to greater job satisfaction
- Makes the accomplishment of organizational goals and objectives easier
- Allows the use of management by exception

Disadvantages

- May result in a lack of goal congruence or suboptimization
- Requires more effective communication abilities
- May create personnel difficulties upon introduction
- Can be extremely expensive
- Requires accepting inappropriate decisions as it is a training ground

Advantages of Decentralization

Decentralization has many personnel advantages. Managers have both the need and the opportunity to develop their leadership qualities, creative problem-solving abilities, and decision-making skills. Decentralized units provide excellent settings for training personnel and for screening aspiring managers for promotion. Managers can be judged on job performance and on the results of their units relative to units headed by other managers; such comparisons can encourage a healthy level of organizational competition. Decentralization also often leads to greater job satisfaction for managers because it provides for job enrichment and gives a feeling of increased importance to the organization. Employees are given more challenging and responsible work that provides greater opportunities for advancement.

In addition to the personnel benefits, decentralization is generally more effective than centralization in accomplishing organizational goals and objectives. The decentralized unit manager has more knowledge of the local operating environment than top management, which leads to (1) reduction in decision-making time, (2) minimization of difficulties resulting from attempts to communicate problems and instructions through an organizational chain of command, and (3) quicker perceptions of environmental changes. Thus, the manager of a decentralized unit is not only in closest contact with daily operations but also is charged with making decisions about those operations.

management by exception
a technique in which managers set upper and lower limits of tolerance for deviations and investigate only deviations that fall outside those tolerance ranges

A decentralized structure also allows implementation of the **management by exception** principle. Top management, when reviewing divisional reports, can address issues that are out of the ordinary rather than dealing with operations that are proceeding according to plans.

An alternative to either centralization or decentralization is outsourcing. By outsourcing, decisions do not need to be made on centralizing or decentralizing. All decisions are made by the supplier or vendor when outsourcing is pursued. Outsourcing was examined in Chapter 10.

Disadvantages of Decentralization

Not all aspects of a decentralized structure are positive. For instance, authority and responsibility for making decisions may be divided among too many individuals, which can result in a lack of *goal congruence* among the organizational units.

(**Goal congruence** exists when the personal and organizational goals of decision makers throughout a firm are consistent and mutually supportive.) In a decentralized company, unit managers are essentially competing with one another since the results of unit activities are compared. Unit managers may make decisions that positively affect their own units but are detrimental to other organizational units or to the whole company. This process results in suboptimization, which is discussed later in the chapter.

A decentralized organization requires more effective methods of communicating plans, activities, and achievements because decision making is removed from the central office. Top management has delegated the authority to make decisions to unit managers but still retains the ultimate responsibility to corporate ownership for the effects of those decisions. Thus, to determine whether operations are progressing toward established goals, top management must be continuously aware of events occurring at lower levels. If decentralization gets totally out of control, top management must be willing to step in and take action. Similarly, if a faculty were constantly in deficit (i.e., if expenses exceeded revenues), the president would have to replace the dean.

Some employees may be disturbed when top management attempts to introduce decentralization policies. Employees may be asked to do too much too soon or without enough training. Furthermore, some top managers have difficulty relinquishing control or are unwilling or unable to delegate effectively.

A final disadvantage of decentralization is that it may be extremely expensive. In a large company, it is unlikely that all subordinate managers have equally good decision-making skills. Thus, the first cost is for training lower-level managers to make better decisions. Second, there is the potential cost of poor decisions. Decentralization implies the willingness of top management to let subordinates make some mistakes.

Another cost of decentralization relates to developing and operating a more sophisticated planning and reporting system. Since top management delegates decision-making authority but retains ultimate responsibility for decision outcomes, a reporting system must be implemented that will provide top management with the ability to measure the overall accountability of the subunits. This reporting system is known as a responsibility accounting system.

Decentralization can also create a duplication of activities that can be quite expensive in terms of both time and money. For example, it is not unusual for an organization to recentralize, in part to unify its resources for greater efficiency and effectiveness.[1]

Responsibility Accounting Systems

Responsibility accounting refers to an accounting system that provides information to top management about the performance of an organizational unit. As decentralization became more prevalent in the business environment, responsibility accounting systems evolved from the increased need to communicate operating results through the managerial hierarchy.

A responsibility accounting system produces **responsibility reports** to assist each successively higher level of management in evaluating the performances of its subordinate managers and their respective organizational units. These reports reflect the revenues and/or costs under the control of a specific unit manager. Any revenues or costs that are not under the control of a specific unit manager should not be shown on his or her responsibility reports. For example, a portion of straight-line depreciation on the company headquarters building may be allocated

goal congruence
a condition that exists when the personal and organizational goals of decision makers throughout the firm are consistent and mutually supportive

LEARNING OBJECTIVE 2

How does responsibility accounting relate to decentralization?

responsibility accounting
an accounting system that provides information to top management about segment or subunit performance

responsibility reports
reflect the revenues and/or costs under the control of a specific unit manager

to the Sales Department. Because the manager of the Sales Department has no control over this cost, it should not be included on the responsibility report of the Sales Department manager. Much of the information communicated on these reports is monetary, although other data may be included. Examples of the latter include proportion of deliveries made on time, number of defects generated by production for the month, and tonnes of waste produced during the month. Deans at multiversities receive monthly reports of actual revenues, expenses, and number of students compared to the budget, and of the research funding received by the faculty's professors.

The number of responsibility reports routinely issued for a decentralized unit depends on how much influence that unit's manager has on the unit's day-to-day operations and costs. If a manager strongly influences all operations and costs of a unit, one report will suffice for both the manager and the unit. Normally, however, some costs are not controlled—or are only partially or indirectly controlled—by the unit manager. In such instances, the responsibility report takes one of two forms. First, a single report can be issued that shows all costs incurred in the unit, separately classified as either controllable or uncontrollable by the manager. Alternatively, separate reports can be prepared for the manager and the unit. The manager's report includes only costs under his or her control, while the unit's report includes all costs.

A responsibility accounting system is the linchpin in making decentralization work effectively. The responsibility reports about unit performance are primarily tailored to fit the planning, controlling, and decision-making needs of subordinate managers. Top managers review these reports to evaluate the efficiency and effectiveness of each unit and each manager.

One purpose of a responsibility accounting system is to "secure control at the point where costs are incurred instead of assigning them all to products and processes remote from the point of incurrence."[2] This purpose agrees with the concepts of standard costing and activity-based costing. In standard costing, variances are traced to the person (or machine) responsible for the variance; for example, the material purchase price variance can generally be traced to the purchasing agent. Activity-based costing attempts to trace as many costs as possible to the activities that caused the costs rather than using highly aggregated allocation techniques.

Control procedures are implemented for the following three reasons:

1. Managers attempt to cause actual operating results to conform to planned results. This conformity is known as **effectiveness**.
2. Managers attempt to cause, at a minimum, the standard output to be produced from the actual input costs incurred. This conformity is known as **efficiency**.
3. Managers need to ensure, to the extent possible, a reasonable utilization of plant and equipment. Utilization is primarily affected by product or service demand. At higher volumes of activity or utilization, fixed capacity costs can be spread over more units, resulting in a lower unit cost. However, demand for the product or service must first be generated before the benefits of spreading the overhead can be realized. Otherwise output is produced that creates holding costs that burden the company.

Responsibility accounting implies that subordinate managers accept the authority given to them by top management and helps them in conducting the five basic control functions shown in Exhibit 11-3. Budgets are used to officially communicate output expectations (sales, production, and so forth) and, through budget appropriations, to delegate the authority to spend. Ideally, subunit managers negotiate

effectiveness
a measure of how well the firm's objectives and goals were achieved; it involves comparing actual output results with desired results

efficiency
the degree to which the relationship between outputs and inputs is satisfactory; performance of a task to produce the best outcome at the lowest cost from the resources used

EXHIBIT 11-3
Basic Steps in a Control Process

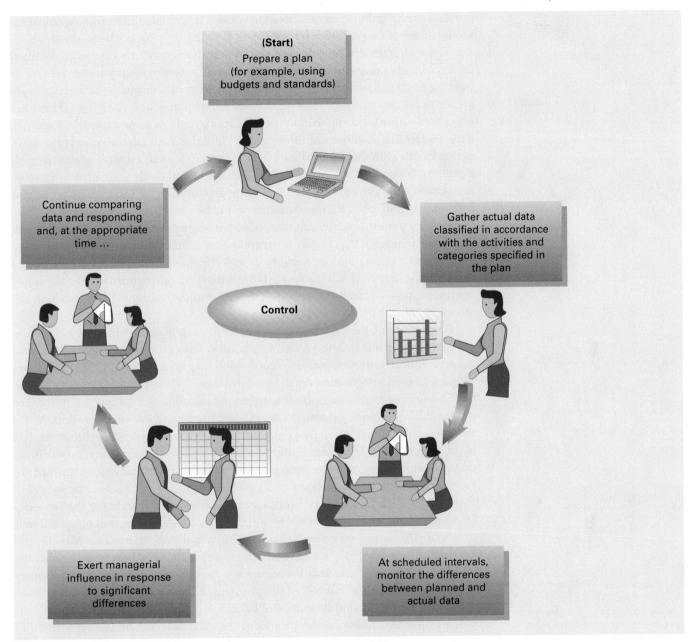

budgets and standards for their units with top management for the coming year. Involvement in the budgeting process is essential for motivating those whose performance will be evaluated on budget-to-actual comparisons.

The responsibility accounting system should be designed so that actual data are captured in conformity with budgetary accounts. During the year, the accounting system records and summarizes data for each organizational unit. Operating reports comparing actual account balances with budgeted, standard, or target amounts are prepared periodically and issued to managers. Because of day-to-day contact with operations, managers should be aware of any significant variances before they are reported, identify variance causes, and attempt to correct causes of the problems. Top managers, on the other hand, may not know about operational variances until they receive responsibility reports. By the time top management receives the reports, problems causing the variances should have been corrected, or subordinate managers should be able to explain why the problems were not or could not be resolved.

The responsibility reports received by top management may compare actual performance against the master budget. Such a comparison can be viewed as yielding an overall performance evaluation, since the master budget reflects management's expectations about sales prices, volume, and mix, as well as costs. However, using the budget for comparison may be inappropriate in some cases. For example, if the budget has an allowance for scrap built into the materials usage estimate, comparing results with the budget figure fails to support a focus on total quality. In such a case, a positive variance relative to the budget should not be judged as favourable performance if significant scrap still is being produced. Establishing a target goal of zero scrap would mean that any variance would be identified as unfavourable.

Perhaps a more appropriate form of responsibility report is that associated with the flexible budget. This report form compares actual information about controllable items (revenues and/or costs) both with the master budget and with amounts based on the achieved activity level. This secondary comparison is more useful for control purposes, since both operating results and budget figures are based on the same level of activity.

Regardless of the comparisons provided, responsibility reports reflect the upward flow of information from operational units to top management. These reports indicate the broadening scope of managerial responsibility. Managers receive detailed information on the performance of their immediate areas of control and summary information on all other organizational units for which they are responsible. Summarizing results causes a pyramiding of information. Reports for the lowest-level units are highly detailed, while reports are less specific at the top of the organization. Upper-level managers desiring information more specific than that provided in summary reports can review the responsibility reports prepared for their subordinates.

Exhibit 11-4 illustrates the March set of performance reports for the Generics Division of Heinrick Chemicals, a fictional Dutch conglomerate. All information is shown in the home office currency of Dutch guilders (Hfl). The Mixing and Preparing Department's actual costs are compared with those in the flexible budget. Data for Mixing and Preparing are then aggregated with data of other departments under the control of the production vice-president. These combined data are shown in the middle section of Exhibit 11-4. In a like manner, the total costs of the production vice-president's area of responsibility are combined with other costs for which the company president is responsible and are shown in the top section of Exhibit 11-4.

Variances should be individually itemized in lower-level performance reports so that the manager under whose supervision those variances occurred has the detail needed to take appropriate corrective action. Under the management by exception principle, major deviations from expectations are highlighted in the subordinate manager's reporting section to assist upper-level managers in making decisions about when to become involved in the subordinate's operations. If no significant deviations exist, top management is free to devote its attention to other matters. In addition, such detailed variance analysis alerts operating managers to items they may need to explain to superiors.

EXHIBIT 11-4

Generics Division March
Performance Reports

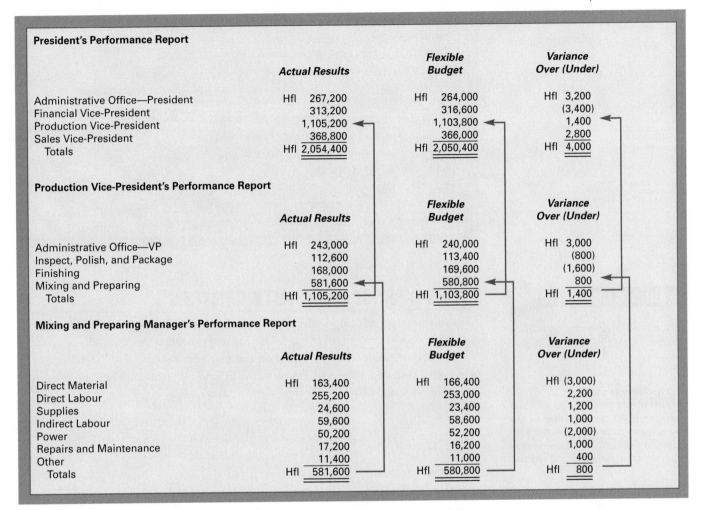

President's Performance Report

	Actual Results	Flexible Budget	Variance Over (Under)
Administrative Office—President	Hfl 267,200	Hfl 264,000	Hfl 3,200
Financial Vice-President	313,200	316,600	(3,400)
Production Vice-President	1,105,200	1,103,800	1,400
Sales Vice-President	368,800	366,000	2,800
Totals	Hfl 2,054,400	Hfl 2,050,400	Hfl 4,000

Production Vice-President's Performance Report

	Actual Results	Flexible Budget	Variance Over (Under)
Administrative Office—VP	Hfl 243,000	Hfl 240,000	Hfl 3,000
Inspect, Polish, and Package	112,600	113,400	(800)
Finishing	168,000	169,600	(1,600)
Mixing and Preparing	581,600	580,800	800
Totals	Hfl 1,105,200	Hfl 1,103,800	Hfl 1,400

Mixing and Preparing Manager's Performance Report

	Actual Results	Flexible Budget	Variance Over (Under)
Direct Material	Hfl 163,400	Hfl 166,400	Hfl (3,000)
Direct Labour	255,200	253,000	2,200
Supplies	24,600	23,400	1,200
Indirect Labour	59,600	58,600	1,000
Power	50,200	52,200	(2,000)
Repairs and Maintenance	17,200	16,200	1,000
Other	11,400	11,000	400
Totals	Hfl 581,600	Hfl 580,800	Hfl 800

In addition to the monetary information shown in Exhibit 11-4, many responsibility accounting systems are now providing information on critical nonmonetary measures of the period's activity. Some examples are shown in Exhibit 11-5. Many of these measures are equally useful for manufacturing and service organizations and can be used along with basic financial measurements in judging performance.

The performance reports of each management layer are reviewed and evaluated by all successive layers of management. Managers are likely to be more careful and alert in controlling operations knowing that the reports generated by the responsibility accounting system reveal financial accomplishments and problems. Thus, in addition to providing a means for control, responsibility reports can motivate managers to influence operations in ways that will reflect positive performance.

The focus of responsibility accounting is people. The people emphasized are the managers responsible for an organizational unit such as a department, division, or geographic region. The subunit under the control of a manager is called a responsibility centre.

EXHIBIT 11-5

Nonmonetary Information for Responsibility Reports

- Departmental/divisional throughput
- Number of defects (by product, product line, supplier)
- Number of orders backlogged (by date, quantity, cost, and selling price)
- Number of customer complaints (by type and product); method of complaint resolution
- Percentage of orders delivered on time
- Manufacturing (or service) cycle efficiency
- Percentage of reduction of nonvalue-added time from previous reporting period (broken down by idle time, storage time, quality control time)
- Number of employee suggestions considered significant and practical
- Number of employee suggestions implemented
- Number of unplanned production interruptions
- Number of schedule changes
- Number of engineering change orders; percentage change from previous period
- Number of safety violations; percentage change from previous period
- Number of days of employee absences; percentage change from previous period

LEARNING OBJECTIVE 3

What are the differences among the four types of responsibility centres?

responsibility centre
the cost object under the control of a manager; in the case of a decentralized company, the cost object is an organizational unit such as a division, department, or geographical region

TYPES OF RESPONSIBILITY CENTRES

Responsibility accounting systems identify, measure, and report on the performance of people who control the activities of responsibility centres. There are four types of **responsibility centres**, based on the manager's scope of authority and type of financial responsibility: cost, revenue, profit, and investment. They are illustrated in Exhibit 11-6 and discussed in the following sections.

EXHIBIT 11-6

Types of Responsibility Centres

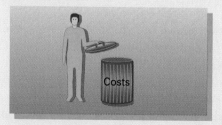

Cost centre—manager is responsible for cost containment.

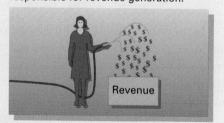

Revenue centre—manager is responsible for revenue generation.

Profit centre—manager is responsible for profit (both revenue generation and cost containment).

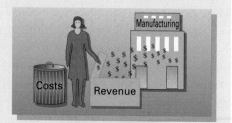

Investment centre—manager is responsible for return on asset base.

Cost Centres

In a **cost centre**, the manager has the authority only to incur costs and is specifically evaluated on the basis of how well costs are controlled. In many cost centres, no revenues are generated because the unit does not engage in any revenue-producing activity. For example, the placement centre in a university may be a cost centre, since it does not charge for the use of its services but does incur costs.

In some cost centres, the costs may be difficult to control because there are many drivers. In other instances, revenues may be associated with a particular subunit, but they either are not under the manager's control or are not effectively measurable. The first type of situation exists in a governmental agency that is provided a specific proration of sales tax dollars but has no authority to levy or collect the related taxes. The second situation could exist in discretionary cost centres, such as a marketing research or a research and development department, in which the outputs (revenues or benefits generated from the cost inputs) are not easily measured. In these situations, revenues should not be included in the manager's responsibility accounting report.

In the traditional manufacturing environment, a standard costing system is generally used, and variances are reported and analyzed. In such an environment, the highest priority in a cost centre is often the minimization of unfavourable cost variances. Top management may often concentrate only on the unfavourable variances occurring in a cost centre and ignore the efficient performance indicated by favourable variances. For example, referring back to Exhibit 11-4, the production vice-president of the Generics Division of Heinrick Chemicals might focus only on the unfavourable material and power variances for the Mixing and Preparing Department while disregarding the favourable variances for the other costs of production. Significant favourable variances should not be ignored if the management by exception principle is to be applied appropriately. Using this principle, all variances—both favourable and unfavourable—that fall outside the preestablished limits for normal deviations should be investigated.

In the Heinrick Chemicals example, Gottfried Menchen, the manager of the Mixing and Preparing Department, should have determined the causes of the variances before filing the report. For instance, it is possible that substandard material was purchased and caused excessive usage. If this is the case, the purchasing agent, not Mr. Menchen, should be held accountable for the variance. Other possible causes for the unfavourable material variance include increased material prices, excess waste, or some combination of all these causes. Only additional inquiry or investigation can determine whether that variance could have been controlled by Menchen. Similarly, the power variance may have resulted from an increase in utility costs.

cost centre
an organizational unit in which the manager has the authority only to incur costs and is specifically evaluated on the basis of how well costs are controlled

Empirical Evidence for Market-Based Transfer Prices

INTERNATIONAL NEWS NOTE

Market-based transfer prices are often used for internally transferred goods and services. The assumption is that such prices encourage efficiency and motivation in internal production. However, this assumption has not been proven adequately in empirical terms using specific production processes.

A recent study of German companies tested whether market-based transfer price systems have stronger efficiency and motivation effects than systems in which prices are not related to market. Seventy-three questionnaires were returned completed. The findings suggest that market-based transfer price systems are perceived as more efficient and "motivational" than those that are not market-based. However, the market prices must be transparent and observable.

SOURCE: Michael Wolff, "Market Price–Based Transfer System: Empirical Evidence for Effectiveness and Preconditions," *Problems and Perspectives in Management* 2 (2007): 66–74.

The favourable direct labour variance should also be analyzed. Mr. Menchen may have used inexperienced personnel who were being paid lower rates. Such a situation might explain both the favourable direct labour variance and, to some extent, the unfavourable direct material variance (because the workers were less skilled and may have overused material). Alternatively, the people working in the Mixing and Preparing Department could simply have been very efficient this period. In this case, Menchen would compliment and reward the efficient employees and might also consider incorporating the improvement as a revised time standard.

Revenue Centres

> **revenue centre**
> an organizational unit in which the manager is accountable only for the generation of revenues and has no control over selling prices or budgeted costs

A **revenue centre** is strictly defined as an organizational unit whose manager is accountable only for the generation of revenues and has no control over costs. In many retail stores, the individual sales departments are considered independent units and managers are evaluated based on the total revenues generated by their departments. Departmental managers, though, may not be given the authority to change selling prices to affect volume, and they often do not participate in the budgeting process. Thus, the departmental managers may have no impact on costs. In general, however, few pure revenue centres exist.

Managers of revenue centres are typically responsible for revenues and also are involved in planning and control related to some, but not necessarily all, single of the centre's costs. Thus, a more appropriate term for this organizational unit is a "revenue and limited cost centre." For example, a sales manager who is responsible for the sales revenues generated in her territory may additionally be accountable for controlling the mileage and other travel-related expenses of her sales staff. She may not, however, be able to influence the types of cars her sales staff obtain, because automobiles are acquired on a fleetwide basis by top management.

Salaries, if directly traceable, are often a cost responsibility of a revenue centre manager. This situation reflects the traditional retail environment in which each sales clerk is assigned to a specific department and is only allowed to check out customers who want to purchase that department's merchandise. Most stores have found such a checkout situation to be detrimental to business, because customers are forced to wait for the appropriate clerk. Clerks in many stores are now allowed to assist all

Individual departments in a large retail store may be treated as cost or revenue centres by the store manager, while the store itself may be treated as a profit or investment centre by corporate headquarters. Such designations reflect the degree of control a manager has over selling prices, costs, and plant assets.

customers with all types of merchandise. Such a change in policy converts what was a traceable departmental cost into an indirect cost. Stores carrying high-cost, high-selling-price merchandise normally retain the traditional system. Managers of such departments are thus able to trace sales salaries as a direct departmental cost.

In analyzing variances from budget, managers in a revenue centre need to consider three possible causes: sales price differences, sales mix differences, and volume differences. A model is expanded below to illustrate the effect of a difference in product sales mix from that which was budgeted.

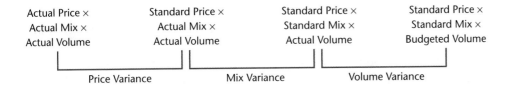

Exhibit 11-7 presents the revenue statistics and variance computations for the Canadian Sales Division of Heinrick Chemicals for a month. The Canadian Sales Division is a wholesaler that sells to retail chains in lot sizes of 1,000 units each.

EXHIBIT 11-7

Variances for a Revenue Centre

Budget	Lots	Lot Price	Revenue	Standard Mix for Budgeted Volume
Vitamins (V)	3,000	$1,400	$4,200,000	3,000 ÷ 6,000 = 50.0%
Hunger suppressant (H)	2,000	1,600	3,200,000	2,000 ÷ 6,000 = 33.3%
Facial cream (F)	1,000	1,100	1,100,000	1,000 ÷ 6,000 = 16.7%
Totals	6,000		$8,500,000	100.0%

Actual Mix for Actual Volume	Lots	Lot Price	Revenue	
Vitamins	3,200	$1,500	$4,800,000	
Hunger suppressant	1,800	1,600	2,880,000	
Facial cream	1,100	1,200	1,320,000	
Totals	6,100		$9,000,000	

Standard Mix for Actual Volume

Vitamins	(6,100 × 0.500) = 3,050			
Hunger suppressant	(6,100 × 0.333) = 2,031			
Facial cream	(6,100 × 0.167) = 1,019			

Actual Price × Actual Mix × Actual Volume	Standard Price × Actual Mix × Actual Volume	Standard Price × Standard Mix × Actual Volume	Standard Price × Standard Mix × Budgeted Volume
V $1,500(3,200) = $ 4,800,000	$1,400(3,200) = $4,480,000	$1,400(3,050) = $4,270,000	$1,400(3,000) = $4,200,000
H $1,600(1,800) = 2,880,000	$1,600(1,800) = 2,880,000	$1,600(2,031) = 3,249,600	$1,600(2,000) = 3,200,000
F $1,200(1,100) = 1,320,000	$1,100(1,100) = 1,210,000	$1,100(1,019) = 1,120,900	$1,100(1,000) = 1,100,000
Totals $9,000,000	$8,570,000	$8,640,500	$8,500,000

	$430,000 F	$70,500 U	$140,500 F
	Price Variance	Mix Variance	Volume Variance

$500,000 F

Total Revenue Variance

Inspection of the results reveals that (1) prices increased (except for hunger suppressants), causing an overall favourable price variance; (2) the actual mix included more of the lower-priced products (vitamins and facial cream) than the standard mix, causing an overall unfavourable mix variance; and (3) the number of lots sold (6,100) was greater than the number of lots budgeted (6,000), causing a favourable volume variance. The Canadian Sales Division's manager is to be commended for good performance.

Profit Centres

profit centre
an organizational unit in which the manager is responsible for generating revenues and planning and controlling all expenses

In **profit centres**, managers are responsible for generating revenues and for planning and controlling all expenses. A profit centre manager's goal is to maximize the centre's net income. Profit centres should be independent organizational units whose managers have the authority to obtain resources at the most economical prices and to sell products at prices that will maximize revenue. If managers do not have complete authority to buy and sell at objectively determined costs and prices, it is difficult to make a meaningful evaluation of the profit centre.

Profit centres are not always manufacturing divisions or branches of retail stores. A dental clinic may view each department (Cleaning, X-Ray, Tooth and Gum Restoration, and Crown Fabrication) as a profit centre, and a university may view faculties as profit centres.

To illustrate the variance computations for a profit centre, assume that Heinrick Chemicals uses 18-wheel trucks to deliver products throughout Western Europe and each truck is considered a profit centre. The budgeted and actual revenues and expenses for "Tour de France," a truck for which Claudette Harfleur is responsible, are shown in Exhibit 11-8. The profit centre should be judged on the F67,250 of profit centre income (in French francs—F), but Harfleur should be judged on the controllable margin of F96,500. Harfleur should point out that her delivery revenues were greater than budgeted because she drove more kilometres than budgeted. Thus, using the master budget as a basis for comparison, it is natural that unfavourable variances would exist for all of the variable costs.

EXHIBIT 11-8

Profit Centre Master Budget Comparisons for August

	Master Budget	Actual	Variance	
Delivery revenues	F 180,000	F 186,000	F 6,000	F
Variable costs:				
Direct labour	F 4,500	F 4,600	F 100	U
Gas and oil	37,800	39,050	1,250	U
Variable overhead	7,740	7,850	110	U
Total	F 50,040	F 51,500	F 1,460	U
Contribution margin	F 129,960	F 134,500	F 4,540	F
Fixed overhead—controllable	(38,400)	(38,000)	400	F
Segment margin—controllable	F 91,560	F 96,500	F 4,940	F
Fixed overhead—not controllable				
by profit centre manager	(27,000)	(29,250)	(2,250)	U
Profit centre income	F 64,560	F 67,250	F 2,690	F

The comparison of actual results to a flexible budget at the actual activity level shown in Exhibit 11-9 provides better information for assessing cost control within the profit centre. Harfleur did a good job controlling the costs of her profit centre; the problem area is related to the noncontrollable fixed overhead. She should investigate the causes for the F2,250 unfavourable variance. Then she and her manager

	Flexible Budget	Actual	Variance	
Delivery revenues	F 186,000	F186,000	F 0	
Variable costs:				
Direct labour	F 4,650	F 4,600	F 50	F
Gas and oil	39,060	39,50	10	F
Variable overhead	7,998	7,850	148	F
Total	F 51,708	F 51,500	F 208	F
Contribution margin	F 134,292	F134,500	F 208	F
Fixed overhead—controllable	(38,400)	(38,000)	400	F
Segment margin—controllable	F 95,892	F 96,500	F 608	F
Fixed overhead—not controllable				
by profit centre manager	(27,000)	(29,250)	(2,250)	U
Profit centre income	F 68,892	F 67,250	F 1,642	U

EXHIBIT 11-9

Profit Centre Flexible Budget Comparisons for August

can discuss any ideas she may have for addressing those causes. It is also possible that the budgeted figure for the noncontrollable fixed overhead is inappropriate because of cost increases for some or all of the items composing that fixed overhead pool.

Investment Centres

An **investment centre** is an organizational unit in which the manager is responsible for generating revenues, planning and controlling costs, and acquiring, using, and disposing of plant assets. The manager performs each of these activities with the aim of earning the highest feasible rate of return on the investment base. Many investment centres are independent, freestanding divisions or subsidiaries of a firm. This independence allows investment centre managers the opportunity to make decisions about all matters affecting their organizational units and to be judged on the outcomes of those decisions.

Assume that Walker Pharmaceuticals (a subsidiary of Heinrick Chemicals) is an investment centre headed by Henri LeBaron. The income statement for the company (in Swiss francs—Fr) is as follows:

Sales	Fr1,613,200
Variable expenses	900,000
Contribution margin	Fr 713,200
Fixed expenses	490,000
Net income	Fr 223,200

investment centre
an organizational unit in which the manager is responsible for generating revenues, planning and controlling costs, and acquiring, disposing of, and using plant assets to earn the highest feasible rate of return on the investment base

The establishment of a national call centre at Canadian Tire has helped to streamline operations, both internally and externally.

IBM Cost Centres into Profit Centres

Louis Gerstner became **IBM's** CEO in 1993. He was recruited from the outside, as IBM's board of directors believed that the company needed to become more innovative if it was to survive and that only an outsider could spur that innovation. The biggest problem facing Gerstner was that the old, mainframe-based business could not compete with increasingly powerful networks of PCs.

Gerstner decided very early that fusion was important. He defined fusion (which he referred to as "convergence") as "the melding of telecommunications, computing, and consumer electronics; or, stated differently, the merger of traditional analog technologies with their emerging digital kin." He anticipated that fusion, along with global connectivity, would create a revolution in the interactions among millions of businesses, schools, governments, and consumers. He expected it to introduce extensive changes.

In the environment he first encountered, the burden was being placed on the customer to integrate hardware, software, and networks. The lack of uniform standards throughout the IT industry made integration especially difficult. Gerstner explained IBM's new innovation as follows: "Before the components reach the consumer, somebody has to sit at the end of the line and bring it all together in a way that creates value. In effect, he or she takes responsibility for translating the pieces into value. I believe that if IBM was uniquely positioned to do or to be anything, it was to be that company."

IBM's new innovation focused on the following: (1) services (consulting and custom programming), (2) systems integration (designing, building, and installing complex information systems), (3) systems operations (in which a vendor runs part or all of a company's information systems), (4) business innovation services (such as supply chain management), (5) strategic outsourcing and application management services, (6) integrated technology services (such as business recovery), (7) network services, (8) learning services, (9) security services, (10) storage services, and (11) wireless services. Specifically, the innovation was to serve customers by providing them with a full set of services.

When Gerstner arrived, IBM was not a service fusionist ("integrator" is IBM's term) or a full-solution company. It was a product company that made and sold products. It serviced its own products, but it did not service any other products. It would integrate, but only its hardware with its software and networks.

Gerstner fused the abilities of IBM's product people (including scientists), thereby turning them into management consultants. In other words, the capacity of IBM employees to develop products and services was offered to clients for a fee. In effect, IBM was converting its cost centres into profit centres. Gerstner realized early that IBM had a unique advantage in the consulting sphere, in that it designed, engineered, and marketed important products. This provided the company with internal abilities, which could be deployed to clients via IBM consultants. No longer would IBM simply supply post-sales support for its products. IBM achieved a powerhouse of knowledge by fusing services to serve customers (again, by turning cost centres into profit centres).

IBM's organizational structure was another area of fusion. When Gerstner arrived, IBM was structured along geographical lines, which he called "geographical fiefdoms." In order to become a global firm capable of serving customers in all parts of the world, and of serving customers who were themselves global, IBM structured itself as a single firm rather than many divisions facing the world. Gerstner described this goal as "to integrate all the parts for our customers." IBM became a single global firm with 12 groups: 11 industrial groups (including banking, government, insurance, and distribution) and a single group covering small- and medium-sized businesses. Gerstner referred to this single-firm structure as an "integrated IBM."

SOURCE: Robert J. Fong and Gary Spraakman. "Design Your Abilities: Dell, GE, IBM, Siebel, and IKEA," Working Paper, School of Administrative Studies, York University, 2006; Louis V. Gerstner, Jr., *Who Says Elephants Can't Dance? Inside IBM's Historic Turnaround* (New York: HarperBusiness, 2002).

LeBaron has the authority to set selling prices, incur costs, and acquire and dispose of plant assets. The plant has an asset base of Fr2,480,000; and thus, the rate of return on assets for the year was 9% (Fr223,200 ÷ Fr2,480,000). In evaluating the performance of Walker Pharmaceuticals, top management would compare this rate of return with the rates desired by Heinrick Chemicals' management and with the rates of other investment centres in the company. Rate of return and other performance measures for responsibility centres are treated in greater depth in Chapter 12.

SUBOPTIMIZATION

Due to their closeness to daily divisional activities, responsibility centre managers should have more current and detailed knowledge about sales prices, costs, and other market information than does top management. Managers of profit and investment centres are encouraged, to the extent possible, to operate those subunits as separate economic entities while making certain that they exist to achieve goals consistent with those of the larger organization of which they are part.

Regardless of size, type of ownership, or product or service being sold, one basic goal for any business is to generate profits. For other organizations, such as charities and governmental entities, the ultimate financial goal may be to break even. The ultimate goal will be achieved through the satisfaction of organizational critical success factors—those items that are so important that, without them, the organization would cease to exist. Most organizations would consider quality, customer service, efficiency, cost control, and responsiveness to change as five critical success factors. If all of these factors are managed properly, the organization should be financially successful. If they are not, sooner or later the organization will fail. All members of the organization—especially managers—should work toward the same basic objectives if the critical success factors are to be satisfied. Losing sight of the overall organizational goals while working to achieve a separate responsibility centre's conflicting goal will result in *suboptimization*.

Suboptimization exists when individual managers pursue goals and objectives that are in their own and/or their segments' particular interests rather than in the company's best interest. As managers of profit and investment centres have great flexibility in regard to financial decisions, these managers must remember that their operations are integral parts of the entire corporate structure. Thus, actions of these organizational units should be in the best long-run interest of both the unit and its parent organization. Unit managers should be aware of and accept the need for goal congruence throughout the organization.

For suboptimization to be limited or minimized, top management must be aware of it and must develop ways to avoid it. One way managers can limit sub-optimization is by communicating corporate goals to all organizational units. Exhibit 11-10 depicts other ways of limiting suboptimization as stairsteps to the achievement of corporate goals. These steps are in no hierarchical order. If any steps are missing, however, the climb toward corporate goals and objectives becomes more difficult for divisional managers.

Companies may define their organizational units in various ways based on management accountability for one or more income-producing factors—costs, revenues, and/or assets. To properly evaluate the accomplishments of segments and their managers, companies will often set a market-based price at which to transfer goods or services between segments. Such prices can help measure a selling segment's revenue and a buying segment's costs.

LEARNING OBJECTIVE 4

What is suboptimization and what are its effects?

suboptimization
a situation in which unit managers make decisions that positively affect their own unit but that are detrimental to other organizational units or to the company as a whole

EXHIBIT 11-10

Performance Measures to Limit
Suboptimization

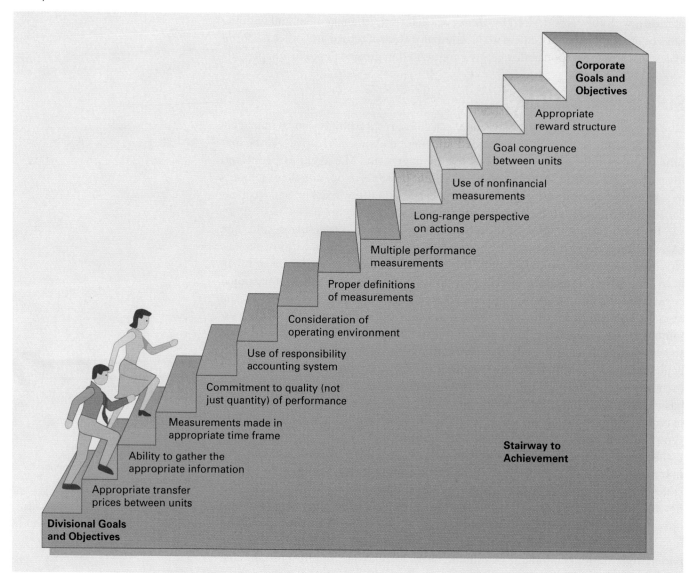

TRANSFER PRICING

Responsibility centres often provide goods or services to other company segments.
These transfers require that a **transfer price** (or charge-back system) be established
to account for the flow of these goods or services within the company. A transfer
price is an internal charge established for the exchange of goods or services
between organizational units of the same company. Internal company transfers
should be presented on external financial statements at the producing segment's
costs. Thus, if transfers are sold at an amount other than cost, the intersegment
profit, expense, and/or revenue must be removed from the accounts for external
financial reporting.

Intracompany transfers should be made only if they are in the best interest of
the whole organization. If both the buying and selling managers have the authority

McCain Foods Limited headquartered in Florenceville, New Brunswick, has plants in various parts of Canada and around the world that manufacture frozen french fries and other quality food products.

to negotiate the transfer price, the following general rules create the limits of the transfer pricing model:[3]

- The maximum transfer price should be no greater than the lowest market price at which the buying segment can acquire the goods or services externally.
- The minimum transfer price should be no less than the sum of the selling segment's incremental production costs plus the opportunity cost of the facilities used. Incremental cost refers to the additional cost of producing a contemplated quantity of output, which generally means variable costs of production. Examples of opportunity cost include forgone contribution margin on alternative products not made and rent on the facilities that would otherwise be available if the company were not making the product that is the subject of the transfer price analysis.

The difference between this model's upper and lower limits is the corporate profit (or savings) generated by producing internally rather than buying externally. The transfer price acts to "divide the corporate profit" between the buying and selling segments. From the company's perspective, any transfer price set between these two limits is generally considered appropriate. If the market price is less than the internal incremental cost, it may be concluded that the competition is significantly more efficient than the firm at making a specific product. In this case, management should consider either discontinuing production of that product or finding ways to make it more efficiently and competitively.

To illustrate use of this model, assume that product K is made by Division A of Heinrick Chemicals Company. Product K has per unit incremental production and opportunity costs of $8 and $5, respectively. The $5 opportunity cost represents the forgone unit contribution margin on a similar product the company would otherwise make. If Division A were to sell product K to Division B, the minimum transfer price would be $13. The same product is available from external suppliers for $11. Heinrick Chemicals' management has two choices. First, it can have Division A stop making product K and, instead, have Division B buy it from the external suppliers.

This decision is reasonable since, compared with those suppliers, Division A does not appear to be cost efficient in its production activities. Stopping production would release the facilities for other, more profitable purposes. Alternatively, management could insist that Division A improve its efficiency and reduce the cost of making product K. Either choice would benefit the company as a whole.

After the transfer price range limits have been determined, management may consider understandability in choosing a price within the range. Managers should be able to comprehend how a transfer price was set and how it will affect their divisions' profits. Most transfer prices are cost-based, market-based, or arrived at through a process of negotiation.

Assume that the Sussex Division (managed by Mr. Henry Higgins) of Heinrick Chemicals manufactures the basic compounds needed to formulate its antioxidant pill for the Montbatton Pharmaceutical Sales Territory (managed by Ms. Julie Pickering). The managers are attempting to establish a transfer price for each lot-size of 1,000 bottles. Sussex Division data (shown in Exhibit 11-11) are used to illustrate various transfer pricing approaches. Note that Sussex Division is capable of supplying all external and internal production needs.

EXHIBIT 11-11

Standard Cost and Other Information About Antioxidant Pills

Standard production cost per lot:		
Direct material (DM)	$160	
Direct labour (DL)	48	
Variable overhead (VOH)	72	
Variable selling and administrative	8	
Total variable costs		$288
Fixed overhead (FOH)*	$ 78	
Fixed selling and administrative*	10	88
Total costs		$376
Normal mark-up on variable cost (50%)		144
List selling price		$520

Estimated annual production: 400,000 lots
Estimated sales to outside entities: 150,000 lots
Estimated intracompany transfers: 250,000 lots

*Fixed costs are allocated to all lots produced based on estimated annual production.

Canadian tax reform could affect transfer prices, if the U.S. lead is followed. The U.S. Senate Finance Committee recently approved a bill that would treat U.S. companies domiciled in tax havens, like Bermuda, as U.S. firms for tax purposes unless they do a meaningful amount of business in their new host country.[4] An example would be a small appliance made in a low-tax country where the domiciled U.S. subsidiary pays $5 for it, only to sell the appliance for $50, to its U.S. parent, which sells it to Wal-Mart for $55. The $45 in income is taxed at a low rate, while the $5 is taxed at the higher U.S. rates. The U.S. Senate Finance Committee wants the entire $50 in profit to be taxed at the higher U.S. rates.

LEARNING OBJECTIVE 6

What are the differences among the various definitions of product cost for transfer pricing?

Cost-Based Transfer Prices

Because of its emphasis on cost, the cost-based method of establishing a transfer price would seem to be logical and appropriate. There are, however, numerous ways to compute cost. Product cost is defined as including direct material, direct labour, variable production overhead, and fixed production overhead. This definition reflects the concept of absorption, or full, costing. In contrast, variable costing includes only those cost components that change in relationship to volume (direct material, direct labour, and variable production overhead) in product cost. Variable costing treats fixed production overhead as a period expense. If cost is to be used as the basis for setting a transfer price, a definition of *cost* must first be agreed on by the managers engaging in the intracompany transfer.

The absorption cost for a 1,000-bottle lot is $358 ($160 DM + $48 DL + $72 VOH + $78 FOH). A transfer price equal to absorption cost provides a contribution toward covering the selling division's fixed production overhead. Such a transfer price does not produce the same amount of income that would be generated if the transferring division sold the goods externally, but it does provide for coverage of all production costs.

A transfer price for a lot size of bottles of antioxidant pills based on variable cost is either $280 or $288. The difference depends on whether variable cost is defined as variable production cost or total variable cost. Using either of these costs as the transfer price will not give Mr. Higgins much incentive to transfer the antioxidant pills internally. Fixed costs of Sussex Division would not be reduced by selling internally and no contribution margin would be generated by the transfers to help cover these fixed expenses.

One final difficulty with using a cost-based transfer price is whether an actual or standard cost should be used. If actual costs are used, inefficiencies in production may not be corrected, since their cost will simply be covered by the buying division.

Transfer Pricing Principles for Intellectual Property

INTERNATIONAL NEWS NOTE

Transfer pricing is the most significant tax issue of our time. It is an inherent feature of the global economy and it is universal, unavoidable, and especially important in managing the knowledge of the economy of which we are integral parts. Although little understood and appreciated, knowledge of transfer price can provide companies with a competitive advantage if used properly.

Transfer pricing is used with transferring property or services from one related member of a multinational enterprise (MNE) to another; specifically, they establish prices among themselves for transactions such as selling goods, providing services, licensing intellectual property (IP), and other commercial transactions. The transferred properties or services provided, of course, have an economic and accounting value.

As MNE members are related, they could be tempted to distort the value of the property or services for their own tax advantage. Thus, a series of rules called the transfer pricing rules was crafted to ensure that the transferred value between related companies is akin to the value that arm's length parties would establish in similar circumstances.

Significant tax advantages can be obtained from the licensing of IP. There are two arenas in which transfer pricing can be applied to IP licensing: property-based licensing and business-based licensing.

Property-based IP licensing is the more traditional approach. The most common form of property-based technology licensing usually occurs when the IP owner simply licenses the technology away in return for a royalty.

Business-based licensing is more sophisticated. It treats licensing as a full-fledged business concern. The business is not merely the IP business per se, but rather it is the licensing business. A licensing business plan requires proper business management. It must be based on knowledge of, and experience in, the business of licensing and in the licensing industry generally.

To apply transfer pricing principles to the business of licensing, it is necessary to separate the property function (the research and development function and the IP it generates) from the business function (crafting and implementing a global licensing program). This can be done quite readily by establishing a subsidiary corporation (commonly called an International Business Corporation or IBC) in another jurisdiction, commonly with a lower tax rate and with the requisite skills in the licensing business.

SOURCE: Ted LeValliant, "Transfer Pricing Principles for Intellectual Property," *CMA Management*, February 2004, pp. 36–38. Reprinted with permission.

But, if standard costs are used, and savings are effected over standard costs, the buying division will be "paying" more than actual cost for the goods.

Market-Based Transfer Prices

To avoid the problems involved in defining cost, some companies simply use a market price approach to setting transfer prices. Market price is believed to be an objective measure of value and simulates the selling price that would exist if the segments were independent companies. If a selling division is operating efficiently relative to its competition, it should ordinarily be able to show a profit when transferring products or services at market prices. An efficiently operating buying division should not be troubled by a market-based transfer price. After all, that is what would have to be paid for the goods or services if the alternative of buying internally did not exist.

Still, several problems may exist with using market prices for intracompany transfers. The first problem is that transfers may involve products that have no exact counterpart in the external market. Second, market price may not be entirely appropriate because of internal cost savings arising from reductions in bad debts, packaging, advertising, and delivery expenditures. Third, difficulties can arise in setting a transfer price when the market is depressed because of a temporary reduction in demand for the product. Should the current depressed price be used as the transfer price, or should the expected long-run market price be used? Last, a question exists as to what is the "right" market price to use. Different prices are quoted and different discounts and credit terms are allowed to different buyers. Thus, it may not be possible to determine the most appropriate market price to charge.

NEGOTIATED TRANSFER PRICES

negotiated transfer price
an intracompany charge for goods or services that has been set through a process of negotiation between the selling and purchasing unit managers

Due to the problems associated with both cost-based and market-based prices, **negotiated transfer prices** are often set through a process of bargaining between the selling and purchasing unit managers. Such prices are normally below the external sales price of the selling unit, above that unit's incremental costs plus opportunity cost, and below the market purchase price for the buying unit. A negotiated price meeting these specifications falls within the range limits of the transfer pricing model.

A negotiated transfer price for the Sussex Division of Heinrick Chemicals would be less than the $520 list selling price or the Montbatton Pharmaceutical Sales Division's buying price, if lower. The price would also be set greater than the $288 incremental (variable) costs. If some of the variable selling costs could be eliminated, the incremental cost would be even less. If Sussex Division could not sell any additional lots of antioxidant pills externally or downsize its facilities, there would be no opportunity cost involved. If neither of these conditions existed, an opportunity cost would have to be determined. This could increase total costs to as much as the $520 list selling price, if all lots could be sold externally.

Authority to negotiate a transfer price implies that division managers have the autonomy to sell or buy products externally if internal negotiations fail. To encourage cooperation between the transferring divisions, top management may consider allowing each party to set a different transfer price.

Dual Pricing

dual pricing arrangement
a transfer price method that allows a selling division to record the transfer of goods or services at a market-based or negotiated price and a buying division to record the transfer at a cost-based amount

Since a transfer price is used to satisfy internal managerial objectives, a **dual pricing arrangement** can be used that allows different transfer prices for the selling and the buying segments. The selling division records the transfer of goods or services at a market or negotiated market price, which provides a profit for that division. The buying division records the transfer at a cost-based amount, which provides a minimal cost for that division. Dual transfer pricing gives managers the most relevant information for decision making and performance evaluation.

Choosing the Appropriate Transfer Price

The final determination of which transfer pricing system to use should reflect the circumstances of the organizational units, as well as corporate goals. No one method of setting a transfer price is best in all instances. Exhibit 11-12 provides the results of a transfer pricing survey of Canadian multinational corporations (MNC) and indicates that transfer pricing is a major concern, especially for income tax reasons. An amazing 95% of the Canadian respondents reported that they had been investigated by the Canada Revenue Agency (CRA), thus suggesting that multinational corporations and other companies should set transfer prices to approximate market prices. Regardless of what method is used, a thoughtfully set transfer price will provide the following advantages:

- A means of encouraging what is best for the organization as a whole
- An appropriate basis for the calculation and evaluation of segment performance
- The rational acquisition or use of goods and services between corporate divisions
- The flexibility to respond to changes in demand or market conditions
- A means of motivating managers in decentralized operations

EXHIBIT 11-12

Survey of Canadian Transfer Pricing Methods

- 68% of Canadian parent respondents believe that transfer pricing is the biggest international tax issue they face over the next two years.
- 88% of Canadian subsidiary respondents believe that transfer pricing is very important to their group at present, and 80% think it will be a major international tax issue for them over the next two years.
- 92% of Canadian subsidiary respondents and 100% of Canadian parent respondents report that they do not include stock option expenses in their cost base.
- Canadian parent respondents report administrative or management services and the transfer or sale of finished goods for resale as transactions that are particularly susceptible to transfer pricing disputes with revenue authorities such as the Canada Revenue Agency.
- 96% of Canada's 25 subsidiary respondents report that they prepared transfer pricing documentation in accordance with the tax rules in Canada.
- 68% of Canadian parent respondents report that revenue authorities appear to be more attuned to transfer pricing issues.
- 84% of Canadian parent respondents have reviewed their current transfer pricing documentation for compliance in light of current revenue authority pronouncements and trends.

SOURCE: "Transfer Pricing: 2003 Global Survey," Ernst & Young.

Setting a reasonable transfer price is not an easy task. Everyone involved in the process must be aware of the positive and negative aspects of each type of transfer price and be responsive to suggestions of change if the need is indicated.

Transfer Prices for Service Departments

Setting transfer prices for products moving between one organizational unit and another is a well-established practice. Instituting transfer prices for services is a less common technique but an effective one for some types of service departments. Examples of services for which transfer prices may be used include computer services, secretarial services, legal services, and maintenance services. If management is

LEARNING OBJECTIVE 7

How and why are transfer prices for services used in organizations?

considering setting a transfer price for a service department, the questions in Exhibit 11-13 should first be answered. The exhibit also presents some suggestions as to how the transfer price should be set. All the questions should be considered simultaneously and the suggestions combined to form a reasonable transfer price.

EXHIBIT 11-13

Setting a Transfer Price for Services

	If Response Is:	
Questions	*Yes*	*No*
Is the service department to be considered a "money maker"?	Set transfer price using market-based, negotiated, or dual pricing.	Set transfer price using cost-based prices.
Does a user department have significant control over the quantity and quality of service used?	Use a base that reflects total quantity of activity of the service department.	Transfer prices are not particularly useful.
Do opportunities exist to use external services rather than internal services?	Use a base that reflects the typical manner in which external purchases are made.	Set transfer price by negotiation or upper level management; use a base that reflects the quantity of activity of the service department.
Is there a reasonable alternative (or surrogate) measure of service benefits provided to users?	Use a base representing total volume of alternative measures produced by the service department.	Transfer prices are not particularly useful.
Are the services provided of a recurring nature?	Use a fixed price for each service used.	Use a price that reflects the degree of use, constrained by whether the user can bear the cost.
Are all services provided of a similar nature?	Use a fixed price based on a single factor of use.	Use a price that reflects the degree of use, constrained by whether user can bear the cost.
Are the services performed typically expensive?	Use market-based or negotiated prices, constrained by whether the user can bear the cost. The base may be more complex than typical.	Use cost-based or negotiated prices. The base should be easy to understand and to compute.

A department planning to use transfer prices for services must decide on a capacity level for use in price development. This decision is equivalent to that made in setting a predetermined overhead rate. For example, a service department may use expected annual capacity or practical capacity. If expected annual capacity is chosen, the transfer price per unit of service will be higher than if practical capacity is chosen. If the service department uses expected annual capacity and performs more services than expected, a favourable volume variance will arise.[5] Users will not necessarily benefit from reduced charges, because the transfer price is not normally changed. Use of practical capacity will, on the other hand, create a lower price. It might also encourage more internal services use and generate ideas as to how to use the additional capacity to fill outside needs. In addition, if the practical capacity level is not achieved, an unfavourable volume variance is noted, and the opportunity cost of underutilization is clearly identifiable.

In developing transfer prices for services, general costs must be allocated to the various departments equitably, and the underlying reason for cost incurrence must be determined. Transfer prices are useful when service departments provide distinct, measurable benefits to other areas or provide services having a specific cause-and-effect relationship. Transfer prices in these circumstances can provide certain advantages (see Exhibit 11-14) to the organization in both the revenue-producing and service departments.

EXHIBIT 11-14

Advantages of Transfer Prices for Services

	User Departments	Provider Departments
User involvement	Because they are being charged for services, user departments may suggest ways in which provider departments can improve services.	Because they are charging for the services they are providing, provider departments may become more aware of the needs of their users and seek to develop services that are more beneficial to user departments.
Cost consciousness	Because they are being charged for services, user departments may restrict usage to those services that are necessary and cost beneficial.	Because they are charging for the services they are providing, provider departments must be able to justify the prices charged and, thus, may maintain more control over costs.
Performance evaluations	Because control over amount of services used exists, user departments can include costs in performance evaluations.	Because transfer prices can generate "revenues" for their departments, provider department managers have more ways to evaluate departmental performance.

First, transfer prices can encourage more involvement between the user and service departments. Users are more likely to suggest ways for the service department to improve its performance, since improved performance could result in lower transfer prices. Service departments are more likely to interact with users to find out the specific types of services that are needed and to eliminate or reduce those that are not cost beneficial.

Second, use of a transfer price for services should cause managers to be more cost conscious. Managers of user departments should attempt to eliminate waste. For example, if an MIS Department charged recipients in other departments for the number of reports received, managers would be less likely to request reports simply to be "on the receiving list," as sometimes occurs. For managers of the service departments, cost consciousness is directed at monitoring the cost to provide services. If excessive costs are incurred, a reasonable transfer price may not cover costs or a high transfer price may not be justifiable to users.

Last, transfer prices can provide information useful in evaluating managerial performance. Responsibility reports for user departments show a service department cost related to the quantity of actual services used. User department managers should be able to justify what services were used during the period. Transfer prices allow service departments to be treated as money-making operations rather than simply cost-generating operations. Responsibility reports of these departments indicate the transfer prices charged and the costs of providing services. Thus, these managers can be held accountable for cost control and profitability. The cost effectiveness of the provider department can then be determined and compared with the cost of outsourcing.

Although transfer prices for services can be effective tools, they do have certain disadvantages. First, there can be, and often is, disagreement among unit managers as to how the transfer price should be set. Second, implementing transfer prices in the accounting system requires additional organizational costs and employee time. Third, transfer prices may not work equally well for all types of service departments. Service departments that do not provide measurable benefits or cannot show a distinct cause-and-effect relationship between cost incurrence and service use by other departments should not use transfer prices. Finally, depending on how the transfer price is set, a transfer price may cause dysfunctional behaviour among the organizational units; for example, certain services may be underutilized or overutilized. A company should weigh the advantages and disadvantages of using transfer prices before deciding whether a transfer pricing system would enhance or detract from organizational effectiveness and efficiency.

LEARNING OBJECTIVE 8

How are transfer prices set in a multinational setting?

TRANSFER PRICING IN A MULTINATIONAL SETTING

Because of the differences in tax systems, customs duties, freight and insurance costs, import/export regulations, and foreign exchange controls, setting transfer prices for products and services becomes extremely difficult when the company is engaged in multinational operations. In addition, as shown in Exhibit 11-15, the internal and external objectives of transfer pricing in multinational companies (MNCs) differ.

EXHIBIT 11-15

Multinational Company Transfer Pricing Objectives

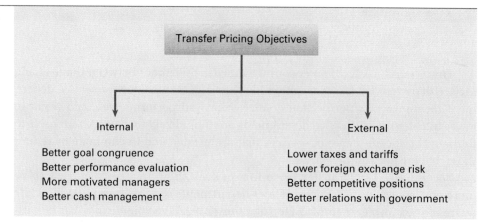

SOURCE: Republished with permission of the Institute of Management Accounting, from Wagdy M. Abdallah, "Guidelines for CEOs in Transfer Pricing Policies," *Management Accounting,* September 1998.

Because of these differences, there is no simple way to determine transfer prices in MNCs. Multinational companies may use one transfer price when a product is sent to or received from one country and a totally different transfer price for the same product when it is sent to or received from another. However, some guidelines as to transfer pricing should be set by the company and followed on a consistent basis. For example, a company should not price transfers to nondomestic subsidiaries in a way that would send the majority of costs to a subsidiary in the country with the highest tax rate unless that pricing method was reasonable and equitable to all subsidiaries. The general test of reasonableness is that transfer prices should reflect unbiased, or "arm's-length" transactions.

As indicated in the following News Note, MNC transfer prices are now being carefully scrutinized by tax authorities in both the home and host countries because such prices determine which country taxes the income from the transfer. The Government of Canada is concerned about both Canadian multinationals operating in low-tax countries and foreign companies operating in Canada. The Government of Canada believes that, in both situations, companies could avoid paying Canadian

CRA Clarifies "Reasonable Efforts" to Determine Arm's Length Transfer Prices

THE CANADA REVENUE AGENCY (CRA) recently released guidance to help taxpayers determine whether they had made "reasonable efforts" to determine and use arm's-length transfer prices or arm's-length allocations. The guidance may also apply to reasonable efforts to match the contributions of participants to their respective expected benefits under a qualifying cost contribution arrangement.

Background

Taxpayers may be subject to a 10% transfer pricing penalty when the net amount of transfer pricing adjustments imposed by the CRA exceeds a specific threshold.

This penalty focuses on the efforts a taxpayer makes to determine an arm's length price; it does not focus solely on the ultimate accuracy of the transfer price. As long as a taxpayer has made "reasonable efforts" to determine and use arm's length prices or allocations, the transfer pricing penalty will not apply.

Rules for Transfer Pricing Documentation

Under rules concerning contemporaneous documentation for non–arm's-length transactions, a taxpayer may be deemed not to have made reasonable efforts to determine and use arm's-length transfer prices or allocations unless the taxpayer has:

- Prepared or obtained records or documents providing a complete and accurate description of several items related to the transactions listed in subsection 247(4) of the Income Tax Act (the Act)
- Prepared or obtained the documentation by the due date
- Provided the documents to the CRA within three months of a written request to do so.

Guidance for Determining Reasonable Efforts

Though the CRA has said that whether a taxpayer has made reasonable efforts to determine and use arm's-length prices or allocations can only be determined case by case, the CRA recently provided general guidance in its Transfer Pricing Memorandum TPM-09.

According to the guidance, the CRA's Transfer Pricing Review Committee will consider several factors when evaluating whether a taxpayer has made reasonable efforts to determine arm's-length transfer prices or allocations. These factors are summarized as follows:

Compliance Versus Accuracy

Generally, "reasonable efforts" requires the taxpayer to consider applying a recommended transfer pricing methodology in accordance with the CRA's hierarchy of recommended methodologies. The taxpayer should explain the choice of the method applied.

Determining whether a taxpayer reasonably selected and applied a specified method is whether the taxpayer made a reasonable search for data. The CRA will assess the degree of this compliance effort against the absolute size of the transactions. As such, it would be reasonable for taxpayers to devote proportionally more effort to finding comparable data for larger transactions than for smaller ones, regardless of their relative importance to the taxpayer's business.

When differences exist between the taxpayer's situation and that of the entities engaged in comparable transactions, it may be difficult to determine the adjustments necessary to eliminate the effects of those differences on transfer prices. Nevertheless, taxpayers should make an effort to identify and make any adjustments required to account for those differences.

Demonstrated Efforts

The use of proper documentation is the most effective way that taxpayers can demonstrate that they have made reasonable efforts to comply with the arm's-length principle. The list of documents in subsection 247(4) of the Act is not intended to be exhaustive. Taxpayers may have to provide additional documentation to satisfy the general determination of reasonable efforts.

The taxpayer should maintain sufficient documentation to establish that it reasonably concluded that, given the available data and the applicable pricing methods, the method chosen provides an arm's-length result. The taxpayer needs to explain all steps taken to ensure compliance with the arm's length principle.

Administrative Burden

When preparing documentation, the taxpayer should attempt to weigh the significance of the transactions in relation to its business against the additional administrative costs required to prepare or obtain such documentation. The obligation of finding comparable transactions for applying the arm's-length principle is not absolute. The cost and likelihood of finding such comparables relative to the significance of the transactions to the taxpayer should be taken into account.

Qualifying Cost Contribution Arrangements

The CRA guidance also addresses "qualifying cost contribution arrangements" (QCCAs). A cost sharing arrangement will not be considered a QCCA if the taxpayer does not make reasonable efforts to match the contributions of the participants to their respective expected benefits. The guidance details items that documentation pertaining to a QCCA should include.

SOURCE: KPMG LLP (Canada), November 20, 2006, No. 2006-07; Found at: http://www.kpmg.ca/en/services/tax/TP60Sec0607.html.

corporate income taxes by using misleading or inaccurate transfer pricing. Thus, the Canada Revenue Agency may be quick to investigate Canadian subsidiaries that operate in low-tax countries or areas and suddenly show unusually high profits. If foreign companies charge their Canadian subsidiaries higher prices than what they would charge subsidiaries in their home country, Canadian taxable income (and thus the tax base) will decline—which may also bring about a CRA review.

As mentioned in Chapter 1, transfers among nations are becoming easier because of trade arrangements such as the European Union, the North American Free Trade Agreement, the General Agreement on Tariffs and Trade, and the World Trade Organization. These arrangements should help reduce the significance of transfer price manipulations through the harmonization of tax structures and reductions in import/export fees, tariffs, and capital movement restrictions.

INTERNATIONAL NEWS NOTE

Transfer Pricing in China

The relevant legislation governing transfer pricing in China stipulates that intercompany transactions and transactions between "associated entities" should be priced using "arm's length principles." Many of the Chinese transfer pricing laws and regulations were formulated largely on the recommendations set out by the Organization for Economic Co-Operation and Development. The arm's length principle is the international standard that the OECD member countries have agreed should be used for determining transfer pricing for tax purposes. The principle requires that a parent company treat its associated enterprises on the same basis as it treats an independent enterprise.

In 1998, China's State Administration of Taxation issued the first comprehensive transfer pricing regulations, known as Circular 59, which regulates both the procedural and substantive aspects of the transfer pricing investigations in China. Generally this allows for the tax bureau to make adjustments to tax payable on companies who do not conduct transactions as independent enterprises. The test of "association" between entities is based on control and ownership. If two entities are regarded as being associated, the firm must classify all related interentity transactions and account for them according to the arm's length principle. This applies to tangible assets, intangible assets, and intercompany service transactions. Should an enterprise fail to conduct business with its related parties at arm's length, and that business results in profit shifting out of China, the local tax bureau may adjust the pricing and tax the deemed income accordingly.

SOURCE: *Shanghai Business Review*, January–February 2004, pp. 14–15.

A multiversity is highly accountable for spending money. As a nonprofit organization, it must balance its budget; generally, it cannot go seriously into debt except to finance capital projects. However, responsibility accounting with regard to revenues and expenses is rather trivial. All of Canada's 10 to 12 multiversities have two main missions. (Those universities are University of British Columbia, University of Alberta, University of Western Ontario, University of Waterloo, McMaster University, University of Toronto, Queen's University, University of Montreal, McGill University, and Laval University. Two others should be added: University of Calgary and University of Ottawa.)

One mission is teaching, the other is research, and those two missions are measured in different ways. Regarding research productivity, the research output of professors is constantly being evaluated by other specialists in conjunction with refereed conferences and journals. Research funding is measured and reported by university and is biased toward those universities with faculties of engineering and medicine. Also, Fellows of the Royal Society of Canada at a given university are counted as another indication of research quality. The ultimate measure is the presence of Nobel laureates on the university's various faculties.

There are few available measures for assessing teaching quality. There are no published reports that reveal how much students have progressed intellectually.

For proper responsibility accounting, multiversities should measure their performance in both research and teaching. A balanced budget does not indicate success with either research nor teaching. Performance measures will be discussed in the next chapter.

SOURCES: Derek Bok, *Our Underachieving Colleges: A Candid Look at How Much Students Learn and Why They Should Be Learning More* (Princeton: Princeton University Press, 2006); George Fallis, *Multiversities, Ideas, and Democracy* (Toronto: University of Toronto Press, 2007).

CHAPTER SUMMARY

1 **When are decentralized operations appropriate?**

Centralization refers to a concentration of management control at high organizational levels, while decentralization refers to the downward delegation of decision-making authority to subunit managers. Thus, a decentralized organization comprises operational units led by managers who have some autonomy in decision making. The degree to which a company is decentralized depends on top management's philosophy and the unit managers' abilities to perform independently. Decentralization provides the opportunity for managers to develop leadership qualities, creative problem-solving abilities, and decision-making skills. It also lets the individual most closely in tune with the operational unit and its immediate environment make the decisions for that unit, and reduces the time spent in communicating and making decisions.

2 **How does responsibility accounting relate to decentralization?**

In a decentralized structure, subunit managers are evaluated in part by use of responsibility reports. Responsibility reports reflect the upward flow of information from each decentralized unit to the top of the organization. Managers receive information regarding the activities under their immediate control and under the control of their direct subordinates. The information is successively aggregated, and the reports allow the application of the management by exception principle.

3 **What are the differences among the four types of responsibility centres?**
Responsibility centres are classified as cost, revenue, profit, or investment. Each classification reflects the degree of authority managers have for financial items within their subunits. The type of responsibility centre also affects the kind of performance measurements that can be used for the centre and its manager.

4 **What is suboptimization and what are its effects?**
Suboptimization occurs when a subunit or separate subordinate responsibility unit loses sight of the overall organizational goals; the effects are a lack of cohesion among responsibility centres.

5 **How and why are transfer prices for products used in organizations?**
Transfer prices are intracompany charges for products exchanged between segments of a company.

6 **What are the differences among the various definitions of product cost for transfer pricing?**
Product transfer prices are typically cost-based, market-based, or negotiated. A dual pricing system that assigns different transfer prices to the buying and selling units may also be used. Management should promote a transfer pricing system that is in the best interest of the whole company, motivates managers to strive for segment effectiveness and efficiency, and is practical.

7 **How and why are transfer prices for services used in organizations?**
Transfer prices for services are used in organizations for charging for services that are provided by one responsibility centre to another. The prices are established to compensate the provider responsibility centre.

8 **How are transfer prices set in a multinational setting?**
Setting transfer prices in multinational enterprises is a complex process because of the differences that exist in tax structures, import/export regulations, customs duties, and other factors associated with international subsidiaries and divisions. A valid transfer price for a multinational firm is one that achieves economic benefit for the entire company and generates support from the domestic and international managers utilizing the system.

Key Terms

Centralization (p. 662)
Cost centre (p. 671)
Decentralization (p. 662)
Dual pricing arrangement (p. 682)
Effectiveness (p. 666)
Efficiency (p. 666)
Goal congruence (p. 665)
Investment centre (p. 675)
Management by exception (p. 664)

Negotiated transfer price (p. 682)
Profit centre (p. 674)
Responsibility accounting (p. 665)
Responsibility centre (p. 670)
Responsibility reports (p. 665)
Revenue centre (p. 672)
Suboptimization (p. 677)
Transfer price (p. 678)

Points to Remember

Transfer Prices (Cost-based, market-based, negotiated, dual)

Assuming both managers have the authority to negotiate transfer price:

      Upper Limit: Lowest price available from external suppliers
      Feasible region for setting a reasonable transfer price
      Lower Limit: Incremental costs of producing and selling the transferred goods
         or services plus the opportunity cost for the facilities used

DEMONSTRATION PROBLEM

Jorgensen Company of Sweden makes duck callers. The firm's annual revenue is SKr14,000,000 (SKr is the symbol for the krona, the currency unit in Sweden). Johan Ericsen, the firm's controller, devised a new budgetary system. Annual budget figures are divided into 12 equal monthly amounts for monthly performance evaluations. Greta Thommasen, vice-president of production, was distressed when she reviewed the following responsibility report for the Forming and Polishing Department for March:

Forming and Polishing Department—Responsibility Report
For the Month Ended March 31

	Actual	*Budget*	*Variance Over (Under)*
Volume in units	3,822	3,600	222
Variable production costs:			
Direct material	SKr119,250	SKr115,200	SKr 4,050
Direct labour	140,650	133,200	7,450
Variable overhead	168,170	159,840	8,330
Total	SKr428,070	SKr408,240	SKr19,830
Fixed production costs:			
Depreciation	SKr 7,200	SKr 7,200	SKr 0
Indirect labour	15,840	16,000	(160)
Insurance	1,150	1,150	0
Taxes	1,440	1,440	0
Other	4,930	4,460	470
Total	SKr 30,560	SKr 30,250	SKr 310
Corporate costs:			
Quality assurance staff	SKr 17,890	SKr 11,520	SKr 6,370
Selling and general	19,560	17,280	2,280
Total	SKr 37,450	SKr 28,800	SKr 8,650
Total costs	SKr496,080	SKr467,290	SKr28,790

Required:

a. Discuss the weaknesses in the report.
b. Revise the report to reduce or eliminate the weaknesses.
c. Variances greater than 10% of budget are considered to be significant enough to be investigated. Identify these.

   (IMA adapted)

Solution to Demonstration Problem

a. There are two major deficiencies in the report:
  1. Responsibility reports for a cost centre should compare actual costs with flexible budget costs. The report presented compares actual costs with static budget costs (which were estimated for 3,600 units, while actual production was 3,822 units). Costs measured at two different activity levels are not comparable for control or evaluation purposes.
  2. The report presented includes corporate costs that are not within the control of the Forming and Polishing Department manager. Some of the fixed production costs are also probably not controllable by the manager of this cost centre, although the problem does not provide enough information to address this concern.

b.

Forming and Polishing Department—Responsibility Report
For the Month Ended March 31

Volume in units	Actual (3,822)		Budget (3,822)		Variance
	Per unit	Total	Per unit	Total	Over (Under)
Variable production costs:					
Direct material	SKr 31.20	SKr 119,250	SKr 32.00	SKr 122,304	SKr (3,054)
Direct labour	36.80	140,650	37.00	141,414	(764)
Variable overhead	44.00	168,170	44.40	169,697	(1,527)
Total	SKr 112.00	SKr 428,070	SKr 113.40	SKr 433,415	SKr (5,345)
Fixed production costs:					
Depreciation		SKr 7,200		SKr 7,200	SKr 0
Indirect labour		15,840		16,000	(160)
Insurance		1,150		1,150	0
Taxes		1,440		1,440	0
Other		4,930		4,460	470
Total		SKr 30,560		SKr 30,250	SKr 310
Total production costs		SKr 458,630		SKr 463,665	SKr (5,035)

c. Only the "other" cost category reflects a variance exceeding 10% of budget. Note that the revised report provides a more realistic and a more favourable view of performance than does the original report.

End-of-Chapter Materials

SELF-TEST QUESTIONS

(SOLUTIONS APPEAR AT THE END OF THE CHAPTER.)

1. Decentralization works best in organizations with all of the following attributes except:
   a. Young
   b. Growing
   c. Large
   d. Top management has high confidence in subordinates

2. Which of the following is a disadvantage of decentralization?
   a. Helps top management recognize and develop managerial talent
   b. Requires more effective communication abilities
   c. Often leads to job satisfaction
   d. Allows the use of management by exception

3. Centralization works best in organizations with all of the following attributes except:
   a. High use of technology
   b. Young
   c. Small
   d. Slow growth rate

4. Responsibility accounting:
   a. Ensures that managers are responsible
   b. Means that a firm uses budgets and plans
   c. Is another word for flexible budgeting
   d. Assists management in evaluating subordinate performance

5. The steps of the control process include all of the following except:
   a. Prepare a plan
   b. Gather actual data
   c. Demand performance from subordinates
   d. Monitor the differences between planned and actual data

6. Responsibility centres include the following:
   a. Cost centres
   b. Revenue centres
   c. Investment centres
   d. All of the above

7. Suboptimization exists when:
   a. Optimization is not known
   b. Individual managers pursue goals that are not the organization's goals
   c. Individual managers pursue the company's goals
   d. Companies are unable to define their optimal goals

8. Transfer prices can be all of the following except:
   a. Cost-based
   b. Revenue-based
   c. Market-based
   d. Negotiated

9. In setting transfer prices with multinational firms, the following should occur:
   a. Transfer prices should be minimized
   b. Transfer prices should be maximized
   c. Transfer prices should reflect non-arm's length transactions
   d. Transfer prices should reflect arm's length transactions

10. Which is not an advantage of transfer prices for services?
    a. Suggest ways in which provider departments cannot improve services
    b. Suggest ways in which provider departments can improve services
    c. User departments may restrict usage
    d. User departments can include costs in performance evaluation

QUESTIONS

1. Differentiate decision-making authority between centrally organized and decentrally organized companies.

2. Would a very young company or a large mature company be more likely to employ decentralized management? Explain.

3. Why do the personality traits of subunit managers affect the success of efforts to decentralize decision making?

4. Some organizational activities are more likely to be decentralized than others. What activities are most likely to be decentralized? least likely? Why?

5. Top managers at Worldwide Manufacturing Company are pondering the possibility of decentralizing control of all foreign operating divisions. The firm has traditionally maintained very tight central control over these operations. What major costs of decentralization should Worldwide's top managers consider in making their decision?

6. What is a responsibility accounting system? What is its role in a decentralized firm?

7. Why is a segment manager's performance evaluated separately from the segment's performance?

8. Describe the four types of responsibility centres. For each type, how can performance be measured?

9. How are variances used by managers in controlling the organization?

10. How is the philosophy of management by exception employed in responsibility accounting systems?

11. Describe how suboptimization is related to the performance measures that are used to evaluate segment managers and segment performance.

12. Is managerial performance always evaluated solely on financial measures? Explain.

13. What is a transfer price? What role does a transfer price play in a decentralized company?

14. What are the high and low limits of transfer prices, and why do these limits exist?

15. A company is considering the use of a cost-based transfer price. What argument favours the use of standard, rather than actual, cost?

16. What practical problems may interfere with the use of a market-based transfer price?

17. What is dual pricing? What is the intended effect of dual pricing on the reported performance of each division affected by the dual price?

18. How can service departments use transfer prices, and what advantages do transfer prices have over cost allocation methods?

19. Explain why determining transfer prices may be more complex in a multinational setting than in a domestic setting.

20. Why do provincial, federal, and foreign taxation authorities scrutinize transfer price determination in multinational companies?

EXERCISES

1. (LO 1, 2, 3, 4, 6) Your roommate has asked you for help in matching each of the lettered items on the left with the appropriate numbered item on the right.

<table>
<tr><td>a.</td><td>Suboptimization</td><td>1.</td><td>Decisions in this type of company are made by division managers</td></tr>
<tr><td>b.</td><td>Dual pricing arrangement</td><td></td><td></td></tr>
<tr><td>c.</td><td>Centralized organization</td><td>2.</td><td>Manager is primarily responsible for generating revenues, controlling costs, and managing assets</td></tr>
<tr><td>d.</td><td>Goal congruence</td><td></td><td></td></tr>
<tr><td>e.</td><td>Profit centre</td><td></td><td></td></tr>
<tr><td>f.</td><td>Decentralized organization</td><td>3.</td><td>Manager is primarily responsible for controlling operating costs</td></tr>
<tr><td>g.</td><td>Cost centre</td><td></td><td></td></tr>
<tr><td>h.</td><td>Investment centre</td><td>4.</td><td>The process of making decisions that may not be in the best interest of the entire firm</td></tr>
<tr><td>i.</td><td>Responsibility centre</td><td></td><td></td></tr>
<tr><td>j.</td><td>Revenue centre</td><td></td><td></td></tr>
<tr><td></td><td></td><td>5.</td><td>Price charged to buying division differs from price paid to selling division</td></tr>
<tr><td></td><td></td><td>6.</td><td>Organizational and personal goals are consistent</td></tr>
<tr><td></td><td></td><td>7.</td><td>Manager is responsible for revenue generation and operating cost control</td></tr>
<tr><td></td><td></td><td>8.</td><td>Manager is primarily responsible for revenue generation</td></tr>
<tr><td></td><td></td><td>9.</td><td>The organizational cost object under the control of a manager</td></tr>
<tr><td></td><td></td><td>10.</td><td>Decisions in this type of company are generally made by top management</td></tr>
</table>

2. (LO 1, 2) Each of the following independent descriptions characterizes some trait of an organization. You have become involved in the formation of a new company and are considering how to structure it.

Required:

For each description below, you have been asked by your investor group to indicate whether the firm would be more likely to adopt a centralized (C) or decentralized (D) control structure.

a. The firm has just been established.

b. A bad decision would have disastrous consequences for the company.

c. The firm is growing very rapidly.

d. The entrepreneurial CEO is the firm's founder and wants to maintain involvement in all aspects of the business.

e. The firm's operations span the globe. Many of the foreign divisions have operations that are very sensitive to volatility in local economic conditions.

f. Top management expresses sincere doubts about the capability of lower-level managers to make sound economic decisions.

3. (LO 1) The local chapter of the Chamber of Commerce has invited you to give an after-dinner speech on selecting an appropriate organizational structure. A friend of yours has suggested a number of issues that might be considered in choosing between a centralized organization and a decentralized one. However, before he can discuss these issues with you, he gets lost in cyberspace and refuses to be disturbed.

Required:

Since your talk is tonight, you need to decide whether each of the following might be a potential advantage (A) of decentralization, a disadvantage (D) of decentralization, or neither (N).

a. Promotion of goal congruence

b. Support of training in decision making

c. Development of leadership qualities

d. Complication of communication process

e. Cost of developing planning and reporting systems

f. Placement of decision maker closer (in time and place) to problem

EXERCISES

g. Speed of decisions
h. Use of management by exception principle by top management
i. Greater job satisfaction
j. Delegation of ultimate responsibility

4. (LO 2) The Tool and Die Department of Metro Manufacturing is structured as a cost centre. Below are selected budget and actual costs of the department:

	Planning Budget	Actual	Flexible Budget
Professional labour	$900,000	$925,000	$1,000,317
Supplies	14,000	15,200	16,200
Materials	114,000	119,350	117,200
Energy	26,000	29,300	32,100
Quality control	172,600	172,000	195,100
Depreciation	250,000	250,000	250,000
Software amortization	90,000	103,000	90,000

Metro has a policy of investigating any variance that differs from the expected amount for the actual level of operations by 5% or more.

Required:

The company accountant has become ill and the CEO has enlisted you to address the following:

a. Which budget amount, planning or flexible, reflects the expected level of cost occurrence for the actual level of operations?
b. Based on your answer in part (a), compute variances for each cost category.
c. Which variances should be investigated further?
d. Which favourable variances, if any, might be of great concern to management? Explain.

5. (LO 3) Namer Industries produces and sells a stainless steel surgical knife. The Marketing Department is evaluated based on a comparison of achieved revenues with budgeted revenues. For the year, the company projected sales to be 410,000 units at an average price of $42. The company actually sold 425,000 knives at an average price of $39.50.

Required:

The Marketing Department manager is upset and has enlisted your help in trying to understand the revenue shortfall.

a. Compute the revenue price and volume variances for the year.
b. The president of Namer is curious as to why you didn't compute a sales mix variance. Write a brief memo explaining to her why a sales mix variance is inappropriate for her company.
c. Based on your computations in part (a), can you determine whether profits were above or below the budget level? Explain.

6. (LO 3) The Sales Department of the Aqua Store is responsible for sales of two principal products: fins and masks. For August, the Sales Department's actual and budgeted sales were as follows:

	Fins		Masks	
	Dollars	Units	Dollars	Units
Budgeted sales	$20,000	4,000	$80,000	4,000
Actual sales	18,000	3,000	69,000	3,000

Required:

The sales manager for the Aqua Store is your friend and has asked you to help her with the following.

a. For August, compute the price variance for the Sales Department of the Aqua Store.
b. Compute the volume variance for the Sales Department for August.
c. Compute the sales mix variance for the Sales Department for August.
d. Explain why you would expect a relatively minor sales mix variance for this company even when substantial variances may arise for sales volume and price.

EXERCISES

7. (LO 3) Fine Leather Products Inc. manufactures two products: women's shoes and baseball gloves. The firm budgeted the following:

	Shoes	Baseball Gloves
Sales	$800,000	$1,800,000
Unit sales price	$40	$30

At the end of the period, managers were informed that total actual sales amounted to 70,000 units and totalled $2,700,000. Shoe sales for the year amounted to 30,000 units at an average price of $35.

Required:
a. Compute the total revenue variance.
b. Compute the price variance.
c. Compute the sales mix variance.
d. Compute the sales volume variance.

8. (LO 3) Cascade Inns evaluates its inns and innkeepers based on a comparison of actual profit with budgeted profit. A budgeted income statement for the Cascade Inn in Saskatoon follows:

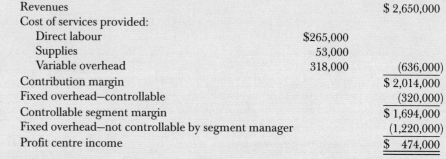

Revenues		$ 2,650,000
Cost of services provided:		
Direct labour	$265,000	
Supplies	53,000	
Variable overhead	318,000	(636,000)
Contribution margin		$ 2,014,000
Fixed overhead—controllable		(320,000)
Controllable segment margin		$ 1,694,000
Fixed overhead—not controllable by segment manager		(1,220,000)
Profit centre income		$ 474,000

Actual revenues generated were $2,900,000. Actual variable costs were: direct labour, 12% of revenues; supplies, 3% of revenues; variable overhead, 14% of revenues. Controllable fixed costs amounted to $330,000, and other fixed overhead costs were $1,425,000.

Required:
a. Prepare an actual income statement.
b. Compute revenue and cost variances.
c. Evaluate the performance of the manager of the Cascade Inn.
d. Evaluate the performance of the Cascade Inn.

9. (LO 5) The Accessory Division, an autonomous segment (profit centre) of All-Canadian Motors, is considering what price to charge for transfers of water pumps to the Large Truck Division of the company. The following data on production cost per water pump have been gathered:

Direct materials	$20.40
Direct labour	4.20
Variable overhead	12.60
Fixed overhead	10.80
Total	$48.00

The Accessory Division sells the water pumps to external buyers for $63. Managers of the Large Truck Division have received external offers to provide comparable water pumps at prices ranging from $55 at one company to $73 at another.

Required:
Top management has engaged you to help in developing a transfer price for these water pumps.
a. Determine the upper and lower limits for the transfer price between the Accessory Division and the Large Truck Division.
b. What is the transfer price if it is equal to full production cost?

EXERCISES

c.   What is the transfer price if it is equal to variable production cost?

d.   Why would the Accessory Division be reluctant to transfer goods at a price equal to variable cost?

10. (LO 5) Bridgeport Corporation has several operating divisions. The Motor Division manufactures motors for ceiling fans and other appliances. The Fan Division manufactures ceiling fans and several other products that require a motor similar to the one produced by the Motor Division. The Motor Division sells 90% of its output externally and transfers the other 10% to the Fan Division. Bridgeport Corporation makes all internal transfers at market price. The Motor Division's cost and revenue structure follows:

Sales price per motor	$75
Variable manufacturing costs	37
Fixed manufacturing costs	14
Variable selling and administration	2
Fixed selling and administration	5

Both per unit fixed cost computations are based on an expected capacity of 200,000 units.

Required:

As a student intern assigned to Bridgeport's finance office, you have been asked to address the following items.

a.   From the perspective of Bridgeport Corporation, what is the variable cost of producing and selling a fan motor?

b.   What is the variable cost of a fan motor from the perspective of the Fan Division?

c.   Under what circumstances would it be desirable for the Fan Division to know the true variable cost of an electric fan motor?

11. (LO 5) Among other products, the Office Supplies Division of Upscale Artifacts Company produces small plastic cases. Of its output, 40% is sold to the Garden Division of Upscale Artifacts Company, and the rest is sold to external parties. All internal transfers occur at a fixed price of $1.25 per unit. Office Supplies Division's expected results for the year are shown next.

	Internal	External
Sales (150,000 units)	$ 75,000	$135,000
Costs:		
Variable	(30,000)	(45,000)
Fixed	(36,000)	(54,000)
Gross profit	$ 9,000	$ 36,000

Office Supplies Division has received an external offer that would enable it to sell, at $1.40 per unit, all the units now scheduled to be sold internally. To accommodate this sale, Garden Division would have to purchase its units externally for $1.70 per unit.

Required:

The two division managers have come to you, the firm's chief accountant, with the following questions.

a.   By what amount will Office Supplies Division's gross profit change if it accepts the offer from the external party?

b.   By what amount will Garden Division's gross profit change if Office Supplies Division accepts the offer from the external party?

c.   Assume Office Supplies Division negotiates a transfer price with Garden Division of $1.40 per unit. However, the additional gross profit (relative to the normal internal sales price) generated for Office Supplies Division by this transfer price will be split between Office Supplies Division and Garden Division. What will be the actual transfer price for each unit after this sharing of profit takes place?

d.   How could a dual pricing system be used to provide an incentive for an internal transfer in this situation?

12. (LO 5) Accessories Division produces a speaker set that is sold to Stereo Division at the market price of $90. Accessories Division does not sell any speakers externally. Annual production and sales are 40,000 sets. The cost of production for a speaker set is shown below:

Variable production costs	$55
General fixed overhead ($12 per hour; 1 hour for production time)	12
Direct fixed overhead ($320,000 ÷ 40,000)	8
Unit cost	75
Variable shipping expenses	4
Total unit cost	$79

General fixed overhead is composed of some allocated production costs relating to the building and the production activities. Discontinuation of speaker production would save Accessories Division $40,000 in annual direct fixed overhead. Accessories Division's management has asked you to address the following items.

Required:
a. Determine the incremental cost of producing one speaker set.
b. Assume Accessories Division is operating at full capacity. What is the appropriate unit cost to be used to set a minimum transfer price for selling speaker sets to Stereo Division? Why is this cost most appropriate?

13. (LO 7) A friend of yours has asked you whether, in relation to using transfer prices for service department costs, each of the following conditions might be a potential advantage (A), a potential disadvantage (D), or neither (N):
a. Can make a service department into a profit centre
b. May reduce goal congruence
c. Can make users and providers more cost conscious
d. Can increase disagreements about how transfer prices should be set
e. Can put all service departments on an equal footing
f. Can cause certain services to be underutilized or overutilized
g. Can improve ability to evaluate performance
h. Can increase communication about what additional services are needed and which can be reduced or eliminated
i. Requires additional cost and employee time commitment

14. (LO 7) The computer operation of Brown Legal Services is in the process of developing a transfer price for its services. Capacity is defined by the computer operation in minutes of computer time. Expected annual capacity for the next year is 600,000 minutes, and full capacity is 800,000 minutes. Costs of the computer area are expected to total $720,000.

Required:
a. What is the transfer price if it is based on expected annual capacity?
b. What is the transfer price if it is based on full capacity?
c. Assume the actual cost of operating the computer area in the next year is $745,000. What is the total variance of that department? What are some possible causes of that variance?

15. (LO 5, 6) Comput Industries is a high-tech company located in the United States. Comput Industries has several subsidiaries, including Cancomput, which is located in Canada, and Heavencomput, which is located in another country with very favourable tax laws. Both responsibility centres are considered profit centres. Cancomput manufactures components used by Heavencomput and sells all its production to this subsidiary. The transfer price has been established by the controller at $135 per component, even if Cancomput can sell the same pieces on the external market for $175.

Required:
a. Briefly explain why Comput Industries is fixing a transfer price below the market price. What are the advantages for the company as a whole?
b. Explain the consequences of the transfer pricing policy on each subsidiary. Explain what change should be made to rectify the situation.
c. Briefly describe *two* other transfer pricing methods that could be used in this situation.

EXERCISES

16. (LO 3, 5) A company has two responsibility centres that are considered to be profit centres. Profit centre A produces an electronic component with the following costs:

Variable production costs	$60/unit
Fixed costs	$10/unit

Profit centre A is operating at full capacity and sells all of its output to outside customers at $82/unit. Profit centre B currently purchases a similar component from an outside supplier for $75/unit. It has determined that the component produced by profit centre A could be used instead, with no adverse effect on the quality of the final product. What is the minimum transfer price at which profit centre A should agree to transfer the component to profit centre B? What would you recommend?

17. (LO 5) Newmarket Corporation has several operating divisions. The Motor Division manufactures motors for ceiling fans and other appliances. The Fan Division manufactures ceiling fans and several other products that require a motor similar to the one produced by the Motor Division. The Motor Division sells 80% of its output externally and transfers the other 20% to the Fan Division. Newmarket Corporation makes all internal transfers at market price. The Motor Division's cost and revenue structure follows:

Sales price per motor	$150
Variable manufacturing costs	73
Fixed manufacturing costs	29
Variable selling and administration	4
Fixed selling and administration	10

Both per unit fixed cost computations are based on an expected capacity of 210,000 units.

Required:

As a student intern assigned to Newmarket Corporation's finance office, you have been asked to address the following items.

a. From the perspective of Newmarket Corporation, what is the variable cost of producing and selling a fan motor?

b. What is the variable cost of a fan motor from the perspective of the Fan Division?

c. Under what circumstances would it be desirable for the Fan Division to know the true full cost of an electric fan motor?

18. (LO 5) The Monitor Division, an autonomous segment (profit centre) of All-Canadian PCs, is considering what price to charge for transfers of monitors to the Assembly Division of the company. The following data on production cost per monitor have been gathered:

Direct materials	$10.20
Direct labour	2.60
Variable manufacturing overhead	6.30
Fixed manufacturing overhead	5.40
Total	$24.50

The Monitor Division sells the monitors to external buyers for $32. Managers of the Assembly Division have received external offers to provide comparable monitors ranging from $27 at one company to $36.50 at another.

Required:

Top management has engaged you to help in developing a transfer price for these monitors.

a. Determine the upper and lower limits for the transfer price between the Monitor Division and the Assembly Division.

b. What is the transfer price if it is equal to full production cost?

c. What is the transfer price if it is equal to variable production cost?

d. Why would the Monitor Division be reluctant to transfer goods at a price equal to variable cost?

EXERCISES

19. (LO 3, 5) The Aurora Company has two responsibility centres that are considered to be profit centres. The Sutton profit centre produces a hardwood component with the following costs:

Variable production costs	$30/unit
Fixed costs	$5/unit

The Sutton profit centre is operating at three-quarter capacity and sells all of its output to outside customers at $41 per unit. The Keswick profit centre currently purchases a similar component from an outside supplier for $38 per unit. Keswick has determined that the component produced by Sutton could be used instead, with no adverse effect on the quality of the final product. Sutton has sufficient capacity to meet the requirements of Keswick. What is the minimum transfer price at which Sutton should agree to transfer the component to Keswick? What would you recommend?

Exercises 15, 16, and 19 are an extract from *Management Accounting 2 Examination*, published by the Certified General Accountants Association of Canada (© CGA-Canada 2002). Reprinted with permission.

20. (LO 3) Electronics Products Inc. manufactures two products: tape recorders and speakers. For the year, the firm budgeted the following:

	Tape Recorders	**Speakers**
Sales	$2,400,000	$3,000,000
Unit sales price	80	60

At the end of the year, managers were informed that total actual sales amounted to 70,000 units and totalled $5,500,000. Tape recorder sales for the year amounted to 30,000 units at an average price of $70.

Required:
a. Compute the total revenue variance.
b. Compute the price variance.
c. Compute the sales mix variance.
d. Compute the sales volume variance.

PROBLEMS

1. (LO 2) Metropolitan Engineering Associates was suffering from a decline in profit because of competitive pressures. One of its responses to declining profitability was to establish a responsibility accounting system. One of the responsibility centres established was the Electrical Engineering Division, which is treated as a cost centre for control purposes. For the first year after responsibility accounting was put in place, the responsibility report for the Electrical Engineering Division contained the following comparisons:

	Budgeted	**Actual**	**Variance**
Variable costs:			
Professional labour	$1,000,000	$ 940,000	$ 60,000 F
Travel	50,000	40,000	10,000 F
Supplies	100,000	90,000	10,000 F
Fixed costs:			
Professional labour	400,000	405,000	(5,000) U
Facilities cost	250,000	265,000	(15,000) U
Insurance	80,000	78,000	2,000 F
Totals	$1,880,000	$1,818,000	$ 62,000 F

For the year the Electrical Engineering Division projected that it would generate $2,000,000 of revenues; it actually generated $1,800,000. The company has consulted with you for help in understanding what is happening. You decide to address the items that follow.

Required:
a. What are the major weaknesses in the responsibility report above?
b. Recast the responsibility report in a more meaningful format for cost control evaluation.

PROBLEMS

c. Metropolitan Engineering Associates utilizes a management by exception philosophy. Using the report prepared in part (b), which costs are likely to receive additional evaluation? Explain.

d. In most organizations, who would you expect to be involved in establishing policies on which variances should be investigated? Explain.

2. (LO 3, 4) On January 1, Tom Clark was promoted to the position of production manager in Seattle Seafood Company. The firm purchases raw fish, cooks and processes it, and then cans it in single-portion containers. The canned fish is sold to several wholesalers specializing in providing food to school lunch programs in the Northwest region of the United States and certain areas in Canada. All processing is conducted in the firm's highly automated plant in Parksville, British Columbia. Performance of the production manager is evaluated on the basis of a comparison of actual costs with standard costs. Only costs that are controllable by the production manager are included in the comparison (all are variable). The cost of fish is noncontrollable. Standard costs per kilogram of canned fish for the year were set as follows:

Direct labour	$0.50
Repairs	0.10
Maintenance	0.60
Indirect labour	0.10
Power	0.20

For the year, the company purchased 2,500,000 kilograms of fish and canned 1,500,000 kilograms. There were no beginning or ending inventories of raw, in-process, or canned fish. Actual costs were:

Direct labour	$600,000
Repairs	160,000
Maintenance	650,000
Indirect labour	155,000
Power	315,000

Required:

As the chief managerial accountant for the company, you have been asked to address the following.

a. Prepare a performance report for Tom Clark.

b. Evaluate Tom Clark's performance based on your report.

c. Tom feels that his performance is so good that he should be considered for immediate promotion to the position of vice-president of operations. Do you agree? Defend your answer.

d. Should additional performance measures (other than standard cost variances) be added to evaluate the production manager's performance? If so, identify the measures you would recommend.

3. (LO 3) Nancy Padgett is a production supervisor at the West Vancouver plant of Alberta Steelworks, which manufactures steel bridge guards. As plant production supervisor, Ms. Padgett is evaluated based on her ability to meet standard production costs. The standard costs to produce a one-metre section of bridge guard are as follows:

Metal		$12.00
Galvanizing ($10 per litre)		2.00
Direct labour ($15 per hour)		3.00
Overhead		
Welding supplies	$0.90	
Utilities	1.10	
Indirect labour	0.80	
Machine maintenance/repairs	0.40	
Equipment depreciation	2.20	
Miscellaneous	0.80	6.20
Total		$23.20

PROBLEMS

In October, the West Vancouver plant produced 35,000 metres of bridge guards. During October, the plant incurred the following costs:

Metal		$507,500
Galvanizing ($9.40 per litre)		65,800
Direct labour ($14.90 per hour)		104,300
Overhead		
Welding supplies	$34,900	
Utilities	38,300	
Indirect labour	25,500	
Machine maintenance/repairs	21,200	
Equipment depreciation	77,000	
Miscellaneous	29,500	226,400
Total		$904,000

Required:

a. For October, management has requested that you compute the variance for each production cost category in the West Vancouver plant.

b. Based on the variances computed in part (a), management has asked you to evaluate the performance of Nancy Padgett. Which variances might deserve closer scrutiny by top management? Explain.

4. (LO 3) David Leno manages the Sales Department at PEI Electric Supply. He is evaluated based on his ability to meet budgeted revenues. He has asked for your help in several ways listed below. For May, Mr. Leno's revenue budget was as follows:

	Price Per Unit	Unit Sales
Floor lamps	$107	960
Hanging lamps	55	2,800
Ceiling fixtures	75	4,240

The actual sales generated by Mr. Leno's department in May were as follows:

	Price Per Unit	Total Sales in Dollars
Floor lamps	$115	$ 93,150
Hanging lamps	50	207,000
Ceiling fixtures	78	315,900

Required:

a. For May, compute the revenue price variance in the Sales Department at PEI Electric Supply.

b. For May, compute the revenue mix variance in the Sales Department at PEI Electric Supply.

c. For May, compute the revenue volume variance in the Sales Department at PEI Electric Supply.

d. Based on your answers to parts (a), (b), and (c), evaluate the performance of Mr. Leno.

e. Assume you are Mr. Leno's supervisor. Why might you want to consider giving Mr. Leno the authority to set the salary and commission structure for thesalespersons?

5. (LO 3) Beth Jackson, the head of the accounting department at Red River College, has felt increasing pressure to raise external monies to compensate for dwindling provincial government financial support. Accordingly, in early January, she conceived the idea of offering a three-day accounting workshop in income taxation for local accountants. She asked Jim Thomas, a tenured tax professor, to supervise the planning for the seminar, which was to be held in late March. In early February, Professor Thomas presented Jackson with the following budgetary plan:

Revenues ($800 per participant)		$ 80,000
Expenses:		
Speakers ($1,000 each)	$10,000	
Rent on facilities	7,200	
Advertising	4,200	
Meals and lodging	36,000	
Departmental overhead allocation	7,000	(64,400)
Profit		$ 15,600

PROBLEMS

Explanation of budget items: The facilities rent of $7,200 is a fixed rental to be paid to a local hotel for use of its meeting rooms. The advertising is also a fixed budgeted cost. Meals expense is budgeted at $10 per person per meal (a total of nine meals are to be provided for each participant); lodging is budgeted at the rate of $90 per participant per night. The departmental overhead includes a specific charge for supplies costing $20 for each participant as well as a general allocation of $5,000 for use of departmental secretarial resources. After reviewing the budget, Jackson gave Thomas approval to proceed with the seminar.

Required:

As Dr. Jackson's assistant, you have been asked to address several issues presented below.

a. Recast the above budget with a flexible budget format.

b. Assume the actual financial results of the seminar were as follows:

Revenues (120 participants)		$ 77,000
Expenses:		
Speakers ($1,550 each)	$ 15,500	
Rent on facilities	8,400	
Advertising	5,800	
Meals and lodging	43,200	
Departmental overhead allocation	7,400	(80,300)
Loss		$ (3,300)

Explanation of actual results: Because registration was running below expectations, the seminar fee was reduced from $800 to $600 for late enrollees, and the advertising expense was increased. These changes caused the number of participants to be larger than expected, so a larger meeting room had to be rented from the local hotel. In budgeting for the speakers, Professor Thomas neglected to include airfare, which averaged $500 per speaker. Recast the actual results in the same format as the flexible budget.

c. Compute variances between the budget and the actual results. Identify and discuss the factors that are primarily responsible for the difference between the budgeted profit and the actual loss on the tax seminar.

d. Evaluate Professor Thomas's management of the tax seminar.

6. (LO 5, 6) Better Homes Products' Canadian operations are organized into two divisions: West and East. West Division sells a component that could be used by East Division in making one of the company's principal products. East Division has obtained three price quotations from external suppliers for the component: $154, $138, and $143. Examination of West Division's accounting records pertaining to the production of the component reveals the following costs: direct materials, $56; direct labour, $44; variable overhead, $18; and fixed overhead, $25.

Required:

As the chief accountant, you have been directed by the CEO to determine the following.

a. What savings (or profits) would be available to Better Homes Products if East Division bought the component internally rather than externally?

b. What would the transfer price be if the two divisions agreed to split the total company savings evenly between them?

c. Assuming dual transfer pricing is used, set the maximum realistic price for West Division and the minimum realistic price for East Division.

7. (LO 5, 6) Two of the divisions of Heavy-Duty Equipment Company are the Motor Division and the Dragline Division. The Motor Division produces motors that are used by both the Dragline Division and a variety of external industrial customers.

For external sales, sales orders are generally produced in 100-unit lots. Based on this typical lot size, the cost per motor is as follows:

Variable production costs	$2,100
Fixed manufacturing overhead	900
Variable selling expenses	300
Fixed selling expenses	420
Fixed general and administrative expenses	640
Total unit cost	$4,360

Motor Division normally has earned a profit margin of 20% on internal sales but has set the external selling price at $5,400. Because a significant number of sales are being made internally, Motor Division managers have now decided that $5,400 is the appropriate price to use for all future transfers to the Dragline Division. Previous transfers have been based on full cost plus the stipulated per unit profit.

When the managers in Dragline Division hear of this change in the transfer price, they become very upset since the change will have a major negative impact on Dragline's net income. Because of competition, corporate management has asked Motor Division to lower its sales price and consider reducing the transfer price. At the same time, Dragline Division management has asked to be allowed to buy motors externally. Bill Bird, Dragline's president, has gathered the following price information in order to help the two divisional managers negotiate an equitable transfer price:

Current external sales price	$5,400
Total variable production cost plus 20% profit margin ($2,100 × 1.2)	2,520
Total production cost plus 20% profit margin ($3,000 × 1.2)	3,600
Unit bid price from external supplier (if motors are purchased in 100-unit lots)	4,800

Required:
Mr. Bird is a former classmate of yours and has asked you to help him analyze the following matters:

a. Discuss advantages and disadvantages of each of the above transfer prices to the selling and buying divisions and to Heavy-Duty Equipment Company. Explain what circumstances would make each of the alternative prices the most appropriate choice.

b. If Motor Division can sell all of its production externally at $5,400 per unit, what is the appropriate transfer price and why?

8. (LO 4, 5) The Accessories Division of Johnson Power Sources manufactures a starter with the following standard costs:

Direct materials	$ 10
Direct labour	60
Overhead	30
Total unit cost	$100

The standard direct labour rate is $30 per hour, and overhead is assigned at 50% of the direct labour rate. Normal direct labour hours are 20,000, and the overhead rate is $5 variable and $10 fixed per direct labour hour.

The starters sell for $150, and the Accessories Division is currently operating at a level of about 16,000 direct labour hours for the year. Transfers in Johnson Power Sources are normally made at market price, although the divisional managers are permitted to negotiate a mutually agreed upon transfer price.

The Motor Division currently purchases 2,000 starters annually from the Accessories Division at the market price. The divisional manager of the Motor Division can purchase the starters from a foreign supplier for $140. Since she is free to select a supplier, she has indicated that she would like to negotiate a new transfer price with the Accessories Division. The manager of the Accessories Division believes that the foreign supplier is attempting to "buy in" by selling the starters at what he considers to be an excessively low price.

Required:
As vice president of finance for Johnson Power Sources, your expertise has been requested in the following matters.

a. From the viewpoint of the firm, should the Motor Division purchase the starters internally or externally? Show calculations and explain.

b. From the viewpoint of the Motor Division, should the starters be purchased internally or externally? Show calculations and explain.

c. Assume that the Accessories Division is presently operating at capacity and could sell the starters that it now sells to the Motor Division to external buyers at its usual price. From the viewpoint of the firm, should the Motor Division purchase the starters internally or externally? Show calculations and explain.

d. If you were the marketing manager of the Motor Division, what concerns might you have regarding the decision to buy internally or externally?

PROBLEMS

9. (LO 5, 6) Irresistible Scents Ltd. manufactures a line of perfume. The manufacturing process is basically a series of mixing operations involving the addition of certain aromatic and colouring ingredients. The finished products are packaged in company-produced glass bottles and packed in cases containing six bottles.

Management feels that the sale of its product is heavily influenced by the appearance of the bottle and has, therefore, devoted considerable managerial effort to the bottle production process. This has resulted in the development of certain unique processes in which management takes considerable pride.

The two areas (perfume production and bottle manufacturing) have evolved almost independently over the years; in fact, rivalry has developed between management personnel about which division is more important to Irresistible Scents. This attitude intensified when the bottle manufacturing plant was purchased intact 10 years ago. No real interchange of management personnel or ideas (except at the top corporate level) has taken place.

Since the Bottle Division was acquired, its entire production has been absorbed by the Perfume Division. Each area is considered a separate profit centre and evaluated as such. As the new corporate controller, you are responsible for the definition of a proper transfer price to use between the bottle production profit centre and the packaging profit centre. At your request, the general manager of the Bottle Division has asked certain other bottle manufacturers to quote a price for the quantities and sizes demanded by the Perfume Division. These competitive prices for cases of six bottles each are as follows:

Volume	Total Price	Price Per Case
2,000,000 cases	$ 8,000,000	$4.00
4,000,000 cases	14,000,000	3.50
6,000,000 cases	20,000,000	3.33

A cost analysis of the internal bottle plant indicates that it can produce bottles at these costs:

Volume	Total Price	Price Per Case
2,000,000 cases	$ 6,400,000	$3.20
4,000,000 cases	10,400,000	2.60
6,000,000 cases	14,400,000	2.40

The above analysis represents fixed costs of $2,400,000 and variable costs of $2 per case.

These figures have given rise to considerable corporate discussion about the proper value to use in the transfer of bottles to the Perfume Division. This interest is heightened because a significant portion of a division manager's income is an incentive bonus based on profit centre results.

The Perfume Division has the following costs in addition to the bottle costs:

Volume	Total Cost	Cost Per Case
2,000,000 cases	$32,800,000	$16.40
4,000,000 cases	64,800,000	16.20
6,000,000 cases	96,780,000	16.13

Market Research has furnished you with the following price–demand relationships for the finished product:

Sales Volume	Total Sales Revenue	Sales Price Per Case
2,000,000 cases	$ 51,000,000	$25.50
4,000,000 cases	91,200,000	22.80
6,000,000 cases	127,800,000	21.30

PROBLEMS

Required:

a. Irresistible Scents has used market-based transfer prices in the past. Using the current market prices and costs, and assuming a volume of 6,000,000 cases, calculate the income for the Bottle Division, the Perfume Division, and Irresistible Scents Ltd.

b. The 6,000,000-case production and sales level is the most profitable volume for which of the following: the Bottle Division, the Perfume Division, or Irresistible Scents Ltd.? Explain your answer.

c. As the corporate controller, answer the following question posed by the president of Irresistible Scents Ltd.: "Why have we structured the bottle operation as a separate division?"

(CMA adapted)

10. (LO 5, 6) Madison Decorative Floors operates with 10 profit centres. Company policy requires all transfers between corporate units to be made at fair market price. Tile Division has been asked to produce 10,000 standard tiles for Consumer Products Division. Tile Division is operating at full capacity and could otherwise sell any output it produces externally. This order represents 10% of the division's capacity, stated in terms of machine hours. Tile Division has quoted a $3.50 price per unit, but Consumer Products Division has found an external company that will make the tiles for $2.80. Since corporate policy states that external market prices must be used, Tile Division will be required to sell the units at $2.80. Tile Division's total variable cost for this specific type of tile is $2.20.

You have just graduated with a business degree, and your dad owns Madison Decorative Floors. He has asked you to help him with the following matters.

Required:

a. What amount of contribution margin will Tile Division earn at the originally quoted price? at the externally quoted price?

b. What effect does the use of the externally quoted purchase price of $2.80 have on Madison Decorative Floors' net income?

c. Some of the time that would be required to produce Consumer Products Division's order could be used instead to produce a special order for an outside company. Discuss how Tile Division management should make the choice between producing the order for Consumer Products Division and producing the outside company's order. What factors should be considered?

d. Should market price always be used to set a transfer price between organizational units? If so, discuss why. If not, discuss why not and when it is appropriate.

11. (LO 5, 6) Industrial Solutions Inc. has several regional divisions, which often purchase from each other. The company is fully decentralized, with divisions buying from and selling to each other or in outside markets. Conveyor Systems Division purchases most of its needs for hydraulic pumps from Hydraulic Division. The managers of these two divisions are currently negotiating a transfer price for the hydraulic pumps for next year. Hydraulic Division prepared the following financial information for negotiating purposes:

Costs of hydraulic pumps as manufactured by Hydraulic Division:

Direct material costs	$120
Direct labour costs	40
Variable overhead costs	30
Fixed overhead costs	50
Fixed selling expenses	30
Fixed administrative expenses	20
Total	$290

Hydraulic Division is currently operating at 70% of its capacity. It is the policy of the division to target a net income to sales ratio of 20%.

The current market price for hydraulic pumps is $260 each. Recently, there has been a drop in price for such products because of industry advances in production technology.

Required:

Answer each of the following questions independently.

a. If Hydraulic Division desires to achieve its goal of a net income to sales ratio of 20%, what should be the transfer price of pumps?

PROBLEMS

b. If Hydraulic Division wants to maximize its income, what transfer price would you recommend that it offer to the Conveyor Systems Division?

c. What is the price that you believe should be charged by Hydraulic Division if overall company profit is to be maximized?

(CMA adapted)

12. (LO 5, 6) CanElectric is a decentralized company with divisions throughout Canada. Each division has its own salesforce and production facilities and is operated autonomously as either a profit or an investment centre. Switch Division has just been awarded a contract for a product that uses a component that is manufactured by Wire Division as well as by outside suppliers. Switch Division uses a cost figure of $3.80 for the component in preparing the bid for the new product. This cost figure was supplied by Wire Division in response to Switch Division's request for the average variable cost of the component.

Wire Division has an active salesforce that is continually soliciting new customers. Its regular selling price for the component needed by Switch Division for the new product is $6.50. Sales of the component are expected to increase. Wire Division management has associated the following costs with the component:

Standard variable manufacturing cost	$3.20
Standard variable selling and distribution expenses	0.60
Standard fixed manufacturing cost	1.20
Total	$5.00

The two divisions have been unable to agree on a transfer price for the component. Corporate management has never established a transfer price because no interdivisional transactions have ever occurred. The following suggestions have been made for the transfer price.

- Regular selling price
- Regular selling price less variable selling and distribution expenses
- Standard manufacturing cost plus 15%
- Standard variable manufacturing cost plus 20%

Required:

a. Compute each of the suggested transfer prices.

b. Discuss the effect each of the transfer prices might have on Wire Division management's attitude toward intracompany business.

c. Is the negotiation of a price between Switch Division and Wire Division a satisfactory method for solving the transfer price problem? Explain your answer.

d. Should the corporate management of CanElectric become involved in this transfer controversy? Explain your answer.

(CMA adapted)

13. (LO 5, 6) Wood Inc., a manufacturer of wood poles, has two responsibility centres, harvesting and sawing, which are both evaluated as profit centres. The harvesting division executes all the harvesting operations and transfers logs to the sawing division, which converts the wood into poles for external clients. When operating at full capacity, the sawing division can convert 10,000 poles. Management is considering replacing this type of wood pole with another type of wood pole that can be sold at a lower price and could allow the firm to operate at full capacity.

The director of the sawing division suggested that the maximum price the division can pay for each log from harvesting is $29.50. Here is the information that supports this suggestion:

Price per pole that the client would pay		$90.00
Direct labour costs	$35.00	
Variable overhead costs	4.50	
Fixed overhead costs	8.50	
Raw material costs (other than logs)	2.50	
	50.50	
Profit margin	10.00	
Total costs		60.50
Maximum price for a log		$29.50

PROBLEMS

The director of the harvesting division disagrees with selling the logs at a price of $29.50. The division is operating at full capacity and sells logs to external clients for $44.50. Moreover, the director says: "My direct costs of labour are $22.50, my variable overhead costs are $4.50, and my fixed overhead costs are $9.00. I can't cut trees for $36.00 and sell them for 29.50."

Required:

a. Assuming production at full capacity, would Wood Inc., as a whole, make a higher contribution margin if logs were transferred to the sawing division for $29.50 per log? Show your calculations.

b. Explain the effect of transferring the logs at $29.50 per log on each division's profit performance.

c. Calculate the minimum and maximum transfer prices that could be used, and recommend an appropriate transfer price. Explain your answer.

14. (LO 5, 6) Yarra Fresh Foods grows and sells large fresh lambs to retail and institutional customers. Yarra has two responsibility centres, farming and selling, which are both evaluated as profit centres. The farming division executes all the farming activities and transfers fresh lamb to the selling division, which packages and delivers the lamb to customers. When operating at full capacity, the selling division can sell 20,000 lambs a day. Management is considering replacing this type of lamb with another type of fresh lamb that can be sold at a lower price and could allow the firm to operate at full capacity.

The director of the selling division suggests that the maximum price the division can pay for each lamb is $39.00. Here is the information that supports this suggestion:

Price per lamb that clients would pay		$110.00
Direct labour costs	$40.00	
Variable overhead costs	6.50	
Fixed overhead costs	10.50	
Raw material costs (other than lambs)	4.00	
	61.00	
Profit margin	10.00	
Total costs		71.00
Maximum price for a lamb		$ 39.00

The director of the farming division disagrees with selling the lambs at a price of $39.00. The division is operating at full capacity and sells lambs to external clients for $54.00. Moreover, the director says: "My direct costs of labour are $32.00, my variable overhead costs are $5.00, and my fixed overhead costs are $9.00. I can't raise lambs for $46.00 and sell them for 39.00."

Required:

a. Assuming production at full capacity, would Yarra, as a whole, make a higher contribution margin if lambs were transferred to the selling division for $39.00 per lamb? Show your calculations.

b. Explain the effect of transferring the lamb at $39.00 per lamb on each division's profit performance.

c. Calculate the minimum and maximum transfer prices that could be used, and recommend an appropriate transfer price. Explain your answer.

Problems 13 and 14 are an extract from *Management Accounting 2 Examination*, published by the Certified General Accountants Association of Canada (© CGA-Canada 2002). Reprinted with permission.

15. (LO 3, 4) The Olds Food Company purchases beef, cooks and processes it, and then packs it in single-portion containers. The beef products are sold to several Canadian retailers specializing in quality prepared foods. All processing is conducted in the firm's highly automated plant in Olds, Alberta. The production manager's performance is evaluated on the basis of a comparison of actual costs with standard costs. Only costs that are controllable by the production manager are included in the comparison (all are variable). The cost of beef is noncontrollable. Standard costs per kilogram of beef for the year were set as follows:

Direct labour	$1.00
Repairs	0.20
Maintenance	1.20
Indirect labour	0.20
Power	0.40

PROBLEMS

For the year, the company purchased 2,500,000 kilograms of beef and out of that (no inventory) processed 1,600,000 kilograms. There were no beginning or ending inventories of raw, in-process, or packaged beef. Actual 2007 costs were:

Direct labour	$1,200,000
Repairs	400,000
Maintenance	1,300,000
Indirect labour	300,000
Power	600,000

Required:

As the chief managerial accountant for the company, you have been asked to address the following.

a. Prepare a performance report for the production manager for the year.

b. Evaluate the production manager's performance based on your report.

c. The production manager believes that his performance is so good that he should be considered for immediate promotion to the position of vice-president of operations. Do you agree? Defend your answer.

d. Should additional performance measures (other than standard cost variances) be added to evaluate the production manager's performance? If so, identify the measures you would recommend.

16. (LO 3) Andrea Jill is a paint supervisor at a Halifax auto body repair shop. As paint supervisor, Ms. Jill is evaluated based on her ability to meet standard production costs. The standard costs to produce a standard car's paint job are given below (assuming 300 cars a month):

Materials		$24.00
Paint ($20 per litre)		8.00
Direct labour ($30 per hour)		30.00
Overhead		
Welding supplies (variable)	$0.90	
Utilities (variable)	1.10	
Indirect labour (fixed)	2.40	
Machine maintenance/repairs (fixed)	0.40	
Equipment depreciation (fixed)	2.20	
Miscellaneous (fixed)	1.00	8.00
Total		$70.00

In October, the Halifax auto body repair shop painted 250 cars. During October, the plant incurred the following costs:

Materials		$ 6,500
Paint ($19.40 per litre)		1,800
Direct labour ($31.90 per hour)		8,300
Overhead		
Welding supplies	$220	
Utilities	270	
Indirect labour	730	
Machine maintenance/repairs	125	
Equipment depreciation	650	
Miscellaneous	313	2,308
Total		$18,908

Required:

a. For October, management has requested that you compute the variance for each production cost category in the Halifax shop.

b. Based on the variances computed in part (a), management has asked you to evaluate the performance of Andrea Jill. Which variances might deserve closer scrutiny by top management? Explain.

17. (LO 4, 5) The Coat Division of Jones Fashions manufactures a winter coat with the following standard costs:

Direct materials	$ 40
Direct labour	60
Overhead	30
Total unit cost	$130

PROBLEMS

The standard direct labour rate is $30 per hour, and overhead is assigned at 50% of the direct labour rate. Normal direct labour hours are 25,000, and the breakdown of the $30 per coat overhead is $10 variable and $20 fixed.

The coats sell for $200, and the Coat Division is currently operating at a level of about 21,000 direct labour hours for the year. Transfers in Jones Fashions are normally made at market price, although the divisional managers are permitted to negotiate a mutually agreed upon transfer price.

The Retail Division currently purchases 3,000 coats annually from the Coat Division at the market price. The divisional manager of the Retail Division can purchase the coats from a foreign supplier for $180. Since she is free to select a supplier, she has indicated that she would like to negotiate a new transfer price with the Coat Division. The manager of the Coat Division believes that the foreign supplier is attempting to "buy in" by selling the coats at what he considers to be an excessively low price.

Required:

As vice president of finance for Jones Fashions, your expertise has been requested in the following matters.

a. From the viewpoint of the firm (Jones Fashions), should the Retail Division purchase the coats internally or externally? Show calculations and explain.

b. From the viewpoint of the Retail Division, should the coats be purchased internally or externally? Show calculations and explain.

c. Assume that the Coat Division is presently operating at capacity and could sell the coats that it now sells to the Retail Division to external buyers at its usual price. From the viewpoint of the firm, should the Retail Division purchase the coats internally or externally? Show calculations and explain.

d. If you were the marketing manager of the Retail Division, what concerns might you have regarding the decision to buy internally or externally?

18. (LO 5, 6) Two of the divisions of Super Chem Company are the Moose Jaw Division and the Swift Current Division. The Moose Jaw Division produces basic chemicals that are used by both the Swift Current Division and a variety of external industrial customers.

For external sales, sales orders are generally produced in 100-litre lots. Based on this typical lot size, the cost per lot is as follows:

Variable production costs	$1,100
Fixed manufacturing overhead	500
Variable selling expenses	200
Fixed selling expenses	220
Fixed general and administrative expenses	340
Total unit cost	$2,360

Moose Jaw Division normally has earned a profit margin of 30% on internal sales but has set the external selling price at $3,300. As a significant number of sales are being made internally, Moose Jaw Division managers have now decided that $3,300 is the appropriate price to use for all future transfers to the Swift Current Division. Previous transfers have been based on full cost plus the stipulated per unit profit.

When the managers in Swift Current Division heard of this change in the transfer price, they became very upset since the change will have a major negative impact on Swift Current's net income. Due to competition, corporate management has asked Moose Jaw Division to lower its sales price and consider reducing the transfer price. At the same time, Swift Current Division management has asked to be allowed to buy the chemicals externally. Bill Bird, Swift Current's president, has gathered the following price information in order to help the two divisional managers negotiate an equitable transfer price:

Current external sales price	$3,300
Total variable production cost plus 30% profit margin ($1,100 × 1.3)	1,430
Total production cost plus 30% profit margin ($1,600 × 1.3)	2,080
Unit bid price from external supplier	3,400

Required:

a. Discuss advantages and disadvantages of each of the above transfer prices to the selling and buying divisions and to Super Chem Company. Explain what circumstances would make each of the alternative prices the most appropriate choice.

b. If Moose Jaw Division can sell all of its production externally at $3,300 per unit, what is the appropriate transfer price and why?

19. (LO 5, 6) Tile Master operates with 10 profit centres. Company policy requires all transfers between divisions to be made at fair market price. The Manufacturing Division has been asked to produce 20,000 standard tiles for Retail Division. The Manufacturing Division is not operating at full capacity; it has a 40,000-tile unused capacity from its total 200,000 capacity. The Manufacturing Division has quoted a $4.50 price per unit, but the Retail Division has found an external company that will make the tiles for $3.70. Since corporate policy states that external market prices must be used, the Manufacturing Division will be required to sell the units at $3.70. The Manufacturing Division's total variable cost for this specific type of tile is $3.10.

Required:

a. What amount of contribution margin will the Manufacturing Division earn at the originally quoted price? at the externally quoted price?

b. What effect does the use of the externally quoted purchase price of $3.70 have on Tile Master's net income?

c. If the order from the Retail Division is accepted, will the Manufacturing Division be able to accept other special orders? For what quantities, at what minimal price?

d. When would market price not be used to set a transfer price between organizational units?

20. (LO 5, 6) EXXPO manufactures and installs information technology equipment and software. It has several divisions, which often purchase from each other. The company is fully decentralized, with divisions buying from and selling to each other or in outside markets. The Consulting Division purchases most of its needs for information storage systems from the Information Storage Division. The managers of these two divisions are currently negotiating a transfer price for information storage systems for next year. The Information Storage Division prepared the following financial information for negotiating purposes:

Costs of information storage systems as manufactured by Information Storage Division:

Direct material costs	$360
Direct labour costs	120
Variable overhead costs	90
Fixed overhead costs	150
Fixed selling expenses	90
Fixed administrative expenses	60
Total	$870

The Information Storage Division is currently operating at 80% of its capacity. It is the policy of the division to target a net income to sales ratio of 15%.

The current market price for information storage systems is $910 each. Recently, there has been an increase in demand for such products due to productivity improvements.

Required:

Answer each of the following questions independently.

a. If the Information Storage Division desires to achieve its goal of a net income to sales ratio of 15%, what should be the transfer price of information storage systems?

b. If the Information Storage Division wants to maximize its income, what transfer price would you recommend that it offer to the Consulting Division?

c. What is the price that you believe should be charged by the Information Storage Division if overall company profit is to be maximized?

(CMA adapted)

PROBLEMS

21. (LO 2, 3) Family Resorts, Inc. is a holding company for several vacation hotels in the Maritimes and Northern Ontario. The firm originally purchased several old inns, restored the buildings, and upgraded the recreational facilities. The inns have been well received by vacationing families, as many services are provided that accommodate children and afford parents time for themselves. Since the completion of the restorations 10 years ago, the company has been profitable.

Family Resorts has just concluded its annual meeting of regional and district managers. This meeting is held each November to review the results of the previous season and to help the managers prepare for the upcoming year. Prior to the meeting, the managers submitted proposed budgets for their districts or regions as appropriate. These budgets have been reviewed and consolidated into an annual operating budget for the entire company. The budget has been presented at the meeting and accepted by the managers.

To evaluate the performance of its managers, Family Resorts uses responsibility accounting. Therefore, the preparation of the budget is given close attention at headquarters. If major changes need to be made to the budgets submitted by the managers, all affected parties are consulted before the changes are incorporated. The following two reports are from the budget booklet that all managers received at the meeting.

Family Resorts, Inc.
Responsibility Summary
($000 omitted)

Reporting Unit: Family Resorts	
Responsible Person: President	
Maritimes	$ 605
Northern Ontario	365
Unallocated costs	(160)
Income before taxes	$ 810
Reporting Unit: Northern Ontario	
Responsible Person: Regional Manager	
Region A	$ 200
Region B	140
Region C	105
Unallocated costs	(80)
Total contribution	$ 365
Reporting Unit: Region C	
Responsible Person: District Manager	
Harbour Inn	$ 80
Camden Country Inn	60
Unallocated costs	(35)
Total contribution	$105
Reporting Unit: Harbour Inn	
Responsible Person: Innkeeper	
Revenue	$ 600
Controllable costs	(455)
Allocated costs	(65)
Total contribution	$ 80

The budget for Family Resorts, Inc. follows.

PROBLEMS

Family Resorts, Inc.
Condensed Operation Budget—Maritime/Northern Ontario Districts
For the Year Ending December 31
($000 omitted)

	Family Resorts	Maritimes	Northern Ontario	Unallo-cated[1]	Region A	Region B	Region C	Unallo-cated[2]	Harbour	Camden Country
Net sales	$ 7,900	$4,200	$3,700		$1,400	$1,200	$1,100		$600	$500
Cost of sales	(4,530)	(2,310)	(2,220)	____	(840)	(720)	(660)	____	(360)	(300)
Gross margin	$ 3,370	$1,890	$1,480		$ 560	$ 480	$ 440		$240	$200
Controllable expenses										
Supervisory expenses	$ 240	$ 130	$ 110		$ 35	$ 30	$ 45	$ 10	$ 20	$ 15
Training expenses	160	80	80		30	25	25		15	10
Advertising expenses	500	280	220	$ 50	55	60	55	15	20	20
Repairs and maintenance	480	225	255	____	90	85	80		40	40
Total controllable expenses	$(1,380)	$ (715)	$ (665)	$(50)	$ (210)	$ (200)	$ (205)	$(25)	$ (95)	$ (85)
Controllable contribution	$ 1,990	$ 1,175	$ 815	$(50)	$ 350	$ 280	$ 235	$(25)	$145	$115
Expenses controlled by others										
Depreciation	$ 520	$ 300	$ 220	$ 30	$ 70	$ 60	$ 60	$ 10	$ 30	$ 20
Property taxes	200	120	80		30	30	20		10	10
Insurance	300	150	150		50	50	50	____	25	25
Total expenses controlled by others	$(1,020)	$ (570)	$ (450)	$(30)	$ (150)	$ (140)	$ (130)	$(10)	$ (65)	$ (55)
Total contribution	$ 970	$ 605	$ 365	$(80)	$ 200	$ 140	$ 105	$(35)	$ 80	$ 60
Unallocated costs[3]	(160)									
Income before taxes	$ 810									

[1]Unallocated expenses include a regional advertising campaign and equipment used by the regional manager.
[2]Unallocated expenses include a portion of the district manager's salary, district promotion costs, and district manager's car.
[3]Unallocated costs include taxes on undeveloped real estate, headquarters expense, legal, and audit fees.

Required:

a. Responsibility accounting has been used effectively by many companies, both large and small.
   i. Define responsibility accounting.
   ii. Discuss the benefits that accrue to a company using responsibility accounting.
   iii. Describe the advantages of responsibility accounting for the managers of a firm.
b. The budget of Family Resorts, Inc. was accepted by the regional and district managers. Based on the facts presented, evaluate the budget process employed by Family Resorts by addressing the following:
   i. What features of the budget preparation process are likely to result in the managers' adopting and supporting the budget process?
   ii. What recommendations, if any, could be made to the budget preparers to improve the budget process? Explain your answer.

(CMA)

PROBLEMS

22. (LO 2, 3) Pittsburgh–Walsh Company (PWC) is a manufacturing company whose product line consists of lighting fixtures and electronic timing devices. The Lighting Fixtures Division assembles units for the upscale and midrange markets. The Electronic Timing Devices Division manufactures instrument panels that allow electronic systems to be activated and deactivated at scheduled times for both efficiency and safety purposes. Both divisions operate in the same manufacturing facility and share production equipment.

PWC's budget for the year ending December 31 was prepared on a business segment basis under the following guidelines:
- Variable expenses are directly assigned to the incurring division.
- Fixed overhead expenses are directly assigned to the incurring division.
- Common fixed expenses are allocated to the divisions on the basis of units produced, which bear a close relationship to direct labour. Included in common fixed expenses are costs of the corporate staff, legal expenses, taxes, staff marketing, and advertising.
- The production plan is for 8,000 upscale fixtures, 22,000 midrange fixtures, and 20,000 electronic timing devices.

Pittsburgh–Walsh Company
Budget for the Year Ending December 31
(amounts in thousands)

| | Lighting Fixtures | | Electronic | |
	Upscale	Midrange	Timing Devices	Totals
Sales	$1,440	$770	$800	$3,010
Variable expenses				
Cost of goods sold	(720)	(439)	(320)	(1,479)
Selling and administrative	(170)	(60)	(60)	(290)
Contribution margin	$ 550	$271	$420	$1,241
Fixed overhead expenses	(140)	(80)	(80)	(300)
Segment margin	$ 410	$191	$340	$ 941
Common fixed expenses				
Overhead	(48)	(132)	(120)	(300)
Selling and administrative	(11)	(31)	(28)	(70)
Net income (loss)	$ 351	$ 28	$192	$ 571

PWC established a bonus plan for division management that requires meeting the budget's planned net income by product line, with a bonus increment if the division exceeds the planned product line net income by 10% or more.

Shortly before the year began, the CEO, Jack Parkow, had a heart attack and subsequently retired. After reviewing the budget, the new CEO, Joe Kelly, decided to close the lighting fixtures midrange product line by the end of the first quarter and use the available production capacity to increase the remaining two product lines. The marketing staff advised that electronic timing devices could grow by 40% with increased direct sales support. Increases above that level and increasing sales of upscale lighting fixtures would require expanded advertising expenditures to increase consumer awareness of PWC as an electronics and upscale lighting fixture company. Kelly approved the increased sales support and advertising expenditures to achieve the revised plan. Kelly advised the divisions that for bonus purposes, the original product line net income objectives must be met, but he did allow the Lighting Fixtures Division to combine the net income objectives for both product lines for bonus purposes.

Prior to the close of the fiscal year, the division controllers were furnished with preliminary actual data for review and adjustment, as appropriate. These following preliminary year-end data reflect the revised units of production amounting to 12,000 upscale fixtures, 4,000 midrange fixtures, and 30,000 electronic timing devices.

PROBLEMS

Pittsburgh–Walsh Company
Preliminary Actuals
for the Year Ending December 31
(amounts in thousands)

	Lighting Fixtures Upscale	Midrange	Electronic Timing Devices	Totals
Sales	$2,160	$140	$1,200	$3,500
Variable expenses				
Cost of goods sold	(1,080)	(80)	(480)	(1,640)
Selling and administrative	(260)	(11)	(96)	(367)
Contribution margin	$ 820	$ 49	$ 624	$1,493
Fixed overhead expenses	(140)	(14)	(80)	(234)
Segment margin	$ 680	$ 35	$ 544	$1,259
Common fixed expenses				
Overhead	(78)	(27)	(195)	(300)
Selling and administrative	(60)	(20)	(150)	(230)
Net income (loss)	$ 542	$ (12)	$ 199	$ 729

The controller of the Lighting Fixtures Division, anticipating a similar bonus plan, is contemplating postponing the recognition of some revenues until next year because the sales are not yet final, and advancing into the current year some expenditures that will be applicable to the first quarter of next year. The corporation would meet its annual plan, and the division would exceed the 10% incremental bonus plateau in the current year, despite the postponed revenues and advanced expenses contemplated.

Required:

a. i. Outline the benefits that an organization realizes from segment reporting.
    ii. Evaluate segment reporting on a variable cost basis versus an absorption cost basis.
b. i. Segment reporting can be developed based on different criteria. What criteria must be present for division management to accept being evaluated on a segment basis?
    ii. Why would the managers of the Electronic Timing Devices Division be unhappy with the current reporting, and how should the reporting be revised to gain their acceptance?
c. Are the adjustments contemplated by the controller of the Lighting Fixtures Division unethical? Explain.

(CMA)

23. (LO 2, 3) Golf course maintenance at the Westlake Country Club is managed by the greenskeeper and treated as a cost centre. Performance measurement is based on a comparison of the budgeted amounts with the actual expenses for the year. The following statement has been prepared by the bookkeeper of the club.

Westlake Country Club
Golf Course Expenses
For the Year Ended December 31

	Budgeted Amount	Actual Expense	Variance
Payroll and payroll taxes	$54,000	$54,500	$ (500)
Sand and gravel	300	500	(200)
Topsoil	1,000	800	200
Fertilizer	5,000	8,500	(3,500)
Fungicide	1,000	1,400	(400)
Grass seed	800	300	500
Parts	2,500	1,800	700
Petroleum products	1,800	3,100	(1,300)
Golf equipment	500	100	400
Uniforms	300	0	300
Training	300	0	300
Equipment rental	2,500	250	2,250
Utilities	3,000	5,100	(2,100)
Depreciation	5,000	5,000	0
Total	$78,000	$81,350	$(3,350)

The budget for the golf course is prepared by the greens committee and Mr. Jim Wallace, the greenskeeper. The budget is approved by the board of directors of the club and is used in evaluating the performance of Mr. Wallace at the end of the year. As a part of this evaluation, the following conversation takes place between Mr. Driver, the president of the club, and Mr. Wallace:

Mr. Driver: Jim, you should realize that the golf course budget represents the best judgments of the greens committee and the board of directors as to how resources should be used on the golf course. It is my opinion that differences between each budgeted amount and the expense incurred should be minor if you operate the course as directed by the committee with the approval of the board. The only items on this report where I view the differences as insignificant are payroll and depreciation. In many areas—such as fertilizer, petroleum products, and utilities—you significantly exceeded the budgeted amounts. To cover up these excesses, you failed to carry out our wishes concerning golf equipment and uniforms, and I can't explain the problem with equipment rental. I have received several complaints from our members about the condition of our markers and ball washers and the appearance of the help on the course. I now see how this is reflected in this report. Besides that, we have had many complaints as to the condition of the course.

Mr. Wallace: My understanding has been that I am to run the golf course and try to remain within the total budget. I can explain all of the differences that show up on this report. The cost of fertilizer, fungicide, petroleum products, and utilities went up significantly this year. Because of this, we only put out a minimum of fertilizer. It was either this or incur a significant budget overrun. The late summer was very dry, which required excessive pumping, and this added to the increased utility cost.

Mr. Driver: Jim, you're telling me that the budget did not allow for any price increases, but I know this is not the case.

Mr. Wallace: I know price increases were built into the budget, but they in no way covered the actual increases for the year. No one could have anticipated the short supply of fertilizer and fungicide that existed this year.

Mr. Driver: You should have limited your expenditures for these items to the amounts in the budget, and you should have bought the new uniforms and golf equipment and started some of the reseeding that was included in your budget.

Mr. Wallace: In my opinion, I did the best job possible to maintain the course, given the economic and weather conditions during the year. These things cannot be anticipated in preparing a budget. I must use my professional judgment in some of these matters. In addition, concerning the depreciation, I have nothing to do with it! It just shows up at the end of each year.

Mr. Driver: I am not sure that that helps the situation.

Required:

a. Explain how Mr. Driver and Mr. Wallace differ in the ways that they interpret the budget and in the ways they believe Mr. Wallace's performance is to be evaluated.

b. Prepare a report suggesting how the differences you identified in part (a) can be reconciled.

c. Do you see any problems with the treatment of depreciation in the budget? Explain.

d. Who should evaluate Mr. Wallace's performance: the greens committee or the board of directors? Explain.

24. (LO 5, 6) P Company consists of three divisions: Eastern, Western, and Southern. Two of the divisions, Eastern and Western, have their own manufacturing *and* marketing facilities. The Southern Division, on the other hand, is engaged *only* in manufacturing. The Southern Division's only product is a part, Part S, which it transfers to the other two divisions. The Southern division operates at *full* capacity with an annual total output of 50,000 units of Part S, which is distributed 60% to Eastern Division and 40% to Western Division. These transfers account for about 30% of the cost of raw materials purchased by each of the two divisions and for about 22% of each division's total manufacturing costs.

Each division prepares its own profit budget at the beginning of the year. When approved by P Company's top management, this budget becomes the basis for evaluating the performance of the division and its manager. The profit budget for the Southern Division reflects the transfer of its budgeted output of Part S to the other two divisions according to the 60% and 40% split. The transfer price is set at budgeted full

PROBLEMS

manufacturing cost plus a 20% mark-up to cover administrative expenses (all fixed) as well as profits. The transfer pricing policy is set by P Company's top management and is applicable to *all* internal transfers between divisions.

P Company's top management has decided to review the existing transfer pricing policy for two reasons. First, the manager of the Southern Division is considering the possibility of using outside salespersons to market Part S externally at 8% commission, unless the existing transfer price policy is changed. To support her case, the manager cites the fact that her division's ROI for the coming budget period will be far less than the 10% competitive rate that P Company's top management requires of the division. Second, the Eastern Division is likely to reject an order from one of its long-time customers unless it can obtain Part S from companywide present policy. The customer is willing to pay $130 per unit for a contract for 2,500 units of Part S, which represents the average monthly demand by the Eastern Division.

P Company's executive vice-president in charge of settling transfer pricing disputes has requested and received from the managers of the Eastern Division and the Southern Division the information given in the exhibit below. With the information in the exhibit, the executive vice-president has instructed the managers of the two divisions to negotiate an acceptable transfer price.

Information provided by Southern Division:

Budgeted manufacturing costs:	
Variable cost per unit	$20.00
Total fixed manufacturing cost	$250,000
Commission (as a percentage of selling price) to be paid to outside salespersons	8%

Information provided by Eastern Division on order for 2,500 units of final product:

Outside market price of Part S	$35.00
Contract price of final product	$130.00
Eastern Division's own budgeted manufacturing costs per unit:	
Variable (excluding cost of Part S)	$95.00
Fixed	$10.00
Budgeted selling and administrative expenses per unit:	
Variable	$2.60
Fixed	$1.40

Required:

a. i. Calculate the transfer price per unit of Part S, using the companywide transfer pricing policy.

  ii. Discuss *two* major weaknesses of the companywide transfer pricing policy.

b. Assume the managers of the Eastern Division and Southern Division are unable to negotiate an acceptable transfer price.

  i. Which one of the following three actions will maximize the short-run total net cash inflow for P company *as a whole*? Please address *each* of the actions, and provide calculations to support your conclusion.

- Action A: The Eastern Division purchases 2,500 units of Part S *internally* at a transfer price of $40 *and* accepts the terms of the contract from the longtime customer.
- Action B: The Eastern Division purchases 2,500 units of Part S *externally* at the market price of $35 per unit *and* accepts the terms of the contract from the longtime customer. (Assume Southern Division cannot sell the equivalent units externally.)
- Action C: The Southern Division decides to sell 2,500 units of Part S to an outside party at the market price of $35 per unit, paying an 8% commission to outside salespersons. Since Part S is not available to the Eastern Division, the Eastern Division cannot accept the terms of the contract from the long-term outside customer. (Assume the Eastern Division is unable to fill the slack with alternative work.)

  ii. Is the action that maximizes the short-run total net cash flow for P Company as a whole dependent on the amount of the internal transfer price? Why or why not?

c. P Company's executive vice president in charge of settling transfer pricing disputes is considering a recommendation to treat the Southern Division as a cost centre instead of an investment centre for the purposes of evaluating both economic and managerial performance.

i.   Discuss some of the strengths and weaknesses of the recommendation.

ii. Discuss some of the major controls that would have to be implemented in the Southern Division (after it has become a cost centre) in order to avoid possible conflicts between the goals of the division and the long-run profit maximization goal of P Company.

Extract from *Management Accounting 2 Examination*, published by the Certified General Accountants Association of Canada (© CGA-Canada 1998). Reprinted with permission.

CASES

1.   Tata Fine Furniture is a chain of 47 retail stores in Quebec and Ontario that sell household furniture. Tata also has three furniture manufacturing plants, located in small Quebec communities. One plant makes a line of wooden bedroom furniture; the other two produce two lines of wooden dining room furniture. The furniture made by these plants is shipped to all 47 stores.

The furniture that Tata makes sells very well at the Tata retail stores because of the quality of wood and assembly. The workers at the three plants are renowned craftspeople with many years—often generations—of experience. All of the output of the three plants is sold to the Tata stores. Indeed, the stores would buy more from the plants, but they are already producing at full capacity. Because demand exceeds supply, some customers have to wait six months for the delivery of Tata furniture. Customers are willing to do so, as Tata's prices are about 10% less than comparable furniture.

The transfer price has been a 30% markup over prime costs for decades, with no complaints by the either the vice president of furniture manufacturing or the vice president of the retail stores. That is, until the past few months. The vice president of furniture manufacturing wants the markup increased from 30 to 80%.

What motivated this request for a transfer price increase was that two months ago, the CEO, the vice president of furniture manufacturing, and the vice president of retail stores agreed to make the plants and stores profit centres. Previously, the plants had been cost centres and the stores had been revenue centres. Now there is concern over the transfer price. They have asked you, the controller, for help.
Required:
Help them.

2.   You and your partner have just graduated from university. She graduated as an electrical engineer; you graduated with a degree in marketing. During your four years at university, the two of you made plans to go into business together. Each of you took courses in entrepreneurship. In your final school year, the two of you developed a business model for a cellphone and communication device superstore. It would carry all makes of both products, including Blackberries and Palm Pilots. Besides the broad and deep product line, Cell Phones, etc. Super Stores would accept trade-ins on new phones and communication devices. The trade-ins would then be reconditioned and sold.

Your business model created a lot of excitement in the business community. It enabled you and your partner to win a competition for best new business idea, retail category. Soon after, many investors and venture capitalists approached you with offers of financing to get your business model implemented. You accepted one offer from the third generation of the Rabbitbrook family. Nat Rabbitbrook made a fortune in the first half of the twentieth century, which was then wasted by the second and third generations. Over the past year, Nat Rabbitbrook III has been able, on the basis of a legal technicality, to recover part of his grandfather's art collection, which had been donated to a provincial art gallery. To celebrate this windfall, he has invested $50 million in Cell Phones, etc. Super Stores for 49% of the common shares.

In about eight months, on July 1, 11 stores will commence operations. Each will be located in a different mall in southern Ontario, and each will have approximately 40 square metres of space. The managers will not be hired until June 1.

It is expected that total sales per store will average $10,000 per square metre per year. COGS is expected to be 60% of sales. Each store will be open 50 weeks a year, from 10 a.m. to 8 p.m. each day except Sunday, when the hours will be 12 noon to 6 p.m. The stores will be staffed each day based on expected sales. It has been estimated that each opening hour will on average cost $35 for employee costs, including benefits and the manager.

All store locations will be rented at an average annual cost of $80 per square metre. The rented space will need to be properly equipped with carpets, shelving, and so forth. These leasehold improvements will cost $100,000 per store and will have a useful life of 10 years.

Inventory will be equal to three months' sales. All sales will be made for cash or equivalent with credit or debit cards. Similarly, all purchases of inventory will be made with cash on delivery in order to obtain the lowest prices. In this way there will be no accounts receivable or accounts payable. However, each store will need an initial cash float for making change.

These store performance estimates have just been completed. Store profitability has yet to be ascertained based on those estimates.

There are six board members. You and your partner have been fortunate in obtaining four experienced board members. Two have been appointed by the Rabbitbrook family. The third is a retired merchandising vice president from the Hudson's Bay Company. The fourth is the CFO of an engineering firm. You and your partner are also directors. The other directors are deeply concerned about profitability and are insisting that you, as the CFO, ensure that there is financial accountability in the form of budgets and regular reporting against those budgets. You agree. You mention to the other board members that during your introductory management accounting course you learned about budgeting and other ways to ensure accountability.

The store managers will be hired in seven months; the stores will open in eight months. Nevertheless, the directors want the system of financial accountability to be established immediately, even before the managers are hired, in order to ascertain the potential profitability and the need for investment.

Required:
As the CFO, address the concerns of the directors.

3. XXZ is a software company that provides high-functioning accounting software and specialized ERP systems to manufacturing firms. About six years ago, XXZ became an application service provider (ASP) for a major automotive parts manufacturer, Sagma. XXZ installed an ERP system at Sagma, and then provided the employees and supervisors necessary to operate it. This arrangement was necessary at the time in order to sell XXZ's version 3.1 of its Internet-based ERP system at Sagma. The contract was for two years, and at the time of its signing, there were no plans to expand into the ERP ASP business.

In effect, Sagma outsourced its ERP operating activities to XXZ. This arrangement was highly satisfactory to Sagma; at the end of the two-year contract, Sagma asked for a 10-year extension. XXZ was obliged to extend the contract, which has not been troublesome to XXZ. The contract has been highly profitable and it has also allowed the testing of the latest products, to the benefit of both XXZ and Sagma.

After the first Sagma contract, other ERP customers requested that XXZ operate their ERP systems. Within three years—with no promotion or sales activity—XXZ was the ASP for 14 major firms. To look after these customers, XXZ has about 4,000 employees located on premises of these customers plus about 500 at the XXZ office to provide common services and management. The business model is straightforward. A contract is negotiated that covers multiple services and multiple performance measures of those services. The contract specifies the required software and equipment, plus employees and managers.

Structurally, the ERP ASP business has been delivered out of the division of the VP sales with assistance from the human resources, programming, and product development units. Revenues less expenses equals the profit contributed to the sales division. There is also a modest charge from XXZ for miscellaneous services. Of course, the costs of the installed XXZ ERP systems are charged to the sales division.

Another 20 or more firms have requested that XXZ provide complete ERP services. Consequently, in observing this highly profitable unplanned business, the XXZ CEO decided that, starting next year, a separate division is needed to market its ASP capability. The 4,000 field employees are expected to grow by 1,000 a year for five years. Each customer site will be a separate responsibility centre. The 500 employees at the XXZ office are expected to grow by 25 employees per year for the same five years.

The CEO appointed Rae Randers to be divisional general manager. She hired five people to fill the senior positions for the division. You have been appointed controller, which is one of the new division's senior positions. One of your tasks is to establish a system of responsibility centres, and to advise the new division general manager how to account for them, how to evaluate them, and how to set up transfer prices for the services provided by the employees at the XXZ office.

Required:

Using the case approach, undertake your assigned task regarding responsibility centres.

ETHICS

1. The British Columbia Division is one of several divisions of North American Products. The divisional manager has a high degree of autonomy in operating the division. British Columbia Division's management staff consists of a division controller, a division sales manager, and a division production manager, all reporting to the division manager. The division manager reports to the executive vice president at corporate headquarters, while the division controller has a functional reporting relationship to the corporate controller.

The members of the management staff of the British Columbia Division have developed good working relationships with each other over the past several years. Regularly scheduled staff meetings are held, and most of the management process is carried out through daily contact among the members of the staff.

An important staff meeting is held each September. At the meeting, management makes decisions required to finalize the annual budget to be submitted to corporate headquarters for the coming calendar year. The fourth-quarter plans are finalized, and the current year's forecasted results are reviewed prior to completion of the budget for the coming year.

For the first time in recent years, the budgeted amounts of the British Columbia Division for next year show no growth and lower profits than the forecast for the current year. A review of the coming year's plans has not uncovered any alternatives that could improve the sales and profits. This unusual situation is of concern to the division manager because he has developed a reputation for producing growing profits. In addition, growth and profits affect the division manager's performance evaluation and annual bonus.

During the meeting in September, the division manager states that he would like to see some of the profits shifted from the current year to the next year. He has heard that another company shifted profits, and believes that the following actions were used to accomplish this objective.

- Shipments made to customers in the last two weeks of December were not billed until January.
- The salesforce was instructed to encourage customers to specify January delivery rather than December wherever possible.
- Abnormally generous amounts were used to establish accruals for warranties, bad debts, and other expenses.
- Raw materials for which title had passed and which were in transit at the end of December were recorded as purchased in December; however, the raw materials were not included in the year-end inventory.
- Sales on account for the last day of December were not recorded until the first business day of January.
- The cleaning and painting of the exterior of the plant was rescheduled to be completed in the current year rather than in the coming year as planned.

The dollar amounts involved in these actions were material and would be material for the British Columbia Division if similar actions were taken. The division manager asks you, the division controller, whether profits would be shifted from the current year to the next year if actions similar to these were carried out at the British Columbia Division.

Required:

What should you do? Please elaborate.

2. A large Canadian corporation participates in a highly competitive industry. To meet this competition and achieve profit goals, the company has chosen the decentralized form of organization. Each manager of a decentralized investment centre is measured on the basis of profit contribution, market penetration, and return on investment. Failure to meet the objectives established by corporate management for these measures is unacceptable and usually results in demotion or dismissal of an investment centre manager.

An anonymous survey of managers in the company has revealed that the managers feel pressure to compromise their personal ethical standards to achieve corporate objectives. For example, at certain plant locations there is pressure to reduce quality control to a level that cannot assure that all unsafe products will be rejected. Also, sales personnel are encouraged to use questionable sales tactics to obtain orders, including gifts and other incentives to purchasing agents.

You, the CEO, are disturbed.
Required:
What should you do? Please elaborate.

(CMA)

3. Egret and Swan are partners in an accounting firm. Egret runs the tax practice and is both a CA and a CMA. Swan is in charge of the management consulting area; his background is in information systems and statistics. Egret and Swan used to be good friends but, since his divorce, Egret believes that everyone is out to take him for everything possible. In addition to their salaries, Egret and Swan receive (1) a bonus based on the profits of their respective practice areas and (2) a share of total profits after expenses. The tax practice has consistently shown higher profits than the consulting area, although consulting revenues are growing and costs are remaining fairly constant.

Recently, Swan asked for some help regarding several of his client engagements in tax matters. Egret also needed some computer assistance from Swan's area. Therefore, they agreed to establish a transfer price for such assistance. The transfer price was to be the cost of service provided. At the end of the year, the tax area showed a very large profit while the consulting area's increase was not so substantial, even though several new clients had been acquired. Egret spent his bonus on a trip to the island of St. Thomas and felt much better when he returned after three weeks. He hoped the following year would be even more profitable, since he was using absorption (full) cost as the basis for transferring his assistance to consulting and Swan was using variable cost as the basis for transferring his assistance to tax.
Required:
You work for Egret. What should you do? Please elaborate.

SOLUTIONS TO SELF-TEST QUESTIONS

1. a, 2. b, 3. a, 4. d, 5. c, 6. d, 7. b, 8. b, 9. d, 10. a

ENDNOTES

1. Matt Murray, "After Long Overhaul, Banc One Now Faces Pressure to Perform," *Wall Street Journal*, March 10, 1998, A1, A10.
2. William W. Cooper and Yuri Ijiri, eds., *Kohler's Dictionary for Accountants*, Englewood Cliffs: Prentice-Hall, 1983, pp. 43–45.
3. These rules are more difficult to implement when the selling division is in a captive relationship and is not able to sell its products outside the corporate entity. In such situations, opportunity cost must be estimated to give the selling division an incentive to transfer products.
4. Ian Karleff, "Tax Haven Earnings at Risk?" *National Post*, August 9, 2002, N1.
5. Volume variances are covered in Chapter 7, on standard costing.

Chapter 12

Measuring and Rewarding Performance

LEARNING OBJECTIVES

After reading this chapter, you should be able to answer the following questions:

1   **Why**
should organizations use multiple performance measures to assess performance?

2   **How**
are return on investment (ROI) and residual income (RI) similar and different?

3   **Why**
has economic value added (EVA) become a popular performance measure?

4   **Why**
are nonfinancial measures important for evaluating performance?

5   **How**
are activity-based costing concepts related to performance measurement?

6   **Why**
is it more difficult to measure performance in multinational firms than in solely domestic companies?

7   **How**
should employee rewards, including compensation, and performance be linked?

8   **How**
do expatriate reward systems differ from those for domestic operations?

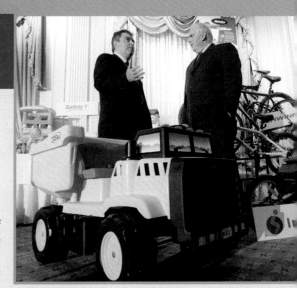

www.dorel.com

Dorel Industries Incorporated

Montreal-based **DOREL INDUSTRIES** is a global manufacturer of consumer products with numerous factories. It specializes in three market segments, for which it produces branded products:

- Juvenile products such as infant car seats, strollers, high chairs, toddler beds, playpens, swings, and infant health and safety aids.
- Home furnishings such as a wide variety of ready-to-assemble furniture for home and office use, as well as metal folding furniture, futons, step stools, ladders, and other imported furniture items.
- Recreational/leisure items such as bicycles, jogging strollers, and other recreational products and accessories.

In a recent year, 72% of Dorel's sales were in the United States, 5% in Canada, and 23% in Europe and elsewhere. It employs about 4,700 people in 15 countries. The company also has eight offices in China, headquartered in Shanghai, to oversee the sourcing, engineering, and logistics of the company's Asian supply chain.

Dorel conducts its business through a variety of sales and distribution arrangements, including these: salaried Dorel employees; individual agents, who carry Dorel's products on either an exclusive or non-exclusive basis; individual specialized agents, who sell products, including Dorel's, exclusively to one customer such as a major discount chain; and sales agencies that employ their own sales forces.

Dorel has two major customers, Wal-Mart Stores and Kmart Corporation. These two retailers represented 47.3% of Dorel's total revenue in a recent year. The company's commitment to providing high-quality, industry-leading service has enabled it to develop successful relationships with major retailers. Dorel has achieved high levels of customer satisfaction by fostering excellent relations between its sales reps and its retail customers. Thus, for example, Dorel has placed a permanent, full-service account team near Wal-Mart's headquarters in Bentonville, Arkansas. Similarly, Dorel has sales teams dedicated exclusively to Kmart and Toys "R" Us. These dedicated sales teams provide its major customers with the assurance that demanding inventory and supply requirements will be met and that any problems will be addressed quickly. The sales teams also provide product and market analysis to help major retailers with product designs and specs.

The trend among Dorel's mass merchant customers is to buy from fewer but larger suppliers. That is, suppliers that can deliver a wide range of products, provide greater security of supply, and offer increased levels of service. Dorel's competitive advantages are basically two: it delivers a wide range of products reliably; and it has a demonstrated commitment to service.

Dorel has succeeded well in carrying out its strategy in a competitive world market. It thinks globally when organizing and coordinating its many brands, its numerous factories, and its extensive network of suppliers.

SOURCE: Dorel Industries Inc. Found at: http://www.secinfo.com/d12K7a.uw.d.htm#1ema (Feb. 15, 2008).

This chapter covers two related sets of topics. First, performance measurement is discussed in the context of the balanced scorecard and more conventional monetary indicators, such as cash flows, return on investment, and residual income. The more innovative nonmonetary and monetary performance measures that are needed by world-class, customer-driven companies are also addressed. Second, a variety of employee rewards that might be used by an organization seeking to balance short-run and long-run interests are presented, along with discussion of the related topics for performance enhancement.

LEARNING OBJECTIVE   1

Why should organizations use multiple performance measures to assess performance?

MEASURING ORGANIZATIONAL AND EMPLOYEE PERFORMANCE

As indicated in previous chapters, people must have benchmarks against which to compare their accomplishments in order to evaluate performance. A benchmark can be monetary, such as a target level of economic value added (EVA), or nonmonetary, such as product defect rate or market share. Whatever measures are used, the following four general rules for performance measurement are appropriate:

- Measures that assess progress toward organizational goals and objectives should be established.
- Persons being evaluated should have some input in developing the performance measurements and should be aware of them.
- Persons being evaluated should have the appropriate skills and should be provided the necessary equipment, information, and authority to be successful under the measurement system.
- Feedback relative to performance should be provided in a timely and useful manner.

In selecting performance measures, missions of specific subunits must be considered. For example, objectives established for newly formed divisions are likely described in terms of sales growth, market share, research and development success,

Multiple performance measures can be used to evaluate the success of any activity—even Winterlude in Ottawa. The city could evaluate the success of this festivity by measures that include visitor spending, hotel occupancy rates, and tonnes of garbage cleaned up.

or rate of new product introductions. For these divisions, the use of profit measures to assess performance is inappropriate. Alternatively, objectives for mature divisions can be couched in terms of profits and cash flows; hence, profit measures are appropriate for evaluating the relative success of mature divisions.

As organizations have a variety of goals and objectives, some of which are related to product life cycle issues, it is unlikely that a single measure or even several measures of the same type will effectively assess organizational progress toward all of those goals and objectives. A primary goal is, by necessity, to be financially solvent. As solvency is determined by the relationship between cash inflows and cash outflows, cash flow is often used as a performance measure. If the organization is profit oriented, a goal of the firm is to provide a satisfactory return to shareholders. This requirement is satisfied by generating a net income considered by the owners to be sufficient, relative to the assets (capital) invested. Accordingly, some measurement of income is used by virtually all businesses to assess performance.

Although financial measures provide necessary indications of performance, they do not address some of the new issues of competitive reality essential to business survival in a global economy. Many companies have established goals relative to customer satisfaction rates, product defect rates, lead time to market, and environmental social responsibility. Such goals are not measured directly by income. Companies producing inferior goods, delivering late, abusing the environment, or, in general, making customers dissatisfied will lose market share and, eventually, be forced out of business. Nonfinancial performance measures can be developed that indicate progress (or lack thereof) toward achievement of the important, long-run critical success factors of world-class companies. As the following quote indicates, selecting performance measures is a crucial organizational decision because the performance measures will determine how, and on what bases, managers and other employees focus their time and attention.

> Performance measures are usually used to track progress towards [a] target. Often the measures become a surrogate for the target itself. When we turn our attention to what gets measured, and only what gets measured, we may overlook avenues of investigation that offer far greater opportunities to achieve [the target].[1]

Nonfinancial indicators are, in effect, surrogate measures of financial performance.

Financial and nonfinancial performance measures can be combined to provide a comprehensive portrayal of organizational and managerial performance. Exhibit 12-1 illustrates a balanced scorecard that ultimately links all aspects of performance to the company's strategies. The balanced scorecard is defined as a performance measurement conceptualization that translates an organization's strategy into clear objectives, measures, targets, and initiatives organized by the four perspectives: financial, customer, internal business processes, and learning and growth. The balanced scorecard provides a set of financial and nonfinancial measures that encompasses both internal and external perspectives. Think of the balanced scorecard as the dials and indicators in an airplane cockpit. For the complex task of navigating and flying an airplane, pilots need detailed information about many aspects of the flight. They need information on fuel, air speed, altitude, bearing, destination, and other indicators that summarize the current and predicted environment. Reliance on a single instrument can be fatal.

It is estimated that a balanced scorecard should have 15 to 25 measures that support a company's strategy and are linked together in the form of cause-and-effect hypothesis statements. Forming these linkages encourages a company to specify how investments in human resources will drive continuous process improvements, increasing customer satisfaction and financial prosperity.

EXHIBIT 12-1

Performance Measurement
"Balanced Scorecard"

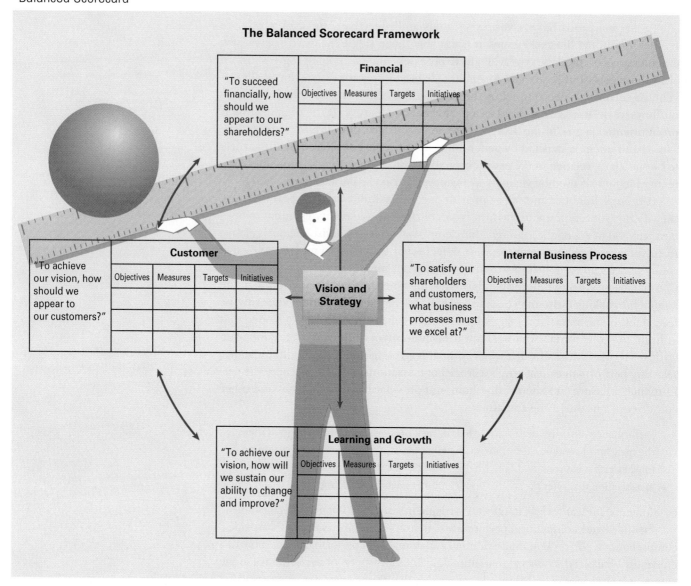

SOURCE: Reprinted from an article appearing in the September 2000 issue of *CMA Management* magazine by Anthony A. Atkinson and Marc Epstein, with permission of Certified Management Accountants of Canada.

What would a balanced scorecard look like for Dell? Peter Brewer, an authority on balanced scorecards, has some suggestions for a balanced scorecard for Dell. Brewer uses Dell's mission statement to create a balanced scorecard.[2] Dell's mission statement, which appears on its website, is "to be the most successful computer company in the world at delivering the best customer experience in markets we serve." From an understanding of Dell and deductive logic, Brewer suggests that the following might be the four balanced scorecard perspectives.

Learning and growth measures might include:

- Training dollars spent per full-time equivalent by customer segment to ensure that well-educated business segment managers provide state-of-the-art advice to customers

- Number of collaborative customer-solution teams that motivate Dell to collaborate with its customers and jointly create technology solutions to fulfill any unmet customer needs
- Number of emerging technologies evaluated inspires Dell's leaders to stay abreast of technology threats and opportunities that may alter the competitive landscape in the future

Internal business process measures might include:
- Percentage of total hours spent in contact with customers at the executive and managerial levels
- Number of customer-initiated product innovations
- Average customer idea ramp-up time

Customer measures might include:
- Customer perception of customized response capability
- Customer perception of stability and first-to-market capability with the latest technology
- Customer retention

Financial measures might include:
- Revenue growth by segment
- Gross margin by segment

The following News Note considers the motivations for using a balanced scorecard to measure performance and why the balanced scorecard includes more than financial measurements.

Regardless of which performance measures are selected, they must be set at levels that will encourage employees to do their best. Such a notion obviously means that individuals who will be evaluated by those measures must know about them. Communication of information is essential in any performance measurement

---

Balanced Scorecard for Foster Brewing International

INTERNATIONAL NEWS NOTE

Fosters is an Australian-based firm with investments in brewing and wines. The measures it uses do more than describe past performance; they also articulate and communicate the company's strategy for ensuring that individual, organizational, and cross-departmental initiatives are aligned. Those measures are listed below:

Financial:
Shareholder equity/total assets (%)
Return on investment (%)
Added value/employee ($)
Market value ($)
Profits from new products or business operations ($)

Process improvement
Inventory turnover (no.)
Improvement in productivity (%)
Administrative expense/employee ($)

Customer
Market share (%)
Brand image index (%)
Satisfied customer index ($)
Annual sales/customer ($)
Customer loyalty index (%)

Learning and growth
Investment in development of new markets ($)
Satisfied employee index (no.)
Marketing expense/customer ($)
Investment in new product support & training ($)
Research and development (number of patents and trademarks)
Knowledge management—tacit and explicit ($ value of estimated values)

SOURCE: Sanjoy Bose and Keith Thomas, "Applying the Balanced Scorecard for Better Performance of Intellectual Capital," *Journal of Intellectual Capital* 4 (2007): 653–65.

process. Individuals must know about and understand the performance measures to be used so that they can make a conscious choice to perform or not perform in a manner consistent with the measurement system. Withholding information about measures will keep employees from performing at their highest level of potential, will be frustrating for them, and will not support feelings of mutual respect and cooperation. In addition, participation in devising performance measures captures the attention of those persons being evaluated and results in a social contract between participants and evaluators. Performance measures should also promote harmonious operations among organizational units. The effects of suboptimization can then be minimized because all employees will be working toward the same goals.

Managers must place individuals in appropriate jobs, because employees who are put in jobs for which they are unsuited are destined to fail. Assuming employees possess basic competencies, they must be given the appropriate tools—including equipment, information, authority, training, and support—to perform their jobs in a manner consistent with the measurement process. Competent individuals or teams of workers having the necessary job tools can be held responsible for their performance. If these tools are unavailable, people cannot be expected to accomplish their tasks.

Employee performance should be monitored and feedback provided on a continuous basis. Positive feedback encourages employees to continue favourable behaviours, while negative feedback creates awareness of problems so that employees can respond with different behaviours.

A dashboard is similar to a balanced scorecard. There are some important differences. Dashboards are generally used to monitor data that are measured frequently.[3] Also, they focus on the organization's health and efficiency. In contrast, scorecards tend to focus on monitoring progress toward strategic goals.

Balanced Scorecard at Hilton Hotels

The balanced scorecard tries to develop a "balanced" perspective, focusing on financial results as well as forward-looking measures that tend to predict future business, such as customer satisfaction and intent to return. The HILTON BSC model consists of five "value drivers":

- Operational effectiveness
- Revenue maximization
- Loyalty (customer, team members, owners)
- Brand management
- Learning and growth

These drivers of value represent the corporate strategic direction for Hilton. Based on these value drivers, Hilton creates property-specific goals called key performance indicators (KPI). For example, as noted above, revenue management is part of Hilton's corporate strategy. Under this value driver, the hotel-level KPI is revenue per available room (RevPAR). Applying an improvement factor to the individual property's actual results creates a property-specific KPI for RevPAR that applies to that specific hotel. The process continues for all the Hilton value drivers. The result: realistic, quantifiable property-specific goals aligned with the overall corporate strategy direction.

Add a proprietary continuous improvement process that, on a corporate level, incorporates tools like Six Sigma (an approach to implementation of a measurement-based strategy that focuses on improvement), root cause analysis, and kaizen (the Japanese business strategy that involves everyone in an organization working together to make improvements). Then add prioritized property-level tools that, through matrix weighting, provide the dimensions of customer importance and "gap to perfection," and you will have an idea of how Hilton strengthens its leadership position.

SOURCE: Dennis Koci, Senior Vice-President of Operations Support, Hilton Hotels Corp.; http://www.hcfsinternational.com/whats_the_score/Whats_the_score.html.

The differences between these two management tools are often unclear. Exhibit 12-2 highlights those differences.

EXHIBIT 12-2
Dashboards and Scorecards:
A Comparison

	Dashboards ...	Scorecards ...
Description	... are up-to-date or real time ... are highly visual (using charts, graphs, and dials) ... are customizable and flexible (end user can refine views for analysis purposes) ... improve efficiency ... help manage resources ... provide daily statistics ... empower decision makers	... support the organizational culture ... communicate vision and strategy ... foster a collaborative environment ... help with transformation ... foster a culture of accountability ... articulate strategy
Purpose	... provide current management information ... track key performance indicators (KPIs) ... link compensation to performance ... conduct variance analyses ... get to the details for root cause analysis ... assist benchmarking ... review daily statistics ... analyze data to understand trends and possibly predict them	... provide management with available information ... communicate vision and strategy ... provide a single collaborative system ... help transform the organization into a strategy-focused one ... help foster a culture of accountability ... help shift the organization's focus from products to customer needs ... tie executive bonuses to achievement of strategy ... link business processes to key initiatives

SOURCE: Raef Lawson, William Stratton, and Toby Hatch, "Scorecards and Dashboards—Partners in Performance," *CMA Management*, December–January 2007, pp. 33–37.

FINANCIAL PERFORMANCE MEASUREMENTS FOR MANAGERS

LEARNING OBJECTIVE 2

How are return on investment (ROI) and residual income (RI) similar and different?

Attempts to use financial measures to evaluate higher-level managerial performance must consider the type of responsibility centre over which the manager has control. If a manager is responsible for only one monetary item (such as in a cost or revenue centre), performance measurements are limited to those relevant to that single monetary measure. Alternatively, profit and investment centre managers are responsible for their centres' revenues and expenses. Given this greater accountability, a greater number of financial measures can be used to evaluate performance.

Cash Flow

Use of accrual-based segment margin or income as a performance measure may divert management's attention from two critical issues—the size and the direction of cash flows. Profit and investment centre managers know that continuous liquidity is essential for their entities to succeed. Thus, another important performance measure is cash flow. The cash flow statement highlights the cash impacts of the three primary categories of business activities: operating, investing, and financing. A cash-based portrayal of operations helps managers to judge an entity's ability to meet current fixed cash outflow commitments, undertake new commitments, and adapt to adverse changes in business conditions. Also, by identifying relationships between segment margin (or net income) and net cash flow from operations, the cash flow statement assists managers in judging the quality of the entity's earnings.

Like segment margin and income, cash flow can be manipulated and relates to the short run rather than the long run. But, as pointed out earlier, adequate cash flow is essential to business success. Inadequate cash flow may indicate poor judgment and decision making on the part of the entity's manager. A variety of financial ratios that include cash flow information—such as the current ratio, acid test ratio, and number of days' collections in accounts receivable—can help managers conduct their functions efficiently and effectively.

Return on Investment

Because they are responsible for generating revenues, controlling costs, and acquiring, using, and disposing of assets, investment centre managers can be evaluated using return on investment. **Return on investment** (ROI) is a ratio that relates income generated by an entity to the resources (or the asset base) used to produce that income. The return on investment formula is:

$$ROI = Income \div Assets\ invested$$

Before the ROI formula can be used effectively, the numerator and denominator must be specifically defined. In Exhibit 12-3 there are questions relative to these definitions—and the answers to and rationale for each, assuming that the entity being measured is an investment centre. The answers would be different if ROI were being calculated for an entire company. The ROI formula can be used to evaluate individual investment centres, as well as to make intracompany, intercompany, and industry comparisons, if managers making these comparisons are aware of and allow for any differences in the entities' characteristics and accounting methods.

return on investment
a ratio that relates income generated by the investment centre to the resources (or asset base) used to produce that income

EXHIBIT 12-3
ROI Definitional Questions and Answers

Question	Preferable Answer	Rationale
Is income defined as segment margin or operating income?	Segment margin	This amount includes only elements controllable by the investment centre manager.
Is income defined on a before-tax or after-tax basis?	Before-tax basis	Investment centres are not taxed separately; if they were, the tax would probably be a different amount.
Is income defined on a before-interest or after-interest basis?	Before-interest basis	Interest rates are generally negotiated based on the company's (not the investment centre's) creditworthiness; if the centre had to borrow funds as an independent entity, the rate might be different.
Should assets be defined as • total assets utilized, • total assets available for use, or • net assets (equity)?	Total assets available for use	The investment centre manager is responsible for all assets, even idle ones.
Should plant assets be included in the asset denominator at • original costs, • depreciated book values, or • current values?	Current values	These values measure the opportunity cost of using the assets.
Should beginning, ending, or average assets be used?	Average assets	Periodic income relates to assets used during the entire period.

Exhibit 12-4 uses data for the Richmond Machine Company to illustrate ROI computations. The company has three product-line divisions: Machinery, Materials Handling, and Tools. All of the divisions are operated as separate investment centres.

EXHIBIT 12-4

Richmond Machine Company Divisional ROI Computation

	Machinery	Materials Handling	Tools	Total
Revenues	$ 6,000,000	$ 967,400	$ 1,771,000	$ 8,738,400
Direct costs:				
Variable	(2,100,000)	(387,000)	(815,500)	(3,302,500)
Fixed (avoidable)	(1,100,000)	(120,000)	(302,000)	(1,522,000)
Segment margin	$ 2,800,000	$ 460,400	$ 653,500	$ 3,913,900
Unavoidable fixed and allocated costs	(725,000)	(92,400)	(153,000)	(970,400)
Operating income	$ 2,075,000	$ 368,000	$ 500,500	$ 2,943,500
Taxes (34%)	(705,500)	(125,120)	(170,170)	(1,000,790)
Net income	$ 1,369,500	$ 242,880	$ 330,330	$ 1,942,710
Current assets	$ 110,000	$ 42,000	$ 90,000	
Plant assets	11,422,000	995,000	8,825,000	
Total asset cost	$ 11,532,000	$ 1,037,000	$ 8,915,000	
Accumulated depreciation	(1,750,000)	(123,000)	(4,568,000)	
Asset book value	$ 9,782,000	$ 914,000	$ 4,347,000	
Liabilities	(4,205,000)	(117,000)	(927,000)	
Net assets	$ 5,577,000	$ 797,000	$ 3,420,000	
ROI: Segment margin	$ 2,800,000	$ 460,400	$ 653,500	
÷ Assets invested*	÷$ 11,532,000	÷$ 1,037,000	÷$ 8,915,000	
= Return on investment	24.3%	44.4%	7.3%	

*Although use of current values would have been preferable, Richmond Machine Company found these values difficult to obtain and had more confidence in the original cost of the assets used.

To provide useful information about individual factors that compose the rate of return, the ROI formula can be restated in terms of profit margin and asset turnover. **Profit margin** is the ratio of income to sales; it indicates what proportion of each sales dollar is not used for expenses and so becomes profit. **Asset turnover**, which is calculated as sales divided by assets, shows the sales dollars generated by each dollar of assets and measures asset productivity. The ROI formula restated in terms of profit margin and asset turnover is called the **Du Pont model**:

$$ROI = \text{Profit margin} \times \text{Asset turnover}$$

As with the original ROI formula, terms must be specifically defined before the formula can be used for comparative or evaluative purposes. This model provides refined information about organizational improvement opportunities. Profit margin can be used to indicate management's efficiency as shown in the relation between sales and expenses. Asset turnover can be used to judge the effectiveness of asset use relative to revenue production. Calculations based on the Richmond Machine Company information are given in Exhibit 12-5. Income and asset base are defined as segment margin and total historical cost. Thus, these computations provide the same answers as those given in Exhibit 12-4.

With the profit margin and asset turnover ratios computed for each division, the division's performance can be evaluated relative to benchmark ratios. The benchmark ratios could be expectations of performance for each division, industry performance levels, or similar ratios for specific competitors. Because the three divisions

profit margin
the ratio of income to sales

asset turnover
a ratio that measures asset productivity; it is the number of sales dollars generated by each dollar of assets during a specific period

Du Pont model
ROI = Profit margin × Asset turnover

EXHIBIT 12-5

Richmond Machine Company
Du Pont Model ROI
Computations

ROI = Profit Margin × Asset Turnover
   = (Income ÷ Sales) × (Sales ÷ Assets)

Machinery:
ROI = ($2,800,000 ÷ $6,000,000) × ($6,000,000 ÷ $11,532,000)
   = 0.467 × 0.520 = 24.3%

Materials Handling:
ROI = ($460,400 ÷ $967,400) × ($967,400 ÷ $1,037,000)
   = 0.476 × 0.933 = 44.4%

Tools:
ROI = ($653,500 ÷ $1,771,000) × ($1,771,000 ÷ $8,915,000)
   = 0.369 × 0.199 = 7.3%

compete in different industries, it would not be appropriate to compare one internal division's performance to the performance of the others.

ROI is affected by management decisions involving sales prices, volume and mix of products sold, expenses, and capital asset acquisitions and dispositions. Return on investment may be increased through various management actions, including (1) raising sales prices, if demand will not be impaired; (2) decreasing expenses; and (3) decreasing dollars invested in assets, especially if those assets are no longer productive. Thus, actions to improve performance should be taken only after all the interrelationships that determine ROI have been considered. A change in one of the component elements can affect many of the others. For instance, a selling price increase can reduce sales volume if demand is elastic with respect to price.

Assessments of whether profit margin, asset turnover, and return on investment are favourable or unfavourable can be made only by comparison of actual results for each component. Valid bases of comparison include expected results, prior results, and results of similar entities. Many companies establish target rates of return either for the company or for each division. These rates are based on the nature of the industry or market in which the company or division operates. Favourable results should mean rewards for investment centre managers.

Unfavourable rates of return should be viewed as managerial opportunities for improvement. Factors used in the computation should be analyzed for more detailed information. For example, if asset turnover is low, additional analyses can be made of inventory turnover, accounts receivable turnover, machine capacity level experienced, and other rate-of-utilization measures. Such efforts should help indicate the causes of the problems so that adjustments can be made. Another measure related to return on investment is the residual income of an investment centre.

Residual Income

residual income
the profit earned that exceeds an amount "charged" for funds committed to a responsibility centre

Residual income (RI) is the profit earned that exceeds an amount "charged" for funds committed to an investment centre. The amount charged for funds is equal to a management-specified target rate of return multiplied by the assets used by the division. The rate can be changed periodically to reflect market rate fluctuations or to compensate for risk. The residual income computation is:

$$\text{Residual income} = \text{Income} - (\text{Target rate} \times \text{Asset base})$$

Perhaps the most significant advantage of residual income over return on investment is that residual income provides a dollar figure of performance rather than a percentage. It is always to a company's advantage to obtain new assets if the assets will earn an amount greater than the cost of the additional investment. Expansion, or additional investments in assets, can occur in an investment centre as long as positive residual income is expected on the additional investment.

Residual income can be calculated for each investment centre of Richmond Machine Company. The company has established 12% as the target rate of return on total historical cost of assets invested and continues to define income as segment margin. Calculations are shown in Exhibit 12-6. The residual income measures provide a clear indication of the relative contributions of the three divisions to the profit of the company. Although the Machinery and Materials Handling divisions are contributing substantial profits to the company, the profit of the Tools Division is insufficient to cover the required return on capital.

Residual income = Income − (Target rate × Asset base)

Machinery:
RI = $2,800,000 − [0.12($11,532,000)] = $2,800,000 − $1,383,840 = $1,416,160

Materials Handling:
RI = $460,400 − [0.12($1,037,000)] = $460,400 − $124,440 = $335,960

Tools:
RI = $653,500 − [0.12($8,915,000)] = $653,500 − $1,069,800 = $(416,300)

EXHIBIT 12-6
Richmond Machine Company
Residual Income Calculations

Limitations of Return on Investment and Residual Income

When used to measure investment centre performance, return on investment and residual income have certain limitations (see Exhibit 12-7) that must be considered by managers.

1. *Problems related to income*
   - Income can be manipulated on a short-term basis by accelerating or delaying the recognition of income and expenses.
   - Because income depends on accounting methods selected, all investment centres must use the same methods if comparisons are to be made.
   - Accrual-based income reflects neither the cash flow patterns nor the time value of money, and these performance dimensions are generally important.

2. *Problems related to the asset base*
   - Some asset investment values are difficult to measure or assign to investment centres, while some other values, such as research and development, are not capitalized.
   - Current managers may be evaluated on decisions over which they had no control, such as decisions by previous managers to acquire some of the assets included in the division's investment base.
   - Inflation causes investment book values to be understated unless they are price-level adjusted.

3. *ROI and RI reflect investment centre performance without regard to companywide objectives, which can result in suboptimization.*

EXHIBIT 12-7
Limitations of ROI and RI

Item 1 problems are common to most accounting-based measurements. However, use of ROI or RI in the new global environment can lead to the significant problems listed in Item 2. For example, intangible assets such as patents are significant keys to competing successfully today. The market values of such assets may differ very substantially from the assets' book values. Furthermore, some intangible assets may simply be ignored by traditional accounting methods, and therefore will be ignored by the analysis. A reputation for high-quality output and a high level of customer loyalty are examples of such assets.

Additionally, ROI and RI are short-term performance measures; consequently, they are better measures of performance for mature divisions than for high-growth divisions. For divisions that have opportunities for high rates of growth, the ROI and RI measures punish managers who currently invest in assets that do not generate returns until future periods.

LEARNING OBJECTIVE 3

Why has economic value added (EVA) become a popular performance measure?

economic value added
EVA = After-tax income − (Cost of capital % × Capital invested)

ECONOMIC VALUE ADDED

Perhaps the most popular trend in performance measurement is the development of measures intended to align the interests of common shareholders and managers more directly. Leading this trend is corporate adoption of the measure known as **economic value added** (EVA). Conceptually similar to RI, EVA is a measure of the income produced above the cost of capital. The major distinction between RI and EVA is that the target rate of return for EVA is applied to the capital invested in the division or firm as opposed to the market value or book value of book assets, which is the measure used for RI. Furthermore, because only after-tax profits are available to shareholders, EVA is calculated based on after-tax income:

$$\text{EVA} = \text{After-tax income} - (\text{Cost of capital \%} \times \text{Capital invested})$$

Capital invested is defined as the market value of total equity and interest-bearing debt. *Cost of capital* is the average cost of capital. For reasons mentioned earlier, the market value of invested capital (generally debt plus owners' equity) can differ considerably from the book or market value of booked assets. As this difference increases, so do the relative benefits of using EVA rather than RI as a performance measure.

It is not uncommon from time to time for the market value of a firm to be significantly higher than the book value of the firm. Accordingly, RI, which is based on a target rate of return applied to the book value of assets, is likely to indicate much better performance than EVA. This point is demonstrated in Exhibit 12-8. Because the invested capital of Richmond Machine Company far exceeds its book

EXHIBIT 12-8

Comparison of RI and EVA for Richmond Machine Company

Invested capital	$45,000,000
Book value of assets	26,484,000*
Required return	12%
Net income (sum of divisions' net incomes from Exhibit 11-3)	$1,942,710

RI = Income − (Target rate × Asset base)
    = $1,942,710 − (0.12 × $26,484,000) = $(1,235,370)

EVA = After-tax income − (Cost of capital % × Capital invested)
    = $1,942,710 − (0.12 × $45,000,000) = $(3,457,290)

*Book value of assets is equal to the sum of asset costs for each of the company's three divisions, as given in Exhibit 12-3 ($11,532,000 + $1,037,000 + $8,915,000) plus an assumed amount of $5,000,000 of corporate assets that are not associated with any of the three divisions.

value of assets, the firm's performance measured by EVA is well below the performance measured by RI.

Despite the growing popularity of the EVA measure, it cannot measure all dimensions of performance, and it is a short-term measure of performance. Accordingly, the EVA measure can discourage investment in long-term projects because such investments drive up the amount of invested capital immediately but increase after-tax profits only at some point in the future. The result is a near-term decrease in EVA. Thus, EVA should be supplemented with longer-term financial performance measures and with nonfinancial performance measures, especially for growth-oriented organizational subunits.

NONFINANCIAL PERFORMANCE MEASURES

The previous two sections discussed the financial measures of the balanced scorecard. This section discusses nonfinancial performance measures, which include the other three parts of the balanced scorecard: customer measures, business process measures, and human resource measures. This section also relates to the sections in Chapter 12, particularly performance measurement. The next chapter deals with the system details of nonfinancial performance measurement, whereas this section deals more with content of nonfinancial performance measures.

Customarily, performance evaluations have been conducted based almost solely on financial results. But top management, in maintaining such a narrow focus, is similar to a hockey player who, in hopes of playing well, concentrates solely on the scoreboard. Both the financial measures and game score reflect the results of past decisions. Success also requires that considerable attention be paid to the individual actions for effective competitiveness—not just the summary performance measure, the score. A hockey player must focus on skating, hitting, passing, and shooting. A company must focus on performing well in activities such as customer service, product development, manufacturing, marketing, and delivery. For a company to improve, its performance measurements must specifically track the causes and occurrences of these activities.

Thus, a progressively designed performance measurement system should encompass both financial and nonfinancial measures, especially those that track factors necessary for world-class status. **Nonfinancial performance measures** (NFPMs) include statistics for activities such as on-time delivery, manufacturing cycle time, set-up time, defect rate, number of unplanned production interruptions, and customer returns. NFPMs have two distinct advantages over financial performance measures:

- Nonfinancial indicators directly measure an entity's performance in the activities that create shareholder wealth, such as producing and delivering quality goods and services to customers.
- As they measure productive activity directly, nonfinancial measures may better predict the direction of future cash flows. For example, the long-term financial viability of some industries rests largely on their ability to keep promises of improved product quality at a competitive price.

nonfinancial performance measures statistics on activities such as on-time delivery, manufacturing cycle time, set-up time, defect rate, number of unplanned production interruptions, and customer returns

Another nonfinancial performance measure is customer experience, defined as the internal and subjective response that customers have to any direct or indirect contact with the company. Successful brands positively shape customer experiences through the value proposition at every stage; this is referred to as customer experience management. A related technique is customer relationship management. As Exhibit 12-9 indicates, customer experience management and customer relationship management differ with regard to subject matter, timing, monitoring, audience, and purpose.

EXHIBIT 12-9

Customer Experience Management Versus Customer Relationship Managements

	Customer Experience Management (CEM)	Customer Relationship Management (CRM)
What	Captures and distributes what a customer thinks about a company	Captures and distributes what a company knows about a customer
When	At points of customer interaction: "touch points"	After there is a record of a customer interaction
How Monitored	Surveys, targeted studies, observational studies, "voice of customer" research	Point-of-sales data, market research, website click-through, automated tracking of sales
Who Uses Information	Business or functional leaders, in order to create fulfillable expectations and better experiences with products and services	Customer-facing groups such as sales, marketing, field service, and customer service, in order to drive more efficient and effective execution
Relevance to Future Performance	Leading: Locates places to add offerings in the gaps between expectations and experience	Lagging: Drives cross-selling by bundling products in demand with ones that are not

SOURCE: Christopher Meyer and Andre Schwager, "Understanding Customer Experience," *Harvard Business Review*, February 2007, pp. 117–126.

Selection of Nonfinancial Measures

The set of nonfinancial performance measures that can be used is quite large because it is limited only by the imaginations of the persons establishing the system. Before establishing the measurement system, though, management should strive to identify the firm's critical success factors. A company's critical success factors may include quality, customer satisfaction, manufacturing efficiency and effectiveness, technical excellence, and rapid response to market demands.

For each success factor chosen, management should target a few attributes of each relevant NFPM for continuous improvement. These attributes should include both short-run and long-run measures to steer organizational activities properly. For instance, a short-range success measure for quality is the number of customer complaints in the current period. A long-range success measure for quality is the number of patents obtained to improve the quality of the company's products.

The nonfinancial measures selected for the performance evaluation system can be qualitative or quantitative. Qualitative measures are often subjective; for example, simple low-to-high rankings may be assigned for job skills, such as knowledge, quality of work, and need for supervision. Although such measures provide useful information, performance should also be compared against a quantifiable standard.

Quantitative performance measures are more effective in creating employee receptiveness and compliance, because such measures provide a defined target at which to aim. These measures must be systematically captured and compared with predetermined standards to assess performance.

Establishment of Comparison Bases

After performance measures have been chosen, managers should establish acceptable performance levels by providing bases against which actual measurement data can be compared. These benchmarks can be developed internally (for example, based on a high-performing division) or can be determined from external sources, such as other companies, regardless of whether they are within the company's industry.

In each area in which a performance measurement is to be made, employees must agree (1) to accept specific responsibility for performance and (2) to be evaluated. A system for monitoring and reporting comparative performance levels should be established at appropriate intervals, as shown in Exhibit 12-10. The exhibit reflects a responsibility hierarchy of performance standards, with the broader issues addressed by higher levels of management and the more immediate issues addressed by lower-level employees. Note also that the lower-level measures are monitored more frequently (continuously, daily, or weekly) while the upper-level measures are investigated less frequently (monthly, quarterly, and annually). Measures addressed

EXHIBIT 12-10

Performance Measurement Factors and Timetables

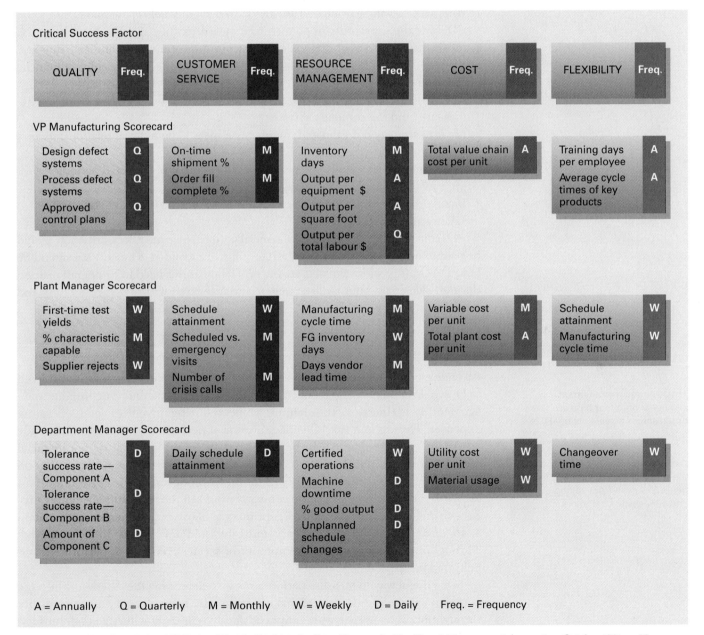

A = Annually   Q = Quarterly   M = Monthly   W = Weekly   D = Daily   Freq. = Frequency

SOURCE: Mark E. Beischel and K. Richard Smith, "Linking the Shop Floor to the Top Floor," *Management Accounting,* October 1991, p. 28. Adapted with permission of the Institute of Management Accountants, Montvale, N.J., USA, www.imanet.org

by middle-level employees (in Exhibit 12-10, the plant manager) are intermediate linkages between the lower-level and upper-level performance measures and require monitoring at intermediate points in time (weekly, monthly, and annually).

A general model for measuring the relative success of an activity compares a numerator representing number of successes with a logical and valid denominator representing total activity volume. For example, market share can be measured as follows:

$$\text{Market share} = \text{Number of units sold by specific firm} \div \text{Total units sold in the industry}$$

Assume an internal division sold 9,000 units during a period in which 48,000 units were sold by all the participants in the industry. The division's market share is 18.75% (9,000 ÷ 48,000). If a competitive benchmark for market share has been set at 20%, success will be evaluated as close to, but slightly below, the mark.

Despite the superiority of nonfinancial measures, they are not always effective. A recent survey of about 300 executives from more than 60 manufacturing and services companies found four reasons for the lack of effectiveness of nonfinancial performance measures:

- Measures not linked to strategy; there must be a causal relationship between the measures and the company's strategy
- Links to strategy not validated; there may appear to be a causal relationship, but it needs to be proven or validated
- Appropriate performance targets not set; the amount of expected periodic improvements needs to be made explicit
- Incorrect measurements; metrics need to be employed that have statistical validity and reliability[4]

Of course, when designing nonfinancial performance measures, attention should be paid to ensure that the above shortcomings are avoided. The NFPMs should be linked to strategy with validated measures. The measures need to be operationalized through challenging but realistic targets and measured with statistical validity and reliability.

Throughput

synchronous management
all endeavours that help an organization achieve its goals

throughput
the rate at which a company generates cash from selling products and services to customers

All endeavours undertaken to help an organization achieve its goals are considered to be **synchronous management** techniques. The intent behind synchronous management is to increase throughput, while reducing inventory and operating expenses. Throughput is a valuable indicator of performance that is gaining wide acceptability. Throughput can be measured in either financial or nonfinancial terms. Defined in nonfinancial terms, **throughput** refers to the number of good units produced and sold by an organization within a time period. An important aspect of this definition is that the company must sell the units and not simply produce them for inventory stockpiles. A primary goal of a profit-oriented organization is to make money, and inventory must be sold for profits to be achieved. Throughput can also refer to the number of services requested, performed, and delivered in a period.

One useful way to measure performance is to determine the extent to which the company is meeting its goal of making money by having rapid and high-quality throughput. Throughput, as mentioned, simply reflects how many good units are produced and sold for each available processing hour. Throughput can also be viewed as a set of component elements, as the Du Pont model, presented earlier, includes components of return on investment. Components of throughput include manufacturing cycle efficiency, process productivity, and process quality yield.

$$\text{Throughput} = \text{Manufacturing cycle efficiency} \times \text{Process productivity} \times \text{Process quality yield}$$

or

$$[\text{Good units} \div \text{Total time}] = [\text{Value-added processing time} \div \text{Total time}] \times$$
$$[\text{Total units} \div \text{Value-added processing time}] \times [\text{Good units} \div \text{Total units}]$$

The manufacturing cycle efficiency is the proportion of total processing time from beginning of production to completion, or service performance that is value-added. This time relates to activities that increase the product's worth to the customer. For instance, assume that the Machinery Division of Richmond Machine Company worked a total of 15,000 hours last month making Product L007. Of these hours, only 6,000 were considered value-added; thus, the division had a manufacturing cycle efficiency of 40%.

Total units started, completed, and sold during the period are divided by the value-added processing time to determine **process productivity**. Assume the Machinery Division produced 30,000 units in the 6,000 hours of value-added processing time and all units were sold. Thus, the division had a process productivity rate of 5.0, meaning that 5.0 units were produced in each value-added processing hour.

process productivity
the total units produced during a period using value-added processing time

But not all units started, completed, and sold during the period are necessarily good units—some may be defective. The proportion of good units produced is the **process quality yield**. Thus, if only 27,000 of the 30,000 units produced by the Machinery Division last month were good units, the division had a 90% process quality yield for the period. This measure reflects the quality of the production process.

process quality yield
the proportion of good units that resulted from the activities expended

The total Product L007 throughput for Machinery Division last month was 1.80 ($0.40 \times 5.0 \times 0.90$); that is, the division produced and sold only 1.80 good units for every hour of total actual processing time—quite a difference from the 5.0 units indicated as process productivity! The division could increase throughput by decreasing nonvalue-added activities, increasing total production and sales of units, decreasing the per unit processing time, or increasing process quality yield.

Quality Indicators

A world-class company that is seeking growth and profitability will do well to systematically measure quality and assess its organizational cost of quality (COQ). Such measures should focus on and be related to actions that add value to products and services for the customer. Exhibit 12-11 presents several examples of quality indicators for each of the four quality classifications, as well as their cost drivers and value-added status.

The only value-added COQ category presented in Exhibit 12-11 is prevention, which eliminates defects from products consumed by consumers. As they cannot be added to products, appraisal costs add no customer value. Internal and external failures add no value for anyone; they simply create unnecessary correction costs that make total costs higher for both the company and the customer. These failure costs are the result of poor quality.

A firm can drive down the costs of appraisal, internal failure, and external failure by investing in prevention. Many prevention measures involve one-time

EXHIBIT 12–11

Cost of Quality (COQ) Measurements

Classifications	Measure	Operational Cost Drivers
Prevention	Prevention cost ÷ Total COQ	Investment in reducing overall COQ operations
Appraisal	Number of inspections	Set-up frequency Tight tolerance operations Complex design
Internal failure	Number of pieces rejected	Machine reliability Tooling age or condition Design error Operator error
External failure	Number of customer complaints	Order entry errors Incorrect assembly instructions Product failure Operator error

SOURCE: Reprinted by permission of the publisher: Michael R. Ostrenga, "Return on Investment through the Cost of Quality," *Journal of Cost Management*, Summer 1991, p. 43; © 1991 by Warren Gorham and Lamont of RIA.

costs that improve quality now and long into the future. Some prevention measures are fairly inexpensive. Such measures are often suggested by the employees engaged in the process. Suggestion programs can be effective in pointing out opportunities for continuous improvement that will benefit employees, customers, and the firm and its owners.

GENERAL NEWS NOTE

Managing for Quality

UNITED TECHNOLOGIES CORPORATION (UTC) is a particularly successful conglomerate. UTC has been among the top five performers in the 30 companies that make up the Dow Jones industrial average for the past three years. Some of its major units include Otis Elevator, Sikorsky helicopter, Carrier (air conditioning), Pratt & Whitney (jet airplane motors), and Chubb (fire detection and security).

Although designated as a conglomerate, all of its business models emphasize internal processes. All these businesses are tied together because they involve basic manufacturing operations that are susceptible to quality improvements, efficiency improvements, and technological improvements. It is the wringing out of incremental gains, rather than new technology, that has enabled UTC to increase efficiency and reduce waste. UTC has five tenets for managing quality

- **Educate.** Teach line workers common-sense techniques to identify quality problems—and give them the authority to work on the solutions.
- **Organize.** Reconfigure the factory floor to make it cleaner, simpler, and more intuitive. Nothing is random; everything has a designed place.
- **Analyze.** Rigorously study the root of every defect and complaint. Then even if it means stopping production, fix the problem once and for all.
- **Track.** Map out every process, make people own it, and reward constant improvements. For every action, ask why and how it could be done better.
- **Lead.** Convert top management into disciples of the process and make proselytizing (i.e., converting others) part of their job. Nonbelievers can head for the exits.

SOURCE: Diane Brady, "The Unsung CEO," *Business Week*, October 25, 2004, pp. 74–84; www.utc.com/profile/quality/; www1.iwon.com/home/careers/company_profile/0,15623,1243,00.html.

ACTIVITY-BASED COSTING AND PERFORMANCE MEASUREMENT

LEARNING OBJECTIVE **5**

How are activity-based costing concepts related to performance measurement?

Choosing appropriate nonfinancial performance measures can significantly help a company focus on activities that create costs. By controlling these activities, the company can more effectively control costs and improve processes.

Activity-based costing is concerned with reducing nonvalue-added activities to increase throughput. Traditional performance measurements in accounting are filled with factors that contribute to nonvalue-added activities. Material and labour standards often include factors for waste and idle time. Predetermined overhead rates are based on estimates of expected capacity usage rather than full capacity usage. Inventories are produced to meet budget expectations rather than sales demand. Detailed explanations of how to treat spoiled and defective unit costs are provided in organizational accounting procedures. Exhibit 12-12 provides some traditional performance indicators and some potential suboptimizing results they may encourage.

Measurement	Action	Result
Purchase price variance	Purchasing increases order quantity to get lower price and ignores quality and speed of delivery	Excess inventory; increased carrying cost; suppliers with the best quality and delivery are overlooked
	Purchasing acquires inferior quality materials to generate positive price variances	Production quality suffers and customers receive inferior goods
Machine utilization percentage	Supervisor requires employees to produce more than daily unit requirements to maximize machine utilization percentage	Excess inventory; wrong inventory
Scrap built into standard cost	Supervisor takes no action if there is no variance (from the lax standard)	Inflated standard; scrap threshold built in
Overhead rate based on expected capacity	Supervisor overproduces WIP or FG to have a favourable fixed overhead volume variance	Excess inventory
Responsibility centre reporting	Management focus is on responsibility centres instead of activities	Missed cost reduction opportunities because common activities among responsibility centres are overlooked

EXHIBIT 12-12
Traditional Performance Measurements and Results

If companies are to move toward world-class operations, nonvalue-added activities must be removed from performance evaluation measurements and value-added activities must be substituted. For example, when a performance measurement is the cost of defective units produced during a period, the original assumption is that management is expecting defects to occur and will accept some stated or implied defect cost. Instead, when the performance benchmark is zero defects, the assumption is that no defects will occur. It seems reasonable that managers would strive harder to eliminate defects under the second measurement than under the first.

As activity-based costing focuses on actions that add value from a customer's viewpoint, this accounting method stresses external performance measurements. Customers define good performance as that which equals or exceeds their expectations as to quality, cost, and delivery. Companies that cannot measure up will find themselves without customers and without a need for financial measures of performance. In this regard, nonfinancial measures are more effective because they can be designed to monitor the characteristics desired by external parties rather than internal financial goals.

Knowing that performance is to be judged according to some external criteria of success should cause companies to begin implementing concepts such as just-in-time inventory and total quality management. The common themes of these concepts are to make the organization, its products, and its processes better and to lower costs to provide better value.

Although some performance measurements, such as zero defects, can be implemented anywhere, companies operating in a multinational environment face more complex issues than do companies operating only in a domestic setting. Thus, multinational companies need to consider some additional factors relative to performance measurement and evaluation.

PERFORMANCE EVALUATION IN MULTINATIONAL SETTINGS

Operating overseas business units is more complex than operating domestic units. In attempting to compare multinational organizational units, differences among cultures and economies are as important as differences in accounting standards and reporting practices. CEOs in Japan take long-term views and make decisions accordingly, whereas Canadian and U.S. CEOs are very short-term oriented and cater to the stock markets. This attitude allows Japanese companies to concentrate on long-run, rather than short-run, business decisions.

The investment base needed to create a given type of organizational unit may differ substantially in different countries. For example, because of the exchange rate and legal costs, it is significantly more expensive for a company to open a Japanese subsidiary than an Indonesian one. If performance measures are based on a concept such as residual income, the Japanese unit will be placed at a distinct disadvantage because of its large investment base. However, the parent company may believe that the possibility of future joint ventures with Japanese organizations—which the parent has specified as a primary corporate goal—justifies the larger investment. The company may wish to handle the discrepancy in investment bases by assigning a lower target rate to compute residual income for the Japanese subsidiary. Such a differential is appropriate because of the lower political, financial, and economic risks.

Income comparisons between multinational units may be invalid because of important differences in trade tariffs, income tax rates, currency fluctuations, and possible restrictions on the transfer of goods or currency. Income earned by a multinational unit may also be affected by conditions totally outside its control, such as government protection of local companies, government aid in some countries, and varying wage rates resulting from differing standards of living, levels of industrial development, or quantities of socialized services. If the multinational subunit adopts the local country's accounting practices, differences in international standards can make income comparisons among units difficult and inconvenient even after the statements have been translated to a single currency basis.

The diverse economic, legal/political, and tax structures of countries have affected the development and practice of accounting. The International Accounting Standards Committee is working to achieve harmonization of accounting standards. However, many of the standards issued to date by this organization reflect compromise positions, allow for a significant number of alternatives, and rely on voluntary compliance. Additionally, as discussed in Chapter 11, managers may be able to transfer goods between segments at prices that minimize profits or tariffs in locations where taxes are high by shifting profits or cost values to more advantageous climates. These transfers must, of course, be made within the constraints of legal, moral, and social responsibility.

Recently, many Western firms have stepped up their investments in China. These firms are struggling with measurement and reward structures that result in efficient operations and retention of managerial talent. In hiring local managers, firms are finding that they must nurture loyalty, or talented individuals will be attracted to rival firms. Thus, measurement of performance must be partly based on the goal of retaining highly qualified local talent.

Given all these difficulties in monitoring the performance of their nondomestic investment centres, companies should use multiple measures that consider both the short run and the long run. Firms should establish flexible systems of measuring profit performance for those units. Such systems should recognize that differences in sales volume, accounting standards, economic conditions, and risk may be outside the control of an international subunit's manager. In such cases, nonfinancial, qualitative factors may become significantly more useful than monetary ones. Performance evaluations can include measures such as market share increases, quality improvements (reduction of defects), establishment of just-in-time inventory systems with the related reduction in working capital, and new product development.

The use of measures that limit suboptimization of resources is vital to the proper management of multinational responsibility centres. No single system is appropriate for all companies or, perhaps, even for all responsibility centres within the same company. The measurement of performance is the measurement of people. Since each person is unique and has multiple facets, the performance measurement system must reflect these individual differences. Once the measurement system is established, people are generally concerned about the way in which that system will affect their personal rewards or compensation.

The increased importance of strategy in management accounting has changed what is measured and what is used for the management of organizations. The earlier focus on financial accounting has shifted to a more balanced approach, as shown in the following News Note.

Performance Measurement Systems: Traditional Versus Contemporary

GENERAL NEWS NOTE

Items	Traditional PMSs	Contemporary PMSs
Basis of system	Accounting standard	Company strategy
Types of measures	Financial	Financial, nonfinancial
Focus of measures	Internal, historical	Internal, external, future
Audience	Middle, top managers	All employees
Shop floor relevance	Ignored	Used
Frequency	Lagging, weekly or monthly	Real time, hourly or daily

BREAKING NEWS

GENERAL NEWS NOTE

Maintenance	Expensive	Relevant, easy
Integration	Ignored	Integration exists
Linkage with reality	Indirect, misleading	Simple, accurate, direct
Local-global relevance	Static; non-varying	Dynamic; situation structure dependent
		Dynamic, situation timing dependent
Stability	Static; non-changing	Flexible/variable Improving
Format	Fixed	Encourage creativity and learning
Purpose	Monitoring	Unstructured
Function	Allocate blame	Supports/stimulates
Decision making	Structured	Derived from strategy
Effect on continuous improvement	Impedes	
Linked to strategy	No/less to strategy	

SOURCE: Thomas Burgess, Tze S. Ong, and Nicky Shaw, "Traditional or Contemporary? The Prevalence of Performance Measurement System Types," *International Journal of Productivity and Performance Management* 7 (2007): 583–602. © Emerald Group Publishing Limited.

---

compensation strategy
a foundation for the compensation plan that addresses the role compensation should play in the organization

RELATING COMPENSATION AND PERFORMANCE

A company should compensate employees in a manner that motivates them to act in ways that result in the company's effectively and efficiently achieving its goals. A rational compensation plan ties its component elements—organizational goals, performance measurements, and employee rewards—together in a cohesive package. The relations and interactions among these elements are shown in Exhibit 12-13.

In this model, strategic organizational goals are determined by the board of directors (the governing body representing shareholder interests) and top management. From these strategic goals, the organization's critical success factors are identified, and operational targets are defined. For example, operational targets could include specified annual net income, unit sales of a specific product, quality measures, customer service measures, or costs.

The board of directors and top management must also decide on a **compensation strategy** for the organization. This strategy should provide a foundation for the compensation plan by addressing the role compensation should play in the organization. The compensation strategy should be made known to everyone, from the board of directors to the lowest-level worker. In an era of cost competitiveness, automatic cost-of-living adjustments and annual pay raises are being reduced or eliminated. Compensation plans need to encourage greater levels of employee performance and loyalty, while lowering overall costs and raising profits. Plans of this kind reflect a pay-for-performance strategy that encourages behaviour essential to achieving organizational goals and maximizing shareholder value.

Pay-for-Performance Plans

Recall that what gets measured gets employees' attention—especially when compensation is involved. Therefore, in structuring a pay-for-performance plan, it is crucial

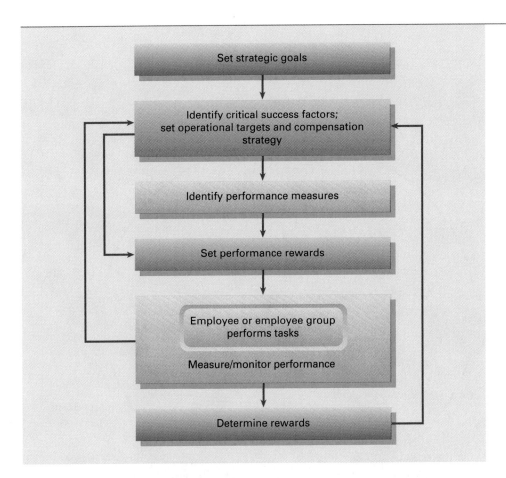

EXHIBIT 12-13
Plan–Performance–Reward
Model

that the defined performance measures be highly correlated with the organization's operational targets. Otherwise, suboptimization may occur and workers can earn incentive pay even though broader organizational objectives are not achieved.

Tying an organization's pay-for-performance plan to goals established in the strategic planning phase is the first step to motivating employees to focus on productivity improvement. The entire package of decisions regarding performance measurements can be referred to as a performance management system, depicted in Exhibit 12-14. When employees meet improvement objectives, rewards follow, and organizational results—such as growth in market share, faster throughput, and greater profits—can be expected. Re-evaluating the performance measurement linkages with the satisfaction of corporate goals completes the cycle.

Traditionally, performance measures have focused on short-run profits without giving adequate attention to long-run performance. If done properly, pay-for-performance criteria should encourage employees to adopt a long-run perspective. To encourage a long-range perspective, many top executives receive a significant portion of their compensation in the form of stock or stock options, and this can work well if the executives are committed to the organization for the long term. If the executives are short-term oriented, they can manipulate the performance of their organization, exercise their options, or sell their shares before the share price falls. This negative aspect has been seen with such firms as Nortel, Enron, and WorldCom.

Since many companies have shifted from evaluating workers by observing their inputs to evaluating them based on their outputs, new problems have been

EXHIBIT 12-14

Performance Management
System

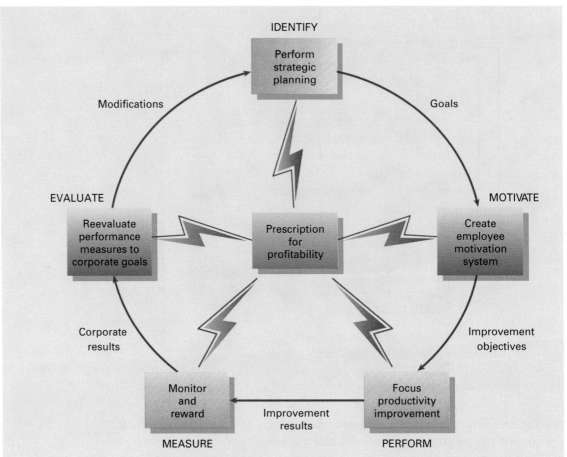

SOURCE: Dan J. Seidner and Glenn Kieckhaefer, "Using Performance Measurement Systems to Create Gainsharing Programs," (Grant Thornton) *Manufacturing Issues,* Summer 1990, p. 9. Reprinted by permission of Grant Thornton LLP.

created in the pay-for-performance relationship for workers as well as managers. Earlier chapters have stressed the importance of evaluating managers and workers only on the basis of controllable factors. Regrettably, most performance measures tend to capture results that are a function of both controllable and noncontrollable factors.

Actual performance results from worker effort, worker skill, and random effects. Random effects include performance measurement error, problems or efficiencies created by co-workers or adjacent workstations, illness, and weather-related production problems. Once actual performance has been measured, it is impossible in many instances to determine the contributions of controllable and noncontrollable factors to the achieved performance. Consequently, the worker bears the risk that a less-than-desirable outcome may result from an uncontrollable cause. Management should seek to identify performance measures that minimize this risk.

At the basic worker level, performance measures should be specific and should usually focus on cost or quality control. At higher organizational levels, the critical success factors under a manager's control and responsibility become more important. Performance measures should, by necessity, be less specific, focus on a longer time horizon, and be more concerned with organizational longevity than with short-run cost control or income. This type of thinking has resulted in shifts in compensation plans to include shares of corporate common stock. When employees become shareholders in their employing company, they tend to develop the same perspective as other shareholders: long-run wealth maximization. However, the plans must be carefully designed to obtain this mutuality of interests, and the participating executives must have more than a minimum degree of integrity.

Inclusion of Subjective Performance Measures

As output is influenced somewhat by noncontrollable factors, one school of thought advocates basing compensation on subjectively assessed intangible measures rather than more objective, performance-related measures. Subjective measures could include items such as leadership skills, flexibility, attitude, ability to work well with colleagues, professional pride, and enthusiasm.

By including subjective measures in the compensation system, management can blend less quantifiable but potentially more important long-range aspects of job performance—such as leadership, responsiveness, pride in work, cooperativeness, and enthusiasm—with more quantifiable but shorter-range considerations.

Compensation Packages

Conventionally, the compensation system has been based primarily on current monetary incentives. Middle managers are paid salaries with the opportunity for raises based on some measure of performance, usually accounting-related, such as segment income, divisional return on investment, or residual income. Lower-level workers are compensated through wages, usually specified by union contract or tied to the minimum wage law, based on the number of hours worked or production level achieved; current or year-end bonuses may be given when performance is above some specified quantitative measure. If provided, worker performance bonuses usually amount to a fairly small sum or percentage of wages. Significant incentive pay is usually limited to top management, and possibly the salesforce, regardless of the levels of employees who may have contributed to increased profits. The reason for linking top management pay to incentives such as earnings and common share performance pay is that there is a direct relation. Lower-level employees have little control over earnings and common share performance.

As with performance measures, an employee's organizational level and current compensation should affect the types of rewards chosen. Individuals at different levels of employment typically view monetary rewards differently because of the relationship of pay to standard of living. Using relative pay scales is essential to recognizing the value of this difference. At lower employee levels, more incentives should be monetary and short-term; at higher levels, more incentives should be nonmonetary and long-term. The system should, however, include some nonmonetary and long-term incentives for lower-level employees and some monetary and short-term incentives for top management. Such a two-faceted compensation system provides lower-paid people with tangible rewards that directly enhance their lifestyles—more money—but also provides rewards (such as stock options) that cause them to take a long-run "ownership" view of the organization. In turn, top managers, who are well paid by most standards, would receive more rewards (stock and stock options) that should cause them to be more concerned about the organization's long-term well-being rather than short-term personal gains.

Incentives

Another consideration in designing compensation packages is to balance the incentives provided for both groups, or teams, and individuals. In automated production systems, workers function more by indirectly monitoring and controlling machinery and are, therefore, less directly involved in hands-on production. Additionally, evolving organizational and managerial philosophies, such as total quality management and implementation of quality circles, have stressed group performance and the performance of work in teams.

Incentive plans for small groups and individuals are often virtually interchangeable. As the group grows larger, incentives must be in place for both the group and the individual. Group incentives are necessary to encourage cooperation among workers. However, if only group incentives are offered, the incentive compensation system may be ineffective because the reward for individual effort goes to the group. The larger the group size, the smaller the individual's share of the group reward becomes. Eventually, individual workers will be encouraged to take a free ride on the group. This situation occurs when individuals perceive their proportional shares of the group reward as insufficient to compensate for their efforts.

A study found that two-thirds of surveyed companies use quantifiable measures of team effectiveness in addition to measures of individual effectiveness.[5] The study also found that subjective, qualitative measures are frequently used to assess the performance of individuals in teams, such as level of cooperation and level of participation in teams.

Motivating Employees

In addition to various forms of monetary compensation, workers may be motivated by nonfinancial factors. Although all employees value and require money to satisfy

Rewards for performance do not always have to be monetary. Sometimes, tokens of appreciation convey an equally satisfying acknowledgment for a job performed well.

basic human needs, other human needs are not necessarily fulfilled with monetary wealth. Employees generally desire some compensation that is not monetary in nature but that satisfies the higher-order social needs of humans. For example, workers and managers are typically more productive in environments in which they believe their efforts to be appreciated. Simple gestures such as compliments and small awards can be used by superiors to formally recognize contributions of subordinates. Allowing subordinates to participate in decisions affecting their own welfare and the welfare of the firm also contributes to making employment socially fulfilling. Such efforts provide assurance to employees that they are serving a productive role in the firm and that superiors are attentive to and appreciative of employee contributions.

Care must also be taken that a company's compensation strategy does not result in suppressing creativity, innovation, risk taking, and proactive assumption and conduct of job responsibilities. If monetary rewards can be withheld when failure occurs, employees who are otherwise industrious and cooperative might avoid taking actions or making proposals that could fail. Fear of failure can be reduced if management creates an atmosphere of employee empowerment in which failure is accepted as part of the progression toward continuous improvement.

Organizational compensation packages must be developed that blend organizational goals with monetary and nonmonetary employee rewards. Only if there is a perception of equity across the contributions and entitlements of labour, management, and capital will the organization be capable of achieving the efficiency to compete in global markets.

GLOBAL COMPENSATION

LEARNING OBJECTIVE 8

How do expatriate reward systems differ from those for domestic operations?

With international operations increasing, policies that compensate expatriate employees and managers on a fair and equitable basis must be developed. Expatriates are parent-company and third-country nationals assigned to a foreign subsidiary or foreign nationals assigned to the parent company. Placing employees in foreign countries requires careful consideration of compensation. What is thought to be a fair and reasonable compensation package in one setting may not be fair and reasonable in another.

Expatriates' compensation packages must reflect labour market factors, cost-of-living considerations, and currency fluctuations, as well as tax consequences. Since expatriates have a variety of financial requirements, these individuals may be paid in the currency of the country where they have been relocated, or in their home currency, or a combination of both. An expatriate's base salary and fringe benefits should typically reflect what he or she would have been paid domestically. This base should then be adjusted for reasonable cost-of-living factors. These factors may be obvious, such as needs similar to those that would exist in the home country (transportation, shelter, clothing, and food), or the need to be compensated for a spouse's loss of employment; or they may be less apparent, such as a need to hire someone in the home country to care for young children or to manage an investment portfolio.

Price-level adjustment clauses are often included in the compensation arrangement to mitigate any local currency inflation or deflation. Regardless of the currency makeup of the pay package, the fringe benefit portion related to retirement must be tied to the home country and should be paid in that currency. These adjustments can be very expensive. For example, Douglas R. Stanton, a Hong Kong–based partner for the consulting firm Towers Perrin Inc., says he knows of one

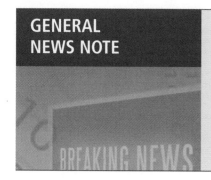

GENERAL NEWS NOTE

A New Compensation Base

According to a July 2001 survey by Hay Group, 84% of companies offering stock option programs said they had no plans to amend their program. The survey also found that flexible pay has become prevalent across hierarchical levels in both public and private sector organizations. Last year, in the private sector, 89% of senior management, 82% of middle management, 65% of technical and support staff, and 46% of blue collar workers qualified for annual bonus programs based on productivity gains and profit sharing.

SOURCE: Gerard Berube, "A New Compensation Base," *CA Magazine*, January–February 2002, p. 6.

company whose expatriate general manager collects compensation equal to a quarter of the firm's revenue in China.[6]

Income taxes are important in expatriates' compensation packages because such individuals may be required to pay taxes in the local country, the home country, or both. Some countries, such as the United States and Great Britain, exempt expatriates from taxation on a specified amount of income earned in a foreign country. If a tax treaty exists and local taxes are paid on the balance of the nonexempt income of an expatriate, those taxes may be credited against the expatriate's home-nation income taxes.

In conclusion, tying the global compensation system to performance measurement is essential because everyone in business recognizes that what gets measured and rewarded is what gets accomplished. Businesses must focus their reward structures to motivate employees to succeed at all activities that will create shareholder and personal value. In this highly competitive age, the new paradigm of success is to provide high-quality products and services at a reasonable price while generating a reasonable profit margin.

Wellington, New Zealand, is the home of this New World grocery store. New World is a chain that stocks McCain's frozen foods. To serve grocery stores such as New World, McCain—of Florenceville, New Brunswick—has processing plants in many parts of the world.

On October 22, 2007, Cognos announced that Dorel Industries had selected Cognos's BI (business intelligence) software to help it optimize operational planning and reporting across all divisions. This software will make it easier for Dorel's senior managers to access and share financial information for timely operations planning and decision making. It will also allow Dorel to replace its current multiple reporting tools with a unified solution, streamline its planning and forecasting, and ensure regulatory compliance.

Specifically, Dorel has acquired Cognos 8 BI to help it track trends, report against key performance benchmarks, and analyze timely information to uncover the root causes of problems. Cognos 8 Controller will automate and structure Dorel's financial consolidation processes and thus deliver validated financial information for internal and external reporting. It will also provide a transparent, accurate, and timely management view of enterprise-wide corporate performance. It is expected that Cognos 8 Controller will contribute to efficiencies in financial statement preparation while also improving internal control. Finally, Dorel will be able to use Cognos 8 Planning (which is wireless capable) to develop consistent and accurate sales and operations budgets to help it prepare up-to-date rolling budgets and forecasts in the most efficient way possible.

SOURCE: http://tsedb.globeinvestor.com/servlet/WireFeedRedirect?cf=GlobeInvestor/tsx/config&date=20071022&archive=cnw&slug=C6585.

CHAPTER SUMMARY

Performance measures should assess progress toward goals and objectives and should be accepted by those being evaluated.

1 **Why should organizations use multiple performance measures to assess performance?**
Using multiple measures of the firm's critical success factors is more effective than using a single performance measure, because organizations have multiple activities that need to perform. Divisional profits and cash flow are frequently used financial performance measures.

2 **How are return on investment (ROI) and residual income (RI) similar and different?**
Two significant financial measures of performance are return on investment and residual income. Return on investment is computed as segment margin, or net income, divided by invested assets. Residual income is the amount of segment margin, or net income, in excess of an amount calculated by use of a pre-established "interest charge" on the asset base. Both ROI and RI provide important information about the efficiency and effectiveness of managers. Neither should be used alone, however, and their inherent limitations, including the fact that they can be manipulated because of their basis in accounting, should be considered.

3 **Why has economic value added (EVA) become a popular performance measure?**
EVA is superior to other short-term financial performance measures because of its close linkage to shareholders' interests. EVA is measured as the difference between net income for a period and the dollar cost of invested capital for a period.

4 **Why are nonfinancial measures important for evaluating performance?**
Financial measures can be effectively coupled with nonfinancial measures to provide a more complete and useful picture of performance. One useful nonfinancial measure is throughput—the nondefective goods or services started, finished, and sold by an organization during a period. When throughput is increased, the company goal of making money is enhanced. Various quality measures have also gained prominence as companies begin to compete more heavily in the global marketplace. These measures focus on activities that add value for the customer.

5 **How are activity-based costing concepts related to performance measurement?**
A focus on activity-based costing and activities will provide a sharper understanding of how to establish nonfinancial performance measures to eliminate nonvalue-added activities.

6 **Why is it more difficult to measure performance in multinational firms than in solely domestic companies?**
Performance measures may be more difficult to establish for multinational units than for domestic units because of differences in taxes, tariffs, currency exchange rates, and transfer restrictions. Because of such differences, top management may wish to consider extending the use of qualitative performance measures.

7 **How should employee rewards, including compensation, and performance be linked?**
Customarily, compensation systems have often been based solely on individual performance and short-run financial results. With operational changes and shifts in managerial philosophies, performance measurements and their related rewards now encompass group success, nonfinancial performance attributes, and long-run considerations. Companies also need to recognize that some top managers' compensation grossly exceeds pay to ordinary workers. Such excesses can be counterproductive, causing a demoralizing effect within the firm, and ultimately, failure to maximize long-term shareholder wealth. Thus, it is important that the compensation strategy and system are linked with the performance measurement system and that together they serve to assure fairness, effectiveness, and efficiency in an organization.

8 **How do expatriate reward systems differ from those for domestic operations?**
Expatriate reward systems differ as they must incorporate greater complexity caused by differences in labour market conditions, cost-of-living considerations, and currency fluctuations.

Key Terms

Asset turnover (p. 731)
Compensation strategy (p. 744)
Du Pont model (p. 731)
Economic value added (p. 734)
Nonfinancial performance measures (p. 735)
Process productivity (p. 739)

Process quality yield (p. 739)
Profit margin (p. 731)
Residual income (p. 732)
Return on investment (p. 730)
Synchronous management (p. 738)
Throughput (p. 738)

Points to Remember

Performance Measurements for Responsibility Centres

- Profit Centre

    Budgeted divisional profits
- − Actual divisional profits
- = Variances (consider materiality)

    Cash inflows
- − Cash outflows
- = Net cash flow (adequate for operations?)
- Investment Centre

    Budgeted investment centre profits
- − Actual investment centre profits
- = Variances (consider materiality)

    Cash inflows
- − Cash outflows
- = Net cash flow (adequate for operations?)

    Return on Investment = Income ÷ Assets Invested (high enough rate?)

  Du Pont model:

$$\text{ROI} = \text{Profit margin} \times \text{Asset turnover}$$
$$= (\text{Income} \div \text{Sales}) \times (\text{Sales} \div \text{Assets})$$
$$(\text{high enough rate?})$$
$$\text{RI} = \text{Income} - (\text{Target rate} \times \text{Asset base})$$

or

$$\text{RI} = \text{Asset base} \times (\text{ROI} - \text{Target rate})$$
$$(\text{positive or negative? high enough amount?})$$
$$\text{EVA} = \text{After-tax income} - (\text{Cost of capital \%} \times \text{Capital invested})$$
$$(\text{positive or negative? high enough amount?})$$

  Measuring Throughput

$$\text{Throughput} = \text{Manufacturing cycle efficiency} \times \text{Process productivity} \times \text{Process}$$
$$\text{quality yield}$$

or

$$[\text{Good units} \div \text{Total time}] = [\text{Value-added processing time} \div \text{Total time}] \times [\text{Total units}$$
$$\div \text{Value-added processing time}] \times [\text{Good units} \div \text{Total units}]$$

Designing a Reward System

It is impossible to design a generic incentive model that would be effective across a variety of firms. However, affirmative answers to the following questions provide guidance as to the applicability of a proposed incentive and reward plan for a particular organization.

1. Will the organizational and subunit objectives be achieved if the proposed compensation structure is implemented?
2. Is the proposed structure consistent with the organizational design, culture, and management philosophy?
3. Are there reasonable and objective performance measures that are good surrogates for the organizational objectives?
4. Are factors beyond employee/group control minimized under the performance measures of the proposed compensation structure?

5. Are there minimal opportunities for employees to manipulate the performance measurements tied to the proposed compensation structure?
6. In light of the interests of managers, workers, and shareholders, is the proposed reward structure fair and does it encourage and promote ethical behaviour?
7. Is the proposed reward structure arranged to take advantage of potential employee/employer tax benefits?
8. Does the proposed reward structure promote harmony between employee groups?
9. Is there an adequate balance between group and individual incentives?

DEMONSTRATION PROBLEM

Meltzer Wholesaling sells a broad line of clothing goods to specialty retail and department stores. For last year, the company's Canadian Division had the following performance targets:

Asset turnover	1.8
Profit margin	8%
Target rate of return on investments for EVA, RI	10%
Income tax rate	25%

Actual information concerning the performance of the Canadian Division for last year follows:

Total assets at beginning of year	$ 4,800,000
Total assets at end of year	7,200,000
Total invested capital (annual average)	11,000,000
Sales	12,000,000
Variable operating costs	5,000,000
Direct fixed costs	6,280,000
Allocated common costs	800,000

Required:

1. For the Canadian Division of Meltzer Wholesaling, compute the segment margin and average assets for the year.
2. Based on segment income and average assets, compute the actual profit margin, asset turnover, and ROI.
3. Evaluate the ROI performance of the Canadian Division.
4. Using your answers from Question 2, compute the Canadian Division's residual income using segment margin.
5. Compute the EVA of the Canadian Division using net income. Why are EVA and RI levels different?
6. Based on the data given in the problem, discuss why ROI, EVA and RI may be inappropriate measures of performance for the Canadian Division.

Solution to Demonstration Problem

1.
Sales	$12,000,000
Variable costs	(5,000,000)
Direct fixed costs	(6,280,000)
Segment margin	$ 720,000

Average assets = ($4,800,000 + $7,200,000) ÷ 2 = $ 6,000,000

2. Profit margin = $\frac{$720,000}{$12,000,000}$ = 6%

Asset turnover = $\frac{$12,000,000}{$6,000,000}$ = 2

ROI = 6% × 2 = 12%

3. The target ROI for the division was 8% × 1.8 = 14.4%. The division generated an ROI of only 12%. Thus, the division did not achieve its target rate of return. The poor performance resulted from the division's failure to achieve the target profit margin. Even though the asset turnover target was exceeded, the ROI fell below the target level because the profit margin was 2% below its target level.

4. RI $= \$720,000 - (0.10 \times \$6,000,000)$
    $= \$720,000 - \$600,000 = \underline{\$120,000}$

5. After-tax income $= \text{Segment margin} - \text{Taxes}$
    $= \$720,000 - (\$720,000 \times 0.25) = \$540,000$
    EVA $= \$540,000 - (0.10 \times \$11,000,000) = \underline{\$(560,000)}$

EVA and RI differ for two reasons. First, RI is based on segment margin, rather than after-tax income; second, RI is based on the book value of investment while EVA is based on the market value of investment.

6. As discussed in the chapter, ROI, RI, and EVA are measures of short-term performance. These measures may be particularly inappropriate for divisions that have long-term missions, such as growth. In this case, the relatively large growth in assets of the Canadian Division from the beginning to the end of the period may indicate that this division is oriented to growth. If so, the ROI and RI measures will provide an incentive contrary to the growth mission.

End-of-Chapter Materials

SELF-TEST QUESTIONS

(SOLUTIONS APPEAR AT THE END OF THE CHAPTER.)

1. Organizations have multiple performance measures for all of the following reasons except:
    a. They have a variety of goals and objectives
    b. They are big
    c. Their products have life cycles
    d. Financial performance measures are not comprehensive

2. The balanced scorecard is best described as:
    a. A performance measurement conceptualization that translates an organization's strategy into clear objectives, measures, targets, and initiatives organized by the four perspectives
    b. An intracompany charge for goods or services that has been through a process of negotiations between the selling and purchasing unit managers
    c. The set of basic assumptions about the organization, its goals, and its business practices; describes an organization's norms in internal and external, as well as formal and informal, transactions
    d. A listing of all tasks necessary to make a unit of product or perform a service and the time allowed for each operation

3. Which is the definition of return on investment?
    a. Assets invested ÷ Income
    b. Profit margin ÷ Asset turnover
    c. Asset turnover ÷ Profit margin
    d. Income ÷ Assets invested

4. The Du Pont model is calculated with:
    a. Assets invested ÷ Income
    b. Profit margin × Asset turnover
    c. Asset turnover ÷ Profit margin
    d. Income ÷ Assets invested

5. Residual income is calculated with:
    a. After-tax income – (Cost of capital % × Capital invested)
    b. Income – (Cost of capital % × Asset base)
    c. Income – (Cost of capital % × Capital invested)
    d. Income – (Target rate × Asset base)

6. Which is a limitation of ROI and RI?
    a. Income can be manipulated on a short-run basis by accelerating or delaying the recognition of income and expenses
    b. Accrual-based income reflects neither the cash flow pattern nor the time value of money, and these performance dimensions are generally important
    c. Some asset investment values are difficult to measure or assign to investment centres, while some other values, such as research and development, are not capitalized
    d. All of the above

7. Which of the following is out of sequence when going from the top to the bottom of the performance pyramid?
    a. Vision
    b. Operations
    c. Market measures, financial measures
    d. Customer satisfaction, flexibility, productivity

8. Throughput is the product of which of the following?
    a. Manufacturing cycle efficiency, process productivity, and process quality yield
    b. Manufacturing cycle efficiency, process productivity
    c. Process productivity, process quality yield
    d. Manufacturing cycle efficiency, process quality yield

9. Of the following cost of quality measures, which relates to appraisal?
   a. Prevention ÷ Total cost of quality
   b. Number of inspections
   c. Number of pieces rejected
   d. Number of customer complaints

10. Which one of the following is not a traditional performance measure?
   a. Purchase price variance
   b. Machine utilization percentage
   c. Customer satisfaction scores
   d. Responsibility centre reporting

QUESTIONS

1. What basic rules should be observed in selecting benchmarks for evaluating managers' performance?

2. Should performance measures be financial, nonfinancial, or both? Justify your answer.

3. What message is conveyed by the phrase "managers devote their attention to activities that get measured"?

4. What are the two primary financial requirements for the success of a profit or investment centre? Why are these important?

5. What is the major difference between a profit centre and an investment centre? How does this difference create a need for different financial performance measures in these two types of centres?

6. Discuss the most appropriate definition of the term "assets invested" in computing return on investment.

7. What is residual income and how is it used to measure divisional performance? How is it similar to and different from the return on investment measure?

8. Describe the circumstances in which use of ROI would likely create a suboptimization problem. Under what circumstances would use of this measure be less likely to create a suboptimization problem?

9. How is economic value added computed? Why is the measure potentially superior to residual income?

10. Modular Office Systems manufactures movable partitions for commercial offices. Recently, the company has become much more concerned with reducing the number of flaws in its completed products. Identify some performance measures that the company could use to monitor the effectiveness of its efforts to improve product quality.

11. What is captured by a throughput measure? Why is throughput defined on the basis of goods sold rather than goods produced?

12. Why is prevention the only value-added cost of quality category?

13. How can activity-based costing concepts be used in designing performance measures?

14. Why is the design of performance measures a more complex task in multinational companies than in single-country operations?

15. To be effective, why must firms link the compensation system to the performance measurement structure?

16. Why is it desirable for chief executives (as well as other managers) to own stock in their companies?

17. What special considerations bear on designing pay plans for expatriates?

18. How do activity-based costing and activity-based management relate to the balanced scorecard?

19. What are United Technologies' five tenets for managing quality?

20. What are four reasons for the lack of effectiveness of nonfinancial performance measures?

EXERCISES

1. (LO 1, 2, 3) Match the numbered definitions with the lettered terms. Definitions may be used more than once or not at all.

a. Throughput
b. Economic value added
c. Synchronous management
d. Residual income
e. Compensation strategy
f. Expatriate
g. Du Pont model
h. Asset turnover
i. Profit margin
j. Process quality yield

1. A parent-company worker in a foreign subsidiary
2. A measure of asset productivity
3. A method of computing ROI as the product of two separate ratios
4. All endeavours that help an organization achieve its goal
5. After-tax profits minus a charge for cost of invested capital
6. Profits that exceed a normal return on assets
7. A ratio of income to sales
8. A ratio of good units to total units
9. A plan for determining the role of compensation in an organization
10. The total good output completed and sold within an operating period

2. (LO 2) Johnson Wholesale Supply of Newmarket comprises three autonomous divisions. Data for each division for the year follow:

	Division 1	Division 2	Division 3
Segment income	$20,000	$ 225,000	$ 150,000
Asset investment	80,000	1,500,000	1,500,000

Compute the return on investment in each division.

3. (LO 2) The managers of Hong Kong Industries are evaluating the use of ROI to measure performance. The managers have gathered the following information for their most recent operating period.

Average assets invested	$ 3,600,000
Revenues	14,400,000
Expenses	13,004,000

Required:
a. Calculate profit margin.
b. Calculate asset turnover.
c. Calculate return on investment using your answers to parts (a) and (b).

4. (LO 2) For the most recent fiscal year, the Pullman Division of Modern Luggage generated an asset turnover ratio of 5 and a profit margin (as measured by the segment margin) ratio of 4% on sales of $4,000,000.
Required:
Compute:
a. Average assets employed by Pullman Division
b. Segment margin
c. ROI

5. (LO 2) Your managerial accounting class has been assigned a case, but the professor has provided only partial information. You have been told that a division of a company has an ROI of 12.5%, average total assets of $3,400,000, and total direct expenses of $1,275,000.
Required:
You have been asked to do the following:
a. Determine segment income.
b. Determine total revenues.
c. Determine asset turnover.
d. Determine profit margin.
e. Prove that ROI is 12.5% from the amounts calculated in parts (a) to (d).

EXERCISES

6. (LO 2) Leduc Law, Inc., has a target rate of return of 14% for its Criminal Law Division. For the year, the Criminal Law Division generated gross fees of $10,000,000 on average assets of $5,000,000. The Criminal Law Division's variable costs were 35% of sales and fixed costs were $3,750,000.

   Required:

   For the year, compute the Division's:
   a. Residual income
   b. Profit margin
   c. Asset turnover
   d. Return on investment

7. (LO 2) North and South Divisions of Western Financial Corp. reported the following data for the year (in thousands):

	North Division	**South Division**
Segment income	$ 30,000	$ 68,000
Investment	180,000	290,000

   Required:
   a. Assuming the firm charges each division 12% of the capital invested, determine the residual income for each division.
   b. Based on the preceding information, which division is more successful? Explain.

8. (LO 2) Sarnia Chemical comprises two divisions. Following is some financial information about each of these divisions.

	Industrial Products	**Consumer Products**
Sales	$4,800,000	$ 8,400,000
Total variable cost	1,200,000	5,460,000
Total fixed cost	2,800,000	1,250,000
Average assets invested	4,000,000	10,000,000

   Required:
   a. What is each division's residual income if the company has established a 14% target rate of return on invested assets?
   b. Which division is more successful? Explain.
   c. What would be each division's residual income if its sales increased by 10% and no other changes occurred? Which division would be more successful if such a sales change occurred? Explain.
   d. Explain why the answers to parts (b) and (c) differed or did not differ.

9. (LO 3) Chancellor Environmental Services Co. relies on the EVA measure to evaluate the performance of certain segment managers. The target rate of return on invested capital for all segments is 16%. One subsidiary, Water Systems, generated after-tax income of $1,800,000 for the year just ended. For the same period, the invested capital in the subsidiary was $12,000,000.

   Required:

   Compute the EVA of Water Systems.

10. (LO 3) Stealth Technology Corporation has a required rate of return of 12% on invested capital. The firm's Laser Division generated an EVA of $4,000,000 last year. The amount of capital invested in Laser Division is $38,000,000.

   Required:
   a. How much after-tax income was generated by Laser Division last year?
   b. As the controller of Stealth Technology Corporation, how could you determine the level of capital investment for a particular division?

11. (LO 3) Mary Jenks is a division manager of Nova Scotia Pneumatic. She is presently evaluating a potential new investment that has the following characteristics:

Capital investment required		$8,000,000
Net annual increase in after-tax divisional income:		
Year 1		800,000
Year 2		800,000
Year 3		1,160,000
Year 4		2,900,000
Year 5		2,700,000

EXERCISES

Ms. Jenks is evaluated and compensated based on the amount of EVA her division generates. More precisely, she receives an annual salary of $350,000 plus a bonus equal to 12% of divisional EVA. Nova Scotia Pneumatic has a required rate of return of 13%.

a. Compute the effect of the new investment on the level of divisional EVA for years 1 through 5.

b. Determine the effect of the new project on Ms. Jenks's compensation for each of the five years.

c. Based on your computations in part (b), will Ms. Jenks want to invest in the new project? Explain.

d. As the CEO of Nova Scotia Pneumatic, would you prefer that Ms. Jenks invest or not invest in the project?

e. What nonfinancial performance measures could be used to supplement EVA as a performance measure that would serve to make Ms. Jenks more long-term oriented?

12. (LO 4) The Waterloo Wave is a chain of microbreweries. The company evaluates its store managers on the basis of both financial and nonfinancial performance measures. One of the nonfinancial measures used is throughput. The following data pertain to the company's store in Moncton. The unit of measurement is litres.

Units started into production	360,000
Total good units completed	270,000
Total hours of value-added processing time	180,000
Total hours	240,000

Required:

a. What was the manufacturing cycle efficiency?

b. What was the process productivity of the store?

c. What was the process quality yield of the store?

d. What was the total throughput per hour?

e. As the production manager of the Waterloo Wave, how could you use the information on the component ratios of throughput to increase performance?

13. (LO 4) For each of the following nonfinancial performance measures, indicate whether the measure captures performance in terms of quality (Q), customer service (CS), resource management (RM), or flexibility (F), and discuss the rationale for your answer.

a. First-time-through rejection rate

b. Percent on-time shipments

c. Manufacturing cycle time

d. Percent good output

e. Percent of units meeting design tolerance

f. Output per labour dollar

g. Number of crisis calls

h. Changeover time

i. Machine downtime

j. Supplier rejects

14. (LO 4) For the past three years, the highest divisional ROI within Lumar Corporation has been generated by the Winch Division, a very high-tech manufacturing division. The segment income and ROI for each year appear below. Lumar Corporation has specified a growth mission for the Winch Division.

	2009	2010	2011
Segment income (thousands)	$200,000	$195,000	$193,500
ROI	20%	23%	27%

Required:

a. Why do you think the Winch Division has been so successful as measured by its ROI?

b. As controller of Lumar Corporation, what change or changes would you recommend to control the continued escalation in the ROI?

c. Assume that Lumar Corporation operates in a very competitive industry and its strategy is based on maintaining market share by delivering the best customer service in the industry. What nonfinancial performance measures could be used to capture Lumar's performance?

EXERCISES

15. (LO 2) Explain how each of the following items will affect the asset turnover ratio of a corporate division if asset amounts are determined by their net book values.
    a.   A new labour contract is negotiated that reduces labour costs by 10%.
    b.   Unused assets are carried on the books. These assets could be sold.
    c.   Obsolete inventory is carried on the books.
    d.   Uncollectible accounts receivable are carried on the books.
    e.   The rate of depreciation on plant and equipment is increased.
    f.   Fixed costs allocated to the division drop by 4%.

16. (LO 4) Managers must be able to deliver both positive and negative feedback to employees. The method of delivering such feedback is often as important as the message in terms of its impact on the affected employee. Discuss how, as a manager, you would deliver critical comments to an employee whose performance is unsatisfactory. How would you deliver feedback to an employee whose performance is superlative?

17. (LO 1 to 6) You have recently been appointed as the chief executive officer (CEO) of a medium-sized, decentralized, national, multiproduct manufacturing and marketing corporation, which employs over 6,000 people. Although revenues have remained constant over the last five years, net income has decreased by over 50% in this period. As a result of this decline in profitability, the share price has decreased 60%.
    Required:
    Identify five management accounting techniques or tools that you will instruct your staff to investigate. For each technique or tool identified, explain what specific benefits you hope to realize. Note that to state that profitability will improve is too general; rather you should explain how the technique leads to this improvement. Be thoughtful and practical in your discussions and be mindful of the type of company of which you are CEO.

    Extract from *Management Accounting Examination*, published by the Certified General Accountants Association of Canada (© CGA-Canada 1999). Reprinted with permission.

18. (LO 3) Anderson Division's performance is measured by economic value added (EVA). The division's capital charge, used to compute its EVA, is $650,000. Data required to convert the division's GAAP income for 2010 to net operating profit after taxes (NOPAT) are as follows:

2010 GAAP income	$ 925,000
EVA-adjusted total capital, December 31, 2009	3,400,000
Research costs in 2010	75,000
Development costs in 2010 expensed under GAAP	37,000
Development costs in 2010 capitalized under GAAP	21,000
Amortization of goodwill attributed to Anderson Division and included in its calculation of GAAP income	27,000

    Assume that R&D costs for 2010 occur on January 1, 2010. Capitalized development costs are amortized over a period of seven years in GAAP income; research and development costs are amortized over the same period in the calculation of EVA.

    What is Anderson Division's 2010 EVA? Show your calculations.
    a. $344,000
    b. $371,000
    c. $398,000
    d. $416,000

    Extract from *Management Accounting 2 Examination*, published by the Certified General Accountants Association of Canada (© CGA-Canada 1999). Reprinted with permission.

19. (LO 1) In their book *The Balanced Scorecard – Translating Strategy Into Action*, Norton and Kaplan asserted that excessive reliance on financial measures leads to overemphasis on external financial reporting, low awareness of operational issues, a lack of understanding of how value is created, and undervaluation of intangible assets such as intellectual capital. They stated that an effective measurement system should focus on four perspectives, which are found in the balanced scorecard.

EXERCISES

Required:
Describe the *four* perspectives found in a properly constructed balanced scorecard.

Extract from *Management Accounting 2 Examination*, published by the Certified General Accountants Association of Canada (© CGA-Canada 2000). Reprinted with permission.

20. (LO 3) A small company in Vancouver sold $788,000 worth of its products last year. Net income represented 24% of sales. Net income after taxes was $240,000 and total capital was $520,000. The weighted average cost of capital was 15% and the required cost of capital was 12%. Calculate the EVA.

Extract from *Management Accounting 2 Examination*, published by the Certified General Accountants Association of Canada (© CGA-Canada 2003). Reprinted with permission.

PROBLEMS

1. (LO 4, 6) Western Division of the Raymond Fabrics Co. produces and markets floor covering products to wholesalers in British Columbia, Alberta, Saskatchewan, and Manitoba. The manager of Western Division is Kara Forrester. Raymond Fabrics evaluates all of its division managers on the basis of a comparison of budgeted profit to actual profit achieved. The profit measure used is pretax income. For 2011, the budgeted income for the Western Division is as shown:

Sales	$12,000,000
Variable costs	(8,400,000)
Contribution margin	$ 3,600,000
Fixed costs	(2,400,000)
Segment income	$ 1,200,000

At the end of 2011, the actual results for Western Division were determined:

Sales	$13,000,000
Variable costs	(9,750,000)
Contribution margin	$ 3,250,000
Fixed costs	(2,410,000)
Segment income	$ 840,000

Required:
a. Assume that you are the controller of Raymond Fabrics. Based on the preceding information, evaluate the performance of the Western Division. What was the principal reason for the poor profit performance?
b. Explain how complete income statements provide a better basis to evaluate the profit performance of a manager than mere comparisons of the bottom lines of the budgeted and actual income statements.
c. Given your answer to part (a), describe some nonfinancial performance measures that could be used by the manager of the Western Division in a strategy to improve divisional profit performance in the next year.

2. (LO 2) Complete Solutions Inc. manufactures various production equipment. Corporate management has examined industry-level data and determined the following industry norms for producers of material handling systems:

Asset turnover	1.6 times
Profit margin	8%

The actual 2011 results for the company's Material Handling Division are summarized below:

Total assets at year-end 2010	$ 9,600,000
Total assets at year-end 2011	12,800,000
Sales	13,440,000
Operating expenses	12,499,200

Required:
a. For 2011, how did the Material Handling Division perform relative to industry norms?
b. As the divisional manager of Material Handling, how would you use the comparison in part (a) to improve performance in the division?

PROBLEMS

3. (LO 2) Johnson, First Star, and Nolan Bay are three companies that operate in the retail clothing industry. Some information on each of these companies for the year follows:

	Johnson	First Star	Nolan Bay
Average total assets	$ 6,300,000	$ 5,400,000	$ 7,200,000
Revenues	12,600,000	16,200,000	14,400,000
Expenses	11,340,000	15,228,000	12,420,000

Required:

a. For each company, calculate profit margin, asset turnover, and return on investment.

b. As an investment analyst, you are going to recommend that stock in one of these companies be purchased by your clients. Which of these companies would you recommend? Why?

c. Do the ratios indicate how any of the companies could improve their performance? How?

4. (LO 2) The 2010 income statement for the Aurora Division of Industrial Services Corp. follows.

Sales	$ 3,200,000
Variable expenses	(1,600,000)
Contribution margin	$ 1,600,000
Fixed expenses	(800,000)
Segment income	$ 800,000

Assets at the beginning of 2010 for Aurora Division were $3,600,000. Because of various capital investments during the year, the division ended 2010 with $4,400,000 of assets. Overall, Industrial Services Corp. experienced a 15% return on investment for 2010. It is company policy to award year-end bonuses to the managers whose divisions show the highest ROIs.

The chief operating officer of Aurora is investigating a new product line for the division. The new line is expected to show the following approximate annual results: sales, $400,000; variable expenses, $200,000; and fixed expenses, $100,000. The product line would require a $620,000 average first-year investment in plant assets.

Required:

a. What was Aurora's 2010 ROI?

b. What is the expected ROI on the new product line?

c. If Aurora had invested in the new product line in 2010 and the expected results had occurred, what would have been the division's ROI?

d. Is the Aurora Division manager likely to want to add the new product line? Would the president of Industrial Services Corp. want Aurora to add the new product line? Discuss the rationale of each of the individuals.

5. (LO 2) The numbers (1–9) in the following table identify missing data for three divisions of Big Creek Industries.

	Package Division	Transport Division	Storage Division
Sales	$2,000,000	$16,000,000	$8,000,000
Segment income	$400,000	(4)	$1,000,000
Profit margin	(1)	15%	(7)
Asset turnover	(2)	1.4	(8)
Average assets	(3)	(5)	$4,000,000
Return on investment	10%	(6)	(9)

Required:

a. Determine the values for each of the missing items.

b. Identify the area where each division's performance is weakest and strongest relative to the other divisions.

PROBLEMS

6. (LO 2) Stolzer Wholesaling sells a broad line of clothing to specialty retail and department stores. For 2010, the company's Canadian Division had the following performance targets:

Asset turnover	1.5 times
Profit margin	8%

Actual information concerning the performance of the Canadian Division in 2010 follows:

Total assets at year-end 2009	$2,400,000
Total assets at year-end 2010	3,600,000
Sales for 2010	6,000,000
Operating expenses for 2010	5,640,000

Required:

a. For 2010, what was the Canadian Division's target objective for ROI? Show calculations.

b. For 2010, did the Canadian Division achieve its target objectives for ROI, asset turnover, and profit margin?

c. Where, as indicated by the performance measures, are the areas that are most in need of improved performance?

d. If the company has an overall target return of 13%, what was the Canadian Division's residual income for 2010?

7. (LO 2, 5) The following are transactions affecting a specific division within a multiple-division company. Indicate whether each described transaction would increase (IN), decrease (D), have no effect (N) on, or have an indeterminate effect (I) on each of the following measures: asset turnover, profit margin, ROI, and RI for the present fiscal year. Each transaction is independent.

Required:

a. The division writes down an inventory of obsolete finished goods through the cost of goods sold expense account. The journal entry is

Cost of Goods Sold	40,000
Finished Goods Inventory	40,000

b. A special overseas order is accepted. The sales price for this order is well below the normal sales price but is sufficient to cover all costs traceable to this order.

c. A piece of equipment is sold for $70,000. The equipment's original cost was $400,000. At the time of sale, the book value of the equipment was $60,000. The sale of the equipment has no effect on product sales.

d. The division fires its research and development manager. The manager will not be replaced during the current fiscal year.

e. The company raises its target rate of return for this division from 12% to 14%.

f. At mid-year, the divisional manager decides to increase scheduled annual production by 2,000 units. This decision has no effect on scheduled sales.

g. Also at mid-year, the division manager spends an additional $150,000 on advertising. Sales immediately increase.

h. The divisional manager replaces a labour-intensive operation with machine technology. This action has no effect on sales, but total annual expenses of the operation are expected to decline by 12%.

8. (LO 2) The Canadian Yacht Company evaluates the performance of its two division managers using an ROI formula. For the forthcoming period, divisional estimates of relevant measures are:

	Pleasure	Commercial	Total Company
Sales	$12,000,000	$48,000,000	$60,000,000
Expenses	10,800,000	42,000,000	52,800,000
Divisional assets	10,000,000	30,000,000	40,000,000

The managers of both operating divisions have the authority to make decisions regarding new investments. The manager of Pleasure Crafts is contemplating an investment in an additional asset that would generate an ROI of 14%, and the manager of Commercial Crafts is considering an investment in an additional asset that would generate an ROI of 18%.

PROBLEMS

Required:

a. Compute the projected ROI for each division disregarding the contemplated new investments.

b. Based on your answer in part (a), which of the managers is likely to actually invest in the asset under consideration?

c. Are the outcomes of the investment decisions in part (b) likely to be consistent with overall corporate goals? Explain.

d. If the company evaluated the division managers' performances using a residual income measure with a target return of 17%, would the outcomes of the investment decisions be different from those described in part (b)? Explain.

9. (LO 3) You are a division manager of Luxwood Design Co. Your performance as a division manager is evaluated primarily on one measure: after-tax divisional segment income less the cost of capital invested in divisional assets. For existing operations in your division, projections for 2011 follow:

Sales	$ 40,000,000
Expenses	(35,000,000)
Segment income	$ 5,000,000
Taxes	(1,500,000)
After-tax segment income	$ 3,500,000

The invested capital of the division is $25,000,000, the required after-tax return on capital is 12%, and the tax rate is 30%.

At this moment, you are evaluating an investment in a new product line that would, according to your projections, increase 2011 pretax segment income by $400,000. The cost of the investment has not yet been determined.

Required:

a. Ignoring the new investment, what is your projected EVA for 2011?

b. In light of your answer in part (a), what is the maximum amount that you would be willing to invest in the new product line?

c. Assuming the new product line would require an investment of $1,100,000, what would be the revised projected EVA for your division in 2011 if the investment were made?

10. (LO 4) Bangor Spool Co. has historically evaluated divisional performance exclusively on financial measures. Top managers have become increasingly concerned with this approach to performance evaluation and are now actively seeking alternative measures. Specifically, they wish to focus on activities that generate value for customers. One promising measure is throughput. To experiment with the annual throughput measure, management has gathered the following historical information on one of its larger operating divisions:

Units started into production	200,000
Total good units completed	130,000
Total hours of value-added processing time	80,000
Total hours	120,000

Required:

a. What is the manufacturing cycle efficiency?

b. What is the process productivity of the division?

c. What is the process quality yield of the division?

d. Based on your answers to parts (a), (b), and (c), what is the total throughput per hour?

e. Which of the previous measures—part (a), (b), or (c)—reflects the possible existence of a production bottleneck? Why?

f. Which of the previous measures—part (a), (b), or (c)—reflects potentially poor quality in the production process as measured by the number of defective units? Why?

11. (LO 2) Fruta Division, one of the investment centres of Wholesale Fruits Inc., had net operating income in 2009 of $360,000. The average assets employed by Fruta during 2009 were $1,800,000. In January of 2010, the division manager of the Fruta Division retired after 15 years to start a bookkeeping business. The chief executive officer (CEO) of Wholesale Fruits appointed you as the new division manager of Fruta. After assuming your new position, you discovered that most of Fruta's manufacturing equipment needed to be replaced. You also found out that at the end of 2009, the previous

division manager had disposed of some of the plant and equipment. In order to increase efficiency, you made a large investment to replace the obsolete equipment and to update the facilities. In 2010, on a total of $4,000,000 of average assets employed, the division reported net operating income of $735,000.

The CEO of Wholesale Fruits uses return on investment (ROI) to evaluate the performance of his division managers. He feels that your performance in running Fruta is not as good as the previous manager's since the 2010 ROI is much lower than it was in 2009.

Required:

a. Calculate the ROI for Fruta in 2009 and 2010.

b. You feel quite strongly that you have done a much better job than the previous manager and suggest to the CEO that he should consider residual income (RI) as an alternative performance measure. Wholesale Fruits' minimum required rate of return is 16%. Calculate the RI for Fruta in 2009 and 2010. If RI were used by the CEO, whose performance would be better?

c. Explain and justify the lower ROI in 2010 compared to that in 2009.

d. You find out that in 2009 the previous manager was presented with an investment opportunity that would have required a $500,000 investment and that would have provided net operating income of $90,000. Explain fully why the previous manager refused to undertake this investment.

e. You had convinced the CEO that RI is a better performance measure than ROI. However, the CEO recently found out that one of your competitors had a net operating income of $5,000,000 on a total of $25,000,000 in average assets employed during 2010. As a result, the CEO is still unhappy with your 2010 performance. Using the same minimum required rate of return as Wholesale Fruits, calculate the RI of this competitor. How are you going to respond to the CEO's criticisms?

Extract from *Management Accounting Examination*, published by the Certified General Accountants Association of Canada (© CGA-Canada 1999). Reprinted with permission.

12. (LO 4) The accountant of SYST Inc. prepared a report on the costs of quality for the last three years. He needs someone to help interpret these results.

SYST INC.
Cost of Quality Report
2008 to 2010

	2008	2009	2010
Amortization of testing equipment	$ 10,000	$ 9,500	$ 8,700
Disposal of defective products	12,000	18,000	22,500
Inspection	11,000	10,500	10,000
Net cost of scrap	5,200	7,100	9,100
Product recalls	8,000	10,500	13,500
Product testing	8,500	8,600	8,000
Quality engineering	4,000	3,800	3,750
Rework labour	6,000	8,100	8,950
Statistical process control	4,500	4,600	4,800
Supplies used in testing	8,750	8,300	7,550
System development	10,500	10,000	9,000
Warranty repairs	10,650	13,050	19,450
Warranty replacements	9,550	10,850	14,250
	$108,650	$122,900	$139,550
Percent of sales	11.44%	12.94%	14.69%

The amount of sales is $950,000 for each year.

Required:

a. Calculate the prevention costs and the external failure costs for every year (2008 to 2010), including the total costs as a percentage of sales.

b. Interpret your answer in part (a), and explain briefly the effect of the results on future sales.

Extract from *Management Accounting 2 Examination*, published by the Certified General Accountants Association of Canada (© CGA-Canada 2003). Reprinted with permission.

PROBLEMS

13. (LO 4) Newbury Inc. manufactures products used in the electronics industry. Sales reached $3,000,000 in 2010. However, Newbury has been struggling with quality problems over the last three years. The chief financial officer (CFO) heard of a new report on quality costs and benchmarking. At the request of the CFO, her assistant has obtained the following information for 2010:

Inspection	$65,890
Labour used to rework products	33,460
Scrap (net cost)	92,500
Downtime due to quality problems	54,450
Cost incurred to test equipment	22,500
Vendor certification	15,000
Customer returns of defective products	89.760
Warranty repairs	33,650
Training (direct labour)	45,000

Required:

a. Prepare a cost of quality report.

b. Explain what benchmarking is and how it could assist Newbury in solving its quality problems.

Extract from *Management Accounting 2 Examination*, published by the Certified General Accountants Association of Canada (© CGA-Canada 2000). Reprinted with permission.

14. (LO 7) LMF Corporation, a heavy machinery manufacturer, has implemented an executive compensation plan that rewards divisional achievement in sales. A divisional director (earning a base salary of $80,000) who exceeds the assigned annual sales target is entitled to the following for one year:

- Use of a luxury car, including a monthly fuel allowance, insurance, and maintenance
- Free use of the exclusive executive dining room for the director and immediate family
- A larger office on a higher floor along a window, plus a $6,000 furniture allowance
- A vacation in Australia with up to four friends or family members, to be taken within the next 12 months
- A cash payment of $15,000 intended to cover any potential taxes

An independent audit recently appraised the value of the above perquisite package at $45,000.

Required:

a. Outline *two* advantages and *two* disadvantages of the above compensation plan.

b. From the firm's perspective, what would be more effective in motivating managers: the compensation package as described, or a straight payment of $50,000? Explain.

Extract from *Management Accounting 2 Examination*, published by the Certified General Accountants Association of Canada (© CGA-Canada 1999). Reprinted with permission.

15. (LO 2, 7) Kappa Company has three divisions: A, B, and C. The vice-president in charge of the best performing division is entitled to a sizeable bonus. The results for the year are now in and each vice-president has claimed to be entitled to the bonus, using some version of return on investment (ROI) or residual income (RI), based on either the net book value (NBV), defined as original/historical cost less accumulated amortization, or gross book value (GBV), defined as original/historical cost *without* any amortization of the asset base.

The vice-presidents based their claims on the following information:

Division	GBV at Start of Year	Net Operating Income
A	$400,000	$47,500
B	380,000	46,000
C	250,000	30,800

All divisions have fixed assets with a 20-year useful life and no terminal value. The fixed assets were purchased 10 years ago. Kappa's cost of capital is 10%. The company's three divisions all use beginning-of-the-year values for invested capital in the ROI or RI calculation. Assume straight-line amortization.

PROBLEMS

Required:
Determine which method for computing performance each vice-president used in order to show that his/her division had the best performance.

Extract from *Management Accounting 1 Examination*, published by the Certified General Accountants Association of Canada (© CGA-Canada 2000). Reprinted with permission.

16. (LO 3) A high-tech company has made profits during the last three years (2008 to 2010). However, the CEO of the company has asked the accounting team to determine the economic value added (EVA) for 2010. The following information was used to compute the EVA for 2010 and prepare the EVA report.

GAAP income	$ 225,000
EVA-adjusted total capital, December 31, 2008	1,450,000
EVA-adjusted total capital, December 31, 2009	1,500,500
Expected EVA-adjusted capital, December 31, 2010	1,650,500
Amortization of goodwill included in the calculation of GAAP income	26,000

Additional information
- Marginal tax rate = 38%
- Cost of equity = 47%
- After-tax cost of debt = 8.7%
- Capital structure is three times more equity than debt
- Amortization period for research and development costs = 6 years

The accountants assumed that the company invested $57,000 in R&D in 2010 and that 25% was capitalized under GAAP. The accounting team determined that EVA for 2007 is $8,241.

EVA Report
Prepared by the accounting team
Year 2010

Calculation of weighted average cost of capital (WACC):
WACC = 0.67(0.38 × 0.087) + 0.33(0.47) = 17.73%

Calculation of net operating profit after taxes (NOPAT):

GAAP income	$225,000
R&D not capitalized	57,000
Deduct 2010 amortization of R&D	(7,125)
Add back amortization for goodwill included in 2010 income	26,000
	$300,875

Calculation of EVA:
EVA = $300,875 − (17.73% × $1,650,500) = $8,241

Required:
a. Identify any errors in the EVA report prepared by the accounting team. Recalculate the EVA that the accounting team has computed and make all changes, if any are necessary, to obtain the accurate amount of EVA. Present the revised calculations.
b. Briefly explain the significance of your calculated EVA result in part (a), and state what actions the CEO of the company can take, in light of the EVA result.

17. (LO 2) National Motors is a major car manufacturer with a wide variety of models, including the most recent one, named *Speed*. The new model uses parts and components from external suppliers as well as from the following divisions of National Motors:
- *Division S:* This division manufactures stainless steel components for the *Speed* model and other models sold by National Motors. Sales of components for the *Speed* model represent 25% of the division's revenue.
- *Division F:* This division produces different wipers that fit a wide variety of car models manufactured by National Motors and other major car manufacturers. Sales of wipers for the *Speed* model are negligible. Division F has total assets of $250,000,000. Last year's revenues were $150,000,000 with operating expenses of $117,500,000.
- *Division D:* This division uses all its capacity to manufacture engines for the *Speed* model. The divisional manager is strictly responsible for choosing the inputs used to produce the engines.

PROBLEMS

National Motors uses return on investment (ROI) to evaluate the performance of the divisional managers. The required rate of return of 14% is the same for all divisions.

At the last meeting of the divisional managers, Mr. Goodman, manager of Division D, was not happy because he thought that he was not evaluated fairly. The chief executive officer of National Motors did not understand how Mr. Goodman's evaluation could be unfair because she thought that ROI was the best measure available to evaluate performance.

Required:

a.   Calculate the residual income for Division F based on last year's results and investment. Show your calculations.

b.   Identify which type of responsibility centre each of the three divisions should be. Briefly explain your reasoning.

c.   Is ROI appropriate to evaluate the performance of Mr. Goodman and Division D? Briefly explain your answer.

Problems 16 and 17 are an extract from *Management Accounting 2 Examination*, published by the Certified General Accountants Association of Canada (© CGA-Canada 2002). Reprinted with permission.

18.   (LO 2) The performance of the division manager of Rarewood Furniture is measured by ROI, defined as divisional segment income divided by gross book value of total divisional assets. For existing operations, the division's projections for the coming year are as follows:

Sales	$ 20,000,000
Expenses	(17,500,000)
Segment income	$ 2,500,000

The gross book value of assets supporting present operations is $12,500,000. Currently, the manager is evaluating an investment in a new product line that would, according to her projections, increase 2010 segment income by $200,000. The cost of the investment has not yet been determined. The company's cost of capital is 10%.

Required:

a.   Calculate ROI for 2010 without the new investment

b.   Assuming that the new product line would require an investment of $1,100,000, calculate the revised projected ROI for the division in 2010 with the new investment. Would the manager likely accept or reject the investment? Explain.

c.   At what investment cost would the manager be indifferent as to whether to make the new investment?

d.   Create a brief numerical example to explain and illustrate how the use of residual income as a performance measure may encourage a manager to accept a project that is in the best interests of the company, but that he or she might otherwise reject. (Hint: Using the above situation as an example might be a way of explanation.)

Extract from *Management Accounting 2 Examination*, published by the Certified General Accountants Association of Canada (© CGA-Canada 2003). Reprinted with permission.

19.   (LO 4) Victoria Turkey Producers Co. has historically evaluated divisional performance exclusively on financial measures. Top managers have become increasingly concerned with this approach to performance evaluation and are now actively seeking alternative measures. Specifically, they wish to focus on activities that generate value for customers. One promising measure is throughput. To experiment with the annual throughput measure, management has gathered the following historical information on one of its larger operating divisions:

Units started into production	390,000
Total good units completed	360,000
Total hours of value-added processing time	170,000
Total hours	240,000

Required:

a.   What is the manufacturing cycle efficiency?

b.   What is the process productivity of the division?

c.   What is the process quality yield of the division?

d.   Based on your answers to parts (a), (b), and (c), what is the total throughput per hour?

e.   Which of the previous measures—part (a), (b), or (c)—reflects the possible existence of a production bottleneck? Why?

f.   Which of the previous measures—part (a), (b), or (c)—reflects potentially poor quality in the production process as measured by the number of defective units? Why?

PROBLEMS

20. (LO 2) M Company is a medium-sized diversified manufacturing company consisting of several divisions. The divisions are of different sizes, ranging from about $5 million to over $120 million in total assets. Each division has its own manufacturing and marketing facilities.

M Company treats each division as an investment centre and uses residual income after tax to evaluate *and* compare the performance of the divisions. For the purpose of calculating the residual income, the rate for the capital charge is the same for *all* divisions and is set by M Company's top management at the beginning of each fiscal year. Again, for the purpose of calculating the residual income, a division's investment base is defined as the difference between its total assets and total current liabilities.

A typical statement of actual and budgeted operating results of one of M Company's divisions, Division X, for 2010 is presented in Exhibit 12-1. Averages of selected balance sheet account balances (actual and budgeted) for Division X for 2010 are presented in Exhibit 12-2.

	Actual	Budget
Sales	$12,000	$11,000
Expenses:		
Direct materials and labour	4,830	4,400
Manufacturing overhead	3,220	2,960
Marketing expenses	1,450	1,500
Administrative expenses	800	700
Income taxes (at 30%)	510	420
Total expenses	10,810	10,020
Net income	$ 1,190	$ 980
Capital charge @ 12%	$ 817	$ 720
Residual income	$ 373	$ 260

EXHIBIT 12-1

Division X: Actual and Budgeted Operating Results for 2010 ($000s)

	Actual	Budget
Current assets:		
Cash	$ 960	$ 880
Accounts receivable	1,910	1,620
Inventories	1,200	1,200
Other current assets	220	300
Plant capital assets (net)	4,500	4,000
Total current liabilities	1,980	2,000

EXHIBIT 12-2

Division X: Averages of Selected Balance Sheet Account Balances for 2010 ($000s)

The following additional information was available for 2010:
- Standard absorption costing was used for product costing. Production volume and sales volume were the same, and there were no changes in inventories of raw materials and work in process during 2010.
- Marketing expenses were all traceable to specific divisions and did not vary with sales volume.
- M Company charges each of the divisions 4% of budgeted sales to cover head office expenses, including company executives, finance, facility management and maintenance, internal audit, and human resources. This charge is included in the budgeted administrative expenses of divisions.
- Company sales are typically to customers outside Canada, although all financial statements are in Canadian funds. During 2010, the budgeted exchange rate was U.S.$1.60 per C$1; however, the actual rate averaged U.S.$1.51 per C$1.

PROBLEMS

- M Company allocated its investment in head office facilities to the divisions. For example, Division X was allocated $250,000 for 2010 and this amount was included in its budgeted plant capital assets.
- Accounts receivable, inventories, and other current assets as well as current liabilities are all traceable to divisions.
- The top management of M Company set the minimum rate for the capital charge at 12% after taxes for 2010.

Required:

a. Is it appropriate for M Company's top management to compare the residual incomes of the different divisions? Why or why not?

b. The division managers have complained that M Company's calculation of residual income understates division performance, because the calculation includes "uncontrollable costs" such as head office expenses, exchange rate fluctuations, and head office facilities. Explain the specific conditions under which M Company's residual income calculation would remain an effective performance measure, notwithstanding the "uncontrollable costs".

c. Each division is charged 4% of budgeted sales for head office expenses. This is a transfer price that makes sure that nondiscretionary head office functions are fully funded companywide. Outline *two* advantages and *two* disadvantages of the transfer pricing method M Company uses to account for head office expenses.

d. Explain *two* alternative approaches for transferring head office expenses. For each alternative, outline *one* advantage and *one* disadvantage of using this method, *relative to the method currently being used*. What changes would you recommend, if any, for transferring head office expenses to divisions?

e. What *specific additional* information would you need in order to do a better job of evaluating the managerial performance of Division X? The information should be useful in determining each of the following:
   - the appropriate key success factors
   - managerial performance with respect to costs, expenses, and revenues

Extract from *Management Accounting 2 Examination*, published by the Certified General Accountants Association of Canada (© CGA-Canada 1999). Reprinted with permission.

21. (LO 1, 2) Raddington Industries produces tool and die machinery for manufacturers. The company expanded vertically in 2009 by acquiring one of its suppliers of alloy steel plates, Reigis Steel Company. In order to manage the two separate businesses, the operations of Reigis are reported separately as an investment centre.

Raddington monitors its divisions on the basis of both unit contribution and return on average investment (ROI), with investment defined as average operating assets employed. Management bonuses are determined based on ROI. All investments in operating assets are expected to earn a minimum return of 11% before income taxes.

Reigis's cost of goods sold is considered to be entirely variable, while the division's administrative expenses are not dependent on volume. Selling expenses are a mixed cost with 40% attributed to sales volume. Reigis's ROI has ranged from 11.8% to 14.7% since 2009. During the fiscal year ended November 30, 2010, Reigis contemplated a capital acquisition with an estimated ROI of 11.5%; however, division management decided that the investment would decrease Reigis's overall ROI.

The 2010 operating statement for Reigis follows. The division's operating assets employed were $15,750,000 at November 30, 2010, a 5% increase over the 2009 year-end balance.

Reigis Steel Division
Operating Statement
For the Year Ended November 30, 2010
($000 omitted)

Sales revenue		$ 25,000
Less expenses:		
Cost of goods sold	$16,500	
Administrative expenses	3,955	
Selling expenses	2,700	(23,155)
Operating income before taxes		$ 1,845

PROBLEMS

Required:

a. Calculate the unit contribution for Reigis Steel Division if 1,484,000 units were produced and sold during the year ended November 30, 2010.

b. Calculate the following performance measures for 2010 for the Reigis Steel Division:
   i. Pretax return on average investment in operating assets employed (ROI)
   ii. Residual income calculated on the basis of average operating assets employed

c. Explain why the management of the Reigis Steel Division would have been more likely to accept the contemplated capital acquisition if residual income rather than ROI had been used as a performance measure.

d. The Reigis Steel Division is a separate investment centre within Raddington Industries. Identify several items that Reigis should control if it is to be evaluated fairly by either the ROI or residual income performance measure.

(CMA)

22. (LO 2, 7) Northstar Offroad Co. (NOC), a subsidiary of Allston Automotive, manufactures go-carts and other recreational vehicles. Family recreational centres that feature go-cart tracks, miniature golf, batting cages, and arcades have increased in popularity. As a result, NOC has been receiving some pressure from Allston Automotive top management to diversify into some of these other recreational areas. Recreational Leasing Inc. (RLI), one of the largest firms that leases arcade games to family recreation centres, is looking for a friendly buyer. Allston Automotive management believes that RLI's assets could be acquired for an investment of $3.2 million and has strongly urged Bill Grieco, division manager of NOC, to consider acquiring RLI.

Grieco has reviewed RLI's financial statements with his controller, Marie Donnelly, and they believe that the acquisition may not be in NOC's best interests. "If we decide not to do this, the Allston Automotive people are not going to be happy," said Grieco. "If we could convince them to base our bonuses on something other than return on investment, maybe this acquisition would look more attractive. How would we do if the bonuses were based on residual income using the company's 15% cost of capital?"

Allston Automotive has traditionally evaluated all of its divisions on the basis of return on investment, which is defined as the ratio of operating income to total assets; the desired rate of return for each is 20%. The management team of any division reporting an annual increase in the return on investment is automatically eligible for a bonus. The management of divisions reporting a decline in the return on investment must provide convincing explanations for the decline to be eligible for a bonus, and this bonus is limited to 50% of the average bonus paid to divisions reporting an increase.

Presented below are condensed financial statements for both NOC and RLI for the fiscal year ended May 31.

	NOC	RLI
Sales revenue	$10,500,000	
Leasing revenue		$ 2,800,000
Variable expenses	(7,000,000)	(1,000,000)
Fixed expenses	(1,500,000)	(1,200,000)
Operating income	$ 2,000,000	$ 600,000
Current assets	$ 2,300,000	$ 1,900,000
Long-term assets	5,700,000	1,100,000
Total assets	$ 8,000,000	$ 3,000,000
Current liabilities	$ 1,400,000	$ 850,000
Long-term liabilities	3,800,000	1,200,000
Shareholders' equity	2,800,000	950,000
Total liabilities and shareholders' equity	$ 8,000,000	$ 3,000,000

Required:

a. Under the present bonus system, how would the acquisition of RLI affect Grieco's bonus expectations?

b. If Grieco's suggestion to use residual income as the evaluation criterion is accepted, how would acquisition of RLI affect Grieco's bonus expectations?

PROBLEMS

   c. Given the present bonus arrangement, is it fair for Allston Automotive management to expect Grieco to acquire RLI?

   d. Is the present bonus system consistent with Allston Automotive's goal of expansion of NOC into new recreational products?

23. (LO 1, 2) Major Currency, the controller of Altoma Meat Products, has become increasingly disillusioned with the company's system of evaluating the performance of profit centres and their managers. The present system focuses on a comparison of budgeted to actual income from operations. Major's concern with the current system is the ease with which the measured income from operations can be manipulated by profit centre managers. The basic business of Altoma Meat Products consists of purchasing live hogs and cattle, slaughtering the animals, and then selling the various meat products and by-products to regional wholesalers and large retail chains. Most sales are made on credit, and all live animals are purchased for cash. The profit centres consist of geographical segments of Altoma Meat Products, and all profit centre segments conduct both production and sales activities within their geographical territories. Following is a typical quarterly income statement for a profit centre, which appears in the responsibility report for the profit centre:

Sales	$ 5,000,000
Cost of goods sold	(3,000,000)
Gross profit	$ 2,000,000
Selling and administrative expenses	(1,500,000)
Income from operations	$ 500,000

Major has suggested to top management that the company replace the accrual income evaluation measure *income from operations* with a measure called *cash flow from operations*. He says that this measure will be less susceptible to manipulation by profit centre managers. To defend his position, he compiles a cash flow income statement for the same profit centre:

Cash receipts from customers	$ 4,400,000
Cash payments for production labour, livestock, and overhead	(3,200,000)
Cash payments for selling and administrative activities	(800,000)
Cash flow from operations	$ 400,000

Required:

   a. If Major is correct about profit centre managers' manipulating the income measure, where are manipulations likely taking place?

   b. Is the proposed cash flow measure less subject to manipulation than the income measure? Explain.

   c. Could manipulation be reduced if both cash flow and income measures were utilized? Explain.

   d. Do the cash and income measures reveal different information about profit centre performance? Explain.

   e. Could the existing income statement be used more effectively in evaluating performance? Explain.

24. (LO 2, 7) Western Chemical Group is a multinational firm that markets a variety of chemicals for industrial uses. One of the many autonomous divisions is the North America Petro-Chemical Division (NAPCD). The manager of NAPCD, Karyn Kravitz, was recently overheard discussing a vexing problem with her controller, William Michaels. The topic of discussion was whether the division should replace its existing chemical-handling equipment with newer technology that is safer, more efficient, and cheaper to operate.

According to an analysis by Mr. Michaels, the cost savings over the life of the new technology would pay for the initial cost of the technology several times over. However, Ms. Kravitz remained reluctant to invest. Her most fundamental concern involved the disposition of the old processing equipment. Because the existing equipment has been in use for only two years, it has a very high book value relative to its current market value. Ms. Kravitz noted that if the new technology were not purchased, the division would expect a segment income of $4 million for the year. However, if the new technology were purchased, the old equipment would have to be sold, and the division could probably sell it for only $1.2 million. This equipment had an original cost of $8 million, and $1.5 million in depreciation has been recorded. Thus, a book loss of $5.3 million ($6.5 million – $1.2 million) would be recorded on the sale.

Ms. Kravitz' boss, Jim Heitz, is the president of the Western Chemical Group, and his compensation is based almost exclusively on the amount of ROI generated by his group, which includes NAPCD. After thoroughly analyzing the facts, Ms. Kravitz concluded, "The people in the Western Chemical Group will swallow their dentures if we book a $5.3 million loss."

Required:

a. Why is Ms. Kravitz concerned about the book loss on disposal of the old technology in her division?

b. What weaknesses in Western Chemical Group's performance pay plan are apparently causing Ms. Kravitz to avoid an investment that meets all of the normal criteria for acceptability (ignoring the ROI effect)?

CASES

1. Dell Incorporated's mission statement, which appears on its Web site, is "to be the most successful computer company in the world at delivering the best customer experience in markets we serve." The present strategy of Dell has three dominant and related characteristics. First, all Dell PCs are custom built or assembled to order and then shipped directly to customers, bypassing wholesalers and retailers. Direct interaction with customers ensures quality service and lower costs. Second, Dell uses just-in-time manufacturing to avoid carrying large stocks of parts, components, and finished goods. JIT reduces costs, particularly with model or technology changes, as it carries only a few days of inventory. Third, although Dell assembles the PCs (and other products) it sells, most parts are outsourced to firms who are the best in the world in what they produce. Michael Dell explains the advantages of outsourcing with the following (paraphrased) story: "If you have a race with 20 players all vying to make the fastest graphics chip in the world, do you want to be the twenty-first player, or do you want to evaluate the field of 20 and pick the best player?"

Clearly, Dell chose to evaluate the suppliers and to pick the world's best for long-term partnerships, which had two advantages, (1) name-brand processors, disk drives, modems, speakers, and multimedia components to enhance quality and performance, and (2) timely deliveries of components because Dell's commitment to purchase specific percentages from each of its long-term suppliers.

For dealing with suppliers, Dell invested significantly in Web site abilities or systems for dealing with suppliers, which were linked to its customers using the Internet and its organizational know-how systems. Dell's network of linked suppliers, or the fusion of its operations with those of its suppliers, makes possible the efficient tailoring of PC products to fit the needs of individual buyers, whether for home use or for a global company. Dell was also quick to benefit from Web-based sales and customer service operations. Customers are served by a telephone or an on-line order taker who actually works for a division of a telephone company. More frequently, the orders are placed by the customer through Dell's Web page. Once placed by telephone or Internet, the order is sent to a coordinator—actually an employee of another company—who in turn passes the order to the relevant Dell assembly plant from among five around the world. At the same time, the coordinator directs the suppliers to ship the parts to the selected plant. The coordinator also directs the parcel courier to go to the respective plant at the predetermined time for pick-up and then delivery of the finished product to the customer.

Required:

Using the case approach, assume you have been hired by Dell to design a balanced scorecard. Design the balanced scorecard for Dell.

2. Doyle Trust was founded in 1899. Now it is the largest trust company in the country, with assets under administration exceeding $152 billion and 8,300 employees worldwide. The only Canadian trust company with an established international network, Doyle Trust operated its first overseas office in London in 1929. Today it has 20 offices overseas.

Doyle Trust also operates 136 loan offices and branches in the Pacific Northwest through its U.S. subsidiary. Through a network and 144 branches across Canada, Doyle Trust provides a wide range of financial products, services, and advice. These include personal and corporate banking services, as well as international investment advice, portfolio management, and administration for private and corporate clients.

The president has described Doyle Trust's compensation and reward system, which establishes, according to him, a mutuality of interest between individual employee and company needs:

> The right people, with the right basic training, living common values, talking a lot and sharing information through technology, put the pieces in place for local empowerment without chaos. Mutuality of self-interest with the interest of the client and shareholder is the glue that makes the strategy work for all stakeholders. Our compensation plans are founded on establishing mutuality between the individual's interest and the company's. For example, the 170 most senior managers have relatively low salaries, but they receive company-provided loans to buy common shares. These senior managers get about half or more of their annual income from Doyle Trust common share dividends and market appreciation of those same shares. Other managers forgo a smaller part of their cash compensation for share options, with the number of options offered being dependent on the manager's performance, not length of service or position. Virtually everyone on the payroll is on a bonus plan of some sort, either individual or team. For example, managers voluntarily ask the company to hold back from 5% to 25% of their base pay to be paid back in multiples from zero to three times the amount withheld, if the company meets its return on equity and profit objectives and the individual meets his or her objectives. Last year Doyle Trust did not meet its financial objectives—the first time in seven years. There was no payout from the bonus plan—irrespective of an individual's meeting his or her personal objectives. If the company does not win, no individual can either. We have found that mutuality of interest implemented through compensation and bonus schemes gives everyone a stake in achieving common objectives, either corporate or business unit. It puts teeth in the "soft" processes of training, values and communications.

Despite senior management's support for the compensation and reward system, employees have recently complained, and this has prompted your consulting firm to be called in to do an evaluation.

Required:

You are a consultant with a major Canadian consulting firm. One of your clients, a major trust company, Doyle Trust, has requested that your firm evaluate its employee compensation and reward systems. Use the case approach.

3. Boating World Limited (BWL) is an Ontario manufacturer of recreational boats and motors. It also operates a marina on Georgian Bay, which is where the company got its start in 1977. Initially a family-operated marina, Boating World expanded into boat repair in the 1980s. Then in 1995, Boating World acquired Rama Boat Engines, a Barrie manufacturer of inboard engines. The three divisions are located at different sites within a five-mile radius. The divisions are independent.

The three divisions are boat building, engine manufacturing, and the marina. Each division has its own general manager, and each is an investment centre. BWL's divisional operating statements are shown in Exhibit 12-1.

EXHIBIT 12-1

Abbreviated Operating
Statements, 2006 Budget ($000)

	Boats	Engines	Marina	Consolidated
Revenue	300,000	250,000	450,000	990,000
Variable costs	160,000	100,000	250,000	505,000
Contribution margin	140,000	150,000	200,000	485,000
Fixed costs	110,000	100,000	167,000	377,000
Pre-tax net income	30,000	50,000	33,000	108,000
Current assets	10,000	12,000	25,000	47,000
Net fixed assets	175,000	180,000	125,000	480,000
Total assets	185,000	192,000	150,000	527,000
ROI	?	?	?	?

CASES

Each of the three divisions is managed by one of your children; you were the founder, and now you have the title of CEO. The boat division is managed by Marta, the engine division by Mory, the marina division by Manuel. The divisions are autonomous except that every year, the engine division sells 25,000 motors at $2,000 each to the boat division. The per unit transfer price is set at a slight discount (about 2%) from market to reflect the cost savings the engine division enjoys when dealing with a sister division. For all intents and purposes, it is the market transfer price.

Though you and your spouse own all the shares of Boating World, your three children receive bonuses under the following formula: $1 million each when divisional ROI exceeds 20%, and $250,000 each when the ROI for the total firm exceeds 20%. This bonus system has worked well since its implementation four years ago. However, even before you calculate the present year's ROIs, Marta has expressed two concerns about how it is calculated for the boat division. First, the market-based transfer price is unfair because it exceeds the total cost for making the engines. The engine division has excess capacity even after selling 2,000 engines to the boat division, so she believes that the transfer price should be based on variable costs. Second, because the extent to which the transfer price exceeds cost is eliminated through consolidation, it should not be allowed from the beginning.

Required:

As the owner and CEO, address Marta's concerns and calculate the bonuses for each of the divisional managers. Use the case approach.

4. As a member of the controller's department at Yoour University, a large Canadian university, you have been asked to develop a balanced scorecard. You have an advantage: you were once a student at Yoour. As you begin to prepare the balanced scorecard, you reflect on Yoour University. Its mission statement:

> The mission of Yoour University is the pursuit, preservation, and dissemination of knowledge. We promise excellence in research and teaching in pure, applied, and professional fields. We test the boundaries and structures of knowledge. We cultivate the critical intellect.
>
> Yoour University is part of Toronto: we are dynamic, metropolitan, and multicultural. Yoour University is part of Canada: we encourage bilingual study, we value tolerance and diversity. Yoour University is open to the world: we explore global concerns.
>
> A community of faculty, students, and staff committed to academic freedom, social justice, accessible education, and collegial self-governance, Yoour University makes innovation its tradition.
>
> *Tentanda Via*: the way must be tried.

Yoour University is known for its interdisciplinary approach to research and scholarship. Twenty research centres cover a broad spectrum of interests—from applied sustainability, to work and society, to refugee studies, to earth sciences. It is a community of more than 3,000 full- and part-time faculty, 1,800 staff, 40,000 undergraduate and graduate students, and 150,000 alumni. Yoour graduates more than 7,000 students annually from its 10 faculties (e.g., Arts, Business, and Education).

The CEO is the president, to whom five vice presidents report. The deans of the 10 faculties report to the vice president, academic. The other vice presidents direct the following portfolios: student services, finance and administration, research and innovation, and advancement (fundraising).

Like all universities, Yoour receives funding from three sources: the provincial government, student fees, and donations. The government funding is based on rules relating mainly to the number of students. Except for a limited number of deregulated programs, fees are largely regulated by the government. Donations depend on the university's ability to raise funds and on the largess of the alumni and the community.

The standard balanced scorecard has four perspectives: financial, customer, internal processes, and learning and growth. In your university setting, unlike in a profit-oriented organization, the financial perspective does not involve shareholders. You are beginning to wonder whether a single balanced scorecard is sufficient.

Required:

Carry out your assignment using the case approach.

CASES

5. Boughtwell Real Estate Investment Trust is a growth-oriented investment trust that owns and manages a complete spectrum of seniors apartment buildings in various cities and towns across Canada. Focused solely on the Canadian marketplace, Boughtwell REIT is currently the second largest participant in the Canadian seniors housing business. It is benefiting strongly from Canada's aging population. Whether it is facilities for empty-nesters catering to mature lifestyles, minimum or basic care facilities, or assisted living, there is a growing market for housing alternatives that offer services, amenities, and independent living arrangements for seniors.

Boughtwell owns and manages seniors housing properties through its indirect subsidiary Boughtwell Master Care LP. The returns come in two forms: (1) rents paid by the tenants, and (2) appreciation of the buildings.

Boughtwell Mastercare manages about 2,000 apartment buildings with the goal of providing an attractive ROI to Boughtwell REIT. To that end, a superintendent is employed in each building. A manager is responsible for approximately 20 superintendents (i.e., buildings). You are a manager, which means that 20 superintendents report to you.

Annual ROI is calculated using the following formula. The example is for a typical building ($000s):

Revenues (rents from all units)	$ 7,000
Less:	
Building operating expenses	2,000
Capital cost allowance (based on historical cost)	1,000
Equals:	
Pre-tax, pre-interest return	4,000
Divided by:	
Investment (working capital plus market value of building)	64,000
Equals ROI	6.3%

The target ROI is 8.5%; thus you are not happy with the performance of your superintendents. In the past, there have been demands to improve the ROI. Instead of improvements, the opposite has occurred. In an attempt to improve the ROI, the superintendents have reduced operating expenses by about $500,000 (from $2.5 million to $2 million). The result has been poorer service: fewer repairs, delays in repairs, and less cleaning. The tenants, obviously, are less satisfied, and as a result the occupancy rate has declined from 80% to 70%. (Occupancy is the number of apartments occupied or rented divided by the total apartments available.) Occupancy should be 95%.

You as the manager report to a vice president, who is displeased with the performance of your 20 apartment buildings. She wants the ROI to be a minimum of 8.5%, and she has committed herself to giving you a bonus on anything you obtain over 8.5%. You tell her that you did demand an 8.5% ROI, but it only led to a reduction in operating expenses and a reduction in the occupancy rate. She responds that you need to use a balanced scorecard to ensure an 8.5% or higher ROI from your 20 apartment buildings.

Required:

Using the case approach, develop a balanced scorecard to improve the ROI for the 20 apartment buildings you manage.

ETHICS

1. As the assistant controller for a forest products firm in Ontario, you help prepare the monthly and annual financial statements. You look after the regular revenues and expenses. Your boss, the controller, reviews your work and looks after special situations. To minimize errors, you review her handling of the special situations. This arrangement has worked well for the two years in which you have been the assistant controller.

For the year just ended, your boss calculated the write-offs from a discontinued branch at $1 million, or 10 cents a share. Your calculations indicate that the write-offs should be $1.5 million, or 15 cents a share. You confront her. She agrees with your calculation but says that the CEO needs the extra 5 cents a share to meet his commitment to the board of directors.

What should you do? Please elaborate.

ETHICS

2. You and two partners operate a management accounting consulting firm. All three of you are CMAs. Your firm hires recent MBA graduates as consultants. Preferably, these newly hired consultants are also CMAs, or at a minimum are with a year of acquiring that designation. One new consultant has just qualified as a CMA. He has asked you to sign his application. You agree. He has worked directly for you on a number of consulting assignments, and on that basis you consider him an outstanding management accountant with obvious partnership potential.

   As you go to sign his application paper, you notice that you are required to have known the candidate for two years. You have known him for only one year.

   What should you do? Please elaborate.

3. As the CFO of a retail firm, you and CEO have been discussing the acceptability of changing a sales practice to pull some of the next year's sales into the current year so that reported current earnings can be pushed up. The CEO wants to move $8 million in sales in order to increase current year earnings per share by 8%, the amount needed for him to get his full bonus from the board of directors.

   You explain to the CEO that on ethics basis you cannot condone the movement of $8 million in sales to the current year. The CEO counters that the $8 million is an immaterial amount.

   How should you reply to this?

SOLUTIONS TO SELF-TEST QUESTIONS

1. b, 2. a, 3. d, 4. b, 5. d, 6. d, 7. b, 8 a, 9. b, 10. c

ENDNOTES

1. Gay Gooderham and Jennifer La Trobe, "Measures Must Motivate," *Cost and Measurement,* October 1997, p. 52.

2. Peter Brewer, "Putting Strategy into the Balanced Scorecard," *Strategic Finance,* January 2002, pp. 44–52.

3. Raef Lawson, William Stratton, and Toby Hatch, "Scorecards and Dashboards— Partners in Performance," *CMA Management,* December–January 2007, pp. 33–37.

4. Christopher D. Ittner and David F. Larcker, "Coming Up Short on Nonfinancial Performance Measurement," *Harvard Business Review,* November 2003, pp. 88–95.

5. Jac Fitz-Enz, "Measuring Team Effectiveness," *HR Focus,* August 1997, p. 55.

6. Bob Hagerty, "Executive Pay (A Special Report)—Asian Scramble: Multinationals in China Hope Lucrative Compensation Packages Can Attract Local Executives They Desperately Need," *Wall Street Journal,* April 10, 1997, R12.

Chapter 13

Management Accounting Systems

LEARNING OBJECTIVES

After reading this chapter, you should be able to answer the following questions:

1 What
is a cost management system?

2 What
is a performance measurement system?

3 What
are the four stages of cost management and performance measurement systems?

4 How
did inventory systems evolve into enterprise resource planning systems?

5 How
do enterprise resource planning systems integrate cost management and performance measurement systems?

6 How
has Wal-Mart's enterprise resource planning system contributed to its outstanding success?

7 How
has the focus of management accounting changed with budgeting?

ON SITE

www.hbc.ca

The Hudson's Bay Company

THE HUDSON'S BAY COMPANY (Hbc) presently operates more than 500 retail outlets across Canada with four banners: The Bay, Zellers, Home Outfitters, and DealsOutlet.ca. As the oldest commercial organization in the world, Hbc has learned that it is necessary to change to survive, and no commercial organization has been more successful at surviving than Hbc.

Hbc was established in 1670 by a charter from King Charles II. Its first century of operation found Hbc firmly ensconced in a few forts and posts around the shores of James Bay and Hudson Bay; Aboriginal peoples brought furs annually to these locations to barter for manufactured goods such as knives, kettles, beads, needles, and blankets. By the late eighteenth century, competition had forced Hbc to expand into the interior, and a string of posts grew up along the great river networks of the west, foreshadowing the modern cities that would succeed them: Winnipeg, Calgary, and Edmonton.

In 1821 Hbc merged with its most successful rival, the North West Company, based in Montreal. The resulting commercial enterprise now spanned the continent all the way to the Pacific Northwest (Oregon, Washington, and British Columbia) and the North (what is now Alaska, Yukon, the Northwest Territories, and Nunavut). The merger also set the pattern of the company's growth, being the first of a series of notable acquisitions.

By the end of the nineteenth century, changing fashion tastes were contributing to the fur trade's decline. Western settlement and the Gold Rush quickly introduced a new type of client to Hbc: one that shopped with cash and not with skins. With the *Deed of Surrender* in 1869 between the Hbc and Canada, the company yielded sovereignty over its traditional territories to the new country and the retail era began. The company's focus shifted as it concentrated on transforming trading posts into saleshops, stocked with a wider variety of goods than ever before.

In 1912, with competition from Eaton's and following advice from one of its directors who was with Harrods department store in London, Hbc began an aggressive modernization program. The resulting original six Hbc department stores—in Victoria, Vancouver, Edmonton, Calgary, Saskatoon, and Winnipeg—are the living legacy of that period.

The growth of retail spurred Hbc into a wide variety of commercial pursuits during most of the twentieth century. The economic downturn of the 1980s caused Hbc to rethink its priorities and, like many other firms, return to its core business. Nonretail businesses were sold off. The pace of retail acquisition increased with takeovers of Zellers (1978), Simpsons (1978), Fields (1978), Robinsons (1979), Towers/Bonimart (1990), Woodwards (1993), and KMart Canada (1998) following in the tradition of Cairns (1921), Morgans (1960), and Freimans (1972).

Competition in the markets in which Hbc contends intensified after 1994 when Wal-Mart entered Canada by acquiring Woolco. Wal-Mart competes on low costs, which are possible because of (a) its large size, which enables it to buy direct from manufacturers at substantial discounts, and (b) its supply chain management, which coordinates via satellite the flow of inventory from suppliers around the world (generally, the manufacturers) to Wal-Mart stores around the world. Wal-Mart has set the standard in Canada, and Hbc must meet that standard in order to survive. Hbc has had to change to meet competition—something it has done throughout its long history.

Early in 2006 an American investor, Jerry Zucker, acquired all of Hbc's common shares. At that point, Hbc ceased to be a public company. In the three months prior to the approval of the acquisition by the Canadian government, Hbc lost more than $50 million, with sales falling as shoppers flocked to cheaper big-box alternatives such as Wal-Mart. That performance indicated that Hbc had not adjusted sufficiently to the new retail environment.

Mr. Zucker was planning to make the Hbc adjust. At the time, he stated: "We are committed to enhancing our customers' shopping experience through a substantially greater focus on service and revitalizing the spirit of the organization."

Unexpectedly and unfortunately Mr. Zucker died. In July 2008, NRDC acquired Hbc with the stated intention of merging it with Lord & Taylor an upscale U.S. department store.

SOURCE: Hbc annual reports, various years, www.hbcheritage.ca, www.hbc.ca

To compete, Hbc has had to establish an enterprise resource planning system (ERP). A management accounting system is a core component of any ERP system. Earlier chapters provided you with numerous ad hoc techniques for controlling costs and measuring performance: variously, Chapter 1 discussed strategy and the value creation chain; Chapter 2, terminology; Chapter 3, cost behaviours; Chapter 4, overhead and job order costing; Chapter 5, process costing; Chapter 6, budgeting; Chapter 7, standards and variances; Chapter 8, activity-based management and costing; Chapter 9, relevant costing; Chapter 10, cost control techniques; Chapter 11, responsibility costing; and Chapter 12, measuring and rewarding performance. Chapter 13 brings these techniques together as a management accounting system, which has two important components. The first of these is a cost management system, which focuses on managing and controlling activity costs. The second is a system for managing and controlling activities that go into the creation of value. After this, the chapter discusses the stages through which organizations evolve in developing cost management and performance measurement systems. For managing organizations, these two systems supplement the financial accounting system. The highest level is when ERP systems incorporate both cost management and performance measurement systems. The subsequent section discusses the Wal-Mart ERP system, a leader in integrating cost management and performance measurement. This chapter also discusses how contemporary ERP organizations use IT and colloboration to increase value creation.

The content of this final chapter is demanding. It requires you to integrate what you have learned in earlier chapters. Moreover, it assumes a contemporary ERP environment, one in which management accounting techniques have been selected on the basis of their ability to create value for strategic-oriented organizations.

COST MANAGEMENT SYSTEM

A **cost management system (CMS)** is a set of formal methods developed for controlling the costs of an organization's activities in its value creation chain relative to its goals and objectives. A CMS is not merely a system for minimizing the costs incurred by an organization. Rather, it should aid an organization in obtaining maximum benefits from incurring costs by helping managers:

- identify the cost of resources consumed in performing significant activities of the organization
- determine the efficiency and effectiveness of the activities performed
- identify and evaluate new activities that can improve the future performance of the organization
- accomplish the three previous objectives in an environment characterized by changing technology[1]

The information generated from the CMS should integrate and benefit all functional areas of the entity. As shown in Exhibit 13-1, the CMS should "improve the quality, content, relevance, and timing of cost information that managers use for decision making."[2]

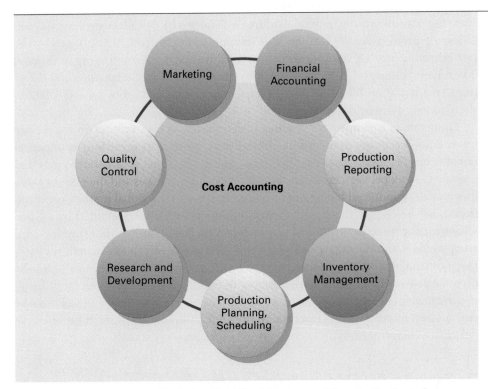

SOURCE: Robert McIlhattan, "The Path to Total Cost Management," *Emerging Practices in Cost Management*, p. 178, Warren, Gorham and Lamont. ©2003 Thomson/RIA, All rights reserved.

EXHIBIT 13-1
A Functionally Integrated Cost Management System

By crossing all functional areas (not simply accounting), a cost management system can be viewed as having five primary goals: (1) to develop reasonably accurate product/service costs; (2) to assess product/service profitability over the entire life of the product/service; (3) to improve understanding of internal processes and activities; (4) to control costs; and (5) to allow the pursuit of organizational strategies.

First and foremost, a CMS should provide the means to develop reasonably accurate product and/or service costs. Thus, the system must be designed to gather information in a manner that allows costs to be traced to products and services. It is not necessary that the system be "the most accurate one, but one which matches benefits of additional accuracy with expenses of achieving additional accuracy. The best system will report approximate, but inaccurate, product costs, with the degree of approximation determined by the organization's competitive, product, and process environment."[3] Traceability has been made easier by improved information technology, such as bar coding and the Internet.

The product/service costs generated by the CMS are the input to managerial processes. These costs are used to plan, prepare financial statements, assess individual products/services and period profitability, establish prices for outputs, and create a basis for performance measurement. If the input costs accumulated and assigned by the CMS are not reasonably accurate, the information output of the CMS will be inappropriate for control and decision-making purposes.

Although product/service profitability may be calculated periodically as a requirement for external reporting, the financial accounting system does not reflect life-cycle information. The CMS should provide information about the life-cycle cost of a product or service. Without life-cycle information, managers will not have a basis to relate costs incurred in one stage of the life cycle to costs and profitability of other stages. For example, managers may not recognize that increasing investment in the development and design stage of the life cycle could provide significant rewards in later stages by minimizing potential future costs caused by design, environmental pollution, or product recall. Further, if development/design cost is not traced to the related product or service, managers may not be able to recognize organizational investment "disasters." Finally, companies should take a long-term view and determine cost based on life-cycle relationships (rather than period-by-period relationships) among prices, profit margins, and costs.

To maintain a competitive position in an industry, an organization must generate information necessary to determine present and future costs regarding its organizational strategies. As discussed in Chapter 1, strategy is the set of long-term plans that provide the link between an organization's goals and objectives and the costs of activities actually conducted by the organization. In the current global market, organizations must be certain that such a linkage exists. Information provided by a CMS allows managers to perform strategic analyses on such issues as determining core competencies and managing organizational resources from a cost–benefit perspective, assessing the positive and negative financial and non-financial factors of investment and operational plans, and engaging in employee empowerment by utilizing new management techniques such as those discussed in Chapters 8 and 9. Thus, the cost management system is essential to the generation of information for effective resource management.

Designing a Cost Management System

Because a CMS is concerned with costs, it has been founded in part on accounting information. All accounting information is generated from one accounting system and one set of accounts. Although existing technology would allow companies to design different accounting systems for different purposes, most companies still rely on a single system to supply all accounting information. Historically, most accounting systems have been focused on providing information for financial accounting purposes, and their informational outputs must be adapted to meet most internal management requirements.

An activity-based costing (ABC) system is an alternative approach that can gather accurate cost information on products and customers. As noted in Chapter 8, ABC is an accounting information system that identifies the various activities performed in an organization and collects costs on the basis of the underlying nature and extent of the activities. ABC has been described as "an economic map of the organization's expenses and profitability based on organizational activities."[4] The concern of ABC is with determining and documenting the activities being undertaken by the organization's resources. With this activity information the costs are calculated for performing activities and processes. ABC also ascertains the activity requirements for producing the organization's products, services, and customers.

Four steps have been identified in developing an ABC system:

1. Develop the activity dictionary or list of activities.
2. Determine how much the organization is spending on each of its activities.
3. Identify the organization's products, services, and customers.
4. Select activity cost drivers that link activity costs to the organization's products, services, and customers.[5]

To be an economic map, an ABC system must, as Step 1, identify the activities being performed by the indirect or overhead costs. For example, the indirect costs related to supervision or ordering parts must be allocated to activities, and the costs of those activities will subsequently be allocated to products, services, and customers. After more than a decade of experience with implementing ABC systems, standard activity dictionaries have been developed that provide a template for determining the appropriate activity classification for nearly all overhead activities. For example, a set of activities for a purchasing function might include (1) developing specifications and obtaining a list of potential vendors; (2) sending specifications to prospective vendors and requesting quotes from them; and (3) reviewing submitted quotes against specifications and awarding orders. Activity dictionaries can vary, containing from as few as 10 activities to hundreds of activities and more, with more activities being related to size and complexity of the organization and the desire for detailed costs.

Step 2 is to attach indirect costs to activities. In effect, this involves attaching the respective indirect costs to the respective activity in the activity dictionary. For example, if the purchasing department has eight activities, the second step would be allocation of the total cost of the purchasing department to each of the activities. The allocation method may be based on asking employees where they spend their work time in percentage terms, by observing where they spend their time, etc.

GENERAL NEWS NOTE

The Dashboard for Managing

The dashboard is becoming very important. What is a dashboard? A dashboard for managing is comparable what you have in a car: it contains all the instruments or views you need to operate the car.

The dashboard is a new technique for pulling together all the information required by senior managers to effectively manage an organization. A number of firms make dashboards, including Net Suite, Salesforce.com, and Hyperion Solutions. A dashboard computerizes decision making. This is not a new idea, but the Internet has increased the effectiveness and efficiency of dashboards. It is estimated that 40% of the 2,000 largest companies use dashboards. Senior managers who use them include Steven A. Ballmer (Microsoft) and Ivan G. Seidenberg (Verizon). Seidenberg has said: "The dashboard puts me and more and more of our executives in real-time touch with the business . . . The more eyes that see the results we're obtaining every day, the higher the quality of the decisions we can make."

Dashboards are based on powerful programs. They provide crucial information for decision making that is often buried deep in the organization. GE's Consumer and Industrial Division tracks the number of orders coming in from each customer every day and compares those figures with targets. It also follows the production of all products, including lightbulbs and dishwashers, to ensure that all production lines are functioning at the planned levels.

SOURCE: Spencer Ante, "Giving the Boss the Big Picture," *BusinessWeek,* February 12, 2006, pp. 48–51.

Step 3 is to identify the activities' products, services, and customers. Products, services, and customers are the intended result of incurring indirect costs for activities. The indirect costs are first allocated to products and services, and then the same costs are allocated to the customers of those products and services.

Finally, in Step 4, the linkages between the activity costs in Step 2 and the products, services, and customers in Step 3 are made with what is called activity cost drivers. Cost drivers are what drive the activity costs in making the products and services for the customers. Activity drivers require substantial judgment. There is no single, obvious, and precise driver for every type of activity cost.

Three generic types of activity drivers form a framework for determining appropriate drivers: transaction, duration, and intensity.[6] Transaction drivers count how often an activity is done (e.g., number of truck tires inspected). Duration drivers represent the amount of time required for the activity (e.g., four hours to inspect a completed diesel motor). Intensity drivers charge directly for the time required for the activity (e.g., the cost to patent the truck transmission was $125,900, which included all legal fees plus out-of-pocket disbursements). To be an effective driver, the change in the driver level must be highly related or, more specifically, correlated with the costs of the activities.

LEARNING OBJECTIVE 2

What is a performance measurement system?

performance measurement system
a major set of financial and, particularly, nonfinancial performance measures for evaluating the performance of a manager, activity, or organizational unit

PERFORMANCE MEASUREMENT SYSTEM

A **performance measurement system** provides economic feedback to managers and operators about process efficiency and effectiveness.[7] ABC systems reveal the activities that must be undertaken to effectively produce products and services. Greater awareness of activities leads to the explicit management of the detailed activities, which is often called activity-based management. This requires nonfinancial information for feedback on activities, which allows for modification in the way activities are carried out in order to improve performance.

A performance measurement system should help managers and operators to comprehend business processes and organizational activities. Only by understanding how an activity is accomplished in terms of nonfinancial performance measures, and the reasons for performance variation, can managers make cost–benefit improvements in products and services. Managers desiring to implement new technology such as installing robotic assembly lines must identify the costs and benefits that will flow from such actions; these assessments can be made only if the managers understand how processes and activities affect the value creation chain.

Cost management systems are not sufficient. Knowing the costs is important and necessary, but managers need to know on an ongoing basis—hourly or at least daily—the efficiency and effectiveness of the performance of activities. Only by efficiently and effectively undertaking all activities can Canadian organizations be competitive in the global market. Activities can be controlled only when the activity is known and its performance monitored against reasonable expectations or standards. The information generated from a performance measurement system should also help managers measure and evaluate human and equipment performance and assess future decision alternatives. Financial and, particularly, nonfinancial measurements captured at different organizational levels can be combined and used for different purposes.

Lastly, to maintain a competitive position in an industry, an organization must generate performance information necessary to define and implement its strategies. Information provided by a performance measurement system allows managers to understand how well activities are being done. A performance measurement system for reporting on activity accomplishments complements a CMS, which reports on

How RONA Is Fine-Tuning Its Financials With Cutting Edge Tools

GENERAL NEWS NOTE

RONA, the hardware, home improvement, and gardening distributor and retailer, took its financial system to a new level by integrating value chain analytics (VCA) software and activity-based management (ABM) software to create route-to-market cost modelling for its substantial supplier base. These additions take cost efficiencies to a new level, and they will likely be adopted by other companies wanting more accurate cost allocations.

RONA managers had a need for such system improvements. They were not able to determine accurate costs. The company had merely used average costs to determine the cost of getting products from suppliers to its stores. The earlier costing system had incorporated RONA's transportation, labour, and other expenses to provide an appropriate cost per supplier. A margin was assigned to cover average costs. However, it was known that some products in the warehouses took more time and thus used more resources, but there was no way to accurately measure these costs. These shortcomings were aggravated by recent acquisitions that increased the supplier base by 1,000 and the number of stores to 535. To supply these stores, the company has 20 different processes in the warehouses, 40,000 SKUs to manage, and more than 3,000 vendors. In addition, the company has had to negotiate with vendors on as many as seven different stocking options.

RONA chose to install two integrated SAS systems—the VCA and the ABM. VCAs describe the relationship from vendor to warehouse or to satellite locations. RONA's 20 different processes are considered. ABM describes what occurs in the warehouse. VCA and ABM give a very accurate cost for a process from vendor to retail outlet. With such a specific breakdown, RONA can look at how each product or product family moves through its distribution system. For instance, one vendor may move everything through the warehouse, whereas it may be cheaper if some items are shipped directly to retail locations. Other items may simply be redirected (cross-docked) at the warehouse and shipped out immediately. Most analysis is done at the product family level, despite the availability of information at the detailed SKU level. The information provided by VCA and ABM allows RONA's management to make decisions on shipments from vendors to stores based on cost information on the various alternative warehouses and direct-to-store routes.

SOURCE: Robert Colman, "Route-to-Market Knowledge," *CMA Management*, February 2004, pp. 14–15.

the cost of activities. Thus, a performance measurement system is essential to the generation of information for effective resource management.

The activities that an organization undertakes should contribute to creating value for customers. The success of an organization in creating value for customers can be ascertained by evaluating or measuring the performance or success in carrying out the activities that create value for customers. The implementation of an ABC system is often an important step in understanding activities. The managing of activities to create customer value or activity-based management is equally important.

FOUR STAGES OF COST MANAGEMENT AND PERFORMANCE MEASUREMENT SYSTEMS

LEARNING OBJECTIVE **3**

What are the four stages of cost management and performance measurement systems?

Four stages have been identified for evolution of cost and performance measurement systems.[8]

Stage I:	Inadequate for financial reporting
Stage II:	Financial reporting-driven
Stage III:	Customized, managerially relevant, standalone
Stage IV:	Integrated cost management, financial reporting, and performance measurement

This sequence of systems or progression in the development of cost and performance measurement systems is premised on the belief that it is most elementary for organizations to accurately report product and other costs for external reporting purposes specified by law. Only after that can organizations develop cost management and performance measurement systems.

Stage I Systems

These relatively simple organizations of the first stage have cost systems that are inadequate for financial reporting. They are not able to record costs accurately and they do not have the means to accurately allocate overhead costs to products and services. Although these systems often exist in new organizations, they also exist in mature organizations that continue to use what is presently called legacy systems. Stage I systems have five characteristics that are consequences of the inability to accurately record and allocate costs:

- extensive amounts of time and resources needed to consolidate different reporting entities within the company and to close the books each accounting period
- unexpected variances at the end of each accounting period when physical inventories are reconciled
- large writedowns of inventory after internal and external audits
- many postclosing adjusting entries to financial accounts
- a general lack of integrity and auditability of the system.

Stage II Systems

Organizations with Stage II systems are able to meet financial reporting requirements and to collect costs accurately by responsibility centres (but not by activities and business processes). In other words, they are adequate for valuing inventory for financial reporting purposes and for preparing periodic financial reports. However, these systems produce highly distorted product costs because traditional allocation systems are used instead of ABC (see Chapter 8 for a discussion). Relatedly they have nonexistent or highly distorted customer costs and performance feedback that is too late, too aggregated, and too financial.

Stage II systems are able, shortly after the end of an accounting period, to prepare complete financial statements that require minimal postclosing adjustments. Product or service costing with Stage II systems reports individual product or service costs with the same simple and aggregate methods used for external financial reporting, to value inventory, and to measure cost of goods sold. The problems with Stage II are:

- the inability to estimate the cost of activities and business processes, and therefore the cost and profitability of products, services, and customers
- the inability to provide useful feedback to improve business processes

These deficiencies are a result of the financial reporting system that is being used for both product costing and performance measurement. Financial reporting systems, although appropriate for external reporting, do not operate at the activity level, which is necessary for accurate costing and performance measurement. Consequently, Stage II systems do not provide adequate information to managers for planning, decision making, and control.

Stage III Systems

When organizations operate at Stage III, they have all of the necessary systems, but the systems are freestanding rather than integrated. Freestanding systems lead to confusion because of inconsistent assessments among the three systems, which are:

- a traditional but well-functioning financial reporting system capable of basic accounting and transaction-capturing functions, such as preparing monthly and quarterly financial statements for external stakeholders
- one or more activity-based costing systems that use data from the financial reporting and other systems to measure the costs of organizational units, customers, products, services, processes, and activities

GENERAL NEWS NOTE

Hbc Adds Precision

Hbc has acquired SAS® Merchandise Intelligence to support its sales activities. The SAS system supports the following components of Hbc's retail performance:

- *Revenue optimization,* to analyze and predict how promotional pricing affects profitability.
- *Merchandise planning,* to increase revenue through improved merchandise selection and allocation.
- *Merchandise forecasting,* to improve accuracy in predicting customer demand.

Hbc's Jerry Zucker says that "improving our merchandise operations to perform more effectively and efficiently is a priority for Hbc's management team. This integrated approach to merchandise planning will not only provide our Company with the ability to better analyze, plan, and manage our business holistically, it will ensure that our customers are able to purchase the products they want, when they want them. By standardizing our planning frameworks, processes, and enabling systems, Hbc is well positioned to drive customer satisfaction levels to new heights."

According to SAS: "Having completely re-engineered its merchandising infrastructure, processes, and performance measures, Hbc selected SAS to provide the technology to drive its merchandising strategy and help coordinate its approach to merchandise planning across all channels of business."

Commenting on the SAS acquisition, Michael Rousseau, the president of Hbc, added: "The partnership between Hbc and SAS will ensure that people, process, and technology work in concert to enhance the experience of our customers. In order to enable best-in-class merchandising at Hbc, we had to find a strategic partner like SAS that had the retail domain expertise and the best retail software applications on the market. The ability to see the complete life cycle of merchandising and have retail intelligence solutions support that integrated view was crucial in our vision for [the SAS software]."

The SAS software has enabled HBC to develop a customer relationship management (CRM) system. Hbc's vice president of CRM and Loyalty (and co–chief privacy officer), Rob Shields, says that SAS's software code is extremely flexible for exploring "because the language is written in a way that is easy to understand and more intuitive than some of the other programming languages. You can create insertions into the code and deletions from the code without having to rewrite the entire programming set. You can save it and go back into it or not if you want. It is a very flexible way of looking at your data. Once it's in SAS, you can export it to spreadsheets or whatever seamlessly without any challenge."

He sees the advantages of CRM coming from what is done with the data. For example, "Often times we were in the position where we thought we were making the right decision and then we said 'Have we looked at what customers that will effect?' or 'What will they buy or stop buying as a result of that because it is a destination purchase?' And we have seen that 'Wow, maybe we shouldn't make the decision because we're going to jeopardize a bunch of things.'"

SOURCE: SAS, http://www.sas.com/industry/retail; Susan Maclean, "HBC Captures the CRM Value of Its Data," *IT World Canada*, September 2007, http://www.itworldcanada.com/a/IT-Focus/054ae9f4-a510-41ea-a56a-3ec23fe473fd.html; Neil Sutton, "HBC Puts IT Smarts into Its Merchandising Strategy," *IT Business*, http://www.itbusiness.ca/it/client/en/Home/News.asp?id=40143&bSearch=True.

- performance measurement systems of various types that provide front-line workers and their superiors with timely, accurate information—financial and nonfinancial—on the efficiency and effectiveness of activities and processes.

These Stage III organizations are often those with satisfactory Stage II financial reporting systems for accurately reporting to external stakeholders. These financial reporting systems are augmented by one or more ad hoc activity-based costing system to provide accurate cost information and are further augmented by one or more ad hoc performance measurement systems.

Stage IV Systems

Rather than separate systems for financial reporting, cost management, and performance measurement, Stage IV organizations have ABC and performance measurement systems that are integrated. Consequently, no fundamental conflict exists between the product costs from the ABC system and the external requirements for financial reporting. The ABC cost drivers are used for assigning overhead costs for both internal decision making and external financial reporting. Any allocations (i.e., nonmanufacturing costs) that do not comply with GAAP, regulatory requirements, or tax rules can be eliminated for external financial reporting. Simple attribute fields for activities can identify these noninventoriable costs for the system to eliminate them from product costs in inventory accounts.

The transition to Stage IV systems is generally facilitated by the installation of enterprise resource planning (ERP) systems that were discussed in Chapter 1. SAP, PeopleSoft, Great Plains, and Oracle are examples of organizations that provide ERP systems.

LEARNING OBJECTIVE 4

How did inventory systems evolve into enterprise resource planning systems?

materials requirement planning system
a computer simulated system that helps organizations plan by coordinating future production output requirements with individual future production input needs using a master production schedule

bill of materials
a document that contains information about product material components, their specifications (including quality), and the quantities needed for production

bottleneck
resource constraint

THE EVOLUTION OF INVENTORY SYSTEMS TO ENTERPRISE RESOURCE PLANNING[9]

ERP systems evolved from various inventory systems. The focus of inventory systems in the 1960s was on inventory control. Companies could afford to carry relatively large amounts of inventory and thus economic order quantity (EOQ)—discussed in Chapter 10—was used.

Companies in the 1970s could no longer afford as much inventory, which led to the introduction of **materials requirement planning** (MRP) **systems**. MRP is a computer simulation system to answer the questions of what, how many, and when inventory items are needed. MRP coordinates the future production output requirements with individual future production input needs using a master production schedule, which is developed from estimated sales information. Once projected sales and production for a product have been estimated, the MRP computer models access the product's **bill of materials** to determine all production components. Quantities needed are compared with current inventory balances. If purchases are necessary, the estimated lead time for each purchase is obtained from supplier information contained in an internal database. The model then generates a time-sequenced schedule for purchase and production of component requirements.

The master production schedule is integrated with the operations flow document to project the workload for each work centre from the master schedule. The workload is compared with the work centre's capacity to determine whether meeting the master schedule is feasible. Potential **bottlenecks**, or resource constraints, are identified so that changes in input factors (such as the quantity of a particular component) can be made. Then the MRP program is run again. This process is repeated until the schedule compensates for all potential bottlenecks in the production system. The ability to systematically and efficiently schedule all parts is a tremendous advantage to those adopting MRP systems.

MRP was good for manufacturers, but once they got these systems, more integration was demanded. Increased power and affordability of information technology led to improvements to MRP in the 1980s that resulted in the next stage of manufacturing systems, the MRP II or **manufacturing resource planning system**. This fully integrated system plans production jobs using the usual MRP method and also calculates resource needs such as labour and machine hours. MRP II involves manufacturing, marketing, and finance in determining the master production schedule, and also incorporates the financial accounting and financial management systems. Although manufacturing is primarily responsible for carrying out the master schedule, it is essential that appropriate levels of resources and sales support be available to make the plan work.

manufacturing resource planning system
a fully integrated system that uses the usual MRP method to plan production jobs and calculate resource needs involving manufacturing, marketing, and finance in determining the master production schedule; it also incorporates the financial accounting and financial management systems

The MRP models extended, rather than eliminated, the economic order concept. EOQ indicates the most economical quantity to order at one time, and MRP indicates which items of inventory to order at what points in time. The EOQ and MRP models are considered push systems of production control because they may cause inventory that is not currently needed to be purchased or produced. Such inventory must be stored—that is, pushed into storage—until needed by a work centre.

Then, in the early 1990s, continuing improvements in information technology allowed MRP to be expanded to incorporate all resource planning for the entire enterprise. Functional units such as product design, information warehousing, materials planning, capacity planning, communications systems, human resources, finance, and project management could now be included in the plan. Thus, the term *enterprise resource planning* (ERP) was coined. Then ERP systems were offered to nonmanufacturing companies that wanted to enhance competitiveness by most effectively using all their assets, including information. Wal-Mart and Hbc are examples of nonmanufacturing companies using ERP systems.

ENTERPRISE RESOURCE PLANNING SYSTEMS

LEARNING OBJECTIVE 5

How do enterprise resource planning systems integrate cost management and performance measurement systems?

Implementing an **enterprise resource planning** (ERP) **system** is a major undertaking. An ERP system has a common database or data warehouse that integrates all systems for all parts of the organization, including, for example, financial, manufacturing, sales, inventory, and human resources. By linking all systems with a data warehouse, an ERP system allows an organization to manage its activities holistically. An ERP system is able to include not just the parts of an organization but also its suppliers and customers. Consequently, an ERP system is able to integrate financial reporting, cost management, and performance measurement along with all other systems in an organization.

enterprise resource planning system
a fully integrated, full-service suite of software with a common database that can be used to plan and control resources across an entire organization

Implementation of an ERP system is a major challenge for all organizations. ERP systems consist of relatively rigid sets of software for processing transactions and information. In implementing an ERP system, there is minimal customization of the software to meet the organization's requirements. Standard software is less prone to errors, and with a shortage of skilled programmers, it is economically more viable to adjust the organization to the software than vice versa. Thus, instead of customizing software, the organization must change its business processes.

Supply Chain Imperatives

There are substantial cost reduction opportunities in a company's supply chain operations. Increases in energy costs have made these cost savings even more apparent. To be effective with supply chain costs, organizations need a high-level overview.

Supply chain leaders, including CANADIAN TIRE, PARMALAT CANADA, and WAL-MART, use "scenario modelling" to help them make the best possible decisions. Scenario modelling encompasses the following:

- Geographical location as it affects customer demand, sources of supply, and distribution centres (DCs).
- Annual inventory movement by distribution centre, sales by outlet, and movements from suppliers to suppliers' DCs to buyers' DCs to retail outlets.
- Costs to conduct the above activities.

The modelling also incorporates customer service and response time. It generates a baseline from which improvements can be measured. Ten questions need to be asked during the process of making a supply chain more efficient:

1. Do we have clear information about our transportation costs from business and information management reports?
2. Do we have contracts in place with our carriers/couriers, and are we able to arrive at a fair market price for those services, through negotiations, to support our business?
3. Do we apply a clear comparative analysis to determine the benefits of various service options to support our transportation strategy?
4. Is the fuel charge that is being assessed to us currently being used as a cost recovery or profit enhancer by our provider?
5. Do we understand the mechanics of the fuel charge and are there ways for us to negotiate different approaches to it?
6. In an environment where we prepay and add freight charges to our customers, are we able to reconcile to our internal general ledger accounts and amounts?
7. Do we understand how cubic- and linear-foot charges are applied by our carriers/couriers, and are there ways for us to negotiate terms?
8. Are there ways to load more into trucks to improve space use?
9. Can we take advantage of loading off-hours and arranging trucks to help offset peak travel and charge times?
10. When we purchase materials or finished goods from suppliers, how are they charging us for the freight portion, and are there different FOB terms that may be more advantageous for us?

SOURCE: Mike Croza, "Supply Chain Imperatives," *CMA Management,* December–January 2006, pp. 34–38, with permission of Certified Management Accountants of Canada.

business process redesign
when an organization changes its business processes

This is called **business process redesign**. There are three basic approaches for ERP business process redesign.[10]

- First, change all processes to achieve the ideal set of business processes. With these changes, there may be difficulties with implementing an ERP system as the new processes may be inconsistent with ERP system requirements.
- Second, accept the ERP design. This allows for fast implementation—and the saving of time, human energy, and money—because issues regarding process redesign are avoided. Generally, with this approach the disadvantage is the lack of flexibility; business processes that use the ERP vendor's design might not be sufficiently appropriate for the organization.
- Third, redesign with the ERP system in mind. This approach is often called "ERP design by default." The advantage of this approach is that for most processes the plain ERP system is adequate. For those few cases where customized software is crucial, the extra cost needs to be incurred.

The third approach, i.e., "(t)he path of least resistence is usually to meet [the ERP system] halfway and not to try to change the software to meet the organization's vision completely, but rather to accept a speedy implementation of 85 to 90% of [the] vision and get on with the business of doing business."

The re-engineering of business processes in conjunction with ERP would involve the elimination of technical and organizational bottlenecks, the improvement in quality of information, the replacement of out-of-date processes and activities, the integration of processes, and the reduction in standalone systems and interfaces.[11] Generally, process redesign is pursued before and after the ERP implementation. **Process re-engineering** (which involves more dramatic changes than process redesign) would need to be done prior to ERP implementation. The elimination of nonvalue-adding work and the automation of low-valuing work will allow employees to undertake truly value-adding work and to dramatically increase productive capacity. There are some common themes for process redesign:

- Forgetting about old business practices
- Organizing around continuous business processes aimed at getting products and services to customers
- Applying increasingly sophisticated information technology[12]

To be effective, an ERP system will contain an extensive **chart of accounts** or codes for accurate recording and tracking of activities and costs. The coding incorporates stable entities of a business, such as divisions, plants, stores, and warehouses. At a lower level there are codes for functions such as finance, production, sales, marketing, and materials management. There are also the traditional financial account codes such as assets, liabilities, revenues, and expenses, and the central ERP feature of coding processes, activities, and sub-activities.

There must be consistency of coding among all entities of an organization in order for all parts to relate to one another. In addition, by coding to the activity and sub-activity levels for entire organizations, the reach of ABC can be expanded via assigning business and corporate-level expenses to activities, as well as assigning brand, product line, and channel support costs. Direct costs are easy to assign to activities; indirect costs are more difficult but once they have been analyzed, it is easier to see how these indirect costs can be traced to activities with cause-and-effect relationships of activity cost drivers to cost objects such as products, services, and customers.

An important characteristic of an ERP system is the coding of activities that allows activity costs to be used to construct ABC for products and services as well as for periodic reporting. The same activity-based costs of an ERP system can be used for financial reporting to external parties. The ABC costs relevant for financial reporting are assigned according to GAAP. For example, manufacturing overhead can be assigned to products and then to the cost of goods sold or inventory. Nonmanufacturing overhead can be assigned as period costs. ABC costs would include marketing overhead, which could not be assigned to products. With ABC, the marketing overhead would be allocated with the relevant cost driver, but with financial accounting the marketing costs would be accumulated functionally as a period cost.

Global electronic commerce associations are recommending that retailers use 14-digit bar codes that accompany the UPC (universal product code).[13] Currently, North American goods have a 12-digit code and 13- or 14-digit codes are used elsewhere. With the existing 12-digit bar code in Canada, the first six digits identify the manufacturer, the next five identify the item, and the last is a check for ensuring correct scanning.

When an organization has an ERP system, it can access daily expenses for activities and processes as well as daily quantities for activity cost drivers. This daily access

process re-engineering
process innovation and redesign aimed at finding and implementing radical changes in how things are made or how tasks are performed to achieve substantial cost, service, or time reductions

chart of accounts
the list of all codes for recording transactions

to information on activity costs and activity drivers is much more efficient than pre-ERP systems, with which businesses often waited a month for the needed information. This feedback relates to costs and also to the cost of operations. Accordingly, ERP activity-based information is the basis of cost management and performance measurement—both are based on the activities that are done to create organizational value. Frequent information or feedback on costs and drivers of those costs facilitates learning, which makes for improved performance and decision making.

As the ERP system incorporates activities in terms of quantities of resources, including labour, a record of resource use is maintained. Therefore, performance can be measured in physical terms and compared to standards, which allows for the calculation of variances. This performance measurement at the activity level serves as a feedback system on efficiency and effectiveness. The confusion of monetary measures is erased, and what is actually happening with the conversion of resources into goods and services can be seen. Performance measurement deals with demand, the success in meeting that demand, delays, defects, backlogs, outputs, etc. More specifically, using the example of a courier company, a performance measure would be "percent of time when the parcels arrived when promised." In contrast, ABC would be concerned with the average cost—based on all variable and fixed costs—of delivering a parcel.

Performance measurement and ABC are complementary. ABC determines the costs of activities in dollar terms. ABC also allows the costs of activities to be compared intra- and interorganizationally. When activity costs exceed expectations, the changes that need to be made involve resource utilization and performance measurement.

With these ERP systems, organizations are becoming linked more and more closely with their suppliers and customers. This requires the exchange of information, which raises problems because there are different ways to classify information. One solution is a new approach to classifying information in the supply chain for subsequent use, called eXtensible Business Reporting Language (XBRL).[14] This is a standard data file structure that tags imformation with common definitions and that establishes rules for that information's use. All users of XBRL use the same terms, structure, and even charts of accounts. The result is that different organizations use comparable classifications, so that information can be electronically moved up and down the value creation chain with ease and accuracy.

WAL-MART'S ENTERPRISE RESOURCE PLANNING SYSTEM

Wal-Mart is now the world's largest company. At $250 billion in sales, Wal-Mart is an outstanding example of a successful retail strategy. Basically, the strategy is to offer customers everyday low prices on a broad assortment of merchandise, which is supported with a focus on store-level execution, rigid expense control, logistics superiority, and a corporate culture that emphasizes personal responsibility.[15] Wal-Mart's competitive advantage came from converging product lines or departments, and then establishing various store types to pursue its growth objectives. Sam Walton, who started with a single 16,000-square-foot store with 22 departments in Rogers, Arkansas, in 1962,[16] developed Wal-Mart into the world's largest retailer, whose store types now include:[17]

- *Wal-Mart Stores*: The national discount retailer offers a wide variety of general merchandise out of 36 departments that include family apparel, health and beauty aids, household needs, electronics, toys, fabrics and crafts, lawn and garden, jewellery, and shoes.

- *Superstores*: The growing demand for one-stop shopping led to Wal-Mart's decision in 1988 to open a full-line grocery department in many of its new stores. These Superstores generally include 36 departments and from 100,000 to 210,000 square feet of retail space. A 109,000-square-foot format that includes innovative features has been particularly popular in recent years.[18]

- *Sam's Clubs*: These members-only warehouse or volume sales outlets have approximately 3,500 different items appealing to local businesses. Merchandise is typically in larger institutional sizes or multipacks of like or assorted items, and includes a complete line of food products and frozen foods, janitorial products, tires, batteries, auto supplies, computers and equipment, etc.

- *Neighborhood Market*: At 42,000 to 55,000 square feet, these stores offer about 28,000 items that include groceries, pharmaceuticals, and general merchandise.

- *International*: Since 1991, Wal-Mart has established more than 1,000 outlets in nine countries. For example, Wal-Mart is already the largest retailer in Canada and Mexico.[19]

- *walmart.com*: The business of selling to customers was brought to the Internet store, which has yet to become a significant part of operations.

- *Specialty Divisions*: These include Tire & Lube Express, Wal-Mart Pharmacy, Wal-Mart Vacations (cruises, vacation packages, car rental and hotel discounts, select theme park tickets), and Wal-Mart's Used Fixture Auctions (allows for the resale of fixtures for reuse in another location).

Outsourcing has contributed to Wal-Mart's success. Private brands have been avoided. With outsourcing, Wal-Mart differentiates itself by reaching back into the value creation chain to influence the goods it acquires, in effect by forcing suppliers to adhere to Wal-Mart's performance and cost expectations, as implied in the following quote:

> Suppliers are treated as part of the family, once they have proved their worth. Nervous newcomers are shown to "the row," a long corridor of drab rooms, each adorned with a notice explaining that Wal-Mart buyers do not accept bribes. It is like a scene from a bazaar: sweaters spill out of suitcases and haggling over prices continues all day. Angel Burgos, from Puerto Rico, wants to sell computers to Wal-Mart: "We were grapes," he sighs, "but now we are raisins. They suck you dry." . . . Proven suppliers, though, feel differently. Through Wal-Mart's proprietary systems, they are given full and free access to real-time data on how their products are selling, store by store. By sharing information that other retailers jealously guard, Wal-Mart allows suppliers to plan production runs earlier and so offer better prices. Procter & Gamble's $6 billion-a-year business with Wal-Mart is so important that the maker of Crest toothpaste has a 150-strong Bentonville office dedicated to it. Andy Jett, a director there, says Europe's retailers are still blind to the competitive edge that partnering with suppliers gives Wal-Mart. "Wal-Mart treats suppliers as extensions of its company. All retailers will eventually work this way," he predicts.[20]

In Canada, Wal-Mart has outsourced logistics and distribution to the U.K.-based Tibbet & Britten, one of the world's 10 largest logistic and supply chain management organizations.

Part of Wal-Mart's success has come from its use of information technology. Low-cost information has been used to link the manufacturers with the stores with minimal inventory in transit and no excess inventory in stores. Even in the late

Wal-Mart's use of ERP has contributed to its success as one of the world's leading retailers.

1980s and early 1990s, Wal-Mart's systems logged every item sold, automatically kept warehouses informed of the merchandise to be ordered, and directed the flow of goods not only to the stores but also to the proper shelves.[21] A related benefit from the low-cost information was Wal-Mart's early adoption of uniform product code (UPC) technology, which is used for point-of-sale electronic scanning for keeping accurate track of product movement.

Wal-Mart's information system, "Retail Link," is an ERP system plus a supply chain management (SCM) system, which integrates its electronic data interchange (EDI) network with an extranet used by Wal-Mart buyers and some 10,000 suppliers to gather and disseminate information about sales and inventory levels in every store.[22] Retail Link allows the world's largest organization to be managed, to grow, and to prosper. It allows Wal-Mart and its suppliers to make decisions to optimize the acquisition and sale of merchandise, control its suppliers, manage multiple product lines, and manage stores around the world.

McKinsey Global Institute (MGI), the research arm of the McKinsey consulting organization, found that Wal-Mart directly and indirectly caused the bulk of U.S. retail trade productivity, which contributed to 0.31 percentage points of the 1.33-percentage-point total growth in the U.S. economy from 1987 to 1999.[23] Wal-Mart maintained a significant productivity advantage over other general merchandiser retailers. Market share for Wal-Mart was 9% in 1987, 27% in 1995, and 30% in 1999. The authors of the MGI report attribute Wal-Mart's success to the improvement in the organization of functions and tasks through enablement by information technology, which is epitomized by Retail Link. Four improvements in Wal-Mart's organization of functions and tasks were noted by MGI:

- the more extensive use of cross-docking and better flow of goods/palleting to maximize in-store labour efficiency, which was enabled by "sScan" or other electronic supply chain management tools
- the use of forecasting tools to better align staffing levels with demand
- the redefining of store responsibilities and cross-training employees through the pooling of labour across aisles and organization of tasks such as price changes on a functional rather than departmental level
- the improvement of productivity measurement and utilization rates at check-out

The MGI authors note that the first two sources are possible because of information technology. The third and fourth sources are the result of continual process improvement and managerial innovation. Furthermore, the authors estimate that information technology contributed approximately one-half of the growth in Wal-Mart's productivity improvement.

Shattering ERP Misconceptions

For most finance people, the reality of moving enterprise resource planning (ERP) applications to an outsourced, Web-based environment is lost in a fog of misconceptions. "How can I control it if it's off-site?" is one of the most popular refrains among executives considering the application service provider (ASP) model. In fact most ERP-as-ASP solutions blend product and service offerings as well as Web and non-Web architectures, and provide little or no drop off in control compared with on-site platforms.

Chief financial officers (CFOs) considering hybrid solutions must correct common misconceptions about ASP solutions and evaluate the value proposition of moving toward an ERP system accessed over the Internet. Then, they can better determine how to expand the ERP footprint within their organization and decide whether that solution should have one or both feet on the Web.

They have many choices. Under the most basic level of ASP service, a company chooses a service provider to run its applications, house and run its IT equipment, and provide continuous access to the software—a "ping, power, and pipe" arrangement. At the other end of the spectrum, "the highest level is when the [ASP] partner purchases all of the equipment, puts the company's applications on it, answers all help desk and tech support calls, and makes all the changes to the application," notes Pete Koltis, an ANDERSEN partner based in Miami. Most of the ERP-via-ASP arrangements are closer to the basic end of the spectrum and require the client company's IT personnel to write any custom reports finance executives need. Koltis says that large ERP software vendors like PEOPLESOFT and ORACLE would rather establish standard, "vanilla" environments that their clients can customize.

Another twist on the ASP model is when a company serves as its own host. Some businesses do not use an external service provider at all but, rather than installing ERP software on every end-user's desktop, provide access to the applications via the Internet or an intranet. This approach lets IT departments centrally manage the software, and the only application end users need on their desktop is a Web browser.

Managing Misconceptions

As CFOs evaluate the array of potential ERP solutions, one myth they must address is the idea that a hosted ERP system must be all-Web or have no Web capabilities. A new breed of accounting applications, called "loosely coupled," offer a mix of locally installed products with services delivered over the Internet. Evidence of such loose couplings appears in recent ERP software releases. And the three largest ERP vendors have all added, or recently enhanced, consulting services.

Many companies that continue to invest in traditional accounting solutions have begun to use Web-based services to optimize their systems. "We have no doubt that we're moving to a Web-based ERP," notes Jean Braaten, financial reporting director of HIRSH INDUSTRIES in Des Moines, Iowa, "but we're not there quite yet." Instead, the consumer durables manufacturer invested in an offline upgrade to its SAP suite while asking Web-based consultants to help it get the most out of the new version.

Similarly prevalent—but false—is the notion that companies must give up control and sacrifice security to use the ASP model. Kyle Lambert, vice president of information solutions for Portland, Ore.-based JOHN I. HAAS INC., the largest domestic grower of hops, recently implemented Oracle's Web-based version 11i. "One of the concerns we heard was 'How are we going to manage systems and software that aren't on-site?'" he says. "Is that going to be secure, and what level of access will we have to those systems and to those boxes?" These questions came mainly from the user community and non-IT executives. "It was a curious statement for them to make because most of them had never seen the boxes in the first place," he adds. "It was truly a perception issue."

Haas' CFO, to whom Lambert reports, previously used a wide-area network (WAN) to access the company's ERP system. "He had always used remote services," Lambert adds. "My staff is located primarily in Yakima, Washington, supporting a number of sites remotely. When I put it in those sorts of contexts, he and other executives became much more comfortable with the concept."

SOURCE: Eric Krell, "Shattering ERP Misconceptions," *Business Finance*, February 2002, pp. 25–26. Reprinted by permission of *Business Finance* magazine, www.bf.mag.com

LEARNING OBJECTIVE 7

How has the focus of management accounting changed with budgeting?

COLLABORATION IN THE VALUE CREATION CHAIN

This chapter, along with Chapter 1, describes the contemporary business environment, in which the firms in a value creation chain are linked together electronically, with increasing functionality from a management accounting perspective. Chapter 1 discussed how various suppliers and buyers, such as aggregators and disseminators, must collaborate to create value for customers. This section provides an example of how electronic linking increases value. Specifically, the example shows how management accounting is focusing more on interfirm activities in addition to intrafirm activities, and on real or physical quantities and not simply dollar quantities.

Representatives of about 20 retail, manufacturing, and software firms, including Wal-Mart and Hbc, have been collaborating on techniques for starting and operating inventory distribution centres. Traditionally, supply chains have had to contend with two distribution centres (see below). This system of two distribution centres is expensive, especially when inventory begins to accumulate in either distribution centre or when there are stock-outs. These inventory imbalances arise because the "partners" are not sharing information on inventory needs. The solution proposed by this group is Collaborative Planning, Forecasting, and Replenishment (CPFR).

Manufacturer → Manufacturer's → Retailer's → Retailer's
                  Distribution   Distribution   Stores
                  Centre   Centre

The CPFR group has a clear purpose: to get suppliers (manufacturers) and buyers (retailers) to "work together to optimize the flow of inventory into the retail distribution centre and out to the store network." A key recommendation of the CPFR group is for suppliers to share the responsibility for distribution centres (DCs). The two partners—the retail buyers and the manufacturer-suppliers—need to use their collective insights to improve the availability of inventory at DCs.

From CPFR's perspective, most consumer products carried by large retail chains today are shipped first to the retailer's DC and from there to stores. Under this traditional replenishment model, the retailer's buyers use independent systems and processes to generate purchase orders for upstream suppliers. These purchase orders are usually submitted by EDI, fax, and Internet for immediate or almost immediate execution. The suppliers fill each purchase order from available inventory, and delivery is arranged through established routes. CPFR sees five inefficiencies in this system:

- The supplier has a limited view of the retailer's demand requirements.
- The buyer may be without category/market insights that would result in better forecasts and orders.
- The two partners forecast their needs independently of each other.
- Supply chain deficiencies encourage both suppliers and buyers to carry buffer stock to avoid unfavourable surprises.
- Supply chain deficiencies lead to adversarial relations between suppliers and buyers.

When it comes to ordering and delivering inventory, the traditional relationship between suppliers and buyers is inefficient—it suffers from a lack of cooperation. To boost efficiency, the partners need to develop a collaborative strategy and a joint business plan, probably on an annual or quarterly basis. They must work together to understand the impact on inventories from planned events and budgets. For example, buyers need to convey plans for events and budgets; when they do, the suppliers can then ensure that appropriate inventories are available when the buyers require them.

When such information is shared, suppliers can ship inventory as required. This information sharing must be ongoing so that the two partners can capture revisions to budgets brought about by changing retail conditions.

Changes during the year to sales, and therefore to inventory expectations, are normal. When buyers do not share information about retail cycles, and instead simply place orders as inventory needs arise, suppliers face problems, for they will not always have inventory on hand in the desired quantities. The result will be inventory deficits. Sharing budgets and inventory forecasts is a way to ensure that suppliers will be able to meet buyers' requirements.

CPFR has a four-step collaboration process for buyers and suppliers:

1. *Strategy and planning.* The buyer (retailer) and supplier (manufacturer) develop a working agreement for sharing information. They also develop a joint business plan.
2. *Demand and supply management.* The buyer presents a monthly sales forecast for at least one year for suppliers to incorporate into their production plans.
3. *Execution.* The buyers generate orders, and the suppliers fill those orders.
4. *Analysis.* The buyer and supplier monitor sales and shipments. In response to variations, they adjust the sales forecasts and order plans. Later, they calculate the performance indicators specified in the agreement and also periodically assess progress toward goals, taking corrective action as necessary.

The CPFR's collaborative planning, forecasting, and replenishment process requires the sharing of detailed information, such as the following:

- What events will take place during a given time period (typically the next 6 to 12 months)?
- When will events take place (i.e., start and end)?
- What brands and SKUs will be included in each event?
- How will the events be classified (e.g., supplier promotion, holiday sale)?
- What tactics will be used with events (e.g., store display details, features, displays, ads)?
- Which store locations will be targeted to participate?
- What pricing and cost sharing arrangements will buyer and supplier make?

The point of sharing detailed information is to ensure that events are designed to achieve optimal performance, which happens when both the buyer and the supplier are prepared to execute their responsibilities carefully. For example, when the buyer informs a supplier about events and products to be promoted, that supplier will be more likely to meet the buyer's requirements.

CPFR takes planning, forecasting, and budgeting to a more detailed level, often expressed as "more data granularity." Sales forecasting starts with past retail point-of-sales (POS) data. Though the concern is with future sales, past sales are used to establish a starting point, especially with regard to daily, weekly, and seasonal patterns. Nevertheless, POS data will be detailed by electronic product codes. POS data can be considered along three dimensions:

- By day and week.
- By location (store, DC, region, etc.). and
- By product (at a detailed code level consistent with ordering).

With CPFR, suppliers can obtain POS data at different levels, the most common being DC-level data summarized by week. With this detailed information on past sales, the retailer can develop forecasts and share them with suppliers. Forecasts consider three elements:

- *Base.* CPFR calls this the "turn" component. It represents regular demand without the effects of particular events.

- *Season.* Many sales are based on repetitive factors such as climate and holidays. These sales need to be considered separately.
- *Promotions.* The impact of special promotions, advertising, and the like should also be considered separately.

Store-level sales forecasting provides a starting point for order planning. Order planning determines what the buyer and supplier must do through a time-phased sequence of orders, shipments, and receipts. Order planning considers two paths. Though no inventory may be held at the retailer's DC level—as with Wal-Mart cross-docking or flow-through—both the DC-to-store path and supplier–to-DC-to-buyer-DC path must be planned. When inventory is held at the DC, the replenishment calculation must be made for the DC-to-store path and subsequently for the supplier-to-DC-to-buyer-DC path.

To be effective, the sales forecast and the order forecast should be linked, equivalent (i.e., the order must proceed the sale), and accurate. Thus, there should be a dynamic synchronized process so that when changes are made to the sales forecast, it automatically modifies the order forecast. Put another way, the two forecasts should be completely interdependent. According to CPFR, these forecasts and the collaboration provide the supplier with the answer to, "What is my customer going to order and when?" CPFR identifies a number of variables that must be considered in order to ensure accurate forecasts:

- On-hand and on-order situations for the buyer.
- Order cycle and order frequency policies.
- Adjustments to inventory policies regarding safety stock requirements—service levels, weeks of supply, and so on.
- Shipping requirements with regard to item minimums and maximums, order minimums and maximums, and so on.
- Lead times.
- Unit translations, such as order packages of 4, 12, 144, and so on.
- Retailer DC-to-DC transfers.

In developing a single shared sales forecast, suppliers can shift from a "build to stock" to a "build to order" approach to inventory replenishment. This approach can greatly reduce dependence on buffer inventory. CPFR says this approach greatly reduces inefficiencies noted at the beginning of this section. It also changes the work on management accountants from static to dynamic forecasts and budgets.[24]

SITE ANALYSIS

The Hudson's Bay Company

Hbc has six related retail businesses—The Bay, Zellers, Home Outfitters, Designer Depot, Fields, and DealsOutlet.ca—and has sought to simplify and have fewer different systems. Consequently, it has developed shared support services to provide its accounting, inventory ordering and delivery, etc. In 1998, it launched a major transformation of its entire infrastructure with the intent of driving customer service issues at the front end and inventory management issues at the back end, and with an overall expense reduction. Hbc formalized a strategy called

"One Hbc" that was to enable it to become a shopping solution to Canadians through the following business model initiatives:

- leveraging the breadth of products and services offered throughout its retail channels
- aligning customer touchpoints, logistics, and retail enablement, creating a common front to the customer through credit cards, loyalty programs, and gift cards
- creating a seamless, cost-effective back office that supports the distinct customer-focused formula

Information technology is a major part of the new business model. Since 2000, Hbc has been shifting from a traditional mainframe-centric approach to one that matched the company's products and customer needs. It created a strategic alliance with IBM and Oracle to work together for the installation of a Retek—a retail-specific application that is an ERP system for retail businesses. It links all aspects of the supply chain from buying product, transportation, storage, store inventory, and sales to increase effectiveness (inventory in stock) and efficiency (transportation and inventory costs). Leading global retailers such as Tesco, Best Buy, Gap Inc., Sainsbury's, Eckerd Corp., and Selfridges have installed Retek.

Retek was introduced at Zellers in 2000. It enabled Zellers to achieve the highest in-stock position in its recorded history while reducing inventory levels. Retek was implemented at The Bay in 2002, also to enhance inventory control and merchandising capabilities. Improvements and refinements are ongoing. Retek has a very detailed chart of accounts for operating the merchandising or inventory systems. The information on physical inventory is joined to the financial chart of accounts through Hbc's Oracle financial ERP system, which has a specialized retail accounting module, an HR module, etc. These two ERP systems allow the financial chart of accounts to be part of a supply chain. To ensure survival, Hbc is competing with its supply chain.

SOURCES: Hbc annual reports, various years, www.hbc.ca, www.cisco.com/en/US/strategy/retail/hudsons_bay.html, www.retek.com/company, www.computerworld.com/managementtopics/management/story/0,10801,71034,00.html.

CHAPTER SUMMARY

Management accountants provide information for managers' planning, controlling, performance-evaluation, and decision-making needs. In the current environment, those duties are being done with ERP systems. Cost management and performance measurement are increasingly part of ERP systems.

1 What is a cost management system?

A cost management system is a set of formal methods developed for controlling the costs of an organization's activities in its value creation chain relative to its goals and objectives. The emphasis is on managing costs, and not on minimizing costs.

2 What is a performance measurement system?

A performance measurement system provides economic feedback to managers and front-line workers about process efficiency and effectiveness. It assists them with comprehending business processes and organizational activities.

3 What are the four stages of cost management and performance measurement systems?

The four stages of cost management and performance measurement systems are: inadequate for financial reporting; financial reporting-driven; customized, managerially relevant, standalone; and integrated cost management, financial reporting, and performance measurement.

4 **How did inventory systems evolve into enterprise resource planning systems?**
For decades economic order quantity had been used to specify optimal order size. Computerized materials requirement planning (MRP) not only specified optimal order sizes, but it also specified the what, how many, and when for inventory. Manufacturing resources planning (MRP II) expanded MRP to include production scheduling. MRP II was further expanded to ERP when all parts of the firms wanted and received electronic linkages to inventory and manufacturing.

5 **How do enterprise resource planning systems integrate cost management and performance measurement systems?**
Enterprise resource planning systems have common databases that integrate all systems for all parts of organizations, including those involved with cost management and performance measurement.

6 **How has Wal-Mart's enterprise resource planning system contributed to its outstanding success?**
Wal-Mart has used its ERP capacity to link all aspects of its operations together, thereby increasing effectiveness and reducing costs.

7 **How has the focus of management accounting changed with budgeting?**
Increasingly, organizations are doing dynamic, interorganizational, and detailed budgeting. Moreover, these budgets are denominated in physical units rather than being restricted to abstract dollar amounts.

Key Terms

Bill of materials (p. 788)
Bottleneck (p. 788)
Business process redesign (p. 790)
Chart of accounts (p. 791)
Cost management system (p. 780)
Enterprise resource planning system
  (p. 789)

Manufacturing resource planning
  system (p. 789)
Materials requirement planning
  system (p. 788)
Performance measurement system
  (p. 784)
Process re-engineering (p. 791)

End-of-Chapter Materials

SELF-TEST QUESTIONS

(SOLUTIONS APPEAR AT THE END OF THE CHAPTER.)

1. Which of the following is not a stage of cost management and performance measurement systems?
    a. Inadequate for financial reporting
    b. Financial reporting driven
    c. Customized, managerially relevant, standalone
    d. Wal-Mart ERP

2. A cost management system and a performance measurement system are:
    a. Complements
    b. Substitutes
    c. Part of a financial accounting system
    d. Stage II systems

3. Which of the following is incorrect regarding Stage IV systems?
    a. ABC is included
    b. Cost management and performance measurement systems are integrated
    c. GAAP statements are prepared
    d. PeopleSoft would not be included

4. What allows an ERP system to tie all types of information together?
   a. Cost management systems
   b. Performance measurement systems
   c. Financial accounting systems
   d. Codes

5. What is used by Wal-Mart to track products that are purchased and sold?
   a. JIT
   b. Uniform product codes
   c. Fields
   d. Rows

6. What is not a theme for process redesign?
   a. Forgetting about old business practices
   b. Organizing around continuous business processes aimed at getting products and services to customers
   c. Applying increasingly sophisticated information technology
   d. Reducing costs

7. Which is not one of the basic approaches for business process redesign when implementing an ERP system?
   a. Re-engineer all processes to achieve an ideal set of business processes
   b. Accept the ERP design
   c. Redesign with the ERP system in mind
   d. Implement a cost management system

8. Which dimension is not for considering POS data?
   a. Time—day and week
   b. Dollar amount
   c. Location—store, DC, region, etc.
   d. Product—at a detailed code level consistent with ordering

9. With detailed information on past sales, forecasts are developed by the retailer (buyer) for sharing with the manufacturer (supplier). Forecasts consider three elements. Which is not one of the three?
   a. Base forecast
   b. Seasonal
   c. Daily
   d. Promotional

10. CPFR has a four-step collaboration process for the buyer and supplier. Which is not one of these steps?
    a. Strategy and planning
    b. Managing
    c. Execution
    d. Analyzing

QUESTIONS

1. How can a cost management system help managers?
2. What are the five primary goals of a cost management system?
3. Identify examples of useful information that could be provided to a cost management system by each of the functional areas shown in Exhibit 13-1.
4. Identify examples of useful information that could be provided to a performance measurement system by each of the functional areas shown in Exhibit 13-1.
5. Why would management be willing to accept "inaccurate" costs from the cost management system? What sacrifices would be necessary to obtain "accurate" costs?
6. What are examples of costs that a cost management system might treat differently for internal and external purposes? Why would these treatments be appropriate?
7. Why would an organization have multiple control systems in place?
8. What is a performance measurement system?
9. Why is a performance measurement system necessary if an organization has a cost management system?
10. How does a performance measurement system help an organization remain competitive?
11. What are the four stages of cost management and performance measurement systems? Be sure to describe each stage.
12. Compare Stage III and Stage IV in regard to the use of enterprise resource planning systems. In which of these stages is there the greatest integration?
13. What are some brands of enterprise resource planning systems?
14. Discuss the database used with enterprise resource planning systems.
15. What are the three basic approaches for enterprise resource planning system business process redesign?
16. What is a chart of accounts? How is a chart of accounts used with an ERP system?

17. What is Wal-Mart's information system called? What does it do?

18. What were the four improvements in Wal-Mart's organization of functions and tasks?

19. What classification of factors is important in designing performance measurement systems? What is that one term that describes these factors?

20. What kind of organizations implement ERP systems?

21. What two distribution centres are discussed by CPFR? Why?

22. What is the basis on which the theory of DC replenishment works?

23. Name the two parts of strategy and planning in CPFR's DC replenishment overview model.

EXERCISES

1. (LO 1, 2, 3, 4, 5, 8) Match each lettered item in the left-hand column with a numbered item in the right-hand column.

a. Cost management system	1. Wal-Mart's information system (i.e., its enterprise resource planning and supply chain management systems)
b. Performance measurement system	
c. Stage II system	
d. Stage III system	2. Collaborative planning, forecasting, and replenishing
e. Business process redesign	
f. Process re-engineering	3. Regular demand without the effects of particular events
g. Retail Link	
h. Base forecast	4. Financial reporting driven
i. CPFR	5. Integrated cost management, financial reporting, and performance measurement
j. Stage IV system	
	6. Customized, managerially relevant, standalone
	7. A formal set of methods for providing feedback about activity or process efficiency
	8. Modest or minor changes to an organization's activities and processes
	9. A formal set of methods for controlling the costs of an organization's activities
	10. Major changes to an organization's activities and processes

2. (LO 1, 2, 3) The following words or phrases describe or are associated with one of the stages of cost management and performance measurement systems. Categorize them as "I" for Stage I, "II" for Stage II, "III" for Stage III, and "IV" for Stage IV.

a. Extensive amounts of time needed to consolidate different reporting entities and to close the books each period

b. All necessary systems, albeit with inconsistency

c. Existence of an ERP system

d. No conflict among the three systems

e. Not able to record costs accurately

f. Simple organization

g. Financial reporting supplemented by *ad hoc* ABC and performance measurement systems

h. Financial reporting used for both product costing and performance measurement

i. Adequate for valuing inventory for financial reporting purposes, but no more

EXERCISES

  j. Completely integrated financial reporting, cost management, and performance measurement

  k. All necessary systems—but freestanding

  l. Able to meet financial reporting requirements, but not able to collect costs accurately by responsibility centre

  m. Traditional cost allocation methods used rather than ABC

  n. Legacy systems

3. (LO 5) Beside each of the following, indicate where the word or phrase refers to business process redesign (BPR) or process re-engineering (PRE).

  a. Accept 80% to 90% of the vision

  b. Forget old business practices

  c. Eliminate technical and organizational bottlenecks

  d. Organize around continuous businesses aimed at getting products and services to customers

  e. Apply increasingly sophisticated information technology

  f. Drastic changes

  g. Accept the ERP design, thus minimal changes

  h. Change all processes to achieve an ideal

  i. Design process with the ERP system in mind

4. (LO 1) Prepare a brief report on how cost management information can (a) help and (b) hinder an organization's progress toward its mission and objectives.

5. (LO 1) In groups of four or five students, develop an activity dictionary for the specific organization where one member of the group worked or works. The organizational subject should be the part of the organization where the student worked or works, and not the entire organization. For example, if the student worked for McDonald's in serving customers, then the subject should be order taking, order preparation, change making, order delivering, etc., activities. Generally, the work of an employee can be classified into six to eight meaningful activities.

6. (LO 2) Assume that you are an accountant who is considering employment with one of two organizations. The first organization is a fast-growing technology organization. Its sales are $500 million per year, with annual sales projected to grow at a rate of 22% over the next five years. The other organization is in a mature industry in which approximately 12 organizations are fiercely competing to maintain market share and profitability. This organization has annual sales of $2 billion. Prepare a brief report in which you discuss how your job focus and daily activities would likely vary between the two organizations.

7. (LO 2) Performance measurement systems are expected to provide information on the efficiency and effectiveness of operations sufficiently and frequently as to allow adjustments to correct shortcomings. For the deli counter of a large grocery store, specify a performance measurement system.

8. (LO 3) Form groups of three or four students to discuss the types of documents and information you would expect to be produced by a Stage I organization. How frequently would this information be produced?

9. (LO 3) Form groups of three or four students to discuss the types of documents and information you would expect to be produced by a Stage II organization. How frequently would this information be produced?

10. (LO 3) Form groups of three or four students to discuss the types of documents and information you would expect to be produced by a Stage III organization. How frequently would this information be produced?

11. (LO 3) Form groups of three or four students to discuss the types of documents and information you would expect to be produced by a Stage IV organization. How frequently would this information be produced?

12. (LO 4) Explain how enterprise resource planning systems developed from materials requirement planning. Be sure to mention the information technology equipment and software used at each key stage.

13. (LO 5) What systems would you expect to be integrated with an ERP system? How does an ERP system facilitate reconciliation among different systems?

14. (LO 5) What is a chart of accounts? Why is it important for an ERP system?

15. (LO 5, 6) Wal-Mart is the world's largest retailer and easily argued to be the world's most successful retailer. How does Retail Link contribute to Wal-Mart's success?

16. (LO 6) In this text, Wal-Mart and Dell have been used as examples of organizations that have pioneered value creation chains that have set the standards for their respective competitors. Specify two or three critical success factors for Wal-Mart. Do the same for Dell.

17. (LO 6) At the present time, how are Canadian retailers reacting to the competition from Wal-Mart? Are they meeting the Wal-Mart competition? What do you expect to be the impact of Wal-Mart for the next decade?

18. (LO 7) Describe how inventory flows from a manufacturer to a retail store. Be sure to mention the location of distribution centres and the methods for minimizing time from manufacturer to sale to a retail customer.

19. (LO 7) What are some characteristics of the relationship between buyers and suppliers that lead to inefficiencies?

20. (LO 7) Describe the CPFR replenishment cycle.

PROBLEMS

The problems included with Chapter 13 draw upon topics from the various chapters of the book and can be found on the instructor and student companion sites at http://www.mallouk3e.nelson.com.

CASES

1. You have been hired by BarCode Extraordinaire Inc., a manufacturer, distributor, and service specialist for point of sale equipment and related software. The president has been concerned with the product costing and performance measurement systems, although the accounting employees are less concerned. As an initial investigation, he has hired you to make some preliminary inquiries about the validity of the product costing practices at BarCode.

After four days of interviews you reach two conclusions. First, the present cost accounting system only allocates manufacturing costs to products. The extensive costs of marketing, selling, distribution, research and development, and general administration are not assigned at all to cost objects such as products, services, and customers. This is because periodic financial reporting does not require or in fact allow these outlays to be assigned to cost objects such as products, services, and customers. For financial reporting purposes, these cash expenditures are treated as period expenses. No attempt is made to causally link them to activities and businesses actually being performed or to cost objects—products, services, and customers—that create the demand for these expenditures.

As there are no financial accounting requirements at all for allocating indirect and support expenses to services produced or customers served, the service part of BarCode's business does not merely suffer from distorted cost numbers; it has no cost numbers at all. There are responsibility centres for services, but there is no understanding of how those costs relate to individual services and customers.

The second problem is that the existing system does not provide adequate information to support organizational continuous learning and improvement. The present competitive environment requires managers and operators to have timely and accurate information to help them make processes more efficient and more customer focused. The existing system prepares and issues summary feedback according to a monthly financial reporting cycle. Due to the complexities and adjustments associated with closing the books, the reports are delayed but only for several days after the close of the accounting period, which is still too late for responsibility centres to take immediate corrective action. A manager remarked: "To understand the problem of delay and aggregated financial information, you could think of the responsibility centre manager as a bowler, throwing a ball at pins every minute. But we do not let the bowler see how many pins he has knocked down with each throw. At the end of the month, we close the books, calculate the total number of pins knocked down during the month, compare this with a standard, and report the total and the variance back to the bowler. If the total number is below standard, we ask the bowler for an explanation and encourage him to do better next period. We are beginning to understand that we will not turn out many world-class bowlers with this type of reporting system."

Required:

As the consultant, use the case approach to complete this assignment.

2. This year was when Manitoba Manufacturing Ltd. turned 40 years of age and when sales exceeded $500 million for the first time. Manitoba Manufacturing makes a range of small household appliances which are sold to Canadian and U.S. retail chains.

Inventory has always been important for Manitoba Manufacturing's success. In the 1960s and the 1970s the focus was on inventory control. The company could afford to keep amounts of "just-in-case" inventory on hand to satisfy customer demand and still stay competitive. Consequently, EOQ techniques of the 1960s and 1970s focused on the most efficient ways to manage large volumes of inventory. In the 1980s, it became increasingly clear that Manitoba Manufacturing could no longer afford the luxury of maintaining large quantities of inventory. This led to the introduction of a materials requirement planning (MRP) system. MRP represented a large step forward in the materials planning process. Manitoba Manufacturing was able, using a master production schedule supported by bill of materials files, to identify the specific materials needed to produce each finished item. A computer was used to calculate gross material requirements, which prompted an activity such as placing an order, cancelling an existing order, or modifying the timing of existing orders. For the first time at Manitoba Manufacturing there was a formal mechanism for keeping inventory priorities valid in a changing manufacturing environment. The ability of the planning system to systematically and efficiently schedule all inventory was a tremendous productivity and quality advantage.

Manitoba Manufacturing began in the late 1980s and the early 1990s to take advantage of the increased power and affordability of available information technology. It was able to connect the movement of inventory with the coincidental financial activity. A manufacturing resources planning (MRP II) system evolved to incorporate the financial accounting system and the financial management system along with the manufacturing and materials management systems. This allowed the company to have a more integrated business system that derived the materials and capacity requirements associated with a desired operations plan, allowed input of detailed activities, translated all this to a financial statement, and suggested a course of action to address those items that were not in balance with the desired plan.

There were few changes in recent years because of the management problems to do with the transition from a family-managed business to a professionally-managed business. At the resolution of these problems, you were hired as the controller. One of your first tasks was to investigate the MRP II system. You have interviewed a large number of the stakeholders, with the following overall assessment:

- Suppliers are requesting to be linked electronically to the MRP II system to facilitate their planning activities.
- Major retail chain customers are requesting, or more precisely demanding, to be linked electronically to facilitate ordering, particularly with the increasingly large number of small and frequently placed orders.

- Internal units such as product design, warehousing, materials planning, capacity planning, communication systems, human resources, finance, and project management want to be electronically connected or, for those already connected, differently connected with the MRP II system.

Required:

As the new controller, use the case approach to address the concerns of the suppliers, major retail customers, and the internal units wanting to be linked (or differently linked) electronically with the existing MRP II system.

3. Andrews Marko is the owner of ComboIE Ltd., which will soon start producing customized equipment that combines previously separate information and entertainment products such as PCs with TVs, CDs, videos, and quality sound systems. In addition to ComboIE, there are a few manufacturers such as Sony that are making product combinations especially with miniaturization technologies. ComboIE plans to assemble this type of product in a major way starting in about six months.

Andrews was very aware of the combination products being made by Sony. These products were increasingly easy to make as the individual components became highly standardized and commoditized. All information and entertainment components such as DVDs, PCs, etc. are widely available. The various housings or platforms to combine the information and entertainment components can be easily obtained from a large number of suppliers. Many of the suppliers who can provide the components in regular size or miniaturized are located in Southeast Asia, mainly China.

All of the products that ComboIE expects to produce could be outsourced, but the problem would be that the various suppliers could easily start manufacturing and selling independently of ComboIE and, in effect, competing with ComboIE. This is the problem that Nike has with suppliers, who often sell products identical to those they made for Nike but at lower prices. Dell prevented that problem by allowing prime suppliers to produce only one component, with a secondary supplier and a backup supplier for the same component. Thus, no supplier produced more than one component. However, this required Dell to have assembly plants for making the final product from components received from numerous suppliers. Consequently, Andrews decided to use the Dell business model of assembly plants near customers. The first ComboIE plant is to be located in Toronto for the assembly of components received from Southeast Asia.

There will be two types of assembly. First, there will be entirely customized products made to the specifications requested by individual customers. These orders will be placed over the Internet by the customer. The exact components will be specified by the customer. ComboIE will respond with a price and expected delivery date. The customer will confirm the order by paying for the requested product with a credit card. When the order is confirmed, the suppliers (who would be under longer-term contracts regarding components, their quality, and prices) will be contacted with the component requirements and the delivery schedule. At the same time, the courier will be contacted for the scheduled pick-up of the completed product. Also at the same time the delivery instructions will be issued to the courier. When the components arrive, the product will be assembled and by the time it is completed, the courier will be there for the pick-up and timely delivery.

The other type of assembly will be orders received from retail chains, who will specify the various combination products, their quantities, and their delivery schedules. These products will be customized, but rather than a batch of one, these batches will be considerably larger. Nevertheless, ComboIE expects each order to contain products unique to that retail chain.

The organization will consist of Andrews Marko as president, with four vice-presidents responsible for assembly, purchasing, sales, and administration, respectively.

Required:

As Andrews Marko, using the case approach, specify the budgeting, costing, and performance measurement systems required at ComboIE.

4. Gordon Oilfield Services provides transportation and field warehousing of drill pipe and casing for the petroleum industry in Alberta and northern British Columbia. It operates a versatile fleet of specialized vehicles and equipment engineered to safely and efficiently handle a broad range of commodities, including oilfield and construction equipment, storage tanks, and oilfield tubular goods. The Gordon fleet consists of approximately 235 truck tractors, 300 trailers, and a fleet of support equipment, including cranes and other specialized lifts. It also offers complete storage and handling, as well as state-of-the-art inventory management of oil well tubular goods. Its strategically located pipe yards offer more than 350 acres of outdoor storage.

   Just over a year ago, Ray Gordon purchased seven separate entrepreneurial firms in the belief that there would be significant advantages to running an integrated oilfield support services business. A year later, the integrated firm has sales exceeding $600 million and profits are low but acceptable. The firm has been divided into six divisions, each with a similar strategy for serving the oil industry, but each serving a different geographical market (Nisku, Grande Prairie, Strathmore, and Brooks in Alberta; Fort St. John and Fort Nelson in BC). Each division provides the following services: (1) pipe storage and transportation, (2) tank moving, and (3) trucking. Gordon's head office is in Edmonton.

   Accounting performance has been mixed. The financial accounting system from one of the prior firms has been adopted by the head office. It is used by each of the six divisions and for consolidation by headquarters. As a result, the firm is able to meet financial reporting requirements to collect costs accurately by responsibility centre. Similarly, the financial accounting system is adequate for valuing inventory for financial reporting purposes and for preparing periodic financial reports. But to the divisions, this system seems to be producing highly distorted service costs. Also, there is little understanding among the divisions regarding service costs, customer costs and performance feedback.

   A larger concern is how difficult it is to track the costs of services provided to customers. The financial accounting system provides costs that are too aggregated and that are generally too late to be useful. The prices obtained for services provided are competitive in the industry; market prices must be accepted. However, there is no indication of how profitable competitively won contracts are because the financial accounting system cannot provide that type of information.

   Ray Gordon thinks there might be shortcomings with the present management accounting system. The entrepreneurs at the seven original companies had all thoroughly understood their businesses; for them, formalized management accounting was not necessary. You have been hired as an expert in management accounting.

   Required:

   As the consulting management accountant, advise Ray Gordon on the accounting requirements for Gordon Oilfield Services. Use the case approach.

5. You are a management accountant. After a few years' work experience, you have joined a major ERP systems firm as a salesperson for accounting and other integrated systems.

   The president of Globawear has asked your firm what it can do to improve Globawear's operations. The two of you meet, and she provides information and answers your questions about her company's present systems.

   Now you are preparing to meet with Globawear's president and her management group to suggest a new system. You need to assess what the prospective client requires. Following is a summary of your initial investigation.

Globawear Limited is a multi-outlet retailer of sports clothing. Presently, it is the country's second largest sports clothing retailer. It was formed only recently, through the acquisition and merger of three separate sports clothing retail firms. Each of these three original firms had positioned itself similarly in the value creation chain. Each had interacted face-to-face with retail customers in shopping mall outlets. Each had acquired the bulk of its inventory from wholesalers. Now, with the larger size of the combined operation, Globawear wants to bypass the wholesalers and deal directly with manufacturers. This will require some changes. Specifically, the manufacturers want multiyear agreements, as they do with all retailers; they also all want orders to arrive electronically with barcode numbers. In the past, all orders with wholesalers had been placed by fax or telephone.

All three of the earlier firms had used the same cash register system, which read the barcodes of clothing items. That system is still being used by Globawear, since it has not been difficult to combine the three separate systems into a single Globawear system.

There is a single and appropriate chart of accounts. The problem is that the cash register system is not connected to the inventory and ordering systems. These different systems need to be reconciled manually. As a result, there are problems with differences among inventory levels, cost of inventory, and cost of goods sold.

As the three earlier firms had a common retail cash register system, they also had a common financial accounting system. That system was a traditional but well-functioning system capable of basic accounting and transaction-capturing functions such as preparing monthly and quarterly financial statements for external stakeholders. The system works well for outlets (i.e., stores) but does not explain gross profitability by product line, mainly because the financial accounting system uses a different database than the cash register system.

There are no performance measurement systems at Globawear. Similarly, its predecessor firms did not have any performance measurement systems. This lack of performance measurement was partly because of the relatively small size of the earlier firms. However, Globawear has grown to the point where it needs performance measurement systems in order to indicate, other than in aggregated financial terms, exactly how its businesses are doing at meeting customer requirements, turning over inventory, and so on. Globawear is now more than large enough to warrant a performance measurement system.

The president of Globawear believes that there could be considerable merit in implementing an ERP and related systems. She is unclear which systems are needed and what benefits would come with ERP and/or related systems.

Required:
Using the case approach, address the concerns of Globawear and its president and make appropriate recommendations for solving those concerns.

6. Flatland Metals Co. produces steel products for a variety of customers. One division of the company is Residential Products Division. This division was created in the late 1940s; its principal products since that time have been galvanized steel components used in garage door installations. The division has been continuously profitable since 1950 and in the last year generated profits of $10 million on sales of $300 million.

However, over the past 10 years, growth in the division has been slow; profitability has become stagnant, and few new products have been developed, as the garage door components market has matured. The president of the company, John Stamp, has asked his senior staff to evaluate the operations of the Residential Products Division and to make recommendations for changes that would improve its operations. The staff uncovered the following facts:

a. Jolene Green, aged 53, has been president of the division for the past 15 years.
b. Ms. Green receives a compensation package that includes a salary of $175,000 annually plus a cash bonus based on achievement of the budgeted level of annual profit.

c.   Growth in sales in the residential metal products industry has averaged 12% annually over the past decade. Most of the growth has occurred in ornamental products used in residential privacy fencing.

d.   Nationally, the division's market share in the overall residential metal products industry has dropped from 12% to 7% during the past 10 years, and it has dropped from 40% to 25% for garage door components.

e.   The division maintains its own information systems. The systems in use today are mostly the same systems that were in place 15 years ago; however, some of the manual systems have been computerized (e.g., payroll, accounts payable, accounting).

f.   The division has no customer service department. A small sales staff solicits and takes orders by phone from national distribution chains.

g.   The major intradivision communication tool is the annual operating budget. No formal statements have been prepared in the division regarding strategies, mission, values, goals, or objectives, or identifying core competencies or critical success factors.

Required:
You have been hired as a consultant for the Residential Products Division. Given the introductory paragraphs, prepare a report in which you identify the major problems in the Residential Products Division regarding cost management and performance measurement, and develop recommendations to address the problems you have identified.

ETHICS

1.   Some people may view an organization's culture as a mechanism to eliminate diversity in the workplace. Is it ethical to attract and retain only individuals who accept an organization's culture and value system? In responding, be sure to discuss the positive and negative aspects of conformity as part of organizational culture.

2.   The underlying assumption with a cost management system is to reduce costs, not just once, but continuously. Organizations such as Wal-Mart, Dell, and Intel have become successful by constantly reducing costs. However, there is also a negative relationship between cost and quality (i.e., as costs are cut, quality suffers). How can you have constantly declining costs without declining quality? In responding, be sure to use the value creation chain in your argument.

3.   Naomi Klein, in her book *No Logo*, observed,
     ... the "part-time" classification is often more a technicality than a reality, with retail employees keeping their part-timers just below the forty-hour legal cutoff for full-time—Laurie Bonang, for instance, clocks between thirty-five and thirty-nine hours a week at Starbucks. For all intents and purposes, she has the duties of a full-time employee, but under forty hours the company does not have to pay overtime or guarantee full-time hours. Other chains are equally creative.

Klein then mentions the practices of Wal-Mart and GAP in employing part-time employees rather than full-time employees.
Required:
Evaluate the extensive use of part-time employees from the perspective of part-time employees and also from the perspective of the shareholders of these organizations.

4.   Stage IV of cost management and performance measurement systems is described as integrated cost management, financial reporting, and performance systems using an enterprise resource planning system. Recently, we have read in the financial press about organizations such as WorldCom and Enron, which manipulated their financial statements to the detriment of shareholders. It is unclear whether such delinquent organizations have a Stage IV cost management and performance measurement

ETHICS
system, but if they did, what would be the consequences of misleading or fraudulent financial reporting on cost management and performance measurement? There could be an impact as cost management and performance measurement are integrated with financial reporting.

SOLUTIONS TO SELF-TEST QUESTIONS

1. d, 2. a, 3. d, 4. d, 5. b, 6. d, 7. d, 8. b, 9. c, 10. b

ENDNOTES

1. Callie Berliner and James A. Brimson, eds., *Cost Management for Today's Advanced Manufacturing*, Boston: Harvard Business School Press, 1988, p. 10.

2. Steven C. Schnoebelen, "Integrating an Advanced Cost Management System into Operating Systems (Part 2)," *Journal of Cost Management*, Spring 1993, p. 60.

3. Robin Cooper and Robert S. Kaplan, *The Design of Cost Management Systems*, Englewood Cliffs, N.J.: Prentice-Hall, 1991, p. 4.

4. Ibid., p. 79.

5. Ibid., pp. 85–99.

6. Ibid., pp. 95–98.

7. Robert S. Kaplan and Robin Cooper, *Cost and Effect: Using Integrated Cost Systems to Drive Profitability and Performance*, Boston: Harvard Business School Press, 1998, p. 2. Note that this outstanding book was used extensively for parts of this chapter.

8. Ibid., pp. 11–27.

9. This section borrows from E.J. Umble, R.R. Half, and M.M. Umble, "Enterprise Resource Planning: Implementation Procedures and Critical Success Factors," *European Journal of Operational Research* 146 (2003): 241–57.

10. Grant Norris, Ian Wright, James R. Hurley, John Dunleavy, and Alison Gibson, *SAP: An Executive's Comprehensive Guide*, New York: Wiley, 1998, pp. 84–86.

11. Subba Rao Siriginidi, "Enterprise Resource Planning in Re-engineering Business," *Business Process Management Journal* 6 (2000): 377.

12. Norris et al., p. 128.

13. Marina Strauss, "Big Chains Set for Globalization 14-Digit Bar Code," *Globe and Mail*, August 19, 2002.

14. Mark O'Connor, "The Information Supply Chain—Changing the Landscape," *CMA Management*, February 2007, pp. 27–32.

15. Mike Troy, "The Super Growth Leaders—Wal-Mart: Global Dominance Puts Half Trillion in Sight," *DSN Retailing Today*, December 10, 2001, pp. 17–18+.

16. Sandra S. Vance and Roy V. Scott, *Wal-Mart: A History of Sam Walton's Retail Phenomenon*, New York: Twayne Publishers, 1994, pp. 43–44.

17. These descriptions are based on information from the Wal-Mart homepage, http://www.walmartstores.com/wmstores/wms.

18. Mike Troy, "Wal-Mart Fills in Markets with 'One-oh-Nine' Footprint," *DSN Retailing Today*, Vol. 39, Issue 17, September 4, 2000, pp. 3, 46.

19. "Business Around the World; Wal-Mart," *The Economist*, Vol. 361, Issue 8251, December 8, 2001, pp. 55–57.

ENDNOTES

20. Ibid.

21. Vance and Scott, pp. 92–93.

22. Barry Janoff, "High-Tech Knowledge," *Progressive Grocer*, December 2000, pp. 45–48.

23. McKinsey Global Institute, *U.S. Productivity Growth 1995–2001: Understanding the Contribution of Information Technology Relative to Other Factors*, October 2001, Chapter 4, sector case studies—retail trade.

24. *Distribution Centre Replenishment Collaboration: Business Process Guide,* Uniform Code Council, Inc.; Voluntary Inter-industry Commerce Standards (VUCS) Association, 2005.

Appendix A

Code of Ethics—Society of Management Accountants of Canada

As professionals and pre-eminent specialists in the field of strategic management accounting, CMAs are bound by the Society's Code of Professional Ethics. This code stipulates and binds them to the highest level of care, duty, and responsibility to their employers and clients, the public, and their fellow professionals.

CODE OF PROFESSIONAL ETHICS

(Section 21 of the Society's By-Law)

All Members will adhere to the following "*Code of Professional Ethics*" of the Society:

(a) A Member will act at all times with:

  (i)   responsibility for and fidelity to public needs;

  (ii) fairness and loyalty to such Member's associates, clients and employers; and

  (iii) competence through devotion to high ideals of personal honour and professional integrity.

(b) A Member will:

  (i)   maintain at all times independence of thought and action;

  (ii) not express an opinion on financial reports or statements without first assessing her or his relationship with her or his client to determine whether such Member might expect her or his opinion to be considered independent, objective and unbiased by one who has knowledge of all the facts; and

  (iii) when preparing financial reports or statements or expressing an opinion on financial reports or statements, disclose all material facts known to such Member in order not to make such financial reports or statements misleading, acquire sufficient information to warrant an expression of opinion and report all material misstatements or departures from generally accepted accounting principles.

(c) A Member will:

  (i)   not disclose or use any confidential information concerning the affairs of such Member's employer or client unless acting in the course of his or her duties or except when such information is required to be disclosed in the course of any defence of himself or herself or any associate or employee in any lawsuit or other legal proceeding or against alleged professional misconduct by order of lawful authority of the Board or any committee of the Society in the proper exercise of their duties but only to the extent necessary for such purpose;

(ii) inform his or her employer or client of any business connections or interests of which such Member's employer or client would reasonably expect to be informed;

(iii) not, in the course of exercising his or her duties on behalf of such Member's employer or client, hold, receive, bargain for or acquire any fee, remuneration or benefit without such employer's or client's knowledge and consent; and

(iv) take all reasonable steps, in arranging any engagement as a consultant, to establish a clear understanding of the scope and objectives of the work before it is commenced and will furnish the client with an estimate of cost, preferably before the engagement is commenced, but in any event as soon as possible thereafter.

(d) A Member will:

(i) conduct himself or herself toward other Members with courtesy and good faith;

(ii) not commit an act discreditable to the profession;

(iii) not engage in or counsel any business or occupation which, in the opinion of the Society, is incompatible with the professional ethics of a management accountant;

(iv) not accept any engagement to review the work of another Member for the same employer except with the knowledge of that Member, or except where the connection of that Member with the work has been terminated, unless the Member reviews the work of others as a normal part of his or her responsibilities;

(v) not attempt to gain an advantage over other Members by paying or accepting a commission in securing management accounting or public accounting work;

(vi) uphold the principle of adequate compensation for management accounting and public accounting work; and

(vii) not act maliciously or in any other way which may adversely reflect on the public or professional reputation or business of another Member.

(e) A Member will:

(i) at all times maintain the standards of competence expressed by the Board from time to time;

(ii) disseminate the knowledge upon which the profession of management accounting is based to others within the profession and generally promote the advancement of the profession;

(iii) undertake only such work as he or she is competent to perform by virtue of his or her training and experience and will, where it would be in the best interests of an employer or client, engage, or advise the employer or client to engage, other specialists;

(iv) expose before the proper tribunals of the Society any incompetent, unethical, illegal or unfair conduct or practice of a Member which involves the reputation, dignity or honour of the Society; and

(v) endeavour to ensure that a professional partnership or company, with which such Member is associated as a partner, principal, director, officer, associate or employee, abides by the Code of Professional Ethics and the rules of professional conduct established by the Society.

Appendix B

Instructions for Writing Cases

Short but integrative cases are included in the end-of-the-chapter materials. There are two purposes for these cases. First, the cases test students with higher level educational objectives. Second, cases integrate the testing across chapters or in other words they integrate course materials. These purposes will be amplified with defining cases and the case method.

Among other testing devices, the back-of-the-chapter materials contain questions, exercises, and problems. The questions ask you to respond with some facts from the chapter. The educational objective of back-of-the-chapter questions is to test students' knowledge and comprehension of management accounting terms. These are the first two of Bloom's educational objectives.

The problems generally ask students to apply a technique from the textbook, say, chapter 5 problem 8 asks the student to apply the weighted average process costing. With the data provided, the task is to apply a specified technique to the data to produce a numerical answer which is marked against a solution containing a single correct answer set. Thus, the educational objective of problems is to test students' ability to apply techniques. Problems in this textbook employ Bloom's third level of educational objectives, application.

The educational objective for cases is to test students on use of management accounting techniques for assessing and solving complex issues. Cases are a description of a situation in an organization which has ramifications for management. The situation is practical in that it has happened or it could happen. In addition, the situation contains issues which are just suboptimal performance. Issues are defined as doing something wrong vis-à-vis what should be done according to good management accounting practices. For example, management accounting, as per this textbook, advocates costing goods being made or services being provided in order to make informed decisions on production and pricing. If an organization in a case does not have a costing system (a management accounting technique), then the fact that there is no costing system is an issue. Cases tend to have multiple issues. There are generally two or three issues in each of the mini cases in the back-of-the-chapter material.

There is a relationship between issues and management techniques. With the above example, the issue was that there was no costing system, which is a management accounting technique. Students are being tested on identifying issues or in other words they are being tested on identifying the lack of existence of or the lack of properly functioning of management accounting techniques. The solution would be to implement an appropriate costing system. Another example would be a growing organization where the budgeting is done after the year begins. Budgeting is to be completed before the year begins to guide the organization. Thus, the late completion of budgeting would be the issue. The solution would be for budgeting to be completed before year end, likely about 15 days prior to the end of the year preceding the budget.

Cases are integrative when they include management accounting techniques from more than one chapter. Thus, the cases integrate across chapters. Integration is more difficult to accomplish in the first two or three chapters because few management accounting techniques have been considered. However, integration becomes easier in later chapters as the techniques to draw from are more plentiful.

Thus, management accounting case is a practice situation which has issues that can be solved with appropriate management accounting techniques. That written situation is called a case question. Good cases provide situations as real as possible. With a case, a student is placed with the "action." The case question provides information on the context and actors. Accordingly cases require students to be active learners.

Cases in this text employ two educational objectives; they are the fourth and fifth in Bloom's taxonomy of educational objectives. The fourth is analysis which is the ability to break content into parts in order to understand the relationship among parts. The fifth, synthesis, is the putting together of parts to form a new whole. For both, management accounting techniques are used; for pulling apart issues or to construct a new solution from parts.

Case questions, as noted, consist of narrative or the case question. This is typically the situation, scenario, or story which includes characters and a setting that will be some component of an organization. Most importantly it contains issues that are revealed in comments made by case characters, findings by case characters, trends, or ratios contained in documents, etc.

Issue identification can be difficult without practice. With practice a student becomes skilled with identifying and linking issues.

A case question contains a "required" in the text, usually at the end, or it may be provided by the instructor. It asks the student to do something. The mini cases in this textbook use requireds that are directed. They explicitly tell the student to do something. In cases used in more senior courses, the requireds will be less directed; students will need to determine what to do.

The case response is the student response to the case question and required. It tends to have three parts: issues, analyses, and recommendations. The issues are the root issues facing the organization that need to be solved. The analysis is an explanation of the apparent issues and how they can be solved by solving the root issues. The apparent issues are casually linked together by the root issues. Thus, solving the root issues will solve all or the most important apparent issues.

The recommendation is the suggested actions to solve the root issues. In that root issues are the major management accounting problems facing organizations, the case approach is a method for solving problems.

SOURCE: G. Spraakman, *Current Trends and Traditions in Management Accounting Case Analysis,* 5th edition, Toronto, Captus, 2007; B.S. Bloom, M.D. Englehart, G.J. Furst, W.H. Hill, and D.R. Krathwohl, *Taxonomy of Educational Objectives: The Classification of Educational Goals,* New York, David McKay Co., 1956.

Appendix C

Present and Future Value Tables

Present and Future Value Tables

TABLE 1 PRESENT VALUE OF $1

Period	1.00%	2.00%	3.00%	4.00%	5.00%	6.00%	7.00%	8.00%	9.00%	9.50%	10.00%	10.50%	11.00%
1	0.9901	0.9804	0.9709	0.9615	0.9524	0.9434	0.9346	0.9259	0.9174	0.9132	0.9091	0.9050	0.9009
2	0.9803	0.9612	0.9426	0.9246	0.9070	0.8900	0.8734	0.8573	0.8417	0.8340	0.8265	0.8190	0.8116
3	0.9706	0.9423	0.9151	0.8890	0.8638	0.8396	0.8163	0.7938	0.7722	0.7617	0.7513	0.7412	0.7312
4	0.9610	0.9239	0.8885	0.8548	0.8227	0.7921	0.7629	0.7350	0.7084	0.6956	0.6830	0.6707	0.6587
5	0.9515	0.9057	0.8626	0.8219	0.7835	0.7473	0.7130	0.6806	0.6499	0.6352	0.6209	0.6070	0.5935
6	0.9421	0.8880	0.8375	0.7903	0.7462	0.7050	0.6663	0.6302	0.5963	0.5801	0.5645	0.5493	0.5346
7	0.9327	0.8706	0.8131	0.7599	0.7107	0.6651	0.6228	0.5835	0.5470	0.5298	0.5132	0.4971	0.4817
8	0.9235	0.8535	0.7894	0.7307	0.6768	0.6274	0.5820	0.5403	0.5019	0.4838	0.4665	0.4499	0.4339
9	0.9143	0.8368	0.7664	0.7026	0.6446	0.5919	0.5439	0.5003	0.4604	0.4419	0.4241	0.4071	0.3909
10	0.9053	0.8204	0.7441	0.6756	0.6139	0.5584	0.5084	0.4632	0.4224	0.4035	0.3855	0.3685	0.3522
11	0.8963	0.8043	0.7224	0.6496	0.5847	0.5268	0.4751	0.4289	0.3875	0.3685	0.3505	0.3334	0.3173
12	0.8875	0.7885	0.7014	0.6246	0.5568	0.4970	0.4440	0.3971	0.3555	0.3365	0.3186	0.3018	0.2858
13	0.8787	0.7730	0.6810	0.6006	0.5303	0.4688	0.4150	0.3677	0.3262	0.3073	0.2897	0.2731	0.2575
14	0.8700	0.7579	0.6611	0.5775	0.5051	0.4423	0.3878	0.3405	0.2993	0.2807	0.2633	0.2471	0.2320
15	0.8614	0.7430	0.6419	0.5553	0.4810	0.4173	0.3625	0.3152	0.2745	0.2563	0.2394	0.2237	0.2090
16	0.8528	0.7285	0.6232	0.5339	0.4581	0.3937	0.3387	0.2919	0.2519	0.2341	0.2176	0.2024	0.1883
17	0.8444	0.7142	0.6050	0.5134	0.4363	0.3714	0.3166	0.2703	0.2311	0.2138	0.1978	0.1832	0.1696
18	0.8360	0.7002	0.5874	0.4936	0.4155	0.3503	0.2959	0.2503	0.2120	0.1952	0.1799	0.1658	0.1528
19	0.8277	0.6864	0.5703	0.4746	0.3957	0.3305	0.2765	0.2317	0.1945	0.1783	0.1635	0.1500	0.1377
20	0.8195	0.6730	0.5537	0.4564	0.3769	0.3118	0.2584	0.2146	0.1784	0.1628	0.1486	0.1358	0.1240
21	0.8114	0.6598	0.5376	0.4388	0.3589	0.2942	0.2415	0.1987	0.1637	0.1487	0.1351	0.1229	0.1117
22	0.8034	0.6468	0.5219	0.4220	0.3419	0.2775	0.2257	0.1839	0.1502	0.1358	0.1229	0.1112	0.1007
23	0.7954	0.6342	0.5067	0.4057	0.3256	0.2618	0.2110	0.1703	0.1378	0.1240	0.1117	0.1006	0.0907
24	0.7876	0.6217	0.4919	0.3901	0.3101	0.2470	0.1972	0.1577	0.1264	0.1133	0.1015	0.0911	0.0817
25	0.7798	0.6095	0.4776	0.3751	0.2953	0.2330	0.1843	0.1460	0.1160	0.1034	0.0923	0.0824	0.0736
26	0.7721	0.5976	0.4637	0.3607	0.2812	0.2198	0.1722	0.1352	0.1064	0.0945	0.0839	0.0746	0.0663
27	0.7644	0.5859	0.4502	0.3468	0.2679	0.2074	0.1609	0.1252	0.0976	0.0863	0.0763	0.0675	0.0597
28	0.7568	0.5744	0.4371	0.3335	0.2551	0.1956	0.1504	0.1159	0.0896	0.0788	0.0693	0.0611	0.0538
29	0.7493	0.5631	0.4244	0.3207	0.2430	0.1846	0.1406	0.1073	0.0822	0.0719	0.0630	0.0553	0.0485
30	0.7419	0.5521	0.4120	0.3083	0.2314	0.1741	0.1314	0.0994	0.0754	0.0657	0.0573	0.0500	0.0437
31	0.7346	0.5413	0.4000	0.2965	0.2204	0.1643	0.1228	0.0920	0.0692	0.0600	0.0521	0.0453	0.0394
32	0.7273	0.5306	0.3883	0.2851	0.2099	0.1550	0.1147	0.0852	0.0634	0.0058	0.0474	0.0410	0.0355
33	0.7201	0.5202	0.3770	0.2741	0.1999	0.1462	0.1072	0.0789	0.0582	0.0500	0.0431	0.0371	0.0319
34	0.7130	0.5100	0.3660	0.2636	0.1904	0.1379	0.1002	0.0731	0.0534	0.0457	0.0391	0.0336	0.0288
35	0.7059	0.5000	0.3554	0.2534	0.1813	0.1301	0.0937	0.0676	0.0490	0.0417	0.0356	0.0304	0.0259
36	0.6989	0.4902	0.3450	0.2437	0.1727	0.1227	0.0875	0.0626	0.0449	0.0381	0.0324	0.0275	0.0234
37	0.6920	0.4806	0.3350	0.2343	0.1644	0.1158	0.0818	0.0580	0.0412	0.0348	0.0294	0.0249	0.0210
38	0.6852	0.4712	0.3252	0.2253	0.1566	0.1092	0.0765	0.0537	0.0378	0.0318	0.0267	0.0225	0.0190
39	0.6784	0.4620	0.3158	0.2166	0.1492	0.1031	0.0715	0.0497	0.0347	0.0290	0.0243	0.0204	0.0171
40	0.6717	0.4529	0.3066	0.2083	0.1421	0.0972	0.0668	0.0460	0.0318	0.0265	0.0221	0.0184	0.0154
41	0.6650	0.4440	0.2976	0.2003	0.1353	0.0917	0.0624	0.0426	0.0292	0.0242	0.0201	0.0167	0.0139
42	0.6584	0.4353	0.2890	0.1926	0.1288	0.0865	0.0583	0.0395	0.0268	0.0221	0.0183	0.0151	0.0125
43	0.6519	0.4268	0.2805	0.1852	0.1227	0.0816	0.0545	0.0365	0.0246	0.0202	0.0166	0.0137	0.0113
44	0.6455	0.4184	0.2724	0.1781	0.1169	0.0770	0.0510	0.0338	0.0226	0.0184	0.0151	0.0124	0.0101
45	0.6391	0.4102	0.2644	0.1712	0.1113	0.0727	0.0476	0.0313	0.0207	0.0168	0.0137	0.0112	0.0091
46	0.6327	0.4022	0.2567	0.1646	0.1060	0.0685	0.0445	0.0290	0.0190	0.0154	0.0125	0.0101	0.0082
47	0.6265	0.3943	0.2493	0.1583	0.1010	0.0647	0.0416	0.0269	0.0174	0.0141	0.0113	0.0092	0.0074
48	0.6203	0.3865	0.2420	0.1522	0.0961	0.0610	0.0389	0.0249	0.0160	0.0128	0.0103	0.0083	0.0067
49	0.6141	0.3790	0.2350	0.1463	0.0916	0.0576	0.0363	0.0230	0.0147	0.0117	0.0094	0.0075	0.0060
50	0.6080	0.3715	0.2281	0.1407	0.0872	0.0543	0.0340	0.0213	0.0135	0.0107	0.0085	0.0068	0.0054

11.50%	12.00%	12.50%	13.00%	13.50%	14.00%	14.50%	15.00%	15.50%	16.00%	17.00%	18.00%	19.00%	20.00%
0.8969	0.8929	0.8889	0.8850	0.8811	0.8772	0.8734	0.8696	0.8658	0.8621	0.8547	0.8475	0.8403	0.8333
0.8044	0.7972	0.7901	0.7832	0.7763	0.7695	0.7628	0.7561	0.7496	0.7432	0.7305	0.7182	0.7062	0.6944
0.7214	0.7118	0.7023	0.6931	0.6839	0.6750	0.6662	0.6575	0.6490	0.6407	0.6244	0.6086	0.5934	0.5787
0.6470	0.6355	0.6243	0.6133	0.6026	0.5921	0.5818	0.5718	0.5619	0.5523	0.5337	0.5158	0.4987	0.4823
0.5803	0.5674	0.5549	0.5428	0.5309	0.5194	0.5081	0.4972	0.4865	0.4761	0.4561	0.4371	0.4191	0.4019
0.5204	0.5066	0.4933	0.4803	0.4678	0.4556	0.4438	0.4323	0.4212	0.4104	0.3898	0.3704	0.3521	0.3349
0.4667	0.4524	0.4385	0.4251	0.4121	0.3996	0.3876	0.3759	0.3647	0.3538	0.3332	0.3139	0.2959	0.2791
0.4186	0.4039	0.3897	0.3762	0.3631	0.3506	0.3385	0.3269	0.3158	0.3050	0.2848	0.2660	0.2487	0.2326
0.3754	0.3606	0.3464	0.3329	0.3199	0.3075	0.2956	0.2843	0.2734	0.2630	0.2434	0.2255	0.2090	0.1938
0.3367	0.3220	0.3080	0.2946	0.2819	0.2697	0.2582	0.2472	0.2367	0.2267	0.2080	0.1911	0.1756	0.1615
0.3020	0.2875	0.2737	0.2607	0.2483	0.2366	0.2255	0.2149	0.2049	0.1954	0.1778	0.1619	0.1476	0.1346
0.2708	0.2567	0.2433	0.2307	0.2188	0.2076	0.1969	0.1869	0.1774	0.1685	0.1520	0.1372	0.1240	0.1122
0.2429	0.2292	0.2163	0.2042	0.1928	0.1821	0.1720	0.1625	0.1536	0.1452	0.1299	0.1163	0.1042	0.0935
0.2179	0.2046	0.1923	0.1807	0.1699	0.1597	0.1502	0.1413	0.1330	0.1252	0.1110	0.0986	0.0876	0.0779
0.1954	0.1827	0.1709	0.1599	0.1496	0.1401	0.1312	0.1229	0.1152	0.1079	0.0949	0.0835	0.0736	0.0649
0.1752	0.1631	0.1519	0.1415	0.1319	0.1229	0.1146	0.1069	0.0997	0.0930	0.0811	0.0708	0.0618	0.0541
0.1572	0.1456	0.1350	0.1252	0.1162	0.1078	0.1001	0.0929	0.0863	0.0802	0.0693	0.0600	0.0520	0.0451
0.1410	0.1300	0.1200	0.1108	0.1024	0.0946	0.0874	0.0808	0.0747	0.0691	0.0593	0.0508	0.0437	0.0376
0.1264	0.1161	0.1067	0.0981	0.0902	0.0830	0.0763	0.0703	0.0647	0.0596	0.0506	0.0431	0.0367	0.0313
0.1134	0.1037	0.0948	0.0868	0.0795	0.0728	0.0667	0.0611	0.0560	0.0514	0.0433	0.0365	0.0308	0.0261
0.1017	0.0926	0.0843	0.0768	0.0700	0.0638	0.0582	0.0531	0.0485	0.0443	0.0370	0.0309	0.0259	0.0217
0.0912	0.0826	0.0749	0.0680	0.0617	0.0560	0.0509	0.0462	0.0420	0.0382	0.0316	0.0262	0.0218	0.0181
0.0818	0.0738	0.0666	0.0601	0.0543	0.0491	0.0444	0.0402	0.0364	0.0329	0.0270	0.0222	0.0183	0.0151
0.0734	0.0659	0.0592	0.0532	0.0479	0.0431	0.0388	0.0349	0.0315	0.0284	0.0231	0.0188	0.0154	0.0126
0.0658	0.0588	0.0526	0.0471	0.0422	0.0378	0.0339	0.0304	0.0273	0.0245	0.0197	0.0160	0.0129	0.0105
0.0590	0.0525	0.0468	0.0417	0.0372	0.0332	0.0296	0.0264	0.0236	0.0211	0.0169	0.0135	0.0109	0.0087
0.0529	0.0469	0.0416	0.0369	0.0327	0.0291	0.0258	0.0230	0.0204	0.0182	0.0144	0.0115	0.0091	0.0073
0.0475	0.0419	0.0370	0.0326	0.0289	0.0255	0.0226	0.0200	0.0177	0.0157	0.0123	0.0097	0.0077	0.0061
0.0426	0.0374	0.0329	0.0289	0.0254	0.0224	0.0197	0.0174	0.0153	0.0135	0.0105	0.0082	0.0064	0.0051
0.0382	0.0334	0.0292	0.0256	0.0224	0.0196	0.0172	0.0151	0.0133	0.0117	0.0090	0.0070	0.0054	0.0042
0.0342	0.0298	0.0260	0.0226	0.0197	0.0172	0.0150	0.0131	0.0115	0.0100	0.0077	0.0059	0.0046	0.0035
0.0307	0.0266	0.0231	0.0200	0.0174	0.0151	0.0131	0.0114	0.0099	0.0087	0.0066	0.0050	0.0038	0.0029
0.0275	0.0238	0.0205	0.0177	0.0153	0.0133	0.0115	0.0099	0.0086	0.0075	0.0056	0.0043	0.0032	0.0024
0.0247	0.0212	0.0182	0.0157	0.0135	0.0116	0.0100	0.0088	0.0075	0.0064	0.0048	0.0036	0.0027	0.0020
0.0222	0.0189	0.0162	0.0139	0.0119	0.0102	0.0088	0.0075	0.0065	0.0056	0.0041	0.0031	0.0023	0.0017
0.0199	0.0169	0.0144	0.0123	0.0105	0.0089	0.0076	0.0065	0.0056	0.0048	0.0035	0.0026	0.0019	0.0014
0.0178	0.0151	0.0128	0.0109	0.0092	0.0078	0.0067	0.0057	0.0048	0.0041	0.0030	0.0022	0.0016	0.0012
0.0160	0.0135	0.0114	0.0096	0.0081	0.0069	0.0058	0.0049	0.0042	0.0036	0.0026	0.0019	0.0014	0.0010
0.0143	0.0120	0.0101	0.0085	0.0072	0.0060	0.0051	0.0043	0.0036	0.0031	0.0022	0.0016	0.0011	0.0008
0.0129	0.0108	0.0090	0.0075	0.0063	0.0053	0.0044	0.0037	0.0031	0.0026	0.0019	0.0013	0.0010	0.0007
0.0115	0.0096	0.0080	0.0067	0.0056	0.0046	0.0039	0.0033	0.0027	0.0023	0.0016	0.0011	0.0008	0.0006
0.0103	0.0086	0.0077	0.0059	0.0049	0.0041	0.0034	0.0028	0.0024	0.0020	0.0014	0.0010	0.0007	0.0005
0.0093	0.0077	0.0063	0.0052	0.0043	0.0036	0.0030	0.0025	0.0020	0.0017	0.0012	0.0008	0.0006	0.0004
0.0083	0.0068	0.0056	0.0046	0.0038	0.0031	0.0026	0.0021	0.0018	0.0015	0.0010	0.0007	0.0005	0.0003
0.0075	0.0061	0.0050	0.0041	0.0034	0.0028	0.0023	0.0019	0.0015	0.0013	0.0009	0.0006	0.0004	0.0003
0.0067	0.0054	0.0044	0.0036	0.0030	0.0024	0.0020	0.0016	0.0013	0.0011	0.0007	0.0005	0.0003	0.0002
0.0060	0.0049	0.0039	0.0032	0.0026	0.0021	0.0017	0.0014	0.0011	0.0009	0.0006	0.0004	0.0002	0.0002
0.0054	0.0043	0.0035	0.0028	0.0023	0.0019	0.0015	0.0012	0.0010	0.0008	0.0005	0.0004	0.0002	0.0002
0.0048	0.0039	0.0031	0.0025	0.0020	0.0016	0.0013	0.0011	0.0009	0.0007	0.0005	0.0003	0.0002	0.0001
0.0043	0.0035	0.0028	0.0022	0.0018	0.0014	0.0012	0.0009	0.0007	0.0006	0.0004	0.0003	0.0002	0.0001

TABLE 2 PRESENT VALUE OF AN ORDINARY ANNUITY OF $1

Period	1.00%	2.00%	3.00%	4.00%	5.00%	6.00%	7.00%	8.00%	9.00%	9.50%	10.00%	10.50%	11.00%
1	0.9901	0.9804	0.9709	0.9615	0.0524	0.9434	0.9346	0.9259	0.9174	0.9132	0.9091	0.9050	0.9009
2	1.9704	1.9416	1.9135	1.8861	1.8594	1.8334	1.8080	1.7833	1.7591	1.7473	1.7355	1.7240	1.7125
3	2.9410	2.8839	2.8286	2.7751	2.7233	2.6730	2.6243	2.5771	2.5313	2.5089	2.4869	2.4651	2.4437
4	3.9020	3.8077	3.7171	3.6299	3.5460	3.4651	3.3872	3.3121	3.2397	3.2045	3.1699	3.1359	3.1025
5	4.8534	4.7135	4.5797	4.4518	4.3295	4.2124	4.1002	3.9927	3.8897	3.8397	3.7908	3.7429	3.6959
6	5.7955	5.6014	5.4172	5.2421	5.0757	4.9173	4.7665	4.6229	4.4859	4.4198	4.3553	4.2922	4.2305
7	6.7282	6.4720	6.2303	6.0021	5.7864	5.5824	5.3893	5.2064	5.0330	4.9496	4.8684	4.7893	4.7122
8	7.6517	7.3255	7.0197	6.7327	6.4632	6.2098	5.9713	5.7466	5.5348	5.4334	5.3349	5.2392	5.1461
9	8.5660	8.1622	7.7861	7.4353	7.1078	6.8017	6.5152	6.2469	5.9953	5.8753	5.7590	5.6463	5.5371
10	9.4713	8.9826	8.5302	8.1109	7.7217	7.3601	7.0236	6.7101	6.4177	6.2788	6.1446	6.0148	5.8892
11	10.3676	9.7869	9.2526	8.7605	8.3064	7.8869	7.4987	7.1390	6.8052	6.6473	6.4951	6.3482	6.2065
12	11.2551	10.5753	9.9540	9.3851	8.8633	8.3838	7.9427	7.5361	7.1607	6.9838	6.8137	6.6500	6.4924
13	12.1337	11.3484	10.6350	9.9857	9.3936	8.8527	8.3577	7.9038	7.4869	7.2912	7.1034	6.9230	6.7499
14	13.0037	12.1063	11.2961	10.5631	9.8986	9.2950	8.7455	8.2442	7.7862	7.5719	7.3667	7.1702	6.9819
15	13.8651	12.8493	11.9379	11.1184	10.3797	9.7123	9.1079	8.5595	8.0607	7.8282	7.6061	7.3938	7.1909
16	14.7179	13.5777	12.5611	11.6523	10.8378	10.1059	9.4467	8.8514	8.3126	8.0623	7.8237	7.5962	7.3792
17	15.5623	14.2919	13.1661	12.1657	11.2741	10.4773	9.7632	9.1216	8.5436	8.2760	8.0216	7.7794	7.5488
18	16.3983	14.9920	13.7535	12.6593	11.6896	10.8276	10.0591	9.3719	8.7556	8.4713	8.2014	7.9452	7.7016
19	17.2260	15.6785	14.3238	13.1339	12.0853	11.1581	10.3356	9.6036	8.9501	8.6496	8.3649	8.0952	7.8393
20	18.0456	16.3514	14.8775	13.5903	12.4622	11.4699	10.5940	9.8182	9.1286	8.8124	8.5136	8.2309	7.9633
21	18.8570	17.0112	15.4150	14.0292	12.8212	11.7641	10.8355	10.0168	9.2922	8.9611	8.6487	8.3538	8.0751
22	19.6604	17.6581	15.9369	14.4511	13.1630	12.0416	11.0612	10.2007	9.4424	9.0969	8.7715	8.4649	8.1757
23	20.4558	18.2922	16.4436	14.8568	13.4886	12.3034	11.2722	10.3711	9.5802	9.2209	8.8832	8.5656	8.2664
24	21.2434	18.9139	16.9355	15.2470	13.7986	12.5504	11.4693	10.5288	9.7066	9.3342	8.9847	8.6566	8.3481
25	22.0232	19.5235	17.4132	15.6221	14.0939	12.7834	11.6536	10.6748	9.8226	9.4376	9.0770	8.7390	8.4217
26	22.7952	20.1210	17.8768	15.9828	14.3752	13.0032	11.8258	10.8100	9.9290	9.5320	9.1610	8.8136	8.4881
27	23.5596	20.7069	18.3270	16.3296	14.6430	13.2105	11.9867	10.9352	10.0266	9.6183	9.2372	8.8811	8.5478
28	24.3164	21.2813	18.7641	16.6631	14.8981	13.4062	12.1371	11.0511	10.1161	9.6971	9.3066	8.9422	8.6016
29	25.0658	21.8444	19.1885	16.9837	15.1411	13.5907	12.2777	11.1584	10.1983	9.7690	9.3696	8.9974	8.6501
30	25.8077	22.3965	19.6004	17.2920	15.3725	13.7648	12.4090	11.2578	10.2737	9.8347	9.4269	9.0474	8.6938
31	26.5423	22.9377	20.0004	17.5885	15.5928	13.9291	12.5318	11.3498	10.3428	9.8947	9.4790	9.0927	8.7332
32	27.2696	23.4683	20.3888	17.8736	15.8027	14.0840	12.6466	11.4350	10.4062	9.9495	9.5264	9.1337	8.7686
33	27.9897	23.9886	20.7658	18.1477	16.0026	14.2302	12.7538	11.5139	10.4664	9.9996	9.5694	9.1707	8.8005
34	28.7027	24.4986	21.1318	18.4112	16.1929	14.3681	12.8540	11.5869	10.5178	10.0453	9.6086	9.2043	8.8293
35	29.4086	24.9986	21.4872	18.6646	16.3742	14.4983	12.9477	11.6546	10.5668	10.0870	9.6442	9.2347	8.8552
36	30.1075	25.4888	21.8323	18.9083	16.5469	14.6210	13.0352	11.7172	10.6118	10.1251	9.6765	9.2621	8.8786
37	30.7995	25.9695	22.1672	19.1426	16.7113	14.7368	13.1170	11.7752	10.6530	10.1599	9.7059	9.2870	8.8996
38	31.4847	26.4406	22.4925	19.3679	16.8679	14.8460	13.1935	11.8289	10.6908	10.1917	9.7327	9.3095	8.9186
39	32.1630	26.9026	22.8082	19.5845	17.0170	14.9491	13.2649	11.8786	10.7255	10.2207	9.7570	9.3299	8.9357
40	32.8347	27.3555	23.1148	19.7928	17.1591	15.0463	13.3317	11.9246	10.7574	10.2473	9.7791	9.3483	8.9511
41	33.4997	27.7995	23.4124	19.9931	17.2944	15.1380	13.3941	11.9672	10.7866	10.2715	9.7991	9.3650	8.9649
42	34.1581	28.2348	23.7014	20.1856	17.4232	15.2245	13.4525	12.0067	10.8134	10.2936	9.8174	9.3801	8.9774
43	34.8100	28.6616	23.9819	20.3708	17.5459	15.3062	13.5070	12.0432	10.8380	10.3138	9.8340	9.3937	8.9887
44	35.4555	29.0800	24.2543	20.5488	17.6628	15.3832	13.5579	12.0771	10.8605	10.3322	9.8491	9.4061	8.9988
45	36.0945	29.4902	24.5187	20.7200	17.7741	15.4558	13.6055	12.1084	10.8812	10.3490	9.8628	9.4163	9.0079
46	36.7272	29.8923	24.7755	20.8847	17.8801	15.5244	13.6500	12.1374	10.9002	10.3644	9.8753	9.4274	9.0161
47	37.3537	30.2866	25.0247	21.0429	17.9810	15.5890	13.6916	12.1643	10.9176	10.3785	9.8866	9.4366	9.0236
48	37.9740	30.6731	25.2667	21.1951	18.0772	15.6500	13.7305	12.1891	10.9336	10.3913	9.8969	9.4449	9.0302
49	38.5881	31.0521	25.5017	21.3415	18.1687	15.7076	13.7668	12.2122	10.9482	10.4030	9.9063	9.4524	9.0362
50	39.1961	31.4236	25.7298	21.4822	18.2559	15.7619	13.8008	12.2335	10.9617	10.4137	9.9148	9.4591	9.0417

11.50%	12.00%	12.50%	13.00%	13.50%	14.00%	14.50%	15.00%	15.50%	16.00%	17.00%	18.00%	19.00%	20.00%
0.8969	0.8929	0.8889	0.8850	0.8811	0.8772	0.8734	0.8696	0.8658	0.8621	0.8547	0.8475	0.8403	0.8333
1.7012	1.6901	1.6790	1.6681	1.6573	1.6467	1.6361	1.6257	1.6154	1.6052	1.5852	1.5656	1.5465	1.5278
2.4226	2.4018	2.3813	2.3612	2.3413	2.3216	2.3023	2.2832	2.2644	2.2459	2.2096	2.1743	2.1399	2.1065
3.0696	3.0374	3.0056	2.9745	2.9438	2.9137	2.8841	2.8850	2.8263	2.7982	2.7432	2.6901	2.6386	2.5887
3.6499	3.6048	3.5606	3.5172	3.4747	3.4331	3.3922	3.3522	3.3129	3.2743	3.1994	3.1272	3.0576	2.9906
4.1703	4.1114	4.0538	3.9976	3.9425	3.8887	3.8360	3.7845	3.7341	3.6847	3.5892	3.4976	3.4098	3.3255
4.6370	4.5638	4.4923	4.4226	4.3546	4.2883	4.2236	4.1604	4.0988	4.0386	3.9224	3.8115	3.7057	3.6046
5.0556	4.9676	4.8821	4.7988	4.7177	4.6389	4.5621	4.4873	4.4145	4.3436	4.2072	4.0776	3.9544	3.8372
5.4311	5.3283	5.2285	5.1317	5.0377	4.9464	4.8577	4.7716	4.6879	4.6065	4.4506	4.3030	4.1633	4.0310
5.7678	5.6502	5.5364	5.4262	5.3195	5.2161	5.1159	5.0188	4.9246	4.8332	4.6586	4.4941	4.3389	4.1925
6.0698	5.9377	5.8102	5.6869	5.5679	5.4527	5.3414	5.2337	5.1295	5.0286	4.8364	4.6560	4.4865	4.3271
6.3406	6.1944	6.0535	5.9177	5.7867	5.6603	5.5383	5.4206	5.3069	5.1971	4.9884	4.7932	4.6105	4.4392
6.5835	6.4236	6.2698	6.1218	5.9794	5.8424	5.7103	5.5832	5.4606	5.3423	5.1183	4.9095	4.7147	4.5327
6.8013	6.6282	6.4620	6.3025	6.1493	6.0021	5.8606	5.7245	5.5936	5.4675	5.2293	5.0081	4.8023	4.6106
6.9967	6.8109	6.6329	6.4624	6.2989	6.1422	5.9918	5.8474	5.7087	5.5755	5.3242	5.0916	4.8759	4.6755
7.1719	6.9740	6.7848	6.6039	6.4308	6.2651	6.1063	5.9542	5.8084	5.6685	5.4053	5.1624	4.9377	4.7296
7.3291	7.1196	6.9198	6.7291	6.5469	6.3729	6.2064	6.0472	5.8947	5.7487	5.4746	5.2223	4.9897	4.7746
7.4700	7.2497	7.0398	6.8399	6.6493	6.4674	6.2938	6.1280	5.9695	5.8179	5.5339	5.2732	5.0333	4.8122
7.5964	7.3658	7.1465	6.9380	6.7395	6.5504	6.3701	6.1982	6.0342	5.8775	5.5845	5.3162	5.0700	4.8435
7.7098	7.4694	7.2414	7.0248	6.8189	6.6231	6.4368	6.2593	6.0902	5.9288	5.6278	5.3528	5.1009	4.8696
7.8115	7.5620	7.3257	7.1016	6.8889	6.6870	6.4950	6.3125	6.1387	5.9731	5.6648	5.3837	5.1268	4.8913
7.9027	7.6447	7.4006	7.1695	6.9506	6.7429	6.5459	6.3587	6.1807	6.0113	5.6964	5.4099	5.1486	4.9094
7.9845	7.7184	7.4672	7.2297	7.0049	6.7921	6.5903	6.3988	6.2170	6.0443	5.7234	5.4321	5.1669	4.9245
8.0578	7.7843	7.5264	7.2829	7.0528	6.8351	6.6291	6.4338	6.2485	6.0726	5.7465	5.4510	5.1822	4.9371
8.1236	7.8431	7.5790	7.3300	7.0950	6.8729	6.6629	6.4642	6.2758	6.0971	5.7662	5.4669	5.1952	4.9476
8.1826	7.8957	7.6258	7.3717	7.1321	6.9061	6.6925	6.4906	6.2994	6.1182	5.7831	5.4804	5.2060	4.9563
8.2355	7.9426	7.6674	7.4086	7.1649	6.9352	6.7184	6.5135	6.3198	6.1364	5.7975	5.4919	5.2151	4.9636
8.2830	7.9844	7.7043	7.4412	7.1937	6.9607	6.7409	6.5335	6.3375	6.1520	5.8099	5.5016	5.2228	4.9697
8.3255	8.0218	7.7372	7.4701	7.2191	6.9830	6.7606	6.5509	6.3528	6.1656	5.8204	5.5098	5.2292	4.9747
8.3637	8.0552	7.7664	7.4957	7.2415	7.0027	6.7779	6.5660	6.3661	6.1772	5.8294	5.5168	5.2347	4.9789
8.3980	8.0850	7.7923	7.5183	7.2613	7.0199	6.7929	6.5791	6.3776	6.1872	5.8371	5.5227	5.2392	4.9825
8.4287	8.1116	7.8154	7.5383	7.2786	7.0350	6.8060	6.5905	6.3875	6.1959	5.8437	5.5277	5.2430	4.9854
8.4562	8.1354	7.8359	7.5560	7.2940	7.0482	6.8175	6.6005	6.3961	6.2034	5.8493	5.5320	5.2463	4.9878
8.4809	8.1566	7.8542	7.5717	7.3075	7.0599	6.8275	6.6091	6.4035	6.2098	5.8541	5.5356	5.2490	4.9898
8.5030	8.1755	7.8704	7.5856	7.3193	7.0701	6.8362	6.6166	6.4100	6.2153	5.8582	5.5386	5.2512	4.9930
8.5229	8.1924	7.8848	7.5979	7.3298	7.0790	6.8439	6.6231	6.4156	6.2201	5.8617	5.5412	5.2531	4.9930
8.5407	8.2075	7.8976	7.6087	7.3390	7.0868	6.8505	6.6288	6.4204	6.2242	5.8647	5.5434	5.2547	4.9941
8.5567	8.2210	7.9090	7.6183	7.3472	7.0937	6.8564	6.6338	6.4246	6.2278	5.8673	5.5453	5.2561	4.9951
8.5710	8.2330	7.9191	7.6268	7.3543	7.0998	6.8615	6.6381	6.4282	6.2309	5.8695	5.5468	5.2572	4.9959
8.5839	8.2438	7.9281	7.6344	7.3607	7.1050	6.8659	6.6418	6.4314	6.2335	5.8713	5.5482	5.2582	4.9966
8.5954	8.2534	7.9361	7.6410	7.3662	7.1097	6.8698	6.6450	6.4341	6.2358	5.8729	5.5493	5.2590	4.9972
8.6058	8.2619	7.9432	7.6469	7.3711	7.1138	6.8732	6.6479	6.4364	6.2377	5.8743	5.5502	5.2596	4.9976
8.6150	8.2696	7.9495	7.6522	7.3754	7.1173	6.8761	6.6503	6.4385	6.2394	5.8755	5.5511	5.2602	4.9980
8.6233	8.2764	7.9551	7.6568	7.3792	7.1205	6.8787	6.6524	6.4402	6.2409	5.8765	5.5517	5.2607	4.9984
8.6308	8.2825	7.9601	7.6609	7.3826	7.1232	6.8810	6.6543	6.4418	6.2421	5.8773	5.5523	5.2611	4.9986
8.6375	8.2880	7.9645	7.6645	7.3855	7.1256	6.8830	6.6559	6.4431	6.2432	5.8781	5.5528	5.2614	4.9989
8.6435	8.2928	7.9685	7.6677	7.3881	7.1277	6.8847	6.6573	6.4442	6.2442	5.8787	5.5532	5.2617	4.9991
8.6489	8.2972	7.9720	7.6705	7.3904	7.1296	6.8862	6.6585	6.4452	6.2450	5.8792	5.5536	5.2619	4.9992
8.6537	8.3010	7.9751	7.6730	7.3925	7.1312	6.8875	6.6596	6.4461	6.2457	5.8797	5.5539	5.2621	4.9993
8.6580	8.3045	7.9779	7.6752	7.3942	7.1327	6.8886	6.6605	6.4468	6.2463	5.8801	5.5541	5.2623	4.9995

TABLE 3 FUTURE VALUE OF $1

Period	3.00%	4.00%	5.00%	6.00%	7.00%	8.00%	9.00%	10.00%	11.00%	12.00%	13.00%	14.00%	15.00%
1	1.0300	1.0400	1.0500	1.0600	1.0700	1.0800	1.0900	1.1000	1.1100	1.1200	1.1300	1.1400	1.1500
2	1.0609	1.0816	1.1025	1.1236	1.1449	1.1664	1.1881	1.2100	1.2321	1.2544	1.2769	1.2996	1.3225
3	1.0927	1.1249	1.1576	1.1910	1.2250	1.2597	1.2950	1.3310	1.3676	1.4049	1.4429	1.4815	1.5209
4	1.1255	1.1699	1.2155	1.2625	1.3108	1.3605	1.4116	1.4641	1.5181	1.5735	1.6305	1.6890	1.7490
5	1.1593	1.2167	1.2763	1.3382	1.4026	1.4693	1.5386	1.6105	1.6851	1.7623	1.8424	1.9254	2.0114
6	1.1941	1.2653	1.3401	1.4185	1.5007	1.5869	1.6771	1.7716	1.8704	1.9738	2.0820	2.1950	2.3131
7	1.2299	1.3159	1.4071	1.5036	1.6058	1.7138	1.8280	1.9487	2.0762	2.2107	2.3526	2.5023	2.6600
8	1.2668	1.3686	1.4775	1.5938	1.7182	1.8509	1.9926	2.1436	2.3045	2.4760	2.6584	2.8526	3.0590
9	1.3048	1.4233	1.5513	1.6895	1.8385	1.9990	2.1719	2.3579	2.5580	2.7731	3.0040	3.2519	3.5179
10	1.3439	1.4802	1.6289	1.7908	1.9672	2.1589	2.3674	2.5937	2.8394	3.1058	3.3946	3.7072	4.0456
11	1.3842	1.5395	1.7103	1.8983	2.1049	2.3316	2.5804	2.8531	3.1518	3.4785	3.8359	4.2262	4.6524
12	1.4258	1.6010	1.7959	2.0122	2.2522	2.5182	2.8127	3.1384	3.4985	3.8960	4.3345	4.8179	5.3503
13	1.4685	1.6651	1.8856	2.1329	2.4098	2.7196	3.0658	3.4523	3.8833	4.3635	4.8980	5.4924	6.1528
14	1.5126	1.7317	1.9799	2.2609	2.5785	2.9372	3.3417	3.7975	4.3104	4.8871	5.5348	6.2613	7.0757
15	1.5580	1.8009	2.0789	2.3966	2.7590	3.1722	3.6425	4.1772	4.7846	5.4736	6.2543	7.1379	8.1371
16	1.6047	1.8730	2.1829	2.5404	2.9522	3.4259	3.9703	4.5950	5.3109	6.1304	7.0673	8.1372	9.3576
17	1.6528	1.9479	2.2920	2.6928	3.1588	3.7000	4.3276	5.0545	5.8951	6.8660	7.9861	9.2765	10.7613
18	1.7024	2.0258	2.4066	2.8543	3.3799	3.9960	4.7171	5.5599	6.5436	7.6900	9.0243	10.5752	12.3755
19	1.7535	2.1068	2.5270	3.0256	3.6165	4.3157	5.1417	6.1159	7.2633	8.6128	10.1974	12.0557	14.2318
20	1.8061	2.1911	2.6533	3.2071	3.8697	4.6610	5.6044	6.7275	8.0623	9.6463	11.5231	13.7435	16.3665

TABLE 4 FUTURE VALUE OF AN ORDINARY ANNUITY OF $1

Period	3.00%	4.00%	5.00%	6.00%	7.00%	8.00%	9.00%	10.00%	11.00%	12.00%	13.00%	14.00%	15.00%
1	1.0000	1.0000	1.0000	1.0000	1.0000	1.0000	1.0000	1.0000	1.0000	1.0000	1.0000	1.0000	1.0000
2	2.0300	2.0400	2.0500	2.0600	2.0700	2.0800	2.0900	2.1000	2.1100	2.1200	2.1300	2.1400	2.1500
3	3.0909	3.1216	3.1525	3.1836	3.2149	3.2464	3.2781	3.3100	3.3421	3.3744	3.4069	3.4396	3.4725
4	4.1836	4.2465	4.3101	4.3746	4.4399	4.5061	4.5731	4.6410	4.7097	4.7793	4.8498	4.9211	4.9934
5	5.3091	5.4163	5.5256	5.6371	5.7507	5.8666	5.9847	6.1051	6.2278	6.3528	6.4803	6.6101	6.7424
6	6.4684	6.6330	6.8019	6.9753	7.1533	7.3359	7.5233	7.7156	7.9129	8.1152	8.3227	8.5355	7.7537
7	7.6625	7.8983	8.1420	8.3938	8.6540	8.9228	9.2004	9.4872	9.7833	10.0890	10.4047	10.7305	11.0668
8	8.8923	9.2142	9.5491	9.8975	10.2598	10.6366	11.0285	11.4359	11.8594	12.2997	12.7573	13.2328	13.7268
9	10.1591	10.5828	11.0266	11.4913	11.9780	12.4876	13.0210	13.5795	14.1640	14.7757	15.4157	16.0853	16.7858
10	11.4639	12.0061	12.5779	13.1808	13.8164	14.4866	15.1929	15.9374	16.7220	17.5487	18.4197	19.3373	20.3037
11	12.8078	13.4864	14.2068	14.9716	15.7836	16.6455	17.5603	18.5312	19.5614	20.6546	21.8143	23.0445	24.3493
12	14.1920	15.0258	15.9171	16.8699	17.8885	18.9771	20.1407	21.3843	22.7132	24.1331	25.6502	27.2707	29.0017
13	15.6178	16.6268	17.7130	18.8821	20.1406	21.4953	22.9534	24.5227	26.2116	28.0291	29.9847	32.0887	34.3519
14	17.0863	18.2919	19.5986	21.0151	22.5505	24.2149	26.0192	27.9750	30.0949	32.3926	34.8827	37.5811	40.5047
15	18.5989	20.0236	21.5786	23.2760	25.1290	27.1521	29.3609	31.7725	34.4054	37.2797	40.4175	43.8424	47.5804
16	20.1569	21.8245	23.6575	25.6725	27.8881	30.3243	33.0034	35.9497	39.1899	42.7533	46.6717	50.9804	55.7175
17	21.7616	23.6975	25.8404	28.2129	30.8402	33.7502	36.9737	40.5447	44.5008	48.8837	53.7391	59.1176	65.0751
18	23.4144	25.6454	28.1324	30.9057	33.9990	37.4502	41.3013	45.5992	50.3959	55.7497	61.7251	68.3941	75.8364
19	25.1169	27.6712	30.5390	33.7600	37.3790	41.4463	46.0185	51.1591	56.9395	63.4397	70.7494	78.9692	88.2118
20	26.8704	29.7781	33.0660	36.7856	40.9955	45.7620	51.1601	57.2750	64.2028	72.0524	80.9468	91.0249	102.4436

(Numbers in parentheses refer to the chapter(s) containing the main discussion of the term.)

A

ABC analysis an inventory control method that separates items into three groups based on annual cost-to-volume usage; items having the highest dollar volume are referred to as A items, while C items represent the lowest dollar volume (10)

Abnormal spoilage units lost in production due to circumstances not inherent in the manufacturing process; these losses are not expected under normal, efficient operating conditions and are accounted for as period costs (5)

Absorption costing a cost accumulation method that treats the costs of all manufacturing components (direct materials, direct labour, variable overhead, and fixed overhead) as inventoriable or product costs; also known as full costing (3)

Accepted quality level a predetermined level of acceptability (5)

Accounting rate of return the rate of accounting earnings obtained on an average capital investment (or initial investment) over a project's life (W14)

Activity a repetitive action, movement, or work sequence performed to fulfill a business function (1, 8)

Activity-based costing an accounting information system that identifies the various activities performed in an organization and collects costs on the basis of the underlying nature and extent of those activities (8)

Activity-based management a discipline that focuses on how the activities performed during the production/performance process can improve the value received by a customer and the profit achieved by providing this value (8)

Activity centre a segment of the production or service process for which management wants a separate report of the costs of activities performed (8)

Activity cost driver a measure of the demands placed on activities and, thus, the resources consumed by products and services; often indicates an activity's output (8)

Actual cost system a method of accumulating product or service costs that uses actual direct materials, actual direct labour, and actual overhead costs (4)

Administrative departments organizational units that perform management activities that benefit the entire organization (4)

Allocate assign indirect or overhead costs based on the use of a cost driver, a predictor, or an arbitrary method (2)

Annuity a series of equal cash flows occurring at equal time intervals (W14)

Annuity due an annuity in which each cash flow occurs at the beginning of the period (W14)

Applied overhead the amount of overhead assigned to WIP Inventory as a result of incurring the activity that was used to develop the application rate; computed by multiplying the quantity of actual activity by the predetermined rate (4)

Appropriation a maximum allowable expenditure for a budget item (6)

Asset turnover a ratio that measures asset productivity; it is the number of sales dollars generated by each dollar of assets during a specific period (12)

Authority the right (usually by virtue of position or rank) to use resources to accomplish a task or achieve an objective; can be delegated or assigned to others (1)

Avoidable costs are costs which can be traced directing to a segment and would disappear if that segment was estimated (9)

B

Backflush costing a costing system that focuses on output and works backward through the system to allocate costs to cost of goods sold and inventory (10)

Batch-level cost a cost that is created by a group of similar things made, handled, or processed at a single time (8)

Benchmarking process of studying the best practices of comparable organizations or their units to improve the organization's own performance and then using those insights to set justified performance expectations (8, 10)

"Benefits-provided" ranking a listing of service departments in an order that begins with the one providing the most service to all other organizational areas; the ranking ends with the service department that provides the least service to all but the revenue-producing areas (4)

Bill of materials a document that contains information about product material components, their specifications (including quality), and the quantities needed for production (7, 13)

Bottleneck resource constraint (13)

Breakeven graph a graphical depiction of the relationships among revenues, variable costs, fixed costs, and profits (or losses) (3)

Breakeven point that level of activity, in units or dollars, at which total revenues equal total costs (3)

Budget the quantitative expression of an organization's commitment to planned activities and resource acquisition and use (6)

Budget committee a group, usually composed of senior management and the chief financial officer, that reviews and approves or makes adjustments to the master budget and/or the budgets submitted from operational managers (6)

Budgeting the process of determining a financial plan for future operations (6)

Budget manual a detailed set of documents that provides information and guidelines about the budgetary process (6)

Budget slack the intentional underestimation of revenues and/or overestimation of expenses (6)

Business model a description of a business's distinguishing operations or mechanisms, functions, and revenues and expenses (1)

Business process redesign when an organization changes its business processes (13)

Business process reengineering process innovation and redesign aimed at finding and implementing radical changes in how things are made or how tasks are performed to achieve substantial cost, service, or time reductions (8)

Business value-added activity an activity that is necessary for the operation of a business but for which a customer would not want to pay (8)

By-products products that have minor sales value as compared with the sales value of the major products and are not separately identifiable as individual products until they have become split-off (9)

C

Canada Revenue Agency the federal government body that collects income taxes; formerly known as Canada Customs and Revenue Agency (W14)

Capital asset an asset used to generate revenues or cost savings by providing production, distribution, or service capabilities for more than one year (W14)

Capital budgeting a process for evaluating proposed long-range projects or courses of future activity for the purpose of allocating limited resources to desirable projects (6, W14)

Capital cost allowance tax depreciation (W14)

Carrying costs the (variable) costs of carrying one unit of inventory in stock for one year; consist of storage, handling, insurance charges, property taxes based on inventory size, possible losses from obsolescence or the like, and opportunity cost (10)

Cash flow the receipt or disbursement of cash (W14)

Centralization an organizational structure in which top management makes most decisions and controls most activities of the organizational units from the organization's central headquarters (11)

Chart of accounts the list of all codes for recording transactions (13)

Compensation strategy a foundation for the compensation plan that addresses the role compensation should play in the organization (12)

Compounding period the time from one interest computation to the next (W14)

Compound interest interest earned in prior periods is added to the original investment so that, in each successive period, interest is earned on both principal and interest (W14)

Concurrent engineering see *simultaneous engineering* (8)

Continuous budget an ongoing 12-month budget that adds a new budget month (12 months into the future) as each current month expires (6)

Continuous loss reductions that occur uniformly during processing (5)

Contribution margin selling price per unit minus all variable production, selling, and administrative costs per unit (3)

Contribution margin ratio contribution margin divided by revenue; indicates what proportion of selling price remains after variable costs have been covered (3)

Control exertion of managerial influence on operations so that they will conform to plans (1)

Conversion the transformation of organizational inputs into outputs (10)

Conversion cost the sum of direct labour and manufacturing overhead that is directly or indirectly necessary for transforming direct (raw) materials and purchased parts into a saleable finished product (2)

Core competency any critical function or activity in which one organization has a higher proficiency than its competitors; the roots of competitiveness and competitive advantage (1)

Correlation a statistical measure of the strength of the relationship between two variables (2)

Cost a monetary measure of the resources given up to acquire a good or service (2)

Cost accounting tools and methods applied to determine the cost of making products or performing services (1)

Cost avoidance a process of finding acceptable alternatives to high-cost items and not spending money for unnecessary goods or services (10)

Cost behaviour the manner in which a cost responds to a change in a related level of activity (2, 10)

Cost centre an organizational unit in which the manager has the authority only to incur costs and is specifically evaluated on the basis of how well costs are controlled (11)

Cost consciousness an organizationwide employee attitude toward cost understanding, cost containment, cost avoidance, and cost reduction (10)

Cost containment the process of attempting, to the extent possible, to minimize period-by-period increases in per-unit variable and total fixed costs (10)

Cost control system a logical structure of formal and informal activities designed to influence costs and to enable management to analyze and evaluate how well expenditures were managed during a period (10)

Cost driver a factor that has a direct cause–effect relationship to a cost (2)

Cost leadership a competitive strategy in which an organization becomes the low-cost producer/provider and is thus able to charge low prices that emphasize cost efficiencies (1)

Cost management system a set of formal methods developed for controlling an organization's cost-generating activities relative to its goals and objectives (13)

Cost object anything to which costs attach or are related (2)

Cost of capital the weighted average rate that reflects the costs of the various sources of funds making up a firm's debt and equity structure (W14)

Cost of goods manufactured the total manufacturing costs attached to units produced during an accounting period (2)

Cost of goods manufactured statement the total cost of the goods that were completed and transferred to Finished Goods Inventory during the period (2)

Cost of goods sold the cost of the products or services sold during the period (2)

Cost of production report a document used in a process costing system; details all manufacturing quantities and costs, shows the computation of cost per equivalent unit of production (EUP), and indicates the cost assignment to goods produced during the period (5)

Cost-plus job a job being billed at cost plus a specified profit margin (4)

Cost pool a grouping of all costs that are associated with the same activity or cost driver (4)

Cost reduction a process of lowering current costs, especially those in excess of necessary costs (10)

Cost–volume–profit analysis the process of examining the relationships among revenues, costs, and profits for a relevant range of activity and for a particular time period (3)

Cycle time the time from when a customer places an order to the time that the product or service is delivered or, using a full life-cycle approach, the time from the conceptualization of a product or service to the time the product or service is delivered to the market/customer (8)

D

Decentralization the downward delegation by top management of authority and decision making to the individuals who are closest to internal processes and customers (11)

Defective unit see *spoilage* (5)

Degree of operating leverage a measure of how a percentage change in sales will affect profits; calculated at a specified sales level as contribution margin divided by income before tax (3)

Dependent variable an unknown variable that is to be predicted by use of one or more independent variables (2)

Differentiation a competitive strategy in which an organization distinguishes its products or services from those of competitors by adding enough value (including quality and/or features) that customers are willing to pay a higher price (1)

Direct cost a cost that is clearly, conveniently, and economically traceable to a particular cost object (2)

Direct costing see *variable costing* (3)

Direct labour the time spent by individuals who work specifically on manufacturing a product or performing a service and whose efforts are conveniently and economically traceable to that product or service; can also be viewed as the cost of the direct labour time (2)

Direct material a readily identifiable, physical part of a product that is clearly, conveniently, and economically traceable to that product (2)

Direct method (of service department allocation) a method that uses a specific base to assign service department costs directly to revenue-producing departments (4)

Discounting the process of removing the portion of a future cash flow that represents interest, thereby reducing that flow to a present value amount (W14)

Discount rate the rate of return on capital investments required by the company; the rate of return used in present value computations (W14)

Dual pricing arrangement a transfer price method that allows a selling division to record the transfer of goods or services at a market-based or negotiated price and a buying division to record the transfer at a cost-based amount (11)

Du Pont model ROI = Profit margin $\times$ Asset turnover (12)

E

Economic order quantity an estimate of the least costly number of units per order that would provide the optimal balance between ordering and carrying costs (10)

Economic value added EVA = After-tax income − (Cost of capital % $\times$ Capital invested) (12)

Effectiveness a measure of how well the firm's objectives and goals were achieved; it involves comparing actual output results with desired results (11)

Efficiency the degree to which the relationship between outputs and inputs is satisfactory; performance of a task to produce the best outcome at the lowest cost from the resources used (11)

Employee time sheet (time ticket) a source document that indicates, for each employee, what jobs were worked on during the day and for what amounts of time (4)

Empowerment all practices that are designed to give workers the training, authority, and responsibility they need to manage their own jobs and make decisions about their work (10)

Enterprise resource planning a fully integrated, full-service suite of software with a common database that can be used to plan and control resources across an entire organization (1, 13)

Environmental constraint any limitation on strategy caused by external cultural, fiscal (such as taxation structures), legal/regulatory, or political situations or by competitive market structures; tends to have long-run rather than short-run effects (1)

Equivalent units of production an approximation of the number of whole units of output that could have been produced during a period from the actual effort expended during that period (5)

Ethical standards norms that represent beliefs about moral and immoral behaviours; norms for individual conduct in making decisions and engaging in business transactions (1)

Expected activity a short-run concept representing the anticipated level of activity for the upcoming year (4)

Expected standard a standard that reflects what is actually expected to occur in a future period (7)

F

Facility-level cost see *organizational-level cost* (8)

FIFO method a method of process costing that computes an average cost per equivalent unit of production using only current production and current cost information; units and costs in beginning inventory are accounted for separately (5)

Financial accounting generation of accounting information for external reporting (1)

Financial budget a budget that reflects the funds to be generated or used during the budget period; includes the cash and capital budgets and the projected or pro forma financial statements (6)

Financing decision a judgment regarding how funds will be obtained to make an acquisition (W14)

Fixed cost a cost that remains constant in total within a specified range of activity (2)

Fixed overhead spending variance the difference between actual and budgeted (planned) fixed overhead (7)

Flexible budget a budget that is a series of financial plans detailing the individual cost factors that comprise total cost (6)

Functional classification a grouping of costs incurred for the same basic purpose (3)

Future value the amount to which one or more sums of money invested at a specified interest rate will grow over a specified number of time periods (W14)

G

Goal a desired result or condition that is expressed in qualitative terms (1)

Goal congruence a condition that exists when the personal and organizational goals of decision makers throughout the firm are consistent and mutually supportive (9, 11)

H

High–low method a technique for separating mixed costs that uses actual observations of a total cost at the highest and lowest levels of activity and calculates the change in both activity and cost; the levels chosen must be within the relevant range (2)

Horizontal price fixing the practice by which competitors attempt to regulate prices through an agreement or conspiracy (10)

Hurdle rate the rate of return deemed by management to be the lowest acceptable return on investment (W14)

I

Idle time storage time and time spent waiting at a production operation for processing (8)

Imposed budget a budget that is prepared by senior management with little or no input from operating personnel, who are simply informed of the budget goals and constraints (6)

Incremental analysis a technique used in decision analysis that compares alternatives by focusing on the differences in their projected revenues and costs (3)

Incremental cost the additional cost of producing or selling a contemplated quantity of output (9)

Incremental revenue the additional revenue resulting from a contemplated sale of a quantity of output (9)

Independent project an investment project that has no specific bearing on any other investment project (W14)

Independent variable a variable that, when changed, will cause consistent, observable changes in another variable; a variable used as the basis of predicting the value of a dependent variable (2)

Indirect cost a cost that cannot be clearly traced to a particular cost object (2)

Inspection time the time taken to perform quality control (8)

Internal rate of return the discount rate at which the present value of the cash inflows minus the present value of the cash outflows equals zero (W14)

Investing decision a judgment regarding which assets an entity will acquire to achieve its stated objectives (W14)

Investment centre an organizational unit in which the manager is responsible for generating revenues, planning and controlling costs, and acquiring, disposing of, and using plant assets to earn the highest feasible rate of return on the investment base (11)

J

JIT manufacturing system acquires components and produces inventory units only as they are needed, minimizes product defects, and reduces lead/setup times for acquisition and production (10)

Job a single unit or group of like units identifiable as being produced to distinct customer specifications (4)

Job order costing system a product costing method used by entities that produce limited quantities of custom-made goods or services that conform to specifications designated by the purchaser (4)

Job order cost sheet a source document that provides virtually all the financial information about a particular job; the set of all job order cost sheets for uncompleted jobs composes the Work in Process Inventory subsidiary ledger (4)

Joint cost the cost incurred, up to the split-off point, for material, labour, and overhead in a joint process (9)

Joint process a process in which one product cannot be manufactured without others being produced (9)

Joint products two or more products that have relatively significant sales values and are not separately identifiable as individual products until the split-off point (9)

Just-in-time a philosophy about when to do something; the *when* is "as needed" and the *something* is a production, purchasing, or delivery activity (7)

K

Kaizan costing a technique used to reduce costs during the manufacturing stage of the total life cycle of a product (10)

Kanban the Japanese word for *card*; another name for just-in-time manufacturing, which originated in Japan from the use of cards to control the flow of materials or units between work centres (10)

Key variable a critical factor believed to be a direct cause of the achievement or nonachievement of organizational goals and objectives; can be internal or external (6)

L

Labour efficiency variance the difference between the number of actual direct labour hours worked and the standard hours allowed for the actual output multiplied by the standard labour rate per hour (7)

Labour rate variance the difference between the total actual direct labour wages for the period and the standard rate for all hours actually worked during the period (7)

Lead time the time from the placement of an order to the arrival of the goods (10)

Least-squares regression analysis a statistical technique for mathematically determining the cost line of a mixed cost that best fits the data set by considering all representative data points; allows the user to investigate the relationship between or among dependent and independent variables (2)

Long-term variable cost a cost that has traditionally been viewed as fixed but that will actually react to some significant change in activity; also referred to as a step fixed cost (8)

M

Make-or-outsource (buy) decision a decision that compares the cost of internally manufacturing a product component with the cost of purchasing it from outside suppliers or from another division at a specified price and, thus, attempts to assess the best uses of available facilities (9)

Management accounting the gathering and application of information used to plan, make decisions, evaluate performance, and control an organization (1)

Management by exception a technique in which managers set upper and lower limits of tolerance for deviations and investigate only deviations that fall outside those tolerance ranges (7, 11)

Manufacturing cycle efficiency value-added production time divided by total cycle time; provides a measure of processing efficiency (8)

Manufacturing resource planning system a fully integrated system that uses the usual MRP method to plan production jobs and calculate resource needs involving manufacturing, marketing, and finance in determining the master production schedule; it also incorporates the financial accounting and financial management systems (13)

Margin of safety the excess of the estimated (budgeted) or actual sales of a company over its breakeven point; can be calculated in units or sales dollars, or as a percentage (3)

Mass customization the relatively low-cost mass production of products to the unique specifications of individual customers; requires the use of flexible manufacturing systems (8)

Master budget the comprehensive set of all budgetary schedules and the pro forma financial statements of an organization (6)

Material price variance the amount of money spent below (F for favourable) or above (U for unfavourable) the standard price for the quantity of materials purchased (7)

Material quantity variance the cost saved (F) or expended (U) because of the difference between the actual quantity of material used and the standard quantity of material allowed for the goods produced or services rendered during the period (7)

Materials requirement planning a computer simulated system that helps organizations plan by coordinating future production output requirements with individual future production input needs using a master production schedule (13)

Materials requisition form a source document that indicates the types and quantities of materials to be placed into production or used in performing a service; causes materials and their costs to be released from the raw materials warehouse and sent to Work in Process Inventory (4)

Method of neglect a method of treating spoiled units in the schedule calculating equivalent units (5)

Mixed cost a cost that has both a variable and a fixed component; it does not fluctuate in direct proportion to changes in activity, nor does it remain constant with changes in activity (2)

Multiple regression regression analysis using two or more independent variables (2)

Mutually exclusive projects a set of proposed investments for which there is a group of available candidates that all perform essentially the same function or meet the same objective; from this group, one is chosen and all others are rejected (W14)

Mutually inclusive projects a set of investment projects that must be chosen as a package (W14)

N

Negotiated transfer prices an intracompany charge for goods or services that has been set through a process of negotiation between the selling and purchasing unit managers (11)

Net present value the difference between the present values of all of the project's cash inflows and cash outflows (W14)

Net present value method an investment evaluation technique that uses discounted cash flow to determine if the rate of return on a project is equal to, higher than, or lower than the desired rate of return (W14)

Nonfinancial performance measures statistics on activities such as on-time delivery, manufacturing cycle time, set-up time, defect rate, number of unplanned production interruptions, and customer returns (12)

Nonvalue-added activity an activity that increases the time spent on a product or service but does not increase its value or worth to the customer (8)

Normal capacity the long-run (5 to 10 years) average activity of the firm that gives effect to historical and estimated future production levels and to cyclical and seasonal fluctuations (4)

Normal cost system a method of accumulating product or service costs that uses actual direct materials and direct labour cost, but assigns overhead costs to Work in Process through the use of a predetermined overhead rate (4)

Normal spoilage units lost due to the nature of the manufacturing process; such losses are unavoidable and represent a product cost (5)

O

Objective a quantitatively expressed result that can be achieved during a preestablished period or by a specified date; should logically measure progress in achieving goals (1)

Operating budget a budget that is expressed in both units and dollars (6)

Operating leverage a factor that reflects the relationship of a company's variable and fixed costs; measures the change in profits expected to result from a specified percentage change in sales (3)

Operations flow document a listing of all tasks necessary to make a unit of product or perform a service and the time allowed for each operation (7)

Opportunity cost the benefit forgone when one course of action is chosen over another (9)

Ordering costs the variable costs associated with preparing, receiving, and paying for an order (10)

Order point the inventory level that triggers the placement of an order (10)

Ordinary annuity an annuity in which each cash flow occurs at the end of the period (W14)

Organizational culture the set of basic assumptions about the organization, its goals, and its business practices; describes an organization's norms in internal and external, as well as formal and informal, transactions (1)

Organizational-level cost a cost incurred to support ongoing operations, which in turn provide available facilities (8)

Organizational structure the way in which authority and responsibility for making decisions is distributed in an organization (1)

Outlier a nonrepresentative point that falls outside the relevant range or that is a distortion of normal costs within the relevant range (2)

Outsource use a source external to the company to provide a service or manufacture a needed product or component (9)

Outsourcing the contracting with outside manufacturers or vendors for necessary goods or services rather than producing the goods or performing services in-house (10)

Overapplied overhead an occurrence that results when the overhead applied to Work in Process is greater than actual overhead (4)

Overhead the expenses of a business such as rent, insurance, and utilities consumed in the production of a product or consumed in the supplying of a service (2)

P

Participatory budget a budget that has been developed through a process of joint decision making by senior management and operating personnel (6)

Payback period the time required to recoup the original investment in a project through its cash flows (W14)

Performance measurement system a major set of financial and, particularly, nonfinancial performance measures for evaluating the performance of a manager, activity, or organizational unit (13)

Period cost a cost that is incurred during an accounting period to support the activities of the company; the cost of resources consumed during the period—an expense (2)

Post-investment audit a comparison of expected and actual project results after a capital investment (W14)

Practical capacity the activity level that could be achieved during normal working hours giving consideration to ongoing, regular operating interruptions, such as holidays, downtime, and start-up time (4)

Practical standards standards that can be reached or slightly exceeded approximately 60% to 70% of the time with reasonable effort by workers (7)

Predetermined overhead rate an estimated constant charge (rate) per unit of activity used to assign overhead costs to production or services (4)

Predictor an activity measure that is accompanied by a consistent, observable change in a cost item (2)

Preference decision a judgment regarding how projects are to be ranked based on their impact on the achievement of company objectives (W14)

Present value the amount that a future cash flow is worth currently, given a specified rate of interest (W14)

Price fixing a practice by which firms conspire to set a product's price at a specified level (10)

Price variance the difference between what was paid and what should have been paid for inputs during the period (7)

Prime cost the total cost of direct materials and direct labour; so called because these costs are most convincingly associated with and traceable to a specific product (2)

Process-based management involves managing processes in order to accomplish objectives (10)

Process costing a method of accumulating and assigning costs to units of production in companies that make large quantities of homogeneous products (5)

Process costing system a product costing system used by companies that produce large amounts of homogeneous products through a continuous production flow (5)

Process-level cost see *product-level cost* (8)

Process map a flowchart or diagram that indicates every step in making a product or providing a service (8)

Process productivity the total units produced during a period using value-added processing time (12)

Process quality yield the proportion of good units that resulted from the activities expended (12)

Process re-engineering process innovation and redesign aimed at finding and implementing radical changes in how things are made or how tasks are performed to achieve substantial cost, service, or time reductions (13)

Product complexity the number of components in a product or the number of processes or operations through which a product flows (8)

Product contribution margin revenue minus variable cost of goods sold (3)

Product cost a cost associated with making or acquiring inventory or providing a service—an asset (2)

Production cost in a manufacturing company, includes costs associated with buying direct materials, paying for direct labour, incurring traceable overhead, and absorbing allocated fixed overhead (10)

Product-level cost a cost created by the need to implement or support a specific product (8)

Product margin the excess of a product's revenues over both its direct variable expenses and any avoidable fixed expenses related to the product; the amount remaining to cover unavoidable direct fixed expenses and common costs and then to provide profits (9)

Product variety the number of different types of products produced (8)

Profitability index a ratio that compares the present value of net cash inflows with the present value of the net investment (W14)

Profit centre an organizational unit in which the manager is responsible for generating revenues and planning and controlling all expenses (11)

Profit margin the ratio of income to sales (12)

Profit–volume graph a graphical presentation of the profit or loss associated with each level of sales (3)

Project future activity, such as the purchase, installation, and operation of a capital asset (W14)

Pull system a production system in which parts are delivered or manufactured only as they are needed (10)

Purchasing cost the quoted purchase price minus any discounts allowed plus shipping charges (10)

Push system a production system in which work centres may purchase or produce inventory that is not currently needed because of lead time or economic order (production) quantity requirements; the excess inventory is stored until it is needed (10)

Q

Quantity variance the difference between the quantity of actual inputs and the standard quantity of inputs for the actual output of the period multiplied by a standard price or rate (7)

R

Recapture occurs when all assets in a class are sold and the proceeds exceed the undepreciated capital cost of the class; the excess is subject to tax (W14)

Red-line system an inventory system in which a single container (or stack) of inventory is available for production needs, and a red line is painted on the inventory container (or the wall, for a stack) at a point deemed to be the reorder point (10)

Regression analysis a statistical procedure used to determine and measure a predictive relationship between one dependent variable and one or more other variables (2)

Regression line a line that represents the cost formula for a set of cost observations fit to those observations in a mathematically determined manner (2)

Relevant cost a cost that is pertinent to or logically associated with a specific problem or decision and that differs between alternatives (9)

Relevant costing a process that allows managers to focus on pertinent facts and disregard extraneous information by comparing, to the extent possible and practical, the differential, incremental revenues and incremental costs of alternative decisions (9)

Relevant range the specified range of activity over which a variable cost remains constant per unit and a fixed cost remains fixed in total (2)

Rent each equal cash flow of an annuity (W14)

Residual income the profit earned that exceeds an amount "charged" for funds committed to a responsibility centre (12)

Responsibility the obligation to accomplish a task or achieve an objective; cannot be delegated to others (1)

Responsibility accounting an accounting system that provides information to senior management about segment or subunit performance (11)

Responsibility centre the cost object under the control of a manager; in the case of a decentralized company, the cost object is an organizational unit such as a division, department, or geographical region (11)

Responsibility reports reflect the revenues and/or costs under the control of a specific unit manager (11)

Return of capital recovery of the original investment (W14)

Return on capital income; equals the discount rate times an investment amount (W14)

Return on investment a ratio that relates income generated by the investment centre to the resources (or asset base) used to produce that income (12)

Revenue centre an organizational unit in which the manager is accountable only for the generation of revenues and has no control over selling prices or budgeted costs (11)

S

Safety stock the quantity of inventory kept on hand by a company to compensate for potential fluctuations in usage or unusual delays in receiving orders (10)

Sales mix the relative combination of quantities of sales of the various products that make up the total sales of a company (9)

Sales price variance the difference between actual and budgeted selling prices multiplied by the actual number of units sold (7)

Sales volume variance the difference between actual and budgeted volumes multiplied by the budgeted selling price (7)

Scarce resources resources that are available only in limited quantity; they create constraints on producing goods or providing services and may include money, machine hours, skilled labour hours, raw materials, and production capacity (9)

Scattergraph a graphic representation of the relationship between variables within a population achieved by plotting each magnitude or item against the coordinates provided (2)

Scrap inputs that do not become part of the outputs but have very minor values (9)

Screening decision a judgment regarding the desirability of a capital project based on some previously established minimum criterion or criteria (W14)

Service departments organizational units that provide one or more specific functional tasks for other internal units (4)

Service variety the number of different types of services provided (8)

Setup costs the direct and indirect labour costs of getting equipment ready for a new production run (10)

Simple interest interest calculated as a percentage of only the original investment, or principal amount (W14)

Simple regression regression analysis using only one independent variable to predict the dependent variable (2)

Simultaneous engineering an integrated approach in which all primary functions and personnel contributing to a product's origination and production are involved continuously from the beginning of a project (8)

Special order pricing determining a sales price to charge for manufacturing or service jobs that are outside the company's normal production or service realm (9)

Split-off point the point at which the outputs of a joint process are first identifiable as individual products (9)

Spoilage unit of product with imperfections that cannot be corrected in an economical way (5)

Spoiled unit see *spoilage* (5)

Standard cost a budgeted or estimated cost to manufacture a single unit of product or perform a single service (7)

Standard cost card a document that summarizes the direct materials and direct labour standard quantities and prices needed to complete one unit of product as well as the overhead allocation bases and rates (7)

Standard costing system a product costing method using unit norms for production costs (7)

Standard quantity allowed a measure of quantity that translates the actual output achieved into the standard input quantity that should have been used to achieve that output (7)

Standards benchmarks or norms against which actual results may be compared (7)

Static budget incorporates anticipated value about volume, prices, and costs that are conceived before the period in question begins (6)

Step cost a variable or fixed cost that shifts upward or downward when activity changes by a certain interval or step (2)

Step method (of service department cost allocation) assigns service department costs to cost objects using a specific base after considering the interrelationships of the service departments and the revenue-producing departments (4)

Strategic alliance an agreement involving two or more firms with complementary core competencies to contribute jointly to the value creation chain (1)

Strategic planning the process of developing a statement of long-range (5 to 10 years) goals for the organization and defining the strategies and policies that will help the organization achieve those goals (6)

Strategy a long-term dynamic plan that fulfills organizational goals and objectives through satisfaction of customer needs or wants within the company's acknowledged operating markets (1)

Suboptimization a situation in which unit managers make decisions that positively affect their own unit but that are detrimental to other organizational units or to the company as a whole (11)

Sunk cost the historical or past cost that is associated with the acquisition of an asset or a resource (9)

Survival triplet the cost/price, quality, and functionality that products need to demonstrate in order to survive and prosper (10)

Synchronous management all endeavours that help an organization achieve its goals (12)

T

Tactical planning the process of determining the specific objectives and means by which strategic plans will be achieved; are short-term (1 to 18 months), single use plans that have been developed to address a given set of circumstances or for a specific time frame (6)

Target costing a process of determining an allowable cost for a product or component that is inferred from projecting a market price for the product and subtracting a required profit margin (10)

Tax shield the amount of the reduction of taxable income provided by Capital Cost Allowance (W14)

Theoretical capacity some estimated absolute maximum potential activity that could occur during a specific time frame (4)

Theoretical standards standards that allow for no inefficiencies of any type; encompass the highest level of rigour and do not allow for normal operating delays or human limitations such as fatigue, boredom, or misunderstanding (7)

Throughput the rate at which a company generates cash from selling products and services to customers (12)

Timeline illustration of the timing of expected cash receipts and payments; cash inflows are shown as positive amounts and cash outflows are shown as negative amounts (W14)

Total contribution margin revenue minus all variable costs regardless of the area of incurrence (production or nonproduction) (3)

Total cost to account for the balance in Work in Process Inventory at the beginning of the period plus all current costs for direct material, direct labour, and overhead (5)

Total quality management a philosophy for organizational management and organizational change that seeks ever-increasing quality (7)

Total units to account for total whole or partial physical units for which the department is responsible during the current period; beginning WIP inventory units plus units started (5)

Transfer price an internal charge established for the exchange of goods and services between organizational units of the same company (11)

Transfer time the time it takes to move products or components from one place to another (move time) (8)

Two-bin system an inventory system in which two containers or stacks of inventory are available for production needs; when production begins to use materials in the second bin, a purchase order is placed to refill the first bin (10)

U

Underapplied overhead an occurrence that results when the overhead applied to Work in Process Inventory is less than actual overhead (4)

Unit-level cost a cost created by the production or acquisition of a single unit of production or the delivery of a single unit of service (8)

Units started and completed the total units completed during the period minus the units in beginning inventory; alternatively, units started minus units in ending inventory (5)

V

Value-added activity an activity that increases the worth of a product or service to the customer and for which the customer is willing to pay (8)

Value-added processing time the time it takes to perform the functions necessary to manufacture a product (8)

Value-added service time the time it takes to perform all necessary service functions for a customer (8)

Value chart a visual representation of the value-added and non-value-added activities and the time spent in all of these activities from the beginning to the end of a process (8)

Value creation chain the set of processes and activities that convert inputs into products and services that have value to the organization's customers (1)

Value engineering a tool used to manage the relationship between product design, product price, and target cost (10)

Variable cost a cost that varies in total in direct proportion to changes in activity (2)

Variable costing a cost accumulation method that includes only variable production costs (direct materials, direct labour, and variable manufacturing overhead) as product or inventoriable costs and treats fixed manufacturing overhead as a period cost; also known as direct costing (3)

Variable cost ratio 100% minus the CM ratio; represents the variable cost proportion of each revenue dollar (3)

Variable overhead efficiency variance the difference between budgeted (planned) variable overhead at actual input activity and budgeted variable overhead at standard input activity allowed (7)

Variable overhead spending variance the difference between actual variable overhead and budgeted (planned) variable overhead based on actual input (7)

Variance any difference between actual and standard costs or quantities (7)

Variance analysis the process of categorizing the nature (favourable or unfavourable) of the differences between standard and actual costs and seeking the reasons for those differences (7)

Vertical integration the extent to which the value creation chain resides within a single firm (1)

Vertical price fixing collusion between producing businesses and their distributors to control the prices at which their products may be sold to consumers (10)

Volume variance the difference between budget (planned) capacity and standard hours allowed for production attained (basically a measure of utilization of the plant facilities) (7)

W

Waste inputs that do not become part of the output (9)

Weighted average method a method of process costing that computes an average cost per equivalent unit of production; combines beginning inventory units with current production and beginning inventory costs with current costs to compute that average (5)

Work-out a management activity designed to take unnecessary work out of the system (10)

Z

Zero-based budgeting a comprehensive budgeting process that systematically considers the priorities and alternatives for current and proposed activities in relation to organizational objectives (6)